Turkey

a Lonely Planet travel survival kit

Tom Brosnahan
Pat Yale

Turkey

5th edition

Published by

Lonely Planet Publications

Head Office: PO Box 617, Hawthorn, Vic 3122, Australia
Branches: 155 Filbert St, Suite 251, Oakland, CA 94607, USA
10 Barley Mow Passage, Chiswick, London W4 4PH, UK
71 bis rue du Cardinal Lemoine, 75005 Paris, France

Printed by

Pac-Rim Kwartanusa Printing
Printed in Indonesia

Photographs by

Chris Barton, Glenn Beanland, Tom Brosnahan, Kim Grant, Paul Steel, Tony Wheeler

Front cover: Carpet from Kayseri (Glenn Beanland)
Title page: Gök Medrese, Sivas (Margaret Jung)

First Published

July 1985

This Edition

September 1996

National Library of Australia Cataloguing in Publication Data

Brosnahan, Tom.
Turkey

5th ed.
Includes index.
ISBN 0 86442 364 0.

1. Turkey – Guidebooks. I. Yale, Pat, 1954–
II. Title. (Series: Lonely Planet travel survival kit).

915.610439

Tom Brosnahan

Tom Brosnahan was born and raised in Pennsylvania, went to college in Boston, then set out on the road. His first two years in Turkey, during which he learned to speak fluent Turkish, were spent as a US Peace Corps Volunteer. He studied Middle Eastern history and the Ottoman Turkish language for eight years, but abandoned the writing of his PhD dissertation in favour of travelling and writing guidebooks.

So far his 30 books for various publishers have sold over two million copies in twelve languages. *Turkey* is the result of over a decade of experience and travel in the country.

Tom Brosnahan is also the author of Lonely Planet's *İstanbul city guide, Guatemala, Belize & Yucatán: La Ruta Maya* and the *Turkish phrasebook*, as well as co-author of *Mexico, Central America on a shoestring* and other Lonely Planet guides.

Pat Yale

Pat Yale first went to Turkey in 1974 in an old van that didn't look as if it would make it past Dover. After graduating she spent several years selling holidays before throwing away sensible careerdom to head overland from Egypt to Zimbabwe. Returning home, she mixed teaching with extensive travelling in Europe, Asia and Central and South America. A full-time writer now, she also helped update Lonely Planet's *Ireland*, *Dublin* and *Britain* guides.

From the Authors

From Tom Turkey is an important travel destination, growing and changing rapidly. If you find new things of interest to travellers, please let me know so I can include them in the next edition. Audio cassettes are available to help you learn some basic Turkish. For details, see the Language section in Facts about the Country.

I'm very grateful for letters; I read each one, and I reply if I can. Send your letter to Lonely Planet Publications, PO Box 617, Hawthorn, Victoria 3122, Australia. If you have access to electronic mail, that's even better. Contact me on CompuServe at 76400,3110, on America Online at TBros, or on the Internet at tbros@infoexchange.com. If you have access to the Internet World Wide Web, browse my Web site at http://infoexchange.com/biz/travelinfo.

In revising this edition I had the help of numerous people. First and foremost is Pat Yale of Bristol, England – an experienced author who revised the Black Sea chapter, much of the Central Anatolia and Eastern Turkey chapters, and part of the Mediterranean chapter. Many thanks for her hard and thorough work.

I must also thank Ms Leyla Özhan, director of the Turkish tourism office in New York City; Mr Mustafa Siyahhan of the Turkish tourism office in Washington DC; Ms Cansen Bekleriz of the tourism office in İstanbul's Sirkeci station, who seems able to answer any question or solve any problem; Mr Ersan Atsür, director of Orion-Tour in İstanbul, who went beyond the call of duty to make travel arrangements; Mr Çelik Gülersoy of the Turkish Touring & Automobile Association for much background information; Lufthansa Airlines, which made it easy to get to Turkey; Mr Süha Ersöz of the Esbelli Evi in Ürgüp; Ms Ann Nevens of the Hotel Empress Zoe in İstanbul; and, as always, the Turkish people (especially the cooks!) who made my research trips so enjoyable.

From Pat As usual, I was overwhelmed by the warmth of Turkish hospitality. Many people helped me along the way but the following were particularly generous in sharing their time and thoughts: Ali Kamil Yalçın in Amasya; Ahmet Diler in Avanos; Adnan Pirikoğlu in Ayder; Ali Baykal in Boğazkale; Zafer Önay and Hasan Elgi in Doğubeyazıt; Nuri Çiçek in Erzurum; Ali Karataş, Dawn Köse, Nico Leyssen and Ruth Lockwood in Göreme; Tovi Grinstein-Diler in Güzelyurt; Mike Belton and Karen McGrath in Kaş; Mustafa Filizmol and Mahir Kaplan in Kayseri; and Mustafa Dramalı in Marmaris. Of the travellers who shared their experiences with me, I'm especially grateful to Filiz Osman, Marcus Pugh, Rosie Jones and Annie Heslop. Many thanks to you all.

Dedication (from Tom)

For Josephine and John – who else?

From the Publisher

This edition of *Turkey* was edited by Susan Noonan with assistance from Michelle Glynn, Cathy Lanigan, Rachel Scully, Diana Saad and Kristin Odijk. Cartography and design were coordinated by Margaret Jung with mapping assistance from Verity Campbell, Indra Kilfoyle, Paul Piaia, Michael Signal, Geoff Stringer and Trudi Canavan. The illustrations were drawn by Margaret, Trudi, Jane Hart and Valerie Tellini.

Thanks to David Kemp and Adam McCrow for the cover design, Kerrie Williams for indexing, Dan Levin for the soft fonts, Chris Love for the climate charts, and the readers' letters team for all their assistance. Finally, special thanks goes to Peter Ward of Peter Ward Book Exports for his help with the bookshops sections, and to Aydin from The Kilim, Victoria St, Richmond, for allowing us to photograph his exhibits.

Thanks

Thanks to those travellers who wrote to us about their experiences in Turkey. These people's names appear at the end of this book.

Warning & Request

Things change – prices go up, schedules change, good places go bad and bad places go bankrupt – nothing stays the same. So if you find things better or worse, recently opened or long since closed, please write and tell us and help make the next edition better.

Your letters will be used to help update future editions and, where possible, important changes will also be included in an Update section in reprints.

We greatly appreciate all information that is sent to us by travellers. Back at Lonely Planet we employ a hard-working readers' letters team to sort through the many letters we receive. The best ones will be rewarded with a free copy of the next edition or another Lonely Planet guide if you prefer. We give away lots of books, but, unfortunately, not every letter/postcard receives one.

Contents

Map Legend

BOUNDARIES

International Boundary
Regional Boundary

ROUTES

Freeway
Highway
Major Road
Unsealed Road or Track
City Road
City Street
Railway
Underground Railway
Tram
Walking Track
Walking Tour
Ferry Route
Cable Car or Chairlift

AREA FEATURES

Parks
Built-Up Area
Pedestrian Mall
Market
Christian Cemetery
Non-Christian Cemetery
Beach or Desert
Reef

HYDROGRAPHIC FEATURES

Coastline
River, Creek
Intermittent River or Creek
Rapids, Waterfalls
Lake, Intermittent Lake
Canal
Swamp

SYMBOLS

CAPITAL — National Capital
Capital — Regional Capital
CITY — Major City
City — City
Town — Town
Village — Village
Place to Stay, Place to Eat
Cafe, Pub or Bar
Post Office, Telephone
Tourist Information, Bank
Bus Station or Terminal, Bus Stop
Museum, Youth Hostel
Caravan Park, Camping Ground
Church, Cathedral
Mosque, Synagogue
Temple, Parking
Hospital, Police Station

Embassy, Petrol Station
Airport, Airfield
Swimming Pool, Gardens
Shopping Centre, Zoo
Winery or Vineyard, Picnic Site
A25 — One Way Street, Route Number
Stately Home, Monument
Castle, Tomb
Cave, Hut or Shelter
Mountain or Hill, Lookout
Lighthouse, Shipwreck
Pass, Spring
Beach, Surf Beach
Archaeological Site or Ruins
Ancient or City Wall
Cliff or Escarpment, Tunnel
Train Station

Note: not all symbols displayed above appear in this book

Introduction

The history of Anatolia, the Turkish homeland, is simply incredible. The world's oldest 'city' was discovered here, at Çatal Höyük in 7500 BC. The Hittite Empire, little known in the west, rivalled that of ancient Egypt, and left behind captivating works of art.

The heartland of classical Hellenic culture is actually in Turkey, including cities such as Troy, Pergamum, Ephesus, Miletus and Halicarnassus. Most modern Turkish cities have a Roman past, and all have a Byzantine one. The Seljuk Turkish Empire could boast of people like Omar Khayyam and Celaleddin Rumi, the poet, mystic and founder of the order of Whirling Dervishes.

In the minds of most western visitors the mention of Turkey conjures up vague stereotypical visions of oriental splendour and decadence, of mystery and intrigue, of sultans and harems, of luxury and wickedness. These outdated stereotypes quickly evaporate once the visitor arrives in the country. The Turkish Republic is democratic, rapidly modernising, secular and western-oriented with a vigorous economy.

The Turks are mostly friendly to foreign visitors, the cuisine is frequently excellent, the cities are dotted with majestic old buildings, and the countryside is often beautiful like a national park. The old stereotype of oriental decadence originated in the Ottoman Empire, when the entire Middle East and much of North Africa was ruled by the Turkish sultan. The great powers of Western Europe coveted the sultan's lands, and put pressure on him by portraying him in the western press as little better than a monster. This negative image built easily on the notion of the 'terrible Turk' left from the days, in the 17th century, when Ottoman armies threatened Vienna and central Europe.

The Turks look back proudly to the times of Mehmet the Conqueror and Süleyman the Magnificent, when the Turkish Empire was rich, powerful and envied by the west. Turks are also fascinated by the depth of history in their homeland, by the progression of kingdoms and empires which fostered a dozen great cultures: Hittite, Hellenic, Hellenistic, Roman, Byzantine, Seljuk, Ottoman and more.

Turks harbour no romantic visions of once again ruling the sultan's vast domains. But with the independence of the Turkic republics of central Asia, Turkey has gained important influence in that region. It is seen as the model for these new countries: a democratic, secular nation-state with a free market economy.

Turkey is a big country, and the variety of things to see and do is enormous – ranging from water sports to mountain trekking, archaeology to night-clubbing, river rafting to raki drinking. Turkey can easily keep you happy for weeks or even months.

Facts about the Country

HISTORY

Turkey's history is astoundingly long, extending for almost 10,000 years.

Earliest Times

The Mediterranean region was inhabited as early as 7500 BC, during Palaeolithic (Old Stone Age) times. By 7000 BC a Neolithic (New Stone Age) city had grown up at what's now called Çatal Höyük, 60 km south-east of Konya. The early Anatolians developed fine wall paintings, statuettes, domestic architecture and pottery. Artefacts from the site, including the wall paintings, are displayed in Ankara's Museum of Anatolian Civilisations.

The Chalcolithic (Stone and Copper Age)

Time Line

7500 BC	Earliest known inhabitants; earliest human community at Çatal Höyük
5000 BC	Stone and Copper Age; settlement at Hacılar
2600-1900 BC	Old Bronze Age; Proto-Hittite Empire in central and south-eastern Anatolia
1900-1300 BC	Hittite Empire, wars with Egypt; the Patriarch Abraham departs from Harran, near Şanlıurfa, for Canaan
1250 BC	Trojan War
1200-600 BC	Phrygian and Mysian invasions, followed by the great period of Hellenic civilisation; Yassı Höyük settlement flourishes; King Midas and King Croesus reign; coinage is invented; kingdoms of Ionia, Lycia, Lydia, Caria, Pamphylia; Empire of Urartu
550 BC	Cyrus of Persia invades Anatolia
334 BC	Conquest of simply everything and everybody by Alexander the Great from Macedon
279 BC	Celts (or Gauls) invade and set up Galatia near Ankara
250 BC	Rise of the Kingdom of Pergamum (Bergama)
129 BC	Rome establishes the Province of Asia ('Asia Minor'), with its capital at Ephesus (near İzmir)
47-57 AD	St Paul's trips in Anatolia
330 AD	Constantine dedicates the 'New Rome' of Constantinople, and the centre of the Roman Empire moves from Rome to the Bosphorus
527-65 AD	Reign of Justinian, greatest Byzantine emperor; construction of Sancta Sophia, greatest church in the world
570-622 AD	Muhammed's birth; revelation of the Koran; flight *(hijra)* to Medina
1037-1109 AD	Empire of the Great Seljuk Turks, based in Iran
1071-1243 AD	Seljuk Sultanate of Rum, based in Konya; life and work of Celaleddin Rumi ('Mevlana'), founder of the Whirling Dervishes
1000s-1200s AD	Age of the Crusades
1288 AD	Birth of the Ottoman Empire, near Bursa
1453 AD	Conquest of Constantinople by Mehmet II
1520-66 AD	Reign of Sultan Süleyman the Magnificent, the great age of the Ottoman Empire; most of North Africa, most of Eastern Europe and all of the Middle East controlled from İstanbul; Ottoman navies patrol the Mediterranean and Red seas and the Indian Ocean
1876-1909 AD	Reign of Sultan Abdülhamid, last of the powerful sultans; the 'Eastern Question' arises: which European nations will be able to grab Ottoman territory when the empire topples?
1923 AD	Proclamation of the Turkish Republic
1938 AD	Death of Atatürk

period saw the building of a city at Hacılar, near Burdur, in about 5000 BC. The pottery here was of finer quality and copper implements, rather than stone or clay ones, were used.

Hittites – the Bronze Age

The Old Bronze Age (2600-1900 BC) was when Anatolians first developed cities of substantial size. An indigenous people now named the Proto-Hittites, or Hatti, built cities at Nesa or Kanesh (today's Kültepe), and Alacahöyük. The first known ruler of Kanesh was King Zipani (circa 2300 BC), according to Akkadian texts. As for Alacahöyük, 36 km from Boğazkale (bo-AHZ-kahl-eh), it was perhaps the most important pre-Hittite city and may have been the first Hittite capital.

The Hittites, a people who spoke an Indo-European language, overran this area and established themselves as a ruling class over the local people during the Middle Bronze Age (1900-1600 BC). The Hittites took over existing cities and built a magnificent capital at Hattuşaş (Boğazkale), 212 km east of Ankara near Sungurlu. The early Hittite Kingdom (1600-1500 BC) was replaced by the greater Hittite Empire (1450-1200 BC). The Hittites captured Syria from the Egyptians (1380-1316 BC), clashed with the great Rameses II (1298 BC), and meanwhile developed a wonderful culture.

Their graceful pottery, ironwork ornaments and implements, gold jewellery and figurines now fill a large section of the Museum of Anatolian Civilisations in Ankara. The striking site of Boğazkale, set in dramatic countryside, is worth a visit, as is the religious centre of Yazılıkaya nearby. The Hittite religion was based upon worship of a sun goddess and a storm god.

The Hittite Empire was weakened in its final period by the cities of Assuwa ('Asia'), subject principalities along the Aegean coast, which included the city of Troy. The Trojans were attacked by Achaean Greeks in 1250 BC – the Trojan War – which gave the Hittites a break. But the *coup de grâce* came with a massive invasion of 'sea peoples' from various Greek islands and city-states. Driven from their homelands by the invading Dorians, the sea peoples flocked into Anatolia by way of the Aegean coast. The Hittite state survived for a few centuries longer in the south-eastern Taurus (Toros) Mountains, but the great empire was dead.

Phrygians, Urartians, Lydians & Others

With the Hittite decline, smaller states filled the power vacuum. Around 1200 BC the Phrygians and Mysians, of Indo-European stock, invaded Anatolia from Thrace and settled at Gordium (Yassı Höyük), 106 km south-west of Ankara. This Hittite city became the Phrygian capital (circa 800 BC). A huge Hittite cemetery and a royal Phrygian tomb still exist at the site. King Midas (circa 715 BC), he of the golden touch, is Phrygia's most famous son.

At the same time (after 1200 BC), the Aegean coast was populated with a mixture of native peoples and Greek invaders. The region around İzmir became Ionia, with numerous cities. To the south was Caria, between modern Milas and Fethiye, a mountainous region whose people were great traders. The Carians sided with the Trojans during the Trojan War. When the Dorians arrived they brought some Greek culture to Caria, which the great Carian king Mausolus developed even further. His tomb, the Mausoleum, was among the Seven Wonders of the Ancient World. Of his capital city, Halicarnassus (modern Bodrum), little remains.

Further east from Caria were Lycia, a kingdom stretching from Fethiye to Antalya, and Pamphylia, the land east of Antalya.

As the centuries passed, a great city grew up at Sardis, in the kingdom of Lydia, 60 km east of İzmir. Sardis dominated most of Ionia and clashed with Phrygia. Lydia is famous not only for Sardis, but for a great invention: coinage. It's also famous for King Croesus, the world's first great coin collector. Lydia's primacy lasted only from 680 to 547 BC, when Persian invaders overran it.

Meanwhile, out east on the shores of salty Lake Van (Van Gölü), yet another kingdom and culture arose. Not much is known about the Urartians who founded the Kingdom of Van (860-612 BC), except that they left interesting ruins and vast, bewildering cuneiform inscriptions in the massive Rock of Van just outside the modern town.

The Cimmerians invaded Anatolia from the west, conquered Phrygia and challenged Lydia, then settled down to take their place amongst the great jumble of Anatolian peoples. In 547 BC the Persians invaded and jumbled the situation even more. Though the Ionian cities survived the invasion and lived on under Persian rule, the great period of Hellenic culture was winding down. Ionia, with its important cities of Phocaea (Foça, north of İzmir), Teos, Ephesus, Priene and Miletus, and Aeolia, centred on Smyrna (İzmir), had contributed a great deal to ancient culture, from the graceful scrolled capitals of Ionic columns to the ideas of Thales of Miletus, the first recorded philosopher in the west.

While the great city of Athens was relatively unimportant, the Ionian cities were laying the foundations of Hellenic civilisation. It is ironic that the Persian invasion which curtailed Ionia's culture caused that of Athens to flourish. On reaching Athens, the Persians were overextended. By meeting the Persian challenge, Athens grew powerful and influential, taking the lead in the further progress of Hellenic culture.

In his short reign, Alexander the Great, King of Macedonia, conquered the entire Middle East from Greece to India initiating an era of Greek territorial monarchies. He is renowned as a great strategist and one of the most skilful generals in history.

Cyrus & Alexander

Cyrus, emperor of Persia (550-530 BC), swept into Anatolia from the east, conquering everybody and everything. Though he subjected the cities of the Aegean coast to his rule, this was not easy. The independent-minded citizens gave him and his successors trouble for the next two centuries.

The Persian conquerors were defeated by Alexander the Great, who stormed out of Macedon, crossed the Hellespont (Dardanelles) in 334 BC, and within a few years had conquered the entire Middle East from Greece to India. Alexander, so it is said, was frustrated in untying the Gordian knot at Gordium, so he cut it with his sword. It seems he did the right thing, as the domination of Asia – which he was supposed to gain by untying the knot – came to be his in record time. His sword-blow proved that he was an impetuous young man.

Alexander's effects on Anatolia were profound. He was the first of many rulers to attempt to meld western and eastern cultures (the Byzantines and the Ottomans followed suit). Upon his death in 323 BC, in Babylon, Alexander's empire was divided among his generals in a flurry of civil wars. Lysimachus claimed western and central Anatolia after winning the Battle of Ipsus in 301 BC, and he set his mark on the Ionian cities. Many Hellenistic buildings went up on his orders. Ancient Smyrna was abandoned and a brand-new city was built several km away, where the modern city stands.

But the civil wars continued, and Lysimachus was slain by Seleucus (king of Seleucid lands from 305 to 280 BC), another of Alexander's generals, at the Battle of Corupedium in 281 BC. Though Seleucus was in turn slain by Ptolemy Ceraunus, the kingdom of the Seleucids, based in Antioch (Antakya), was to rule a great part of the Middle East for the next century.

Meanwhile the next invaders, the Celts (or Gauls) this time, were storming through Macedonia on their way to Anatolia in 279 BC where they established the Kingdom of Galatia. The Galatians made Ancyra (Ankara) their capital and subjected the Aegean cities to their rule. The foundations of parts of the citadel in Ankara date from Galatian times.

While the Galatians ruled western Anatolia, Mithridates I had become king of Pontus, a state based in Trebizond (Trabzon) on the eastern Black Sea coast. At its height, the Pontic Kingdom extended all the way to Cappadocia in central Anatolia.

Still other small kingdoms flourished at this time, between 300 and 200 BC. A leader named Prusias founded the Kingdom of Bithynia and gave his name to the chief city: Prusa (Bursa). Nicaea (İznik, near Bursa) was also of great importance. And in southeastern Anatolia an Armenian kingdom grew up, centred on the town of Van. The Armenians, a Phrygian tribe, settled around Lake Van after the decline of Urartian power.

A fellow named Ardvates who ruled from 317 to 284 BC and was a Persian satrap (provincial governor) under the Seleucids, broke away from the Seleucid Kingdom to found the short-lived Kingdom of Armenia. The Seleucids later regained control, but lost it again as Armenia was split into two kingdoms, Greater and Lesser Armenia. Reunited in 94 BC under Tigranes I, the Kingdom of Armenia became very powerful for a short period (83-69 BC). Armenia finally fell to the Roman legions not long afterwards.

But the most impressive and powerful of Anatolia's many kingdoms at this time was Pergamum. Gaining tremendous power around 250 BC, the Pergamene king picked the right side to be on, siding with Rome early in the game. With Roman help, Pergamum threw off Seleucid rule and went on to challenge King Prusias of Bithynia (186 BC) and also King Pharnaces I of Pontus (183 BC).

The kings of Pergamum were great warriors, governors and also mad patrons of the arts, assembling an enormous library which rivalled that of Alexandria's. The Asclepion, or medical centre, at Pergamum was flourishing at this time, and continued to flourish for centuries under Roman rule. Greatest of the Pergamene kings was Eumenes II (197-159 BC), who ruled an enormous empire stretching from the Dardanelles to the Taurus Mountains near Syria. He was responsible for building much of what's left on Pergamum's acropolis, including the grand library.

Roman Times

The Romans took Anatolia almost by default. The various Anatolian kings couldn't refrain from picking away at Roman holdings and causing other sorts of irritation, so finally the legions marched in and took over. Defeating King Antiochus III of Seleucia at Magnesia (Manisa, near İzmir) in 190 BC, the Romans were content for the time being to leave 'Asia' (Anatolia) in the hands of the kings of Pergamum. But the last king, dying without an heir, bequeathed his kingdom to Rome (133 BC). In 129 BC, the Romans established the province of Asia, with its capital at Ephesus.

An interesting postscript to this period is the story of Commagene. This small and rather unimportant little kingdom in east-central Anatolia, near Adıyaman, left few marks on history. But the one notable reminder of Commagene is very notable indeed: on top of Nemrut Dağı (NEHM-root dah-uh, Mt Nimrod), Antiochus I (62-32 BC) built a mammoth, cone-shaped funerary mound framed by twin temples filled with huge stone statues portraying himself and the gods and goddesses who were his 'peers'. A visit to Nemrut Dağı, from the nearby town of Kahta, is one of the high points of a visit to Turkey.

Roman rule brought relative peace and prosperity for almost three centuries to

Anatolia, and provided the perfect conditions for the spread of a brand-new, world-class religion.

Early Christianity

Christianity began in Roman Palestine (Judaea), but its foremost proponent, St Paul, came from Tarsus in Cilicia, in what is now southern Turkey. Paul took advantage of the excellent Roman road system to spread the teachings of Jesus. When the Romans drove the Jews out of Judaea in 70 AD, Christian members of this Diaspora may have made their way to the numerous small Christian congregations in the Roman province of Asia.

On his first journey in about 47-49 AD, Paul went to Antioch, Seleucia (Silifke), and along the southern coast through Pamphylia (Side, Antalya) and up into the mountains. First stop was Antioch-in-Pisidia, today called Yalvaç, near Akşehir. Next he went to Iconium (Konya), the chief city in Galatia; Paul wrote an important 'Letter to the Galatians' which is now the ninth book of the New Testament.

From Iconium, Paul tramped to Lystra, 40 km south, and to Derbe nearby. Then it was back to Attaleia (Antalya) to catch a boat for Antioch. His second journey took him to some of these same cities, and later northwest to the district of Mysia where Troy (Truva) is located; then into Macedonia.

Paul's third trip (53-57) took in many of these same places, including Ancyra, Smyrna and Adramyttium (Edremit). On the way back he stopped in Ephesus, capital of Roman Asia and one of the greatest cities of the time. Here he ran into trouble because his teachings were ruining the market for silver effigies of the local favourite goddess, Cybele/Diana. The silversmiths led a riot, and Paul's companions were hustled into the great theatre for a sort of kangaroo court. Luckily, the authorities kept order: there was free speech in Ephesus; Paul and his companions had broken no laws; they were permitted to go freely. Later on this third journey Paul stopped in Miletus.

Paul got his last glimpses of Anatolia as he was being taken to Rome as a prisoner for trial on charges of inciting a riot in Jerusalem (59-60). He changed ships at Myra (Demre); further west, he was supposed to land at Cnidos, at the tip of the peninsula west of Marmaris, but stormy seas prevented this.

Other saints played a role in the life of Roman Asia as well. Tradition has it that St John retired to Ephesus to write the fourth gospel near the end of his life, and that he brought Jesus' mother Mary with him. John was buried on top of a hill in what is now the town of Selçuk, near Ephesus. The great, now ruined basilica of St John marks the site. As for Mary, she is said to have retired to a mountaintop cottage near Ephesus. The small chapel at Meryemana ('Mother Mary') is the site of a mass to celebrate her Assumption on 15 August.

The Seven Churches of the Revelation were the Seven Churches of Asia: Ephesus (Efes), Smyrna (İzmir), Pergamum (Bergama), Sardis (Sart, east of İzmir), Philadelphia (Alaşehir), Laodicea (Goncalı, between Denizli and Pamukkale) and Thyatira (Akhisar). 'Church' of course meant congregation, so don't go to these sites looking for the ruins of seven buildings.

The New Rome

Christianity was a struggling faith during the centuries of Roman rule. By 250 AD, the faith had grown strong enough and Roman rule so unsteady that the Roman emperor Decius decreed a general persecution of Christians. Not only this, but the empire was falling to pieces. Goths attacked the Aegean cities with fleets and later invaded Anatolia. The Persian Empire again threatened from the east. Diocletian (284-305) restored the empire somewhat, but continued the persecutions.

When Diocletian abdicated, Constantine battled for succession, which he won in 324. He united the empire, declared equal rights for all religions, and called the first ecumenical council to meet in Nicaea in 325.

Meanwhile, Constantine was building a great city on the site of Hellenic Byzantium. In 330 he dedicated it as New Rome, his capital city; it came to be called Constantinople. The emperor died seven years later in Nicomedia (İzmit, Kocaeli), east of his capital. On his deathbed he adopted Christianity.

Justinian

While the barbarians of Europe were sweeping down on weakened Rome, the eastern capital grew in wealth and strength. Emperor Justinian (527-65) brought the eastern Roman, or Byzantine, Empire to its greatest strength. He reconquered Italy, the Balkans, Anatolia, Egypt and North Africa, and further embellished Constantinople with great buildings. His personal triumph was the Church of the Holy Wisdom, or Sancta Sophia, which remained the most splendid church in Christendom for almost 1000 years, after which it became the most splendid mosque.

Justinian's successors were generally good, but not good enough, and the empire's conquests couldn't be maintained. Besides, something quite momentous was happening in Arabia.

Birth of Islam

Five years after the death of Justinian, Muhammed was born in Mecca. In 612 or so, while meditating, he heard the voice of God command him to 'recite'. Muhammed was to become the Messenger of God, communicating his holy word to people. The written record of these recitations, collected after Muhammed's death into a book by his family and followers, is the Koran.

The people of Mecca didn't take to Muhammed's preaching all at once. In fact, they forced him to leave Mecca, which he did, according to tradition, in the year 622. This 'flight' (*hijra* or *hegira*) is the starting-point for the Muslim lunar calendar.

Setting up house in Medina, Muhammed organised a religious commonwealth which over 10 years became so powerful that it could challenge and conquer Mecca (624-30). Before Muhammed died two years later, the Muslims (adherents of Islam, 'submission to God's will') had begun the conquest of other Arab tribes.

The story of militant Islam is one of history's most astounding tales. Fifty years after the Prophet's ignominious flight from Mecca, the armies of Islam were threatening the walls of Constantinople (669-78), having conquered everything and everybody from there to Mecca, plus Persia and Egypt. The Arabic Muslim empires that followed these conquests were among the world's greatest political, social and cultural achievements.

Muhammed was succeeded by caliphs, or deputies, whose job was to oversee the welfare of the Muslim commonwealth. His close companions got the job first, then his son-in-law Ali. After that, two great dynasties emerged: the Umayyads (661-750), whose empire was based in Damascus, and the Abbasids (750-1100), who ruled from Baghdad. Both continually challenged the power and status of Byzantium.

The Coming of the Turks

The history of the Turks as excellent soldiers goes back at least to the reign of the Abbasid caliph Al-Mutasim (833-42). This ruler formed an army of Turkish captives and mercenaries that became the empire's strength, and also its undoing. Later caliphs found that their protectors had become their masters, and the Turkish 'praetorian guard' raised or toppled caliphs as it chose.

The Seljuk Empire

The first great Turkish state to rule Anatolia was the Great Seljuk Turkish Empire (1037-1109), based in Persia. Coming from Central Asia, the Turks captured Baghdad (1055). In 1071, Seljuk armies decisively defeated the Byzantines at Manzikert (Malazgırt), taking the Byzantine emperor as a prisoner. The Seljuks then took over most of Anatolia and established a provincial capital at Nicaea. Their domains now included today's Turkey, Iran and Iraq. Their empire developed a distinctive culture, with especially beautiful architecture and design; the Great Seljuks also produced Omar Khayyam (died 1123). Politically, however, the Great Seljuk Turkish Empire declined quickly, in the style of Alexander the Great's empire, with various pieces being taken by generals.

A remnant of the Seljuk Empire lived on in Anatolia, based in Iconium. Called the Seljuk Sultanate of Rum ('Rome', meaning Roman Asia), it continued to flourish, producing great art and great thinkers until it was overrun by the Mongol hordes in 1243. Celaleddin Rumi or 'Mevlana', founder of the Mevlevi (Whirling) Dervish order, is perhaps the Sultanate of Rum's outstanding thinker.

The Crusades

These 'holy wars', created to provide work for the lesser nobles and riffraff of Europe, proved disastrous for the Byzantine emperors. Although a combined Byzantine and crusader army captured Nicaea from the Seljuks in 1097, the crusaders were mostly an unhelpful, unruly bunch. The Fourth Crusade (1202-04) saw European ragtag armies invade and plunder Christian Constantinople. This was the first and most horrible defeat for the great city, and it was carried out by 'friendly' armies.

Having barely recovered from the ravages of the crusades, the Byzantines were greeted with a new and greater threat: the Ottomans.

Founding of the Ottoman Empire

In the late 13th century, Byzantine weakness left a power vacuum which was filled by bands of Turks fleeing westwards from the Mongols. Warrior bands, each led by a warlord, took over parts of the Aegean and Marmara coasts. The Turks who moved into Bithynia, around Bursa, were followers of a man named Ertuğrul. His son, Osman, founded a principality (circa 1288) which was to grow into the Osmanlı (Ottoman) Empire.

The Ottomans took Bursa in 1326. It served them well as their first capital city. But they were vigorous and ambitious, and by 1402 they moved the capital to Adrianople (Edirne) because it was easier to rule their Balkan conquests from there. Constantinople was still in Byzantine hands.

The Turkish advance spread rapidly to both east and west, despite some setbacks. By 1452, under Mehmet the Conqueror, they were strong enough to think of taking Constantinople, capital of eastern Christendom, which they did in 1453. Mehmet's reign (1451-81) began the great era of Ottoman power.

Süleyman the Magnificent

The height of Ottoman glory was under Sultan Süleyman the Magnificent (1520-66). Called the 'Lawgiver' by the Turks, he beautified İstanbul, rebuilt Jerusalem and expanded Ottoman power to the gates of Vienna in 1529. The Ottoman fleet under Barbaros Hayrettin Paşa seemed invincible, but by 1585 the empire had begun its long and celebrated decline. Most of the sultans after Süleyman were incapable of great rule. Luckily for the empire, there were very competent and talented men to serve as grand viziers, ruling the empire in the sultans' stead.

Süleyman I, sultan of the Ottoman Empire between 1520 and 1566, was known also as Sultan the Magnificent or the Lawgiver. He undertook several military campaigns which saw the empire grow, and built the naval strength of the empire to seemingly invincible levels. He was also responsible for building many public works – mosques, aqueducts, bridges – particualy in İstanbul, the capital of the empire.

KIM GRANT

TOM BROSNAHAN

TOM BROSNAHAN

TOM BROSNAHAN

Top Left: A woman performs needlework in the popular holiday resort of Kaş.
Top Right A çaycı (tea waiter) serves Turkish tea, a hearty and full-flavoured brew.
Bottom Left: A *piyangocu* (lottery–ticket seller) in İstanbul.
Bottom Right: A dignified haji quenches your thirst in İstanbul's Hippodrome.

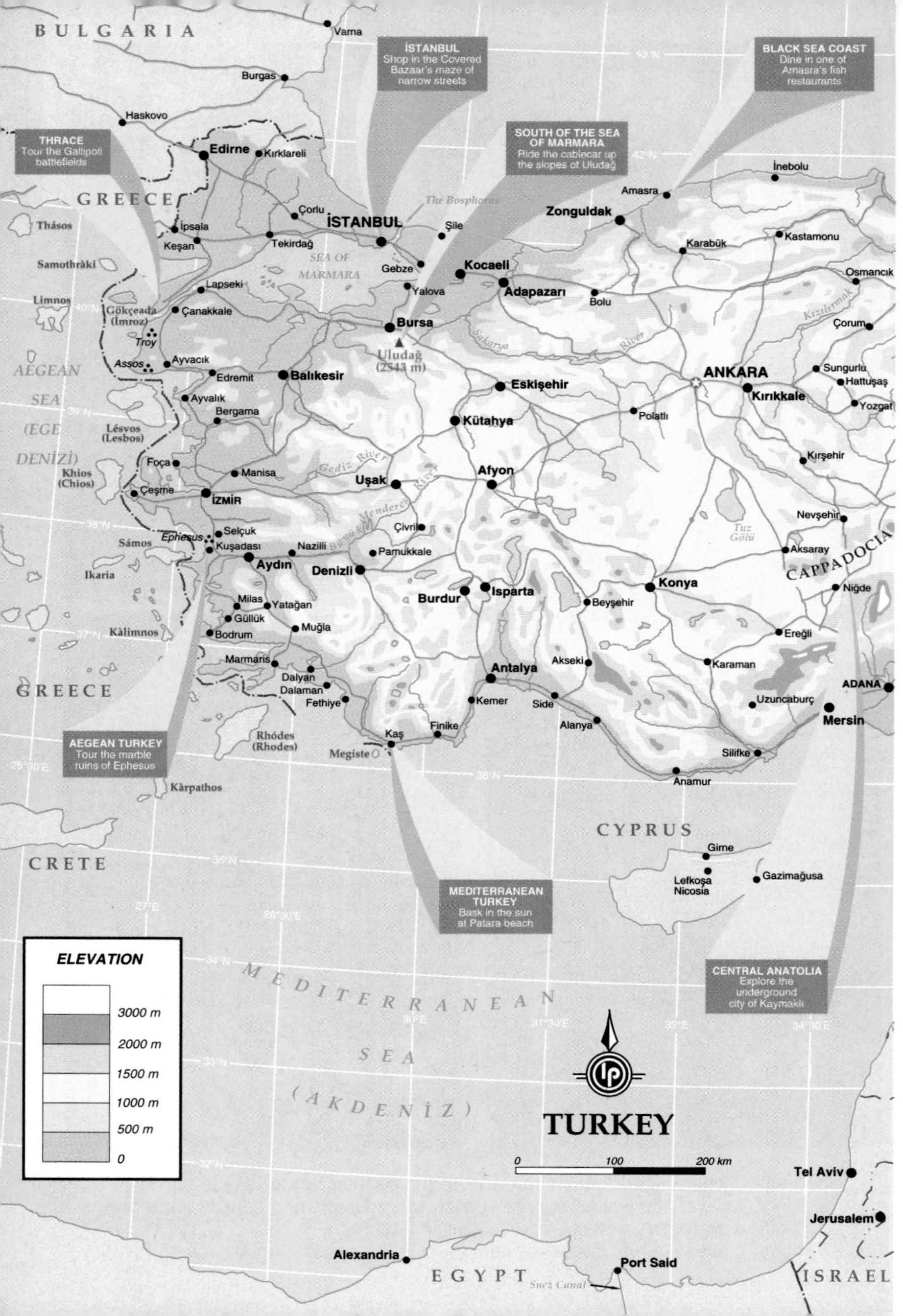

TURKEY
ISTANBUL
Shop in the Covered Bazaar's maze of narrow streets
BLACK SEA COAST
Dine in one of Amasra's fish restaurants
THRACE
Tour the Gallipoli battlefields
SOUTH OF THE SEA OF MARMARA
Ride the cablecar up the slopes of Uludağ
AEGEAN TURKEY
Tour the marble ruins of Ephesus
MEDITERRANEAN TURKEY
Bask in the sun at Patara beach
CENTRAL ANATOLIA
Explore the underground city of Kaymaklı
ELEVATION
3000 m
2000 m
1500 m
1000 m
500 m
0
0
100
200 km
BULGARIA
GREECE
CYPRUS
CRETE
EGYPT
ISRAEL
AEGEAN SEA (EGE DENİZİ)
MEDITERRANEAN SEA (AKDENİZ)
SEA OF MARMARA
CAPPADOCIA
The Bosphorus
Varna
Burgas
Haskovo
Edirne
Kırklareli
Çorlu
İSTANBUL
Şile
İpsala
Keşan
Tekirdağ
Gebze
Yalova
Kocaeli
Adapazarı
Bolu
Zonguldak
Amasra
İnebolu
Karabük
Kastamonu
Osmancık
Çorum
Lapseki
Çanakkale
Gökçeada (İmroz)
Troy
Assos
Ayvacık
Edremit
Balıkesir
Bursa
Uludağ (2543 m)
Eskişehir
ANKARA
Kırıkkale
Sungurlu
Hattuşaş
Yozgat
Polatlı
Kütahya
Ayvalık
Bergama
Foça
Manisa
Kırşehir
Uşak
Afyon
Çeşme
İZMİR
Nevşehir
Selçuk
Ephesus
Kuşadası
Nazilli
Çivril
Pamukkale
Aydın
Denizli
Tuz Gölü
Aksaray
Konya
Niğde
Burdur
Isparta
Beyşehir
Milas
Yatağan
Güllük
Bodrum
Muğla
Ereğli
Marmaris
Dalyan
Dalaman
Fethiye
Antalya
Akseki
Karaman
Kemer
Side
Alanya
Uzuncaburç
ADANA
Mersin
Kaş
Finike
Megiste
Silifke
Anamur
Thásos
Samothràki
Limnos
Lésvos (Lesbos)
Khios (Chios)
Sámos
Ikaria
Kàlimnos
Rhódes (Rhodes)
Kàrpathos
Girne
Lefkoşa Nicosia
Gazimağusa
Tel Aviv
Jerusalem
Alexandria
Port Said
Suez Canal
Gediz River
Menderes River
Sakarya River
Kızılırmak
43°N
42°N
40°N
39°N
38°N
37°N
36°N
35°N
34°N
33°N
32°N
25°30'E
27°E
28°30'E
30°E
31°30'E
33°E
34°30'E

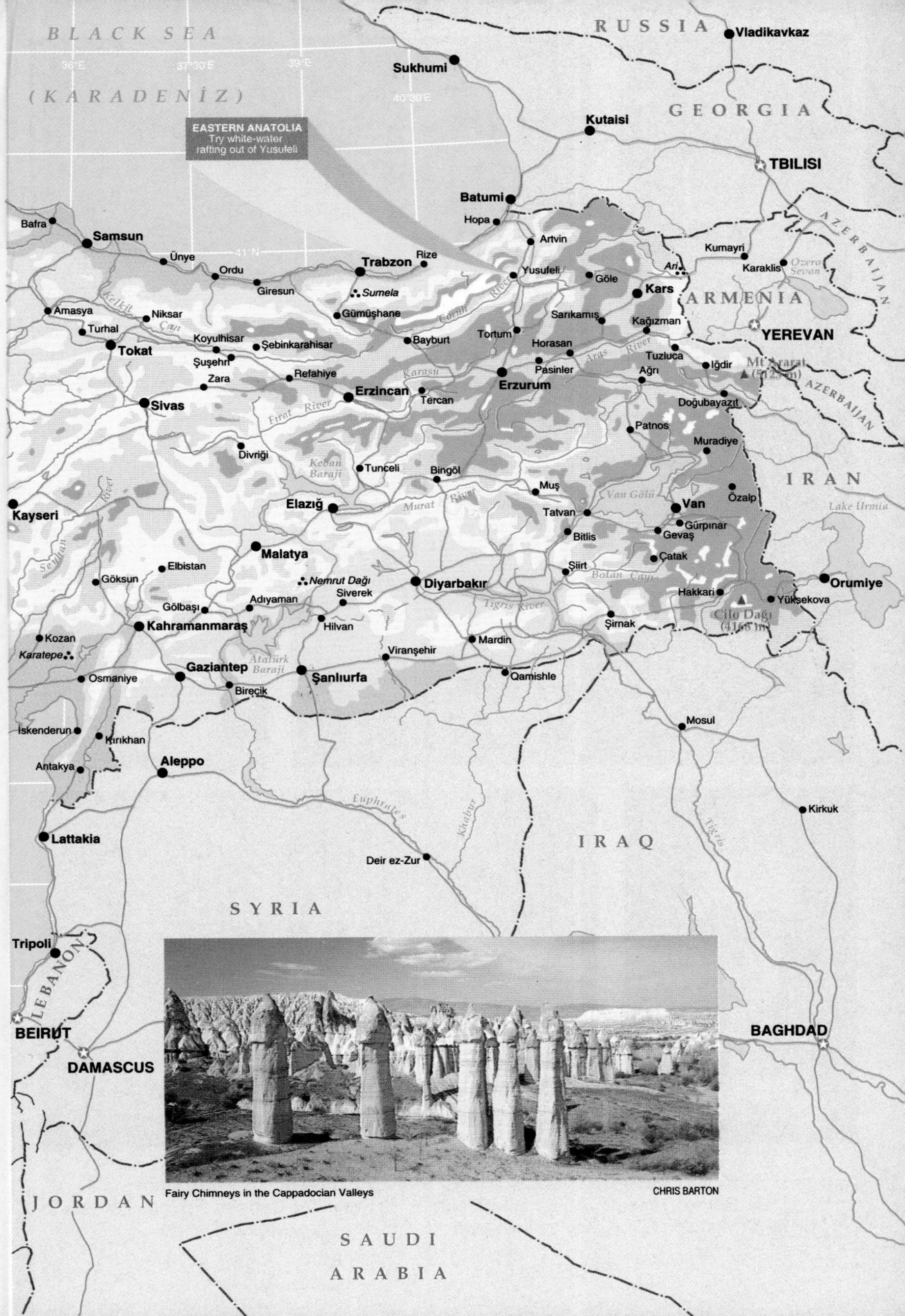

Fairy Chimneys in the Cappadocian Valleys

TOM BROSNAHAN

TOM BROSNAHAN

TOM BROSNAHAN

TOM BROSNAHAN

TOM BROSNAHAN

TOM BROSNAHAN

A	B
C	D
E	F

A: Marble torsos in the Side Museum
B: Roman mosaic, Antakya Museum
C: Mosaic ceiling, Kariye Museum
D: Stone head, Nemrut Dağı
E: Statue of Cybele, Ephesus Museum
F: Funerary stone, Aizanoi

The Later Empire

By 1699, Europeans no longer feared an invasion by the 'terrible Turk'. The empire was still vast and powerful, but it had lost its momentum and was rapidly dropping behind the west in terms of social, military, scientific and material progress. In the 19th century, several sultans undertook important reforms. Selim III, for instance, revised taxation, commerce and the military. But the Janissaries (members of the sultan's personal guard) and other conservative elements resisted the new measures strongly, and sometimes violently.

For centuries, the non-Turkish ethnic and religious minorities in the sultan's domains had lived side by side with their Turkish neighbours, governed by their own religious and traditional laws. (The head of each community – chief rabbi, Orthodox patriarch, etc was responsible to the sultan for the community's well-being and behaviour.) But in the 19th century, strong currents of ethnic nationalism flowed eastward from Europe. Decline and misrule made nationalism very appealing. The subject peoples of the Ottoman Empire revolted, often with the direct encouragement and assistance of the European powers. After bitter fighting in 1832, the Kingdom of Greece was formed; the Serbs, Bulgarians, Rumanians, Albanians, Armenians and Arabs would all seek their independence soon after.

As the empire broke up, the European powers (Britain, France, Italy, Germany, Russia) hovered in readiness to colonise or annex the pieces. They used religion as a reason for pressure or control, saying that it was their duty to protect the Catholic, Protestant or Orthodox subjects from misrule and anarchy. The holy places in Palestine were a favourite target, and each power tried to obtain a foothold here for colonisation later.

The Russian emperors put pressure on the Turks to grant them powers over all Ottoman Orthodox subjects, whom the Russian emperor would thus 'protect'. The result of this pressure was the Crimean War (1853-56), with Britain and France fighting on the side of the Ottomans against the Russians.

In the midst of imperial dissolution, western-style reforms were proposed in an attempt to revivify the moribund empire and make it compatible with modern Europe. Mithat Paşa, a successful general and powerful grand vizier, brought the young crown prince Abdülhamid II (1876-1909) to the throne along with a constitution in 1876. But the new sultan did away both with Mithat Paşa and the constitution, and established his own absolute rule.

Abdülhamid modernised without democratising, building thousands of km of railways and telegraph lines, and encouraging modern industry, keeping watch on everything through an extensive spy network. But the empire continued to disintegrate, with nationalist insurrections in Crete, Armenia, Bulgaria and Macedonia.

The younger generation of the Turkish elite watched bitterly as the country fell apart, then organised into secret societies bent on toppling the sultan. The Young Turk movement for western-style reforms gained enough power by 1908 to force the restoration of the constitution. In 1909, the Young Turk-led Ottoman parliament deposed Abdülhamid and put his weak-willed, indecisive brother Mehmet V ('Vahdettin') on the throne.

In its last years, though a sultan still sat on the throne, the Ottoman Empire was ruled by three members of the Young Turks' Committee of Union & Progress, named Talat, Enver and Jemal. Their rule was vigorous, but harsh and misguided, and it only worsened an already hopeless situation. When WWI broke out, they made the fatal error of siding with Germany and the Central Powers. With their defeat, the Ottoman Empire collapsed. İstanbul and several other parts of Anatolia were occupied, and the sultan became a pawn in the hands of the victors.

The victorious Allies had been planning, since the beginning of the war, how they would carve up the Ottoman Empire. They even promised certain lands to several different peoples or factions in order to get their support for the war effort (as when Palestine was promised both to Jews and Arabs). With

Gazi Osman Paşa

Gazi Osman Paşa was born into a relatively poor Tokat family in 1832 but grew up to become one of Turkey's most famous soldiers, serving in the army in Thessaly, Crete, Bosnia-Herzegovina and Yemen. After a great victory in the Ottoman-Serbian War of 1875-76 he became a marshal.

Later when the Russians crossed the Danube during the Ottoman-Russian War, Osman was ordered to defend Plevne in Bulgaria. He did this by surrounding the town with earthworks and attempting to sit out a five-month siege by a Russian force twice the size of his own. When the siege showed no sign of lifting, he was forced to try and fight his way out of Plevne. Taken captive with serious injuries, he was treated as a great hero by a Russian tsar astonished at his fortitude.

Equally impressed, Sultan Abulhamid II bestowed the title of Gazi (Conqueror) on him, together with a sword encrusted with diamonds. Osman became commander-in-chief and then marshal of the Sultan's household.

Gazi Osman Paşa died in İstanbul in 1900 but there's hardly a Turkish town which doesn't commemorate him in a street name. ■

the end of the war, these promises came due. With more promises than territory, the Allies decided on the dismemberment of Anatolia itself in order to get more land with which to satisfy the ambitions of the victorious countries. The choicest bits of Anatolia were to be given to Christian peoples, with the Muslim Turks relegated to a small land-locked region of semi-barren steppe.

The Turkish Republic

The situation looked very bleak for the Turks as their armies were being disbanded and their country taken under the control of the Allies. But a catastrophe turned things around.

Ever since gaining independence in 1831, the Greeks had entertained the *Megali Idea* (Great Plan) of a new Greek empire encompassing all the lands which had once had Greek influence – in effect, the refounding of the Byzantine Empire. During WWI, the Allies had offered Greece the Ottoman city of Smyrna. King Constantine declined for various reasons, even though his prime minister, Eleutherios Venizelos, wanted to accept. After the war, however, Alexander became king, Venizelos became prime minister again, and Britain encouraged the Greeks to go ahead and take Smyrna. On 15 May 1919, they did.

The Turks, depressed and hopeless over the occupation of their country and the powerlessness of the sultan, couldn't take this: a former subject people capturing an Ottoman city and pushing inland with great speed and ferocity. Even before the Greek invasion, an Ottoman general named Mustafa Kemal had decided that a new government must take over the destiny of the Turks from the powerless sultan. He began organising resistance on 19 May 1919. The Greek invasion was just the shock needed to galvanise the people and lead them to his way of thinking.

The Turkish War of Independence lasted from 1920 to 1922. In September 1921 the Greeks very nearly reached Ankara, the nationalist headquarters, but in desperate fighting the Turks held them off. A year later, the Turks began their counteroffensive and drove the Greek armies back to İzmir by 9 September 1922.

Victory in the bitterly fought war made Mustafa Kemal even more of a national hero. He was now fully in command of the fate of the Turks. The sultanate was abolished and, after it, the Ottoman Empire. A Turkish republic was born, based in Anatolia and eastern Thrace. The treaties of WWI, which had left the Turks with almost no country, were renegotiated.

Ethnic Greeks in Turkey and ethnic Turks in Greece were required to leave their ancestral homes and move to their respective ethnic nation-states; Greeks from İzmir moved into the houses of Turks in Salonika, whose owners had moved to İzmir, and so forth. Venizelos even came to terms with Kemal, signing a treaty in 1930.

Atatürk's Reforms

Mustafa Kemal undertook the job of completely remaking a society. After the republic was declared in 1923, a constitution was adopted (1924); polygamy was abolished and the fez, mark of Ottoman backwardness, was prohibited (1925); new, western-style legal codes were instituted, and civil (not religious) marriage was required (1926); Islam was removed as the state religion, and the Arabic alphabet was replaced by a modified Latin one (1928). In 1930, Constantinople officially became İstanbul, and other city names were officially Turkified (Angora to Ankara, Smyrna to İzmir, Adrianople to Edirne etc). Women obtained the right to vote and serve in parliament in 1934.

In 1935, Mustafa Kemal sponsored one of the most curious laws of modern times. Up to this time, Muslims had only one given name. Family names were purely optional. So he decided that all Turks should choose a family name, and they did. He himself was proclaimed Atatürk, or 'Father Turk', by the Turkish parliament, and officially became Kemal Atatürk.

Atatürk lived and directed the country's destiny until 10 November 1938. He saw WWII coming, and was anxious that Turkey stay out of it. His friend and successor as president of the republic, İsmet İnönü, succeeded in preserving a precarious neutrality. Ankara became a hotbed of Allied-Axis spying, but the Turks stayed out of the conflict.

Recent Years

In its early years, Atatürk's Republican Peoples' Party was the only political party allowed. But between 1946 and 1950 true democracy was instituted, and the opposition Democratic Party won the election in 1950.

By 1960 the Democratic Party had acquired so much power that the democratic system was threatened. The army, charged by Atatürk to protect democracy and the constitution, stepped in and brought various Democratic Party leaders to trial on charges of violating the constitution. The popular Peron-like party leader, Adnan Menderes, was executed, though all other death sentences were commuted. Elections were held in 1961.

In 1970 there was a polite coup d'état again because the successor to the Democratic Party had overreached its bounds. High-ranking military officers entered the national broadcasting headquarters and read a short message, and the government fell.

Under the careful watch of those same officers, democracy returned and things went well for years, until political infighting and civil unrest brought the country to a virtual halt in 1980. On the left side of the political spectrum, Soviet-bloc countries pumped in arms and money for destabilisation and, it is claimed, supported Armenian terrorist elements who murdered Turkish diplomats and their families abroad. On the right side of the spectrum, fanatical Muslim religious groups and a neo-Nazi party caused havoc. In the centre, the two major political parties were deadlocked so badly in parliament that for months they couldn't even elect a parliamentary president.

The economy was in bad shape, inflation was 130% per year, the law-makers were not making laws, and crime in the streets by the fringe elements of left and right was epidemic. The military stepped in again on 12 September 1980, much to the relief of the general population, and restored civil, fiscal and legal order, but at the price of strict control and some human rights abuses.

The constitution was rewritten so as to avoid parliamentary impasses. In a controlled plebiscite, it was approved by the voters. The head of the military government, General Kenan Evren, resigned his military commission (as Atatürk had done) and became the country's new president. The old political leaders, seen by the new government to have been responsible for the breakdown of society, were tried (if they had committed crimes) or excluded from political life for 10 years, though many returned to politics before this time was up.

In 1983, elections under the new constitution

Atatürk

It won't take you long to discover the national hero, Kemal Atatürk. Though he died on 10 November 1938, his picture is everywhere in Turkey – a bust or statue (preferably equestrian) is in every park, quotations from his speeches and writings are on every public building. He is almost synonymous with the Turkish Republic.

The best popular account of his life and times is Lord Kinross's *Atatürk: The Rebirth of a Nation.* Kinross portrayed Atatürk as a man of great intelligence and even greater energy and daring, possessed by the idea of giving his fellow Turks a new lease of life. In contrast to many leaders, he had the capability of realising his obsession almost single-handedly. His achievement in turning a backward empire into a forward-looking nation-state was taken as a model by former Egyptian president Nasser, the shahs of Iran and other Islamic leaders.

Early Years In 1881, a boy named Mustafa was born into the family of a minor Turkish bureaucrat living in Salonika – now the Greek city of Thessaloniki, but at that time a city in Ottoman Macedonia. Mustafa was smart and a hard worker at school. His mathematics teacher was so impressed that he gave him the nickname Kemal (excellence). The name Mustafa Kemal stuck with him as he went through a military academy and the war college, and even as he pursued his duties as an officer.

Military Career He served with distinction and acquired a reputation as something of a hothead, perhaps because his commanders were not as bold as he was. By the time of the battle at Gallipoli in WWI, he was a promising lieutenant colonel of infantry.

The defence of Gallipoli, which saved Constantinople from British conquest (until the end of the war, at least), was a personal triumph for Mustafa Kemal. His strategic and tactical genius came into full play. His commanders had little to do but approve his suggestions; he led with utter disregard for his own safety. A vastly superior British force (including Anzacs from Australia and New Zealand) was driven away, and Mustafa Kemal became an Ottoman folk hero.

Though he was promoted to the rank of *paşa* ('pasha', general), the powers-that-be wanted to keep him under control. They saw him as a 'dangerous element', and they were right. When the war was lost and the empire was on the verge of being disarmed and dismembered, Mustafa Kemal Pasha began his revolution.

The Revolution He held meetings and congresses to rally the people, began to establish democratic institutions and held off several invading armies (French, Italian and Greek). He did all of this at the same time with severely limited resources. Several times the whole effort almost collapsed, and many of his friends and advisors were ready to ride for their lives out of Ankara. But Kemal never flinched and was always ready to dare the worst.

He was skilful and fortunate enough to carry it through. Many great revolutionary leaders falter or fade when the revolution is won. Atatürk lived 15 years into the republican era, and he had no doubts about what the new country's course should be. He introduced reforms and directed the country's progress with surprising foresight. ■

were held, and the centre-right Anavatan Partisi (Motherland Party), the one less favoured by the military caretakers, won handily. The new prime minister was Turgut Özal, a former World Bank economist, who instituted economic liberalisations and precipitated a business boom which lasted through the 1980s. Özal's untimely death in April 1993 removed a powerful, innovative force from Turkish politics. (For details of current politics, see Political Parties under Government in this chapter.)

GEOGRAPHY

Most first-time visitors come to Turkey expecting to find deserts, palm trees and camel caravans. In fact, the country is geographically diverse, with snow-capped mountains, rolling steppe, broad rivers, verdant coasts and rich agricultural valleys.

It's interesting to note that Ankara, the country's capital, is at a latitude similar to that of Naples, Lisbon, Beijing, and Philadelphia. The southernmost shore of Turkey is similar in latitude to Tokyo, Seoul, Gibraltar and San Francisco.

Distances

Turkey is big: the road distance from Edirne on the Bulgarian border to Kars on the Armenian one is over 1700 km. From the Black Sea shore to the Mediterranean coast it's almost 1000 km. Now, 1000 km on flat ground might take only one very long day to drive, but Turkey has many mountain ranges which can lengthen travel times considerably.

Geographic Statistics

Turkey is between 35° and 42° north latitude, and 25° and 44° east longitude. It covers 779,452 sq km and has borders with Armenia, Bulgaria, Georgia, Greece, Iran, Iraq and Syria. The coastline totals almost 8400 km – the Aegean coastline alone is 2800 km long. As for mountains, the highest is Ağrı Dağı (Mt Ararat) at 5165m. Uludağ (Mt Olympus) near Bursa is 2543m high. During imperial times, snow and ice could be taken from Uludağ, sailed across the Sea of Marmara, and presented to the sultan in İstanbul to cool his drinks.

CLIMATE

Going from west to east, here's the lay of the land. See also the climate graphs on the following page. For temperature conversion, see the table at the back of the book.

Marmara

The Marmara region includes eastern Thrace from Edirne to İstanbul, with rolling steppe and low hills good for grazing, some farming and industry. The peninsula of Gelibolu (Gallipoli) forms the north shore of the Çanakkale Boğazı (the Dardanelles or Hellespont). On the southern shore of the Sea of Marmara are low hills and higher mountains (including Uludağ). The land is very rich, excellent for producing fruit such as grapes, peaches and apricots. Average rainfall is 668 mm; temperature extremes are 40.5°C maximum and -16.1°C minimum. This is Turkey's second most humid region, with an annual average of 73% humidity.

Aegean

Fertile plains and river valleys, low hills and not-so-low mountains make up the Aegean region. The ancient river Meander, now called the Menderes, is a good example of the Aegean's rivers. When you see it from the heights of ruined Priene, you'll know where the word 'meander' comes from. When travelling, the Aegean region presents constantly changing views of olive, fig and fruit orchards on hillsides, and broad tobacco and sunflower fields in the valleys. The maximum temperature is 42.7°C, the minimum is -8.2°C. Average humidity is 69%; average annual rainfall is 647 mm.

Mediterranean

The Mediterranean coast is mountainous without much beach between Fethiye and Antalya, but then opens up into a fertile plain between Antalya and Alanya before turning into mountains again. All along the south coast mountains loom to the north. The great

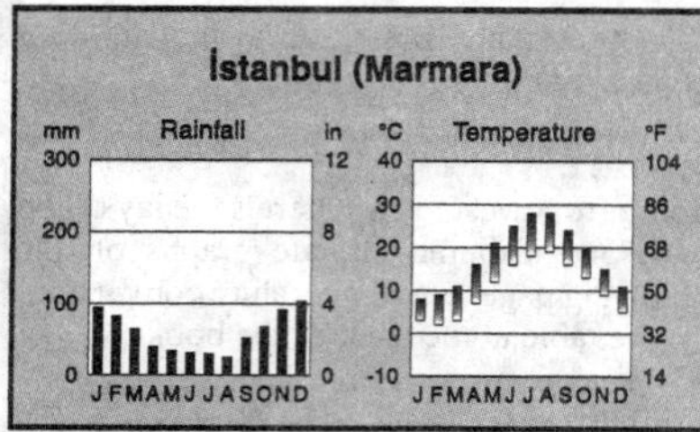

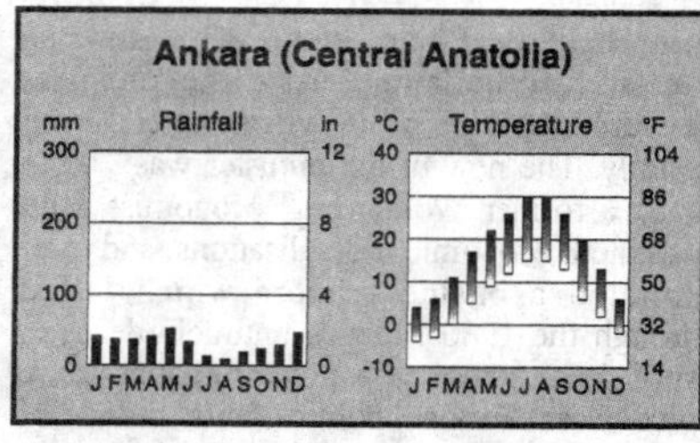

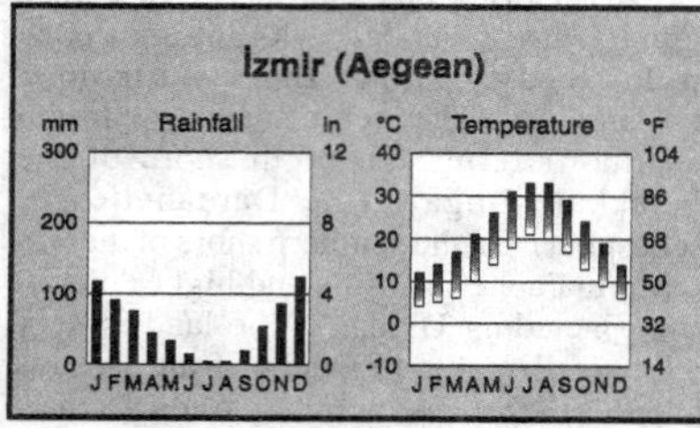

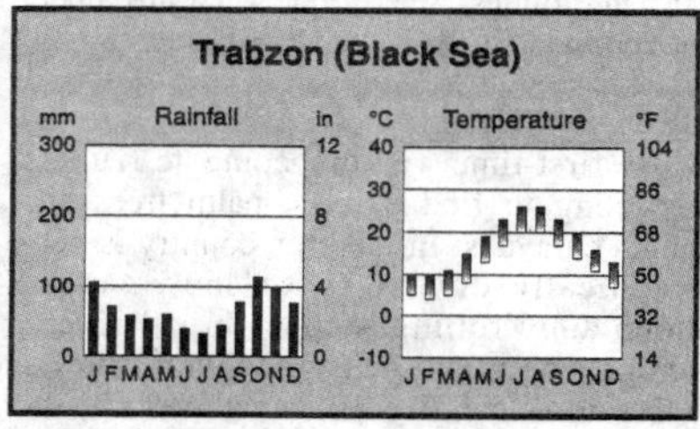

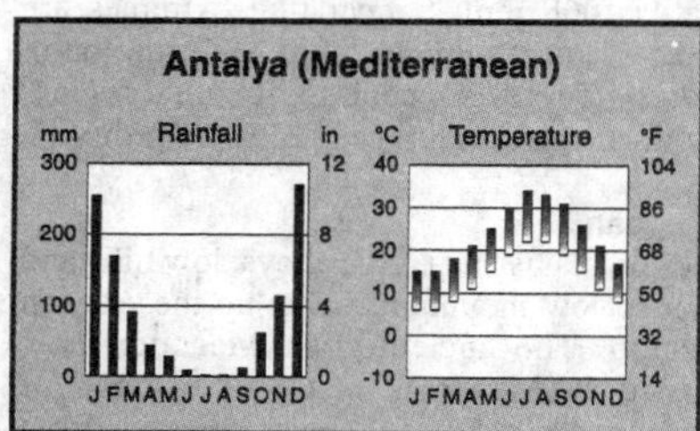

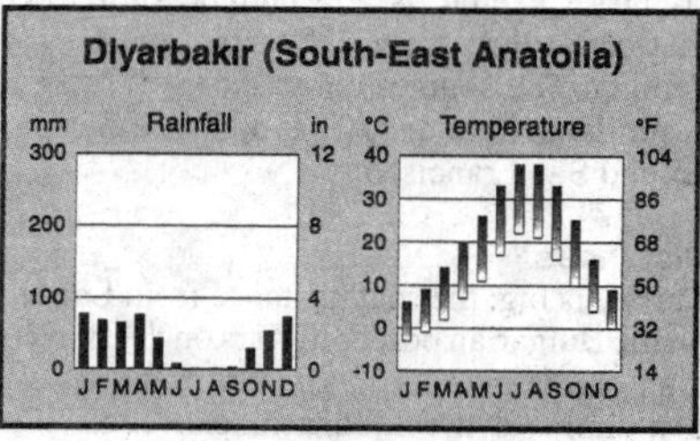

Taurus range stretches all the way from Alanya east to Adana. Temperatures at Antalya are a few degrees warmer than at İzmir. The eastern Mediterranean coast is always very humid. The maximum temperature is 44.6°C, and the minimum is -4.6°C. Annual precipitation is 777 mm; average humidity is 69%.

Central Anatolia

The Turkish heartland of Central Anatolia is a vast high plateau broken by mountain ranges, including some volcanoes with snow-capped peaks. The land is mostly rolling steppe, good for growing wheat and grazing sheep. Ankara's elevation is 900m above sea level. In summer, Ankara is hot and dry; in winter, it's chilly and often damp. Late spring and early autumn are perfect. The maximum temperature is 40°C, the minimum is -24.9°C. Annual rainfall is a low 382 mm; average humidity is 62%.

Black Sea

The Black Sea coast, 1700 km long, has a climate you might not expect to find in this part of the world. Rainfall is two to three times the national average, and temperatures are moderate. You will see hazelnut groves (on which the economy depends heavily), cherry orchards and tobacco fields. This is where cherries originated, getting their name in Roman times: the root word of 'cherry' is the Latin *cerasus* (Turkish: *kiraz).* The cattle on the outskirts of every town provide milk, cream and butter famous throughout Turkey. At the eastern end of the Black Sea coast, the mountains come right down to the sea, and the slopes are covered with tea plantations. Rainfall and humidity are highest here. All in all, the Black Sea coast is like central Europe, but pleasantly warmer. The maximum temperature is 40.5°C, the minimum is -8°C. Annual rainfall is 781 mm and average humidity is 72%.

South-East Anatolia

The region of south-east Anatolia is of rolling steppe with outcrops of rock. The major rivers are the Tigris (Dicle) and the Euphrates (Fırat), both of which have their sources in Turkey. With 576 mm rainfall per year, it is very dry and hot in summer, with maximum temperatures reaching 46.5°C. Minimums are around -12°C. Average humidity, at 52%, is the lowest in Turkey. The climate produces bumper crops if there's water. The mammoth GAP hydroelectric project now provides irrigation water in abundance.

Eastern Anatolia

A mountainous and somewhat forbidding zone, this is a wildly beautiful region like no other in Turkey. The average temperature is a cool 9.5°C, but varies between a hot 38°C and a daunting -43.2°C. It's cold out here except from June to September. The rainfall is average for Turkey, about 560 mm per year. The people are not as rich as in other regions, but they do well enough grazing sheep, growing wheat and producing a few other crops.

ECOLOGY & ENVIRONMENT

Turkey is one of those countries straddling the environmental dilemma. Much of the country still lives in the pre-pollution era of frugal living, home-made goods and dung-cake fuel, but urban dwellers are well into the lifestyle of quickly changing fashion and disposable everything. Village dwellers are just leaving the era when environmental concern was not necessary, and urbanites are just discovering it as a major problem.

There is an environmental movement in Turkey, and it is making some progress. Some cities attempt to recycle glass and metal, and Bosphorus restaurants now seem to refrain from disposing of food waste right into the water. Sewage treatment plants are being built, but as these projects are expensive and Turkey is hardly a rich country, it will take time. At least vessels – including yachts – in Turkish waters are prohibited by law from emptying waste into the seas, though it still happens because of insufficient enforcement.

The best thing that you, the traveller, can do to help the cause of environmental protection in Turkey is to set a good example and encourage local efforts. Despite the insufficient number of rubbish bins, don't litter, and if you see others littering, suggest that they dispose of it properly. Complain to local tourism offices about litter on beaches or sewage near swimming areas. Ask for non-smoking buses, even if it's plain that none exist on your route.

Remember always that you are a guest in Turkey, and that Turkey does not yet have anywhere near the financial resources or technical expertise – or force of public concern – for these issues as exists in the western countries. A superior, preachy attitude may do more harm than good, but acting the part of environmental advocate will hasten the adoption of similar attitudes by the Turks.

FLORA & FAUNA

Once cloaked in dense forest, after millennia of woodcutting Anatolia is now largely denuded. The government encourages conservation and reforestation, but the great forests will never return. The Mediterranean coast west of Antalya, the Black Sea area and north-eastern Anatolia still have forests of considerable size. Elsewhere, the great swaths of wild flowers which cover the rolling steppes in spring make fine splashes of colour.

Because of Turkey's temperate climate,

domesticated plants such as apples, apricots, bananas, cherries, citrus fruit, cotton, date palms, grapes, sugar beet, sunflowers and tobacco thrive. The long roots of deliciously sweet *kavun* melons go deep into the dry soil of the Anatolian Plateau to find water. Turkey grows much of the world's supply of hazelnuts (filberts), and a large volume of pistachios and walnuts. Of the cash crops, cotton is king, and grains such as wheat and barley are important.

Turkey has similar animal life to that in the Balkans and much of Europe: bears, deer, jackals, lynx, wild boars, wolves and rare leopards. Besides the usual domestic animals such as cattle, horses, donkeys, goats and several varieties of sheep (including the fat-tail), there are camels and water buffalo. (Though most yoghurt is made from cow's milk, that from sheep's milk is richer, and that from water buffalo's milk is richer still.)

Turkish shepherds are proud of their big, powerful and fierce Kangal sheep dogs which guard the flocks from hungry wolves. The breed is now controlled, and export is only allowed under licence. The same goes for the beautiful Van cats, with pure white fur and different-coloured eyes – one blue, one green.

Bird life is exceptionally rich, with many eagles, vultures and storks, as well as rare species such as the bald ibis, now nearly extinct except for a few birds which visit Birecik, between Gaziantep and Şanlıurfa, each year. In several parts of the country reserves have been set aside as *kuş cenneti* (bird paradises).

Turkey's coastal waters have rich varieties of fish, shellfish and other sea creatures, though overfishing and pollution are now serious problems.

GOVERNMENT & POLITICS

Parliament

Turkey is a parliamentary democracy. The Turkish Grand National Assembly (TGNA), elected by all citizens over 19 years of age, is the direct descendant of the congress assembled by Atatürk during the War of Independence to act as the legitimate voice of the Turkish people in place of the sultan.

President & Prime Minister

The president, elected by the TGNA from among its members, serves for one seven-year term and is supposed to be 'above politics', and symbolise the nation. He or she is the head of state, with important executive powers and responsibilities. The true head of government, who decides its policies and directions, is the prime minister. However, recent presidents (Özal and Demirel) have informally expanded the powers of the presidential office and have been accused at times of having used the office with partisan effect.

The prime minister is appointed by the president to form a government, and thus is almost always the head of the majority party, or of a likely coalition.

The judiciary, though theoretically independent, has in many instances been influenced by current government policies.

Political Parties

Though the Turks are firm believers in democracy, the tradition of popular rule and responsibility is relatively short. Real multi-party democracy came into being only after WWII (compared to England's tradition of almost 800 years). Turkish democracy has had its ups and downs.

Mid-Century Atatürk's Republican People's Party (CHP) enjoyed one-party rule until after WWII, when multi-party democracy became a reality. In the first elections the CHP lost out to the right-wing Democratic Party (DP), which attempted to control the government as closely as the CHP had before the war by grabbing extra-constitutional power. The Turkish armed forces, entrusted by Atatürk's legacy as guarantors of the Turkish constitution, intervened.

After the military intervention of 1960, the Democratic Party was banned, but its party faithful simply formed a successor, the similarly centre-right Justice Party (AP), and did as well in the elections against the centre-left CHP.

1960s Under the watchful eye of the military, the CHP and AP governed as a coalition until 1965, when the AP won a parliamentary majority on its own, and its leader, Süleyman Demirel, began his first term as prime minister. He stepped down at the insistence of the military in 1971 as left-right violence and parliamentary deadlock threatened public order.

1970s In 1973 a revivified CHP under Bülent Ecevit won election and formed a government, but was soon forced into coalition with the small far-right religious National Salvation Party (MSP).

During the 1970s the CHP and AP locked horns in parliament, both having around 40% of the votes. The smaller parties farther out on the political spectrum thus gained inordinate influence – their few votes making the difference between winning or losing a parliamentary vote. The Islamic fundamentalist MSP, the fascistic Nationalist Action Party (MHP), and the leftist Turkish Workers Party (TİP) all traded their support for control of various government ministries through which to push their agendas. The result was widespread civil violence and government paralysis.

1980s The bloodless military coup of September 1980 saw the dissolution of all former political parties and the exclusion from politics of their leaders (especially Ecevit and Demirel). In the elections of 1983, the armed forces supported a new centrist party formed of their supporters, but the new centre-right Motherland Party (ANAP) led by Turgut Özal won.

Özal was a financial technocrat and former World Bank economist who had helped the military to revivify the economy after the 1980 intervention. His

Army Days

To the Turks, military service is an honourable duty with a long and glorious history.

The Turkish people trace their lineage all the way back to the ancient Turkish states in Dzungaria around 2000 BC, but the earliest great Turkish empire dependent upon military prowess was that of the Huns around 220 BC. Through the Göktürks (552-745 AD), the Avars (565-835 AD), the Uygurs (745-940), the Karahanlıs (940-1040), the Ghaznavids (962-1187), the Great Seljuks (990-1157), and the Ottomans (1281-1922), Turkey's armed forces retained a central role in government and society. In other societies such as the Arab and Mameluke empires, Turks formed the military caste. To be a Turk is to be a soldier, at least at some point.

Turkey was neutral during WWII, and the Turkish contingent with the United Nations forces during the Korean War was highly praised for its discipline, courage and tenacity.

In republican Turkey, every Turkish male is required to spend 18 months in the army. Despite it being an honourable duty, few Turkish men look forward to it. Most men do their military service when they are 18 but there are several ways in which the moment can be put off. Deferment is allowed, for example, if you are a student or if your brother is already doing his military service. However, conscientious objection is not an option and if a man cannot produce proof that he's done his time by age 32, then he will find it almost impossible to get a job.

Useful social as well as military purposes are served by army service. It's not unusual to see army troops doing clean-up or gardening duty at archaeological sites, or planting new forests.

The government also uses compulsory military service as a mechanism for social leavening. Young men from the comfortable, developed western provinces are usually shipped off to serve in the rugged east, while country boys from poor eastern villages are posted to cosmopolitan İstanbul, İzmir, or the tourist resorts.

Because of the current PKK insurgency in the south-east, being a Turkish soldier is not just a temporary interruption to a young man's career. Thousands of conscripts have come home in body bags. ■

policies produced a boom in economic development, but also high inflation and charges of corruption. Throughout the decade his policies were challenged by several 'new' parties: the Social Democrat Populist Party (SHP), an heir to the CHP; the Democratic Left Party (DSP), another heir to the CHP led secretly by Ecevit, who was still under political exclusion; the True Path Party (DYP), successor to Demirel's Justice Party; and the Prosperity (or Welfare) Party (RP), successor to the religious MSP.

Late in 1989, Turgut Özal was elected to the presidency. He remained active in ANAP politics, however, running the country through figurehead prime minister Yıldırım Akbulut. This was against at least the spirit if not the letter of the constitution, and raised eyebrows in political and military circles.

1990s In the hotly contested elections of February 1992 ANAP gained only about a third of the vote, losing the plurality to the durable Süleyman Demirel, back from political exclusion, and his DYP. The centre-right True Path formed an unlikely coalition with the centre-left SHP under Professor Erdal İnönü (son of general, prime minister and president, the late İsmet İnönü) to form a government.

Demirel brought a new vigour to the government after almost a decade of Motherland leadership.

With Özal's untimely death due to heart disease in April 1993, Demirel was elected to be the ninth president of the Turkish Republic. In June 1993, President Demirel asked Professor Tansu Çiller, the economics minister, to form a government, thereby making her Turkey's first female prime minister, an anomaly in a parliament which is overwhelmingly male.

Recent Years Prime Minister Çiller earned high marks from international bankers for making progress in privatising Turkey's money-losing state enterprises, leftovers from the statist policies of Atatürk of 60 years ago. Despite her modest progress in this, the economy worsened as the government seemed to lack any strong, clearly defined economic plan – and it continued to run huge deficits. Turkey's commercial, industrial, agricultural and tourism sectors boomed producing record profits, but the lira continued to slide in a constant devaluation against harder currencies.

In the summer of 1995 Çiller's government lost a vote of confidence in parliament when its coalition partner, upset over the government's unwillingness to raise the minimum wage, withdrew. September and October were one long political crisis as Çiller, now caretaker, attempted to form a new government, ultimately forming a new coalition with Mr Deniz Baykal of the Republican Peoples' Party (CHP) as foreign minister and deputy prime minister to take the country to early elections.

The elections of 24 December 1995 were a wake-up call against politics as usual: the upstart religious-right Welfare Party (RP) won a plurality of 23%, which was seen as a protest vote against the ineffective policies and tedious political wrangles of the mainstream Motherland Party (20%) and Çiller's True Path Party (19%). Prof Necmettin Erbakan, the RP leader, was given the mandate to form a coalition, but neither of the other big parties would join him.

In March 1996, President Demirel gave the nod to caretaker prime minister Çiller, who formed a coalition with erstwhile bitter political rival Mesut Yilmaz of Motherland. Yilmaz and Çiller plan to alternate in the prime ministership, with Yilmaz taking the office for the first year, Çiller for the following two years, then Yilmaz again for one year, and after that someone else, should the coalition go to full term.

ECONOMY

Turkey has a strong agricultural base to its economy, being among the handful of countries which are net exporters of food. Wheat, cotton, sugar beet, sunflowers, hazelnuts, tobacco, fruit and vegetables are abundant. Sheep are the main livestock, and Turkey is the biggest wool producer in Europe.

However, manufactured goods now dominate exports and much of the economy. Turkey builds motor vehicles, appliances, consumer goods and large engineering projects, and exports them throughout the region. In the first half of 1995, Turkey's exports grew by 29.5%, giving it the fourth-highest export growth rate in the world.

However, the economy is still dragged down by the heavy weight of the 'state economic enterprises' (KITs), government-controlled corporations subject to subsidies, political influence, payroll-padding and corruption. In 1994, six of the 10 largest corporations were KITs, refining and selling petroleum products and petrochemicals; generating and distributing electricity; making and selling salt, tobacco products and alcoholic beverages; and refining and marketing sugar. The government is also involved in the marketing of agricultural products including grain, hazelnuts and tea; in coal and steel production; in transportation and broadcasting and many other industries.

Tourism is now among the most important sectors of the Turkish economy, bringing in billions of dollars in foreign currency earnings. In 1995, tourism increased 20% from already-high 1994 levels as almost eight million visitors came to Turkey – over one million in August alone.

There is still a large Turkish workforce in the industries of Europe, particularly those of Germany, which sends home remittances.

POPULATION & PEOPLE

Turkey has a population approaching 60 million, the great majority being Sunni Muslim Turks.

Turks

The Turkic peoples originated in central Asia, where they were a presence to be reckoned with as early as the 4th century AD. The Chinese called them *Tu-küe*, which is perhaps the root of our word 'Turk'. They were related to the *Hiung-nu*, or Huns.

The normally nomadic Turks ruled several vast empires in central Asia before being pushed westward by the Mongols. Various tribes of the Oğuz Turkic group settled in Azerbaijan, northern Iran and Anatolia.

At first they were shamanist, but at one time or another these early Turks followed each of the great religions of the region including Buddhism, Nestorian Christianity, Manichaeism and Judaism. During their western migrations they became more familiar with Islam, and it stuck.

Having begun their history as nomadic shepherds, the Turks used their skills with horses to become excellent soldiers. With the expansion of the Arab Empire into Turkish lands, the Turks used their renowned military prowess first to gain influence, and later to gain control. To this day most Turks are proud of their military traditions, and military prowess, courage and discipline are widely admired.

Kurds

Turkey has a significant Kurdish minority estimated at 10 million. Some ethnologists believe that the Kurds, who speak an Indo-European language, are closely related to the Persians, and that they migrated here from northern Europe centuries before Christ.

Turkey's sparsely populated eastern and south-eastern regions are home to perhaps six million Kurds and minorities of Turks, Armenians and others. Four million Kurds live elsewhere throughout the country, more or less integrated into greater Turkish society. (Yilmaz Güney's film *Yol (The Road)*, winner of the best film award at Cannes in 1982, explores the dilemmas of a Kurd from a traditional family integrated into modern, urban Turkish society. Unfortunately, the subtitles do not do the script justice, and anti-Turkish trailers were added by the foreign distributor.)

Though virtually all of Turkey's Kurds are Muslims and physically similar to the Turks, they jealously guard their language, culture and family traditions.

Separatism Since the collapse of the Ottoman Empire, the Kurds have periodically aspired to their own ethnic nation-state with revolts. Some dream of a Greater Kurdistan encompassing the millions of Kurds in neighbouring regions of Iran, Iraq and Syria. Fearing that Kurdish separatism could tear the country apart, the government in Ankara pursued a policy of assimilation. Officially, there were no 'Kurds', only 'mountain Turks', and all were equal citizens of the republic. The Kurdish language and other overt signs of Kurdish life were outlawed.

In recent years the Kurdish question has come to the fore again. During the 1980s, Kurdistan Workers Party (PKK) guerrillas, based in neighbouring Syria, Iraq and Iran and supported clandestinely by the PLO, made hundreds of raids into south-eastern Turkey killing thousands of civilians and Turkish troops. The resulting military crackdown embittered many Turkish Kurds, but also brought the matter of Turks and Kurds to the national agenda. Some say Kurdish separatists fear that the vast South-East Anatolia Project (GAP) will bring prosperity to a historically poor region, thereby ruining their chances of ever founding an independent Kurdistan.

In 1988, Iraqi armed forces made a deadly chemical-weapon attack on the Iraqi Kurdish village of Halabja, sending thousands of refugees fleeing across the border to safety in Turkey. After the Gulf War of 1991, fearing similar attacks, three million Iraqi Kurds fled towards Turkey, threatening to overwhelm its eastern provinces.

The plight of the Kurds drew the attention of Europe and the USA, and resultant publicity led to a softening of Ankara's restrictions: Kurdish conversation and songs are now legal, and other measures such as Kurdish-language radio and TV broadcasts are being debated. But just as many Kurds are now beginning to imagine the delights of independence, their Turkish compatriots are imagining the disaster of the Turkish homeland dismembered. With the violent chaos of the former Soviet Caucasian republics and Yugoslavia in mind, one can only hope that the Kurds and Turks find some peaceful *modus vivendi*.

Other Islamic Peoples

Turkey's coasts are home to small ethnic or linguistic groups such as the Laz and Hemşin peoples along the Black Sea coast, and the Yörüks and Tahtacıs along the eastern Mediterranean coast.

Jews

The small Jewish community of about 24,000 people is centred in İstanbul (20,000), with smaller communities in Ankara, Bursa, İzmir and other cities. The Turkish Jewish community is the remnant of a great influx which took place in the 16th century when the Jews of Spain (Sephardim) were forced by the Spanish Inquisition to flee their homes. They were welcomed into the Ottoman Empire, and brought with them knowledge of many recent European scientific and economic discoveries and advancements. In 1992 they celebrated 500 years of peaceful life among the Turks.

Armenians

The Armenians are thought by some to be descended from the Urartians (518-330 BC), but others think they arrived from the Caucasus area after the Urartian state collapsed.

Armenians have lived in eastern Anatolia for millennia, almost always as subjects of some greater state such as the Alexandrine empire, or of the Romans, Byzantines, Persians, Seljuks or Ottomans. They lived with their Kurdish and Turkish neighbours in relative peace and harmony under the Ottoman *millet* system of distinct religious communities. But when this system gave way to modern ethnic nationalism, they suffered one of the greatest tragedies in their history.

Rebellion As ethnic groups on the fringes of the empire rose in rebellion and won their independence, the Armenians followed. Unlike other peoples, however, the Armenians lived in the Muslim heartland, where they were sometimes a plurality but never a majority. (The tragic ethnic wars of the early 1990s in the former Soviet Union and Yugoslavia arose from similarly confused ethnic situations.)

By the 1890s there were constant rebellions and Armenian terrorist attacks on Ottoman government buildings and personnel, which were inevitably answered with ferocious repression by the police and army. The revolutionaries hoped that if they triggered atrocities, the Christian powers of Europe would be persuaded to come to their aid, opening the way to independence. None of the powers, however, would allow any other to gain an advantage in the dismantling of the Ottoman Empire. Also, the tsar, like the sultan, did not want the creation of an independent Armenian state carved from his territory. The Armenians became the hopeless victims of their own small numbers, European power politics, and the Ottomans' alarm at the dissolution of their once-mighty country.

As the terrorist incidents continued, the Armenians' erstwhile Turkish and Kurdish neighbours turned against them violently. On 26 August 1896, Armenian revolutionaries seized the Ottoman Bank building in İstanbul, threatening to blow it up. Though they were unsuccessful, the incident provoked widespread massacres in the capital and elsewhere in which thousands of innocent Armenians died. The European powers raised their voices in protest, but again put no effective pressure on the sultan to stop the atrocities.

The restoration of the Ottoman constitution in 1908 provided a brief respite as all Ottoman peoples saw hope of living in harmony. But ethnic rivalries surfaced again quickly as Ottoman Bulgaria declared independence and Austria seized the former Ottoman provinces of Bosnia-Herzegovina. More Armenian demonstrations provoked massacres at Adana in April 1909. Albania and Arabia rose in revolt. War broke out with Italy, Bulgaria, Serbia and Greece. The Ottoman grand vizier was assassinated. The Ottoman Turks felt beleaguered on all sides.

WWI As WWI approached, a triumvirate of Young Turks named Enver, Talat and Jemal seized power. When war broke out, the Christian Orthodox Armenians of eastern Turkey were seen (with some justification) as a 'fifth column' sympathetic to the advancing Russian army.

On 20 April 1915 the Armenians of Van rose in revolt, massacred the local Muslims, took the *kale* (fortress) and held it until the Russian army arrived. Four days after the beginning of the Van revolt, on 24 April 1915 (now commemorated as Armenian Martyrs' Day) the Ottoman government began the deportation of the Armenian population from the war zone to Syria. Hundreds of thousands of Armenians (mostly men) were massacred in the process, the rest (mostly women and children) were marched to Syria in great privation.

With the Russian victories a short-lived Armenian Republic was proclaimed in north-eastern Anatolia, and the victorious Armenians repaid defeated local Muslims with massacres in kind. But an offensive by the armies of Mustafa Kemal's Turkish nationalist Ankara government reclaimed Kars and Ardahan.

On 3 December 1920, the Ankara government concluded a peace treaty with the Armenian government in Erivan, now a Soviet republic. By the end of the war, the Armenian population of Anatolia had been reduced to insignificant numbers, mostly in the major cities.

The Aftermath The Armenians who survived the cataclysm, and their descendants in the Diaspora, blame both the Ottoman government and the Turkish people as a whole for the tragedy, labelling it genocide. The Turks, while admitting that massacres occurred, deny that there was an official policy of genocide, claim that many Armenians were indeed traitorous, and that many if not most Armenian casualties were the result of civil war, disease and privation rather than massacre. Republican Turks dissociate themselves from the actions of the Ottoman government, pointing out that they themselves (or, more correctly, their parents and grandparents) fought to overthrow it.

Historians and pseudo-historians on both sides trade accusations and recriminations, dispute the actual number of casualties, the authenticity of incriminating historical documents, and the motives and actions of the other side. In the 1970s, Armenian terrorist assassinations of Turkish diplomats and their families raised the level of recrimination and bitterness.

Armenians say they want the Turks to recognise and acknowledge the tragedy, and to provide compensation, perhaps even territory. Turks say they sympathise with the Armenians' great loss, but that those who were responsible are long dead, and those living today had nothing to do with it and cannot be held responsible, and thus compensation is inappropriate. It is an impasse likely to endure for generations.

Other Christian Peoples

As for Christian Turkish citizens, ethnic Greeks number fewer than 100,000 and live mostly in İstanbul. Assyrian Orthodox Christians, sometimes called Jacobites, trace their roots to the church founded by Jacob Baradeus, the 6th-century bishop of Edessa (today called Şanlıurfa). Their small community has its centre south of Diyarbakır, in and around Mardin and the Tur Abdin.

EDUCATION

The Turkish Republic provides five years of compulsory primary *(İlkokul)* and middle-school *(Ortaokul)* education for all children aged from seven to 12 years. Secondary, *lise* (high school, *lycée*), and vocational or technical education is available at no cost to those who decide to continue. Specialised schools are available for the blind, the deaf, the mentally retarded, orphans and the very poor. There are also numerous licensed private schools, *kolej* (colleges, like high schools) and universities which charge tuition fees.

Turkey has 29 government-funded universities to which students are admitted through a central placement system. At Ankara's Middle East Technical University and Bilkent University, and at İstanbul's Boğaziçi (Bosphorus) University, English is the language of instruction.

ARTS

Ottoman Art

Art under the Ottomans was very different from art in the Turkish Republic. Until 1923 and the founding of the republic, all mainstream artistic expression conformed (more or less) to the laws of Islam, which forbade representation of any being 'with an immortal soul' (ie animal or human). Sculpture and painting as known in the west did not exist – with the notable exception of Turkish miniature painting, which was for the upper classes.

Instead of painting and sculpture, Islamic artists worked at arabesque decoration, faïence, filigree, geometric stained glass, gilding, pottery and metalworking, glass-blowing, marquetry, repoussé work, calligraphy and illumination, textile design (including costumes and carpets), horticulture and landscape gardening. Turks may have invented the art of marbling paper, which is still practised today. Ottoman architecture is outstanding.

Most of these arts reached their height during the great age of Ottoman power from the early 16th to the late 18th centuries. Turkish museums are full of examples of them: delicate coloured tiles from İznik, graceful glass vases and pitchers from İstanbul, carved wooden mosque doors, glittering illuminated Korans, intricate jewellery and sumptuous costumes.

By the late 19th century educated Ottomans were taking up landscape and still-life painting in European styles.

Literature before the republic was also bound up with Islam. Treatises on history, geography and science were cast in religious terms. Ottoman poets, borrowing from the great Arabic and Persian traditions, wrote sensual love poems of attraction, longing, fulfilment and ecstasy about the search for union with God.

Republican Art

Under the republic, Atatürk encouraged

Pages from an 18th-century Turkish prayer book. Most of the arts in Turkey reached their height during the great age of Ottoman power from the early 1500s to the late 1700s, during which time artistic expression conformed with the laws of Islam which forbade representation of any being 'with an immortal soul'.

European-style artistic expression. The government opened official painting and sculpture academies, encouraging this 'modern' secular art over the religious art of the past.

In this century, Turkish artists and writers have been in touch with European and US trends in the arts. Some have followed slavishly, others have borrowed judiciously, mixing in a good portion of local tradition and inspiration. By the 1970s and 80s, Turkish painting had become vigorous enough to support numerous different local schools of artists whose work is shown by museums, galleries, collectors and patrons.

By the late 19th century some Ottoman writers were adapting to European forms. With the foundation of the republic, the ponderous cadences of Ottoman courtly prose and poetry gave way to use of the vernacular. Atatürk decreed that the Turkish language be 'purified' of Arabic and Persian borrowings. This, and the introduction of the new Latin-based Turkish alphabet, brought literacy within the reach of many more citizens. Several Turkish writers, including Nazım Hikmet, Yashar Kemal and Orhan Pamuk, have been translated into other languages and have met with critical and popular acclaim abroad.

Folk Arts & Crafts

Turkish carpet-making transcends the boundaries of folk art and fine art. Embroidery and lace-making are still practised in rural Turkey, as they have been for centuries. Primitive landscape painters once used horse-drawn wagons and carts as their venue; now it's the wood-panelled sides of trucks.

Turkish artisans also craft decorated wooden spoons, lathe-turned wooden items, lamps and stoves in tinplate, onyx and alabaster carvings, pottery and glass. Almost no-one leaves the country without a blue-and-white *nazar boncuğu* (evil-eye charm), usually of glass but now also of plastic.

Music

There are many kinds of Turkish music, almost all of them unfamiliar to foreign ears. Ottoman classical, religious (particularly *Mevlevi)* and some folk and popular music uses a system of *makams*, or modalities, an exotic-sounding series of tones similar in function to western scales. In addition to the familiar western whole- and half-tone intervals, much Turkish music uses quarter-tones, unfamiliar to foreign ears and perceived as 'flat' until the ear becomes accustomed to them.

Though Ottoman classical music sounds ponderous and lugubrious to the uninitiated, much Turkish folk music as played in the villages is sprightly and immediately appealing. *Türkü* music, of which you'll hear lots on the radio, falls somewhere in between: traditional folk music as performed by modern singers who live in the city.

The 1000-year-old tradition of Turkish

Top of the Turkish Pops

Rock music in Turkey is as faddy and ephemeral as anywhere else. The flavour of 1995, for example, was **Tarkan**, the George Michael of Turkish pop who rocketed to teenybop fame on the back of his *Acayıpsın* (*You're Shameful*) album but who has yet to prove he's a stayer. But alongside the shooting stars there are also many well-established artists whose back catalogues remain as popular as those of the Stones and Springsteen.

Queen of 1990s pop was **Sezen Aksu**, a singer-songwriter whose memorable melodies were typified by the 1991 album *Gülümse* (*Smile*). Well enough established to take risks, in 1995 she branched out with the more experimental *Işik Doğudan Yükselir* (*The Light Rises in the East*) which draws on Turkey's regional musical traditions.

As well as performing her own songs, Aksu writes for other singers, notably for **Sertab Erenler** whose *Lâl* (*Ruby*) was another big seller of the 90s. In 1995 Aksu and Erenler were in the vanguard of a cultural movement aimed at healing Turkey's political wounds by persuading big-name acts to perform in eastern venues.

A longer established performer who lent his voice to this same enterprise is protest singer **Zülfü Livaneli**, a singer and *saz* player who is also well known in Turkey as a journalist with left-wing sympathies; in the 1994 elections he was narrowly defeated for the post of mayor of İstanbul by the Refah Party candidate. Since Livaneli's music often incorporates western instrumentation, it's fairly accessible to non-Turkish audiences. His songs are often covered by other musicians, not least by his daughter Aylin, and he has recorded with Greek musicians Maria Farandouri and Mikis Theodorakis in an effort to heal another set of political wounds.

More alien to western ears is the style of music known as *arabesk* which, as its name implies, puts an Arabic spin on home-grown Turkish traditions. The mournful themes (if not the melodies) of this music have led to it being compared to Greek *rembetika* and until the advent of independent radio and TV in the 1990s, the authorities kept arabesk off the airwaves. In any case, until recently it wasn't at all cool to like a style of music associated, as the *Virgin Guide to World Music* puts it, 'with *gazinos* and the sound systems of taxis'. However, arabesk now attracts a homosexual following which sits rather oddly alongside its more traditional macho audience.

Playing to that traditional audience is the hugely successful Kurdish singer **İbrahim Tatlises**, a burly, moustachioed former construction worker from Urfa whose life seems positively dull compared to those of arabesk's artier practitioners. In 1980 **Bulent Ersoy**, for example, underwent a sex-change operation, following which her music was banned. The ban lifted in 1988 and Ersoy started performing live again – only to be shot at by a member of the right-wing Grey Wolves (an offshoot of the neo-fascist National Action Party) when she refused to sing a nationalist anthem. Despite being blinded in one eye when her fiancé threw acid in her face, the singer **Bergen** recorded several extremely popular arabesk songs...only to be shot dead by the same fiancé on his release from jail! ■

troubadours *(aşık)*, still very much alive as late as the 1960s and 70s, is now dying out in its pure form – killed off by radio, TV, video and audio cassettes. But the songs of the great troubadours – Yunus Emre (1238?-1320?), Pir Sultan Abdal (16th century) and Aşık Veysel (died 1974) – are still popular and often performed and recorded.

Unfortunately, the sorts of Turkish music which are most easily comprehensible to foreign ears are the fairly vapid *taverna* styles, and the local popular songs based on European and US models. Though this music can be fun, it is also fairly mindless and forgettable. Perhaps the best is Adnan Ergil's series of audio cassettes entitled *Turkish Folk Guitar*.

Finally, there's western music. Most of the groups and singers popular in Europe and the USA are popular in Turkey as well – everyone from Pearl Jam to Pavarotti. Western classical symphony, chamber music, opera and ballet have a small but fiercely loyal following in Turkey. Government-funded orchestras, dance groups and opera companies, supported by visiting artists, keep them satisfied.

Film

Cinema appeared in Turkey just a year after the Lumière brothers presented their first cinematic show in 1895. At first it was only foreigners and non-Muslims who watched movies, but by 1914 there were cinemas run by and for Muslims as well.

The War of Independence inspired actor Muhsin Ertuğrul, Turkey's cinema pioneer, to establish a film company in 1922 and make patriotic films. Comedies and documentaries followed. Within a decade Turkish

Yilmaz Güney: Film-Maker Behind Bars

Outside Turkey, the country's best known film-maker must surely be Yilmaz Güney whose *Yol*, although banned in Turkey, won the *Palme d'Or* at the 1982 Cannes Film Festival. That the film was banned in Turkey was hardly surprising, given its director's history of run-ins with the law. What is more surprising is that the film was actually written and part-directed from his prison cell.

Yilmaz Güney was born in a Kurdish village near Adana in 1937. Despite his humble origins, he supported himself through law and economics courses at university with a series of odd jobs and later began writing articles and short stories which fell foul of the law for their allegedly subversive slant. In 1958 Güney started work as an actor-scriptwriter but was quickly imprisoned for political offences.

While in jail Güney wrote a novel about the experiences of poor peasant families like his own. Released from prison, he earned his living as the handsome anti-hero of a series of low-budget action movies, making his directing debut in 1966. But by 1971 he was back in prison, this time accused of harbouring left-wing terrorists.

In 1975 Güney was given a 19-year jail sentence for murdering a magistrate in a café brawl, a crime which a nephew later claimed to have committed.

Astonishingly, he continued to run Güney Films from prison. *Sürü* (*The Herd*, 1978), his poignant film about the misadventures of a herder taking his sheep to Ankara to sell them, was scripted in a room shared with 80 other men. The one Turkish cinema which risked showing it was bombed and forced to close.

Moved to a tougher prison in 1979, Güney began work on *Yol* (*The Road*), which told the grim stories of five men on home leave from prison. The script was smuggled out of the jail, and in 1981 Güney himself escaped, fleeing to Switzerland to complete the editing. *Yol* won joint first prize at the 1982 Cannes Film Festival alongside Costas-Gavras' *Missing*. Ignoring this acclaim, the Turkish authorities promptly banned it, not least because some of its dialogue was in Kurdish, at the time a prohibited language.

Having failed to extradite Güney from Europe, the Turks stripped him of his citizenship. With French backing, Güney completed one last film, *Duvar* (*The Wall*, 1983), which tried to explain the events leading up to a revolt in the children's dormitory of Ankara Prison in 1976. In 1984 he died of cancer in Paris.

The ban on his films has now been lifted. ■

films were winning awards in international competitions, even though a mere 23 films had been made.

After WWII the industry expanded rapidly with new companies and young directors. Lütfi Akad's *Kanun Namına* (*In the Name of the Law*, 1952), Turkey's first colour film, brought realism to the screen in place of melodrama, and won first prize at the first Turkish film festival held a year later.

By the 1960s, Turkish cinema was delving deeply into social and political issues. Metin Erksan's *Susuz Yaz* (*Dry Summer*, 1964) won a gold medal at the Berlin Film Festival and another award in Venice. Yılmaz Güney, the fiery actor-director, directed his first film *At, Avrat, Silah* (*Horse, Woman, Gun*) in 1966, and starred in Lütfi Akad's *Hudutların Kanunu* (*The Law of the Borders*) after he had written the script.

The 1970s brought the challenge of television, dwindling audiences, political pressures and unionisation of the industry. The quality of films continued to improve, and social issues such as Turkish workers in Europe were treated with honesty, naturalism and dry humour. By the early 1980s, several Turkish directors were well recognised in Europe and the USA. Among current directors, Tunç Başaran, Zülfü, Halit Refiğ and Ömer Kavur bear watching.

SOCIETY & CONDUCT

At first glance, much of Turkish society is highly Europeanised. Men and women march off to jobs in city offices and shops, farmers mount their tractors for a day in the fields, and bureaucrats belly up to typewriters and computer keyboards. But Turkish traditions are different from those of Europe, and glimpses of traditional attitudes and behaviour often come through.

Liberal western attitudes born of Atatürk's reforms are strongest in the urban centres of the west and along the coasts, among the middle and upper classes. Westerners will feel quite comfortable amongst these Turks, who look to western culture as the ideal, and accept the validity of other religious beliefs alongside their own.

The working and farming classes, particularly in the east, are more conservative, traditional and religious. There is a small but growing segment of 'born again' Muslims, fervent and strict in their religion but otherwise modern. Though always polite, these Turks may give you the feeling that east is east and west is west, and that the last echo of crusaders versus Saracens has not yet died away.

Hospitality is an honoured tradition in Turkey, from the shopkeeper who plies you with tea, coffee or soft drinks to the village family which invites you to share their home and meals for the customary three days. Commercialism has begun to corrupt traditional hospitality in tourist areas, producing the shady carpet merchant who lays on the friendliness with a trowel only to sell you shoddy goods at inflated prices. Don't let the carpet touts make you lose sight of true Turkish hospitality, which is a wonderful thing.

Customs & Practices

Under the Ottoman Empire (from the 14th century to 1923), Turkish etiquette was highly organised and very formal. Every encounter between people turned into a mini-ceremony full of the flowery romance of the east.

Though the Turks have adapted to the informality of 20th-century life, you'll still notice vestiges of this courtly state of mind. Were you to learn Turkish, you'd find dozens of polite phrases – actually rigid formulas – to be repeated on cue in many daily situations. Some are listed in the Language section. Use one of these at the proper moment, and the Turks will love it.

Turks are very understanding of foreigners' different customs, but if you want to behave in accordance with local feelings, use all the polite words you can muster, at all times. This can get laborious, and even Turks complain about how one can't even get out the door without five minutes of politenesses. But even the complainers still say them.

Also note these things: don't point your

The Hat Law

You wouldn't think a law saying that all men must wear a hat (instead of a fez) could have the impact of a revolution...or at least you wouldn't until you discover the outcry that greeted Atatürk's introduction of the Hat Law in 1925.

In early 20th century Turkey, all men wore maroon-coloured felt fezzes and had done so since this style of headgear had been introduced as a replacement for 'old-fashioned' turbans a century earlier. But as a young man growing up in Macedonia Mustafa Kemal (Atatürk) had been laughed at for his fez and came to see it as exemplifying Ottoman Turkey's backwardness.

Thus one of his first acts as president of the new Turkish Republic was to abolish the fez. So sudden was the change that Turkey didn't have enough hats in store to cover all the heads now needing them. There was a rush to snap up second-hand bowlers, and unscrupulous European retailers took the opportunity to offload outmoded and wholly inappropriate hats on unsuspecting Turks. Reports exist of burly İzmir cobblers and blacksmiths going about their daily business clad in pink hats complete with feathers and ribbons. The press had a field day, too, with articles explaining how to wear these uncustomary items of apparel.

But if all that sounds fun, what followed was much less so as people rioted against the new law and some men refused point-blank to remove their fez. In some cases the penalty for resistance was death: men were actually hanged in Erzurum, Giresun, Rize and Maraş for refusing to put on a hat. Others received hefty jail sentences.

For more on the Hat Law and the upset it caused, read Jeremy Seal's witty *A Fez of the Heart.* ■

finger directly towards any person. Don't show the sole of your foot or shoe towards anyone (ie so they can see it). Don't blow your nose openly in public, especially in a restaurant; instead, turn or leave the room and blow quietly. Don't pick your teeth openly, but cover your mouth with your hand. Don't do a lot of kissing or hugging with a person of the opposite sex in public. All of the above actions are considered rude.

Mosque Etiquette Always remove your shoes before stepping on a mosque's carpets, or on the clean area just in front of the mosque door. This is not a religious law, just a practical one. Worshippers kneel and touch their foreheads to the carpets, and they like to keep them clean. If there are no carpets, as in a saint's tomb, you can leave your shoes on.

Wear modest clothes when visiting mosques, as you would when visiting a church. Don't wear tatty blue jeans, shorts (men or women) or any gear which worshippers might find outlandish. Women should have head, arms and shoulders covered, and wear modest dresses or skirts, preferably reaching to the knees. At some of the most visited mosques, attendants will lend you long robes if your clothing doesn't meet a minimum standard. The loan of the robe is free, though the attendant will probably indicate where you can give a donation to the mosque. If you donate, chances are that the money actually will go to the mosque.

Visiting Turkish mosques is generally very easy, though there are no hard and fast rules. Most times no-one will give you any trouble, but now and then there may be a stickler for propriety guarding the door, and they will keep you out if your dress or demeanour is not acceptable.

Avoid entering mosques at prayer time, (ie at the call to prayer – dawn, noon, mid-afternoon, dusk and evening, or 20 minutes thereafter). Avoid visiting mosques at all on Fridays, especially morning and noon. Friday is the Muslim holy day.

When you're inside a mosque, even if it is not prayer time, there will usually be several people praying. Don't disturb them in any way; don't take flash photos; don't walk directly in front of them.

Everybody will appreciate it if you drop some money into the donations box.

Body Language Turks say 'yes' *(evet*, eh-VEHT) by nodding forward and down.

To say 'no' *(hayır*, HAH-yuhr), nod your

Lese-Majesty

At the beginning of the 20th century, the western image of the Ottoman Turks was of a decadent, sombre, ignorant and incompetent people. This western image, which replaced that of the 'Terrible Turk' once there was no longer a threat that Turkey would conquer Europe, was based on a little truth, a lot of politics, and a good dose of religious and ethnic prejudice.

Atatürk's success in holding off the Allied powers from dismembering Turkey, and his republican reforms, gave Turks a new, positive image of themselves as pro-European and modern in outlook.

Atatürk was the right man at the right time, and many Turks believe that without this particular man there is no way Turkey could be what it is today. Rather, it might have ceased to exist; at the least, it would be like one of its Islamic neighbours, with less material and social progress, and no real grounding in democratic traditions. The Turks look around them at their Islamic neighbours and think themselves lucky to have had a leader of such ability and foresight.

This all means something to the visitor. There is a law against defaming the national hero, who is still held in the highest regard by most Turks (excluding the religious right), and similar laws against showing disrespect to other patriotic symbols such as the Turkish flag. You won't see cartoons or caricatures of Atatürk, and no-one mentions him in jest. A slight or jest directed toward Atatürk, the Turkish flag, the Turkish Republic or any other national symbol may be interpreted as a serious case of lese-majesty, and should be avoided. ■

head up and back, lifting your eyebrows at the same time. Or just raise your eyebrows: that's 'no'.

Another way to say 'no' is *yok* (YOHK): literally, 'It doesn't exist (here)', or 'We don't have any (of it)' – the same head upward, raised eyebrows applies.

Remember, when a Turkish person seems to be giving you an arch look, they're only saying 'no'. They may also make the sound 'tsk', which also means 'no'. There are lots of ways to say 'no' in Turkish.

By contrast, wagging your head from side to side doesn't mean 'no' in Turkish; it means 'I don't understand'. So if a Turkish person asks you, 'Are you looking for the bus to Ankara?' and you shake your head, they'll assume you don't understand English and will probably ask you the same question again, this time in German.

There are other signs that can cause confusion, especially when you're out shopping. For instance, if you want to indicate length ('I want a fish this big'), don't hold your hands apart at the desired length, but hold out your arm and place a flat hand on it, measuring from your fingertips to the hand. Thus, if you want a pretty big fish, you must 'chop' your arm with your other hand at about the elbow.

Height is indicated by holding a flat hand the desired distance above the floor or some other flat surface such as a counter or table top.

If someone – a shopkeeper or restaurant waiter, for instance – wants to show you the stockroom or the kitchen, they'll signal 'Come on, follow me' by waving a hand downward and towards themselves in a scooping motion. Waggling an upright finger would never occur to them, except perhaps as a vaguely obscene gesture.

RELIGION

The Turkish population is 99% Muslim, mostly of the Sunni creed; there are groups of Shiites in the east and south-east. As non-Muslim groups make up less than 1% of the population, to talk about Turkish religion is to talk about Islam.

The story of Islam's founding is covered in the History section.

Principles of Islam

The basic beliefs of Islam are these: God (Allah) created the world and everything in it pretty much according to the biblical account. In fact, the Bible is a sacred book to Muslims. Adam, Noah, Abraham, Moses and Jesus were prophets. Their teachings and revelations are accepted by Muslims, except for Jesus' divinity and his status as saviour. Jews and Christians are called 'People of the Book', meaning those with a revealed religion that preceded Islam. The Koran prohibits enslavement of any People of the Book. Jewish prophets and wise men, and Christian saints and martyrs, are all accepted as holy in Islam.

However, Islam is the 'perfection' of this earlier tradition. Though Moses and Jesus were great prophets, Muhammed was the greatest and last, *the* Prophet. To him, God communicated his final revelation, and entrusted him to communicate it to the world. Muhammed is not a saviour, nor is he divine. He is God's messenger, deliverer of the final, definitive message.

Muslims do not worship Muhammed, only God. In fact, *Muslim* in Arabic means, 'one who has submitted to God's will'; *Islam* is 'submission to God's will'. It's all summed up in the Ezan, the phrase called out from the minaret five times a day and said at the beginning of Muslim prayers: 'God is great! There is no god but God, and Muhammed is his Prophet'.

The Koran

God's revelations to Muhammed are contained in the *Kur'an-i Kerim*, the Holy Koran. Muhammed recited the *Suras* (verses or chapters) of the Koran in an inspired state. They were written down by followers, and are still regarded as the most beautiful, melodic and poetic work in Arabic literature, sacred or profane. The Koran, being sacred, cannot be translated. It exists in its true form in Arabic only.

The Islamic Commonwealth

Ideally, Islam is a commonwealth, a theocracy, in which the religious law of the Koran is the only law – there is no secular law. Courts are religious courts. In Turkey and several other Muslim countries, this belief has been replaced by secular law codes. By contrast, Ayatollah Khomeini attempted to do away with secular law and return to the exclusive use of Islamic law in the Islamic Republic of Iran. In Saudi Arabia, religious law of the strict Wahhabi sect rules as well.

Religious Duties & Practices

To be a Muslim, one need only submit in one's heart to God's will and perform a few basic and simple religious duties:

One must say, understand and believe, 'There is no god but God, and Muhammed is his Prophet'.
One must pray five times daily: at dawn, at noon, at mid-afternoon, at dusk and after dark.
One must give alms to the poor.
One must keep the fast of Ramazan, if capable of doing so.
One must make a pilgrimage to Mecca once during one's life, if possible.

Muslim prayers are set rituals. Before praying, Muslims must wash hands and arms, feet and ankles, head and neck in running water; if no water is available, in clean sand; if there's no sand, the motions will suffice. Then they must cover their head, face Mecca and perform a precise series of gestures and genuflections. If they deviate from the pattern, they must begin again.

In daily life, a Muslim must not touch or eat pork, nor drink wine (interpreted as any alcoholic beverage), and must refrain from fraud, usury, slander and gambling. No sort of image of any 'being with an immortal soul' (ie human or animal) can be revered or worshipped in any way.

Islam has been split into many factions and sects since the time of Muhammed. Islamic theology has become very elaborate and complex. These tenets, however, are still the basic ones shared by all Muslims.

LANGUAGE

Turkish is the dominant language in the Turkic language group which also includes such less-than-famous tongues as Kirghiz, Kazakh and Azerbaijani. Once thought to be related to Finnish and Hungarian, the Turkic languages are now seen as comprising their own unique language group. You can find people who speak Turkish, in one form or another, from Belgrade all the way to Xinjiang in China.

In 1928, Atatürk did away with the Arabic alphabet and adopted a Latin-based alphabet much better suited to easy learning and correct pronunciation. He also instituted a language reform to purge Turkish of abstruse Arabic and Persian borrowings, in order to rationalise and simplify it. The result is a logical, systematic and expressive language which has only one irregular noun *(su*, 'water'), one irregular verb *(etmek*, 'to be') and no genders. It is so logical, in fact, that Turkish grammar formed the basis for the development of Esperanto, an artificial international language.

Word order and verb formation are very different from those belonging to the Indo-European languages, which makes Turkish somewhat difficult to learn at first despite its elegant simplicity. Verbs, for example, consist of a root plus any number of modifying suffixes. Verbs can be so complex that they constitute whole sentences in themselves, although this is rare. The standard example for blowing your mind is *Afyonkarahisarlılaştıramadıklarımızdanmısınız?* ('Aren't you one of those people whom we tried – unsuccessfully – to make resemble the citizens of Afyonkarahisar?'). It's not the sort of word you see every day.

Turks don't expect any foreigner to know Turkish, but if you can manage a few words it will be appreciated. For their part, they'll try whatever foreign words they know, usually English or German, but some French, Danish, Dutch or Swedish as well.

Lonely Planet's *Turkish phrasebook* has words and phrases for travellers. Ask for it at your bookshop.

For the meanings of common terms used in this guide, and Turkish words and phrases you might encounter on signs, please refer to the Glossary at the end of this book.

Turkish Audio Cassettes

An audio cassette is a big help in learning correct pronunciation. I've made a 90-minute audio cassette (TSK 05) which helps you learn Turkish. I also have another cassette (TKPB 01) which is keyed to the *Turkish phrasebook.* For either cassette, please send your name and address, the stock number of the cassette you would like, and a cheque or money order payable to Tom Brosnahan for US$12 or UK£8 per cassette to Turkish Cassette, c/o Tom Brosnahan, PO Box 563, Concord, MA 01742-0563 USA. Fast letter-mail ('1st-class') postage is included in the price. If you can't find the Lonely Planet *Turkish phrasebook* at your bookshop, send US$5 or UK£3.50 to me at the address above. I'll send you one by letter mail.

Note that this address is for orders **only**. Please send all other correspondence to me via a Lonely Planet office (for addresses, see the back of the title page at the front of this book).

Pronunciation

Despite daunting oddities such as the soft 'g' (ğ) and undotted 'i' (ı), Turkish is phonetic and quite simple to pronounce. Here are some tips on correct pronunciation. Most letters in Turkish are pronounced as they appear. Here are the tricky ones, the vowels and the exceptions.

a short as in '**a**rt' or long as in '**ba**r'
â denotes a faint 'y' sound in preceding consonant, eg *Lâleli* is pronounced *lyaah-leh-LEE*
e as in 'f**e**ll'
i as in 's**ee**'
ı pronounced as 'uh'
o as in the British 'h**o**t'
ö as the 'ur' sound in the British 'f**ur**'
u as in 'm**oo**'
ü as the 'ew' sound in 'f**ew**' but without the 'y' sound before it
c as in '**j**et'
ç as in '**ch**urch'
g always hard as in '**g**et'
ğ silent; lengthens preceding vowel; ignore it!
h never silent; always as in '**h**alf'
j as the 's' in 'plea**s**ure'
s as in 'stre**ss**', never 'z' as in 'ea**s**e'
ş as in '**sh**ow'

v soft, almost like a 'w'
w only in foreign words
x only in foreign words; Turks use 'ks' instead

An important point for English speakers to remember is that each Turkish letter is pronounced; there are no vowel combinations (diphthongs) or double-letter sounds as in English. Thus the name *Mithat* is pronounced *'meet-HOT'*, not like the English word 'methought', and *meshut* is *'mess-HOOT'*.

Basics

Yes.	*Evet.*
No.	*Hayır.*
I hear you/I get it.	*Ha!*
Please.	*Lütfen.*
Thanks.	*Teşekkürler/Sağ Ol/ Mersi.*
Thanks very much.	*Çok teşekkür ederim.*
You're welcome.	*Bir şey değil.*
Pardon.	*Pardon.*
Pardon me.	*Affedersiniz.*
and	*ve*
Help yourself.	*Buyurun(uz).*
friend	*arkadaş*
What?	*Ne?*
How?	*Nasıl?*
Who?	*Kim?*
Why?	*Niçin/Neden?*
When?	*Ne zaman?*
What's this?	*Bu ne?*

Greetings

Hello.	*Merhaba.*
Good morning/day.	*Günaydın.*
Good evening.	*İyi akşamlar.*
Good night.	*İyi geceler.*
Goodbye. (said by the person departing)	*Allaha ısmarladık.*
Bon voyage. (said by the person staying; literally 'Go smiling')	*Güle güle.*
Stay happy. (alternative to goodbye)	*Hoşça kalın.*

Civilities

May it contribute to your health!
Afiyet olsun!
(said to someone sitting down to a meal)

May your life be spared!
Başınız sağ olsun!
(said to someone who has just experienced a death in the family)

May your soul be safe from harm!
Canınız sağ olsun!
(said to someone who has just accidentally broken something)

May it be in your past!
Geçmiş olsun!
(said to someone who is ill, injured, or otherwise distressed)

May it last for hours!
Saatler olsun!
(said to someone who just emerged from a bath or shower, a shave or a hair cut. It's a corruption of *sıhhatler olsun*)

In your honour/To your health!
Şerefinize!

Small Talk

What is your name?	*Adınız ne?*
My name is ...	*Adım ...*
How are you?	*Nasılsınız?*
I'm fine, thank you.	*İyiyim, teşekkür ederim.*
Very well.	*Çok iyiyim.*
Where are you from?	*Nerelisiniz?*
How old are you?	*Kaç yaşındasınız?*
I'm ...(number of years)	*... yaşındayım*

Language Difficulties

Do you speak English?
İngilizce biliyor musunuz?

I understand.
Anlıyorum.

I don't understand.
Anlamıyorum.

What does it mean?
Ne demek?

Could you speak more slowly please?
Lütfen daha yavaş konuşunuz?

Accommodation

Where is a (cheap, clean) hotel?
(Ucuz, temiz) bir otel nerede?

I/We want a ...	*... istiyorum/ istiyoruz.*
double room	*İki kişilik oda*
twin-bed room	*Çift yataklı oda*
single room	*bir kişilik oda*
triple room	*üç kişilik oda*

It's very noisy.
Çok gürültülü.
What does it cost?
Kaç para?
Where is the toilet?
Tuvalet nerede?
Where is the manager?
Patron nerede?

room with bath	*banyolu oda*
room without bath	*banyosuz oda*
room with shower	*duşlu oda*
room with washbasin	*lavabolu oda*
quiet room	*sakin bir oda*

Getting Around

Where is a/the ... ?	*... nerede?*
railway station	*Gar/istasyon*
bus station	*Otogar*
boat/ship dock	*iskele*
ticket office	*bilet gişesi*

I want a ticket to ...
... bir bilet istiyorum.
When does it depart/arrive?
Ne zaman kalkar/gelir?
How many hours does it take?
Kaç saat sürer?

airplane	*uçak*
airport	*havaalanı*
bus	*otobüs/araba*
direct	*direk(t)*
indirect (change buses)	*aktarmalı*
ship	*gemi*
train	*tren*
sleeping car	*yataklı vagon*
1st class	*birinci sınıf*
2nd class	*ikinci sınıf*
one-way trip	*gidiş*
return/round-trip	*gidiş-dönüş*
reserved seat	*numaralı yer*
student (ticket)	*öğrenci (bileti)*
full fare (ticket)	*tam (bileti)*
left luggage	*emanetçi*
map	*harita*
timetable	*tarife*

Directions

left	*sol*
right	*sağ*
straight on	*doğru*
here	*burada*
there	*şurada*
over there	*orada*
near	*yakın*
far	*uzak*

Around Town

Towns are marked by blue signs with white lettering; villages are marked by white signs with black lettering. Yellow signs with black lettering mark sights of touristic interest. Yellow signs with blue lettering have to do with village development projects.

Where is a/the ...?	*... nerede?*
bank	*Banka*
... embassy	*Büyükelçilik ...*
market	*Çarşı*
post office	*Postane (PTT)*
restaurant	*Lokanta*
tourist office	*Turizm bürosu*

What is the exchange rate?
Kur ne?
Where can I change a travellers' cheque?
Nerede seyahat çeki bozdurabilirim?
I 'd like some stamps.
Birkaç pul istiyorum.

Open	*Açık*
Closed	*Kapalı*

Shopping

Do you have ...?	*... var mı?*
Give me ...	*... bana verin*

I want this/that.	*Bu(nu) /Şu(nu) istiyorum.*
Which?	*Hangi?*
How much/many?	*Kaç/kaç tane?*
How many liras?	*Kaç lira?*
I'll give you ...	*... vereceğim*
shopping district	*çarşı*
covered bazaar	*kapalı çarşı*
bookshop	*kitapçı*
chemist/pharmacy	*eczane*
tailor	*terzi*

Health & Emergencies

Please call a/an/the ...	*... çağırın.*
ambulance	*cankurtaran/ ambulans*
doctor	*doktor/hekim*
police	*polis*
Help me.	*Yardım edin.*
I'm ill.	*Hastayım.*
My ... hurts.	*... ağrıyor.*
hospital	*hastane*
dispensary	*sağlık ocağı*

I'm allergic to penicillin.
Penisiline karşı alerjim var.

Time & Days

What time is it?	*Saat kaç?*
It's 8 o'clock.	*Saat sekiz.*
At what time?	*Saat kaçta?*
day	*gün*
week	*hafta*
today	*bugün*
tomorrow	*yarın*
yesterday	*dün*
Sunday	*Pazar*
Monday	*Pazartesi*
Tuesday	*Salı*
Wednesday	*Çarşamba*
Thursday	*Perşembe*
Friday	*Cuma*
Saturday	*Cumartesi*

Cardinal Numbers

0	*sıfır*
¼	*çeyrek*
½	*yarım* (used alone)
½	*buçuk (used with a whole number)*
1	*bir*
2	*iki*
3	*üç*
4	*dört*
5	*beş*
6	*altı*
7	*yedi*
8	*sekiz*
9	*dokuz*
10	*on*
11	*on bir*
12	*on iki*
13	*on üç*
20	*yirmi*
30	*otuz*
40	*kırk*
50	*elli*
60	*altmış*
70	*yetmiş*
80	*seksen*
90	*doksan*
100	*yüz*
200	*iki yüz*
1000	*bin*
2000	*iki bin*
10,000	*on bin*
1,000,000	*milyon*

Facts for the Visitor

PLANNING

When to Go

Spring and autumn are best, roughly from April to June and from September to October. The climate is perfect on the Aegean and Mediterranean coasts then, as well as in İstanbul. It's cooler in Central Anatolia, but not unpleasantly so. Normally, there is little rain between May and October except along the Black Sea coast. If you visit before mid-June, you will avoid the mosquitoes which can be a plague in some areas.

Most lodging-places and restaurants in coastal resorts close from late October to early April, though a few remain open year-round.

The best months for water sports are July and August. But the water is fine in May, June, September and October too.

In the hottest months on the coasts you may have to take a siesta during the heat of the day between noon and 3 pm. Get up early in the morning, clamber around the local ruins, then after lunch and a siesta come out again for *piyasa vakti*, promenade time, when everyone strolls by the sea, sits in a café, and watches the sunset.

If you plan a trip to eastern Turkey, go there in late June, July, August or September. As a general rule, you should not venture into the east before mid-May or after mid-October unless you're prepared, as there may be snow, perhaps even enough to close roads and mountain passes. Unfortunately, the trip to eastern Turkey in high summer usually includes passing through the south-east, which is beastly hot at that time.

See The Calendar in this chapter for further weather information and details of religious festivals and other special events.

Maps

Turkish-produced maps often lack detail or contain inaccuracies, so you'd be well advised to bring a good map from home. Lonely Planet is now producing, what I have never found previously, a fully accurate *Turkey travel atlas* which covers the entire country.

If you buy a Turkish one, get the Turkish Touring & Automobile Association's *East Turkey* and/or *West Turkey* at 1:850,000, for about US$4 each. They divide the country at Kayseri and do not show the railways. Don't trust these maps for back roads, though, particularly in the east.

Of the British maps, the Bartholomew *Euromap Turkey* (two sheets) covers the country at 1:800,000 for about US$10 per sheet; the *AA/ESR Tourist Map Turkey* is also good. It covers the whole of the country at a scale of 1:2,000,000; the south-west coast at 1:750,000; and includes street plans of İstanbul, İzmir and several tourist resorts. The French *Turquie* (Série Internationale No 331) by Recta Foldex covers the entire country at 1:1,600,000. Germany produces several good series, including the Reise und Verkehrsverlag's *Euro-Atlas* series which covers the country in two sheets, eastern and western Turkey at 1:800,000. They also have some city maps, including a detailed street plan of İstanbul. Kümmerly + Frey has a fairly good sheet which covers the entire country, as does Hallwag.

For İstanbul, the city publishes a very detailed map book called the *Şehir Rehberi* from time to time (latest at the time of writing is the 1989 edition), but it's difficult to find. More easily available is the *İstanbul A-Z Rehber-Atlas* sold in many foreign-language and tourist-oriented bookshops for about US$10.

What to Bring

In the hottest months from mid-June to mid-September, you'll need light cotton summer clothes, and a light sweater or jacket for the evenings or to wear up on the Central Anatolian Plateau. You won't need rain gear at all, except perhaps on the Black Sea coast. You would do better to duck between the showers rather than haul rain gear during your entire trip just for a possible day or two of rain on the Black Sea coast.

In spring and autumn, summer clothing will still be OK, but the evenings will be cooler. If you plan to travel extensively in Central Anatolia (to Ankara, Konya, Cappadocia or Nemrut Dağı), pack a heavier sweater and perhaps a light raincoat.

Winter wear – for December to March – is woollens and rain gear. Though it doesn't get really cold along the Mediterranean coast, it does get damp, rainy and chilly in most of the country, including along the south coast. İstanbul and İzmir get dustings of snow; Ankara gets more. Nemrut Dağı and the eastern region are frigid and covered in snow.

Formal or Informal? How does one dress in a Muslim country? In this one, men dress pretty much as they would for Europe; women should dress on the conservative side.

In the height of summer, no-one will really expect men to have a coat and tie, even when visiting a government official. Women should avoid clothing that is particularly revealing.

For the rest of the year, Turks tend to dress formally in formal situations such as at the office or in a good restaurant or nightclub, but informally at other times. Neat and tidy dress is still admired here. Tatty or careless clothes, a sign of nonchalance or independence in other societies, are looked upon as tatty or careless in Turkey. T-shirts and shorts are the mark of the summer tourist.

Anyone can visit a Turkish mosque so long as they look presentable. Clothes must be neat – no shorts or sleeveless shirts on either men or women; women require skirts of a modest length (knees) and a headscarf.

SUGGESTED ITINERARIES

Any itinerary is an expression of interest, energy, time and money. You can see a lot of the country if you spend from six to eight weeks, but if your time is limited, here are some suggestions. These are *minimal* times – moving fast.

Less than a Week (three to five days)

İstanbul, with an overnight trip to İznik and Bursa, or Troy and the Dardanelles.

Basic One-Week Itinerary (seven to nine days)

İstanbul (two nights), Bursa (one night), Dardanelles and Troy (one night), Bergama, İzmir and Kuşadası (two nights) with excursions to Ephesus, Priene, Miletus, Didyma; return to İstanbul (one night). Spend any extra time in İstanbul.

Two Weeks

Add an excursion from Kuşadası via Aphrodisias to Pamukkale and Hierapolis (one to two nights); also take a loop excursion to Ankara, Konya and Cappadocia. Visit the Hittite cities. If you have time left over, spend a day or two on the Turquoise Coast (Kaş, Antalya, Side, Alanya).

Three Weeks

Add a yacht cruise or coastal highway excursion from Kuşadası south to Bodrum (Halicarnassus), Marmaris, Fethiye, Kaş, Finike, Kemer and Antalya; or second-best, an excursion along the Black Sea coast. Another option is a tour to the south-east – Şanlıurfa, Mardin and Diyarbakır – best done at a time other than blazing-hot July and August.

Eastern Tour

A 14 to 21-day tour for mid-May to early October only: a circuit beginning in Ankara or Cappadocia going to Adıyaman and Nemrut Dağı (Mt Nimrod), Diyarbakır, Van, Doğubeyazıt and Mt Ararat, Erzurum, Kars, Artvin, Hopa, Rize, Trabzon, Samsun, Amasya, and returning to Ankara via Boğazkale (Hattuşaş).

HIGHLIGHTS

In İstanbul, don't miss Topkapı Palace, Aya Sofya, the Blue Mosque and the Kariye Museum. The battlefields of Gallipoli, on the Dardanelles, are particularly moving. Many visitors find Troy disappointing, but not so Ephesus, which is the best-preserved classical city on the Mediterranean.

Seljuk Turkish architecture, earlier than Ottoman, is particularly fine. Alanya, Konya, Sivas and Erzurum have many good Seljuk buildings.

Beaches are best on the southern Aegean and central Mediterranean coasts at Pamucak (near Ephesus), Bodrum, Patara, Antalya, Side and Alanya.

The improbable 'lunar' landscapes of Cappadocia, riddled with troglodyte dwellings and churches cut from the rock, are perhaps the single most visually impressive feature in all Turkey.

More adventurous travellers prefer eastern Turkey and the Black Sea coast to the western regions. The east is wilder, rougher, and less accustomed to (or jaded by) foreigners. The scenery is spectacular.

TOURIST OFFICES

Local Tourist Offices

Every Turkish town of any size has a Tourism Information Office run by the Ministry of Tourism and marked by the fan-like Hittite sun figure. Some are staffed by willing and often helpful people with more or less knowledge about the area; others are attended by time-servers who see tourists with questions as interruptions in their otherwise somnolent and comfortable daily routine. There may also be an office operated by the city or provincial government, or by a local tourism association (Turizm Derneği).

If you need help and can't find an office, ask for the Belediye Sarayı (Municipality). They'll rummage around for someone who speaks some English, and will do their best to solve your problem. Locations of tourist offices are given in each chapter for each Turkish city and town.

Representatives Abroad

Here are details of some Turkish tourism offices and diplomatic missions abroad:

Australia
: Turkish Tourism Office, Suite 101, 280 George St, Sydney 2000 NSW (☎ (61-2) 9223 3055, fax 9223 3204)

Austria
: Turkische Botschaft Informationsabteilung, Singerstrasse 2/8, 1010 Wien (☎ (43-1) 512 2128, fax 513 8326)

Belgium
: Conseiller de l'Information, rue Montoyer 4, 1040 Bruxelles (☎ (32-2) 513 8230, fax 511 7951)

Canada
: 360 Albert St, Suite 801, Ottawa ON K1R 7X7 (☎ (613) 230 8654, fax 230 3683)

Denmark
: Turkish Embassy Information Counsellor Bureau, Vesterbrogade II A, 1620 Copenhagen V (☎ (45-31) 223 100, fax 229 068)

Finland
: Turkish Information Office, Mikonkatu 6 C 18, 00100 Helsinki (☎ (35-80) 666 044, fax 666 061)

France
: Turquie, Service d'Information, 102, avenue des Champs-Elysées, 75008 Paris (☎ (33-1) 4562 2610, fax 4563 8105)

Germany
: Informationsabteilung des Türkischen Generalkonsulats, Tauentzienstrasse 7, 10789 Berlin (☎ (49-30) 214 3752, fax 214 3952)
: Informationsabteilung des Türkischen Generalkonsulats, Karlsplatz 3/1, 80335 München (☎ (49-89) 59 49 02, fax 550 4138)

Israel
: Turkish Information Office, 1 Ben Yehuda St, 63801 Tel Aviv (☎ (972-3) 517 6157, fax 517 6303)

Italy
: Ambasciata di Turchia, Ufficio Informazione, Piazza della Republica 56, 00185 Roma (☎ (39-6) 487 1190, fax 488 2425)

Japan
: Turkish Tourism & Information Office, 233-6, Jingumae Shibuya-Ku, Tokyo (☎ (81-3) 3470 6380, fax 3470 6037)

Kuwait
: P O Box 15518, Değeyah, 35456 Kuwait (☎ (965) 242 4248, fax 242 4298)

Netherlands
: Turkish Embassy, Information Counsellor's Office, Herengracht 451, 1017 BS Amsterdam (☎(31-20) 626 6810, fax 622 2283)

Singapore
: 20-B Nassim Road, Singapore 1025 (☎ (65) 732 9702, fax 732 8032)

Spain
: Oficina de Información y Turismo de Turquía, Plaza de España, Torre de Madrid, Planta 13, Oficina 3, 28008 Madrid (☎ (34-1) 559 7014, fax 547 6287)

Sweden
: Turkiska Statens Informationsbyra, Kungsgatan 3, S-11143 Stockholm (☎ (46-8) 679 8320, fax 611 3828)

Switzerland
: Türkisches Generalkonsulat, Talstrasse 74, 8001 Zürich (☎ (41-1) 221 0810, fax 212 1749)

UK
: Turkish Tourism & Information, 170-173 Piccadilly, 1st Floor, London W1V 9DD (☎ (44-71) 355 4207, fax 491 0773)

USA

Office of the Information Attaché, Turkish Consulate-General, Turkish Center, 821 United Nations Plaza, New York NY 10017 (☎ (1-212) 687 2194, fax 599 7568)

Turkish Information Office, 1717 Massachusetts Ave NW, Suite 306, Washington DC 20036 (☎ (202) 429 9844, fax 429 5649)

VISAS & DOCUMENTS

Passport

Citizens of Australia, Canada, Ireland, Japan, New Zealand and virtually all the countries of Western Europe need only a valid passport for stays up to three months. Make sure your passport has at least three months' validity remaining, or you may not be admitted.

Visas

Visas are required for many visitors, and the list lengthens as the Turkish government discovers what easy money it is. In effect, it's a travel tax. When obtaining visas at the border or airport, seek out the separate visa sales desk (often – infuriatingly – unmarked) before getting in the line for passport control. Otherwise you will wait in line only to be told to go and get your visa then get back in line.

UK and Hong Kong passport holders need a visa, obtainable in advance at a Turkish consulate, or at the border with no trouble, for UK£10. Make sure your passport is good for at least another three months, and carry a cash UK£10 note (British, not Scottish) to pay for the visa.

Citizens of the USA must also purchase a visa, obtainable in advance at a Turkish consulate, or at the border with no difficulty for US$20. Have a US$20 bill for this purpose.

If you're planning to travel to Turkey through Bulgaria, you may need a transit visa. (See Bulgaria in the list of consulates and embassies below).

Residence Permit

If you plan to stay in Turkey more than three months, you might want to apply for a residence permit *(ikamet tezkeresi)*. Contact a tourist office or tourism police office. You will need to show means of support: savings, a steady income from outside the country, or legal work within the country (see Work in this chapter). Most people staying for a shorter period, or working without a valid permit (as short-term private tutors of English, for example), cross the border into Greece for a day or two every three months rather than bother with the residence permit.

Driving Licence & Permits

Drivers must have a valid driving licence; an International Driving Permit is useful, but not normally required. Your own national driving licence should pass all right. Third-party insurance, such as a Green Card, valid for the entire country (not just for Thrace or European Turkey), or a Turkish policy purchased at the border is obligatory.

International Health Card

You need proof of vaccination against infectious diseases only if you are coming from an endemic or epidemic area.

Special Discounts

Holders of International Student Identity Cards (ISICs) are admitted to museums at sharply reduced fees, usually half-price. In fact, it's a good idea to show your student card before you show your money in almost every payment situation.

Students with ISICs get discounts of 10% on the Turkish State Railways and on Turkish Maritime Lines ships. Turkish Airlines, which used to give very good student discounts, does not do so any more. However, the airline does offer a 10% 'family discount' to any husband-and-wife couple, with or without children.

Turkey is part of the Wasteels and Inter-Rail Youth discount schemes for rail, so if you have one of these cards, it will save you money on Turkish train fares.

Those over 65 years of age receive free admission to most archaeological and historical sites and museums. Show your passport to prove that you are of the 'Golden Age' *(Altın Yaş)*.

EMBASSIES

Foreign Representatives in Turkey

The following countries have embassies and/or consulates in Turkey:

Australia *(Avustralya)*
Ankara Embassy: Nene Hatun Caddesi 83, Gaziosmanpaşa, Ankara (☎ (312) 436 1240, fax 445 0284)
İstanbul Consulate: Tepecik Yolu 58, 80630 Etiler, İstanbul (☎ (212) 257 7050, fax 257 7054) open from 8.30 am to 12.30 pm weekdays

Austria *(Avusturya)*
Ankara Embassy: Atatürk Bulvarı 189, Kavaklıdere (☎ (312) 434 2172, fax 418 9454)
İstanbul Consulate: Köybaşı Caddesi 46, 80870 Yeniköy (☎ (212) 262 4984, fax 262 2622)
İzmir Honorary Consulate: Şehit Fethibey Caddesi 41/704 (☎ (232) 483 6123, fax 484 8127)

Belgium *(Belçika)*
Ankara Embassy: Nenehatun Caddesi 100, Gaziosmanpaşa (☎ (312) 436 1653, fax 436 7143)
İstanbul Consulate: Sıraselviler Caddesi 73, Taksim (☎ (212) 243 3300, fax 243 5074)
İzmir Honorary Consulate: Atatürk Caddesi 228/12 (☎ (232) 421 8647, fax 422 4161)

Bulgaria *(Bulgaristan)*
Ankara Embassy: Atatürk Bulvarı 124, Kavaklıdere (☎ (312) 426 7456, fax 427 3178)
İstanbul Consulate: Zincirlikuyu Caddesi 44, Ulus, Levent (☎ (212) 2269 0478, 269 2216)
Have a photo (colour or B&W) of yourself, or get one taken at the Koray Foto shop, 2 Ulus Şehitler Sokak 45, Deniz Sitesi (on the ground floor), 70m from the consulate for US$1. Jump to the head of the queue and ask for a white English-language visa form. Fill it in, then get in the queue. Transit visas good for 36 hours cost US$22. Tourist visas valid for three months and good for a 30-day stay in Bulgaria cost US$35 for normal three-day delivery, or US$50 for express 30-minute delivery.
To get to the consulate, take bus No 56 or 210 behind the Sultanahmet tourist office to Beşiktaş, get out and take bus No 58UL, 58U1 or 58U2 to Zincirlikuyu, a 90-minute trip in all.

Canada *(Kanada)*
Ankara Embassy: Nenehatun Caddesi 75, Gaziosmanpaşa (☎ (312) 436 1275/9, fax 446 4437)
İstanbul Honorary Consulate: Büyükdere Caddesi 107/3, Bengun Han, 3rd floor, Gayrettepe (☎ (212) 272 5174)

Denmark *(Danimarka)*
Ankara Embassy: Kırlangıç Sokak 42, Gaziosmanpaşa (☎ (312) 427 5258, fax 468 4559)
İstanbul Consulate: Bilezik Sokak 2, 80040 Fındıklı (☎ (212) 245 0385, fax 249 4434)
İzmir Honorary Consulate: Akdeniz Caddesi, Reyent İşhanı (☎ (232) 489 5401, fax 425 5388)

Egypt *(Mısır)*
Ankara Embassy: Atatürk Bulvarı 126, Kavaklıdere (☎ (312) 426 6478, fax 427 0099)
İstanbul Consulate: Bebek Sarayı, Cevdetpaşa Caddesi 173, Bebek (☎ (212) 263 6038, 265 2440, fax 257 4428)

Finland *(Finlandiya)*
Ankara Embassy: Galipdede Sokak 1/20, Farabi (☎ (312) 426 5921, fax 468 2507)
İstanbul Honorary Consulate: Dördüncü Levent (☎ 282 8164)
İzmir Honorary Consulate: 1881 Sokak No 30/32, Balçova (☎ (232) 259 8845, fax 285 4177)

France *(Fransa)*
Ankara Embassy: Paris Caddesi 70, Kavaklıdere (☎ (312) 468 1154, fax 467 9434)
İstanbul Consulate: İstiklal Caddesi 8, Taksim (☎ (212) 243 1852, fax 249 9168)

Germany *(Almanya)*
Ankara Embassy: Atatürk Bulvarı 114, Kavaklıdere (☎ (312) 426 5451/65, fax 426 6959)
İstanbul Consulate: İnönü (Gümüşsuyu) Caddesi, Selim Hatun Camii Sokak 46, Ayazpaşa, Taksim (☎ (212) 251 5404, fax 249 9920)
İzmir Consulate: Atatürk Caddesi 260 (☎ (232) 421 6995, fax 463 4023)

Greece *(Yunanistan)*
Ankara Embassy: Ziya-ur-Rahman Sokak (Karagöz Sokak) 9-11, Gaziosmanpaşa (☎ (312) 436 8861, fax 446 3191)
İstanbul Consulate: Turnacıbaşı Sokak 32, Ağahamam, Kuloğlu, Beyoğlu (☎ (212) 245 0596, fax 252 1365)

India *(Hindistan)*
Ankara Embassy: Cinnah Caddesi 77/A, Çankaya (☎ (312) 438 2195, fax 440 3429)
İstanbul Honorary Consulate: Cumhuriyet Caddesi 257/3, Harbiye (☎ (212) 296 2128, fax 230 3697)
İzmir Honorary Consulate: Anadolu Caddesi 37-39, Koyuncuoğlu Han, Salhane (☎ (232) 486 1064, fax 435 0549)

Iran *(İran)*
Ankara Embassy: Tahran Caddesi 10, Kavaklıdere (☎ (312) 429 4320)
İstanbul Consulate: Ankara Caddesi 1/2, Cağaloğlu (☎ (212) 513 8230)

Ireland *(İrlonda)*
İstanbul Honorary Consulate: Cumhuriyet Caddesi 26/A, Pegasus Evi, Harbiye (☎ (212) 246 6025, fax 248 0744)

Iraq *(Irak)*
Ankara Embassy: Turan Emeksiz Sokak 11, Gaziosmanpaşa (☎ (312) 426 6118, 426 3907)

İstanbul Consulate: Halide Edip Adıvar Mahallesi, İpekböceği Sokak 1 (☎ (212) 230 2930/3, fax 234 5726)
The İstanbul consulate usually issues transit visas a day after submission of your passport, upon receipt of a letter of recommendation from your embassy or consulate, and payment of a fee of US$50.

Israel *(İsrail)*
Ankara Embassy: Mahatma Ghandi Caddesi 85, 06700 Gaziosmanpaşa (☎ (312) 446 3605, fax 426 1533)
İstanbul Consulate: Valikonağı Caddesi 73/4, Nişantaşı (☎ (212) 225 1040, fax 225 1048)

Italy *(Italya)*
Ankara Embassy: Atatürk Bulvarı 118, Kavaklıdere (☎ (312) 426 5460, fax 426 5800)
İstanbul Consulate: Palazzo di Venezia, Tomtom Kaptan Sokak 15, 80073 Galatasaray (☎ (212) 243 1024, 251 3294, fax 252 5879)
İzmir Consulate: 1377 Sokak 2/1, Mutlu Apt, Alsancak (☎ (232) 463 6696, fax 421 2914)

Japan *(Japon)*
Ankara Embassy: Reşit Galip Caddesi 81, Gaziosmanpaşa (☎ (312) 446 0500/3, fax 437 1812)
İstanbul Consulate: İnönü Caddesi 24, Ayazpaşa, Taksim (☎ (212) 251 7605, fax 252 5864)

Jordan *(Ürdün Kraliyeti)*
Ankara Embassy: Dedekorkut Sokak 18, Çankaya (☎ (312) 446 0500)
İstanbul Honorary Consulate: Valikonağı Caddesi 63, Nişantaşı (☎ (212) 230 1222, fax 241 4331)

Lebanon *(Lübnan)*
Ankara Embassy: Cinnah Caddesi 11/3, Çankaya (☎ (312) 426 3729)
İstanbul Consulate: Saray Apt 134/1, Teşvikiye (☎ (212) 236 1365, fax 227 3373)

Netherlands *(Holanda)*
Ankara Embassy: Köroğlu Sokak 16, Gaziosmanpaşa (☎ (312) 446 0470, fax 446 3358)
İstanbul Consulate: İstiklal Caddesi 393, Tünel, Beyoğlu (☎ (212) 251 5030, fax 251 9289)
İzmir Honorary Consulate: Cumhuriyet Meydanı, Meydan Apt 11/2 (☎ (232) 463 4980, fax 422 0690)

New Zealand *(Yeni Zelanda)*
Ankara Embassy: Kızkulesi Sokak 42/1, Gaziosmanpaşa (☎ (312) 446 0768, 446 0732, fax 445 0557)

Norway *(Norveç)*
Ankara Embassy: Kelebek Sokak 20, Gaziosmanpaşa (☎ (312) 437 9950, 437 6430)
İstanbul Honorary Consulate: Rıhtım Caddesi 89, Frank Han, Kat 3, Karaköy (☎ (212) 249 9753, fax 251 3173)
İzmir Honorary Consulate: 1378 Sokak No 4/1, Kordon İşhanı 2/201 (☎ (232) 463 3290, fax 422 0690)

Poland *(Polonya)*
İstanbul Consulate: Büyük Çiftlik Sokak 5/7, Yücel Ap, Nişantaşı (☎ (212) 232 0361)

Russian Federation *(Rusya)*
Ankara Embassy: Karyağdı Sokak 5, Çankaya (☎ (312) 439 2122/3, fax 438 3952)
İstanbul Consulate: İstiklal Caddesi 443, Tünel, Beyoğlu (☎ (212) 244 2610, 244 1693, fax 249 0107)
Aeroflot travel agency (☎ (212) 225 0290), Mete Caddesi, Taksim, İstanbul, can issue you a 10 to 15-day tourist visa for US$70, but you must submit a letter of recommendation from your embassy and four photos. Aeroflot will insist that they book accommodation for your entire stay.

South Africa *(Güney Afrika)*
İstanbul Consulte: Esentepe (☎ (212) 275 4793)

Spain *(İspanya)*
Ankara Embassy: Abdullah Cevdet Sokak 9, Çankaya (☎ (312) 438 0392/3/4, fax 439 5170)
İstanbul Consulate: Valikonağı Caddesi 33, Başaran Apt, Harbiye (☎ (212) 225 2153, fax 262 6530)
İzmir Honorary Consulate: Cumhuriyet Bulvarı 109, Alsancak (☎ (232) 489 7996, fax 484 3873)

Sweden *(İsveç)*
Ankara Embassy: Katip Çelebi Sokak 7, Kavaklıdere (☎ (312) 428 6735, fax 468 5020)
İstanbul Consulate: İstiklal Caddesi 497, Tünel, Beyoğlu (☎ (212) 243 5770, fax 252 4114)
İzmir Honorary Consulate: 1378 Sokak No 4/1, Kordon İşhanı 2/201, Alsancak (☎ (232) 422 0138, fax 422 0690)

Switzerland *(İsviçre)*
Ankara Embassy: Atatürk Bulvarı 247, Çankaya (☎ (312) 467 5555, fax 467 1199)
İstanbul Consulate: Hüsrev Gerede Caddesi 75/3, 80200 Teşvikiye (☎ (212) 259 1115, fax 259 1118)

Syria *(Suriye)*
Ankara Embassy: Abdullah Cevdet Sokak 7, Çankaya (☎ (312) 438 8704, 439 4588)
İstanbul Consulate: Mecidiyeköy (☎ (212) 275 4396)

UK *(İngiltere, Birleşik Krallığı)*
Ankara Embassy: Şehit Ersan Caddesi 46/A, Çankaya (☎ (312) 427 4310, fax 468 3214)
İstanbul Consulate: Meşrutiyet Caddesi 34, Tepebaşı, Beyoğlu (☎ (212) 252 6436, 244 7540 fax 245 4989)
İzmir Vice Consulate: Mahmut Esat Bozkurt Caddesi, 1442 Sokak No 49 (☎ (232) 463 5151, fax 421 2914)

USA *(Amerika Birleşik Devletleri, Amerika)*
Ankara Embassy: Atatürk Bulvarı 110, Kavaklıdere (☎ (312) 468 6110, fax 467 0019)
Adana Consulate: Atatürk Caddesi at Vali Yolu (☎ (322) 453 9106)

USA *cont*

İstanbul Consulate: Meşrutiyet Caddesi 104-108, Tepebaşı, Beyoğlu (☎ (212) 251 3602, fax 252 7851)

İzmir Consular Agent: Turkish American Association, Şehit Nevres Bulvarı 23, Alsancak (☎ (232) 421 3643)

CUSTOMS

Upon entering the country, customs inspection is often very cursory for foreign tourists. There may be spot-checks, but you probably won't have to open your bags.

Arrival

A verbal declaration is usually all you need; the major airports use the red and green channel system. You can bring in up to one kg of coffee, five litres of liquor and two cartons (400) of cigarettes. Things of exceptional value (jewellery, unusually expensive electronic or photographic gear etc) are supposed to be declared, and may be entered in your passport to guarantee that you will take the goods out of the country when you leave.

Vehicles Automobiles, minibuses, trailers, towed watercraft, motorcycles and bicycles can be brought in for up to three months without a carnet or triptyque (a customs licence allowing the temporary importation of a motor vehicle). (See also Driving Licence & Permits in Visas & Documents in this chapter).

Departure

It is illegal to buy, sell, possess or export antiquities! Read on.

You may export valuables (except antiquities) that have been registered in your passport on entry, or that have been purchased with legally converted money. For souvenirs, the maximum export limit is US$1000 of all items combined; if two or more similar items are exported, a licence may be required. Also, you may need to show proof of exchange transactions for at least these amounts. Save your currency exchange slips, and have them ready for the customs officer who will confront you after passport control, as you make your way to your departing flight.

Your bags may well be searched when you leave the country (both for customs and security reasons), and questions may be asked about whether or not you are taking any antiquities with you. Only true antiquities well over a century old are off limits, not newer items or the many artful fakes. If you buy a real Roman coin from a shepherd boy at an archaeological site, can you take it home with you? Legally not. What happens if you get caught trying to smuggle out a significant piece of ancient statuary? Big trouble.

Turkey is one of those countries with treasure-troves of antiquities, some of which are smuggled out of the country and fed into the international contraband art market. The Turkish government takes vigorous measures to defend its patrimony against theft. Antiquity smuggling, like drug smuggling, is a dirty business. Don't do anything that makes you look like you're a part of it.

Arrival Home

British readers have written to warn that you should get official-looking receipts from Turkish shopkeepers for any expensive item you purchase to take home to the UK. British customs officers may expect you to underdeclare, asking 'What did you *really* pay?'. If you budge from your original price (as on the receipt), they'll read you the riot act, and you'll have to cough up some duty. If you try to smuggle dutiable goods through the 'green' channel and are caught, they may offer you a choice: pay a fine equal to the price you paid for the goods abroad, or face criminal prosecution. In any country it is best to make a full and honest declaration to avoid expensive unpleasantness.

MONEY

Costs

All costs in this guide are given only in US dollars as prices in Turkish liras (TL) would be hopelessly out of date before the book even emerged from the printer.

In recent years, inflation has been 75 to

100% per annum, and the Turkish lira has been subjected to a slow, creeping devaluation which offsets this inflation and keeps the actual cost for foreign visitors low. Indeed, you may find some of the prices in this guide to be higher than the amounts you'll actually pay. The situation is volatile, and prices can fluctuate from month to month, or even week to week.

Turkey is Europe's low-price leader, and you can travel on as little as US$15 to US$20 (average) per day using buses and trains, staying in pensions, and eating one restaurant meal daily. For US$20 to US$45 per person per day you can travel more comfortably by bus and train, staying in one and two-star hotels with private baths, and eating most meals in average restaurants. For US$45 to US$75 per day you can move up to three and four-star hotels, take the occasional airline flight, and dine in restaurants all the time. If you have over US$100 per person to spend, you can travel luxury class. Costs are highest in İstanbul, lowest in small eastern towns off the tourist track.

Here are some average costs:

Single/double room in small pension – US$8 to US$18
Single/double room with bath in one-star hotel – US$15 to US$30
Three-course meal in simple restaurant – US$6
Loaf of bread – 25c
Bottle of beer (from a shop) – 95c
Litre of petrol/gasoline – 70 to 90c
100 km by express train (1st class) – US$2.20 to US$2.70
100 km by bus – US$2.25 to US$2.75
Local telephone call – 10c
Turkish Daily News – 80c

Price Adjustments Government entities such as the Turkish State Railways, Turkish Maritime Lines and the Ministry of Culture (which administers many of the country's museums) may set prices in the beginning of the year, and then adjust them only every three or four months – if at all – throughout the year. Thus a 400,000 TL museum admission ticket might cost you US$6 in January, but only US$4 or even US$3 later in the year. For this reason, many prices in this guide must be looked upon as approximate.

Private enterprises tend to adjust prices more frequently and many in the travel industry such as Turkish Airlines, Turkish Maritime Lines' international routes, rental car firms and the more expensive hotels quote prices not in liras but in US dollars or in Deutschmarks.

Travellers' Cheques

Turkish banks, shops and hotels often see it as a burden to change travellers' cheques (including Eurocheques), and may try to get you to go elsewhere. You must often press the issue. The more expensive hotels, restaurants and shops will more readily accept the cheques, as will car rental agencies and travel agencies, but not at good rates of exchange. Generally it's better to change cheques to Turkish liras at a bank, although some banks may charge a fee (see Commissions later in this section).

Exchange Receipts Save your currency exchange receipts *(bordro)*. You may need them to change back Turkish liras at the end of your stay, and to show to the customs officer if you've purchased expensive souvenirs such as carpets or jewellery. Turkish liras are worth less outside the country, so you won't want to take any with you.

Credit & Cash Cards

Big hotels, the more expensive shops and car rental agencies usually will accept your credit card. Make sure in advance because not all establishments accept all cards. If you have American Express, Visa, Diners Club, MasterCard, Access and Eurocard, you're probably equipped for any establishment that takes cards. If you only have one or two cards, ask. Turkish Airlines, for instance, may accept only Visa, MasterCard, Access and Eurocard. The Turkish State Railways doesn't accept credit cards at present, but it may soon do so. A souvenir shop may accept all major cards.

A few shopkeepers may still require you to pay the credit card fee, from 3 to 7%, or the charges (up to US$10) for making credit card arrangements *(provizyon)* with a bank. They may assume that any price haggled for is for cash.

ATMs Automated teller machines (ATMs, cash points etc) are common in Turkish cities, towns and resorts. Virtually all offer instructions in English, French, German and Turkish, and will pay out Turkish liras when you insert your major credit card (especially Visa). The daily limit on payouts is the equivalent of about US$250 per day.

Most machines also accept bank cash (debit) cards in principle, if not in fact. The specific machine you use must be reliably connected to one of the major cashpoint networks such as Cirrus or Plus Systems. Look for stickers with the logos of these services affixed to the machine. If the connection is not reliable, you may get a message saying that the transaction was refused by your bank (which may not be true), and your card will be returned to you. Try another machine.

All major Turkish banks – Akbank, Garanti Bankası, İş Bankası, Pamukbank, Yapı Kredì and Ziraat Bankası – and some smaller banks, have ATMs connected to the Visa system, allowing you to take cash advances on your Visa credit card. Akbank, Pamukbank and Yapı Kredi also claim to have the most machines connected to Plus Systems, so that you can withdraw money from your bank account with your bank cash card. I've found Yapı Kredi cash points to be the most convenient and reliable.

International Transfers

The PTT (post office) in Turkey handles postal money orders, and this is fine for small amounts. For large amounts, you'd do better with a bank.

Banks can wire money in a matter of a day or two (usually), for a fee of US$20 to US$40 per transfer. Sometimes the transfer fee is a percentage of the amount transferred. Have your passport with you when you go to receive your money.

Currency

The unit of currency is the Turkish *lira*, or TL, which was called the Turkish pound (LT) in Ottoman times. The lira is supposedly divided into 100 *kuruş* (koo-ROOSH), but inflation of roughly 70 to 100% per year has rendered the kuruş obsolete. Soon the Turkish government will have to drop at least three, and possibly more zeros from the currency.

Coins are 1000, 2500, 5000, 10,000 and, as time goes on, ever higher denominations. Banknotes come as 10,000, 20,000, 50,000, 100,000, 250,000, 500,000, one million etc. With all those zeros, it's often difficult to make sure you're giving the proper notes – or getting them in change. Beware shopkeepers and taxi drivers who may try to give you a 50,000-lira note in place of a 500,000, or a 100,000 note instead of a one million.

When the government eliminates some zeros on the currency, the confusion will be far greater as old lira notes with all the zeros will remain in circulation with the new notes, at least for a time. Take your time and be sure of amounts.

Currency Exchange

With inflation at 100% in Turkey, the value of the lira drops daily. The rates given below will seem prehistoric by the time you arrive. When this guide went to press the rates were:

A$1	=	62,000TL
CN$1	=	57,000TL
DM1	=	50,800TL
NZ$1	=	53,500TL
UK£1	=	118,100TL
US$1	=	77,900TL

Changing Money

Wait until you arrive in Turkey to change your home currency (cash or travellers' cheques) into Turkish liras. Exchange bureaus in other countries (eg the UK, USA) usually offer terrible rates of exchange. When in doubt, check the foreign exchange listings in the business section of any important daily newspaper, or call a commercial bank. A proper tourist exchange rate will be only a few percentage points less than – and may well be better than – this published rate.

With the value of the Turkish lira constantly dropping, it's wise to change money every few days rather than all at once at the beginning of your visit.

You will always need your passport when you change travellers' cheques in Turkey, and you may need it when you change cash as well.

Many tourist shops, travel agencies, expensive restaurants and most hotels accept foreign currency, though they often give bad rates of exchange. In the past, most post office (PTT) branches would give you liras for foreign cash, but not always for travellers' cheques. At present, a dispute with the banks has stopped PTTs from acting as exchange houses, but that may change.

Banks & Exchange Offices Banks are open from 8.30 am till noon, and from 1.30 to 5 pm, Monday to Friday. Outside those times it can be difficult to change money, so plan ahead, and anticipate holidays such as Şeker Bayramı and Kurban Bayramı (see Business Hours and Holidays & Special Events in this chapter).

There are currency exchange desks open long hours at the major entry points to Turkey by road, air and sea. The rate at these points will be pretty close to the one in town, so it's a good idea to change some money when you enter – US$25 or US$50 at least.

Most banks will change money for you. Look for a sign on or near the front door reading 'Kambiyo – Exchange – Change – Wechsel', which says it all. In the large cities, big banks have branches everywhere, even within 100m of one another, and exchange facilities may be limited to the more convenient branches. If a particular branch can't change your money, clerks will direct you to one which can.

In many cities, non-bank currency exchange offices handle much of the exchange business. They prefer to change cash – and may even require that it be US dollars or Deutschmarks – but may change travellers' cheques if you pressure them.

Procedures Changing money, either banknotes or travellers' cheques, can take anywhere from two to 20 minutes, depending upon the bank and how cumbersome its procedures are. Sometimes a clerk must type up a form with your name and passport number, you must sign it once or twice, then it must be countersigned by one or two bank officers before you get your money. Always take your passport when changing money at a bank, and be prepared to wait a while.

Commissions Some banks charge a fee for changing travellers' cheques (though not for changing cash notes). To find out before you begin, ask *Komisyon alınır mı?* (koh-meess-YOHN ah-luh-NUHR muh, 'Is a commission taken?'). Sometimes the teller will scribble some figures on the back of the form, then pay out your liras several thousand short, saying this is a commission, but will give no receipt. Don't let them do this.

Black Market

There is no currency black market as the Turkish lira is fully convertible.

Tipping

Restaurants In the cheapest places tipping is not necessary, though some people do leave a few coins in the change plate. In more expensive restaurants, tipping is customary.

Some places will automatically add a service charge *(servis ücreti)* of 10 or 15% to your bill, but this does not absolve you from the tip, oddly enough. The service charge goes into the pocket of the *patron* (owner). Turks will give around 5% to the waiter directly, and perhaps the same amount to the maıtre d'.

If service is included, the bill may say *servis dahil* (service included). Still, a small tip is expected. In any situation, 5 to 10% is fine. Only in the fancy foreign-operated hotels will waiters expect those enormous 15 to 20% US-style tips. In the very plain, basic restaurants you needn't tip at all, though the price of a soft drink or a cup of coffee is always appreciated.

Hotels In the cheapest hotels there are few services and tips are not expected. In most hotels, a porter will carry your luggage and show you to your room. For doing this he'll expect about 2 or 3% of the room price. So if your room costs US$30, give about 60c to US$1. For any other chore done by a porter, a slightly smaller tip is in order.

Taxis Taxi drivers may look for a tip from you (especially on trips to the airport), but that's only because you're a foreigner and foreigners tip taxi drivers. Turks don't tip taxi drivers, though they often round off the metered fare. Thus, if the meter reads 280,600TL, it's quite common to give the driver 300,000TL. Conversely, if the fare is 310,000TL, the driver may happily accept 300,000TL and wave off the extra coins.

A driver of a *dolmuş* – a cab or minibus that departs only when all seats are filled – never expects a tip or a fare to be rounded upwards.

Hairdressers In barbershops and hairdressers, pay the fee for the services rendered (which goes to the shop), then about 10% to the person who cut your hair, and smaller tips to the others who provided service, down to the one who brushes stray locks from your clothing as you prepare to leave (5% for that).

Turkish Baths In a Turkish bath, or *hamam*, there will be fees for the services, and in baths frequented mostly by Turks these will be sufficient. In tourist-oriented baths these prices may be an order of magnitude higher (US$20 instead of US$2!), in which case you may assume that service is included.

If staff in a non-tourist bath approach you as you are leaving, share out 20 to 30% of the bath fees among them.

Sleeping Cars If you take a sleeping compartment on a train, the porter will come around near the end of the trip, request an official service charge of 10% of the sleeping car charge, give you a receipt for it, and hope for a small additional tip of around 5%.

Other Situations There are other situations in which a tip is indicated, but these must be handled delicately. For instance, at a remote archaeological site, a local guardian may unlock the gate and show you around the ruins. The guardian will probably have official admission tickets, which you must pay for. If that's all they do, that's all you pay. But if they go out of their way to help you, you may want to offer a tip. They may be reluctant to accept it, and may refuse once or even twice. Try at least three times. They may well need the money, but the rules of politeness require several refusals. If they refuse three times, though, you can assume that they truly want to help you only for friendship's sake. Don't press further, for this will insult their good intentions.

In many of these situations, a token gift will be just as happily received as a cash tip. If you have some small item, particularly something distinctive from your home country, you can offer it in lieu of money.

Taxes & Refunds

There is a Value Added Tax (VAT) on most goods and services in Turkey. When leaving the country, tourists can claim the VAT paid on larger purchases. (See Value Added Tax under Things to Buy in this chapter).

POST & COMMUNICATIONS

Postal and telegraph services in Turkey are handled by the Posta Telgraf office, usually known as the PTT (peh-teh-TEH, *posta, telefon, telgraf*). However, the telephone service has been privatised (see following). To find a post office, look for the distinctive yellow signs with black 'PTT' letters. For hours of operation, see Business Hours in this chapter.

Letter boxes and postal vehicles are yellow as well. Every town has a PTT, usually close to the main square. Go there to buy stamps, send letters, faxes and telegrams, or to make telephone calls if no other phone is available. It's best to post letters in the post office slots rather than in a letter box. The *Yurtdışı* slot is for mail to foreign countries, *Yurtiçi* is for mail to other Turkish cities, and *Şehiriçi* is for mail within the city.

Many of the larger train and bus stations in Turkey have their own branch PTTs.

Count your change carefully when buying stamps. Short-changing foreigners is common in some PTTs.

Anyone asking for stamps for Australia will invariably be asked *Avusturya Avustralya?* (Austria or Australia?) The two words are quite similar in Turkish, and every clerk's response is Pavlovian. Get used to it.

Postal Rates

The constant creeping devaluation of the Turkish lira results in frequent rises in postal rates. Ask at the post office to find out current rates.

Sending Mail

Express Mail The PTT now operates an express mail, courier-type service called *acele posta servisi* (AH-jeh-leh POHSS-tah sehr-vee-see) or APS, which competes with international express carriers such as DHL, Federal Express and United Parcel Service. If you must have something reach its destination in the fastest, most secure possible manner, ask for this. Don't confuse this courier service with the traditional *ekspres* (special delivery) service, which is slower.

Parcels To mail packages out of the country, or to receive dutiable merchandise, you must have your package opened for customs inspection, and you may have to endure a bit of frustrating red tape. (In İstanbul you may have to go to the special Paket Postahane (Parcel Post Office) near Karaköy.) Have paper, box, string, tape and marker pens with you when you go.

If you want to make certain that a parcel will get to its destination intact, send it by APS (see above) or at least *kayıtlı* (by registered mail).

Receiving Mail

Addresses Turkish postal addresses are usually written with the name of the main street first, then the minor street and then the name and number of the building. For example:

Bay Mustafa Adıyok
Geçilmez Sokak, Bulunmaz Çıkmazı
Lüks Apartımanı No 23/14
80200 Tophane
İSTANBUL

In this example, *Bay* means 'Mr'; for 'Mrs', 'Ms' or 'Miss', use *Bayan*, pronounced like the English phrase 'buy an...'. The next line has the name of a largish street, 'Geçilmez Sokak', followed by the name of a smaller street, alley, or dead end, 'Bulunmaz Çıkmazı', which runs off it. The third line has the name of an apartment building, 'Lüks Apartımanı'. As for the numbers, the first one, '23', is the street number of the building; the second, '14', is the apartment or office number within the building. The district, 'Tophane', comes next, then the city. *Kat* in an address means floor, as in Kat 3, '3rd floor' (4th floor up if you count street level as the 1st floor).

The address can be written more simply when the desired building is on a large, well-known street. For example:

Bay Mustafa Adıyok
Büyük Caddesi No 44/10
80090 Taksim
İSTANBUL

In some cases, the district of the city is put at the beginning of the second line, eg 'Taksim, Büyük Caddesi No 44/10'. In any case, you've got to be familiar with the district names to find a certain address.

Turkey has a system of five-digit postal codes *(posta kodu)*. Use the postal code if you have it.

Poste Restante If you are having mail sent, have it addressed this way:

(Name)
Poste Restante
Merkez Postahane
(District)
(City, Province)
TURKEY

Merkez Postane means Central or Main Post Office, which is where you should go to pick up your mail, passport in hand. The poste restante desk often keeps more limited hours than others, and may close for lunch.

Telephone

Türk Telekom, a private company, is taking control of Turkey's telephone network from the government post office, so service – already useful – should improve.

You pay for a call with a *jeton* (zheh-TOHN, token), or perhaps several, or a *telekart* debit card. Calls are measured in usage units, each of which costs about US$0.10; a local call of several minutes' duration costs one usage unit.

Tokens Jetons come in three sizes. The small one-usage-unit *(küçük jeton*, kew-CHEWK zheh-TOHN) costs about 10c and is for local calls. The middle-sized five-usage-unit *(normal jeton*, nohr-MAHL), costing around 40c, is useful mostly for long-distance calls within Turkey. The large 10-usage-unit *(büyük jeton*, bew-YEWK), about 85c, is necessary for international calls. Currently one buys jetons at the post office, or from a disabled person (often in a wheelchair) outside a PTT or near a rank of public telephones, but this may change as Türk Telekom sets up its own sales points.

Telekarts Telephone debit cards are currently sold at post offices, but other sales points will undoubtedly arise as the phone system is privatised. Telekarts come in values of 30, 60, 100, 120, or 180 telephone usage units.

Special telekart phones take only these cards, inserted in a slot in the centre of the front panel. As you call, your telephone usage is electronically deducted from the value of the card. These phones are not yet found everywhere in Turkey; you'll see them mostly in the heavily frequented tourist areas. Try to find them, because they are easier to use than jeton phones.

There are two types of telekarts, and they are not interchangeable (each works in a separate type of phone). The newer and more useful cards – because they work in more phones – are the yellow-and-black laminated paper ones bearing coloured pictures of touristic scenes on the back. The older red-and-silver plastic-and-metal cards are being phased out; avoid them unless you've already located a phone which accepts them.

Long-Distance Calls Rates for local and intercity domestic calls are moderate, but international calls can be quite expensive: almost £1 per minute to the UK, US$3 per minute to the USA, and even higher to Australia. Reduced rates are in effect from midnight to 10 am, and on Sunday. Beware of hotel surcharges, which can be as high as 100%. Perhaps the best strategy is to make a quick call, give the other person the telephone number and a time at which you can be reached, and have them call you back.

If you make an international call from a phone office, be sure to get a receipt. Fiddling the bills is common as you see no meter

Special Telephone Services

AT&T customers can use the company's USADirect service from Turkey. Though expensive (US$2.45 for the first minute, US$1.38 for each additional minute, and US$2.50 surcharge to charge the call to your AT&T credit card), it is less expensive than calling via the Turkish PTT system. In my experience you can only use jeton phones (not telekart phones) when using USADirect. To use the service, insert jetons as for a local call, and dial ☎ 0-0-8001 2277. It seems that this service only works from İstanbul; calls from other cities are cut off after a few seconds.

MCI offers a similar service called MCI World Reach. To access the service in Turkey, call ☎ 0-0-8001 1177. US Sprint's similar service, called the Sprint Express, is accessible on ☎ 0-0-8001 4477. ■

and can't tell what a call will cost. Clerks are less willing to fiddle with an official receipt with an amount and their name on it.

To make a long-distance call from a jeton phone, look for the little round light in the last box, to the right of the pictorial instructions above the push buttons. When this light goes out, push '0'. Then, when you hear the intercity long-distance tone, push the buttons for the city code and the local number. For international calls, push '0' twice, then the country code, followed by the city code and local number. For instance for London, after pushing '0' twice, push '44', then the area code (71), then the number. For Melbourne, dial thus: 0-0-61-3 plus the local number. For the USA and Canada, dial 0-0-1 plus area code plus the local number. It can take as long as 60 seconds for the connection to be made.

As you talk, watch that little round red light on top, and listen for chimes on the line. Both are indications that it's time to deposit another jeton or telekart.

Telephone Etiquette Turks answer the phone by saying *Alo?* (from 'hello'), a word which is defined in Turkish dictionaries as 'Word said when answering the telephone' because it is never used otherwise. Turks may also say *Buyurun!* (roughly, 'at your service'). When speaking to a Turk in whatever language, he or she is liable to say *hah!* now and then. This means 'yes', 'I agree', 'all right' or 'just so'.

Fax, Telegraph & Email

Turks are addicted to fax machines. Most businesses including hotels, car rental companies and airlines have them. If you must make reservations in advance, this is the fastest and often the cheapest way. Usually you can send a fax in English, German or French and the recipients will have someone translate it and reply in the same language.

Most cities have post offices with fax *(faks)* facilities, but PTT red tape turns a simple matter into a half-hour procedure. You must write your message on an official form which the PTT retains (so keep a copy if you need one). The cost is about the same as for a short phone call (it takes about a minute to send a page). You can often send a fax simply and quickly from your hotel, but the rate may be higher than from the PTT.

Most city PTTs also have telex machines, which operate by a similar procedure. If all else fails, a simple telegram to North America may cost from US$15 to US$20, less to Europe, more to Australasia.

The Internet snakes its way through Turkey, but access points are still few, slow and often difficult to access. If you are a Compuserve subscriber you can access that service through 9600 bps nodes in Ankara (modem (312) 468 8042) and İstanbul (modem (212) 234 5168).

BOOKS

Everyone from St Paul to Mark Twain and Agatha Christie has written about Turkey. The books mentioned below have not been published in all countries by the same publisher, so publication information is not given. The titles used for some books may even change from country to country. Bookshops and libraries index books by author and title, so you should be able to locate those available in your country.

Lonely Planet

Besides this guide to Turkey, Lonely Planet has other titles which may assist you.

Lonely Planet's *Turkish phrasebook* is truly a language survival kit, as it contains words and phrases useful to real-life situations. Besides including all the common words and phrases needed during travel, it covers the unmentionable situations in which you need to know the word for tampon or condom. An audio cassette to aid you in learning pronunciation is available from the author (see the earlier Turkish Language section for details).

An essential tool for hikers going to Turkey is Lonely Planet's *Trekking in Turkey* by Marc Dubin & Enver Lucas. It does not duplicate any of the information given in this book, but rather supplements it with detailed information on the best places to hike, the finest mountains to climb, and the perfect places to camp. If you want trail maps, details on hiring guides for the trek up Mt Ararat, facts on traditional village life, and lists of essential trekking gear, this is the book in which to find them.

I have never found a fully accurate travel atlas of Turkey, so Lonely Planet is producing one. LP's *Turkey travel atlas*, one in a growing series, covers the entire country.

If you're travelling with children, look at Lonely Planet's *Travel with Children* by Maureen Wheeler. It provides comprehensive information about what you can do to prepare yourself and enjoy your trip.

Guidebooks

This book was written to tell you just about everything you'd need to know on a first or even subsequent trip to Turkey. Other excellent guides exist, however, each with its own special interest.

For the literary-minded, *Istanbul – a traveller's companion* (1987) by Laurence Kelly is a delight. The editor has combed through the writings of two millennia and collected the choicest bits, by the most interesting writers, relating to Byzantium, Constantinople and İstanbul. History, biography, diary and travellers' observations are all included.

Otherwise, the most interesting travel guides on Turkey are those published by the Redhouse Press of İstanbul. Founded under the Ottoman Empire as part of a US missionary effort, the Redhouse Press now does an admirable job of publishing dictionaries, guidebooks and general works designed to bridge the gap between the Turkish and English-speaking realms. Some of the Redhouse guides have been translated into German, French and Italian. Though only a few Redhouse books turn up in bookshops outside Turkey, you'll find them readily within the country itself, in decent editions at moderate prices. A good example of a Redhouse work is *Biblical Sites in Turkey* (1982) by Everett C Blake & Anna G Edmonds. It has colour photos, maps and costs about US$8. Other guides cover İstanbul and day trips from it.

Travel

Mary Lee Settle's *Turkish Reflections* (1991) is a travelogue rich with history and personal impression, fluently written by an acclaimed US novelist. To write this book, she cruised through Turkey in a chauffeur-driven Mercedes Benz; but her observations are deepened by her earlier years of residence in Turkey.

The published diaries and accounts of earlier travellers in Turkey provide fascinating glimpses of Ottoman life. One of the more familiar of these is Mark Twain's *Innocents Abroad*. Twain accompanied a group of wealthy tourists on a chartered boat which sailed the Black Sea and eastern Mediterranean over a century ago. Many of the things he saw in İstanbul haven't changed much.

A Fez of the Heart by Jeremy Seal is the account of the author's recent journeys throughout Turkey in search of Turks who still wear the fez. Despite its unfortunate title it's a witty, entertaining inquiry into resurgent Islam and what it means to be a 'modern' Turk.

Neal Ascherson's *Black Sea* is a long essay on that region by the talented *Independent on Sunday* journalist. *A Traveller's History of Turkey* by Richard Stoneman is also worth a look.

A more modern account of a foreigner's life in Turkey is *Scotch & Holy Water* (1981) by John D Tumpane. The author lived in Turkey for eight years as an employee of a US company, and has written a humorous and sympathetic account of his Turkish friends and adventures.

History

The Ottoman Centuries by Lord Kinross covers the greatness of the empire without weighing too heavily on your consciousness. At US$20, the paperback reads easily and has many illustrations and maps.

Professors Stanford & Ezel Kural Shaw's excellent and authoritative *History of the Ottoman Empire & Modern Turkey* comes in two volumes. Volume One is *Empire of the Gazis: The Rise & Decline of the Ottoman Empire 1280-1808*; Volume Two is *Reform, Revolution & Republic: The Rise of Modern Turkey 1808-1975*.

The Emergence of Modern Turkey by Bernard Lewis is a scholarly work covering Turkey's history roughly from 1850 to 1950, with a few chapters on the earlier history of the Turks.

Gallipoli by Alan Moorhead is the fascinating story of the battles for the Dardanelles, which figured so significantly in the careers of Atatürk and Winston Churchill, and in the histories of Australia and New Zealand.

The Harvest of Hellenism by FE Peters details Turkey's Hellenic heritage. *Byzantine Style & Civilisation* by Sir Steven Runciman is the standard work on the later Roman Empire.

The thorny subject of the Armenian tragedy is rarely dealt with in a purely scholarly fashion. Turkish and Armenian writers and scholars regularly issue 'proofs' that the other side is ignoring facts, or falsifying records, or refusing to admit the 'truth' as they see it. When a dispassionate account of the Turkish-Armenian conflict is presented, the authors may find themselves to be *persona non grata* with one side or the other. (When the Shaws' *History of the Ottoman Empire & Modern Turkey* was published, Armenian zealots fire-bombed their home and forced them into hiding for a time.)

It is certainly true that the more one learns on this subject, the more confusing it all becomes as rumour, fiction, press release, memory, questionable statistic, hyperbole and propaganda are all put forth as absolute truth. One work which has been favourably received by the unbiased scholarly community as a dispassionate summary of Turkish-Armenian disputes is Professor Michael M Gunter's *Pursuing the Just Cause of Their People: A Study of Contemporary Armenian Terrorism* (1986). Though most of the book deals with the modern problem of terrorism, the first chapter is an admirably brief and straightforward summary of both the Turkish and Armenian positions on this historical quandary.

General

Biography *Atatürk, The Rebirth of a Nation* by Lord Kinross (JPD Balfour) is essential reading for anyone who wants to understand the formation of the Turkish Republic and the reverence in which modern Turks hold the father of modern Turkey. It's well written and more exciting than many novels. The US edition is *Atatürk: A Biography of Mustafa Kemal*.

For a fascinating look into the last years of the Ottoman Empire and the early years of the Turkish Republic, read İrfan Orga's *Portrait of a Turkish Family*. First published in 1950 and recently republished with an afterword by the author's son, it's an absorbing portrait of a family trying to survive the collapse of an old society and the birth of a new one.

Anthropology For a good overview of life during the great days of the empire, look in a library for *Everyday Life in Ottoman Turkey* by Raphaela Lewis.

Archaeology *Ancient Civilisations & Ruins of Turkey* by Ekrem Akurgal is a detailed and scholarly guide to many of Turkey's ruins 'from Prehistoric Times until the End of the Roman Empire'. The book has 112 pages of photographs and is a good, readable English translation of the original. This is the best handbook for those with a deep interest in classical archaeology.

George Bean (1903-77) was the grand old man of western travel writers on Turkish antiquities. His four books with maps, diagrams and photos cover the country's greatest wealth of Greek and Roman sites in depth, but in a very readable style. These four works were written as guidebooks to the ruins. They contain plenty of detail, but not so much that the fascination of exploring an ancient city or temple is taken away.

If you'd like to go deeply into a few sites, but not make the investments of time, energy and money necessary to cover the entire coast from Pergamum to Silifke, just buy Bean's *Aegean Turkey*. It covers İzmir and its vicinity, Pergamum, Aeolis, sites west of İzmir to Sardis, Ephesus, Priene, Miletus, Didyma, Magnesia on the Menderes River and Heracleia.

Other books by George Bean include:

Lycian Turkey (1978), which covers the Turkish coast roughly from Fethiye to Antalya, and its hinterland.

Turkey Beyond the Meander (1980), which covers the region south of the Menderes River, excluding Miletus, Didyma and Heracleia (covered in *Aegean Turkey)* but including sites near Bodrum, Pamukkale, Aphrodisias and Marmaris, and to the western outskirts of Fethiye.

Turkey's Southern Shore (1979), which overlaps with *Lycian Turkey* a bit, and covers eastern Lycia, Pisidia and Pamphylia, or roughly the coast from Finike east to Silifke.

Besides these archaeological guides, you'll find shorter, locally produced guides on sale at each site. Most include colour photographs but of varying quality. The text, however, is often badly translated, or else doesn't go into much depth. Look closely before you buy.

Food *Eat Smart in Turkey: How to Decipher the Menu, Know the Market Foods & Embark on a Tasting Adventure*, written by Joan & David Peterson, is a delightful in-depth look at the history, practice and enjoyment of Turkish cuisine.

Fiction Everybody knows about Agatha Christie's *Murder on the Orient Express*, and so they should. It has some scenes in Turkey itself, though most of the train's journey was through Europe and the Balkans. In any case, it helps to make vivid the 19th-century importance of the Turkish Empire.

Among Turkish authors, the one with the world-class reputation is Yaşar Kemal, whom some compare to Kazantzakis. Kemal's novels often take Turkish farming or working-class life as their subject matter, and are full of colourful characters and drama. There are translations in English (done by Kemal's wife) of *Memed, My Hawk* and *The Wind from the Plains* and several others.

Orhan Pamuk is a young Turkish novelist who now has a worldwide following. *The White Tower* and *The Black Book* are his two best known works in English.

Many modern 'harem' novels trade on the romance (real or wildly imagined) of the sultan's private household. Most are facile. The exception is *The Bride of Suleiman* (1981) by Aileen Crawley. The author, who lives in Northern Ireland, has written a historically faithful and absorbing fictionalised account of the relationship between Hürrem Sultan ('Roxelana') and her husband Süleyman the Magnificent, greatest of the Ottoman sultans. She brings alive the life of the Ottoman Empire during its golden age.

Arts & Crafts *Turkish Traditional Art Today* by Henry Glassie (1993) is a masterful, scholarly, detailed yet superbly entertaining survey of traditional Turkish arts such as calligraphy, carpet-weaving, pottery, metal- and woodworking.

Dictionaries Several companies publish Turkish-English pocket dictionaries, including Langenscheidt and McGraw Hill.

For a more detailed dictionary, look to *The Concise Oxford Turkish Dictionary*. Similar in scope and easier to find in Turkey is the *Portable Redhouse/Redhouse Elsözlüğlu* this 500-page work on thin paper was actually intended for Turkish students learning English, but it does the job well when you graduate from the pocket dictionary.

Turkish Grammar by Geoffrey L Lewis is the best general grammar. If a grammar book can be said to read like a novel, this one does.

However, the most useful thing to have is not a dictionary, but a good phrasebook. (See Lonely Planet earlier in this section.)

Bookshops

Major cities and most of the resort towns have bookshops which sell some foreign-language books, newspapers and magazines. See each city section for details.

NEWSPAPERS & MAGAZINES

Local daily newspapers are produced by up-to-date computerised methods in lurid colour. A few decades ago, İstanbul could boast more than a dozen Turkish-language dailies, two in Greek, one in Armenian, one in French and two in Ladino Spanish (spoken by Jews who came from Spain to the Ottoman Empire in the Middle Ages). As everywhere, the number of dailies is dwindling.

Of prime interest to visitors is the *Turkish Daily News*, an English-language daily newspaper published in Ankara and sold for US$0.60 in most Turkish cities where tourists go. It is the cheapest source of English-language news in print. The big international papers such as the *International Herald Tribune, Le Monde, Corriere della Sera, Die Welt* etc are on sale in tourist spots as well, but are much more expensive (US$2 for the *Herald Tribune*). Check the date on any international paper before you buy it. If it's more than a day or two old, look elsewhere.

Large-circulation magazines including *The Economist, Newsweek, Time, Der Spiegel* and the like, are also sold in tourist spots.

If you can't find the foreign publication you want, go to a big hotel's newsstand or check at a foreign-language bookshop.

RADIO & TV

TRT, for Türkiye Radyo ve Televizyon, is a quasi-independent government broadcasting service modelled on the BBC. Western classical and popular music, along with Turkish classic, folk, religious and pop music, are played regularly on both AM (medium-wave) and FM channels. Short news broadcasts in English, French and German are given each morning and evening.

The BBC World Service is often receivable on AM as well as on short-wave. The Voice of America broadcasts in English on AM, relayed from Rhodes, each morning. The rest of the AM band is a wonderful babel of Albanian, Arabic, Bulgarian, Greek, Hebrew, Italian, Persian, Romanian and Russian.

TRT broadcasts in colour from breakfast time till midnight on four TV channels. Independent Turkish-language stations relayed from Europe by satellite include Star 1, SHOW TV and TeleOn. The familiar Los Angeles-made series and many of the films are dubbed in Turkish. Occasionally you'll catch a film in the original language. In addition to the Turkish channels, many of the larger and more expensive hotels have satellite hook-ups to receive European channels, with programmes mostly in German, but often including the European service of CNN, NBC Super-Channel, and/or the BBC.

PHOTOGRAPHY

Film is moderately expensive in Turkey (24 Kodacolor prints about US$10, plus developing). Kodachrome slide (*diapositive*, transparency) film is difficult to find, and cannot be developed in Turkey, though the simpler E-6 process films such as Ektachrome, Fujichrome and Velvia are readily available and speedily processed in city photo shops.

Do not photograph anything military, whether or not you see signs reading *Foto çekmek yasak(tır)* or *Fotoğraf çekilmez* (No Photography). In areas off the tourist track, it's polite to ask *Foto çekebilir miyim?* ('May I take a photo?') before taking close-ups of people.

For camera repair, one reader recommends Mr Nazmi Kılıçer (☎ (1) 511 4259, 527 7935), Babiali Caddesi, Başmusahip Sokak 19/1, Gün Han, 34410 Cağaloğlu, İstanbul. Although he iş a Hasselblad specialist, he repairs all sorts of cameras.

TIME

Turkish time is East European Time, two hours ahead of Coordinated Universal Time (UTC/GMT), except in the warm months, when clocks are turned ahead one hour. Daylight saving ('summer') time usually begins at 1 am on the last Sunday in March, and ends at 2 am on the last Sunday in September.

When it's noon in İstanbul, Ankara or Erzurum, the time elsewhere is:

city	*winter*	*summer*
London	10 am	10 am
Paris, Rome	11 am	11 am
Perth, Hong Kong	6 pm	5 pm
Sydney	8 pm	7 pm
Auckland	10 pm	9 pm
Los Angeles	2 am	2 am
New York	5 am	5 am

ELECTRICITY

Electricity in Turkey is supplied at 220 volts, 50 cycles, as in Europe. Plugs *(fiş*, FEESH) are of the European variety with two round prongs, but there are two sizes in use. Most common is the small-diameter prong, so if you have this you'll be fine. The large-diameter, grounded plug, used in Germany and Austria, is also in use, and you'll find some outlets (or points, *priz*, PREEZ in Turkish) of this type. Plugs for these won't fit the small-diameter outlets.

Adaptors are not easily available. You've got to rig something up yourself unless you've brought an adaptor from Europe and it happens to be the right one. (Adaptors for the flat-prong North American-style plugs are sold in many electrical shops. If you have these plugs, and 220-volt appliances, you're unusual and in luck.)

WEIGHTS & MEASURES

Turkey uses the metric system. For those accustomed to the British-US systems of measurement, conversion information can be found at the back of this book.

LAUNDRY

There are few coin-operated automatic laundries in Turkey yet, but getting laundry *(çamaşır*, chahm-mah-SHUR) done is a simple matter. At any hotel or pension, ask at the reception desk, or just short-circuit it and ask a housekeeper. They'll quickly find someone to do laundry. Agree on a price in advance. The classier the hotel, the more exorbitant their laundry rates. Even so, the rates are no higher than at home.

Allow at least a day to get laundry done. It may be washed in a machine or by hand, but it may be dried on a line, not in a drying machine. In summer, drying takes no time at all. If you wash a T-shirt at 10.30 am in İzmir and hang it in the sun, it'll be dry by 11 am.

By the way, the word çamaşır also means 'underwear' in Turkish. This can be confusing at times.

Dry-cleaning shops *(kuru temizleme*, koo-ROO tehm-eez-lem-MEH) are found here and there in big cities, usually in the better residential sections or near luxury hotels.

Service is similar to that in Europe and the USA: fast service takes an hour or two if you're willing to pay 50% more; otherwise, overnight or two-day service is normal practice. Prices are moderate to expensive, and you'll save money by taking the garments there yourself rather than having the hotel staff do it.

HEALTH

Travel health depends on your predeparture preparations, your day-to-day health care while travelling and how you handle any medical problem or emergency that does develop. While the list of potential dangers can seem quite frightening, with a little luck, some basic precautions and adequate information, few travellers experience more than upset stomachs. However, if you do happen to get sick the information on various diseases may be useful.

Medical services are fairly well distributed in Turkey, though they are often very basic and sometimes inept. Some doctors in the larger cities speak English, French or German, and have studied in Europe or the USA. Your embassy or consulate may be able to recommend a good doctor or dentist (see Embassies in this chapter).

For minor problems, it's customary to ask at a pharmacy *(eczane*, edj-zahn-NEH) for advice. Sign language usually suffices to communicate symptoms, and the pharmacist/chemist will prescribe on the spot. Even 'prescription' drugs (except the most danger-

Hit the Internet
Lonely Planet provides up-to-date information for travellers on health issues on the Internet. For all you need to know about pre-departure planning, keeping healthy, women's health and diseases and ailments, check out http://www.lonelyplanet.com/health/health.htm. Lonely Planet's site can also direct you to other relevant on-line health information.

The US Public Health Service's Centers for Disease Control and Prevention in Atlanta, Georgia, can also provide current health information through the three Internet sites it maintains.

The CDC site is at http://www.cdc.gov/travel/travel.html. Look for the Middle East region. You may also be interested in the item called Information Networks and Other Information Sources.

There's more information available by file transfer protocol (ftp) at ftp.cdc.gov, and at the CDC Gopher site at gopher://gopher.cdc.gov/ under Traveler's Health. ■

ous or addictive ones) are often sold without a prescription. It's useful to know that there are almost as many female pharmacists in Turkey as male, so when you need to explain embarrassing problems you can usually find a sympathetic soul of your own gender.

Though Turkey manufactures most modern prescription medicines, don't risk running out of your medicine. If you take a drug regularly, bring a supply. If your medicine is available in Turkey, it may be less expensive here than at home. Take the prescription or better still part of the packaging showing the generic rather than the brand name (which may not be locally available). It is wise to have a legible prescription or letter from your doctor with you to show that you legally use the medication.

Predeparture Preparations

Health Insurance A travel insurance policy to cover theft, loss and medical problems is a wise idea. There are many policies and your travel agent may have recommendations. The international student travel policies handled by STA or other student travel organisations are usually good value. Some policies offer lower and higher medical-expense options, but the higher one is chiefly for countries like the US with extremely high medical costs. Check the small print:

- Some policies specifically exclude 'dangerous activities' which can include scuba diving, motorcycling, even trekking. If these activities are on your agenda you don't want that sort of policy.
- You may prefer to take out a policy which pays doctors or hospitals directly rather than one where you have to pay first and claim later. If you have to claim later make sure you keep all documentation. Some policies ask you to call back (reverse charges) to a centre in your home country where an immediate assessment of your problem is made.
- Check that the policy covers ambulances or an emergency flight home. If you have to stretch out you will need two seats and somebody has to pay for them!

Medical Kit It is wise to carry a small, straightforward medical kit. A possible medical kit list includes:

- Aspirin, acetaminophen, paracetamol – for pain or fever
- Antihistamine (such as Benadryl) – useful as a decongestant for colds and allergies (especially useful in preventing ear infection from air travel with these conditions), or to ease the itch from insect bites or stings and to help prevent motion sickness. There are several antihistamines on the market, all with different pros and cons (eg a tendency to cause drowsiness), so it's worth discussing your requirements with a pharmacist or doctor. Antihistamines may cause sedation and interact with alcohol so care should be taken when using them.
- Antibiotics – useful if you're travelling well off the beaten track, but they must be prescribed and you should carry the prescription with you.
- Loperamide (eg Imodium) or diphenoxylate (Lomotil) – for severe diarrhoea; prochlorperazine (eg Stemetil) or metraclopramide (eg Maxalon) for nausea and vomiting. Anti-diarrhoea medication should not be given to children under the age of 12.
- Rehydration mixture – for treatment of severe diarrhoea, this is particularly important if travelling with children, but is recommended for everyone.
- Antiseptic for cuts and grazes
- Calamine lotion or Stingose spray – to ease irritation from bites or stings

- Bandages and Band-aids (sticking plaster) – for minor injuries
- Scissors, tweezers and a digital thermometer (mercury thermometers are prohibited by airlines)
- Insect repellent containing 15 to 25% of the compound DEET (which is very important along the Turkish coasts from July to September), sunblock cream, suntan lotion, chapstick and water purification tablets

Vaccinations Legally, you need no special inoculations before entering Turkey, unless you're coming from an endemic or epidemic area. However, polio, tetanus, diptheria, typhoid and hepatitis A are all present; vaccinations should be considered by most travellers.

You should also consider taking anti-malarials if you intend to stay in tropical areas of Turkey for any length of time. Rabies, Hepatitis B and TB also exist in Turkey.

Hepatitis B Anyone anticipating contact with blood or other bodily secretions, either as a health-care worker or through sexual contact with the local population, should have this vaccination.

Rabies Vaccination should be considered by those who will be travelling for a month or longer (especially if they are cycling, handling animals, caving, travelling to remote areas) or children (who may not report a bite).

Tuberculosis TB risk should be considered for people travelling more than three months. As most healthy adults do not develop symptoms, a skin test before and after travel, to determine whether exposure has occurred, may be all that is required. However, vaccination is recommended for children who will be travelling more than three months.

For up-to-date information on recommended innoculations and precautions, contact your local health authorities. You can also get good current information via the Internet's World Wide Web from the US Centers for Disease Control and Prevention's site at http://www.cdc.gov/. Choose the 'Travelers' Health' menu to access guidelines for international travel.

In the UK, contact the Medical Advisory Service for Travellers Abroad (MASTA) of the London School of Hygiene and Tropical Medicine (☎ (0891) 224100). You answer a set of questions on your destination and means of travel, and will be sent a health brief with precautions to be taken. The phone line is open 24 hours a day; charges are 37p off-peak and 49p peak.

In the USA, contact the US Public Health Service's Centers for Disease Control and Prevention (☎ & fax (404) 332 4559).

In Australia, contact the Traveller's Medical and Vaccination Centre in Sydney (☎ (02) 9221-7133), 2nd Floor, Dymocks Building, 428 George St, or in Melbourne (☎ (03) 9602-5788), 2nd Floor, 393 Little Bourke St.

Food & Water

Travellers in Turkey experience a fair amount of travellers' diarrhoea ('the Sultan's Revenge'). Any experienced traveller knows that getting sick from food is mostly by chance, but there are still a few things you can do to improve your chances.

Dining Precautions Choose dishes that look freshly prepared and sufficiently hot. You can go into almost any Turkish kitchen (except in the very posh places) for a look at what's cooking. In fact, in most places that's what the staff will suggest, the language barrier being what it is. Except for grilled meats, Turkish dishes tend to be cooked slowly for a long time, just the thing to kill any errant bacteria. But if the dishes don't sell on the day they're cooked, they might be saved, and the oil may congeal and become harder to digest.

As for grilled meats, these may be offered to you medium rare. They'll probably be all right, but if they really look pink, send them back for more cooking (no problem in this). The words you'll need are *biraz daha pişmiş* (beer-ahz da-HAH peesh-meesh) for 'cooked a bit more', and *iyi pişmiş* (ee-EE peesh-meesh) or *pişkin,* (peesh-KEEN) for 'well done'.

Beware of milk products, and dishes

which contain milk that has not been properly refrigerated. Electricity is expensive in Turkey, and many places will scrimp on refrigeration temperature. If you want a rice pudding *(sütlaç)* or some such dish with milk in it, choose a shop that has lots of them in the window, meaning that a batch has been made recently. In general, choose things from bins, trays, cases, pots etc that are fairly full. If you make a point of eating some yoghurt every day, you'll keep your digestive system in excellent condition.

Drinking Precautions Drink bottled spring water whenever possible. It's sold everywhere in clear plastic bottles in sizes of one-third of a litre, 1.5 and three litres. Check the date of manufacture on the bottle, and don't buy water that's been around for a while as it may taste of the plastic. Check that the seal of the bottle hasn't been tampered with.

Tap water in Turkey is chlorinated, but it is not certain to be safe, and it rarely tastes good.

A roadside *çeşme* (CHESH-meh, fountain or spring), may bear the word *içilmez* (eech-eel-MEHZ, 'not to be drunk'), or *içilir* (eech-eel-LEER, 'drinkable'), or *içme suyu* (EECH-meh soo-yoo, 'drinking water'), or *içilebilir* (EECH-eel-eh-bee-LEER, 'can be drunk'), but I'd avoid these if possible unless you think you really know what's upstream from them.

Alternatives to spring water include *maden suyu*, naturally fizzy mineral water, and *maden sodası* (or just *soda)*, artificially carbonated mineral water. The latter just has bigger bubbles, and more of them, than the former. Both come from mineral springs, and both are truly full of minerals. The taste is not neutral. Some people like it, some don't. It's supposed to cleanse your kidneys and be good for you.

Packaged fruit juice *(meyva suyu)*, soft drinks, beer and wine are reliably pure, except in rare cases.

Infectious Diseases

Diarrhoea A change of water, food or climate can all cause the runs; diarrhoea caused by contaminated food or water is more serious. Despite all your precautions you may still get a mild bout of travellers' diarrhoea but a few rushed toilet trips with no other symptoms is not indicative of a serious problem. Moderate diarrhoea, involving half-a-dozen loose movements in a day, is more of a nuisance. Dehydration is the main danger with any diarrhoea, particularly for children where dehydration can occur quite quickly. Fluid replacement remains the mainstay of management. Weak black tea with a little sugar, soda water, or soft drinks allowed to go flat and diluted 50% with water are all good. With severe diarrhoea a rehydrating solution is necessary to replace minerals and salts. Commercially available ORS (oral rehydration salts) are very useful; add the contents of one sachet to a litre of boiled or bottled water. In an emergency you can make up a solution of eight teaspoons of sugar to a litre of boiled water and have salted cracker biscuits at the same time. You should stick to a bland diet as you recover.

Lomotil or Imodium can be used to bring relief from the symptoms, although they do not actually cure the problem. Only use these drugs if absolutely necessary – eg if you *must* travel. For children under 12 years Lomotil and Imodium are not recommended. Under all circumstances fluid replacement is the most important thing to remember. Do not use these drugs if the person has a high fever or is severely dehydrated.

In certain situations antibiotics may be indicated:

- Watery diarrhoea with blood and mucous. (In this situation, gut-paralysing drugs like Imodium or Lomotil should be avoided.)
- Watery diarrhoea with fever and lethargy.
- Persistent diarrhoea not improving after 48 hours.
- Severe diarrhoea, if it is logistically difficult to stay in one place.

The recommended drugs (adults only) would be either norfloxacin 400 mg twice daily for three days or ciprofloxacin 500 mg twice daily for three days.

The drug bismuth subsalicylate has also

been used successfully. It is not available in some countries. The dosage for adults is two tablets or 30 ml and for children it is one tablet or 10 ml. This dose can be repeated every 30 minutes to one hour, with no more than eight doses in a 24-hour period.

The drug of choice in children would be co-trimoxazole (Bactrim, Septrin, Resprim) with dosage dependent on weight. A five-day course is given.

Giardiasis The parasite causing this intestinal disorder is present in contaminated water. The symptoms are stomach cramps, nausea, a bloated stomach, watery, foul-smelling diarrhoea and frequent gas. Giardiasis can appear several weeks after you have been exposed to the parasite. The symptoms may disappear for a few days and then return; this can go on for several weeks.

Dysentery This serious illness is caused by contaminated food or water and is characterised by severe diarrhoea, often with blood or mucus in the stool. There are two kinds of dysentery. Bacillary dysentery is characterised by a high fever and rapid onset; headache, vomiting and stomach pains are also symptoms. It generally does not last longer than a week, but it is highly contagious.

Amoebic dysentery is often more gradual in the onset of symptoms, with cramping abdominal pain and vomiting less likely; fever may not be present. It is not a self-limiting disease: it will persist until treated and can recur and cause long-term health problems.

Hepatitis Hepatitis (*sarılık*, SAH-ruh-luhk) is a general term for inflammation of the liver. The discovery of new strains has led to a virtual alphabet soup, with hepatitis A, B, C, D, E, G and others. Travellers shouldn't be too paranoid about this apparent proliferation of hepatitis strains; hep C, D, E and G are fairly rare (so far) and following the same precautions as for A and B should be all that's necessary. Hepatitis A is the most common form of this disease and is spread by contaminated food and water.

Hepatitis B is transmitted through contact with infected blood, usually by means of transfusions, unsterile needles or other medical or dental equipment, but also through contact with open lesions.

Hepatitis C is spread like B. It is a concern because it seems to lead to liver disease more rapidly than hepatitis B. There is no available vaccine.

Hepatitis E (also called Non-A, Non-B) is spread like A, but no cases have yet been reported in Turkey. The virus is being researched, but there is not yet a vaccine.

The chief symptoms of hepatitis are fatigue, loss of energy, a yellow cast to the eyes and skin, and odd-coloured brownish urine. You should seek medical advice, but in general there is not much you can do apart from resting, drinking lots of fluids, eating lightly and avoiding fatty foods. People who have had hepatitis must forego alcohol for six months after the illness as hepatitis attacks the liver and it needs that amount of time to recover.

Typhoid Typhoid fever is another gut infection that travels the faecal-oral route – ie contaminated water and food are responsible. Vaccination against typhoid is not totally effective and it is one of the most dangerous infections, so medical help must be sought.

In its early stages typhoid resembles many other illnesses: sufferers may feel like they have a bad cold or flu on the way, as early symptoms are a headache, a sore throat, and a fever which rises a little each day until it is around 40C or more. The victim's pulse is often slow relative to the degree of fever present and gets slower as the fever rises – unlike a normal fever where the pulse increases. There may also be vomiting, diarrhoea or constipation.

In the second week the high fever and slow pulse continue and a few pink spots may appear on the body; trembling, delirium, weakness, weight loss and dehydration are other symptoms. If there are no further complications, the fever and other symptoms will slowly diminish during the third week. However, you must get medical help before this because pneumonia (acute infection of the lungs) or peritonitis (perforated bowel) are common complications, and because typhoid is very infectious.

The fever should be treated by keeping the victim cool and dehydration should also be watched for.

Worms These parasites are most common in rural, tropical areas and a stool test when you return home is not a bad idea. They can be present on unwashed vegetables or in undercooked meat and you can pick them up through your skin by walking in bare feet. Infestations may not show up for some time, and although they are generally not serious, if left untreated they can cause severe health problems. A stool test is necessary to pinpoint the problem and medication is often available over the counter.

Tuberculosis (TB) There is a world-wide resurgence of Tuberculosis. It is a bacterial infection which is usually transmitted from person to person by coughing but may be transmitted through consumption of unpasteurised milk. Milk that has been boiled is safe to drink, and the souring of milk to make yoghurt or cheese also kills the bacilli. Typically many months of contact with the infected person are required before the disease is passed on. The usual site of the disease is the lungs, although other organs may be involved. Most infected people never develop symptoms. In those who do, especially infants, symptoms may arise within weeks of the infection occurring and may be severe. In most, however, the disease lies dormant for many years until, for some reason, the infected person becomes physically run down. Symptoms include fever, weight loss, night sweats and coughing.

Sexually Transmitted Diseases (STDs)
Sexual contact with an infected sexual partner spreads these diseases. While abstinence is the only 100% preventative, using condoms is also effective. Gonorrhoea, herpes and syphilis are the most common of these diseases; sores, blisters or rashes around the genitals, discharges or pain when urinating are common symptoms. Symptoms may be less marked or not observed at all in women. Syphilis symptoms eventually disappear completely but the disease continues and can cause severe problems in later years. The treatment of gonorrhoea and syphilis is with antibiotics.

There are numerous other sexually transmitted diseases, for most of which effective treatment is available. However, there is no cure for herpes and there is also currently no cure for AIDS.

HIV/AIDS HIV, the Human Immunodeficiency Virus, may develop into AIDS, Acquired Immune Deficiency Syndrome. HIV is a major problem in many countries. Any exposure to blood, blood products or bodily fluids may put the individual at risk. In Turkey transmission is mostly through contact between homosexual or bisexual males, or via contaminated needles shared by IV drug users. Vaccinations, acupuncture, tattooing and ear or nose piercing can be potentially as dangerous as intravenous drug use if the equipment is not clean. If you do need an injection, be absolutely certain that the syringe used is sterile. The best course is to buy a new syringe *(şırınga)* from a pharmacy and ask the doctor to use it. Apart from abstinence, the most effective preventative is always to practise safe sex using condoms. It is impossible to detect the HIV-positive status of an otherwise healthy-looking person without a blood test.

Fear of HIV infection should never preclude treatment for serious medical conditions. Although there may be a risk of infection, it is very small indeed.

Insect-Borne Diseases
Malaria This serious disease is spread by mosquito bites. Officially, malaria is present in south-east Anatolia from Mersin on the Mediterranean coast eastward to the Iraqi border, but the highest danger is in the muggy agricultural area called Cukurova

north of Adana, and in the newly-irrigated areas around Şanlıurfa, where the incidence of malaria has skyrocketed from 8600 cases in 1990 to approximately 100,000 cases in 1995.

If you just pass through, or spend most of your time in cities, the danger is lower; but if you plan to spend lots of time in rural areas and camp out, you're at significant risk and should consider taking chloroquine tablets weekly (consult a doctor first). At present there are no known chloroquine-resistant strains of mosquitoes in this area. I have visited south-east Anatolia repeatedly without taking medicine and have never had a problem, but you must make your own decision.

Symptoms include headaches, fever, chills and sweating which may subside and recur. Without treatment malaria can develop more serious, potentially fatal effects.

Antimalarial drugs do not prevent you from being infected but kill the parasites during a stage in their development.

The main messages are:

Primary Prevention This must always be in the form of mosquito-avoidance measures. The mosquitoes that transmit malaria bite from dusk to dawn and during this period travellers are advised to:

- wear light coloured clothing
- wear long pants and long sleeved shirts
- use mosquito repellents containing the compound DEET on exposed areas (overuse of DEET may be harmful, especially to children, but its use is considered preferable to being bitten by disease-transmitting mosquitoes)
- avoid highly scented perfumes or aftershave
- use a mosquito net – it may be worth taking your own

Drugs While no antimalarial is 100% effective, taking the most appropriate drug significantly reduces the risk of contracting the disease.

Diagnosis No-one should ever die from malaria. It can be diagnosed by a simple blood test. Symptoms range from fever, chills and sweating, headache and abdominal pains to a vague feeling of ill-health, so seek examination immediately if there is any suggestion of malaria.

Contrary to popular belief, once a traveller contracts malaria he/she does not have it for life. Two species of the parasite may lie dormant in the liver but they can also be eradicated using a specific medication. Malaria is curable, as long as the traveller seeks medical help when symptoms occur.

Filariasis This is a mosquito-transmitted parasitic infection which is found in Turkey. There is a range of possible manifestations of the infection, depending on which filarial parasite species has caused the infection. These include fever, pain and swelling of the lymph glands; inflammation of lymph drainage areas; swelling of a limb or the scrotum; skin rashes and blindness. Treatment is available to eliminate the parasites from the body, but some of the damage they cause may not be reversible. Medical advice should be obtained promptly if the infection is suspected.

Typhus Typhus is spread by ticks, mites or lice. It begins with fever, chills, headache and muscle pains followed a few days later by a body rash. There is often a large painful sore at the site of the bite and nearby lymph nodes are swollen and painful. Treatment is with tetracycline, or chloramphenicol under medical supervision.

Tick typhus is spread by ticks. Seek local advice on areas where ticks pose a danger and always check your skin carefully for ticks after walking in a danger area such as a tropical forest. A strong insect repellent can help, and serious walkers in tick areas should consider having their boots and trousers impregnated with benzyl benzoate and dibutylphthalate.

Women's Health

Gynaecological Problems Poor diet, lowered resistance due to the use of antibiotics for stomach upsets and even contraceptive pills can lead to vaginal infections when travelling in hot climates. Maintaining good personal hygiene, and wearing skirts or loose-fitting trousers and cotton underwear will help to prevent infections.

Yeast infections, characterised by a rash, itch and discharge, can be treated with a vinegar or lemon-juice douche, or with yoghurt. Nystatin, miconazole or clotrimazole suppositories are the usual medical prescription. Trichomoniasis and gardnerella are more serious infections; symptoms are a smelly discharge and sometimes a burning sensation when urinating. Male sexual partners must also be treated, and if a vinegar-water douche is not effective medical attention should be sought. Metronidazole (Flagyl) is the prescribed drug.

Pregnancy Most miscarriages occur during the first three months of pregnancy, so this is the most risky time to travel as far as your own health is concerned. Miscarriage is not uncommon, and can occasionally lead to severe bleeding. The last three months should also be spent within reasonable distance of good medical care. A baby born as early as 24 weeks stands a chance of survival, but only in a good modern hospital. Pregnant women should avoid all unnecessary medication, but vaccinations and malarial prophylactics should still be taken where possible. Additional care should be taken to prevent illness and particular attention should be paid to diet and nutrition. Alcohol and nicotine, for example, should be avoided.

Doctors, Dentists & Hospitals

You can find good doctors and dentists in Turkey's big cities, as well as hospitals *(hastane*, hahs-tah-NEH) and clinics *(klinik*, klee-NEEK). Government-supported hospitals are called *devlet hastanesi*, and you can find them by following the standard international road sign with a large 'H' on it. See the chapter or section about each city for details.

Clinics run by the Red Crescent (Kızılay, the Turkish equivalent of the Red Cross) are marked by a red crescent. *İlk yardım* on one of these signs means 'first aid', which may or may not be competent; a *sağlık ocağı* is a simple dispensary. All hospital and clinic costs are controlled by the government, and are quite low, even at private hospitals.

In every city and town of any size you will see signs marking the medical offices of doctors and giving their specialities.

A *tıbbi doktor*, medical doctor, might specialise in *dahili*, internal medicine; *göz hastalıkları*, eye diseases; *kadın hastalıkları*, gynaecological ailments or *çocuk hastalıkları*, paediatric (children's) ailments. An *Operatör* is a surgeon.

By the way, half of all the physicians in Turkey are women. Female patients might prefer to see a woman doctor: if a woman visits a male doctor, it's customary to have a companion present during any physical examination or treatment. There is not always a nurse available to serve in this role.

Care in provincial Turkish hospitals is sometimes not of the highest standard in terms of comfort, convenience or facilities. But medical care often depends upon the particular staff members (doctors and nurses) involved. The quality varies. The lower staff echelons may be low paid and trained on the job. As a foreigner, you will probably be given the best possible treatment and the greatest consideration.

Accidents

It's worth mentioning that highway traffic accidents claim thousands of lives annually in Turkey. See Driving in the Getting Around chapter for details.

TOILETS

In most public conveniences you are asked to pay a small fee of US$0.10 to US$0.20. Virtually every hotel above the lowest class, most apartments, many restaurants, train stations and airports have the familiar raised-bowl commode toilet. The Turkish version is equipped with facilities for washing the user's bottom (always with the left hand): a spigot and can on the floor nearby or, much more conveniently, a little copper tube snaking up the back and right to the spot where it's needed. As washing is the accustomed method of hygiene, toilet paper – used by Turks mostly for drying – is considered a dispensable luxury and may not be provided. In the government-rated hotels there should be paper. In public toilets, if there's no attendant, there will be no paper. It's a good idea to carry enough paper or tissues with you at all times.

You may also meet with the traditional flat 'elephant's feet' toilet, a porcelain or concrete rectangle with two oblong foot-places and a sunken hole. Though daunting, it has much to recommend it: doctors say that the squatting position aids in the swift and thorough accomplishment of the business at hand; and since only your shod feet contact the vessel, it is more sanitary than bowl toilets.

So much for science. The first time you use it, you'll feel awkward (and older readers have found it difficult to arise from the squat). Don't despair. Think of the generations of magnificent Ottoman sultans and gracious harem ladies who did it this way. Take a tip from them: don't let all of the stuff fall out of your pockets when you squat.

Sometimes the plumbing is not built to take wads of paper, and the management will place a wastepaper basket or can next to the toilet for used paper. Signs in Turkish will plead with you not to throw the paper down the toilet. If the toilet doesn't flush when you pull the handle, use the usually provided bucket or plastic container of water to do the job.

Serviceably clean public toilets can be found near the big tourist attractions. In other places, it depends. Look first. Every mosque has a toilet, often smelly and very basic, but it may be better than nothing, depending upon the urgency of Nature's call.

WOMEN TRAVELLERS

Ms Pat Yale, my assistant in the preparation of this guide, gives this advice to women travellers in Turkey:

Attitudes to Women

As in most Muslim countries, western women travellers often attract the sort of attention they never would at home. Since Turkey is basically friendly and welcoming, much of this attention will be perfectly pleasant. (Though one black female traveller wrote to say that she was stared at by everyone, all the time, as Turks are not used to seeing black people.) Inevitably, however, some of it won't be, and many women write to Lonely Planet complaining about verbal and physical harassment.

There are many reasons why this might be. It's easiest to heap all the blame on the men...and certainly when you're being relentlessly pursued after asking to be left alone, you may think they richly deserve all the blame. But unfortunately some tourist women haven't helped matters by refusing to acknowledge the deep cultural divisions that exist and adjust their holiday behaviour accordingly. It may be wrong, but when Turkish men see western women drinking heavily, dressing skimpily and engaging in what are clearly non-marital affairs, sometimes with locals, they all too easily conclude that that's what we're all after. Turkish tabloid newspapers then exacerbate matters by publishing pictures of half-naked foreigners with text suggesting we're all yearning to get to grips with Turkish men.

Social Customs

If you want to avoid problems, it helps to understand – and perhaps follow – Turkish social custom. Things may be easing up in the big cities, but in general young women don't go out shopping without friends or mother. College-aged women usually stroll with friends. Women in their prime look purposeful, ignore catcalls and don't walk on lonely streets after dark. Physical contact between women and men outside their immediate family is taboo. Even smiling at a man can be misconstrued as flirtation.

Countermeasures

That said, it's very difficult to lay down hard and fast rules that will protect you. Obviously how you dress has some bearing on the problem, particularly as you travel farther east to areas where most women are still covered up. However, I have been mauled when clothed from head to toe. At the very least keep your torso, legs and upper arms covered – no shorts or skimpy T-shirts.

Wearing a wedding ring and carrying

photos of a husband and children can be helpful...and who's to stop you inventing same even if they don't exist? Wearing dark glasses to avoid eye contact can also be helpful.

If approached by a Turkish man in circumstances that you don't appreciate, you could try ignoring him. You could also try saying *Ayıp!* (ah-YUHP) which means 'shameful', but some men won't take kindly to being called shameful when they're sure you'll find them irresistible.

On the Road

Ironically the habitual segregation of Turkish society can actually help tourist women. Men and unrelated women are not expected to sit beside each other on public transport, and you'll often see an extraordinary rigmarole going on to separate the sexes on crowded dolmuşes. When you buy a bus ticket, the ticket agent will automatically put you next to another woman or leave the other seat empty. Some buses even have single seats near the driver set aside for women. That said, we have received letters from women who have been hassled by bus conductors, especially on night buses. If anything like that happens to you, it would be a good idea to complain loudly to the bus conductor and/or the driver. You should certainly complain when you reach your destination. If you don't, you risk adding substance to the belief that western women don't mind these things.

Women should avoid sitting in the front seat of a taxi next to the driver if at all possible. The driver may believe it is an invitation to greater intimacy. It is not advisable for women to hitchhike in Turkey, especially alone. (See Hitching in Getting Around.)

At the Hotel

When it comes to finding a hotel, women travellers may have to accept that the cheapest flea-pits may not be the best places to stay. It's not that anything will happen to you in them; more that it's hard to feel comfortable in a place where conversation in the lobby invariably comes to a halt every time you cross the threshold. If men bang on your door at night, make your annoyance plain in the morning before you leave.

In Restaurants

When looking for somewhere to eat, the magic word to look out for is *aile*, meaning wife, or husband and wife, or family. Restaurants often have a separate *aile salonu* and tea gardens may also have a separate *aile* section. Disliking the idea of segregation, western women often ignore these areas, especially as *aile salonus* are often less immediately inviting than the main dining rooms. However, if you're alone they do offer you protection and indicate that you want to be treated with respect.

Love & Marriage

It would be easy to run away with the idea that every approach made by a Turkish man to a western woman amounts to harassment. In fact many Turkish men are extremely charming and countless women fall in love during their trip. There's nothing wrong with that, of course, except that there have been disquieting instances of tourist women giving large sums of money to their lovers, to pay for visas and air tickets out of Turkey that never materialise. Turks are also as likely as men anywhere to be economical with the truth about their precise marital status. However starry-eyed you may be, you should never forget the safe sex message, especially in the resort areas where gross promiscuity is commonplace.

Safety

It's important to remember that most female tourists would be at much greater risk of serious assault in their home countries than in Turkey, where social taboos against sexual assault and rape remain strong. But as Turkish society takes on western ways, the bad comes along with the good. A particularly nasty multiple rape and murder, involving tourists near Alanya in 1995, shocked the Turkish public and announced to all that western-style crime was starting.

A Final Word

Whatever happens, try not to get paranoid and let stupid hassles ruin your trip. Provided you dress and behave sensibly, most men will treat you hospitably, with kindness and generosity.

DISABLED TRAVELLERS

Turkey has severely limited accessibility for disabled travellers. Though local people will go out of their way to help a disabled traveller get around, with few exceptions the arrangements will be ad hoc.

Airlines and the top hotels and resorts have some provisions for wheelchair access, and ramps are beginning to appear (ever so slowly) in a few other places. But you should expect general difficulty.

A good source of information on accessible travel is the Royal Association for Disability and Rehabilitation (RADAR, ☎ (171) 250 3222), 12 City Forum, 250 City Road, London EC1V 8AF, UK.

TRAVEL WITH CHILDREN

For lots of practical information and advice on how to make travel as stress-free as possible, for both children and parents, consult Lonely Planet's *Travel with Children*. It is a complete guide to what to take, being on the road, health issues and also includes stories of other people who have travelled with their children, including in Turkey.

Your child *(çocuk)* or children *(çocuklar)* will be very well received in Turkey and, given the high Turkish birthrate, they'll have lots of company.

Child safety seats are available from all large, and many small, car rental companies at a small extra daily charge. It's best to request a child seat in advance, when you reserve your car.

Disposable baby diapers *(bebek bezi)* are readily available for infants *(bebek)*. The best brand is *Ultra Prima,* sold in pharmacies according to the baby's weight in kg. A packet of 24 costs about US$6.

Ultra-pasteurised milk is sold everywhere. Some baby foods in individual jars may also be found, but it's usually better to rely on the willingness and ingenuity of hotel and restaurant staff to make up special dishes for small children. You might also want to carry a small portable food mill, on sale in pharmacies and children's products shops at home, to purée vegetables, fruits and meats.

The larger hotels and resorts can arrange for daycare *(kreş)* and baby-sitting services; the seaside resorts often have extensive children's play and activity equipment. Public parks sometimes have basic play equipment.

The market for childhood products and services is not as elaborately developed in Turkey as in Europe or America, but Turks are handy at improvising anything which may be needed for a child's safety, health or enjoyment.

DANGERS & ANNOYANCES

Turkey is a safe country relative to most of the world; however, if you plan on travelling in the east, read the warnings about Kurdish activity at the start of the Getting Around and Eastern Anatolia chapters.

General crime, however, is not a big problem in Turkey – yet. In fact, you may feel safer here than at home.

Police

The blue-clad officers, both men and women, are part of a national force designated by the words *Polis* (poh-LEES) or *Emniyet* (ehm-nee-YEHT, security). They control traffic, patrol highways and attend to other police duties in cities and towns. Under normal circumstances you will have little to do with them. If you do encounter them, they will judge you partly by your clothes and personal appearance. If you look tidy and 'proper', they'll be on your side. If you're dressed carelessly, they may subject you to bureaucratic tedium.

Other blue-clad officers with special peaked caps are called *belediye zabıtası*, municipal inspectors or market police. These officers are the modern expression of an age-old Islamic custom of special commercial police who make sure a loaf of bread weighs what it should, that 24-carat gold is indeed 24 carats, that scales and balances don't cheat the customer. You'll see these officials patrolling the markets and bazaars, and if you have a commercial problem they'll be glad to help, though they may not speak much of a foreign language.

Soldiers in the standard Turkish army uniforms may be of three types. Without special insignia, they're regular army. With a red armband bearing the word 'jandarma', they're gendarmes who keep the peace, catch criminals on the run, stop smuggling etc. If the soldiers have white helmets emblazoned with the letters 'As İz', plus pistols in white holsters connected to lanyards around their necks, they're Askeri İnzibat, or military police who keep off-duty soldiers in line.

Most of these soldiers are draftees inducted into the enormous Turkish army, put through basic training, and sent out to guard-jobs that are usually pretty unexciting. They look ferocious – life in the Turkish army is no joke – but basically they are hometown boys waiting to get out. Every single one of them can tell you the precise number of days he has left to serve. Any request from a foreign tourist for help or directions is received as though it were a marvellous privilege.

Theft & Robbery

Theft is not much of a problem, and robbery (mugging) even less, but don't let Turkey's relative safety lull you. Take normal precautions.

Precautions include keeping track of your wallet or other valuables on crowded buses and trains and in markets; not leaving valuables in your hotel room, or at least not in view; and not walking into unknown parts of town when nobody else is around. There are isolated reports of bags being quietly slashed in İstanbul's Covered Market, and of distract, bump and grab thefts in similar crowded places in the major cities.

Actually, the biggest danger of theft is probably in dormitory rooms and other open accommodation where other foreigners can see what sort of camera you have (and can guess its value pretty accurately), or where you stash your money.

Gassing happens mostly on trains in the Balkans (ie not in Turkey) when thieves spray anaesthetic gas into your train compartment as you sleep, then enter and relieve you of all your stuff. One reader of this guide, suitably alerted to the danger of gassing, left the compartment window open a bit (it was a cold night) and tried to stay awake, but the gas worked anyway and the thieves got all his stuff.

In İstanbul there's a nightclub shakedown racket aimed at single men which amounts to robbery. Here's how it works: you're strolling along İstiklal Caddesi or Cumhuriyet Caddesi in the evening. You stop to look in a shop window. A well-dressed man or a couple of men approach and chat about this and that. They offer to buy you a drink in a nightclub nearby. You're given a seat next to some 'girls', and even if you protest at this point, it's too late. They say the girls' drinks are on your bill. If you resist paying an amount which conveniently equals the entire contents of your wallet, you are escorted to the back office and convinced forcibly to pay up. Moral: single men should not accept invitations from unknown Turks in large cities without sizing the situation up very carefully.

Disputes

In general, Turks view foreigners as cultured, educated and wealthy – even if many foreign visitors don't deserve such a view. This means that you will sometimes be given special consideration, jumped to the heads of queues, given the best seat on the bus etc.

Thus, in a dispute, if you keep your cool and act dignified, you will generally be given the benefit of the doubt. If it is thought you have powerful friends, you will definitely be given that benefit.

It's difficult to imagine a dispute involving a foreigner coming to the point of blows, as Turks are slow to anger. Don't let it happen. A Turk rarely finds it necessary to fight, but if he does, he wants to win, *whatever* the cost. Knowing that horrible things could happen, bystanders will pull two

The Turkish Knockout

I'm receiving an increasing number of reports of theft by drugging. Thieves befriend travellers, usually single men, and offer them drinks which contain powerful drugs which cause the victims to lose consciousness quickly. When the victim awakes hours later, they've been stripped of everything except their clothes and a terrible hangover.

The perpetrators of this sort of crime usually work in pairs or trios. They befriend you and travel with you, perhaps even for a day or two. One report was of foreign (non-Turkish) thieves from a Middle East country befriending a British subject and riding by bus with him across the country to İstanbul. The thieves offered him a soda in Gülhane Parkı. When the victim awoke his camera, wallet and passport were gone, as was his luggage from the hotel where they were all staying.

Another team – Turks this time – works out of Ankara's otogar. They look for travellers on their way to Cappadocia and start a conversation. They mention that, by coincidence, they're going to Ürgüp as well. They buy their own tickets and join you on the bus. When you arrive at your destination, they break open a bottle of ayran (the yoghurt drink), they each take a sip, then they offer it to you. How they get the drugs in after they drink is a mystery, but the effect on the victim is powerful and virtually immediate. One sip knocks you out for half a day.

A variation perpetrated by impatient thieves is to offer you the drink (tea, soda, whatever) on the bus, you 'fall asleep', and they get off at the next town with all your gear.

This scheme is difficult to defeat, as Turks are generally very hospitable, and it is a Turkish custom to offer visitors drinks. Here are some things you can do to protect yourself:

- If you are a single male traveller, be suspicious of pairs or trios of other males (usually aged 18 to 28 years) who befriend you, whether Turkish or foreign. Be especially suspicious if they ask you where you are going, then travel with you.
- If you are at all suspicious of new-found friends, eat and drink only from your own supplies or those bought fresh in sealed containers from the hand of a waiter or shopkeeper. A true Turkish friend may offer to pay for drinks to satisfy the requirements of traditional hospitality. They needn't deliver the drinks themselves.
- If your new travelling companions insist on staying with you at the same lodging, start thinking of how to get away. Suggest that you want to take their picture as a souvenir, and see how they react.
- If you must, cite 'allergy'(*alerji*) as your reason for not accepting a drink. Or 'accidentally' spill the drink. And if your new 'friends' accuse you of insulting their generosity, get out of the situation quickly – to the police if necessary. If there is no police station near, try a bank or other location with a security officer.

A variation was described by a female reader who claims that an over-friendly local in the village of Tevfikiye (next to Troy) drugged her husband in the course of a 'friendly' evening of drinking with them, in order to get her alone and pressure her for sex. ■

quarrelling men apart, even if they've never seen them before.

In the case of women travellers in disputes with Turks, you should know that Turkish men feel acutely any insults to their manhood, and will retaliate. Insults to them can include being shouted at or browbeaten by a woman who is not (in their eyes) unquestionably of a higher social status. In general, keep it all formal.

Lese-Majesty

There are laws against insulting, defaming or making light of Atatürk, the Turkish flag, the Turkish people, the Turkish Republic etc. Any difficulty will probably arise from misunderstanding. At the first sign that you've inadvertently been guilty of lese-majesty, be sure to make your apologies, which will be readily accepted (see the boxed story on lese-majesty in Facts about the Country).

Natural Hazards

Earthquakes Turkey sometimes has bad ones. The big quakes only seem to hit every eight or 10 years, though, and the same thing happens in many parts of the world, so it's up to Allah.

Undertows & Riptides At some of the swimming areas, particularly in the Black Sea near İstanbul, this is a real danger. Undertows can kill you by powerfully pulling you beneath the surface, and a riptide does the same by sweeping you out to sea so that you exhaust yourself trying to regain the shore. There may be no signs warning of the danger. Lifeguards may not be present, or may be untrained or not equipped with a boat. Don't trust to luck. You can't necessarily see these hazards or predict where they will be.

In either situation, remain calm, as panic can be fatal. Don't exhaust yourself by trying to swim straight back to the beach from a rip, because you'll never make it. Rather, swim to the left or right to escape the rip area, and make for land in that direction. These dangers are usually a problem only on long stretches of open-sea beach with surf. In coves and bays, where waves are broken or diverted by headlands, you probably won't be in danger.

Insects, Snakes & Other Animals Turkey has mosquitoes, scorpions and snakes. You will not see many of them, but be aware, as you tramp around the ruins on the Aegean and Mediterranean coasts in particular, that such beasts do live here and may be nearby, at least in summer. There are also wild boar and wolves about, though you won't encounter these unless you hike deep into the bush.

The Imperial Auto

As a pedestrian, give way to cars and trucks in all situations, even if you have to jump out of the way. The sovereignty of the pedestrian is unrecognised in Turkey. If a car hits you, the driver (if not the law courts) will blame you. This does not apply on a recognised crossing controlled by a traffic officer or a traffic signal. If you've got a 'Walk' light, you've got the right of way. Watch out, all the same. Know that every Turkish driver considers you, a pedestrian, as merely an annoyance composed of so much vile protoplasm. A dispute with a driver will get you nowhere and may escalate into an even bigger problem.

Cigarette Smoke

If you're offended by cigarette smoke, you will have some unpleasant moments in Turkey. Though the local cancer prevention society fields a brave effort to stop smoking, this is the land of aromatic Turkish tobacco, and smoking is a national passion. The movement for no-smoking areas in public places is gaining ground, but it will be a long battle.

In general, position yourself near a fresh-air source if possible. And help in my campaigns to have separate smoking and no-smoking areas: if you do not smoke, ask for the no-smoking *(sigarasız)* section whenever you board a bus. (Turkish Airlines domestic flights are all no-smoking – in principle.)

Noise

Noise is a source of great annoyance in cities and larger towns. Choose hotel rooms keeping noise in mind.

Among the most persistent and omnipresent noises is that of the call to prayer, amplified to ear-splitting levels. In the good old days before microphones and amplifiers, it must have been beautiful to hear the clear, natural voices of the muezzins calling from a hundred minarets, even before dawn, when the first call is given. Now you hear a cacophony of blaring noise five or more times a day. If there's a minaret right outside your hotel window, you'll know it.

Also, Turks are addicted to nightlife and think nothing of staying up until 1 or 2 am in the middle of the week, so watch out for highly amplified bands and singers. Nightclub noise is particularly insulting when you have spent good money to upgrade your accommodation only to find that the better the hotel, the louder its nightclub. In some resorts (such as Bodrum), atomic-powered discos rock the entire town until dawn, making sleep virtually impossible. Indeed, the governor of Muğla, the province in which Bodrum is located, typified the problem: when confronted with a noise complaint, he responded 'If they don't like noise and nightlife, why did they come to Bodrum?'

When in doubt, ask *Sakin mi?* (sah-KEEN mee, 'Is it quiet here?').

Air Pollution

In winter, air pollution is a problem in the big cities. In Ankara it is a serious problem, rivalling that of Tokyo and Mexico City. The traditional heating fuel is lignite (soft brown coal), which produces enormous clouds of heavy, choking particles.

The situation is improving as Ankara and İstanbul convert their thousands of furnaces to burn clean natural gas imported by pipeline from Russia. But air quality in winter may still be substandard for a while. If you find your nose running, your eyes watering and itching, and your head aching, that's the pollution. The heating season lasts from 15 October to 1 April. In summer there is some pollution from cars, but it's no worse than in other big cities.

BUSINESS HOURS

The following are opening hours in Turkey:

Archaeological Sites
: Sites are open from 8 or 9 am to 5 or 6 pm (some later) every day, with no break for lunch.

Banks
: Open from 8.30 am to noon and 1.30 to 5 pm, Monday to Friday.

Covered Markets
: İstanbul's Grand Bazaar and covered markets in other cities are open from Monday to Saturday from 8 am to 6.30 pm.

Grocery Shops & Markets
: Open from Monday to Saturday from 6 or 7 am to 7 or 8 pm. On Sunday most markets close, though one or two grocers open in each neighbourhood.

Mosques
: Most are open all the time. If a mosque is locked, there is usually a *bekçi* (guardian) with a key somewhere nearby. Avoid visiting mosques at prayer time (at or within 20 minutes after the call to prayer). Avoid visiting on Friday, the Muslim holy day, particularly in the morning.

Museums
: Museums open from 8.30 or 9.30 am to noon or 12.30 pm, then (in some cases) they close for lunch, reopening at 1 or 1.30 pm and remaining open until 5 or 5.30 pm, perhaps later in the summer. Museums are closed on Monday, with the exception of Topkapı Palace in İstanbul which is closed on Tuesday.

Offices
: Government and business offices may open at 8 or 9 am, close for lunch, and reopen around 1.30 pm, remaining open until 4 or 5 pm. During the hot summer months in some cities the working day begins at 7 or 8 am and finishes at 2 pm. Also, during the holy month of Ramazan the working day is shortened.

Post Offices
: Main post offices in large cities tend to be open every day from 8 am to 8 pm for most services (stamp sales, telephone jeton and card sales, telegrams, fax etc), and the telephone centres may be open until midnight. However, windows may be open only from 8.30 am to noon and 1.30 pm to 5 or 6 pm for other services such as poste restante and parcel service. Smaller post offices have more limited hours: 8.30 am to 12.30 pm and 1.30 to 5.30 pm, and may be closed part of Saturday, and all day Sunday.

Restaurants
: Most restaurants serve food continuously from 11 am to 11 pm or later. Many open early (6 or 7 am) for breakfast. The exceptions are a few restaurants in bazaars, business and financial districts which serve primarily office workers and serve only lunch.

Shops
: Open Monday to Saturday, 9 am to noon and 1.30 or 2.30 pm to 6 or 7 pm or even later; many don't close for lunch.

Tourist Offices
: Usually Monday to Friday from 8.30 am to noon or 12.30 pm, and 1.30 to 5.30 pm, longer in summer in popular tourist locations.

THE CALENDAR

Religious Festivals

The official Turkish calendar is the western, Gregorian one used in Europe, but religious festivals are celebrated according to the Muslim lunar Hijri calendar. As the lunar calendar is about 11 days shorter than the Gregorian, the Muslim festivals arrive that many days earlier each year.

Actual dates for Muslim religious festivals are not completely systematic. Rather, they are proclaimed by Muslim authorities after the appropriate astronomical observations and calculations have been made, and then the civil authorities decide how many days should be public holidays. To help you know what's going on, the approximate dates of all major festivals for the near future are listed below.

Muslim days, like Jewish ones, begin at sundown. Thus a Friday holiday will begin on Thursday at sunset and last until Friday at sunset.

For major religious and public holidays there is also a half-day vacation for 'preparation', called *arife*, preceding the start of a festival. Shops and offices close about noon, and the festival begins at sunset.

Friday is the Muslim Sabbath, but it is not a holiday. Mosques and baths will be crowded, especially on Friday morning. The day of rest, a secular one, is Sunday.

Only two religious holidays are public holidays: Şeker Bayramı and Kurban Bayramı.

Ramazan The Holy Month, called Ramadan in other Muslim countries, is similar in some ways to Lent. For the 30 days of Ramazan, a good Muslim lets *nothing* pass the lips during daylight hours: no eating, drinking, smoking, or even licking a postage stamp.

A cannon shot, and these days a radio announcer, signal the end of the fast at sunset. The fast is broken traditionally with flat pide bread if possible. Lavish dinners are given and may last far into the night. Before dawn, drummers circulate through town to awaken the faithful so they can eat before sunrise.

During Ramazan, restaurants may be closed from dawn till nightfall, and in conservative towns it's bad form for anyone – non-Muslims included – to smoke, munch snacks or sip drinks in plain view. Business hours may change and be shorter. As non-Muslims, it's understood that you get to eat and drink when you like, and in the big cities you'll find lots of non-fasting Muslims right beside you, but it's best to be discreet and to maintain a polite low visibility.

The 27th day of Ramazan is **Kadir Gecesi**, the Night of Power, when the Koran was revealed and Muhammed was appointed to be the Messenger of God.

The fasting of Ramazan is a worthy, sacred act and a blessing to Muslims. Pregnant or nursing women, the infirm and aged, and travellers are excused, according to the Koran, if they feel they cannot keep the fast.

Şeker Bayramı Also called Ramazan Bayramı or İd es-Seğir, this is a three-day festival at the end of Ramazan. *Şeker* (shek-EHR) is sugar or candy. During this festival children traditionally go door to door asking for sweet treats, Muslims exchange greeting cards and pay social calls, and everybody enjoys drinking lots of tea in broad daylight after fasting for Ramazan. The festival is a national holiday when banks and offices are closed and hotels, buses, trains and aeroplanes are heavily booked.

Kurban Bayramı The most important religious and secular holiday of the year, Kurban Bayramı (koor-BAHN, sacrifice) is equivalent in importance to Christmas in Christian countries.

The festival commemorates Abraham's near-sacrifice of Isaac on Mt Moriah (Genesis 22; Koran, Sura 37). In the story, God orders Abraham to take Isaac, the son of his old age, up to Mt Moriah and sacrifice him.

Abraham takes Isaac up the mountain and lays him on the altar, but at the last moment God stops Abraham, congratulates him on his faithfulness, and orders him to sacrifice instead a ram tangled in a nearby bush. Abraham does so.

Following the tradition today, 2.5 million rams are sacrificed on Kurban Bayramı in Turkey each year. For days beforehand you'll see herds of sheep parading through streets or gathered in markets. Every head of household who can afford a sheep buys one and takes it home. Right after the early morning prayers on the actual day of Bayram, the head of the household slits the sheep's throat. It's then flayed and butchered, and family and friends immediately cook up a feast. A sizeable portion of the meat is distributed to the needy, and the skin is often donated to a charity; the charity sells it to a leather products company.

Lots of people take to the road, going home to parents or friends. Everybody exchanges greeting cards. At some point you'll probably be invited to share in the festivities.

Kurban Bayramı is a four-day national holiday which you must plan for. Banks may be closed for a full week, though one or two branches will stay open in the big cities to serve foreigners. Transportation will be packed, and hotel rooms, particularly in resort areas, will be scarce and expensive.

Minor Festivals During minor religious festivals mosques are illuminated with strings of lights, and special foods are prepared.

Regaip Kandili This is the traditional date for the conception of the Prophet Muhammed. You'll see packets of small, sweetish *simit* bread rings, wrapped in coloured paper, for sale on the streets.

Miraç Kandili This is the celebration of Muhammed's miraculous nocturnal journey from Mecca to Jerusalem and to heaven astride a winged horse named Burak.

Berat Kandili This festival has various meanings in different Islamic countries.

Mevlid-i Nebi The 12th of the Hijri month of Rebi ul-evvel is the anniversary of the Prophet's birth (in 570 AD). There are special prayers and foods, and mosque illuminations.

Annual Holidays & Events

The following is a month-by-month list of holidays and special events in Turkey.

January

It's rainy and cold throughout the country in January, with high air pollution in the cities – not usually a pleasant time to visit. Eastern Turkey is in the icy grip of winter; Ankara and the rest of the Anatolian Plateau may be covered in snow.

Religious Festivals – Ramazan, the holy month which changes lots of schedules, is from 10 January to 8 February in 1997, 30 December 1997 to 28 January 1998, 19 December 1998 to 17 January 1999, and 8 December 1999 to 6 January 2000. Kadir Gecesi, the Night of Power, is celebrated on 27 Ramazan, which falls on these dates: 26 January 1998, 15 January 1999 and 4 January 2000. Ramazan is followed by the three-day celebration of Şeker Bayramı each year.

1 – New Year's Day is a public holiday. Decorations in shops, exchanges of gifts and greeting cards, make it a kind of surrogate Christmas, good for business.

Mid-January – Camel-wrestling festival in the village of Selçuk, next to Ephesus, south of İzmir.

February

In February it rains almost everywhere and is chilly and cheerless. The only fun to be had is indoors or at the ski slopes on Uludağ near Bursa, in the Beydağları mountains near Antalya, on Erciyes near Kayseri, or at Palandöken near Erzurum.

Religious Holidays – Kadir Gecesi is celebrated on 5 February 1997 and Şeker Bayramı from 9 to 11 February 1997 (public holiday period).

March

Still rainy in most of the country, though there may be some good periods on the south Aegean and Mediterranean coasts. It's still bitterly cold in the east.

Religious Festivals – Kurban Bayramı, the four-day holiday which disrupts Turkish schedules for a week, is celebrated from 28 March to 1 April 1999 and 16 to 20 March 2000.

April

April can be delightful throughout the country, except in the east, where it's still cold. There may be some rain, but in any case the wild flowers will be out on the Anatolian Plateau. The waters of the Aegean and Mediterranean are approaching a comfortable temperature for swimming. The south-east (Gaziantep, Urfa, Mardin, Diyarbakır), so torrid and parched in high summer, is very pleasant now, but there may still be snow on top of Nemrut Dağı. April is when the bus tours begin in earnest.

Religious Festivals – Kurban Bayramı is celebrated from 17 to 21 April 1997 and 8 to 12 April 1998.

20-30 – Manisa Power Gum Festival, when a traditional remedy called *mesir macunu* or *kuvvet macunu* (power gum), said to restore health, youth and potency, is concocted and distributed in Manisa, near İzmir.

23 – The big national holiday, National Sovereignty Day, when the first Grand National Assembly, or republican parliament, met in Ankara in 1920. It's also Children's Day, an international children's festival, with kids from all over the world, held in Ankara.

Late April-Early May – Tulip festival held in Emirgan, the Bosphorus suburb of İstanbul.

May

May usually brings perfectly beautiful weather throughout the country, with little chance of rain, though it's still chilly out east. May is a good month to visit the hot, dry south-east. This month begins the tourist season in earnest, and also includes important public holidays. Sound and light shows begin at the Blue Mosque in İstanbul and last until October. In Konya, the javelin-throwing game of *cirit* (jirid), played on horseback, takes place every Saturday and Sunday until October.

1st Week – Selçuk Ephesus Festival of Culture & Art at Selçuk, south of İzmir, features folk dances, concerts and exhibits, some in the Great Theatre at Ephesus.

19 – Youth & Sports Day, held to commemorate Atatürk's birthday (1881).

29 – In İstanbul, celebrations remember the takeover of the city from the Byzantines in 1453.

Last Week – Festival of Pergamum at Bergama, north of İzmir, which features drama in the ancient theatre, folk dancing and handicraft exhibits.

June

The weather is perfect throughout the country, but getting hot. There is little rain except along the Black Sea coast.

Religious Festivals – Mevlid-i Nebi, the Prophet's birthday, is celebrated on 26 June 1999 and 15 June 2000.

1st Week – The International Mediterranean Festival takes place in İzmir usually at this time.

4-5 – Traditional rose-growing competition at Konya, when roses grown in the region are judged.

7-13 – Music & Art Festival at Marmaris, with musical performances, folk dances and exhibitions.

2nd Week – Traditional Kırkpınar Oiled Wrestling Competition held at Edirne and Festival of Troy at Çanakkale, on the Dardanelles near Troy.

3rd Week – The Kafkasör Festival, in a *yayla* (alpine pasture) takes place near Artvin in north-eastern Turkey – a true country festival featuring local dances, crafts, foods, and fights between bulls in rut.

Late June-Mid-July – World-class International İstanbul Festival of the Arts, with top performers in music and dance, and special exhibitions.

July

The weather is hot, the sky is always blue, the sea water is warm, and everything is crowded with holiday-makers, both Turkish and foreign.

Religious Festivals – Mevlid-i Nebi, the Prophet's birthday, is celebrated on 28 July 1996, 18 July 1997 and 7 July 1998. The İstanbul Festival continues until mid-July.

1 – Denizcilik Günü (Navy Day), when mariners, ships and various maritime pursuits are celebrated.

5-10 – Nasreddin Hoca celebrations (in Akşehir, his traditional birthplace) are held in honour of the semi-legendary, humorous master of Turkish folklore legends and tales.

7-12 – At Bursa, the Folklore & Music Festival is one of Turkey's best folk-dancing events of the year; the Bursa Fair (trade & tourism) starts about the same time.

29-31 – Music, Folklore & Water Sports Festival in Foça, north of İzmir

August

It's hot, sunny and crowded. This is the best time to be in eastern Turkey, when the weather is fine and crowds are smaller than along the western beaches. Sound and light shows begin at the Anıt Kabir, Atatürk's mausoleum, in Ankara.

15 – A special mass at the House of the Virgin Mary (Meryemana) near Ephesus celebrates the Assumption of the Virgin Mary. The Catholic archbishop of İzmir says mass.

15-18 – Çanakkale Troy Festival at Çanakkale, with folk dances, music, tours of Mt Ida and Troy.

Mid-August – Haci Bektaş Veli commemoration at the town of that name in Cappadocia.

20 August-9 September – The biggest festival is the İzmir International Fair. For a month the city's hotels are packed and transportation is crowded. The fair has amusements, cultural and commercial-industrial displays.

30 August – Zafer Bayramı (zah-FEHR, Victory), commemorating the decisive victory at Dumlupınar of the republican armies over the invading Greek army during Turkey's War of Independence in 1922. Towns and cities celebrate their own Kurtuluş Günü (Day of Liberation) on the appropriate date commemorating when Atatürk's armies drove out the foreign troops during July and August 1922.

September

The weather is still hot and fine, moderating a bit towards the end of the month. Swimming is still wonderful, crowds are still fairly heavy, and the bus tours begin to make a comeback. Sound and light shows continue at the Anıt Kabir in Ankara. The İzmir Fair goes on until 9 September.

1-9 – Bodrum Culture & Art Week, featuring Turkish classical music concerts in Bodrum Castle, art exhibits and water sports shows.

2-4 – Kırşehir Ahi Evran Crafts & Folklore Festival at Kırşehir, when Turkish handicrafts are displayed and modelled in shows.

9 – In İzmir it's Kurtuluş Günü, or Liberation Day, with lots of parades, speeches and flags.

11-12 – Çorum Hittite Festival with crafts shows, musical performances and tours of Hittite archaeological sites at Çorum near Ankara.

15-18 – Cappadocia Festival, a grape harvest and folklore festival highlighting the 'fairy chimneys' and underground cities of Cappadocia.

22-30 – Konya hosts a culinary contest.

Mid or Late September – At Diyarbakır, there's the Watermelon Festival. One year when I attended, everybody was disappointed because the prize-winning watermelon weighed in at a mere 32 kg. A bad year, they said – no rain.

October

The weather is perfect again, and crowds are diminishing, though bus tours start again in earnest, after a lull during high summer. The rains begin sometime in mid or late October. There may also be freak snowstorms on the Anatolian Plateau. Sound and light shows are supposed to continue in İstanbul at the Blue Mosque, but check in advance.

Religious Festivals – Regaip Kandili is celebrated on 23 October 1998, 15 October 1999 and 6 October 2000. Miraç Kandili is on 25 October 2000.

1-9 – The 'Golden Orange' Film & Art Festival is held in Antalya, with a competition for best Turkish film of the year. There are other exhibits.

21-29 – During Turkish Troubadours' Week at Konya bards who continue the traditional poetic forms hold contests in repartee, free-form composition and riddles.

29 – Cumhuriyet Bayramı (Republic Day), commemorates the proclamation of the republic by Atatürk in 1923. It's the biggest civil holiday, with lots of parades and speeches.

November

The weather is very pleasant, with cool to warm days and chilly nights, but one must dodge the rain. If your luck holds, you can have a marvellous late-year beach holiday.

Religious Festivals – Regaip Kandili is celebrated on 12 November 1996 and 7 November 1997; Berat Kandili is on 23 and 24 November 1999 and 12 and 13 November 2000; Miraç Kandili is on 27 November 1997, 16 November 1998 and 5 November 1999. Ramazan begins on 28 November 2000.

10 – The most important day of the month, it is the day Atatürk died in 1938. At precisely 9.05 am, the moment of his death, the entire country comes to a screeching halt for a moment of silence. Literally everything stops in its tracks (you should too), just for a moment. Car horns and sirens blare. In schools, in the newspapers (the names of which are normally printed in red, but are all in black on this day), on radio and TV, the national hero's life and accomplishments are reviewed.

December

The weather is chilly throughout the country, though milder along the Mediterranean coast. You must expect some, perhaps heavy, rain. There are few visitors; some museums close some exhibits for renovation. In rare years, the warmth and pleasantness of a good November will stretch into early December.

Religious Festivals – The holy month of Ramazan is from 28 November to 27 December 2000. Kadir Gecesi, the Night of Power, is commemorated on 24 December 2000. Şeker Bayramı is from 28 to 30 December 2000. Berat Kandili is celebrated on 25-26 December 1996, 15-16 December 1997, and 4-5 December 1998.

All Month – Camel wrestling occurs at various locations in the province of Aydın, south of İzmir.

6-8 – St Nicholas Festival, when commemorative ceremonies are held in the 4th-century church of St Nicholas, the original Santa Claus, in Demre near Antalya.

14-17 (approximately) – The Mevlana Festival, honouring Celaleddin Rumi, the great poet and mystic who founded the Mevlevi order of Whirling Dervishes, held in Konya. Hotel space is tight, so try to pin down a room in advance, or be prepared for a room below your normal standard.

ACTIVITIES

Water Sports

Water sports are big in Turkey because of the beautiful coasts and beaches. Yachting, rowing, water-skiing, snorkelling, diving (with or without scuba gear) and swimming are well represented. Because of the many antiquities in the depths off the Turkish coasts, scuba diving is regulated. Diving shops in Marmaris, Bodrum and other coastal towns can provide details. Turkish divers are very safety conscious, so bring your diving credentials to dive to the depth you want to explore.

Mountain Climbing

Mountain climbing *(dağcılık*, DAAH-juh-LUHK) is practised by a small but enthusiastic number of Turks, and Turkey has plenty of good, high mountains for it. For complete information, with addresses of outfitters, guides and Turkish climbing clubs, buy a copy of *Trekking in Turkey* (see Lonely Planet in the Books section in this chapter).

Skiing

There is decent skiing on Uludağ, near Bursa, at a few resorts in the Beydağları mountain range near Antalya, on Mt Erciyes near Kayseri, and at Palandöken near Erzurum. Except at Bursa, facilities are basic, even primitive, but equipment can be rented at the slopes. The reward for true skiers is on the slopes: at Palandöken, the snow is good for nine months of the year.

Cycling

Cycling through Turkey is possible, and mostly delightful. For details, see the Getting Around chapter.

WORK

You can extend your time in Turkey by getting a job. Most people who do this teach English at one of the many private colleges or schools in İstanbul or Ankara. Others work at one of the publication offices such as at the *Turkish Daily News*.

It's best to obtain a work visa *(çalışma vizesi)* from the Turkish embassy or consulate (in person or by mail; it takes from three weeks) in your home country before you leave. Submit the completed visa form, your passport, two photos of yourself, your proof of employment (a contract or letter from your employer) and the required fee. Your passport will be returned with the visa stamped inside.

If you're not at home and you want a work visa, apply for it outside Turkey. The Turkish consulate in Komotini in Greece, an 11-hour overnight bus ride from İstanbul, is used to such requests. It usually grants the visa within a few hours. If you plan to make a special trip, check to make sure the consulate will be open and issuing work visas when you arrive. Your own consulate or a Greek consulate may be able to tell you (see Embassies in this chapter).

Once you arrive in Turkey on a work visa, you must obtain a 'pink book', a combined work permit and residence permit, from the Yabancılar Polisi (Foreigners' Police). In İstanbul they're in Cağaloğlu behind the İstanbul Valiliği on Ankara Caddesi. Your employer may do this for you. If not, apply with your passport, two more photos, and the US$40 processing fee. They should have your pink book ready in two or three days. The pink book, which takes over from the visa in your passport, is renewable every year, as long as you show proof of continued employment.

TURKISH CARPETS

Turkey is famous for its beautiful carpets and kilims and wherever you go you'll be spoilt for choice as to what to buy. Unfortunately, the carpet market is highly competitive and the hard-sell antics of some dealers have tended to bring it into disrepute, putting many visitors off venturing into the shops. This is a great shame because there are certainly some great purchases to be made...especially if you concentrate on finding something you really like rather than on unearthing a 'bargain'.

An Age-Old Art

Turkish women have been weaving carpets for a very long time. These beautiful, durable, eminently portable floor coverings were a nomadic family's most valuable and practical 'furniture', warming and brightening the clan's oft-moved homes.

The oldest known carpet woven in the Turkish double-knotted *Gördes* style dates from sometime between the 4th and 1st centuries BC.

It is thought that hand-woven carpet techniques were introduced to Anatolia by the Seljuks in the 12th century. Thus it's not surprising that Konya, the Seljuk capital, was mentioned by Marco Polo as a centre of carpet production in the 13th century.

Traditional Patterns

Traditionally, village women wove carpets for their own family's use, or for their dowry. Knowing they would be judged on their efforts, the women took great care over their handiwork, hand-spinning and dyeing the wool, and choosing what they judged to be the most interesting and beautiful patterns.

The general pattern and colour scheme of old carpets was heavily influenced by local traditions and the availability of certain types of wool and colours of dyes. Traditional patterns were memorised, and women usually worked with no more than 18 inches of the carpet visible. But each artist imbued her work with her own personality, choosing a motif or a colour based on her own artistic preferences, and even events and emotions in her daily life.

Old carpets incorporate all sorts of symbols which can be 'read' by those in the know. At a glance two carpets might look identical, but closer examination reveals the subtle differences that give each old Turkish carpet its individuality, and much of its charm.

In the 19th century, the European rage for Turkish carpets spurred the development of carpet companies. The companies, run by men, would deal with customers, take orders, purchase and dye the wool according to the customers' preferences, and contract local women to produce the finished product. The designs might be left to the women, but more frequently were provided by the company based on the customers' tastes. Though well made, these carpets lost some of the originality and spirit of the traditional work.

Carpet Weaving Today

These days the picture is more complicated. Many carpets are made not according to local traditions, but to the dictates of the market. Weavers in eastern Turkey might make carpets in popular styles native to western Turkey. Long-settled villagers might duplicate the wilder, hairier and more naive *yörük*, or nomad, carpets. The shopkeeper may tell you about these adaptations.

Village women still weave carpets but these days most of them work to fixed contracts for specific shops. In 95% of cases they work to a pattern and are paid for their final effort rather than for each hour of work. A carpet made to a fixed contract may still be of great value to its purchaser. However, the selling price should be lower than for a one-off piece.

Other carpets are the product of division of labour, with different individuals responsible for dyeing and weaving. What such pieces lose in individuality and rarity is often more than made up for in quality control. Most silk *Hereke* carpets are mass produced in this way but to standards that make them some of the most sought-after of all Turkish carpets.

Fearing that old carpet making methods would be lost forever, the Ministry of Culture now sponsors a number of projects to revive traditional weaving and dyeing methods in western Turkey. Some carpet shops will have stocks of these 'project carpets' which are usually of high quality with prices reflecting that fact.

Carpets and loom outside a shop in Göreme, Cappadocia

CHRIS BARTON

Kilims, Sumaks & Cicims

A good carpet shop will have a range of pieces made by a variety of techniques. Besides the traditional pile carpets, they may offer double-sided flat-woven mats such as kilims. Some traditional kilim motifs are similar to patterns found at the prehistoric mound of Çatal Höyük, testifying to the very ancient traditions of flat-woven floor coverings in Anatolia. Older, larger kilims may actually be two narrower pieces of similar but not always identical design stitched together. As this is now rarely done, any such piece is likely to be fairly old.

Other flat-weave techniques include *sumak*, a style originally from Azerbaijan in which coloured threads are wrapped round the warp. In Turkey the sumak technique was only used for saddlebags, so big sumak pieces must be from elsewhere in the Turkic world. Some sumaks are decorated with naive animal patterns and are often (but fantastically) called 'Noah's Ark carpets'. *Cicims* are kilims with small, lively patterns embroidered on top of them.

GLENN BEANLAND

Top: Detail of a Turkish carpet

Bottom: Carpet weaver, Göreme, Cappadocia

CHRIS BARTON

Carpets From Other Countries

As well as Turkish carpets, many carpet shops sell pieces from other countries, especially from neighbouring Iran and from the ex-Soviet Republics of Azerbaijan and Uzbekistan. If it matters to you that yours is actually from Turkey, bear in mind that Iran favours the single knot and Turkey the double, or Gördes, knot. Turkish carpets also tend to have a higher pile and more dramatic designs than their Iranian cousins.

TOM BROSNAHAN

Top: Carpet shop, Side, Antalya

Bottom: Detail of a kilim, Kayseri

GLENN BEANLAND

A Carpet-Buyer's Primer

When deciding whether to buy a particular carpet, follow some of the tests below.

A good-quality, long-lasting carpet should be 100% wool (*yüz de yüz yün*): check the warp (the lengthwise yarns), weft (the crosswise yarns) and pile (the vertical yarns knotted into the matrix of warp and weft). Is the wool fine and shiny, with signs of the natural oil still present? More expensive carpets may be of a silk and wool blend. Cheaper carpets may have warp and weft of mercerised cotton. You can tell by checking the fringes at either end, which are in fact the ends of the warp yarns. If the fringe is of cotton or 'flosh' (mercerised

TOM BROSNAHAN

Top: Carpet shop, Grand Bazaar, İstanbul

Bottom: Colourful kilim, Kayseri

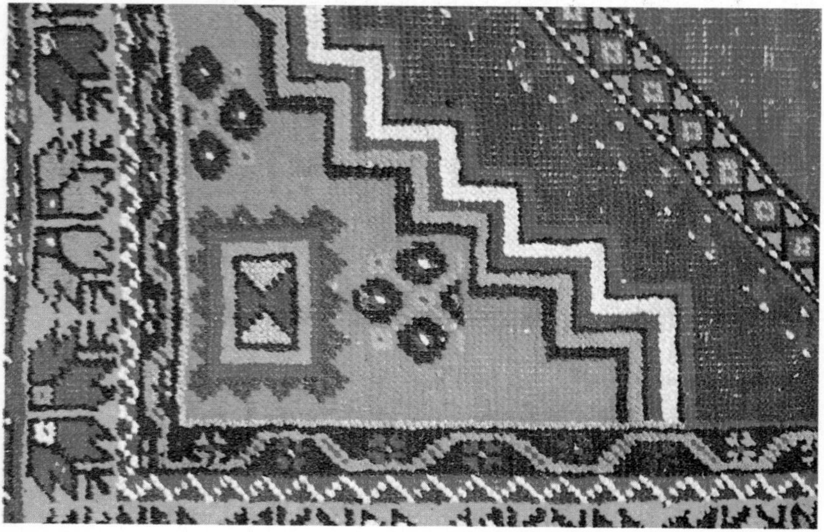

GLENN BEANLAND

cotton...sometimes misleadingly called 'floss silk'), you shouldn't pay for wool. Another way to identify the material of the warp and weft is to turn the carpet over and look for the fine, frizzy fibres common to wool, but not to cotton. Some connoisseurs of fine carpets will pluck some of these fine fibres and burn them to see if they smell like wool, silk, or nylon. But bear in mind that just being made of wool doesn't guarantee a carpet's quality. If the dyes and design are ugly, even a 100% woollen carpet can be a bad buy.

Check the closeness of the weave by turning the carpet over and inspecting the back. In general, the tighter the weave and the smaller the knots, the higher the quality and durability of the carpet. But bear in mind that the oldest carpets sometimes had quite thick knots, so consider the number of knots alongside the colours and the quality of the wool.

Compare the colours on the back with those on the front. Spread the nap with your fingers and look at the bottom of the pile. Are the colours brighter there than on the surface? Slight colour variations could occur in older carpets when a new batch of dye was mixed, but richer colour deep in the pile is often an indication that the surface has faded in the sun. Natural dyes don't fade as readily as chemical dyes. There is nothing wrong with chemical dyes, which have a long history of their own. But natural dyes and colours tend to be preferred and so fetch higher prices. Don't pay for natural if you're getting chemical.

New carpets can be made to look old, and damaged or worn carpets can be rewoven (good work, but expensive), patched or even painted. Rub a wet handkerchief on the top of the carpet. If colour comes off on it, it could suggest that the dyes are runny or that a worn carpet has been retouched with watercolours. There is nothing wrong with a dealer offering you a patched or repainted carpet provided they point out these defects and price the piece accordingly, but it would be dishonest to offer you cheap goods at an inflated price. On the other hand, some red *Bokhara* carpets will continue to give off colour even though they're of better quality than cheap woollen carpets which don't.

Look at the carpet from one end, then from the other. The colours will be different because the pile always leans one way or the other. Take the carpet out into the sunlight and look at it there. Imagine where you might put the carpet at home, and how the light will strike it.

Pricing & Payment

When it comes to choosing what to buy, there's no substitute for spending time comparing what's on offer in different shops and developing an 'eye' for what you really like. You also need to be realistic about your budget. These days carpets are such big business that true bargains are hard to come by unless there is something (like gigantic size) that makes them hard to sell for their true value.

Carpet prices are determined by age, material, quality, condition, demand in the market, the enthusiasm of the buyer, and the debt load of the seller. Bear in mind that if you do your carpet shopping on a tour or when accompanied by a guide, the price will be hiked by up to 35% to cover somebody's commission.

It may be wiser to go for something small but of high quality rather than for a room-sized cheapie. Another way to make the money stretch further is to opt for one of the smaller items made from carpet materials: old camel bags and hanging baby's cradles opened out to make rugs; *sofras* or rugs on which food would be eaten; decorative grain bags; cushion covers; even the bags which once held rock salt for animals.

Some dealers will take personal cheques, but all prefer cash. An increasing number of shops take credit cards but some may require you to pay the credit card company's fee and the cost of the phone call to check your creditworthiness. A few dealers will let you pay in instalments.

If you can't provide proof of employment (ie if you're working illegally), you may still be able to get a three-month residence permit if you can show bank deposits in Turkey totalling more than about US$200. You may or may not be able to renew a three-month permit, at the whim of the officer.

When all else fails, leave the country for a day or two to Greece, Bulgaria or Cyprus, and get a new 90-day tourist visa as you return to Turkey. This may only be possible a few times, however, as the immigration officer will become suspicious of too many recent Turkish stamps in your passport.

ACCOMMODATION

Camping

Using your own equipment and bedding, it is sometimes possible to sleep on the roof of a pension or hotel, or camp in the garden, for a minimal fee of US$2 to US$4 per person, which includes use of bathing and other hotel facilities. In seaside areas and near major attractions such as Cappadocia, you'll see signs marking small, scruffy *kampink* areas which often have few facilities, but may be cheap, especially if you haggle. The fancier camping grounds near seaside resorts have all facilities – showers, shops, swimming pools, gardens, games – but charge almost as much as cheap hotels.

Camping outside recognised camping grounds by the roadside is often more hassle than it's worth as the police may come and check you out, the landowner may wonder what's up, and curious villagers may decide that they'd rather sit and watch you than the *Dynasty* reruns on the TV.

Another way to save lodging money is to take night buses or trains on long hauls.

Hostels

As the lowest priced hotels and pensions are already rock-bottom, there is no extensive system of hostels in Turkey. The term *yurt* (hostel or lodge) or *ö'renci yurdu* (student hostel) usually defines an extremely basic and often dingy dormitory lodging intended for low-budget Turkish students from the provinces who are attending university classes. These are not normally affiliated with the International Youth Hostel Federation, and often they are not conveniently located near the major sights, though they may open their doors to foreign students in the summertime.

Hotels

The cheapest hotels in Turkey are rated by each local municipality. These are the basic places that provide bed, heat, light and water. They are used mostly by working-class Turkish men travelling on business. Virtually all hotels above this basic standard are rated by the Ministry of Tourism according to a star system. One-star hotels are just a step above the cheap places rated by the municipalities. At the top, rating five stars, are the international-class places, such as the Hiltons, Hyatts, Kempinskis, Ramadas and Sheratons.

In this guide, hotels are listed according to price, except in places with only a few hotels which must be used by all visitors regardless of preference.

Bottom End Lodgings in this group are priced from US$4 per bed in a small town up to US$20 or US$25 for a double room in a large city. For Turks, these are the *otels* (hotels) used by farmers in town for the market, workers in town looking for a job, or the *pansiyons* (pensions) used by working-class families on holiday at the seaside. Not surprisingly, the most difficult place to find a truly cheap, good, low-budget room is İstanbul. In most other cities good, cheap beds can be found fairly easily. In out-of-the-way villages the price for a bed is surprisingly low.

Rooms priced below about US$10 do not usually have a private shower or toilet in the room, but may have a *lavabo* (sink). Above that price, in small towns you may get private facilities. Cold-water showers are usually free, as they should be. Hot-water showers may cost between US$1 and US$2 in lodgings where a fire must be built in the hot-water heater. If there is solar water-heating, hot showers are often free, but the water may only be warm, as the solar tanks are generally uninsulated in the off season. On cloudy days, or if everyone else has preceded you to the showers, expect tepid water. With solar water-heating, plan to shower in the evening when the water is hottest, rather than in the morning.

At the lowest prices, the rooms will be quite bare and spartan, but functional. Hotels may quote prices per bed rather than per room. For privacy, you may have to pay for all of the beds in the room. If you find used sheets on the bed, request clean ones; the owner has got to change them sometime, and it may as well be for you. Say *Temiz çarşaf lazım* (teh-MEEZ chahr-SHAHF lyaa-zuhm, 'Clean sheets are necessary'). Bedbugs are not unheard of; let me know of any bug banquets you host so I can warn other readers.

Middle Turkey has lots of modern and comfortable hotels rated at one to three stars by the Ministry of Tourism. Facilities in this range include lifts, staff capable of speaking a smattering of German, French and English, rooms with a private shower or bath and toilet, perhaps balconies from which you can enjoy the view, and maybe guarded car parks. Prices in this range are from US$20 to US$90.

A one-star hotel will have these facilities and little else, and will price its double rooms with a bath at around US$20. A two-star hotel will probably have a restaurant and bar, a TV lounge, obsequious staff, and some pretensions to décor and architecture. Double rooms with a private bath would be priced from US$25 to US$60.

A three-star hotel may provide colour TVs and mini-bar refrigerators in all guest rooms, and may have haughty but multilingual staff, a swimming pool, nightclub, pastry shop, or other special facilities as well. Double rooms with a bath would be priced from US$40 to US$90. Fairly prosperous Turks look upon a hotel room in this range as quite luxurious accommodation.

Top End Hotels at the top end are priced from US$90 to US$250 and up for a double room.

Hotels of an international standard, such as the Hiltons, Sheratons, Kempinskis, Ramadas, Hyatts, Swissötels etc, are rated at five stars and are mostly to be found in the largest cities (İstanbul, Ankara, İzmir, Adana) and in the most famous tourist destinations (Antalya, Cappadocia). Just below the international chains in luxury are the Turkish chain hotels such as Dedeman, Merit and others, rated at four or five stars. These hotels sometimes provide almost the same degree of luxury as some of the top places, but at prices around 20 to 40% lower.

Besides these very expensive places, Turkey has a number of smaller, very comfortable hotels where you'll enjoy more personal and attentive service at much lower prices. These four-star luxury hotels may not have swimming pools, health clubs, ballrooms and convention centres, but they have most of the comforts an individual traveller would normally require. Prices for a double room range from US$90 to US$150.

Boutique Hotels In some tourist towns old Ottoman mansions, caravanserais or other historic buildings have been refurbished or even completely rebuilt, and equipped with modern conveniences. Charm, atmosphere and history are the attractions here, and they are provided in abundance at prices ranging from US$75 to US$175 for a double room, breakfast included. Because of their unique character, these hotels may not be rated according to the star system. Most would rate three or four stars if they were.

Choosing a Hotel

The following are some points to watch.

Inspect the Rooms For bottom-end and middle lodgings, don't judge a hotel by its façade, tell the reception clerk you'd like to see a room. A staff member will invariably be appointed to show you one or several rooms.

In the middle range of Turkish hotels there is a tendency to put money into the lobby rather than into the rooms, and so looking at the lobby does not give you an accurate idea of the quality of the guest quarters.

Know the Price Prices should be posted prominently at the reception desk. Sometimes the posted prices will be above what the proprietor actually expects to get for a room. Unless the hotel or pension is obviously quite full and very busy, you may be able to haggle for a lower price.

Please keep in mind when you haggle that pension and cheap hotel owners must be able to make some money to stay in business. A few travellers make a habit of haggling forcefully even if the price (say, US$3 for a tidy bed with clean sheets in a safe dorm room) is already rock bottom. This may only lead to unpleasantness and even bitterness. It certainly doesn't promote understanding between Turks and foreigners. If the price represents good value for money, it's best to pay it with a smile.

Whether you haggle or not, make sure you understand the price. Is it per bed *(beher yatak*, beh-HEHR yah-TAHK) or per room *(oda fiyatı*, OH-dah fee-yah-tuh)? Is breakfast *(kahvaltı)* included *(dahil)* or excluded *(hariç)*? Is there an extra fee for a hot shower *(duş ücreti*, DOOSH urj-reh-tee)? Is the tax included *(vergi dahil*, vehr-GEE dah-HEEL)? It usually is (and should be) except at the most expensive hotels.

Beware of Noise Turkish cities and towns are noisy places, and you will soon learn to choose a hotel and a room with quiet in mind. In this guide I have done some of the work for you by recommending mostly the quieter places, but you will have to be aware when you select your room. The front rooms in a hotel, those facing the busy street, are usually looked upon as the most desirable by the hotel management, and are sometimes priced higher than rooms at the rear. Take advantage of this: take a room at the back. Ask for *sakin bir oda* (sah-KEEN beer oh-dah, 'a quiet room') and pay less.

Water Pressure In some cities, and particularly in summer, there may be temporary water problems. Water may be cut off for several hours at a time, though many hotels have roof tanks which do away with this problem. The other problem with water pressure is when the pressure remains high, but the fixtures are not in good repair, and the toilet tinkles all night.

Hot Water Except in the fanciest hotels, do not trust hot water to come out of the left-hand tap and cold water out of the right-hand one. Every time you settle into a hotel room, or use a shower, experiment with the taps. It means nothing that the left-hand one is marked in red, it may yield cold water, while the right-hand one, marked in blue, gives hot water. In the same bathroom, the sink may be marked correctly and the shower incorrectly. It's a daily struggle. Open both taps and let them run full force for a minute or so, close them, then open one and next the other to see what you get. If both are cold, let them run a few minutes more and check again. Still cold? OK, now it's time to complain to the management.

As for hot water, it's often difficult to find in summer in the cheaper hotels, unless they have solar water-heaters. Many small hotels have only a single furnace for both hot water and central heating, and they really don't want to run that furnace in summer. Since the summers are warm, even hot, this doesn't present much of a problem. Early spring and late autumn are another matter, though. Every desk clerk will say, 'Yes, we have hot water', but when you try to take a shower the new fact will be, 'Ah, the furnace just this minute broke down!'

Believe it or not, the most dependable hot water is in the cheapest pensions, because in these places the owner builds a little fire in the bottom of the hot-water tank 30 minutes before your shower appointment, and you bathe in as much steaming water as you want. The extra charge for this luxury is US$1 to US$2.

An alternative, fairly dependable hot-water method is the *şofben* (SHOHF-behn), or flash heater. This type runs on gas, and flashes into action as soon as you turn on the hot-water tap. It's activated by water flowing through the hot-water pipe. Obviously this sort of heater is not dependent on a central furnace, but it does have other problems. Gas pressure must be sufficient to heat the water, which it sometimes is not; and the flow of water must be strong enough to activate the şofben, which it sometimes is not. Often it's a balancing act, keeping the flow of water fast enough to activate the heater, yet slow enough to make sure the water remains hot.

Lifts If you push the wrong button on the lift/elevator, you'll never get to the right place. 'Ç' stands for *çağır* (call) which is what you want to do to the lift – call it to where you are. 'G' is for *gönder* (send), and if you push this one, you'll send the lift to the end of its run (usually to the ground floor). A little illuminated 'M' means the lift is *meşgül* (engaged); wait until the light goes out before pushing 'Ç'. If there's a little illuminated 'K', it means the car is *katta* (positioned at your floor). 'Z' or *zemin* in lift parlance means ground floor; this is the button to push to get there. If you push '1', you'll end up on the 1st floor above ground level. If the ground floor button is not 'Z' it's probably 'L' for *lobi.*

If you stay in hotels with lifts, at least once you will have the idiotic feeling that comes when you press the 'Ç' button only to have the lift respond 'K', meaning, 'The car's already here, stupid. Just pull the door open and get in'.

Electricity Electricity may go off for short periods in some locations. This is not much of a problem, however. What is a problem is the lack of reading lights in all but the more expensive hotels. Your bedside lamp will never have more than a 25-watt bulb in it. Apparently Turks don't read in bed. However, you may find a *gece lambası* in your room, a low-wattage bulb, perhaps even one in a lurid colour, perhaps high on the wall. The function of this 'night light' (as the term translates) is to give an eerie glow to the room so that you do not sleep in total darkness.

Unmarried Couples Unmarried couples sharing rooms usually run into no problems, even though the desk clerk sees the obvious when taking down the pertinent information from your passports onto the registration form. By law, Turkish men are forbidden to share rooms with women to whom they are not married, and if there is a doubt must produce a marriage certificate. The cheaper the hotel, the more traditional and conservative its management tends to be. Very simple hotels which are clean and 'proper' want to maintain their reputations. If you look clean and proper, and act that way, there should be no trouble.

FOOD

It is worth travelling to Turkey just to eat. Turkish cuisine is the very heart of eastern Mediterranean cooking, and it demands fresh ingredients and careful preparation. The ingredients are often simple but of high quality. Turkish farmers, herders and fishers bring forth a wealth of superb produce from this agriculturally rich land and its surrounding seas. Turkey is one of only seven

Popular dishes in Turkey include fried, grilled or poached fish, grilled meats and kebaps. Vegetarianism is not prevalent and it can be difficult to find vegetable alternatives to meat dishes. Salads, cheeses and pilavs are possibilities.

A Taste of Honey

As you journey around Turkey you will no doubt spot the lines of blue and white beehives lined up by the roadside, tended by their careful owners in space-age-looking suits.

Turkish honey comes in several delicious varieties which are well worth sampling. First, there's *çam balı* (CHAHM bah-luh), a pine-scented honey from young forest growth which is rich, dark and full-flavoured. A variation is *siyah çam balı*, black-pine honey, with a rich deep flavour and a colour almost as dark as molasses.

Then there's *portakal*, or orange-blossom honey, which is very light-coloured and thin textured, with a light, sweet flavour. *Akasya balı* comes from locust-tree blossom. Slightly darker and more flavoursome is *çiçek*, or flower honey. Finally there's *oğul balı*, or virgin honey, the first honey from a new swarm.

A popular Turkish breakfast consists of half a loaf of bread with a pat of butter which you mix with honey and spread on the bread. In western Turkey, Marmaris is a particularly good place for honey sampling. In eastern Turkey, Kars is the place. ■

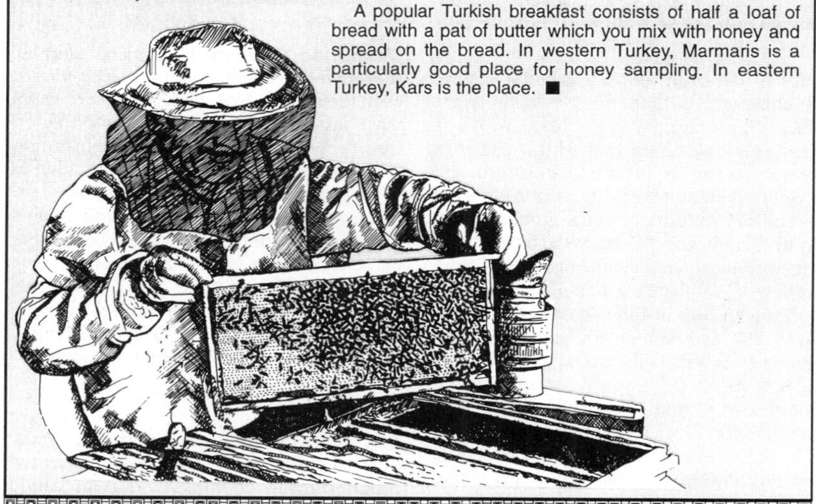

countries on earth which produces a surplus of food.

The variety of dishes found in restaurants is not as great as that found in home kitchens. And when you'd like a change from charcoal-grilled lamb, you'll rarely find an Indonesian or Mexican or Indian or Japanese restaurant just around the corner. Despite the extent of the Ottoman Empire the Turks did not trade extensively with other nations during the 18th and 19th centuries, and never received an influx of foreign populations and cuisines. This is changing, though. Some Chinese restaurants have opened, Japanese ones are sure to follow, and you can now – for better or worse – get authentic Yankee hamburgers and pizza in the larger cities.

Saving Money

Several tips can save you lots of money on food. Firstly, order as you eat. There is no need to order your entire meal at the beginning, except perhaps in the international hotels. Secondly, don't overeat with your eyes. Thirdly, eat bread. Turkish sourdough bread is delicious, fresh, plentiful and cheap. Many Turkish dishes are served with savoury sauces; dip and sop your bread and enjoy. Fourthly, don't accept any plate of food which you have not specifically ordered. For example, in İstanbul's Çiçek

Pasajı, near Galatasaray Square, itinerant vendors may put a dish of fresh almonds on your table. They're not a gift. They'll show up on your bill at a higher than average rate. If you haven't ordered it, ask *İkramiye mi?* ('Is it a gift?') or *Bedava mı?* ('Is it free?'). If the answer is no, say *İstemiyorum* ('I don't want it').

Finally, always ask prices in advance and check your restaurant bill for errors. As tourism has come to Turkey, so has the common sin of ripping off the tourist. The traditional Turkish practice of figuring the bill, then turning it over, folding it in half and writing the total on the back has the look of a ripoff. It's not necessarily so, but you should feel no embarrassment in opening the bill, redoing the addition, and questioning any items, including obscure *kuver* (cover) and *servis* (service) charges. If you don't get an itemised bill, by all means ask for one.

Restaurants

Restaurants *(restoran/lokanta)* are everywhere, and most are open early in the morning until late at night. Most are very inexpensive, and although price is always some determinant of quality, often the difference between a US$6 meal and a US$15 meal is not great, at least as far as flavour is concerned. Service and ambience are fancier at the higher price.

In any restaurant in Turkey there is a convenient sink *(lavabo)* so that you can wash your hands before eating. Just say the word and the waiter will point it out.

Also, if you're a woman or are travelling with a woman, ask for the *aile salonu* (family dining room, often upstairs) which will be free of the sometimes oppressive all-male atmosphere to be found in many cheap Turkish eateries.

Many Turkish waiters have the annoying habit of snatching your plate away before you're finished with it. This may be due to a rule of eastern etiquette which holds that it is impolite to leave a finished plate sitting in front of a guest. If a waiter engages in plate-snatching, say *Kalsın* ('Let it stay').

Full Service This is the familiar sort of restaurant with white tablecloths and waiter service. It may be open for three meals a day, and will probably be among the more expensive dining places. They usually serve spirits, wine and beer, and are sometimes called *içkili* (literally, 'serving drinks') because of this.

Hazır Yemek Literally, 'ready food', these are sometimes arranged as a *self-servis* cafeteria. Although all restaurants offer some dishes prepared in advance, these places specialise in an assortment of dishes, prepared in advance, kept warm in a steam table. Usually no alcoholic beverages are served in these places, but occasionally, if you order a beer, the waiter will run to a shop nearby and get one for you.

Décor may be nonexistent and the letters on the front window may only say *Lokanta*, but the welcome will be warm, the food delicious and very cheap.

With your meal you will receive as much fresh bread as you can eat, for a nominal charge.

Kebapçı & Köfteci Two other sorts of restaurant are the *kebapçı* (keh-BAHP-chuh) and *köfteci* (KURF-teh-jee). A kebapçı is a person who cooks *kebap* (roast meat). A köfteci roasts *köfte*, meatballs of minced (ground) lamb made with savoury spices. Though they may have one or two ready-food dishes, kebapçı and köfteci restaurants specialise in grilled meat, plus soups, salad, yoghurt and perhaps dessert.

Kebapçıs can be great fun, especially the ones that are fireside *(ocakbaşı*, oh-JAHK bah-shuh). Patrons sit around the sides of a long rectangular firepit and the kebapçı sits enthroned in the middle, grilling hundreds of *şiş kebap* and *şiş köfte*, which is köfte wrapped around a flat skewer. *Adana köfte* (ah-DAHN-nah) is the same thing, but spicy hot. The chef hands them over as they're done, and they are eaten with flat bread, a salad and perhaps *ayran* (ah-yee-RAHN), a drink of yoghurt mixed with spring water. Alcoholic beverages are not usually served.

Pideci For those on an adventurer's low budget, the Turkish *pideci* (pizza place) is a godsend. At a pideci, the dough for flat bread is patted out and shaped something like a boat, then dabbed with butter and other toppings, baked in a wood-fired oven, and served at once. It's fresh, delicious, inexpensive, sanitary and nutritious. As for toppings, if you want cheese say *peynirli* (pehy-neer-LEE); if you want eggs, say *yumurtalı* (yoo-moor-tah-LUH); *kıymalı* or *etli* means with minced lamb. In some parts of Turkey a pide (pizza) with meat is called *etli ekmek*. Alcoholic beverages are usually not served in pidecis.

Ask *Buralarda bir pideci var mı?* ('Is there a pideci around here?').

Pastane *Pasta* in Turkey is pastry, not noodles, which are usually designated by some Turkicised Italian name such as *makarna* or *lazanya*. Turkish *pastanes* (pastry shops) generally have supplies of *kuru pasta* (dry pastry) such as biscuits of various sorts, and *yaş pasta* (moist pastry) meaning cakes, crumpets, and syrup-soaked baked goods. Soft drinks are served, and tea and coffee are sometimes available. Some pastanes serve baklava, the many-layered nut-and-honey sweet; others leave this to separate shops called *baklavacıs*.

Most pastanes serve breakfast, either from their normal stock or as a *komple kahvaltı* of bread, butter, honey or jam, egg, olives, cheese and coffee or tea. In Kars, out by the Armenian frontier, you can have great gobs of the excellent local honey to mix with butter and spread on fresh bread.

Büfe & Kuru Yemiş Besides restaurants, Turkey has millions of little snack stands and quick-lunch places known as *büfe* (bew-FEH, buffet). These serve sandwiches, often grilled, puddings, portions of *börek* (bur-REHK, flaky pastry), and perhaps *lahmacun* (LAHH-mah-joon), an Arabic soft pizza made with chopped onion, lamb and tomato sauce.

A *kuru yemiş* (koo-ROO yeh-MEESH) place serves dried fruits and nuts and a dozen other good things. Prices are displayed – usually per kg.

İstanbul's Egyptian Market (Mısır Çarşısı) in Eminönü has several kuru yemiş shops which also sell *pestil* (pehs-TEEL), fruit which has been dried and pressed into flat, flexible sheets (sometimes called 'fruit leather' in English). Odd at first, but delicious, it's also relatively cheap and comes made from *kayısı* (apricots), *dut* (mulberries) and other fruits.

Hotel Restaurants These, in general, do not offer good value in Turkey. You may want to have breakfast in a hotel restaurant for convenience (or because breakfast has been included in the room price), but most other meals should be taken in independent, local places. There are exceptions, of course, as in those remote towns where the one good hotel in town also has the one good restaurant.

Meals

Breakfast In a hotel or pastry shop, breakfast *(komple kahvaltı*, kohm-PLEH-kahvahl-TUH) consists of fresh, delicious *ekmek* (ek-MEHK, Turkish bread) with jam or honey, butter, salty black olives, sliced tomatoes and cucumbers and cheese, as well as *çay* (CHAH-yee, tea). In my experience, Turkish bread and tea are usually fresh and good, but the other ingredients are often of poor quality or stale.

You can always order an egg *(yumurta*, yoo-moor-TAH). Soft-boiled is *üç dakikalık* (EWCH dahk-kah-luhk), hard-boiled is *sert* (SEHRT), and fried eggs are *sahanda yumurta* (sah-hahn-DAH yoo-moor-tah). Bacon is difficult to find as any pork product is forbidden to Muslims.

When breakfast is included in the room rate, the desk clerk will say *Kahvaltı dahil* (kah-vahl-TUH dah-HEEL).

After a week or so of standard Turkish breakfasts (and a few bad ones), I generally do what many working-class Turks do. I go to a lokanta for breakfast and have a bowl of hot soup which, with lots of fresh bread, makes quite a delicious breakfast for a very low price. If that's not for you, try a lokanta or pastane serving *su böreği* (SOO bur-reh-yee), a many-layered noodle-like pastry with white cheese and parsley among the layers, served warm.

Hot, sweetened milk *(sıcak süt*, suh-JAHK sewt) is also a traditional breakfast drink, replaced in winter by *sahlep* (sah-LEHP), which is hot, sweetened milk flavoured with tasty orchid-root *(Orchis mascula)* powder and a sprinkle of cinnamon.

Lunch The midday meal *(öğle yemeği)*. In summer, many Turks wisely prefer to eat a big meal at midday and a light supper in the evening.

Dinner The evening meal can be a repeat of lunch, a light supper, or a sumptuous repast. In fine weather the setting might be outdoors.

Hors d'Oeuvres

Meze, or hors d'oeuvres, can include almost anything. You can easily – and delightfully – make an entire meal of meze. Often you will be brought a tray from which you choose what you want: *zeytin* (olives), *turşu* pickled vegetables), *patates tava* (french fries/chips) or light potato fritters called *patates köfte*. Other mezes you might choose include:

beyaz peynir
white cheese
börek
flaky pastry
etli
with meat (hot)
kabak dolması
stuffed squash/marrow
patlıcan salatası
aubergine/eggplant puree
pilaki/piyaz
cold white beans vinaigrette
tarama salatası
red caviar in mayonnaise
yaprak dolması/yalancı dolması
stuffed vine leaves
zeytinyağlı
with olive oil

Soup

soup	*çorba*
broth with mutton	*haşlama*
chicken soup	*tavuk çorbası*
egg and lemon soup	*düğün çorbası*
fish soup	*balık çorbası*
lentil soup	*mercimek çorbası*
lentil & rice soup	*ezo gelin çorbası*
mutton broth (with egg)	*et suyu (yumurtalı)*
tripe soup	*işkembe çorbası*
trotter soup	*paça*
tomato soup	*domates çorbası*
vegetable soup	*sebze çorbası*
vermicelli soup	*şehriye çorbası*
yoghurt and barley soup	*yayla çorbası*

Salads

Each of the salads will be followed by the word *salata* or *salatası* on a menu. You may be asked if you prefer it *sirkeli* (with vinegar) or *limonlu* (with lemon juice). Most salads (except *söğüş)* come with olive oil. If you don't like hot peppers, say *bibersiz*, though this often doesn't work.

beyin
sheep's brain salad, usually the whole brain served on lettuce – food for thought
cacık
pronounced 'jah-JUHK' – yoghurt thinned with grated cucumber, then beaten and flavoured with a little garlic and a dash of olive oil
patlıcan salatası
puréed eggplant, perhaps mixed with yoghurt. The best has a faintly smoky, almost burnt flavour from the charcoal grilling of the eggplant.
pilaki
broad white beans and sliced onions in a light vinegar pickle, served cold
karışık (çoban)
chopped mixed salad
yeşil
green salad
Amerikan/Rus
mayonnaise, peas, carrots

turşu
pickled vegetables
patlıcan
roast aubergine/eggplant puree
marul
romaine lettuce
söğüş
sliced vegetables, no sauce
domates salatalık
tomato and cucumber salad

Main Courses

Fish The fish is marvellous all along the coast, especially in the Aegean region. Ankara has some excellent fresh fish restaurants, too. A menu is of no use when ordering fish *(balık)*. You must ask the waiter what's fresh, and then ask the approximate price. The fish will be weighed, and the price computed at the day's per-kg rate. Sometimes you can haggle.

Aegean tuna	*trança*
anchovy (fresh)	*hamsi*
black bream	*karagöz*
bluefish	*lüfer*
caviar	*havyar*
crab	*yengeç*
grey mullet	*kefal*
lobster	*istakoz*
mackerel	*uskumru*
mussels	*midye*
plaice	*pisi*
red coralfish	*mercan*
red mullet	*barbunya*
roe/red caviar	*tarama*
sardine (fresh)	*sardalya*
sea bass	*levrek*
shrimp	*karides*
sole	*dil balığı*
swordfish	*kılıç*
trout	*alabalık*
turbot	*kalkan*
tunny/bonito	*palamut*

Meat & Kebap In *kebap*, the meat *(et)* is always lamb – ground or in chunks. Preparation, spices and extras (onions, peppers, bread) make the difference among the kebaps. Some may be ordered *yoğurtlu*, with a side-serving of yoghurt. After the plate has been brought to your table, a waiter comes with savoury tomato sauce and pours a good helping on top. Then another waiter comes with browned butter, which goes on top of the sauce. This stuff is addictive. If you want any sort of kebap or köfte well done, say *iyi pişmiş* or *pişkin*.

patlıcan kebap
aubergine/eggplant and meat
sığır
beef
tavuk/piliç
chicken
şatobriyan
chateaubriand
çerkez tavuğu
chicken in walnut sauce
pirzola
cutlet (usually lamb)
bursa kebap
döner with tomato sauce
etli pide/ekmek
flat bread with minced lamb
köfte
grilled minced lamb patties
böbrek
kidney
tas kebap
lamb stew
kağıt kebap
lamb and vegetables in paper
ciğer
liver
güveç
meat and vegetable stew
(süt) kuzu
(milk-fed) lamb
karışık ızgara
mixed grill (lamb)
kuzu pirzolası
charcoal grilled lamb chops
tandır kebap
pit-roasted lamb
domuz
pork (forbidden to Muslims)
koç yumurtası
ram's 'eggs' (testicles)

orman kebap
roast lamb with onions
tavuk/piliç şiş
roast skewered chicken
şiş kebap
roast skewered lamb
bonfile
small fillet beefsteak
Adana kebap
spicy-hot roast köfte
tavuk/piliç döner
spit-roasted chicken slices
döner kebap
spit-roasted lamb slices
pastırma
sun-dried, spiced beef
çöp kebap
tiny bits of skewered lamb
dana
veal
saç kavurma
wok-fried lamb
şinitzel
wienerschnitzel

There are numerous fancy kebaps, often named for the places where they originated. Best is *Bursa kebap* (BOOR-sah), also called *İskender kebap*, since it was invented in the city of Bursa by a chef named İskender (Alexander). Of the other fancy kebaps, *Urfa kebap* comes with lots of onions and black pepper; *Adana kebap* is spicy hot, with red pepper the way the Arabs like it.

Cheese Although there are some interesting peasant cheeses – such as *tulum peynir* (a salty, dry, crumbly goats' milk cheese cured in a goatskin bag) and a dried cheese which looks just like twine – they rarely make it to the cities and almost never to restaurant tables. What you'll find is the ubiquitous *beyaz peynir* (bey-AHZ pey-neer), white sheep's milk cheese. To be good, this must be full-cream *(tam yağlı)* cheese, not dry and crumbly and not too salty or sour. You may also find *kaşar peynir* (kah-SHAHR pey-neer), a firm, mild yellow cheese which comes fresh *(taze,* tah-ZEH) or aged *(eski,* ess-KEE).

Vegetables

vegetable	*sebze*
cabbage	*lahana*
carrot	*havuç*
cauliflower	*karnabahar*
cucumber	*salatalık*
green beans	*taze fasulye*
marrow/squash	*kabak*
okra	*bamya*
onion	*soğan*
peas	*bezelye*
peppers	*biber*
potato	*patates*

Cream from Contented Cows

The claim to fame among Turks of Afyon in the Aegean Hinterland is not its opium, but its clotted cream *(kaymak)*.

The story is this: Afyon's opium farmers rarely use the drug themselves, but they use every other part of the plant. The poppy seeds are sprinkled on bread and pastries, the tender leaves are good in salads and the left-over opium plants are fed to the cattle. The cattle become very contented and produce rich cream in abundance.

Early each morning, near the Ot Pazarı Camii just a few blocks from Hükümet Meydanı, you can see the dairy farmers carrying their cylindrical kaymak containers. Brokers and restaurant-owners meet them in front of the mosque and haggle over prices for the precious cream, carefully protected in flat circular dishes of glass or plastic. Later in the day, the kaymak will end up atop a serving of *kadayıf* (crumpet in syrup), in kaymaklı baklava, or even stuffed in lokum (Turkish delight).

The popularity of eating kaymak on, in and with sweets may have inspired many locals to open confectioners' shops, *şekerleme*. Afyon has dozens of them, concentrated on Millet Caddesi off Hükümet Meydanı, and at the otogar. ■

radish	*turp*
red beans	*barbunye*
spinach	*ıspanak*
tomato	*domates*
white beans	*kuru fasulye*

Desserts

Turkish desserts tend to be very sweet, soaked in sugar syrup. Many are baked, such as crumpets, biscuits or shredded wheat.

Baklava comes in several varieties: *cevizli* is with chopped walnut stuffing; *fıstıklı* is with pistachio nuts; *kaymaklı* is with clotted cream. Sometimes you can order *kuru baklava*, 'dry' baklava which has less syrup. True baklava is made with honey, not syrup, and though the home-made stuff may contain honey, the store-bought stuff rarely does.

The standard unsweetened dessert, available in most restaurants, is *krem karamel* (crème caramel or flan).

Chicken is an ingredient in two dessert puddings *(tavuk göğsü* and *kazandibi)*, and you wouldn't know it from looking at or even eating them.

As an alternative to sweet desserts, Turkish fruits are superb, especially in midsummer when the melon season starts, and early in winter when the first citrus crop comes in. *Kavun* is a deliciously sweet, fruity melon.

apple	*elma*
apricot	*kayısı*
banana	*muz*
cherry	*kiraz*
fig	*incir*
fruit	*meyva/meyve*
grapefruit	*greyfurut*
grapes	*üzüm*
morello (sour) cherry	*vişne*
orange	*portakal*
peach	*şeftali*
pear	*armut*
pomegranate	*nar*
quince	*ayva*
strawberries	*çilek*
tangerine, mandarin	*mandalin*
watermelon	*karpuz*

Vegetarian

Vegetarianism is not prevalent in Turkey. Turkish cuisine does have many dishes in which meat is used merely as a flavouring rather than as a principal element. However, if you wish to avoid meat utterly, you will have to choose carefully.

I can't eat any meat.	*Hiç et yiyemem.*
I can't even eat meat juices.	*Et suyu bile yiyemem.*
Do you have any dishes without meat?	*Etsiz yemek var mı?*

Kosher Food

Turkey's small Jewish community lives in the largest cities. Some kosher food is available to them, but there are virtually no kosher restaurants, groceries or butchers serving the traveller. This may change due to the current boom in visitors from Israel, who head mostly for İstanbul and Antalya.

DRINKS

Nonalcoholic Drinks

When waiters ask *İçecek?* or *Ne içeceksiniz?*, they're asking what you'd like to drink. You will find the usual range of soft drinks. Shops and restaurants often sign exclusive distribution contracts with one company or the other, so you will find either Coke or Pepsi but rarely Coke and Pepsi. Turks just order *kola* and take what comes.

Fruit juice is a favourite refresher, and can be excellent. The good fruit juices tend to come in glass bottles and may be so thick that you'll want to dilute them with spring water.

fruit juice	*meyva suyu*
sour cherry	*vişne*
peach	*şeftali*
apricot	*kayısı*
strawberry	*çilek*
hot milk and tapioca root	*sahlep*
lemonade	*limonata*
milk	*süt*
fizzy mineral water	*maden sodası*
mineral water	*maden suyu*
spring water	*menba suyu*

thick millet drink	*boza*
yoghurt drink	*ayran*

Water Turks are connoisseurs of good water *(su)*, and stories circulate of old people able to tell which spring it came from just by tasting it. Spring water is served everywhere, even on intercity buses. The standard price for a 1.5-litre bottle of any brand, sold in a grocery, probably chilled, is around US$0.75. If you order it in a restaurant there will be a mark-up of 100 to 300%.

Tap water is supposedly safe to drink because it is treated, but it's not as tasty or as trustworthy as spring water. (For more information on water, see Food & Water in the Health section.)

Tea & Coffee The national drink is not really Turkish coffee as you might expect, but *çay* (tea). The Turks drank a lot of coffee when they owned Arabia, because the world's first (and best) coffee is said to have come from Yemen. With the collapse of the Ottoman Empire, coffee became an imported commodity. You can get Turkish coffee anywhere in Turkey, but you'll find yourself drinking a lot more çay.

The tea plantations are along the eastern Black Sea coast, centred on the town of Rize. Turkish tea is hearty and full-flavoured, served in little tulip-shaped glasses which you hold by the rim to avoid burning your fingers. (If you need a lot, order a *duble*, which will come in a drinking glass.) Sugar is usually added; milk is often available, though milk in tea is a foreign custom. If you want your tea weaker, ask for it *açık* (ah-CHUK, clear); for stronger, darker tea, order *koyu* or *demli* (dark).

For a real tea-drinking and talking session, Turks go to an outdoor tea garden and order a *semaver* (samovar) of tea so they can refill the glasses themselves, without having to call the *çaycı* (CHAH-yee-juh, tea-waiter).

Traditional herbal teas are infusions such as *adaçay* (island tea), made from coastal sage, and *ıhlamur* (linden-flower tea), perfumed and soothing. *Papatya çayı* is camomile tea.

A few years ago a brand-new beverage, *elma çay* (apple tea) was introduced, and it caught on quickly. Tourists love it as much as Turks do, and you may even see street vendors selling packets of it for tourists to take home with them. It's caffeine-free and slightly tart, with a mild apple flavour. There are other, similar fruit-flavoured teas as well. Surprisingly, the list of ingredients yields no mention of fruit, only sugar, citric acid, citrate, food essence and vitamin C.

As for Turkish coffee *(kahve)* you must order it according to sweetness – the sugar is mixed in during the brewing, not afterwards. You can drink it *sade*, without sugar; *az*, if you want just a bit of sugar; *orta*, with a middling amount; *çok* or *şekerli* or even *çok şekerli*, with lots of sugar. Nescafé is readily found throughout Turkey but tends to be expensive, often around US$0.70 per cup.

coffee	*kahve*
coffee and milk	*Fransız*
instant coffee	*neskafe*
Turkish coffee	*Türk kahvesi*
American coffee	*Amerikan kahvesi*

Alcoholic Drinks

Strictly observant Muslims don't touch alcoholic beverages at all, but in Turkey the strictures of religion are moderated by the 20th-century lifestyle.

Beer *Bira* is served almost everywhere. Tuborg makes light or pale *(beyaz*, bey-AHZ) and dark *(siyah*, see-YAH) beer in Turkey under licence. A local company with a European brewmaster is Efes Pilsen, which also makes light and dark beer claimed by many to be Turkey's best. The light is a good, slightly bitter pilsener. Marmara is a new brand on the market, not easily found.

As with Coke and Pepsi, shops and restaurants sign exclusive contracts for one brand, so just order bira as you will rarely get a choice, except in the most expensive places.

Beer is available in returnable bottles, and also in disposable cans at a higher than average price. You'll save money, get better flavour, and not contribute to the litter problem if you buy bottled beer.

beer	*bira*
dark	*siyah*
light	*beyaz*
draught ('keg')	*fıçı bira*

Wine Turkish wines are surprisingly good and delightfully cheap. Tekel makes all kinds in all price ranges. Güzel Marmara is the cheap white table wine. Buzbağ (BOOZ-baah) is a hearty Burgundy-style wine with lots of tannin. Restaurants seem to carry mostly the wines of the two big private firms, Doluca (DOHL-oo-jah) and Kavaklıdere (kah-vakh-LUH-deh-reh). You'll find the more expensive Villa Doluca wines in most places. Kavaklıdere wines include the premium white named Çankaya and the medium-range wines named Kavak (white), Dikmen and Yavak (red) and Lal (rosé/blush).

In recent years, Turkish vineyards have begun producing some good varietal wines as well.

wine	*şarap*
red	*kırmızı*
rose	*roze*
sparkling	*köpüklü*
white	*beyaz*

Strong Liquor The favourite ardent spirit in Turkey is *rakı* (rah-KUH), an aniseed-flavoured grape brandy similar to the Greek ouzo, French pastis and Arab arak. Turkish rakı is made by Tekel, the state liquor company. The standard is Yeni Rakı. Kulüp Rakısı is somewhat stronger, with a bit more anise. Altınbaş is the strongest, with the highest anise content.

It's customary (but not essential) to mix rakı with cool water, half-and-half, perhaps add ice, and to drink it with a meal.

Tekel also makes decent *cin* (JEEN, gin), *votka* and *kanyak* (kahn-YAHK, brandy). When ordering kanyak, always specify the *beş yıldız* or *kaliteli* (five-star or quality) stuff, officially named Truva Kanyak. The regular kanyak is thick and heavy, the five-star much lighter.

There is a Tekel *viski* (VEES-kee, whisky) named Ankara. You might try it once. Vermouth is *vermut*.

For after-dinner drinks, better restaurants will stock the local sweet fruit-brandies, which are nothing special.

Imported spirits are available from shops in the larger cities. Though they are much more expensive than local drinks, they may not cost much more than what you'd pay at home. Hotels and restaurants usually mark up the prices of imported spirits hugely.

ENTERTAINMENT

İstanbul, Ankara and İzmir have opera, symphony, ballet and theatre. Many smaller towns have folk dance troupes. Every Turkish town has at least one cinema and one nightclub with live entertainment.

The seaside resorts throb each warm evening to the sounds of seemingly innumerable clubs and discos.

SPECTATOR SPORT

Turks are sports enthusiasts. Football (soccer), basketball and wrestling are the favoured sports. Every city of any size has a large football stadium which fills up on match days.

The famous oiled wrestling matches, where brawny strongmen in leather breeches rub themselves down with olive oil and grapple with equally slippery opponents, take place each June in Edirne. Another purely Turkish sight is the camel-wrestling matches held in the province of Aydın, south of İzmir, in the winter months. Konya is the setting for *cirit*, the javelin-throwing game played on horseback.

THINGS TO BUY

Most shops and shopping areas close on Sunday. For details, see Business Hours in this chapter.

Haggling

For the best buy in terms of price and quality, know the market. Spend some time shopping for similar items in various shops, asking prices. Shopkeepers will give you pointers on what makes a good *kilim* (flat-woven mat), carpet, meerschaum pipe or alabaster carving. In effect, you're getting a free course in product lore. This is not at all unpleasant, as you will often be invited to have coffee, tea or a soft drink as you talk over the goods and prices.

You can, and should, ask prices if they're not marked, but you should not make a counter-offer unless you are seriously interested in buying. No matter how often the shopkeeper asks you, 'OK, how much will you pay for it?', no matter how many glasses of tea you've drunk at their expense, don't make a counter-offer if you do not plan to buy. If the shopkeeper meets your price, you should buy. It's considered very bad form to haggle over a price, agree, and then not buy.

Some shopkeepers, even in the 'haggle capital of the world' (İstanbul's Covered Market), will offer a decent price and say, 'That's my best offer'. Many times they mean it, and they're trying to do you a favour by saving time. How will you know when they are, and when it's just another haggling technique? Only by knowing the market, by having shopped around. Remember, even if they say, 'This is my best offer', you are under no obligation to buy unless you have made a counter-offer, or have said, 'I'll buy it'.

It's perfectly acceptable to say a pleasant goodbye and walk out of the shop, even after all that free tea, if you cannot agree on a price. In fact, walking out is one of the best ways to test the authenticity of the shopkeeper's price. If they know you can surely find the item somewhere else for less, they'll stop you and say, 'OK, you win, it's yours for what you offered'. And if they don't stop you, there's nothing to prevent you from returning in a half-hour and buying the item for what they quoted.

If any shopkeeper puts extraordinary pressure on you to buy, walk out of the shop, and consider reporting the shop to the Market Police (see Belediye Zabıtası under Police in the Dangers & Annoyances section).

Commissions

Read and believe: *if Turks accompany you into a shop, they will expect commissions from the shopkeeper on any purchase you make*. Your guide may be a wonderful person, the owner of your pension, a cheery and engaging soul, but after you buy and depart, the guide will take a cut. This is money that comes out of your pocket. It's better to go alone and strike a bargain on your own, because then you have a better chance of getting a lower price from the shopkeeper, who will have no commission to pay.

In the most touristed places, some personable young Turks and foreigners make their living chatting you up, helping you find your way around, and eventually leading you to a shop (usually a carpet shop) and 'helping' you to buy a carpet at a greatly inflated price.

Value Added Tax

Turkey has a Value Added Tax (VAT), called Katma Değer Vergisi or KDV, added to and hidden in the price of most items and services, from souvenirs to hotel rooms to restaurant meals. Most establishments display a sign saying *Fiatlarımızda KDV Dahildir* (VAT is included in our prices). Thus, it is rare that the VAT is added to your bill separately, and you should be suspicious if it is.

There is a scheme whereby tourists can reclaim the amount paid in VAT on larger purchases such as leather garments, carpets etc. Not all shops participate in the scheme, so you must ask if it is possible to get a KDV İade Özel Fatura (keh-deh-VEH ee-ah-DEH err-ZEHL fah-too-rah, 'Special VAT Refund Receipt'). Ask for this during the haggling rather than after you've bought. The receipt can – in principle – be converted to cash at a bank in the international departures lounge at the airport (if there is a bank open, which there usually isn't), or at your other point of exit from Turkey. Or, if you submit the form to a customs officer as you leave the country, the shop will (one hopes) mail a refund cheque to your home after the government has completed its procedures (don't hold your breath).

To increase your chances of actually getting the refund, make a photocopy or two of the KDV İade Özel Fatura in advance and, when you're leaving Turkey, take along a stamped envelope addressed to the shop where you bought the goods. Have the KDV form and the photocopy stamped by the customs officer at the airport, then mail the photocopy from the airport to the shop. Enclose a note requesting refund of the tax and giving your address to which the refund cheque should be sent. In some cases it can take as long as four months for the cheque to arrive. Keep the other photocopy for your own records.

Shipping Parcels Home

If practicable, carrying your parcels with you is the best idea, as you may escape extra duty payments when you return to your home country; parcels arriving separately may be dutiable. If you decide to ship something home from Turkey, don't close up your parcel before it has been inspected by a customs or postal official, who will check to see if you are shipping antiquities out of the country; take packing and wrapping materials with you to the post office. Wrap it very securely and insure it. Sending it by registered mail is not a bad idea, either. Unless you buy from a very posh shop (eg in one of the luxury hotels), it's best to ship your own parcels. At least one reader has had the sad experience of buying a beautiful kilim and agreeing to have the shopkeeper ship it, only to discover that the kilim shipped was not the one bought, but a much cheaper item.

Alabaster

A translucent, fine-grained variety of either gypsum or calcite, alabaster is pretty because of its grain and colour, and because light passes through it. You'll see ashtrays, vases, chess sets, bowls, egg cups, even the eggs themselves carved from the stone.

Antiques

Turkey has a lot of fascinating stuff left over from the empire: vigorous peasant jewellery, water-pipe mouthpieces carved from amber, old Korans and illuminated manuscripts, Greek and Roman figurines and coins, tacky furniture in the Ottoman Baroque style. However, *it is illegal to buy, sell, possess or export any antiquity*, and you can go to prison for breaking the law. All antiquities must be turned over to a museum immediately upon discovery. (See Departure under Customs in this chapter for details.)

Ceramics

The best Turkish ceramics were made in İznik and Kütahya in the 17th and 18th centuries. These tiles from the great days are now museum-pieces, found in collections throughout the world.

Today most of the tile-making is done in Kütahya in the Aegean hinterland. For the very best ceramics, you must go there (see Kütahya in the Aegean Hinterland section of the Aegean Turkey chapter for more information on buying ceramics). Souvenir shops will also have attractive, handmade tiles,

A ceramic mosque lamp. Most ceramic-work is now done in Kütahya in the Aegean hinterland. Scholars from all over the world flock to Kütahya to attend the International Faïence & Ceramics Congress.

A skirting tile from the Ramazan Efendi Camii in İstanbul. İznik faïence (tin-glazed earthenware) is a feature of many of İstanbul's mosques.

plates, cups and bowls. They're not really high-fired so they're vulnerable to breaks and cracks, but they can be quite attractive and useful even so.

The real, old İznik tiles from the 16th and 17th centuries qualify as antiquities and cannot be exported. If you go to İznik, you will find a reviving tile industry on a small scale. Some of the items are quite pretty and reasonably priced.

Avanos, in Cappadocia, is a centre for simple but attractive red clay pottery, made from deposits taken from the neighbouring Kızılırmak (Red River).

Copper

Gleaming copper vessels will greet you in every souvenir shop you peep into. Some are old, sometimes several centuries old. Most are handsome, and some are still eminently useful. The new copperware tends to be of lighter gauge; that's one of the ways you tell new from old. But even the new stuff will have been made by hand.

'See that old copper water pipe over there?' my friend Alaettin asked me once. We were sitting in his impossibly cluttered, closet-sized shop on İstanbul's Çadırcılar Caddesi, just outside the Covered Market. 'It dates from the time of Sultan Ahmet III (1703-30), and was used by the *Padişah* (sultan) himself. I just finished making it yesterday.'

Alaettin was a master coppersmith, and had made pieces for many luminaries, including the late Nelson Rockefeller. His pieces might well have graced the sultan's private apartments – except that the sultanate was abolished in 1922. He charged a hefty price for his fine craftwork but not for the story, which was the gift-wrapping, so to speak.

Copper vessels should not be used for cooking in or eating from unless they are tinned inside: that is, washed with molten tin which covers the toxic copper. If you intend to use a copper vessel, make sure the interior layer of tin is intact, or negotiate to have it tinned *(kalaylamak)*. If there is a *kalaycı* shop nearby, ask about the price of the tinning in advance, as tin is expensive.

Inlaid Wood

Cigarette boxes, chess and *tavla* (backgammon) boards and other items will be inlaid with different coloured woods, silver or mother-of-pearl. It's not the finest work, but it's pretty good. Make sure there is indeed inlay. These days, alarmingly accurate decals exist. Also, check the silver: is it silver, or aluminium or pewter? Is the mother-of-pearl actually 'daughter-of-polystyrene'?

Jewellery

Turkey is a wonderful place to buy jewellery, especially antique. None of the items sold here may meet your definition of 'chic', but window-shopping is great fun. Jewellers' Row in any market is a dazzling strip of glittering shop windows filled with gold. In the Covered Market, a blackboard sign hung above Kuyumcular Caddesi (Street of the Jewellers) bears the daily price for unworked gold of so-many carats. Serious gold-buyers should check this price, watch carefully as the jeweller weighs the piece in question, and then calculate what part of the price is for gold and what part for labour.

Silver is another matter. There is sterling silver jewellery (look for the hallmark), but nickel silver and pewter-like alloys are much more common. Serious dealers don't try to pass off alloy as silver.

Leather & Suede

On any given Kurban Bayramı (Sacrifice Holiday), over 2.5 million sheep get the axe in Turkey. Add to that the normal day-to-day needs of a cuisine based on mutton and lamb and you have a huge amount of raw material to be made into leather items.

Shoes, bags, cushions, jackets, skirts, vests, hats, gloves and trousers are all made from soft leather. This is a big industry in Turkey, particularly in and around the Grand Bazaar. So much leather clothing is turned out that a good deal of it will be badly cut or carelessly made, but there are lots of fine pieces as well.

The only way to assure yourself of a good piece is to examine it carefully, taking time. Try it on just as carefully; see if the sleeves are full enough, if the buttonholes are positioned well, if the collar rubs. If something is wrong, keep trying others until you find what you want.

Made-to-order garments can be excellent or disappointing, as the same tailor who made the ready-made stuff will make the ordered stuff; and will be making it fast because the shopkeeper has already impressed you by saying 'No problem. I can have it for you tomorrow'. It's better to find something off the rack that fits than to order it, unless you can order without putting down a deposit or committing yourself to buy (this is often possible).

Leather items and clothing are standard tourist stuff, found in all major tourist destinations.

Meerschaum

If you smoke a pipe, you know about meerschaum. For those who don't, meerschaum ('sea foam' in German; *lületaşı* in Turkish) is a hydrous magnesium silicate, a soft, white, clay-like material which is porous but heat-resistant. When carved into a pipe, it smokes cool and sweet.

Over time, it absorbs residues from the tobacco and turns a nut-brown colour. Devoted meerschaum pipe smokers even have special gloves for holding the pipe as they smoke, so that oil from their fingers won't sully the fine, even patina of the pipe.

The world's largest and finest beds of meerschaum are found in Turkey, near the city of Eskişehir. Miners climb down shafts in the earth to bring up buckets of mud, some of which contain chunks of the mineral. Artful carving of this soft stone has always been done, and blocks of meerschaum were exported to be carved abroad as well. These days, however, the export of block meerschaum is prohibited because the government realised that exporting uncarved blocks was the same as exporting the jobs to carve them. So any carved pipe will have been carved in Turkey.

You'll marvel at the artistry of the Eskişehir carvers. Pipes portraying turbaned paşas, wizened old men, fair maidens and mythological beasts, as well as many pipes in geometrical designs, will be on view in any souvenir shop.

Pipes are not the only things carved from meerschaum these days. Bracelets, necklaces, pendants, earrings and cigarette holders all appear in souvenir shops.

When buying, look for purity and uniformity in the stone. Carving is often used to cover up flaws in a piece of meerschaum. For pipes, check that the bowl walls are uniform in thickness all around, and that the hole at the bottom of the bowl is centred. Purists buy uncarved, plain pipe-shaped meerschaums that are simply but perfectly made.

Prices for pipes vary, but should be fairly low. Abroad, meerschaum is an expensive commodity, and pipes are luxury items. Here in Turkey meerschaum is cheap, the services of the carver are low-priced, and nobody smokes pipes. If you can't get the pipe you want for US$10 to US$20, or at least only half of what you'd pay at home, then you're not working at it hard enough.

Getting There & Away

You can get to Turkey by air, rail, road or sea.

AIR

İstanbul's Atatürk airport is the country's busiest. Other international airports are at Ankara, İzmir, Adana (down near the Syrian border), Antalya and Dalaman (on the south-western Mediterranean coast).

Most foreign visitors arrive in İstanbul because air traffic is most frequent there and it is also the first place tourists want to see. İzmir has its Menderes airport south of the city on the road to Ephesus. Antalya and Dalaman receive mostly charter flights filled with vacationers headed for the south coast.

Turkish Airlines (Türk Hava Yolları or THY, symbol TK) has flights to and from New York, most major cities in Europe, the Middle East and North Africa, and several routes to the Far East.

İstanbul Airlines (symbol IL) has flights between Turkey and Austria, Belgium, Denmark, Eire, France, Germany, Holland, Italy, Spain, Turkish Cyprus and the UK.

All the fares mentioned here are subject to change, but they will give you an idea of what to expect. For more details of air travel to/from Turkey see the Getting There & Away sections under the individual Turkish destinations.

Greece

Olympic Airlines and Turkish Airlines share the Athens-İstanbul route, offering at least four flights per day in summer. Fares for the 70-minute flight are US$222 one way, US$314 for a round-trip excursion (fixed-date return) ticket.

Elsewhere in Europe

Both Turkish Airlines and İstanbul Airlines fly to Turkey from many points in Europe. Most Turkish Airlines flights go to the airline's hub in İstanbul, while İstanbul Airlines (ironically) flies nonstop from Europe to cities such as Adana, Antalya, Dalaman and İzmir. İstanbul Airlines' fares tend to be lower than those of the major carriers, but flights are fewer.

The normal one-way fare from London to İstanbul is UK£300 (US$570) and up, but there are fixed-date return (excursion) fares as low as UK£180 (US$280). Peak-season (summer) excursion fares are higher, but there are still bargains to be had. British Airways and Turkish Airlines fly the route nonstop, and most other European airlines do it with one stop. Check also the schedules and fares of Tarom of Rumania, and Pakistan International Airlines (PIA).

Don't neglect the European and Turkish charter lines such as Condor (German) and Air Alfa (Turkish), which fly to Turkey from more than a dozen European centres, often for round-trip fares as low as US$200.

Middle East

Middle Eastern flights by Turkish Airlines include the following weekly nonstop flights to and from İstanbul: three from Bahrain, two from Beirut, one from Dubai, two from Kuwait, three from Teheran, three from Tripoli and one from Tunis.

Details of some other services to İstanbul from various Middle Eastern cities follow.

Amman Turkish Airlines and Royal Jordanian share the traffic, with about three flights per week. The nonstop 2½-hour flight costs US$260 one way. It costs from US$290 to US$360 for a round-trip excursion ticket.

Cairo EgyptAir and Turkish Airlines have flights about four days per week, charging from US$333 to US$373 one way. It costs from US$368 to US$450 for a round-trip excursion ticket on the nonstop, two-hour flight.

Damascus Syrian Arab Airlines and Turkish Airlines make the 2½-hour flight four days per week and charge from US$241 to US$277 one way, from US$316 to US$326 for a round-trip excursion.

Nicosia (Turkish Side) Turkish Airlines operates nonstop flights connecting Ercan airport (ECN) in Nicosia (Lefkoşa in Turkish) with Adana (four flights weekly), Ankara (five flights weekly), Antalya (one flight weekly), İstanbul (daily, twice daily in summer) and İzmir (four flights weekly). Fares are subsidised and very reasonable.

In Nicosia, contact Turkish Airlines at Osman Paşa Caddesi 32 (☎ (392) 227 1061, fax 228 6152).

İstanbul Airlines (☎ (392) 228 3576, fax 228 3644) on Osman Paşa Caddesi, Mirata Apartımanı 4 and at Ercan airport (☎ (392) 231 4 714, fax 231 4715), flies between Nicosia, Antalya (four flights weekly), Dalaman (one flight weekly), İzmir (two flights weekly) and İstanbul (daily), at fares lower than Turkish Airlines'.

Tel Aviv El Al and Turkish Airlines share the traffic with daily nonstop flights to/from İstanbul for US$336 one way and US$506 for a round-trip excursion. Turkish Airlines also has twice weekly nonstop flights between Tel Aviv and Antalya, Dalaman and İzmir.

Azerbaijan

Turkish Airlines runs nonstop flights between Baku and İstanbul thrice weekly.

India

Numerous airlines, including Air India, British Airways, Delta, KLM, Lufthansa, Olympic and Turkish Airlines will take you on various routes between New Delhi and İstanbul. One-way fares are a high US$700, with round-trip excursions (fixed-date return) costing only US$795. For cheap fares, try contacting Aeroflot to see what it offers via Moscow.

The USA

Airlines Of the airlines serving the US-Europe-İstanbul route, Lufthansa has perhaps the best route and schedule structures, which is not surprising as Lufthansa ranked second in terms of the number of international passengers flown worldwide in 1994.

Lufthansa flights depart 121 times weekly from 10 American cities – Atlanta, Boston, Chicago, Dallas/Fort Worth, Houston, Los Angeles, Miami, New York/Newark, San Francisco and Washington DC – bound for its hub in Frankfurt. Lufthansa's code-sharing agreement with United Airlines makes it easy to reach any of these gateway cities from 46 other cities in the USA. Once in Frankfurt, you can connect with any of several daily Lufthansa nonstop flights to Ankara, İstanbul or İzmir.

Turkish Airlines operates daily nonstop flights in summer on the New York-İstanbul route in both directions. Pakistan International Airlines has a one-stop service from Toronto and also from New York to İstanbul with an even lower excursion fare, but some passengers find the service less than luxurious. Of the major US airlines, only Delta flies directly to İstanbul.

Fares Coach-class fares are US$625 to US$1100 and up, one way; excursion fares range from US$850 to US$1250 and up depending upon season, stopovers etc. From Chicago you pay from US$779 to US$854 one way and US$950 to US$1330 for a round-trip excursion. Fares from San Francisco or Los Angeles are normally from US$984 to US$1000 one way and from US$1194 to US$1444 for a round-trip excursion. You can pay an astounding US$6870 to go 1st class with all the trimmings.

Special Fares From New York and Chicago, particularly during the summer months, group fares to İstanbul are sold by various tour operators. You do not have to be part of a group, nor do you have to take a tour or pay for nights in a hotel. You pay only for the flight (which is on a regular, scheduled airline, not a charter), but you get your ticket at a special low group rate. There may be some restrictions, perhaps such as having to stay more than seven nights and less than 180 nights. From New York, fares are about US$400 to US$600 one way, US$700 to US$850 round trip. Turkish Airlines usually has the lowest fares.

It's best to pay for these cheapie flights with a credit card so that if something goes wrong, you don't lose your money. For more information contact a travel agent.

Consolidators Consolidators, called bucket shops in some other countries, buy blocks of seats at wholesale prices from major airlines, then sell them to the general public at retail, often at significant discounts. Though some are incompetent or crooked, most consolidators are legitimate companies.

You can often buy consolidator tickets from your travel agency, which will put its own markup on the ticket, but it'll still be cheaper than standard fares. Buying through a travel agency often helps to avoid the less reliable consolidators.

Whether you buy your ticket through a travel agency or direct from the consolidator, be sure to pay for it with a credit card. If for some reason your ticket or flight doesn't materialise, you can legally refuse to pay the credit card charge. If you pay in cash or by cheque and the consolidator goes bankrupt or disappears, your money is gone.

One consolidator which I have used is the Euram Flight Center (☎ (202) 789 2255, (800) 848 6789), 1522 K Street, NW, Suite 406, Washington DC 20005. You can find others by checking the small ads boasting of cheap flights in the travel sections of newspapers in other cities.

Australia

There are direct flights from Australia to İstanbul offered by Malaysian Airlines (via Kuala Lumpur and Dubai) and Singapore Airlines (via Singapore and Dhahran) with round-trip fares for about A$1800. Cheaper are Middle Eastern Airlines, Gulf Air and Egypt Air with round-trip fares for about A$1600. There are also connecting flights via Athens, London, Rome, Amsterdam or Singapore on Thai International, British Airways, Olympic, Alitalia, KLM, Turkish Airlines and Qantas.

All these airlines regularly have specials (usually during the European low season of mid-January to the end of February and the start of October to mid-November) with most offering fares for A$1500 or less. Usually these specials must be booked and paid for reasonably quickly.

If you can get a cheap fare to London, you might do well once you're there to look for a cheap flight to Turkey.

Another way to get to Turkey from Australia is to fly to Athens and take a boat to one of the islands (Lesbos, Chios, Samos, Kos or Rhodes) and then a ferry to the Turkish mainland. If you don't want to arrive as far north as İstanbul or if you're interested in travelling that way, it's a good option. However, new taxes mean it's no longer a cheap way to get there and it takes longer.

LAND

Greece

From Greece, the major road goes to Kastanéai (Greece) and Pazarkule (Turkey), seven km south-west of Edirne on the Meriç River (mehr-EECH, Maritsa), two km past the Turkish village of Karaağaç to a border post originally meant to serve the railway line.

The frontier, as determined by the Treaty of Lausanne (1923), left the Turkish line passing through Greece on its way to Edirne! A bypass line was built in the 1970s, though. The problem here is that the Greeks have declared the border area a military zone and do not permit anyone to walk in it without a military escort, so you will probably have to take a Greek taxi (US$6, two minutes) to the actual border, which is midway in the one-km-wide wasteland which separates the two border posts. On the Turkish side, you can walk to and from Pazarkule. These small border posts are open during daylight hours.

From Pazarkule, or from the nearby train station, you will probably have to take a Turkish taxi (US$5, 15 minutes) into town as there is not much traffic and hitching is not too easy, though you may be lucky.

If you are crossing from Turkey into Greece, do so as soon after 8 am as possible in order to catch one of the few trains or buses from Kastanéai heading south to Alexandroûpolis.

Bulgaria

If you're travelling overland from Bulgaria see the Edirne section for border-crossing and travel details. Transit visas obtained at Bulgarian consulates in Turkey and valid for 36 hours cost US$22; tourist visas valid for three months and good for a 30-day stay in Bulgaria cost US$35 for normal three-day delivery, or US$50 for express 30-minute delivery.

Georgia

The Turkish-Georgian border crossing at Sarp is now open to all travellers, not just to Turks and Georgians. For details see the Black Sea chapter.

Iran

Once you accept the cultural peculiarities of the Islamic Revolution, travel in Iran can be enjoyable. The people are mostly friendly and helpful. To visit or travel through Iran you must have a visa, theoretically obtainable from an Iranian embassy or consulate, but this may depend on the fluctuating currents of international relations.

It may take anywhere from a week to a month or more to obtain a visa. You may first have to obtain a visa for the country you will enter when you leave Iran; you may be asked to show a bus or airline ticket out of Iran. Be prepared for some Middle Eastern bureaucratic hassles. See the Visas & Embassies section in the Facts for the Visitor chapter, and contact your embassy in Ankara for details on current availability and requirements for visas.

The border crossing may take as little as one hour. You may be asked to pay an unofficial fee (ie, a bribe) by the Iranian officials. The Bank Melli branch at the border changes cash dollars or pounds or travellers' cheques into Iranian rials (tomans). It may not change Turkish liras, but you may be able to exchange liras at banks farther into Iran.

From Doğubeyazıt (see also that section), you can catch a minibus to the Iranian frontier. From the border you can take a taxi to Maku, then an Iran Peyma bus from Maku to Tabriz.

Syria

Syrian visas are not normally issued at the border, but this depends partly upon your nationality and partly upon current regulations. If you plan to travel to Syria and other Middle Eastern countries, plan ahead and obtain the necessary visas in your home country, in İstanbul or in Ankara.

Bus

Turkish bus companies operate frequent passenger services to and from Turkey.

Athens For a bus to İstanbul, go to the train station (OSE Hellenic Railways Organisation, Plateia Peloponisu), from which the buses depart.

Varan Turizm (☎ (30-1) 513 5768) operates daily buses to and from İstanbul via Thessaloniki, as does Ulusoy (☎ (30-1) 524 0519, fax 524 3290), also at the Peloponese Railway Station. The trip takes about 20 hours and costs about US$70 from Athens, US$45 from Thessaloniki, one way.

Elsewhere in Europe Ulusoy and Varan also operate luxury buses on routes to and from Europe. Going by bus is often faster, safer and more comfortable than the now-neglected trains, and comparable in price. But once you add the cost of meals and the time involved (between 30 and 45 hours), the price of a flight doesn't look too bad.

One-way fares to İstanbul are US$175 from Frankfurt, US$155 from Munich, and US$110 from Vienna. Round-trip fares are discounted about 20%. The major discomfort on the trip may be cigarette smoke.

Some addresses follow:

Frankfurt

Ulusoy Turizm, Deutsche Touring GmbH, Römerhof 17 (☎ (49-69) 790 350, fax 704 714)

İstanbul

Ulusoy Turizm, İnönü Caddesi 59, Taksim (☎ (212) 244 1271, 244 2823)

Varan Turizm, İnönü Caddesi 29/B, Taksim (☎ (212) 243 1903, 244 8457)

Munich

Ulusoy Turizm, Deutsche Touring Stadtbüro, Starnberger Bahnhof, Arnulfstrasse 3 (☎ (49-89) 591 824, fax 596 133)

Vienna

Ulusoy Turizm, Südbahnhof, Argentinierstrasse 267 (☎ (43-1) 505 0644)

Varan Turizm, Südbahnhof, Südtirolerplatz 7 (☎ (43-1) 504 6593, fax 504 3550)

Syria For details of bus services to/from Syria and other Middle Eastern countries see also the Adana, Antakya and Ankara Getting There & Away sections.

Direct daily buses connect Antakya, at the eastern end of Turkey's Mediterranean coast, with the Syrian cities of Aleppo (105 km, four hours, US$20) and Damascus (465 km, eight hours, US$35), and with Amman in Jordan (675 km, 10 hours, US$42).

Travel times to these cities do not include border-crossing formalities, which may add several hours to the trip. Get your visas in advance to hasten formalities.

For travel in Syria, you may need to obtain a visa from a Syrian consulate before you reach the border. Dolmuşes run frequently from the southern end of Antakya's bus station to the Turco-Syrian border stations at Reyhanlı (for Aleppo) and Yayladağ (for Lattakia and Beirut) throughout the day.

Israel & Egypt It's possible to bus between Israel or Egypt and Turkey via Amman, Damascus and Antakya. See Getting There & Away in the Antakya section of the Mediterranean Chapter for more info.

Train

Fares Rail tickets generally cost more than bus tickets. If you're young, you can take advantage of the Wasteels BIGE Youth Train, with special low fares. In İstanbul, buy your tickets at window *(gişe)* No 5 in Sirkeci train station.

The Inter-Rail Youth Pass is now valid for all of Turkey's railways, but it may not be valid in Bulgaria (check for current regulations). Thus if you travel on the Inter-Rail pass, you may have to go around Bulgaria by taking the Belgrade to Edirne route via

The *Orient Express*

The fabled *Orient Express*, which first ran between Paris and Constantinople in 1883, was removed from the timetables and the rails in 1977 and replaced by the İstanbul Express to Munich.

In the 1960s and 1970s, there was little romance left on the famed *Orient Express* route from Paris (Gare de l'Est) via Lausanne, Milan, Venice, Trieste, Belgrade, Sofia and Edirne to İstanbul. The trains were not well kept, and were always many hours – even days – late. Now, with the Bosnian War, even these have ceased to run.

When armed conflict does not make rail travel through the Balkans impossible, the *Orient Express* lives on in special excursion trains with various names, but the fares for these deluxe tours cost between US$2500 and US$5500 one way. These packages include transportation from European points to İstanbul aboard restored railway coaches, with lectures and optional side-trips. By the way, the train which now bears the name *Orient Express* goes nowhere near İstanbul on its run between London and Venice. ■

Thessaloniki, which can take a long 55 hours from Munich. The alternative is to pay full fare through Bulgaria for the 39-hour *İstanbul Express* trip.

Dangers For several years I received reports of thieves who sprayed sleeping gas under compartment doors at night, and when the occupants were knocked out, stripped them of their valuables; it happened to close friends of mine. One reader even left the windows open to dilute the gas, and tried to stay awake, but they still got his stuff.

Greece The 1400-km journey on the *Atina Ekspresi* (Athens Express) takes 24 hours, departing from İstanbul late in the evening, arriving in Thessaloniki late in the afternoon the next day, and Athens very late in the evening. From Athens, the train leaves at breakfast time, arrives in Thessaloniki after lunch, and gets to İstanbul at breakfast time the next morning. There's a change of trains at Thessaloniki.

Munich, Vienna, Moscow & Bucharest When it's running, the daily *İstanbul Express* from Munich departs each evening at dinner time, reaches Belgrade at breakfast time, Sofia at dinner time, and İstanbul at breakfast time on the third day, taking about 35 hours (if it's on time).

The train hauls sleeping and couchette *(kuşet)* coaches, a restaurant car and (three days weekly) auto-train *(oto-kuşet)* carriages so you can take your car with you. The auto-train service runs Tuesday, Friday and Saturday from Munich; Wednesday, Thursday and Sunday from İstanbul. The fare for a car and driver from Munich to İstanbul (one way) is from US$660 to US$900; round-trip fares are discounted about 12%.

A second train, the *Skopje-İstanbul Express*, departs from Munich later each evening, reaching Sofia in about 25½ hours. At Sofia it is met by the *Sofia Express* from Moscow and Bucharest before continuing to İstanbul overnight, arriving around lunch time, 38 hours after having left Munich, 37 hours after having left Moscow.

A nightly train from Vienna connects with the *İstanbul Express* at Zagreb, departing from Vienna after dinner, arriving in Zagreb several hours after midnight. You reach İstanbul in the morning after two nights on the train. (For more details, see the İstanbul Getting There & Away section.)

Armenia The railway line from Ankara to Erzurum goes on to Kars and, in good times, goes as far as the Armenian frontier, with a connecting train to Moscow.

At the time of writing, two trains run daily from Kars to the Armenian border at Doğu Kapı. The slow *Akyaka Postası* departs from Kars each Friday afternoon for Ahuryan, just across the border in Armenia, returning to Kars in the early evening each Tuesday. You should obtain an Armenian visa from a consulate before proceeding to the border.

Iran The *Doğu Ekspresi* to Tatvan and Van continues once a week into Iran, with a connection to Tabriz and Tehran. See the Van section for details.

Car

Car ferries (see the Sea section) from Italy and Cyprus can shorten driving time considerably. No special car documents are required for visits of up to three months. The car will be entered in the driver's passport as imported goods, and must be driven out of the country by the same visitor within the time period allowed. Do not drive someone else's car into Turkey.

Normally, you cannot rent a car in Europe and include Turkey (or many other Eastern European countries) in your driving plans. If you want to leave your car in Turkey and return for it later, the car must be put under customs seal, usually a tedious process.

For stays longer than three months, or for any other information regarding car travel in Turkey, contact the Turkish Touring and Automobile Association (Türk Turing ve Otomobil Kurumu) (☎ (90-212) 282 8140, fax 282 8042), Oto Sanayi Sitesi Yanı, Seyrantepe, 4 Levent, İstanbul.

The E 80 highway makes its way through

the Balkans to Edirne (see also that section) and İstanbul, then onward to Ankara.

Insurance Your Green Card third-party insurance must be endorsed for all of Turkey, both European and Asian, not just the European portion (Thrace). If it is not, you will be required to buy a Turkish insurance policy at the border.

SEA

Several shipping lines operate car and passenger ferries from Italy, Greece and Turkish Cyprus to Turkey in summer, and small ferries shuttle between the Greek islands and the Turkish mainland. A hydrofoil service operates in high summer between Rhodes and Fethiye.

Italy (& Greece)

Turkish Maritime Lines Turkish Maritime Lines (Denizyolları, or TML) operates comfortable car/passenger ferries from Venice to Çeşme, İzmir and Antalya.

Per-person one-way fares range from US$236 to US$286 for a Pullman seat to US$494 to US$636 for a berth in a luxury cabin; the fare for each of two berths in a B-class cabin with shower and WC is US$386 to US$493. The higher price is for voyages in the busy summer months; three meals and port tax are included in these examples.

The cost for taking a car is US$207 to US$250, one-way, port tax included.

Venice-İzmir The m/f *Ankara* departs İzmir each Wednesday year-round at 4 pm, arriving in Venice on Saturday at 11 am, departing Venice for İzmir the same day at 9 pm, arriving on Tuesday at noon.

Venice-Çeşme From late June through September, the m/f *İskenderun* departs Çeşme, 85 km west of İzmir, every Wednesday at 6 pm, arriving in Venice on Saturday at 10 am, departing the same day for İzmir at 8 pm, arriving back in Çeşme on Tuesday at noon.

Venice-Antalya From mid-June to early October, the m/f *Samsun* departs Antalya, on Turkey's Mediterranean coast, every Wednesday at noon, arriving in Venice on Saturday at 10 am, departing the same day for İzmir at 4 pm, arriving back in Antalya on Tuesday at 2 pm.

For more information, contact TML at the following addresses:

İstanbul
: Türkiye Denizcilik İşletmeleri, Rıhtım Caddesi, Karaköy (☎ (212) 244 2502, fax 251 9025)

İzmir
: Türkiye Denizcilik İşletmeleri Acenteliği, Yeniliman, Alsancak (☎ (232) 421 1484, fax 421 1481)

London
: Sunquest Holidays Ltd, 23 Princes St, London W1R 7RG (☎ (171) 499 9992, fax 499 9995)

Venice
: Bassani SpA, Via 22 Marzo 2414, 30124 Venezia (☎ (41) 522 9544, fax 520 4009)

European Seaways European Seaways operates car ferries from Brindisi and Bari via Mykonos to Çeşme from March to December. For complete information, contact these agencies:

Bari
: Pan Sped Srl, stazione Marittima, Corso de Tullio 26, 70126 Bari, Italy (☎ (080) 523 0420, fax 521 1989)

Brindisi
: Il Globbo Viaggi, Corso Garibaldi 97, 72100 Brindisi, Italy (☎ (831) 27 66 84, fax 25991)

Çeşme
: Karavan Shipping, Belediye Dükkanları 3, by the harbour (☎ (232) 712 7230, fax 712 8987)

Corfu
: Vaba Travel, Ethnikis Antistassis St 26, 49100 Corfu, Greece (☎ (661) 21904, fax 21906)

Igoumenitsa
: Katsios Shipping, Ethnikis Antistassis St 55-A, Igoumenitsa, Greece (☎ (665) 22409, fax 22590)

Mykonos
: Mykonos Travel, Mykonos Port, 84600 Mykonos, Greece (☎ (289) 22232, fax 23985)

Med Link Lines Med Link Lines operates ferries on the route Brindisi-Igoumenitsa-Patras-Çeşme from April to September. Fares tend to be lower than on TML or Stern, and there are reductions for students travelling in Deck, Pullman or C-class cabins (four to eight beds). For information, contact MLL at:

Brindisi
 Discovery Shipping Agency, 49 Corso Garibaldi, 72100 Brindisi, Italy (☎ (831) 52 76 67, fax 56 40 70)

Çeşme
 Karavan Shipping, Belediye Dükkanları 3, by the harbour (☎ (232) 712 7230, fax 712 8987)

Cologne
 Viamare seetouristik, Apostelnstrasse 9, 50667 Köln, Germany (☎ (221) 257 3781, fax 257 3682)

Igoumenitsa
 Eleni Pantazi, 8 December St No 27, Greece (☎ (665) 26833, fax 26111)

Patras
 George Giannatos, Othonos Amalias St 15 (☎ (061) 62 30 11, fax 62 33 20)

Stern Ferrylines Stern Ferrylines GmbH (☎ (721) 85 62 31, fax 85 89 65), Sophienstrasse 126, 76135 Karlsruhe, Germany, operates car ferries between the Italian ports of Bari and Brindisi and Çeşme, departing Bari on Saturday and Wednesday, departing Çeşme on Monday and Friday. Departures from Brindisi are on Sunday or Wednesday, from Çeşme on Monday or Thursday. Round-trip fares range from US$272 to US$315 for deck class, US$296 to US$371 for a Pullman seat, up to US$679 to US$786 for a berth in a luxury cabin. In Çeşme, contact Maskot Turizm Seyahat (☎ (232) 712 7654, fax 712 8435), İnkilap Caddesi 93/19.

Greek Islands

With the boom in Turkish tourism, the traffic from the Greek islands to the Turkish mainland is intense in the warm months. From time to time, the Greek government issues regulations designed to make it difficult for travellers to go from Greece to Turkey. You may have to contend with these.

Previous efforts have included making it difficult to obtain information on boats to Turkey: the law stated that only one sign no greater than a piece of typing paper could be displayed, and only in the window of the agency selling tickets. In general it is very difficult to obtain information on transport from Greece to Turkey while in Greece. The best in the Athens area is to be had from the ferry offices at the port in Piraeus.

Greek regulations may require that passengers on trips originating in Greece must travel on Greek-flag vessels, which means that you may not be allowed to hop aboard a convenient Turkish vessel for your trip from the Greek islands to the Turkish mainland. (If you've come over from Turkey for the day, you may return on the Turkish boat.)

The most recent regulation raised port taxes for travellers to Turkey to unconscionable heights – several times the actual boat fare. The Turkish government and tourism sector – and travellers – protested at once. The Greek taxes were lowered, but are still unconscionably high, about US$25 per person on some crossings.

There are numerous regular ferry services, with more being added each year (see following). The cheapest, most frequent and convenient are Samos to Kuşadası and Rhodes to Marmaris. The most expensive and hassled is Lesbos to Ayvalık.

The procedure is this: once you've found the ticket office, buy your ticket a day in advance. You may be asked to turn in your passport the night before the trip. The next day, before you board the boat, you'll get it back.

Here are the routes, fares and ticket agencies from Greece. For details on travelling from Turkey, see the section on each departure port (eg Ayvalık, Çeşme, Kuşadası etc).

Lesbos to Ayvalık Both Greek and Turkish boats make this run daily in summer (from late May or early June to September). The rest of the year boats operate about once or twice a week, weather permitting. The passage is now so expensive (US$50 one way, US$65 same-day round trip) that few people choose to use it. If you're coming from Greece (ie not returning to Turkey after a day trip), you must also pay an outrageous 4000-drachmae Greek port tax.

Chios to Çeşme In high summer (1 July to

10 September) there are daily boats. From 4 to 30 June and 11 to 30 September boats run on Tuesday, Thursday, Friday and Sunday. From 1 May to 3 June and in October boats run on Tuesday, Thursday and Sunday. From 16 to 30 April, boats run on Tuesday and Thursday. From 1 November to 15 April, boats run on Thursday only. The voyage lasts about 45 minutes.

A one-way fare between Çeşme and Chios is US$25, to go there and back in a day costs US$30, making for a nice day excursion. An open-date round trip costs US$35. An exorbitant Greek port tax of US$18 is levied on each passenger as well. Children aged from four to 12 years get a 50% reduction in fare (but not tax). Motorcycles, cars, even caravans, minibuses and buses can be carried on some of the ferries. The fare for a car is US$60 or US$80, depending upon length.

Samos to Kuşadası Boats sail between the Greek island of Samos and Turkish Kuşadası, near Ephesus. Services go from Samos town (daily at 8.30 am and 5 pm, a 30-minute trip) and Pythagorion (thrice weekly in summer at 8.30 am, a 45-minute trip). In spring and autumn there are four trips weekly from the town of Samos.

There is no scheduled service in winter, though this may change; check with a travel agency in Samos or Kuşadası for the latest information. The voyage costs US$35 one way, US$55 for a round trip good for a year. Some agencies discount these tickets, so ask, and flash your student card if you have one.

Kos to Bodrum Hydrofoils (20 minutes) and ferries (50 minutes) carry passengers and cars across to Kos daily from May to September. Buy tickets (US$22.50 one way, US$29 same-day round trip) at least a day in advance. Limited ferry service (usually two or three days per week, weather permitting) continues right through the winter.

Rhodes to Bodrum Hydrofoils (two hours) depart Bodrum for Rhodes at 8.30 am on Monday and Thursday from May to September. The return trip departs Rhodes at 4 pm. Buy tickets (US$45 one way, US$50 same-day round trip) from Bodrum Express a day in advance.

Rhodes to Marmaris This is the busiest ferry service of all, with numerous boats flying Greek or Turkish flags competing for business. The Rhodes ticket office is the ANKA Travel Centre (☎ (241) 25 095), 13 Odos Galias, near the New Market. It is open from 8.30 am to 2 pm and 5.30 to 9.30 pm in summer, closed on Sunday. In Turkey, buy your tickets at any travel agency.

Hydrofoils operate to Rhodes daily in summer, taking 45 minutes to reach Rhodes Town. Tickets cost US$41 one way, US$44 same-day return and US$56 open-date return. Entering Turkey from Rhodes on a one-way ticket you'll have to pay a US$10 port tax. Returning from Rhodes to Turkey, people needing a visa will have to buy a new one if they've stayed overnight but not if they went on a day trip.

In high summer boats also run to and from Rhodes three times a week, taking 2½ hours for the voyage. Turkish boats depart from Marmaris in the morning, returning from Rhodes in the late afternoon; Greek boats depart from Rhodes in the morning, returning from Marmaris in the late afternoon. Some of these ferries are capable of carrying cars as well as passengers. Most places selling hydrofoil tickets also sell boat tickets (US$30 one way, US$33 same-day return, US$44 open-date return) and these too must be booked at least a day in advance.

At other times of the year there may be fewer boats but you can depend on at least two a week except during stormy weather.

Rhodes to Fethiye In high summer a hydrofoil service operates between Rhodes and Fethiye on the Turkish Mediterranean coast on Tuesdays and Thursdays. A one-way ticket costs US$47, a day return US$71 and an open return US$93.

Cyprus

You should be aware that relations between the Greek Cypriot-administered Republic of

Cyprus and the Turkish Republic of Northern Cyprus (TRNC) are not good, and that the border between the two regions will probably be closed. Also, if you enter the TRNC and have your passport stamped you will later be denied entry to Greece. The Greeks will reject only a stamp from the Turkish Republic of Northern Cyprus, *not* a stamp from Turkey proper. Have the Turkish Cypriot official stamp a piece of paper instead of your passport.

Famagusta to Mersin Turkish Maritime Lines operates a car ferry service between Mersin and Famagusta. See the Mersin section for details.

Kyrenia to Taşucu Kyrenia (Girne in Turkish) and Taşucu, near Silifke, are connected by daily hydrofoil and car-ferry service. See the Taşucu section for details.

Georgia

Travel between Trabzon and Batumi (Georgia) by hydrofoil is possible but frustrating. First you must get a visa from the former USSR consulate in Trabzon 200 metres south-east from the south-east corner of Atatürk Alanı (look for the police guard booth). For more details see the Trabzon section.

After obtaining your visa, you must get boat tickets down by the harbour. The boat may or may not leave on time, and may or may not have a place for you. Many swindlers work the rackets concerning these boats and tickets to ride on them. One hopes the situation will soon improve.

LEAVING TURKEY

Turkey levies a tax of about US$12 on visitors departing by air. The tax is customarily included in the cost of your ticket.

Don't have any antiquities in your luggage. If you're caught smuggling them out, you'll probably go to jail.

WARNING

The information in this chapter is particularly vulnerable to change: prices for international travel are volatile, routes are introduced and cancelled, schedules change, special deals come and go, and rules and visa requirements are amended. Airlines and governments seem to take a perverse pleasure in making price structures and regulations as complicated as possible.

You should check directly with the airline or travel agent to make sure you understand how a fare (and ticket you may buy) works. In addition, the travel industry is highly competitive and there are many lurks and perks.

The upshot of this is that you should get opinions, quotes and advice from as many airlines and travel agents as possible before you part with your hard-earned cash. The details given in this chapter should be regarded as pointers and are not a substitute for your own careful, up-to-date research.

Getting Around

Turkey has an elaborate public transport system, as Turks love to travel all the time. Turkish Airlines connects all the major cities and resorts. The railway network, though limited, is useful on a few major routes. And the bus system is a marvel, with big, modern coaches going everywhere, all the time, at reasonable prices.

AIR

Domestic Air Services

Turkish Airlines Türk Hava Yolları (THY, Turkish Airlines; symbol: TK), the state-owned airline waiting reluctantly for privatisation, has the major route network in Turkey. When you fly THY, ask about the 10% discount for couples or parent(s) with child(ren) travelling together, and discounts for youth (aged from 12 to 24 years), seniors (60 years and over), and those on their honeymoon or wedding anniversary.

THY flights serve these cities and towns: Adana, Ankara, Antalya, Batman, Bodrum, Çanakkale, Dalaman, Diyarbakır, Elazığ, Erzincan, Erzurum, Gaziantep, İstanbul, İzmir, Kars, Kayseri, Malatya, Muş Samsun, Siirt, Sivas, Şanlıurfa, Trabzon and Van. Hubs are İstanbul and Ankara. To go from Dalaman to Diyarbakır, for example, you will connect at İstanbul or Ankara.

İstanbul Airlines İstanbul Hava Yolları (symbol: IL) operates a few flights between its namesake city and Adana, Ankara, Antalya, Dalaman, İzmir and Trabzon, as well as on international routes to Austria, Belgium, Denmark, Eire, France, Germany, Holland, Italy, Spain, Turkish Cyprus and the United Kingdom. The domestic flights are essentially feeder operations for the international routes, so most flights operate only once or twice per week.

Prices are usually lower than those of THY. You can make reservations through the reservations centre in İstanbul at Firuzköy Yolu No 26, Avcılar (☎ (212) 509 2121, fax 593 6035) and buy tickets at the airport. (See each city section for details on each local office.) Discounts include 10% for families, youth fares (12 to 24 years), and seniors over 60 years of age.

Check-in Procedures

It's a good idea to get to the airport *at least* 45 minutes before flight departure to allow time for security checks and normal confusion. Signs and announcements are not always provided or understandable, so you need to keep asking to make sure you end up at the proper destination.

Also, you need to make sure that your checked baggage is tagged and sent off to the plane. Sometimes when you hand it over to the agents, they just assume you want them to keep it for you until you return.

At the time of writing, there was open seating on most domestic flights; you are not assigned a specific seat number, but may sit wherever you choose. No smoking is allowed on domestic flights, but this is not always observed.

Security

As you approach the airport perimeter, your bus or taxi will be stopped and spot-checked by police looking for terrorists. On a bus, your passport and ticket will be inspected.

As you enter the terminal, you will have to put your luggage through an x-ray machine. Before you leave the terminal you will be frisked for weapons and your hand baggage will be searched. Don't try to carry even a pocketknife aboard, as it will probably be found, and you certainly won't be allowed to carry it on the plane. Rather, pack it in your checked luggage.

As you approach the aircraft, all passengers' luggage will be lined up, and you will be asked to point out your bag. It will then be put on board. This is to prevent someone from checking in a bag with a bomb inside it, then not boarding the plane. If you forget to point out your bag to the baggage handler, it may not be loaded on board and may be regarded with distrust, or even destroyed.

BUS

The bus and the *dolmuş* (minibus) are the most widespread and popular means of transport in Turkey. Buses go literally everywhere, all the time. Virtually every first-time traveller in Turkey comments on the convenience of the bus system.

The bus service runs the gamut from plain and inexpensive to comfortable and moderately priced. It is so cheap and convenient that many erstwhile long-distance hitchhikers opt for the bus. The eight-hour, 450-km trip between İstanbul and Ankara, for example, costs only US$12 to US$20, depending on the bus company.

Though bus fares are open to competition among companies, and even to haggling for a reduction, the cost of bus travel in Turkey works out to around US$2.25 to US$2.75 per 100 km – a surprising bargain.

The best companies, offering smooth service at a higher than average price on national routes, are Kamil Koç, Metro, Ulusoy and Varan. Many other more regional companies offer varying levels of service, some quite good, others less so.

The Otogar

Most Turkish cities and towns have a central bus station called variously *otogar*, *otobüs garajı*, *otobüs terminalı*, *santral garaj* or *şehir garajı* (city garage). In each city, I'll use the term the locals use. Besides intercity buses, the otogar often handles minibuses to outlying districts or villages. A few small towns have only a collection of bus line offices rather than a proper station.

Otogars are often equipped with their own PTT branches, telephones with an international service, restaurants, snack stands, pastry shops, tourism information booths and left-luggage offices *(emanet)*.

Buying Tickets

Though you can often just walk into an otogar and buy a ticket for the next bus out, it's wise to plan ahead. At the least, locate the companies' offices and note the times for your destination a day in advance. This is especially important along the south-east Mediterranean coast and the east, where long-distance bus traffic is less frequent than in other parts of the country.

Some bus companies will grant you a reduction on the fare if you show your ISIC student card. This may not be official policy, but just an excuse for a reduction – in any case you win.

The word for 'tomorrow', very handy to know when buying bus tickets a day in advance, is *yarın* (YAHR-uhn). Bus departure times will be given using the 24-hour clock system, eg 18.30 instead of 6.30 pm.

When you enter an otogar you'll see lots of people and baggage, buses and minibuses, and rows of little ticket offices. Touts will invariably approach asking where you're bound. Competition on some routes is stiff. In most cases, more than one company will run to your desired destination; the cities and towns served by the company will be written prominently at that company's ticket office. Let the touts lead you to the office they work for, but then check other ticket offices, asking when the company's next bus leaves.

Please also join my crusade (holy war?) against smoke-filled buses. Whenever you buy an intercity bus ticket in Turkey, ask for a *sigara içilmez otobüsü* (see-GAH-rah ee-cheel-MEHZ oh-toh-bur-sur, a 'no smoking' bus). Most of your enquiries will elicit a sad smile and a *maalesef* ('unfortunately...'), indicating that there aren't any no-smoking buses on that route yet. But Turks are quick to recognise demand for a service, and future travellers may not have to suffer so much.

Once you've bought a ticket, getting a refund can be difficult, though it's possible. Exchanges for other tickets within the same company are easier.

Seat Selection Plan your seat strategy. Don't leave it up to the ticket agent. All seats are reserved, and your ticket will bear a specific seat number. The ticket agent often has a chart of the seats in front of them, with those already sold crossed off. Look at the chart, and indicate your seating preference.

Preferable seats are in the middle of the bus; seats over the wheels are liable to be cramped and give an unsmooth ride. You also want to get a seat on the side of the bus which will not get full sun. Turks, it seems, are constitutionally opposed to air draughts of any strength, even (or perhaps especially) on a sweltering hot day. The ventilation or air-con system of the bus may be excellent, but it may not be turned on. On a four-hour summer afternoon trip from Ankara to Konya, for instance, you'll be too warm if you're on the right-hand (western) side of the bus, while the seats on the left (eastern) side will remain comfortable.

However, unless you adore inhaling cigarette smoke, you may prefer to seize one of the front seats (Nos 1 to 4) near the driver's open window, perhaps the only fresh-air source on the bus. The problem with the front seats, however, is that they are most vulnerable in case of a traffic accident. Some buses now have *sigarasız* (no smoking) sections, and some companies (usually the more expensive ones such as Ulusoy and Varan) operate no-smoking buses on some routes. Ask.

Bus seat configurations are not uniform, but here are some hints. On the Mercedes 0302 bus, avoid if possible the front rows over the wheels and the last three rows (usually Nos 33 to 43); seats Nos 9 to 28 are the best, but on the shady side. On the single-deck Neoplan bus, wheel seats are Nos 5 to 8 and Nos 33 to 36; Nos 31 to 32 are right by the rear door, and Nos 45 to 48 are right on top of the motor. Avoid these. On the double-decker Neoplan bus, lower deck seats are Nos 53 to 72; you should avoid wheel seats Nos 57 to 60, and rear seats Nos 69 to 72; all of the upper deck seats are good, though Nos 31 to 36 and Nos 39 to 40 are next to the door.

About Bus Travel

A bus trip in Turkey is usually a fairly pleasant experience, if it's not too long. Buses are big, modern and comfortable. As Turks are great cigarette smokers, you may encounter a significant amount of smoke on the trip.

Once en route, your fellow passengers will be curious about where you come from, what language you speak, and how you're enjoying the country. Passengers near you may offer you cigarettes as an ice-breaker, hoping to strike up a conversation. There's no stigma in refusing. Say *Hayır, teşekkür ederim, içmem* ('No, thank you, I don't smoke') or, if this is a mouthful, just *İçmem* (eech-MEHM) with a smile. Turks, like most people, think it laudable that someone doesn't smoke (or has given up smoking). Besides, the offer was intended as a politeness, a welcome and a conversation opener. It serves this purpose whether you smoke or not. It's polite to exchange at least a few sentences.

Shortly after you head out, the *yardımcı* (assistant, also called the *muavin)* will come through the bus with a bottle of lemon cologne with which to refresh their *sayın yolcular* (honoured passengers). They'll dribble some cologne into your cupped hands, which you then rub together, and then rub on your face and hair, ending with a sniff to clear your nasal passages. You may not be used to the custom, but if you ride buses in Turkey much you will get used to it quickly, and probably love it.

Water is provided at no charge on virtually all buses. Signal to the yardımcı and ask *Su, lütfen* ('Water, please'). On the best lines it is cool, bottled spring water; on the worst, tap water of questionable potability served from a common cup.

You can also join in my fresh-air campaign. Summon the yardımcı/muavin and say *çok sıcak!* ('choke' suh-jahk, 'It's very hot'). Indicate the ventilation system and say *Havalandırma açın!* (hah-vah-lahn-duhr-MAH ah-chun, 'Open the ventilation system'). If you can't manage that, just point to it here, in the book, and let the yardımcı read it. Sometimes this works.

Stops will be made every 1½ hours or so for the toilet, snacks or meals and the inevitable *çay*. At some stops children rush onto the bus selling sweets, nuts, sandwiches and the like, or a waiter from the teahouse (buses always stop at a teahouse) may come through to take orders. Most people, however, welcome the chance to stretch their legs.

Keep your bus ticket until you reach your absolutely final destination. In some cases, companies have *servis arabası* (sehr-VEES ah-rah-bah-suh, service cars) – a minibus service that will shuttle you from the bus station into the city at no extra charge, provided you can show a ticket for the company's line.

You can save money by taking night buses on long hauls (eight or 10 hours or more). Cigarette smoke will be less, the bus will be cooler, and you will save money on a hotel room. You miss the scenery, though.

Dolmuş or Minibus

A dolmuş (DOHL-moosh, 'filled') is a Turkish minibus *(minibüs* or *münübüs)*, Fiat taxi, or huge old US car serving as a shared cab.

A dolmuş departs as soon as every seat (or nearly every seat) is taken. You can catch one from point to point in a city, or from village to village, and in some cases from town to town.

Though dolmuşes on some routes operate like buses by selling tickets in advance (perhaps even for reserved seats), the true dolmuş does not. Rather, it is parked at the point of departure (a town square, city otogar or beach) and waits for the seats to fill up.

The dolmuş route may be painted on the side of the minibus, or on a sign posted next to the dolmuş, or in its window; or a hawker may call out the destination. When the driver is satisfied with the load, the dolmuş heads off.

Fares Fares are collected en route or at the final stop. Often the fare is posted on the destination sign, whether it's on a signpost or in the vehicle's window. If it's not, watch what other passengers to your destination are paying and pay the same, or ask. Though passengers to intermediate stops sometimes pay a partial fare, on other routes the driver (or the law) may require that you pay the full fare. In either case, prices are low, though slightly more than for a bus on the same route.

Dolmuş Etiquette Here are some rules of dolmuş etiquette. If your stop comes before the final destination, you may do some shuffling to ensure that you are sitting right by the door and not way up the back. Also, a woman is expected to sit with other women whenever possible. If this is not possible, she should choose a side seat, not a middle seat between two men, for her own comfort and 'protection'. If a man and a woman passenger get into the front of a car, for instance, the man should get in first and sit by the driver (contrary to everything his mother taught him about letting the lady go first), so that the woman is between 'her' man and the door. This is not a gesture against women, but rather the opposite, to show respect for their honour.

Collection of fares will begin after the car starts off, and the driver will juggle and change money as he drives. This thrilling practice costs no extra. If you're still not sure about your fare, hand over a bill large enough to cover the fare but small enough not to anger the driver, who will never have enough change and will not want a large bill. Should there be any doubt about fares or problem in payment (rare), you can always settle up at the last stop.

To signal the driver that you want to get out, say *İnecek var* (ee-neh-JEK vahr, 'Someone wants to get out') or *Sağda* (SAAH-dah, 'On the right', meaning 'Please pull over to the kerb'.) Other useful words are *durun* (DOOR-oon, stop) and *burada* (BOO-rah-dah, here).

TRAIN

Turkish State Railways (TC Devlet Demiryolları, TCDD or DDY) runs services to many parts of the country on lines laid out by German companies which were supposedly paid by the km. Some newer, more direct lines have been laid during the republican era, shortening travel times for the best express trains.

It's not a good idea to plan a train trip all

Trains from İstanbul (Haydarpaşa)
(Daily unless otherwise noted)

Train	*Type*	*Departs*	*Arrives*	*Notes*
Başkent	Super	10 am	Ankara 5.10 pm	Fastest train
Fatih	Super	1.15 pm	Ankara 8.40 pm	
Toros	Express	8.55 am	Adana 6.50 pm	
Boğaziçi	Express	2.55 pm	Ankara 11.10 pm	
Doğu	Express	11.55 pm	Ankara 9.52 am	To Kars; always late
Güney	Express	8 pm	Ankara 5.54 am	Runs four days per week to Diyarbakır & Kurtalan
Vangölü	Express	8 pm	Ankara 5.54 am	Runs three days per week to Tatvan
Anadolu	Express	10 pm	Ankara 7.18 am	1st, 2nd, kuşet
Ankara	Express	10.30 pm	Ankara 7.35 am	All sleeping cars
Mavi Tren	Blue Train	11.50 pm	Ankara 8.02 am	
İç Anadolu Mavi	Blue Train	11.30 pm	Karaman 2.25 pm	Via Konya
Meram	Express	6.30 pm	Konya 8.10 am	
Pamukkale	Express	5.30 pm	Denizli 7.27 am	
Marmara	Boat-Train	8 am	İzmir 8 pm	Except Friday & Sunday

Trains from Ankara
(Daily unless otherwise noted)

Train	*Type*	*Departs*	*Arrives*	*Notes*
Başkent	Super	9.50 am	İstanbul (Haydarpaşa) 5.05 pm	Fastest train
Fatih	Super	1 pm	İstanbul (Haydarpaşa) 8.35 pm	
Boğaziçi	Express	8.10 pm	İstanbul (Haydarpaşa) 4.25 am	
Doğu	Express	2.55 pm	İstanbul (Haydarpaşa) 00.10 am	From Kars; always late
Güney	Express	5.30 pm	İstanbul (Haydarpaşa) 4 am	From Kurtalan & Diyarbakır; often late
Vangölü	Express	8 pm	İstanbul (Haydarpaşa) 4 am	From Tatvan; often late
Anadolu	Express	10 pm	İstanbul (Haydarpaşa) 7.17 am	Seats & kuşets
Ankara	Express	10.30 pm	İstanbul (Haydarpaşa) 8 am	Sleeping cars only
Mavi Tren	Blue Train	11.30 pm	İstanbul (Haydarpaşa) 7.45 am	
İzmir	Express	6.15 pm	İzmir (Basmane) 9.35 am	
İzmir Mavi	Blue Train	9.50 pm	İzmir (Basmane) noon	

the way across Turkey in one stretch. Turkey is a big country, and the cross-country trains are a lot slower than the buses. For example, the *Vangölü Ekspresi* from İstanbul to Lake Van (Tatvan), a 1900-km trip, takes almost two full days – and that's an express! The bus would take less than 24 hours. Train travel between Ankara, İzmir and İstanbul is another matter, however. The top trains on these lines are a pleasure to ride on, whether by night or day.

Whenever you take an intercity train in Turkey, you'd do well to take only *mavi tren* (blue train), *ekspres* or *mototren* trains. These are fairly fast, comfortable, and often not too much more expensive than the more cramped and smoky (but often faster) bus. *Yolcu* (passenger) and *posta* (mail) trains, however, are laughably slow and dilapidated, and should be avoided by all but sociologists wanting a long and intimate look at Turkish country life.

Note that Turkish train schedules indicate *stations*, not cities; the station name is usually, but not always, the city name. Thus you may not see İstanbul on a schedule, but you will see Haydarpaşa and Sirkeci, the Asian and European stations in İstanbul. For İzmir, the stations are Basmane and Alsancak. I'll mention the station names in this guide where appropriate.

Top Trains

Full information on trains is given in Getting There & Away for each city section, but here are the top trains running to the three major cities. All are daily unless otherwise noted.

Başkent Ekspresi The Capital Express, pride of the Turkish State Railways, makes the run between İstanbul and Ankara in just over seven hours, the fastest train of all. It's an air-conditioned, super-1st-class day train between İstanbul (Haydarpaşa) and Ankara with Pullman seats, video, and meals served at your seat, airline-style.

Fatih Ekspresi Named for Mehmet the Conqueror (Fatih), this train is similar to the *Başkent* in comfort, speed and price.

Mavi Tren 'Blue Trains' are comfortable expresses with 1st-class Pullman-style seats only.

Anadolu Ekspresi This nightly couchette and coach train between Ankara and İstanbul (Haydarpaşa) hauls Pullman and couchette *(kuşetli)* cars.

Ankara Ekspresi Sleeping compartments on this nightly all-sleeping-car express between Ankara and İstanbul (Haydarpaşa) cost US$30/45 a single/double.

Marmara Ekspresi Car ferries depart İstanbul at 8 am for Bandırma (four hours, US$8), daily except Friday and Sunday, connecting with daily motor-trains (5½ hours, US$6) between Bandırma and İzmir (Basmane). The boat-train transfer at Bandırma takes from one to two hours. Trains depart İzmir (Basmane) at 8 am daily for Bandırma as well.

İzmir Ekspresi This nightly coach train departs İzmir (Basmane) at 6 pm, arriving in Ankara at 9.17 am; departure from Ankara is at 6.15 pm, arriving in İzmir at 9.35 am. The one-way fare is US$10/7 in 1st/2nd-class.

İzmir/Ankara Mavi Tren The nightly coach and sleeping car Ankara Blue Train departs İzmir (Basmane) at 7.30 pm, arriving in Ankara at 9.35 am. The İzmir Blue Train departs Ankara at 9.50 pm, arriving in İzmir at noon. The one-way fare is US$13; sleeping compartments cost US$32 for one person, US$55 for two people, US$75 for three. Table d'höte dinner on board costs from US$6 to US$10.

Fares

Normal train fares are cheaper than or the same as bus fares for the same journey; the top trains are usually a bit more expensive than the bus. Train fares are set by the railway bureaucracy, however, and are not revised as frequently as bus fares. Thus with the creeping devaluation of the lira, you may find trains cheaper than buses if you ride several months after the last price-fixing.

The table shows fares (in US dollars) on the top trains. The low sleeping-car fare is for a berth in a shared three-bed compartment; highest is for a private compartment.

Buying Tickets

Most seats on the best trains, and all sleeping compartments, must be reserved. As the best trains are popular, particularly the sleeping-car trains, you should make your reservation and buy your ticket as far in advance as possible. A few days will usually suffice, except at holiday times (see The Calendar in the Facts for the Visitor chapter). Weekend trains, between Friday evening and Monday morning, seem to be busiest.

If you can't buy in advance, check at the station anyway. There may be cancellations, even at the last minute.

Though Turkish State Railways now has

Train Fares

Route	*Full Fare*	*Sleeping Car Fare*	*Student Fare*	*Return Fare (Full)*
Ankara-Adana	$13	$22-$28	$10	$20
Ankara-Erzurum	$15	$32-$45	$12	$26
Ankara-İstanbul	$12-$15	$30-$45	$9-$12	$19-$26
Ankara-İzmir	$13-$15	$32-$45	$10-$12	$20-$26
İstanbul-Edirne	$5	–	$4	$8.50
*İstanbul-İzmir	$14	–	$11	$28

(All fares are in US dollars.) *This is the full fare for the entire journey by train and boat.

a computerised reservations system, it is usually impossible to book sleeping-car space except in the city from which the train departs. You can buy tickets at the train station, at many post offices (PTTs) in the major cities, and at some travel agencies.

Turkish words useful in the train station are given in the Turkish Language Guide at the back of this book.

Classes of Travel Most of the best trains, and the short-haul *mototrens* (motor-trains) and rail-buses now have only one class of travel. Coaches on the top trains *(Başkent* and *Fatih Ekspresi*, *Mavi Tren)* usually have Pullman reclining seats; the normal expresses usually have European-style compartments with six seats. The very slow trains and those in the east often have 1st and 2nd-class coaches with compartments.

Sleeping accommodation is of three classes. A *kuşetli* (couchette) wagon has six-person compartments with seats which rearrange into six shelf-like beds at night; you sleep with strangers. *Örtülü kuşetli* means the couchettes have bedding (sheets, pillows, blanket), and there may be only four beds per compartment, so two couples travelling together can get an almost private compartment. A *yataklı* wagon has European-style sleeping compartments capable of sleeping up to three people. Price depends upon the number of occupants: per person cost is lowest when three share, highest if you want a compartment all to yourself.

Discounts & Passes Inter-Rail passes are valid on the Turkish State Railways' entire network; Eurail passes are not valid on any of it.

Full fare is called *tam*. Round-trip (return) fares, called *Gidiş-Dönüş*, are discounted by 20%. Student *(öğrenci* or *talebe)* fares discounted by 20 to 30% are offered on most routes (show your ISIC). If you are under 26 years of age or over 55, you can buy a Tren-Tur card which allows you one month's unlimited rail travel. Ask at Sirkeci Station in İstanbul, or at the station in Ankara. Families *(aile)* travelling together are entitled to a 20 to 30% discount; disabled persons get 30% off, press card holders 50% off.

Cancellation Penalties If you decide not to travel and you seek a refund for your rail ticket up to 24 hours before the train's departure, you must pay a cancellation fee of 10% of the ticket price. Within 24 hours of departure the fee rises to 25%. After the train has departed the fee is 50%.

CAR

Having a car in Turkey, whether owned or rented, gives you unparalleled freedom to enjoy the marvellous countryside and coastline. If you can manage it, car travel in Turkey is rewarding despite the drawbacks.

Road Rules

In theory, Turks drive on the right and yield to traffic approaching them from the right. In practice, Turks drive in the middle and yield to no-one. You must accustom yourself to drivers overtaking you on blind curves. If a car approaches from the opposite direction, all three drivers stand on their brakes and trust to Allah.

The international driving signs are there but rarely observed. Signs indicating *otoyols* (motorways, expressways) are green. Maximum speed limits, unless otherwise posted, are 50 km/h in towns, 90 km/h on highways; and 130km/h maximum, 40 km/h minimum on otoyols. The death toll from speeding is so high that the government carries out a publicity campaign which exhorts drivers to tame the 'Trafik Canavarı' (Motoring Monster) within them, to drive considerately, at a safe speed.

As there are only a few divided highways and many two-lane roads are serpentine, you must reconcile yourself to spending some hours sniffing the stinky diesel exhaust of slow, seriously overladen trucks. At night you will encounter cars without lights or with lights missing; vehicles stopped in the middle of the road; and oncoming drivers who flash their lights just to announce their advent.

Driving Permits

You don't really need an International Driving Permit (IDP) when you drive in Turkey, despite what some travel books say. Your home driving licence, unless it's something unusual (say, from Upper Volta), will be accepted by traffic police and by car rental firms. If you'd feel more secure against bureaucratic hassle by carrying an IDP, you can get one through your automobile club in your home country.

Road Safety

The quality of Turkish highways is passable. The Türkiye Cumhuriyeti Karayolları (Turkish Republic Highways Department or TCK) undertakes ambitious improvements constantly, but despite its efforts most roads still have only two lanes, perhaps with overtaking lanes on long uphill grades. Otoyols (expressways/motorways) run from the Bulgarian border near Edirne to İstanbul and Ankara, and south from İzmir to Aydın.

In eastern Turkey, with its severe winter weather, roads are easily destroyed by frost, and potholes are a tyre-breaking nuisance any time of year.

The expressways are often busy but not impossible; the lesser highways can be busy or pleasantly traffic-free. City streets are usually thronged.

Turkish drivers are not particularly discourteous out on the highway, but they are impatient and incautious. They drive at high speed. They have an irrepressible urge to overtake you.

In the cities *düzensizlik* – disorder – is universal. In addition to the customary and very appropriate *Allah Korusun* ('May God Protect Me') emblazoned somewhere on every Turkish car, bus and truck, imagine the additional motto *Önce Ben* ('Me First').

Kısmet (Fate)

Many local drivers, it seems, believe in *kısmet* (fate). If Turkish drivers, careering along slippery highways in cars with smooth tyres and accelerator pedals flat to the floor and their minds engaged in heated conversation, swerve to avoid an errant sheep and crash into trees, that's kısmet, and it can't be helped. Moderating speed, getting better tyres, wearing safety belts or paying attention to the road are not really options, as kısmet will get you if it's going to, no matter what you do. So why bother?

Whether because of kısmet or not, Turkey's accident rate is one of the highest in the world. In the last decade around 80,000 people have lost their lives, and a million have been injured in traffic accidents, most often because of driver error. On Turkey's highways in the average day, 15 people are killed. Almost every family in the country has been touched by the tragedy.

If you drive, be extremely cautious and defensive. When travelling by bus, it's good to give preference to the better companies with newer equipment, better-trained and more experienced drivers, and stricter policies regarding vehicular safety. ■

To survive on Turkey's highways, drive very defensively, avoid driving at night, and *never* let emotions affect what you do.

Fuel

Fuel stations are everywhere, operated by some familiar international companies (BP, Shell, Mobil) and unfamiliar Turkish ones (Türk Petrol, Petrol Ofisi). Many never close, others stay open long hours, so refuelling is usually no problem. All the same, it's a good idea to have a full tank when you start out in the morning across the vast spaces of central and eastern Anatolia.

Benzin (gasoline/petrol) comes as *normal, süper* and *kurşunsuz* (the last being unleaded, which is not found easily outside the major cities and the heavily touristed western region). Normal costs about US$0.70 per litre (US$2.65 per US gallon); süper, about US$0.80 per litre (US$3.02 per US gallon); kurşunsuz, about US$0.85 per litre (US$3.21 per US gallon). *Dizel* (diesel) costs about US$0.55 per litre (US$2.08 per US gallon).

Spares & Repairs

Turkey's equivalent of the Automobile Association (UK) and American Automobile Association (USA) is the Türkiye Turing ve Otomobile Kurumu (TTOK), the Turkish Touring & Automobile Association (☎ (212) 282 8140, fax 282 8042), Oto Sanayi Sitesi Yanı, Seyrantepe, 4 Levent, İstanbul. It is useful for driving aids (maps, lists of repair shops, legal necessities) as well as for repairs and advice on repairs.

Spare parts for most cars may be available, if not readily so, outside the big cities. European models (especially Renaults, Fiats and Mercedes-Benz) are preferred, though ingenious Turkish mechanics contrive to keep all manner of huge US models – some half a century old – in daily service.

If you have a model with which Turkish mechanics are familiar (such as a Mercedes, simple Renault or Fiat), repairs can be swift and very cheap. Don't be afraid of little roadside repair shops, which can often provide excellent, virtually immediate service, though they (or you) may have to go somewhere else to get the parts. The Sanayi Bölgesi (industrial zone) on the outskirts of every city and town has a row of repair shops.

It's always good to get an estimate of the repair cost in advance. Ask *Tamirat kaç para?* ('How much will repairs cost?'). For tyre repairs find a *lâstikçi* (tyre-repairer). Repair shops are closed on Sunday, but even so, if you go to the repair shop district of town (every town has one) and look around, you may still find someone willing and able to help you out.

Traffic Police

Trafik Polisi in black-and-white cars (usually Renaults) and blue uniforms set up checkpoints on major highways in order to make sure that vehicle documents are in order, that you are wearing your seatbelt, and that vehicle safety features are in working condition. They busy themselves mostly with trucks and buses, as that is where lie the greatest possibilities for supplemental income. They'll usually wave you on, but you should slow down and prepare to stop until you get the wave.

If you are stopped, officers may ask for your car registration, insurance certificate and driving licence. They may ask you to turn on your headlights (high and low beam), hoot your horn, switch on your turning signals and windscreen wipers etc, to see that all are working properly. They'll certainly ask your nationality, and try to chat, because one of the reasons you've been stopped was to break the monotony of checking trucks by throwing in a curious foreigner. If they seem to be requesting money, refuse to understand.

Rental

Renting a car is expensive, but gives you freedom. If you share the cost among several people, renting can be reasonable.

Minimum age is generally 19 or 21 years for the cheapest cars, 24 for some larger cars, and 27 for the best. You must have a major credit card to pay with, or you will be required to make a large cash deposit.

Cars may be rented in Adana, Alanya, Ankara, Antalya, Bodrum, Bursa, Çeşme, Dalaman, Gaziantep, İstanbul, İzmir, Kuşadası, Marmaris, Mersin, Samsun, Side and Trabzon from the larger international rental firms (Avis, Budget, Dollar, Europcar, Hertz, Inter-Rent, Kemwel, National) or from smaller local ones. Rentals may also be picked up in most other cities by prior arrangement.

Avis has the most extensive and experienced network of agencies and staff, and the highest prices. Some firms will be happy to deliver your car to another place, or arrange for pick-up, at no extra charge; others will charge you.

You should not be afraid to try (with caution) one of the small local agencies. Though there is no far-flung network for repairs and people in these places have little fluency in English, they are friendly, helpful and charge from 10 to 20% less than the large firms, particularly if you're willing to haggle a bit.

The most popular rental cars are the Fiat 124 (Serçe), a small four-passenger car with limited space and power; Fiat 131 (Şahin), more powerful and comfortable; Fiat 131SW (Kartal), still more powerful and comfortable; and Fiat Mirafiori (Doğan), big enough for five. Of the Renaults, the 12TX is similar to the Fiat 131, but more economical with fuel; the Renault 9 is larger and more powerful, the 12 STW, better still. All of these cars have standard gear shift. Only the most expensive cars (big Fords, Mercedes etc) have automatic transmission and air-conditioning.

Costs Rental cars are very expensive in Turkey, partly due to huge excise taxes paid when the cars are purchased. Total costs of a rental arranged on the spot in Turkey during the busy summer months, for a week with unlimited km, including full insurance and tax, might be from US$400 to US$700. If you reserve a car in advance from your home country, however, prices may be up to 30% lower. Ask your travel agent to shop around, or to set up a fly-drive arrangement. Kemwel and Autoeurope are two firms which have had low prices in the past, but shop around.

If you rent from abroad, the Collision Damage Waiver (CDW) is usually included in the all-inclusive price quoted to you. The CDW is not a bad thing to have, because a renter is liable not merely for damage, but for rental revenue lost while the car is being repaired or, in the case of a stolen car (uncommon in Turkey), until the car is recovered.

The normal CDW does not cover damage to the car's glass (windscreen, side windows, head and tail lamps etc) nor to its tyres. Yet another charge of US$3 to US$5 per day is required to pay for this. If you do not pay this charge and encounter these misfortunes, it's usually best and cheapest to arrange for repair or replacement yourself, en route.

Note that in most cases you do not need the personal injury insurance, as your health insurance from home should cover any medical costs.

When you look at a rental company's current price list, keep in mind that the daily or weekly rental charge is only a small portion of what you will actually end up paying, unless it includes unlimited km. The charge for km normally ends up being higher, per day, than the daily rental charge. By the way, the 15% value-added tax (KDV) should be included in the rental, insurance and km prices quoted to you. It should not be added to your bill as an extra item.

Any traffic fines you incur will be charged to you. Normally, the company charges your credit card.

Safety & Accidents Child safety seats are usually available from the larger companies if you order them at least 48 hours in advance. Rental costs about US$5 per day.

If your car incurs any damage at all, or if you cause any, do not move the car before finding a police officer and asking for a *kaza raporu* (accident report). The officer may ask you to submit to an alcohol test. Contact your car rental company within 48 hours.

Your insurance coverage may be void if it can be shown that you were operating under the influence of alcohol or other drugs, were speeding, or if you did not submit the required accident report within 48 hours.

MOTORCYCLE

Motorcycles and mopeds are becoming more popular in Turkey because they are cheaper to buy and to run than cars. These days, Austrian and German mopeds are the popular items. Motorcycles tend to be large old Czechoslovak Jawa models that make a distinctive hollow putt-putt sound.

You can bring your motorcycle to Turkey and have a fine time seeing the country. Spare parts will probably be hard to come by, so bring what you may need, or rely on the boundless ingenuity of Turkish mechanics to find, adapt or make you a part. Or else be prepared to call home, have the part flown in, and endure considerable hassles from customs.

BICYCLE

Though Turks use bicycles primarily as utilitarian vehicles to go short distances, long-distance bicycling for sport is being introduced by foreign cyclers. You can cycle pleasurably through Turkey, though you may want to bring your own bike, as renting and selling good bikes is not yet widespread.

The pleasures are in the spectacular scenery, the friendly people, the easy access to archaeological sites and the ready availability of natural camping sites both official and unofficial. The best routes are those along the coasts, particularly the western Mediterranean coast between Marmaris and Antalya. You may be wheeling merrily along, overtaken by a truck loaded with fruit, and handed some on the run by the laughing children who have just picked it. Some of the best routes are the unpaved coastal roads not marked on many maps.

On the minus side, you must watch out for the occasional inattentive driver: have a rearview mirror on your bike. Also, maps available in Turkey are sometimes incorrect on such things as grades and altitudes, so search out a suitable map before leaving home (see Maps in the Facts for the Visitor chapter).

As a cyclist, you may find your relations with Turks somewhat extreme. Along the road, some children not used to cyclists may toss stones. This is often more of an annoyance than a danger, and as cyclists become more familiar sights it should subside. In hotels and pensions, and on those occasional bus and train rides, you may find people so accommodating and helpful in storing your valuable cycle 'safely' that lights, carriers and reflectors may get damaged unintentionally, so supervise and say *yavaş yavaş* (yah-VAHSH yah-VAHSH, 'slowly') frequently.

Whenever you stop for a rest or to camp, the rural staring squads of the curious will appear, instantly, as if by magic. You may find, like the royal family, that constant scrutiny, even if friendly, can be wearisome.

You can usually transport your bike by air, bus, train and ferry, sometimes at no extra charge.

Here are some tips on equipment and repairs. You cannot depend upon finding spare parts, so bring whatever you think you may need. Moped and motorcycle repair shops are often helpful, and if they can't do the repairs they will seek out someone who can. High-pressure pumps are not yet available in Turkey; fuel-station pumps may or may not go to 90 psi (high pressure). Inner tubes of 69 cm by three cm are available, but not everywhere; most of the tubes sold are larger, and they won't fit 69 cm by 2½ cm rims because of the large valve seat. Be prepared for frequent chain maintenance because of the effects of dust and mud.

HITCHING

Hitching is never entirely safe in any country in the world, and we don't recommend it. Travellers who decide to hitch should understand that they are taking a small but potentially serious risk. However, many people do choose to hitch, and the advice that follows should help to make the journey as fast and safe as possible.

When you hitchhike *(otostop)*, Turkish

custom requires that you offer to pay for your ride, though these days some drivers pick up foreign hitchers for the curiosity value. The amount is more or less equivalent to the bus fare on the same route. (Say *Borcum kaç?*, bohr-JOOM kahtch, 'How much do I owe you?' as you prepare to get out.) Overcharging hitchhikers has not been a big problem.

Long-distance hitchhiking, though possible in Turkey, is not all that common. The bus and minibus network is so elaborate and cheap that most people opt for that, figuring that if bus fares must be paid, bus comforts might as well be enjoyed. Private cars are not as plentiful as in Europe, and owners here are not as inclined to pick up hitchers.

Short-distance hitching is somewhat different. As the country is large and vehicles not so plentiful outside the towns, short-distance country hops are the norm. If you need to get from the highway (where the bus dropped you) into an archaeological site (Ephesus, Troy or wherever), you hitch a ride with whatever comes along. Again, private cars are the least amenable, but delivery vans, heavy machinery, oil tankers, farm tractors etc are all fair game. You should still offer to pay for the ride; in most cases your offer will be declined (though appreciated), because you are a 'guest' in Turkey.

The signal used in hitchhiking is not an upturned thumb. In Turkey, you face the traffic, hold your arm out towards the road, and wave your hand and arm up and down as though bouncing a basketball.

Women Hitchhikers

When it comes to women hitchhiking, Turkey is like the rest of the world, perhaps a bit more so: it is seldom done, and you really should not do it, especially alone. A Turkish woman would rather die than hitchhike; she'd feel like she was offering herself to every man in every car that picked her up. With buses so cheap, why set yourself up for hassles?

Hitching as a couple is usually OK, but avoid vehicles with more than one or two men in them. Two women hitching together is preferable to one alone. If you're determined to hitch, take the normal precautions: don't accept a ride in a car or truck which is already occupied by men only (especially if it's only one man, the driver). Look for vehicles carrying women and/or children as well as men. Be appreciative and polite, but cool, dignified and formal, to the driver who picks you up. Avoid hitching across long, empty spaces, and never hitch at night.

BOAT

Turkish Maritime Administration (Türkiye Denizcilik İşletmeleri), also called Turkish Maritime Lines (TML) operates car and passenger ferry services from İstanbul eastward along the Black Sea coast and southward along the Aegean coast, as well as passenger services in the Sea of Marmara and shuttle services across the Dardanelles and the Bay of İzmit. These services may be privatised in the near future, in which case terms of service may change.

Ferry

Car and passenger ferries save you days of driving. Even if you have no car, they offer the opportunity to take mini-cruises along the Turkish coasts. Room on these ships is usually in hot demand, so reserve as far in advance as possible through one of TML's agents (see below), or directly with the İstanbul Karaköy office by fax.

İstanbul to İzmir The İstanbul-İzmir car ferry service operates each weekend throughout the year, departing İstanbul's Sarayburnu dock each Friday at 5.30 pm, arriving in İzmir on Saturday at 11.45 am. Departure from İzmir is on Sunday at 2 pm, arriving in İstanbul on Monday at 9 am.

One-way fares (per person) range from Pullman seats for US$35 to deluxe cabin berths for US$150; a two-berth, B-class cabin would cost US$160 a double. Should you want to use your cabin as a hotel room on Saturday night in İzmir, the cost ranges from US$45 a double for the cheapest cabin to US$165 a double for deluxe, with a two-berth, B-class cabin costing US$95.

Meals are extra, at US$7 for breakfast, US$15 for lunch and US$15 for dinner. Fare for a car is US$60 one way, less than half that for a motorcycle.

İstanbul to Trabzon Car ferries operate each week from early June to mid-September, departing from İstanbul on Monday at 2 pm, stopping briefly in Sinop, arriving in Samsun on Tuesday at 6.30 pm and departing at 8.30 pm, arriving in Trabzon on Wednesday at 9.30 am.

The boat continues to Rize, returning to Trabzon and departing on the return voyage to İstanbul at 4.30 pm on Wednesday. The returning ferry stops briefly at Giresun, Samsun and Sinop, arriving back in İstanbul on Friday at 2 pm.

Per-person fares between İstanbul and Trabzon are US$45 for a Pullman seat, US$50 to US$120 for cabin berths; meals cost US$7 for breakfast, US$15 for lunch or dinner extra. Cars cost US$56; motorcycles, US$25.

İstanbul to Bursa If you're headed from İstanbul to Bursa, you'll doubtless want to take the speedy and enjoyable hydrofoil trip across the Sea of Marmara and the Bay of İzmit to Yalova, where you catch the bus for İznik or Bursa. Details of this route are given in the South of the Sea of Marmara chapter.

There is also a car ferry service every half-hour between Gebze (Eskihisar docks), on the coast east of Üsküdar, and Topçular, east of Yalova on the Sea of Marmara's southern shore. A similar car ferry shuttles between Hereke and Karamürsel, farther east. The drive (or bus ride) east around the Bay of İzmit is long, boring, congested and the scenery's ugly. Take one of these ferries instead.

Sea of Marmara Services

The *Marmara Ekspresi* boat-train runs between İstanbul and İzmir five days a week. See the previous Top Trains section of this chapter.

LOCAL TRANSPORT

Airport

Transport to and from each airport in Turkey is covered within the section on each city.

Bus

Turkish cities have lots of buses, but they are usually crowded to capacity. Buses run by the city government often have *(city-name) belediyesi* (municipality) marked on them. Most municipal buses now work on a ticket system, and you must buy a ticket *(otobüs bileti*, or simply *bilet*, bee-LEHT) at a special ticket kiosk. These kiosks are at major bus termini or transfer points; some shops may sell them as well, and scalpers may hang around bus stops selling them for a marked-up price.

Dolmuş

Dolmuşes, minibuses or sedans, operate in many cities, and are usually faster, more comfortable and only slightly more expensive than the bus (and still very cheap). Intracity dolmuş stops are near major squares, terminals or intersections, and you'll have to ask: (name of destination) *dolmuş var mı?* (DOHL-moosh VAHR muh). If you are in Laleli or Aksaray in İstanbul, for instance, and you want to get to Taksim Square, you ask, *Taksim dolmuş var mı?* Someone will point you to the dolmuş stop on Atatürk Bulvarı.

Often there is not a direct dolmuş route from where you are to where you're going. Maps of the system don't exist. If the person you ask hesitates, they're probably trying to tell you that you must take one dolmuş to a certain point, and then another.

Once you know a few convenient routes, you'll feel confident about picking up a dolmuş at the kerb. In the larger cities, stopping-places are regulated and sometimes marked by signs with a black 'D' on a blue-and-white background reading *Dolmuş İndirme Bindirme Yeri* (Dolmuş Boarding and Alighting Place). You'll see minibuses, old US cars and new little Turkish-made cars stopping.

A true city dolmuş has a solid-colour band,

usually yellow or black, painted horizontally around the car just below the windows. Sometimes taxis with a black-and-yellow chequered band operate like the dolmuş. You've got to be careful. If you climb into an empty car, the driver might assume (honestly, or for their own benefit) that you want a taxi, and will charge you the taxi fare. Always ask, *Dolmuş mu?* (dohl-MOOSH moo? 'Is this a dolmuş?') when you climb into an empty car.

Taxi

Taxis in most cities have digital meters and routinely use them. If yours doesn't, mention it right away by saying, *Saatiniz* (saa-AHT-EE-NEEZ, 'Your meter'). The starting rate is about US$0.70, more late at night. The average taxi ride costs from US$2 to US$3 during the day time, 50% more at night.

With the flood of tourists arriving in Turkey, some taxi drivers – especially İstanbul's many crooks-on-wheels – have begun to demand flat payment from foreigners. In some cases the driver will actually offer you a decent fare, and will then pocket all the money instead of giving the owner of the cab their share. But most of the time the driver will offer an exorbitant fare, give you trouble, and refuse to run the meter. Find another cab and, if convenient, report them to the police.

A woman should not sit in the front seat next to the driver unless there is no other available seat. The driver may misunderstand the gesture as an invitation to greater intimacy.

Ferry & Sea Bus

Public intracity sea transport is by ferryboat and *deniz otobüsü* ('sea bus').

Traditional ferries steam up, down and across the Bosphorus and the Bay of İzmir, providing city dwellers with cheap, convenient transport, views of open water and (in summer) fresh cool breezes.

Sea buses are faster, enclosed craft which ply certain routes heavily used by commuters.

These are not nostalgic transport but vital elements of each city's transport system. You should take the ferry in each city at least once, sipping tea while enjoying the cityscapes from the decks. The ferries can be crowded during rush hours but there's always air and scenery; and while buses sit trapped in traffic the ferries glide through the water effortlessly, at speed.

TOURS

As Turkey's tourist boom continues, the number of companies offering guided tours of cities or regions expands apace. A travel agency and tour operator of long standing and excellent reputation is Orion-Tour (☎ (212) 248 8437, fax 241 2808), Halaskargazi Caddesi 284/3, Marmara Ap, 80220 Şişli, İstanbul. Orion's multilingual staff can arrange almost any sort of travel in Turkey, from flight reservations and airport transfers to guided tours and yacht cruises.

Along with legitimate operators, the sleazy ones are moving in, so you should be careful when choosing a tour company.

The actual tour you get depends greatly on the competence, character and personality of your particular guide; but it's difficult to pick a tour by guide rather than company, so you must go by the tour company's reputation.

The best course of action is to ask at your hotel for recommendations. Other foreign visitors may be able to give you tips about which companies to use and which to avoid. Watch out for the following rip-offs:

- a tour bus that spends the first hour or two of your 'tour' circulating through the city to various hotels, picking up tour participants;
- a tour that includes an extended stop at some particular shop (from which the tour company or guide gets a kickback);
- a tour that includes a lunch which turns out to be mediocre.

Most of the time, it is a lot cheaper and quicker to see things on your own by bus, dolmuş, or even taxi. Tours can cost from US$20 to US$40 per person; you may be able to hire a taxi and driver for the entire day for less than that, after a bit of haggling.

İstanbul

For many centuries this city was the capital of the civilised world. Even though in 1922 Ankara became the capital of the newly proclaimed Turkish Republic, İstanbul continued to be the Turkish metropolis. It remains the country's largest city (with about 12 million residents) and port, its business and cultural centre and the first destination for Turkish and foreign tourists alike.

Although İstanbul has yielded some of its pre-eminence to up-and-coming towns such as Ankara, İzmir and Antalya, it remains, without doubt, the heartbeat of the Turkish spirit. The Turks are proud of Ankara, their modern, 20th-century capital, but it is İstanbul, the well-worn but still glorious metropolis, which they love. Its place in the country's history, folklore, commerce and culture is unchallenged.

No matter how you arrive in İstanbul, you'll be impressed. The train skirts the southern coast of the Thracian peninsula, following the city walls until it comes around Seraglio Point and terminates right below Topkapı Palace. Buses come in along an expressway built on the path of the Roman road. Flying in on a clear day may reveal the great mosques and palaces, the wide Bosphorus (Boğaziçi) and the narrower Golden Horn (Haliç), all in a wonderful panorama.

But nothing beats 'sailing to Byzantium' – gliding across the Sea of Marmara while watching the slender minarets and bulbous mosque domes rise on the horizon. Even Mark Twain, who certainly had control of his emotions, waxed rhapsodic in his *Innocents Abroad* on the beauties of arriving by sea. Today, though fumes from fossil fuels may obscure the view, it's still impressive. If you take the boat-train from İzmir via Bandırma, or the ferry from Bursa and Yalova, you'll approach the city by sea.

İstanbul has grown ferociously in the past two decades, and now sprawls westward beyond the airport, 23 km from the centre, northward halfway to the Black Sea, and eastward deep into Anatolia. And it is crowded. However, both the Bosphorus, the strait which connects the Black Sea and the Sea of Marmara, and the narrower Golden Horn, a freshwater estuary, help to create a sense of openness and space. More than that, the Bosphorus provides an uncrowded maritime highway for transport to various sections of the city. For several thousand years before the construction of the Bosphorus Bridge in 1973, the only way to go between the European and Asian parts of the city was by boat. The second Bosphorus bridge, named Fatih Köprüsü, north of the

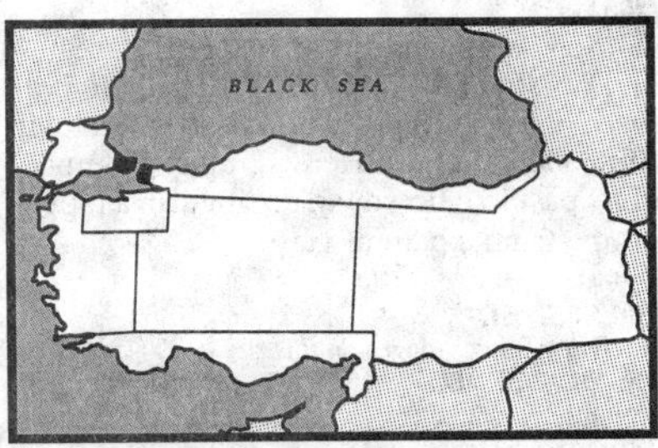

Highlights

- Strolling through Topkapı Palace, especially the Treasury and Harem
- Listening to sound echo in the vastness of Sancta Sophia
- Viewing the glittering Byzantine mosaics of the Kariye Müzesi
- Cruising up the Bosphorus on the special excursion ferryboat
- Touring the opulent vastness of Dolmabahçe Palace
- Shopping in the Covered Bazaar's maze of narrow streets
- Walking the length of untouristy Uzunçarşı Caddesi
- Joining the crowds strolling along İstiklal Caddesi, day or night

first one at Bebek/Beylerbeyi, was finished in 1988. A third bridge, farther north, is planned, and a metro is being developed.

HISTORY

With a past spanning 3000 years, the greatest part of İstanbul's fascination comes from its place in history and the buildings that remain from ancient times. Here's a quick summary of its past to help you to distinguish a hippodrome from a harem.

1000-657 BC
Ancient fishing villages on this site.
657 BC-330 AD
Byzantium, a Greek city-state, later subject to Rome.
330-1453 AD
Constantinople, the 'New Rome', capital of the Later or Eastern Roman (Byzantine) Empire – reached its height in the 12th century.
1453-1922
İstanbul, capital of the Ottoman Turkish Empire – reached the height of its glory in the 16th century.
1922-84
Ankara becomes the capital of the Turkish Republic. İstanbul continues to be the country's largest city and port, and its commercial and cultural centre.
1984 to the Present
İstanbul begins to enjoy a renaissance as 'capital of the East'. A new municipal government undertakes vast schemes to modernise and beautify the city and attract international business operations. New parks, museums and cultural centres are opened, old ones are restored and refurbished.

Early Times

The earliest settlement, Semistra, was probably around 1000 BC, a few hundred years after the Trojan War and in the same period that kings David and Solomon ruled in Jerusalem.

It was followed by a fishing village named Lygos, which occupied Seraglio Point where Topkapı Palace stands today. Later, around 700 BC, colonists from Megara (near Corinth) in Greece settled at Chalcedon (now Kadıköy) on the Asian shore of the Bosphorus.

Byzantium

The first settlement to have historic significance was founded by another Megarian colonist, a fellow named Byzas. Before leaving Greece, he asked the oracle at Delphi where he should establish his new colony. The enigmatic answer was 'Opposite the blind'. When Byzas and his fellow colonists sailed up the Bosphorus, they noticed the colony on the Asian shore at Chalcedon. Looking to their left, they saw the superb natural harbour of the Golden Horn on the European shore. Thinking, as legend has it, 'Those people in Chalcedon must be blind', they settled on the opposite shore, on the site of Lygos, and named their new city Byzantium. This was in 657 BC.

The legend might as well be true. İstanbul's location on the waterway linking the Sea of Marmara and Black Sea, and on the 'land bridge' linking Europe and Asia, is still of tremendous importance today, 2600 years after the oracle spoke.

Byzantium submitted willingly to Rome and fought Rome's battles for centuries, but finally got caught supporting the wrong side in a civil war. The winner, Septimius Severus, razed the city walls and took away its privileges in 196 AD. When he relented and rebuilt the city, he named it Augusta Antonina.

Constantinople

Another struggle for control of the Roman Empire determined the city's fate for the next 1000 years. Constantine pursued his rival Licinius to Augusta Antonina, then across the Bosphorus to Chrysopolis (Üsküdar). Defeating his rival in 324 AD, Constantine solidified his control and declared this city to be 'New Rome'. He laid out a vast new city to serve as capital of his empire, and inaugurated it with much pomp in 330 AD. The place which had been first settled as a fishing village over 1000 years earlier was now the capital of the world, and would remain so for almost another 1000 years.

The Later Roman, or Byzantine, Empire lasted from the re-founding of the city in 330 AD to the Ottoman Turkish conquest in 1453, an impressive 1123 years. Much remains of ancient Constantinople, and you'll be able to visit churches, palaces, cisterns and the Hippodrome during your stay.

IMPERIAL MOSQUES

In 1453, when the victorious armies of Mehmet the Conqueror poured through the great walls of vanquished Constantinople, they found a depopulated city. Foreseeing the inevitable fall of the Byzantine capital, many of its citizens had long since fled to Greece or Europe, and large tracts of the city were abandoned and derelict.

Mehmet the Conqueror, seeing himself as the legitimate successor to the Roman (Byzantine) emperors by right of conquest, sought to repopulate the great metropolis and make it a capital city worthy of his empire. One way in which he and his successors carried out this task was by building imperial mosques.

When a sultan built an imperial mosque, it quickly became the centre of a new quarter. Workers poured in, residences and workshops were built, and ancillary services such as shops quickly appeared. The building of a mosque took years, at the end of which time the quarter would be fully populated.

Each imperial mosque had a *külliye*, or collection of charitable institutions, clustered around it. These might include a hospital, insane asylum, orphanage, soup kitchen, hospice for travellers, religious school, library, baths and a cemetery in which the mosque's imperial patron, his family and other notables could be buried.

The distinctive domes (left) of İstanbul's Blue Mosque (Sultan Ahmet Camii) and its main portal (right)

TONY WHEELER

TOM BROSNAHAN

TURKEY'S WOODEN HOUSES

These days most Turkish towns are vanishing fast beneath a blanket of ugly brick and concrete. It wasn't always like this, of course, and in the 19th century most towns and villages boasted fine wooden houses. Enthusiasts for such houses will find much to please them in Afyon, Amasya or Tokat, but the crème de la crème when it comes to wooden housing must be Safranbolu, declared a World Heritage Site by UNESCO primarily on the basis of its civic architecture.

Ottoman wooden houses were generally two or three-storied, with the upper storeys jutting out over the lower ones on carved corbel brackets. Their timber frames were filled with adobe and then plastered with a mixture of mud and straw. Sometimes, particularly in the villages, the houses were left like that but in towns they were usually given a finish of plaster or whitewash, with decorative flourishes in plaster or wood. The wealthier the owner, the fancier the decoration.

Lower storey windows often had ornamental grilles fitted to them, while the upper ones were fitted with fretwork. The houses of the wealthy sometimes had a stained-glass skylight above the door. Many houses had double doors wide enough to let carts through into a courtyard. Often they had fine metal door-knockers.

Inside, the larger houses had 10 to 12 rooms, divided into *selamlık* (men's quarters) and *haremlik* (women's quarters). Rooms were often decorated with built-in niches and cupboards, and had fine plaster fireplaces with *yaşmaks* or conical hoods. Sometimes the ceilings were extraordinarily elaborate; the ceiling of the Paşa Odası of Tokat's Latifoğlu Konağı, for example, is thought to be emulating a chandelier in wood.

The houses rarely had much furniture beyond the low benches, or *sedir*, around the walls. Families ate on the floor around tables which could be put away at the end of the meal. Bedding was kept in the cupboards during the day and brought out at night. Washing facilities were usually concealed inside closets.

Regarding such houses as old-fashioned, noisy and expensive to maintain, most modern Turks prefer to move into apartment blocks. But a conservation movement is gradually taking hold, and government aid may eventually be forthcoming to help people maintain these houses.

Street scene, Bosphorus

KIM GRANT

In fact, there's more of Constantinople left than anyone knows about. Any sort of excavation reveals streets, mosaics, tunnels, water and sewer systems, houses and public buildings. Construction of a modern building may be held up for months while archaeologists investigate – an unmitigated disaster to a modern real-estate developer!

The Conquest What westerners refer to as 'The Fall of Constantinople' was to Muslims 'The Conquest of İstanbul'. Though the Byzantine Empire had been moribund for several centuries, the Ottomans were quite content to accept tribute from the weak Byzantine emperor as they progressively captured all the lands surrounding his well-fortified city. By the time of the Conquest, the emperor had control over little more than the city itself and a few territories in Greece.

When Mehmet II, 'the Conqueror' *(Fatih)*, came to power in 1451 as a young man, he needed an impressive military victory to solidify his dominance of the powerful noble class. As the Ottomans controlled all of Anatolia and most of the Balkans by this time, it was obvious that the great city should be theirs. Mehmet decided it should be sooner rather than later.

Mehmet II (the Conqueror) was responsible for the Conquest of İstanbul (or the Fall of Constantinople) in 1453. Mehmet's entry into the city is commemorated annually on 29 May in İstanbul.

The story of the Conquest is thrilling, full of bold strokes and daring exploits, heroism, treachery and intrigue. Mehmet started with the two great fortresses on the Bosphorus. Rumeli Hisar, the larger one, was built in an incredibly short four months on the European side. Anadolu Hisarı, the smaller one on the Asian side built half a century earlier by Yıldırım Beyazıt, was repaired and brought to readiness. Together they controlled the strait's narrowest point.

The Byzantines had closed the mouth of the Golden Horn with a heavy chain to prevent Ottoman boats from sailing in and attacking the city walls on the north side. In another bold stroke, Mehmet marshalled his boats at a cove (now covered by Dolmabahçe Palace) and had them transported overland on rollers and slides, by night, up the valley (where the Hilton now stands) and down the other side into the Golden Horn at Kasım Paşa. He caught the Byzantine defenders completely by surprise and soon had the Golden Horn under control.

The last great obstacle was the mighty bastion of land walls on the western side. No matter how heavily Mehmet's cannons battered them by day, the Byzantines would rebuild them by night and, come daybreak, the impetuous young sultan would find himself back where he'd started. Then he received a proposal from a Hungarian cannon founder named Urban who had come to offer his services to the Byzantine emperor for the defence of Christendom against the infidels. Finding that the emperor had no money, he went to Mehmet and offered to make the most enormous cannon ever. Mehmet, who had lots of money, accepted the offer, and the cannon was cast and tested in Edirne.

The first shot, which terrified hundreds of peasants, sent a huge ball 1.5 km, where it buried itself two metres in the ground. The

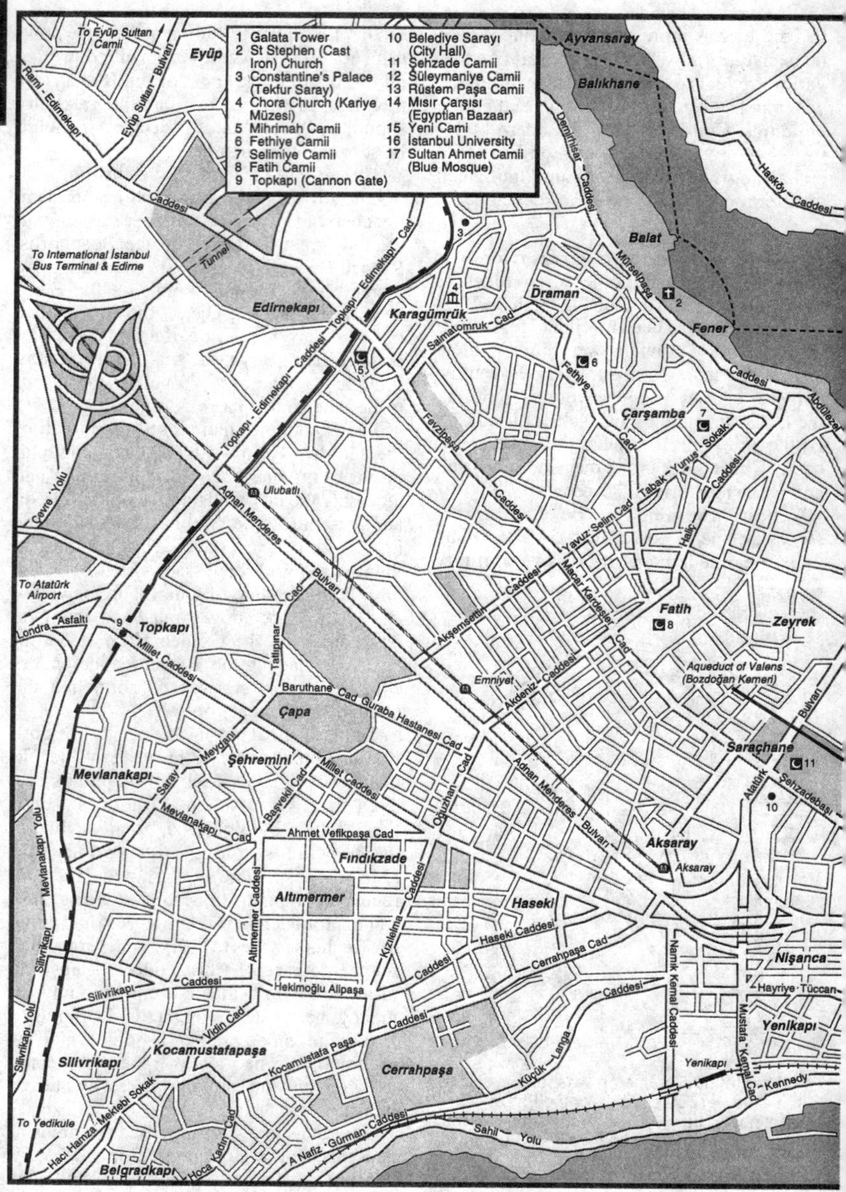
1 Galata Tower
2 St Stephen (Cast Iron) Church
3 Constantine's Palace (Tekfur Saray)
4 Chora Church (Kariye Müzesi)
5 Mihrimah Camii
6 Fethiye Camii
7 Selimiye Camii
8 Fatih Camii
9 Topkapı (Cannon Gate)
10 Belediye Sarayı (City Hall)
11 Şehzade Camii
12 Süleymaniye Camii
13 Rüstem Paşa Camii
14 Mısır Çarşısı (Egyptian Bazaar)
15 Yeni Cami
16 İstanbul University
17 Sultan Ahmet Camii (Blue Mosque)
To Eyüp Sultan Camii
Eyüp
Eyüp Sultan Bulvarı
Rami - Edirnekapı Caddesi
Ayvansaray
Balıkhane
Demirhisar Caddesi
Hasköy Caddesi
Balat
Mürselpaşa Caddesi
Fener
Abdülezel
To International İstanbul Bus Terminal & Edirne
Tunnel
Edirnekapı
Topkapı - Edirnekapı Caddesi
Karagümrük
Draman
Salmatomruk Cad
Fethiye Cad
Çarşamba
Fevzipaşa Caddesi
Tabak Yunus Sokak
Yavuz Selim Cad
Haliç Caddesi
Çevre Yolu
Ulubatlı
Adnan Menderes Bulvarı
Macar Kardeşler Cad
To Atatürk Airport
Londra Asfaltı
Topkapı
Tatlıpınar Cad
Akşemsettin Caddesi
Fatih
Zeyrek
Millet Caddesi
Emniyet
Akdeniz Caddesi
Aqueduct of Valens (Bozdoğan Kemeri)
Baruthane Cad
Guraba Hastanesi Cad
Çapa
Saraçhane
Mevlanakapı
Saray Meydanı
Şehremini
Başvekil Cad
Oğuzhan Cad
Atatürk Bulvarı
Şehzadebaşı
Mevlanakapı Cad
Ahmet Vefikpaşa Cad
Aksaray
Fındıkzade
Mevlanakapı Yolu
Altımermer Caddesi
Altımermer
Kızlelma Caddesi
Haseki
Haseki Caddesi
Namık Kemal Caddesi
Nişanca
Silivrikapı Yolu
Cerrahpaşa Cad
Silivrikapı Caddesi
Hekimoğlu Alipaşa
Hayriye Tüccarı
Vidin Cad
Kocamustafa Paşa Caddesi
Yenikapı
Silivrikapı
Kocamustafapaşa
Mustafa Kemal Cad
Cerrahpaşa
Küçük Langa
Kennedy
To Yedikule
Hacı Hamza Mektebi Sokak
A Nafiz Gürman Caddesi
Sahil Yolu
Belgradkapı
Hoca Kadın Cad

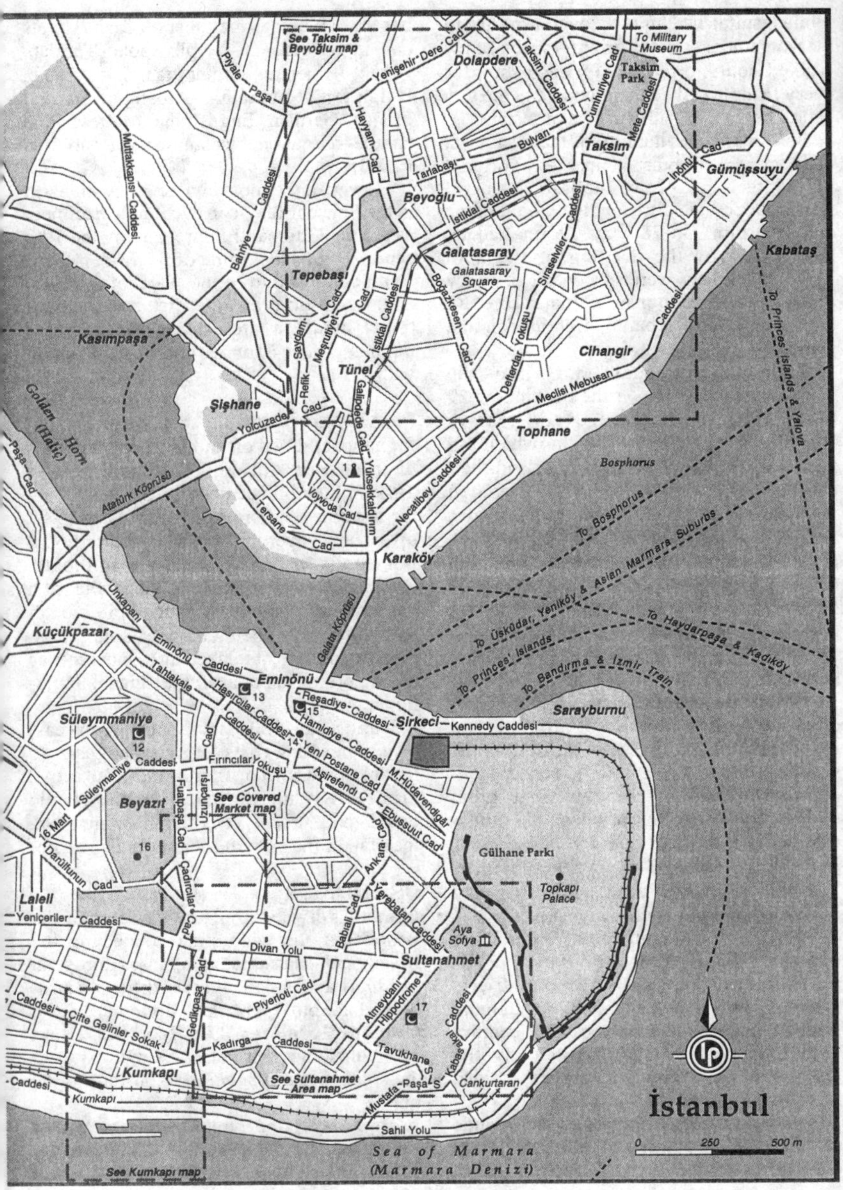
İstanbul
See Taksim & Beyoğlu map
To Military Museum
Yenişehir Dere Cad
Dolapdere
Taksim Caddesi
Cumhuriyet Cad
Taksim Park
Mete Caddesi
Piyale Paşa
Hayyam Cad
Bulvarı
Tarlabaşı
Taksim
Cad
İnönü
Gümüşsuyu
Muttakkapısı Caddesi
Caddesi
Bahriye
Beyoğlu
İstiklal Caddesi
Galatasaray
Galatasaray Square
Sıraselviler Caddesi
Kabataş
Tepebaşı
Meşrutiyet Cad
Cad
İstiklal Caddesi
Boğazkesen Cad
Yokuşu
Caddesi
To Princes' Islands & Yalova
Kasımpaşa
Saydam
Refik
Cad
Tünel
Defterdar
Cihangir
Meclisi Mebusan
Golden Horn (Haliç)
Şişhane
Galipdede Cad
Yolcuzade
Tophane
Paşa Cad
Atatürk Köprüsü
Yüksekkaldırım
Voyvoda Cad
Necatibey Caddesi
Bosphorus
Tersane
Cad
To Bosphorus
Karaköy
To Üsküdar, Yeniköy & Asian Marmara Suburbs
Unkapanı
To Haydarpaşa & Kadıköy
Küçükpazar
Eminönü Caddesi
Galata Köprüsü
To Princes' Islands
Tahtakale
Eminönü
To Bandırma & İzmir Train
Hasırcılar Caddesi
Reşadiye Caddesi
Sirkeci
Kennedy Caddesi
Sarayburnu
Süleymmaniye
Caddesi
Hamidiye Caddesi
Cad
Yeni Postane Cad
Fırıncılar Yokuşu
Aşirefendi C
M. Hüdavendigâr
Süleymaniye Caddesi
Beyazıt
Uzunçarşı
See Covered Market map
Fuatpaşa Cad
Ebussuut Cad
Ankara Cad
Gülhane Parkı
16 Mart
Darülfünun
Cad
Çadırcılar Cad
Topkapı Palace
Laleli
Yerebatan Caddesi
Babıali Cad
Yeniçeriler Caddesi
Aya Sofya
Divan Yolu
Sultanahmet
Gedikpaşa Cad
Piyerloti Cad
Atmeydanı Hippodrome
Caddesi
Caddesi
Çifte Gelinler Sokak
Kadırga Caddesi
Tavukhane S
Akbıyık Caddesi
Kabasakal
Kumkapı
See Sultanahmet Area map
Mustafa Paşa S
Cankurtaran
Caddesi
Kumkapı
Sahil Yolu
Sea of Marmara (Marmara Denizi)
See Kumkapı map
0
250
500 m
1
12
13
14
15
16
17

jubilant sultan had his new toy transported to the front lines and set to firing. A special crew worked hours to ready it for each shot, for every firing wrecked the mount, and the gun had to be cooled with buckets of water.

Despite the inevitability of the Conquest, the emperor refused surrender terms offered by Mehmet on 23 May 1453, preferring to wait in hope that Christendom would come and save him. On 28 May the final attack began, and by the evening of the 29th Mehmet's troops were in control of every quarter. The emperor, Constantine XI Dragases, died in battle, fighting on the walls.

Mehmet's triumphant entry into 'the world's greatest city' on the evening of 29 May is commemorated every year in İstanbul. Those parts of the city which did not resist his troops were spared, and their churches guaranteed. Those that resisted were sacked for the customary three days, and their churches turned into mosques. As for Sancta Sophia, the greatest church in Christendom (St Peter's in Rome, though larger, was not begun until 1506), it was converted immediately into a mosque.

İstanbul

The Ottoman Centuries Mehmet the Conqueror began at once to rebuild and repopulate the city. He saw himself as the successor to the glories and powers of Constantine, Justinian and the other great emperors who had reigned here. He built a mosque (Fatih Camii) on one of the city's seven hills, repaired the walls and made İstanbul the administrative, commercial and cultural centre of his growing empire.

Süleyman the Magnificent (1520-66) was perhaps İstanbul's greatest builder. His mosque, the Süleymaniye (1550), is İstanbul's largest. Other sultans added more grand mosques, and in the 19th century numerous palaces were built along the Bosphorus: Çirağan, Dolmabahçe, Yıldız, Beylerbeyi and Küçük Su.

As the Ottoman Empire grew to include all of the Middle East and North Africa as well as half of Eastern Europe, İstanbul became a fabulous melting pot. On its streets and in its bazaars, people spoke Turkish, Greek, Armenian, Ladino, Russian, Arabic, Bulgarian, Rumanian, Albanian, Italian, French, German, English and Maltese. The parade of national costumes was no less varied.

However, the most civilised city on earth in the time of Süleyman eventually declined, as did the Ottoman Empire, and by the 19th century it had lost some of its former glory. But it continued to be the 'Paris of the East' and, to reaffirm this, the first great international luxury express train ever run, the famous *Orient Express*, connected İstanbul with Paris.

Republican İstanbul Atatürk's campaign for national salvation and independence was directed from Ankara. The founder of the Turkish Republic decided to get away from the imperial memories of İstanbul and to set up the new government in a city which could not easily be threatened by gunboats. Robbed of its importance as the capital of a vast empire, İstanbul lost much of its wealth and glitter. From being the East's most cosmopolitan place, it relaxed into a new role as an important national, rather than international, city.

During the 1980s İstanbul began to reassume something of its former role. Easier to live in than Cairo or Beirut, more attractive than Tel Aviv, more in touch with the Islamic world than Athens, it is fast becoming the 'capital' of the eastern Mediterranean again.

ORIENTATION

İstanbul is divided from north to south by the Bosphorus, the wide strait connecting the Black and Marmara seas, into European *(Avrupa)* and Asian *(Asya)* portions. European İstanbul is further divided by the Golden Horn into Old İstanbul (Eski İstanbul, sometimes called the Old City) to the south and Beyoğlu (BEY-oh-loo) to the north.

Three days is the minimum time necessary for a meaningful visit to this city; a week is better. The sights below are organised with the most important and accessible sights first, and the lesser ones after.

Eski İstanbul

The Old City is ancient Byzantium/Constantinople/İstanbul, called Stamboul by 19th-century travellers. It's here, from Seraglio Point (Sarayburnu) jutting into the Bosphorus to the mammoth land walls some seven km westward, that you'll find the great palaces and mosques, hippodromes and monumental columns, ancient churches and the Grand Bazaar, called the Covered Market *(Kapalı Çarşı)* in Turkish. The best selection of bottom-end and middle-range hotels is also here, with a few top-end places as well.

Beyoğlu

North of the Golden Horn is Beyoğlu, the Turkish name for the two ancient cities of Pera and Galata, or roughly all the land from the Golden Horn to Taksim Square. Here you'll find the Hilton, the Sheraton, the Pera Palas and other luxury hotels; airline offices and banks; the European consulates and hospitals; and Taksim Square, the hub of European İstanbul.

Under the Byzantines, Galata (now called Karaköy, KAHR-ah-keuy) was a separate city built and inhabited by Genoese traders.

Under the sultans, the non-Muslim European population of Galata spread up the hill and along the ridge, founding Galata's sister city of Pera. In modern times this part of the city has been the fastest growing and has stretched far beyond the limits of old Galata and Pera. The name Beyoğlu still refers to just those two old cities. Beyoğlu is good for a walking tour, especially along İstiklal Caddesi, formerly known as the Grande Rue de Péra.

Eski İstanbul and Beyoğlu are connected by the Galata Köprüsü (Galata Bridge) at the mouth of the Golden Horn. Just east of the bridge are the docks for Bosphorus ferryboats.

Asian İstanbul

The Asian part of the city, on the eastern shore of the Bosphorus, is of less interest to tourists, being mostly dormitory suburbs such as Üsküdar (EU-skeu-dahr, Scutari) and Kadıköy (KAH-duh-keuy). One landmark you'll want to know about is Haydarpaşa Station (Haydarpaşa İstasyonu), right between Üsküdar and Kadıköy. This is the terminus for Anatolian trains, which means any Turkish train except the one from Europe via Edirne. If you're headed for Ankara, Cappadocia or any point east of İstanbul, you'll board at Haydarpaşa.

The Bosphorus

The Bosphorus is lined with more suburbs, some of which are quite charming and worth a walk around. You should plan to spend at least one day exploring the strait.

INFORMATION

Tourist Offices

There are Ministry of Tourism offices at Atatürk Airport (☎ (212) 663 6363, fax 663 0793) in the international arrivals area, at the north-western end of the Hippodrome in Sultanahmet (☎ (212) 518 1802, fax 518 1802), open from 9 am to 5 pm daily, and at Sirkeci railway station (☎ (212) 511 5888).

In Beyoğlu, there is an office at the Karaköy Yolcu Salonu (Karaköy International Maritime Passenger Terminal) (☎ (212) 249 5776); another in Elmadağ in the Hilton Hotel arcade (☎ (212) 233 0592), just off Cumhuriyet Caddesi, two long blocks north of Taksim Square on the right-hand side of the street (open from 9 am to 5 pm, closed on Sunday). Yet another office is in the regional Directorate of Tourism (☎ (212) 243 2928, fax 252 4346), more or less opposite the British Consulate-General at Meşrutiyet Caddesi 57, Tepebaşı.

Automobile Club

The Türk Turing ve Otomobil Kurumu (Turkish Touring & Automobile Association; ☎ (212) 280 4449, 282 7874), Birinci Oto Sanayi Sitesi Yanı, Dördüncü Levent, about seven km north of Taksim Square, provides information on car insurance and import permits, and has a breakdown service and repair facilities. The association and its longtime director, Mr Çelik Gülersoy, have been prime movers in efforts at historical restoration and beautification in İstanbul and several other Turkish cities.

Foreign Consulates

For details of the many consulates in İstanbul, see the Facts for the Visitor chapter.

Money

For general information on banks, see the Money section in the Facts for the Visitor chapter. Remember that you can usually change money (preferably cash) at PTT branches; see Post & Communications for locations. Currency exchange booths at Atatürk Airport's international arrivals area are open whenever flights arrive.

Most bank ATMs allow withdrawals only in Turkish liras, but the larger branches of Türkiye İş Bankası will usually allow you to withdraw money via ATM in US dollars as well, which is useful if you're trying to build up your dollar reserves for travel to another country. An alternative is to withdraw liras and convert them to dollars at a non-bank currency exchange office (döviz bürosu) offering good selling rates for dollars.

İstanbul has an ever-growing number of döviz bürosus. They offer faster service than banks, longer opening hours, and usually do not charge a commission. The rates are worse at bureaux heavily used by tourists, such as those in Sultanahmet (Arkent Döviz) and the Grand Bazaar. Better rates are offered in Taksim, Şişli, Eminönü, and other areas where Turks change money.

Entel Döviz (☎ 513 8284), on Ankara Caddesi opposite Sirkeci station, gives decent rates of exchange. A nearby alternative is Koçkaya Döviz (☎ 522 5353), Muradiye Caddesi, Kale İş Hanı 12.

Bamka Döviz (☎ 253 5500), Cumhuriyet Caddesi 23 near Aydede Caddesi, two blocks north of Taksim across the boulevard from Pizza Hut, is open every day from 8 am to 8 pm. Çetin Döviz (☎ 252 6428), İstiklal Caddesi 39, Beyoğlu, across from the French Consulate a block off Taksim, does not offer as good a rate as Bamka. Fast Forex (☎ 293 0024), Meşrutiyet Caddesi 22, Galatasaray, near the British consulate, has English-speaking staff. The cheapest rate in town is at Aktif (☎ 230 1961), on the west side of Şişli Meydanı, two km north of Taksim, but there's usually a long queue.

Post & Communications

İstanbul's Main Post Office *(Merkez Postane)* is several blocks west of Sirkeci train station on Yeni Postane Sokak. It's open daily from 8 am to 8 pm, though many services such as poste restante have more restricted hours and close at lunch time. The phone centre, however, is open until midnight. There are other convenient PTT branches near Taksim Square at Cumhuriyet Caddesi, Taksim Gezi Dükkanları, on İstiklal Caddesi in Galatasaray, in Aksaray and in the Covered Market near the Havuzlu Lokantası please show on map.

The telephone area code for European İstanbul is 212; numbers given in this section which do not include an area code are preceded by 212. The area code for Asian İstanbul is 216.

Travel Agencies

Travel agents on the northern side of Divan Yolu in Sultanahmet specialise in budget flights, but can also arrange bus and train tickets. There are more such agencies downhill from Aya Sofya along Alemdar Caddesi on the way to Gülhane Park.

Ms Filiz Bingöl at the Overseas Travel Agency (☎ 513 4175, fax 513 4177), Alemdar Caddesi 16, Sultanahmet, is a Turkish-Australian woman whom readers of this guide have found particularly helpful.

Backpackers Travel Agency (☎ 638 6343, fax 638 1483), Yeni Akbıyık Caddesi 22, is right among the hotels and pensions of Cankurtaran.

The fancier travel agencies and airline offices are in the districts called Elmadağ and Harbiye, north of Taksim Square along Cumhuriyet Caddesi between the Divan and Hilton hotels.

A travel agent/tour operator which gives good service with English-speaking staff is

Orion-Tour (☎ 248 8437, fax 241 2808), Halaskargazi Caddesi 284/3, Marmara Apartımanı, Şişli, about two km north of Taksim. Orion (pronounced OR-yohn in Turkish) can arrange flights, cruises (including private or group yacht charters), transfers to and from the airport, city tours of İstanbul and other major cities, and private or group tours anywhere in Turkey.

Bookshops

In general, the place to find foreign-language books is in and around Tünel Square, at the southern end of İstiklal Caddesi. The big luxury hotels all have little bookshops or news-stands.

Robinson Crusoe (☎ 293 6968), İstiklal Caddesi 389, Tünel, has two floors of books and a good selection, including many in European languages.

Dünya Aktüel (☎ 249 1006), İstiklal Caddesi 469, Tünel, has Turkish, French and English books and periodicals. Dünya also operates shops at the Hilton, Holiday Inn, Mövenpick and Swissôtel hotels.

The Metro Kitabevi (☎ 249 5827), İstiklal Caddesi 513, facing Tünel Square, sells guidebooks and maps. The nearby ABC Kitabevi (☎ 293 1629), on Tünel Square, has mostly language-learning aids, but some other books as well.

Pandora (☎ 245 1667), Büyükparmakkapı Sokak 3, Taksim, off İstiklal Caddesi, has a good collection of books on Turkish and Ottoman history, Turkish literature in English and Lonely Planet books.

Librairie de Péra (☎ 245 4998), Galip Dede Caddesi 22, Tünel, is an antiquarian shop with old books in Turkish, Greek, Armenian, Arabic, French, German, English etc.

Eren (☎ 251 2858), Sofyalı Sokak 34, Tünel, has old and new history and art books and maps.

Alman Kitabevi (☎ 244 7731), İstiklal Caddesi, Tünel, sells German-language books (mostly religious and language-learning materials).

Fransız/İtalyan/İspanyol Kitabevi (☎ 249 0099), Meşelik Sokak 12-14, in the Sekban Han building, sells French, Italian and Spanish-language books.

Aypa (☎ 516 0100), Mimar Mehmet Ağa Caddesi 19, Sultanahmet, just down the hill from Aya Sofya and the Blue Mosque on the way to the hotels and pensions of Cankurtaran (see map), has guides, maps and magazines in English, French and German.

Dilmen Kitabevi (☎ 527 9934), Sahaflar Çarşisi 20, has a good selection of titles on Turkey and Turkish history in English.

Karum (☎ 241 7988), Akkavak Sokak 19/21/1 Nişantaşi, has a good selection of art books, art prints and posters.

Remzi Kitabevi (☎ 234 5475), Rumeli Caddesi 44, Nişantaşi is a top quality general English language bookshop with a wide selection on all subjects. Worth a special visit! Equally good is their other shop (☎ 282 0245) in the new Akmerkez Shopping Centre in Etiler (a northern suburb of İstanbul).

Sahaflar Çarşısı, the used-book bazaar, is great fun for browsing. It's just west of the Covered Market across Çadırcılar Caddesi, sandwiched between that street and the Beyazıt Camii. Among the shops here, one of the best is the Üniversiteli Kitabevi (☎ (212) 511 3987, fax (216) 345 9387), at No 5, with a modern outlook and the most current books published in Turkey. The Zorlu Kitabevi (☎ 511 2660, fax 526 0495), at No 22, specialises in books about İstanbul, old documents and maps.

Libraries

The American Library (☎ 251 2675), next to the US Consulate at Meşrutiyet Caddesi 108, Tepebaşı, is being scaled back to a reference library due to government budget cuts. It's open Monday through Friday from noon to 4 pm.

Atatürk Library (☎ 251 7972), Mete Caddesi 45, Taksim, is open daily from 8.30 am to 7 pm, with a good selection of periodicals.

The British Council Library (☎ 249 0574), İstiklal Caddesi 151-253, Beyoğlu, in the Örs Turistik İş Merkezi building, is open

Tuesday through Friday from 10 am to 5.45 pm and Saturday from 10 am to 1.30 pm.

The Women's Library (☎ 534 9550), near the ferry dock in Fener on the south-west side of the Golden Horn, is open from 9 am to 5.30 pm; closed Sunday. The library, housed in an historic building, acts as a women's resource centre, with a programme of cultural and special events of interest to women.

Laundry

If you don't do your own laundry, ask for prices at your hotel. Alternatives in Sultanahmet include:

Hobby Laundry (☎ 513 6150), Caferiye Sokak 6/1, Sultanahmet, adjoining the Yücelt Interyouth Hostel and opposite Aya Sofya. Posted hours are 9 am to 8 pm every day, actual hours may be different. The charge is US$1.50 per kg to wash (minimum two kg), about US$0.50 per kg to dry, but 'dry' means dampish. Attendants take your clothes and run the machines.

Active Laundry, Dr Emin Paşa Sokak 14, off Divan Yolu beneath the Arsenal Youth Hostel (see map), charges US$1.50 per kg to wash, US$0.50 to dry, and is open daily.

Sultan Laundry, İncili Çavuş Çıkmazı 21, opposite the Hotel Nomade and around the corner, charges similar rates.

İstanbul has numerous dry-cleaning shops *(kuru temizleme)*, usually open every day except Sunday from 8 am to 7 pm. Bring items in early for same-day service. Two blocks westward uphill from the southern end of the Hippodrome in Sultanahmet is Doğu Expres (☎ 526 0725), Peykhane Sokak 61 (also called Üçler Sokak). In Tepebaşı, try Reforma Kuru Temizleme (☎ 243 6862), Meşrutiyet Caddesi 131, near the Büyük Londra Oteli. West of Taksim down the hill towards Dolmabahçe is Cevat Kuru Temizleme (☎ 249 0578), İnönü Caddesi 30.

Medical Services

For details of health concerns in Turkey, see Health in the Facts for the Visitor chapter. You should contact your country's consulate in İstanbul or embassy in Ankara (see Embassies in the Facts for the Visitor chapter). They may have advice about suitable doctors, dentists, hospitals, and other medical care. İstanbul has several private hospitals which provide good quality care at low government-controlled prices. These include:

Amerikan Bristol Hastanesi, Güzelbahçe Sokak, Nişantaşı (☎ 231 4050), about two km north-east of Taksim, with US administration and a dental clinic

Florence Nightingale Hospital, Abidei Hürriyet Caddesi 290, Çağlayan, Şişli (☎ 231 2021), about four km north of Taksim

Intermed Check-up Centre, Teşvikiye Caddesi, Bayar Apt 143, Nişantaşı (☎ 225 0660), about two km north of Taksim

International Hospital, İstanbul Caddesi 82, Yeşilyurt (☎ 663 3000), west of the centre on the shore near the airport

La Paix ('Lape') Hastanesi, Büyükdere Caddesi 22-24, Şişli, (☎ 246 1020), with French administration

Alman Hastanesi, Sıraselviler Caddesi 119, Taksim (☎ 293 2150), a few hundred metres south of Taksim on the left-hand side, with German administration

Emergency

In case of hassles, stolen or lost documents and the like, you might get some help from the Tourism Police (☎ 527 4503), Yerebatan Caddesi 2, Sultanahmet, opposite Yerebatan Saray (the 'Sunken Palace' cistern). They have some multilingual staff and some experience with foreigners.

If you have a personal crisis – financial, physical, psychological, emotional – and need someone to talk to about it, dial the İstanbul Blue Line on ☎ 638 2626. Multilingual staff will help you to find a solution.

Turkey has national emergency numbers which can be dialled from any phone without charge:

Ambulance	112
Fire	110
Police	155

Admission Hours & Days

Most museums are closed on Monday, but Topkapı Palace is closed on Tuesday instead. Dolmabahçe Palace is closed on both

Monday and Thursday. The Covered Market (Kapalı Çarşı) is closed on Sunday.

Mosques are open every day. Avoid visiting mosques right after the call to prayer (wait 30 minutes) and on Friday morning (the Muslim Sabbath), when congregations assemble for prayers and sermons.

Holders of an International Student Identity Card are admitted free or at reduced rates to sites controlled by the Ministry of Tourism and Ministry of Culture.

OLD İSTANBUL

In the Old City, Topkapı Palace is right next to Aya Sofya, which is right next to the Blue Mosque, which is right on the Hippodrome, which is right next to the Cistern Basilica, which is only a few steps from the museum complex, which is right next to Topkapı Palace. You can spend at least two days just completing this loop. Start with the palace, which is among the world's great museums.

Topkapı Palace

Topkapı Sarayı (TOHP-kahp-uh) was the residence of the sultans for almost three centuries. Mehmet the Conqueror built the first palace shortly after the Conquest in 1453, and lived here until his death in 1481. Sultan after sultan played out the drama of the Ottoman sovereign here until the 19th century. Mahmut II (1808-39) was the last emperor to occupy the palace. After him, the sultans preferred to live in new European-style palaces – Dolmabahçe, Çirağan, Yıldız – which they built on the Bosphorus.

Foreigners called Topkapı the *Seraglio*, an Italian word. Mozart's famous opera *Abduction from the Seraglio* is performed in the palace every summer from late June to early July during the International İstanbul Festival.

Topkapı Palace (☎ 512 0480) is open from 9.30 am to 5 pm (till 7 pm during July and August); closed on Tuesday. Admission to the palace costs US$6, half-price for students; you will buy a separate ticket for the Harem (tours every 30 minutes from 10 am to noon and 1 to 4 pm, US$2.50) at the Harem entrance as you begin the tour.

I suggest that you head straight for the Harem when you enter the palace, note the tour times posted on the board by the entry, buy your ticket, and return in time to catch the next tour. In summer this may not work; the crowds are so thick and the tour groups so numerous that individual travellers sometimes are out of luck as the groups book all of the Harem tours in advance. You may want to ask at the Harem ticket booth about scheduling a special tour with a private guide for about US$10 for a group of six or so.

It will take you the better part of a day to explore Topkapı Palace. You should be at the door when it opens if you plan to visit in the busy summer months. Though it's tempting to nip into Aya Sofya for a look as you go by on your way to Topkapı, I strongly recommend that you resist the urge. Aya Sofya has been there for 1500 years, and it will be there when you come out of Topkapı.

Court of the Janissaries Topkapı grew and changed with the centuries, but its basic four-courtyard plan remained the same. As you pass through the great gate behind Aya Sofya, you enter the First Court (Birinci Avlu), the Court of the Janissaries. On your left is the former **Aya İrini Kilisesi**, or Church of Divine Peace (☎ 520 6952), Sarayiçi 35, now a concert hall where recitals are given during the International İstanbul Festival.

There was a Christian church here from earliest times, and before that, a pagan temple. The early church was replaced by the present one during the reign of the Byzantine emperor Justinian in the 540s, so the church you see is as old as Aya Sofya. When Mehmet the Conqueror began building his palace, the church was within the grounds and thus couldn't be used for worship. Ironically, it was used as an arsenal for centuries, then as an artillery museum.

Janissaries, merchants and tradespeople could circulate as they wished in the Court of the Janissaries, but the Second Court was different. The same is in a way true today, because you must buy your tickets before entering the Second Court. The ticket booths

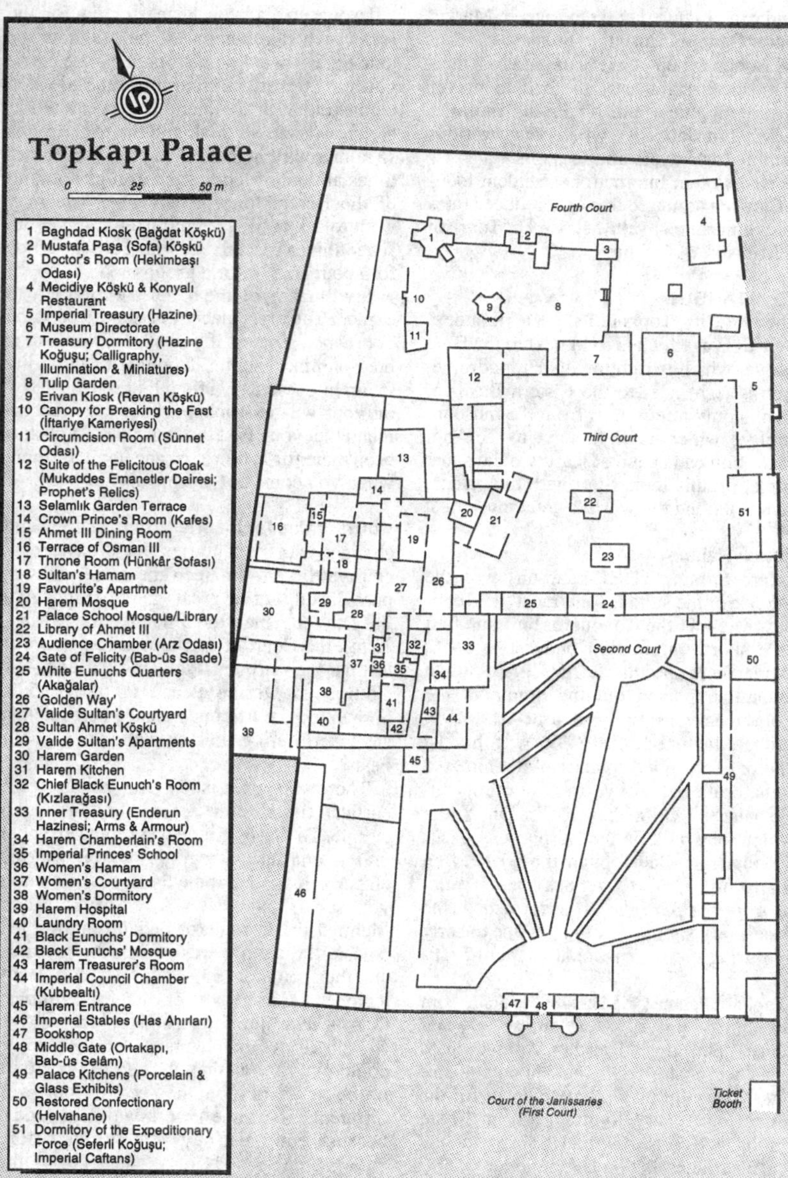
Topkapı Palace
0 25 50 m
1 Baghdad Kiosk (Bağdat Köşkü)
2 Mustafa Paşa (Sofa) Köşkü
3 Doctor's Room (Hekimbaşı Odası)
4 Mecidiye Köşkü & Konyalı Restaurant
5 Imperial Treasury (Hazine)
6 Museum Directorate
7 Treasury Dormitory (Hazine Koğuşu; Calligraphy, Illumination & Miniatures)
8 Tulip Garden
9 Erivan Kiosk (Revan Köşkü)
10 Canopy for Breaking the Fast (İftariye Kameriyesi)
11 Circumcision Room (Sünnet Odası)
12 Suite of the Felicitous Cloak (Mukaddes Emanetler Dairesi; Prophet's Relics)
13 Selamlık Garden Terrace
14 Crown Prince's Room (Kafes)
15 Ahmet III Dining Room
16 Terrace of Osman III
17 Throne Room (Hünkâr Sofası)
18 Sultan's Hamam
19 Favourite's Apartment
20 Harem Mosque
21 Palace School Mosque/Library
22 Library of Ahmet III
23 Audience Chamber (Arz Odası)
24 Gate of Felicity (Bab-üs Saade)
25 White Eunuchs Quarters (Akağalar)
26 'Golden Way'
27 Valide Sultan's Courtyard
28 Sultan Ahmet Köşkü
29 Valide Sultan's Apartments
30 Harem Garden
31 Harem Kitchen
32 Chief Black Eunuch's Room (Kızlarağası)
33 Inner Treasury (Enderun Hazinesi; Arms & Armour)
34 Harem Chamberlain's Room
35 Imperial Princes' School
36 Women's Hamam
37 Women's Courtyard
38 Women's Dormitory
39 Harem Hospital
40 Laundry Room
41 Black Eunuchs' Dormitory
42 Black Eunuchs' Mosque
43 Harem Treasurer's Room
44 Imperial Council Chamber (Kubbealtı)
45 Harem Entrance
46 Imperial Stables (Has Ahırları)
47 Bookshop
48 Middle Gate (Ortakapı, Bab-üs Selâm)
49 Palace Kitchens (Porcelain & Glass Exhibits)
50 Restored Confectionary (Helvahane)
51 Dormitory of the Expeditionary Force (Seferli Koğuşu; Imperial Caftans)
Fourth Court
Third Court
Second Court
Court of the Janissaries (First Court)
Ticket Booth

The Janissaries

The word 'janissary' comes from the Turkish *yeni çeri*, 'new levies'. These soldiers were personal servants of the sultan, 'owned' by him, fed and paid regularly by him, and subject to his will. They were full-time soldiers, an innovation in an age when most soldiers – and all soldiers in Europe – were farmers in spring and autumn, homebodies in winter, and warriors only in summer.

In a process termed *devşirme*, government agents went out from İstanbul into the towns and villages of the Balkans to round up 10-year-old boys from Christian families for the sultan's personal service. Having one's son taken by the devşirme was undoubtedly a blow to the family, who would probably lose his love and labour forever. The boy would be instructed in Turkish, converted to Islam, and enrolled in the sultan's service.

The imperial service was a meritocracy. Those of normal intelligence and capabilities went into the Janissary corps, the sultan's imperial guard. The brightest and most capable boys went into the palace service, and many eventually rose to the highest offices, including that of grand vizier. This ensured that the top government posts were always held by personal servants of the sultan. These top government and military officers would often remember their birthplaces, and would lavish benefits such as public works projects (mosques, bridges, schools etc) upon them.

Topkapı's large Court of the Janissaries, stretching from the church to the Ortakapı, is now a shady park, but in the old days this was where the sultan's elite corps of guards gathered to eat the hearty pilav provided by him. When they were dissatisfied with the sultan's rule (which meant his treatment of them), they would overturn the great cauldrons of pilav as a symbol of revolt, after which the sultan's hours were numbered.

By the early 19th century, the Janissary corps had become unbearably corrupt and self-serving, and a constant threat to the throne. The reforming sultan Mahmut II, risking his life, his throne and his dynasty, readied a new, loyal European-style army, then provoked a revolt of the Janissaries in the Hippodrome and brought in his new army to wipe them out, ending their 350-year history in 1826. ■

are on your right as you approach the entrance. Just past them is a little fountain where the imperial executioner used to wash the tools of his trade after decapitating a noble or rebel who had displeased the sultan. The head of the unfortunate was put on a pike and exhibited above the gate you're about to enter.

Ortakapı & Second Court The Ortakapı (Middle Gate, Gate of Greeting or Bab-üs Selâm) led to the palace's Second Court, used for the business of running the empire. Only the sultan and the *valide sultan* (queen mother) were allowed through the Ortakapı on horseback. Everyone else, including the grand vizier, had to dismount. The gate you see was constructed by Süleyman the Magnificent in 1524, utilising architects and workers he had brought back from his conquest of Hungary.

To the right after you enter is a map and model of the palace to help you get your bearings.

Within the second courtyard is a beautiful, park-like setting. Topkapı is not a palace on the European plan – one large building with outlying gardens – but rather a series of pavilions, kitchens, barracks, audience chambers, kiosks and sleeping quarters built around a central enclosure, much like a fortified camp.

The great **palace kitchens**, on your right, hold a small portion of Topkapı's vast collection of Chinese celadon porcelain. Beyond the celadon are the collections of European and Ottoman porcelain and glassware. The last of the kitchens, the Helvahane in which all the palace sweets were made, is now set up as a kitchen, and you can easily imagine what went on in these rooms as the staff prepared food for the 5000 inhabitants of the palace.

On the left side of the Second Court is the ornate **Kubbealtı** ('beneath the cupola') or Imperial Council Chamber, marked by the squarish tower which is among the palace's most distinctive architectural features.

Beneath this tower is where the grand vizier met with the Imperial Divan (council) on matters of state. The sultan did not participate in these discussions, but sometimes attended them sitting behind a screen and listening.

Next to the Kubbealtı, to the right, is the armoury *(silahlar)* exhibit of fearsome Ottoman and European weaponry.

Harem The entrance to the Harem, open only from 10 am to 4 pm, is just behind the Kubbealtı. Tour times and languages are listed on a board at the Harem ticket office. Make sure the guide will be speaking a language that you understand. Refreshments are served to those waiting for the tour from a little snacks and drinks stand.

Fraught with legend and romance, the Harem is usually imagined as a place where the sultan could engage in debauchery at will. In fact, these were the imperial family quarters, and every detail of Harem life was governed by tradition, obligation and ceremony.

Every traditional Muslim household had two distinct parts: the *selamlık* (greeting room) where the master greeted friends, business associates and tradespeople; and the *harem* (private apartments), reserved for himself and his family. The Harem, then, was something akin to the private apartments in Buckingham Palace or the White House.

The women of the Harem had to be foreigners, as Islam forbade enslaving Muslims, Christians or Jews (Christians and Jews could be enslaved in the Balkans – as with the janissaries' devşirme: see the aside on Janissaries – due to a loophole in Islamic law, or if taken as prisoners of war, or if bought as slaves in a legitimate slave market). Besides prisoners of war, girls were bought as slaves (often sold by their parents at a good price), or received as gifts from nobles and potentates. A favourite source of girls was Circassia, north of the Caucasus Mountains in Russia, as Circassian women were noted for their beauty, and parents were often glad to give up their 10-year-old girls in exchange for hard cash.

Upon entering the Harem, the girls would be schooled in Islam and Turkish culture and language, the arts of make-up, dress, comportment, music, reading and writing, embroidery and dancing. They then entered a meritocracy, first as ladies-in-waiting to the sultan's concubines and children, then to the sultan's mother and finally, if they were the best, to the sultan himself.

Ruling the Harem was the valide sultan, the mother of the reigning sultan. She often owned large landed estates in her own name and controlled them through black eunuch servants. She was allowed to give orders directly to the grand vizier. Her influence on the sultan, on the selection of his wives and concubines, and on matters of state, was often profound.

The sultan was allowed by Islamic law to have four legitimate wives, who received the title of *kadın* (wife). If a wife bore him a child, she was called *haseki sultan* if it was a son; *haseki kadın* if it was a daughter. The Ottoman dynasty did not observe primogeniture, so in principle the throne was available to any imperial son. Each lady of the Harem contrived mightily to have her son proclaimed heir to the throne, thus assuring her own role as the new valide sultan.

As for concubines, Islam permits as many as a man can support in proper style. The Ottoman sultans had the means to support many, sometimes up to 300, though they were not all in the Harem at the same time. The domestic thrills of the sultans were usually less spectacular, however. Mehmet the Conqueror, builder of Topkapı, was the last sultan to have four official wives. After him, sultans did not officially marry, but instead kept four chosen concubines without the legal encumbrances, thereby saving themselves the embarrassments and inconveniences suffered by another famous Renaissance monarch, King Henry VIII of England.

The Harem was much like a small village with all the necessary services. About 400 or 500 people lived in this section of the palace at any one time. Not many of the ladies stayed in the Harem all their lives: the sultan

Life in the Cage

Imperial princes were brought up in the Harem as children, taught and cared for by its women and servants.

In the early centuries of the empire, Ottoman princes were schooled as youths in combat and statecraft by direct experience: they practised soldiering, fought in battles and were given provinces to administer. But as the Ottoman dynasty did not observe primogeniture (succession of the firstborn), the death of the sultan regularly resulted in a fratricidal bloodbath as his sons battled it out amongst themselves for the throne. In the case of Beyazıt II, his sons began the battles even before the sultan's death, realizing that to lose the battle for succession meant death for themselves. The victorious son, Selim, even forced Beyazıt to abdicate, and may even have had him murdered as he went into retirement.

Fratricide was not practised by Ahmet I, who could not bring himself to murder his mad brother Mustafa. Instead, he kept him imprisoned in the Harem, beginning the tradition of *kafes hayatı* (cage life). This house arrest, adopted in place of fratricide by later sultans, meant that princes were prey to the intrigues of the women and eunuchs, corrupted by the pleasures of the Harem, ignorant of war and statecraft, and thus usually unfit to rule if and when the occasion arose. Luckily for the empire in this latter period, there were able grand viziers to carry on.

In later centuries the dynasty abandoned kafes hayatı and adopted the practice of having the eldest male in the direct line assume the throne. ■

might grant them their freedom, after which they would often marry powerful men who wanted the company of these supremely graceful and intelligent women, not to mention their connections with the palace.

The *kızlarağası* (kuhz-LAHR-ah-ah-suh, chief black eunuch), the sultan's personal representative in administration of the Harem and other important affairs of state, was the third most powerful official in the empire, after the grand vizier and the Şeyh-ul İslâm (supreme Islamic judge).

Tour Much of the Harem was constructed during the reign of Süleyman the Magnificent (1520-66), but much more was added or reconstructed over the years.

The modest door through which you enter was for tradespeople who brought their wares here to the black eunuch guards. The tile work in the second room is some of Turkey's finest: the green and yellow colours are unusual in İznik faïence (tin-glazed earthenware). A corridor leads past the rooms of the black eunuchs who guarded the sultan's ladies. In the early days white eunuchs were used, but black eunuchs sent as presents by the Ottoman governor of Egypt later took control. As many as 200 lived here, guarding the doors and waiting on the women.

The sultan, as he walked these corridors, wore slippers with silver soles. As no woman was allowed to show herself to the 'imperial regard' without specific orders, the clatter of the silver soles warned residents of the sultan's approach so they could disappear from his sight. This rule no doubt solidified the valide sultan's control, as *she* got to choose which girls would be presented to the sultan.

Around a small courtyard were the private apartments of the sultan's four kadıns. A larger courtyard beyond was the domain of the valide sultan – the centre of power in the Harem – to which each new sultan came after his accession to the throne to receive the allegiance and congratulations of the people of the Harem.

The sultan's private Turkish bath is next. His mother and his four wives each had their own private bath. Other private baths went to the lady responsible for discipline in the Harem and to her assistant, the treasurer. Below that rank the women shared common baths.

Next on the tour are several of the sultan's private chambers, originally built by Sinan,

Süleyman the Magnificent's great architect, but the present décor dates from the 18th century.

There is also a 17th-century room with a beautifully decorated fireplace, and a reception room with a fountain. Here the sultan received the ladies of the Harem, or his married female relatives – sisters, cousins and aunts. The fountain obscured the sounds of their conversation so that no-one, in this hotbed of intrigue, could eavesdrop.

Sultan Ahmet I (1603-17), builder of the Blue Mosque, added a nice little library. In 1705 his successor Ahmet III added the pretty dining room with the bowls of fruit painted on the walls.

The **Veliaht Dairesi** is the legendary *kafes* (see the boxed story 'Life in the Cage'), the apartment of the crown prince, where he was kept secluded from the world. Note the ingenious little fountains in the windows and the leather-domed ceiling. Next to the crown prince's suite are the sumptuous rooms of his mother, the haseki sultan.

The tour exits into the third courtyard.

Third Court If you enter the Third Court through the Harem, and thus by the back door, you should head for the main gate into the court. Get the full effect of entering this holy of holies by going out through the gate, and back in again.

This gate, the **Bab-üs Saade**, or Gate of Felicity, also sometimes called the Akağalar Kapısı (Gate of the White Eunuchs), was the entrance into the sultan's private domain. As is common with oriental potentates, the sultan preserved the imperial mystique by appearing in public very seldom. The Third Court was staffed and guarded by white eunuchs, who allowed only very few, very important people in. As you enter the Third Court, imagine it alive with the movements of imperial pages and white eunuchs scurrying here and there in their palace costumes. Every now and then the chief white eunuch or the chief black eunuch would appear, and all would bow deferentially. If the sultan walked across the courtyard, all activity stopped until the event was over.

An exception to the imperial seclusion was the ceremony celebrating a new sultan's accession to the throne. After girding on the sword of Osman, which symbolised imperial power, the new monarch would sit enthroned before the Bab-üs Saade and receive the obeisance, allegiance and congratulations of the empire's high and mighty.

Before the annual military campaigns in summertime, the sultan would also appear before this gate bearing the standard of the Prophet Muhammed to inspire his generals to go out and win one for Islam.

During the great days of the empire, foreign ambassadors were received on days when the Janissaries were to get their pay. Huge sacks of silver coins were brought to the Kubbealtı. High court officers would dispense the coins to long lines of the tough, impeccably costumed and faultlessly disciplined troops as the ambassadors looked on in admiration.

Today the Bab-üs Saade is the backdrop for the annual performance of Mozart's *Abduction from the Seraglio* during the International İstanbul Festival in late June and early July.

Just inside the Bab-üs Saade is the **Arz Odası**, or Audience Chamber, constructed in the 16th century but refurnished in the 18th century. Important officials and foreign ambassadors were brought to this little kiosk to conduct the high business of state. An ambassador, frisked for weapons and held on each arm by a white eunuch, would approach the sultan. At the proper moment, he knelt and kowtowed; if he didn't, the eunuchs would urge him ever so forcefully to do so.

The sultan, seated on the divans whose cushions are embroidered with over 15,000 seed pearls, inspected the ambassador's gifts and offerings *(pişkeş)* as they were passed through the small doorway *(pişkeş kapısı)* on the left. Even if the sultan and the ambassador could converse in the same language (sultans in the later years knew French, and ambassadors often learned Turkish), all conversation was with the grand vizier. The sultan would not deign to speak to a foreigner, and only the very highest Ottoman officers were allowed to address the monarch directly.

Right behind the Arz Odası is the pretty little **Library of Ahmet III** (1718). Walk to the right as you leave the Arz Odası, and enter the rooms of the Seferli Koğuşu (Dormitory of the Expeditionary Force), which now house the rich collections of imperial robes, kaftans and uniforms (Padişah Elbiseleri) worked in thread of silver and gold. Textile design reached its highest point during the reign of Süleyman the Magnificent, when the imperial workshops produced cloths of exquisite design and work.

Next along on the same side are the chambers of the **Imperial Treasury** (Hazine), packed with an incredible number and variety of objects made from or decorated with gold, silver, rubies, emeralds, jade, pearls and diamonds. Look for the tiny figurine of a sultan sitting under a canopy, his body one enormous pearl. Next to him, a black eunuch's pantaloons are also one pearl.

The Kaşıkçının Elması, or Spoonmaker's Diamond, is an 86-carat rock surrounded by several dozen smaller stones. First worn by Mehmet IV at his accession to the throne in 1648, it is the world's fifth-largest diamond. There's also an uncut emerald weighing 3.26 kg, and the golden dagger set with three large emeralds which was the object of Peter Ustinov's criminal quest in the movie *Topkapi*.

Also be sure to see the gold throne given by Nadir Shah of Persia to Mahmud I (1730-54). Other thrones are almost as breathtaking.

Next door to the Treasury is the **Hayat Balkonu**, or the Balcony of Life. From here the breeze is cool and there's a marvellous view of the Bosphorus and the Sea of Marmara.

Suite of the Felicitous Cloak Opposite the Treasury is another set of wonders, the holy relics in the **Hırka-i Saadet**, or Suite of the Felicitous Cloak, nowadays called the Mukaddes Emanetler Dairesi (Sacred Safekeeping Rooms). These rooms, sumptuously decorated with İznik faïence (don't miss the harmonious dome), constituted a holy of holies within the palace. Only the chosen could enter the Third Court, but entry into the Hırka-i Saadet rooms was for the chosen of the chosen, and only on special ceremonial occasions.

These rooms contain the cloak of the Prophet Muhammed, his battle standard, two of his swords, a hair from his beard, a tooth, his footprint and a letter in his own handwriting.

The 'felicitous cloak' itself resides in a golden casket in a special alcove along with the battle standard. During the empire, this suite of rooms was opened only once a year so that the imperial family could pay homage to the memory of the Prophet on the 15th day of the holy month of Ramazan. Even though anyone, prince or commoner, faithful or infidel, can enter the rooms now, you should respect the sacred atmosphere by observing decorous behaviour.

Notice also the carved door from the Kaaba in Mecca and, hanging from the ceiling, gilded rain gutters from the same place.

Between the Treasury and the Hırka-i Saadet is the Hazine Koğuşu, or Treasury Barracks, with exhibits of Turkish and Islamic bibliographic arts, including calligraphy and illumination; and portraits of the sultans (Padişah portreleri)

Other exhibits in the Third Court include the **Ağalar Camii**, or Mosque of the Eunuchs, another little **library**, Turkish miniature paintings, imperial monograms, seals and arms, calligraphy, and portraits of the sultans. In the room with the seals, notice the graceful, elaborate *tuğra* (TOO-rah, monogram) of the sultans. The tuğra, placed at the top of any imperial proclamation, contains elaborate calligraphic rendering of the names of the sultan and his father, eg 'Abdülhamid Khan, son of Abdülmecit Khan, Ever Victorious'.

Fourth Court Four imperial pleasure domes occupy the north-easternmost part of the palace, sometimes called the gardens, or Fourth Court. The **Mecidiye Köşkü**, built by

Abdülmecit (1839-61), was designed according to 19th-century European models. Beneath it is the Konyalı Restaurant, which fills up by noon. If you want to dine here, arrive by 11.30 am, or after 2 pm.

In the other direction (north-east) is the **Mustafa Paşa Köşkü**, or Kiosk of Mustafa Pasha, sometimes called the Sofa Köşkü. Also here is the room of the *hekimbaşı*, or chief physician to the sultan, who was always one of the sultan's Jewish subjects.

During the reign of Sultan Ahmet III (1703-30), known as the Tulip Period because of the rage for these flowers which spread through the upper classes, the gardens around the Sofa Köşkü were filled with tulips. Little lamps would be set out among the hundreds of varieties at night. A new variety of the flower earned its creator fame, money and social recognition. Tulips had been grown in Turkey from very early times, having come originally from Persia. Some bulbs were brought to Holland during the Renaissance. The Dutch, fascinated by the possibilities in the flower, developed and created many varieties, some of which made their way back to Turkey and began the tulip craze there.

Up the stairs at the end of the tulip garden are two of the most enchanting kiosks. Sultan Murat IV (1623-40) built the **Revan Köşkü**, or Erivan Kiosk, in 1635 after reclaiming the city of Yerevan (now in Armenia) from Persia. He also constructed the **Bağdat Köşkü**, or Baghdad Kiosk, in 1638 to commemorate his victory over that city. Notice the İznik tiles, the inlay and woodwork, and the views all around.

Just off the open terrace with the wishing well is the **Sünnet Odası**, or Circumcision Room, used for the ritual which admits Muslim boys to manhood. (Circumcision is usually performed when the boy is nine or 10.) The outer walls of the chamber are graced by particularly beautiful tile panels.

Imperial Stables Though closed for renovation at my last visit, the stables (Has Ahırları) may be open by the time you visit. If so, enter from the Second Court, just to the north-west of the main entrance (Ortakapı). Go down the cobbled slope.

The stables are now a museum for the carriages, saddles and other horse-related gear used by the sultans. The usual collection of gold-encrusted coaches, diamond-studded bridles etc fill the rooms. One gets the impression that the imperial lifestyle was at least soft, even though it had its complications.

As you leave the palace proper through the Ortakapı, you can walk to your right and down the slope along Osman Hamdi Bey Yokuşu to the archaeological museums, or straight to Aya Sofya. I'll assume, for the moment, that you're heading for Aya Sofya, only a few steps away.

Soğukçeşme Sokak

Just after you leave the tall gate of the Court of the Janissaries, take a look at the ornate little structure on your left (presently under restoration). It's the **Fountain of Ahmet III**, built in 1728 by the sultan who so favoured tulips. It replaced a Byzantine fountain at the same spring.

The ornate gate across the road from the fountain was the one by which the Sultan would enter Aya Sofya for prayers. It led to the Hünkâr Mahfili, or Imperial Loge, which you'll see inside.

The gate is at the beginning of Soğukçeşme Sokak (Street of the Cold Fountain), to the right, a street entirely restored by the Turkish Touring & Automobile Association (Turing). The houses clinging to the palace walls are the Ayasofya Pansiyonlar, or Sancta Sophia Pensions. At the far (western) end of the street is the entrance to the Restaurant Sarnıç, or Cistern Restaurant, in a restored Byzantine cistern, and across the street from it the Konuk Evi, a new hotel and garden restaurant built in the old İstanbul manner. (For details, see Places to Stay and Places to Eat.)

Aya Sofya (Sancta Sophia)

The Church of the Divine Wisdom (Sancta Sophia in Latin, Hagia Sofia in Greek, Aya Sofya in Turkish) was not named for a saint, but for Holy (sancta, hagia) Wisdom (sophia). Aya Sofya (☎ 522 1750) is open daily except Monday from 9.30 am to 4.30 pm (to 7 pm in July and August); the galleries are open from 9.30 to 11.30 am and from 1 to 4 pm. Admission costs US$6, half-price for students.

Emperor Justinian (527-65) had the church built as yet another effort to restore the greatness of the Roman Empire. It was constructed on the site of Byzantium's acropolis, which had also been the site of an earlier Sancta Sophia destroyed in the Nika riots of 532. Justinian's church was completed in 548 and reigned as the greatest church in Christendom until the conquest of Constantinople in 1453.

A lot can happen to a building in 14 centuries, especially in an earthquake zone, and a lot has certainly happened to Aya Sofya. Ignore, if you can, the clutter of buttresses and supports, kiosks, tombs and outbuildings which hug its massive walls, and the renovations which are filling the interior with scaffolding.

It is not enough to 'see' Aya Sofya. You must experience it as its architects, Anthemius of Tralles and Isidorus of Miletus, intended.

In Justinian's time, a street led uphill from the west straight to the main door. Today entry is from the south-west side. Pay your admission fee and walk to the terrace before the main entrance. Here are the sunken ruins of a Theodosian church (404-15), and the low original steps. Now enter the church slowly, one step at a time, and watch what happens: at first there is only darkness broken by the brilliant colours of stained-glass windows. As your eyes adjust to the dark, two massive doorways appear within, and far beyond them in the dim light, a semi-dome blazing with gold mosaics portraying the Madonna and Child – she as Queen of Heaven. Take a few steps and stop just inside the threshold of the first door: the

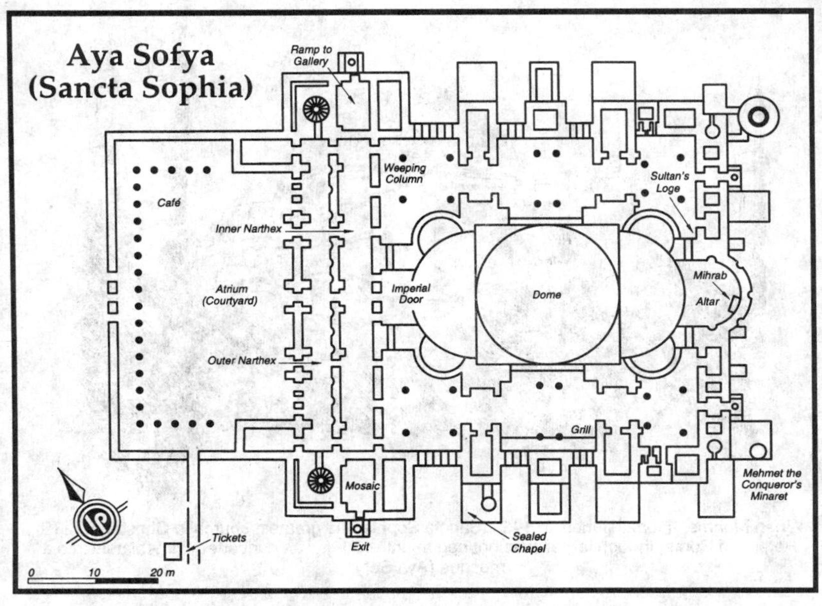

far mosaic is clear and beautiful, and the apse beneath it makes a harmonious whole.

Look up from where you are standing now to see a gorgeous mosaic of Christ as Pantocrator (Ruler of All) above the third and largest door, visible except for the august expression on the face.

Take a few more steps and the face of the Pantocrator becomes visible. Look deep into the church again, and you'll see that the semi-dome of the Madonna and Child is topped by another semi-dome, and above that is the famous, gigantic main dome of the church; at the same time, you are facing the Pantocrator in all His majesty.

Walk through the second door and towards the immense Imperial Door, and you are surprised to see that the 'gigantic main dome' is in fact only another semi-dome: halfway to the Imperial Door, a row of windows peeks out above the larger semi-dome and betrays the secret. As you approach the Imperial Threshold the real, magnificent main dome soars above you and seems to be held up by nothing. Justinian, on entering his great creation for the first time almost 1500 years ago, came this far and exclaimed, 'Glory to God that I have been judged worthy of such a work. Oh Solomon! I have outdone you!'

During its years as a church (almost 1000), only imperial processions were permitted to enter through the central, Imperial Door. You can still notice the depressions in the stone by each door just inside the threshold where imperial guards stood. It was through the Imperial Door that Mehmet the Conqueror came in 1453 to take possession for Islam of the greatest religious edifice in the world. Before he entered, historians tell us, he sprin-

When Mehmet II took İstanbul in 1453, Sancta Sophia, the greatest church in Christendom (St Peter's in Rome, though larger, was not begun until 1506), was converted immediately into a mosque (Aya Sofya).

kled earth on his head in a gesture of humility. Aya Sofya remained a mosque for almost 500 years. In 1935 Atatürk proclaimed it a museum.

There are bigger buildings, and bigger domes, but not without modern construction materials such as reinforced concrete and steel girders. The achievement of the architects is unequalled. The dome, constructed of special hollow bricks made in Rhodes from a unique light, porous clay, was a daring attempt at the impossible. The sense of air and space in the nave and the apparent lack of support for the dome made the Byzantines gasp in amazement. Indeed, it almost was impossible, because the dome lasted only 11 years before an earthquake brought it down in 559.

Over the centuries it was necessary for succeeding Byzantine emperors and Ottoman sultans to rebuild the dome several times, to add buttresses and other supports and to steady the foundations. The dome is supported by massive pillars incorporated into the interior walls. In order to appreciate how this works, compare it with the Blue Mosque. And for an acoustic thrill, stand right beneath the centre of the dome and clap your hands.

The Ottoman chandeliers, hanging low above the floor, combined their light with the rows of little oil lamps which lined the balustrades of the gallery and even the walkway at the base of the dome. When all were lit, it must have been an impressive sight.

Justinian ordered the most precious materials for his church. Note the matched marble panels in the walls, and the breccia columns. The Byzantine emperor was crowned while seated in a throne placed within the square of inlaid marble in the main floor. The nearby choir gallery is an Ottoman addition, as is the *mihrab* (prayer niche), which shows the faithful the direction in which Mecca lies. The large alabaster urns were added by Sultan Murat III (1574-95) as a place where worshippers could perform their ritual ablutions before prayer.

The large medallions inscribed with gilt Arabic letters were added in the mid-19th century. Calligraphy is a highly prized art in Islam, and these medallions were done by Mustafa İzzet Efendi, a master calligrapher of the time. The inscriptions are the names of God (Allah), Muhammed and the early caliphs Ali and Abu Bakr.

The curious, elevated kiosk, screened from public view, is the **Hünkar Mahfili** or Sultan's Loge. Ahmet III (1703-30) had it built so he could come, pray, and go unseen, preserving the imperial mystique.

In the side aisle to the left of the Imperial Door is the 'weeping column', with a copper facing pierced by a hole. Legend has it that those who put their finger in the hole and make a wish will see it come true if the finger emerges moist.

Mosaics Justinian filled his church with gorgeous mosaics. The Byzantine church and state later went through a fierce civil war (726-87) over the question of whether images were to be allowed or not. The debated biblical passage was Exodus 20:4:

> Thou shalt not make unto thee any graven image, or any likeness of anything that is in heaven above, or that is in the earth beneath, or that is in the water under the earth: Thou shalt not bow down thyself to them, nor serve them.

Though the Bible seems clear, images (icons, mosaics, statues) were very popular, and the iconoclasts ('image-breakers') were defeated. It's interesting to speculate whether iconoclastic Islam, militant and triumphant at this time, had any influence on Byzantine theology.

When the Turks took Constantinople there was no controversy. The Koran repeatedly rails against idolatry, as in Sura 16:

> We sent a Messenger into every nation saying, Serve God and give up idols.

Consequently Islamic art is supposed to have no saints' portraits, no pictures of animals, fish or fowl, nor anything else with an immortal soul, and the mosaics had to go. Luckily they were covered with plaster rather than destroyed. Restoration work is still going on.

From the floor of Aya Sofya you can see several saints' portraits high up in the semicircles of the side walls. The best are in the galleries, reserved for female worshippers in Byzantine times. Climb to the galleries by a switchback ramp which starts at the northern end of the narthex.

Some of the work, though partially lost, is superb. The best mosaics are in the southern gallery. Most famous of all is the beautiful Deesis, dating from the early 14th century. Christ is at the centre, with the Virgin Mary on one side, John the Baptist on the other.

Be sure to go all the way to the far ends of the galleries. At the apse end of the south (right-hand) gallery are portraits of emperors, with a difference. The Empress Zoe (1028-50), for instance, had three husbands. When her portrait was put here in mosaic her husband was Romanus III Argyrus, but he died in 1034. So when she married Michael IV in that year, she had Romanus's portrait taken out and Michael's put in, but Michael didn't last long. In 1042 his portrait was removed to make way for that of Constantine IX Monomachus. Constantine outlived Zoe, so it is his portrait that you see today. The inscription reads, 'Constantine, by the Divine Christ, Faithful King of the Romans'.

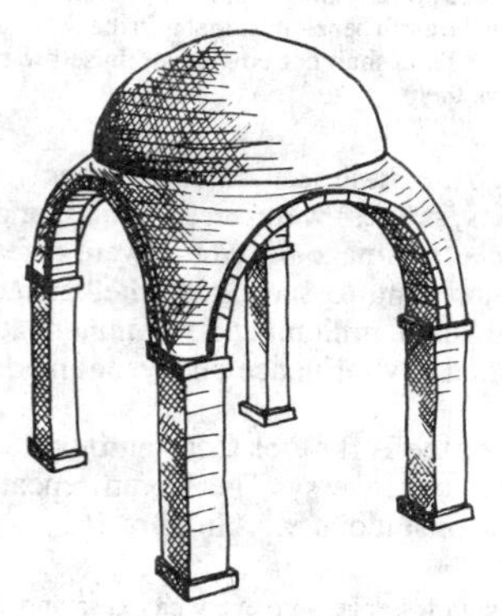

A Byzantine dome from Aya Sofya (Sancta Sophia) in İstanbul. The development of the domed space was probably the major achievement of Byzantine architecture. In contrast to Roman church architecture which focused on the altar, the Byzantine architecture, by use of the dome, focuses attention upwards and outwards.

As you leave Aya Sofya, pass all the way through the corridor-like narthex and through the door at the end of it. Then turn and look up. Above the door is one of the church's finest mosaics, a Madonna and Child dating from the late 10th century; on the left, Constantine the Great offers her the city of Constantinople; on the right, Justinian offers her Sancta Sophia.

Upon exiting the museum, the fountain to the right was for Muslim ablutions. Immediately to your left is the church's baptistery, converted after the Conquest to a tomb for sultans Mustafa and Ibrahim. Other tombs are clustered behind it: those of Murat III, Selim II, Mehmet III and various princes. The minarets were added by Mehmet the Conqueror (1451-81), Beyazıt II (1481-1512) and Selim II (1566-74).

Baths of Lady Hürrem Every mosque had a Turkish steam bath nearby. Aya Sofya's is across the road to the left (east) of the park with the fountain. It's the Haseki Hürrem Hamamı, or Turkish baths of Lady Hürrem, built by the great Sinan in 1556 on the site of earlier Byzantine baths, and now fixed up as a government-run carpet gallery and shop, the Turkish Handwoven Carpets Sale Centre (☎ 511 8192). It's open daily except Tuesday from 9.30 am to 5 pm; admission is free.

Designed as a 'double hamam' with identical baths for men and women, the centre wall dividing the two has now been breached by a small doorway. Both sides have the three traditional rooms: first the square frigidarium for disrobing (on the men's side, this has a pretty marble fountain and stained-glass windows); then the long tepidarium for washing, and finally the octagonal caldarium for sweating and massage. In the caldarium, note the four *eyvan* niches and the four semi-private washing rooms. The *göbektaşı* (hot platform) in the men's bath is inlaid with coloured marble.

The carpet shop, by the way, offers guaranteed quality and fixed prices, but some readers of this book have found its prices surprisingly high.

The Blue Mosque

There used to be palaces where the Blue Mosque now stands. The Byzantine emperors built several of them, stretching from near Aya Sofya all the way to the site of the mosque. You can see a mosaic from one of these palaces, still in place, in the Mosaic Museum (described later).

Sultan Ahmet I (1603-17) set out to build a mosque that would rival and even surpass the achievement of Justinian. He came close to his goal. The Sultan Ahmet Camii (Mosque of Sultan Ahmet or Blue Mosque) is a triumph of harmony, proportion and elegance, and its architect, Mehmet Ağa, achieves the sort of visual experience on the exterior which Aya Sofya has on the interior.

As at Aya Sofya, you must approach the Blue Mosque properly in order to appreciate its architectural mastery. Don't walk straight from Aya Sofya to the Blue Mosque through the crowd of touts. Rather, go out to the middle of the Hippodrome and approach the mosque from its front.

Walk towards the mosque and through the gate in the peripheral wall. Note the small dome atop the gate: this is the motif Mehmet Ağa uses to lift your eyes to heaven. As you walk through the gate, your eyes follow a flight of stairs up to another gate topped by another dome; through this gate is yet another dome, that of the *şadırvan* (ablutions fountain) in the centre of the mosque courtyard. As you ascend the stairs, semi-domes come into view, one after another: first the one over the mosque's main door, then the one above it, and another, and another. Finally the main dome crowns the whole, and your attention is drawn to the sides, where forests of smaller domes reinforce the effect, completed by the minarets, which lift your eyes heavenward.

The layout of the Blue Mosque is classic Ottoman design. The forecourt contains an ablutions fountain in its centre. The portico around three sides could be used for prayer, meditation or study during warm weather.

The Blue Mosque is such a popular tourist sight that admission is controlled so as to preserve its sacred atmosphere. Only worshippers are admitted through the main door; tourists must use the north door, and are not admitted at prayer times. At the north door an attendant will take your shoes; if your clothing is immodest by local standards, you'll be lent a robe. There's no charge for this, but you may be asked to make a donation for the mosque, to which the money will actually go.

Though the stained-glass windows are replacements, they still create the luminous effects of the originals. The semi-domes and the dome are painted in graceful arabesques. The 'blue' of the mosque's name comes from the İznik tiles which line the walls, particularly in the gallery (which is not open to the public).

You can see immediately why the Blue Mosque, constructed between 1606 and 1616, over 1000 years after Aya Sofya, is not as daring as Aya Sofya. Four massive pillars hold up the dome, a less elegant but sturdier solution to the problem.

Note also the imperial loge, covered with marble latticework, to the left; the piece of the sacred Black Stone from the Kaaba in Mecca, embedded in the mihrab; the grandfather clock, useful as prayers must be made at exact times; and the high, elaborate chair *(mahfil)* from which the *imam*, or teacher, gives the sermon on Friday. The *mimber*, or pulpit, is the structure with a curtained doorway at floor level, a flight of steps and a small kiosk topped by a spire. From this mimber of skilfully carved, fine marble, the destruction of the Janissary corps was proclaimed in 1826 (see the Topkapı Palace section).

Mosques built by the great and powerful usually included numerous public-service institutions. Clustered around the Sultan Ahmet Camii were a *medrese* (theological school); an *imaret* (soup kitchen) serving the poor; a hamam so that the faithful could wash on Friday, the holy day; and shops, the rent from which supported the upkeep of the mosque. The tomb *(türbe)* of the mosque's great patron, Sultan Ahmet I, is on the north side facing the fountain park (open for visits daily except Monday and Tuesday from 9.30 am to 4.30 pm). Buried with Ahmet are his brothers, Sultan Osman II and Sultan Murat IV.

Textile Museum Up the stone ramp on the Blue Mosque's north side is the Carpet and Kilim Museum (Halı ve Kilim Müzesi, ☎ 528 5332), with displays of some of the country's finest. It's open from 9 am to 4 pm, closed Sunday and Monday; admission costs US$1.

Mosaic Museum When archaeologists from the University of Ankara and the University of St Andrew's (in Scotland) dug at the back (east) of the Blue Mosque in the mid-1950s, they uncovered a mosaic pavement dating from early Byzantine times, circa 500 AD. The pavement, filled with wonderful hunting and mythological scenes and emperors' portraits, was a triumphal way which led from the Byzantine emperor's palace, which stood where the Blue Mosque now stands, down to the harbour of Boucoleon. The dust and rubble of 1500 years have sunk the pavement considerably below ground level.

Other 5th-century mosaics were saved providentially when Sultan Ahmet had shops built on top of them. The row of shops, called the **Arasta**, was intended to provide rent revenues for the upkeep of the mosque. Now they house numerous souvenir vendors, a little teahouse, and the entrance to the Mosaic Museum. The museum is open daily except Tuesday from 9 am to 5 pm, for US$1.

After you've paid your admission fee, descend to the walkways around the sunken mosaics. The intricate work is impressive, with hunters, beasts, maidens and swains. Note the ribbon border with heart-shaped leaves which surrounds the mosaic. In the westernmost room is the most colourful and dramatic picture, that of two men in leggings carrying spears and holding off a raging tiger. If you can convince the custodian to wipe the mosaics with a wet cloth, the colours will become much more vivid.

The Hippodrome

The Hippodrome was the centre of Byzantium's life for 1000 years and of Ottoman life for another 400. It was the scene of countless political and military dramas during the long life of this city.

History In Byzantine times, the rival chariot teams of 'Greens' and 'Blues' were politically connected. Support for a team was the same as membership in a political party, and a team victory had important effects on policy. A Byzantine emperor might lose his throne as the result of a post-match riot.

Ottoman sultans kept an eye on activities in the Hippodrome. If things were going badly in the empire, a surly crowd gathering here could signal the start of a disturbance, then a riot, then a revolution. In 1826, the slaughter of the debased and unruly Janissary corps was carried out by the reformer sultan, Mahmut II. Almost a century later, in 1909, there were riots here which caused the downfall of Abdülhamid II and the repromulgation of the Ottoman constitution.

Though the Hippodrome might be the scene of their downfall, Byzantine emperors and Ottoman sultans outdid one another in beautifying it. Many of the priceless statues carved by ancient masters have disappeared. The soldiers of the Fourth Crusade sacked Constantinople, a Christian ally city, in 1204, tearing all the bronze plates from the stone obelisk at the Hippodrome's southern end in the mistaken belief that they were gold. The crusaders also stole the famous 'quadriga', or team of four horses cast in bronze, which now sits atop the main door to St Mark's Church in Venice.

Monuments Near the northern end of the Hippodrome, the little gazebo in beautiful stonework is actually **Kaiser Wilhelm's fountain**. The German emperor paid a state visit to Abdülhamid II in 1901, and presented this fountain to the sultan and his people as a token of friendship. According to the

Ottoman inscription, the fountain was built in the Hijri (Muslim lunar calendar) year of 1316 (1898-99 AD). The monograms in the stonework are those of Abdülhamid II and Wilhelm II.

The impressive granite obelisk with hieroglyphs is called the **Obelisk of Theodosius**, carved in Egypt around 1500 BC. According to the hieroglyphs, it was erected in Heliopolis (now a suburb of Cairo) to commemorate the victories of Thutmose III (1504-1450 BC). The Byzantine emperor, Theodosius, had it brought from Egypt to Constantinople in 390 AD. He then had it erected on a marble pedestal engraved with scenes of himself in the midst of various imperial pastimes. Theodosius' marble billboards have weathered badly over the centuries. The magnificent obelisk, spaced above the pedestal by four bronze blocks, is as crisply cut and shiny as when it was carved from the living rock in Upper Egypt 3500 years ago.

South of the obelisk is a strange **spiral column** coming up out of a hole in the ground. It was once much taller and was topped by three serpents' heads. Originally cast to commemorate a victory of the Hellenic confederation over the Persians, it stood in front of the temple of Apollo at Delphi from 478 BC until Constantine the Great had it brought to his new capital city around 330 AD. Though badly bashed up in the Byzantine struggle over the place of images in the church (called the Iconoclastic Controversy), the serpents' heads survived until the early 18th century. Now all that remains of them is one upper jaw in the Archaeological Museum.

The level of the Hippodrome rose over the centuries, as civilisation piled up its dust and refuse here. The obelisk and serpentine column were cleaned out and tidied up by the English troops who occupied the city after the Ottoman defeat in WWI.

No-one is quite sure who built the large **rough-stone obelisk** at the southern end of the Hippodrome. All we know is that it was repaired by Constantine VII Porphyrogenetus (913-59), and that the bronze plates were ripped off during the Fourth Crusade.

Turkish & Islamic Arts Museum

The Palace of İbrahim Paşa (1524) is on the western side of the Hippodrome. Now housing the Türk ve İslam Eserleri Müzesi, or Turkish & Islamic Arts Museum (☎ 522 1888), it gives you a glimpse into the opulent life of the Ottoman upper class in the time of Süleyman the Magnificent. İbrahim Paşa was Süleyman's close friend, son-in-law and grand vizier. His wealth, power and influence on the monarch became so great that others wishing to influence the sultan became envious. After a rival accused İbrahim of disloyalty, Süleyman's favourite, Hürrem Sultan (Roxelana), convinced her husband that İbrahim was a threat. Süleyman had him strangled.

The museum is open from 10 am to 5 pm daily; closed on Monday. Admission costs US$3. Labels are in Turkish and English. A video show on the 1st floor gives you a quick summary of Turkish history, and explains the sultan's tuğra (monogram) and *ferman* (imperial edict). The coffee shop in the museum is a welcome refuge from the press of crowds and touts in the Hippodrome.

Highlights among the exhibits, which date from the 8th and 9th centuries up to the 19th century, are the decorated wooden Koran cases from the high Ottoman period; the calligraphy exhibits, including fermans with tuğras, Turkish miniatures, and illuminated manuscripts. You'll also want to have a look at the *rahles*, or Koran stands, and the many carpets from all periods.

The lower floor of the museum houses ethnographic exhibits. At the entry is a black tent *(kara çadır)* like those used by nomads in eastern Turkey. Inside the tent is an explanation of nomadic customs, in English. Inside the museum building are village looms on which carpets and kilims are woven, and an exhibit of the plants and materials used to make natural textile dyes for the carpets. Perhaps most fascinating are the domestic interiors, including those of a *yurt* (Central Asian felt hut), a village house from

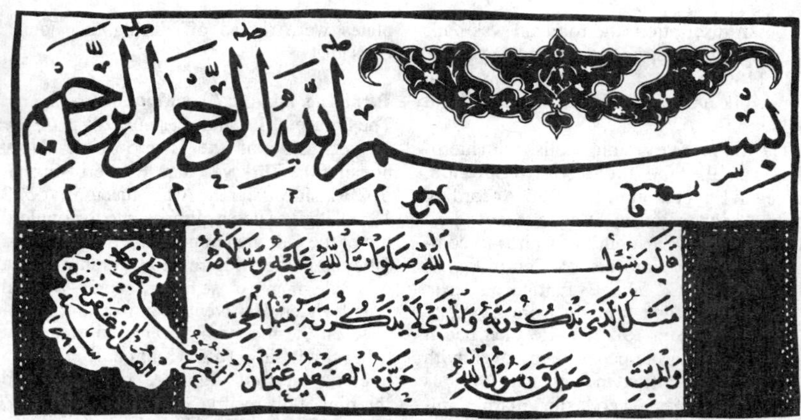

A 17th century *murakka* (decorative page of Arabic writing composed of various pieces of writing patched together) in the Turkish & Islamic Arts Museum. The top line reads 'In the Name of God, the Omnipotent, the All-Merciful'.

Yuntdağ, and a late 19th-century house from Bursa. One display shows women shopping for cloth; another, a scene of daily life in an İstanbul home of the early 20th century.

The buildings behind and beside İbrahim Paşa's palace are İstanbul's law courts and legal administration buildings.

South of the Hippodrome

Take a detour into the district's back streets for a look at a feat of Byzantine engineering and two exquisite small mosques.

Facing south, with the Blue Mosque on your left, go to the end of the Hippodrome and turn left, then right, onto Aksakal Sokak. Soon you'll be able to recognise the filled-in arches of the **Sphendoneh**, a feat of Byzantine engineering, on your right. The Sphendoneh supported the southern end of the Hippodrome.

Follow the curve of the street around to the right and onto Kaleci Sokak. The next intersecting street is Mehmet Paşa Sokak; turn left to the **Küçük Aya Sofya Camii**, or 'Little' Sancta Sophia. If the mosque is not open, look around or signal to a boy on the street and the guardian will come with the key.

Justinian and Theodora built this little church sometime between 527 and 536. Inside, the layout and décor are typical of an early Byzantine church, though the building was repaired and expanded several times during its life as a mosque after the Conquest. Repairs and enlargements to convert the church to a mosque were added by the chief white eunuch Hüseyin Ağa around 1500. His tomb is to the left as you enter.

Go north on Mehmet Paşa Sokak, back up the hill to the neighbouring **Sokollu Mehmet Paşa Camii**. This one was built during the height of Ottoman architectural development in 1571 by the empire's greatest architect, Sinan. Though named for the grand vizier of the time, it was really sponsored by his wife Esmahan, daughter of Sultan Selim II. Besides its architectural harmony, typical of Sinan's great works, the mosque is unique because the medrese is not a separate building but actually part of the mosque structure, built around the forecourt.

If the mosque is not open, wait for the guardian to appear. When you enter, notice the harmonious architecture, the coloured marble, and the beautiful İznik tiles, some of the best ever made. The mosque contains four fragments from the sacred Black Stone in the Kaaba at Mecca: one above the entrance framed in gold, two in the mimber, and one in the mihrab. The marble pillars by the mimber revolve if the foundations have been disturbed by earthquake – an ingenious signalling device.

Walk back up the hill on Suterazisi Sokak to return to the Hippodrome.

Yerebatan Saray

On the north side of Divan Yolu is a little park with a stone pillar rising from it. The pillar is part of an ancient aqueduct. Beneath the park, entered by a doorway on its north side (on Yerebatan Caddesi) is the Yerebatan Saray (Sunken Palace), or Cistern Basilica (☎ 522 1259). Admission, from 9 am to 5.30 pm, costs US$2.50.

Yerebatan Saray, built in 532 AD, is not a basilica but a Byzantine cistern 70m wide and 140m long, its roof supported by 336 columns. Coloured lights, recorded western classical music (Mozart, Vivaldi), a maze of walkways, carp in the waters, and even two cafés have been added as tourist enhancements.

The cistern was built by Justinian the Great (527-65), who was incapable of thinking in small terms. Columns, capitals and plinths from ruined buildings were among those used in its construction. Note the two blocks carved with Medusa heads supporting columns in the north-west corner.

The exit from Yerebatan Saray is onto Alemdar Caddesi.

Gülhane Park & Sublime Porte

Walk downhill from Yerebatan Saray along Alemdar Caddesi with Aya Sofya on your right. Just past a big tree in the middle of the road, the street turns left, but just in front of you is the arched gateway to Gülhane Parkı.

Before entering the park, look to the left. That bulbous little kiosk built into the park walls at the next street corner is the **Alay Köşkü**, or Parade Kiosk, from which the sultan would watch the periodic parades of troops and trade guilds which commemorated great holidays and military victories.

Across the street from the Alay Köşkü (not quite visible right from the Gülhane gate) is a gate leading into the precincts of what was once the grand vizierate, or Ottoman prime ministry, known in the west as the Sublime Porte. Today the buildings beyond the gate hold various offices of the İstanbul provincial government.

Gülhane Park was once the palace park of Topkapı; admission costs less than US$0.25. There's a small zoo here, and also the **Tanzimat Müzesi** (☎ 512 6384), open daily from 9 am to 5 pm. 'Tanzimat' (Reorganisation) was the name given to the political and societal reforms planned by Sultan Abdülmecit in 1839 and carried out through

The Sublime Porte

In Islamic societies, and in other societies with strong clan roots, it was customary for the chief or ruler to adjudicate disputes and grant favours. Petitioners wishing justice or favours would appear at the door of the chief's tent, house, or palace, and await the chance to protest their claims.

When a western ambassador arrived at the sultan's door, or 'porte', he was looked on as just another petitioner asking favours. In response to an embassy, the sultan would often issue a proclamation which began with the words, 'The ambassador of (country) having come to my sublime porte...' Thus the term 'Sublime Porte' was adopted by European embassies to mean the Ottoman state as personified by the sultan in his palace.

In later centuries, when the grand vizier was the active head of government, ambassadors reported not to the palace but to the grand vizierate, and the term Sublime Porte (or simply 'the Porte') came to mean not the sultan's door but the grand vizierate as functioning head of the Ottoman government. ■

the middle of the 19th century. Museum exhibits trace their progress.

At the far (north) end of the park, up the hill, is a flight of steps used as seats, and a small tea garden. Few tourists know about this quiet refuge, where you can sip a bracing glass of tea or a cool drink, gaze at the Bosphorus, and shake off the stresses of travel.

Archaeological Museums

İstanbul's archaeological museums are between Gülhane Park and Topkapı. As you pass beneath the arched gateway from Alemdar Caddesi into Gülhane, bear right and walk up the slope along a cobbled road, Osman Hamdi Bey Yokuşu, which then turns to the right. After the turn, a gate on the left leads to the İstanbul Archaeological Museum, Tiled Kiosk and Museum of the Ancient Orient.

You can also reach the museum complex from Topkapı. As you come out of the Ortakapı gate from the palace, walk into the Court of the Janissaries, then turn right and walk down the hill before you get to Aya İrini.

Admission to the complex (closed Monday) costs US$3. The Archaeological Museum (☎ 520 7740) is open daily from 9.30 am to 5 pm (last ticket sold at 4.30 pm), but the Museum of the Ancient Orient is open only from 9.30 am to noon, and the Tiled Kiosk from 1 to 5 pm, so plan your visit accordingly.

These museums were the palace collections, formed during the 19th century and added to greatly during the republic. While not immediately as dazzling as Topkapı, they contain a wealth of artefacts from the 50 centuries of Anatolia's history.

The **Museum of the Ancient Orient** (Eski Şark Eserler Müzesi) holds the gates of ancient Babylon in the time of Nebuchadnezzar II (604-562 BC), clay tablets bearing Hammurabi's famous law code (in cuneiform, of course), ancient Egyptian scarabs, and artefacts from the

The Alexander sarcophagus at İstanbul's Archaeological Museum, exquisitely carved in high relief, is now known not to have been Alexander's, but is nonetheless impressive as a work of art.

Assyrian and Hittite empires. It is a rich collection.

The Ottoman Turkish inscription over the door of the **Archaeological Museum** (Arkeoloji Müzesi) reads 'Eser-i Atika Müzesi', or Museum of Ancient Works. The neoclassical building houses an extensive collection of Hellenic, Hellenistic and Roman statuary and sarcophagi. Signage is in Turkish and English.

A Roman statue in archaic style of the daemonic god Bes greets you as you enter. Turn left to see the ancient monolithic basalt sarcophagus of King Tabnit of Egypt, its former occupant having been transferred to a neighbouring glass case. Nearby, the famous marble Alexander sarcophagus, exquisitely carved in high relief, is now known not to have been Alexander's, but is nonetheless impressive as a work of art.

In a long room behind the entrance hall is a mock-up of the facade of the Temple of Athena at Assos (Behramkale). Erected in 525 BC, it was the first and only temple of the Archaic Period designed in the Doric order. The frieze depicted hunting and banquet scenes, and battles of the centaurs. Some bits of the original frieze have been incorporated here; other bits are in the Louvre and in Boston.

On the mezzanine level above the Temple of Athena is an exhibition called 'İstanbul Through the Ages', tracing the city's entire history, concentrating on its most famous buildings and public spaces: Archaic, Hellenistic, Roman, Byzantine and Ottoman.

To the right of the entrance hall are the statuary galleries. In Greek and Roman architecture, sculpture was an important element in the decoration of building facades and public spaces. Artisans at Anatolia's three main sculpture centres – Aphrodisias, Ephesus and Miletus – turned out thousands of beautiful works, the best of which have been collected here and arranged by period: Archaic, Persian, Hellenistic and Roman.

The museum's 2nd and 3rd floors were closed for renovation.

The **Tiled Kiosk** (Çinili Köşk) of Sultan Mehmet the Conqueror is the oldest surviving non-religious Turkish building in İstanbul, constructed in 1472 not long after the Conquest. Though once completely covered in fine tile work, only the tile work on the facade remains. The kiosk, once an imperial residence, now houses an excellent collection of Turkish faïence including many good examples of İznik tiles from the period in the 17th and 18th centuries when that city produced the finest coloured tiles in the world.

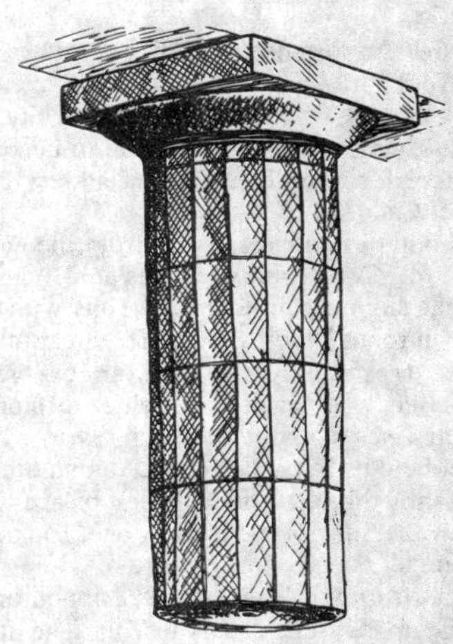

Example of a Doric column. Doric is the first of the classical Greek orders of architecture. The Doric order is most easily recognised by its sturdy proportions and simple capitals. There are examples of Archaic, Hellenistic, Roman, Byzantine and Ottoman architecture on display at the 'İstanbul through the Ages' exhibition at the Archaeological Museum.

Divan Yolu

Divan Yolu, the Road to the Imperial Council, is the main thoroughfare of the Old City. Starting from the Hippodrome and Yerebatan Saray on the city's first of seven hills, it heads due west, up another hill, past the Covered Market, through Beyazıt Square and past İstanbul University to Aksaray

Square. Turning north a bit, it continues to the Topkapı (Cannon Gate) in the ancient city walls. In its progress through the city, its name changes from Divan Yolu to become Yeniçeriler Caddesi, Ordu Caddesi and Millet Caddesi.

This thoroughfare, dating from the early times of Constantinople, was laid out by Roman engineers to connect the city with the Roman roads heading west. The great milestone from which all distances were measured was near the tall shaft of stones which rises above Yerebatan Saray. The street held its importance in Ottoman times, as Mehmet the Conqueror's first palace was in Beyazıt Square, and his new one, Topkapı, was under construction.

Start from Aya Sofya and the Hippodrome and go up the slope on Divan Yolu. The little **Firuz Ağa Camii** on the left, built in 1491, was commissioned by the chief treasurer to Beyazıt II (1481-1512). The style is the simple one of the early Ottomans: a dome on a square base with a plain porch in front.

Just behind Firuz Ağa Camii are the ruins of the **Palace of Antiochus** (5th century), now mere ruined foundations.

The first major intersection on the right is that with Babiali Caddesi. Turn right onto this street until you reach Nuruosmaniye Caddesi; a block to the right is **Cağaloğlu Square**, once the centre of İstanbul's newspaper and book publishing industry. Most of the newspaper publishers have moved to large, modern buildings outside the city walls, though some of the smaller book publishers survive here. The **Cağaloğlu Hamamı** is just off the square, on the right (see the Entertainment section for details).

If instead you turn left (south) from Divan Yolu, you'll be on Klodfarer Caddesi, named for the Turcophile French novelist Claude Farrère. It leads to a large open area beneath which lies the Byzantine cistern now called **Binbirdirek**, or 'A Thousand-and-One Columns'. A door (often locked) in the park opens onto stairs leading down to the pitch-black cistern through an accumulation of trash; unfortunately Binbirdirek is not in a condition to receive visitors these days.

Back on Divan Yolu, the impressive enclosure right at the corner of Babiali Caddesi is filled with **tombs** of the Ottoman dynasty. The first one to be built was that of Sultan Mahmut II (1808-39), the reforming emperor who wiped out the Janissaries and revamped the Ottoman army. Several of Mahmut's successors, including sultans Abdülaziz (1861-76) and Abdülhamid II (1876-1909), chose to be buried here as well.

Right across Divan Yolu from the tombs is a small stone **library** built by the Köprülü family in 1659. The Köprülüs rose to prominence in the mid-17th century and furnished the empire with a succession of grand viziers, generals and grand admirals for centuries. They administered the empire during a time when the scions of the Ottoman dynasty fell well below the standards of Mehmet the Conqueror and Süleyman the Magnificent.

At the corner of Türbedar Sokak is the **Press Museum** (Basın Müzesi), Divan Yolu 84, open from 10 am to 5.30 pm (closed Sunday), without charge. The old printing presses will interest some, the lively *Müze Café* will interest more as it serves cappuccino (US$1.75), tea (US$0.50), Turkish coffee, sahlep (US$1.25), pastries and light meals of soups, salads and sandwiches.

Stroll a bit further along Divan Yolu. On the left, the curious tomb with wrought-iron grillework on top is that of Köprülü Mehmet Paşa (1575-1661). Across the street, that strange building with a row of streetfront shops is actually an ancient Turkish bath, the **Çemberlitaş Hamamı** (1580).

The derelict, time-worn column rising from a little plaza is one of İstanbul's most ancient and revered monuments. Called **Çemberlitaş** (The Banded Stone or the Burnt Column), it was erected by Constantine the Great (324-37) to celebrate the dedication of Constantinople as capital of the Roman Empire in 330. This area was the grand Forum of Constantine, and the column was topped by a statue of the great emperor himself. In an earthquake zone erecting columns can be a risky business. This one has survived, though it needed iron bands for support within a century after it was built. The statue crashed to the ground almost 1000 years ago.

The little **mosque** nearby is that of Atik Ali Paşa, a eunuch and grand vizier of Beyazıt II.

Beyond Çemberlitaş along Divan Yolu, on the right (north) side in the graveyard and courtyard of the Atik Ali Paşa Medresesi is the *İlesam Lokalı*, a club formed by the enigmatically-named Professional Union of Owners of the Works of Science and Literature. Touted as a 'traditional mystic water pipe and tea garden', it almost lives up to its billing. Tables and chairs are set out in the shady graveyard, and low benches covered with kilims in the medrese courtyard. Try a water pipe *(nargile,* US$1) or a glass of tea or cup of coffee. Some of the other patrons may speak some English.

Just on the other side of Bileyciler Sokak from İlesam is a similar place, the *Erenler Nargile Salonu*, in the courtyard of the Çorlulu Ali Paşa Medresesi and to the right. Most of the other people in this lofty türbe-like structure will either be absorbed in the racing forms or in watching a horserace on television.

The Covered Market

İstanbul's Kapalı Çarşı (Covered Market or Grand Bazaar) is 4000 shops and several km of streets, mosques, banks, police stations, restaurants and workshops open daily except Sunday from 8.30 am to 6.30 pm. Today it is very touristy, with touts badgering bus tour groups and the ubiquitous eastern European clothing merchants everywhere.

Starting from a small *bedesten* (warehouse) built in the time of Mehmet the Conqueror, the bazaar grew to cover a vast area as neighbouring shopkeepers decided to put up roofs and porches so that commerce could be conducted comfortably in all weather. Great people built *hans*, or caravanserais, at the edges of the bazaar so that caravans could bring wealth from all parts of the empire, unload and trade right in the bazaar's precincts. Finally, a system of locked gates and doors was provided so that the entire mini-city could be closed up tight at the end of the business day.

Though tourist shops now crowd the bazaar, it is also still a place where an İstanbullu (citizen of İstanbul) may come to buy a few metres of printed cloth, a gold bangle for a daughter's birthday gift, an antique carpet or a fluffy sheepskin. Whether you want to buy or not, you should see the bazaar (remember that it's closed on Sunday). Also, I've had a report from a reader that his flight bag was slashed while strolling in the bazaar, and again while walking down the busy market streets to the Egyptian Market. Guard your belongings.

Turn right off Divan Yolu at the Çemberlitaş and walk down Vezir Hanı Caddesi. The big mosque before you is **Nuruosmaniye Camii** (Light of Osman Mosque) built between 1748 and 1755 by Mahmut I and his successor Osman III, in the style known as Ottoman Baroque. It's one of the earliest examples of the style.

Turn left through the mosque gate. The courtyard of the mosque is peaceful and green but with a constant flow of pedestrian traffic heading to and from the bazaar.

Out the other side of the courtyard, you're standing in Çarşıkapı Sokak (Bazaar Gate St) and before you is one of several doorways into the bazaar. The gold emblem above the doorway is the Ottoman armorial emblem with the sultan's monogram.

Inside the bazaar, the street you're on is called **Kalpakçılarbaşı Caddesi**. It's the closest thing the bazaar has to a main street. Most of the bazaar is down to your right in the maze of tiny streets and alleys, though you will want to take a left turn up the steps and into the **Kürkçüler Çarşışı**, the Furriers Bazaar. Street names refer to trades and crafts: Jewellers St, Pearl Merchants St, Fez Makers St. Though many trades have died out, moved on or been replaced, there are several areas that you should see.

Start with a stroll through the **Sandal Bedesteni**, the municipal auction hall and pawn shop. **Kuyumcular Caddesi**, the second street on the right as you walk along Kalpakçılarbaşı Caddesi, is Jewellers St,

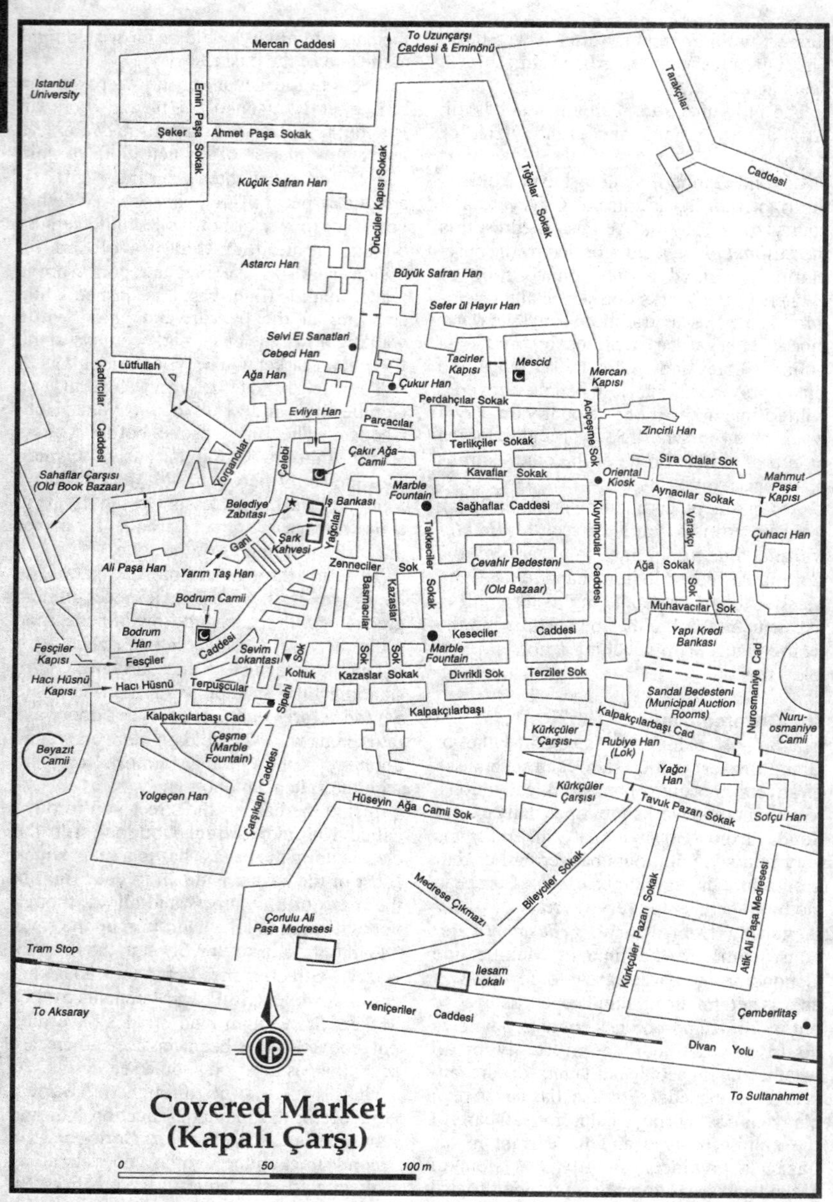

Covered Market (Kapalı Çarşı)

aglitter with tonnes of gold and gems. The Furriers Bazaar now houses shops selling leather clothing and other goods, but it's still an interesting corner of the bazaar. You should of course have a look in the **Old Bazaar** at the centre of the bazaar, dating from the 15th century. This is sometimes called the Cevahir Bedesteni (Jewellery Warehouse). I'd also recommend explorations into one or more of the hans which adjoin the bazaar. A particularly pretty one is the **Zincirli Han** at the far (north) end of Jewellers St, on the right.

By the way, no-one will mind if you wander into any of these hans for a look around. In fact, you may well be invited to rest your feet, have a glass of tea and exchange a few words.

The bazaar has numerous inexpensive little restaurants and 'cookshops' (marked 'lokanta' or 'lok' on the map). See the Places to Eat section for details.

Uzunçarş Caddesi There is another interesting route you can follow by starting from within the bazaar. Near the western end of Kalpakçılarbaşı Caddesi, Sipahi Sokak heads north, changes names to become Feraceciler Sokak (Cloakmakers St), then becomes Yağcılar Caddesi (Oil Merchants St). You'll see the Şark Kahvesi on your left, then some steps up to a *mescit* (small mosque). Continue straight on, past shops and han entrances to Örücüler Kapısı (Gate of the Darners). Cross a main street named Mercan Caddesi (to the left) and Çakmakçılar Yokuşu (to the right), and continue on Uzunçarşı Caddesi (Longmarket St).

'Longmarket St' lives up to its name: one long market of woodturners' shops, luggage merchants, shops selling guns and hunting equipment, bakeries for simits, second-hand clothing merchants and the like. Stroll down the hill into the market district of Tahtakale, near the Egyptian Market and Galata Bridge, and to the small, exquisite Rüstem Paşa Camii. See the section on Eminönü for more information.

Old Book Bazaar Exit the bazaar by walking to the western end of Kalpakçılarbaşı Caddesi. Once outside, turn right onto Çadırcılar Caddesi, then left through a doorway and you'll enter the Sahaflar Çarşısı, or Old Book Bazaar. Go up the steps and along to the shady little courtyard. Actually, the wares in the shops are both new and old. Of the new, most are in Turkish. Of the old, many are in other languages. It's unlikely that you'll uncover any treasures here, but you can certainly find a curiosity or two.

The book bazaar dates from the Byzantine Empire. Many of the booksellers are members of a dervish order called the Halveti after its founder, Hazreti Mehmet Nureddin-i Cerrahi-i Halveti. Their *sema* (religious ceremony) includes chanting from the Koran, praying, and rhythmic dancing and breathing to the accompaniment of classical Turkish liturgical music. As with all dervish orders, the sema is an attempt at close knowledge of and communion with God. The Mevlevi dervishes attempt it by their whirling dance, the Halveti through their circular dance and hyperventilation. Don't, however, expect to wander into a den of mystics. What you'll see are normal Turkish booksellers who just happen to be members of this dervish order.

Out the north gate of the Sahaflar Çarşısı is a daily flea market; on Sunday the flea market expands and spills out into Beyazıt Square.

Beyazıt & İstanbul University

The Sahaflar Çarşısı is right next to **Beyazıt Camii**, or Mosque of Sultan Beyazıt II (1481-1512). Beyazıt used an exceptional amount of fine stone in his mosque, which he built in 1501-06 on a plan similar to that of Aya Sofya, but smaller. It's well worth a look.

The main street here, which started out as Divan Yolu, is now called Yeniçeriler Caddesi. It runs past Beyazıt Square, officially called Hürriyet Meydanı (Freedom Square), though everyone knows it simply as Beyazıt. The plaza is backed by the impressive portal of İstanbul University.

Under the Byzantines, this was the largest of the city's many forums, the **Forum of Theodosius**, built by that emperor in 393. Mehmet the Conqueror built his first palace here, a wooden structure which burnt down centuries ago. After Mehmet built Topkapı, he used his wooden palace as a home for ageing harem women.

The grand gates, main building and tall tower of the university were originally built as the Ottoman War Ministry, which explains their grandiose and martial aspect.

The small building at the western side of the square is now the **Beyazıt Hat Sanatları Müzesi**, or Beyazıt Calligraphy Museum, open from 9.30 am to 4 pm every day, for US$0.50 admission. Though you may not be fascinated by Ottoman calligraphy, the building, once a theological college, is certainly worth a look.

Laleli & Aksaray

As you continue west along the main street, now named Ordu Caddesi (Army or 'Horde' Ave), notice the huge broken marble columns decorated with peacock-tail designs on the left-hand side of the roadway. These were part of the decoration in the Forum of Theodosius. There was a monumental arch hereabouts.

A bit further along, on the right, are more university buildings, and beyond them the hotel district of Laleli. Stay on Ordu Caddesi and, just past the big Merit Hotel, you'll come to the **Laleli Camii**, an Ottoman Baroque mosque built in 1759-63 by Sultan Mustafa III. The ornate Baroque architecture houses a sumptuous interior. Underneath the mosque are shops and a plaza with a fountain. These were partly to produce rent for the upkeep of the mosque, partly to show off the architect's skill and cunning.

Continue down the hill on Ordu Caddesi and you will enter the confused clamour of Aksaray Square, where there's nothing particularly interesting. The **Valide Camii** on the square's north-west side is an ornate late Ottoman work built in 1871 by Valide Sultan Pertevniyal, mother of Sultan Abdülaziz. When it's clean it looks like a white wedding cake among the drab structures of Aksaray, but exhaust fumes have sullied it and traffic flyovers block a full view.

Süleymaniye Camii

The Süleymaniye Camii, or Mosque of Sultan Süleyman the Magnificent, directly north of (behind) the university, is İstanbul's largest mosque. Facing the university portal in Beyazıt, go to the left along Takvimhane Caddesi to reach the mosque, which is open every day, but the impressive tombs are usually inaccessible on Monday and Tuesday, the caretaker's 'holiday'.

The Süleymaniye Camii crowns one of İstanbul's hills, dominating the Golden Horn and providing a magnificent landmark for the entire city. This, the grandest of all Turkish mosques, was built between 1550 and 1557 by the greatest, richest, and most powerful of Ottoman sultans, Süleyman I (1520-66), 'The Magnificent'.

Süleyman the Magnificent was a great builder who restored the mighty walls of Jerusalem (an Ottoman city from 1516) and built countless other monuments throughout his empire. He was the patron of Mimar Sinan (MEE-mahr see-NAHN), Turkey's greatest architect. Though the smaller Selimiye Camii in Edirne is generally counted as Sinan's masterpiece, the Süleymaniye is without doubt his grandest work.

Most visitors enter the mosque precincts by a side door. Though this is the most convenient entrance coming from Beyazıt, the effect of entering from the north-west side and seeing the four towering minarets and the enormous billowing domes is far better.

Inside, the mosque is breathtaking in its size and pleasing in its simplicity. There is little decoration except for some very fine İznik tiles in the mihrab, gorgeous stained-glass windows done by one İbrahim the Drunkard, and four massive columns, one from Baalbek, one from Alexandria and two from Byzantine palaces in İstanbul. The painted arabesques on the dome are 19th-century additions, recently renewed. Sinan, ever challenged by the technical accomplishments of Aya Sofya, took the floorplan of that

TONY WHEELER

TOM BROSNAHAN

TOM BROSNAHAN

Top: One of the most pleasant ways to travel around İstanbul is by ferry.
Middle: Süleymaniye Mosque dominates İstanbul's Golden Horn.
Bottom: Fishing on the Marmara shore. Ancient fishing villages were established in İstanbul as early as 1000 BC.

TONY WHEELER

TONY WHEELER

TOM BROSNAHAN

Top Left: A man sells fish from his boat near the Galata Bridge, İstanbul.
Top Right: Emperor Justinian's Sancta Sophia was completed in 548 and reigned as the greatest church in Christendom until the conquest of Constantinople in 1453.
Bottom: Fishing skiffs ply the Bosphorus at sunset, İstanbul.

The Süleymaniye Camii (Mosque of Sultan Süleyman the Magnificent), İstanbul's largest mosque, crowns one of İstanbul's hills, dominating the Golden Horn and providing a magnificent landmark for the entire city.

church, adapted it to the needs of Muslim worship, and used it here.

The *külliye* (mosque complex; see also the boxed story on Imperial Mosques) of the Süleymaniye is particularly elaborate, with the full complement of public services: soup kitchen, hostel, hospital, theological college etc. Near the south-east wall of the mosque is the cemetery. Ask for the *bekçi* (BEHK-chee, caretaker) so you can see the *türbeler* (tombs) of Süleyman and his wife Haseki Hürrem Sultan (known in the West as Roxelana), and of his architect, Mimar Sinan. The tombs are high points of rich, high Ottoman decoration. The İznik tiles in Hürrem's tomb are particularly fine.

Places to Eat Several little eateries are in the row of souvenir shops outside the mosque enclosure to the south-west, including the *Beydağı* and *Kanaat Lokantası* restaurants for full meals, and the *Sanus Büfe* for pizza, soft drinks and other light fare.

For upscale meals, try *Darüzziyafe* (☎ 511 8414), Şifahane Caddesi 6, in the imaret (soup kitchen) opposite the mosque's main portal. Constructed as part of the külliye, the building has a courtyard surrounded by porches and centred on a fountain. The court is used for dining in fine weather, and several rooms opening onto it have changing art exhibits. The menu is Ottoman with mid-range prices, such as soup for US$2.50, meze plates for US$3, main courses for US$5 to US$8, and full meals for US$10 to US$18.

Şehzadebaşı Caddesi

Aqueduct of Valens Walk along Süleymaniye Caddesi, which goes south-west from the mosque, and turn right onto

Şehzadebaşı Caddesi. You can see remnants of the high Bozdoğan Kemeri, or Aqueduct of Valens, on the left side of the street. It's not really certain that the aqueduct was constructed by the Emperor Valens (364-78), though we do know it was repaired in 1019, and in later times by several sultans. After the reign of Süleyman the Magnificent, parts of it collapsed, but restoration work was begun in the late 1980s.

Şehzade Camii On the south side of the aqueduct is the Şehzade Camii, the Mosque of the Prince. Süleyman had it built between 1544 and 1548 as a memorial to his son Mehmet, who died in 1543. It was the first important mosque to be designed by Mimar Sinan, who spent the first part of his long career as a military architect. Among the many important people buried in tile-encrusted tombs here are Prince Mehmet, his brothers and sisters, and Süleyman's grand viziers, Rüstem Paşa and İbrahim Paşa.

Gazanfer Ağa Medresesi If you have a few minutes to spare, walk west on Şehzadebaşı Caddesi. The dusty modern building on the left is the Belediye Sarayı, İstanbul's Municipality or city hall. Turn right (north) and pass under the aqueduct, then take your life in your hands and cross Atatürk Bulvarı. Just on the other side of the street is the former medrese of Gazanfer Ağa (1599), now the **İstanbul Karikatür ve Mizah Müzesi** (Cartoon & Humour Museum). Turkish cartoon artistry is lively and politically important. Though the exhibits may not hold much interest for you, the pleasant sunny courtyard, with its fountain, grapevines, café and toilets, is an excellent place for a rest-stop. Hours are from 10 am to 6 pm daily except Sunday; admission is free.

THE GOLDEN HORN

The Golden Horn, or Haliç, is İstanbul's historic harbour, shipyard and city-centre waterway. Bordered by forests, fields and palaces in the 18th century, by the mid-20th century it had become a poisonous sewer of industrial waste lined with dilapidated warehouses and workshops.

An ambitious programme of beautification was carried out during the 1980s under Mayor Bedreddin Dalan. The shores were stripped of ugly buildings and landscaped as parks, and the dumping of most wastes into the water was stopped.

Many of the districts along the Golden Horn are heavy with history. Eminönü , with its Egyptian Bazaar, New Mosque and Galata Bridge, was the main customs entry point and market throughout Byzantine and Ottoman times. Fener (Phanar), to the north-west, is the seat of the Ecumenical Orthodox Patriarchate, and was once home to many wealthy and powerful Ottoman Greeks. Balat and Hasköy were once populated heavily by Jews. Between Balat and Fener stands one of the city's most intriguing architectural curiosities: the Bulgarian Church of St Stephen, constructed completely of cast iron.

A limited ferry service still operates on the Haliç between Eminönü and Eyüp, and boaters still ferry passengers from one side to the other as they have done for centuries, but bus and taxi transport has taken much of the trade from these more leisurely forms of transport.

Eminönü

No doubt you've already seen Eminönü. The view of the Galata Bridge, crowded with ferries and dominated by the Yeni Cami (YEHN-nee jahm-mee, New Mosque), also called the Pigeon Mosque because of the ever present flocks of these birds, is a favourite for advertisements and magazine articles about İstanbul. The Yeni Cami sits comfortably and serenely in the midst of the bustling Eminönü district as the traffic, both vehicular and pedestrian, swirls around it. Visitors to İstanbul find themselves passing through Eminönü frequently.

Eminönü is the inner city's transportation hub. Bosphorus and Marmara ferries dock here, Galata Bridge traffic passes through, and Sirkeci Station is nearby.

Galata Bridge In Byzantine times the

Golden Horn provided a perfect natural harbour for the city's commerce. Suppliers of fresh vegetables and fruits, grain and staple goods set up shop in the harbour. Until a decade ago, their successors in İstanbul's wholesale vegetable, fruit and fish markets performed the same services, in the same area to the west of the Galata Bridge in Eminönü. With the drive to clean up and beautify the Golden Horn, the wholesale markets have been moved to the outskirts of the city.

Until June 1992 the Galata Bridge, which crosses the mouth of the Golden Horn, was a 19th-century structure which floated on pontoons. Ramshackle fish restaurants, tea-houses and hookah joints filled the dark recesses beneath the roadway, while an intense stream of pedestrian and vehicular traffic passed above.

The pontoon bridge blocked the natural flow of water and kept the Golden Horn from flushing itself of pollution, so it was replaced by a new bridge which allows the water to flow.

At the time of writing the new bridge had yet to acquire the shops and restaurants expected to occupy its nether portions.

Still picturesque and interesting is the retail market district which surrounds the Egyptian Market. But before wandering into this maze of market streets, take a look inside the Yeni Cami.

Yeni Cami The Yeni Cami imperial mosque was begun in 1597, commissioned by Valide Sultan Safiye, mother of Sultan Mehmet III (1595-1603). The site was earlier occupied by a community of Karaite Jews, radical dissenters from orthodox Judaism. When the valide sultan decided to build her grand mosque here, the community was moved to Hasköy, a district farther up the Golden Horn which still bears traces of the Karaite presence.

The valide sultan lost her august position when her son the sultan died, and the mosque was completed six sultans later in 1663 by Valide Sultan Turhan Hatice, mother of Sultan Mehmet IV (1648-87).

In plan, the Yeni Cami is much like the Blue Mosque and the Süleymaniye Camii, with a large forecourt and a square sanctuary surmounted by a series of half-domes crowned by a grand dome. The interior is richly decorated with gold, coloured tiles and carved marble. The mosque and its tiles are 'late', past the period when Ottoman architecture was at its peak. The tilemakers of İznik were turning out slightly inferior products by the late 17th century. Compare these tiles to the ones in the Rüstem Paşa Camii, which are from the high period of İznik tile work. Only in İstanbul would a 400-year-old mosque be called 'New'.

Egyptian (Spice) Market The Mısır Çarşısı (MUH-suhr chahr-shuh-shuh, Egyptian Market) is also called the Spice Bazaar because of its many spice shops. A century or two ago, its merchants sold such things as cinnamon, gunpowder, rabbit fat, pine gum, peach-pit powder, sesame seeds, sarsaparilla root, aloe, saffron, liquorice root, donkey's milk and parsley seeds, all to be used as folk remedies.

Gunpowder, for instance, was prescribed as a remedy for haemorrhoids: you'd boil a little gunpowder with the juice of a whole lemon, strain off the liquid, dry the powder and swallow it the next morning with a little water on an empty stomach. It was also supposed to be a good cure for pimples when mixed with a little crushed garlic. Whatever its values as a pharmaceutical, it was finally banned from the market because the shops in which it was sold kept blowing up.

The market was constructed in the 1660s as part of the Yeni Cami complex, the rents from the shops going to support the mosque's upkeep and its charitable activities. These included a school, baths, hospital and public fountains.

Enter the market (open Monday to Saturday from 8.30 am to 6.30 pm, closed Sunday) through the big armoured doors which open onto Eminönü Square. Just inside the doors, to the left, is the little stairway which leads up to the Pandeli restaurant (see the Places to Eat section).

Strolling through the market, the number of shops selling tourist trinkets is increasing annually, though there are still some shops which sell *baharat* (bah-hah-RAHT, spices) and even a few which specialise in the old-time remedies. Some of the hottest items are bee pollen and royal jelly, used to restore virility. You'll see also shops selling nuts, candied fruits, chocolate and other snacks. Try some *incir* (een-JEER, figs) or *lokum* (low-KOOM, Turkish delight). Fruit pressed into sheets and dried (looks like leather) is called *pestil*. It's often made from apricots or mulberries, and is delicious and relatively cheap. Buy 50 or 100g to start with.

When you come to the crossroads within the market, you have a choice. I'd suggest you turn left, see the rest of the market, then return to the crossroads and take the street to the right.

Walking east in the market, turn left again at the first opportunity, and you'll leave the bazaar and enter its busy courtyard, backed by the Yeni Cami. This is the city's major market for flowers, plants, seeds and songbirds. There's a toilet to your left, down the stairs, subject to a small fee. To the right, across the courtyard, is the **tomb of Valide Sultan Turhan Hatice**, founder of the Yeni Cami. Buried with her are no less than six other sultans, including her son Mehmet IV, plus dozens of imperial princes and princesses.

Now, back at that crossroads within the bazaar, take the right turn and exit through another set of armoured doors. Just outside the doors is another crossroads of bustling market streets. You can always smell coffee here, because right across the intersection is the shop of Kurukahveci Mehmet Efendi. Clerks wrap customer's parcels with lightning speed (they take great pride in this), and there always seems to be a queue of people waiting to make a purchase. To the right, down towards the Golden Horn, is a small fish market and a few butchers' shops. Up to the left, the shops and street pedlars sell mostly household and kitchen items.

Head out the bazaar doors and straight across the intersection. This is **Hasırcılar Caddesi,** Mat Makers St. Shops along it sell fresh fruits, spices, nuts, condiments, knives and other cutlery, coffee, tea, cocoa, hardware and similar retail necessities. The colours, smells, sights and sounds make this one of the liveliest and most interesting streets in the city.

Rüstem Paşa Mosque Walk a few short blocks along Hasırcılar Caddesi from the Egyptian Bazaar to the Rüstem Paşa Camii. It's easy to miss as it is not at street level: look for a stone doorway and a flight of steps leading up; there is also a small marble fountain and plaque.

At the top of the steps is a terrace and the

Maşallah

In İstanbul's Egyptian Bazaar you may see a shop which specialises in the white outfits boys wear on the day (usually Sunday) of their circumcision *(sünnet)*. The white satin suit is supplemented with a spangled hat and red satin sash emblazoned with the word *Maşallah* (MAH-shah-lah, 'What wonders God has willed!').

Circumcision, or the surgical removal of the foreskin on the penis, is performed on a Turkish Muslim lad when he is between eight and 10 years old, and marks his formal admission into the faith, as does confirmation in Christianity and bar mitzvah in Judaism.

On the day of the operation the boy is dressed in the special suit, visits relatives and friends, and leads a parade – formerly on horseback, now in cars – around his neighbourhood or city attended by musicians and merrymakers. You may come across these lads while visiting the Eyüp Sultan Camii, one of Islam's holiest places, where they often stop on the way to their circumcision.

The simple operation, performed in a hospital or clinic in the afternoon, is followed by a celebration with music and feasting. The newly circumcised lad attends, resting in a bed, as his friends and relatives bring him gifts and congratulate him on having entered into manhood. ■

mosque's colonnaded porch. You'll notice at once the panels of İznik faïence set into the mosque's facade. The interior is covered in similarly gorgeous tiles, so take off your shoes (women should also cover their head and shoulders) and venture inside. This particularly beautiful mosque was built by Sinan for Rüstem Paşa, son-in-law and grand vizier of Süleyman the Magnificent. Ottoman power, glory, architecture and tilework were all at their zenith when the mosque was built in 1561.

After your visit to the mosque, you might want to spend some more time wandering the streets of this fascinating market quarter. Tahtakale, as it's called, is synonymous with buying and selling anything and everything, including the bizarre and the illegal. Informal money changers here will give you the best rate for your foreign currency, but be careful of people out to con you and petty thieves if you do change money here.

If you need a goal during your walk, head up the hill (south) on Uzunçarşı Caddesi, which begins right near the Rüstem Paşa Camii and ends at the Covered Market.

Fener

Fener (fehn-EHR; Greek: *Phanar*, lantern or lighthouse) was the centre of Greek life in Ottoman İstanbul, and is still the seat of the Ecumenical Orthodox patriarchate.

Ecumenical Orthodox Patriarchate The Ecumenical patriarch is a ceremonial head of the Orthodox churches, though most of the churches – in Greece, Cyprus, Russia and other countries – have their own patriarchs or archbishops who are independent of İstanbul. Nevertheless, the 'sentimental' importance of the patriarchate, here in the city which saw the great era of Byzantine and Orthodox influence, is considerable.

These days the patriarch is a Turkish citizen of Greek descent nominated by the church and appointed by the Turkish government as an official in the Directorate of Religious Affairs. In this capacity he is the religious leader of the country's Orthodox citizens and is known officially as the Greek Patriarch of Fener (Fener Rum Patriği).

To find the patriarchate *(patrikhane)*, go inland from the Fener ferry dock on the Golden Horn, and ask the way. The patriarchate has been in this district since about 1600.

The **Church of St George**, within the patriarchate compound, is a modest place, built in 1720, but the ornate patriarchal throne may date from the last years of Byzantium. In 1941 a disastrous fire destroyed many of the buildings but spared the church.

Selimiye Camii Looming above the central stretch of the Golden Horn is the mosque of Yavuz Selim (Selim I, 1512-20). Sultan Selim 'the Grim' laid the foundations of Ottoman greatness for his son and successor, Süleyman the Magnificent. Though he ruled for a very short time, Selim greatly expanded the empire's territory, solidified its institutions and filled its treasury. He came to power by deposing his father, Beyazıt II (1481-1512), who died 'mysteriously' soon thereafter. To avoid any threat to his power, and thus the sort of disastrous civil war which had torn the empire apart in the days before Mehmet the Conqueror, Selim had all his brothers put to death, and in the eight years of his reign he had eight grand viziers beheaded.

But his violence was in the interests of empire-building, at which he was a master. He doubled the empire's extent during his short reign, conquering part of Persia and all of Syria and Egypt. He took from Egypt's decadent, defeated rulers the title Caliph of Islam, which was borne by his successors until 1924. In his spare time he wrote poetry in Persian, the literary language of the time.

Selim's imperial mosque was built mostly during the reign of his son Süleyman. It is especially pretty, with lots of fine, very early İznik tiles (the yellow colour is a clue to their 'earliness') and a shallow dome similar to that of Aya Sofya. Selim's tomb behind the mosque is also very fine. Among the others buried nearby are Sultan Abdülmecit (1839-61) and several children of Süleyman the Magnificent.

Church of St Stephen The Church of St Stephen of the Bulgars, between Balat and Fener on the Golden Horn, is made completely of cast iron, as is most of its interior decoration. The building is unusual, and its history even more so.

The church is not normally open for visits, but well-dressed visitors arriving during or after services on Sunday morning may well be invited in for a look round.

During the 19th century the spirit of ethnic nationalism swept through the Ottoman Empire. Each of the many ethnic groups in the empire wanted to rule its own affairs. Groups identified themselves on the bases of language, religion and racial heritage. This sometimes led to problems, as with the Bulgars.

The Bulgars, originally a Turkic-speaking people, came from the Volga in about 680 AD and overwhelmed the Slavic peoples living in what is today Bulgaria. They adopted the Slavic language and customs, and founded an empire which threatened the power of Byzantium. In the 9th century they were converted to Christianity.

The Orthodox Patriarch, head of the Eastern church in the Ottoman Empire, was an ethnic Greek; in order to retain as much power as possible, the patriarch was opposed to any ethnic divisions within the Orthodox church. He put pressure on the sultan not to allow the Bulgarians, Macedonians and Rumanians to establish their own religious groups.

The pressures of nationalism became too great, however, and the sultan was finally forced to recognise some sort of autonomy for the Bulgars. He established not a Bulgarian patriarchate, but an 'exarchate'. The Bulgarian exarch would be 'less important' than, but independent of, the Greek Orthodox patriarch. In this way the Bulgarians would get their desired ethnic recognition and would get out from under the dominance of the Greeks, but the Greek Patriarch would allegedly suffer no diminution of his glory or power.

St Stephen's is the Bulgarian exarch's church. The Gothic structure was cast in Vienna, shipped down the Danube on 100 barges, and assembled in İstanbul in 1871. A duplicate church erected in Vienna, the only other copy, was destroyed by aerial bombing during WWII.

Balat

The quarter on the Golden Horn called Balat used to house a large portion of the city's Jewish population. Spanish Jews driven from their country by the judges of the Spanish Inquisition found refuge in the Ottoman Empire in the late 15th and early 16th centuries. The quincentenary (500th anniversary) of their migration to Ottoman lands was celebrated in 1992. As the sultan recognised, they were a boon to his empire: they brought news of the latest western advances in medicine, clockmaking, ballistics and other means of warfare. The refugees from the Inquisition set up the first printing presses in Turkey. Like all other religious 'nations' within the empire, the Jewish people were governed by a supreme religious leader, the Chief Rabbi, who oversaw their adherence to biblical law and who was responsible to the sultan for their good conduct.

Balat used to have dozens of synagogues, of which two remain for worship: the recently restored Ahrida and the nearby Yanbol. Admission is by guided tour only. Contact a local tour company for information.

Many of the city's Jewish residents have long since moved to more attractive quarters or emigrated to Europe or Israel, leaving a community of some 12,000 here. There is still one İstanbul newspaper published in Ladino Spanish, the language brought by the immigrants in Renaissance times and still remembered, if not actively spoken, in this city today.

Eyüp

The district of Eyüp, once a village outside the walls, is named for the standard-bearer of the Prophet Muhammed. The most pleasant way to reach Eyüp is on a Golden Horn ferry, boarded at Galata Bridge (Eminönü side) or at one of the little landing stages along the route westward. Otherwise, take bus 55 (Taksim to Eyüp Üçşehitler) or bus 99 (Eminönü to Alibeyköyü), and get off at the 'Eyüp' stop. There are also dolmuşes: Edirnekapı to Eyüp, Topkapı to Eyüp, Aksaray to Eyüp, or Aksaray to Alibeyköyü.

History Eyüp Ensari (Ayoub in Arabic, Job in English) fell in battle here while carrying the banner of Islam during the Arab assault and siege of the city in 674-78. Eyüp had been a friend of the Prophet and a revered member of Islam's early leadership. His tomb and the Eyüp Sultan Camii are very sacred places for most Muslims, ranking after Mecca, Medina and Jerusalem.

Ironically, Eyüp's tomb was first venerated by the Byzantines after the Arab armies withdrew, long before the coming of the Turks.

When Mehmet the Conqueror besieged the city in 1453, the tomb was no doubt known to him, and he undertook to build a grander and more fitting structure to commemorate it. A legend persists, though, that the tomb had been lost and was miraculously rediscovered by Mehmet's Şeyh-ül-İslam (Supreme Islamic Judge). Perhaps both are true. If the tomb was known to Mehmet Fatih and his leadership, but not to the common soldiers, it could be used for inspiration – have it miraculously 'rediscovered', and the army would take it as a good omen for the holy war in which they were engaged.

Whatever the truth, the tomb has been a very holy place ever since the Conquest. Mehmet had a mosque built here within five years of his victory, and succeeding sultans came to it to be girded with the Sword of Osman, the Ottoman equivalent of coronation, signifying their power and title as *padişah* (king of kings) or sultan. Mehmet's mosque was levelled by an earthquake in 1766, and a new mosque was built on the site by Sultan Selim III in 1800.

Visiting the Tomb & Eyüp Sultan Camii From the open space next to the complex, enter the great doorway to a large courtyard, then to a smaller court shaded by a huge, ancient plane tree. Note the wealth of brilliant İznik tilework on the walls here. To the left, behind the tilework and the gilded grillework, is Eyüp's tomb; to the right is the mosque. Be careful to observe the Islamic proprieties when visiting: decent clothing (no shorts for men), and modest dresses for women, who should also have their head, shoulders and arms covered. Take your shoes off before entering the small tomb enclosure, rich with silver, gold, crystal chandeliers and coloured tiles. Try not to stand in front of those at prayer; act respectfully; don't use a camera.

Across the court from the tomb is the Eyüp Sultan Camii (Mosque of the Great Eyüp). The Baroque style of the mosque – gilding, marble, windows, calligraphy and other decoration lavished on it – is elegant and even simple, if Baroque can ever be described as simple. The mosque is open long hours every day, free; avoid visiting on Friday and on Muslim holy days, when the mosque and tomb will be very busy with worshippers. For a snack or lunch, there are little pastry shops and snack stands on Kalenderhane Caddesi across from the mosque.

As the Eyüp Sultan Camii is such a sacred place, many important people including lots of grand viziers wanted to be buried in its precincts. Between the mosque-tomb complex and the Golden Horn you will see a virtual 'village' of octagonal tombs. Even those who were not to be buried here left their mark. The Valide Sultan Mihrişah, Queen Mother of Selim III, built important charitable institutions such as schools, baths and soup kitchens. Sokollu Mehmet Paşa, among the greatest of Ottoman grand viziers, donated a hospital which still functions as a medical clinic to this day.

Feshane About 500m south of the Eyüp Sultan Camii on the Golden Horn shore stands the Feshane (FESS-hah-neh, fez factory). Built in the mid-19th century to manufacture the distinctive headgear of the Ottomans, the Feshane was converted to other textile production when Atatürk's reforms did away with the fez in 1925. The factory, after being abandoned in the 1980s, was restored by the late philanthropist Dr Nejat Eczacıbaşı, former head of Turkey's largest pharmaceutical company, who provided the funds and the inspiration to restore and modernise the landmark building.

The Feshane was meant to become İstanbul's Museum of Contemporary Art (Çağrılı Sanat Müzesi), with a permanent collection of works by Turkish artists and space for changing exhibits. With Dr Eczacıbaşı's untimely death in 1994, however, the project remains uncompleted.

Pierre Loti Café Up the hill to the north of the mosque is a café where 'Pierre Loti' (Louis Marie Julien Viaud, 1850-1923) used to sit and admire the city. Loti pursued a distinguished career in the French navy, and at the same time became his country's most celebrated novelist. Though a hard-headed mariner, he was also an inspired and incurable romantic who fell in love with the graceful and mysterious way of life he discovered in Ottoman İstanbul.

Loti set up house in Eyüp for several years and had a love affair, fraught with peril, with a married Turkish woman whom he called Aziyadé (the title of his most romantic and successful novel). He was transferred back to France and forced to leave his mistress and his beloved İstanbul, but he decorated his French home in Ottoman style and begged Aziyadé to flee and join him. Instead, her infidelity was discovered and then she 'disappeared'.

Pierre Loti's romantic novels about the daily life of İstanbul under the last sultans introduced millions of European readers to Turkish customs and habits, and helped to counteract the politically inspired Turkophobia then spreading through Europe.

Loti loved the city, the decadent grandeur of the empire, and the fascinating late-medieval customs of a society in decline. When he sat in this café, under a shady grapevine, sipping *çay* (tea), he saw a Golden Horn busy with caiques, schooners and a few steam vessels. The water in the Golden Horn was still clean enough to swim in, and the vicinity of the café was all pastureland.

The café which today bears his name may not have any actual connection to Loti, but it occupies a spot and enjoys a view which he must have enjoyed. It's in a warren of little streets on a promontory surrounded by the Eyüp Sultan Mezarlığı (Cemetery of the Great Eyüp), just north of the Eyüp mosque. The surest way to find it is to ask the way to the café via Karyağdı Sokak. Walk out of the mosque enclosure, turn right, and walk around the mosque complex keeping it on your right until you see the street going uphill into the cemetery. There's a little sign, 'Pierre Loti'. Hike up the steep hill on Karyağdı Sokak for 15 minutes to reach the café. If you take a taxi, it will follow a completely different route because of one-way streets. At my last visit, tea was US$0.45, soft drinks were about twice as much. They serve a few snacks and sandwiches as well.

Hasköy

The north bank of the Golden Horn is of less historical interest, except for the imperial lodge at Aynalıkavak in the district of Hasköy.

Aynalıkavak Kasrı İstanbul's imperial lodges *(kasrs)* are less impressive but more charming than its many palaces. Designed to a more human scale, kasrs were built not to impress visitors but to please the monarchs themselves. Among the least frequently visited is Aynalıkavak Kasrı, an early 19th-century hunting lodge in the district called Hasköy, on the northern shore of the Golden Horn about six km from Karaköy.

Several centuries ago an imperial naval arsenal was established at Kasımpaşa, southeast of Hasköy, and near it a shipyard *(tersane)*. The collection of imperial hunting lodges and pleasure kiosks at Hasköy became known as the Tersane Palace, after the shipyard. A wooden palace was built on this site by Sultan Ahmet III (1703-30), and restored by Selim III (1789-1807). What you see today is mostly the work of Sultan Mahmut II (1808-39).

With its Lale Devri (Tulip Period, early 18th century) decoration and Ottoman furnishings, the pavilion is a splendid if dusty place giving a vivid impression of the life-style of the Ottoman ruling class at the turn of the 19th century, when Hasköy was a thriving Jewish neighbourhood. Some rooms – much the most comfortable – are furnished in Eastern style, others in the less commodious European style which was then penetrating the sultan's domains.

Selim III composed poetry and music in one of its eastern rooms; futon-like beds were tucked away into cabinets during the day. The Bekleme Salonu (Waiting Room) has the only extant Tulip Period ceiling. Of the European-style rooms, one is filled with sumptuous mother-of-pearl furniture. There's a small museum of Turkish musical instruments on the lower level.

The only practical way to reach it is by taxi (US$3 from Beyoğlu). Tell the driver to take you to the Hasköy Polis Karakolu (police station) or the Şükrü Urcan Spor Tesisleri (athletic facilities), which are well known. A minute's walk south-east of the Hasköy police station along Kasımpaşa-Hasköy Yolu brings you to Aynalıkavak Kasrı (☎ 250 4094), open from 9.30 am to 4 pm (closed Monday and Thursday); admission costs less than US$1, with reductions for students. The pavilion's gardens and grounds provide a welcome respite from the city's concrete landscape.

Koç Industrial Museum The Rahmi M Koç Industrial Museum (☎ 256 7153), Hasköy Caddesi 27, Sütlüce, was founded by the current head of the Koç industrial group, one of Turkey's most prominent conglomerates, to exhibit artefacts from İstanbul's industrial past. Exhibits include models of trains, cars, steam engines, ships – and even a fully recreated ship's bridge. It's open from 10 am to 5 pm, closed Monday.

The *Café du Levant* (☎ 250 8938), on the museum's grounds, is a surprisingly elegant French bistro serving lunch and dinner at moderate prices daily except Monday.

WESTERN DISTRICTS

From early times the heart of this ancient city has been near the tip of Seraglio Point. As the city grew over the centuries, its boundaries moved westward. That process continues.

There are several points of interest farther west, and if you have at least four days to tour İstanbul you should be able to see all the centre's essential sights and still have time for these outlying ones. They include the Fatih Camii, the Church of the Holy Saviour in Chora (Kariye Müzesi), famous for its Byzantine mosaics, the Palace of Constantine Porphyrogenetus (Tekfur Saray), several other mosques, the mammoth city walls, and Yedikule, the Fortress of the Seven Towers. You can combine a tour of these sites with some of those in the Golden Horn section easily.

Fatih Camii

The Mosque of the Conqueror is just west of the Aqueduct of Valens, on Fevzi Paşa Caddesi. Catch a dolmuş from Aksaray or Taksim to the town hall (ask for the Belediye Sarayı, behl-eh-DEE-yeh sar-rah-yuh) near the Aqueduct and walk five blocks; or you can catch any bus that has 'Fatih' or 'Edirnekapı' listed on its itinerary board.

The Fatih Camii was the first great imperial mosque to be built in İstanbul following the Conquest. For its location, Sultan Mehmet the Conqueror chose the hilltop site of the ruined Church of the Apostles. The mosque complex, finished in 1470, was enormous and included in its külliye 15 charitable establishments – religious schools, a hospice for travellers, a caravanserai etc. The mosque you see, however, is not the one he built. The original stood for nearly 300 years before toppling in an earthquake in 1766. It was rebuilt, but to a completely different plan. The exterior of the mosque still bears some of the original decoration; the interior is not all that impressive.

While you're here, be sure to visit the tomb of Mehmet the Conqueror behind the mosque. His wife Gülbahar, whose tomb is next to the sultan's, is rumoured to have been a French princess.

Mihrimah Camii

When you're finished at the Fatih mosque, go back to Fevzi Paşa Caddesi and catch a bus or dolmuş headed north-west towards Edirnekapı. Get out just before the city walls at the Mihrimah Camii, a mosque built by Süleyman the Magnificent's favourite daughter, Mihrimah, in the 1560s. The architect was Sinan, and the mosque marks a departure from his usual style. The inevitable earthquakes worked their destruction, and the building has been restored several times, most recently around 1900. Mihrimah married Rüstem Paşa, Süleyman's brilliant and powerful grand vizier (his little tile-covered mosque is down by the Egyptian Market). You can visit her tomb on the south-east side of the mosque.

Cross the road from the Mihrimah Camii and, still inside the walls, head north towards the Golden Horn. You'll see signs, and children pointing the way, to the Chora church.

Chora Church

If we translate the original name *(Chora)* of this building, it would be called 'Church of the Holy Saviour Outside the Walls' or 'in the Country', because the first church on this site was indeed outside the walls built by Constantine the Great. But just as London's church of St Martin-in-the-Fields is hardly surrounded by bucolic scenery these days, the Church of the Holy Saviour was soon engulfed by Byzantine urban sprawl. It was enclosed within the walls built by the Emperor Theodosius II in 413, less than 100 years after Constantine. So the Holy Saviour in the Country was 'in the country' for about 80 years, and has been 'in the city' for 1550 years.

It was not only the environs of the church which changed: for four centuries it served as a mosque (Kariye Camii), and is now a museum, the Kariye Müzesi (☎ 523-3009). It is open daily from 9.30 am to 4.30 pm, closed Tuesday; admission costs US$3. You reach it by taking any Edirnekapı bus along Fevzi Paşa Caddesi.

The building you see is not the original church-outside-the-walls. Rather, this one was built in the late 11th century, with repairs and restructuring in the following centuries. Virtually all of the interior decoration – the famous mosaics and the less renowned but equally striking mural paintings – dates from about 1320. Between 1948 and 1959 the decoration was carefully restored under the auspices of the Byzantine Society of America.

The **mosaics** are breathtaking, and follow the standard Byzantine order. The first ones are those of the dedication, to Christ and to the Virgin Mary. Then come the offertory ones: Theodore Metochites, builder of the church, offering it to Christ. The two small domes of the inner narthex have portraits of all Christ's ancestors back to Adam. A series outlines the Virgin Mary's life, and another, Christ's early years. Yet another series concentrates on Christ's ministry. Various saints and martyrs fill the interstices.

In the nave are three mosaics: of Christ, of the Virgin as Teacher, and of the Dormition (Assumption) of the Blessed Virgin – turn around to see this one, it's over the main door you just entered. The 'infant' in the painting is actually Mary's soul, being held by Jesus, while her body lies 'asleep' on its bier.

South of the nave is the parecclesion, a side chapel built to hold the tombs of the church's founder and his relatives, close friends and associates. The frescoes appropriately deal with the theme of death and resurrection. The striking painting in the apse shows Christ breaking down the gates of Hell and raising Adam and Eve, with saints and kings in attendance.

Tekfur Saray

From Kariye, head west to the city walls, then north again, and you'll soon come to the Palace of Constantine Porphyrogenetus, the Tekfur Saray (tehk-FOOR sar-rah-yuh). It's nominally open on Wednesday, Thursday and Sunday from 9 am to 5 pm, but you can usually just wander in on any day. The caretaker may appear and sell you a ticket for US$0.25.

Though the building is only a shell these days, it is remarkably preserved for a Byzantine palace built in the 14th century. Sacred buildings often survive the ravages of time because they continue to be used even though they may be converted for use in another religion. Secular buildings, however, are often torn down and used as quarries for building materials once their owners die. The Byzantine palaces which once crowded Sultanahmet Square are all gone; so is the great Palace of Blachernae, which adjoined the Tekfur Saray. Only this one remains.

The caretaker may put a ladder against the wall for you, so you can climb up onto the walls for a view of the palace, the city walls, the Golden Horn, and much of the city.

The City Walls

Since being built in the 5th century, the city walls have been breached by hostile forces only twice. The first time was in the 13th century, when Byzantium's 'allies', the armies of the Fourth Crusade, broke through and pillaged the town, deposing the emperor and setting up a king of their own. The second time was in 1453 under Mehmet the Conqueror. Even though Mehmet was ultimately successful, he was continually frustrated during the siege as the walls withstood admirably even the heaviest bombardments by the largest cannon in existence at the time.

The walls were kept defensible and in good repair until about a century ago, when the development of mighty naval guns made such expense pointless: if İstanbul was going to fall, it would fall to ships firing from the Bosphorus, not to soldiers advancing on the land walls.

During the late 1980s, the city undertook to rebuild the major gates for the delight of tourists. Debates raged in the Turkish newspapers over the style of the reconstruction. Some said the restorations were too theatrical, while others said that if the walls never actually did look like that, perhaps they *should* have. Anyway, the work allows you to imagine what it must have looked like in the Middle Ages. The gates which have been completed include the Topkapı, Mevlanakapı and Belgrat Kapısı.

For a look at the most spectacular of the defences in the walls see Yedikule (later in this section).

Heading north, you can make your way on foot to the Golden Horn at Balat or Ayvansaray and then take a bus, dolmuş or ferry to Eyüp. Otherwise, return to the Kariye Müzesi and make your way through the maze of streets to the Fethiye Camii, where there are more magnificent Byzantine mosaics. From the Fethiye Camii it's only a few minutes' walk (three short blocks – ask for directions) to the seat of the Ecumenical Orthodox Patriarchate.

Fethiye Camii

Fethiye Camii (Mosque of the Conquest) was built in the 12th century as the Church of the Theotokos Pammakaristos or Church of the Joyous Mother of God. To reach it, ask someone to point you towards Draman Caddesi; follow this street until it changes names to become Fethiye Caddesi, then look left (north) to see the mosque, set in the midst of an open space.

The original monastery church was added to several times over the centuries, then converted to a mosque in 1591 to commemorate Sultan Murat III's victories in Georgia and Azerbaijan. Before its conversion it served as the headquarters of the Ecumenical Orthodox Patriarch (1456-1568); Mehmet the Conqueror visited to discuss theological questions here with Patriarch Gennadios not long after the conquest of the city. They talked things over in the side chapel known as the parecclesion, which has been restored to its former Byzantine splendour; the rest of the building remains a mosque. Visit the parecclesion to see the wonderful mosaics showing Jesus, the Apostles, the Virgin Mary, St John the Baptist, angels and saints. Entry to the parecclesion costs US$1; it is open daily from 9.30 am to 4.30 pm, closed on Tuesday.

Yedikule

If you arrived in İstanbul by train from

Europe, or if you rode in from the airport along the seashore, you've already had a glance of Yedikule, the Fortress of the Seven Towers, looming over the southern approaches to the city.

The fortress is open every day from 9.30 am to 5 pm; admission costs US$1.

History Theodosius I built a triumphal arch here in the late 4th century. When the next Theodosius (408-50) built his great land walls, he incorporated the arch. Four of the fortress' seven towers were built as part of the Emperor Theodosius' walls; the other three, inside the walls, were added by Mehmet the Conqueror. Under the Byzantines, the triumphal arch became known as the **Golden Gate**, and was used for triumphal state processions into and out of the city. For a time, its gates were indeed plated with gold. The doorway was sealed in the late Byzantine period.

In Ottoman times the fortress was used for defence, as a repository for the imperial treasury, a prison and a place of execution. Diplomatic practice in Renaissance times included chucking into loathsome prisons the ambassadors of countries with which yours didn't get along. For foreign ambassadors to the Sublime Porte, Yedikule was that prison. Latin and German inscriptions still visible in the Ambassadors' Tower bring the place's history to light. It was also here that Sultan Osman II, a 17-year-old youth, was executed in 1622 during a revolt of the Janissary corps. The kaftan he was wearing when he was murdered is now on display in Topkapı Palace's costumes collection.

Visiting Yedikule & the Walls The best view of the city walls and of the fortress is from the **Tower of Sultan Ahmet III**, near the gate in the city wall. It is possible to walk along the land walls from the Sea of Marmara past Yedikule, even making some of the walk atop the walls. The district is not the safest, however, and I know of at least one robbery attempt, so it's best to go in a group and to take the normal precautions.

Right down at the shoreline, where the land walls meet the Sea of Marmara, is the **Marble Tower**, once part of a small Byzantine imperial seaside villa.

Getting There & Away Yedikule is a long way from most other sights of interest in İstanbul and involves a special trip. Situated where the great city walls meet the Sea of Marmara, it's accessible by cheap train from Sirkeci. Take any *banliyö* train and hop off at Yedikule, then walk around to the entrance in the north-east. You can take bus 80 ('Yedikule') from Eminönü, Sultanahmet and Divan Yolu, but the ride may take the better part of an hour if there's any sort of traffic.

BEYOĞLU

Beyoğlu (BEY-oh-loo) is fascinating because it holds the architectural evidence of the Ottoman Empire's frantic attempts to modernise and reform itself, and the evidence of the European powers' attempts to undermine and subvert it. The Ottomans were struggling for their very existence as a state; the Europeans were struggling for domination of the entire Middle East so as to control its holy places, its sea lanes through the Suez Canal to India, and especially its oil, already important at that time.

New ideas walked into Ottoman daily life down the streets of Pera which, with Galata, makes up Beyoğlu). The Europeans, who lived in Pera, brought new fashions, machines, arts and manners, and rules for the diplomatic game. The Old City across the Golden Horn was content to sit tight and continue living in the Middle Ages with its oriental bazaars, great mosques and palaces, narrow streets and traditional values. But Pera was to have telephones, underground trains, tramways, electric light and modern municipal government. The sultans followed Pera's lead. From the reign of Abdülmecit (1839-61) onwards, no sultan lived in Mehmet the Conqueror's palace at Topkapı. Rather, they built opulent European-style palaces in Pera and along the shores of the Bosphorus to the north.

The easiest way to tour Beyoğlu is to start from its busy nerve-centre: Taksim Square.

You can get a dolmuş directly to Taksim from Aksaray or Sirkeci; there are buses as well.

History

Sometimes called the New City, Beyoğlu is 'new' only in a relative sense. There was a settlement on the northern shore of the Golden Horn, near Karaköy Square, before the birth of Jesus. By the time of Theodosius II (408-50), it was large enough to become an official suburb of Constantinople. Theodosius built a fortress here, no doubt to complete the defence system of his great land walls, and called it Galata (gah-LAH-tah), as the suburb was then the home of many Galatians.

During the height of the Byzantine Empire, Galata became a favourite place for foreign trading companies to set up business. To this day, it still harbours the offices of many non-Muslim businesses and foreign representatives.

The word 'new' actually applies more to Pera, the quarter above Galata, running along the crest of the hill from the Galata Tower to Taksim Square. This was built up only in later Ottoman times.

In the 19th century, the European powers were waiting eagerly for the 'Sick Man of Europe' (the decadent Ottoman Empire) to collapse so that they could grab territory and spheres of influence. All the great colonial powers – the British, Russian, Austro-Hungarian and German empires, France and the kingdom of Italy – maintained lavish embassies and tried to cajole and pressure the Sublime Porte into concessions of territory, trade and influence.

The embassy buildings, as lavish as ever, still stand in Pera. Ironically, most of the great empires which built them collapsed along with that of the Ottomans. Only the British and French survived to grab any of the spoils. Their occupation of Middle Eastern countries under League of Nations 'mandates' has given us the Middle East we have today.

Taksim Square

'Taksim' could mean 'my taxi' in Turkish, but it doesn't; after a look at the square, you may wonder why not. Rather, it is named after the *taksim* (tahk-SEEM, distribution point) in the city's water-conduit system. The main water line from the Belgrade Forest, north of the city, was laid to this point in 1732 by Sultan Mahmut I (1730-54), and the branch lines lead from the taksim to all parts of the city.

The first thing you'll notice in the elongated 'square' is the **Atatürk Kültür Merkezi**, or Atatürk Cultural Centre (sometimes called the Opera House), the large building at the eastern end. In the summertime, during the International İstanbul Festival, tickets for the various concerts are on sale in the ticket kiosks here, and numerous performances are staged in its various halls.

At the opposite end of the square is the **Cumhuriyet ve İstiklal Abidesi**, Monument to the Republic & Independence, one of the earliest monuments erected during the time of the republic. It was done by an Italian sculptor in 1928. Atatürk, his assistant and successor İsmet İnönü and other revolutionary leaders appear prominently on the monument set in a circular garden circumnavigated by the İstiklal Caddesi tram.

To the south of the square is the luxury Marmara Hotel. To the north is the **Taksim Gezi Yeri**, Taksim Park or Promenade, with the Inter-Continental Hotel at its northern end.

North of Taksim

From the roundabout, Cumhuriyet Caddesi (Republic Ave) leads north past streetside cafés and restaurants, banks, travel agencies, airline offices, nightclubs and the Divan and İstanbul Hilton hotels to the districts of Harbiye, Nişantaşı and Şişli.

Military Museum A km north of Taksim in Harbiye is the Askeri Müzesi (☎ 248 7115), open Wednesday to Sunday from 9 am to noon and 1 to 5 pm; admission costs US$1.50. Concerts by the Mehter, the medieval Ottoman Military Band, are at 3 and 4 pm. To reach the museum, walk north out of

Taksim Square along the eastern side of Cumhuriyet Caddesi (by Taksim Park) and up past the Hilton. When you come to Harbiye, the point where Valikonağı Caddesi bears right off Cumhuriyet Caddesi, you'll see the gate to the Military Museum on your right.

The museum, within a military complex, has two parts. Entering from Cumhuriyet Caddesi, you'll come first to the new section. On the ground floor are displays of weapons, a 'heroes' gallery' *(şehit galerisi)* with artefacts from fallen Turkish soldiers of many wars, displays of Turkish military uniforms through the ages, and many glass cases holding battle standards, both Turkish and captured. The captured ones include Byzantine, Greek, British, Italian, Austro-Hungarian, and Imperial Russian. Perhaps the most interesting of the exhibits are the *sayebanlar*, or imperial pavilions. These luxurious cloth shelters, heavily worked with thread of silver and gold, jewels, precious silks and elegant tracery, were the battle headquarters for sultans during the summer campaign season.

The upper floor of the new section has fascinating displays of Ottoman tents, more

PLACES TO STAY

1 Divan Oteli
2 Hyatt Regency Istanbul
3 Inter-Continental Hotel
4 Hotel İstanbul Kervansaray
5 Hotel Eresin
6 Hotel Nippon
7 Otel Avrupa
9 Crystal Hotel
10 Hotel Lamartine
12 Riva Otel
35 The Marmara Hotel
46 Family House
50 Savoy Hotel
53 Dilson Hotel
55 Keban Hotel
83 Hotel Emperyal
96 Büyük Londra Oteli
101 Pera Palas Oteli
102 Hotel Pullman Etap İstanbul
103 Yenişehir Palas
111 Hotel Richmond & Patisserie Lebon

PLACES TO EAT

8 Lebanese Restaurant
11 Çin Lokantası
19 Pizza Hut
26 McDonald's
39 C Fischer Restaurant
45 Great Hong Kong Restaurant
49 Çetin Restaurant & Büfe Snack Stands
52 Pehlivan Restaurant
59 Hacı Baba Restaurant
62 Sohbet Ocakbaşı Restaurant
65 Kaktüs Café
66 Cadde-i Kebir Café
67 Borsa Fast Food Kafeteryası
68 Hacı Abdullah Restaurant
69 Meşhur Sultanahmet Köftecisi & Kristal Köftecisi
71 Afacan Restaurant
73 Nature & Peace
76 Ada Lokantası
78 Tarihi Cumhuriyet Meyhanesi & Other Tavernas
79 Mercan Restaurant
80 Şütte Delicatessen
82 Çiçek Pasajı
98 Garibaldi Restaurant
105 Çati Restaurant
107 Karadeniz Pide Salonu
108 Yakup 2 Restaurant
114 Four Seasons (Dört Mevsim) Restaurant

OTHER

13 Yeşilköy-Ataköy-Florya-Hava Limanı Dolmuş
14 Bakırköy Dolmuş
15 Bamka Döviz Exchange Office
16 Sarıyer Dolmuş
17 Karaköy-Eminönü-Sirkeci Dolmuş
18 Kadıköy Şişli-Beşiktaş Dolmuş
20 Türkiye İş Bankası
21 Air France Ticket Office
22 Turkish Airlines Ticket Office
23 Yapı Kredi Bankası
24 Topkapı Dolmuş
25 Aksaray Dolmuş
27 Aeroflot Ticket Office
28 PTT
29 Pamukkale & Nev Tur Bus Ticket Office
30 Kadıköy-Bostancı Dolmuş
31 Toilets
32 Cumhuriyet Anıtı (Republic Monument)
33 Tourism Information Office
34 Taksim Gazete Bayii Newsstand
36 Atatürk Cultural Centre
37 Japanese Consulate
38 Ulusoy Bus Ticket Office
40 Kamil Koç Bus Ticket Office
41 Metro Bus Ticket Office
42 Varan Bus Ticket Office
43 As Turizm & Hakiki Koç Bus Ticket Offices
44 German Consulate General
47 Beşiktaş-Dolmabahçe Dolmuş
48 French Consulate
51 Maksim Gazino Nightclub & Taksim Sahnesi Theatre
54 Aya Triyada Greek Orthodox Church
56 Rumanian Consulate
57 Andon Pera Bar
58 Belgian Consulate
60 Akbank & Aksanat Cultural Centre
61 Fitaş Sinemasi
63 Ziraat Bankası
64 Türkiye İş Bankası
70 Ağa Camii
72 Yapı Kredi Bankası
74 Vakko Department Store
75 Ali Muhiddin Hacı Bekir Confectionery
77 Sinema Rüya
81 British Consulate General
84 PTT
85 British Council Office
86 Tourism Information Office
87 Galatasaray Square
88 Galatasaray Lisesi
89 Toilets
90 Yapı Kredi Bankası
91 Panaya Isodyon Greek Orthodox Church
92 Telephone Centre
93 Greek Consulate
94 Tarihi Galatasaray Hamamı
95 Church of San Antonio di Padua
97 Odakule Office Bldg & Armenian Church
99 Robinson Crusoe Bookshop
100 Palais de France
104 Netherlands Consulate General
106 American Consulate General
109 Church of St Mary Draperis
110 Russian Consulate General
112 Dünya Aktüel Bookshop
113 Swedish Consulate
115 Tünel (Undeground Train)
116 Divan Edebiyatı Müzesi (Whirling Dervish Museum)
117 Christ Church (Anglican)

imperial pavilions, and a room devoted to Atatürk who was, of course, a famous Ottoman general before he became founder and commander-in-chief of the Turkish republican army, and first president of the Turkish Republic.

To reach the old section of the Military Museum, walk out of the new section, turn right, and walk down the hill past displays of old cannon, then turn right again and climb the steps into the museum. Signs along the way read 'To the Other Departments'. The cannons, by the way, include Gatling guns bearing the sultan's monogram, cast in Vienna.

The old section is where you really feel the spirit of the Ottoman Empire. It has exhibits of armour (including cavalry), uniforms, field furniture made out of weapons (chairs with rifles for legs etc), and a Türk-Alman Dostluk Köşesi (Turco-German Friendship Corner) with mementoes of Turkish and German military collaboration before and during WWI. Some of the exhibits here are truly amazing. My favourites are the great chain that the Byzantines spread across the mouth of the Golden Horn to keep Mehmet the Conqueror's ships out during the battle for Constantinople in 1453; and a tapestry woven by Ottoman sailors (who must have had lots of time on their hands) showing the flags of all of the world's important maritime nations.

Perhaps the best reason to visit the Military Museum is for a little concert by the Mehter. The Mehter, according to historians, was the first true military band in the world. Its purpose was not to make pretty music for dancing, but to precede the conquering Ottoman paşas into vanquished towns, impressing upon the defeated populace that everything was going to be different now. They would march in with a steady, measured pace, turning all together to face the left side of the line of march, then the right side. With tall Janissary headdresses, fierce moustaches, brilliant instruments and even kettledrums, they did their job admirably.

Around Taksim Square

To the south-west, two streets meet before entering the square. Sıraselviler Caddesi goes south and İstiklal Caddesi goes south-west. The famous **taksim**, a small octagonal stone building, is to the south-west of the Republic Monument, just to the right of İstiklal Caddesi.

Nestled in the small triangle formed by the two mentioned streets, rising above the shops and restaurants which hide its foundations, is the **Aya Triada Kilisesi**, or Greek Orthodox Church of the Holy Trinity. If it's open, as it is daily for services, you can visit. Walk along İstiklal Caddesi and turn left.

Now head down İstiklal Caddesi for a look at the vestiges of 19th-century Ottoman life. The restored turn-of-the-century tram runs from Taksim via Galatasaray to Tünel for US$0.35. It's fun, but it runs too seldom to be very useful, and is always crowded.

İstiklal Caddesi

Stretching between Taksim Square and Tünel Square, İstiklal Caddesi (ees-teek-LAHL, Independence Ave) was formerly the Grande Rue de Péra. It was the street with all the smart shops, several large embassies and churches, many impressive residential buildings and a scattering of tea shops and restaurants. Renovation efforts in the past decade have restored much of the street's appeal. It's now a pedestrian way, which in Turkey means that there are fewer cars, not no cars.

As you stroll along İstiklal, try to imagine it during its heyday a century ago, peopled by frock-coated merchants and Ottoman officials, European officers in uniform, women with parasols, and lightly veiled Turkish women.

Just out of Taksim Square, the first building on the right is the former French plague hospital (1719), for years used as the **French Consulate General** in İstanbul. There's a French library here as well.

İstiklal Caddesi is packed with little restaurants and snack shops, bank branches, clothing stores, itinerant pedlars, shoppers and strollers. If you have the time, take a few detours down the narrow side streets. Any one will reveal glimpses of Beyoğlu life. The street names alone are intriguing: Büyükparmakkapı Sokak, 'Gate of the Thumb St'; Sakızağacı Sokak, 'Pine-Gum Tree St'; Kuloğlu Sokak, 'Slave's Son St'.

A few streets before coming to Galatasaray Square, look on the left for Suterazisi Sokak. Turn into this street, and at its end you'll find the **Tarihi Galatasaray Hamamı**, or Historic Galatasaray Turkish Bath. The bath is one of the city's best, with lots of marble decoration, comfy little cubicles for resting and sipping tea after the bath, pretty fountains and even a shoeshine service. However, the staff are very hungry for tips, and this can result in an unpleasant bathing experience. If you go, you'll enjoy it more if you don't go alone; best of all, go with a Turkish friend. The women's section of the bath, by the way, is not nearly so elegant or pleasant as the men's.

Galatasaray Square Halfway along the length of İstiklal Caddesi is Galatasaray (gah-LAH-tah-sah-rah-yee) Square (really an intersection, named for the imperial lycée you can see behind the huge gates on your left. This building once housed the country's most prestigious school, established in its present form by Sultan Abdülaziz in 1868, who wanted a place where Ottoman youth could hear lectures in both Turkish and French. Across İstiklal Caddesi from the school is the Galatasaray post office.

Çiçek Pasajı Before coming into Galatasaray square, turn right into the Çiçek Pasajı (chee-CHEHK pah-sah-zhuh, or Flower Passage). This is the inner court of the 19th-century 'Cité de Péra' building which symbolised Pera's growth as a 'modern' European-style city. For years the courtyard held a dozen cheap little restaurant-taverns. In good weather beer barrels were rolled out onto the pavement, marble slabs were balanced on top, wooden stools were put around, and enthusiastic revellers filled the stools as soon as they hit the ground.

In the late 1980s parts of the Cité de Péra building collapsed. In rebuilding, the venerable Çiçek Pasajı was 'beautified', its makeshift barrelhead slabs and stools replaced by comfortable, solid wooden tables and benches, the broken pavement with smooth tiles, all topped by a glass canopy to keep out foul weather. The clientele is better behaved now, and its smattering of adventurous tourists has become a significant proportion. It's a favourite destination for local guys who have picked up foreign women and want to show them some tame İstanbul nightlife. The Çiçek Pasajı is still OK for an evening of beer drinking, food and conversation, but prices are relatively high.

Pick a good place, pull up a stool and order a mug of beer, *beyaz* (pale) or *siyah* (dark). For something stronger, ask for *Bir kadeh rakı* (BEER kah-deh rah-KUH), 'a shot of rakı'. As for food, printed menus, even if you can find them, mean little here. If you already know a few Turkish dishes you like, order them, but ask prices first. Otherwise, the waiter will lead you to the kitchen so you can see what's cooking. As you eat and drink, at least three nearby revellers will want to know where you are from; when you tell them, the response is always *Çok iyi*, 'Very good!'

Many regulars have now abandoned the Çiçek Pasajı to the tourists and their attendant carpet and leather-apparel touts, opting instead to dine at little *meyhanes* (tavernas) deeper in the market. (See Places to Eat for some suggestions.)

Balık Pazar Walk out of the courtyard to neighbouring Sahne Sokak, turn right, then look for a little passage off to the left. This is the Avrupa Pasajı, the 'European Passage', a small gallery with marble paving and shops selling upscale goods. In Pera's heyday it was elegant, a state which recent restoration has done much to recreate.

Sahne Sokak is the heart of Beyoğlu's Balık Pazar (fish market), actually a general-purpose market with a good number of fish merchants. Small stands sell midye (skewered mussels) fried in hot oil, others grilled kokoreç (lamb intestines packed with more lamb intestines). I recommend the mussels, but get a skewer that's been freshly cooked.

Farther up Sahne Sokak, Duduodaları Sokak leads off to the left and down to the British Consulate General (more of that in a moment). Continuing along Sahne Sokak, though, near this junction on your right is the entrance to the Üç Horan Ermeni Kilisesi, the Armenian Church of Three Altars. You can visit if the doors are open.

Past the Armenian church, Sahne Sokak changes names to become Balık Sokak. Leading off to the right from Balık Sokak is Nevizade Sokak, lined with meyhanes where the old-time life of the Çiçek Pasajı continues, untrammelled by the glossy overlays of tourist İstanbul. Feel free to wander in and have a meal and a drink. (See Places to Eat for suggestions.)

Unless you want to continue down the slope among the fishmongers on Balık Sokak, turn back and then right into Duduodalari Sokak, and stroll down this little street past fancy food shops, butchers', bakers', and greengrocers' shops to the British Consulate General.

At the end of the market street you emerge into the light. Right in front of you is Meşrutiyet Caddesi, and on the corner here are the huge gates to the **British Consulate General**, an Italian palazzo built in 1845 to plans by Sir Charles Barry, architect of London's Houses of Parliament.

Walk past the British Consulate General along Meşrutiyet Caddesi, which makes its way down to the Pera Palas Oteli and the American Consulate General. Watch for an iron gate and a small passage on the left, leading into a little courtyard with a derelict lamp post in the centre. Enter the courtyard, turn right up the stairs, and you'll discover the Greek Orthodox **Church of Panaya Isodyon**. It's quiet and very tidy, hidden away in the midst of other buildings. The doors are open to visitors most of the day.

When you've seen the church, go down the stairs *behind* it (not the stairs you came up). Turn right, and just past the church property on the right-hand side you will see the entrance to the **Yeni Rejans Lokantası**, or New Regency Restaurant. Founded, as legend would have it, by three Russian dancing girls who fled the Russian Revolution, the restaurant is still operated by their Russian-speaking descendants.

This area of Beyoğlu was a favourite with Russian émigrés after the revolution. The Yeni Rejans, by the look of it, was a cabaret complete with orchestra loft and grand piano. Lunch and dinner are still served except on Sunday. Though in vogue with İstanbul's intelligentsia, service is far from good and prices are high for what you get.

When you go out the restaurant door and down the steps, turn right, then left along the narrow alley called Olivia Han Pasajı, and this will bring you back to İstiklal Caddesi.

Back on İstiklal Caddesi Across İstiklal, Caddesi notice the large Italian Gothic church behind a fence. The Franciscan **Church of San Antonio di Padua** was founded here in 1725; the red brick building dates from 1913.

Cross over to the church, turn right, and head down İstiklal Caddesi once more. After the church you will pass Eskiçiçekçi Sokak on the left, then Nuriziya Sokak. The third street, a little cul-de-sac, ends at the gates of the **Palais de France**, once the French embassy to the Ottoman sultan. The grounds are extensive and include the chapel of St Louis of the French, founded here in 1581, though the present chapel building dates from the 1830s. You can get a better look at the palace and grounds another way: read on.

A few steps along İstiklal Caddesi brings you to the pretty **Netherlands Consulate General**, built as the Dutch embassy in 1855 by the Fossati brothers, formerly architects to the Russian tsar. The first embassy building here dated from 1612. Past the consulate, turn left down the hill on Postacılar Sokak. The **Dutch Chapel**, on the left, is now the home of the Union Church of İstanbul, a multinational English-speaking Protestant congregation.

The narrow street turns right, bringing you face to face with the former Spanish Embassy. The little chapel, founded in 1670, is still in use though the embassy is not.

The street then bends left and changes

names to become Tomtom Kaptan Sokak. At the foot of the slope, on the right, is the **Palazzo di Venezia**, once the embassy for Venice, now the Italian Consulate. Venice was one of the great Mediterranean maritime powers during Renaissance times, and when Venetian and Ottoman fleets were not madly trading with one another, they were locked in ferocious combat.

To the left across the open space is a side gate to the Palais de France. Peek through the gates for another, better view of the old French embassy grounds, then slog back up that hill to İstiklal Caddesi.

Continuing along İstiklal Caddesi, the **Church of St Mary Draperis**, built in 1678 and extensively reconstructed in 1789, is behind an iron fence and down a flight of steps. This entrance is rarely open, though a side entrance may be.

Past the church, still on the left-hand side, is the grand **Russian Consulate General**, once the embassy of the tsars, built in 1837 to designs by the Fossati brothers. After designing several embassies, they were employed by the sultan to do extensive restorations on Sancta Sophia.

Now take a detour: turn right (north-west) off İstiklal Caddesi along Asmalımescit Caddesi, a narrow, typical Beyoğlu street with some antique shops, food shops, suspect hotels and little eateries. After 50m the street intersects Meşrutiyet Caddesi. To the left of the intersection is the American Library & Cultural Center, and just beyond it the pretty marble mansion which was first the US embassy, now the American Consulate General. Built as a pleasure palace for a rich man's mistress, it is now heavily fortified. A new consulate, more easily defensible, is to be built on a site up the Bosphorus.

Pera Palas Oteli The Pera Palas, opposite the American consulate, was built in the 1890s by Georges Nagelmackers, the Belgian entrepreneur who founded the Compagnie Internationale des Wagons-Lits et Grands Express Européens in 1868. Nagelmackers, who had succeeded in linking Paris and Constantinople by luxury train, found that once he got his esteemed passengers to the Ottoman imperial capital there was no suitable place for them to stay. So he built the hotel here in the section today called Tepebaşı. It opened in the 1890s, advertised as having 'a thoroughly healthy situation, being high up and isolated on all four sides', and 'overlooking the Golden Horn and the whole panorama of Stamboul'.

The Pera Palas Oteli is a grand place, with huge public rooms, a pleasant bar, a good but very pricey pastry shop, and a birdcage lift. Atatürk stayed here; his luxurious suite on the 2nd floor (room 101) is now a museum, preserved as it was when he used it (ask at the reception desk). Once you've taken a turn through the hotel, and perhaps had a drink in the bar or tea in the salon (not for the budget-minded), walk back up Asmalımescit Caddesi toward İstiklal Caddesi.

Just before reaching İstiklal, turn right onto Sofyalı Sokak, a typical Beyoğlu back street with backgammon and bridge parlours, small eateries, and shops selling a range of goods from antiques to electrical equipment.

Near Tünel Square Back on İstiklal Caddesi, you will notice, on your left, the **Royal Swedish Consulate**, once the Swedish embassy. Across İstiklal, the large pillared building was the Russian embassy before the larger building on İstiklal was built.

Beside the Swedish consulate, turn left downhill on Şahkulu Bostanı Sokak. At the base of the slope turn left, then right onto Serdari Ekrem Sokak to find the Anglican sanctuary of **Christ Church** (☎ 244 4828) at No 82. Designed by CE Street (who did London's Law Courts), its cornerstone was laid in 1858 by Lord Stratford de Redcliffe, known as 'The Great Elchi' (*elçi*: ambassador) because of his paramount influence in mid-19th-century Ottoman affairs. The church, dedicated in 1868 as the Crimean Memorial Church, is the largest of the city's Protestant churches. It had fallen into disrepair, but was restored and renamed in the mid-1990s. Ring the bell and with luck the caretaker will admit you for a look around.

Back up on İstiklal Caddesi, the road curves to the right into Tünel Square.

Tünel

İstanbul's short underground railway, the Tünel, was built by French engineers in 1875. It allowed European merchants to get from their offices in Galata to their homes in Pera without hiking up the steep hillside. Until the 1970s, the carriages were of dark wood with numerous coats of bright lacquer, and the signs within read, in Turkish, 'It is Requested that Cigarettes not be Smoked in the Cars'. A modernisation programme replaced them with rubber-tyred Paris metro-type steel trains in which the signs read 'No Smoking'.

The fare is US$0.40. Trains run as frequently as necessary during rush hours, about every five or 10 minutes at other times.

In Tünel Square, stop for a rest at *Café Gramofon* (☎ 293 0786), which echoes the style of the restored trams with its turn-of-the-century décor. Sandwiches, pastries, light meals and drinks are served all day every day.

Galata Mevlevihanesi Though the main road (İstiklal Caddesi) bears right as you come into Tünel Square, you should continue walking straight on along Galipdede Caddesi. On the left is the **Museum of Divan Literature** (Divan Edebiyatı Müzesi, ☎ 245 4141), originally a meeting-place for Mevlevi (Whirling) Dervishes, and preserved as such.

The museum is open from 9.30 am to 5 pm, closed on Monday. Admission costs US$0.75. The dervishes still occasionally whirl here, usually on the last Sunday of each month. Ask for current times and dates.

Dervish orders were banned in the early days of the republic because of their ultra-conservative religious politics, and this hall, once the Galata Whirling Dervish Monastery (Galata Mevlevi Tekkesi), now holds exhibits of *hattat* (Arabic calligraphy) and *Divan* (Ottoman) poetry.

The Whirling Dervishes took their name from the great sufi mystic and poet, Celaleddin Rumi (1207-73), called *Mevlana* (Our Leader) by his disciples. Sufis seek mystical communion with God through various means. For Mevlana, it was through a *sema* (ceremony) involving chants, prayers, music and a whirling dance. The whirling induced a trancelike state which made it easier for the mystic to seek spiritual union with God.

The Mevlevi *tarikat* (order), founded in Konya during the 13th century, flourished throughout the Ottoman Empire and survives in Konya even today. Like several other orders, the Mevlevis stressed the unity of humankind before God regardless of creed.

In Ottoman times, the Galata Mevlevihanesi (Whirling Dervish Hall) was open to all who wished to witness the sema, including foreign, non-Muslim visitors.

This modest frame *tekke* (a place where dervishes hold religious meetings and ceremonies) was restored between 1967 and 1972, but the first building here was erected by a high officer in the court of Sultan Beyazıt II in 1491. Its first *şeyh* (sheik, or leader) was Muhammed Şemai Sultan Divani, a grandson of the great Mevlana. The building burned in 1766, but was repaired that same year by Sultan Mustafa III.

In the midst of the city, this former monastery is an oasis of flowers and shady nooks. As you approach the building, notice the little graveyard on the left and its stones with graceful Ottoman inscriptions. The shapes atop the stones reflect the headgear of the deceased, each hat denoting a different religious rank. Note also the tomb of the sheik by the entrance passage, and the *şadırvan* (ablutions fountain).

Inside the tekke, the central area was for the whirling sema. Several times a year Mevlevi groups from Konya (now supposedly organised as 'social clubs') come to perform the sema here. In the galleries above, visitors sit and watch. Separate areas were set aside for the orchestra and for female visitors (behind the lattices).

Mevlâna & the Whirling Dervishes

In Celaleddin Rumi (Mevlâna to his followers), the Sultanate of Rum produced one of the world's great mystic philosophers. His poetic and religious work, mostly in Persian, the literary language of the day, is some of the most beloved and respected in the Islamic world.

Mevlâna was born in 1207 in Balkh, near Mazar-i Sharif in modern Afghanistan. His family fled the impending Mongol invasion by moving to Mecca and then to the Sultanate of Rum, reaching Konya by 1228. His father, Baha'uddin, was a noted preacher and Rumi became a brilliant student of Islamic theology. After his father's death in 1231, he studied in Aleppo and Damascus, returning to live in Konya by 1240.

In 1244 he met Mehmet Şemseddin Tebrizi, called Şemsi Tebrizi, one of his father's Sufi (Muslim mystic) disciples. Tebrizi had a profound effect on Rumi, who became devoted to him. Jealous of his overwhelming influence on their master, an angry crowd of Rumi's own disciples put Tebrizi to death in 1247. Stunned by the loss, Rumi withdrew from the world to meditate and, in this period, wrote his great poetic work, the *Mathnawi* (called *Mesnevi* in Turkish). He also wrote many *ruba'i* and *ghazal* poems, collected into his 'Great Opus', the *Divan-i Kebir*.

His ecumenical teachings were summed up in this beautiful verse:

Come, come again, whoever, whatever you may be, come
Heathen, fire worshipper, sinful of idolatry come;
Come even if you broke your penitence a hundred times;
Ours is not the portal of despair and misery, come.

Rumi died late in the day on 17 December 1273, the date now known as his 'wedding night' as he was finally united with Allah. His son, Sultan Veled, organised his followers into the brotherhood called the Mevlevi, or Whirling Dervishes.

Though the Mongol invasion put an end to Seljuk sovereignty in Anatolia, the Mevlevi order prospered. In the centuries following Mevlâna's death, over 100 dervish lodges were founded throughout the Ottoman domains in Turkey, Syria and Egypt, and numerous Ottoman sultans were Sufis of the Mevlevi order.

Under the Ottoman Empire, dervish orders exerted considerable influence on the country's political, social and economic life. In most cases their world-view was monarchist, arch-conservative and xenophobic. Committed to democracy and the separation of religion and state, Atatürk saw the dervishes as an obstacle to advancement for the Turkish people, so in 1925 he had the dervish orders proscribed. Many of the monasteries were converted into museums. The shrine of Mevlâna opened as a museum in 1927.

Though outlawed, several of the dervish orders survived as fraternal religious brotherhoods. The dervishes were revived in Konya in 1957 as a 'cultural association' intended to preserve a historical tradition. The annual festival of Mevlâna is officially encouraged as a popular rather than a religious event. Groups of dervishes are also sent on cultural exchange tours to other countries, performing the ceremony from Hawaii to Helsinki.

These days the dervishes may not be interested in politics but it would be naive to see them just a 'cultural association'. Young novices are recruited at puberty and devotion to the principles of the order can still be lifelong. Konya's dervishes whirl today to celebrate a great tradition and, as they have been doing for over 700 years, to worship and to seek mystical union with God. ■

Don't neglect the exhibits of calligraphy, writing instruments and other paraphernalia associated with this highly developed Ottoman art.

Back on Galipdede Caddesi Leaving the mevlevihane, turn left down Galipdede Caddesi, lined with shops selling books, Turkish and European musical instruments, plumbing supplies and cabinetmakers' necessities such as wood veneers. The hillside is covered with winding streets, passageways, alleys of stairs and European-style houses built mostly in the 19th century. There are also older 'Frankish' houses giving a glimpse of what life was like for the European émigrés who came to make their fortunes centuries ago.

A few minutes' walk along Galipdede Caddesi will bring you to Beyoğlu's oldest landmark, the Galata Tower.

Galata Tower

The cylindrical Galata Tower (Galata Kulesi, ☎ 245 1160) was the highpoint in the Genoese fortifications of Galata, and has been rebuilt many times. Today it holds a forgettable restaurant/nightclub as well as a memorable **panorama balcony** open to visitors from 9 am to 9 pm every day, for US$1.

In the shadow of the tower are woodworking shops, turners' lathes, workshops making veneer and other materials for interior decoration, and a few dusty antique stores. During the 19th century Galata had a large Sephardic Jewish population, but most of this community has now moved to more desirable residential areas. **Neve Shalom Synagogue**, a block north-east of the Galata Tower towards Şişhane Square on Büyük Hendek Caddesi, was the site of a brutal massacre by Arab gunmen during the summer of 1986. Now restored, it is used by İstanbul's Jewish community for weddings, funerals and other ceremonies.

From the Galata Tower, continue downhill on the street called Yüksek Kaldırım to reach Karaköy.

Karaköy

In order to avoid 'contamination' of their way of life, both the later Byzantine emperors and the Ottoman sultans relegated European traders to offices and residences in Galata, now called Karaköy. Under the later Byzantines, Genoese traders took over the town. Today Karaköy still harbours many shipping and commercial offices and banks, as well as small traders.

As you approach the Galata Bridge from Karaköy, the busy ferry docks and also the docks for Mediterranean cruise ships are to your left. To your right is a warren of little streets filled with hardware stores and plumbing-supply houses. Scattered throughout this neighbourhood are Greek and Armenian churches and schools and a large Ashkenazi synagogue, reminders of the time when virtually all of the empire's businesspeople were non-Muslims.

At the far end of the square from the Galata Bridge, right at the lower end of Yüksek Kaldırım, Voyvoda Caddesi (also called Bankalar Caddesi) leads up a slope to the right towards Şişhane Square. This street was the banking centre during the days of the empire, and many merchant banks still have headquarters or branches here. The biggest building was that of the Ottoman Bank, now a branch of the Turkish Republic's Central Bank. On 26 August 1896, Armenian revolutionaries seized the Ottoman Bank building and threatened to blow it up if their demands were not met. They were not, and the terrorists surrendered, but anti-Armenian riots following the incident caused many Armenian casualties.

Karaköy has busy bus stops, dolmuş queues and the lower station of the Tünel. To find the Tünel station descend into the hubbub of the square from Yüksek Kaldırım, and turn into the next major street on the right, Sabahattin Evren Caddesi. The Tünel is a few steps along this street, on the right, in a concrete bunker.

THE BOSPHORUS

The strait which connects the Black Sea and Sea of Marmara, 32 km long, from 500m to three km wide and 50 to 120m (average 60m) deep, has determined the history not only of İstanbul, but of the empires governed from this city.

In Turkish, the strait is the Boğaziçi, from *boğaz*, throat or strait, and *iç*, inside or interior: 'within the strait'. In earlier centuries it was one of the city's strongest defences. Until the age of armoured gunboats, the city was never seriously threatened from the sea.

The Bosphorus provides a convenient boundary for geographers. As it was a military bottleneck, armies marching from the east tended to stop on the eastern side, and those from the west on the western. So the western side was always more like Europe, the eastern more like Asia. Though the modern Turks think of themselves as Europeans, it is still common to say that Europe ends and Asia begins at the Bosphorus.

Except for the few occasions when the Bosphorus froze solid, crossing it always meant going by boat – until 1973. Late in that year, the Bosphorus Bridge, the fourth-longest in the world, was opened to travellers. For the first time in history there was a firm physical link across the straits from Europe to Asia. (Interestingly, there had been a plan for a bridge during the late years of the Ottoman Empire, but nothing came of it.)

Traffic was so heavy over the new bridge that it paid for itself in less than a decade. Now there is a second bridge, the Fatih Köprüsü (named after Mehmet the Conqueror, Mehmet Fatih), just north of Rumeli Hisar. A third bridge, even farther north, is already in the works.

History

Greek legend recounts that Zeus, unfaithful to his wife Hera in an affair with Io, tried to make up for it by turning his erstwhile lover into a cow. Hera, for good measure, provided a horsefly to sting Io on the rump and drive her across the strait. In ancient Greek, *bous* is cow, and *poros* is crossing place, giving us Bosphorus: the place where the cow crossed.

From earliest times the Bosphorus has been a maritime road to adventure. It is thought that Ulysses' travels brought him through the Bosphorus. Byzas, founder of Byzantium, explored these waters before the time of Jesus. Mehmet the Conqueror built two mighty fortresses at the strait's narrowest point so as to close it off to allies of the Byzantines. Each spring, enormous Ottoman armies would take several days to cross the Bosphorus on their way to campaigns in Asia. At the end of WWI, the defeated Ottoman capital cowered under the guns of Allied frigates anchored in the strait. When the republic was proclaimed, the last sultan of the Ottoman Empire snuck quietly down to the Bosphorus shore, boarded a launch, and sailed away to exile in a British man-of-war. And when Kemal Atatürk died, his body was taken aboard a man-of-war at Seraglio Point for the first part of its journey to Ankara.

Touring the Bosphorus

You could spend several days exploring the sights of the Bosphorus: five Ottoman palaces, four castles, Üsküdar and other Asian suburbs, and several interesting small towns, but one day will do in a pinch.

The essential feature of any Bosphorus tour is a cruise along the strait, though visits to particular buildings are best done by land, so a trip combining travel by both land and sea is best. Begin your explorations with a ferry cruise for a general view, then visit selected sites by bus and taxi.

A Bosphorus Cruise Though tour agencies and luxury hotels have private boats for cruises on the Bosphorus, it's considerably cheaper to go on one of the daily ferries. Traditionally operated by the government-controlled Denizyolları (Turkish Maritime Lines), the ferry network is slated for privatisation, so some of this information may have changed by the time you arrive.

Special Bosphorus cruise trips are operated twice daily on summer weekdays and Saturdays, and five times a day on summer Sundays and holidays. If you can't afford the time for the whole trip, you can get off at one of the four stops en route.

Reading the Ferry Schedule The special cruise ferries are called 'Boğaziçi Özel Gezi Seferleri'. Look for this heading on the schedules, which are posted in the waiting area of each ferry dock. By tradition, European ports of call are printed on the schedules in black, Asian ports in red.

Times will be close to the following, but check to be sure. Eminönü departures are on summer weekdays at 10.30 am, 12.30 and 2.10 pm; on Sundays and holidays they're at 10 and 11 am, noon, 1.30 and 3 pm. In winter,

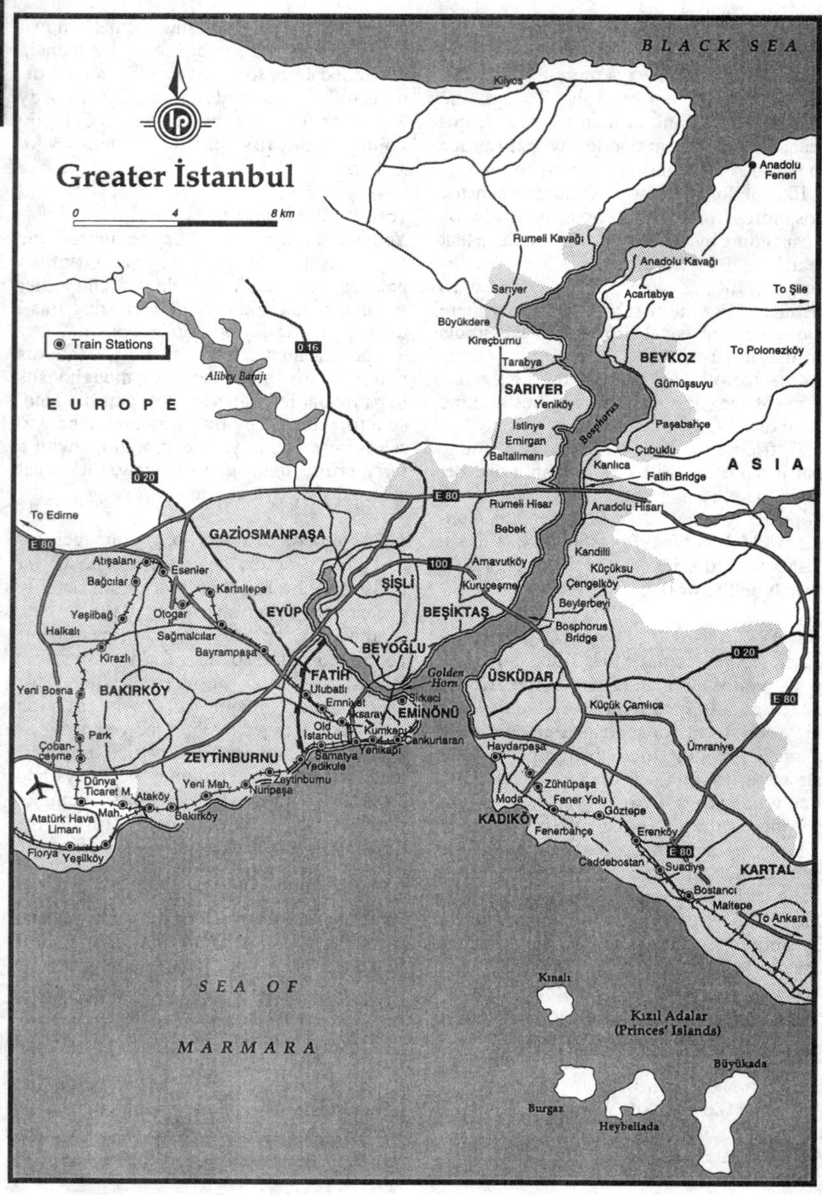
Greater İstanbul
0
4
8 km
Train Stations
BLACK SEA
EUROPE
ASIA
SEA OF MARMARA
Kilyos
Anadolu Feneri
Rumeli Kavağı
Anadolu Kavağı
Sarıyer
Acartabya
To Şile
Büyükdere
Kireçburnu
Tarabya
SARIYER
Yeniköy
İstinye
Emirgan
Baltalimanı
BEYKOZ
To Polonezköy
Gümüşsuyu
Paşabahçe
Çubuklu
Kanlıca
Fatih Bridge
Bosphorus
Alibey Barajı
To Edirne
Rumeli Hisar
Anadolu Hisarı
Bebek
GAZİOSMANPAŞA
Arnavutköy
Kuruçeşme
Kandilli
Küçüksu
Çengelköy
Beylerbeyi
Bosphorus Bridge
Atışalanı
Esenler
Bağcılar
Kartaltepe
Yeşilbağ
Otogar
Halkalı
Sağmalcılar
Bayrampaşa
Kirazlı
EYÜP
ŞİŞLİ
BEŞİKTAŞ
BEYOĞLU
FATİH
Golden Horn
ÜSKÜDAR
Yeni Bosna
BAKIRKÖY
Ulubatlı
Emniyet
Aksaray
Sirkeci
EMİNÖNÜ
Küçük Çamlıca
Park
Old İstanbul
Kumkapı
Cankurtaran
Yenikapı
Haydarpaşa
Ümraniye
Çobançeşme
ZEYTİNBURNU
Samatya
Yedikule
Zeytinburnu
Nuripaşa
Yeni Mah.
Dünya Ticaret M.
Ataköy
Mah.
Bakırköy
Zühtüpaşa
Moda
Fener Yolu
Göztepe
KADIKÖY
Fenerbahçe
Erenköy
Atatürk Hava Limanı
Florya
Yeşilköy
Caddebostan
Suadiye
KARTAL
Bostancı
Maltepe
To Ankara
Kınalı
Kızıl Adalar (Princes' Islands)
Büyükada
Burgaz
Heybeliada
E 80
O 16
O 20
100

there are daily departures at 10.30 am and 1.30 pm. Anadolu Kavağı departures are on summer weekdays at 1.30, 3 and 5.10 pm; Sunday departures are at 12.30, 1.30, 2.30, 4 and 5.30 pm. In winter daily departures are at 3 and 5.10 pm.

The fare for the 1¾-hour cruise from Eminönü to Anadolu Kavağı, or vice versa, is US$4. Buy your ticket only from a ticket-seller in a booth; ignore the touts. Prices are printed on all tickets. Save your ticket to show the ticket-collector when you leave the ferry at your destination. The special cruise ferries call at only five docks: Beşiktaş on the European shore, Kanlıca on the Asian shore, Yeniköy and Sarıyer on the European shore, and Anadolu Kavağı on the Asian shore (the turn-around point).

If you visit in the cooler months and the special ferries aren't running, look at the schedule for the heading 'Boğaz'a Gidiş' (To the Bosphorus), and also 'Boğaz'dan Geliş' (From the Bosphorus), for long-distance boats that make good substitutes. The boats run southward down the Bosphorus in the morning rush hour, and northward up the Bosphorus in the evening.

The special cruise ferries are popular, and they fill up early and quickly. It's a good idea to get to the dock 30 minutes or more before departure time to seize a seat. Keep the sun in mind when you choose your place; you may want some shade as you head north.

Cross-Bosphorus Ferries At several points along the Bosphorus, passenger ferries run between the European and Asian shores, allowing you to cross easily from one side to the other. If you can't catch one of these ferries, you can often hire a boater to motor you across the Bosphorus for a few dollars.

Southernmost are the routes from Eminönü, Kabataş and Beşiktaş in Europe to Üsküdar in Asia. See Sights on the Asian Shore for details.

Another ring route is from Kanlıca to Anadolu Hisarı on the Asian shore, thence across the Bosphorus to Bebek on the European shore. Departures from Kanlıca are at 8.30, 9.30, 10.30 and 11.30 am, and 12.30, 2.30, 4, 5.15 and 6.15 pm. The voyage to Bebek takes 25 minutes and costs US$0.50.

Other ring ferries run from İstinye on the European side to Beykoz and Paşabahçe on the Asian side. Yet another ring ferry operates from Sarıyer and Rumeli Kavağı in Europe to Anadolu Kavağı in Asia.

Sights on the European Shore

If you've cruised up the Bosphorus on a ferry, catch any bus or dolmuş headed south. Mention the name of your destination ('Rumeli Hisar' for example) to the driver so they know where to stop.

Coming from Aksaray, Sultanahmet or Eminönü to visit the sights along the Bosphorus, your best bet is to take a bus or dolmuş to reach Dolmabahçe, one km down the hill from Taksim Square. From Taksim, the downhill walk is short (about 10 minutes) and pleasant with views of the Bosphorus and the palace. Starting in Taksim Square, walk towards the Atatürk Cultural Centre (Opera House). As you stand facing it, the tree-lined, divided street on your right is İnönü Caddesi, formerly called Gümüşsuyu Caddesi. It leads directly to Dolmabahçe. On the right-hand side of İnönü Caddesi, just out of Taksim, are dolmuşes going to Beşiktaş, which will drop you at Dolmabahçe if you want to ride.

Coming from other parts of the city, catch a bus that goes via Eminönü and Karaköy to Beşiktaş. Any bus heading out of Karaköy along the Bosphorus shore road will take you to Dolmabahçe. Get off at the Kabataş stop. Just north of the stop is the Dolmabahçe mosque, and beyond it the palace.

Dolmabahçe Palace For centuries the padişah, the Ottoman sultan, had been the envy of other monarchs. Cultured, urbane, sensitive, courageous; controller of vast territories, great wealth and invincible armies and navies, he was the Grand Turk. The principalities, city-states and kingdoms of Europe, Africa and the Near East stood in fear of a Turkish conquest. Indeed, the Turks conquered all of North Africa, parts

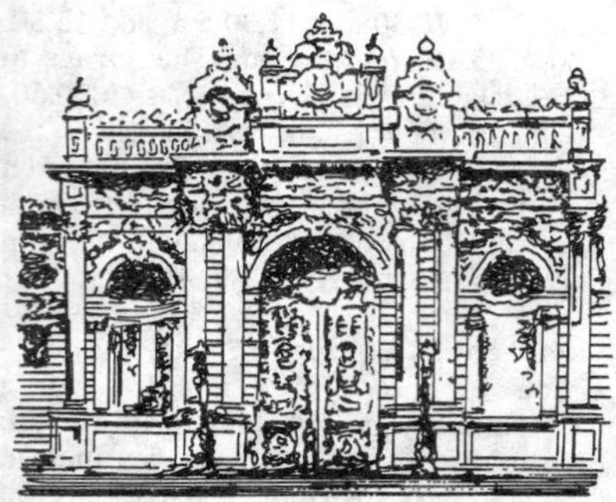

In building Dolmabahçe ('filled in garden'), Sultan Abdülmecit was hoping to create a 'European-style' marble palace. The result is partly European, partly oriental. It is an example of the turn towards European models and ways of doing things which occurred in the 19th century.

of southern Italy, and eastern Europe to the gates of Vienna. The opulent Dolmabahçe Palace might be seen as an apt expression of this Ottoman glory – but it's not.

History Dolmabahçe was built between 1843 and 1856, when the homeland of the once-mighty padişah had become the 'Sick Man of Europe'. His many peoples, aroused by a wave of European nationalism, were in revolt; his wealth was mostly mortgaged to, or under the control of, European bankers; his armies, while still considerable, were obsolescent and disorganised. The western, European, Christian way of life had triumphed over the eastern, Asian, Muslim one. Attempting to turn the tide, 19th-century sultans turned to European models, modernising the army and civil service, granting autonomy to subject peoples, and adopting – sometimes wholesale – European ways of doing things.

The name Dolmabahçe, 'filled-in garden', dates from the reign of Sultan Ahmet I (1607-17), when a little cove here was filled in and an imperial pleasure kiosk built on it. Other wooden buildings followed, but all burned to the ground in 1814. Sultan Abdülmecit, whose favourite architects were scions of an Armenian family named Balyan, wanted a 'European-style' marble palace. What he got is partly European, partly oriental, and certainly sumptuous and heavily overdecorated.

Admission & Tours Look for the ornate **clock tower** between Dolmabahçe Camii and the palace. The gate near the clock tower is the one you enter. The palace is open from 9 am to noon and from 1.30 to 4.30 pm, closed Monday and Thursday. Admission costs US$5. There is a camera fee, but you should leave your camera at the door rather than pay the fee as the palace interior is too dark to photograph (even with fast film) and flash and tripod are not allowed. Rather, take your photos from the small garden near the clock tower. The palace gardens are very pretty. The fence along the Bosphorus and the palace facade go on for almost half a km.

You must take a guided tour which lasts between 60 and 90 minutes. Get here and get in line early: even so, you may queue for an hour in high summer because of the crowd. Make sure the palace tour leader will be speaking a language you understand, though what the guide has to say is not always worth hearing.

Touring the Palace The tour passes through opulent public and private rooms, into a harem with steel doors, past numerous Sèvres vases and Bohemian chandeliers, and up a staircase with a crystal balustrade. One room was used by the fat Sultan Abdülaziz (1861-76) who needed an enormously large bed. The magnificent throne room, used in 1877 for the first meeting of the Ottoman Chamber of Deputies, has a chandelier that weighs over 4000 kg.

Don't set your watch by any of the palace clocks, all of which are stopped at 9.05 am, the moment at which Kemal Atatürk died in Dolmabahçe on the morning of 10 November 1938. You will be shown the small bedroom which he used during his last days. Each year on 10 November, at 9.05 am, the entire country observes a moment of silence in commemoration of the republic's founder.

Dolmabahçe's **Aviary & Art Gallery** (Kuşluk ve Sanat Galerisi) is on the inland side of the palace, entered from Dolmabahçe Caddesi from 9.30 am to 4 pm (closed Monday and Thursday). This section of the palace, of less interest, was the aviary, with its birdhouse and cages now restored, and a pretty garden restaurant added. The art gallery is a single corridor over 100m long lined with paintings by 19th and 20th-century Ottoman artists (many of them from the nobility).

Maritime Museum When you've finished at the aviary and gallery, turn right (north) and walk for five minutes to the suburb of **Beşiktaş**, sometimes called Barbaros Hayrettin Paşa. The Deniz Müzesi, or Maritime Museum, is on the Bosphorus shore just south of the flyover in Beşiktaş. Among its exhibits are an outdoor display of cannons (including Selim the Grim's 21-tonne monster) and a statue of Barbaros Hayrettin Paşa (1483-1546), the famous Turkish admiral known also as Barbarossa who conquered North Africa for Süleyman the Magnificent. The admiral's tomb, designed by Sinan, is close by.

History Though the Ottoman Empire is most remembered for its conquests on land, its maritime power was equally impressive. During the reign of Süleyman the Magnificent (1520-66), the eastern Mediterranean was virtually an Ottoman lake. The sultan's navies cut a swath in the Indian Ocean as well. Sea power was instrumental in the conquests of the Aegean coasts and islands, Egypt and North Africa. Discipline, well-organised supply and good ship design contributed to Ottoman victories.

However the navy, like the army and the government, lagged behind the west in modernisation during the later centuries. The great battle which broke the spell of Ottoman naval invincibility was fought in 1571 at Lepanto, in the Gulf of Patras off the Greek coast. (Cervantes fought on the Christian side and was badly wounded.) Though the Turkish fleet was destroyed, the sultan quickly produced another, partly with the help of rich Greek shipowners who were his subjects.

Admission There are two parts to the museum (☎ 261 0040), one entered from the main road, the other from the Bosphorus shore. You must pay an admission fee for each part. It is open from 9.30 am to 5 pm, closed on Monday and Tuesday. Admission costs US$1 in each part.

Exhibits In the Bosphorus section of the museum, be sure to see the sleek, swift imperial barges in which the sultan would speed up and down the Bosphorus from palace to palace (in those days the roads were not very smooth or fast). Over 30m in length but only two metres wide, with 13 banks of oars, the barges were obviously the rocket boats of their day. The ones with latticework screens were for the imperial ladies. There's also a war galley with 24 pairs of oars.

You may also be curious to see a replica of the *Map of Piri Reis*, an early Ottoman map (1513) which purports to show the coasts and continents of the New World. It's assumed that Piri Reis (Captain Piri) got hold of the work of Columbus for his map. The original map is in Topkapı Palace; this one is on the wall above the door as you enter the Bosphorus section. Copies are on sale.

Places to Eat A Beşiktaş restaurant in the middle range is *Hanedan* (☎ 260 4854), near the ferry terminal, just north of the Maritime Museum. Seafood is the speciality, but meats and traditional dishes are cheaper. It's clean and pleasant, and you'll pay about US$8 to US$10 for a meal.

Ihlamur Kasrı Sheltered in a narrow valley inland to the north of Dolmabahçe Palace and the Maritime Museum is the Ihlamur Kasrı (UHH-lah-moor kahss-ruh), or Kiosk of the Linden Tree (☎ 261 2991), surrounded by a maze of twisting streets.

The park and its two small, ornate imperial pavilions are open from 9.30 am to 4 pm every day except Monday and Thursday.

Admission to the park and kiosks costs US$0.75, or US$0.25 if you just want to stroll through the park. The fee for using a camera is US$6. The easiest way to find this place in its maze of streets is to take a taxi which, from Dolmabahçe or Beşiktaş, should cost only US$1 or so. Bus 26 (from Dikilitaş to Eminönü) departs from Eminönü, stops at Karaköy, Dolmabahçe and Beşiktaş, before heading inland to the Ihlamur stop and continuing to Dikilitaş (DEE-kee-LEE-tahsh), which is not far past Ihlamur. Other buses are 26A, 26B or 26C.

Once a quiet, sheltered valley neighbouring the imperial palaces of Yıldız and Dolmabahçe, the site now hums with the noise of traffic and is surrounded by modern apartment blocks. It's not difficult to imagine, however, what it must have been like when these two miniature palaces stood here alone, in the midst of a forest. Near the entry gate the park is open and formal, with grassy lawns, ornamental trees and a quiet pool. To the right behind the Maiyet Köşkü the gardens are more rustic, shady and cool, with naturalistic spring-like fountains.

As you enter, look across the pool to find the **Merasim Köşkü**, or Sultan's Kiosk, built on the orders of Sultan Abdülmecit between 1849 and 1855 by Nikogos Balyan, of the family of imperial architects. As you enter, a guide will approach to offer you a free guided tour. Up the marble stairway and through the ornate door is the Hall of Mirrors, with crystal from Bohemia and vases from France. The Baroque décor includes patterns of shells, flowers, vines, fruits and lots of gold leaf.

The music room which is to the right of the entrance has precious Hereke fabrics on the chairs and an enamelled coal-grate fireplace painted with flowers. Similarly beautiful fireplaces ornament the other rooms; the music rooms walls are faux-marble.

The main appliance in the Imperial Water Closet is of the traditional flat Turkish type, demonstrating that in here even the sultan was dethroned.

The room to the left of the entrance was a reception salon with a sofa-throne and faux-marble decoration of plaster with gold flecks. The tour ends downstairs, where displays of photographs show details of the restoration work carried out in the 1980s.

The **Maiyet Köşkü**, or Retinue Kiosk, was for the sultan's suite of attendants, guests or harem. It's now a teahouse serving tea, coffee and snacks (for around US$2). Downstairs are toilets and a shop selling books and other publications.

Çirağan Palace Unsatisfied with the architectural exertions of his predecessor at Dolmabahçe, Sultan Abdülaziz (1861-76) built his own grand residence at Çirağan on the Bosphorus shore, only a km north of Dolmabahçe, replacing an earlier wooden palace. The architect was the self-same Balyan as for Dolmabahçe. The sultan didn't get to live here much, however. Instead, it served as a detention place for his successor, the mentally unbalanced Sultan Murat V, who was deposed before he had even reigned a year. Later the palace housed the Ottoman Chamber of Deputies and Senate in 1909, but in 1910 it was destroyed by fire under suspicious circumstances.

From the Maritime Museum and the flyover in Beşiktaş, you can walk north for 10 minutes, or catch a bus or dolmuş heading north along the shore, to reach the entrance to Yıldız Park (bus stop Galatasaray Lisesi). Before you reach the entrance, you'll be passing Çirağan Palace on your right. The palace, now restored as the posh Çirağan Palace Hotel Kempinski, is hidden from the road by a high wall, though you can get a glimpse of it through the huge gates. If you're dressed like an affluent tourist you can even go in and take a turn around the sumptuous hotel and its grounds.

Yıldız Palace & Park Sultan Abdülhamid II (1876-1909), who succeeded Murat V, also had to build his own palace. He added considerably to the structures built by earlier sultans in Yıldız Park, on the hillside above Çirağan.

The park is open from 9 am to 6 pm every

day; admission costs US$0.25 for pedestrians, US$1 for cars (including taxis). If you come to the park by taxi, have it take you up the steep slope to the Şale Köşkü. You can visit the other kiosks on the walk down. A taxi from Taksim Square to the top of the hill might cost around US$5 or US$6.

The park, with its kiosks, had become derelict, but was beautifully restored by Turing in the 1980s, under lease from the city government. In 1994 a newly elected city government declined to renew the lease, and the park is now rapidly returning to its earlier state of neglect.

The park began life as the imperial reserve for Çirağan Palace, but when Abdülhamid built the Şale Köşkü, largest of the park's surviving structures, the park served that palace. Under Abdülhamid, the park was planted with rare and exotic trees, shrubs and flowers, and was provided with carefully tended paths and a superior electric lighting and drainage system.

Pavilion & Malta Kiosks As you toil up the hill along the road, near the top of the slope to the left you'll see the Çadır Köşkü (Pavilion Kiosk), an ornate kiosk built between 1865 and 1870 as a place for the sultan to enjoy the view, rest from a walk, and have a cup of tea or coffee.

To the right (north) as you hike up the road from the gate are two greenhouses, the **Kış Bahçesi** (Winter Garden) and the **Yeşil Sera** (Green Nursery), and the Malta Köşkü. The Malta Kiosk (☎ 260 2752), restored in 1979, is now a café serving refreshments, alcoholic drinks and light meals. The view from here is the best in the park, much better than that at the Çadır Köşkü. If you sit down to a plate of grilled lamb and then finish up with something sweet, your bill will add up to US$4 to US$6.

Also to the right is the **Yıldız Porselen Fabrikası**, or Yıldız Porcelain Factory, constructed to manufacture dinner services for the palace. It still operates and is open to visitors.

Chalet Kiosk At the very top of the hill, enclosed by a lofty wall, is the Şale Köşkü, a 'guesthouse' put up in 1882 and expanded in 1898 by Abdülhamid for use by Kaiser Wilhelm II of Germany during a state visit. You must pay a separate admission fee of US$4 to see the Chalet Kiosk (☎ 258-3080) which is open from 9.30 am to 4 pm daily and is closed on Monday.

I expect the Kaiser had enough space to move in, as the 'chalet' has 64 rooms. After his imperial guest departed, the sultan became quite attached to his 'rustic' creation, and decided to live here himself, forsaking the more lavish but less well-protected palaces on the Bosphorus shore. Abdülhamid was paranoid, and for good reason. Fate determined that his fears would come true. He was deposed, left this wooden palace in April 1909 and boarded a special train which took him to house arrest in Ottoman Salonika (today Thessaloniki, in Greece). He was later allowed by the Young Turks' government to return to İstanbul and live out his years in Beylerbeyi Palace, on the Asian shore of the Bosphorus.

This place was to be associated with more dolorous history. The last sultan of the Ottoman Empire, Mehmet V (Vahideddin), lived here until, at 6 am on 11 November 1922, he and his first chamberlain, bandmaster, doctor, two secretaries, valet, barber and two eunuchs accompanied by trunks full of jewels, gold and antiques, boarded two British Red Cross ambulances for the secret journey to the naval dockyard at Tophane. There they boarded the British battleship HMS *Malaya* for a trip into exile, ending the Ottoman Empire forever. On the way to the quay one of the tyres on the sultan's ambulance went flat; while it was being changed, the 'Shadow of God on Earth' quaked, fearing that he might be discovered.

In the republican era, the Chalet Kiosk has served as a guesthouse for visiting heads of state, including Charles de Gaulle, Pope Paul VI and the Empress Soraya of Iran. As you enter the palace, a guide will approach you to give you the tour, which is required.

The first section you visit was the original chalet, built in 1882. The first room on the tour was used by Abdülhamid's mother for her religious devotions, the second was her guest reception room, with a very fine mosaic tabletop. Then comes a women's resting room, and afterwards a tearoom with furniture marked with a gold star on a blue background, which reminds one that this is the 'star' *(yıldız)* palace.

In 1898 the chalet was expanded, and the older section became the harem (with steel doors), while the new section was the selamlık. In the selamlık are a bathroom with tiles from the Yıldız Porcelain Factory, and several reception rooms, one of which has furniture made by Abdülhamid himself, an accomplished woodworker. The grand hall of the selamlık is vast, its floor covered by a 7½-tonne Hereke carpet woven just for this room. So huge is the rug that it had to be brought in through the far (north) wall before the building was finished and the wall was closed.

Ceremonial Kiosk Other buildings at Yıldız include the Merasim Köşkü, or Ceremonial Kiosk and barracks. Part of the kiosk was restored in 1988 and opened as the **İstanbul Şehir Müzesi** (İstanbul City Museum), open daily except Thursday from 9 am to 4.30 pm; admission costs US$1. It's reached from Barbaros Bulvarı, the road along the south side of the park, not from within the park itself.

Yıldız Palace Museum The carpentry shop *(marangozhane)* at Yıldız, where Sultan Abdülhamid II liked to lay down the burdens of rank and office, pick up chisel and malet and make furniture, is now a museum (☎ 258 3080, extension 280; closed Monday and Tuesday). It houses rare porcelain vases and urns, and some of the sultan's joinery projects.

Onward Transport After seeing Yıldız, you can take a bus or dolmuş north to Bebek and Rumeli Hisar, or return to Beşiktaş to catch a shuttle ferry over to Üsküdar, on the Asian side, in order to continue your sightseeing. The ferries operate every 15 or 20 minutes in each direction, from 6 am to midnight. There are also boats between Üsküdar and Eminönü. Ferries going to Eminönü may bear the sign 'Köprü' or 'Bridge', meaning the Galata Bridge.

Ortaköy Literally 'middle village', this Bosphorus suburb has an interesting ethnic history in which church, synagogue and mosque coexist peacefully in its narrow streets. Today it is a trendy gathering-place for the young and hip, with art galleries, chic café-bars, and boutiques selling antiques, carpets and jewellery. On warm Sundays artisans display their wares in the narrow streets in an impromptu arts-and-crafts show.

At the water's edge by the ornate mosque called the **Ortaköy Camii** are terrace cafés with open-air tables and views of the Bosphorus and the mosque. Officially named the Büyük Mecidiye Camii, the eclectic-Baroque mosque is the work of Nikogos Balyan, architect of Dolmabahçe Palace, who designed it for Sultan Abdülmecit in 1854. Within the mosque hang several masterful examples of Arabic calligraphy executed by the sultan, who was an accomplished calligrapher.

Get out of the bus or dolmuş at Osmanzade Sokak, near the doorway to the Etz Ahayim Synagogue, and walk eastward. *İlhami'nin Yeri* (İlhami's Place), on the left, is a full-service restaurant specialising in seafood. Meat, fish and kalamar (squid) dishes are usually available for about US$2.50 to US$4 each. Osmanzade Sokak has other café-bar-restaurants as well.

The streets near Osmanzade Sokak have more browsing, eating and drinking possibilities. On Yelkovan Sokak, look for the *Çardak Café* and the *Café-Bar Maria*, serving cappuccino at outdoor tables in summer, sıcak şarap (mulled wine) in winter.

On Hazine Sokak, *Alaturka* (☎ 258 7924) was among the first café-bars to open after Ortaköy's renaissance. Here you can have light meals such as gözleme (folded pastry with filling), mantı (Turkish ravioli) or salad bar for about US$2.50; no alcohol is served.

Andon (☎ 260 8298), Yelkovan Sokak 10,

is a café-bar in which to see, be seen, and meet the locals.

İskele Caddesi has several places to eat and enjoy. *Myott* (☎ 258 9317), İskele Caddesi 14, is popular for its light meals and strong dark-roast Italian coffee. The *Sis Bar* (☎ 259 4858), İskele Caddesi 4/6, features loud rock music until 4 am on weekends.

Bebek & Rumeli Hisar Bebek is a prosperous suburb of İstanbul with a surprising foreign and academic presence because of Boğaziçi Üniversitesi (Bosphorus University). A ring ferry service here joins Bebek with Kanlıca and Anadolu Hisarı on the Asian shore.

Just north of Bebek is Rumeli Hisar, the Fortress of Europe. The fortress is open from 9.30 am to 5 pm daily; closed on Monday. Admission costs US$2.50, half-price on Sundays and holidays. Within the walls are park-like grounds, an open-air theatre and the minaret of a ruined mosque. Stairs lead up to the ramparts and towers.

Here at the narrowest part of the Bosphorus, Mehmet the Conqueror had this fortress built in a mere four months during 1452, in preparation for his planned siege of Byzantine Constantinople. To speed its completion in line with his impatience to conquer Constantinople, Mehmet the Conqueror ordered each of his three viziers to take responsibility for one of the three main towers. If the tower's construction was not completed on schedule, the vizier would pay with his life, or so legend has it. Not surprisingly, the work was completed on time, with Mehmet's three generals competing fiercely with one another to finish.

Once completed, Rumeli Hisar, in concert with Anadolu Hisarı on the Asian shore just opposite, controlled all traffic on the Bosphorus, and cut the city off from resupply by sea from the north.

The mighty fortress's useful military life lasted less than one year. After the conquest of Constantinople, it was used as a glorified Bosphorus toll booth for a while, then as a barracks, later as a prison, and finally as an open-air theatre, but never again as a fortress.

Above the town you'll notice the New England 19th-century-style architecture of the **Boğaziçi Üniversitesi** (Bosphorus University) on a hilltop above the town of Bebek. Founded as Robert College in the mid-19th century by the American Board of Foreign Missions, the college had an important influence on the modernisation of political, social, economic and scientific thought in Turkey. Though donated by the board to the Turkish Republic in the early 1970s, instruction is still in English and Turkish.

Places to Eat Just north of Rumeli Hisarı on the shore is *Han Karaca* (☎ 265 2968), Yahya Kemal Caddesi 10, with fine Bosphorus views, excellent fish and squid, and a plethora of mezes; avoid shrimp which are, as everywhere in Turkey, very expensive for what you get. Expect to pay US$12 to US$24 per person with rakı.

'S' Restoran (☎ 287 0150), Vezirköşkü Sokak 2, Bebek, is on the upper floor of a fuel station on the coast road. Don't let this put you off, the imaginative Chinese, French, Russian and Turkish dishes are excellent, as is the view of the Bosphorus. Make reservations for lunch (from noon to 4 pm) or dinner (7 pm to midnight); closed on Sunday. Dinner for two can cost as high as US$75 – higher if you're reckless.

Emirgan & Yeniköy Each spring a **tulip festival** takes place in Emirgan, a wealthy suburb north of the Fatih Bridge. North of Emirgan, at İstinye, is a cove with a dry dock. A ring ferry service runs from İstinye to Beykoz and Paşabahçe on the Asian shore and will soon be replaced by a third Bosphorus bridge.

On a point jutting out from the European shore is Yeniköy, first settled in classical times. This place later became a favourite summer resort, indicated by the lavish 19th-century Ottoman *yalı*, or seaside villa, of the one-time grand vizier, Sait Halim Paşa. Not too many of these luxurious wooden villas survive. Fire destroyed many. Economics and desire for modern conveniences caused many others to be torn down before preservation laws were promulgated. Today it is against the law to remove a yalı from the Bosphorus – it must either be repaired or rebuilt.

İstinye Continue northward from Bebek, under the Fatih Bridge, to the village of İstinye and the famous restaurant called *Süreyya* (☎ 263 8385), İstinye Caddesi 26. The cuisine is superb and varied, with Russian, Turkish and continental dishes to choose from. Chicken Kiev is a favourite here, but there's also good borsch and various French-inspired dishes. Hours are from noon to 3 pm and from 8 pm to midnight, reservations are essential, and dinner for two can hit US$100 unless you're careful.

Tarabya Originally called Therapeia for its healthful climate, the little cove of Tarabya has been a favourite summer watering place for İstanbul's well-to-do for centuries. Little restaurants specialising in fish ring the cove. North of the village are some of the old summer embassies of foreign powers. When the heat and fear of disease increased in the warm months, foreign ambassadors and their staff would retire to palatial residences, complete with lush gardens, on this shore. The region for such embassy residences extended north to the village of Büyükdere.

Places to Eat On the south side of the cove is the *Garaj Restaurant* (☎ 262 0032), Yeniköy Caddesi 30, where the fish is fresh and in vast array, but the waiters have a tendency to load your table (and your bill) with items you did not order. A delicious seafood lunch or dinner here costs from US$18 to US$30 per person, wine, tax and tip included.

On the north side of the cove, the inland side of the road is lined solidly with little seafood restaurants. All have streetside tables, but the traffic makes these unpleasant at times.

Palet 1 (☎ 262 0118), Kefeliköy Caddesi 110, is small and overdecorated, but it dares to be different by offering seafood souffle, shrimp in a Mexican barbecue sauce, octopus in a cheese sauce, and even paella. In trying these exotic items, I would not expect authenticity, though they will be tasty enough. A fish dinner is about US$15 or US$20 per person, meat about half that, all included. The Palet's sister establishments, *Palet 2* and *Palet 3*, provide additional seating when Palet 1 is heavily booked.

Sarıyer The villagers of Sarıyer have occupied themselves for most of their history by fishing in the currents of the Bosphorus. Fishing is still a pastime and a livelihood here, and Sarıyer is justly noted for its several good fish restaurants. Turn right as you leave the ferry dock, stay as close to the shore as possible, and you will soon come to the village's active fish market and several fish restaurants – both cheap and expensive. Dolmuşes for the beach at **Kilyos** leave from a point just to the north of the ferry dock.

Dolmuş minibuses link Sarıyer and Taksim Square (US$1). The stop in Taksim is on Mete Caddesi north of the Gezi Oteli, east of the Hyatt and Inter-Continental hotels.

Sadberk Hanım Museum Of particular interest in Sarıyer is the Sadberk Hanım Museum (☎ 242 3813), Piyasa Caddesi 27-29, Büyükdere, a private museum of Anatolian antiquities and Ottoman heirlooms from one of Turkey's richest families. If you come to Sarıyer by ferry, look to the left as you leave the dock, and you will see a yellow wooden house on the shore road about 300m to the south – that's the museum. It's open in summer from 10.30 am to 6 pm, in winter from 10 am to 5 pm; it's closed on Wednesday all year. Admission costs US$1. Plaques are in English and Turkish.

Sadberk Hanım, who gathered the collections now housed in the museum, was the wife of Mr Vehbi Koç, one of the country's foremost businesspeople, who made much of his fortune as the Turkish agent for many international firms such as Coca-Cola, Avis and IBM. After her death in the 1970s, the family established the museum in this graceful old Bosphorus yalı, once the summer residence of Manuk Azaryan Efendi, an Armenian who was speaker of the upper house of the Ottoman parliament.

The original museum building houses artefacts and exhibits from Turkey's Islamic past. The non-Islamic collections are displayed in a separate building at the rear.

In my opinion, the most fascinating of the museum's collections are those in the original yalı, dating from Ottoman times: worry beads of solid gold; golden, bejewelled tobacco boxes and watches (one bears the sultan's monogram in diamonds); beautiful Kütahya pottery; even a table that once belonged to Napoleon (he's pictured on it, surrounded by his generals). A number of rooms in the great old house have been arranged and decorated in Ottoman style – the style of the ruling class, obviously. There's a sumptuous maternity room with embroidered cloth and lots of lace, a salon with all the paraphernalia of the Ottoman coffee ceremony, and a third set up as a circumcision room. A display case holds a fine collection of Ottoman spoons (the prime dining utensil) made from tortoiseshell, ebony, ivory and other precious materials.

The collections in the new building include very choice artefacts dating from as early as the 6th century BC, and continuing through Roman and Byzantine times. There is also a well-chosen collection of Chinese celadon ware from the 14th to 16th centuries, later Chinese blue-and-white porcelain, and some 18th-century Chinese porcelain made specifically for the Ottoman market.

Places to Eat *Mücahit Körfez Balık Lokantası*, Orta Çeşme Caddesi, is upscale, with live fish in aquaria, fresh fish laid out on beds of crushed ice, baskets of live crabs and lobsters, buckets of shellfish and shrimp. Try to get a table next to the windows overlooking the Bosphorus, choose a fish, determine the price, then order wine, soup or mezes and salads. Expect to pay from US$25 to US$40 per person, all in, for dinners based on fish in season. Lobster and fish out of season can be breathtakingly expensive.

There's also *Aquarius* (☎ 271 3434), Cami Arkası, in the old fish market, in a setting that's certainly appropriate. It's open daily from noon to midnight, and charges from US$28 to US$30 for a full meal.

Rumeli Kavağı North of Rumeli Kavağı, the village farthest north on the European shore, is a military zone. The sleepy little town gets most of its excitement from the arrival and departure of ferries. There is a little public beach named **Altınkum** near the village.

Kilyos From Sarıyer you can get a bus (No 151, US$0.50) or dolmuş ('Sarıyer-Kilyos', US$0.65) to Kilyos, on the Black Sea coast. The 20-minute ride takes you up into the hills past posh villas built by Arab oil potentates and traders, and little impromptu open-air roadside restaurants featuring *kuzu çevirme* (spit-roasted lamb). I can recommend the lamb highly. These places are usually open every day in high summer, but only on weekends in the off season. Prices range from low to moderate.

There are some little pensions, hotels and guesthouses in Kilyos, open during the summer for beach fanciers. The best beach is the fenced one in front of the Turban Kilyos Moteli, open daily in warm weather from 8 am to 6 pm; it's very crowded on summer weekends, but not bad during the week. You can use it without staying at the motel if you pay US$3.50 per person; a private changing cabin for two costs US$7.50. Parking costs US$2, so if you drive, park elsewhere in the village and walk over to the beach.

If you go to Kilyos for swimming, keep in mind that the waters of the Black Sea are fairly chilly. More importantly, there is a deadly undertow on many beaches. Swim only in protected areas or where there is an attentive lifeguard, and don't swim alone.

Places to Stay On summer weekends all Kilyos lodgings are likely to be filled from advance reservations. You will have a better chance of finding a room if you plan your visit for the middle of the week, reserve ahead, or visit outside the high season (which lasts from mid-July to the end of August).

Yuva Motel (☎ (212) 201 1043), Kilyos, İstanbul, near the beach, has a few rooms with views of the sea. All rooms have little porches, but the rooms on the sea side of the motel are preferable. The price for a small double room with private shower, breakfast included, is US$28.

Yalı Pansiyon (☎ (212) 201 1018), Kilyos, İstanbul, is a tidy little place at the eastern end of the beach. The rooms are simple, neat and clean, but have no running water; washing facilities are down the hall. Rooms on the lower level, with no sea view, cost US$24 a double; upstairs, with sea views, the price is US$32 a double. The upstairs rooms have one double and one single bed each, perfect for a couple with one child. The pension's kitchen facilities are available for your use.

The two-star *Kilyos Kale Hotel* (☎ (212) 201 1818, fax 201 1823), Kale Caddesi 78, is up the hill from the centre of the village. This modern, comfortable hotel has 36 rooms with bath, many of which have beach and sea views; there's a fine view from the restaurant as well. Rooms cost US$30/40 a single/double; add US$4.50 more per person for breakfast, US$10 per person for breakfast and dinner, or US$13 per person for all three meals.

Gurup Hotel (☎ (212) 201 1194, fax 201 1266), Kale Caddesi 21/1, has a nice hillside location with fine views of the sea and the beach, a sunny patio and a vine-covered restaurant. It's a small place with two stars, 42 rooms, each with twin beds, a private shower and grape-vine-covered porch with sea view (in late summer you can pick the grapes). The aptly named Gurup (abundant) is a favourite with British holiday groups. You must take breakfast and dinner with your room; the price for room and half board is US$44 a double.

The two-star *Kilyos Erzurumlu Motel* (☎ (212) 201 1003, fax 201 1108), Kale Caddesi 77, is next door to the Kilyos Kale Hotel. It's somewhat older but tidy and quiet. Rooms have splendid views and cost US$40 a double with breakfast.

The largest hostelry in Kilyos is the *Kilyos Moteli* (☎ (212) 201 1480, fax 201 1028), right on the beach. Formerly run by the quasi-governmental Turban chain, the hotel is now being transferred to private control; prices and other details may change. At present, the several two-storey motel buildings hold 144 rooms. Prices depend upon the number of beds, the position of the building (whether it's nearer or farther from the beach), and the season of the year. In high summer prices range from US$45 to US$50 a single, US$68 to US$78 a double, breakfast and dinner included.

Getting There & Away Kilyos is an hour's drive (35 km) north of the Galata Bridge. To get there from Taksim Square, you can take bus 40 ('Taksim-Sarıyer') and then bus 151 ('Sarıyer-Kilyos') for a total cost of US$0.85, or a dolmuş minibus from Taksim to Sarıyer (US$1) and another dolmuş from Sarıyer to Kilyos, for only a little more. Catch the Sarıyer dolmuş at the northern end of Mete Caddesi, just past the Hotel Gezi.

Sights on the Asian Shore

The Asian shore of the Bosphorus has a number of possibilities for interesting excursions, with the advantage that you will meet far fewer tourists than in European İstanbul.

Crossing the Bosphorus To reach the Asian shore, hop on the Üsküdar ferry from Eminönü (Dock No 2), which runs every 20 minutes between 6 am and midnight, even more frequently during rush hours, for US$0.50. A similar, frequent ferry service operates between Beşiktaş and Üsküdar. From Kabataş, just south of Dolmabahçe Palace, ferries run to Üsküdar every 30 minutes on the hour and half-hour from 7 am to 8 pm. There are also city buses and dolmuşes departing from Taksim Square for Üsküdar. The ferries are faster and much more enjoyable, though.

If you take the ferry to Üsküdar, you'll

notice **Leander's Tower**, called the Kız Kulesi (Maiden's Tower) in Turkish, to the south just off the Asian mainland. The tower was a toll booth and defence point in ancient times; the Bosphorus could be closed off by means of a chain stretching from here to Seraglio Point. The tower has really nothing to do with Leander, who was no maiden, and who swam not the Bosphorus but the Hellespont (Dardanelles), 340 km from here.

The tower is subject to the usual legend: oracle says maiden will die by snakebite; concerned father puts maiden in snake-proof tower; fruit vendor comes by in boat, sells basket of fruit (complete with snake) to maiden; maiden gets hers. The legend seems to crop up wherever there are offshore towers and maidens. Anyway, it's a pretty tower, and an İstanbul landmark.

Another landmark is the tall spear of a television tower on Büyük Çamlıca hilltop, a lookout you can visit from Üsküdar.

A landmark especially for travellers is the German-style **Haydarpaşa Station**, south of Üsküdar, the city's terminus for Asian trains. During the late 19th century, when Kaiser Wilhelm was trying to charm the sultan into economic and military cooperation, he gave him the station as a little gift.

You will also notice the large **Selimiye Barracks** (Selimiye Kışlası), a square building with towers at the corners. It dates from the early 19th century, when Selim III and Mahmut II reorganised the Ottoman armed forces along European lines. Not far away is the **Selimiye Camii** (1805). That other highly ornamented building, very storybook Ottoman, was formerly a rest home for ageing palace ladies. It's now a school.

Üsküdar Üsküdar (ER-sker-dahr) is the Turkish form of the name Scutari. Legend has it that the first ancient colonists established themselves at Chalcedon, the modern Kadıköy, south of Üsküdar. Byzas, bearing the oracle's message to found a colony 'opposite the blind', thought the Chalcedonites blind to the advantages of Seraglio Point as a town site, and founded his town on the European shore. Still, people have lived on this, the Asian shore, longer than they've lived on the other.

Today Üsküdar is a busy dormitory suburb for İstanbul, and you will enjoy several hours' browsing through its streets, markets and mosques.

For a meal, try the *Kanaat Restaurant* near the Mihrimah Sultan Camii on the north side of the main square. Founded in 1933, it still serves good food at low prices. A full meal of meze, şiş kebap, pilav and drinks need cost only US$5 per person.

Üsküdar Mosques As you leave the ferry dock in Üsküdar, the **main square**, Hakimiyet-i Milliye Meydanı, is right before you. North-east of the square behind the dolmuş ranks and near the ferry landing is

Florence Nightingale

During the Crimean War (1853-56), when Britain and France fought on the Ottoman side against the Russian Empire, Üsküdar's Selimiye Barracks served as a military hospital. It was here that the English nurse Florence Nightingale, horrified at the conditions suffered by the wounded, established with 38 companion nurses the first model military hospital with modern standards of discipline, order, sanitation and care. In effect, her work at the Selimiye Barracks laid down the norms of modern nursing, and turned nursing into a skilled, respected profession. A small museum (☎ (216) 343 7310) in the barracks, open from 9 am to 5 pm on Saturday (other days by appointment), is dedicated to her work. ■

the **Mihrimah Sultan Camii** (1547), sometimes called the İskele Camii (Dock Mosque), designed by Sinan for Süleyman the Magnificent's only daughter. To the south of the square is the **Yeni Valide Camii**, or New Queen Mother's Mosque (1710), built by Sultan Ahmet III for his mother. It resembles the Rüstem Paşa Camii near the Egyptian Market in Eminönü. Built late in the period of classical Ottoman architecture, it is not as fine as earlier works.

West of the square, overlooking the harbour, is the **Şemsi Paşa Camii** (1580), also designed by Sinan. After you have explored downtown Üsküdar a bit, head up to the Çamlıca hilltops.

Büyük Çamlıca The hilltop park, highest point in İstanbul at 261m, has long been enjoyed by İstanbul's nobility, poets and common folk.

Once favoured by Sultan Mahmut II (1808-39), by the late 1970s it was a dusty (or muddy), unkempt car park threatened by illegal and unplanned construction. In 1980 the municipal government leased the land to the Turing, which landscaped the hilltop and built a coffee-house restaurant such as Mahmut might have enjoyed. The plan was a great success, yielding a park to be enjoyed by locals as well as visitors.

Unfortunately, the municipal government which came to power in 1994 did not renew the lease, and the park has suffered noticeably without the careful maintenance of Turing.

To reach the hilltop from Üsküdar's main square, you can take a taxi (US$2.50 to US$3) all the way to the summit, or a dolmuş most of the way. For the latter, walk to the dolmuş ranks in front of the Mihrimah Sultan Mosque, take a dolmuş headed for Ümraniye, and ask for Büyük Çamlıca. The dolmuş will pass the entrance to Küçük Çamlıca and drop you off shortly thereafter in a district called Kısıklı. The walk uphill following the signs to the summit takes from 20 to 30 minutes, depending on your speed and stamina.

At the car park you'll find the **Museum of Illuminating & Heating Appliances** (Aydınlatma ve Isıtma Araçları Müzesi), which might well escape your interest, even though it has its own café and gift shop.

Once at the top you can rest and marvel at the view (and the crowds, if it's a weekend). From Büyük Çamlıca the Bosphorus is laid out like a map, with its twists and turns, and the minaretted skyline of Old İstanbul looks just like the picture postcards.

Neighbouring **Küçük Çamlıca** hilltop, with its tea garden, is not quite as fancy as its loftier sibling, and is thus more likely to be quiet on weekends.

Tiled Mosque The Çinili Cami (CHEE-nee-lee jah-mee) is Üsküdar's jewel, a small and unassuming building harbouring a wealth of brilliant İznik faïence on its interior walls.

It's a neighbourhood mosque in the quarter called Tabaklar, up the hillside a way from Üsküdar's main square. It can be tricky to find on your own (a 30-minute walk); a taxi costs less than US$2. If you're descending from Büyük Çamlıca, a taxi is the way to go.

To get there on foot from Üsküdar's main square, walk out of the square along the main street south, Hakimiyet-i Milliye Caddesi. Turn left (south-east) onto Toptaşı Caddesi and follow it for several blocks to Valide İmareti Sokak, on the left. Take this street up to Çinili Cami Sokak and the mosque.

It's unprepossessing from the outside: just a shady little neighbourhood mosque with the usual collection of bearded old men sitting around. Inside, it is brilliant with İznik faïence, the bequest of Mahpeyker Kösem (1640), wife of Sultan Ahmet I (1603-17) and mother of sultans Murat IV (1623-40) and İbrahim (1640-48). As it is used heavily by local people for prayer, be properly dressed and on your best behaviour when you visit, and avoid visiting on Friday.

Beylerbeyi Palace Both shores of the Bosphorus have their Ottoman palaces. The grandest on the Asian side is Beylerbeyi, a few km north of Üsküdar. Catch a bus or dolmuş north along the shore road from

Üsküdar's main square, and get out at the Çayırbaşı stop, just north of Beylerbeyi and the Asian pylons of the Bosphorus Bridge.

Beylerbeyi Palace (☎ (216) 321 9320) is open from 9.30 am to 5 pm, closed on Monday and Thursday; admission for the obligatory guided tour costs US$3; camera permits (no flash or tripod) cost US$6, and are a waste of money.

The entrance to the palace is down a long, vaulted stone passage which used to be a vehicular tunnel on the coast road; traffic was rerouted when the Bosphorus Bridge was built. The tunnel is now a gallery for small exhibits. At its southern end is a beautiful small garden with a bamboo grove, and the entrance to the palace.

Today the palace, for all its grandeur, is a bit musty, but still impressive, particularly on a sunny afternoon when golden light floods the rooms. The tour goes too fast. Soon you are overwhelmed by Bohemian crystal chandeliers, Sèvres and Ming vases and sumptuous carpets.

Every emperor needs some little place to get away to, and 30-room Beylerbeyi Palace was the place for Abdülaziz (1861-76). Mahmut II had built a wooden palace here, but like so many other wooden palaces it burned down. Abdülaziz wanted stone and marble, so he ordered Serkis Balyan to get to work on Beylerbeyi Palace. The architect came up with an Ottoman gem, complete with fountain in the entrance hall, and two little tent-like kiosks in the sea wall. The sultan provided much of the decorating expertise himself.

Abdülaziz spent a lot of time here, as did other monarchs and royal guests, for this was, in effect, the sultan's guest quarters. Empress Eugénie of France stayed here on a long visit in 1869. Other royal guests included Nasruddin, Shah of Persia; Nicholas, grand duke of Russia; and Nicholas, king of Montenegro. The palace's last imperial 'guest' was none other than the former sultan, Abdülhamid II, who was brought here to spend the remainder of his life (from 1913 to 1918), having spent the four years since his deposition in 1909 in Ottoman Salonika. He had the dubious pleasure of gazing across the Bosphorus at Yıldız, and watching the great empire which he had ruled for over 30 years crumble before his eyes.

Küçüksu Lodge If Beylerbeyi Palace was a sultan's favourite retreat, Küçüksu was preferred for picnics and 'rustic' parties. Sultan Abdülmecit was responsible for building the Küçüksu Kasrı, an ornate lodge, actually a tiny palace, in 1856. Earlier sultans had wooden kiosks here, but architect Nikogos Balyan, son of the designer of Dolmabahçe, produced a Rococo gem in marble. The Büyük Göksu Deresi (Great Heavenly Stream) and Küçük Göksu Deresi (Small Heavenly Stream) were two brooks which descended from the Asian hills into the Bosphorus. Between them was a flat, fertile delta, grassy and shady, just perfect for picnics, which the Ottoman upper classes enjoyed here frequently. Foreign residents, referring to the place as 'The Sweet Waters of Asia', would often join them.

Take a bus or dolmuş along the shore road north from Beylerbeyi to reach Küçüksu Kasrı (☎ (216) 332 0237), open from 9.30 am to 5 pm, closed on Monday and Thursday; admission costs US$2.

Anadolu Hisarı North of Küçüksu, in the shadow of the Fatih Bridge is the castle and village of Anadolu Hisarı. This small castle, built by Sultan Beyazıt I in 1391, was repaired and strengthened as the Asian strong-point in Mehmet the Conqueror's stranglehold on Byzantine Constantinople. Anadolu Hisarı is a fraction the size of its great European counterpart, Rumeli Hisar. You're free to wander about the ruined walls.

Kanlıca The Fatih Bridge soars across the Bosphorus just north of Rumeli Hisar and Anadolu Hisarı. North of the bridge are more small Asian Bosphorus towns, including Kanlıca, famous for its yoghurt. The **mosque** in the shady town square dates from 1560. High on a promontory above the town, overlooking the Bosphorus, is an Art-Nouveau villa built by the khedive of Egypt to be his summer cottage during visits to İstanbul. Here's a bit of its history:

Having ruled Egypt for centuries, the Ottomans lost control to an adventurer named Muhammed Ali, who took over the government of Egypt and defied the sultan in İstanbul to dislodge him. The sultan, unable to do so, gave him quasi-independence and had to be satisfied with reigning over Egypt rather than ruling. The ruling was left to Muhammed Ali and his line, and the ruler of Egypt was styled *hıdiv*, 'khedive' (not 'king', as that would be unbearably independent). The khedives of Egypt kept up the pretence of Ottoman suzerainty by paying tribute to İstanbul.

The Egyptian royal family, which looked upon themselves as Turkish and spoke Turkish rather than Arabic as the court language, often spent their summers in a traditional yalı on the Bosphorus shore. In 1906, Khedive Abbas Hilmi built himself a palatial villa on the most dramatic promontory on the Bosphorus, a place commanding a magnificent view. The Egyptian royal family occupied it into the 1930s, after which it became the property of the municipality.

Restored by Turing after decades of neglect, the **Khedive's Villa** (Hıdiv Kasrı) served as a hotel, restaurant and tea garden much to the delight of İstanbullus and tourists alike. But the property was on lease to Turing from the city, and when a new city government took over in 1994, it declined to renew the lease. At the time of writing the villa sits empty and unused, a frightful waste of a historic treasure.

The villa is a few minutes by taxi (US$1.50) uphill from Kanlıca or Çubuklu. To walk, go north from Kanlıca's main square and mosque and turn right at the first street (Kafadar Sokak) which winds up to the villa car park in 15 or 20 minutes.

A much nicer walk is the one up from Çubuklu through the villa's grounds. Take a bus or dolmuş north to the stop marked 'Çubuklu Dalgıç Okulu' (a naval installation). Just north of the stop is a fire station (look for signs saying 'Dikkat İtfaiye' and 'İstanbul Büyükşehir Belediye Başkanlığı İtfaiye Müdürlüğü Çubuklu Müfrezesi'). Walk in the gate and to the right of the fire station, then up the winding forest road to the villa, a 20 to 30-minute walk.

Places to Eat *Körfez Restaurant* (☎ (216) 413 4314), Körfez Caddesi 78 in Kanlıca, is good for special occasions. Call for reservations, then meet the restaurant's boat on the European shore for the ride across. The speciality here is sea bass baked in salt, and it also does a famous zucchini (marrow) salad. Lunch is served from noon to 3 pm, dinner from 7 pm to midnight (closed Monday), for US$28 to US$38 per person, all in.

Paşabahçe & Beykoz North of Çubuklu, the town of Paşabahçe has a large glassware factory whose products you have no doubt already used, perhaps unwittingly.

In Beykoz, legend says that one of Jason's Argonauts, Pollux by name, had a boxing match with the local king, Amicus. Pollux was the son of Leda (she of the swan); Amicus was a son of Poseidon. Pollux won.

At Hünkar İskelesi, farther north, is a former imperial palace now not open to the public.

From Beykoz, a road heads eastward towards the Polish village of Polonezköy and the Black Sea beach resort of Şile. Much of the land along the Bosphorus shore north of Beykoz is in a military zone, and you may be denied entry. You can, however, reach the village of Anadolu Kavağı by ferry, either on the Bosphorus touristic cruise from Eminönü or from Sarıyer and Rumeli Kavağı on the European shore.

Anadolu Kavağı Perched above the village are the ruins of Anadolu Kavağı, a medieval castle with seven massive towers in its walls. First built by the Byzantines, it was restored and reinforced by the Genoese in 1350, and later by the Ottomans. As the straits are narrow here, it was a good choice for a defensive site to control traffic. Two more fortresses, put up by Sultan Murat IV, are north of here.

Anadolu Kavağı is the final stop on the special cruise-ferry route, and the land to the north is in a military zone. If you have a picnic lunch, climb up to the fortress, which provides a comfortable picnic location with spectacular views. Check the ferry schedules before you decide to spend time here, however. You may not want to wait three or more hours for a ferry to get you out.

Polonezköy What's a Polish village doing in İstanbul? Polonezköy is a quaint and dying anachronism, a relic of 19th-century politics and the Crimean War.

Founded in 1842 as Adampol, it was named for Prince Adam Jerzy Czartoryski (1770-1861), once the Imperial Russian foreign minister and later head of a short-lived Polish revolutionary government (1830-31). When the revolution failed, he bought land in the Ottoman Empire for some of his former soldiers. In 1853 Russia provoked war with the Ottoman Empire; England, France and Sardinia joined the Ottomans in battling the Russians in the Crimea. The men of Adampol organised a regiment of Ottoman Cossacks and fought with such bravery that Sultan Abdülmecit exempted them and their heirs from taxation.

A generation ago, Polish was still the lingua franca in the village, but with modern media, the language and customs of old Poland are dying out. Once Poles in a time warp, the people of Polonezköy are now Turkish citizens of Polish ancestry. Even so, the 'Polish Pope' John Paul II visited the village in 1979.

For more than a century, city people would come here for the delicious and authentic Polish farm food: wild mushrooms, wild boar, omelettes with eggs from free-range chickens, excellent fruit. Farmhouses provided simple lodgings as well as meals, and this attracted another, non-culinary clientele: lovers who, unable to show a marriage licence, could not shack up in İstanbul's hotels.

Alas, Polonezköy has lost much of its charm. Simple meals and lodgings are still available, but at relatively high prices; lovers still make up a hefty segment of the trade. Transport is a problem also; it's only easily reachable if you have your own vehicle. If you do, stop and take a turn through the village, have a look at the tiny church, and ponder the vicissitudes of history.

Şile Seaside getaways from İstanbul tend to be disappointing. Ataköy and Florya, on the Sea of Marmara, are crowded and citified. Kilyos is small and crowded. But Şile, 72 km north-east of Üsküdar on the Black Sea coast, has long sand beaches and a fairly laid-back atmosphere – at least on weekdays.

Buses (US$2.50) depart from the western side of Üsküdar's main square on the hour from 9 am to 4 pm on the two-hour journey.

Known as Kalpe in classical times, Şile was a port of call for ships sailing east from the Bosphorus. As an important port, it was visited by Xenophon and his Ten Thousand on their way back to Greece from their disastrous campaign against Artaxerxes II of Persia in the 4th century BC. Unable to find ships to sail them to Greece, Xenophon and his men marched to Chrysopolis (Üsküdar) along the route now followed by the modern road.

Şile's other claim to fame is *Şile bezi*, an open-weave cotton cloth with hand embroidery, usually made up into shirts and blouses which are wonderfully cool in the summer heat.

Numerous hotels provide accommodation, with highest prices on weekends. The *Kumbaba Hotel* (☎ (216) 711 1038), two km south of town, is among the oldest yet still the most congenial, with 40 rooms for US$50 to US$70 a double. They have a camping ground as well. The similarly priced two-star *Değirmen Hotel* (☎ (216) 711 5048, fax 711 5248), Plaj Yolu 24, has two stars, 76 rooms, restaurants and bars, and overlooks the beach. The aptly-named *Resort Hotel* (☎ (216) 711 3627, fax 711 4003), Uzunkum, Ağlayan Kaya Mevkii, is the four-star lodging.

As İstanbul expands, so do the getaway spots on its outskirts. If Şile is too busy for you, hop on the bus to the village of Ağva, less than an hour eastward on the coast. Accommodation is limited, but there are good possibilities for camping – and peace and quiet.

THE PRINCES' ISLANDS

The Turks call the Princes' Islands, which lie about 20 km south-east of the city in the Sea of Marmara, the Kızıl Adalar, 'Red Islands'. Most İstanbullus get along with 'Adalar'

(The Islands), however, as it's obvious which ones they mean.

It's convenient to have islands near a big city, as they serve all sorts of useful purposes. In Byzantine times, so the story goes, refractory princes, deposed monarchs and others who were a threat to the powers that be were interned here. A Greek Orthodox monastery and seminary on Heybeliada turned out Orthodox priests until the 1970s.

In the 19th century the empire's business community of Greeks, Jews and Armenians favoured the islands as summer resorts. The population was heavily non-Muslim up to the end of the empire. Many of the pretty Victorian holiday villas and hotels built by these wealthy Ottoman subjects survive, and make the larger islands, Büyükada and Heybeliada, charming places.

Touring the Islands

Hydrofoils and ferries depart from İstanbul's Kabataş docks for the trip to the islands. The summer schedules heavily favour commuters, with frequent morning boats from the islands and frequent evening boats from the city. But you'll have no trouble getting a convenient boat if you check the schedules in advance. Board the vessel and seize a seat at least half an hour before departure time unless you want to stand.

The fastest way to reach the islands is by hydrofoil (22 minutes, US$5, or US$3.50 for students), operating between Kabataş and Büyükada. There are 11 departures from Kabataş on weekdays, six on weekend days.

Cheaper and more leisurely (50 minutes) are the conventional ferries to the islands, which depart from Kabataş on weekdays at 9.30 am, 2, 6.30 and 7.30 pm in summer for US$3.50 (US$2.50 for students). The first two boats go to Heybeliada first, then Büyükada before continuing to Yalova on the southern shore of the Sea of Marmara; the 6.30 boat goes only to Heybeliada and Yalova, and the 7.30 boat stops at Kınalı, Burgaz and Heybeliada before continuing to Yalova. There are also ferries from Eminönü to the islands.

Perhaps the best plan is to take the cruise out on the conventional ferry at 9.30 am, then return by hydrofoil.

The ferry steams away from Kabataş, with good views all around. To the right is a magnificent panorama of Topkapı Palace, Aya Sofya and the Blue Mosque; to the left, Üsküdar, Haydarpaşa and Kadıköy. Along the southern coast of Asia are more suburbs of İstanbul, some of them industrial. Before coming to the bigger islands, you'll pass the small ones named Kınalı and Burgaz. Heybeliada is next. Finally, you disembark at Büyükada.

Büyükada

The first thing you will notice about this delightful place is that cars are not allowed. Except for the necessary police, fire and sanitation vehicles, transportation is by bicycle, horse-drawn carriage and foot. It's wonderful!

Something you may not notice, but that you should be aware of, is that there is no naturally occurring fresh water on the islands; it must be brought in tanks from the mainland.

Walk from the ferry to the clock tower and the main street. The business district, with some fairly expensive restaurants, is to the left. For a stroll up the hill and through the lovely old houses, bear right. If you need a goal for your wanderings, head for the Greek Monastery of St George, in the 'saddle' between Büyükada's two main hills.

Horse-drawn carriage tours of the island are available. You can take either the 'long tour' *(büyük tur)* for about US$12, or the 'short tour' *(küçük tur)* which gives you a look mostly at the town, not the shores or hills, for US$8. You may have to haggle.

Between the islands of Büyükada and Heybeliada there are fairly frequent ferries making the 15-minute trip.

Places to Stay & Eat Hotels on the island move inexorably up-market, but the many restaurants range from cheap to moderate in price.

Right next to the clock tower, the *Hotel Princess* (☎ (216) 382 1628, fax 382 1949), charges US$60/80 a single/double in summer, breakfast and swimming pool fee included. An extra bed costs US$20.

The *Splendid Otel* (☎ (216) 382 6950), up the hill from the clock tower along Çankaya Caddesi, is a perfect if faded Ottoman Victorian period piece, complete with grand dames taking tea on the terrace each afternoon. A room with Victorian-era comforts (the baths have been upgraded, though) costs US$100 per couple, all three meals included.

Heybeliada

Called Heybeli for short, the small island of Heybeliada holds the Turkish Naval Academy. Within the academy grounds is the grave of Sir Edward Barton (died 1598), ambassador of Queen Elizabeth I to the Sublime Porte. Much less touristed than Büyükada, it's a delightful place for walking in the pine groves and swimming from the tiny (but still crowded) beaches. There's not much accommodation if you don't have your own villa (or an invitation to a friend's), but there are several restaurants with good food and decent prices.

Prime lodging here is the *Merit Halki Palace* (☎ (216) 351 8890, fax 351 8483), Refah Şehitleri Caddesi 88, a restored Ottoman Victorian gingerbread villa with 45 rooms, all comforts, and premium prices over US$100 a double per night.

Burgaz & Kınalı

Two smaller islands are also accessible by ferry, but offer less reward for the trouble. Burgaz has a church, a synagogue, and the home of the late writer Sait Faik, which is now a museum; but it's mostly for the well-to-do İstanbullus who have summer villas here.

Kınalı, flat and fairly featureless, is even more a site for these summer villas, and is favoured by Armenian families. If you stop here to have a meal (there are no hotels), you'll probably be the only foreigner in sight.

PLACES TO STAY

İstanbul is well provided with hotels in all categories, particularly in the middle price range. If the first hotel you look at is full, there will be several others nearby. But Turkish tourism is booming, and by late afternoon in August, all may be close to full.

The prices given here were carefully researched, but they may rise or fall according to İstanbul's volatile hotel situation.

As everywhere in Turkey, the appearance of the lobby tells you little about the rooms. Look at several if possible, and choose the best. If the first one you see won't do, ask *Başka var mı* (BAHSH-kah VAHR-muh, Are there others?).

Sultanahmet is the best place to look for a bottom-end or middle-range hotel room, particularly if you favour a restored Ottoman-mansion hotel. Camping areas are in the beach sections named Ataköy and Florya. Taksim Square has many modern upper-middle-range hotels as well as most of the top-end places; Beşiktaş, to the north of Taksim, has the rest of the luxury hotels.

Places to Stay – bottom end

Student Hostels In the summer (July and August), several university dormitories open their doors to foreign students. These dorms tend to be extremely basic and cheap. They're not for all tastes, but if you want to look into one, ask for the latest information from the Tourism Information Office in Sultanahmet, right at the northern end of the Hippodrome.

Hotels Among the hotels in this section are those which will provide you with a dormitory bed for as little as US$6 or US$8 per person, and those offering double rooms with private toilet, sink and hot-water shower for as much as US$40. Mostly though, these places have simple but adequate double rooms with a sink or private shower for US$20 to US$30.

Many hotels in this area are run by carpet merchants, who may be tedious in their efforts to get you to buy a rug. If you're interested, don't let yourself be pressured as you look and ponder. If you're not interested, it's best to make this perfectly clear to the ruggies at the outset.

Hotels – Sultanahmet & Cankurtaran The Blue Mosque (Sultan Ahmet Camii) gives its name to the quarter surrounding it. This is İstanbul's premier sightseeing area, so the hotels here, and in the adjoining neighbourhoods to the south and east named Cankurtaran and Çatladıkapı, are supremely convenient. Unless otherwise noted, the postal code for these hotels is 34400 Sultanahmet.

Cankurtaran The quiet residential district east of Aya Sofya and the Blue Mosque is Cankurtaran, accessible on foot from Sultanahmet (downhill behind the expensive Yeşil Ev hotel along Tevkifhane Sokak), or by banliyö train from Sirkeci to the Cankurtaran station.

A walking tour of the lodgings in this district follows.

Hotel Park (☎ (212) 517 6596, fax 518 9602), Utangaç Sokak 26, a few steps farther along Tevkifhane Sokak, is one of the best deals in the district with 11 rooms (five with shower) priced from US$14/22 a single/double with sink, US$20/30 with shower. Rooms have been modernised, and there's a nice roof garden with a view of the Sea of Marmara.

Hotel Side Pansiyon (☎ & fax (212) 517 6590), Utangaç Sokak 20, next to the Hotel Park, has 25 plain but pleasant rooms, many large, five with showers. Rates are from US$14 to US$20 a single, US$18 to US$26 a double; higher priced rooms have private facilities.

Alibaba Guest House (☎ (212) 518 0030, fax 638 3061), Tevikfhane Sokak 12, has decent double rooms for US$20 with sink, US$25 to US$30 with shower, but the street-level carpet shop is its *raison d'être*, so the pressure will be on for you to buy a rug, not just rent a room.

Continue down Tevkifhane Sokak to Kutlugün Sokak and turn left.

Guesthouse Berk (☎ (212) 516 9671, fax 517 7715), Kutlugün Sokak 27, is comfortable, congenial, family-run, dependable, and a good choice for single women. The half-dozen rooms all have private bath and cost US$35/45.

Yusuf Guesthouse (☎ (212) 516 5878, fax 517 7287), İshakpaşa Caddesi, Kutlugün Sokak 3, is next door to the Valide Sultan Konağı and charges US$14 a double for clean but cramped rooms – some without windows – and difficult plumbing.

Walk downhill on Adliye Sokak to Akbıyık Caddesi to find more pensions. There's a street market on Akbıyık on Wednesday.

Star Hostel (☎ (212) 638 2302), Akbıyık Caddesi 18, has doubles with shower for US$20, and a public laundry as well.

Across the street, the *Orient Youth Hostel* (☎ (212) 517 9493, fax 518 3994), Akbıyık Caddesi 13, is a friendly place popular with backpackers. The atmosphere is one drawing card, the other is the price: US$3.50 for a bunk in a dorm, or US$12 a double for a room with sink. It's actually two buildings; the front one has common loos on every floor, and showers on all but the ground floor; the back only on the ground and 2nd floors.

Alaaddin Guest House (☎ (212) 516 2330, fax 638 3104), Akbıyık Caddesi 32, is newish, tidy and convenient, with US$40 double rooms with shower and the requisite rooftop terrace.

Alp Guesthouse (☎ (212) 517 9570, fax 518 5728), Adliye Sokak 4, is a clean, simple family-run place with double rooms priced at US$35, private shower and breakfast included.

Off Yerebatan Caddesi Another few cheap hotels are a short walk north-west from Aya Sofya along Yerebatan Caddesi to Salkımsöğüt Sokak, on the right. This area is not as desirable as Cankurtaran.

Elit Hotel (☎ (212) 511 5179, 519 0466, fax 511 4437), Salkımsöğüt Sokak 14, has 12 clean, simple, fairly quiet rooms with private facilities, above a carpet shop. The price is US$30 a double. The adjoining *Hotel Ema* is a bit more expensive.

Down Salkımsöğüt Sokak a few more steps the street narrows. At this point, on the right, is the *Hotel Anadolu* (☎ (212) 512 1035), Salkımsöğüt Sokak 3, 34000 Cağaloğlu, perhaps the oldest hotel in the quarter, but also the quietest. By the front door are a few little tables overlooking a car park, a good place to sip a tea or write a letter. The rooms are tiny and just have sinks, but beds are priced at only US$12 a double, hot showers are free, and there's no carpet shop.

Beside Aya Sofya Right beside Aya Sofya, running along its western side, is Caferiye Sokak. The *Yücelt Interyouth Hostel* (☎ (212) 513 6150/1), Caferiye Sokak 6/1, is literally across the street from the front door of Aya Sofya. Though called a hostel, it's a cheap hotel with restaurant, bulletin board, TV room, terrace, and Turkish bath. Doubles with sink cost US$18, rooms with three or four beds go for US$8 per person, and dormitory beds (eight to a room) cost US$6 each. Some readers enjoy this place, others complain.

Divan Yolu, the Hippodrome & Çemberlitaş *Arsenal Youth Hostel* (☎ (212) 513 6407), Dr Emin Paşa Sokak 12, by the Tarihi Park Hamamı, has dorm rooms with four beds each at US$6 per bed, and showers down the hall.

The friendly *Hotel Nomade* (☎ (212) 511 1236, fax 513 2404), Divan Yolu, Ticarethane Sokak 15, is just a few steps off busy Divan Yolu. French is spoken here, and the price is US$45 a double with private shower. It's a good place for single women travellers.

Hipodrom Pansiyon (☎ (212) 516 0902), Üçler Sokak 9, is simple but convenient, just a few steps up Üçler Sokak from the south-western corner of the Hippodrome. Waterless rooms go for US$20 a double, US$26 a triple.

Türkmen Hotel & Pansiyon (☎ (212) 517 1355, fax 638 5546), Binbirdirek, Dizdariye Çeşmesi Sokak 27, Çemberlitaş, is a modern nondescript but friendly place on a quiet back street a bit out of the way. Double rooms in the pension have private showers, but no toilets, and are priced at US$16; in the hotel, nicer rooms with toilet, sink and shower are US$30.

Piyerloti Pansiyon (☎ (212) 517 8070), Piyerloti Caddesi, Kadırga Hamamı Sokak 4, Çemberlitaş, is a bit out of the way, but undeniably cheap at US$10 a double in camp beds, US$12 in regular beds, in waterless rooms. Beds in six-bed dormitories go for US$5 each. The historic Kadırga Hamamı (built in 1724) is right across the street, and there's a bakery nearby for breakfast goods. The staff are helpful, and the clientele international. To find this pension, take the tram up Divan Yolu to the Çemberlitaş stop, then walk south to Piyerloti Caddesi, and south-west to Kadırga Hamamı Sokak.

Hotels – Taksim & Tepebaşı A few inexpensive hostelries exist amidst the banks, airline offices, nightclubs and towering luxury hotels of Taksim Square. The postal code is 80090 Taksim.

One such place is the *Otel Avrupa* (☎ (212) 250 9420), Topçu Caddesi 32, Talimhane, at Şehit Muhtarbey Caddesi. It's a converted apartment house with an entrance at street level, a cheerful breakfast room one flight up, and guest rooms of varying sizes priced at US$25/40, breakfast included, on the upper floors.

Camping İstanbul's camping areas are ranged along the shore in Florya, Yeşilköy and Ataköy near the airport, about 20 km from Aya Sofya. They have good sea-view locations and average prices of US$8 for two persons in a tent. All are served by the frequent commuter trains *(banliyö trenleri)* which run between Sirkeci Station and the western suburb of Halkalı for less than a dollar.

Ataköy Mokamp (☎ (212) 559 6000, fax 559 6007), in the Ataköy Tatil Köyü (holiday village) complex with bar, restaurant, swimming pools and other services, charges US$10 for two in a tent (try to get a site – *sahile yakın*, sah-heel-EH yah-kuhn – near the shore) and away from the highway. Ataköy is accessible by banliyö tren from

Sultanahmet Area

Kapalı Çarşı (Covered Market)
Vezir Hanı Caddesi
Gedikpaşa Cad
0 100 200 m
Emin Sinan
Hamamı Sok
Taşdirek Çeşme Sok
Caddesi
Göktaş Sok
Saraylıçi Sok
Neviye Sok
Piyerloti
Pertev Paşa Sok
Katip Sinan Camii Sok
Dizdariye
Kadırga Hamamı Sok
Kadırga Limanı Caddesi
Mehmet Paşa
To Kumkapı
Kadırga Meydanı Sok
Çimenlik Sok
Dönüş Sokak
Şahsuvarbey Sk
Yusuf Aşkın Sok
Cinci Meydanı Sok

PLACES TO STAY

6 Ayasofya Pansiyonları
7 Konuk Evi & Conservatory Restaurant
9 Hotel Anadolu
10 Elit Hotel
11 Hotel Ema
12 And Otel
13 Yücelt Interyouth Hostel & Hobby Laundry
25 Hotel Nomade
29 Arsenal Youth Hostel
33 Sipahi Hotel
40 Hotel Halı
45 Four Seasons Hotel
46 Yusuf Guesthouse & Valide Sultan Konagı
48 Hotel Empress Zoe
49 Barut's Guesthouse
50 Alp Guesthouse
51 Green Hotel
52 Orient Youth Hostel
53 Konyalı Hostel
54 Sultan Tourist Hostel
55 İlknur Pansiyon
57 Hotel Armada
58 Otel Obelisk
59 Hotel Sümengen
60 Hotel Historia
61 Hotel Avicenna
62 Alaaddin Guest House
63 Star Hostel & Laundry
65 Guesthouse Berk
66 Petit Palace
67 Alibaba Guest House
68 Hotel Park
69 Hotel Side Pansiyon
74 Ottoman House
75 Yeşil Ev
89 Pension Rose
91 Hotel Sokullu Paşa
92 Hotel Yeni Ayasofya
93 Hipodrom Pansiyon
94 Hotel Alzer
95 Hotel Turkoman
96 Hotel Ferhat
101 Türkmen Hotel & Pansiyon
103 Küçük Ayasofya Hotel
105 Piyerloti Pansiyon
106 Hotel Sidera
107 Hotel Turkuaz
108 Hotel Amber

PLACES TO EAT

4 Taverna-Restaurant Sarnıç
16 Cafeterya Medusa
20 Sultan Pub
21 Pudding Shop
22 Can Restaurant & Sultanahmet Köftecisi
23 Meşhur Halk Köftecisi Selim Usta
24 Rumeli Café
26 Meşhur Halk Köftecisi
27 Tarihi Halk Köftecisi
30 Akdeniz Lokanta & Karadeniz Pide ve Kebap Salonu
31 Konak Restaurant
36 Dedem Börekçisi
42 Sultan Sofrası
64 Backpackers' Underground Café
70 Mehtap Aile Tea Garden
73 Rami Restaurant
77 Derviş Aile Çay Bahçesi
83 Doy Doy Restaurant
97 Lezzet Lokantası
98 Karadeniz Aile Pide Salonu
100 Yeni Birlik Lokantası

OTHER

1 Nuruosmaniye Camii
2 Cağaloğlu Hamamı
3 Gülhane Park
5 Aya İrini (Hagia Eirene Church)
8 Caferağa Medresesi Handicrafts Centre

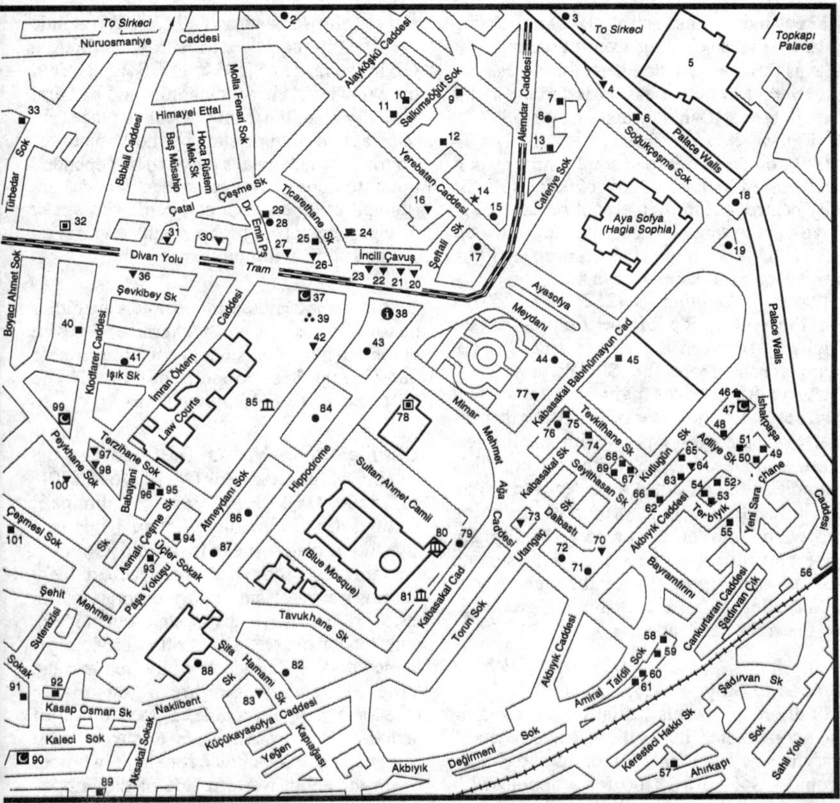

14 Tourism Police
15 Talatpaşa Konağı (Historic House)
17 Yerebatan Saray (Cistern Basilica)
18 Imperial Gate, Topkapı Palace
19 Fountain of Ahmet III
28 Tarihi Park Hamamı
32 Imperial Tombs
34 Basın Müzesi (Press Museum)
35 Çemberlitaş Hamamı
37 Firuz Ağa Camii
38 Tourism Information Office
39 Palace of Antiochus Ruins
41 Binbirdirek Cistern
43 Kaiser Wilhelm's Fountain
44 Haseki Hürrem Hamamı (Carpet Shop)
47 İshak Paşa Camii
56 Cankurtaran (Sultanahmet) Train Station
71 Magnaura Palace Restoration
72 Aypa Bookshop
76 Istanbul Handicrafts Centre
78 Tomb of Sultan Ahmet I
79 Arasta
80 Textile Museum
81 Mosaic Museum
82 Tarihi Şifa Hamamı
84 Obelisk of Theodosius
85 Turkish & Islamic Arts Museum
86 Spiral Column
87 Rough-Stone Obelisk
88 Sphendoneh
90 Küçük Aya Sofya Camii
99 Keçicizade Fuat Paşa Camii
102 Sokollu Mehmet Paşa Camii
104 Kadırga Hamamı

Sirkeci and by Eminönü-Ataköy and Taksim-Ataköy buses. Coming from the airport, the Havaş bus does not stop here; the closest stop is several km farther east at Bakırköy, so it's best to take a 10-minute taxi ride for US$3.

Florya Turistik Tesisleri (☎ (212) 574 0000), on the shore road south of the airport and west of Yeşilköy, is over 20 km from the city centre, but more pleasant because of it. Two-person tent sites cost US$8. Transport is by banliyö treni (the station is 500m away), or by Taksim-Florya bus.

Londra Kamping (☎ (212) 560 4200) is on the south side of the Londra Asfaltı highway between the airport and Topkapı gate across from the Süt Sanayi (milk factory). Right on the highway is a truck fuel and service station, but behind it, farther off the road, are grassy plots with small trees. You won't escape the noise and pollution completely here, but it's not an impossible location. To reach it you must be going eastward from the airport towards Topkapı gate and turn into the *servis yolu* (service road); watch carefully for the sign. About 300m after the turn, the camping ground is on the right-hand side.

Places to Stay – middle

Middle-range hotels, usually newer buildings constructed during the past two decades, vary in size from 30 to 80 rooms and charge from US$40 to US$100 for a double with private shower and/or bath; many include breakfast in the price. Most rooms, though, fall in the range of US$45 to US$65. Except for a few hotels in Sultanahmet and Taksim, virtually all of these middle-range places are rated at two or three stars by the Ministry of Tourism, which means they can be depended upon to have lifts, restaurants and bars (though often empty), and staff who speak foreign languages. Many rooms come with TV and some with minibar.

Sultanahmet Middle-range hotels are either historic buildings with character – even Ottoman-style mansions – or comfortable but characterless modern buildings. The postal code is 34410 Sultanahmet.

Ottoman-Style Hotels The lobby of the small *Hotel Empress Zoe* (☎ (212) 518 2504, 518 4360, fax 518 5699, emzoe@ibm.net), Akbıyık Caddesi, Adliye Sokak 10, is in a Byzantine cistern next to an old Ottoman hamam. The rooms above, reached by a narrow staircase, are simply decorated with taste and character; baths are small but modern, with lots of marble. The rooftop bar-lounge-terrace affords fine views of the sea and the Blue Mosque. Prices are a reasonable US$40/55 a single/double, a good breakfast included. Run by American expatriate Ann Nevens, it's a fine choice for single women.

On the south-western side of the Hippo-

And/Or

The *And Otel* (☎ (212) 512 0208, fax 512 3025), Yerebatan Caddesi, Cami Çıkmazı 46, 34410 Sultanahmet, a short distance west of Yerebatan Saray, is owned by the taxi-drivers' association. İstanbul's cabbies operate an elaborate scheme whereby travellers who come into the city in taxis are told that the hotel at which they've made reservations is 'full up,' or has 'burned down,' or some other untruth. The driver will even have a friend 'call your hotel to check on your reservation.' The friend, of course, calls another friend who's in on the joke. Posing as the hotel reception clerk, he declares that your hotel has no record of the reservation. So the taxi driver settles you in at the And Otel and takes a cut of the profits.

The And Otel offers rooms with bath for US$80/125 a single/double, breakfast included, though I was quoted US$60 a double when I asked. The location is convenient, and the view from the top floor restaurant of the Golden Horn and Bosphorus is good. There's actually nothing wrong with the And Hotel except its unconscionable promotion tactics, and the fact that its posted prices are too high. But if you have reservations elsewhere, go there. ■

drome, the comically narrow *Hotel Alzer* (☎ (212) 516 6262, fax 516 0000), At Meydanı 72, has a cosy Ottoman-style lounge and 20 small bath-equipped guest rooms – some of which look onto the Hippodrome – for US$65 a single, US$75 to US$90 a double, breakfast included.

Up the hill a few steps off the Hippodrome, the *Hotel Turkoman* (☎ (212) 516 2956, fax 516 2957), Asmalı Çeşme Sokak, Adliye Yanı 2, is a 19th-century building with the feeling of a private club. The 12 bath-equipped rooms have names, not numbers, are simply but tastefully decorated, and cost US$60/70/85 a single/double/triple. Take your breakfast (included in the rates) on the roof terrace with fine views of the Hippodrome, Blue Mosque, and Museum of Turkish and Islamic Arts, which is right next door.

At the bottom of Suterazisi Sokak is the *Küçük Ayasofya Hotel* (☎ (212) 516 1988, fax 516 8356), Mehmet Paşa Sokak 25, a modern building made to look like a 19th-century house. The helpful English-speaking manager, Mr Vural Orun, obviously enjoys hosting foreign visitors, and often offers substantial discounts from the posted rates of US$45/65, with breakfast included. All rooms have private shower, phones and central heating.

Hotel Sokullu Paşa (☎ (212) 518 1790/1/2, fax 518 1793), Mehmet Paşa Sokak 5/7, Küçük Ayasofya, is a larger, grander restored Ottoman house with its own small terrace and hamam. Rooms are small and close together but otherwise suitable, with some nice old-time touches. Rates are US$90/110, breakfast included, but they'll cut price quickly if not full.

Nearby, go east (downhill) along Mehmet Paşa Sokak to find the *Hotel Yeni Ayasofya* (☎ (212) 516 9446, fax 513 7622), Küçük Ayasofya Caddesi, Demirci Reşit Sokak 28. Another nicely renovated house in a quiet residential area charging US$50/70 for its rooms with shower, and likewise the staff are ready to haggle with you for lower rates. It's very quiet here.

At the bottom of the hill from the Hippodrome, somewhat out of the way, the *Hotel Sidera* (☎ (212) 516 8185, fax 518 7262), Kadırga Meydanı, Dönüş Sokak 14, Kumkapı, is a newly restored Ottoman mansion, very quiet, charging excellent value-for-money rates of US$55/75 for its bath-equipped rooms. Just around the corner, the *Hotel Turkuaz* (☎ (212) 518 1897, fax 517 3380), Cinci Meydanı 36, Kadırga, is among the most authentic of the restored Ottoman mansion hotels with lots of old-time charm, only 14 rooms (all with private shower), a very un-Ottoman roof bar, and prices at the top of our middle range.

The Cankurtaran district has many restored mansion hotels. Walk down Mimar Mehmet Ağa Caddesi behind the Blue Mosque to Amiral Tafdil Sokak to find the following.

Hotel Sümengen (☎ (212) 517 6869, fax 516 8282), Amiral Tafdil Sokak 21, is an Ottoman town house with its own marble-covered Turkish bath, an airy and light restaurant with excellent views of the Sea of Marmara, an ornate lobby with parquet floors and Turkish carpets everywhere. On the top floor is an open-air terrace with the same fine views of the Sea of Marmara. The 30 guest rooms are small with tiny showers and twin or double beds. A few of the rooms have views of the sea but many rooms open only onto corridors, giving their inhabitants little privacy. Rates are US$70/90/110 a single/double/triple, breakfast included. Turkish baths cost US$10 extra.

Just to the left of the Sümengen stands the *Otel Obelisk* (☎ (212) 517 7173, fax 517 6861), Amiral Tafdil Sokak 17/19, a less appealing restored mansion with Ottoman period furnishings, a roof terrace with Marmara view, and identical prices. I've had a complaint about treatment of women in the Turkish bath, though.

To the right of the Sümengen are two more restored hotels. The *Hotel Historia* (☎ (212) 517 7472, fax 516 8169), Amiral Tafdil Sokak 23, is the newest 'old Ottoman mansion' on this street. All 27 rooms have bathtubs as well as showers, and rent for US$70/90. There's a marble-clad hamam as well.

The *Hotel Avicenna* (☎ (212) 517 0550, fax 516 6555), Amiral Tafdil Sokak 31-33, to the right of the Historia, is a step up in comfort from the other three, with lots of shiny marble but slightly higher prices than the others in this group. Though Ottoman on the outside, it is more modern on the inside, with satellite TV, a roof-terrace café-bar, and 49 small though pleasant rooms for US$90/110, breakfast included. You can often get a reduction if they're not full.

Pensions *Barut's Guesthouse* (☎ (212) 517 6841, fax 516 2944), İshakpaşa Caddesi 8, is a 23-room pension run by artists Hikmet and Füsun Barut (Hikmet Bey specialises in the old Turkish craft of paper marbling). The lobby, furnished with Turkish carpets, is a good place for tea and conversation, as is the small breakfast terrace (with water view) on the top floor. Guest rooms are a bit disappointing, with creaky plumbing, but the family atmosphere is exceptional. Rates are $36/44 for a single/double and US$55/66, a triple/quad.

Modern Hotels Across Akbıyık Caddesi from the Empress Zoe is the modern *Green Hotel* (☎ & fax (212) 638 6600), Akbıyık Caddesi 5, with a popular medium-priced ground-floor restaurant, a roof terrace, and clean rooms for US$40/50, with breakfast. They're ready to haggle off season.

Hotel Ferhat (☎ (212) 516 9642, fax 516 9650), Terzihane Sokak 9, Binbirdirek, looks much fancier than its three-star rating would warrant. There's lots of shiny marble, helpful staff, a restaurant and bar, and 64 up-to-date air-con rooms with bath. Rates are US$60/80/100 a single/double/triple.

Hotel Halı (☎ (212) 516 2170, fax 516 2172), Klodfarer Caddesi 20, Çemberlitaş, uphill to the north-west of the Hippodrome, is a good choice at an even lower price. Clean and bright, it charges US$48/65 for its rooms with bath, breakfast included.

Sipahi Otel (☎ (212) 527 9261, fax 527 3402), Divan Yolu, Türbedar Sokak 20, up from the Basın Müzesi (Press Museum), is an old but quiet and recently refurbished building with 57 rooms conveniently located midway between Sultanahmet and the Grand Bazaar. Rates are US$18 a double in rooms with sink, US$21 with shower. Breakfast costs extra.

The *And Otel* (☎ (212) 512 0208, fax 512 3025), Yerebatan Caddesi, Cami Çıkmazı 46, 34410 Sultanahmet, a short distance west of Yerebatan Saray, is owned by the taxi-drivers' association. It offers rooms with bath for US$80/125, breakfast included, though I was quoted US$60 a double when I asked. The location is convenient, and the view from the top floor restaurant of the Golden Horn and Bosphorus are good.

Aksaray-Laleli The districts of Aksaray and Laleli, 2.5 km west of Sultanahmet, are packed with one-to three-star hotels at decent prices. But virtually all of the patrons are Eastern European small merchants shopping for Turkish-made apparel, especially blue jeans and leather goods. If you're not in the garment trade, you may find the constant bustle of shopping and the huge bundles of goods stacked in hotel lobbies, hallways and lifts a bit tedious. If hoteliers here speak a foreign language, it's most probably Polish, Serbo-Croat, Romanian or Russian.

Taksim Airline offices, foreign banks and luxury hotels are mostly near Taksim Square, postal code 80090 Taksim. The area also has nearly a dozen modern four-star hotels charging US$100 to US$130 for comfortable double rooms with private bath, TV, minibar and air-conditioning. All are fairly quiet and have lifts, bars and restaurants, 24-hour room service (of sorts) and English-speaking personnel. Most customers are here on business or organised tours. Breakfast is included in these prices:

Hotel Lamartine
: Lamartin Caddesi 25 (☎ (212) 254 6270, fax 256 2776) has 58 rooms for US$80/100 a single/double.

Riva Otel
: Aydede Caddesi 8 (☎ (212) 256 4420, fax 256 2033) charges US$80/100 a single/double and has its own currency exchange office.

Hotel Eresin
Topçu Caddesi 34 (☎ (212) 256 0803, fax 253 2247) is older but well maintained, with rooms for US$95/120/140 a single/double/triple.

Crystal Hotel
Recep Paşa Caddesi 9 (☎ (212) 237 8500, fax 237 9480) is among the newest ones, with rates for its 72 rooms of US$90/120 a single/double.

Hotel İstanbul Kervansaray
Şehit Muhtar Caddesi 61 (☎ (212) 235 5000, fax 253 4378) just around the corner from the Hotel Eresin, has a quiet location and charges US$110/140 a single/double for its rooms.

Hotel Nippon
Topçu Caddesi 10 (☎ (212) 254 9900, fax 250 4553) has 94 rooms, is a bit more expensive, and is often filled by tour groups.

Savoy Hotel
Sıraselviler Caddesi 29 (☎ (212) 252 9326, fax 243 2010) has 90 rooms on 10 floors with posted prices of US$110/130 a single/double, but I was quoted US$70/90 when I asked.

Keban Hotel
Sıraselviler Caddesi 51-A (☎ (212) 252 2505, fax 243 3310) is similar, with rates of US$110/130 a single/double.

Dilson Hotel (DEEL-sohn)
Sıraselviler Caddesi 49 (☎ (212) 252 9600, fax 249 7077) has 115 quite comfortable rooms with views of Taksim Square expensively priced at US$120/140 a single/double, and a pastry shop in addition to its restaurant.

Family House
Kutlu Sokak 53, 80090 Gümüşsuyu (☎ (212) 249 7351, fax 249 9667) has five three-room apartments for rent in a quiet, well-kept building. The owner-manager, Mr Atıl Erman, is available to answer any question or solve any problem. Apartments have two single beds and one double bed, telephone, colour TV with video hook-up, kitchen with refrigerator, two-burner gas cooker and utensils. In summer it's US$80 per day, US$500 per week for up to four people. To find Family House, walk down İnönü Caddesi from Taksim, turn right, walk beneath the large red Chinese gate and down the steps, then down another flight, following the Family House signs.

Tepebaşı Between Galatasaray Square and Tünel Square, west of İstiklal Caddesi, the district of Tepebaşı (TEH-peh-bah-shuh) was the first luxury hotel district in the city. The main road through Tepebaşı is Meşrutiyet Caddesi. To get there from Taksim, take the restored tram along İstiklal Caddesi to Galatasaray, or go by taxi or dolmuş; you may have to use a dolmuş that goes past Tepebaşı (say, to Aksaray) and pay the full fare. You can catch a bus along Tarlabaşı Bulvarı (TAHR-la-bash-uh), just out of Taksim near the Air France office. Coming from Karaköy, take the Tünel to the top station and walk the several blocks to the hotels.

The three-star *Yenişehir Palas* (☎ (212) 252 7160, fax 249 7507), Meşrutiyet Caddesi, Oteller Sokak 1/3, 80050 Tepebaşı, is a hotel of eight floors with no views but in a convenient location. Its 138 comfortable rooms with bath, TV and minibar go for US$45/60, breakfast included.

Büyük Londra Oteli (☎ (212) 245 0670, fax 245 0671), Meşrutiyet Caddesi 117, 80050 Tepebaşı, dates from the same era as the Pera Palas Oteli, but has much smaller rooms and bathrooms, and is a bit the worse for wear. But it does preserve some of the Victorian-era glory (in the public rooms at least) at a price which includes a significant nostalgia mark-up. A room with shower costs US$80 with one double bed, US$90 with two beds, breakfast included.

Right next to the British Consulate is the new, modern, four-star *Hotel Emperyal* (☎ (212) 293 3955, fax 252 4370), Meşrutiyet Caddesi 38, 80050 Tepebaşı, offering good value for money at US$80/100.

Places to Stay – top end

The centre of the posh hotel district is certainly Taksim Square, but there are numerous luxury hotels in other parts of the city as well. Prices range from US$125 to US$300 and higher for a double, but most rooms cost from US$140 to US$180. At the big international hotels, try not to pay the 'normal' published rates ('rack rates'), which are quite high. Often these hotels offer special packages; ask when you make reservations. The big international chains usually allow children (of any age) to share a double room with their parents at no extra charge or, if two rooms are needed, they charge only the single rate.

Sultanahmet Turing has restored historic buildings throughout the city, including several Ottoman mansions next door to Aya Sofya and the Blue Mosque.

Yeşil Ev (☎ (212) 517 6785, fax 517 6780), Kabasakal Caddesi 5, 34400 Sultanahmet, is an Ottoman house rebuilt by Turing with 22 rooms furnished with period pieces and antiques in fine taste. To its right is the İstanbul Handicrafts Centre, a restored Ottoman medrese in which the rooms that were once student cells are now shops. Behind the hotel is a lovely shaded garden-terrace restaurant. It costs US$95/125/165 a single/double/triple or US$200 for the Pasha's Room, with its own private Turkish bath. Breakfast, service and tax are included in the rates.

Not far from the Yeşil Ev, behind Aya Sofya against the walls of Topkapı Palace, is a row of Ottoman houses, the *Ayasofya Pansiyonları* (☎ (212) 513 3660, fax 513 3669), Soğukçeşme Sokak, 34400 Sultanahmet, which have also been rebuilt and refitted by Turing. The 58 rooms with private baths are in 19th-century Ottoman style with brass or antique wooden beds, glass lamps, Turkish carpets and period wall hangings. Prices are from US$70 to US$80 a single, US$90 to US$100 a double, US$120 to US$130 a triple, breakfast included. The cheaper rooms are at the back, with little light. The complex's dining rooms provide good food and moderate prices. The reception desk, by the way, is at the north-western end of the street, on the way to Gülhane Park.

Konuk Evi (☎ (212) 514 0120, fax 514 0213), Soğukçeşme Sokak, 34400 Sultanahmet, at Caferiye Sokak, was built in 1992. It duplicates a historic mansion which stood on this site during the reign of Sultan Abdülhamit, but now has all the modern hotel conveniences. Besides the 20 guest rooms with bath, there is a garden, conservatory restaurant and, right next door, the Caferağa Medresesi Handicrafts Centre. Prices are US$90/125/160 a single/double/triple, breakfast included.

Valide Sultan Konağı (Queen Mother's Mansion) (☎ (212) 517 6558, fax 638 1460), Kutlugün Sokak 1, 34400 Cankurtaran, at the intersection of Kutlugün Sokak and İshakpaşa Caddesi, is another boutique hotel in Ottoman style. Its 17 rooms have air-con, TV, minibar, personal safe, and prices of US$90/120, breakfast included.

Among the newer hotels in the district is the *Hotel Armada* (☎ (212) 638 1370, fax 518 5060), Ahırkapı Sokak, right beside the city walls, and a 10-minute walk from the Blue Mosque. Though decorated in a style best termed updated Ottoman, it is a new building with modern facilities and rooms priced at US$99/108, breakfast included.

The Four Seasons hotel chain is scheduled to manage the grand five-star hotel being built directly south of Aya Sofya. Knowing Four Seasons, it will be among the city's finest. Call Four Seasons in your home country for information and rates.

Taksim The *Divan Oteli* (dee-VAHN) (☎ (212) 231 4100, fax 248 8527), Cumhuriyet Caddesi 2, Elmadağ, 80200 Taksim, has built an enduring reputation as a small European-style hotel with excellent cuisine and personal service by well-trained multilingual staff. The location, two blocks from Taksim Square near the Hilton, Hyatt and Inter-Continental, is very convenient. Rooms cost US$133 to US$144 a single, US$175 to US$185 a double. Breakfast is an alarming US$12.50 extra.

A bit farther from Taksim along Cumhuriyet Caddesi is the *İstanbul Hilton* (☎ (212) 231 4650, fax 240 4165), Cumhuriyet Caddesi, 80200 Harbiye, set in its own spacious 14-acre park with tennis courts, swimming pool, and all other luxury services. The site is the best in İstanbul, and the experienced staff are the envy of many other top hotels. Guest rooms are in several locations, with varied décor and special services, and so the price range is broad: from US$170 to US$215 a single, US$205 to US$260 a double, tax and service included.

The 360-room *Hyatt Regency Istanbul* (☎ (212) 225 7000, fax 225 7007), Taşkışla Caddesi, 80090 Taksim, in an excellent city-centre location, is among the city's newest and finest luxury hotels. Though thoroughly modern, it is tastefully and artistically designed with something of the feel of a vast Ottoman mansion. The several restaurants, jazz bar and casino are always busy. Rooms cost US$210 to US$270 a single, US$240 to US$300 a double, the top prices being for Regency Club rooms.

The Marmara (☎ (212) 251 4696, fax 244 0509), 80090 Taksim, towers over the busy square and offers splendid views of the Old City, Beyoğlu and the Bosphorus from its upper floors. The 432 guest rooms are priced from US$175 to US$200 a single, US$200 to US$250 a double, buffet breakfast included.

Tepebaşı The *Hotel Pullman Etap İstanbul* (☎ (212) 251 4646, fax 249 8033), Meşrutiyet Caddesi, 80050 Tepebaşı is a modern 22-storey tower. The 200 simple rooms have satellite TV and minibar; some have splendid views of the Golden Horn, the Old City and the Bosphorus. Rates are US$130/165, breakfast included.

Hotel Richmond (☎ (212) 52 5460, fax 252 9707), İstiklal Caddesi 445, 80670 Tünel, right next to the palatial Russian consulate, is the only hotel on İstiklal. Behind and around its 19th-century facade, the Richmond is all modern and quite comfortable, with 101 full-service rooms priced at US$127/159, breakfast included. If you want to stay amidst the romance of old Pera, this is the place.

Bosphorus *Conrad Istanbul* (☎ (212) 227 3000, fax 259 6667), Yıldız Caddesi, 80700 Beşiktaş, has earned a reputation for having the most accommodating, best trained staff in the city. Off Barbaros Bulvarı just west of Yıldız Palace, the Conrad's 620 rooms and suites have fine Bosphorus views and all the luxuries. Hotel services run the gamut from indoor and outdoor swimming pools to in-room faxes (on request) to a casino. Rates range from US$165 to US$275 a single, US$220 to US$290 a double, tax included.

Swissôtel Istanbul The Bosphorus (☎ (212) 259 0101, fax 259 0105), Bayıldım Caddesi 2, Maçka, 80680 Beşiktaş, capitalises upon its magnificent Bosphorus views: the lobby, restaurant and guest rooms all benefit. Lavish use of marble gives it a luxury feel, and all services give it luxury for real. Rates for the 600 rooms range from US$175 to US$290 a single, US$195 to US$320 a double, tax included. One drawback: you must take taxis almost everywhere.

Çirağan Palace Hotel Kempinski İstanbul (☎ (212) 258 3377, fax 259 6687), Çirağan Caddesi 84, 80700 Beşiktaş, is a modern 312-room luxury hotel annexe built next to the historic Cirağan Palace, on the shore at

The Pera Palas

The *Pera Palas Oteli* (PEH-ra pa-LAHS) (☎ (212) 251 4560; fax 251 4089), Meşrutiyet Caddesi 98-100, 80050 Tepebaşı, fills up regularly with individual tourists and groups looking to relive the great age of Constantinople. The public salons and bar amply fulfill the nostalgia need, though the indifferent service and mediocre restaurant are strong reminders that things were better here a century ago.

The Pera's 145 rooms are varied, from the high-ceilinged guest chambers with period furnishings and bathrooms to match, to the cramped upper-floor servants' quarters and uninspiring annexe rooms. Rooms with bath and breakfast are priced at US$120/180 a single/double in the hotel, US$70/100 in the annexe. You're paying a substantial premium for nostalgia here, much of which you can enjoy at huge savings just by having a coffee in the grand salon or a drink at the bar.

The Pera Palas' ingenious promoters claim that Agatha Christie stayed in room 411 when she visited İstanbul, though reliable sources affirm that she stayed at the once prime but now long-gone Tokatliyan Hotel on İstiklal Caddesi. However, there is no disputing that the great Atatürk preferred room 101, a suite which, kept just as he used it, is now a museum (ask at the reception desk for admission). ■

the foot of the Yıldız Palace park. Destroyed by fire in 1911, the rebuilt marble palace holds meeting rooms, VIP suites, a ballroom, casino, restaurants and boutiques. East-facing rooms enjoy fine Bosphorus views, but west-facing 'park-view' rooms look onto a stone wall. All luxury services are available, and prices are İstanbul's highest: from US$200 to US$320 a single, and from US$235 to US$360 a double, tax included. Nothing is within easy walking distance, making taxis a necessity for every excursion.

PLACES TO EAT

Good food has been a Turkish passion for centuries. The fearsome Janissary corps, the sultan's shock troops, were organised along the lines of a kitchen staff. Their habit of signalling revolt was to overturn the cauldrons which held their dinner of pilav, the message to the sovereign being, 'If you call this food, we have confidence in neither your taste buds nor your leadership'.

Small hazır yemek (ready-food steam table) restaurants, kebapçıs and pidecis, described in the bottom-end section, charge from US$2 to US$3 for a simple main-course lunch to perhaps US$5 or US$6 for a several-course tuck-in. They do not normally serve alcoholic beverages.

Middle-range restaurants with white tablecloths, waiters and alcoholic beverages charge from US$8 to US$20 for a three-course meal with wine, beer or rakı.

A meal costing more than US$30 is a rarity in Turkey except in a few trendy eateries (where spending a lot is the whole point) and five-star hotels. A US$50 per-person dinner bill would be looked upon by most Turks as insane and outrageous.

Places to Eat – bottom end

Sultanahmet The most obvious restaurants in Sultanahmet, those along Divan Yolu, offer decent food in pleasant surroundings, but prices are high by Turkish standards.

Köftecis Divan Yolu's köftecis were traditionally where the district's workers ate cheap, filling, tasty lunches. Now touristed, their prices have risen, but the köfte (grilled lamb meatballs) and şiş kebap are still good. Order by the 'porsyon' (portion): 'bir porsyon' (BEER porss-yohn, one portion) if you're not overly hungry, 'bir buçuk porsyon' (BEER boo-CHOOK, one and a half) if you are, and 'duble porsyon' (DOOB-leh, double) if you're ravenous. An order of köfte, a plate of salad, bread and a glass of ayran (a yoghurt drink) should cost around US$3.

Meşhur Halk Köftecisi Selim Usta (Chef Selim, Famous Popular Köfte-maker), Divan Yolu 12/A, is a classic Turkish workers' eatery which has somehow survived in the midst of this touristy area. It's crowded, noisy and always busy because the food's good and cheap.

Another, similar place named *Meşhur Halk Köftecisi* is up Divan Yolu a short distance away.

Yet another is the *Tarihi Halk Köftecisi* (Historic Popular Köfte-maker) nearby at 28 Divan Yolu.

Down the street towards Aya Sofya is the *Sultanahmet Köftecisi*, also good.

Hazır Yemek Restaurants Divan Yolu has numerous steam table restaurants and grills, all priced higher than equivalent restaurants outside the tourist zone. Most do not serve alcoholic beverages.

The famous *Pudding Shop*, where the drop-out generation of the 1960s kept alive and happy on various nutritious, tasty, inexpensive puddings, is still in operation, though it has become self-conscious and gone upscale in price. A meal taken for nostalgia's sake might cost US$4 to US$6, a sandwich and soft drink less. Breakfast is also expensive.

A few doors down Divan Yolu, overlooking the small park atop Yerebatan Saray, is the *Sultan Pub* (☎ 526 6347), Divan Yolu 2. The upper floor holds a middle-range restaurant, but the ground-floor café serves sandwiches and drinks for US$5 or so. It's a favourite place to meet and talk.

Up the street from the Pudding Shop is the *Can Restaurant*, a cafeteria-style place with better food and lower prices than the Pudding Shop. It's also generally preferred to the nearby *Vitamin (VEE-tah-meen) Restaurant* (☎ 526 5086), Divan Yolu 16, at which you must check your bill carefully.

Up Divan Yolu about a block, on the south side, is the *Dedem Börekçisi,* Divan Yolu 21, a streetside booth selling savoury börek filled with cheese made from white sheep's milk, eaten either hot or cold. You order by weight, so you can have as much as you like; a normal serving is 200g, 250g if you're quite hungry. With a soft drink, lunch would cost less than US$2.

Near Dedem, the Çamlık Restaurant, once recommended in this book, is now overpriced, but across Divan Yolu the *Konak Restaurant* (☎ 526 8933), Divan Yolu 66-68, has fresher food though, like the others, it's more expensive than average, with two courses and a drink coming to about US$5.

For a light meal and a drink in the evening, the popular place is the *Cafeterya Medusa*, on Yerebatan Caddesi near the corner with Şeftali Sokak just a block from the Yerebatan Saray. The open-air terrace is often filled with travellers. Have a pizza or another snack, plus a drink, for about US$4.

Going off the beaten track even a block gets you more value for money.

At the south-western end of the Hippodrome, walk up Peykhane Sokak to the *Yeni Birlik Lokantası* (☎ 517 6465) at No 46, a large, light ready-food restaurant favoured by lawyers from the nearby law courts. Meals are available for US$2.50 to US$4; no alcohol.

Try also the *Lezzet Lokantası* and *Karadeniz Aile Pide Salonu*, two cheap, simple places on Terzihane Sokak; and the *Akdeniz Lokanta* and *Karadeniz Pide ve Kebap Salonu* a half block north of Divan Yolu.

Cafés For refreshments and snacks, the place to go to is the *Sultan Sofrası*, a café-restaurant facing the Hippodrome on its north-west side, good for people-watching. Most of the food served is snacks and sandwiches. A drink and a sandwich should cost less than US$2. Directly across the Hippodrome from the Sultan Sofrası, hugging the wall of the Blue Mosque, is another small *teahouse* under the same management.

If you prefer shade to sun, seek out the *Derviş Aile Çay Bahçesi* (Dervish Family Tea Garden), Kabasakal Caddesi 2/1 near the Yeşil Ev Hotel. In the cool, dark shadows cast by big old trees, this pleasant café offers tea, coffee and small sandwiches for less than US$1. Try peynirli tost, a cheese sandwich mashed in a vice-like sandwich cooker. Prices are posted.

The *Mehtap Aile Tea Garden* on Kutlugün Sokak sits right atop the Magnaura Palace of the Byzantines, slowly being restored, decade by decade.

Sirkeci & Hocapaşa There is a serviceable – if a bit pricey – restaurant called the *Orient Express* right in Sirkeci train station, and lots of good small restaurants nearby in the neighbourhood called (HO-ja pah-shah).

Leave the train station by the main (west) door, turn left and walk up the slope on Ankara Caddesi, turning into the third little street on the left. This will bring you to İbni Kemal Caddesi, the Hoca Paşa Camii, and over a dozen small restaurants with tables out in the narrow, shady pedestrian-only street.

There's variety: *Ali Bey Köfte Piyaz* features grilled lamb meatballs and piyaz (white beans vinaigrette), as does the *Namlı Rumeli Köftecisi. Meşhur Tarihi Hocapaşa Pidecisi* serves Turkish pizza, fresh, good and cheap for as little as US$1.50. *Kasap Osman* (Osman the Butcher) specialises in Bursa-style İskender kebap and other grills, as do the *Kebapçı Kardeşler* (Kebap-making Brothers). The *Yıldız Lokantası* is a steam-table place with a variety of surprisingly tasty stews and grills. A full meal need cost no more than US$2 to US$4. Fresh fruit for afters is available from sidewalk vendors.

Boza Facing the plaza in Eminönü, to the left of the Yeni Cami, is the *Vefa Bozacısı*. Boza (a thick millet drink) is all they serve here from October to June; from June to October they switch to refreshing white grape juice called şıra. A fortifying glass of boza, favourite drink of the Ottoman Janissary corps, costs US$0.50, şıra the same; they serve snacks as well. Prices are posted prominently.

Fish Sandwiches About the cheapest way to enjoy fresh fish from the waters round İstanbul is to buy a fish sandwich from a boatman. Go to the Eminönü end of the old Galata Bridge, and on both sides of the bridge, tied to the quay railing between the ferry docks, are boats bobbing in the water. In each boat, two men cook fish on a grill or griddle. The quick-cooked fish is slid into a slit quarter-loaf of bread, and costs about US$1. I've never been disappointed, nor made sick, by one of these. Seeing a fire in a boat is cool, too.

Covered Market Within the Kapalı Çarşı, the *Sevim Lokantası*, on Koltuk Kazazlar and Kahvehane sokaks, was founded (a sign states proudly) in 1945. Take a seat in the little dining room or sit at a table set out in one of the little streets and order one or two plates of food. The bill shouldn't exceed US$4.

You will no doubt pass the *Şark Kahvesi* (SHARK kahh-veh-see, Oriental Café), at the end of Fesçiler Caddesi, always filled with locals and tourists. The arched ceilings betray its former existence as part of a bazaar street; some enterprising kahveci (coffee-house owner) walled up several sides and turned it into a café. On the grimy walls hang paintings of Ottoman scenes and framed portraits of sultans and champion Turkish freestyle wrestlers. A cup of Turkish coffee, a soft drink or a glass of tea costs less than US$1; Nescafé is overpriced.

Taksim The cheapest eats in Taksim are at the büfes right between Sıraselviler and İstiklal Caddesis. Look for the prominent *Çetin Restaurant* at İstiklal 1, and the büfes are just to the left. They serve fresh-squeezed fruit juices, döner sandwiches (both lamb and chicken) etc for about US$1 each. The Çetin, by the way, specialises in rotisserie chicken, ranks and rows of spitted birds revolving slowly. The upstairs terrace is the place to dine in fair weather.

A few steps down İstiklal from the Çetin is the *Pehlivan Restaurant*. This bright, plain place has the standard cafeteria line, steam

Turkish Delight

For a traditional Ottoman treat, walk through the archway to the left of the Yeni Cami in Eminönü, and turn left onto Hamidiye Caddesi. One short block along, on the right-hand (south) side of the street near the corner with Şeyhülislam Hayri Efendi Caddesi, is the original shop of *Ali Muhiddin Hacı Bekir* (☎ 522 0666), inventor of Turkish delight.

History notes that Ali Muhiddin came to İstanbul from the Black Sea mountain town of Kastamonu and established himself as a confectioner in the Ottoman capital in the late 18th century. Dissatisfaction with hard candies and traditional sweets led the impetuous Ali Muhiddin to invent a new confection that would be easy to chew and swallow. He called his soft, gummy creation *rahat lokum*, the 'comfortable morsel'. 'Lokum', as it soon came to be called, was an immediate hit with the denizens of the imperial palace, and anything that goes well with the palace goes well with the populace.

Ali Muhiddin elaborated on his original confection, as did his offspring (the shop is still owned by his descendants), and now you can buy lokum made with various fillings: *cevizli* (JEH-veez-LEE, with walnuts), *şam fıstıklı* (SHAHM fuhss-tuhk-LUH, with pistachios), *portakkallı* (POHR-tah-kahl-LUH, orange-flavoured), or *bademli* (BAH-dehm-LEE, with almonds). You can also get a çeşitli (CHEH-sheet-LEE, assortment). Price is according to weight; a kg costs US$3 to US$9, depending upon variety. Ask for a free sample by indicating your choice and saying *Deneyelim!* (DEH-neh-yeh-LEEM, 'Let's try it').

During the winter, a cool-weather speciality is added to the list of treats for sale. Helvah, a crumbly sweet block of sesame mash, is flavoured with chocolate or pistachio nuts or sold plain. Ali Muhiddin Hacı Bekir has another, more modern shop on İstiklal Caddesi between Taksim Square and Galatasaray. ■

tables and low prices. Don't take too much; three dishes is plenty. Fill up at lunch or dinner for US$4.

Elsewhere around Taksim, the local *McDonald's* hamburger restaurant, always packed, is on the east side of Cumhuriyet Caddesi near the Turkish Airlines office, along with *Pizza Hut* and several streetside cafés. They may all be razed or relocated as work on İstanbul's Metro progresses.

İstiklal Caddesi *Afacan Restaurant*, 88 İstiklal, just past İmam Adnan Sokak, is similar to the aforementioned Pehlivan, with prices posted in the front window and the food on display. *Borsa Fast Food Kefeteryası*, 89 İstiklal, is modern, bright and popular with Turkish youth – especially the dondurma (ice cream) kiosk. Grills (US$2 to US$3) are the speciality, and beer is served.

Continuing along İstiklal Caddesi takes you past several little side streets. Perhaps the best and most plentiful food for the lowest price in the Taksim area is at the *Ada Lokantası* (☎ 245 1633), at Büyükparmakkapı Sokak 25, the third street on the left coming from Taksim. Open daily from early morning to late evening, it's easy to fill up for US$2 to US$4. Büyükparmakkapı Sokak, by the way, is a colourful introduction to the local street life of Beyoğlu, with a shoe-repair shop, barber shop, bridge salon, record shop, sporting goods shop and cheap nightclubs. Look also for *Nature & Peace* (☎ 252 8609), at No 21, a shop selling herbs, spices, village, whole and natural foods. The café serves up meals on the spot.

On the north side of İstiklal Caddesi, opposite Büyükparmakkapı Sokak, is Mis Sokak and the *Sohbet Ocakbaşı*, at No 9/1. Ocakbaşı means 'right at the grill' which is where you sit in this type of restaurant. The speciality here is Kozan kebap, a spicy shish from south-eastern Turkey where the Arabic influence is strong. A full meal can cost under US$6. Sohbet is best in the summer when tables are set out on the street.

Walk from Taksim until you see the Ağa Camii (on the right), the only little mosque on the street. Behind the Ağa Camii on Mahyacı Sokak you'll find the *Meşhur Sultanahmet Köftecisi* (☎ 244 1355) and the *Kristal Köftecisi* (☎ 245 8462), serving cheap grilled meatballs, lahmacun (Arabic pizza) and pide.

Tepebaşı & Tünel Just north of Galatasaray there's the Balık Pazar (fish market), actually a full food market spread out in two little streets, Sahne and Duduodaları, next to the touristy Çiçek Pasajı. There you'll find a few simple eateries to fill your needs.

The cheapest is *Mercan*, a simple eatery spanning Sahne Sokak. The speciality is midye tavası, mussels deep-fried on a skewer for about US$0.30, a bit more for a sandviçli (in bread); the favoured beverage is draught beer.

This is a prime area for picnic assembly, with greengrocers, 'şarküteri' (charcuterie, delicatessen) shops and bakeries offering cheeses, dried meats such as pastırma, pickled fish, olives, jams and preserves, and several varieties of bread including wholegrain. *Şütte* (☎ 244 9292), Duduodaları Sokak 21, is regarded by many locals as the best of the delis.

For a light lunch or snack near the Pera Palas Oteli, go to the *Karadeniz Pide Salonu* behind and to the left of the Etap İstanbul Hotel, where you can get a fresh pide with butter and cheese for US$1. No alcohol is served.

Places to Eat – middle

Sultanahmet Among the favourites here is *Rami* (☎ 517 6593), Utangaç Sokak 6, set up in a restored house behind the Blue Mosque. The several dining rooms are decorated with Impressionist-style paintings by Turkish painter Rami Uluer (1913-1988), but the favoured spot is the rooftop terrace. Phone for advance reservations to get a table with the full view of the Blue Mosque, then order some of the Ottoman specialities such as Hünkâr Beğendi (grilled lamb and rich aubergine purée) or kağıt kebap (lamb and vegetables cooked in a paper pouch). With drinks, a meal costs about US$20 to US$28 per person.

The indefatigable Turing has established

four restaurants within a few steps of Aya Sofya. The *Yeşil Ev* hotel's garden restaurant has a very pretty setting and decent food.

At the intersection of Caferiye and Soğukçeşme sokaks is the *Taverna-Restaurant Sarnıç* (☎ 512 4291), set up in a vast old Roman cistern. The baronial fireplace hardly belongs in a sunken stone cistern, but the rosy glow is welcome on rainy evenings. The menu is among the most interesting and original in the city. Meals cost from US$20 to US$30 per person with drinks, tax and tip. It's open Wednesday to Sunday from 11.30 am to 11 pm.

Just across the street from the Sarnıç, next to the Konuk Evi hotel, is its *Conservatory Restaurant* (☎ 513 3660), a glass greenhouse with an open-air terrace serving light meals and snacks. Have a beer and a cheese plate (US$6), assorted böreks (US$3.50) or an omelet (US$4).

Sultan Pub (☎ 526 6347), Divan Yolu 2, between the Pudding Shop and the small park atop Yerebatan Saray, has a café-bar on the ground floor and a nicer restaurant one flight up. A full meal upstairs, with wine or beer, costs between US$8 and US$12.

Topkapı Palace Everyone who visits Topkapı Palace has a problem: since it can take almost a whole day to see the palace properly (including the Harem), where does one eat lunch? There is a restaurant in the palace, the *Konyalı Restaurant* (☎ 513 9696), all the way down at the northern end; find the Mecidiye Köşkü, and the restaurant is below. You'll find tables inside and outside under an awning, with very fine views of Üsküdar, the Bosphorus and the Sea of Marmara.

Food and service are decent, though prices are higher than you'd find outside the palace. Even so, the restaurant is always crowded at lunch time. Arrive by 11.30 am to beat the lunch rush, or come later in the afternoon. For a meal of soup, şiş kebap, salad and drink with tax and tip included, figure on paying about US$12 to US$18.

If it's just a good seat, a sandwich and a cool drink you're looking for, go to the café terrace just below the restaurant, where there are even better views, and a snack won't set back your budget so much.

The only other food in the palace is at the little snacks-and-drinks stand by the entrance to the Harem.

Covered Market Though most Covered Market eateries are low budget, at the *Havuzlu Lokantası* (☎ 527 3346), Gani Çelebi Sokak 3, prices are in the moderate range of US$8 to US$10 for a meal. The food is about the same as at the bottom-end places in this area, but you get a lofty dining room made of several bazaar streets walled off for the purpose long ago, and a few tables set out in front of the entrance by a little stone pool (havuzlu means 'with pool'), which I suspect was a deep well centuries ago. Waiter service here is more polite and unhurried, though slow when there are tour groups. To find the Havuzlu, follow the yellow-and-black signs and ask for the PTT, which is next door.

Taksim *Hacı Baba Restaurant* (ha-JUH bah-bah, ☎ 244 1886), at İstiklal Caddesi 49, has a pleasant terrace with tables overlooking the courtyard of the Aya Triada Greek Orthodox church next door. The menu is long and varied, food good, and service usually competent; some English is spoken. Have a look in the kitchen to help you choose your meal. You'll pay from US$8 to US$20 per person for a full lunch or dinner with wine or beer.

Three other good full-service restaurants are a short walk from the square, down the hill on İnönü Caddesi by the Atatürk Cultural Palace.

Near the top of İnönü Caddesi on the right-hand side is a large Chinese gateway and beyond it down the stairs is the *Great Hong Kong Restaurant* (☎ 252 4268), İnönü Caddesi 12/B, a small but quite nice restaurant serving an assortment of Chinese dishes for about US$20 to US$30 per person with drinks. It's open for lunch (11 am to 3 pm) and dinner (6 to 11.30 pm) daily.

Continue down the hill on the left-hand side of the tree-lined street and around the curve until you see the huge rectangular bulk of the German Consulate General on the opposite side of the road. These restaurants are more or less opposite the consulate.

The *C Fischer Restaurant* (☎ 245 2576, 245 3375), İnönü Caddesi 51/A, is the latest expression of a famous old İstanbul dining place which caters mostly to German diplomats at lunchtime; it can be cavernously empty in the evening. The menu lists Turkish and continental dishes including lamb şiş kebap, tiny lamb chops (pirzola), beef tournedos and wienerschnitzel. The traditional starter course at Fischer's is savoury borsch, and for a sweet, apple strudel or palaçinka (crêpes filled with fruit jam). Lunch or dinner at the Fischer costs US$8 to US$15 per person, with wine or beer, tax and tip included.

North of Taksim is the *Lebanese Restaurant* (☎ 250 2071), Lamartin Caddesi 41, a relatively new addition to the city's very limited list of foreign eateries. First reports on food and service are good, and prices are moderate.

Very nearby is the *Çin Lokantası* (Chinese Restaurant, ☎ 250 6263), Lamartine Caddesi 17, İstanbul's original Chinese dining spot opened in 1957. The old favourites are served, having been adapted to tastes unfamiliar with the real thing. Lunch (about US$10) and dinner (about US$18 to US$25 per person) are served daily except Sunday.

İstiklal Caddesi & Galatasaray *Hacı Abdullah* (☎ 293 8561), Sakızağacı Caddesi 17, beside the Ağa Camii (İstiklal Caddesi's only mosque), is a Beyoğlu institution, having been in business a century. Its dining rooms are simple but tasteful, its Turkish and Ottoman cuisine outstanding, with a varied menu of traditional dishes otherwise rarely found in restaurants. Service is friendly, single women are welcomed, and a full meal with soft drink (no alcohol is served) costs US$4 to US$10.

At Galatasaray, 700m along, the big Galatasaray Lycée rises on the south side of the street. On the north side (at İstiklal Caddesi 172) is an entrance to the Çicek Pasajı, the 'Flower Passage', a collection of taverna-restaurants open long hours every day in the courtyard of a historic building.

This used to be a jolly place where locals gathered for drinking, singing and good, cheap food. It has now been tarted up for tourists, and while the food can still be good, prices and the hassle factor have increased dramatically. Prices are twice as high as elsewhere, overcharging and bringing unordered items are commonplace. If you must eat here (and it *can* be enjoyable) ask prices, don't accept unordered items, and be cautious with locals who chat you up and propose outings or nightclubs, which may turn into ripoffs.

The locals who used to eat in the Çiçek Pasajı have moved on to the meyhanes (tavernas) deeper in the market. Walk along Sahne Sokak into the market to the first street on the right, Nevizade Sokak. There are at least eight restaurants here with streetside tables in fine weather charging about US$1 to US$1.75 for plates of meze, about twice that for kebaps. Alcohol is served enthusiastically. The *Tarihi Cumhuriyet Meyhanesi* is amongst the nicest ones.The *Çağlar Restaurant* (☎ 249 7665) is at No 6 and the *Kadri'nin Yeri* (☎ 243 6130) nearby. My favourite, however, is the *İmroz Restaurant* (☎ 249 9073), Nevizade Sokak 24, down at the end of the row on the right. Run by a Turk and a Greek from the island of İmroz (Gökçeada, Imbros), it specialises in fish and other island dishes.

Tepebaşi & Tünel Popular with the diplomatic set at lunch time is the *Dört Mevsim* (Four Seasons) (☎ 293 3941), İstiklal 509, almost in Tünel Square. Under English management, it is well located to draw diners from the US, UK, Dutch, Russian and Swedish consulates. The food is continental with several delicious concessions to Turkish cuisine; preparation and service are first-rate. Lunch is served from noon to 3 pm, dinner from 6 pm to midnight; closed Sunday. If you order the fixed menu at lunch, you might pay US$10, drink and tip included. Ordering from the regular menu at dinner may bring your bill to US$20 or US$25 per person.

Çatı Restaurant (☎ 251 0000), İstiklal

Caddesi, Piremeci Sokak 20/7, is on the 7th (top) floor of a building on a small side street which runs between İstiklal and Meşrutiyet. Though the view is vestigial at best, the greenhouse-style dining room is pleasant, the food quite good and not expensive. Try the Çatı Böreği for an appetiser; it's halfway between a Turkish börek and a turnover, made with cheese. Main courses are mostly Turkish, with a few European specialities. Expect to spend from US$10 to US$15 per person. If you don't like syrupy organ music, come early for dinner. It's open for lunch and dinner every day.

Yakup 2 Restaurant (yah-KOOP ee-KEE, ☎ 249 2925), Asmalımescit Caddesi 35/37, is popular with local artists, musicians, actors and professors. It hasn't been fancied up for tourists, so the décor is minimal but the food is quite good and moderately priced. Strike up a conversation with those at a neighbouring table; they may well speak a foreign language. Full meals with wine, beer or rakı cost about US$8 to US$15. It's open every day for dinner, and for lunch daily except Sunday.

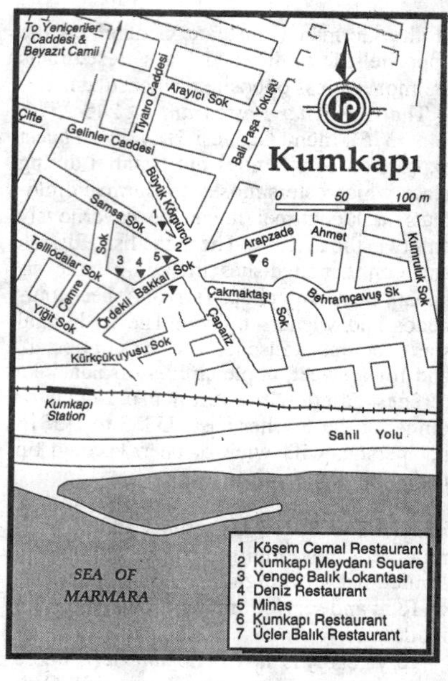

Sirkeci & Eminönü Here, at the Egyptian Market, a famous old restaurant has been serving for decades.

Pandeli (☎ 527 3909), over the main entrance (facing the Galata Bridge) of the Mısır Çarşışı, is a series of small chambers covered in beautiful faïence. Only lunch is served (from Monday to Saturday), and seafood is the speciality, but grilled meats are served as well. In recent years the food has not improved though prices have risen steeply. They even charge you to hang up your coat. Though beautiful, it has become too famous for its own good, so you may spend upwards of US$16 to US$20 for a complete meal.

Places to Eat – top end

Taksim The dining room at the *Divan Oteli* (☎ 231 4100), serves continental and Turkish cuisine in posh surroundings at decent prices, about US$35 to US$40 per person for a fine meal, all in. *Divan Pub*, adjoining, is still fairly fancy but significantly cheaper. The speciality here is excellent Turkish döner kebap.

ENTERTAINMENT

For many first-time visitors, the name 'İstanbul' conjures up Hollywood-Baroque images of mysterious intrigues in dusky streets, sultry belly dancers undulating in smoky dens, and dangerous liaisons from the sublime to the bestial. As with most aged stereotypes, the reality is somewhat different.

News of performances and concerts is carried in the *Turkish Daily News*. There is also limited information of coming events in *The Guide*, a bi-monthly booklet given away in some hotel lobbies, and sold (US$2.50) at some bookshops.

İstanbul's major venues for concerts and performances of dance and opera are the Atatürk Cultural Centre (☎ (212) 251 5600,

Kumkapı Fish Restaurants

In Byzantine times, the fishers' harbour called Kontoscalion was due south of Laleli. The gate into the city from that port came to be called Kumkapı by the Turks. The harbour has been filled in and the gate is long gone, but the district is still filled with fishers who moor their boats in a more modern version of the old harbour. Each evening the narrow streets of the neighbourhood resound to the footsteps of people hungry for fish. In fine weather restaurant tables crowd the narrow streets, and happy diners clatter plates and cutlery between bolts of pungent rakı.

In recent years the scene has become a bit too hectic for some visitors, with touts pushing menus at you as you approach. Ignore them, find a seat, order carefully (and don't accept anything you haven't ordered), and you'll enjoy yourself. Expect to part with US$18 to US$30 unchanged per person for the meal, appetisers, salads, wine, sweet, tax and tip all included.

Seasonal Fish Here are a few tips on seasons. From March to the end of June is a good time to order *kalkan* (turbot), *uskumru* (mackerel), and *hamsi* (fresh anchovies), but from July to mid-August is spawning season for many species, and fishing them is prohibited. In high summer, these are the easiest to find in the markets and on the restaurant tables: *çinakop* (a small bluefish), *lüfer* (medium-size bluefish), *palamut* (bonito), *tekir* (striped goatfish: *Mullus surmuletus*), *barbunya* (red mullet: *Mullus barbatus*), and *istavrit* (scad, horse mackerel).

Restaurant Suggestions Kumkapı has dozens of seafood restaurants, many operated by Turkish citizens of Greek or Armenian ancestry. Among the favourite things to order is swordfish şiş kebap, chunks of fresh fish skewered and grilled over charcoal, but there are fish soups and stews, fish poached with vegetables, pan-fried fish and pickled fish.

Typical of Kumkapı's seafood eateries is *Minas* (MEE-nahss) (☎ 522 9646) at Samsa Sokak 7, facing the square. Minas is not one of the cheaper places; you can dine for less elsewhere. If you're not in the mood for seafood but would like to explore Kumkapı in any case, come for a kebap, and you'll spend a mere US$8 or so.

Also facing the square is *Köşem Cemal Restaurant* (☎ 520 1229), Samsa Sokak 1, with similar prices, cuisine and advantages. Here there are white tablecloths, good careful service and a mixed clientele of Turks and tourists. Upstairs is another pleasant dining room.

Ördekli Bakkal Sokak, the street which runs from the train station to Kumkapı Meydanı (as the little square is named), has another half-dozen good seafood restaurants, including *Üçler Balık Restaurant* (☎ 517 2339), Ördekli Bakkal Sokak 3, just off the square. The *Deniz Restaurant* (☎528 0858), Ördekli Bakkal Sokak 12/A, seems to make it difficult for customers to find out prices in advance. Yet other side streets hold more restaurants. Two that have been recommended to me are the *Yengeç Balık Lokantası* (☎ 516 3227), Telliodalar Sokak 6, and the *Kumkapı Restaurant* (☎ 522 6590), Üstad Sokak 7.

Getting There & Away You can get to Kumkapı by one of three methods. From Laleli, Beyazıt or the Covered Market, walk. Just opposite the Beyazıt Camii in Beyazıt Square, on the south side of Yeniçeriler Caddesi, is the beginning of Tiyatro Caddesi. Follow this street south for 10 short blocks (for the last block, it veers to the left), and you'll find yourself in Kumkapı's main square.

You can also take a taxi, but it may be a bit expensive as the driver might choose to cruise all the way around the old city in order to enter this congested district from the sea side; figure on US$3 or so from Sultanahmet, US$5 or US$6 from Taksim.

The cheapest way to go is by train from Sirkeci Station. Enter the station, bear to the right and buy a ticket at one of the kiosks marked 'Banliyö' for US$0.40, and board any of the electric commuter trains on the right-hand platforms. Most will be for Halkalı, but in fact any train will do, as they all pass Kumkapı. The trains are run-down, but the ride is short.

You will round Seraglio Point, offering marvellous views of the Sea of Marmara and Topkapı Palace, and stop briefly at Cankurtaran Station before pulling into Kumkapı Station. Leave the train and the station, and walk down the most prominent street, which is Ördekli Bakkal Sokak (Grocer with a Duck St).

By the way, the next station on the railway line after Kumkapı is Aksaray (Yenikapı). You can use the train to come and go from that district as well, for the same fare. ■

fax 245 3916) in Taksim Square; the Cemal Reşit Rey Konser Salonu (☎ (212) 240 5012), on Gümüş Sokak just north of the İstanbul Hilton and east of the Military Museum; and the former Aya İrini church in the First Court of Topkapı Palace.

Outdoor venues for summer performances include the Open-Air Theatre (Açık Hava Tiyatrosu) just north of the İstanbul Hilton, and Rumeli Hisar, north of Bebek on the Bosphorus.

International İstanbul Festival

This, the most prominent entertainment event in İstanbul, begins in late June and continues to mid-July. World-class performers – soloists and virtuosos, orchestras, dance companies, rock and jazz groups – give recitals and performances in numerous concert halls, historic buildings and palaces. The highlight is Mozart's *Abduction from the Seraglio* performed in Topkapı Palace, with the Sultan's private Gate of Felicity as the backdrop. Check at the box offices in the Atatürk Cultural Centre for schedules, ticket prices and availability, or contact the festival office (☎ (212) 260 4533, 260 9072, fax 261 8823), İstanbul Kültür ve Sanat Vakfı, Yıldız Kültür ve Sanat Merkezi, 80700 Beşiktaş, İstanbul.

Folklore

Turks are enthusiastic folklore fans, and many are still close enough in tradition to their regional dances to jump in and dance along at a performance. University groups, good amateur companies and professionals all schedule performances throughout the year. The Turkish Folklore Association usually has something going on. For current offerings, ask at a Tourist Information Office or at one of the larger hotels.

High Culture

There are symphony, opera and ballet seasons, and occasional tour performances by the likes of Jean-Pierre Rampal or Paul Badura-Skoda. Many but not all of these performances are given in the Atatürk Cultural Centre. The box offices have schedules, as do many of the luxury hotels.

Theatre

The Turks are enthusiastic theatre-goers, and as a people they seem to have a special genius for dramatic art. The problem, of course, is language. If you're a true theatre buff you might well enjoy a performance of a familiar classic, provided you know the play well enough to follow the action without the benefit of dialogue in your native language.

Theatres are concentrated in Beyoğlu along İstiklal Caddesi and near Taksim Square. The İstanbul Theatre Festival, with performances by Turkish and foreign casts, takes place in May.

Cinema

For current listings, buy the *Turkish Daily News* on Friday to get their special *Weekend* supplement.

İstiklal Caddesi between Taksim and Galatasaray is the centre of İstanbul's cinema *(sinema)* district, with many foreign films being shown. The advent of television has put many cinemas out of business, and some of the survivors screen the racier movies, plus the much-beloved Turkish melodramas.

Many first-run foreign feature films make it to İstanbul, and you will be able to enjoy them at bargain prices.

Look on the cinema posters or ask at the box office to see if the film is in the original language, *Orijinal* (ohr-zhee-NAHL), or dubbed in Turkish, *Türkçe*.

There are three general seating areas, and you pay according to which you choose: *koltuk* (kohl-TOOK), on the floor in the mid-section to the rear; *birinci* (beer-EEN-jee), on the floor near the screen; and *balkon* (bahl-KOHN), in the balcony where the young lovers congregate. If you're going to the cinema to watch the film, ask for koltuk.

When possible, buy your tickets a few hours in advance. Tickets cost from US$1.75

to US$2.50. Also, the usher will expect a small tip for showing you to your seat.

Beyoğlu Along İstiklal Caddesi, look for these:

Aksanat Kültür Merkezi (Aksanat Cultural Centre), İstiklal Caddesi 16-18, in the Akbank building on İstiklal just out of Taksim (☎ 252 3500); movies and films of musical and theatrical performances
Alkazar Sinema Merkezi, İstiklal Caddesi 179 (☎ 245 7538)
Atlas, İstiklal Caddesi 209, Kuyumcular Pasajı (☎ 243 7576)
Beyoğlu, İstiklal Caddesi 140, Halep Pasajı (☎ 251 3240)
Dünya, İstiklal Caddesi 24-26, Fitaş Pasajı (☎ 252 0162)
Emek, İstiklal Caddesi, Yeşilçam Sokak 5 (☎ 293 8439)
Fitaş & Fitaş Cep, İstiklal Caddesi 24-26, Fitaş Pasajı (☎ 249 0166); four cinemas in one
Sinepop, İstiklal Caddesi, Yeşilçam Sokak 22 (☎ 251 1176)

Şişli Cumhuriyet Caddesi goes north from Taksim past the Hilton to Harbiye, where it changes names to become Halaskargazi Caddesi. From Harbiye northward through Osmanbey to Şişli Square (about two km) are several more cinemas:

Kent, Halaskargazi Caddesi 281 (☎ 241 6203)
Nova Baran, Nova Baran Plaza (☎ 240 3558)
Site, Halaskargazi Caddesi 291 (☎ 247 6947)

Çemberlitaş In Old İstanbul, on Yeniçeriler Caddesi between Sultanahmet and Beyazıt, is the Şafak cinema (☎ 516 2660), in the Darüşşafaka Pasajı, with three screens.

Café-Bars

Sultanahmet Best by far is *Rumeli Café* (☎ 512 0008), Ticarethane Sokak 8, İncili Çavuş Çımazı 3, a few steps off Divan Yolu in a little dead-end alley. Decorated by a Greek and run by a Turk, it's atmospheric, friendly and decently priced, with an extensive menu of light meals and snacks, and coffees and drinks from numerous countries. There's live music on weekends. It's open daily from 9 to 1 am, with a discount at happy hour (6 to 9 pm).

Beyoğlu Two nice little café-bars are *Kaktüs* (☎ 249 5979), a half-block south off İstiklal at İmam Adnan Sokak 4, and *Cadde-i Kebir*, directly across the street. Kaktüs is lighter, noisier, more active, with a longer menu. Cadde-i Kebir is quieter; snacks (çerez) and light meals are served. At either place, beer is US$1.50, raki US$2. There are sidewalk tables at both.

Two-thirds of the way along İstiklal toward Tünel, right next to the Odakule office tower, is *Garibaldi* (☎ 249 6895), a restaurant-bar with live music (jazz, smooth or Turkish pop) many nights starting around 8.30 pm. The specialities here are steaks and the extensive salad bar.

Just north of the Hilton at 239 Cumhuriyet Caddesi is *Pub Avni* (☎ 246 1136), a neighbourhood bar with a nightly crowd of middle-aged regulars, American and European recorded music, and a variety of snacks and full meals; closed Sunday.

Discos & Rock Clubs

Most discos and rock clubs are near Taksim Square.

Andromeda (☎ 230 4628), Yedikuyular Caddesi, Duvardibi Sokak 4, Elmadağ, is currently the biggest, best and flashiest. There's a cinema club as well. From the Divan Oteli, cross Cumhuriyet Caddesi and go west along Yedikuyular Caddesi to the first street on the right, which is Duvardibi Sokak.

Other music-and-dance clubs are located along Sıraselviler Caddesi, south out of Taksim. For rock, try *Kemancı* and *Mandala*, two side-by-side in the Taksim Sitesi building at Siraselviler Caddesi 69, a block south of Taksim on the left-hand (east) side. *Andon Dancing*, open from 9.30 pm to 2 am, is part of the popular Andon Pera (☎ 251 0222) café-bar at Sıraselviler Caddesi 89/2, just a short walk farther along the street.

Jazz Bars

The *Kehribar* (☎ 231 4100) in the Divan Oteli is smooth and luxurious, with excellent music and expensive drinks. Next door in the Hyatt Regency Istanbul, it's *Harry's Jazz*

Bar (☎ 225 7000), with a similar reputation. Also try the *Tepe Lounge Bar* (☎ 251 4696) at the Marmara hotel in Taksim, where there's jazz from 10.30 pm to 1 am.

For Turkish music, try the friendly *Jasmine* café-bar (☎ 252 7266), Akarsu Sokak 10, off İstiklal between Taksim and Galatasaray, open from 3 pm to 2 am.

Nightclubs

Nightclubs with entertainment are mostly in Beyoğlu and along the Bosphorus shores. In the Old City there are several Ottoman theme restaurants which offer dinner and an 'Ottoman' show including belly dancers and folk troupes. The larger, more expensive clubs are tame – and hardly authentic – but safe, as are the clubs in the big hotels. You may get ripped off in smaller clubs.

Kervansaray (☎ 247 1630), Cumhuriyet Caddesi 30, Harbiye, on the north side of the İstanbul Hilton arcade, is a good club of long standing with decent food and drinks and a good show at top prices of around US$35 to US$50 per person. It's popular with tour groups.

Belly dancing is a feature of several Ottoman theme restaurants in İstanbul.

A similar club is *Maksim* (☎ 293 4110), Sıraselviler Caddesi 37, just out of Taksim to the right of the Hotel Savoy. Maksim has a set menu (US$40) which includes dinner and a show (8.30 or 11.30 pm).

Casinos

Many of the large luxury hotels, including the Çirağan Palace Kempinski (☎ 259 0700), Conrad (☎ 227 3000), Hyatt Regency (☎ 225 7000), Istanbul Hilton (☎ 231 0300), Marmara (☎ 251 4696) and Swissôtel The Bosphorus (☎ 227 8721), have casinos where you can play slot machines, blackjack, roulette, and other games of chance. All have metal detectors at the door to keep out firearms, which are especially popular among Turkish gamblers.

A traditional Turkish *gazino*, by the way, has nothing to do with gambling. Rather, gazinos are open-air nightclubs popular in the summertime. A few still survive along the European shore of the Bosphorus. You won't find much belly dancing here, just Turkish popular singers, dinner and drinks. If the name of the place has the word 'aile' in it, as in Bebek Aile Gazinosu, it means the proprietor wants to appeal to a respectable, mixed crowd and avoid all-male or heavy-drinking audiences.

Night Cruises

About the cheapest yet most enjoyable nighttime activity in İstanbul is to take a Bosphorus ferry somewhere. It doesn't really matter where, as long as you don't end up on the southern coast of the Sea of Marmara or out in the Princes' Islands. Catch one over to Üsküdar or any town up the Bosphorus, and enjoy the view, the twinkling lights, the fishing boats bobbing in the waves, the powerful searchlights of the ferries sweeping the sea lanes. Have a glass of tea (a waiter will bring it round regularly). Get off anywhere, and take a bus or dolmuş home if you can't catch a ferry back directly.

Perhaps the easiest ferry to catch for this

Nightlife Ripoffs

Foreigners, especially single foreign males, are targets for a classic İstanbul ripoff which works like this:

You're a single male out for a stroll in the afternoon or evening. A well-spoken, well-dressed Turk strikes up a conversation, and says he knows 'a good place where we can have a drink and chat' or 'a great nightspot' etc. You enter, sit down, and immediately several women move to your table and order drinks. When they come, you're asked to pay – anywhere from US$100 to however much money you have with you. It's a mugging, and if you don't pay up they take you into the back office and take it from you.

An exotic variation is a single foreign male having a drink and a meal at the Çiçek Pasajı. Several Turkish friends strike up a conversation, then suggest you all take a taxi to another place. In the taxi, they forcefully relieve you of your wallet.

How do you avoid such ripoffs? As most Turks are generous, hospitable, curious and gregarious, it's difficult to know when an invitation is genuine (as it most often is) or the prelude to a ripoff. Tread carefully if there's any reason for suspicion. As for nightclub recommendations, take them from a trusted source, such as your hotel clerk. ■

purpose is the one from Eminönü to Üsküdar. Just go to Eminönü's Üsküdar dock, buy two jetons (for the voyages out and back), and walk aboard. From Üsküdar, just come back; or wait for one of the frequent ferries to Beşiktaş or Kabataş, from whence you can catch a bus or dolmuş back to your part of town.

A similar ride is the one to Haydarpaşa or Kadıköy, from Karaköy. These two Asian suburbs are the only destinations for ferries from these docks, so you can't end up way off somewhere. Return boats bring you back to Karaköy. The voyage takes 20 minutes in each direction.

Turkish Baths

A visit to the hamam can be wonderful: cleansing, refreshing, relaxing, and sociable.

The tradition of the steam bath was passed from the Romans to the Byzantines, and from them to the Turks, who have fostered it ever since. Islam's emphasis on personal cleanliness resulted in the construction of hundreds of hamams throughout İstanbul. Many of these survive, and continue their historic function.

Traditionally, men and women bathed separately, and bath attendants had to be of the same gender as their clients. Baths were taken frequently – especially on a Friday, the Muslim Sabbath – and prices were low.

Tourism has changed the tradition radically. Some of the finest old baths have raised prices dramatically, meaning that only tourists can afford them. Service has fallen as prices have risen, so you must shop carefully for your Turkish bath experience. For a description of taking a Turkish bath, see the Facts for the Visitor chapter.

In İstanbul, the price for the entire experience can be US$3 or US$4 in a local bath if you bring your own soap, shampoo and towel, and bathe yourself; from US$8 to US$10 for an assisted bath; from US$16 to US$25 at a 'historic' bath, including a perfunctory massage. Tips will be expected all around.

After you're all done, you'll be utterly refreshed, hyper-clean, and almost unable to walk due to the wonderful relaxation of muscles, mind and spirit.

Fancy Tourist Baths Cağaloğlu Hamamı (jaa-AHL-oh-loo) (☎ 522 2424), on Yerebatan Caddesi at Babiali Caddesi, just 200m from Aya Sofya near Cağaloğlu Square, was built over three centuries ago. It boasts (without evidence) that King Edward VIII, Kaiser Wilhelm II, Franz Liszt and Florence Nightingale have all enjoyed its pleasures, no doubt at the same time. Hours are from 7 am to 10 pm (men) or 8 am to 9 pm (women). Service seems to have improved, and hassles reduced, in recent years.

The other famous bath is the Tarihi Galatasaray Hamamı (☎ 244 1412) in Beyoğlu at the end of Suterazi Sokak, a little street going south-east from İstiklal Caddesi, just north of Galatasaray. Look for the sign on İstiklal Caddesi that points the way. The men's section is filled with gleaming marble and bath attendants hungry for tips; the women's section has less marble, but the same sort of service.

Local Baths If it's just a bath you're interested in, ask at your hotel for directions to a *mahalli hamam* (neighbourhood bath) where locals go. Neighbourhood baths will treat you much better for much less money than the touristy baths, though as more foreigners patronise these local baths they may suffer the same fate. Here are some suggestions near Sultanahmet:

Tarihi Park Hamamı – a small and unpretentious place at Doktor Emin Paşa Sokak 10; turn off Divan Yolu opposite the Hippodrome.

Kadırga Hamamı – on Kadırga Hamamı Sokak, just off Piyerloti Caddesi near the Piyerloti Pansiyon (see Places to Stay for directions).

Tarihi Hocapaşa Hamamı – at İbni Kemal Caddesi 23 near the Hocapaşa mosque near Sirkeci train station; the area is described in Places to Eat.

Tarihi Çemberlitaş Hamamı – on Yeniçeriler Caddesi (Divan Yolu) at Çemberlitaş

In Beyoğlu, look for the Tarihi Ağa Hamamı, very near the Galatasaray Hamamı on Turnacıbaşı Sokak. If you find another good, untouristy hamam, please write and let me know. And if your experience at any of the aforementioned baths is bad, let me know so I can warn other readers.

THINGS TO BUY

İstanbul has it all, and prices for craft items are not necessarily higher than at the village source. Leather apparel offers good value, but you must shop around, get to know the market a bit, and inspect your prospective purchase carefully for flaws and bad craftwork.

Carpets

There must be as many carpet shops as there are taxis. The carpet shop touts become exceedingly tedious very early in your visit, but a Turkish carpet – a good one at a fair price – is a beautiful and durable souvenir.

The carpet shops of longstanding are in and around the Covered Market. Their proprietors and sales personnel are more knowledgeable and less pushy than those at the newly opened shops in Cankurtaran and other hotel areas.

The government-run carpet shop in the Haseki Hürrem Hamamı between Aya Sofya and the Blue Mosque, described previously, is a safe choice, with guaranteed quality and fixed prices.

If you haggle for a carpet, at least shop around and get to know price levels a bit. Beware of this scam:

> You make friends with a charming Turk, or perhaps a Turkish-American or Turkish-European couple. They recommend a friend's shop, so you go and have a look. There's no pressure to buy. Indeed, your new friends wine and dine you (always in a jolly group with others), paying for everything. Before you leave İstanbul you decide to buy a carpet. You go to the shop, choose one you like, and ask the price. So far so good; if you can buy that carpet at a good price, everything's fine. But if the owner strongly urges you to buy a 'better' carpet, more expensive because it's 'old' or 'Persian' or 'rare', or 'makes a good investment', beware. You may return home with it to find you've paid many times more than the carpet is worth. If the shopkeeper ships the carpet for you, the cheap carpet which arrives may not be the expensive carpet you bought.

Make sure that *you* choose the carpet, inspect it carefully, compare prices for similar work at other shops, then buy and take it with you or ship it yourself; don't have the shopkeeper ship it.

Leather Apparel

The traditional leather apparel centre is the Kürkçüler Çarşısı section of the Covered Market, but today the leather shops fill street after street in the Beyazıt, Laleli and Aksaray districts.

The best way to be assured of quality is to

shop around, trying on garments in several shops. Look especially for quality stitching and lining, sufficient fullness of sleeve and leg, and care taken in the small things such as attaching buttons and zippers.

Handicrafts

Although the Covered Market has a great deal of general tourist ware, a few shops specialise in high-quality handicrafts. One such is Selvi El Sanatları (☎ 527 0997, fax 527 0226), Yağlıkçılar Caddesi 54, Kapalı Çarşı. The speciality here is Kütahya faïence, and not just the *turist işi* (tourist-ware) sold in most shops. Many of the tile panels, vases, plates and other items here are fine, artistic Kütahya ware.

Several historic medreses (theological colleges) have been restored and turned into handicrafts bazaars. İstanbul Handicrafts Centre is just to the right of the Yeşil Ev hotel on Kabasakal Caddesi, between Aya Sofya and the Blue Mosque.

More lively and interesting, with a café for hot and cold drinks, is the Caferağa Medresesi Handicrafts Centre on Caferiye Sokak, facing Aya Sofya. Shops set up in the old student cells offer carpets, jewellery, leather goods, embroidery, calligraphy and Turkish miniature paintings.

For posher shops, head north-east from Eminönü along the Golden Horn to the Golden Horn Handicrafts Centre (☎ 512 4270), on Ragıp Gümüşpala Caddesi. An ancient four-storey Genoese-Ottoman prison called the Zindan Han has been converted into a beautiful but pricey shop selling jewellery, leather and fine art. There's a restaurant with a view of the Golden Horn as well.

Shopping Malls

Grandest of them all is, of course, the Kapalı Çarşı, described earlier. Almost as popular and enjoyable is pedestrianised İstiklal Caddesi from Taksim Square to Tünel Square, lined with boutiques and places to eat.

Several modern American-style malls have opened as well.

Modern shopping malls were conceived in an automobile-based society with abundant, inexpensive suburban land on which to build sprawling buildings surrounded by vast expanses of car park – just the opposite of İstanbul. Here land is expensive, streets are narrow, and parking is nearly impossible.

Many of the shops in the new malls are branches of the same retailers you're used to at home, at similar prices, so they offer little acquisitive thrill to foreign visitors.

Newest and poshest of İstanbul's malls is the Akmerkez (☎ (212) 282 0170) in Etiler, well north of Taksim, west of Bebek. When you get tired of shopping at Ralph Lauren and Benetton, take sustenance from the supermarket, or relax in one of the cinemas.

İstanbul's first mall was the Galleria (gah-LEHR-ree-yah, ☎ 559 9560), on the Marmara shore road at Ataköy, west of the city walls. The bonus here is the small indoor ice-skating rink in winter.

GETTING THERE & AWAY

All roads lead to İstanbul. As the country's foremost transportation hub, the question is not how to get there (see the Getting There & Away chapter at the front of this book), but how to negotiate the sprawling urban mass when you arrive. Here is the information you may need on arrival.

Air

Atatürk (Yeşilköy) Airport's terminal, not even a decade old, is already insufficient to handle the volume of airborne traffic. A new terminal is already in the works.

The Ministry of Tourism maintains an information office in the international arrivals terminal. There is also a hotel-reservation desk in the arrivals terminal, but some readers of this guide have written to say that they always recommend the same expensive, inconvenient hotel to everyone, regardless of their preference. This may change, so check anyway.

Also in the arrivals terminal are various currency exchange offices operated by Turkish banks. If you change money here, count your money carefully and make sure it agrees with the total on the exchange slip. These guys will often short-change you by several percent, relying upon your confusion as a new arrival to get away with it. Also, don't accept an excuse that they 'have no small change'. It's their business to have the proper change.

Before you pass through customs, you might want to take the opportunity to buy duty-free goods at the shops in the baggage claim area.

For examples of airfares from İstanbul to other Turkish cities, see the introductory Getting Around chapter. For details on transport to and from İstanbul's Atatürk Airport, see the Getting Around section further in this chapter.

Airline Offices Most of the offices are on Cumhuriyet Caddesi between Taksim Square and Harbiye, in the Elmadağ district, but Turkish Airlines has offices around the city. Travel agencies can also sell tickets and make reservations. Some addresses follow:

Aeroflot
- Mete Caddesi 30, Taksim (☎ 243 4725)

Air France
- corner of Cumhuriyet & Tarlabaşı Caddesis, Taksim (☎ 237 3000)
- Atatürk Airport (☎ 663 0600)

Alitalia
- Cumhuriyet Caddesi 12/4, Elmadağ (☎ 231 3391)
- Atatürk Airport (☎ 663 0577)

American Airlines
- Cumhuriyet Caddesi 47/2, Elmadağ (☎ 237 2003)

British Airways
- Cumhuriyet Caddesi 10, Elmadağ (☎ 234 1300)
- Atatürk Airport (☎ 663 0574)

Delta Airlines
- in the Hilton arcade (☎ 231 2339)
- Atatürk Airport (☎ 663 0752)

El Al
- Rumeli Caddesi 4/1, Nişantaşı (☎ 246 5303)
- Atatürk Airport (☎ 663 0810)

Finnair & Gulf Air
- Cumhuriyet Caddesi 26, Elmadağ (☎ 234 5130)

Iberia
- Topçu Caddesi 2/2, Elmadağ (☎ 237 3104)
- Atatürk Airport (☎ 663 0826)

İstanbul Airlines
- Elmadağ/Harbiye Ticket Office, Cumhuriyet Caddesi 289 (☎ (212) 231 7526, fax 246 4967)
- Atatürk Airport, international routes (☎ 663 0664, fax 663 2712); domestic routes (☎ 574 4271, fax 663 2713)

Japan Air Lines
- Cumhuriyet Caddesi 141/6, Elmadağ (☎ 241 7266)

KLM
- Abdi İpekçi Caddesi 8, Nişantaşı, north-east of Harbiye (☎ 230 0311)
- Atatürk Airport (☎ 663 0603)

Lot
- Cumhuriyet Caddesi 91/2, Elmadağ (☎ (212) 240 7927, fax 246 7626)

Lufthansa
- Maya Akar Center, Büyükdere Caddesi 100-102, Esentepe (☎ 288 1050)
- Atatürk Airport (☎ 663 0594)

Malev
- Cumhuriyet Caddesi 141, Elmadağ (☎ (212) 248 8153/241 0909, fax 230 2034)
- Atatürk Airport (☎ 663 0589)

Olympic Airways
- Cumhuriyet Caddesi 203, Elmadağ (☎ 246 5081)
- Atatürk Airport (☎ 663 0820)

Qantas Airways
- Cumhuriyet Caddesi 155/1, Elmadağ (☎ (212) 240 5032/246 3466, fax 241 5552)

Sabena
- Topçu Caddesi 2/1, Taksim (☎ 254 7254)
- Atatürk Airport (☎ 663 0824)

SAS
- Cumhuriyet Caddesi 26/A, Elmadağ (☎ 246 6075)
- Atatürk Airport (☎ 663 0818)

Singapore Airlines
- Halaskargazi Caddesi 113, Harbiye (☎ (212) 232 3706, fax 248 8620)
- Atatürk Airport (☎ 663 0710)

Swissair
- Cumhuriyet Caddesi 6, Elmadağ (☎ 231 2850)
- Atatürk Airport (☎ 663 6778)

Trans World Airlines
- Cumhuriyet Caddesi 193, Elmadağ (☎ 234 5327)

Turkish Airlines
- reservations (☎ (212) 663 6363, fax 240 2984)
- Aksaray Ticket Office, Mustafa Kemal Paşa Caddesi 27 (☎ (212) 518 6840)
- Harbiye Ticket Office, Cumhuriyet Caddesi 199-201, across from the Hilton (☎ (212) 225 0556)
- Sirkeci Ticket Office, Hamidiye Caddesi, Doğubank İşhanı 26 (☎ (212) 511 7170)
- Taksim Square Ticket Office, Cumhuriyet Caddesi, in the Taksim Gezi Yeri shops (☎ (212) 252 1106)

Bus

The International Istanbul Bus Terminal (☎ (212) 658 0505, fax 658 2858), Uluslararası İstanbul Otogarı,), called simply the Otogar, is in the western district of Esenler, just south of the expressway and about 10 km west of Sultanahmet or Taksim. With 168 ticket offices, restaurants, mosques and shops, it is a town in itself, and one of the world's largest bus terminals. For Turkish travellers, this is the domestic equivalent of London-Heathrow or New York-JFK.

Buses depart the Otogar for virtually all cities and towns in Turkey and to neighbouring countries including Azerbaijan, Bulgaria, Greece, Iran, Romania, Saudi Arabia, Syria, and other destinations in Eastern Europe and the Middle East. The top national lines, giving premium service at somewhat higher prices, are As Turizm (office 117), Bosfor Turizm (127), Pamukkale (43), Ulusoy (128) and Varan (15). Other lines are smaller regional or local lines which may have more frequent service and less polished service at lower prices.

Except in busy holiday periods, you can usually just come to the Otogar, spend 30 minutes shopping for tickets, and be on your way to your destination at a good price within the hour. There is no easy way to find the best bus company and the best fare; you've got to go from one office to another asking for information and looking at the buses parked at the *perons* (gates) out the back.

Metro trams, municipal buses and taxis connect the Otogar with the city centre and the airport. See Getting Around, following, for details.

There is another bus terminal on the Asian shore of the Bosphorus at Harem (☎ (216) 333 3763), north of Haydarpaşa train station. If you're arriving from the east, by all means get out at Harem and take the car ferry to Sirkeci; it'll save you two hours' crawl through traffic to the main Otogar, then the Metro ride back to the centre. If you're heading east you can save some time and hassle by taking the car ferry from Sirkeci to Harem and getting the bus there. But the selection of buses, seats, routes and companies is nowhere near as big at Harem as at the main Otogar in Esenler.

Bus Ticket Offices Bus company offices are found clustered at the north-east end of the Hippodrome in Sultanahmet, in Laleli on Ordu Caddesi, near Sirkeci Station on Muradiye Caddesi, and in Taksim on Mete and İnönü Caddesis.

The biggest selection is in Taksim. Pamukkale (☎ 249 2791) is at Mete Caddesi 16; Nev Tur (☎ 249 7961), with buses to Cappadocia, is nearby. Down the hill along İnönü are Varan (☎ 249 1903, 251 7481), at İnönü Caddesi 29/B, a premium line with routes to major Turkish cities and to several points in Europe (including Athens); Kamil Koç (☎ 257 7223), İnönü Caddesi 31; As Turizm and Hakiki Koç lines (☎ 245 4244); and Ulusoy (☎ 249 4373), İnönü Caddesi 59.

Fares & Travel Times Here are some examples of bus fares and travel times from İstanbul. Fares vary among companies, and sometimes can be reduced by haggling or by showing a student card. Departures to major cities and resorts are very frequent.

Alanya – 840 km, 14 hours, US$20 to US$26
Ankara – 450 km, six hours, US$15 to US$24
Antakya – 1115 km, 20 hours, US$23 to US$31
Antalya – 725 km, 12 hours, US$17 to US$24
Artvin – 1352 km, 24 hours, US$34 to US$40
Ayvalık – 570 km, nine hours, US$16 to US$21
Bodrum – 830 km, 14 hours, US$22 to US$28
Bursa – 230 km, four hours, US$9
Çanakkale – 340 km, six hours, US$11 to US$14
Denizli (for Pamukkale) – 665 km, 10 hours, US$15 to US$20
Edirne – 235 km, four hours, US$4
Erzurum – 1276 km, 22 hours, US$21 to US$30
Fethiye – 980 km, 15 hours, US$26 to US$32
Gaziantep – 1150 km, 20 hours, US$27 to US$35
İzmir – 605 km, nine hours, US$16 to US$24
Kaş – 1090 km, 17 hours, US$28 to US$34
Konya – 660 km, 11 hours, US$18 to US$24
Kuşadası – 700 km, 11 hours, US$17 to US$24
Marmaris – 900 km, 15 hours, US$20 to US$27
Nevşehir (Cappadocia) – 725 km, 10 to 12 hours, US$17 to US$24
Side – 790 km, 14 hours, US$20 to US$25
Trabzon – 1110 km, 19 hours, US$25 to US$38

Train

Sirkeci Station All trains from Europe terminate at Sirkeci Garı (SEER-keh-jee, ☎ (212) 527 0051), next to Eminönü in the shadow of Topkapı Palace. The station has a small post office and currency exchange booth, as well as a restaurant and café. If Ms Cansen Bekleriz is on duty in the tourism office (☎ 511 5888), you'll get good answers to questions and information requests.

The north facade of the building was where passengers entered to board the fabled *Orient Express* to Paris. The new main (west) station door is a boring modern structure.

Right outside the station's west door is the tram up the hill to Sultanahmet, Beyazıt, Laleli and Aksaray.

If you're headed for Taksim, go out the station door and turn right. Walk towards the sea and you'll see the Eminönü bus ranks to your left. Catch a bus to Taksim from here, or a dolmuş from the inland end of the pedestrian overpass.

Departures Trains depart Sirkeci for the following destinations:

train	*destination*	*departs*	*arrives*
Balkan Ekspresi	Budapest	10 am	2.13 pm*
Belgrade Ekspresi	Belgrade	9.20 pm	6.07 am*
Baker Ekspresi	Bucharest	10 pm	2.25 pm
Express	Edirne	3.10 pm	9.15 pm
Express	Edirne	8.15 am	2.20 pm
Kiev Ekspresi	Kiev (& Moscow)	5.30 pm	6.40 pm*
Selenic Ekspresi	Thessaloniki	11.40 pm	4.41 pm

* arrival two days after departure

Haydarpaşa Station Haydarpaşa Garı (☎ (216) 336 0475, 348 8020), on the Asian shore of the Bosphorus, is the terminus for trains to and from Anatolia and points east and south.

Ferries (US$0.50, 20 minutes) run every 15 to 30 minutes between Karaköy (at the northern end of Galata Bridge) and Haydarpaşa.

Ignore anyone who suggests that you take a taxi to Haydarpaşa. The ferry is cheap, convenient, pleasant and speedy. Taxis across the Bosphorus are expensive and slow.

Departures The major trains departing from Haydarpaşa for Ankara, with fares, are detailed in the introductory Getting Around chapter. Here are details of other trains:

Güney & Van Gölü Ekspresi
The *Anadolu Ekspresi*, described in the Getting Around chapter, connects at Ankara with the *Güney Ekspresi*, departing from Ankara on Monday, Wednesday, Friday and Saturday via Kayseri, Sivas and Malatya to Diyarbakır and Kurtalan; and with the *Van Gölü Ekspresi*, which departs from Ankara on Tuesday, Thursday and Sunday via Kayseri, Sivas, Malatya, Elazığ and Muş to Tatvan on Lake Van. If you plan to take these trains, remember that you must leave İstanbul the day before (eg to connect with the *Güney Ekspresi* at Ankara on Monday morning, you must take the *Anadolu Ekspresi* from Haydarpaşa on Sunday evening).

Doğu Ekspresi
Though this train departs from Haydarpaşa on time at 11.55 pm, it is usually late thereafter on its long trip via Ankara, Sivas, Erzincan and Erzurum to Kars near the Armenian border. It is a long and not particularly pleasant trip, but it is certainly cheap, costing only US$25/18 in 1st/2nd class for the 2½-day trip across the country. There are coaches only, no sleeping accommodation.

İç Anadolu Mavi Tren
This train departs at 11.30 pm via Eskişehir and Afyon to Konya (US$16; couchette US$20), and arrives at 12.35 pm the next day before continuing to Karaman, arriving at 2.25 pm.

Marmara Ekspresi
Ferries depart Sarayburnu (Seraglio Point) just east of Sirkeci daily except Friday and Sunday at 8 am bound for Bandırma (four hours, US$8) on the south coast of the Sea of Marmara. From Bandırma trains run to İzmir (Basmane) in about 5½ hours (US$6). Note that the trains between İzmir and Bandırma run every day, but the ferries only five days per week.

Meram Ekspresi
The Meram departs daily at 6.30 pm via Eskişehir and Afyon, arriving in Konya at 8.10 am. The fare to Konya is US$13/9 in 1st/2nd class; for sleeping compartments, total fares are US$38/58/82 for singles/doubles/triples.

Pamukkale Ekspresi
The nighttime Pamukkale Express departs daily at 5.30 pm, arriving in Denizli at 7.27 am. Fares are US$12/9 in 1st/2nd class; for sleeping compartments, total fares are US$38/58/82 for singles/doubles/triples.

Toros Ekspresi
: This train departs from Söğütlüçeşme Station on Tuesday, Thursday and Saturday at 8.55 am, and heads for the south-east, arriving in Adana at 6.50 am the next morning. Fares to Adana are US$18/14 in 1st/2nd class; for sleeping compartments, total fares are US$32/52/72 a single/double/triple.

Car

The E80 Trans-European Motorway from Europe passes north of Atatürk Airport, then crosses the Bosphorus on the Fatih Bridge. Exit signs direct you to various districts of the city.

For a scenic entrance to the city, leave the expressway at the airport and follow signs for Yeşilköy or Ataköy, which will take you to the shore of the Sea of Marmara so you can drive into the city along the water's edge. You'll pass the city walls near Yedikule, the Fortress of the Seven Towers and the Marble Tower, as well as the city's southern wall, which will be on your left as you drive. Across the Bosphorus are Üsküdar, Haydarpaşa and Kadıköy, with the large four-square Selimiye Barracks acting as a landmark. Turn left onto Mustafa Kemal Caddesi for Aksaray and Laleli; or continue around Seraglio Point. For Cankurtaran and the hotels near Sultanahmet, turn left and pass through the walls following signs to the Hotel Armada, but then turn right and climb the hill. If you stay on the shore road it will take you to Sirkeci, Eminönü and the Galata Bridge.

Car Rental The best car rental rates are usually those you arrange from home before travelling to Turkey. See the introductory Getting Around chapter for details.

The well-known international car-rental firms have desks at Atatürk Airport and downtown, mostly near Taksim Square and the Elmadağ district just a few blocks to the north.

Avis
: Atatürk Airport international arrivals hall (☎ 663 0646) and domestic arrivals hall (☎ 573 1452, fax 663 6672)
: Reservations centre (☎ (212) 257 7670, fax 263 3918)
: İstanbul Hilton arcade office (☎ 241 7896, fax 231 6244)
: Beyazıt office, Ordu Caddesi, Haznedar Sokak 1 (☎ 516 6109, fax 516 6108)

Budget
: Atatürk Airport international arrivals hall (☎ 663 0858, fax 663 0724)
: Reservations Centre, Cumhuriyet Caddesi 13/1, just north of Taksim Square (☎ (212) 253 9200, fax 256 2611)
: Office, Cumhuriyet Caddesi 19/A, Gezi Apartımanı (☎ (212) 253 9200, fax 237 2919)

Europcar
: Esin Turizm, Topçu Caddesi 1, 80090 Talimhane, a few short blocks north of Taksim Square and only steps west of Cumhuriyet Caddesi (☎ (212) 254 7799, fax 255 5928). It represents Europcar and Inter-Rent and also has an office at Atatürk Airport in the international arrivals hall (☎ 663 0746, fax 663 6830)

Hertz
: Atatürk Airport international arrivals hall (☎ 573 5987)
: Cumhuriyet Caddesi 295, north of Taksim in Harbiye (☎ 234 4300)

Sun Rent a Car
: A local firm with a good reputation and offices in major cities and resorts; reservations centre, Cumhuriyet Caddesi 26, Elmadağ, just north of Taksim Square (☎ (212) 246 0815, fax 240 8351)

Boat

Sarayburnu Ships to and from Bandırma on the *Marmara Ekspresi* boat-train route (see above) between İstanbul and İzmir dock at Sarayburnu, one km east of the Galata Bridge, north and east of Sirkeci Station. The entrance to the dock area is near Milady's Restaurant and the Atatürk statue.

Karaköy Cruise liners dock at Karaköy, near the Yolcu Salonu (YOHL-joo sahl-oh-noo), or International Maritime Passenger Terminal on Rıhtım Caddesi. The Ministry of Tourism has an information office (☎ 249 5776) in the Yolcu Salonu, near the front (street) doors.

This international dock is next to the Karaköy ferry dock and only 100m east of the Galata Bridge. Bus and dolmuş routes to Taksim pass along Kemeraltı Caddesi, a few short blocks north-west of the Yolcu Salonu. For destinations in the Old City such as Sultanahmet, Laleli and Aksaray, go to the western side of Karaköy Square itself, right at the end of the Galata Bridge. You'll have to find the pedestrian underpass to get to the dolmuş and bus stops.

Kabataş Ferries and hydrofoils to and from Yalova and the Princes' Islands dock at Kabataş (KAH-bah-tahsh), about two km north of Karaköy on the Bosphorus shore, just south of the Dolmabahçe palace and mosque. As you leave the dock at Kabataş, buses and dolmuşes heading left will be going to Karaköy and the Old City; those travelling right will be going to Taksim or north along the Bosphorus shore.

GETTING AROUND

Even though several wide boulevards have been cut through the city's medieval street pattern, they are insufficient to move the glut of cars, trucks and buses quickly. Transport by road often creeps.

Transport by sea is far more pleasant and speedy, but with the completion of the Bosphorus bridges the ferry service was severely curtailed. Now the ferries are advantageous on only a handful of routes.

The Airport

Free shuttle buses leave the airport's international terminal for the domestic terminal every 20 minutes or so throughout the day. Just walk out of the international arrivals terminal and look for the Havaş shuttle bus.

Airport to City The fastest way to get into town from the airport is by taxi (from 20 to 30 minutes, US$10 to US$20); the fare depends upon what part of the city you're headed for and whether it's night or day.

A far cheaper but less speedy alternative is the Havaş airport bus (from 35 to 60 minutes, US$2.75), which departs from the international terminal, stops at the domestic terminal, then goes into the city, stopping at Bakırköy (Cevizlik), and on Mustafa Kemal Paşa Bulvarı in Aksaray (near Laleli), before ending its run in Beyoğlu at Taksim Square. Buses leave every half-hour from 5.30 to 10 am, every hour from 10 am to 2 pm, every half-hour from 2 to 8 pm, and every hour from 9 to 11 pm; there are no buses between 11 pm and 5.30 am.

You can cut the cost down to US$1 if you take the No 96 red-and-beige İETT city bus to Yenikapı, a few blocks south of Aksaray, but the nine buses per day leave only about every 1½ hours. Catch the bus at the bus stop by the big taxi-parking area more or less between the two terminals (ask for the *belediye otobüsü*).

For only slightly more, find two or three other thrifty travellers and share a taxi (US$4 total; make sure the driver runs the meter) from the airport to the Yeşilköy banliyö tren istasyonu, the suburban railway station in the neighbouring town of Yeşilköy. From here, battered trains (US$0.50) run every half-hour or less to Sirkeci Station. Get off at Yenikapı for Aksaray and Laleli, at Cankurtaran for Sultanahmet hotels, or at Sirkeci for Beyoğlu. Another way to get to the suburban train line is to take the Metro south (from the Dünya Ticaret Merkezi (World Trade Centre) station just east of the airport) to Ataköy and transfer.

City to Airport You must check in *at least* 30 minutes before departure time for domestic flights, and it's not a bad idea to check in 45 to 60 minutes before. For international flights, you should be in line at the check-in counter at least an hour before take-off, and as it can take a half-hour just to get through the first security check and into the terminal building, you should plan to arrive at the airport 1½ or two hours before departure time. After check-in, you must go through passport control, customs, and another security check before boarding. If the aircraft is large, the officials will have to process about 400 passengers at once.

If you're staying in Old İstanbul and you have plenty of time (45 minutes to an hour) for the return trip to the airport, catch bus 96 (US$0.50) on the east side of Mustafa Kemal Paşa Bulvarı south of Aksaray, across the street from McDonald's. Departures are at 7, 8.40, 10.15 and 11.45 am, and 1.35, 2.45, 4.05, 5.55 and 7.40 pm. Otherwise, get on a suburban train ('Halkalı', US$0.50) at Sirkeci, Cankurtaran or Yenikapı, and get out at Yeşilköy, then take a taxi (US$4) to the airport.

Several private services run minibuses to the airport, advertising their services at budget-priced hotels in and around Sultanahmet. One such company is Bekir Turizm (☎ (212) 529 2328, fax 586 4670), Vezir Caddesi 15, Odabaş, Çapa, which charges US$3.50 per seat. Reserve your seat in advance for pick-up from your hotel; minibuses run every two hours. But allow lots of time for the trip: the minibus may spend an hour circulating through the city collecting all the passengers before heading out to the airport (30 to 45 minutes).

If you're staying in Beyoğlu, the cheapest and most convenient way to the airport is the Havaş bus (US$2.75) from Taksim Square. It also stops on Mustafa Kemal Bulvarı south of Aksaray Square to pick up passengers. There are also dolmuşes to the airport (Hava Limanı) from the Yeşilköy-Ataköy-Florya-Hava Limanı dolmuş stand on Şehit Muhtar Bey Caddesi two blocks north of Taksim.

A taxi to the airport costs US$10 to US$20.

Airport to Bus Terminal The Dünya Ticaret Merkezi (World Trade Centre) Metro station is just east of the airport. From it, Metro trains run north to the Otogar station right in the midst of the International İstanbul Bus Terminal.

Bus

Bus Terminals If you arrive at the Otogar in Esenler, take the Metro east toward Aksaray or Yenikapı. In Aksaray, board the other tram to Sultanahmet and Sirkeci.

To get to the Harem bus terminal, take the car ferry from Sirkeci. An alternative is to take a ferry from Karaköy to Haydarpaşa or Kadıköy, then catch a dolmuş northward along the shore to Harem; they run very frequently. You can also take a ferry from Eminönü, Kabataş or Beşiktaş to Üsküdar, then a dolmuş or bus south 2.5 km to Harem.

City Buses Red-and-beige İETT city buses are useful, but slow and usually packed solid. Fares are US$0.50 per ride, around half-price for students, but you may need a Turkish student ID card to get the discount. Fares are paid on a ticket system (see the introductory Getting Around chapter). Hawkers near the major bus stops usually sell tickets for a markup of 20% for your convenience. On the kerb side of each bus is a list of stops along the route.

Most buses require one ticket for passage (look for *Tek* or *Bir Bilet Geçerlidir* in the windscreen), others on longer routes require two tickets (*Çift* or *İki Bilet Geçerlidir*).

Some buses fill to capacity right at the departure point, leaving no room for passengers en route. If you're jammed in the middle of the bus when your stop comes, shout *İnecek var!* (een-neh-JEK vahr, 'Someone needs to get out!').

Dolmuş

For a definition of 'dolmuş', see the Getting Around chapter. Unlike city buses, dolmuşes are rarely overcrowded. Major dolmuş termini of use to tourists are Taksim and Aksaray. You will have to ask a passerby or shopkeeper to locate the dolmuş stops, which are often unmarked.

Metro

İstanbul's Metro system will be under construction for a decade more, but several useful lines are already in service. The fare is US$0.50.

The main line goes from Aksaray northwestward along Adnan Menderes Bulvarı (formerly Vatan Caddesi) through the Bayrampaşa and Sağmalcılar districts to the bus terminal in Esenler, then turns southwestward to pass the airport, terminating at Ataköy on the Sea of Marmara, where it meets the suburban train line.

The Sirkeci-Halkalı suburban train line follows the Sea of Marmara shore south-westward from Seraglio Point to the south-western suburbs. At Ataköy it links to the main Metro line. The suburban trains (*banliyö treni*) are decrepit but serviceable and cheap.

A shorter tram line goes from Aksaray along Ordu Caddesi/Yeniçeriler Caddesi/ Divan Yolu through Beyazıt to Sultanahmet and Sirkeci.

In Beyoğlu, a restored early 20th-century tram runs along İstiklal Caddesi between Taksim and Tünel squares, but is too small and infrequent to be of great use.

The 7.8-km-long Taksim to 4 Levent underground line is presently under construction. The tunnels have been excavated and the stations built. The laying of the tracks and electrification are scheduled to be completed by the end of 1997.

Tünel

İstanbul's little underground train, the Tünel, runs between Karaköy and the southern end of İstiklal Caddesi called Tünel Meydanı (Tünel Square). The fare is US$0.35. There are only two stations on the line, the upper and lower, so there's no getting lost. Trains run every five or 10 minutes from early morning until about 10 pm.

Car

It makes no sense to drive in İstanbul. If you have a car, park it and use public transport, except perhaps for excursions up the Bosphorus. If you plan to rent a car, do so when you're ready to leave İstanbul. (For addresses of car rental agencies see the Getting There & Away section earlier in this chapter.)

Taxi

Taxis are plentiful, as are honest drivers, though the dishonest ones seem to congregate in touristic areas.

All taxis have digital meters, and it is an offence punishable by a large fine to take a passenger but to refuse to run the meter, or to demand a flat fare in place of the metered fare. Still, such practices are common on trips originating from touristic areas (see the warning under Taxi in the Getting Around chapter). Some drivers also take advantage of the many zeros on Turkish currency to charge you 10 times what the meter reads.

The base rate (drop rate, flag fall) is about US$1 during the daytime *(gündüz)*; the night-time *(gece)* rate is 50% higher. A daytime trip between Aksaray and Sultanahmet costs about US$1.25; between Taksim and Karaköy about US$2.25; between Taksim and Sultanahmet about US$4, between Sultanahmet and the airport about US$10 to US$12.

Older meters have tiny red lights marked with these words to show which rate is being used. Newer meters, with LCD displays, flash 'gündüz' or 'gece' when they are started. Future meters will supposedly have time-of-day clocks built in so that the driver cannot use the 'gece' rate during the daytime. and you should be careful that the driver is not running the night-time rate on his meter during the day. But even this will not stop creative cheaters:

> One driver I used found that if he whacked a certain spot on the instrument panel of his car after starting, the meter would skip from 'gündüz' to 'gece', thereby increasing his profit by 50%. One can hardly fail to notice a driver beating violently on his vehicle, and also that the fare is unusually high: I saw the 'gece' light was on and deducted 33% from the final fare.

Ferry

Without doubt the nicest way to travel any considerable distance in İstanbul is by ferry. You will (and should) use the boats whenever possible.

Founded as the state-owned Şirket-i Hayriye (The Beneficial Company) in Ottoman times, the Turkish Maritime Lines City Routes administration (Denizyolları Şehir Hatları), which runs İstanbul's ferryboats, is about to be sold to private investors. Routes, schedules and fares may change greatly if and when this happens.

The major ferry docks are at Eminönü, Karaköy and Kabataş. Short ferry rides (under 30 minutes) cost US$0.50, most longer ones (up to an hour) US$1. Buy your tokens from the agent in the booth; if you buy them from the men who stand around outside the ferry docks hawking them, you may pay four times the fare.

Schedules At each dock is a framed copy of

the *tarife* (tah-ree-FEH, timetable) outlining the service. It's only in Turkish, so I'll give you the necessary translations. Each route *(hat* or *hattı)* is designated by the names of the principal stops. Please note that the tarife has two completely different parts, one for weekdays *(normal günleri)* and Saturday *(Cumartesi)*, and another for Sunday *(Pazar)* and holidays *(bayram günleri)*. Make sure you're looking at the proper part.

Special Touristic Excursions The ferry most tourists use is the Eminönü-Kavaklar Boğaziçi Özel Gezi Seferleri (Eminönü Special Touristic Excursion, US$5) up the Bosphorus. These ferries depart from Eminönü daily at 10.35 am, 12.35 and 2.10 pm each weekday, arriving at Sarıyer, on the European shore about three quarters of the way up the Bosphorus, at 11.50 am, 1.50 and 3.30 pm respectively. The schedule is fuller on Sunday and holidays, with boats departing from Eminönü at 10 and 11 am, noon, 1.30 and 3 pm. Hold onto your ticket; you need to show it to re-board the boat for the return trip.

Departures from Sarıyer for the trip back down the Bosphorus are at 2.20, 3.10 and 5.50 pm on weekdays.

These special voyages go all the way to Rumeli Kavağı and Anadolu Kavağı (1¾ hours), but you may want to go only as far as Sarıyer, then take a dolmuş or bus back down, stopping at various sights along the way. The boats fill up early, so buy your ticket and walk aboard at least 30 or 45 minutes prior to departure to get a seat.

Karaköy to Haydarpaşa/Kadıköy To get to the Asia train station at Haydarpaşa, or for a little cruise around Seraglio Point (good for photos of Topkapı Palace, Aya Sofya and the Blue Mosque) and across the Bosphorus, catch a boat from the ferry dock in Karaköy; they depart every 15 minutes (every 20 minutes on weekends). If you're going to the station, be sure it's a Hyadarpaşa boat. The trip over to Haydarpaşa or Kadıköy and back will take about an hour, and cost about US$1 for the round trip.

Eminönü/Kabataş to Üsküdar Ferries depart from Eminönü every 15 minutes between 6 am and midnight for Üsküdar, even more frequently during rush hour. From Kabataş, just south of Dolmabahçe Palace, ferries run to Üsküdar every 30 minutes on the hour and half-hour from 7 am to 8 pm. A similarly frequent ferry service operates between Beşiktaş and Üsküdar.

Cross-Bosphorus Ferry Other ferry routes link the eastern and western shores of the Bosphorus, running from breakfast time to dinner time. Here are the routes: Bebek-Kanlıca-Anadolu Hisarı-Kandilli (about every hour); Yeniköy-Beykoz (about every half-hour, with a few boats calling at İstinye and Paşabahçe); Sarıyer-Rumeli Kavağı-Anadolu Kavağı (about every hour). If you don't catch one of these boats, you can always hire a boater as a private water taxi to take you across from one shore to the other.

Hydrofoil

Called *deniz otobüsü* (sea-buses), hydrofoils run from Old İstanbul to the Asian suburbs on the north Marmara shore, and from Kabataş to the Princes' Islands and Yalova (the port for Bursa). For details, see Getting There & Away in the Yalova section of the South of the Sea of Marmara chapter.

Hydrofoil trips cost about twice as much as traditional ferries, but are much faster and more comfortable. Here are the main docks and routes:

Eminönü – occasional service to Büyükada in the Princes' Islands
Kabataş – most frequent service to the Princes' Islands and Yalova
Karaköy – to Bostancı, an Asian suburb on the Sea of Marmara shore
Yenikapı – planned to be the Old City's major hydrofoil port

On Foot

With an overburdened public transport system, walking can often be faster and more rewarding. The street scenes are never dull, and the views from one hill to the next can be extraordinary. While walking, watch out for broken pavement, bits of pipe sticking a few cm out of the pavement, and all manner of other obstacles.

Don't expect any car driver to stop for you, a pedestrian, in any situation. Automobiles seize the right of way virtually everywhere, and drivers of these marvellous and expensive machines become furiously annoyed with pedestrians who assert ridiculous and specious claims to right of way and safety. The infant, the halt, the lame, the aged, the infirm and all the rest flee before the onslaught of the automobile. Step lively, or you'll be hit.

Thrace

The land to the north of the Aegean Sea was called Thrace by the Romans. Today this ancient Roman province is divided between Turkey, Bulgaria and Greece, with Turkey holding the easternmost part. Turkish Thrace (Trakya) is not particularly exciting except for its chief city, Edirne.

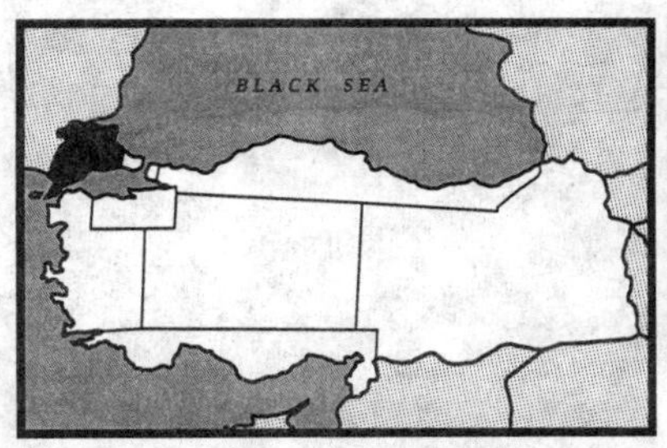

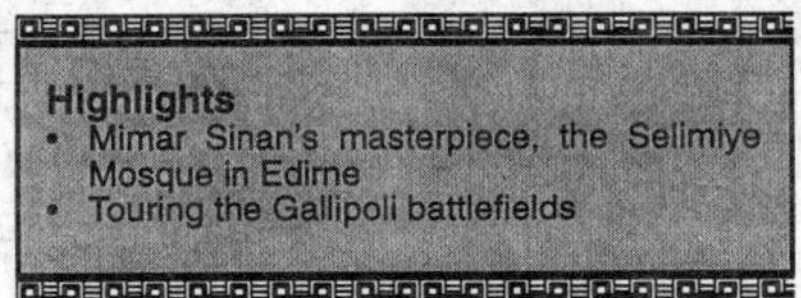

Highlights

- Mimar Sinan's masterpiece, the Selimiye Mosque in Edirne
- Touring the Gallipoli battlefields

EDİRNE

A glance at the map seems to tell you all about Edirne (eh-DEER-neh, altitude 40m, population 115,000): it's a stopping point on the road to İstanbul. But because of its history, Edirne (formerly Adrianople), has several of the finest Turkish mosques, and you really should see them.

If you're coming from İstanbul, you can make the 250-km trip to Edirne (2½ hours) and back to İstanbul in a day.

History

The Roman emperor Hadrian founded Edirne in the 2nd century as Hadrianopolis, a forward defence post for Constantinople. The town's name was later shortened by Europeans to Adrianople, then changed again by the Turks to Edirne.

It played a very important role in the early centuries of the Ottoman Empire which grew from a small Turkish emirate in north-western Anatolia. By the mid-1300s, the emirate of the Ottomans with its capital at Bursa had become very powerful, but not enough to threaten the mighty walls of Constantinople. Bent on further conquest, the Ottoman armies crossed the Dardanelles into Thrace, skirting the great capital. Capturing Adrianople in 1363, they made it their new capital and base of operations for military campaigns in Europe.

For almost 100 years, this was the city from which the Ottoman sultan would set out on his campaigns to Europe and Asia. When, at last, the time was ripe for the final conquest of the Byzantine Empire, Mehmet the Conqueror set out from Edirne on the road to Constantinople. Even after this great city was captured, and became the Ottoman capital, Edirne played an important role in Ottoman life and society, for it was still a forward post en route to other conquests in Europe.

When the Ottoman Empire disintegrated after WWI, the Allies decided to grant all of Thrace to the Greek kingdom. Constantinople was to become an international city. In the summer of 1920, Greek armies occupied Edirne. But Atatürk's republican armies were ultimately victorious and the Treaty of Lausanne left Edirne and eastern Thrace to the Turks. Edirne returned to its role as 'the town on the way to İstanbul'.

Edirne is largely disregarded by tourists, which has helped preserve its Turkish character and appeal. While the towns along the Aegean and Mediterranean coasts are clogged with foreigners and with vast new European-style building projects, Edirne attracts the discerning few who come to enjoy the harmony and history of its mosques, covered bazaars, bridges and caravanserais, and the easy pace of life.

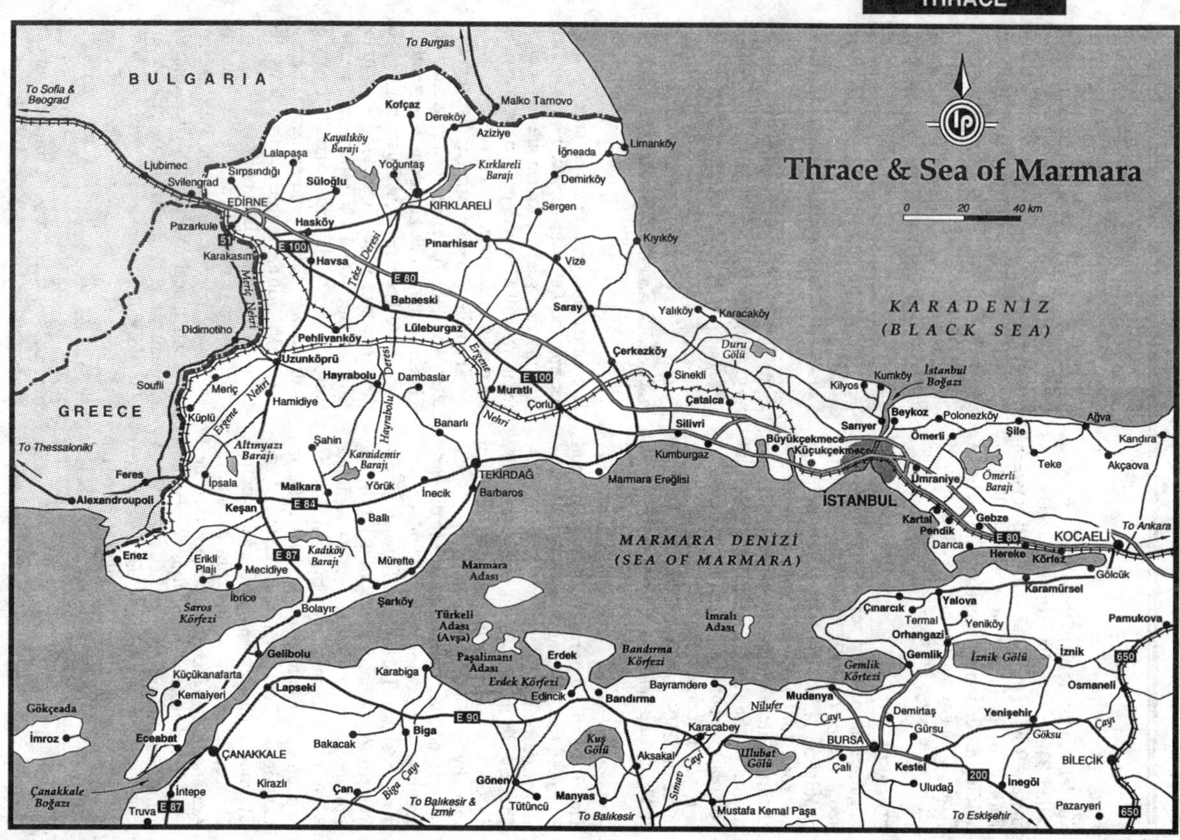
Thrace & Sea of Marmara
0
20
40 km
KARADENİZ
(BLACK SEA)
MARMARA DENİZİ
(SEA OF MARMARA)
BULGARIA
GREECE
To Sofia & Beograd
To Burgas
To Thessaloniki
To Ankara
To Eskişehir
To Balıkesir
To Balıkesir & İzmir
EDİRNE
KIRKLARELİ
TEKİRDAĞ
İSTANBUL
KOCAELİ
BURSA
ÇANAKKALE
BİLECİK
Ljubimec
Svilengrad
Pazarkule
Karakasım
Sırpsındığı
Lalapaşa
Süloğlu
Kayalıköy Barajı
Hasköy
Havsa
Kofçaz
Yoğuntaş
Dereköy
Aziziye
Malko Tarnovo
Kırklareli Barajı
İğneada
Demirköy
Limanköy
Sergen
Kıyıköy
Vize
Pınarhisar
Babaeski
Lüleburgaz
Saray
Çerkezköy
Yalıköy
Karacaköy
Sinekli
Çatalca
Duru Gölü
Silivri
Kumburgaz
Marmara Ereğlisi
Çorlu
Muratlı
Ergene Nehri
Banarlı
Barbaros
Dambaslar
Hayrabolu
Hayrabolu Deresi
Teke Deresi
Meriç Nehri
Pehlivanköy
Uzunköprü
Hamidiye
Şahin
Karaidemir Barajı
Yörük
İnecik
Ballı
Mürefte
Şarköy
Malkara
Kadıköy Barajı
Bolayır
Gelibolu
Keşan
Mecidiye
İbrice
Erikli Plajı
Saros Körfezi
Altınyazı Barajı
İpsala
Meriç
Küplü
Didimotiho
Soufli
Feres
Alexandroupoli
Enez
Gökçeada
İmroz
Çanakkale Boğazı
Eceabat
Kemalyeri
Küçükanafarta
Truva
İntepe
Kirazlı
Lapseki
Bakacak
Çan
Biga
Biga Çayı
Karabiga
Gönen
Tütüncü
Manyas
Kuş Gölü
Erdek
Erdek Körfezi
Edincik
Bandırma
Bandırma Körfezi
Aksakal
Bayramdere
Karacabey
Simav Çayı
Mustafa Kemal Paşa
Uluabat Gölü
Nilufer Çayı
Mudanya
Çalı
Marmara Adası
Türkeli Adası (Avşa)
Paşalimanı Adası
İmralı Adası
Gemlik
Gemlik Körtezi
Çınarcık
Termal
Yalova
Yeniköy
Orhangazi
İznik
İznik Gölü
Demirtaş
Gürsu
Kestel
Uludağ
Yenişehir
İnegöl
Göksu Çayı
Osmaneli
Pazaryeri
Pamukova
Karamürsel
Gölcük
Körfez
Hereke
Gebze
Darıca
Pendik
Kartal
Ümraniye
Ömerli
Ömerli Barajı
Polonezköy
Beykoz
İstanbul Boğazı
Kumköy
Kilyos
Sarıyer
Büyükçekmece
Küçükçekmece
Şile
Teke
Ağva
Kandıra
Akçaova
E 80
E 100
E 84
E 87
E 90
200
650
51

Orientation

The centre of town is Hürriyet Meydanı, or Freedom Square, at the intersection of the two main streets, Saraçlar/Hükümet Caddesi and Talat Paşa Caddesi. Just north-east of the square is the Üçşerefeli Cami. Going east along Talat Paşa Caddesi and north-east along Mimar Sinan Caddesi will bring you to Edirne's masterpiece, the Selimiye Camii. On the way to the Selimiye, you'll pass the Eski Cami. South of Hürriyet Square is the Ali Paşa Çarşısı, Edirne's largest covered bazaar.

The *otogar* (bus station) is two km south-east of the Eski Cami on the old highway (D 100) to Istanbul. The main dolmuş station downtown is next to the Eski Cami and the Hotel Kervansaray.

Information

The Ministry of Tourism's Office (☎ (284) 225 1518, 213 9208, fax 225 2518), Hürriyet Meydanı 17, is just off the main square, a half-block south-west of the Üçşerefeli Cami. They can help with lodging, transport and money-changing questions.

The provincial tourism office (Edirne İl Turizm Müdürlüğü) is farther west along Talat Paşa Caddesi, the road to the Bulgarian border at Kapıkule. There's yet another office at the Kapıkule border post (☎ (284) 238 2019, fax 238 2009).

Edirne's postal code is 22100.

Banks You can change foreign currency at Araz Döviz, to the right of the central tourism office. If you have a bank card, you may be able to withdraw cash from the ATM (cash machine) at the Akbank across the street from the same tourism office. The Garanti Bankası across Maarif Caddesi from the tourism office has another machine tied to the international banking networks, as does the Yapı Kredi Bankası next to the PTT, and the Ziraat Bankası in the market off Saraçlar Caddesi.

Consulates & Visas The Bulgarian Consulate (☎ (284) 225 1069) is on Talat Paşa Asfaltı on the way to the otogar, open Monday to Friday from 9 am to 12.30 pm. A transit visa good for 30 hours costs US$12 for many nationalities; if you buy it at the border it will cost US$16. Visas for longer stays are more expensive.

The Greek Consulate (☎ (284) 225 1074), is in the Kaleiçi district on Cumhuriyet Caddesi, open Monday to Friday from 9 am to 12.30 pm.

Üçşerefeli Cami

The principal reason to stop in Edirne is to see mosques, so start from Hürriyet Meydanı with the Üçşerefeli Cami.

The name means 'mosque with three galleries (balconies)'. Actually it's one of the mosque's four minarets which has the three balconies. The minarets, built at different times, are all wonderfully varied.

Enter at the far end of the courtyard rather than through a side gate. That way you can enjoy the full effect of the architect's genius. The courtyard at the Üçşerefeli (EWCH-sheh-reh-feh-LEE) with its *şadırvan* (ablutions fountain) was a prototype for the courtyards of the Ottoman mosques built in later centuries.

Construction of this mosque was begun in 1440 and finished by 1447. It exemplifies a transition from the Seljuk Turkish type of architecture of Konya and Bursa to a truly Ottoman style, which would be perfected later in İstanbul. The Seljuks were greatly influenced by the Persian and Indian styles prevalent in their empire to the east. The Ottomans learned much from the Seljuk Turks, but also from the Byzantines, for whom İstanbul's Sancta Sophia (with its wide, expansive dome covering a great open space) was the purest expression of their ideal. After the Ottomans took Constantinople in 1453, they assimilated the architecture of Sancta Sophia into their tradition and the transition from Seljuk to pure Ottoman accelerated.

In the Seljuk style, smaller domes are mounted on square rooms. But at the Üçşerefeli, the wide (24m) dome is mounted on a hexagonal drum and supported by two walls and two pillars. Keep this transitional

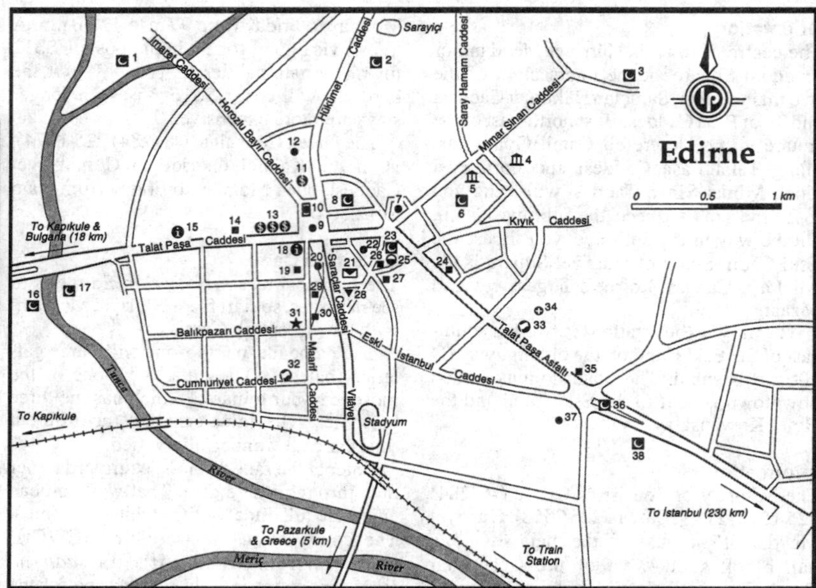

PLACES TO STAY

14 Sultan Oteli
19 Otel Anıl
24 Kervan Oteli
26 Otel Şaban Açıkgöz
27 Hotel Kervansaray
29 Park Hotel
30 Efe Hotel
35 Balta Hotel

PLACES TO EAT

28 Aile Restaurant

OTHER

1 Beyazıt II Külliyesi
2 Beylerbeyi Camii
3 Muradiye Camii
4 Archaeological Museum
5 Turkish & Islamic Arts Museum
6 Selimiye Camii
7 Belediye
8 Üçşerefeli Cami
9 Hürriyet Meydanı
10 Sokullu Mehmet Paşa Hamamı
11 Central Bank
12 Vilâyet
13 Banks
15 Provincial Tourism Information Office
16 Gazimihal Camii
17 Şahmelek Camii
18 Tourism Information Office
20 Ali Paşa Çarşısı
21 PTT
22 Bedesten
23 Eski Cami
25 Dolmuş (Minibus Station)
31 Emniyet Müdürlüğü (Police Station)
32 Greek Consulate
33 Bulgarian Consulate
34 Devlet Hastanesi (Hospital)
36 Ayşekadın Camii
37 Ekmekçioğlu Ahmet Paşa Kervansarayı
38 Kadı Bedrettin Camii

style in mind as you visit Edirne's other mosques which reflect earlier or later styles.

Across the street from the mosque is the **Sokollu Mehmet Paşa Hamamı** or Turkish baths, built in the late 1500s and still in use. Designed by the great Mimar Sinan for Grand Vizier Sokollu Mehmet Paşa, it is a *çifte hamam* (twin baths) with identical but separate sections for men *(erkekler kısmı)*, and women *(kadınlar kısmı)*. Opening hours are from 6 am to 10 pm. Simple admission costs US$2.25, washing by an attendant US$3.50, a massage US$6.

Eski Cami

Now head back to Hürriyet Meydanı, and walk east on Talat Paşa Caddesi to the Eski Cami or Old Mosque. On your way you'll pass the bedesten (covered market) on your right, this one dating from 1418. Behind it to the east is the Rüstem Paşa Hanı, a grand caravanserai built 100 years after the bedesten.

The Eski Cami (1414) exemplifies one of two principal mosque styles used by the Ottomans in their earlier capital, Bursa. Like Bursa's great Ulu Cami, the Eski Cami has rows of arches and pillars supporting a series of small domes. Inside, there's a marvellous mihrab and huge calligraphic inscriptions on the walls. The columns at the front of the mosque were lifted from some Roman building, a common practice over the centuries.

In 1995, extensive renovation was begun on the Eski Cami, but much of it remains open to visitors.

Selimiye Camii

Up the hill to the north-east past the Eski Cami stands the Selimiye mosque, the finest work of the great Ottoman architect Mimar Sinan – or so the architect himself considered it. Constructed for Sultan Selim II (1566-74) and finished just after his death, it is smaller than Sinan's earlier (1557), tremendous Süleymaniye mosque in İstanbul, but more elegant and harmonious. Crowning its small hill, it can be seen from a good distance across the rolling Thracian landscape.

To appreciate its excellence you must enter it from the west as the architect intended. Walk up the street and through the courtyard; don't enter it through the shops below.

Sinan's genius guided him in designing a building which inspires serenity, harmony and a feeling of being centred in those who enter it. Architectural elements are placed symmetrically, often in matching pairs, as with the side windows in the courtyard which match, one side with the other. Inside, the broad and lofty dome is supported unobtrusively by pillars, arches and external buttresses. This was done so well that the interior is surprisingly spacious and the walls, because they bear only a portion of the dome's weight, can be filled with windows, thus admitting plentiful light to the wide, airy, light space for prayer.

Centred beneath the main dome is the kürsü, or platform, and centred beneath that is a small fountain which gives the soothing sound of running water to the quiet interior.

As you might expect, the interior furnishings of the Selimiye are exquisite, from the delicately carved marble mimber to the outstanding İznik faïence in and around the mihrab.

In contrast to the many 'twinnings' (pairs of windows, columns, etc), the north side of the mosque (near the Türk-İslam Eserleri Müzesi) has playful groupings of threes – arches, domes, niches, etc; and even triads of pairs (windows).

Part of the Selimiye's excellent effect comes from its four slender, very tall (71m) minarets. The fluted drums of the minarets add to the sense of height. You'll notice that each is *üçşerefeli*, or built with three balconies – Sinan's respectful acknowledgment, perhaps, to his predecessor, the architect of the Üçşerefeli Cami.

The Selimiye had its share of supporting buildings – religious schools, libraries etc. However, all that survive are a medrese (theological seminary) and a gallery of shops, called the arasta, beneath the mosque. The shops have been restored and are still in use; rents are dedicated to the upkeep of the mosque, as they have been for over 400 years. The medrese now houses the **Turkish & Islamic Arts Museum** (Türk-İslam Eserleri Müzesi), open daily except Monday from 8 am to noon and 1 to 5 pm, for US$1. Collections are eclectic and inclusive, from weapons and chain mail through dervish arts and crafts to the Balkan Wars, locally-made stockings, kitchen utensils, etc. All labels are in Turkish only.

Archaeological Museum

The town's main museum, the Archaeological Museum (Arkeoloji ve Etnoloji Müzesi) – across the street from the Selimiye Camii and a few steps north-east of the Türk-İslam Eserleri Müzesi is open from 8 am to noon and 1 to 5 pm, for US$1.50.

In front of the museum are several *dolmens* and *menhirs* (standing stones), as well as replicas of wattle-and-daub huts such as may have been used by the region's Stone Age inhabitants.

The museum, though small, has an interesting and varied collection: prehistoric, Roman and Byzantine artefacts; textiles including embroidery and weaving; farm implements; dioramas; and even a carriage from Ottoman times.

Muradiye Camii

A short walk (10 to 15 minutes) north-east of the Selimiye and the museum along Mimar Sinan Caddesi brings you to the Muradiye Camii, a mosque built on the orders of Sultan Murat II and finished in 1436 and once the centre of a Mevlevi (Whirling Dervish) lodge. Its T-shaped plan with twin *eyvans* (niche-like rooms) is reminiscent of the Yeşil Cami in Bursa, and its fine İznik tiles remind one that Bursa (near İznik) was the first Ottoman capital and Edirne, the second. Turkish mosque architecture would change dramatically after the Turks conquered Constantinople (1453) and studied Sancta Sophia. The small cupola atop the main dome is unusual.

In the small cemetery is the tombstone of Şeyhülislâm Musa Kâzım Efendi, the empire's chief Islamic judge, who fled the British occupation of İstanbul after WWI, and died here in 1920.

The mosque is usually locked except at prayer times; listen for the call to prayer and walk to the mosque to arrive after most worshippers have left but before the door is locked.

From the front of the Muradiye, the green lowland meadow of Sarayiçi (see following) is visible less than one km's walk away.

Sarayiçi & Beyazıt II Külliyesi

On the outskirts of Edirne, Sarayiçi, once the sultans' private island hunting preserve, is now the site of the annual Kırkpınar oiled wrestling matches or Tarihi Kırkpınar Yağlı Güreş Festivali (yah-LUH gew-RESH, oiled wrestling). Just over a kilometre from it is the stately, but somewhat forlorn, mosque complex of Sultan Beyazıt II. A morning's pleasant five km excursion on foot takes you to both sites.

If you're a mosque maven, start by following the directions (above) to the Muradiye Camii, then continue to the grassy lowland swath of Sarayiçi, clearly visible from the Muradiye's hilltop perch, and onward to the Beyazıt II complex. If not, walk along Hükümet Caddesi from Hürriyet Meydanı past the Üçşerefeli Cami (on your right), and turn left immediately after its Turkish bath. Walk one block and bear right at the ornate little fountain. This street is Horozlu Bayır Caddesi; it changes names later to İmaret Caddesi, and takes you right to the bridge (1488) across the Tunca to the Beyazıt II complex.

Beyazıt II Külliyesi Edirne's last great imperial mosque is that of Sultan Beyazıt II (1481-1512), on the far side (north-west of the town) of the Tunca River (TOON-jah).

Building mosque complexes was the way the Ottomans populated and expanded their cities. A site would be chosen on the outskirts of a populated area and workers employed for construction. Many of the workers and their families would settle near the mosque construction, thereby attracting necessary services (grocers, cookshops, tailors, etc) on which they would spend their pay. The scheme seems not to have worked for the Beyazıt complex (the İkinci Beyazıt Külliyesi), built from 1484 to 1488, as it remains on Edirne's outskirts, unpopulated and little used, after 500 years.

The architect of the complex, one Hayrettin, did a creditable job, though he was obviously no Sinan. The mosque's style is between that of the Üçşerefeli and the Selimiye, moving back a bit rather than advancing: its large prayer hall has one large dome, more like in Bursa's mosques, but it has a courtyard and şadırvan like the Üçşerefeli Cami's. Though of a high standard, Hayrettin's work can't compare with the Selimiye, built less than a century later.

The mosque's külliye is extensive and includes a *tabhane* (hostel for travellers), medrese, bakery, *imaret* (soup kitchen), *tımarhane* (insane asylum) and *darüşşifa* (hospital). These buildings were fully restored in the late 1970s, though time has impacted again.

Eski Saray A pleasant one-km walk upriver (east) from the Beyazıt II Külliyesi are the ruins of the Eski Saray (Old Palace). The shortest and most scenic route is to walk along the raised flood-control levee; cars can follow a curving (and longer) paved road.

Begun by Sultan Beyazıt II in 1450, this palace once rivalled İstanbul's Topkapı in luxury and size. Today, little is left but a few ruins: a kitchen, a hamam, etc, some of which is off limits in a military zone.

Sarayiçi East of Eski Saray, across a branch of the Tunca, is Sarayiçi ('Within the Palace'). This scrub-covered island, once the sultans' hunting preserve, is the site of the famous annual Kırkpınar oiled wrestling matches.

Next to the rather drab modern stadium is a stone tower with a pointed roof, the **Kasr-i Adalet** (Justice Hall, 1561), dating from the time of Süleyman the Magnificent, with two stones in front of it. On one stone, the *Seng-i Hürmet* (Stone of Respect), petitioners would put their petitions to the sultan to be collected by his staff. On the other, the *Seng-i İbret* (Stone of Warning), would be displayed the heads of high court officers who had lost the sultan's confidence in a major way.

If you've made it all the way to Sarayiçi, look for the Kanuni Köprüsü to get you back to the south bank of the Tunca. Bear right coming off the bridge, and the road will lead you to Hükümet Caddesi, and eventually to Hürriyet Meydanı.

The Old Town (Kaleiçi)

While you're here, don't forget to take a stroll through the old town of Edirne to discover some scenes of Turkish daily life. The Old Town, called Kaleiçi ('Within the Fortress') by the locals, was the original medieval town with streets laid out on a grid plan. Some fragments of Byzantine city walls are still visible at the edges of the grid, down by the Tunca River. The Old Town, bounded by Saraçlar Caddesi and Talat Paşa Caddesi, is basically the area behind and to the west of the Ali Paşa Çarşısı.

Places to Stay – bottom end

Edirne has several good places to stay at reasonable prices.

Behind the Tourism Information Office near Hürriyet Meydanı, along Maarif Caddesi, are several grand old town houses which have been converted into fairly dingy but cheap budget hotels.

The *Otel Anıl* (☎ (284) 225 1482), Hürriyet Meydanı, Maarif Caddesi 8, is among the better places with simple but acceptable waterless rooms costing US$12 a double. Bathrooms are down the hall; showers here have electric shower heads for heating the water.

Next door to the Anıl, but not nearly so clean or suitable, is the *Konak Hotel* (☎ (284) 212 1348), Hürriyet Meydanı, Maarif Caddesi 6. Rooms here are also waterless; some have five or six beds, renting for US$4 per person.

Camping Open from April to mid-October, the *Fifi Mocamp* (☎ (284) 225 1554), Demirkapı Mevkii, is eight km east of town on the old İstanbul road (D 100). It has a full range of hook-ups and services for tents and caravans, and even a few motel rooms available for rent the year round.

Places to Stay – middle

Near the Konak and the Anıl hotels, just a block behind the tourism office, the *Park Hotel* (☎ (284) 225 4610, fax 225 4635), Maarif Caddesi 7, is clean, comfortable and

Oiled Wrestling

The origins of *Yağlı güreş* (oiled wrestling) are lost in legend, but it's thought that matches have been held near Edirne for at least six centuries.

According to the best-known version of the tale, Süleyman Paşa, son of Orhan Gazi, the second Ottoman sultan, crossed the Dardanelles in the mid-14th century bent on conquest. His vanguard consisted of 40 enthusiastic warriors who wrestled at rest stops to break the monotony of the march through Thrace. At a meadow in Ahırköy, near Edirne, they wrestled until only two remained standing. These two, unwilling to yield, wrestled long into the night and finally died of exhaustion. They were buried where they fell. The next day a spring of clear, cold water sprang up at the spot and was named *Kırkpınar*, or Forty Springs for the forty warriors.

A Wrestlers' Lodge was soon thriving in Edirne. Matches were held indoors in winter, and in summer outdoors in the Kırkpınar meadow, which is today just across the border in Greece. The highpoint of the year was the three-day series of matches held during the traditional spring festival of Hıdrellez.

These days hundreds of amateur wrestlers from all over Turkey gather in early June at Sarayiçi. Clad only in knickers of goat or calf leather, they slather themselves with olive oil, then chant:

Allah Allah illallah
May we prosper
Our patron is Hamza the wrestler
Our ancestors were wrestlers
Two valiant men take the field
One is blonde, one dark
Both are keen to win the prize
Do not despair when down
Do not boast when up
When above, do not loosen your grip
Meet leg trip with leg trip
Offer a prayer to Muhammed
I hastened to the spring
May Allah be with you both

After this the *cazgır*, or master of ceremonies, offers a prayer, and introduces the matches. Then the *davul* (folk bass drum) and *zurna* (Turkish double-reed instrument) begin the frenetic music which will play throughout the festival. The wrestlers go through the traditional warm-up routine *(peşrev)* consisting of a series of exaggerated arm-swinging steps and gestures.

Wrestlers are organized into 11 classes, from *teşvik* (encouragement) to *baş güreşler* (head wrestlers), with the winner in each class being designated a *başpehlivan*, or master wrestler. On the last day of the festival, the başpehlivans wrestle for the supreme honour. Finally only two are left, and these compete for the top prize, the coveted gold belt, and a small cash prize. With victory comes fame, honour, and the opportunity to make money endorsing commercial products.

Folk-dancing exhibitions, musical performances and crafts displays are organised as part of the festivities, and these begin on Tuesday. The wrestling begins on Friday, with the başpehlivan chosen on Sunday. For exact dates and ticket information, contact the tourism offices in Edirne. ■

convenient. Rooms cost US$13/20 a single/double for a room with bath, breakfast included. Try to get a room off Maarif Caddesi, which has some traffic.

A few metres down the street at Maarif Caddesi 13, the *Efe Hotel* (☎ (284) 213 6166, fax 212 9446) has an air-conditioned lobby, lobby bar, and newish rooms with shower and TV (but without air-con) for US$15/24.

The *Otel Şaban Açıkgöz* (☎ (284) 213 1404, fax 213 4516), Tahmis Meydanı Çilingir Caddesi 9 is near the park next to the Eski Cami. Relatively new and – for Edirne – upscale, they charge US$19/27 for fairly quiet rooms with shower and TV.

The top hotel right in the centre is the three-star, 83-room *Sultan Oteli* (☎ (284) 225 1372; fax 225 5763), Talat Paşa Caddesi

170, a half-block west of the central tourism office. It's several decades old but nicely renovated. Rooms with shower and TV are priced at US$32/38.

The two-star, 80-room *Balta Hotel* (☎ (284) 225 5210, fax 225 3529), Talat Paşa Asfaltı 97, halfway from the otogar to Hürriyet Meydanı has the disadvantages of being a longish walk from Hürriyet Meydanı, facing a noisy street, and having rooms which catch the heat of the afternoon sun. Rooms are priced at US$30/38 with breakfast included.

The 100-room *Hotel Kervansaray* (☎ (284) 225 2195, fax 212 0462), Eski Cami Yanı, facing the park next to the Eski Cami is in fact an Ottoman caravanserai. It was built for Rüstem Paşa, a grand vizier of Süleyman the Magnificent's, who ordered its construction in about 1550. The camel caravans on the road between Europe, İstanbul and points farther east rested here for the night, their valuable freight safe within the building's massive stone walls and great armoured doors.

Despite its romantic history, the hotel depends more on its billiards room and nightclub for profits. The club can be noisy, which is why the rooms are seldom occupied. The price is US$42 a double.

Places to Eat

Edirne has many small eateries, especially *köftecis* (serving grilled lamb patties) and *ciğercis* (serving fried liver), but very few formal restaurants.

Among the brightest and best is the *Serhad Köftecisi* on Saraçlar Caddesi just off Hürriyet Meydanı, selling those good grilled Turkish meatballs with yoghurt, salad, bread and drink for US$3 or so. The similar *Serhad 11* is a bit farther along, around the corner to the left.

The *Edirne Lokantası*, another good köfteci which also has some sulu yemekler (stews), is east of the Serhad near the Hotel Şaban Açıkgöz. Köfte, bread and a plate of stewed green beans costs less than US$4 with a soft drink.

Down the street from the Edirne Lokantası, *Dost'un Yeri* serves stews, kebaps and beer for slightly higher prices; but, like all Edirne eateries, it's still quite cheap.

For fancier meals with alcoholic drinks, try the restaurant in the Hotel Sultan, or the *Çatı Lokantası* across the street from the hotel. Another possibility is the *Aile Restaurant*, Saraçlar Caddesi, Belediye İş Hanı, which has been open for decades. To find it, walk south from Hürriyet Meydanı along Saraçlar Caddesi, looking for the building named Belediye İş Hanı on the left-hand side; it's just past the PTT. The entrance is on the side street by the post office. Climb the stairs to the upper level where you'll find a simple dining room with windows overlooking Saraçlar Caddesi. Kebaps, stews and other traditional Turkish dishes are served, and a meal need cost no more than US$5 or US$7 per person.

Getting There & Away

For consulates, see Information (above).

Bulgarian Border Crossing On the highway from Svilengrad, Bulgaria, you come to the busy border post of Kapıkule (18 km west of Edirne), open 24 hours. After the formalities, you enter the town by crossing the river Tunca at the Gazi Mihal Bridge and passing some fragments of Byzantine city walls. City bus 1 runs along the route from Kapıkule to the centre of Edirne; there are dolmuşes on this route as well, but both are infrequent in the early morning and late at night. By the way, you may be required to hitch a ride or rent a taxi (ie not walk) on the Bulgarian side.

Greek Border Crossing The major road goes to Kastanies (Greece) and Pazarkule (Turkey), seven km south-west of Edirne on the Meriç River (mehr-EECH, Maritsa), two km past the Turkish village of Karaağaç to a border post originally meant to serve the railway line. The frontier, as determined by the Treaty of Lausanne (1923), left the Turkish line passing through Greece on its way to Edirne! (A bypass line was built in the 1970s).

The Greeks have declared the border area a military zone and do not permit anyone to walk in it without a military escort, so you will probably have to take a Greek taxi (US$6, two minutes) to the actual border, which is mid-way in the one-km-wide no-man's-land which separates the two border posts. On the Turkish side, you can usually walk to and from Pazarkule. These small border posts are usually open during daylight hours, but if relations between the two countries are not good (which is common) they may be open only in the morning. Ask at the tourism office, or plan to arrive at the border after 9 but before 11 am.

From Pazarkule, or from the nearby train station, you will probably have to take a Turkish taxi (US$5, 15 minutes) into town as there is not much traffic and hitching is not too easy, though you may be lucky. From Edirne, connections are frequent, fast and easy to İstanbul, less frequent to points south (see following).

If you are crossing from Turkey into Greece, do so as soon after 9 am as possible in order to catch one of the few trains or buses from Kastanies south to Alexandroùpoli, whence there are better connections. Or consider crossing farther south at İpsala/Kipi on the E 84/110 highway.

Road The E 80 highway between Europe and Edirne follows closely the Via Ignatia, the ancient road which connected Rome and Constantinople. It travels along the river valleys past Niš and Sofia, on between the mountain ranges of the Stara and Rhodopi to Plovdiv, and along the Maritsa riverbank into Edirne. The city stands alone on the gently undulating plain, snuggled into a bend of the Tunca River.

After Edirne, the old Edirne-İstanbul highway (D 100) heads east into the rolling, steppe-like terrain of eastern Thrace towards İstanbul, still following the Via Ignatia. The E 80 Avrupa Otoyol (expressway) is far preferable in terms of condition, speed and safety. The toll of about US$3.50 to İstanbul is a small price to pay.

Bus Buses to İstanbul depart Edirne's Otobüs Garajı, two km from the Eski Cami on the outskirts of town every 20 minutes or so throughout the day, taking under three hours to make the 235-km journey; tickets cost US$5.75. Take a city bus or dolmuş from the Eski Cami to the Otobüs Garajı.

The terminus in İstanbul is the new Uluslararası İstanbul Otogar (İstanbul International Bus Station) in Esenler, from which you can take the Metro to Aksaray and change to the tram for Sultanahmet, or a city bus to Taksim Square.

Heading south from Edirne, there are at least five buses daily to Çanakkale, though some require a transfer at Keşan.

Train If you're coming to Turkey by train, get off. Don't miss Edirne. The onward trip to İstanbul by bus is much faster in any case.

If you are leaving Turkey for Europe, note that the daily westbound *İstanbul Express* passes through Edirne each morning around breakfast time (usually between 8 and 9 am). Get up-to-date schedule information from the tourism office.

Edirne has two train stations: the city station (Edirne Garı), and the one at Kapıkule on the Bulgarian border. There is also the station at Uzunköprü 60 km to the south. (Uzunköprü is the last station in Turkey on the route via Alexandroùpoli to Athens.)

Train service between Edirne and İstanbul is slow and inconvenient. The train departs from İstanbul's Sirkeci Station at 3.40 pm, arriving in Edirne about six hours later. The train station is out of town, reachable by dolmuş, bus or taxi. Tickets on the run from Edirne to İstanbul cost US$4 one way, with a 10% discount for students. You'd be better off taking the bus.

East of Edirne

The ride to İstanbul is largely uneventful, even though this part of the country has had

Midnight Express

It's interesting to note that the original *Midnight Express* ran between İstanbul and Edirne through Greece. When the Ottoman Empire collapsed, the new Turkish-Greek border was drawn so that the old railway line was partly in Greece. Greek border police would board when the train entered Greek territory and get off when it re-entered Turkish territory.

During the 1960s and 70s there was a slow, late-night train on this run. Foreigners convicted of drug-related offences in Turkey would be released by the Turkish government while their convictions were being appealed. They'd be given all of their possessions except their passports, and told in a whisper about the *Midnight Express*.

They'd climb aboard in İstanbul and jump off the train in Greece, where Greek border police would pick them up and jail them. They'd call their consulate, arrange for a new passport, be let out of jail and sent on their way. This system allowed the Turkish government to meet the US government's demands that it be strict with drug smugglers, but it avoided the expense and bother of actually incarcerating the convicted smugglers. In the late 1970s, the Turkish State Railways built a bypass line and the Greek corridor route was abandoned. The truth of the *Midnight Express* is quite different from that portrayed in the politically-inspired anti-Turkish movie of the same name, in which a convicted drug-smuggler is magically transmuted into a suffering hero. ■

a tumultuous history. Enemy armies from the west intent on seizing Constantinople/İstanbul passed easily over this rolling countryside. In 1877 the Russians held all of Turkish Thrace, and got to within a few km of İstanbul's city walls. During WWI, Allied armies marched this way; in WWII Thrace was heavily militarised by the Turks to fend off the Germans and to protect Turkey's fragile neutrality. A Turkish friend tells the story of his time on the line in Thrace:

> It was late in a bitter winter. The wolves found little to eat in the countryside, and began coming dangerously close to our outpost. Ammunition was very scarce, but we asked permission to use a few rounds to defend ourselves against the wolves. Our commander said, 'You are Turkish soldiers. Use your bayonets'.

Havsa The first town along the İstanbul road is Havsa (population 10,000), a town of some importance during Ottoman times. The **Sokollu Kasım Paşa Külliyesi** is a mosque complex designed by Sinan and built in 1576-77 on orders of the son of Sokollu Mehmet Paşa, a grand vizier under Sultan Süleyman the Magnificent.

Lüleburgaz About 75 km east of Edirne is the market town of Lüleburgaz (population 56,000), the ancient Arcadiopolis. Unremarkable in itself, Lüleburgaz holds the fine **Sokollu Mehmet Paşa Camii**, a mosque built on the orders (1549) of Sokollu Mehmet Paşa, the *beylerbey* of Rumeli (governor of European Turkey) and later grand vizier to Sultan Süleyman the Magnificent. The mosque was part of a larger complex which was finally completed in 1569. Incorporated into the mosque's design is a *medrese* (theological college). Across the street, the hamam is ruined and now used for storage, but the *arasta* (rows of shops) which surround it are still in use.

Lüleburgaz is not a tourist town, so anyone and everyone stands ready to help you if you need help, or to ignore you if you don't. Useful services such as bus ticket offices, restaurants, pastry shops and cheap hotels are all within a few minutes' walk of the Sokollu Mehmet Paşa Camii.

The *Hotel Sürücü* (☎ (288) 417 1451), İstanbul Caddesi 6, is a half-block from the mosque and charges US$11 for a double room with private shower. The *Hotel Şentürk* (☎ (288) 417 2112, fax 412 5541), İstanbul Caddesi 12, a block farther east across from the park, is a bit newer and better. Up two flights of stairs are rooms with shower and TV which cost US$6/12/15 for a single/double/triple. On the eastern outskirts of the town on the D 100, you'll find the *Hotel Yaman*

(☎ (288) 414 1613, fax 414 1523). It offers four-star comforts at a three-star price of US$25 a double, breakfast included.

Çorlu Though wonderfully ancient, having been founded by the Phrygians around 1000 BC, Çorlu (population 75,000) has little to show for its long history. A farmers' market town at best, it was a way-station on the İstanbul-Edirne road and thus received its share of mosque-building, as well as a caravanserai and hamam. The **Sultan Süleyman Camii** (1521) is its most noteworthy old building. A few small hotels and restaurants provide for travellers.

Tekirdağ Once known for its luxuriant vineyards and excellent wines, Tekirdağ (population 85,000), once called Rodosto, today is a bustling modern place with little to hold your interest. Traces of Early Bronze Age life have been found in the vicinity.

The tourism office (☎ & fax (282) 261 2083) is at Atatürk Bulvarı 65, on the waterfront street next to the Eski İskele (old dock).

The Ottomans – particularly Süleyman the Magnificent's grand vizier Rüstem Paşa – left Tekirdağ a legacy of great buildings, including the mosque, bedesten and medrese named after Rüstem.

Also here is the **Rakoczi Museum** (☎ (282) 261 2082) on Barbaros Caddesi just in from the waterfront near the centre of the town. Prince Francis II Rakoczy (1676-1735) led rebellious Hungarians in their struggle against Hapsburg repression in the early 1700s. Forced to flee in 1711, he went into exile in Poland, then France, and finally in Turkey, where he died. Rakoczy's remains were returned to Hungary in 1906, and his Tekirdağ home (1720-35) became a museum in 1932.

East & West of Tekirdağ Most maps show the road east of Tekirdağ, leading to Silivri and İstanbul, as a major highway. In fact, it is very narrow for the volume of traffic that must pass through, so you should expect some slow going.

West of Tekirdağ the coast road is passable as far as Kumbağ, but then degenerates to a track, very rough and not recommended except for the adventurous. The better road heads due west to İnecik and Keşan. About 48 km west of Tekirdağ a rough road heads south over the mountains to Ballı, Gölcük and Şarköy (32 km). The latter is a seaside resort for those from İstanbul and a handful of enterprising Europeans, with a decent beach and several typically noisy Turkish nightclubs.

South of Edirne

If you've come from İstanbul, it might make sense to head due south after looking around Edirne and go directly to the Dardanelles and Troy. There are few direct buses between Edirne and Çanakkale; most probably you will have to change buses at Keşan (see following). By doing this you miss the ferry cruise across the Sea of Marmara as well as the delightful cities of İznik (ancient Nicaea) and Bursa, the first Ottoman capital. So if you've got the time, head back to İstanbul and catch a ferry to Yalova, first stop on your explorations of the south Marmara shore.

Uzunköprü About 36 km south of Havsa along E 87/D 550 is the farming town of Uzunköprü (population 36,000). Named 'Long Bridge' for its Ottoman viaduct, 1270m long with 173 arches, Uzunköprü has the nearest train station to the border on the line connecting İstanbul and Athens. You can catch the daily train to Athens here, but transport is much easier and more convenient via either Edirne to the north or İpsala to the south.

The Long Bridge itself, begun in 1427 and finished in 1443, is still in use as the town's main access road from the north, a monument to the durability of Ottoman construction. Its southern end is in the town centre, where there are simple, cheap hotels including the *Hotel Ergene*, and basic eateries. At present, buses load and unload in the centre, though a new otogar is under construction on the highway.

İpsala & Keşan İpsala is the main border-crossing point between Turkey and Greece, on the E 84/D 110 highway; the Greek station is named Kipi. Both stations are open 24 hours a day.

The actual Turkish border station is five km west of the town of İpsala, reachable by taxi (US$4). There is a tourism office (☎ & fax (284) 616 1577) at the border station. If you're coming from Greece, go straight through İpsala to Keşan (US$2 by dolmuş, US$12 by taxi), from which bus connections to Edirne, İstanbul, Gelibolu and Çanakkale are easier.

Keşan's otogar (Belediye Terminalı) is on the E 87/D 550 south of the E 84/D 110, but most minibuses terminate at a lot just off the main square, 2.5 km south-east and uphill from the intersection of these two highways, and 2½ km east of the otogar. Keşan's main square has several köftecis, restaurants and pastanes, and, to the left of the Hükümet Konağı (government headquarters), is the *Şapçı Döviz* for currency conversion.

GALLIPOLI PENINSULA

The slender peninsula which forms the north-western side of the Çanakkale Boğazı (Dardanelles), across the water from Çanakkale, is called Gelibolu in Turkish. For a millennium it has been the key to İstanbul: the navy that could force the straits had a good chance of capturing the capital of the Eastern world. Many fleets have tried to force the straits. Most, including the mighty Allied fleet mustered in WWI, have failed.

Today the Gallipoli battlefields are peaceful places covered in scrubby brush, pine forests, and farmers' fields. But the momentous battles fought here nearly a century ago are still alive in the memories of many people, both Turkish and foreign.

On the hillside by Kilitbahir, clearly visible from Çanakkale on the far shore, are gigantic letters spelling out the first few words of a poem by Necmettin Halil Onan commemorating the momentous 1915 struggle for Gallipoli:

Dur yolcu! Bilmeden gelip bastığın
bu toprak bir devrin battığı yerdir.
Eğil de kulak ver, bu sessiz yığın
bir vatan kalbinin attığı yerdir.

Traveller, halt! The soil you tread
once witnessed the end of an era.
Listen! In this quiet mound
there once beat the heart of a nation.

History

Since Byzantine times the straits have been well defended. The Ottomans maintained numerous fortresses: Seddülbahir and Kumkale at the southern end of the straits; Çamburun and Karaburun, and Bigalı and Nara within the straits; Bozcaada on the island at the southern mouth; Çimenlik in the town of Çanakkale, and Kilitbahir, the 'Lock on the Sea', on the Gallipoli side across from Çanakkale.

With the intention of capturing the Ottoman capital and the road to Eastern Europe during WWI, Winston Churchill, British First Lord of the Admiralty, organised a naval assault on the straits. A strong Franco-British fleet tried first to force them in March 1915 but failed. Then, in April, British, Australian, New Zealand and Indian troops were landed on Gallipoli, and French troops near Çanakkale. Both Turkish and Allied troops fought desperately and fearlessly, and devastated one another. After nine months of ferocious combat but little progress, the Allied forces were withdrawn.

The Turkish success at Gallipoli was partly due to bad luck and bad leadership on the Allied side, and partly due to the timely provision of reinforcements coming to the aid of the Turkish side under the command of General Liman von Sanders. But a crucial element in the defeat was that the Allied troops happened to land in a sector where they faced Lieutenant-Colonel Mustafa Kemal (Atatürk).

Though a relatively minor officer, he had General von Sanders' confidence. He

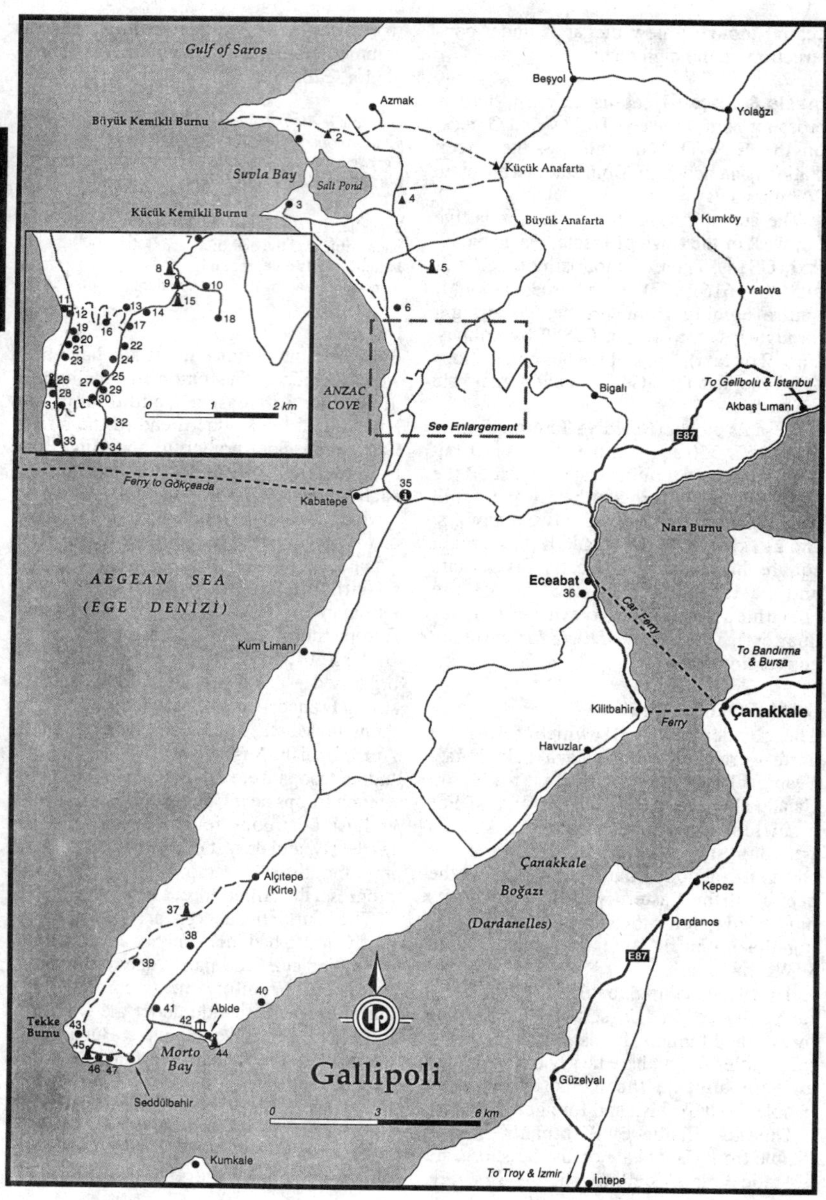

Gulf of Saros
Beşyol
Azmak
Yolağzı
Büyük Kemikli Burnu
Küçük Anafarta
Suvla Bay
Salt Pond
Kücük Kemikli Burnu
Büyük Anafarta
Kumköy
Yalova
ANZAC COVE
See Enlargement
Bigalı
To Gelibolu & İstanbul
Akbaş Lımanı
E87
Ferry to Gökçeada
Kabatepe
Nara Burnu
AEGEAN SEA
(EGE DENİZİ)
Eceabat
Car Ferry
Kum Limanı
To Bandırma & Bursa
Kilitbahir
Ferry
Çanakkale
Havuzlar
Çanakkale
Boğazı
(Dardanelles)
Alçıtepe
(Kirte)
Kepez
Dardanos
Tekke Burnu
Abide
Morto Bay
Seddülbahir
Gallipoli
Güzelyalı
Kumkale
To Troy & İzmir
İntepe
0 1 2 km
0 3 6 km

1 Büyük Kemikli Picnic Area & Beach
2 Hill 10
3 Lala Baba
4 Green Hill
5 Hill 60 New Zealand Memorial
6 7th Field Ambulance Cemetery
7 Kocaçimentepe
8 Chunuk Bair New Zealand Memorial
9 Conkbayırı Mehmetçik Memorials
10 Place where Atatürk Spent the Night of 9-10 August 1915
11 Lala Baba Cemetery
12 Embarkation Pier Cemetery
13 Mehmet Çavuş Cemetery
14 Düztepe (10 Alay Cephesi)
15 Talat Göktepe Monument
16 The Nek
17 Baby 700 Cemetery & Mesudiye Topu
18 Kemalyeri (Scrubby Knoll, Turkish HQ)
19 New Zealand No 2 Outpost Cemetery
20 No 2 Outpost Cemetery
21 Canterbury Cemetery
22 57th Regiment (57 Alay) Cemetery
23 Arıburnu Cemetery
24 Quinn' Post (Bomba Sırt) & Yüzbaşı Mehmet Şehitliği
25 Courtney Steele's Post
26 Anzac Memorial
27 Johnston's Jolly
28 Anzac Cove
29 Kırmızı Sırt (125 Alay Cephesi)
30 Lone Pine (Kanlı Sırt) Cemetery
31 Shrapnel Valley (Korkudere) & Plugge's Plateau Cemeteries
32 Kanlı Sırt Kitabesi
33 Beach (Hell Spit) Cemetery
34 Mehmetçiğe Saygı Anıtı
35 Kabatepe Information Centre & Museum
36 Gelibolu Tarihi Milli Park (GallipolNational Historic Park), Ziyaretçi Merkezi (Park Visitors' Centre) & Picnic Area
37 Twelve Tree Copse Cemetery & NZ Memorial
38 Redoubt Cemetery
39 Pink Farm Cemetery
40 Kerevizdere Picnic Area
41 Skew Bridge Cemetery
42 French Memorial & Museum
43 Lancashire Landing Cemetery
44 Çanakkale Şehitleri Abidesi Memorial
45 Cape Helles British Memorial
46 İlk Şehitler & Yahya Çavuş Memorials
47 'V' Beach Cemetery

guessed the Allied battle plan correctly when his commanders did not, and stalled the invasion by bitter fighting which wiped out his division. Though suffering from malaria, he commanded in full view of his troops and of the enemy, and miraculously escaped death several times. At one point a piece of shrapnel tore through the breast pocket of his uniform, but was stopped by his pocket watch (now in the Çanakkale Military & Naval Museum). His brilliant performance made him a folk hero and paved the way for his promotion to pasha (general).

The Gallipoli campaign lasted for nine months, until January 1916, and resulted in huge numbers of casualties on both sides. The British Empire suffered over 200,000 casualties, with the loss of some 36,000 lives.

French casualties of 47,000 were over half of the entire French contingent. Of the half-million Turkish troops who participated in the battle, one out of every two became a casualty, with more than 55,000 dead. There are now 31 war cemeteries on the peninsula, as well as several important monuments.

Orientation

Gallipoli is a fairly large area to tour, especially without your own transport. It's over 35 km as the crow flies from the northernmost battlefield to the southern tip of the peninsula. The two best bases for a visit are Çanakkale on the eastern shore, and Gelibolu on the western. Eceabat, 45 km south-west of Gelibolu, though closer to the battlefields, has mostly emergency accommodation.

Ferries run from Kilitbahir and Eceabat across the Dardanelles to Çanakkale (for details, see Getting There & Away in the Çanakkale section of the Aegean Turkey chapter).

The principal battles took place on the western shore of the peninsula near Anzac Cove and Arıburnu, and in the hills just to the east. Anzac Cove is about 12 km from Eceabat, 19 km from Kilitbahir, and 57 km from Gelibolu. If your time is limited or if you're touring by public transport, head for these places first.

Transport & Tours

With your own transport you can tour the battlefields easily in a day or less. Touring by public transport is possible, but dolmuşes serve only certain sites or nearby villages, and you must expect to do some waiting and walking. In summer, hitchhiking greatly facilitates getting around on your own, but in other seasons traffic may not be sufficient. The most important group of monuments and cemeteries, from Lone Pine uphill to Chunuk Bair, can be toured on foot, an excellent idea in fine weather.

Joining an organised tour is a good idea as you save time and trouble, and get the benefit of a guide who can relate the history and explain the battles. Some readers have complained that tours go too fast, and allow too little time at the beach, so you'd be well advised to talk with other travellers who have just taken a tour and find out what they recommend. Most tours include a picnic and some time at a Gallipoli beach for swimming. Tours are organised by several agencies in Çanakkale, and in the town of Gelibolu on the Gallipoli Peninsula. (See the sections on those towns for details.)

Gelibolu

Coming from Edirne or Keşan, or from İstanbul along the northern shore of the Sea of Marmara, the little town of Gelibolu (population 17,000) can provide transport connections, a meal or a bed.

Orientation The centre of Gelibolu is right by the docks for the car ferry to Lapseki, and everything you may need is within 100m of here. The stone tower which looms above the ancient harbour is a remnant of the Byzantine town of Kallipolis, which gave the present town and peninsula their name. It's now the Piri Reis Museum and Gelibolu Promotion Centre, named for the famous Turkish cartographer, with changing exhibits and free admission. The otogar is in the shadow of the tower.

Information Go to the Gelibolu Promotion Centre in the stone tower. The PTT has a yellow-and-black kiosk right at the docks where you can convert currency and buy stamps. Across the road is a Yapı Kredi ATM. Other banks are along Yukarı Çarşı Sokak, the town's main shopping street, which starts opposite the Hotel Yılmaz (by the Emlak Bankası) and goes uphill.

Gallipoli Tours Several companies run tours of the Gallipoli battlefields. From the Yılmaz Hotel, for instance, tours depart at 8.30 am, returning at 3.30 pm, for US$18 per person.

Places to Stay Best in town is the newish two-star *Hotel Oya* (☎ (286) 566 0392), Miralay Şefik Aker Caddesi, 100m from the ferry docks, with shower-equipped rooms for US$12/18/22 a single/double/triple.

A block away is the older *Hotel Yılmaz* (☎ (286) 566 1256), Liman Meydanı 6, priced identically. The Yılmaz also operates the somewhat grotty *Anzac Pension* across the street, charging US$6/10/14 for quite cheerless, waterless rooms. A better, quieter choice is the nearby *Otel Yelkenci* (☎ (286) 566 1022), Liman Meydanı, charging US$14 for a double. The *Otel Hakan* (☎ (286) 566 2424), facing the bus station on the main square, has been refurbished and now gives the Yılmaz some competition.

About 12 km south of Gelibolu on the road to Eceabat is the two-star, 48-room *Hotel Boncuk* (☎ (286) 576 8292, fax 576 8158), on the shore, charging US$24 a double. *Cennet Camping & Motel*, 19 km south of Gelibolu, is better for camping than motel accommodation, with some shady sites. *Derya Camping*, across the road, is not as good.

Camping Obidi, 1.5 km from the bus station off the road south-west to Eceabat and Kilitbahir (follow the signs), is on the shore, has some shade, and can be pleasant for a night or two.

Places to Eat Amidst the hotels at the centre

are many small restaurants, kebapçıs and büfes serving everything from stand-up snacks to sit-down dinners with white table-cloths and wine.

The best views and breeze are at the *Café Nezih* next to the Denizyolları ferryboat ticket office by the docks, but they serve only drinks and snacks. For full meals, the *İmren, Boğaz* and *Liman* restaurants near the Otel Yelkenci are best in the evening, with nice views, tables on the pavement, and fish menus (sardalya or fresh sardines are the local speciality). Expect to spend from US$8 to US$12 here. The *Gelibolu Restaurant* is fancier, with prices for full dinners somewhat higher.

As usual, the farther you go from the sea, the lower the prices. Just east of the Hotel Yılmaz is the *Çakırlar Can Restaurant* with white tablecloths but moderate prices. To the left of that is the *İpek Urfa Kebap Salonu* for kebaps.

Walk up Yukarı Çarşı Sokak, a shopping street which begins by the Emlak Bankası opposite the Hotel Yılmaz, to find even cheaper places; no alcohol is served though. The *Yarımada Lokantası* has lots of ready food, a nice garden dining area, and full meals for US$4. A bit farther up the hill are several pastanes (pastry shops), and also *Fenerli Mustafa'nin Yeri*, another good, cheap, ready-food restaurant.

Entertainment Dining near the water is the prime evening entertainment here, but if you just want to sit, drink and nibble at lower prices, walk inland from the ferry docks past the cafés on the left, then turn left. This street, heading south toward Eceabat, has three small *birahanes* (beer halls).

Getting There & Away Gelibolu's otogar is just inland from the ancient harbour, next to the stone tower. Dolmuşes or buses run hourly via Eceabat to Kilitbahir; there are ferries from both these towns to Çanakkale. To get to the Gallipoli battlefields, go to Eceabat, then look for a dolmuş (or hitch a ride) to Kabatepe. Details of services follow:

Balıkesir – change at Çanakkale
Bursa – change at Çanakkale
Çanakkale – 49 km plus ferry ride, less than two hours, US$3.75: take the Gelibolu-Lapseki ferry and catch a bus or minibus going to Çanakkale; or take the minibus to Eceabat or Kilitbahir and then the ferry to Çanakkale
Eceabat – 45 km, 50 minutes, US$2.25; hourly buses or minibuses
Edirne – three hours, US$8; three direct buses daily; or take one of the frequent buses to Keşan and change
İstanbul – 288 km, 4½ hours, US$8 to US$10; hourly buses from 7 am to 7 pm, plus some later buses
İzmir – 384 km, 6½ hours, US$9 to US$11; frequent buses
Keşan – 100 km, two hours, US$5.50; frequent buses
Kilitbahir – 52 km, one hour, US$2.75; hourly minibuses

The Gelibolu-Lapseki car ferry departs from Gelibolu at 1, 6.30, 7.30, 8.15, 9 and 11 am, noon, and 1, 2, 3, 4, 5, 6, 7, 8, 9, 10 and 11 pm and midnight. Departures from Lapseki are at 2, 6.30, 7.30 and 8.15 am, then every hour on the hour until midnight. The fare is 50c per person, US$1.50 for a bicycle or moped, US$8 for a car. If you miss this boat, you can go south-west to Eceabat (45 km, one hour) and catch the similar car ferry, or to Kilitbahir seven km farther on and catch the small private ferry, which can take a few cars as well, and charges less than the other ferries. See the Çanakkale section for details.

Eceabat

The small town of Eceabat (population 4500) exists for the car ferries to Çanakkale and for the Gallipoli National Park headquarters and visitors centre, two km south of the town. For details on the car ferries to Çanakkale, see that section.

The *Saros Otel* (☎ (286) 814 1065, fax 814 2330), near the ferry dock, is the best if you must stay, with bath-equipped double rooms for US$16. Mr Anıl Dinç, a taxi driver at the Saros Otel, can take you around the Gallipoli battlefields.

Also facing the ferry dock are the *Hotel Ece* and *Hotel Boss*, noisy and nothing special but useful in emergencies; the *Atlantik Restaurant* for cheap meals and the *Saros Restaurant-Bar* in the Hotel Ece for slightly more up-market food and drink; and the Yılmaz bus company ticket office.

Buses or minibuses run hourly north-east to Gelibolu (45 km, one hour). In summer there are several dolmuşes daily to the ferry dock at Kabatepe (10 km, 15 minutes) on the western shore of the peninsula, and these can drop you at the national park's Kabatepe information centre and museum, or at the base of the road up to Lone Pine and Chunuk Bair. Dolmuşes also run down the coast to Kilitbahir, from whence there are dolmuşes south to Abide at the southern tip of the peninsula.

Kilitbahir

The small hamlet of Kilitbahir at the foot of the Kilitbahir castle hosts the small private ferry from Çanakkale, which arrives at a dock just north-east of the castle walls. There are a few small teahouses and restaurants, but Kilitbahir is essentially a pass-through place. Dolmuşes and taxis await the ferry to shuttle you north-west to Eceabat (seven km), or south-west via Alçıtepe (19.5 km) to Çanakkale Abidesi ('Abide', 28 km).

Gallipoli National Park

Gallipoli National Historic Park (Gelibolu Tarihi Milli Park) covers much of the peninsula and all of the significant battle sites. Park headquarters is two km south-west of Eceabat (five km north-east of Kilitbahir) at the Ziyaretçi Merkezi (Visitors Centre); there's a picnic ground here as well.

In the national park there are several different signage systems: the normal Turkish highway signs, those erected by the national park administration, and those posted by the Commonwealth War Graves Commission. This leads to confusion because the foreign troops had a completely different nomenclature for battlefield sites to the Turks, and the Turkish battlefield markings do not necessarily agree with the ones erected by the highway department. In the text below and on the Gallipoli map I've put both English and Turkish names.

There are camping grounds at Kabatepe, Kum Limanı and Seddülbahir, and simple accommodation at Kum Limanı, Seddülbahir and Abide.

Tours of the battlefields are arranged by companies and individuals in Gelibolu and Çanakkale. See those sections for details.

Three km north of Eceabat a road marked for Kabatepe and Kemalyeri heads west.

Kabatepe Information Centre & Museum

The Kabatepe Tanıtma Merkezi, nine km from Eceabat and a km or so east of the village of Kabatepe, holds a small museum (US$0.50) with period uniforms, soldiers' letters, rusty weapons and other battlefield finds such as the skull of a luckless Turkish soldier with a ball lodged right in the forehead.

The road uphill to Lone Pine (Kanlı Sırt) and Chunuk Bair (Conkbayırı) begins 750m west of the Information Centre. Anzac Cove is 3.5 km from the Information Centre.

Kabatepe Village The small harbour here was the object of the Allied landing on 25 April 1915, but in the pitch dark of early morning the landing craft were swept northwards by currents to the steep cliffs of Arıburnu – a bit of bad luck which was crucial to the course of the campaign. Today there is little here but the dock for ferries to the Turkish Aegean island of Gökçeada.

Anzac Cove & Beaches Going west from the Information Centre, it's three km to the **Beach Cemetery**, and another 90m to where a road goes inland to the Shrapnel Valley & Plugge's Plateau cemeteries.

Another 400m along is Anzac Cove (Anzac Koyu). The ill-fated Allied landing was made here on 25 April 1915, beneath and just south of the Arıburnu cliffs. The Allied forces were ordered to advance inland, but met with fierce resistance from the Ottoman forces under Mustafa Kemal (Atatürk), who had foreseen the landing here and was prepared. After this first failed effort, the Anzacs concentrated on consolidating and expanding the beachhead, which they did until June while awaiting reinforcements.

In August a major offensive was staged in an attempt to advance beyond the beachhead and up to the ridges of Chunuk Bair and Sarı Bair, and resulted in the bloodiest battles of the campaign, but little progress was made.

Anzac Cove is marked by a Turkish monument, another 300m along, which repeats Atatürk's famous words uttered in 1934 for the Anzac troops:

> Those heroes that shed their blood and lost their lives...you are now lying in the soil of a friendly country. Therefore rest in peace. There is no difference between the Johnnies and the Mehmets to us where they lie side by side here in this country of ours.... You, the mothers, who sent their sons from far away countries, wipe away your tears; your sons are now lying in our bosom and are in peace. After having lost their lives on this land they have become our sons as well.

As a memorial reserve, the beach here is off-limits to swimmers and picnickers.

Beyond Anzac Cove a few hundred metres is the **Arıburnu Cemetery** and, 750m farther along, the **Canterbury Cemetery**. Less than a km farther along the seaside road are the cemeteries at the **No 2 Outpost**, set back inland from the road, and the **New Zealand No 2 Outpost**, right next to the road. The **Embarkation Pier Cemetery** is 200m beyond the No 2 Outpost.

Lone Pine to Chunuk Bair Retrace your steps and follow the signs up the hill for Lone Pine (Kanlı Sırt), perhaps the most poignant and affecting of all the Anzac cemeteries. It's just under three km from the junction with the beach road to Lone Pine, and another three km uphill to the New Zealand Memorial at Chunuk Bair.

This area, which saw the most bitter fighting of the campaign, was later cloaked in pines, but a disastrous forest fire in 1994 denuded the hills. Reforestation efforts are under way.

Mehmetçiğe Saygı Anıtı The first monument, on the right-hand side of the road 1200m up from the junction, is to 'Mehmetçik' (Little Mehmet), the Turkish 'Johnnie' or 'G I Joe' for his contribution to national defence. Another 1200m brings you to the Kanlı Sırt Kitabesi, the inscription monument (in Turkish) detailing the battle of Lone Pine from the Turkish viewpoint.

Lone Pine At Lone Pine, 400m uphill from the Kanlı Sırt Kitabesi, the trees which shaded the cemetery were swept away by the fire in 1994, leaving only one: a lone pine planted years ago as a memorial from the seed of the original tree which had stood here during the battle. The small tombstones carry touching epitaphs: 'Only son', 'He died for his country' and 'If I could hold your hand once more just to say well done'.

Johnston's Jolly to Quinn's Post As you progress up the hill, you quickly come to understand the ferocity of the battles here. At some points the trenches were only a few metres apart. The order to attack meant certain death to all who followed it, and virtually all – on both the Ottoman and Allied sides – did as they were ordered.

At **Johnston's Jolly** (Kırmızı Sırt/125 Alay Cephesi), 200m beyond Lone Pine, at Courtney Steele's Post, another 300m along, and especially at Quinn's Post (Bomba Sırt, Yüzbaşı Mehmet Şehitliği), another 400m uphill, the trenches were separated only by the width of the modern road. On the eastern side at **Johnston's Jolly** is the Turkish monument to the soldiers of the 125th Regiment who died here on 'Red Ridge'. At **Quinn's Post** is the memorial to Sergeant Mehmet, who fought with rocks and his fists after he ran out of ammunition; and the Captain Mehmet Cemetery.

57 Alay (57th Regiment) Just over one km uphill from Lone Pine is another monument to Mehmetçik on the west side of the road and, on the east side, the cemetery and monument for officers and soldiers of the Ottoman 57th Regiment, which was sacrificed to the first Anzac assaults. The cemetery, built only a few years ago, has a surprising amount of religious symbolism for a Turkish Army site, as the republican army has historically been steadfastly secular. The statue of an old man showing his granddaughter the battle sites portrays veteran Hüseyin Kaçmaz, who fought in the Balkan Wars, in the Gallipoli campaign and in the War of Independence at the fateful Battle of Dumlupınar. He died in 1994 at the age of 110.

Mehmet Çavuş A hundred metres uphill past the 57th Regiment cemetery, a road goes west to The Nek and the monument to Mehmet Çavuş (another Sergeant Mehmet). It's 300m uphill to Baby 700 Cemetery.

Baby 700/Mesudiye Topu About 300m uphill from the road to The Nek is the Baby 700 Cemetery and the cannon called the Mesudiye Topu.

Düztepe 10 Alay Cephesi Another 1.5 km uphill brings you to this monument, which marks the spot where the Ottoman 10th Regiment held the line. The views of the strait and the surrounding countryside are very fine.

Talat Göktepe Monument One km farther along from Düztepe is the monument to Talat Göktepe, Chief Director of the Çanakkale Forestry District, the 'martyred forester' who died at the age of 50 fighting the forest fire which ravaged these hills on 25 July 1994.

Chunuk Bair At the top of the hill, 600m past the Talat Göktepe Monument, is a 'T' intersection. A right turn takes you east to the spot where Atatürk spent the night of 9 to 10 August, and to **Kemalyeri** (Scrubby Knoll), his command post. A left turn leads after 100m to **Chunuk Bair** (Conkbayırı), the first objective of the Allied landing in April 1915, and now the site of the New Zealand memorial.

As the Anzac troops made their way up the scrub-covered slopes, Group Commander Mustafa Kemal (Atatürk) gave this famous order to the troops of his 57th Infantry Regiment: 'I order you not just to attack, but to die. In the time it takes us to die, other troops and commanders will arrive to take our places.' The 57th was wiped out, but held the line and inflicted equally heavy casualties on the Anzacs below.

Chunuk Bair was also at the heart of the struggle from 6 to 9 August 1915, when 28,000 men died on this ridge. The peaceful pine grove of today makes it difficult to imagine the blasted wasteland of almost a century ago, when bullets and bombs mowed down men and trees as the fighting went on day and night with huge numbers of casualties. The Anzac attack on 6 August was deadly but the attack on the following day was of a ferocity which, according to Atatürk, 'could scarcely be described'.

On the western side of the road is the **New Zealand memorial** and some **reconstructed Turkish trenches** *(Türk Siperleri)*. A sign indicates the spots at which Mustafa Kemal (Atatürk) stood, known to every Turkish schoolchild: the spot where shrapnel would have hit his heart, but was stopped by his pocket watch (Atatürk'ün saatinin parçaladığı yeri); where he watched the progress of the battle (Savaş gözetleme yeri); and where he gave the order to attack (Atatürk'ün taarruz emrini verdiği yer).

To the east a side road leads up to the **Turkish Conkbayırı Memorial**, five gigantic tablets with inscriptions (in Turkish) describing the progress of the battle.

Beyond Chunuk Bair the road leads to Kocaçimentepe, less than two km along.

Kabatepe to Seddülbahir A road goes south from near the Kabatepe Information Centre past the side road to **Kum Limanı,** where there is a good swimming beach and the *Hotel Kum* and *Kum Camping* (☎ (286) 814 1466, fax 814 1917), just over six km south-west of the Information Centre. It has comfortable shower-equipped rooms for US$35 in summer, and camping places with some shade for US$5. This is the place to stop for a swim; if you're on a guided tour, you will probably swim here.

From Kabatepe it's about 12 km to the village of **Alçıtepe**, formerly known as Kirte. In the village, signs point out the road south-west to **Twelve Tree Copse** and **Pink Farm** cemeteries, and north to the Turkish **Sargı Yeri cemetery** and **Nuri Yamut monument**.

Heading south, the road passes the **Redoubt Cemetery**. About 5.5 km south of Alçıtepe, just south of the **Skew Bridge Cemetery**, the road divides, the right fork for the village of Seddülbahir and several Allied memorials. **Seddülbahir**, 1.5 km from the intersection, is a sleepy farming village with a few small pensions, including the *Helles Panorama*,*Evim*,*Kale* and *Fulda*, a PTT, a ruined Ottoman/Byzantine fortress, army post, and a small harbour.

Follow the signs for Yahya Çavuş Şehitliği to reach the **Helles Memorial**, one km beyond the Seddülbahir village square.

The initial Allied attack was two-pronged, with the southern landing being here at the tip of the peninsula on 'V' Beach. Yahya Çavuş (Sergeant Yahya) was the Turkish officer who led the first resistance to the Allied landing on 25 April 1915, causing heavy casualties. The cemetery named for him (**Yahya Çavuş Şehitliği**) is between the Helles Memorial and 'V' Beach.

Lancashire Landing cemetery is off to the north along a road marked by a sign; another sign points south to **'V' Beach**, 550m downhill. Right next to the beach is the *Mocamp Seddülbahir*, with tent and caravan sites and a few pension-like rooms.

From the Helles Memorial there are fine views of the straits, with ships cruising placidly up and down. A half million men died or were wounded in the dispute over which ships should (or should not) go through.

Retrace your steps to the road division and go east following signs for Abide and/or Çanakkale Şehitleri Abidesi (Çanakkale Martyrs' Memorial) at Morto Bay. Along the way you pass the **French Memorial & Museum** and the simple little *Abide Motel*, less than two km west of the Turkish War Memorial. At the foot of the monument hill is a fine pine-shaded picnic area.

The **Çanakkale Şehitleri Abidesi** commemorates all of the Turkish soldiers who fought and died at Gallipoli. It's a gigantic four-legged stone table almost 42m high surrounded by landscaped grounds which stands above a war museum (admission US$0.50). Exhibits include interesting bits of metal turned up by farmers' ploughs, including English forks and spoons, soldiers' seals and medals, scimitars, French bayonets and machine guns. The poem inscribed on the side of the memorial translates:

Soldiers who have fallen on this land defending this land!
Would that your ancestors might descend from the skies to kiss your pure brows.
Who could dig the grave that was not too small for you?
All of history itself is too small a place for you.

The most touching exhibit is a letter (in Ottoman Turkish) from a young officer who had left law school in Constantinople to volunteer in the Gallipoli campaign. He writes to his mother in poetic terms about the beauty of the landscape and of his love for life. Two days later he died in battle.

THRACE

South of the Sea of Marmara

The southern shore of the Sea of Marmara is a land of small villages surrounded by olive groves, orchards, sunflower fields, rolling hills and rich valleys. During the time of the Ottoman Empire the choice olives for the sultan's table came from here, and snow from the slopes of Bursa's Uludağ (the Bithynian Mt Olympus) cooled his drinks. The region's few cities are of moderate size and significant interest.

You can enjoy this region and its sights in only two days: catch an early boat from İstanbul to Yalova, make a quick tour of İznik (ancient Nicaea) and spend the night in Bursa. After seeing the sights of Bursa, the next morning catch a bus westward to Çanakkale. You'll reach that town on the Dardanelles in time for a late supper.

Spending from three to five days is more realistic if you want to do justice to all this, and also to enjoy the mineral baths of Termal and Çekirge.

Plan to spend some of your extra time in Bursa, where the mosques and museums are particularly fine (this was the Ottomans' first capital city, before Edirne and İstanbul). You can also ride a cable car to the top of Uludağ, which is snowcapped for most of the year, and offers skiing in winter.

On your way to Bursa, you may pass through the port of Yalova on the Sea of Marmara.

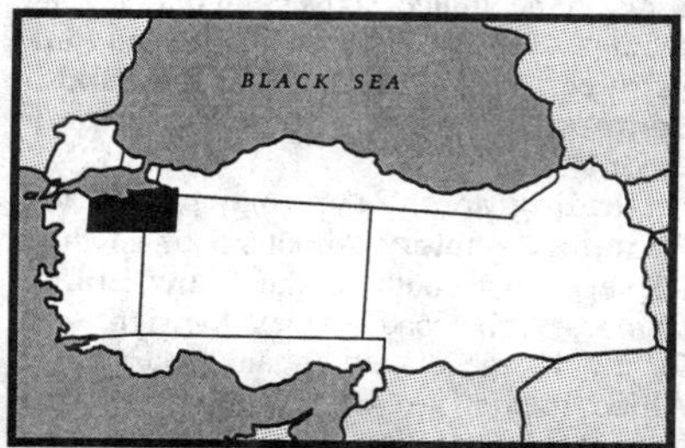

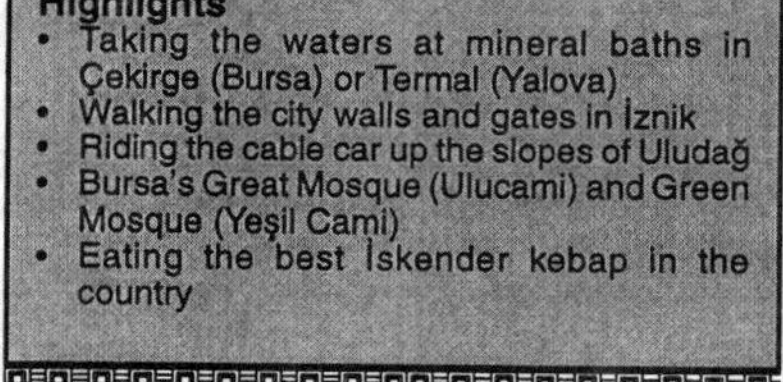
Highlights
- Taking the waters at mineral baths in Çekirge (Bursa) or Termal (Yalova)
- Walking the city walls and gates in İznik
- Riding the cable car up the slopes of Uludağ
- Bursa's Great Mosque (Ulucami) and Green Mosque (Yeşil Cami)
- Eating the best İskender kebap in the country

YALOVA

Yalova (population 60,000) is a farming and transportation centre. The highway between the industrial cities of Bursa and Kocaeli (formerly İzmit) passes near here, as does the hydrofoil-ferry/bus link between Bursa and İstanbul. It's a pleasant enough town, with a few modest hotels and restaurants, most within two blocks of the ferry dock. Everything else you'd need is here as well, including banks, chemists etc.

There's nothing to detain you in Yalova. Head for the spa at Termal, the ancient city of Bursa or İznik without delay.

Places to Stay

Should you need to stay, try the moderately-priced *Hotel Ülke* (☎ (216) 814 1680, fax 813 3232), Yalı Caddesi 17, on the sea front with fine water views and a good restaurant on the top floor. Doubles with private facilities cost US$45.

Getting There & Away

Bus On arrival in Yalova, as you walk from the wharf you will see a traffic circle centred on an enormous statue of Atatürk. Just off the dock to the left are rows of buses and minibuses. Buses to İznik and Bursa leave about every 30 minutes. The fare is US$2.50 to İznik, US$3 to Bursa.

Yalova city bus 4 (Taşköprü-Termal) will take you to Termal for 50c; a dolmuş charges 65c. Coming off the ferry, walk to the traffic circle with the statue and turn right, walk a block and the parking area is on the left.

TOM BROSNAHAN

TOM BROSNAHAN

Top: Kız Kulesi (Leander's Tower) was a toll booth and defence point in ancient times.
Bottom: One of the hundreds of rooms in the harem (imperial family's private apartments) in Topkapi Palace.

TOM BROSNAHAN

TOM BROSNAHAN

TOM BROSNAHAN

Top Left: Lone Pine Cemetery & Memorial, Gallipoli. This area saw the most bitter fighting of the campaign and this cemetery is perhaps the most poignant.
Top Right: A huge replica of the wooden Trojan horse of Homer's *Iliad*.
Bottom: A ferry passes Kilitbahir Castle on its way across the Dardanelles to Çanakkale.

Boat To reach Yalova, Termal, İznik and Bursa from İstanbul, board a hydrofoil (*deniz otobüsü*, for US$6 or US$3.50 for students) at Kabataş, just south of Dolmabahçe Palace, and whiz across the Sea of Marmara to Yalova in about an hour, then continue by bus to Termal, İznik or Bursa. Hydrofoils depart from Kabataş Monday through Friday at 8.35 and 11 am, and 1.45, 4.10 and 6.25 pm; and on weekends at 9.15 and 11.35 am, and 2.45 and 5.45 pm.

Return voyages from Yalova to Kabataş depart weekdays at 7.30 and 9.45 am, and 12.40, 3, 5.15 and 7.30 pm; on weekends departures are at 10.30 am, 1.30, 4.15 and 7 pm.

There are also slower, cheaper conventional ferries between Kabataş and Yalova.

An alternative route, involving slightly less expense but more time and bother, is to take a ferry (50c) from Karaköy to Haydarpaşa, then a suburban train (40c) from Haydarpaşa south-eastward to Kartal, and from Kartal a hydrofoil (US$3.50, or US$1.75 for students) to Yalova. Hydrofoils depart from Kartal for Yalova nine times on weekdays between 7 am and 7.45 pm; on weekends there are 13 departures between 8.30 am and 7.45 pm.

Car Ferry If you're driving, do yourself a favour and take the car ferry from Eskihisar (near Darıca, south-west of Gebze) south across the Bay of İzmit to Topçular, on the south shore east of Yalova. You'll save yourself 100 km of driving along chaotic roads through an industrial wasteland. Ferries run every 30 minutes round the clock on the 25-minute voyage; the fare for car and driver is US$10.

TERMAL

Twelve km west of Yalova, off the road to Çınarcık, is Termal (tehr-MAHL), a spa. The baths here take advantage of hot, mineral-rich waters that gush from the earth and were first exploited in Roman times. The Ottomans used the baths from the 1500s and Abdülhamit II repaired and refurbished them in 1900 in gaudy Ottoman Baroque style to celebrate the 25th anniversary of his accession to the throne.

Atatürk added a simple but comfortable spa hotel. In the midst of the tourism boom, the simple hotels here were upgraded to deluxe comforts and prices.

You can come just to stroll through the shady gardens and have a look at the facilities, or you can come to bathe or stay the night.

Things to See & Do

The gardens and greenery at Termal are worth the trip, and Atatürk had a small house here, which is now a museum. There are also some excellent baths. At the Valide Banyo you get a locker for your clothes, then take a shower and enter a pool. An admission charge of around US$1 gets you 1½ hours of bathing. Soap and shampoo cost extra, so bring your own. The Sultan Banyo is even grander and much pricier at US$3/4 a single/double; you can rent a swimsuit here. The Kurşunlu Banyo features an open-air pool for US$2, an enclosed pool and sauna for US$2.50, and small private cubicles for US$2/2.50 a single/double.

Places to Stay

The villages several km from the centre of Termal have numerous modest little pensions charging from US$7 to US$10 per person for rooms with or without running water. You may find yourself hitchhiking in, or waiting for the infrequent buses and dolmuşes.

Simple but decorous as befits a health resort, both the *Turban Yalova Termal Hotel* (☎ (216) 835 7400, fax 835 7413) and the *Çınar Oteli* (same telephone) charge from US$50 to US$75 a single, US$65 to US$90 a double, breakfast included. The front rooms are the more expensive. Off-season rates are from 25 to 30% lower, but do not include breakfast.

Places to Eat

Termal has several restaurants and cafés, but all are fairly pricey, a mere cup of Nescafé costing over US$1.

İZNİK

The road from Yalova to İznik (population 18,000) runs along fertile green hills punctuated by tall, spiky cypress trees, passing peach orchards, cornfields and vineyards. The journey of 60 km takes about one hour.

As you approach İznik you may notice fruit-packing plants among the orchards. You will certainly have admired the vast İznik Gölü (İznik Lake). Watch for the great Byzantine city walls: one entrance to the city is through the old İstanbul Kapısı (İstanbul Gate) on Atatürk Caddesi, which leads directly to the centre and the ruined Sancta Sophia (Aya Sofya) Church, now a museum.

History

This ancient city may have been founded around 1000 BC. We know that it was revitalised by one of Alexander the Great's generals in 316 BC. Another of the generals, Lysimachus, soon got hold of it and named it for his wife Nikaea. It became the capital city of the province of Bithynia.

Nicaea lost some of its prominence with the founding of Nicomedia (today's Kocaeli, formerly İzmit) in 264 BC, and by 74 BC the entire area had been incorporated into the Roman Empire.

Nicaea flourished under Rome; the emperors built new walls, temples, theatres and baths. But invasions by the Goths and the Persians brought ruin by 300 AD.

Ecumenical Councils With the rise of Constantinople, Nicaea took on a new importance. In 325 AD, the First Ecumenical Council was held here to condemn the heresy of Arianism. During Justinian's reign, Nicaea was grandly refurbished and embellished with new buildings and defences, which served the city well a few centuries later when the Arabs invaded. Like Constantinople, Nicaea never fell to its Arab besiegers.

In 787 AD yet another Ecumenical Council, the seventh, was held in Nicaea's Sancta Sophia Church. The deliberations solved the problem of iconoclasm: henceforth it would be church policy not to destroy icons. Theologians who saw icons as 'images', prohibited by the Bible, were dismayed. But Byzantine artists were delighted, and went to work on their art with even more vigour.

Nicaea and Constantinople did, however, fall to the crusaders. During the period from 1204 to 1261 when a Latin king sat on the throne of Byzantium, the true Byzantine emperor Theodore Lascaris reigned over the 'Empire of Nicaea'. When the crusaders cleared out, the imperial capital moved back to Constantinople.

The Turks The Seljuk Turks had a flourishing empire in Central Anatolia before 1250, and various tribes of nomadic warriors had circulated near the walls of Nicaea during those times. In fact, Turkish soldiers had served as mercenaries in the interminable battles which raged among rival claimants to the Byzantine throne. At one point, a Byzantine battle over Nicaea ended with a Turkish emir as its ruler.

It was Orhan, son of Osman and first true sultan (1326-61) of the Ottoman Empire, who conquered İznik on 2 March 1331. The city soon had the honour of harbouring the first Ottoman theological school. Proussa (Bursa) had fallen to the Ottomans on 6 April 1326, and became their first capital city. In 1337 they took Nicomedia and effectively blocked the Byzantines from entering Anatolia.

Sultan Selim I (1512-20), a mighty conqueror nicknamed The Grim, rolled his armies over Azerbaijan in 1514 and took the Persian city of Tabriz. Packing up all of the region's artisans, he sent them westward to İznik. They brought with them a high level of expertise in the making of coloured tiles. Soon İznik's kilns were turning out faïence which is unequalled even today. The great period of İznik faïence continued almost to 1700. At one point, artisans were sent to Tunisia, then an Ottoman possession, to begin a high-quality faïence industry there.

The art of coloured tile-making is being revived in İznik today, but nowhere near the scale of the trade in Kütahya. Though new tiles make good purchases, 17th and 18th-

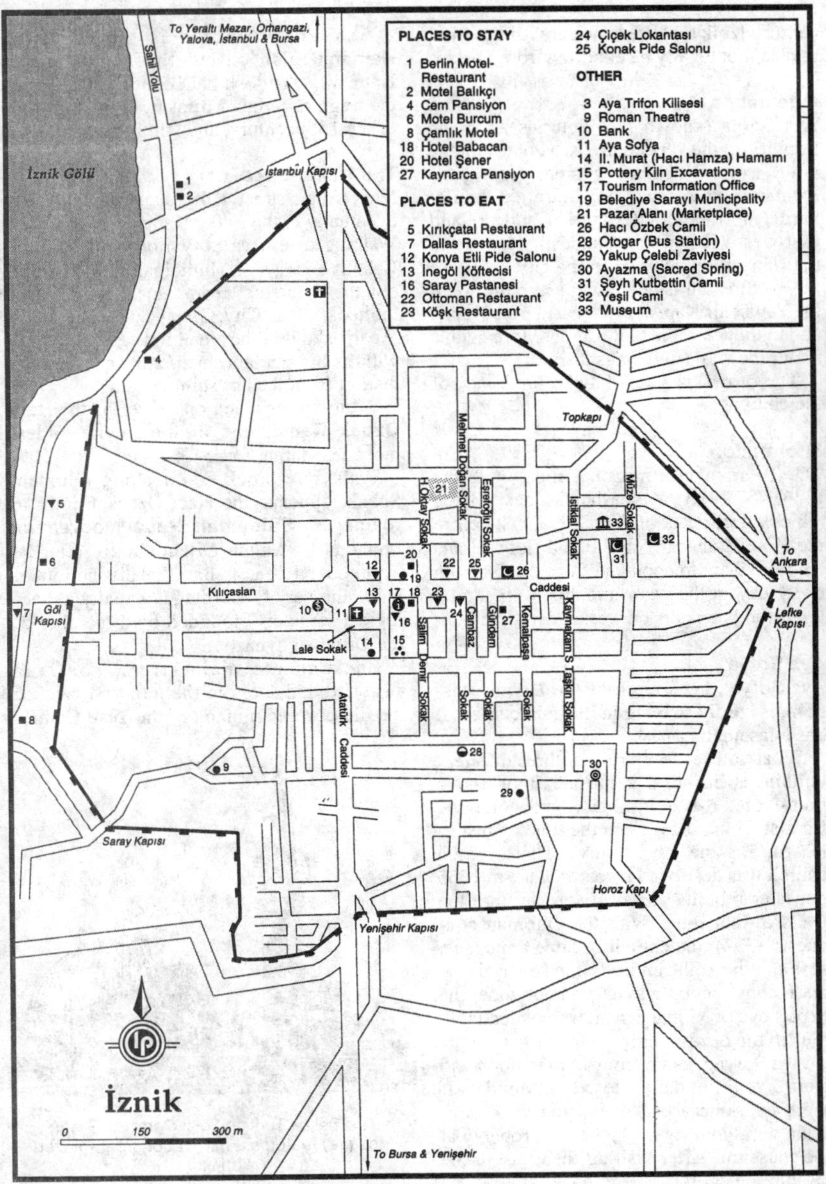

SOUTH OF THE SEA OF MARMARA

century İznik tiles are considered antiquities, and cannot legally be exported from Turkey.

Orientation

Aya Sofya (known for centuries as Hagia Sophia), at the very centre, is a good vantage point from which to consider the town's Roman layout: two dead-straight boulevards, north-south (Atatürk Caddesi) and east-west (Kılıçaslan Caddesi), leading to the four principal gates in the city walls. To the north is the İstanbul Kapısı, to the south the Yenişehir Kapısı, to the east Lefke Kapısı and to the west, the Göl Kapısı. More details about the walls and gates follow.

The otogar is a few blocks south-east of the church.

Information

The Tourism Information Office (☎ & fax (224) 757 1933), Kılıçaslan Caddesi 130, is a block north-east of Aya Sofya, just before the Hotel Babacan, on the 2nd floor. Hours are from 9 am to noon and from 1 to 5.30 pm every day in the warm months, with shorter hours (and no hours on weekends) off season.

Aya Sofya

Aya Sofya, the Church of the Divine Wisdom, is hardly striking in its grandeur, but it has a fascinating past.

What you see is the ruin of three different buildings. Inside is a mosaic floor and a mural of Jesus with Mary and John the Baptist which dates from the time of Justinian (during the 6th century). That original church was destroyed by earthquake in 1065 but later rebuilt. Mosaics were set into the walls at that time. With the Ottoman conquest (1331), the church became a mosque. A fire in the 16th century ruined everything, but reconstruction was carried out under the expert eye of Mimar Sinan, who added İznik tiles to the decoration.

Aya Sofya is open from 9 am to noon and from 2 to 5 pm daily, closed on Monday. If there's no-one about when you visit, continue with your tour. The key is probably at the museum. After visiting there, ask to be let into the church.

Behind Aya Sofya is the **II. Murat Hamamı**, also called the Hacı Hamza Hamamı, a Turkish bath constructed during the reign of Sultan Murat II, in the first half of the 15th century, and still in operation.

The Main Street

İznik's main street, Kılıçaslan Caddesi, leads eventually to the Lefke Kapısı (Lefke Gate). Walking from Aya Sofya, on the left is the Belediye Sarayı or Municipality, with a sign out the front that reads (in Turkish) 'Our motto is, Clean City, Green City'. The motto is carried out in the small but agreeable park with its big poplars shading the commercial district from the hot summer sun.

A bit farther along on the left is the **Hacı Özbek Camii**, one of the town's oldest mosques, dating from 1332.

Walk one block south along Gündem Sokak, opposite the Hacı Özbek Camii, to reach the **Süleyman Paşa Medresesi**. Founded by Sultan Orhan shortly after he captured Nicaea, it has the distinction of being the very first college (actually a theological seminary) founded by a member of the Ottoman dynasty.

Back on the main street, continue eastward and soon, to the left, you can see the tile-covered minaret of the Yeşil Cami.

The Seljuk Turkish Yeşil Cami (or Green Mosque) features a minaret of green-glazed bricks.

SOUTH OF THE SEA OF MARMARA

Yeşil Cami

Built in the year that Columbus discovered America (1492), the Yeşil Cami, or Green Mosque, has Seljuk Turkish proportions influenced more by Persia (the Seljuk homeland) than by İstanbul. The green-glazed bricks of the minaret foreshadowed the tile industry that arose a few decades after the mosque was built. Sultan Selim, impatient to have a tile industry of his own, simply moved a large number of artisans from Tabriz.

Archaeological Museum

Across the road from the Yeşil Cami is the Nilüfer Hatun İmareti, or Soup Kitchen of Lady Nilüfer (1388), now set up as the town's museum. Opening hours are from 8.30 am to noon and 1 to 5 pm, closed Monday (usually). Admission costs US$1.25.

Begun in 1388, it was built by Sultan Murat I for his mother, Nilüfer Hatun, who was born a Byzantine princess but was married off to Orhan, second sultan of the Ottoman state, to cement a diplomatic alliance.

Though intended as a place where the poor could come for free food, it now dispenses culture to the masses. The front court is filled with marble statuary, bits of cornice and column, and similar archaeological flotsam and jetsam. In the lofty, cool halls are exhibits of İznik faïence, Ottoman weaponry, embroidery and calligraphy, and several items from the city's Roman past. Many of the little signs are in French and English, but you'll need to know the word *yüzyıl* (century), as in XVI Yüzyıl (16th century).

While at the museum, enquire about a visit to the **Yeraltı Mezar** (underground tomb), a Byzantine tomb on the outskirts. You must have a museum official accompany you with the key; there is a small charge for admission, and the official should receive a small tip. Also, you will have to haggle with a taxi driver for a return-trip price.

The little tomb, discovered by accident in the 1960s, has delightful Byzantine murals covering walls and ceiling. There is another tomb nearby, but it's not really worth the bother or expense to see.

Across the road to the south of the museum is the **Şeyh Kutbettin Camii** (1492), in ruins.

City Walls

Return to Kılıçaslan Caddesi and continue east to the **Lefke Kapısı**. This charming old monument is actually three gates in a row, all dating from Byzantine times. The middle one has an inscription which tells us it was built by Proconsul Plancius Varus in 123 AD. It's possible to clamber up to the top of the gate and the walls here, a good vantage point for inspecting the ancient walls.

Outside the gate is an **aqueduct**, and the **tomb of Çandarlı Halil Hayrettin Paşa** (late 1300s), with the graves of many lesser mortals nearby.

Lefke, now a small town called Osmaneli, was a city of considerable size in Byzantine times.

Re-enter the city through the Lefke Kapısı, and turn left. Follow the walls south and west to the **Yenişehir Kapısı**. On the way you will pass near the ruined **Church of the Koimesis**, on the west side of Kaymakam S Taşkın Sokak, which dates from about 800 AD. Only some bits of the foundation remain, but it is famous as the burial place of the Byzantine emperor Theodore I Lascaris. When the crusaders took Constantinople in 1204, Lascaris fled to Nicaea and established his court here.

Lascaris built Nicaea's outer ring of walls, supported by over 100 towers and protected by a wide moat. No doubt he didn't trust the crusaders, having lost one city to them. The emperor died and was buried here, and when the court finally returned to the city on the Bosphorus in 1261, it was under the leadership of Michael VIII Palaeologus. Lascaris never made it back to his beloved capital.

Half a block east of the church is an ayazma *(aghiasma)* or **sacred fountain**, also called a *yeraltı çeşme* (underground spring).

After admiring the Yenişehir Kapısı, start towards the centre along Atatürk Caddesi. Halfway to Aya Sofya, a road on the left leads to the ruins of a Roman theatre. Nearby is the

Saray Kapısı, or Palace Gate, in the city walls. Sultan Orhan had a palace near here in the 1300s.

The Lake

Make your way to the lakeshore where there are teahouses and restaurants, as well as a bathing beach. The water tends to be weedy, and chilly except in high summer.

Places to Stay – bottom end

The few hotels in İznik may fill up with Turks from nearby cities on summer weekends, and you may need to reserve a room in advance.

İznik has a few modest hostelries good for a one-night stay. *Kaynarca Pansiyon* (☎ (224) 757 1753, fax 757 1723), Gündem Sokak 1, run by the irrepressible Ali Bulmuş, is clean, simple and central, charging US$6/10/15 a single/double/triple.

In the centre, just across the street from the Belediye, is the plain, fairly drab *Hotel Babacan* (☎ (224) 757 1211) at Kılıçaslan Caddesi 104. Thirty of the rooms come with sinks and are priced at US$8/10 a single/double. With private shower, the prices are US$13/16.

A bit newer, and thus nicer, are the *Cem Pansiyon* (☎ (224) 757 1687) and the *Pension Café Murat* (☎ (224) 757 2651), on the Sahil Yolu (shore road) in the north-west part of town facing the lake. Both charge US$9/13 a single/double.

Camping Motel Burcum and Çamlık Motel (see following) have very basic camping areas.

Places to Stay – middle

Motel Burcum (☎ (224) 757 1011) has verdant grounds and tidy rooms, some with views of the lake, for US$18 a double, breakfast included. Get a room on the 2nd or 3rd floor if you want that view. You can camp in the garden for a few dollars per night.

The *Çamlık Motel* (CHAHM-luhk) (☎ (224) 757 1631), at the southern end of the lake-front road, has good rooms and a restaurant, with prices identical to those at the Burcum. There is camping here as well, and it's perhaps a bit quieter.

Berlin Motel-Restaurant (☎ (224) 757 3355, fax 757 4333), Sahil Yolu 36, north-west of the centre, offers adequate rooms, a well-stocked bar, a popular restaurant, and loud entertainment till midnight some nights. Rates are a fairly high US$18/25 a single/double, with bath.

Hotel Şener (☎ (224) 757 1338, fax 757 2280), Belediye Arkası, H Oktay Sokak 7, prides itself on being the fanciest hotel in the centre, with a lift, lounge, restaurant, and comfortable rooms going for US$12/19/28 a single/double/triple with shower.

Places to Eat

On Kılıçaslan Caddesi, look for the *Konya Etli Pide Salonu*, serving good, cheap, freshly made Turkish-style pizzas for US$1.25 to US$2.50, depending upon toppings. Arab-style lahmacun costs less than 70c per portion. Farther along, the *Köşk* just east of the Belediye on the opposite side of the street, has stews and grills, as does the nearby *Çiçek*, and the *Ottoman Restaurant* farther east at Kılıçaslan Caddesi 137, with full meals for US$4 or less. The *Konak Pide Salonu* east of the Ottoman is cheaper still.

There are also several pastahanes here, including the *Saray Pastanesi*, good for breakfast, tea or a snack.

The lakeside restaurants are the most pleasant and popular for a meal if the weather is fine, and Turkish patrons will enjoy themselves here for hours each evening. Unlike the simple restaurants along Kılıçaslan Caddesi, alcoholic beverages are served in the lakeshore places. Expect to spend about US$8 to US$12 for a full meal, less for a light supper.

Dallas Restaurant, named for the US television series, is just south of where Kılıçaslan Caddesi meets the lake, with a pleasant waterfront position. *Kırıkçatal* (Broken Fork) is north of the Motel Burcum, and has a longstanding reputation. There's live entertainment, Turkish-style, at the *Berlin Motel-Restaurant* even farther north.

Getting There & Away

Bursa has a much better selection of hotels and restaurants than İznik. Unless you are unusually interested in İznik, take one of the hourly buses from İznik's otogar to Bursa. Don't wait until too late in the day, however, as the last bus heads out at 6 or 7 pm on the 1½-hour trip. A ticket costs from US$2 to US$2.75, depending upon the company.

BURSA

Bursa, with a population of one million, has a special place in the hearts of the Turks. It was the first capital city of the enormous Ottoman Empire and, in a real sense, the birthplace of modern Turkish culture. The city, at an altitude of 155m, has its pretty parts despite its industrial base.

History

Called Prusa by the Byzantines, Bursa is a very old and important city. It was founded – according to legend, by Prusias, king of Bithynia – before 200 BC; there may have been an even older settlement on the site. It soon came under the sway of Eumenes II of Pergamum, and thereafter under direct Roman control.

Bursa grew to importance in the early centuries of Christianity, when the thermal baths at Çekirge were first developed on a large scale and when a silk trade was founded here. The importation of silkworms and the establishment of looms began an industry which survives to this day. It was Justinian (527-65) who really put Bursa on the map. Besides favouring the silk trade, he built a palace for himself and bathhouses in Çekirge.

With the decline of Byzantium, Bursa's location near İstanbul drew the interest of would-be conquerors, including the Arab armies (circa 700 AD) and the Seljuk Turks. The Seljuks, having conquered much of Anatolia by 1075, took Bursa with ease that same year, and planted the seeds of the great Ottoman Empire to come.

With the arrival of the First Crusade in

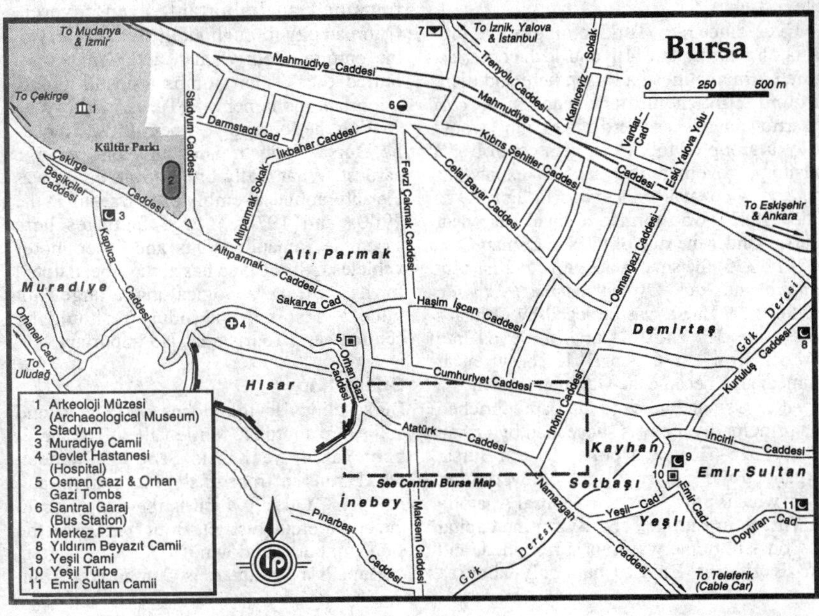

Karagöz
Bursa is traditionally regarded as the 'birthplace' of the Turkish Karagöz shadow-puppet theatre. The puppets – cut from camel hide, treated with oil to promote translucency, and brought to life with coloured paint – are manipulated behind a white cloth onto which their images are cast by a light behind them.

Legend has it that one of the construction foremen working on Bursa's Ulu Cami was a hunchback called Karagöz (Black-eye). He and his straight-man Hacivat indulged in such humorous antics that the other workers abandoned their tasks to watch. This infuriated the sultan, who had the two miscreants put to death. Their comic routines (many of them bawdy) live on in the Karagöz shadow-puppet theatre, a Central Asian tradition brought to Bursa from where it spread throughout the Ottoman lands.

Once commonly performed in tea and coffee houses, salons and parks throughout the empire, it has long since been supplanted by television, but performances are occasionally organised by Şinasi Çelikkol of the Karagöz antiques shop (see Bedesten). ■

1097, Bursa reverted to Christian hands, though it was to be conquered and reconquered by both sides for the next 100 years. When the rapacious armies of the Fourth Crusade sacked Constantinople in 1204, the Byzantine emperor fled to İznik and set up his capital there. He succeeded in controlling the hinterland of İznik, including Bursa, until the capital was moved back to Constantinople in 1261.

Ever since the Turkish migration into Anatolia during the 11th and 12th centuries, small principalities had risen here and there around Turkish military leaders. A *gazi* (warrior chieftain or 'Hero of the Faith') would rally a group of followers, gain control of a territory, govern it and seek to expand its borders. One such prince was Ertuğrul Gazi (died 1281), who formed a small state near Bursa. Under the rule of his son Osman Gazi (1281-1326) the small state grew to a nascent empire and took Osman's name *(Osmanlı*, 'Ottoman'). Bursa was besieged by Osman's forces in 1317 and was finally starved into submission on 6 April 1326 when it immediately became the Ottoman capital.

After Osman had expanded and enriched his principality, he was succeeded by Orhan Gazi (1326-61) who, from his base at Bursa, expanded the empire to include everything from what is now Ankara in Central Anatolia to Thrace in Europe. The Byzantine capital at Constantinople was thus surrounded, and the Byzantine Empire had only about a century to survive. Orhan took the title of sultan (lord), struck the first Ottoman coinage and near the end of his reign was able to dictate to the Byzantine emperors. One of them, John VI Cantacuzene, was Orhan's close ally and later even his father-in-law (Orhan married the Princess Theodora).

Even though the Ottoman capital moved to Adrianople (Edirne) in 1402, Bursa remained an important, even revered, Ottoman city throughout the long history of the empire. Both Osman and Orhan were buried there; their tombs are still proud, important monuments in Turkish history.

With the founding of the Turkish Republic, Bursa's industrial development began in earnest. What really brought the boom was the automobile assembly plants, set up in the 1960s and 1970s. Large factories here assemble Renaults, Fiats and other motor vehicles. Also, Bursa has always been noted for its fruit; it was logical that a large fruit juice and soft drink industry should be centred here. Tourism is also important.

Orientation

Bursa clings to the slopes of Uludağ and spills down into the fertile valley. The major boulevards are Kıbrıs Şehitler Caddesi, which runs in front of the bus station, and Atatürk Caddesi, which is the main axis in the commercial district. Both run across the slope, not up and down it.

Bursa's main square is Cumhuriyet Alanı

(Republic Square), with its equestrian statue of Atatürk. Most people refer to the square as Heykel (hey-KEHL, statue), and this is what you will see on the illuminated signs atop dolmuşes which wait near the bus station to take you to the city centre.

Bursa's main street, Atatürk Caddesi, runs west from Heykel to the Ulu Cami (oo-LOO jah-mee, Great Mosque), a distance of about 700m. This is the business section, the centre of Bursa. Heavy traffic makes it almost impossible to cross the street, so use the pedestrian subways *(altgeçidi*, underpass), each of which bears a name (see following).

To the north-west, Atatürk Caddesi becomes Cemal Nadir Caddesi, then Altıparmak Caddesi, then Çekirge Caddesi. It leads to the spa suburb of Çekirge, about a 10-minute ride away.

South-east of Heykel, Namazgah Caddesi crosses the Gök Deresi stream trickling along the bottom of a dramatic gorge. Just after the stream, Yeşil Caddesi branches off to the left to the Yeşil Cami, after which it changes names to become Emir Sultan Caddesi.

From Heykel and Atatürk Caddesi you can get dolmuşes and buses to all other parts of the city.

Information

The Tourism Information Office (☎ (224) 251 1834, fax 220 1848) is beneath Atatürk Caddesi at the northern entrance to the Orhan Gazi Altgeçidi pedestrian subway, facing the Koza Han and Orhan Gazi Camii across the little park. Staff are well-informed and helpful, particularly to readers of this guide-book. There is also a small information booth in the Santral Garajı (bus station).

Bookshops TAŞ Kitapçılık & Yayıncılık

Nasreddin Hodja...Storyteller Supreme

You won't be long in Turkey before you spot a picture of a bearded man in an outsize turban riding backwards on a donkey. This is Nasreddin Hodja, a medieval joker whose witty moralising stories are as familiar to Turkish children as Aesop's fables are to Europeans.

Strangely enough, almost nothing is known about the man to whom almost 500 stories are attributed. There are even some who claim that there was no such living man outside the 'hero' of the stories.

Assuming Hodja is a real character, it seems likely that he was born the son of an imam around 1208 in the village of Hortu in Sivrihisar. As an adult he may have served time as a judge, as an imam, as a university professor and as a dervish. He probably died in 1284 in Akşehir, near Konya. His stories first turn up in a book called *Saltukname*, produced in 1480 and incorporating other folk tales and legends as well.

A typical Nasreddin Hodja story is written in a clipped prose style and concludes with an epigram intended to make people think. Themes are taken from daily life: cooking, riding a donkey, visiting a Turkish bath. Some so-called Nasreddin Hodja stories were clearly written by other people, and new 'Nasreddin Hodja' stories are still produced today.

The following tale is typical:

Hodja went to Bursa market to buy a pair of trousers. Having selected a pair, he was just about to pay when he spotted a robe and decided to take that instead.

As he walked towards the door, the shopkeeper called out that he hadn't paid for the robe. Hodja pointed out that he had returned the pair of trousers.

'But you hadn't paid for those either,' he was reminded.

'What a strange man you are,' Hodja exclaimed. 'You expect me to pay for a pair of trousers I didn't buy.'

It's also typical of Hodja humour that his tomb in Akşehir has a padlocked gate on one side, although the other three sides are unfenced. What's more, the date inside is written backwards.

Every 5 to 10 July an International Nasreddin Hodja Festival is held in Akşehir. The Association of Turkish Caricaturists also runs an annual international Nasreddin Hodja competition. ■

(☎ 222 9453), Adliye Karşısı, Kültür Sokak 8/A, just a few steps uphill from Heykel, has Penguin books and a number of other English titles as well as some English-language newspapers and periodicals.

Emir Sultan Camii

You can see most of Bursa's sights in one full day, though a leisurely tour will take a little more time. Start with the city's most famous architectural monuments, east of the city centre. You can go by dolmuş (look for the Emir Sultan dolmuş stand on the north side of the square), or by bus 18 (Emir Sultan-Heykel-Santral Garajı). You'll pass by the Yeşil Cami and Yeşil Türbe before coming to the Emir Sultan Camii, but this way you can walk downhill, not up.

This mosque is a favourite of Bursa's pious Muslims. Rebuilt by Selim III in 1805 and restored in the early 1990s, it echoes the romantic decadence of Ottoman Rococo style. The setting, next to a large hillside cemetery surrounded by huge trees and overlooking the city and valley, is as pleasant as the mosque itself.

Yıldırım Beyazıt Camii

Gazing across the valley from the Emir Sultan Camii, you'll see the two domes of the Yıldırım Beyazıt Camii, the Mosque of Beyazıt the Thunderbolt. It was built earlier (in 1391) than Bursa's famous Yeşil Cami, and forms part of the same architectural evolution. You can walk through the city to this mosque if you like, but go and see the Yeşil Cami first. Dolmuşes (Heykel-Beyazıt Yıldırım or Heykel-Fakülte) depart from Heykel and pass near the mosque.

Next to the Yıldırım Beyazıt Camii is its medrese, once a theological seminary, now a public health centre. Here also are the tombs of the mosque's founder, Sultan Beyazıt I, and his son İsa. This peaceful spot gives one no sense of the turbulent times which brought Beyazıt to his death.

Yıldırım Beyazıt (Sultan Beyazıt I, 1389-1402) led his Ottoman armies into Yugoslavia and Hungary, and captured even more of Anatolia for the Ottomans. But he was brought down by Tamerlane, who defeated him and took him prisoner at the Battle of Ankara in 1402. Beyazıt died a year later in captivity, and Tamerlane marched all the way to İzmir and Bursa. With this blow, the Ottoman Empire all but collapsed.

Yeşil Cami

After the disastrous victories of Tamerlane, Beyazıt's sons argued over the succession to the weakened Ottoman throne. The civil war between them lasted for 10 years until 1413, when one son, Mehmet Çelebi, was able to gain supreme power. Six years after becoming sultan, Mehmet I (1413-21) ordered his architect Hacı İvaz to begin construction on Bursa's greatest monument, the Yeşil Cami or Green Mosque. It was finished in 1424.

The mosque is a supremely beautiful building in a fine setting and represents a turning point in Turkish architectural style. Before this, Turkish mosques echoed the style of the Great Seljuks which was basically Persian, but in the Yeşil Cami a purely Turkish style emerges. Notice the harmonious façade and the beautiful carved marble work around the central doorway. As you enter, you will pass beneath the sultan's private apartments into a domed central hall. The rooms to the left and right, if not being used for prayer, were used by high court officials for transacting government business. The room straight ahead, with the 15-metre-high mihrab, is the main prayer room. Greenish-blue tiles on the interior walls gave the mosque its name.

Much of Bursa, including the Yeşil Cami, was destroyed in an earthquake in 1855 but the mosque was restored, authentically, by 1864.

Just inside the mosque's main entrance, a narrow stairway leads up to the **hünkar mahfili**, or sultan's loge, above the main door. The loge is sumptuously tiled and decorated. This is where the sultan actually lived (or at least it was one of his residences), with his harem and household staff in less plush quarters on either side. The caretaker used to choose single travellers or couples, give them a conspiratorial wink, and lead them up for a peek, after which he would receive a tip. Somebody higher up must have caught on, as he no longer seems to be doing it.

Yeşil Türbe

Sharing the small park surrounding the Yeşil Cami is the Yeşil Türbe, or Green Tomb. It's not green, of course. The blue exterior tiles were put on during restoration work in the 1800s; the lavish use of tiles inside is original work, however. The tomb is open from 8.30 am to noon and 1 to 5.30 pm for free; no need to remove your shoes.

The most prominent tomb is that of the Yeşil Cami's founder, Mehmet I (Çelebi). Others include those of his children. The huge tiled mihrab here is very impressive. Take a walk around the outside of the tomb to look at the tiled calligraphy above several windows.

After seeing the mosque and the tomb, you might want to take a rest and have something to drink at one of the cafés on the east side of the mosque, which have wonderful views of the valley, though you pay a premium for them.

Turkish & Islamic Arts Museum

Down the road a few steps from the Yeşil Cami is its medrese, now called the Türk ve İslam Eserleri Müzesi. The building is in the Seljuk style of religious schools, and is open from 8.30 am to noon and 1 to 5 pm, closed on Monday; admission costs US$1.25, half-price for students.

Start to the right to see a recreation of an Ottoman *sünnet odası* (circumcision room), then, in the *eyvan* or niche-like hall, an exhibit of ceramics from the Seljuk period (12th and 13th centuries), İznik ware from the 14th to 18th centuries, and more modern Kütahya ware (18th to 20th centuries).

Next comes an exhibit of Karagöz shadow puppets. It's thought that these painted camel-hide puppets originated in China and Mongolia, and were brought to the Middle East by the Turks.

After Karagöz, museum displays include costumes, carpets, jewellery, metalwork and arms; *dergah* (dervish-hall) musical instruments, turbans and other paraphernalia; illuminated Korans, carpet weaving and embroidery.

Bat Pazarı

From the plaza at Heykel, walk down the hill on the east (right) side of İnönü Caddesi one very long block. Cross Kirişkızı Sokak and turn right onto the next street, Kayhan Caddesi, to enter a warren of little streets called the Bat Pazarı (Goose Market), or, more appropriately, the Demirciler Çarşısı (Ironmongers' Market). The one thing you won't find here today are geese, but you will find ironmongers' shops and pedlars of old clothes, carpets, rope, utensils, potions and just about everything else. This market section is lively and colourful, perfect for photographing. When you snap a shot of the blacksmith at his forge, chances are he will ask you to send him a copy. It's only fair; you should try to do so.

Bedesten

After a half-hour stroll through the Bat Pazarı, head back to İnönü Caddesi and ask someone to point the way to the Bedesten or Covered Bazaar. Cross İnönü Caddesi and head into the side streets, following the directions given. The actual covered market is surrounded by a network of small shopping streets.

The Bedesten was originally built in the late 1300s by Yıldırım Beyazıt, but the earthquake of 1855 brought it down. The reconstructed Bedesten retains the look and feel of the original, though it is obviously much tidier. This is not a tourist trap; most of the shoppers are local people. As you wander around, look for the **Eski Aynalı Çarşı**, which, though now a market, was originally built as the Orhangazi Hamamı (1335), the Turkish bath of the Orhan Camii Külliyesi. The domed ceiling with many small lights shows this.

In the Eski Aynalı Çarşı is a shop called Karagöz (☎ 221 8727), open daily except Sunday, and run by a man named Şinasi Çelikkol. Şinasi specialises in quality goods (copper and brass, carpets and kilims, knitted

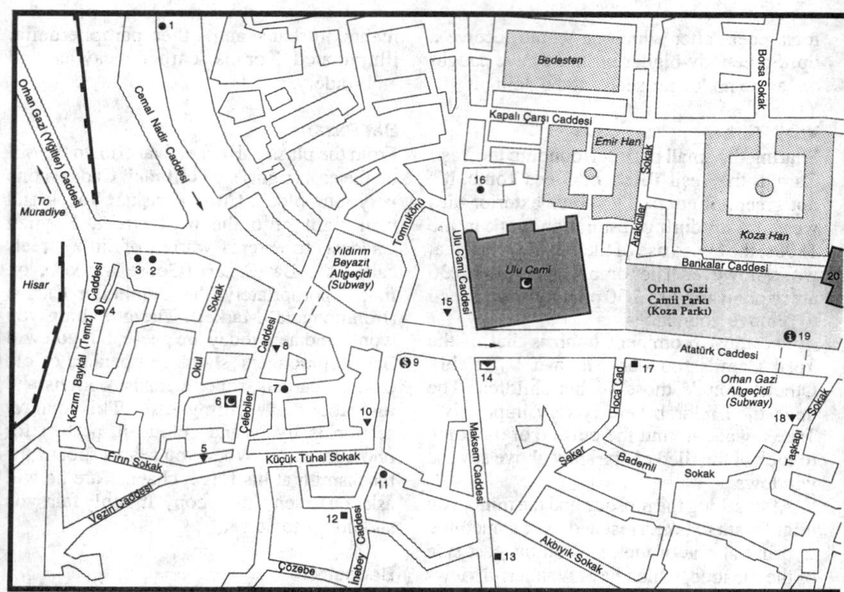

PLACES TO STAY

12 Otel Çamlıbel
13 Hotel Dikmen
17 Kent Hotel
26 Hotel Bilgiç
29 Hotel Çeşmeli
40 Hotel İpekçi

PLACES TO EAT

5 Yeşil İnci Lokantası
8 Alış Izgara & Tahtakale Lokantası
10 Şehir Lokantası
15 Ömür Köftecisi
18 Hacıbey Kebapçısı
21 Çiçek Izgara
23 Kebabçı İskenderoğlu Nurettin
24 İnegöl Köftecisi & Kamil Koç Co Bus Tickets
30 Okyanus Fırın Salonu
38 Adanur Hacıbey
39 Kebapçı İskender

OTHER

1 Ottomantur (Turkish Airlines)
2 Uludağ Co Bus Tickets
3 Çakır Ağa Hamamı (Turkish Bath)
4 Muradiye Dolmuş
6 Mecnundede Camii
7 Tahtakale Çarşısı (Market)
9 Türkiye Emlak Bankası
11 Tarihi İnebey Hamamı (Turkish Bath)
14 PTT
16 Ulu Cami Hamamı (Turkish Bath)
19 Tourism Information Office
20 Belediye Sarayı (Municipality)
22 Çiçek Pazarı (Flower Market)
25 Katlı Otopark
27 Emir Sultan Dolmuş Stand
28 Dolmuşes to Teleferik (Cable Car)
31 TAŞ Kitapçılık & Yayıncılık Bookshop
32 Vilayet (Government Building)
33 Heykel
34 Dolmuşes to Molla Arap
35 Ahmet Vefik Paşa Tiyatrosu (Theatre)
36 Dolmuşes to Muradiye, Santral Garaj & Çekirge
37 TC Ziraat Bankası
41 Bat Pazarı

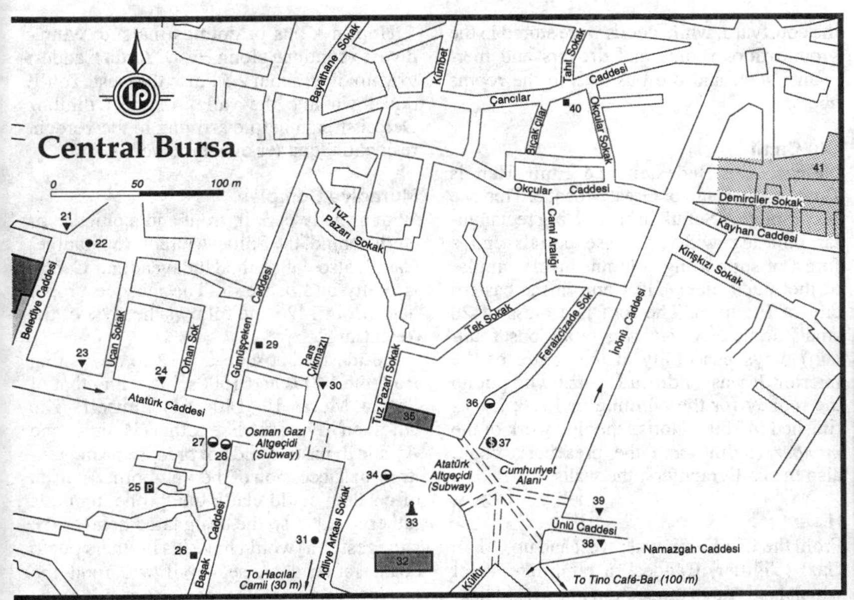

gloves and embroidery, old jewellery etc) at fair prices, as did his father Rafet before him. This is the place to find the delightful Karagöz shadow puppets. Cut from flat, dried camel leather, painted in bright colours and oiled to make them translucent, the puppets are an authentic Turkish craft item.

Şinasi Bey periodically organises performances of the shadow plays in English for groups, charging several dollars for admission. If you're interested, ask at the shop about the next shows. If one is not scheduled, he may give you a brief idea of how the shadow-puppet theatre works right in his shop.

Koza & Emir Hans

The raising of silkworms is a cottage industry in Bursa. Each April, villagers buy the worms from their cooperatives, take them home and raise them on mulberry leaves. After a month the worms spin their cocoons and are soon ready for the trip to the **Koza Han** or Silk Cocoon Caravanserai, just outside the Bedesten's eastern entrance, built in 1490 and lively with cocoon dealers in June and also in September when there is a second harvest.

When you visit, you may well see huge sacks of the precious little white cocoons being haggled over by some of the 14,000 villagers who engage in the trade. In the centre of the Koza Han's courtyard is a small mosque constructed by Yıldırım Beyazıt in 1493, restored by the guild of silk traders in 1948, and again in 1985 by the Aga Khan. The product of all this industry, *ipek* (silk cloth), is for sale in the Bedesten.

Another place you ought to visit in the Bedesten is the **Emir Han**, adjoining the north-east corner of the Ulu Cami, a caravanserai used by many of Bursa's silk brokers today as it has been for centuries. There's a lovely fountain in the centre of the courtyard, and a tea garden for refreshments. Camels from the silk caravans used to be corralled in the courtyard, while goods were stored in the ground-floor rooms and drovers and merchants slept and did business in the rooms above.

Ulu Cami

Next to the Bedesten and Emir Han is Bursa's Ulu Cami or Great Mosque. This one is completely Seljuk in style, a big rectangular building with immense portals and a forest of supporting columns inside, similar to the much older Ulu Cami in the eastern city of Erzurum. The roof is a mass of 20 small domes. A *şadırvan* (ablutions fountain) plays peacefully at the centre of the interior. It was Yıldırım Beyazıt who put up the money for the building in 1396; it was finished in 1399. Notice the fine work of the *mimber* (pulpit) and the preacher's chair, also the calligraphy on the walls.

Hisar

From the Ulu Cami, walk west and up Orhan Gazi (Yiğitler) Caddesi, a ramp-like street which leads up to the section known as Hisar (Fortress). This section, the oldest in Bursa, was once enclosed by stone ramparts and walls, bits of which survive.

'Muradiye', dolmuşes run from Heykel and from the foot of Kazım Baykal (Temiz) Caddesi; by bus, hop in bus 1-A, 'Muradiye-Heykel' or any bus with 'Dev. Hst.' (Devlet Hastanesi) or 'Muradiye' on its signboard. Get off at the 'Tophane' stop. (The Devlet Hastanesi, by the way, is a large government hospital just west of the tombs of sultans Osman and Orhan.)

Near a sign which reads 'İstiklal Savaşı Şehitler', in a little park near the edge of the cliff overlooking Cemal Nadir Caddesi and the valley, are the **tombs of sultans Osman and Orhan**, founders of the Ottoman Empire. The originals were destroyed in the earthquake of 1855 and rebuilt in Ottoman Baroque style by Sultan Abdülaziz in 1868. The tomb of Orhan Gazi was built on the foundations of a small Byzantine church, and you can see some remnants of the church's floor. The park here is attractive, as is the view of the city.

Hop in a bus or dolmuş marked 'Muradiye' to continue along Hasta Yurdu Caddesi to Muradiye, about 2.5 km to the west. You'll dip down into the valley of the Cılımboz Deresi stream before arriving in the verdant residential quarter of Muradiye.

Muradiye Complex

With a shady park in front and a quiet cemetery behind, the Sultan Murat II (Muradiye) Camii, also called the Hüdavendigar Camii, is pretty and peaceful. The mosque proper dates from 1426 and follows the style of the Yeşil Cami.

Beside the mosque are 12 tombs dating from the 1400s and 1500s, including that of Sultan Murat II (1404-51) himself. The Ottoman dynasty, like other Islamic and Asiatic dynasties, did not practise primogeniture, or succession of the first-born. Any son of a sultan could claim the throne upon his father's death, so the designated heir (or the strongest son) would have his brothers put to death rather than see civil war rend the empire. Many of the occupants of tombs here, including all the *şehzades* (imperial sons), died at the hands of their close relatives.

Tomb-visiting may not be high on your list of priorities but you should see the beautiful decoration in some of the tombs. The superb decoration on the woodwork porch of the **Murat II Türbesi** contrasts with the rest of the tomb's austerity. The sultan's tomb has an opening to the sky so that his grave could be washed by the rain, and his unadorned sarcophagus has no lid, following common Muslim custom rather than imperial tradition. The tomb's architect did add a bit of Byzantine grandeur by borrowing some old Corinthian columns, but he used capitals as both capitals and plinths.

The beautiful coloured İznik tilework in the gaudy **Cem Türbesi** celebrates Cem Sultan (1459-95), the youngest son of Sultan Mehmet the Conqueror. Cem reigned for 18 days, but was chased from the throne by Beyazıt II and fled to Europe, where he became a hostage of the pope and a pawn in Ottoman-European diplomacy.

The İznik tiles in the **Şehzade Mustafa Türbesi** are as fine as those in the Rüstem Paşa Camii in İstanbul. Mustafa (1515-53), son of Süleyman the Magnificent, was governor of Amasya when Süleyman's wife Roxelana intrigued against him, causing the sultan to order his execution – which he soon regretted bitterly.

The **Şehzade Ahmet Türbesi** is elegant in its simplicity of light and dark blue tiles framed by a vine-patterned blue-and-white border. The stained glass window is restrained as well. Ahmet's mother Bülbül Hatun is buried beside him.

Also here is the **Tarihi II Murat Hamamı**, or Historic Turkish Bath of Sultan Murat II, still in use (see Mineral Baths, following).

Across the park from the mosque and tombs is an old Ottoman house (the sign says '17 Y. Y. Osmanlı Evi Müzesi', or '17th-century Ottoman House Museum'. Visit for a fascinating glimpse into the daily life of the Ottoman nobility. Carpets and furnishings are all authentic. Hours are from 8.30 am to noon, and 1 to 5 pm, closed on Monday; admission costs US$1.

Kültür Parkı

Bursa's Kültür Parkı (kewl-TEWR pahr-kuh) or Cultural Park, is laid out to the north of the Muradiye complex, down the hill some distance. You can reach it from Heykel by any bus or dolmuş going to Çekirge (see the following Getting Around section). Besides offering a pleasant stroll, the Kültür Parkı is good for lunch in one of its shady outdoor restaurants (see Places to Eat).

The park also houses the **Bursa Archaeological Museum**. Bursa's history goes back to the time of Hannibal (200 BC), and Roman artefacts are preserved here. The collection is nice, but not at all exceptional. If you've seen another good Turkish collection, this is more of the same. Find the bus stop named 'Arkeoloji Müzesı', and enter the park by the gate nearby. The museum (US$2) is open from 9 am to noon and 1 to 5 pm, closed Monday.

Mineral Baths

The warm, mineral-rich waters which spring from the slopes of Uludağ have been famous for their curative powers since ancient times. Today the ailing and the infirm come here for several weeks at a time, take a daily soak or two in the tub, and spend the rest of the time chatting, reading or dining. Most people stay in hotels which have their own mineral bath facilities. There are independent baths *(kaplıca)* as well, some of historical importance.

Baths will be crowded on Friday, the Muslim holy day, as local people clean up for it.

The **Yeni Kaplıca** (☎ 236 6955), Mudanya Çaddesi 10, on the north-west side of the Kültür Parkı, is a bath renovated in 1522 by Sultan Süleyman the Magnificent's grand vizier, Rüstem Paşa, on the site of a much older one built by Justinian. Besides the Yeni (New) baths, you'll find the Kaynarca (Boiling) limited to women, and the Karamustafa, which has facilities for family bathing. All baths in the complex are open from 6 am to 11 pm (last admission at 10 pm).

Perhaps the most attractive place is the **Eski Kaplıcaları** or Old Baths, right next door to the Kervansaray Termal Hotel on the eastern outskirts of Çekirge. Beautifully restored, the baths now cater to an up-market clientele of business travellers, tourists and local notables who stay at or socialise in the hotel.

The bathing rooms are covered in creamy marble; in the hot room on the men's side there's a plunging pool (I haven't seen the women's side); use of the nice swimming pool downstairs is subject to a hefty additional charge. The cool room has lounge chairs for relaxing, and a bar with waiter service.

Prices are higher here than at unrestored local baths, but the building is beautiful, though service is fairly inattentive. Hours are daily from 7 am to 11 pm for men, from 7.30 am to 11 pm for women. There's an entry fee of US$4, and a similar fee to have an attendant wash you; the cost of soap is additional,

The Hamam Experience

The history of steam baths goes back millenniums and many of Turkey's natural spas were enjoyed by the ancient Greeks and Romans. Turks built beautiful, elaborate baths (*hamams*) to serve their communities, partly because Islam demands high standards of personal hygiene, and partly because bathing is such a pleasure.

Public baths used to be required because private homes didn't have bathing facilities. Everybody, rich and poor alike, went to the baths. For a workman, it was simply to get clean. For a high-born woman, it was a ritual of attendants and polite courtesies, and many museums display the gorgeous gold-embroidered towels, mother-of-pearl pattens and lovely accessories she would have taken with her.

Most Turkish towns still have hamams of varying degrees of fanciness, although they are becoming scarcer in the west as homes acquire plumbed-in bathrooms. The custom of going to the hamam continues because the public facilities are so much grander than what is available at home, and because, for Turks, it is still a social occasion. To steam clean, have a massage, relax, watch television, sip tea and chat with friends is looked upon as wonderful, affordable luxury.

What happens in a hamam? Well, you will be shown to a cubicle *(camekan)* where you can undress, store your clothes, lock up your valuables and wrap the cloth that's provided (the *peştemal*) round you. An attendant *(tellak)* will lead you through to the hot room where you sit and sweat for a while.

Then you have to make a choice. It's cheapest to wash yourself with the soap *(sabun)*, shampoo *(şampuan)* and towel *(havlu)* you brought with you. The hot room will be ringed with individual basins which you fill from the taps above before sluicing the water over yourself with a plastic scoop. You should try not to get soap into the water in the basin, and avoid splashing your neighbours, especially on a Friday when someone who has completed their ritual wash would have to start all over again if soaked by an infidel.

But it's far more enjoyable to let an attendant wash you. In the hot room you'll be doused with warm water and then scrubbed with a coarse cloth mitten *(kese)*, loosening dirt you never suspected you had. Afterwards you'll be lathered with a sudsy swab, rinsed off and shampooed.

When all this is done you'll be offered the chance of a massage, an experience worth having at least once during your trip. Some massages are carried out on the floor or a table but often you'll be spread out on the great marble bench (or *göbektaşı*) beneath the dome. In touristy areas (other than İstanbul) the massage is likely to be pretty cursory and unless you're prepared to pay the extra for an 'oil massage' you may be disappointed. Elsewhere, however, a Turkish massage can be an unforgettable, if occasionally rough, experience.

The massage over, you'll be led back to the cold room, there to be swathed in towels and taken to your cubicle for a rest. Tea, coffee, soft drinks and beer are usually available.

Traditional hamams have separate sections for men and women or admit men and women at separate times. As the number of baths declines, it's usually the ones for women that go first as there is some ambivalence about how desirable it is for women to be out of the home. Opening hours for women are almost invariably more restricted than for men.

Bath etiquette dictates that men should keep the peştemal on at all times, washing their own private parts without ever removing this modesty wrap. In the women's section, the amount of modesty expected varies considerably: in some baths total nudity is fine, in others it would be a blunder to remove your knickers. Play safe by keeping your underwear on under your peştemal until inside the hot room when you can remove what looks appropriate. Women also wash their own private parts. If you want to shave your legs or armpits, you should do this in the outer warm room rather than in the bath.

In touristy areas, most hamams are happy for foreign men and women to bathe together, usually for a premium price. In traditional hamams women are washed and massaged by other women. No Turkish woman would let a male masseur near her, but while Turkish men continue to frequent baths used by tourists, the Turkish women vanish and with them go the masseuses.

Sexual activity has no place in the traditional bath ritual. Women who accept a masseur should have their massage within view of their male companions or friends. At the first sign of impropriety, they should protest loudly. ■

so figure on spending US$15 for the works, including massage and tips. You can bring your own soap and wash yourself for little more than the basic entry fee.

For a simpler, less expensive bath in the centre of Bursa, try the Çakır Ağa Hamamı, at the corner of Atatürk Caddesi and Kazım Baykal (Temiz) Caddesi, just west of the Tahtakale/İnebey district. Posted prices are US$2 for a wash, another dollar or so for soap and scrub, US$3 for a massage, or the works for US$7 or so.

Next to the Muradiye mosque is the Tarihi II Murat Hamamı (that's İkinci Murat), open to men on Friday and Sunday, to women all other days, from 10 am to 6 pm.

Places to Stay

Though there are a few hotels in the centre of town, many of Bursa's best lodgings in terms of both quality and price are in the western suburb of Çekirge. I'll mention those in Bursa's centre first, then those in Çekirge. Hotels atop Uludağ are mentioned in that section following the Bursa section.

Places to Stay – bottom end

Near the Santral Garaj You can find a very cheap room in Bursa near the Santral Garajı (bus station), in the centre, or in Çekirge, but you must choose carefully. Hotels near the bus station tend to be horribly noisy and not well kept.

I strongly recommend that you look for lodgings away from the bus station. Walk out the front door of the bus station and cross Kıbrıs Şehitler Caddesi, the big avenue. There are several hotels here, but they are noisy and expensive. Turn left, then right, and walk along this small street (Şirin Sokak) to the *Mavi Ege Oteli* (☎ (224) 254 8420), Fırın Sokak 17. The *Blue Aegean* is utterly basic but undeniably cheap at US$6/9 a single/double. Some rooms have sinks. Check the sheets and have the management change them if they've been used.

A few steps up the street from the Mavi Ege is Celal Bayar Caddesi (formerly Gazcılar Caddesi) and two better lodgings. *Hotel Belkis* (☎ (224) 254 8322), Celal Bayar Caddesi 168, charges the same as the Mavi Ege, but has nicer rooms; there's no running water in the rooms, though. *Öz Uludağ Hotel*, a few doors to the left (west) of the Belkis is not as comfortable.

The *Otel Geçit* (☎ (224) 254 1032), Celal Bayar Caddesi 175, charges only US$15 for a double room with shower. The hotel even has a lift, and central heating. Again, the only advantage here is closeness to the buses. For only slightly more you can have much better accommodation near Heykel.

Central Bursa The Tahtakale/İnebey district just south of the Ulu Cami is an interesting area with many narrow streets and historic houses. Some of the houses are being restored, and will no doubt soon be turned into expensive shops and moderately priced 'boutique' hotels. There's a good produce market here as well.

The traditional lodging choice here is the *Otel Çamlıbel* (CHAHM-luh-behl) (☎ (224) 221 2565), İnebey Caddesi 71, a renovated place with these advantages: a quiet location, rooms with constant hot water and good cross-ventilation, a lift and a few parking places in front of the hotel. Rates are US$13/17/21 a single/double/triple with private shower; breakfast costs extra.

Readers of this guide have also liked the *Hotel İpekçi* (☎ (224) 221 1935), Çancılar Caddesi 38, about four blocks north of Heykel, where a quiet double room with shower costs under US$10.

Çekirge Most Çekirge hotels have their own facilities for 'taking the waters'. You may find that the bathtub or shower in your hotel room runs only mineral water, or there may be separate private or public bathing-rooms in the basement of the hotel. One day's dip in the mineral waters is no great thrill. The therapeutic benefits are supposedly acquired over weeks. All the same, you may find that a soak in a private tub is included in the price of the room, even in the very cheapest hotels, so take advantage of it.

Çekirge's main street is I. Murat Caddesi

(Birinci Murat Caddesi). For all of the Çekirge hotels, get a bus or dolmuş from Heykel or along Atatürk Caddesi.

The *Yeşil Yayla Oteli* (☎ (224) 236 8026), Çekirge Caddesi, behind the Yıldız Hotel at the upper end of the village just off the main road, is old-fashioned and simple, charging US$14 a double for rooms with sink, but free use of the mineral baths.

The *Hotel Eren* (☎ & fax (224) 236 8099), Birinci Murat Caddesi, Camii Aralığı 2, is behind the more visible Ada Palas. It has usable, quiet rooms with showers, and a terrace in front, and charges US$14/22 a single/double for a room with private shower.

Places to Stay – middle

Central Bursa In central Bursa noise is a big problem, but the best hotels are off the main streets in any case.

My favourite is the *Hotel Çeşmeli* (☎ (224) 224 1511), Gümüşçeken Caddesi 6, just a few steps north of Atatürk Caddesi near Heykel. Friendly, simple, fairly quiet, very clean, run by God-fearing Muslims and conveniently located, it charges US$18/22 a single/double for a room with shower and breakfast. This is a good choice for women travellers.

If the Çeşmeli is full (as it often is), you'll be directed to the nearby *Hotel Bilgiç* (☎ (224) 224 3190, fax 224 7633), on the south side of Atatürk Caddesi at Başak Caddesi 30, one block south-west of Heykel. The décor is an amusing melange of Art Deco and Art Nouveau which you may never get used to, but the hotel has usable and fairly quiet rooms, and decent prices of US$17/21 a single/double with shower.

Hotel Dikmen (☎ (224) 224 1840, fax 224 1844), Maksem (Fevzi Çakmak) Caddesi 78, is farther west, then south. This 50-room, three-star hotel's lobby is pleasant, with a small enclosed garden terrace, complete with fountain, at the back; a lift takes you up to your room. Rooms with little luxuries such as bathtubs, TVs and mini bars rent for US$34/44 a single/double, slightly cheaper without the frills. Remember to ask for *sakin bir oda* (a quiet room). The hotel is about 50m uphill on the street which begins beside the PTT.

Çekirge The *Ada Palas* (☎ (224) 233 3990, fax 236 4656), in front of Hotel Eren, charges US$28 for a double with shower, breakfast included; there's a mineral bath on each floor.

Places to Stay – top end

In the centre of Bursa there's the nominally three-star *Kent Hotel* (☎ (224) 223 5420, fax 224 4015), Atatürk Caddesi 69. All 64 rooms have air-con, private showers, mini bars and satellite TVs, and cost US$65/80/96 a single/double/triple, tax and service included.

The three-star *Termal Hotel Gönlü Ferah* (☎ (224) 233 9210, fax 233 9218), I. Murat Caddesi 24, is in the very centre of the village. Some of the 62 rooms have fine views over the valley. The ambience here is 'European spa', the service experienced. Rates are US$50/70 a single/double with breakfast.

Next door, the *Hotel Dilmen* (☎ (224) 233 9500, fax 235 2568), I. Murat Caddesi, rates four stars, boasts a garden terrace restaurant/bar, an exercise room with sauna and mineral-water baths, and 100 posh rooms with TVs and mini bars. Rates are US$70/90 a single/double on the panoramic side, breakfast included.

Bursa's most famous spa hotel is the five-star, 173-room *Hotel Çelik Palas* (☎ (224) 233 38 00, fax 236 19 10), Çekirge Caddesi 79. Given its name in 1935 by Atatürk himself, the hotel had been a favourite resort for the Turkish leader and his peers; King Idris of Libya was taking the waters here when he was ousted by Colonel Muammar Gaddafi. Set in pretty grounds, the hotel consists of a historic older building dating from between the wars, and a newer section. The décor is an odd combination of modern and traditional elements.

All 173 rooms have air-con and bathrooms with separate mineral-water taps. The Çelik Palas's mineral-water bath facilities are the most sumptuous in town, with lots of marble and tile, stained glass and a huge circular pool. Though not on a par with the great spa hotels of Europe, it is quite comfortable. Rates range from US$90 to US$138 a single, from US$110 to US$165 a double.

Çekirge's other five-star hotel is the 211-room *Hotel Kervansaray Termal* (☎ (224) 233 9300, fax 233 9324), Çekirge Meydanı. The design is updated Art Deco. The Eski Kaplıcaları mineral baths adjoin the hotel, which is on the eastern outskirts of Çekirge. Rooms cost US$90/125 a single/double.

Places to Eat

Bursa's culinary specialities include fresh fruit (especially peaches in season), candied chestnuts (kestane şekeri) and two types of roast meat. Bursa kebap, or İskender kebap, is the most famous, made from döner kebap laid on a bed of fresh pide bread and topped with savoury tomato sauce and browned butter. The other speciality is İnegöl köftesi, a type of very rich grilled meatball which is actually the speciality of the nearby town called İnegöl. You will see several restaurants which specialise in these dishes exclusively, called Bursa kebapçısı or İnegöl köftecisi.

The following places to eat are arranged according to the type of food, location and style of place.

Bursa Kebapçıs Cost differences among restaurants of the same class are small due to fixed municipal prices. A *bir porsyon* (one-serving) plate of kebap with yoghurt costs US$5 or US$6, soft drink included (alcohol is not normally served at kebapçıs). Add US$2 if you order *bir buçuk porsyon* (1½ portions). All these places are open seven days a week from 11 am until 9 or 10 pm.

The owners of *Kebapçı İskender* (☎ 221 4615), Ünlü Cadde 7, half a block south-east of Heykel, claim to be descended from the eponymous İskender Usta himself. The elaborate Ottomanesque façade and semi-formal waiters belie moderate prices (US$6.50 for 1½ portions of Bursa kebap with yoghurt, plus a soft drink). This place is usually packed with locals.

Directly across Ünlü Caddesi is *Adanur Hacıbey* (☎ 221 6440), a simpler place where the Bursa kebap comes with a dab of smoky aubergine purée on the side. Price is the same as at Kebapçı İskender. Remember, after your kebap is served, don't begin eating until the waiter brings the tomato sauce and browned butter.

The original *Hacıbey Kebapçısı* (☎ 222 6604), Taşkapı Sokak 4/11, is just south of

İskender Kebap

Roast lamb and mutton have been staples of the Turkish diet for millennia, and it does not take an overly fertile imagination to picture nomadic Turkish warriors skewering chunks of mutton on their swords and roasting it over a campfire 1500 years ago. Melted fat would drip into the fire causing flare-ups, smoking and burning the meat.

Along comes İskender Usta (Chef Alexander), a cook in Bursa. In 1867 he had the idea to build a vertical grill, fill it with hot coals, and put the meat-packed sword on its point next to the grill. This way the fat would baste the meat rather than char it. He sliced the meat off in thin strips as it was cooked.

Like *lokum* (Turkish delight) and the sandwich, this simple innovation was an instant success. Why any of these culinary inventions took centuries to appear is a mystery.

Today *döner kebap* (revolving roast) is Turkey's national dish, served everywhere from street corners to posh dining rooms. Many of the specially made döner grills even continue the symbolism of the sword, with a miniature hilt at the top.

İskender used lamb and mutton from sheep fed on the wild spices (especially thyme) of Uludağ. To compound his fame, he laid the slices of lamb on a bed of flat pide bread, and topped the whole with savoury tomato sauce and browned butter.

The dish's popularity has spread throughout the country and indeed the world, but it's still best in Bursa. The city's most prominent İskender kebapçıs claim direct descent – in both blood and method – from the original İskender Usta. ■

the Koza Parkı. Two floors of narrow rooms have marble floors, beautiful tiled walls and dark polished woodwork. Waiters in waistcoats serve politely and efficiently, and the kebap is very good.

Bursa kebap was invented in a small restaurant now called *Kebabcı İskenderoğlu Nurettin* (Iskender's Son) at Atatürk Caddesi 60, between Heykel and the Ulu Cami. The surroundings are basic and simple, the kebap good but unremarkable.

İnegöl Köfteci For İnegöl köftesi, try the *İnegöl Köftecisi*, Atatürk Caddesi 48, on the corner of the little side street. Besides the plain – rich – grilled meatballs, they make variations stuffed with onions or cheese. A full lunch need cost only US$5.

Other Grills *Çiçek Izgara* (☎ 221 6526), Belediye Caddesi 15, a block from the Koza Park behind (north of) the half-timbered Belediye building, does not specialise in Bursa kebap, but serves excellent grills in a white tablecloth setting that's especially comfortable for single women. Prices range from US$2.50 for köfte to US$7 for the big mixed grill; a bonfile (small beef filet steak) costs US$4.50.

Okyanus Fırın Salonu, on Pars Çıkmazı, the side street between the Vakıfbank and Atatürk Caddesi 44, is shiny and modern, specialising in Konya fırın kebap, rich joints of roasted mutton. A filling meal costs US$6.

The *Ömür*, on the western side of the Ulu Cami, is in the historic arasta (the complex of shops attached to a mosque). As always, prices are posted. The grills range from köfte through şiş kebap and some of the regional variations. Meat, salad and soft drink go for about US$4.50 to US$6.

Hazır Yemek Ready-food restaurants have steam tables and pre-cooked soups, stews, pilavs and stuffed vegetables. Many close by 7 pm.

The Tahtakale/İnebey district is a particularly good place to look for a good, cheap meal. The *Şehir Lokantası*, İnebey Caddesi 85, a half-block up the hill from Atatürk Caddesi, has the advantages of being near the Çamlıbel Hotel, and serving hazır-yemek (ready-food) meals for around US$3.

Further up the street from the Şehir, turn right (west) and walk to the market area known as the *Tahtakale Çarşısı*. To the north-west, at Çelebiler Caddesi 18, is the *Alış Izgara* and the adjoining *Tahtakale Lokantası*. But my favourite is a bit farther south. Walk uphill on Çelebiler Caddesi two blocks to a T-intersection, turn right and walk half a block to the *Yeşil İnci Lokantası*, a very tidy and pleasant restaurant with a separate 10-table *aile salonu* (ladies' dining room). The 'Green Pearl' stays open later than many other local eateries, serving ready food accompanied by its own freshly baked pide bread. You need spend no more than US$4 to fill up.

Kültür Parkı Strolling around the Cultural Park is pleasant, and having a meal here is more so. The *Seljuk Restaurant* (☎ 220 9695) is good, quiet, shady and not overly expensive, with three-course meals for US$7 to US$9.

Çekirge The more expensive hotels in Çekirge have their own dining rooms. Besides these, there's the *Sezen Restaurant* (☎ 236 9156), on Çekirge Caddesi to the right of the Ada Palas Hotel. The food is fine and the prices fairly low, at US$5 or US$6 for a full meal.

Markets The Tahtakale Çarşısı is the nicest and most convenient market area in central Bursa. Walk west from the Ulu Cami along Atatürk Caddesi to the subway (pedestrian underpass) named Yıldırım Beyazıt Altgeçidi. From the south end of the subway, go left or right a few steps, then south along a narrow street to the market area.

Another market lies downhill (north) of the Çiçek Pazarı (Flower Market) behind Koza Parkı and the Belediye.

Cafés *Café Koza*, above Koza Parkı on Atatürk Caddesi near the Ulu Cami is Bursa's central people-watching place, but it's not cheap. A simple tea costs US$0.60, coffee twice as much.

Tino Café-Bar is at Setbaşı, the place 2½ short blocks south-east of Heykel where Namazgah Caddesi crosses the Gök Deresi gorge. Enter the Setbaşı Pasajı on the north side of the road and take the stairs on the right side down to the bar, which has a small terrace overlooking the gorge. Alcohol is served.

Entertainment

Bursa's equivalent of İstanbul's Kumkapı district is Sakarya Caddesi, a small street lined with meyhanes, some of them serving fish. The street is on the north side of the Hisar district, just south of Altıparmak Caddesi. To find it, take a bus or dolmuş from Heykel bound for Çekirge and get out at the Çatal Fırın bus stop across from the Sabahettin Paşa Camii. Cross to the south side of Altıparmak Caddesi and walk west into Sakarya Caddesi. If you're walking, go downhill from the Ulu Cami along Atatürk/Altıparmak on the Hisar side of the road; it's less than 10 minutes.

This was once the main street of Bursa's Jewish quarter, which throve from 1492 until recent times. There are still several operating synagogues on the street, most notably the 500-year-old Geruş Havrası (visits by special arrangement only).

Sakarya Caddesi's fame was made by one Arap Şükrü who opened a restaurant here decades ago. It was so popular and successful that, as with İskender and his kebap, Arap Şükrü's descendants have gone into the business. The street, now generally known as Arap Şükrü Sokak, has no less than five restaurants with that name, all run by relatives or descendants. Among them, perhaps the favourite, is *Arap Şükrü Yılmaz* (☎ (221 9239) at Sakarya Caddesi 4. Fish is the speciality, but grills are always served, and a full meal with rakı, beer or wine need cost no more than US$10 per person.

Most of the clientele of these restaurants are male, but women usually feel comfortable at the *Hanzade Bar-Restaurant* (☎ 221 0052), at Sakarya Caddesi 43, which is among the nicest places.

Things to Buy

I've already mentioned those Bursa exclusives, silk cloth (especially scarves), handknitted woollen mittens, gloves and socks, Karagöz shadow puppets and candied chestnuts. Other good items are thick Bursa Turkish towels (some say they were invented here, for those taking the waters). If you have lots of room in your luggage, buy a *bornoz*, a huge thick, heavy terry-cloth bathrobe.

Getting There & Away

The best way to reach Bursa is by ferry and bus. Air service is limited by the small airport size. (If the air base at Yenişehir is privatised, service will increase.) The train line bypasses Bursa inconveniently to the east, going between Adapazarı, Bozüyük and Eskişehir.

Air Sönmez Holding Hava Yolları at Bursa's airport (☎ (224) 246 5445); in İstanbul (☎ (212) 573 9323, 573 7240 ext 712) runs flights from Bursa to İstanbul at 8.30 am and 3 pm from Monday to Friday, and 9 am Saturday, for US$45 each way. Return flights from İstanbul to Bursa run at 9.30 am and 4 pm on weekdays, 10.30 am on Saturday; no flights on Sunday. A bus departs from the Ottomantur office 45 minutes prior to flight time.

In Bursa, tickets can be bought at Ottomantur (☎ (224) 210 099, 222 097, fax 218 948), Cemal Nadir Caddesi, Kızılay Pasajı, Çakırhamam, a few minutes' walk downhill from the Ulu Cami.

Bus For information on reaching Bursa from İstanbul or Yalova, see the previous Yalova section. For local transport, see the Getting Around section, which follows this one.

You will probably arrive in Bursa by bus or minibus from the ferry dock at Yalova, or from İznik. These services come into Bursa's otogar, officially called the Santral Garajı.

When the time comes to leave Bursa, go to the otogar. The fastest way to İstanbul is a bus to Yalova, then a hydrofoil to İstanbul's Kabataş docks. To do this, be sure to get a bus that departs at least 90 minutes before the scheduled hydrofoil departure. (See the Yalova section for details.)

If you plan to take a bus all the way to İstanbul, be careful when you buy your ticket. Buses designated *karayolu ile* (by road) take four hours and drag you all around the Bay of İzmit; those designated *feribot ile* take you to Topçular, east of Yalova, and drive aboard the car ferry to Eskihisar, a much quicker and more pleasant way to go. You must also determine whether your chosen bus terminates its journey at İstanbul's Harem bus station on the Asian shore, or at the Yeni Otogar in Esenler; some buses stop at both.

For other destinations, buy your ticket in advance to ensure a good seat and departure time. Here are some routes from Bursa:

Afyon – 290 km, 4½ hours, US$10; eight buses daily
Ankara – 400 km, 5½ hours, US$12; hourly buses
Bandırma – 115 km, two hours, US$4; 12 buses daily
Çanakkale (for Troy and Gallipoli) – 310 km, five hours, US$10; a dozen buses daily
Erdek – 135 km, 2¼ hours, US$4.75; three buses daily
Eskişehir – 155 km, 2½ hours, US$6.50; hourly buses
İstanbul – 230 km, four to five hours *karayolu ile* (by road) or 2½ hours *feribot ile* (by car ferry: 135 km by road plus 25 minutes by sea), US$8.50 to US$10; hourly buses
İzmir – 375 km, six hours, US$6; hourly buses
İznik – 82 km, 1½ hours, US$2 to US$2.75; hourly buses until 6 or 7 pm
Kütahya – 200 km, three hours, US$8; several buses daily
Yalova – 60 km, 70 minutes, US$3; minibuses every 30 minutes (see the Yalova section)

Getting Around

Bus Station Transport In front of Bursa's Santral Garajı is a big street named Kıbrıs Şehitler Caddesi; a few metres west of the bus station it intersects with Fevzi Çakmak Caddesi. Here you will find dolmuşes, taxis and city buses. For the city buses, you will need to buy a US$0.40 ticket *before* you board the bus. Look for the ticket kiosk. Bus 18 goes from the Garaj via Heykel to Emir Sultan.

You will most likely be looking for transport to the centre of town and its hotels, or to the hotels at Çekirge. To reach Heykel, walk out the front door of the otogar, cross the street, and look for the rank of cars filling up with people; most of these dolmuşes bear rooftop signs for Heykel (US$0.50), though it actually terminates at the Koza Parkı on Atatürk Caddesi. Take this to get to the Ulu Cami and Tahtakale/İnebey as well. If your luggage takes up a seat, you'll have to pay for it. Paying dolmuş fare for two travellers and two backpacks may exceed a taxi fare.

City Buses Bursa's city buses (US$0.40) are useful and go to many sites you'll want to reach. A main bus stop with three *perons* (gates or platforms) is in front of Koza Parkı on Atatürk Caddesi. Here are bus-route translations followed by descriptions of the bus routes:

Catch a bus marked...	*to get to...*
Devlet Hastanesi (Dev. Hst)	Hisar, Orhan Gazi & Osman Gazi tombs (Koza Park Peron 3)
Emir Sultan	Yeşil Cami, Emir Sultan (Koza Park Peron 3)
Muradiye	Hisar, Muradiye
S Garaj	Santral Garajı (bus station) (Koza Park Peron 3)
Sigorta	Kültür Parkı, Eski Kaplıca baths (Koza Park Peron 2)
SSK Hast(anesi)	Kültür Parkı, Çekirge (Koza Park Peron 2)
Yeşil	Heykel, Setbaşı, Yeşil Cami (Koza Park Peron 3)

Bus 1
travels the entire 'tourist route' through the city from Emir Sultan

Bus 1-A
travels between Muradiye and Heykel

Bus 3 (3-A, 3-B, 3-C etc)
goes to and from the Teleferik, the cable car up Uludağ

Bus 18
travels between Heykel and Emir Sultan

Dolmuşes In Bursa, sedans operate as dolmuşes along with the minibuses. The destination is indicated by the illuminated sign on the roof. The minimum fare is US$0.45.

From Heykel, dolmuşes depart for most parts of the city. See the map of central Bursa for routes and departure points. Other useful routes are mentioned previously in the text.

Taxis As everywhere in Turkey, taxis are readily available and not wildly expensive. In Bursa, a ride halfway across the city from the bus station to Heykel, Muradiye or Tahtakale costs less than US$2.

AROUND BURSA

Typical villages in the region of Bursa are worth a visit if you have time and an interest in Turkish ethnography. You can go on your own or by tour. Mr Uğur Çelikkol at Karagöz Turizm-Seyahat Acentası (travel agency; ☎ (224) 221 8727, fax 220 5350) reachable through the Karagöz Antique Shop in the Eski Aynalı ÇarŞi (see Bedesten section, earlier), organises guided trips to most of these villages at reasonable prices.

Cumalı Kızık

It is said that Osman Gazi, founder of the Ottoman Empire, founded seven villages for his seven sons and their brides about 700 years ago on lands just east of Bursa. Five of the villages, built before the Ottoman conquest of Bursa, survive to this day and retain many features of Ottoman domestic architecture.

The village of Cumalı Kızık, set on the slopes of Uludağ amidst fruit and nut orchards, is registered as a national monument and protected from development. Transportation is difficult without your own vehicle. Go 12 km eastward from Bursa along the main road to İnegöl and Ankara, then 3.5 km south to Cumalı Kızık. Facilities are limited, so you might want to bring a picnic.

The other four old villages, all south of the Bursa-Ankara highway, are Hamamlı Kızık, not far from Cumalı Kızık; Dere Kızık, farther east; and Fidye Kızık and Değirmenlı Kızık, closer to Bursa.

Güneybudaklar With your own vehicle, go west from Bursa, and on the outskirts turn south on the road marked for Keles. The road winds around Uludağ and climbs its southern slopes, passing through the wine-making village of Misi before reaching a road, 45 km from Bursa, marked for Güneybudaklar. The village, three km north of the main road, was founded some 500 years ago by Turcoman nomads on the site of a Roman-Byzantine settlement. The land around is planted with strawberries and other fruits, beans, potatoes, wheat and barley. Flocks graze on the rich mountain grasses while the women of the village weave colourful cloths at their looms. There are few tourists and no services, but you can stop, enjoy the views and the air, and have a satisfying glass of tea before retracing your way to Bursa.

ULUDAĞ

In the ancient world, a number of mountains bore the name Olympus. Uludağ (Great Mountain) was on the outskirts of the ancient city of Bithynia (now Bursa), so this was the Bithynian Olympus.

The gods no longer live on top of Uludağ, but there is a *teleferik* (cable car), a selection of hotels, a national park, cool forests and often snow. Even if you don't plan to hike to the summit (three hours each way from the hotel zone) or to go skiing (in winter only), you might want to take the cable car up for the view and a draught of the cool, fresh air. You can also reach the top by dolmuş.

Skiing

Though a fairly sleepy place in summer, the hotel and ski area on Uludağ comes to life during the ski season from late December to March. Hotels have equipment to rent: boots and skis cost about US$8 per day. Each hotel also has its own ski lift, so when you buy a day pass, you are buying it for that lift alone. If you want to try other slopes, buy only a few rides on any particular lift.

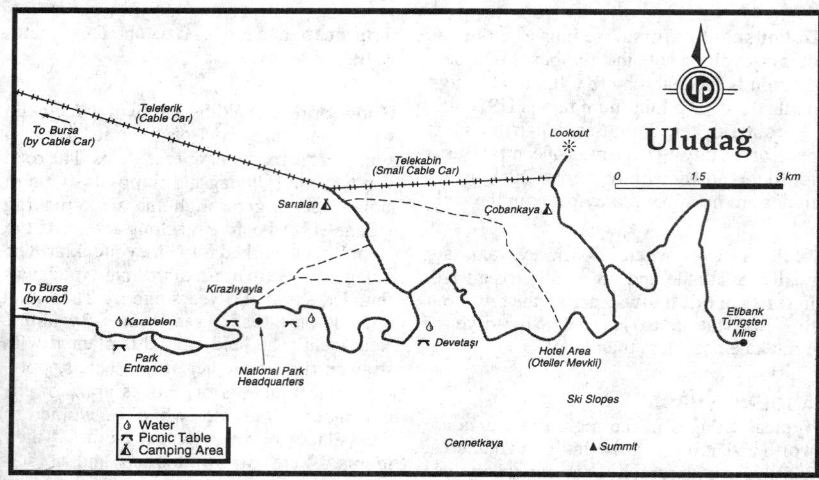

Places to Stay

More than a dozen inns and hotels are scattered about the mountaintop. All are meant for skiers, so they close for much of the year. A few places stay open all the time, though they have little business in summer unless they can schedule a commercial meeting.

Among the better places to stay is the 80-room, three-star *Beceren Hotel* (BEH-jeh-REHN) (☎ (224) 285 2111, fax 285 2119). For US$40 a double you get a room with bath and satellite TV. For US$60 two people can have a room and all three meals in summer. Prices almost double in winter, but all three meals are included.

The 22-room *Hotel Aydın Yıldız* (☎ (224) 285 2140, fax 285 2142), farthest up the road on the right, offers good value during the ski season. Rooms and meals are simple but acceptable, and the price is US$75 a double, meals included.

The four-star status address on the mountain is the 127-room *Kervansaray Uludağ Hotel* (☎ (224) 285 2187, fax 285 2193), where comfortable, though not really luxurious, rooms cost US$75/100 a single/double. Services include a swimming pool, sauna, casino and disco.

Getting There & Away

Cable Car For a summer visit to Uludağ, getting there is most of the fun. Take a Bursa city bus 3 (3-A, 3-B, 3-C etc), a dolmuş from Heykel, or a taxi to the lower terminus of the teleferik, called Teleferuç (☎ 221 3635) – a 15-minute ride from Heykel at the city's eastern edge. In summer when crowds abound, the cable cars depart when full or at least every 30 to 45 minutes, weather and winds permitting. The trip to the top takes about 30 minutes and costs US$5 each way, half-price on Wednesday.

The cable car stops at an intermediate point named Kadıyayla, from where you continue upward to the terminus at Sarıalan (sah-RUH-ah-lahn) at an altitude of 1635m. From Sarıalan, there is a smaller cable car *(telekabin)* which runs to Çobankaya, but it's not worth the time or money.

At Sarıalan there are a few snack and refreshment stands, a national-park camping area (always full, it seems), some walking trails *(patika)* and the occasional dolmuş to the hotel zone (called the *Oteller Mevkii)*, six km farther up the mountain slope. That's all there is to do, except enjoy the scenery.

Dolmuş Dolmuşes depart from Bursa's otogar to the hotel zone on Uludağ several times daily in summer, more frequently in winter, for about US$6 each way, which is more than the cable car. On the winding, 22-km trip you pass the İnkaya Çınarı, a gigantic ancient plane tree about three km beyond Çekirge. The tree, set in a little park, is said to have been alive when the Ottomans conquered Bursa in 1326.

At the 11 km marker you must stop and pay an entry fee for the national park of 50c per person, US$1.50 for a car and driver. The hotel zone is 11 km farther up from the national park entrance. Almost half of the entire 22 km is on rough granite-block pavement.

The return ride can be difficult in summer as there are few dolmuşes or taxis in evidence. In winter there are usually plenty, and they are eager to get at least some fare before they head back down, so you may be able to get back to Bursa for less – haggle.

BANDIRMA

The port town of Bandırma with 80,000 residents has an ancient history, but nothing to show for it. What you see is a 20th-century creation which might well be nicknamed *Betonbol* (Concreteville). It has little to offer the tourist except the junction between the İzmir to Bandırma rail line and the Bandırma to İstanbul ferry line. You'd do well to pass straight through, but if you must stop, there are hotels and restaurants enough.

Orientation

Bandırma's bus station is several km southeast of the centre, out by the main highway; get a *servis arabası* (shuttle bus) to reach the centre. (There is a separate, small bus station west of the centre for buses to Erdek and Gönen.)

If you arrive by train or boat, walk east for one km to reach the main square.

From the main square, the main road going east is İnönü Caddesi, which has most of the services you may want, including cheap hotels and restaurants, and bus ticket offices. The Kamil Koç ticket office is right across from the Hotel Marmara. Behind it down the side street are several others, including As Turizm, Uludağ, Doğan Körfez, and Yılmaz.

Kuşcenneti Milli Parkı

Though Bandırma will not hold your interest for very long, bird fanciers will want to make a detour to Kuşcenneti Milli Parkı (Bird Paradise National Park). This 64-hectare reserve on the shores of Kuş Gölü (Bird Lake, the ancient Manias), 20 km due south of Bandırma, boasts from two to three million feathered visitors, of 255 different varieties, each year.

The best times to visit are in spring (from April to June) and autumn (from September to November) when the birds are making their annual migration. In high summer and mid-winter there is little to see. Avoid weekends, when it's very crowded and noisy – the birds do. Bring binoculars if you have them.

From the Bandırma-Bursa highway, turn south following signs to Aksakal. After three km, turn west following signs for the park, which is two km farther along. Admission costs US$1 (half-price for students).

The Visitors Centre has exhibits – reminiscent of 19th-century natural history museums – of stuffed birds in simulated habitats. From the centre, walk along the patika to the observation tower for the view over the lake.

No camping or picnicking is permitted. For lodgings, you could try the simple *Gölbaşı Pension-Restaurant*, one km to the south in the village of Sığırcıatik.

Places to Stay

There are several cheap hotels on and east of the main square on İnönü Caddesi. Facing the square is the *Sahil Hotel* (☎ (266) 712 4485), İnönü Caddesi 10, a simple and convenient place favoured by Turkish businessmen. It offers rooms for US$7/9 a single/double with sink, US$12/14 a single/double with private shower.

Farther east, the *Marmara Otel* (☎ (266) 712 2080), İnönü Caddesi 44, is simpler and cheaper.

Özdil Hotel (☎ (266) 712 2200), east of the square near the water, facing the Haydar Çavuş Camii, is quieter as it is off the main street. Rates are about the same. *Otel İstanbul* a few doors away is a rock-bottom choice.

Hotel Eken (☎ (266) 718 0840, fax 712 5355), Uğur Mumcu Caddesi 9, is a half-block west of the main square up the hill: you'll see the sign. It's the only hotel of this class in the region, and has 78 clean, fairly simple rooms with tiny bathrooms (mini-tubs), as well as a sauna, hairdresser and TV lounge. Rooms cost US$35/48 a single/double. The nightclub is guaranteed to keep you awake until at least midnight.

Places to Eat

Around the main square are several good places for a meal. At the beginning of İnönü Caddesi, try the *Saray Lokantası* (popular with locals) and *Moby Dick Restaurant* (aimed at attracting foreigners). Simpler, cheaper places are to be found farther east along İnönü Caddesi. Right next door to the Özdil Hotel is the *Mercan Tandır Kebap & Izgara Salonu*, specialising in tandır kebap, a stew of meat and vegetables baked in an earthenware crock.

Getting There & Away

For information on the *Marmara Ekspresi*, the train/boat connection between İstanbul and İzmir, see the Getting Around chapter at the front of this book under Train.

Bandırma is midway on the run between Bursa (115 km, two hours, US$4.50; 12 buses daily) and Çanakkale (195 km, three hours, US$6.50; 12 buses daily). There are also buses southward to Balıkesir and points beyond. For route, schedule and fare information, ask at the otogar, or at the bus-company ticket offices on İnönü Caddesi.

For information on the cities south of Bursa and Bandırma, see the Aegean Turkey chapter under Aegean Hinterland.

Aegean Turkey

Turkey's Aegean region is one of the country's richest in many ways. Agriculture has been important here for millennia, and the many small to medium-sized cities support light manufacturing and commerce. The number, variety and state of preservation of the region's ancient ruins is incomparable. The coast offers excellent opportunities for water sports.

The Aegean coast, once a beautiful procession of ancient ruins, fishing villages, golden wheat fields and fig and olive orchards, has fallen prey to rash development, but if you look beyond the teeming coastal highway, the beautiful Aegean coast is still there. Çanakkale is the best base for visits to the Gallipoli battlefields and to Troy. Assos (Behramkale) is an out-of-the-way village built on an ancient city. Ayvalık is a booming resort town with beaches, seafood restaurants and panoramas of the Aegean islands. At Bergama, the ancient Pergamum, you should see the impressive ruins of the acropolis, where parchment was invented, and the Asclepion, an early medical centre. Dikili, Çandarlı and Foüa are ancient coastal towns inhabited for centuries which have now become less well known seaside resorts.

South of İzmir the main attractions are the many Ionian cities, including Ephesus, the best-preserved classical city in the Mediterranean, and also Priene, Miletus, Didyma, Labranda and several others. The resort towns of Selçuk and Kuşadası can serve as bases for visits to these sites.

At the southern end of the Aegean coast is the resort and yachting port of Bodrum, with its crusader castle, just across the water from the Greek island of Kos.

Inland from the coast (several hours eastward by bus), the cities of the Aegean hinterland are much less visited by tourists, and – despite their lack of coastline – this makes them all the more appealing for travellers wanting to see the 'real' Turkey. Eskişehir, Balıkesir, Kütahya, Afyon, Denizli and Pamukkale, Isparta and Eğirdir all have their good points. Whether you stop for the night or just for some tea, these cities yield interesting experiences and lasting memories.

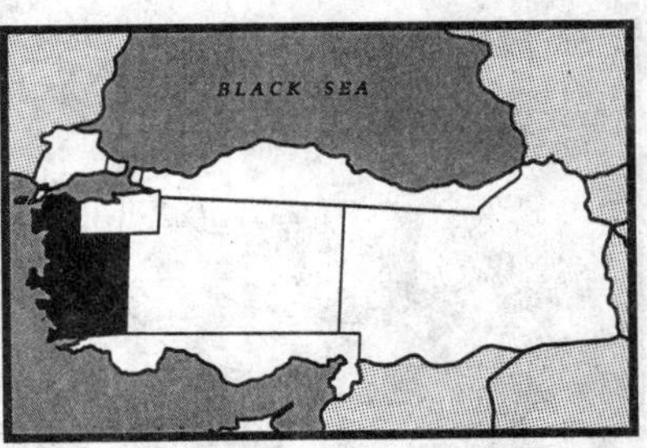

Highlights

- Touring the marble ruins of Ephesus
- Standing in the steep hillside theatre of Pergamum
- The crusader Castle of St Peter at Bodrum, now the Museum of Underwater Archaeology
- Relaxing in the warm calcium-laden waters at Pamukkale
- Shopping for Turkish faïence in Kütahya
- A seaside dinner at sunset in Gümüşlük, near Bodrum
- Sampling clotted cream and Turkish Delight in Afyon

Here's what you'll find on the coastal highway (E24/D550), starting at the Dardanelles.

AEGEAN TURKEY

North Aegean

ÇANAKKALE

As it has been for centuries, Çanakkale (population 55,000) is still a crossroads. Pilgrims, conquering armies and trade caravans stopped here before or after crossing the

Dardanelles, and many travellers still stop here for visits to the Gallipoli battlefields (described at the end of the Thrace chapter) and to the ruins of ancient Troy.

History

The Çanakkale Boğazı (Strait of Çanakkale, Hellespont, Dardanelles) is only about 1.4 km wide at its narrowest point, offering the best opportunity for travellers – and armies – to cross between Europe and Asia Minor.

King Xerxes I of Persia crossed the strait here on a bridge of boats in 481 BC, as did Alexander the Great a century and a half later. In Byzantine times the strait was used as the first defensive point for Constantinople.

By 1402 the strait was under the control of the Ottoman sultan, Beyazıt I, providing the means for the Ottoman armies to cross to – and conquer – the Balkans. Mehmet II, the Conqueror, fortified the strait as part of his grand and ultimately successful plan to conquer Constantinople (1453).

During the 19th century, England and France competed with Russia for influence over the 'Sick Man of Europe' (the Ottoman Empire) and its strategic sea-passages linking the Black, Marmara and Aegean seas.

In WWI, the strait was seen as the key to an Allied conquest of İstanbul and thus all of the Ottoman domains. Though the Allies were ultimately victorious, they failed to force the Dardanelles. By the terms of the treaties of Sévres (1920) and Lausanne (1923) the strait was to be demilitarised, but as WWII approached, the Montreux Convention (1936) permitted Turkey to remilitarise it.

Turkey maintained a precarious neutrality during WWII, allowing both Allied and Axis shipping to pass through, but when the course of the war seemed certain in January 1945, Allied supply ships were allowed through on their way to Russia.

Orientation & Information

The heart of Çanakkale is its docks, and the town has grown from the docks inland. An Ottoman clock tower, the town's symbol, stands just west of the docks, and makes a convenient landmark for hotel searches. Hotels, restaurants, banks and bus ticket offices are within a few hundred metres of the docks. The otogar is one km inland, as is

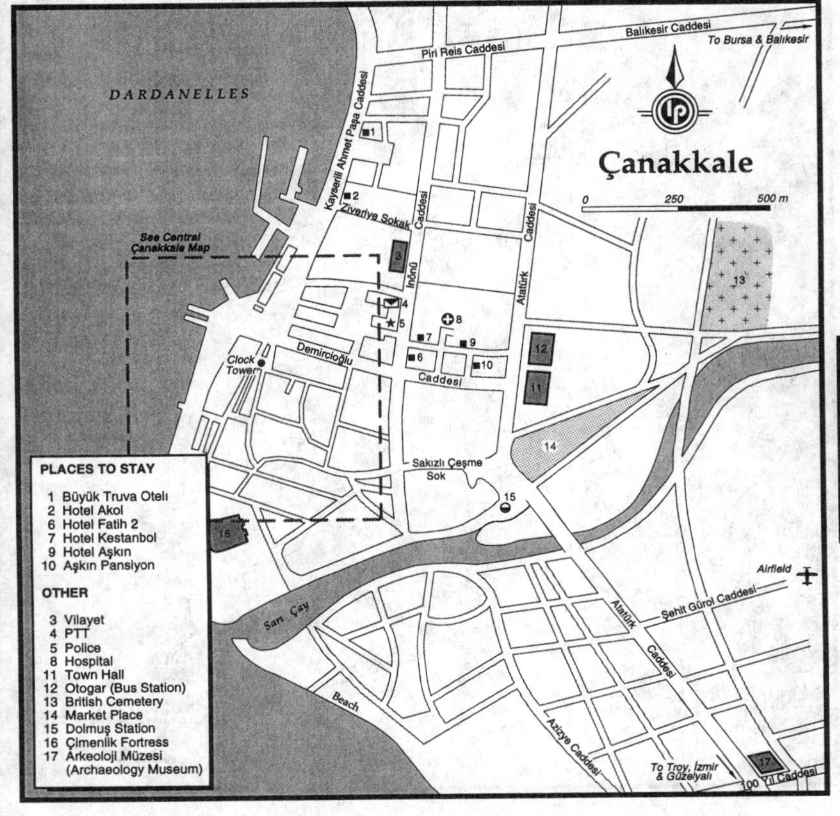

AEGEAN TURKEY

the dolmuş station for Troy; the Archaeology Museum is just over two km away.

From the otogar, turn left, walk to the first turning to the right (Demircioğlu Caddesi) and follow signs straight to the 'Feribot'. Just before the docks on the left (west) is the vaguely Teutonic clock tower, Saat Kulesi, restored in 1995. To reach the market area *(çarşı)*, walk behind the clock tower.

The Tarihi Yalı Hamamı (Turkish bath) is a few short blocks south of the clock tower (see the Central Çanakkale map).

The town's Tourism Information Office (☎ & fax (286) 217 1187) is in a little booth near the quay, between the clock tower and the ferry docks. Çanakkale's postal code is 17100.

Cannon Monument

On the broad main street in the town's centre is a monument constructed of old WWI cannons. The words on the plaque translate as 'Turkish soldiers used these cannons on 18 March 1915 to ensure the impassability of the Çanakkale strait'.

Military & Naval Museums

In the military zone at the southern end of the

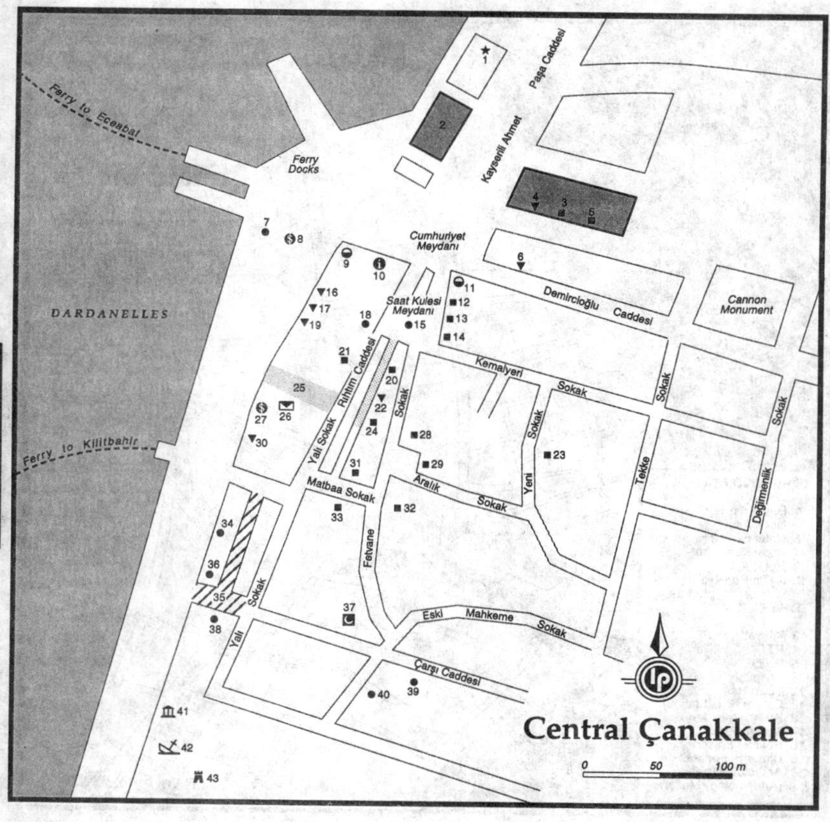

quay are the Military Museum (Çanakkale Askeri Müzesi) and Naval Museum (Çanakkale Deniz Müzesi), set in a park surrounding the Çimenlik fortress (kale). The park is open daily from 9 am to 10 pm; the museums are open daily except Monday and Thursday from 9 to 11 am and from 2.30 to 7.30 pm. Admission is free to the park, US$0.50 to the museums (half-price for students).

Beside the Naval Museum is a mock-up of the minelayer *Nusrat*, which had a heroic role in the Gallipoli campaign. The day before the Allied fleet was to steam through the straits, Allied minesweepers proclaimed the water cleared. At night the *Nusrat* went out, picked up loose mines and relaid them, helping to keep the Allies from penetrating the straits the next day.

There's also a small museum with memorabilia of Atatürk and the battles of Gallipoli.

Çimenlik Kalesi, the impressive fortress, was built by Mehmet the Conqueror in the mid-15th century, and is still considered active in the defence of the straits. Examine the cannons left from various wars which surround the stone walls; many were made in French, English and German foundries.

Archaeology Museum

Çanakkale's Arkeoloji Müzesi is on the southern outskirts of town, just over two km south-east of the clock tower, on the road to Troy. Opening hours are from 10 am to 5 pm; closed on Monday. Admission costs US$2. City buses (to İntepe or Güzelyalı) and dolmuşes (same destinations) run past the museum from the centre of town.

The museum's exhibits are arranged chronologically, starting with prehistoric fossils and continuing with Bronze Age and later artefacts. Perhaps the most interesting exhibits are those from Troy, labelled (in Turkish and English) by 'city', that is: Troy I, Troy II etc; and the exhibits from Dardanos, the ancient town near Çanakkale. Don't miss the glass case of bone pins and small implements near the exit.

Gallipoli Tours

Running tours of the Gallipoli battlefields (see the Gallipoli Peninsula section in the Thrace chapter) is a lucrative business for people in Çanakkale, and any hotel can reserve a place for you. In recent years, prices have risen and quality fallen, so it's a good idea to ask other travellers who have

PLACES TO STAY

- 2 Otel Anafartalar
- 3 Otel Yaldız
- 5 Koç Pansiyon
- 12 Umut Otel
- 13 Hotel Anzac
- 14 Erdem Oteli
- 20 Hotel Küçük Truva
- 21 Hotel Bakır
- 23 Yellow Rose Pension Yetimoğlu
- 24 Hotel Konak
- 28 Hotel Kervansaray
- 29 Hotel Efes
- 31 Otel Fatih
- 32 Can Oteli
- 33 Avrupa Pansiyon

PLACES TO EAT

- 4 Trakya Restaurant No 2
- 6 Trakya Restaurant No 1
- 16 Çekiç
- 17 Rıhtım
- 19 Bizim Entellektüel
- 22 Gaziantep Aile Kebap ve Pide Salonu
- 30 Şehir Restaurant

OTHER

- 1 Police
- 7 Ferry Ticket Office & PTT Exchange Office
- 8 Türkiye Emlak Bankası
- 9 Bus Ticket Office
- 10 Tourism Information Office
- 11 Kamil Koç & Yılmaz Bus Ticket Offices
- 15 Saat Kulesi (Clock Tower)
- 18 Troy-Anzac Tours
- 25 Park
- 26 Branch PTT
- 27 Etibank
- 34 Gümrük (Customs) Office
- 35 Teahouses
- 36 Belediye Halk Gazinosu (Nightclub)
- 37 Yalı Camii
- 38 Tea Garden
- 39 Tarihi Yalı Hamamı (Men's Entrance)
- 40 Tarihi Yalı Hamamı (Women's Entrance)
- 41 Askeri Müzesi (Military Museum)
- 42 Minelayer Nusrat
- 43 Çimenlik Kalesi

The Hellespont

Hellespont, the ancient name of the Çanakkale Boğazı (Dardanelles) is the product of a classical myth.

A king of Thessaly named Athamas, tired of Nephele, his wife, set her aside in favour of Princess Ino of Thebes. Ino, who had a son by Athamas, set to work to eliminate Nephele's son Phryxus, and daughter Helle, so that her own son might inherit Athamas' crown. She secretly parched all of the kingdom's seed corn before the spring sowing, resulting in a disastrous harvest – or, rather, no harvest at all.

The king sent a messenger to the nearest oracle asking what he should do to relieve this terrible distress. As the messenger returned, Ino intercepted, bribed and threatened him to forget what the oracle had said in favour of her own pronouncement. And so it was that the messenger told Athamas that Phryxus must die in sacrifice to the gods before the corn would grow again.

With the boy on the altar about to go under the knife, Hermes, in answer to Nephele's prayer, sent a golden-fleeced flying ram to save him. Phryxus and Helle leapt on the ram's back and were whisked into the sky and across the strait which separates Europe from Asia. During the flight, Helle fell off and drowned in the strait, which was named Hellespont (Helle's Sea) in her memory.

Phryxus continued his flight, finally landing in Colchis at the eastern end of the Unfriendly (Black) Sea, where he sacrificed the ram in honour of Zeus, giving its priceless golden fleece to King Aeetes, who permitted Phryxus to marry one of his daughters. The golden fleece was placed in a sacred grove under the watchful eye of a sleepless dragon, obviously a set-up so that Jason would later have a quest worthy of his heroism.

The strait's other name, Dardanelles, comes from the ancient town of Dardanus, the ruins of which were discovered between Çanakkale and Güzelyalı on its Asian shore. The town was named for Dardanus, son of Zeus and the Pleiad Electra, who founded Troy and the Trojan race, or Dardani.

The Hellespont was also the setting for the legend of Hero and Leander. Leander, a youth from Abydos (Çanakkale) fell in love with Hero, a priestess in the Temple of Venus at Sestos (Kilitbahir). Each night Leander would plunge into the chill waters of the Hellespont and swim to the European shore, guided by a torch which Hero held up in the temple tower. One stormy night the torch was blown out by the wind and Leander, without guidance, was exhausted trying to find the shore, and drowned. Hero, in despair at finding his body on the shore, threw herself from her tower.

The myth was thought to be an impossible exaggeration until Lord Byron, ever the romantic, arrived in 1807 to prove it possible. Born lame, he had no trouble swimming and completed the crossing to incredulous acclaim. He later used Abydos as the setting for his verse tale *The Bride of Abydos* (1813). Since Byron, many others have come to swim the Hellespont, including the American ambassador to Turkey, William Macomber, in 1975. ■

already taken a tour whether the company they used provided good value for money. If you have a whole day and are not averse to hiking, you can visit the most important sites by yourself on foot and by dolmuş, though you'll miss the guide's often interesting commentary. In either case, you might want to take in the movie *Gallipoli*, shown from bootleg (and often poor quality) videotapes in a number of hotels around town.

The typical four-hour (morning or afternoon) battlefield tour includes transport by car or minibus, driver and guide, lunch and a swim from a beach on the western shore. It costs from US$14 to US$20 per person, depending upon the company and the number of people signed up to go. Most tour participants complain that tours do not allow enough time at each site.

Troy-Anzac Tours (☎ (286) 217 5847, 217 5049, fax 217 0196), Saat Kulesi Meydanı 6, Çanakkale, facing the clock tower, has been in business the longest and seems the most reliable. Another good one is Down Under Tours. Ana Tours, heavily promoted by the problematic Anzac House, has disappointed some readers.

Special Events

The great battles of Gallipoli are commem-

TOM BROSNAHAN

The Temple of Zeus in Aizanoi dates from the reign of Hadrian (117-38 AD) and was dedicated to the worship of Zeus and the Anatolian fertility goddess, Cybele.

TOM BROSNAHAN

TOM BROSNAHAN

TOM BROSNAHAN

Top: A winged victory from the Gate of Hercules at Ephesus, once the capital of Roman Asia Minor.
Bottom Left: Ottoman gravestones bear stone turbans denoting the rank of the deceased.
Bottom Right: Crusader inscriptions, Castle of St Peter, Bodrum, Aegean Turkey.

orated each year during March (usually from the 12th to 19th). The biggest celebrations are on 18 March, 'Victory Day', the anniversary of the great naval battle which began the Gallipoli campaign. Australian, British, French and New Zealand representatives usually take part. Hotels, particularly the better ones, are often full during the ceremonies.

For a week in mid-August, the Çanakkale Troya Festivali brings dance and musical troupes to town. Art and craft exhibits, sports and chess tournaments and an underwater rubbish-pickup contest fill the days.

Places to Stay

Çanakkale has a good, if small, selection of hotels in all price ranges. There are also comfortable hotels in a seaside setting at Güzelyalı on the road to Troy, and a few small places in the village of Tevfikiye right next to the ruins of Troy.

Places to Stay – bottom end

The hotels in the centre of town are clustered near the clock tower. Check the sheets for signs of previous occupancy before you take a room.

Hotel Efes (☎ (286) 217 4687), behind the clock tower on Fetvane Sokak at Aralık Sokak 5, is modern and charges US$6/9 a single/double without running water. *Hotel Akgün* (☎ (286) 217 3049), across the street from the Efes, is similar, as are the *Erdem Oteli* (☎ (286) 217 4986) and *Umut Otel* (☎ (286) 217 6473) nearer to the clock tower.

The quaint old *Hotel Kervansaray* (☎ (286) 217 8192), Fetvane Sokak 13, between the Hotel Efes and the clock tower, is the 200-year-old former home of a Turkish paşa. Run by a God-fearing Muslim family, it has a garden with a fountain and drab rooms for US$6/9 a single/double without running water, or US$15 a triple with shower. No alcoholic drinks, please.

Hotel Konak (☎ (286) 217 1150), Fetvane Sokak 14, boasts central heating and constant hot water (so they say). Prices for waterless rooms are US$6/9 a single/double; with shower, US$6/10/14 a single/double/triple.

The *Avrupa Pansiyon* (☎ (286) 217 4084), Matbaa Sokak 8, is quiet but a bit higher in price at US$13 for a double with shower. If the Avrupa is full, try the *Hotel Fatih*, directly opposite, which shares the advantage of the quiet location.

Yellow Rose Pension Yetimoğlu (☎ (286) 217 3343), Yeni Sokak 5, 50m south-east of the clock tower, is tidy, with a quiet garden, washing machine and kitchen for guests' use, English-language TV and flyscreens on the windows. Prices are US$9/14 a single/double with bath.

Koç Pansiyon (☎ (286) 217 0121), Kızılay Sokak, on the south-east side of the Otel Yaldız, is tiny, neat and quiet, and priced at US$14 a double with shower.

The family-run *Otel Fatih 2* (☎ (286) 217 7884), İnönü Caddesi 149 across from the PTT, charges US$8 for a bathless double.

Otel Aşkın (☎ & fax (286) 217 4956), Hasan Mevsuf Sokak 53, only one short block from the bus station, charges US$14 for its double rooms with private shower, breakfast included. Its sister establishment, the nearby *Aşkın Pansiyon* (same phone), offers waterless doubles for US$8.

Camping There are several small camping places 16 km from Çanakkale along the Troy road at Güzelyalı, including *Mocamp Trova* and *Camping Dardanel.*

Places to Stay – middle

You can't miss the two-star, 70-room *Otel Anafartalar* (☎ (286) 217 4454, fax 217 4457), İskele Meydanı, on the north side of the ferry docks. The front rooms in this seven-floor structure have good views of the water and cost US$28/36 a single/double with bath and breakfast. The hotel has a pleasant seaside restaurant (see Places to Eat, following) and a convenient location.

Anzac Hotel (☎ (286) 217 7777, fax 217 2018), Saat Kulesi Meydanı 8, more or less facing the clock tower, is a newish, modern two-star lodging with 27 rooms, all with showers (some with tubs) going for US$24/30 a single/double – good value, comfortable rooms, prime location.

The three-star *Büyük Truva Oteli* (☎ (286) 217 1024, fax 217 0903), Mehmet Akif Ersoy Caddesi 2, on the waterfront 200m north of the docks, has 66 rooms which are comfortable without being fancy. Rates are US$40/50/65 a single/double/triple, breakfast included, for a room with TV, minibar, and private shower or tub-and-shower combination.

The 35-room *Hotel Bakır* (bah-KUHR) (☎ (286) 217 2908, fax 217 4090), Yalı Sokak 12, is very near the clock tower. A clean if old and well-used room with shower and view of the straits costs US$24/30/42 for a single/double/triple, with breakfast included.

Just a block east of the ferry docks is the one-star, 33-room *Otel Yaldız* (☎ (286) 217 1793, 217 1069), Kızılay Sokak 20, on a side street. It is a comfortable enough place offering rooms with private shower for US$17 with a double bed, US$20 with twin beds.

Hotel Kestanbol (☎ (286) 217 0857, fax 217 9173), Hasan Mevsuf Sokak 5, inland a few blocks and across the street from the Emniyet Sarayı (police station), is a modern one-star place with 26 rooms, all with bath, costing US$18/25 a single/double including breakfast. It's quiet and proper, with a rooftop bar that's pleasant on summer evenings.

Tour groups stay at the four-star, 129-room *Hotel Akol* (☎ (286) 217 9456, fax 217 2897), Kordonboyu, on the waterfront north of the docks. Rooms with bath cost US$48/65 a single/double. Services include a swimming pool, several restaurants and bars, a disco, and satellite TV (with CNN) in guest rooms.

There are more three-star hotels in the seaside suburb of Güzelyalı, 16 km southwest of Çanakkale off the road to Troy, of which the best are the *Tusan Hotel* (☎ (286) 232 8210, fax 232 8226) and the *İris Otel* (☎ (286) 232 8100, fax 232 8028).

AEGEAN TURKEY

Places to Eat – bottom end

Çanakkale has inexpensive places to eat throughout town. Look along the main street or past the clock tower for köfteci and pideci shops. At a pideci, fresh flat pide bread is topped with whole eggs, cheese or minced lamb, dabbed with butter and baked. It's delicious, filling and cheap, with the price depending on the toppings. Ask for pide yumurtalı (with eggs), peynirli (with cheese) or kıymalı (with ground lamb).

A typical place is *Gaziantep Aile Kebap ve Pide Salonu*, a few steps behind the clock tower, good for kebaps. A meal of soup, pide or köfte, bread and a soft drink should cost about US$4.

On the main square just in from the ferry docks, *Trakya Restaurant* (☎ (286) 217 7257) is bright and cheerful, always with a selection of ready food in the steam tables. It's supposedly open 24 hours a day.

Places to Eat – middle range

The most enjoyable places to dine are those right along the quay to the north and south of the ferry docks as you face the water. *Rıhtım*, to the south, is one place of long standing, as are *Bizim Entellektüel* (Our Intellectuals' Restaurant) and *Çekiç*. A meal of an appetiser, fried or grilled fish, salad and a bottle of beer might cost from US$10 to US$14. Be sure to ask prices, as bill-fiddling is a tradition at these places.

On the north side, the seaside restaurant at the *Otel Anafartalar* is quite popular. Prices are posted prominently.

Getting There & Away

Bus Çanakkale's otogar is one km east of the ferry docks and clock tower. Walk straight inland from the docks and when you must turn, turn left; the otogar is 100m or so along, on the right. For transport to Troy (30 km), see that section, following.

You can buy bus tickets at the otogar or at the bus company offices on the main street, in the centre of Çanakkale near the ferry docks.

For information on buses to, from and around Gallipoli, see the Gallipoli Peninsula section in the Thrace chapter. Details of some daily bus services from Çanakkale follow:

Ankara – 700 km, 10 hours, US$17; several buses
Behramkale (Assos) – 100 km, two hours (or more, depending upon dolmuşes), US$6; many buses; change to dolmuş at Ayvacık
Ayvalık – 200 km, 3½ hours, US$8; many buses
Bandırma – 195 km, three hours, US$6.50;12 buses
Bursa – 310 km, five hours, US$10; a dozen buses
Edirne – 230 km, 3½ hours, US$8; five direct buses, or change at Keşan
Gelibolu – 49 km plus ferry ride, less than two hours, US$3.75: take a bus or minibus north-east to the Lapseki-Gelibolu ferry or take the ferry to Eceabat or Kilitbahir and then the minibus to Gelibolu
Lapseki – 33 km, 45 minutes, US$1.50; take a Gönen, Bandırma or Bursa-bound bus, but make sure you'll be allowed to get off at Lapseki
İstanbul – 340 km, six hours, US$9 to US$12; 12 buses
İzmir – 340 km, six hours, US$9 to US$11; many buses
Truva (Troy) – 30 km, 35 minutes, US$2; frequent dolmuşes in summer

Boat Two ferries serve Çanakkale, connecting it with Kilitbahir and Eceabat; both carry cars as well as passengers. For information on the Gelibolu-Lapseki car ferry, see Gelibolu in the Gallipoli Peninsula section of the Thrace chapter.

The Çanakkale-Eceabat car ferries are large vessels which take about 25 minutes to cross in good weather. From 6 am to 11 pm boats run in each direction every hour on the hour. There are also boats at midnight and 2 and 4 am from Eceabat and at 1, 3 and 5 am from Çanakkale. Fares are US$0.50 per person, US$1.50 per bicycle, and US$8 per car.

The Çanakkale-Kilitbahir ferry is a much more modest affair, a small boat which takes mostly passengers but manages to take a handful of cars aboard as well. There is only one boat, and it departs from near the Hotel Bakır, to the south-west of the main docks. It runs an irregular schedule, but crosses in only 15 minutes for fares lower than the big boat to Eceabat.

TROY

The approach to Troy (Truva), 30 km from Çanakkale, is across low, rolling grain fields, with villages here and there. This is the Troad of ancient times, all but lost to legend until German-born Californian entrepreneur and amateur archaeologist Heinrich Schliemann (1822-90) excavated it in 1871. The poetry of Homer was at that time assumed to be based on legend, not history, but Schliemann got permission from the Ottoman government to dig here at his own expense. He uncovered four superimposed ancient towns and went on to make notable excavations at other Homeric sites.

History

The first people lived here during the Early Bronze Age. The cities called Troy I to Troy V (3000-1800 BC) had a similar culture, but Troy VI (1800-1275 BC) took on a new character, with a new population of Indo-European stock related to the Mycenaeans. The town doubled in size and carried on a prosperous trade with Mycenae. It also held the key, as defender of the straits, to the prosperous trade with Greek colonies on the Black Sea. Troy VI is the city of Priam which engaged in the Trojan War. A bad earthquake brought down the walls in 1275 BC and hastened the Achaean victory.

This heroic Troy was followed by Troy VII (1275-1100 BC). The Achaeans may have burned the city in 1240 BC; an invading Balkan people moved in around 1190 BC and Troy sank into a torpor for four centuries. It was revived as a Greek city (Troy VIII, 700-300 BC) and then as a Roman one (Troy IX, 300 BC-300 AD). At one point Constantine the Great thought of building his new eastern Roman capital here, but he chose Byzantium instead. As a Byzantine town, Troy didn't amount to much.

Now for Homer's history of Troy. In the *Iliad*, this is the town of Ilium. The battle took place in the 13th century BC, with Agamemnon, Achilles, Odysseus (Ulysses), Patroclus and Nestor on the Achaean (Greek) side, and Priam with his sons Hector and Paris on the Trojan side. Homer alludes to no

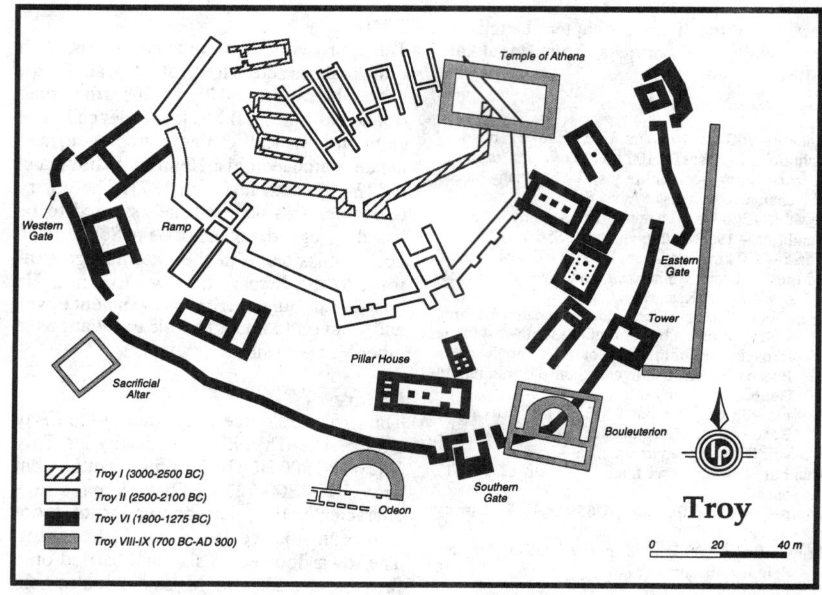

commercial rivalries as cause for the war. Rather, he says that Paris kidnapped the beautiful Helen from her husband Menelaus, King of Sparta, and the king asked the Achaeans to help him get her back.

The war went on for a decade, during which Hector killed Patroclus and Achilles killed Hector. When the time came for Paris to kill Achilles, he was up to the task. Paris knew that Achilles' mother had dipped her son in the River Styx, holding him by his heel, and had thus protected Achilles from wounds anywhere that the water had touched. So Paris shot Achilles in the heel.

Even this carnage didn't end the war, so Odysseus came up with the idea of the wooden horse filled with soldiers. That's the way Homer reported it.

One theory has it that the earthquake of 1275 BC gave the Achaeans the break they needed, bringing down Troy's formidable walls and allowing them to battle their way into the city. In gratitude to Poseidon, the Earth-Shaker, they built a monumental wooden statue of his horse. Thus there may well have been a real Trojan horse, even though Homer's account is less than fully historical.

The last people to live here were Turkish soldiers and their families, subjects of the emir of Karası, in the 14th century. After them, the town disappeared.

Ruins of Troy

The window *(gişe)* where you buy your admission ticket (US$2.50, plus US$0.75 per car) is 500m before the site. The ruins are open from 8 am to 5 pm daily.

A huge replica of the wooden Trojan horse catches your eye as you approach Troy, and so it should, as it was put here so you'd have something distinctive to photograph. Before the hokey horse, the complaint about Troy was that there's little that's eye-catching.

The Excavation Information Centre, to the right of the path, was the house used by earlier archaeological teams. Today it holds exhibits on the work under way. There's a small bookshop on the other side of the path.

The excavations by Schliemann and others have revealed nine ancient cities, one on top of another, dating back to 3000 BC.

The identifiable structures at Troy are marked by explanatory signs. Notice especially the walls from various periods, the **bouleuterion** (council chamber) built at about Homer's time (circa 800 BC) and the **Temple of Athena** from Troy VIII, rebuilt by the Romans. Also, don't miss the beautiful views of the Troad, particularly over towards the straits. On a clear day you can see the Çanakkale Martyrs' Memorial on the far shore, and ships passing through the Dardanelles. You can almost imagine the Achaean fleet beached on the Troad's shores, ready to begin a battle that would be remembered over 3000 years later.

Tevfikiye

Just half a km before the archaeological site is the village of Tevfikiye, with a hotel, drink stands, restaurants, souvenir shops, and replicas of Schliemann's cabin and the Trojan treasure.

By far most visitors stay in Çanakkale and visit Troy in passing, leaving their gear at the gişe or at a restaurant. If you feel the need to stay, the *Deniz Pansiyon*, 600m farther east deep in the village (follow the signs) is tidy and relatively cheap at US$12 for two in a waterless room. The *Hotel Hisarlık* is reasonably comfortable but a bit overpriced at US$25 a double in high summer. The *İlion Restaurant* below is a bus tour favourite. There are alternatives: the *Dinü*, which is among the best, and the *Helena* and *Helen*.

Getting There & Away

In Çanakkale, walk straight inland from the ferry docks and turn right onto the Troy road; the dolmuş station for minibuses to Tevfikiye and Troy is several hundred metres along by a small bridge, about one km total from the docks.

Dolmuşes go to Troy (30 km, 35 minutes, US$2) every 30 to 60 minutes in high summer. If you'd prefer a tour, contact Troy-Anzac Tours (☎ (286) 217 5847, 217 5049,

Frank Calvert, Discoverer of Troy

Heinrich Schliemann is usually given the credit for rediscovering Troy, but according to Dr Susan Heuck Allen it was Frank Calvert (1828-1908), a Malta-born British expatriate and sometime American consul at the Dardanelles, owner of much of the land around the site, who really rediscovered Troy.

In 1859 Calvert, an amateur archaeologist, published a pioneering excavation report on his work at Hanay Tepe, a prehistoric site near Troy. He later moved on to Pınarbaşı, believing it to be the site of Troy. By 1863, however, he was convinced that the hill on his land called Hisarlık, identified in 1812 as the site of the Roman city of Ilium Novum, was the site of Troy. He began to excavate by digging a trench, in which he found numerous artefacts from several periods.

Calvert applied to the British Museum for support in his excavations, but was turned down. He continued his excavations in a small way, but was hampered by financial difficulties and family responsibilities.

In 1868 Calvert was visited by Heinrich Schliemann, who had been excavating for Troy at Pınarbaşı in vain. Convinced by the artefacts which Calvert had uncovered that this was Troy, Schliemann began to excavate on Calvert's land at Hisarlık. The two men later had a falling out, but Calvert continued to support Schliemann's work for the sake of science, and Schliemann continued to fund Calvert's own explorations elsewhere in exchange for the benefit of Calvert's knowledge.

Schliemann, a peerless self-promoter, saw to it that his name was inscribed in the history books as the discoverer of Troy, but it was Frank Calvert who made Schliemann's success possible. In the 20th century, Calvert's priceless collection of artefacts from Troy and nearby sites was dispersed to museums in Çanakkale, London, and Boston and Worcester, Massachusetts. ■

fax 217 0196), Saat Kulesi Meydanı 6, in Çanakkale.

If you plan to visit Troy and then head south, you should try to buy a ticket on a southbound bus a day in advance, let the ticket seller know you want to be picked up at Troy, do your sightseeing at Troy, then be out on the main highway in plenty of time to catch the bus. Without a ticket, you can hitch out to the highway from Troy and hope a bus will come by, and that it will have vacant seats. This often works, though it entails some waiting and some uncertainty regarding seat availability.

If you're coming from the south, ask to be let out on the highway at the access road to Troy, which is 4.5 km north of the big Geyikli/Çimento Fabrikası crossroads. From the highway it's five km west to Troy. Hitch, or wait for a dolmuş.

ÇANAKKALE TO ASSOS

Heading south from Çanakkale and Troy on the main highway (as the buses do), there is little to stop for until you reach the town of **Ayvacık** (population 6000), from which dolmuşes run 19 km west to Assos (Behramkale). If you have your own transport, consider taking a much more interesting side road through the western part of the Biga Peninsula, which takes you to little-visited minor ruins and soon-to-be discovered beaches which are good for camping, while they last.

Some 4.5 km south of the Troy road is a paved if narrow road heading west and marked for Alexandria Troas and Apollo Smintheon. After passing the cement factory the road proceeds south-west to the small towns of Geyikli and Oduniskelesi. **Geyikli**, 24 km along, has a few simple restaurants and basic hotels.

Bozcaada

Bozcaada, formerly known as Tenedos, has always been known to Anatolian oenophiles for its wines (Dimitrakopulo, Doruk, Talay) and to soldiers for its defences. A huge medieval fortress towers over the north-eastern tip of the island, and vineyards blanket its sunny slopes. The island has the advantage of being small (about five or six km across) and easy to explore, and the disadvantage of being too small to host much accommodation. Rooms and beds are usually filled by İstanbullus with reservations in summer, so advance bookings are essential unless you just plan to come for the day.

Ferries depart from the mainland village of Yükyeri İskelesi, five km west of Geyikli, south of Troy; look for the access road (and a sign) in Geyikli. Boats depart in the morning and afternoon for US$0.75 per passenger, US$10 per car. There may be additional boat services in high summer. There's not actually a lot to do on the island, so you may want to make it a day trip.

On Bozcaada, poke around the enormous fortress, then hike across the island to the beaches for a dip.

Alexandria Troas

Five km south of Oduniskelesi the road passes right through the widely scattered ruins of Alexandria Troas near the village of Dalyan. (Some signs read 'Alexandria (Truva)', but this is not Troy.)

Antigonus, one of Alexander the Great's generals, took control of this land after the collapse of the Alexandrian empire and founded the city of Antigoneia in 310 BC in his own honour. He was later defeated in battle by Lysimachus, another of Alexander's generals, who took the city and renamed it in honour of his late commander. An earthquake later destroyed much of the city.

Nowadays dolmuşes run infrequently between Ezine, on the main highway, and Dalyan.

Archaeologists have identified bits of the city's theatre, palace, temple, agora, baths, necropolis, harbour and city walls amidst the farmers' fields. But for most visitors Alexandria Troas is a mood, a place which, like so many places in Turkey, conjures up that feeling of great antiquity disappearing beneath the slowly grinding wheels of time. Don't make a special trip here, but if you pass by, do stop and climb a ruined wall for the view.

Neandria When Antigonus founded the city of Antigoneia, he forced the inhabitants of nearby Neandria, settled around 700 BC, to move to his new city and populate it. The ruins of Neandria, 1.5 km north-east of the village of Kayacık and 500m inland from the sea, offer nothing to the casual visitor today, but archaeologists have discovered here the oldest Aeolian temple with a clearly distinguishable plan.

Gülpınar

Three km south of Alexandria Troas are the **hot springs of Kestanbol Kaplıcaları** (13 km south of Geyikli), with a small bath-house. Continue south 32 km to Gülpınar, a small farming town with no services but for a fuel station. This was once the ancient city of Khrysa, famous for its Ionic temple to Apollo and mice. Cretan colonists who had come to this area had been told by an oracle that they should settle where they were attacked by 'the sons of the earth'. They awoke to find mice chewing on their equipment, so they settled here and built a temple to the 'Lord of the Mice' (Smintheion). The **Apollo Smintheion**, 400m down a steep hill from the centre of the town, has some bits of marble column on top of a short flight of steps. The cult statue of the god, now disappeared, had mice carved in marble at its feet, in accordance with an old legend. Reliefs on the temple's walls illustrated scenes from the *Iliad*.

Babakale & Akliman

In Gülpınar a road going west is marked for Babakale (Lekton), nine km away. Three km along it is the road to Akliman, a coastal settlement with a nice long beach backed by olive groves, and several good, cheap camping places and motels. About six km farther on is Babakale, with a small village clustered at the base of a ruined fortress overlooking a long sweep of sea. A new yacht and fishing harbour is being completed, and the first touristic hotels – the Karayel and Ser-Tur – have been opened, with undoubtedly many more to follow. Some İstanbullus have already fixed up stone village houses (and one windmill) as villas.

From Gülpınar the road east to Assos (25 km) passes through a half-dozen small villages. From some, unpaved roads head down to the shore where there is sure to be some beach shack with a primitive toilet and perhaps fresh water for the ever-increasing number of camper-van owners who have discovered this road.

ASSOS (BEHRAMKALE)

Called Assos in ancient times, the ruins and the Turkish village of Behramkale share a gorgeous setting west of Ayvacık, overlooking the Aegean and the nearby island of Lesbos (Midilli, MEE-dee-lee in Turkish).

It's 73 km from Çanakkale along the main highway (E87/D550) to Ayvacık (not to be confused with nearby Ayvalık), a bus ride of under two hours. From Ayvacık, dolmuşes run the 19 km to Behramkale, and it's often possible to hitch as well.

Assos makes a brave sight as you approach, its craggy summit surrounded by huge remnants of a mighty wall. The main part of the village and the acropolis ruins are perched at the top, but down the far (sea) side of the hill at the *iskele* (wharf), a tiny cluster of stone buildings clings to the cliff in a romantic and unlikely setting. The beach is of pebbles, short and narrow, but there's many km of wider beach at **Kadırga**, four km to the east.

History

In its long history, Assos has flourished as a port, agricultural town and centre for Platonic learning.

The Mysian city of Assos was founded in the 8th century BC by colonists from Lesbos, who later (530 BC) built its great temple to Athena. The city enjoyed its greatest prosperity and renown under the rule of Hermeias, a one-time student of Plato who also ruled the Troad and Lesbos. Hermeias encouraged philosophers and savants to live in Assos, including Aristotle, who lived here from 348 to 345 BC and ended up marrying Hermeias' niece, Pythia. Assos' glory period came to an end with the advent of the Persians, who tortured Hermeias to death.

Alexander the Great drove the Persians out, but Assos' importance was challenged by the ascendancy of Alexandria Troas to the north. From 241 to 133 BC, Assos was ruled by the kings of Pergamum.

St Paul visited Assos briefly during his third missionary journey (53-57 AD) through Asia Minor, walking here from Alexandria Troas to meet Luke and others before taking a boat to Lesbos.

In Byzantine times the city dwindled to a village, which it remained during the rule of the Ottomans and remains today. Excavations continue on the impressive ruins, tourists both Turkish and foreign crowd the iskele, and the local people plough their fields and tend their olive trees awaiting the day when a developer will buy their land at a fat price and make them rich.

Things to See

There's a fine **Ottoman hump-back bridge**, built in the 14th century, to the left of the road as you approach the village. When you get to a fork in the road, go left up to the village proper, or right to see the massive city walls, necropolis and iskele.

Taking the village road, you wind up to a small square with a few shops and restaurants. Continue upwards on the road, and you'll come to a small square with a teahouse and a bust of Atatürk. At the very top of the hill there is a spectacular view, which you can enjoy after fending off villagers eager to sell you examples of the local embroidery. Entrance to the site costs US$2, and it's open from 8 am to 5 pm (till 7 pm in summer).

The **Murad Hüdavendigar Camii** (1359-89), the obvious mosque at the site, is a simple pre-Ottoman work – a dome on squinches set on top of a square box of a room – accomplished before Turks and Turkish architects had conquered Constantinople and assimilated the lessons of Sancta Sophia. The lintel above the entrance bears Greek crosses and inscriptions, a reminder that the Byzantine emperor was still on his throne when this mosque was built with parts permanently borrowed from a local 6th-century church.

The principal sight on top of the hill (altitude 228m) is the **Temple of Athena**, built in a mixed Doric-Ionic style, and now partly reconstructed. Its short, tapered columns with plain capitals are hardly elegant, and the concrete reconstruction hurts more than helps. The site and the view are, as with so many ancient cities, spectacular and well worth the admission fee.

By taking the right fork of the entry road, you'll reach the city's main entrance gate and the best-preserved section of the **city walls**, among the most impressive classical fortifications in Turkey; and the **necropolis**, or cemetery. Assos' sarcophagi ('flesh-eaters') were famous: according to Pliny the stone itself was caustic and 'ate' the flesh off the deceased in 40 days.

Just 2.5 km past the fork, on a block-paved road which winds down the cliff side, is the iskele, the most picturesque spot in Assos. There are lodging and eating possibilities here, and crowds of bodies in summer.

Places to Stay

In high summer, virtually all lodging-places require that you take yarım pansiyon (half-pension, breakfast and dinner) with your room. The room prices are 35% lower in the off season (April, May and October), without the half-pension requirement, so the double room which costs US$60 (with two meals) in August may be priced at US$25 in early October. All of the hotels here are atmospheric old stone buildings right next to the sea. For reservations, write to the hotel, Behramkale/Ayvacık, 17860 Çanakkale or, better, fax.

Places to Stay – bottom end

The cheapest way to stay in Assos is to camp in the olive groves just east (inland) where there are a few primitive *camping grounds* charging about US$2 per person.

In the iskele area, *Dost Camping* (☎ (286)

721 7096) has campsites among the fig and olive trees for US$5.50 (two persons in a tent), and a vine-shaded restaurant. *Şen Camping* below it is second-best.

There are many more *camping grounds* among beachfront olive groves at Kadırga, four km to the east, and beyond it along the road which ultimately rejoins the coastal highway at Küçükkuyu.

The upper town, near the Temple of Athena, has some pensions, including the very simple *Athena Pansiyon*, the *Sidar Pansiyon* (☎ (286) 721 7047) and, near the top of the hill, the *Halıcı Han Pansiyon*. All charge what the traffic will bear, which is usually about US$12 for a waterless double in summer.

Assos Şen Pansiyon (☎ (286) 721 7076) has a roof restaurant with good views and interesting architectural information on the Assos ruins. Most of their double rooms with shower, breakfast and dinner cost US$55 in high summer, but they also have some simpler waterless, viewless, fairly claustrophobic rooms in another building for US$25 a double, two meals included.

Places to Stay – middle

Behram Hotel (☎ (286) 721 7016, fax 721 7044) has about the best hotel restaurant, as well as comfortable shower-equipped rooms at US$28/44 a single/double in summer, two meals included.

Hotel Assos Kervansaray (☎ (286) 721 7093, fax 721 7200) is the most popular place, beautifully kept, with three-star comforts. Rates are US$40/60 a single/double in season, two meals included.

Hotel Yıldız Saray (☎ (286) 721 7025, fax 721 7169), has rooms with partial sea views for US$60 a double, two meals included.

Hotel Nazlıhan (☎ (286) 721 7064, fax 721 7387), beyond the jandarma post, has been nicely restored. The rooms and baths are quite small but attractive. Rates are US$28 a double with sea view, slightly less without.

Hotel Assos (☎ (286) 721 7017, fax 721 7249), right on the harbour, has a popular restaurant and charges from US$60 a double for its comfy air-con rooms in summer, two meals included.

There are many more hotels on the beach at Kadırga, four km east, though reaching them is difficult without your own wheels.

The *Troy Otel* (☎ (286) 721 7154, fax 721 7241) has four-star comforts for US$70 a double, breakfast and dinner included.

Several km farther east, perched on a terrace overlooking the sea, the *Assos Terrace Motel* (☎ (286) 762 9885, fax 762 9884) has comfortable rooms with excellent views for US$40 a double with two meals.

Places to Eat

Most hotels require that you take breakfast and dinner with your room in July and August, which is just as well as there are only a few independent restaurants. Dost Camping's *restaurant* is perhaps the cheapest, and quite pleasant. The fancy *Fenerli Han Restaurant* by the Nazlıhan Hotel has a beautiful seaside setting and a set-price dinner for about US$10, plus drinks and tip.

Getting There & Away

Dolmuşes depart from Ayvacık hourly in high summer for Assos. In the off season, they are less frequent, perhaps only a few times per day. If you visit during the off season (which I recommend), leave from Ayvalık or Çanakkale early in the day, get to Ayvacık as soon as possible, then hang out on the road to Assos to catch a dolmuş or hitch a ride.

ASSOS TO AYVALIK

The road east from Assos and Kadırga follows the coast to rejoin the main coastal highway at Küçükkuyu, then continues round the Bay of Edremit. Along the way at **Altınoluk** the highway passes a motley collection of hotels, motels and beachfront eateries which, though right on the water, are subject to road noise. Seaside accommodations are somewhat better at **Akçay** and **Ören**, off the highway. At Akçay there's a fine five-km-long beach with sulphur springs issuing from parts of it; the beach at Ören is nine km long.

Inland is the farming centre of **Edremit** (population 37,000), called Adramyttium in classical times, but with nothing to draw you today. Ayvalık, your most likely destination, is 130 km (over two hours) south-east of Assos and 110 km (two hours) south-east of Ayvacık, by road.

AYVALIK

Across a narrow strait from the Greek island of Lesbos, Ayvalık (population 30,000) is a seaside resort, fishing town, olive oil and soap-making centre, and a terminus for boats to and from Lesbos. The coast here is cloaked in pine forests and olive orchards, the offshore waters sprinkled with 23 islands.

Orientation & Information

The town of Ayvalık is small and manageable, but with some inconveniences: the otogar is 1.5 km north of the centre and the Tourism Information Office (☎ & fax (266) 312 2122) is a km south of the main square around the curve of the bay, opposite the yacht harbour. There is an information kiosk

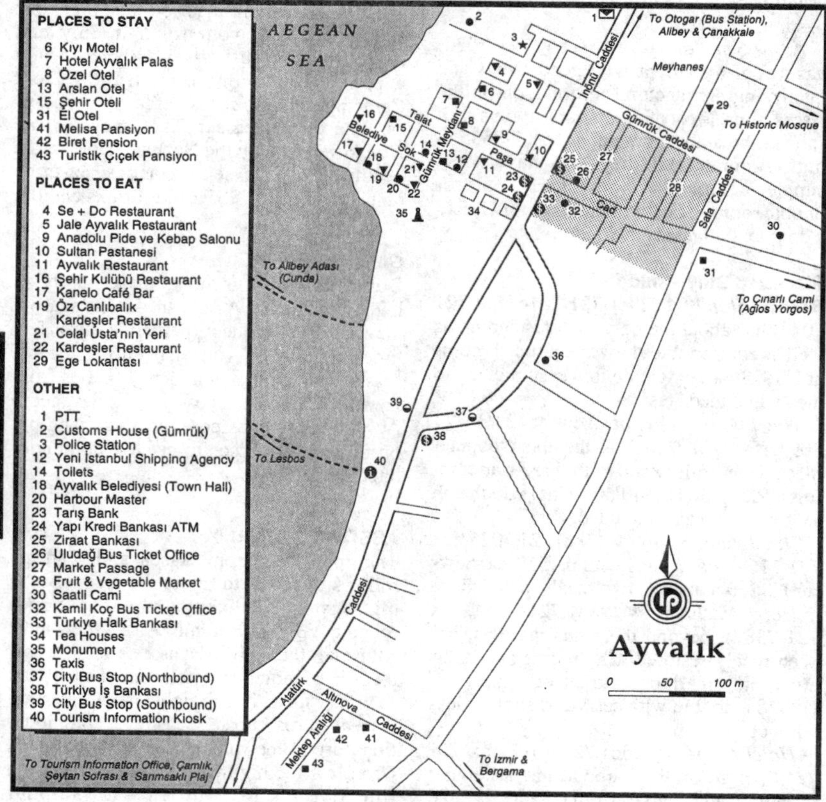

on the waterfront at the south side of the main square staffed by Ayvalık Tourism Association personnel in summer.

Three km farther to the south are the areas called Çamlık and Orta Çamlık, with a scattering of pensions and camping areas popular with Turks on holiday. Eight km south of the centre is Sarımsaklı Plaj (Garlic Beach), incorporated as the municipality of Küçükköy, also called Plajlar (The Beaches). Sarımsaklı is a nice if not spectacular beach lined with hotels, motels and pensions. Alibey Adası (Alibey Island), sometimes called Cunda, is 8.3 km north-west of Ayvalık centre by road, or 15 minutes by boat.

Things to See & Do

Now about 350 years old, Ayvalık ('quince-orchard') was inhabited by Ottoman Greeks until after WWI. When the nations of the former Ottoman Empire decided to exchange minority populations, Ayvalık's Turkish-speaking Greeks went to Greece, and Greek-speaking Turks came here from Lesbos, the Balkans and Crete. A few locals still speak some Greek, and most of the town's mosques are converted Orthodox churches. The **Saatli Camii**, or Mosque with a Clock, was once the church of Agios Yannis (St John); the **Çınarlı Camii** used to be the Agios Yorgos (St George) church.

In summer, boats (15 minutes, US$0.40) depart from the centre of town near the Ayvalık Tourism Society kiosk for **Alibey Adası**, an island just across the bay where there are seaside restaurants, abandoned, ruinous Greek churches, and hundreds of condominiums advertised in Turkish, English and German. A causeway links the island to the mainland, so you can go by city bus or taxi any time of the year, but this isn't nearly so much fun as taking the boat.

The quay is crowded with day-cruisers eager to take you on a daytime or evening sail around the dozens of islands in the bay. Competition is fierce in high summer, with most cruises priced at US$5 to US$7 with a meal.

Another goal for excursions is **Şeytan Sofrası** (Devil's Dinner table), a hilltop south of the town, from which the view is magnificent. There's a snack stand. As no bus or dolmuş runs here regularly, you'll have to walk, hitch (unlikely) or take a taxi.

City buses run through the centre of town from the bus station south to the beach at Sarımsaklı Plaj (Plajlar). Dolmuş minibuses (US$0.35) depart for the beach from the fifth side street south of the main square.

Places to Stay

Pensions, camping areas and little hotels line the road south eight km to Sarımsaklı Plaj, where there are numerous beach resort hotels. Other, quieter camping areas are on the island of Alibey Adası; take the city bus of that name. The hotels in the town centre are convenient and simple. Prices quoted below are for July and August; at any other time, discounts are in order.

Places to Stay – bottom end

The most interesting lodging is the *Taksiyarhis Pansiyon* (☎ (266) 312 1494), İsmetpaşa Mahallesi, Mareşal Çakmak Caddesi 71, a renovated Ottoman house about a five-minute walk east of the PTT behind the former Taxiarkhis church. The owners (he's Austrian, she's Turkish) lovingly restored the priest's house, with five guest rooms, two shared bathrooms, two terraces, good views, and a kitchen for guests' use. At US$25 a double with breakfast, it's often full in summer, so reserve in advance if possible.

Turistik Çiçek Pansiyon (☎ (266) 312 1201), on Mektep Aralığı, is about 200m south of the main square, a half-block east off the main road. It has lots of fluorescent lights and simple, clean rooms with showers for US$11/14 a single/double, breakfast included. The *Biret Pansiyon* (☎ (266) 312 2175), at the other end of Mektep Aralığı, and the *Melisa Pansiyon* around the corner take the overflow.

There are a few small cheap old-style hotels in the warren of little streets just north of the main square, the cheapest of which is the *Özel Otel* (☎ (266) 312 1372), with

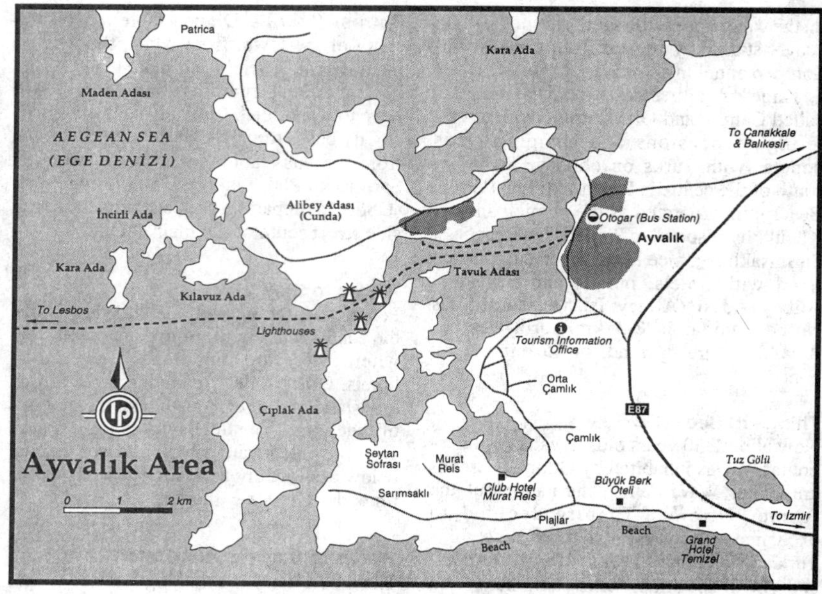

waterless double rooms for US$12. The noisy *Şehir Oteli* nearby awaits renovation.

El Otel (☎ (266) 312 2217) is one long block east of the main street near the main square, at Vehbibey Mahallesi, Sefa Caddesi 3 in the midst of the market. It's clean and correct, run by God-fearing types who will rent you a room with shower for US$11/15/19 a single/double/triple.

For more comfort at higher prices, try the *Hotel Ayvalık Palas* (☎ (266) 312 1064, fax 312 1046), Gümrük Meydanı, which is new and modern and charges US$15/24 for a single/double with shower and breakfast. A few steps away, the renovated *Motel Kıyı* (☎ (266) 312 6677), Gümrük Meydanı 18, charges US$18/26/34 a single/double/triple for rooms with shower. Front rooms have water views. The 20-room *Arslan Otel* (☎ (266) 312 6888) was opened in 1995 and charges US$24 for a bright, clean double with shower and breakfast.

Over on Alibey Adası, the *Günay Motel* (☎ (266) 327 1048) is set back from the waterfront. It is quiet, simple and reasonably priced at US$18 for a double with shower; breakfast costs extra.

Camping The best camping is on Alibey Adası, with the camping grounds located inconveniently – but quietly – outside the village. The ubiquitously advertised *Ada Camp* (☎ (266) 312 1211) is three km to the west, as is *Ortunü Hidden Paradise*. The *Cunda Motel-Camping* is here as well.

At the southern end of Çamlık, on the way to Sarımsaklı Plaj, there's a national forest camping ground *(Orman Kampı)* and several private camping grounds.

Places to Stay – middle

Sarımsaklı The resort hotels in Ayvalık are pleasant and not expensive. One is near Çamlık on the way to Şeytan Sofrası, the others are on Sarımsaklı Plaj.

Club Hotel Murat Reis (moo-RAHT reh-yeess) (☎ (266) 324 1456, fax 324 1457) is set apart in its own pine grove with its own beach at the foot of Şeytan Sofrası. This gives it an air of splendid isolation except for the tour groups which come and go daily. You will need your own car for transport, or will have to depend upon taxis. Double rooms including a bath cost US$55 with breakfast, US$65 with breakfast and dinner, or US$80 (for two) with all meals included.

Down on Sarımsaklı Plaj, a mere 50m from the water, are numerous good hotels. The 100-room *Otel Ankara* (☎ (266) 324 1195, fax 324 0022) has rooms with balcony and bath at US$40 a single and from US$50 to US$60 a double, breakfast included. The hotel has a card-and-game room, bar, café, and terrace restaurant.

Büyük Berk Oteli (☎ (266) 324 1045, fax 324 1194), right next to the Ankara, is a modern building with lots of facilities, including a swimming pool and water-sports paraphernalia, disco, children's playground, billiard and table-tennis room. The 112 guest rooms have private baths, balconies (some with sea views) and prices of US$47 to US$65 a double, breakfast included.

The Büyük Berk has two sister establishments, the fancier *Hotel Club Berk* and the *Hotel Zeytinci* (same phone as Büyük Berk), with even more comfortable and up-to-date guest rooms, a posh lobby done in black marble, golden travertine and soft grey textiles. All of the Büyük Berk's facilities are shared with the newer hotels, though the Club Berk does have its own small swimming pool. Room prices are the same at all three places.

Places to Stay – top end

Alibey The village on Alibey Adası has several new hotels, including the four-star *Hotel Florium* (☎ (266) 312 9628, fax 322 9631), at the end of the causeway as you reach the island. Comfortable double rooms cost US$75 with breakfast.

Sarımsaklı At the western end of the beach, not far from the north-south highway, the five-star *Grand Hotel Temizel* (☎ (266) 324 2000, fax 324 1274) is the class act, with 164 rooms equipped with satellite TV, minibars, air-con, balconies and even hair dryers. Water sports, six bars and a disco, a health club and casino – all the services are yours for US$80 to US$90 a single, US$85 to US$100 a double, breakfast included.

Places to Eat

Ayvalık Most restaurants now put out signboards listing prices, at least in the busy summer months.

Right on the main square are numerous teahouses, with views of the harbour.

The narrow streets north of the harbour have several small, simple restaurants with good food and low prices. The *Ayvalık Restaurant* (☎ 312 6759) has good soups and stews which, with bread, make a filling meal for US$3 or so. *Celal Usta'nin Yeri* is similar. The *Anadolu Pide ve Kebap Salonu* (☎ 312 6759) serves Turkish pizza for about the same. The nearby *Sultan Pastanesi* is good for biscuits or pastries.

Ege Lokantası, inland at the market, remains cheap while the waterfront places are more up-market. They have lots of good cheap steam-table fare ready to eat at any hour of the day. Nearby in the narrow market streets are various meyhanes, the Turkish equivalent of tavernas. These places are patronised by local men and have good food and lots of drinks at non-touristy prices.

The *Se & Do Restaurant* (☎ 312 1418), on Gümrük Meydanı near the Motel Kıyı, specialises in seafood but serves meat as well, with meals costing up to about US$10.

Out on the quay by the main square are several waterfront seafood restaurants, including the *Öz Canlıbalık, Kardeşler* and *Şehir Kulübü*, with spacious, airy dining rooms and nicely lit terraces with sea views. The price for a full dinner rounds out to about US$10 or US$12 per person for meat, somewhat more for fish, drinks included.

Alibey One of the reasons people visit Ayvalık is to take the boat out to Alibey Adası and have lunch or dinner there. You can expect to spend from US$12 to US$18 per person for a full seafood dinner with wine.

The promenade is all restaurants, mostly named after the owner: *Günay'ın Yeri* (Günay's Place), *Arif'in Yeri* (Arif's Place etc). Cheapest among them, and still good, is Günay'ın Yeri at the east end of the promenade. In general, those farther east are a bit cheaper, but it's easy to check in any case as they all have signboards with prices. If you come in the off season, it's best to patronise the busiest one, which will have the freshest food.

Getting There & Away

Bus Ayvalık is served by the frequent bus service running up and down the Aegean coast between Çanakkale and İzmir, but you may have to hitchhike in from the highway. See the following Getting Around section.

To leave Ayvalık, you can buy bus tickets at offices in the main square. Check departure times and availability early in the day as few buses depart in the evening. Here are details of services from Ayvalık to:

Assos (Behramkale, via Ayvacık) – 130 km, over two hours, US$6; many buses to Ayvacık
Bergama – 50 km, 45 minutes, US$3; many buses to highway junction, few into town
Bursa – 300 km, 4½ hours, US$9; a dozen buses daily, continuing to İstanbul or Ankara
Çanakkale – 200 km, 3½ hours, US$8; many buses
İzmir – 240 km, 3½ hours, US$6.50; many buses

AEGEAN TURKEY

Boat The passage by sea between Ayvalık and Lesbos is now so expensive (US$50 one-way, US$65 same-day round trip) that few people choose to use it. If you're coming from Greece (ie not returning to Turkey after a day trip), you must also pay an outrageous 4000-drachmae Greek port tax. Turkish boats make the two-hour voyage to Lesbos on Tuesday and Thursday at 9 am in summer. Usually you must buy your ticket and hand over your passport for paperwork a day in advance of the voyage, whether you are departing from Turkey or from Greece.

For information and tickets, contact one of the several shipping agencies in the warren of little streets north and west of the main square, including the Yeni İstanbul Shipping Agency (☎ (266) 312 6123) and the Jale Ayvalık Tur Shipping Agency (☎ (266) 312 2740, fax 312 2470).

Getting Around

Buses along the highway will drop you at the northern turn off for Ayvalık, exactly five km from the centre, unless the bus company specifically designates Ayvalık Otogar as a stop. From the highway you must hitchhike into town; drivers of most vehicles will understand your situation and stop to give you a lift. If you are dropped in town, it will be at the Şehirlerarası Otobüs Garajı (Intercity Bus Garage), which is 1.5 km (15 or 20 minutes' walk) north of the main square. City buses marked 'Ayvalık Belediyesi' run all the way through the town from north to south and will carry you from the bus station to the main square, south to the Tourism Information Office, and farther south to Çamlık, Orta Çamlık and Sarımsaklı, for US$0.35.

DİKİLİ

Travelling 41 km south from Ayvalık along the coast road, there is a turn off on the right for Dikili (population 20,000), four km west of the coastal highway, and 30 km west of Bergama. A wharf capable of serving ocean liners brings the occasional Aegean cruise ship to Dikili to see the ruins at Bergama. But mostly Dikili is a summer resort for families from İstanbul and İzmir.

The town's main beach (of course, dark sand) starts about 600m north of the main square and goes west for about one km. The PTT is a few steps north of the main square, towards the beach. The otogar is 400m north of the main square and 200m south of the beach.

Places to Stay

Özdemir Pansiyon (☎ (232) 671 1295), 100m north of the main square along the main street, is good if you expect to spend only a night or two and want to do it cheaply; likewise the *Güneş Pansiyon* (☎ (232) 671 1847), a bit farther north from the Özdemir, then east (inland) 100m (follow the signs).

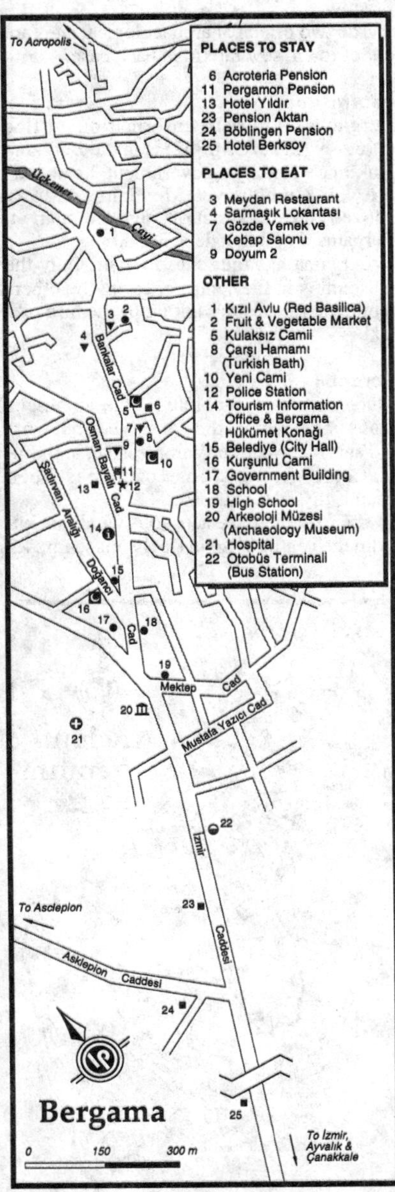

Either charges about US$6 per person. The *Dikili Pansiyon*, farther north and a bit inland (there are no street names in this new section yet) is much newer, and costs just a bit more.

Getting There & Away

Though there are direct buses between İzmir and Dikili via Çandarlı, most long-distance bus traffic goes via Bergama. Take one of the frequent minibuses to Bergama (35 minutes, US$1.25) for connections with more distant points.

BERGAMA (PERGAMUM)

Modern Bergama (BEHR-gah-mah, population 50,000), in the province of İzmir, is an agricultural market town in the midst of a well-watered plain. There has been a town here since Trojan times, but Pergamum's heyday was during the period after Alexander the Great and before Roman domination of all Asia Minor. At that time, Pergamum was one of the richest and most powerful small kingdoms in the Middle East.

History

Pergamum owes its prosperity to Lysimachus and his downfall. Lysimachus, one of Alexander the Great's generals, controlled much of the Aegean region when Alexander's far-flung empire fell apart after his death in 323 BC. In the battles over the spoils Lysimachus captured a great treasure, which he secured in Pergamum before going off to fight Seleucus for control of all Asia Minor. But Lysimachus lost and was slain in 281 BC, so Philetarus, the commander he had posted at Pergamum to protect the treasure, set himself up as governor.

Philetarus was a eunuch, but he was succeeded by his nephew Eumenes I (263-241 BC), and Eumenes was followed by his adopted son Attalus I (241-197 BC). Attalus took the title of king, expanded his power and made an alliance with Rome. He was succeeded by his son Eumenes II (197-159 BC), and that's when the fun began.

Eumenes II was the man who really built Pergamum. Rich and powerful, he added the library and the Altar of Zeus to the hilltop city, and built the 'middle city' on terraces halfway down the hill. The already famous medical centre of the Asclepion was expanded and beautified as well.

The Pergamum of Eumenes II is remembered most of all for its library. Said to have held more than 200,000 volumes, it was a symbol of Pergamum's social and cultural climb. Eumenes was a mad book collector. His library came to challenge the world's greatest in Alexandria (700,000 books). The Egyptians were afraid Pergamum and its library would attract famous scholars away from Alexandria, so they cut off the supply of papyrus from the Nile. Eumenes set his scientists to work, and they came up with *pergamen* (Latin for 'parchment'), a writing surface made from animal hides rather than pressed papyrus reeds.

The Egyptians were to have their revenge, however. When Eumenes died, he was succeeded by his brother Attalus II (159-138 BC). Things went pretty well under him, but under Attalus II's son Attalus III (138-133 BC) the kingdom was falling to pieces. Attalus III had no heir so he willed his kingdom to Rome. The Kingdom of Pergamum became the Roman province of Asia in 129 BC.

In the early years of the Christian era the great library at Alexandria was damaged by fire. Marc Antony, out of devotion to Cleopatra, pillaged the library at Pergamum for books to replace those of the Egyptian queen.

Orientation

Almost everything you'll need in Bergama is between the Otobüs Terminali to the south-west and the market to the north-east, including cheap hotels, restaurants, banks and the Archaeology Museum. All but the cheapest hotels are located west of the bus station away from the centre towards the coastal highway.

The centre of town, for our purposes, is the Archaeology Museum on the main street which, by the way, is called İzmir Caddesi, İzmir Yolu, Cumhuriyet Caddesi, Hükümet Caddesi, Bankalar Caddesi, or Uzun Çarşı Caddesi, depending upon whom and where you ask.

The two principal archaeological sites are out of town, several km in each case.

Information

Bergama's Tourism Information Office (☎ & fax (232) 633 1862) is in the Bergama Hükümet Konağı (government headquarters) in Cumhuriyet Meydanı, midway between the bus station and the market. Bergama's postal code is 35700.

Bergama has four sites to visit. Only the museum is in the centre of town; the others require some healthy hiking or the hire of a taxi.

Acropolis

Much of what was built by the ambitious kings of Pergamum did not survive, but what did survive is certainly impressive, and dramatically sited. Some of it has been beautifully restored.

The road up to the acropolis winds six km from the centre of town (ie the museum; 4.3

km from the Red Basilica), around the north and east sides of the hill, to a car park at the top. Next to the car park are some souvenir and soft-drink stands, and a ticket seller (US$2.50, parking US$0.70). You can visit the acropolis any day from 9 am to 5 pm (till 7 pm in summer); the road is open from 8.30 am to 5.30 pm (till 7.30 pm in summer). If you walk up you can take a shortcut along the path up through the ruins. It's steeper but shorter.

While you're up here on the acropolis, don't forget to look for the Asclepion, across the valley to the west, on the north edge of town near an army base. You'll also see the ruins of a small theatre, a larger theatre and a stadium down in the valley.

The main structures on the acropolis include (of course) the **library** as well as the marble-columned **Temple of Trajan**, rebuilt by the German Archaeological Institute. The great **theatre** is impressive (10,000 seats) and unusual. Pergamum borrowed from Hellenistic architecture, but in the case of the theatre made major modifications. To take advantage of the spectacular view and to conserve precious building space on top of the hill, it was decided to build the theatre into the hillside. Hellenistic theatres are usually more rounded, but because of this one's location, rounding was impossible, so it was increased in height instead.

Below the stage of the theatre is the ruined **Temple of Dionysus**. The **Altar of Zeus**, south of the theatre, shaded by evergreen trees, is in an idyllic setting. Most of the building is now in Berlin, taken there (with the sultan's permission) by the 19th-century German excavators of Pergamum. Only the base remains.

The Hellenistic theatre at Pergamum, with 10,000 seats, is among the steepest and narrowest in the Classical world.

Otherwise, several piles of rubble on top of the acropolis are marked as the **palaces of Attalus I and Eumenes II**, and there is an **agora** as well as fragments of the defensive **walls**.

Walk down the hill from the Altar of Zeus, through the **Middle City**, and you will pass the **Altar & Temple of Demeter, gymnasium** or school, **Lower Agora** and **Roman bath**. The path down is not well marked.

Asclepion

The Asclepion of Pergamum was not the first nor the only ancient medical centre. In fact, this one was founded by Archias, a citizen of Pergamum who had been treated and cured at the Asclepion of Epidaurus in Greece. But Pergamum's centre came to the fore under Galen (131-210 AD), who was born here, studied in Alexandria and Greece as well as in Asia Minor, and set up shop as physician to Pergamum's gladiators.

Recognised as perhaps the greatest early physician, Galen added considerably to the knowledge of the circulatory and nervous systems, and also systematised medical theory. Under his influence, the medical school at Pergamum became renowned. His work was the basis for all Western medicine well into the 16th century. Around 162 AD, he moved to Rome and became personal physician to Emperor Marcus Aurelius.

There are two roads to the Asclepion, the handier being the one from the centre of town (see map). The other is at the western edge of town on the way to the highway. By the latter road, the ruins are 3.5 km from the Archaeology Museum, or about two km from the Otobüs Terminali. This road passes through a large Turkish military base; don't take photos, and be off the road by dusk.

Asclepion opening hours and fees are the same as at the acropolis.

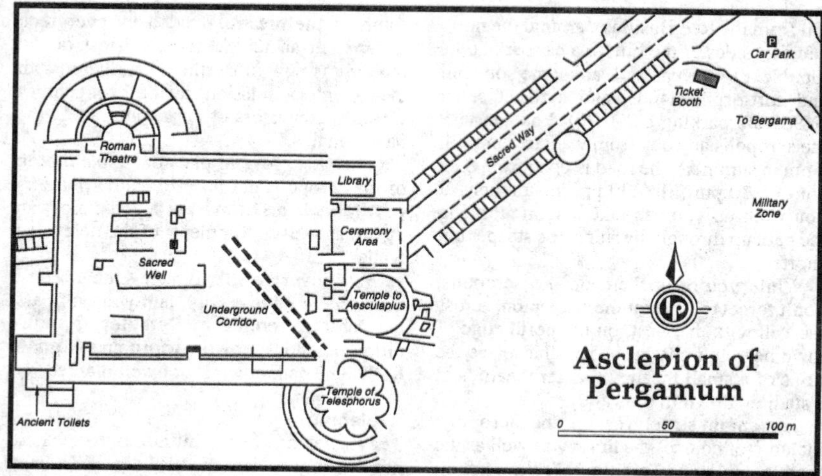

As you walk around the ruins, you'll see bas-reliefs or carvings of a snake, the symbol of Aesculapius, god of medicine. Just as the snake shed its skin and gained a 'new life', so the patients at the Asclepion were supposed to 'shed' their illnesses.

Diagnosis was often by dream analysis. Treatment included massage and mud baths, drinking sacred waters, and the use of herbs and ointments.

A **Sacred Way** leads from the car park to the centre. Signs mark a **Temple to Aesculapius, library** and **Roman Theatre**. Take a drink of cool water from the **Sacred Well**, then pass along the vaulted underground corridor to the **Temple of Telesphorus**.

It is said that patients slept in the temple hoping that Telesphorus, another god of medicine, would send a cure, or at least a diagnosis, in a dream. Telesphorus, by the way, had two daughters named Hygeia and Panacea.

Sights in Town

In the town centre next to the hillside tea gardens is the **Arkeoloji Müzesi** (Archaeology Museum). It has a substantial collection of artefacts for so small a town, and an excellent ethnology section as well. It's open every day from 9 am to noon and 1 to 7 pm in summer (to 5.30 pm in winter); admission costs US$2.50.

The **Kızıl Avlu** (KUH-zuhl ahv-loo), Red Basilica or Red Courtyard, 150m north-east of the Meydan Restaurant, was originally a temple (built in the 2nd century AD) to Serapis, an Egyptian god. Admission costs US$2.50; opening hours are from 9 am to noon and 1 to 5 pm (till 7 pm in summer). It was converted to a Christian basilica by the Byzantines and now holds a small mosque, proving the theory that sacred ground tends to remain sacred even though the religion may change. You'll notice the curious red flat-brick walls of the large, roofless structure if you take the main road to the acropolis, or you can see it from on top of the acropolis. You can walk to the Kızıl Avlu, or stop your taxi there on your way to or from the acropolis.

Çarşı Hamamı

Bergama's central Turkish bath is used by tourists and locals alike, and charges about US$2, a mere fraction of the inflated İstanbul bath prices.

Places to Stay – bottom end
First choice is the family-run *Acroteria Pension* (☎ (232) 633 2469, 632 1047, fax 633 1720), Bankalar Caddesi, Çarşı Hamamı Yanı 11, down a narrow alley just east of the Çarşı Hamamı (follow the signs). Tidy small rooms with tiny showers cluster around a quiet, vine-shaded court. The family provides informative tips, tea and meals on demand. Double rooms cost US$15 in summer.

A hundred metres west on the opposite side of the main street, *Pergamon Pension* (☎ (232) 633 2395), Bankalar Caddesi 3, Polis Karakolu Yanı, is a distant second choice, an old stone house right next to the city's police station. Doubles without running water cost US$8, those with shower are US$12. Avoid the 'large room' with five beds, which is subject to kitchen smells. There's a restaurant with fountain in the courtyard.

Just off Cumhuriyet Meydanı is the *Hotel Yıldır* (☎ (232) 633 6483), entered by Çatal Çıkmazı to the left of the Tekel building. It's not at all as grand as it looks from the outside. The hotel (more like a pension) is on the 2nd floor, is quieter than some, and charges US$18 for a double with private shower.

Manolya Pension (☎ (232) 633 4488, 633 2583), Tanpınar Sokak 5, is managed by the people who run the Manolya Pastanesi on the corner of the main street just outside the bus station. Ask at the pastane for price and availability, then follow the signs 400m. The owner is fairly helpful.

Pension Aktan (☎ (232) 663 4000), İzmir Caddesi 18, is on the main road 120m southwest of the bus station (towards İzmir), on the right-hand side. It's clean and friendly, and charges US$18 for a double room with twin beds and shower.

Böblingen Pension (☎ (232) 633 2153), Asklepion Caddesi 2, run by the Altın family who spent many years in Germany, is quiet, cheap and friendly, charging US$15 for a double. Follow the main street west towards the highway, turn right on the road to the Asclepion, and look up to the right to see the pension.

Camping *Hotel Berksoy* (see following) and, just west of it, *Bergama Camping* have sites for tents, caravans and camper vans. Sometimes a cheaper place will pop up for a brief life nearer to the coastal highway.

Places to Stay – middle
Bergama's nicest place to stay is the three-star, 57-room *Hotel Berksoy* (☎ (232) 633 2595, fax 633 5346), PK (PO Box) 19, two km west of the centre on the road out to the main highway. Set back from the road in verdant grounds, it's a motel-style building with a restaurant, bar, tennis court and swimming pool for US$55 a double in season, breakfast included. Staff tend to be glum, though.

Just west of the Berksoy, the *Hotel İskender* (☎ (232) 633 2123, fax 633 1245) is a standard three-star high-rise, newer than the Berksoy and charging a bit more.

Between the Berksoy and the bus station are several more hotels, including the three-star *Asude Hotel* (☎ (232) 663 1669, 663 3067, fax 663 3143), İzmir Caddesi 93, with slightly cheaper rates. Its 52 rooms have satellite TVs and minibars, but some are noisier than the Berksoy's.

The 20-room *Hotel Serapion* (☎ (232) 633 2663), İzmir Caddesi 75, rates two stars and posts prices of US$35/40 a single/double, but eagerly offers doubles for US$30 if it's not busy. The older, somewhat faded *Efsane Hotel* (☎ (232) 632 6350, fax 632 6353), İzmir Caddesi 86, across the road, rates two stars for its 22 bath-equipped rooms, and charges about the same.

The 42-room *Tusan Bergama Moteli* (☎ (232) 633 1173), Çatı Mevkii, near the junction of the highway and the road into town, is Bergama's oldest touristic hotel but is still nice. It has a restaurant and a quiet location in the middle of nowhere. Rooms with a bath cost US$24/35 a single/double; breakfast costs another US$4.

Places to Eat
There are several small eateries near the Pergamon and Acroteria pensions and the Çarşı Hamamı on the main street. *Gözde*

Yemek ve Kebap Salonu has tidy streetside tables and an assortment of ready foods and grills. The *Adil Lokanta ve Kebap Salonu,* across the street and up the steps in the shady parklet called the Eski Bahçıvan Pazarı, is even more pleasant, and cheaper. *Doyum 2 Lokantası,* on the main street a few steps to the west, is modern and has a longer menu. Any of these places can provide a good three-course meal for US$4 to US$6.

About 400m north-east of these restaurants and 150m before the Red Basilica is a small plaza (meydan). *Meydan Restaurant* is the one with the pleasant vine-shaded front terrace, serving shish or döner kebap for US$2, and half a roasted chicken for US$2.75.

Across the plaza from the Meydan is the *Sarmaşık Lokantası,* a villagers' place without streetside tables, but with good hearty hazır yemek stews and lower prices. For more cheap places, walk south-west along the main street to find simpler places such as *Şen Kardeşler* and *Çiçek Sever Kebap Salonu,* where full meals cost US$3 or US$4.

The *Bergama Restaurant,* midway between the bus station and the museum, is used by tour groups. It's more expensive, but it also is familiar with foreigners' wishes.

At the acropolis and Asclepion there are soft drinks for sale, but no food.

Getting There & Away

Whether you approach Bergama from the north or south, check to see if your bus actually stops *in* Bergama at the Otobüs Terminali. Any bus will drop you along the highway at the turn off to Bergama, but you will have to hitchhike seven km into town in this case. Hitching is pretty easy, except in the evening.

Ask the driver, *Bergama otogarına gidiyor musunuz?* (BEHR-gah-mah oh-toh-GAHR-uh-NAH gee-dee-YOHR moo-soo-nooz, 'Do you go to Bergama's bus terminal?') Be advised that many drivers will nod *Evet!* (Yes!), and then blithely drop you out at the highway.

The main Otobüs Terminali is on the main street at the west end of the centre. There is a supplemental minibus station off the east end of the main street near the Kızıl Avlu.

Following are the major routes. Note that bus traffic dies down dramatically in late afternoon and evening, so if you're headed onward, check schedules and reserve your seat earlier in the day. Several bus companies have ticket offices on the main street not far from the Tourism Information Office.

Ayvalık – 50 km, 45 minutes, US$3; many buses from highway junction, few from Bergama's Otobüs Terminali

Dikili – 30 km, 35 minutes, US$1.50; frequent minibuses

İstanbul – Though there are a few direct night buses between Bergama and İstanbul, it is far cheaper and, surprisingly, quicker to travel via İzmir.

İzmir – 100 km, 1¾ hours, US$4; Pamukkale runs buses almost every half-hour; Bergama municipal buses ('Bergama Belediyesi') run eight times daily

Buses to other destinations are not all that frequent. In winter, you may find yourself changing buses in İzmir or Balıkesir to get to Ankara, Bursa or İstanbul.

Getting Around

On Foot Bergama can be a tiring town if you aren't used to walking. Here are some distances from the Otobüs Terminali:

To Museum – 200m
To Tourism Information Office – 400m
To Acroteria Pension – 700m
To Meydan Restaurant – one km
To Kızıl Avlu (Red Basilica) – 1.2 km
To Asclepion – two km
To Acropolis – 6.2 km

If you're in good shape and don't mind walking, but you have limited time, find others to share a taxi to the top of the acropolis, then walk down the hill to the Kızıl Avlu. Walking down through the various levels of the ruined city is the best way to see the site in any case. From the Kızıl Avlu, walk through the market district into town, have lunch and take a taxi, or hitch, or walk to the Asclepion, depending upon your budget, your level of fatigue and your schedule.

Taxi Tours The standard taxi-tour rates (per car) from town are:

Acropolis – one way: US$5
Acropolis – one hour's waiting, then return to town: US$10
Acropolis – one hour's waiting, then to Kızıl Avlu (short stop), to museum (15 minutes' waiting), to Asclepion (30 minutes' waiting), then return to town: US$21

Taxis for hire cluster near the Tourism Information Office and near the market by the Meydan Restaurant.

ÇANDARLI

The comely little resort town of Çandarlı, dominated by a small but stately Genoese castle, is 11 km west of the main highway, and 18.5 km south of Dikili. The castle and the village at its feet are on a peninsula which juts southward into the Aegean. It ranks very high on my list of pleasant places for a few days' quiet beach-and-sea time. Local tourism fills most of the small pensions and hotels in high summer, while the village shops cater to the owners of the villas on the outskirts. Most of the town's lodgings close in late October until April.

The main square, the weekly Friday market and the commercial section of the village are to the east of the castle; most hotels and pensions are to the west, facing the uncrowded coarse-sand beach. The PTT is on the market square, a few dozen metres south of the main square.

Places to Stay

Near the main square on the eastern side of the castle, *Kaya Pension* (☎ (232) 673 3058) is central but noisy, with beds for US$7 per person, breakfast included. Get a room high up, with less noise and better views. The bus stop is right near the Kaya.

Hotel Diamond (☎ (232) 673 3893, fax 673 3894), Vali Şentürk Caddesi 17, obvious in the centre, is modern and comfy with a seaside restaurant and shower-equipped rooms for US$26 a double, breakfast included.

Walk across the peninsula along the main road near the bus stop and you'll reach the beach near the *Otel Samyeli* (☎ (232) 673 3428, 673 3461), simple but bright and clean, with sea views from some rooms, for US$22 a double with breakfast.

Inland a block from the Samyeli are several cheaper places, among them the very basic *Gül Pansiyon*. Follow the signs along İncirli Çeşme Sokak behind the Samyeli to the *Bağış Pansiyon* (☎ (232) 673 2459), with no sea views but a nice courtyard and a low price of US$16 a double, breakfast included.

The *Senger Pansiyon* (☎ & fax (232) 673 3117), down to the left on the waterfront as you face the Samyeli, is run by a family which spends its winters in Germany. Attractive, well-kept rooms cost the same. The Senger restaurant is quite good as well.

Near the Senger, the *Oral Pansiyon* (☎ & fax (232) 673 3122) is older, friendly, and cheaper at US$18 a double with private shower and breakfast.

In the other direction along the beach, towards the tip of the peninsula, the *Martı Motel* (☎ (232) 673 3441) is simple, with a verdant terrace restaurant and views of the sea. The *Philippi Pansiyon* (☎ (232) 673 3053), 200m south of the Martı, is a better choice: a modern house with a little terrace café and obliging owners. The rate for either place is US$28 a double, breakfast and dinner included.

Places to Eat

Locals prefer the little restaurants around the main square which, though not as pleasant as the 'touristic' places to the west, are cheaper. The *Temiz Ocak Pide Salonu* ('Tidy Hearth'), between the Kaya Pansiyon and the market, serves pides for less than US$2 at a few streetside tables. *Çarşı Lokantası*, to the right of the PTT facing the market square, serves good cheap grilled meats. Otherwise, try the pension and hotel restaurants, especially the Senger.

Getting There & Away

Sebat Otobüsleri runs buses between Çandarlı and İzmir and Dikili several times daily. It also operates several daily minibuses to and from Bergama.

FOÇA

Old Ottoman-Greek stone houses line a sinuous shore crowded with fishing boats. On a hill in the town a Genoese fortress (1275) continues its slow centuries of crumbling. Turkish sailors in nautical whites crowd the cheaper cafés, while the more expensive ones are a babble of European languages. This is Foça (FOH-chah, population 12,000), sometimes called Eski Foça, a pleasant resort town which resembles Kuşadası in the 1970s, before Kuşadası exploded into hyper-tourism.

Eski Foça, the ancient Phocaea, was founded before 600 BC and flourished during the 5th century BC. During their golden age, the Phocaeans were famous mariners, sending swift vessels powered by 50 oars into the Aegean, Mediterranean and Black seas. They were also great colonists, having founded Samsun on the Black Sea as well as towns in southern Italy, Corsica, France and Spain.

Little remains of the ancient city: a ruined theatre, some bits of wall, and a monumental tomb *(anıt mezarı)* seven km east of the town (west of the town of Bağarası) on the way to the İzmir highway.

In recent centuries this was an Ottoman Greek fishing and trading town, but it's now a middle-class Turkish resort with yachts bobbing in the harbour and holiday villas being built on the outskirts. Harbour seals cavort in the bay, enjoying local efforts aimed at their well-being. Several fountains in the centre are renowned for the sweetness of their water, indicated by the lines of people waiting to fill plastic bottles at them.

Orientation & Information

Foça's circular bay is partially divided by a peninsula which juts in from the south-east, dividing the eastern part of the bay into the 'Small Sea' *(Küçük Deniz)* to the north and the 'Big Sea' *(Büyük Deniz)* to the south.

The bus station, on the eastern edge of the Büyük Deniz, is only a few metres south of the main square. Walk north through the square with its Tourism Information Office (☎ (232) 812 1222; open 8.30 am to 7 pm, weekends 10 am to 1 pm and 3 to 7 pm), PTT and shady park. Pass the PTT (☎ 812 1000) keeping it on your right to find the town's restaurants (350m from the bus station) and pensions (600 to 700m from the bus station), along the eastern shore of the Küçük Deniz. Foça's postal code is 35680.

Foça's Castles

West of the Küçük Deniz, Aşıklar Caddesi passes before some modern apartment blocks as it rounds the peninsula which holds the fortress called **Beşkapılar** (Five Gates), built by the Genoese, repaired by the Ottomans, and partially restored in recent times. On the south-west side is the *Amfitiyatro Çay Bahçesi*, a tea garden set up in an ancient odeon.

Another fortress, the **Dışkale** (External Fortress) guards the approaches to the town from its perch at the end of the peninsula which shapes the south-western arc of the bay.

North to Yeni Foça

The road north from Eski Foça to Yeni Foça passes several camping grounds, resort hotels and holiday villa clusters, offering dramatic sea views, small coves and beaches, and numerous opportunities for rough or organised camping and/or swimming and water sports.

Yeni Foça, 25 km north of Foça and 12 km west of the Çanakkale-İzmir highway, has a few old stone houses, many more new houses, hotels, condos and holiday villages, and a sand-and-pebble beach, all ranged around a picture-perfect bay which must have been created by nature expressly for water sports.

Places to Stay

Most of Foça's lodgings are little pensions charging between US$7 and US$12 for a double room, and small hotels charging up to US$30 for double rooms with bath. Here is what you'll encounter as you walk north from the bus station.

Hotel Kaan, a few steps from the bus

station, is cheap at US$7 a double, but run-down and not very comfortable or quiet. Keep walking, and go along the waterfront street (Sahil Caddesi).

Hotel Karaçam (☎ (232) 812 1416, fax 812 2042), Sahil Caddesi 70, is an Ottoman house (1881) fixed up, fairly comfortable, with friendly management and the advantages of a roof-terrace bar, streetside café, fancy furniture in the lobby, and lots of cats. A few of the 22 rooms have water views. Rates are US$28/38 a single/double in season, breakfast included. The adjoining *Villa Dedem* (☎ (232) 812 2838, fax 812 1700) at No 66 is similar.

Walk inland near Sinbat's Café to find the *Pansiyon Bir* (☎ (232) 812 1108), 187 Sokak 6, a quiet family-run lodging charging US$14 a double with private shower.

Ensar Aile Pansiyonu (☎ (232) 812 1777, fax 812 1401), İsmetpaşa Mahallesi, 161 Sokak 15, is a modern building one block inland from the water, charging US$12 a double for its 14 rooms with private showers. The housekeeping could be better here. The adjoining 13-room *Siren Pansiyon* (☎ (232) 812 2660) is similar. *Hotel Melaike* (☎ (232) 812 2414, fax 812 1887), 32 Sokak 4, at the end of the street, is modern, quiet, and charges US$22 a double with shower. There are no water views here.

Sempatik Hotel Güneş (☎ (232) 812 2195), 206 Sokak No 11, is nice, new, comfy, and as the name indicates, 'sympathetic'. Rates for the rooms, done in stucco and honey-coloured pine, are US$22 a double.

Even farther along, *Hotel Celep* has plain rooms with bath for US$20 a double, and its own very popular restaurant with water views. Near the Celep are several other pensions, including the *İyigün Café-Pension* across the street, which charges US$6 per person and also has its own restaurant. At the northern end of the street is the *Fokai Pansiyon* (☎ (232) 812 1765), right on the water.

Camping The coast north of Foça is sculpted into small coves with sandy beaches, mostly backed by holiday condominium developments, but a few have camping places. The closest is the *Belediye Halk Plajı* (Municipal Beach), three km north of Eski Foça.

Farther up the coast are smaller, less well organised private camping grounds, the nicest of which is the *Yeni Pınar Camping*, six km north of Foça, with electrical and water hook-ups in an olive grove on the beach, and no condos nearby. Less than four km farther north (10 km from Foüa), *Acar Camping* is set on a beautiful beach. Another 3.5 km brings you to the unfortunately-named Club Pollen, a hillside full of holiday flats, but a km beyond it there's a small cove with some fishing industry. Finally, 17 km north of Foça and four km before reaching Yeni Foça, the *Azak Restaurant*, set on its own cove, has places for campers.

Places to Eat

For cheap fare, try the *Sahil Pide Salonu* on the south-west side of the bus station, popular with sailors at Foça's naval base because it's the cheapest place in town. *Zümrüt*, facing the main square, is also cheap, with meat stews for US$1.50 or so, but *Julianna's Restaurant* next door is more popular, especially with foreigners. The *İmren Restaurant*, two short blocks to the north, is cheaper still, with good sulu yemekler (stews), making a two-course meal possible for US$3. For grills, try the neighbouring *Rumeli Köftecisi*, which also has a few outside tables.

Be sure to ask prices first at any of the restaurants along the water, particularly if you are ordering fish. All waterfront restaurants – *Gaziantep, Sinbat's, Yengeç, Celep, Gemici, Foça*, all in a row – charge from US$12 to US$20 for a full fish dinner, half that for meat. The Celep was best by far at my last visit; try the chocolate pudding with vanilla ice cream. All are particularly good for sunset dining.

Getting There & Away

Hanedan-Plajlar dolmuşes (US$0.50) run through the town periodically in the summer, ferrying passengers between the town centre and the northern beach (Belediye Halk Plajı).

Foça is 83 km south of Bergama, 73 km

south of Çandarlı, 70 km north-west of İzmir, and 25 km west of the İzmir-Çanakkale highway. Virtually all bus traffic is to and from İzmir (hourly buses in summer, 1¼ hours, US$2), with a stop midway in Menemen (37 km, 35 minutes, US$1.25). If you're bound for somewhere other than İzmir (Manisa in particular), it's best to change buses in Menemen rather than to wait out on the highway.

MANİSA

A road goes east 30 km to the town of Manisa (mah-NEES-ah, population 160,000), the ancient town of Magnesia ad Sipylus. It's a modern little city with an ancient past. An early king was Tantalus, from whose name we get the word 'tantalise'. The early, great Ottoman sultans favoured it as a residence, and for a while the province of Manisa was the training ground for promising Ottoman princes.

During the War of Independence, retreating Greek soldiers wreaked terrible destruction on the town. After they passed through, Manisa's 18,000 historic buildings had been reduced to only 500.

Orientation & Information

Doğu Caddesi is the main street in the commercial district. The historic mosques are only a few hundred metres to the south along İbrahim Gökçen Caddesi. The train station is less than one km north-east of the centre; the otogar, 600m north-west.

Manisa's Tourism Information Office (☎ (236) 231 2541, fax 232 7423) is in the Özel İdare İşhanı building, Yarhasanlar Mahallesi, Doğu Caddesi 14/3.

Things to See

As you might expect, there are several old mosques, among them the **Muradiye Camii** (1586) with nice tilework. The adjoining building, constructed originally as a soup kitchen, is now the **Manisa Müzesi** (open from 9 am to noon and 1 to 5 pm, closed on Monday), with the standard collections, including some fine mosaics from the ruins of Sardis. Near the museum is the ancient **tomb of Saruhan Bey**. The **Sultan Camii** (1572) has some gaudy painting, but an agreeable hamam next door. Perched on the steep hillside above the town centre is the **Ulu Cami** (1366), ravished by the ages, and not as impressive as the view from the teahouse next to it. Other historic mosques in town are the **Hatuniye** (1490) and the **İlyas Bey** (1363).

Special Events

On four days around the spring equinox (21 March) each year, Manisa rejoices in the Mesir Şenlikleri, a festival celebrating *Mesir macunu* (power gum). Legend says that over 450 years ago, a local pharmacist named Merkez Müslihiddin Efendi concocted a potion to cure a mysterious ailment of Hafza Sultan, mother of Sultan Süleyman the Magnificent. The queen mother, delighted with her swift recovery, ordered that the amazing elixir be distributed to the people of Manisa at her expense. In fact, the Ottomans had a long-standing custom of eating spiced sweets at *Nevruz*, the Persian new year (spring equinox).

Hafza Sultan's bank account is long closed, so the municipal authorities pick up the tab for the 10 tonnes of Mesir, mixed from sugar and 40 spices and ingredients. Townsfolk in period costumes re-enact the mixing of the potion, then throw it from the dome of the Sultan Camii. Mesir is credited by locals with improving the circulation, calming the nerves, stimulating hormones, increasing appetite, immunising one against poisonous stings and bites, and doubling tourist revenue.

Places to Stay

The 34-room, two-star *Hotel Arma* (☎ (236) 231 1980), Doğu Caddesi 14, has a restaurant, clean rooms and prices of US$20/28 a single/double. Other than the Arma and the four-star *Büyük Saruhan* (☎ (236) 233 2380. fax 233 2648), Nusret Köklü Caddesi 1 in Laleli, there are few decent places to stay. Everyone, whatever their business, stays in İzmir and drives to Manisa for the day.

Into İzmir

Coming from Manisa, the road passes through the suburb of **Bornova**, once the summer residence of wealthy Levantine traders. Some of their mansions still stand, most now converted for public use as municipal offices, schools and the like. The Aegean University (Ege sniversitesi) is here as well. İzmir city buses run from Bornova to the centre of İzmir.

İZMİR

İzmir (EEZ-meer, population two million), with its distinct Mediterranean ambience, is Turkey's third-largest city and its major port on the Aegean. Its setting is certainly dramatic, sprawling around a great bay and backed by mountains to the east and south. Most of the city is quite modern, with broad boulevards radiating from a series of hubs. The streets are lined with stucco-and-glass apartment and office blocks, and dotted with shady streetside cafés, though here and there the red-tile roof and bull's-eye window of a 19th-century warehouse hide in the shadow of an office tower. When you come upon an old mosque – so common in other Turkish cities – it doesn't really seem to belong in İzmir.

Most of the remains from İzmir's long and eventful history have been swept away by war, fire and earthquake. If you're passing through, you can enjoy a day here seeing its few antiquities and museums, exploring its labyrinthine bazaar, strolling by the palm-shaded cafés along its waterfront, and enjoying the sweeping views from its 2000-year-old castle.

History

İzmir owes its special atmosphere, indeed its entire appearance, to an eventful and turbulent history. What you see today is new because it has risen from the ashes of Ottoman İzmir since 1923, when a Greek invasion and a disastrous fire razed most of the city. Before that year, İzmir was Smyrna, the most western-like and cosmopolitan of Turkish cities, where more citizens were Christian and Jewish than Muslim, and there were thousands of foreign diplomats, traders, merchants and sailors. Its connections with Greece and Europe were close and continuous. To the Turks it was 'Infidel Smyrna'.

İzmir's commercial connections with Europe began in 1535, but the city is far older. The first settlement, at Bayraklı near the eastern end of the bay, was built by Aeolians in the 10th century BC, but there were probably people here as far back as 3000 BC. The city's name comes from the goddess Myrina, the prevalent deity before the coming of the Aeolians who also worshipped Nemesis. Famous early citizens of Smyrna included the poet Homer, the founder of western literature, who lived before 700 BC.

The city began its history of war and destruction early, for the Aeolians were overcome by the Ionians, who in turn were conquered by the Lydians from Sardis. Around 600 BC, the Lydians destroyed the city and it lay in ruins until the coming of Alexander the Great (356-323 BC).

Alexander the Great re-founded Smyrna on Mt Pagus, now called Kadifekale (kah-dee-FEH-kah-leh, Velvet Fortress), in the centre of the modern city. He erected the fortification which, much repaired over the ages, still crowns the hill.

Smyrna's luck changed during the struggles over the spoils of Alexander's empire. The city sided with Pergamum, the Aegean power-to-be. Later, it welcomed Roman rule and benefited greatly from it. When an earthquake destroyed the city in 178 AD, Emperor Marcus Aurelius sent money and men to aid in the reconstruction. Under Byzantium, the later Roman Empire, it became one of the busiest ports along the coast.

As Byzantium's power declined, various armies including the Arabs, Seljuk Turks, Genoese and crusaders marched in, and often out again. When Tamerlane arrived in 1402 he destroyed the city, true to form, but after he left, the Ottomans took over in 1415 and things began to look better.

In 1535, Süleyman the Magnificent signed the Ottomans' first-ever commercial treaty (with François I of France), which permitted foreign merchants to reside in the sultan's dominions. After that humble start, İzmir became Turkey's most sophisticated commercial city. Its streets and buildings took on a quasi-European appearance, and a dozen languages were spoken in its cafés. Any worthwhile merchant was expected to be fluent in Arabic, English, French, German, Greek, Italian and Turkish, and it didn't hurt to know Armenian, Ladino Spanish or Russian as well.

The Ottoman Empire was defeated along with Germany in WWI, and the victorious Allies sought to carve the sultan's vast dominions into spheres of influence. Some Greeks had always dreamed of re-creating the long-lost Byzantine Empire. In 1920, with Allied encouragement, the Greeks took a gamble, invaded İzmir, seized Bursa and headed towards Ankara. In fierce fighting on the outskirts of Ankara, where Atatürk's provisional government had its headquarters, the foreign forces were stopped, then turned around and pushed back. The Greek defeat turned to a rout and the once-powerful army, half its ranks taken prisoner, scorched the earth and fled to ships waiting in İzmir. The day Atatürk took İzmir, 9 September 1922, was the moment of victory in the Turkish War of Independence. (It's now the big local holiday.)

A disastrous fire broke out during the final mopping-up operations and destroyed most of the city. Though a tragedy, it allowed a modern city of wide streets to rise from the ashes.

Orientation

İzmir has wide boulevards and an apparent sense of orderliness, but it is in fact somewhat difficult to negotiate. This is because the numerous roundabouts (traffic circles), with their streets radiating like spokes from a hub, don't give you the sense of direction a street grid does.

The city's two main avenues run parallel to the waterfront. The waterfront street is officially Atatürk Caddesi, which is what you will see in written addresses, but locals call it the Birinci Kordon (beer-EEN-jee kohr-DOHN, First Cordon). Just inland from it is Cumhuriyet Bulvarı (joom-hoor-ee-YEHT bool-vahr-uh, Republic Blvd), the İkinci Kordon (ee-KEEN-jee, Second Cordon).

The city's two main squares are along these two parallel avenues. The very centre is Konak Meydanı (Government House Square). Here you will find the municipality buildings, the Ottoman clock tower (İzmir's symbol), the little Konak Camii mosque decorated with coloured Kütahya tiles, and a dock for ferries to Karşıyaka, the suburb across the bay.

Konak also has an entrance to the bazaar. Anafartalar Caddesi, the bazaar's main street, winds through İzmir's most picturesque quarters all the way to the Basmane Garı train station. The Basmane area holds dozens of small and medium-priced hotels and restaurants, and many intercity bus ticket offices.

The other main square, Cumhuriyet Meydanı, holds an equestrian statue of Atatürk. It is about a km north of Konak along the two kordons. The PTT, Tourism Information Office, Turkish Airlines office, car-rental offices and expensive hotels are near here.

The section called Çankaya (CHAN-kah-yah) is two long blocks inland, south-east of Cumhuriyet Meydanı.

Another İzmir landmark is the Kültür Parkı (kewl-TEWR pahr-kuh), the city's Culture Park, site of the annual İzmir International Fair. When it's not fair time the grounds provide a pleasant, shady place to walk, sit and rest in, as well as some amusements.

Finally, the hill directly behind the main part of town is crowned by Kadifekale, the 'Velvet Fortress'.

Information

Tourist Offices The Tourism Information Office (☎ (232) 484 2148, fax 489 9278), Gaziosmanpaşa Bulvarı 1/D, is next to Turkish Airlines in the Grand Hotel Efes building. Opening hours are from 8.30 am to

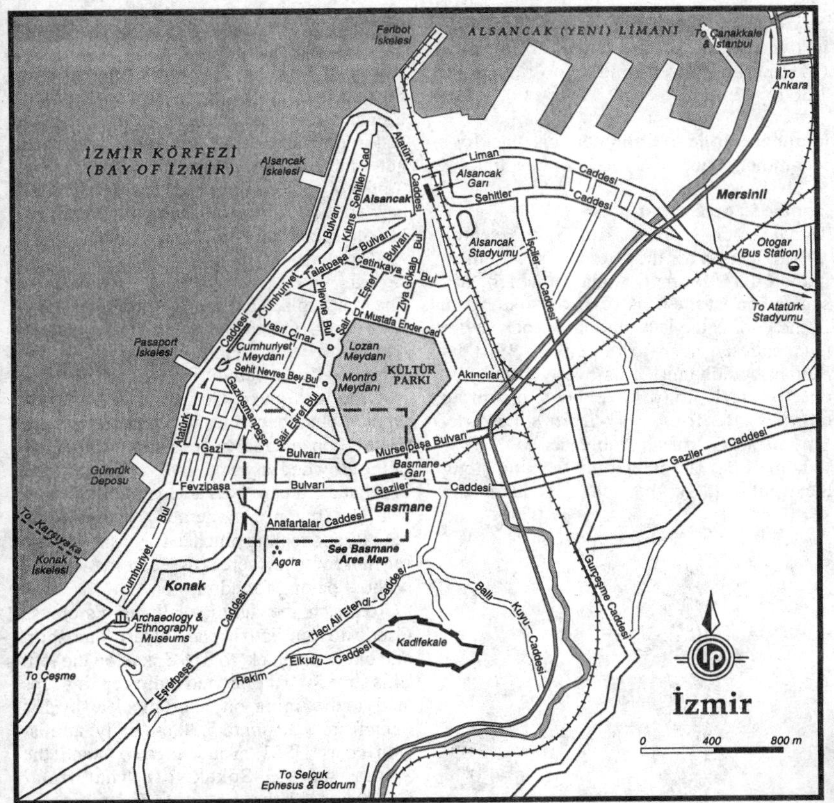

7 pm daily from June to October, till 5.30 pm and closed on Sunday in the off season. There's also an office at Adnan Menderes airport (☎ (232) 251 5480, fax 251 1950). The bus station has a small office as well.

The Tourism Police can be reached on ☎ (232) 421 8652.

Consulates For addresses of foreign consulates, see Embassies in the Facts for the Visitor chapter.

Money Many banks have offices in Konak; Akbank and Türkiye İş Bankası have ATMs here, and there is an İş Bankası ATM in Basmane Garı. You can exchange currency at the PTT on Cumhuriyet Meydanı as well. Bamka Döviz is a currency exchange office on the corner of 1369 and 1364 Sokaks, 1½ blocks west of the little hotels on 1369 Sokak.

Bookshops Try Dünya Aktüel Kitabevi (☎ (232) 463 6877) for foreign periodicals and a few books.

English-language periodicals can be read at the Türk-Amerikan Derneği (Turkish-American Association, ☎ 421 5206), Şehit

Nevres Bey Bulvarı 23-A, at 1379 Sokak, just north-east of the Grand Hotel Efes. Opening hours are Monday to Friday from 1.30 to 6.30 pm.

Medical Services Call your consulate for a recommendation of a doctor or hospital.

Konak & the Bazaar

The heart of İzmir is Konak, the central district named for the Ottoman government mansion (Hükümet Konağı) which still stands here at the back of a park-like plaza. In the park is the late-Ottoman **clock tower** *(saat kulesi)* given to the city in 1901 by Sultan Abdülhamit II. Its overly ornate orientalist style may have been meant to compensate for *gavur İzmir*'s ('infidel Smyrna's') European ambience.

İzmir's bazaar, entered by walking along the right wall of the konak, is large and fascinating. An hour or two of exploration along **Anafartalar Caddesi**, the main street, is a must. You can also enter the bazaar at Basmane, or from Eşrefpaşa Caddesi near Çankaya after your visit to the Agora. Get lost in the bazaar, and when you're ready to get out, ask for directions to Basmane, Çankaya or Konak. Note that virtually all bazaar shops close on Sunday, and there's little to see on that day.

In Konak, İzmir's central district, is the late Ottoman clock tower given to the city in 1901 by Sultan Abdülhamit II.

Agora

The marketplace built on the orders of Alexander was ruined in an earthquake in 178 AD, but there is much remaining from the Agora as it was rebuilt by Marcus Aurelius just after the quake. Corinthian colonnades, vaulted chambers and a reconstructed arch fill this conspicuously open spot in the midst of the crowded city, and give you a good idea of what a Roman 'bazaar' looked like.

If you're only moderately interested in agoras, and feeling pinched for cash, you can see most of what there is to see from the street without paying for admission.

To reach the agora, walk up Eşrefpaşa Caddesi from Fevzipaşa Bulvarı, one short and one long block, to 816 Sokak on the left. This street of bakeries and radio-repair shops leads to the Agora, one short block away. It's open from 8.30 am to 5.30 pm daily; admission costs US$1. You can also reach the Agora via 943 Sokak, off Anafartalar Caddesi near the Hatuniye Camii in the bazaar. Follow the signs.

Archaeology & Ethnology Museums

These two museums are in Bahri Baba Park, just a short walk up the hill from Konak, along the road up to Kadifekale called the Varyant. The entrance is positioned on the one-way road which brings traffic down the hillside so, to reach the museums, walk up that way. If you walk up the road for uphill traffic, you'll walk all the way around the museums but you won't be able to enter.

The two museums are open from 9 am to noon and 1 to 5 pm, closed Monday; admission costs US$1 per museum.

The Arkeoloji Müzesi is in a modern

River God statue, İzmir Archaeology Museum. The museum has fine exhibits of Egyptian, Greek and Roman statuary.

building. You enter on a floor with quite fine exhibits of Egyptian, Greek and Roman statuary, then move to an upper level dedicated to terracotta objects, tools and vessels, glassware, metalwork and jewellery of silver and gold. The lower level has tomb statuary and sarcophagi, and also the head of a gigantic statue of Domitian which once stood at Ephesus. Be sure to see the beautiful frieze from the mausoleum at Belevi (250 BC), south of İzmir, and also the high relief of Poseidon and Demeter dating from 200 AD. All plaques in the museum are in English and Turkish.

Perhaps of even more interest is the Etnoğrafya Müzesi, in the old stone building next door. Once İzmir's Department of Public Health, this interesting old building now houses colourful displays demonstrating the folk arts, crafts and customs of the city and its surrounding province. You'll learn about camel wrestling, the potter's craft as practised here, the important craft of tin-plating whereby toxic copper vessels were made safe for kitchen use, felt-making, embroidery, and wood-block printing for scarves and cloth. You can even see how those curious little blue-and-white 'evil eye' beads are made; this craft goes back hundreds, perhaps even thousands, of years.

Other exhibits include an Ottoman chemist's shop, a fully decorated salon from a 19th-century Ottoman residence, an Ottoman bridal chamber, a circumcision celebration room from the same period and a kitchen. Carpet-making is explained, and there are displays of armour, weapons and local costumes.

Kadifekale

The time to ride up the mountain is an hour before sunset. Catch a city bus south of Konak (it may say only 'K Kale' on the sign) and allow 15 or 20 minutes for the ride. The view on all sides is spectacular. Look inside the walls, and even climb up on them if you like. Just on sunset, the muezzins give the call to prayer from İzmir's minarets, and the wave of sound rolls across the city as the lights twinkle on.

Near the gate in the walls are a few little terrace teahouses where you can have a seat and a tea, soft drink or beer.

Other Sights

As you make your way around town, you will certainly see the **equestrian statue of Atatürk** in Cumhuriyet Meydanı. It symbolises Atatürk's leadership as he began the counteroffensive from Ankara during the War of Independence. His battle order to the troops on the first day of the offensive (26 August 1922) read 'Soldiers, your goal is the Aegean'.

The **Kültür Parkı**, or Culture Park, is a pleasant place for a quiet walk or picnic away from the city bustle. In late August and early September, the fairgrounds hold centre stage in this city, during the İzmir International Fair.

Had it with the crowded, noisy city? Head down to the ferry dock on the waterfront in Konak, and board a ferry for the ride over to **Karşıyaka**, on the far side of the bay. The view is beautiful, the air fresh and cool. The voyage over and back takes an hour, perhaps 75 minutes, and the whole trip costs less than US$1.

Special Events

From mid-June to mid-July, performances of music and dance are organised under the rubric of the International İzmir Festival.

Venues are often Çeşme and Ephesus as well as İzmir. Check with the İzmir Kültür Vakfı (İzmir Culture Foundation), Mahmut Esat Bozkurt Caddesi 4-6, Alsancak, or the Tourism Information Office for current performances and locations.

The annual İzmir International Fair is an amusement and industry show which takes place from 20 August to 9 September. Hotel space can be tight during the fair.

Places to Stay

İzmir has lots of hotels at all prices. A few steps from Basmane Garı are dozens of small, cheap hotels, and a good selection of mid-priced places. The top-end hotels are near Cumhuriyet Meydanı.

Places to Stay – bottom end

The quarter named Akıncı (also called Yenigün) is bounded by Fevzipaşa Bulvarı, Basmane Meydanı, Anafartalar Caddesi and Eşrefpaşa Caddesi. Right next to Basmane (BAHS-mah-NEH), İzmir's main train station, it's a low-budget traveller's dream come true. Several entire streets are lined with cheap places to stay and equally cheap places to eat. The Basmane Hamamı, adjoining the Basmane mosque facing the station, is a convenient Turkish bath. Bus ticket offices for your onward journey are only 50m away in 9 Eylül (doh-KOOZ ey-LURL) Meydanı. The better bus companies have shuttle buses to take you between 9 Eylül and the otogar.

AEGEAN TURKEY

1296 Sokak For the cheapest places, walk out the front door of Basmane station, turn left, cross the large street and walk up shady Anafartalar Caddesi. Take the first small street on your right, which is 1296 Sokak, lined with small hotels, some in new buildings, others in once-grand old İzmir houses with coloured glass, fancy woodwork and mosaic floors, now somewhat dilapidated. The cheapest of these charge about US$7 for a waterless double room. Prices go as high as US$12 for a room with private shower. The hotels seem to improve in quality and fall in price the farther you walk. Look at several rooms before making your choice.

In the Bazaar Several other hotels are in the midst of the bazaar. Walk along Anafartalar Caddesi through the bazaar to the Hatuniye Camii (also called the Kuşlu Cami). Just past it, on the right, is the *Otel Saray* (☎ (232) 483 6946), Anafartalar Caddesi 635, Tilkilik. It's a backpackers' favourite charging US$14 for a clean double room with sink, opening onto a small enclosed central courtyard. Get a room on the upper floor if you can.

You can actually do better at the *Otel Hikmet* (☎ (232) 484 2672), 945 Sokak 26, Tilkilik/Dönertaş, up the side street opposite the Hatuniye Camii. It's a step up in quality and down in price, with newer, clean double rooms with sinks and showers costing US$13; toilets are down the hall, not in the rooms.

1368 & 1369 Sokaks Should you want a slightly better class of hotel, go out the Basmane station door and straight down the right-hand side of Fevzipaşa Bulvarı to the three-star Hotel Hisar. Turn right onto 1368 Sokak, which is lined with over a dozen little hotels charging about US$12 to US$18 for a double room with a private shower. Most give you a choice of rooms with or without private shower, and most are relatively quiet. Prices tend to rise and fall with room availability. Look at several before you choose.

Readers' Recommendation Readers of this guide have also found the *Çakıroğlu Family Pension* (☎ (232) 892 2582), Atatürk Mahallesi, Kubilay Sokak (369 Sokak) 9, to offer good value, with clean shower-equipped double rooms for US$10. Make sure you get a room with a window to the outside.

Another pension that's found favour is the *International House Pension* (☎ (232) 484 6719) at Mithatpaşa Caddesi 435, a five-minute bus ride from Konak, or a US$2 taxi ride. Run by an engaging couple named Cassie and Özer Ataol, the charge is US$4 to US$10 per person for bed and breakfast, with hot showers and cooking and washing facilities available.

Places to Stay – middle

Basmane Of the moderately priced hotels in

the Basmane area, the quietest and best is the marble-fronted *Hotel Baylan* (☎ (232) 483 1426, fax 483 3844), 1299 Sokak 8. Accommodating staff, clean, modern (if quite small) air-con rooms with shower and TV, private car park and good prices of US$35/53 a single/double (breakfast included) make this two-star, 33-room place the first choice. They'll even give you a 10% discount if you show them this guidebook. Walk up 1296 Sokak and enter through the car park, or turn left onto 1299 Sokak by the Otel Gümüş Palas.

Tanık Otel (☎ (232) 441 2007/8/9, fax 483 1119), 1364 Sokak 13, Çankaya, is also rated two-star. It's grander but a bit farther from Basmane. Walk down Gazi Bulvarı two blocks to find this 36-room hotel charging US$35/50 a single/double with breakfast. Rooms have bathroom, TV and sound insulation, but avoid rooms on busy, noisy Gazi Bulvarı all the same.

Down Fevzipaşa Bulvarı a block from the station is the 63-room *Hotel Hisar* (☎ (232) 484 5400, fax 425 8830), Fevzipaşa Bulvarı 153 (or 1368 Sokak 2), an older but still serviceable three-star place featuring rooms with bath, TV, minibar and air-con for US$30/40 a single/double, breakfast included.

Just around the corner, 1368 Sokak might as well be called Zeybek Sokak after Mr Ömer Zeybek, the rags-to-riches entrepreneur who owns the two-star, 36-room *Hotel Zeybek* (☎ (232) 489 6694, fax 483 5020), 1368 Sokak 5, and the *Grand Hotel Zeybek* (☎ (232) 441 9590, fax 484 6791), facing it across the narrow street. He also owns an adjoining modern baths (sıhhi banyo) and a restaurant here. In the Zeybek, the tiny guest rooms have TVs, fans and bathrooms (some with small tubs), and cost US$32/40 a single/double. The Grand Zeybek charges US$36/50 a single/double for a grander room, breakfast included.

Cumhuriyet Meydanı The three-star, 73-room *Otel Karaca* (☎ (232) 489 1940, fax 483 1498), Necati Bey Bulvarı, 1379 Sokak 55, 35210 Alsancak, is between the Hilton and the Büyük Efes. The quiet yet convenient location, comfortable, modern rooms with TVs and minibars, and English-speaking staff make this a long-time favourite of NATO military and diplomatic families. Rooms cost US$55/75 a single/double, breakfast included.

The three-star, 78-room *Hotel Ismira* (☎ (232) 445 6060, fax 445 6071), Gaziosmanpaşa Bulvarı 28 across from the Hilton, is new, well located, and reasonably priced at US$40/55 a single/double.

Otel İzmir Palas (☎ (232) 421 5583, fax 422 6870), on Vasıf Çınar Bulvarı 2 just off Atatürk Bulvarı, 35210 Alsancak, is a short walk north of Cumhuriyet Meydanı. Well located in the centre, it is a comfy three-star, 148-room place, with sea views from many rooms. Prices are good: US$65/81/95 a single/double/suite officially, but I was quoted a price 30% lower when I asked. The good Deniz Restaurant adjoins.

Otel Marla (☎ (232) 441 4000, fax 441 1150), Kazım Dirik Caddesi 7, 35210 Pasaport, advertises 'five-star comforts at three-star-prices'. Its 68 rooms almost meet this claim, with marble vanities in the baths, trendy décor, satellite TVs, minibars and air-con. The location is quiet, yet only a block from Cumhuriyet Meydanı. Rates are US$50/70/90 for a single/double/suite.

Places to Stay – top end

As you enter İzmir, you can't help noticing the *İzmir Hilton* (☎ (232) 441 6060, fax 441 2277), Gaziosmanpaşa Bulvarı 7, 35210 İzmir, which soars 40 storeys above the centre, the tallest building by far. Its 381 rooms and suites have all the luxuries. There are two tennis courts, two squash courts and an indoor pool. Within the same complex is a shopping centre and car park. Rooms cost from US$110 to US$155 a single, from US$120 to US$180 a double, with tax included. This is İzmir's best.

The five-star, 127-room *Pullman Etap İzmir Hotel* (☎ (232) 489 4090, fax 489 40 89) faces Cumhuriyet Meydanı at Cumhuriyet Bulvarı 138. Part of the worldwide French chain, its air-con, minibar and TV-equipped rooms cost US$115/150/170 a single/double/triple in high summer.

There's another Etap, the four-star *Pullman Etap Konak* (☎ (232) 489 1500, fax 489 1709), Mithatpaşa Caddesi 128, 35260 Konak, just south-west of Konak on the way to the archaeology and ethnography museums. It's smaller (76 rooms) and a bit cheaper. Many rooms have fine sea views.

İzmir's newest four-star is the *Ege Palas* (☎ (232) 463 9090, fax 463 8100), Cumhuriyet Bulvarı 210, 35220 Alsancak, rising 20 storeys above northern Alsancak. Close to Alsancak's café and nightlife, its 109 rooms cost US$100/150 a single/double for a sea view, about 10% less for a land view.

The 400-room *Grand Hotel Efes* (Büyük Efes Oteli, ☎ 484 4300, fax 441 5695), Gaziosman Paşa Bulvarı 1, faces out to sea across Cumhuriyet Meydanı, the city's prime hotel location. For decades it was İzmir's best, but it has not kept up with the competition and now seems to concentrate on revenues from weddings, receptions, and its casino. Double rooms cost US$150 to US$165.

Places to Eat – bottom end

The lowest priced meals are to be found in the same areas as the lowest priced hotels.

Basmane If you're in a hurry, there are four noisy restaurants right across from Basmane station at the beginning of Anafartalar Caddesi. Though hardly atmospheric, they're good for a quick, cheap meal before boarding a train: *Aydın-Denizli-Nazilli*, which fries up local fish (get a freshly-fried one) for US$2; *Ödemiş Azim* and *Ankara*, with good, ready-food stews; and *Tokat* for soups and cheap pide.

On 1296 Sokak are several cheap kebapçıs, including the *Güneydoğu Kebap Salonu*, with meals for US$4 or less. There are also several small eateries at the beginning of Anafartalar Caddesi across from the Basmane Hamamı Turkish bath. But the restaurants on 1368 and 1369 sokaks, just across Fevzipaşa Bulvarı, are much more pleasant and many serve alcohol.

1368 & 1369 Sokaks The *Güzel İzmir Restaurant* (☎ 484 0501), 1368 Sokak 8/B, in front of the hotel of the same name, has kebaps and steam-table dishes, streetside tables and lowish prices. A three-course meal costs about US$5 or US$6.

A few steps away at the junction of 1368 and 1369 Sokaks, the *Marmara Börekçisi* serves large portions of flaky börek and freshly baked pide for about US$2.50, soft drink included.

On 1369 Sokak, look for the similarly cheap *İnci Kebap, Pide ve Lahmacun Salonu* – the restaurant's name is its menu.

Other good choices are farther along 1369 Sokak. A block west on the right-hand side is the *Dört Mevsim Et Lokantası* at 51/A, specialising in meats. The owner, cellular phone in hand, will urge you to take a seat and fill up for about US$5 or US$6.

Anafartalar Caddesi If you're staying at the Hotel Hikmet or Otel Saray, try the modern *Konya Lezzet Lokantası*, on Anafartalar between the two hotels. The *Nazilli Pide Salonu* at Anafartalar 543, closer to Konak, has cheap fresh pide. For a good breakfast, try the *Meşhur Trakya Mandırası*, Anafartalar Caddesi 451.

Vegetarian Food The *Vejeteryan Restaurant*, İzmir's only, is a tiny place at 1375 Sokak 11, a block north of Şehit Nevres Bey Bulvarı, near the Turkish-American Association (ask for the Türk-Amerikan Derneği) and the American Hospital.

Near Konak Enter the bazaar along Anafartalar Caddesi from Konak. At 66, the courtyard of the Meserret building holds the *Meserret Kafeterya*, İzmir's answer to a shopping mall food court, with prices posted prominently. Across the street at 61, in the courtyard of the dilapidated 19th-century Yeni Şükran Oteli, is the *Şükran Lokantası*. It's a bazaar merchants' hang-out which serves booze and food in the atmospheric courtyard. Expect to pay from US$8 to US$10 for a full dinner; it's closed on Sunday.

The teeming bazaar has an assortment of other eateries, including several cheap, quick pidecis.

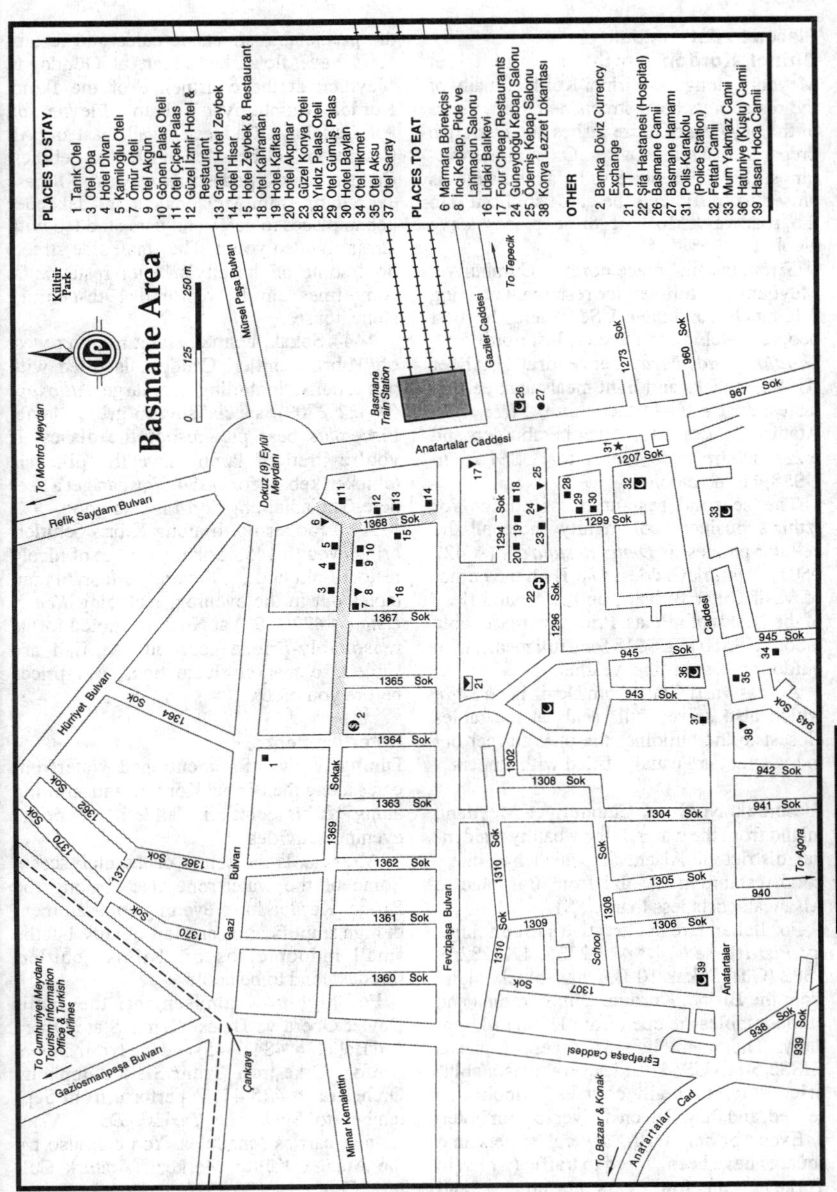

AEGEAN TURKEY

Places to Eat – middle

Birinci Kordon North of Cumhuriyet Meydanı along the Birinci Kordon, many of the restaurants have streetside tables, views of the bay, lots of meze dishes and fresh fish prepared in various ways. On summer evenings, this is the place to be as the street is closed to traffic and the cafés spill out into the roadway. Most of these places serve alcohol.

Sisim, the first place north of Cumhuriyet Meydanı, is a full-service restaurant offering full meals for under US$10 and the best people-watching in the city. Just north of it, *Gördüm* and *Niray* serve draught beer (US$2), snacks and light meals at streetside tables. Just a bit farther north, *Pizzeria Z*, Atatürk Caddesi 186, serves hamburgers and pizza at streetside tables for US$1.25 to US$8, but no alcohol.

The seafood restaurant of choice for İzmir's business community (note all the cellular phones) is *Deniz Restaurant* (☎ 422 0601), Atatürk Caddesi 188-B on the corner of Vasıf Çınar Bulvarı, on the ground floor of the Otel İzmir Palas. Prices are reasonable (about US$10 to US$18 for a full meal), with outdoor tables in fine weather.

Across Vasıf Çınar from Deniz is *La Sera*, which also serves full meals at the tables closest to the building; the ones farther out in the street are usually filled with sippers.

Alsancak North of Cumhuriyet Meydanı, inland from the water, is the wealthy residential district of Alsancak, which has many good restaurants. A taxi from Basmane to Alsancak costs less than US$1.

For Italian fare in attractive surroundings, try *Pizza Venedik* (☎ 422 2735, 422 1826), 1382 (Gül) Sokak 10-B, a half-block inland from the Birinci Kordon. Dining rooms and outdoor tables are open from 11 am to 11 pm daily. The menu lists 16 types of pizzas (US$2.50 to US$4) and several reasonably-priced Italian main courses. Alcohol is served, and they'll even deliver to your hotel.

Even farther north, several streets and squares have been closed to traffic (which in Turkey means fewer cars, not no cars) and the predictable streetside cafés and restaurants have flourished. Start at Gündoğdu Meydanı at the confluence of the İkinci Kordon (Cumhuriyet Bulvarı), Plevne and Ali Çetinkaya Caddesis, walk east on Ali Çetinkaya and bear left on Kıbrıs Şehitleri Caddesi, also a pedestrian way. You'll pass everything from McDonald's and İskender kebap places to cafés and bars studded with İzmir's gilded youth. The small side streets hold some of the city's better restaurants, sometimes amidst restored 19th-century stone houses.

1444 Sokak, a small street running west off Kıbrıs Şehitleri Caddesi, is filled with restaurants, including the large *Altınkapı* (☎ 422 2709), specialising in grilled lamb. Placemats bear pictures of the dishes. If you're tired of lamb, have the piliç şiş (chicken kebap) for US$4. You can get a beer here. The adjoining *Sofra* is also good.

A bit farther north along Kıbrıs Şehitleri brings you to 1453 Sokak, a street of nicely restored old houses. Several restaurants put tables out in the evening, including *Kemal Usta* (☎ 422 3190) at No 20/A, noted for its reasonably-priced seafood. As fish are subject to market fluctuations, ask prices before you order.

Entertainment

Dining at the aforementioned waterfront cafés along the Birinci Kordon, and strolling along Kıbrıs Şehitleri Caddesi, are prime evening activities.

Alsancak is the centre of the club scene. Some of the waterfront places along the Birinci Kordon have evening entertainment of high amplification and low quality, but the small indoor clubs off Kıbrıs Şehitleri Caddesi tend to be cooler.

For highbrow amusement, the İzmir Devlet Opera ve Balesi (İzmir State Opera and Ballet, ☎ 484 6445) and the İzmir Devlet Senfoni Orkestrası (İzmir State Symphony Orchestra, ☎ 425 4115) perform from September to May. The *Turkish Daily News* usually carries schedules. You can also try the Atatürk Kültür Merkezi (Atatürk Cultural Centre, ☎ 484 8526) in Konak.

Getting There & Away

Air For information on flights and fares, see the Getting Around chapter at the front of this book. For airport transport, see the following Getting Around section. The information number at Adnan Menderes airport is ☎ (232) 274 2626.

Turkish Airlines (THY, ☎ (232) 484 1220, for reservations 425 8280, fax 483 6281) is in the row of shops in the Grand Hotel Efes at Gaziosmanpaşa Bulvarı 1, open from 8.30 am to 7.30 pm (until 5.30 pm on Sunday). At Adnan Menderes airport the THY number is ☎ (232) 274 2424.

İstanbul Airlines (☎ (232) 489 0541, fax 445 5768), Gaziosmanpaşa Caddesi 2-E, is across the street from the Grand Hotel Efes and Turkish Airlines. It can also be contacted at Menderes airport (☎ (232) 274 2076, fax 274 2156).

Details of the offices of foreign airlines, all close to Cumhuriyet Meydanı follow:

Air France
: Halit Ziya Bulvarı, 1353 Sokak 1, two blocks south of the Tourism Information Office (☎ (232) 425 9004)

Austrian Airlines
: Şair Eşref Bulvarı, 1371 Sokak 5, Çankaya (☎ (232) 425 8020)

British Airways
: Şair Eşref Bulvarı, 1371 Sokak 3/B, Çankaya (☎ (232) 441 3829, fax 441 6284)

KLM
: Menderes airport (☎ (232) 251 3423, 251 3087)

Lufthansa
: Atatürk Caddesi 244, north of Cumhuriyet Meydanı (☎ (232) 422 3622)

Swissair
: Cumhuriyet Meydanı 11/2, on the south side of the square (☎ (232) 421 4757)

Bus Buses arrive at İzmir's otogar (☎ (232) 486 2263), a mammoth and seemingly chaotic establishment almost three km north-east of the city's centre. Buses roar around outside while throngs of passengers move through the interior past rows of shops selling snacks, trinkets and lemon cologne. There's a small Tourism Information Office and complaints office near the terminal's main gate; ask for the Turizm Ofisi (too-REEZM oh-fee-see). If you're at the otogar to buy a ticket to another city, ask for directions to the *bilet gişeleri* (bee-LEHT gee-sheh-leh-ree, ticket windows).

The larger bus companies provide shuttle service (*servis arabası*) between the otogar and 9 Eylül Meydanı next to Basmane. For other transport to and from the otogar, see the following Getting Around section.

In the city centre, bus companies have ticket offices around 9 Eylül Meydanı: Aydın, Dadaş, Hakiki Koç, İzmir Seyahat, Kamil Koç, Karadeveci, Kent, Kontur, Metro, Pamukkale, Uludağ, Vantur and other companies. The premium companies Pamukkale, Ulusoy and Varan have offices on Gaziosmanpaşa Bulvarı opposite the entrance to the Grand Hotel Efes.

Here are details on travel from İzmir to:

Ankara – 600 km, eight hours, US$18; buses at least every hour

Antalya – 550 km, nine hours, US$18; buses at least every two hours

Bergama – 100 km, one hour, US$4; Pammukale company buses every half-hour from 6 am to 7.30 pm; also several Bergama municipality ('Bergama Belediyesi') buses

Bodrum – 250 km, four hours, US$10; buses every hour in summer

Bursa – 375 km, six hours, US$12; hourly buses

Çanakkale – 340 km, six hours, US$12; buses at least every two hours

Çeşme (for Chios) – 85 km, 1½ hours, US$3; frequent buses (at least hourly) depart from a separate bus station in Üçkuyular, 6.5 km south-west of Konak; take a Balçova minibus from Konak to Üçkuyular

Denizli – 250 km, four hours, US$10; buses every hour

İstanbul – 610 km, eight hours, US$16 to US$25; buses at least every hour

Konya – 575 km, eight hours, US$17; buses at least every two hours

Kuşadası – 95 km, 1½ hours, US$3.25; buses at least every 30 minutes from 6.30 am to 7 pm in summer

Marmaris – 320 km, six hours, US$12; buses at least every two hours

Sardis – 90 km, 1¼ hours, US$3; buses for Salihli (get off at Sartmustafa) at least every 30 minutes

Selçuk (for Ephesus) – 80 km, 1¼ hours, US$3; buses every 15 minutes from 6.30 am to 7 pm in summer

Trabzon – 1375 km, 22 hours, US$38; several buses daily
Van – 1600 km, 28 hours, US$45; several buses daily

Train Most intercity trains come into Basmane Garı (Basmane Station, ☎ (232) 484 8638; for reservations 484 5350), from where there are buses to other sections, and numerous hotels close by. İzmir's other terminus, Alsancak Garı (☎ (232) 421 0114), at the northern end of the city near the port, is mostly for commuter and suburban lines, including frequent trains to Adnan Menderes airport.

For information on trains, don't ask at the prominent Anahat ('Main Lines') ticket kiosk in Basmane, they'll be cross. Rather, consult the agent at Danışma (Information, there's a sign), who has all the schedules in his head.

Here's how to reach these destinations; all train services are daily unless otherwise noted:

Afyon
: Some Ankara-bound trains from Basmane stop at Afyon. Ask at Danışma. A rail-bus *(ray otobüsü)* departs Basmane for Afyon daily at 10.55 pm.

Ankara
: The fastest and most comfortable train is the *Ankara Mavi Tren*, departing from Basmane at 7.30 pm, arriving in Ankara at 9.35 am. The one-way fare is US$13; sleeping compartments cost US$32 for one person, US$55 for two people, US$75 for three. Table d'hôte dinner on board costs from US$6 to US$10. The next best train is the *İzmir Ekspresi*, departing from Basmane at 6 pm, arriving in Ankara at 9.17 am. The one-way fare is US$10/7 in 1st/2nd-class.

Balıkesir
: *Marmara Ekspresi* trains to and from Bandırma (see following) stop in Balıkesir, as do some Ankara-bound trains.

Bandırma
: The *Marmara Ekspresi* departs Basmane daily at 8 am for Bandırma (US$6) on the Sea of Marmara. From Bandırma, a connecting ship (US$8) then sails to İstanbul; but there are no ships on Friday or Saturday.

Denizli (Pamukkale)
: Express trains depart from Basmane for Denizli (near Pamukkale) at 8.15 am (arriving at 1.42 pm), 3.15 pm (arriving at 10 pm), and 6.05 pm (arriving at 11.28 pm), stopping at Adnan Menderes airport, Selçuk (for Ephesus and Kuşadası), Aydın, and Nazilli (for Aphrodisias). The one-way fare is US$4, US$3 for students.

Eskişehir
: All Ankara-bound trains stop at Eskişehir, a major railway switching station. In addition, the *Ege Ekspresi* (Aegean Express) departs İzmir each morning at 6.40 am for Eskişehir.

Kütahya
: All Ankara-bound trains stop at Kütahya.

İstanbul
: See Bandırma, above.

Manisa
: All trains bound for Bandırma/İstanbul and Ankara stop at Manisa. In addition, rail-buses depart Basmane for Manisa at 2.40 and 6.30 pm daily.

Selçuk (Ephesus)
: The three Denizli-bound trains and the Söke-bound trains (departing at 6.46 and 10.40 pm), all from Basmane, stop at Selçuk. The one-way fare is US$1.50 (US$1.10 for students).

Besides all these trains, there are also daily trains to Alaşehir (7.45 pm), Ödemiş (4.10 pm), Söke (6.46 and 10.40 pm) and Uşak (7 am), and banliyö trains to Karşıyaka, across the bay.

Boat The İstanbul-İzmir car ferry service operates each weekend throughout the year. See the Getting Around chapter at the front of this book for details. Also, see the Getting There & Away chapter at the front of this book for information on car-ferry service between İzmir and Venice, Italy.

Should you be lucky enough to arrive in İzmir by sea, the city will present itself to you wonderfully as you glide by, and your ship will come into Alsancak Limanı (Alsancak Harbour, ☎ & fax (232) 421 1484), also called Yeni Liman (New Harbour), at the northern tip of Alsancak. The harbour is about equidistant (two km) from the otogar and the centre of the city, Konak. For transport, turn left as you leave the dock area and walk the block to Alsancak train station, from which buses (US$0.50) and taxis (US$3) take you to the centre.

Getting Around

The airport You can travel between the centre of İzmir and Adnan Menderes airport (25 km south of the city near Cumaovası on the road to Ephesus and Kuşadası) by airport bus, city bus, intercity bus, commuter train or express train.

Havaş airport buses leave for the half-hour trip from the Turkish Airlines (THY) office about 90 minutes before each Turkish Airlines departure. If you're not flying THY, ask for the schedule and catch a bus that leaves at least 90 minutes before your domestic departure, or two hours before an international departure; the bus fare is US$2.

City buses trundle – fairly slowly – between Menderes airport and Montrö Meydanı, at the Kültür Parkı end of Şehit Nevres Bey Bulvarı, every half-hour throughout the day for even less, but the trip takes twice as long.

A taxi between İzmir and Menderes airport can cost between US$15 and US$30, depending upon your haggling abilities and whether or not the driver actually runs the meter (which he should).

There are more or less hourly suburban trains (US$0.50) which connect Menderes airport with Alsancak Garı, and a few intercity trains to and from Basmane. Here's the schedule, which is, of course, subject to change but rarely seems to do so. All trains departing İzmir do so from Alsancak Garı unless otherwise noted:

From İzmir	*From Menderes airport*
5.05 am	5.42 am
5.50	6.32
7.10	7.50
8.15*	--
8.40	9.17
10.40	11.17
11.44	12.22 pm
12.30 pm	1.12
1.30	2.12
2.30	3.12
3.15*	--
3.30	4.12
4.30	5.12
5.45	6.24
6.05*	--
6.43	7.29
6.46*	--
8.30	9.12
10.10	10.59
10.40*	

*Express train to Denizli departing/arriving Basmane Garı

The Otogar If you've come on one of the bigger bus lines, there may be a servis arabası to take you to 9 Eylül Meydanı at no extra charge; ask as you descend from your bus, *Servis arabası var mı?* Otherwise, take a city bus *(şehir otobüsü)* No 50, 51 or 52, 'Yeni Garaj-Konak', which stops at Alsancak Garı and Çankaya as well. Find the tourism and complaints office, go out the gate nearby, turn right, walk to the bus shelter, and buy a ticket at the kiosk.

Minibus dolmuşes depart from in front of this bus rank. Most convenient is the dolmuş marked 'Çankaya-Mersinli', which will take you to the bus ticket offices at 9 Eylül Meydanı, just a few steps from Basmane Garı, then to Çankaya.

If you're arriving in İzmir by bus from the south, ask to be let out at Tepecik (TEH-peh-jeek), which is 700m east of Basmane Station, and closer to the centre than the otogar. Minibuses and dolmuşes run from Tepecik along Gaziler Caddesi to Basmane.

If you're arriving in İzmir by train from the north, get out at Çınarlı station, the penultimate stop, and walk the 300m to the otogar.

To get to Çeşme, catch any bus or dolmuş bound westward from Konak to Güzelyalı, Altay Meydanı or Balçova, and get out at Güzelyalı/Altay Meydanı to board a bus bound for Çeşme.

Bus & Dolmuş City buses painted red-and-beige or silver-and-blue lumber along the major thoroughfares. Two major termini/transfer points are at Montrö Meydanı by the Kültür Parkı, and at Konak in front of the Atatürk Kültür Merkezi. The buses are run by several different administrations. On ESHOT buses, easily recognisable by signs on the front and/or sides, you must have bought a ticket from a kiosk in advance. On İZULAŞ buses you can pay cash on the bus.

Dolmuş minibuses connect the centre with outlying districts as well.

İzmir Metro Ground was broken in 1992 for İzmir's underground train system. The first line of the Metro, 9.2 km in length, is planned to connect Basmane with Konak, then run west along the shore via Üçyol to Altay Meydanı in Güzelyalı, the beginning of the Çeşme Otoyol (highway) where buses leave for Çeşme. But construction is not in progress, and the project is the subject of intense political debate and intrigue.

Car Rental The large international franchises and many small local companies rent cars in İzmir. There's a cluster of offices on Şehit Fethi Bey Caddesi, the street between the Grand Hotel Efes and the İkinci Kordon, near the Otel Anba; and on the İkinci Kordon north of Cumhuriyet Meydanı.

Some addresses of the offices follow:

Avis
  Şair Eşref Bulvarı 18-D (☎ (232) 441 4417, fax 441 4420)
  İzmir Hilton (☎ 441 6016)
  Menderes airport (☎ & fax 274 2172)
Budget
  Şair Eşref Bulvarı 22/1 (☎ (232) 441 9224, fax 441 9375)
Europcar/Interrent
  Esin Turizm, Şehit Fethi Bey Caddesi 122-F (☎ (232) 441 5141, fax 483 0031); this is among Turkey's biggest agencies.
Hertz
  Menderes airport (☎ (232) 274 2193)
Yes Rent a Car
  1377 Sokak 8-B (☎ (232) 422 7107, fax 422 2499)
Zafer Rent a Car
  Akdeniz; Caddesi 8, Anba İşhanı (☎ (232) 484 6096, fax 483 0904)

Taxi It's best to take taxis from a *durak* (taxi stand), or to have your hotel call one. These tend to be more reliable drivers who are less likely to cheat you.

SARDIS (SART) & SALİHLİ

The phrase 'rich as Croesus' made its way into language early, in the 6th century BC to be precise. Croesus (560-546 BC) was the king of Lydia, and Sardis was its capital city. It was here that one of humankind's most popular and valuable inventions appeared: coinage. No doubt the Greeks thought Croesus rich because he could store so much wealth in such a small place. Rather than having vast estates and far-ranging herds of livestock, Croesus kept his wealth in his pockets, and they were deep pockets at that.

History

For all his wealth, Croesus was defeated and captured by Cyrus and his Persians, after which he leapt onto a funeral pyre, proving that even he, Croesus, couldn't take it with him.

The Lydian Kingdom had dominated much of the Aegean area before the Persians came. Besides being the kingdom's wealthy capital, Sardis was a great trading centre, obviously because coinage facilitated trade.

After the Persians, Alexander the Great took the city in 334 BC and embellished it even more. The inevitable earthquake brought its fine buildings down in 17 AD, but it was rebuilt by Tiberius and developed into a thriving provincial Roman town. It became part of the Ottoman Empire at the end of the 14th century.

Orientation

There are actually two small villages at Sardis, nestled in a valley rich in vineyards (for sultanas, not wine grapes), olive groves, melon fields and tobacco fields. **Sartmustafa** (SART-MOOS-tah-fah) is the village on the highway, with a few teahouses and grocery shops. **Sartmahmut** (SART-mah-MOOT) is north of the highway, clustered around the train station. The station is precisely one km north of the highway.

During the day the farmers come into town, park their tractors in front of the teahouses, sit down for a few glasses and discuss the crops. In early August the harvest is in progress, and little stalls by the roadside, attended by children, sell huge bunches of luscious, crisp, sweet sultanas to passers-by.

The teahouses and eateries at the crossroads on the highway are where you wait to catch a bus back to İzmir.

The Archaeological Sites

The ruins of Sardis are scattered throughout the valley which lies beneath the striking ragged mountain range to the south. Two concentrations of ruins are of interest.

Just east of the village (away from İzmir), on the north side of the highway, lies the most extensive part of the ruins, open virtually all the time during daylight hours, every day, for US$3.

Buy your ticket at the little booth, then enter the ruins along the **Marble Way** past rows of **Byzantine-era shops**. Many of them once belonged to Jewish merchants and artisans, as they backed onto the wall of the great synagogue. Note the elaborate drainage system, with pipes buried in the stone walls. Some of the shops have been identified from inscriptions. There's a restaurant, Jacob's Paint Shop, an office, a hardware shop, the shop of Sabbatios and the shop of Jacob, an elder of the synagogue. At the end of the Marble Way is an inscription on the marble paving-stones done in either 17 or 43 AD, honouring Prince Germanicus.

Turn left from the Marble Way and enter the **synagogue**, impressive because of its size and beautiful decoration. It has lots of fine mosaic paving, and coloured stone on its walls. A modern plaque lists donors to the Sardis American Excavation Fund, who supported the excavations carried out between 1965 and 1973.

The striking restored façade to the right of the synagogue is that of the **gymnasium**. Note especially the finely chiselled inscriptions in Greek, and the serpentine fluting on the columns. Behind the façade is a swimming pool and rest area.

Just over one km south of the village (take the road beside the teahouses) is the **Temple of Artemis**, a once-magnificent building which was actually never completed. Today only a few columns stand, but the temple's plan is clearly visible and quite impressive. Next to the temple is an **altar** used since ancient times, refurbished by Alexander the Great and later by the Romans. Clinging to the south-eastern corner of the temple is a small brick **Byzantine church**. From archaic times until the Hellenistic, Roman and Byzantine periods, this was a sacred spot, no matter what the religion was.

Organised Tours

Local travel agencies in İzmir operate full-day tours to Sardis and Manisa for about US$35, lunch included.

Places to Stay & Eat

Snacks are available at the crossroads in Sartmustafa. For full meals and hotel rooms, catch any bus going east from Sart along the E96/D300 to Salihli (nine km).

Salihli (population 71,000) is a local farming town with an otogar, open-air marketplace, and three suitable hotels all together just south of the highway.

The *Hotel Yener* (☎ (236) 712 5003, fax 713 1457), Zafer Mahallesi, Dede Çelik Sokak 7, is a block south of the otogar across the open-air marketplace. Clean double rooms with shower cost US$12. The *Toros Restaurant* shares the ground floor and terrace with the hotel. A sign at the hotel door says 'We accept no drunken customers'.

A block farther south is the *Otel Berrak* (☎ (236) 713 1452, fax 713 1457), Belediye Caddesi 59. Though under the same ownership as the Yener, the Berrak rates two stars, is much more comfortable, and charges US$30 to US$35 for a double room with shower.

Finally, just east of the city hall (Belediye Sarayı), the large *Otel Akgül* was under construction and may be available when you arrive.

Getting There & Away

Sardis is 90 km east of İzmir along the Ankara road. In high summer, start out early so you're not tramping around the ruins in the heat of the day, which can be oppressive.

Bus Buses depart frequently – at least every 30 minutes – for the 90-km, 1¼-hour trip from İzmir's otogar. You needn't buy a ticket in advance, just go out to the bus station and buy a ticket for the next bus to Salihli (US$3). Tell them you want to get out at Sart.

Dolmuş minibuses run between Sartmustafa and Manisa, the provincial capital, for US$1.75 per ride.

Train There are several daily trains from İzmir (Basmane) which stop here; they are slower than the buses. Take the bus out to Sardis, but then ask in town about trains returning to İzmir, as you may find one at a convenient time.

ÇEŞME

The name of this town and resort area (population 100,000), 85 km due west of İzmir, means 'fountain' or 'spring' *(Çeşme,* CHESH-meh). From the town, it's only about 10 km across the water to the Greek island of Chios. The ferries to the Greek islands are the main reason people go to Çeşme, though the fast-growing resort area encircling the town is popular with weekend-trippers from İzmir.

Çeşme is a pleasant seaside town, but the land to the east of it is rolling steppe, a foretaste of Anatolia, though this barrenness subsides as one approaches İzmir, giving way to wheat fields, lush orchards, olive groves and tobacco fields. About 23 km east of Çeşme is the pretty **Uzunkuyu Piknik Yeri**, a roadside picnic area in a pine forest. About 50 km east of Çeşme one passes the official city limits of İzmir, a full 30 km west of Konak Meydanı.

Orientation

Çeşme is right on the coast. Ilıca, a seaside resort town six km to the east of Çeşme, has lots of hotels in all price ranges. Dolmuşes run between Ilıca and Çeşme frequently (US$1), but unless you want to spend all your time at the beach you're better off staying in Çeşme proper.

Çeşme's otogar is less than one km south of the main square and the fortress. Everything you need is very near the main square on the waterfront, with its inevitable statue of Atatürk. The Tourism Information Office, Customs House (Gümrük), ferry ticket offices, bus ticket offices, restaurants and hotels are all here, or within two blocks.

Information

The Tourism Information Office (☎ & fax (232) 712 6653) is down by the dock at İskele Meydanı 6. Hours in summer are 8.30 am to 7 pm, on weekends 9 am to noon and 1 to 5 pm.

The Çeşme Film Festival is held annually during the third week in August.

Fortress & Museum

Çeşme's Genoese fortress was repaired by Sultan Beyazıt, son of Sultan Mehmet the Conqueror, to defend the coast from attack by pirates and by the Knights of St John of Jerusalem based on Rhodes. It is now the **Çeşme Fortress & Museum** (Çeşme Kalesi ve Müzesi), open every day from 8.30 am to noon and from 1 to 5 pm. Admission to the castle is free, but the museum costs US$1.50. The entrance is up the hill on the right-hand side as you face the fort from the main square.

Most of the castle's interior is empty, with the exception of the north tower, which is now the exhibition space featuring archaeological finds from the area, many relating to Çeşme's maritime history, others from nearby Erythrae. Feel free to climb up to the castle's battlements for a look around. In the evening it's pleasant to dine at the *Castle Restaurant* (☎ 712 8339) and enjoy the sunset, especially on your last night in Turkey before leaving by ferry for Greece. A full dinner costs US$10 to US$15.

Facing the main square, with its back to the fortress, is a **statue of Cezayirli Gazi Hasan Paşa** (1714-90), together with a lion which symbolises his temperament. As a boy he was captured in a battle on the Iranian border, sold into slavery by the Ottoman army and bought by a Turkish tradesman who raised him with his own sons. Having joined the Janissary corps at the age of 25, he began a brilliant military, naval and political career which included fierce battles with the Russian fleet off Çeşme. He retired an extremely wealthy man, having served as the sultan's grand vizier and having built public monuments, fountains and mosques on Lesbos, Lemnos, Chios, Kos and Rhodes (all were Ottoman islands at the time).

Caravanserai & Church

Çeşme's caravanserai dates from 1528,

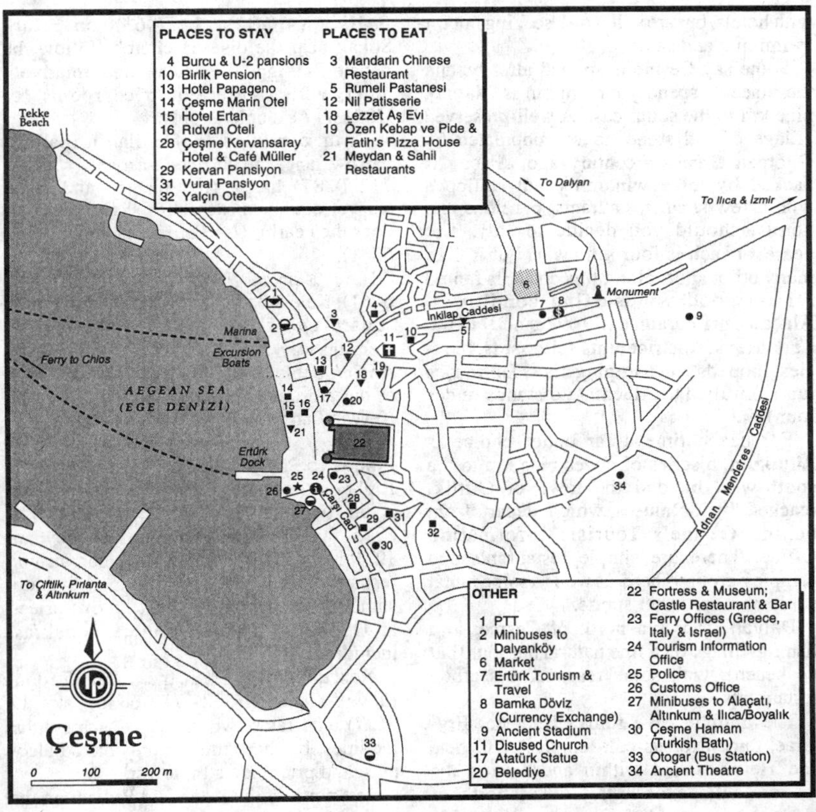

during the reign of Süleyman the Magnificent, but has been restored and converted into a hotel, with limited success. It's worth taking a look round.

On İnkilap Caddesi is the ruined orthodox church of Ayios Haralambos, now used for shows and exhibitions.

Plaza Time

In the evening the people of Çeşme still observe the old Mediterranean custom of *piyasa vakti* ('plaza time'): dressing up and coming down to the main square for a stroll, a glass of tea, a bit of conversation and some people-watching. That's nightlife in Çeşme, and it's pleasant enough. The men, some with their wives, will linger in the seaside restaurants and teahouses.

Excursions

Boats moored along Çeşme's waterfront make day excursions up and down the coast, stopping at good spots for a swim. The cost is around US$15 per person, lunch included.

The best beaches are at **Boyalık,** 1.5 km east of Çeşme's main square, and **Ilıca**, six km east. Both beaches are heavily developed with hotels, but are still worth seeking out for swimming and sun.

Some say Çeşme is spoiled already, and the place to spend your time in is **Alaçatı**, nine km to the south-east. A well-preserved village of old stone houses populated by Ottoman Greeks a century ago, Alaçatı is backed by three windmills and equipped with a few small restaurants, pensions and hotels, should you decide to stay. The nearest beach is four km away, but it, like many other spots along this coast, is famed for its good windsurfing conditions. Alaçatı Surf Paradise (Sörf Cenneti) in the Çark Mevkii district rents sailboards, bicycles, mopeds and camping sites. Dolmuşes run from Ilıca to Alaçatı, a distance under four km.

For beach time a far better choice is **Altınkum**, a series of coves nine km to the south-west beyond the town of Çiftlik, reached by dolmuşes which depart from behind Çeşme's Tourism Information Office. There are simple restaurants and camping grounds here, as well as some rental equipment for water sports.

Dalyan, four km north of Çeşme, is a fishing village on a fine natural harbour (but no beach), with some reasonable seafood restaurants.

The unimpressive ruins of ancient Erythrae, famed for its cult temples of Cybele and Hercules, are within and around the modern village of **Ildır**, 27 km north of Çeşme. A few small fish restaurants provide sustenance.

Places to Stay

Çeşme has several inexpensive pensions and hotels, several moderately priced hotels, a restored caravanserai and a luxury resort. All charge more than normal, and many lodgings are often booked solid in the summer season. The accommodation situation in Çeşme is thus not particularly good in any respect.

Places to Stay – bottom end

Several good pensions are in the midst of the action just off İnkilap Caddesi. The *Birlik Pension* (☎ (232) 712 7463), on Ertürk Sokak near the disused church (follow the pension's signs), is clean and relatively quiet, with shower-equipped rooms for US$13/17 a single/double.

On the opposite side of İnkilap in a parallel narrow lane, the *Burcu Pansiyon* (☎ (232) 712 0387) has a fine terrace and good shower-equipped rooms for slightly less, as does the nearby *U-2 Pansiyon* (☎ (232) 712 6381).

The *Kervan Pansiyon* (☎ (232) 712 6061), Kale Sokak 64, just south of the main square and the docks past the Çeşme Kervansaray Hotel, charges US$13/17 a single/double, though you get less for it than at the aforementioned places. Just past the Kervan Pansiyon is the town's hamam.

Places to Stay – middle

Right on the shore, facing the main square, is the two-star *Hotel Ertan* (☎ (232) 712 6795, fax 712 7852), Cumhuriyet Meydanı 12. It has a lift, open-air terrace bar, air-con restaurant and 60 guest rooms with bath, some of them facing the sea, a bit overpriced at US$48/60 a single/double, breakfast included.

Next door to the Ertan, the newer 35-room *Rıdvan Oteli* (☎ (232) 712 6336, fax 712 7627) also rates two stars and has similar facilities, but here most rooms have balconies, and prices are a bit lower.

Just north of the Ertan and Rıdvan on the water, the *Çeşme Marin Otel* (☎ (232) 712 7579, fax 712 6484), Hürriyet Caddesi 10, offers even better value, with shower-equipped rooms for US$38/48 a single/double, breakfast included.

Parla Apart Otel (☎ (232) 712 6366), Musallah Mahallesi, Kabadayı Sokak 27, run by an energetic woman named Çiğdem, rents clean, modern double rooms for US$25, small apartments (lounge, bedroom, kitchen and bath) for US$32 – great value. The cheaper *Vural Pansiyon*, just behind the Kervan Pansiyon, is under the same competent management.

The *Yalçın Otel* (☎ (232) 712 6981, fax 712 0623), Musalla Mahallesi, Kale Sokak

38, is perched on the hillside overlooking the town. Its 16 pleasant new rooms, all with private showers, some with excellent views, cost US$18/25/32 a single/double/triple.

Hotel Papageno (☎ (232) 712 8327, fax 712 0105), 16 Eylül Mahallesi, 1 Yalı Sokak 11, is new, modern, clean, comfortable, relatively quiet and decently priced at US$25 a double with shower, breakfast included.

Çeşme Kervansaray Hotel (☎ (232) 712 7177, fax 712 6491), just south of the main square, dates from the time of Süleyman the Magnificent. Restored a decade ago, it is currently not very busy. The posted price of US$80 for a double room is quickly reduced to US$55, and perhaps even lower, if you hesitate. If the Turkish Night show is to be held the night of your stay, go elsewhere or be kept awake by the racket.

Places to Eat

Çeşme's restaurants are all fairly cheap, but some are cheaper and better than others. Virtually all restaurants post their prices prominently. For a local taste treat, try the sakızlı dondurma (sah-kuhz-LUH dohn-door-mah), ice cream flavoured with pine resin, the same stuff they put in Greek retsina wine. It tastes like you think it will. If you like retsina, you may like this weird incarnation of the flavour.

By the old church are numerous small eateries, including *Özen Kebap ve Pide*, which serves grills and Turkish pizza, which is also the speciality of *Fatih's Pizza House*. Both places have outdoor tables by the church. Behind the church are more cheap places, including *Ali's Restaurant*.

On İnkilap Caddesi, the *Lezzet Aş Evi* (Flavour Cook-House) is among the cheapest eateries in town, with vegetable plates for US$1, and salçalı köfte for US$1.25. I fear the Lezzet may be driven out by rising rents on this main street.

Nearby, the *Nil Patisserie* serves pastries and excellent baklava (small portions, though) for US$1 to US$2, and has a few streetside café tables. The cheaper *Rumeli Pastanesi* on İnkilap specialises in the local reçel (jellies and preserves), which include bitter orange (turunç), fig (incir), hazelnut (fındık), lemon-flower (limon çiçeği), pinegum (sakız), quince (ayva), rose (gül) and watermelon (karpuz).

Café Müller, just south of the Çeşme Kervansaray Hotel, serves waffles (plain, US$0.75), and excellent filter coffee. The *Sevim Café* in front of the Kervansaray, has outdoor tables which suffer a bit from traffic noise, but is a good place for a sunset drink.

Chinese restaurants have been popping up in Turkish coastal resorts. The cuisine is usually not authentic but worth a try for a change of palette. Çeşme's is the *Mandarin Chinese Restaurant* (☎ 712 0329), just inland from the marina, with main course dishes priced from US$6 to US$12.

The *Castle Restaurant & Bar* (☎ 712 8339), in a tower of the fortress, among the more romantic locales, is described above under 'Fortress-Museum.'

Down on the waterfront at the main square, the *Meydan* and *Sahil* restaurants have the best location but higher prices (posted): pizza is US$3.75, şiş kebap and similar simple grills US$5; fish is substantially more. Both restaurants have outdoor tables, some facing the square, others the sea.

Getting There & Away

The Çeşme-İzmir otoyol (expressway) is now open to Zeytinler, 25 km east of Çeşme, but it should be completed all the way to Çeşme by the time you arrive, alleviating the weekend traffic jams which used to clog the narrow coastal road.

AEGEAN TURKEY

Bus It's simple. Çeşme Turizm buses and minibuses make the 85-km, 1¼-hour run into the big city every 15 minutes or so from 6 am to 6 pm, for US$2. You can buy onward tickets for Ankara or İstanbul, but your bus will still stop in İzmir.

At the İzmir end of the run, Çeşme-bound buses operate out of a separate terminal in sükuyular, a neighbourhood six km west of Konak, not from İzmir's main otogar. From Üçkuyular, you take a 'Konak-Balçova' dolmuş into the city centre.

Ferry – Chios You've probably come to Çeşme on your way to or from the Greek island of Chios.

In high summer (1 July to 10 September) there are daily boats; the Monday boat connects at Chios with a boat for Piraeus, arriving in time to connect with a boat to Israel.

From 4 to 30 June and 11 to 30 September boats run on Tuesday, Thursday, Friday and Sunday.

From 1 May to 3 June and in October boats run on Tuesday, Thursday and Sunday.

From 16 to 30 April, boats run on Tuesday and Thursday.

From 1 November to 15 April, boats run on Thursday only.

Departure is at 9 am (returning at 6 pm) on Tuesday and Thursday; departing at 4 pm and returning at 6 pm on other days.

A one-way fare between Çeşme and Chios is US$25, same-day return costs US$30, making for a nice day trip. An open-date round trip costs US$35. An exorbitant Greek port tax of US$18 is levied on each passenger as well. Children aged from four to 12 years get a 50% reduction in fare (but not tax). Motorcycles, cars, even caravans, minibuses and buses can be carried on some of the ferries. The fare for a car is US$60 or US$80, depending upon length.

It's a good idea to buy your ticket at least a day in advance, if possible. For details, reservations and tickets, contact the Ertürk Travel Agency (☎ (232) 712 6768, fax 712 6223), Beyazıt Caddesi 7/8; or Maskot Turizm Seyahat (☎ (232) 712 7654, fax 712 8435), İnkilap Caddesi 93/19, or at the harbour (☎ (232) 712 0206).

These agencies can also provide information about onward connections by sea and air from Chios to other Aegean islands, Athens, Bari, Brindisi and Venice. From Chios there are usually close connections with ships for Athens (Piraeus), Lesbos, Samos and Thessaloniki, as well as direct flights from Chios to Athens, Samos, Mykonos and Venice.

Çeşme is also served by direct car/passenger ferries to and from Italy. See the Getting There & Away chapter at the front of this book for details.

Getting Around

Of the local car-rental agencies, Ertürk Rent a Car (☎ (232) 712 6768, fax 712 6223), Beyazıt Caddesi 7/8, has perhaps been in business the longest.

SOUTH TO EPHESUS

The route from Çeşme via Seferihisar and Gümüldür to Pamucak beach, Ephesus, Selçuk and Kuşadası (about 150 km) follows shallow river valleys, passes through farming towns, then skirts the coast at points. The region has a dozen ancient cities (Colophon, Claros, Notion, Teos) in an advanced state of ruin; a few of them are of no great interest except to archaeologists.

There are at present no direct buses between Çeşme and Selçuk. You must take a bus to Urla and transfer to a Seferihisar dolmuş. Coming from Selçuk, catch a minibus to Seferihisar (72 km). From Seferihisar, dolmuşes and city buses run west to Sığacık (4.5 km) and Akkum (7.2 km) every few hours.

Sığacık

Sığacık is a yet-to-be-discovered little port village backed by a crumbling castle. Judging from the number of *Emlak* (real-estate) offices that have opened, it won't remain undiscovered for long. At present most people pass through Sığacık quickly on their way to the white sands of Akkum, just to the west over the hills.

The centre of Sığacık village is Atatürk Meydanı, the park bordered by the PTT, teahouses and restaurants. The *Burü Restaurant* is right over the yacht harbour, as is the fancier *Liman Restaurant*, just off the square by the fortress. For a good view of the town, go around the harbour to the *Deniz Restaurant*, on the road to Akkum. For lodging, there's the *Burg Pansiyon* (☎ (232) 745 7464), Atatürk Meydanı 14, a modern building in traditional dark-wood-and-white-stucco style charging US$15 for a double with shower. Some rooms have harbour views. *Liman Pansiyon* (☎ (232) 745 7462), Akkum Caddesi 19, is a clean family-run place with a pide salonu downstairs charging the same prices. The nearby *Deniz Moteli* (☎ (232) 745 2533) is a bit fancier.

Akkum

Two km around the bay and over the hills is the turn off westward to Akkum, another 700m along. The protected cove and dependable winds are exploited by dozens of sailboarders in summer, and two small but smooth sand beaches, Büyük Akkum and Küçük Akkum, backed by olive groves, accommodate non-sailing companions.

For accommodation, there is the 230-room *Neptun Holiday Village Windsurf Center* (☎ (232) 745 7455, fax 745 3038), the sailboarders' hotel behind Büyük Akkum, but bookings are made – and all hotel rooms filled – from Germany. The other accommodation backing the beach is the *Belediye Tesisleri*, run by the Seferihisar town government. Other, small independent hotels are under construction, so you should be able to find a place to stay by the time you arrive. Small restaurants provide sustenance.

Teos

Scattered amidst the farmers' fields and olive groves 3.2 km from Akkum are the ruins of ancient Teos. The few fluted column bases and chunks of marble rubble only hint that this was once a major Ionian city, home of the poet Anacreon and noted for its devotion to Dionysus and the pleasures of the cup and the table.

From Akkum, go up to the road and turn right to reach the **Teos Orman İçi Dinlenme Yeri**, 1100m east of the turn off, a pine-shaded picnic grove run by the forestry department. Entry costs a fraction of a dollar per person, about US$1 per car.

Another 600m along, the road splits: the left fork goes to the ruins of Teos (800m); the right, to the Teos-Emeksiz Plajı, a *Çadırlı Kamp-Günnübirlik Plaj* (beach, day-use and tent-camping ground), one km over the hill.

Ephesus Region

Of Turkey's hundreds of ancient cities and classical ruins, Ephesus is the grandest and best preserved, and indeed the best-preserved classical city on the Mediterranean.

History

This was Ionia. Around 1000 BC, colonists from Greece arrived on these shores, fleeing an invasion by the Dorians. The Ionian culture flourished, and its cities exported these cultural refinements back to Greece.

Example of an Ionic capital. The spiralled Ionic order is common in ancient Ionia (around modern İzmir) where the order originated.

The history of Ionia is much the same as that of İzmir, with the original Ionian league of cities being conquered by the Lydians of Sardis, then the Persians, then Alexander. They prospered until their harbours silted up, or until the predominance of İzmir siphoned off their local trade.

Ephesus (Efes) was a great trading and religious city, centre for the cult of Cybele, the Anatolian fertility goddess. Under the influence of the Ionians, Cybele became Artemis, the virgin goddess of the hunt and the moon, and a fabulous temple was built in her honour. When the Romans took over and made this the province of Asia, Artemis became Diana and Ephesus became the Roman provincial capital. Its Temple of Diana was counted among the Seven Wonders of the World.

As a large and busy Roman town with ships and caravans coming from all over, it had an important Christian congregation very early. St Paul visited Ephesus and later wrote the most profound of his epistles to the Ephesians.

Statue of Diana the Huntress, the Roman incarnation of Artemis. The Temple of Artemis at Ephesus was among the Seven Wonders of the World.

Ephesus was renowned for its wealth and beauty even before it was pillaged by Gothic invaders in 262 AD, and it was still an important enough place in 431 AD for a church council to be held there. Much of the city remains for you to see. As for the other Ionian ports, sometimes a sleepy Turkish village rose among the ruins, sometimes not. Today several of those once-sleepy villages are bustling seaside resort towns.

Orientation

The region around Ephesus is rich in attractions. The city itself is an archaeological zone, but only three km away is Selçuk, a town of 25,000 people, where you catch buses and dolmuşes, have meals and find a bed. On a hilltop 10 km south of Selçuk is Meryemana, the House of the Virgin Mary. About seven km from Selçuk, past Ephesus, is the Aegean coast and Pamucak beach, a four-km-long, wide swath of dark sand.

Farther south along the coast, 20 km from Selçuk, is Kuşadası, a resort town of 50,000 people, a port for Aegean cruise ships doing the Greek islands route, and the dock for boats to Samos. Inland 15 km from Kuşadası and about 35 km due south of Selçuk is the farming town of Söke, a transportation point on the way to the nearby archaeological sites of Priene, Miletus and Didyma.

It is easy to spend at least three days seeing the sights in this region. Plan a day for Selçuk and Ephesus, another for Priene, Miletus and Didyma, and a third for Kuşadası and the beaches.

Places to Stay

If you'd rather save money than spend time in a bustling beach resort, make your base in Selçuk, the town three km from the Ephesus ruins. If you must have a beach close by, stay in Kuşadası, 20 km to the south-west.

Selçuk is closer to Ephesus proper and has a large number of inexpensive pensions. Kuşadası is closer to Priene, Miletus and Didyma, and has a greater number and variety of lodgings, especially in the higher price ranges, but is bigger, noisier and more hectic. See Places to Stay under each town heading.

Getting There & Away

İzmir is the transportation hub for the region, so you may pass through there to continue north or east by bus or train.

Air Adnan Menderes airport, beyond İzmir's southern limit, is only slightly more than a half-hour's ride from Selçuk. Ephesus has an airstrip currently used only for air taxi, training and paragliding flights.

Bus Bus traffic to and through Selçuk and Kuşadası is fast and frequent. Direct services run from İzmir's otogar to:

Selçuk – 80 km, one hour, US$2.25; buses every 15 minutes from 6.30 am to 7 pm in summer
Kuşadası – 100 km, 1⅔ hours, US$2.50; buses at least every 30 minutes from 6.30 am to 7 pm in summer
Söke – 125 km, two hours, US$3

Selçuk is a stopping-place for many buses

travelling between İzmir and Denizli, Pamukkale, Marmaris, Bodrum, Fethiye, Antalya and other south-western points. Kuşadası has lots of direct bus services to İzmir, some direct bus services to Denizli, Pamukkale and other cities farther on, and minibus dolmuş services to beaches and archaeological sites near Kuşadası.

Train Three trains make the İzmir to Denizli run daily in each direction. Confirm these times locally before you travel. Note also that these trains may be hot, crowded and not on time.

Fares are US$1 (express train) between İzmir and Menderes airport, US$2 between İzmir and Selçuk, US$5 between İzmir and Denizli, and US$3 between Selçuk and Denizli. Most travellers prefer taking the dolmuş to Menderes airport instead of the train, as the dolmuş is faster and more dependable.

Car Rental It's simple but expensive to rent a car in İzmir or Kuşadası. The big international companies as well as many small local ones offer cars at varying rates. You will probably have to return the car to the same city. If you give it up in Antalya or Ankara, you may have to pay a hefty charge to get the car back to its home base. See the Getting Around chapter for more information.

SELÇUK

Once a modest farming town with a sideline in tourism, Selçuk has been transformed by Turkey's tourism boom of the 1980s. Tourism is now the driving force in the local economy, though the lush fields of cotton and tobacco and the orchards of apples and figs surrounding the ever-growing town attest to the continuing efforts of the farmers.

Orientation

Ayasoluk Hill, with its castle, is north-west of the centre. Cengiz Topel Caddesi, the pedestrian way which is the heart of the commercial and tourist district, runs from an elaborate round fountain at the intersection with the main road to the Selçuk train station. A few hundred metres south of the fountain on the main road is the bus station. On the west side of the main road is a shady park, and west of it the famous Ephesus Museum. On the south side of the park is the Tourism Information Office.

Information

Selçuk's Tourism Information Office (☎ & fax (232) 892 6945), Agora Çarşısı 35, will help you find accommodation.

The PTT on Cengiz Topel Caddesi is open 24 hours every day, and will change cash, travellers' cheques or Eurocheques anytime. Ziraat Bankası has an office with ATM on Cengiz Topel Caddesi; İş Bankası and Akbank have ATMs on Namık Kemal Caddesi, a block north. There are foreign exchange offices along Cengiz Topel Caddesi as well.

Selçuk's postal code is 35920.

Note If you park a car near the Tourism Information Office, Ephesus Museum, St John Basilica, or a few other touristy places in Selçuk you may be approached by a man wanting to collect a parking fee of up to US$1.50. Ask for a *bilet* (ticket) or *makbuz* (receipt) and if he doesn't have a book of them, and doesn't give you one, ignore him. If he does show you his receipts, move your car and park a few blocks away for free.

Ayasoluk Hill

Before going to Ephesus, take an hour or two to visit the ancient buildings in Selçuk. The best place to start is the **St John Basilica** on top of the hill; look for signs pointing the way to St Jean.

It is said that St John came to Ephesus at the end of his life and wrote his Gospel here. A tomb built in the 4th century AD was thought to be his, so Justinian erected this magnificent church above it in the 6th century. Earthquakes and scavengers for building materials had left the church a heap of rubble until a century ago when restoration began. Virtually all of what you see is restored. The church site is open every day from 8 am to 5.30 pm (later in summer) for

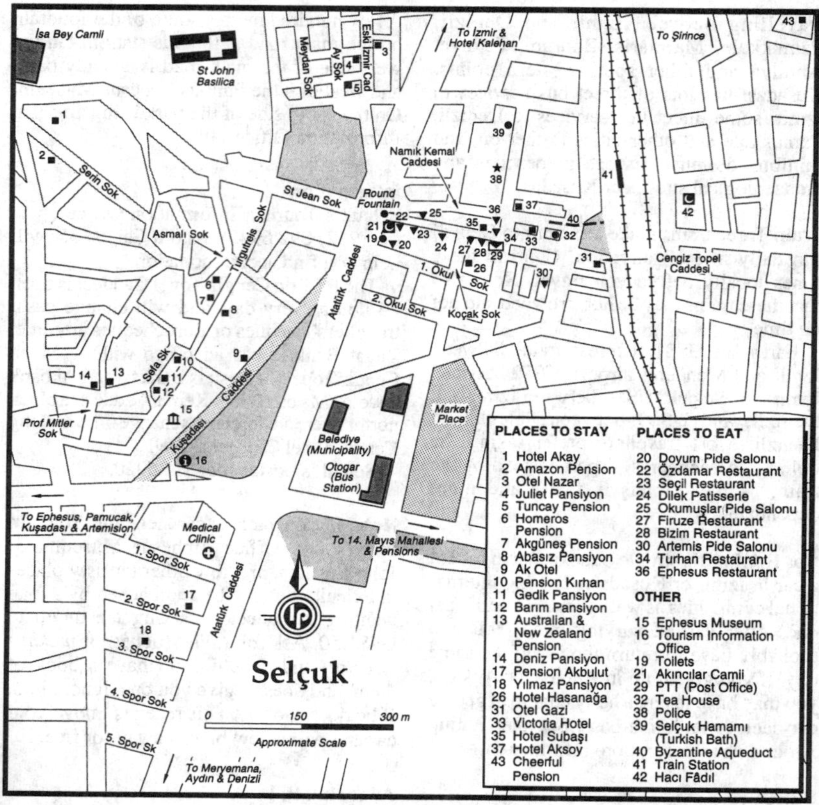

US$2.50. Parking at the entrance costs almost as much, so park a block or two away.

This hill, including the higher peak with the fortress, is called Ayasoluk. The view is attractive. Look west: at the foot of the hill is the **İsa Bey Camii**, built in 1307 by the Emir of Aydın in a transitional style which was post-Seljuk and pre-Ottoman. Keep a picture of it in your mind if you plan to venture deep into Anatolia for a look at more Seljuk buildings.

Beyond the mosque you can see how the Aegean Sea once invaded this plain, allowing Ephesus to prosper from maritime commerce. When the harbour silted up, Ephesus began to lose its famous wealth.

Early in the town's existence it had earned money from pilgrims coming to pay homage to Cybele or Artemis. The many-breasted Anatolian fertility goddess had a fabulous temple, the **Artemision**, to the south-west of the St John Basilica. A sign on the road to Ephesus marks the spot today, and you can see a re-erected column and the outline of the foundation. When you visit the huge temple at Didyma you can get an idea of what the great temple looked like, as the one at Didyma is thought to be similar.

By the way, the **citadel** on top of the hill to the north of the St John Basilica was originally constructed by the Byzantines in the 6th century, rebuilt by the Seljuks and restored in modern times. A small Seljuk mosque and a ruined church are inside.

Ephesus Museum

Don't miss the beautiful museum in the centre of Selçuk, just a few steps from the Tourism Information Office, open from 8.30 am to noon and 1 to 7 pm for US$3.50 (students half-price, those over 65 free). The collection is a significant one, and its statuary, mosaics and artefacts are attractively displayed. Don't miss the small, exquisite figure of the Boy on a Dolphin in the first room, the several marble statues of Cybele/Artemis with rows of egg-like breasts representing fertility, and several effigies of Priapus, the phallic god. There are also good mosaics and frescoes. Beyond the courtyard is the ethnographic section set up in an *arasta* (arcade) concentrating on traditional Turkish and Ottoman life with tools, costumes and a *topuk ev* (tent-like dwelling) used by Turkic nomads.

Other Sites

Selçuk has some **tombs** and a little **mosque** dating from the Seljuk period just south of the bus station. On Namık Kemal Caddesi are the remains of a **Byzantine aqueduct**, now a favourite nesting place for storks. Eggs are laid in late April or May, and the storks are in residence into September.

Special Events

The Ephesus Festival, held during the second week of May, brings world-class performers to the Great Theatre at Ephesus and other venues. From mid-June to mid-July, performances of music and dance are organised under the rubric of the International İzmir Festival, with some performances at Ephesus.

Places to Stay – bottom end

Selçuk has almost 100 small pensions, and the Tourism Information Office will help you find one with rooms available.

The pension and carpet-shop touts in Selçuk have reached the rank of a pestilence. Touts at the bus station will badger you to follow them to one or another of the pensions, and will then badger the owner for a commission, thereby raising your price. Some touts will even promise to lead you to the pension of your choice, but will then lead you instead to some other from which it will be easier to extract a commission. Most pension owners dislike the touts (for obvious reasons); you'd do well to seek out a pension on your own with the help of this book.

If a bus station tout does own a pension, at some point they will tell you about a friend or relative with a carpet shop. Some will nag you tediously to shop for carpets.

Pension and cheap hotel maximum prices are set by the town government, so in high season pensions compete not on price but on such extras as cheap home-made meals, views, and rooms with private facilities. When business is slow, they compete on price as well.

Pensions fall into several groups according to location. Cheapest but most remote are those east of the centre in the section called Zafer Mahallesi, across the railway tracks and up the hill, a 10 or 15-minute walk from the centre; and north-east of Ayasoluk Hill, reached by going north along the main road towards İzmir, then left. The most convenient and congenial, but also a bit more expensive, are those in the sections called Atatürk Mahallesi and İsabey Mahallesi, on the hill behind (north and west of) the museum. Finally, there are a few smaller pensions on the south side of the Ephesus road.

Rooms in these modest, friendly, cheap places cost from $US6 to US$8 a single, US$8 to US$12 a double without bath; or from US$8 to US$10 a single, US$12 to US$15 a double with private shower. In some cases it's possible to sleep on the roof or camp in the garden for US$2 to US$3 per person. Many are run by women, which makes them good choices for female travellers.

Behind the Museum Facing the museum, walk up the street to the right of it. You will find the *Pension Kırhan* (☎ (232) 892 2257),

Turgutreis Sokak 7, with four rooms in a convenient location.

Farther along Turgutreis Sokak, *Abasız Pansiyon* (☎ (232) 892 1367), Turgutreis Sokak 13, is very friendly, with nine rooms, some with views. *Akgüneş Pension* (☎ (232) 892 3869), Turgutreis Sokak 14, across the street, has eight rooms, all with bath. It is run by hard-working Mrs Hamdullah ('Jesse') Akın.

Follow the signs to find the popular *Homeros Pension* (☎ (232) 892 3995), Asmalı Sokak 17, with lots of character and a nice terrace and rooftop bar with a panoramic view. The Homeros is high enough to get a cooling breeze on very hot days.

Back down Turgutreis Sokak past the Kırhan are two more pensions: the *Gedik Pansiyon* (☎ (232) 892 2452), Turgutreis Sokak 5, with 11 rooms, some with showers, and some singles; and beyond it, the *Barım Pansiyon* (☎ (232) 892 1927), Turgutreis Sokak 34, has lots of fancy brick and iron work, and six clean rooms.

Just to the right of the Pension Kırhan, Sefa Sokak winds uphill to the *Australian & New Zealand Pension* (☎ (232) 892 1050), Profesör Mitler Sokak 17, run by the Toparlak family who spent 12 years Down Under. The common facilities are clean, and you're allowed to use the kitchen and washing machine. Surprise! They also own a carpet shop. The five-room *Deniz Pansiyon* (☎ (232) 892 1741), Sefa Sokak 9, just beyond the Australian, takes the latter's overflow.

The quiet *Amazon Pension* (☎ (232) 892 3215), Serin Sokak 8, near the İsa Bey Camii and Hotel Akay, has seven bathless rooms and a pretty garden courtyard where breakfast is served. Ms Seval Demirel-Molenaar runs the popular *Vardar Pension* (☎ (232) 891 4967, fax 891 4099), Sahabettin Dede Caddesi 9, with 15 rooms sharing baths and a nice dining terrace where breakfast and dinner are served. Seval Hanım speaks some Dutch, English, French, German and Japanese, and stresses that she does not employ touts at the bus station, though she herself sometimes meets buses.

East of Ayasoluk Hill East of Ayasoluk Hill and the castle, west of the main road, are several other pensions and hotels. *Tuncay Pension* (☎ (232) 892 1260), Ay Sokak 3, is the best choice here, with cool, quiet, clean rooms, and a washing machine for guests' use.

South of the Ephesus Road South of the Ephesus road and west of the main street is a quiet neighbourhood of unremarkable modern apartment blocks. Some of the apartments have been converted to small pensions. *Yılmaz Pension* (☎ (232) 892 2163), 3 Spor Sokak 2, is typical, with three bathless rooms. *Pension Akbulut* (☎ (232) 892 1139), 2 Spor Sokak 4, has five quiet rooms with shared facilities.

East of the Centre The aptly named *Cheerful Pension* (☎ (232) 892 2732), Zafer Mahallesi, Çimenlik Sokak 3, is a distance from the centre, but has eight bathless rooms and gives excellent service.

In 14 Mayıs Mahallesi, farther up the hill and to the right, is the *Yayla Pension* (☎ (232) 892 2903), İnce Sokak 19. The 10 rooms have showers and toilets, and some have balconies. The view, and the home-cooked meals (by arrangement) are worth the walk. English is spoken by the friendly family proprietors. The nearby *Zümrüt Pension* (☎ (232) 892 1887), İnce Sokak 13, is simpler but cheaper, and just as welcoming.

Camping On the west side of Ayasoluk Hill 200m beyond the İsa Bey Camii, *Garden Motel & Camping* (☎ (232) 892 1163) offers grassy campsites in the shade of aspen trees and (surprise!) a carpet shop. At US$7 for a two-person tent, it's only a bit cheaper than the cheapest pensions, but the setting is nice. There's also camping at Pamucak (see following).

Places to Stay – middle

Selçuk has several simple one and two-star hotels in quiet locations with private facilities. Breakfast is usually included in the price.

First choice is the atmospheric, 50-room *Otel Kalehan* (☎ (232) 892 6154, fax 892 2169), İzmir Caddesi, on the main road just north of the Shell station. Built to resemble an old Turkish house (actually, group of houses), it's decorated in antiques, local crafts and textiles. Rooms, set back from the noisy road around a small swimming pool and verdant terrace, are of differing levels of comfort and price. The better ones have showers, mini-fridges and air-con, and cost US$30/50/70 a single/double/triple. Some have bathtubs. The restaurant is quite good. The owner, Mr Erol Ergir, comes from an old Ottoman family, and has put many historic mementoes on display.

The 16-room *Hotel Akay* (☎ (232) 892 3172, fax 892 3009), İsa Bey Camii Karşısı, Serin Sokak 3, is near the İsa Bey Camii and thus well away from the noise of the town. The simple guest rooms are built around an interior court and reached by walkways, motel-style. All rooms have tiled baths with telephone booth-style showers, and cost US$16/25 a single/double, breakfast included. There's a rooftop restaurant with views.

North of the centre is the simple *Otel Nazar* (☎ (232) 892 2222, fax 891 4016), Eski İzmir Caddesi 14. The enthusiastic owner will show you his tidy rooms and castle-view roof terrace, and rent them to you for US$25 a double, breakfast included, with reductions for stays of several days.

There are also several hotels on and off Cengiz Topel Caddesi between the fountain and the train station. The two-star *Victoria Hotel* (☎ (232) 892 3203), Cengiz Topel Caddesi 4, has a good restaurant on the ground floor and a lift to take you up to your room. The 14 small rooms cost US$25 a double, breakfast included, in the high summer season. Some rooms have views of the storks' nests in the old aqueduct, with storks in residence from mid-April to September.

Hotel Subaşı (☎ (232) 892 6359), Cengiz Topel Caddesi 12 across from the PTT, is comfortable. Owner Ziya Subaşı and his French wife live in Paris most of the year, but run the hotel from April to October. All 16 rooms have baths and cost US$22 a double; breakfast costs extra.

Otel Gazi (☎ (232) 892 6467), at Cengiz Topel Caddesi 1, facing the bust of Atatürk on the little plaza right by the train station, is in the centre of the action. A terrace café, out the front is good for people-watching, and the rooftop bar is perfect for breakfast. Rooms with bath and balcony cost US$22 a double, breakfast included.

A half-block south of Cengiz Topel Caddesi, *Hotel Hasanağa* (☎ (232) 892 6317), Koüak Sokak 5, is a second choice if the others are full. It has 23 quiet rooms, all with private baths, going for US$22 a double. *Hotel Aksoy* (☎ (232) 892 6040), Namık Kemal Caddesi 2, is among the oldest hotels in town, and shows it in some places, but charges US$20 a double. Some rooms have private showers and stork views.

The two-star *Ak Otel* (☎ (232) 892 2161, fax 892 3143), Kuşadası Caddesi 14, is owned by a Turkish family which spent many years in Belgium. It has 60 rooms in two buildings, all with showers. Rooms at the back are quieter. Rates are US$15/25 a single/double, breakfast included, but they'll haggle if not busy.

Places to Eat

Selçuk's restaurant prices, while not as high as Kuşadası's, are higher than those in İzmir or İstanbul. Out of season, they drop considerably. On average, soups cost US$1.25, meze from US$1.50 to US$2, meat dishes from US$2.50 to US$4. The simple pide and köfte places may not serve alcohol.

A speciality of this region is çöp şiş ('splinter kebap'), bits of lamb or beef skewered on a sliver of bamboo and grilled on charcoal.

All the restaurants along Cengiz Topel Caddesi between the highway and the train station have streetside tables in good weather, and most display prices prominently.

Bottom End Some pensions will prepare home-cooked meals for you – great food at low prices. For cheap pide, try the *Artemis Pide Salonu*, a half-block south of the tea garden at the eastern end of Cengiz Topel Caddesi, where Turkish-style pizza costs US$1.50 to US$2.50. Another is *Okumuşlar Pide Salonu* on Namık Kemal Caddesi, across from the Akbank. The *Kodalak Restaurant* at the bus terminal serves cheap stews, but ask prices before you order. The bus station's *Efes Pastanesi* provides snacks for the bus.

Middle Range On Cengiz Topel Caddesi, the *Özdamar Restaurant*, facing the fountain, and next to it the *Seçil*, are perennially popular. For puddings and baklava, try the *Dilek Patisserie*, a bit farther along, where four chunks of baklava and a glass of fizzy water cost US$1.50.

In the next block, the *Firuze* and the *Bizim* restaurants are a bit simpler, and may have slightly lower prices, as may *Tat*.

The family-run *Ephesus Restaurant*, on Namık Kemal Caddesi near the Hotel Aksoy and the İş Bankası, serves beef çöp şiş with rice, salad and bread for US$4, within view of the storks nesting in the old aqueduct.

The restaurant in the *Hotel Victoria* serves a good variety of food from spaghetti to şiş kebap at value-for-money prices.

Even if you aren't staying at the *Hotel Kalehan*, you can drop in for their excellent evening table d'hôte dinner, a carefully-prepared three-course meal for under US$8 with a simple main course, US$10 with a fancier one, plus drinks.

The *Hotel Akay*, near the İsa Bey Camii, has a pleasant roof restaurant on a quiet street.

By the train station there are some shaded tea gardens where you can sit, sip tea and watch the storks on top of the aqueduct from April to September.

For a sweet treat, drop in for a taste at *Tadım Şekerleme* (☎ 892 3999), near the PTT behind the Emlak Bankası, No 37/C (follow the signs). A 125g package of Turkish Delight costs less than US$1, and you can choose from 40 different types, from the fruity to the creamy. Mr Hikmet Çeliker, the confectioner, makes candied chestnuts as well.

Entertainment

Sipping and talking are the main evening entertainments in Selçuk. Besides the restaurants along Cengiz Topel Caddesi, there's the *Ekselans Bar*, 1. Okul Sokak 18/1, with outdoor tables and, next to it, the currently more popular *Pink Bistro Bar*.

The local Turkish bath is the Selçuk Hamamı, north of the Hotel Aksoy and the police station. Traditionally, women bathe on Friday, but in fact the manager will make allowances. If female foreigners or a mixed group show up when it's not busy, you may have the place to yourselves. The fee is still US$2.50 for a simple wash, US$8 for the works.

Getting Around

Bus Selçuk's bus station is across from the Tourism Information Office. Service is mostly local. Most long-distance services start somewhere else (İzmir, Kuşadası, Bodrum) and pick up passengers on the way through. There are dolmuş minibus services to Kuşadası, Pamucak, Şirince, Söke, and other nearby points.

Details of some of the main bus services follow:

Ephesus – three km, five minutes, US$0.50; frequent minibuses in summer, but it's also pleasant to walk (see the following)

İzmir – 80 km, 1¼ hours, US$2.25; buses every 15 minutes from 6.30 am to 7 pm in summer

Kuşadası – 20 km, 30 minutes, US$0.80; minibuses run frequently in summer, with the last minibus departing from Selçuk at 8.30 pm, from Kuşadası at 9 pm. After hours, look for a more expensive taxi lurking near the Tourism Information Office

Pamucak – seven km, 10 minutes, US$0.70; last minibus departs well before sunset; a taxi costs US$8

Minibus Tours For details of minibus tours to Priene, Miletus, Didyma and Altınkum (Yenihisar), see that section, following. If the tours are not running, or if you'd rather go on your own, catch a bus or minibus to Söke. From there, minibuses run to points throughout the region, including to Priene, Didyma and Altınkum. Going on your own is cheaper but can take much more time.

Taxi Taxi drivers charge about US$3 per car to take you the three km to the Ephesus ruins, and about US$10 to Meryemana and back. For US$18 per car, they'll take you to the main ruins, wait, take you to Meryemana, and return you to Selçuk. Perhaps the best plan is to take a taxi to Meryemana for a short visit, then have it drop you at Ephesus' south entrance so you can walk downhill through the ruins rather than up. You'll get as long a visit as you want, after which you can walk the three km back to Selçuk.

EPHESUS

Ephesus is the best-preserved classical city on the eastern Mediterranean, and among the best places in the world to get a feel for what life was like in Roman times. Needless to say, it is a major tourist destination.

In high summer it gets very hot here. It's best to start your tramping early in the morning, then retire to a shady restaurant for lunch at the peak of the heat. If your interest in ancient ruins is slight, a half-day may suffice, but real ruins buffs will want to continue their explorations in the afternoon as well. Take a water bottle as drinks at the site are more expensive.

It's three km from the Tourism Information Office in Selçuk to the admission gate at Ephesus, a pleasant 30 to 45-minute walk along a shady lane at the side of the highway. The lane, actually the old road, is named after Doktor Sabri Yayla, who had the foresight to plant the trees earlier in the century.

Admission to the archaeological site costs US$6, half-price for students and free for those over 65; parking costs US$1.25. The site is open from 8.30 am to 5.30 pm (till 7 pm in summer) every day.

History

Earliest Times According to a legend related by Athenaeus, Androclus, son of King Codrus of Athens, consulted an oracle about where he should found a settlement in Ionia. The oracle answered, in typically cryptic style, 'choose the site indicated by the fish and the boar'.

Androclus sat down with some fishermen near the mouth of the Cayster River and Mt Pion (Panayır Dağı), the hill into which Ephesus' Great Theatre was later to be built. As they grilled some fish for lunch, one of the fish leapt out of the brazier, taking with it a hot coal which ignited some shavings, which in turn ignited the nearby brush. A wild boar hiding in the brush ran in alarm from the fire; the spot at which it was killed by the fishermen became the site of Ephesus' temple of Athena.

For many years thereafter the wild boar was a symbol of the city. Until the 1970s it was still common to see wild pigs in scrub thickets near Ephesus.

In ancient times the sea came much farther inland, almost as far as present-day Selçuk, even lapping at the feet of Mt Pion. The first settlement, of which virtually nothing remains, was built on the hill's northern slope, and was a prosperous city by about 600 BC. The nearby sanctuary of Cybele/Artemis, the Anatolian mother-goddess, had been a place of pilgrimage since at least 800 BC and may – let's face it – have had more to do with the selection of the site than the fish and the pig.

Croesus & The Persians Ephesus prospered so much that it aroused the envy of King Croesus of Lydia, who attacked it around 600 BC. The Ephesians, who had neglected to build defensive walls, stretched a rope from the temple of Artemis to the town, a distance of 1200m, hoping thus to place themselves under the protection of the goddess. Croesus responded to this quaint defensive measure by giving some of his famous wealth for the completion of the temple, which was still under construction. But he destroyed the city of Ephesus and relocated its citizens inland to the south side of the temple, where they rebuilt and lived through classical times.

Neglecting again (or perhaps forbidden) to build walls, the Ephesians were tributaries

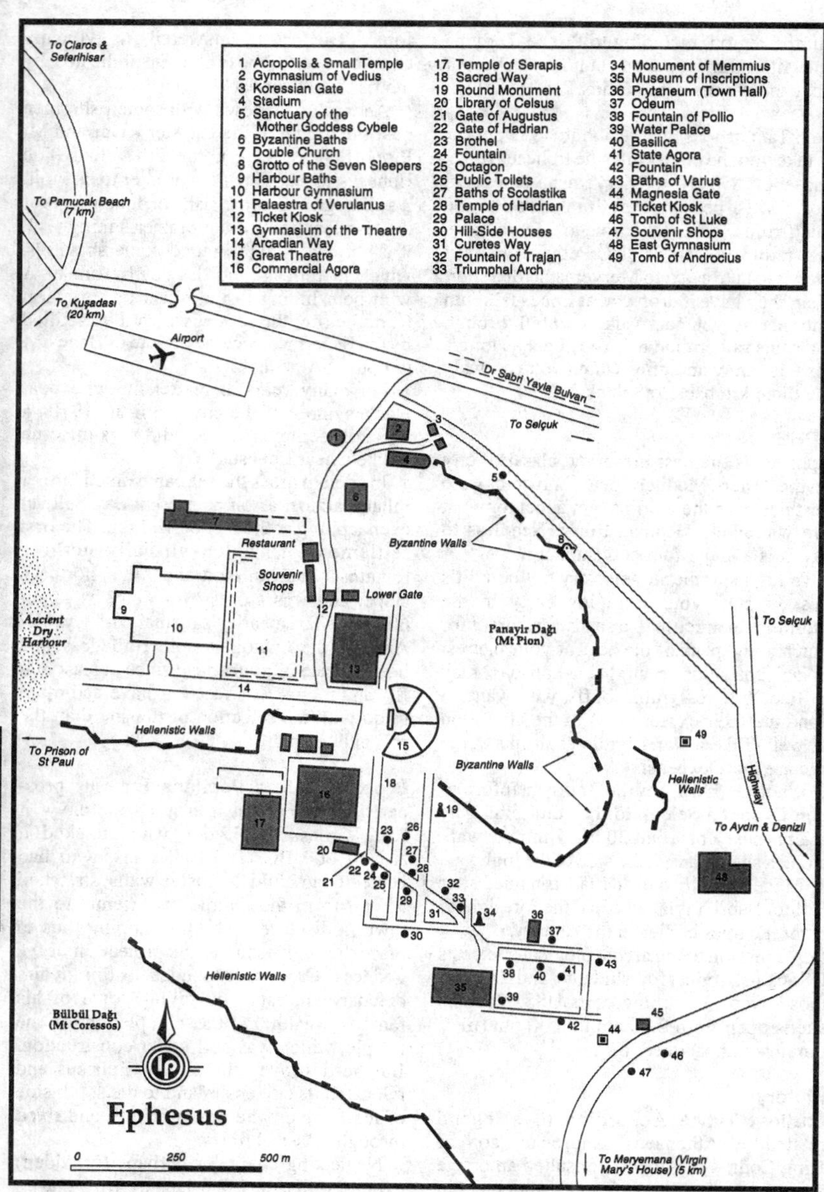
1 Acropolis & Small Temple
2 Gymnasium of Vedius
3 Koressian Gate
4 Stadium
5 Sanctuary of the Mother Goddess Cybele
6 Byzantine Baths
7 Double Church
8 Grotto of the Seven Sleepers
9 Harbour Baths
10 Harbour Gymnasium
11 Palaestra of Verulanus
12 Ticket Kiosk
13 Gymnasium of the Theatre
14 Arcadian Way
15 Great Theatre
16 Commercial Agora
17 Temple of Serapis
18 Sacred Way
19 Round Monument
20 Library of Celsus
21 Gate of Augustus
22 Gate of Hadrian
23 Brothel
24 Fountain
25 Octagon
26 Public Toilets
27 Baths of Scolastika
28 Temple of Hadrian
29 Palace
30 Hill-Side Houses
31 Curetes Way
32 Fountain of Trajan
33 Triumphal Arch
34 Monument of Memmius
35 Museum of Inscriptions
36 Prytaneum (Town Hall)
37 Odeum
38 Fountain of Pollio
39 Water Palace
40 Basilica
41 State Agora
42 Fountain
43 Baths of Varius
44 Magnesia Gate
45 Ticket Kiosk
46 Tomb of St Luke
47 Souvenir Shops
48 East Gymnasium
49 Tomb of Androcius
To Claros & Seferihisar
To Pamucak Beach (7 km)
To Kuşadası (20 km)
Airport
Dr Sabri Yayla Bulvarı
To Selçuk
Byzantine Walls
Restaurant
Souvenir Shops
Lower Gate
Ancient Dry Harbour
Panayir Dağı (Mt Pion)
To Selçuk
Hellenistic Walls
To Prison of St Paul
Byzantine Walls
Hellenistic Walls
Highway
To Aydın & Denizli
Hellenistic Walls
Bülbül Dağı (Mt Coressos)
Ephesus
0
250
500 m
To Meryemana (Virgin Mary's House) (5 km)

of Croesus' Lydia and, later, of the Persians. They then joined the Athenian confederacy, but later fell back under Persian control.

Rebuilding the Temple In 356 BC the temple of Cybele/Artemis was destroyed in a fire set by one Herostratus, who claimed to have done it – like so many modern-day lunatics – in order to go down in history, which he did.

The Ephesians planned a new, even grander temple, the construction of which was well under way when Alexander the Great arrived in 334 BC. Alexander, much impressed by the plans, offered to pay the entire cost of construction if only it would be dedicated in his name. The Ephesians declined his generous offer, saying that it was not fitting for one god to make a dedication to another. When the temple was finished, it was recognised as one of the seven wonders of the world, together with the Mausoleum at Halicarnassus (Bodrum), the Egyptian pyramids, the Colossus of Rhodes, the statue of Zeus at Olympia, the lighthouse at Alexandria, and the hanging gardens of Babylon.

Under Lysimachus After Alexander's death, Ionia came under the control of Lysimachus, one of his generals. As the Cayster brought more silt into the harbour, it became clear that the city would have to move westward or die a commercial death. Lysimachus, unable to convince the Ephesians to budge, blocked the sewers of the old city during a downpour. Their houses flooded, and the Ephesians reluctantly moved to a site on the west side of Mt Pion, where the Roman city now stands.

Little survives of Lysimachus' city, though it finally got a defensive wall almost 10 km long which served it well during the following centuries as it allied itself first with the Seleucid kings of Syria, then with the Ptolemies of Egypt, later with King Antiochus, then Eumenes of Pergamum, and finally with the Romans. Long stretches of the wall survive atop Bülbül Dağı (Mt Croesus), the high ridge on the south side of Ephesus, as does a prominent square tower, nicknamed 'St Paul's Prison', on a low hill to the west.

Roman Ephesus Roman Ephesus, the ruins of which lie before you, boasted that it was the 'first and greatest metropolis of Asia', with a population approaching 250,000. It became the Roman capital of Asia Minor, honoured and beautified by succeeding emperors. With its brisk sea traffic, rich commerce and right of sanctuary in the precincts of the temple of Artemis, it drew many immigrants of various nations and creeds. St

Demetrius the Silversmith

St Paul lived at Ephesus for three years, perhaps in the 60s AD. According to the Bible (Acts 19:24-41), his mission was so successful that the trade in religious artefacts for the Artemis cult dropped off precipitously.

Hurt by the slump, a silversmith named Demetrius, who made silver Artemis shrines, gathered a group of other artisans who had lost business. At first they grumbled about the effects of Paul's preaching on their incomes, but they soon sought a higher rationale and blamed Paul's preaching for a loss of respect for the goddess herself.

Rumours spread throughout the city that someone was being disrespectful of Artemis. People flooded into the Great Theatre, sweeping along several of Paul's Christian travelling companions. Paul, set on entering the theatre (perhaps to give the sermon of his life to a packed house), was dissuaded from doing so by his disciples.

Unclear on the cause of the uproar, the mob in the theatre shouted 'Great is Artemis of the Ephesians!' for an hour before the secretary of the city council calmed them down enough to speak. The Christians, having broken no law, were released and the uproar subsided, but Paul left Ephesus shortly thereafter for Macedonia. ■

John came here, it is said with the Virgin Mary, followed by St Paul, whose Letter to the Ephesians was written to people he had known from his three-year stay here.

Its prosperity from commerce and temple pilgrimage was unrivalled, but the Cayster continued to bring silt down into the harbour. Despite great works by Attalus II of Pergamum, who rebuilt the harbour, and Nero's proconsul, who dredged the harbour, the silting continued. Emperor Hadrian had the Cayster's course diverted, but the harbour continued to silt up, ultimately pushing the sea back to Pamucak, four km to the west. Cut off from its commerce, Ephesus lost its wealth. By the 6th century AD, when the Emperor Justinian was looking for a site for the St John basilica, he chose Ayasoluk Hill in Selçuk, which became the centre of the city from then on.

A Walking Tour

As you walk into the site from Dr Sabri Yayla Bulvarı, a road to the left is marked for the Grotto of the Seven Sleepers, on the north-east side of Mt Pion just over a km away.

Grotto of the Seven Sleepers According to legend, seven persecuted Christian youths fled from Ephesus in the 3rd century AD and took refuge in this cave. Agents of the Emperor Decius, a terror to Christians, found the cave and sealed it. Two centuries later an earthquake broke down the wall, awakening the sleepers, and they ambled back to town for a meal. Finding that all of their old friends were long dead, they concluded that they had undergone a sort of resurrection – Ephesus was by this time a Christian city. When they died they were buried in the cave, and a cult following developed.

The grotto is actually a fairly elaborate Byzantine-era **necropolis** with scores of tombs cut into the rock. You must pay an extra admission charge to enter (at least in season), which many people feel is hardly worth it.

Gymnasium of Vedius & Stadium Back on the entry road you pass the Gymnasium of Vedius (2nd century AD) on your left, which had exercise fields, baths, toilets, covered exercise rooms, a swimming pool and a ceremonial hall. Just south of it is the Stadium, dating from about the same period. Most of its finely cut stones were taken by the Byzantines to build the citadel and walls of the castle atop Ayasoluk hill. This 'quarrying' of pre-cut building stone from older, often earthquake-ruined structures continued through the entire history of Ephesus.

Double Church The road comes over a low rise and descends to the car park, where there are teahouses, restaurants, souvenir shops, a PTT and banks. To the right (west) of the road are the ruins of the Church of the Virgin Mary, also called the Double Church. The original building was a Museum – a Hall of the Muses – a place for lectures, teaching and educated discussions and debates. Destroyed by fire, it was rebuilt in the 4th century AD as a church, later to become the site of the third Ecumenical Council (431 AD) which condemned the Nestorian heresy. Over the centuries several other churches succeeded to the site, somewhat obscuring the plan of the original church.

Arcadian Way As you walk down a lane bordered by evergreen trees, a few colossal remains of the **Harbour Gymnasium** are off to the right (west) before you reach the marble-paved Arcadian Way, or Arcadiane. This, the grandest street in Ephesus, had water and sewer lines beneath the marble flags, 50 streetlights along its colonnades, shops along its sides, and near its western (harbour) end a **Nymphaeum** (fountain and pool) and triumphal columns. It was and is a grand sight. Its builder was the Byzantine emperor Arcadius (395-408).

Great Theatre At the east end of the Arcadian Way is the Great Theatre, of Hellenistic design, skilfully reconstructed by the Romans between 41 and 117 AD, which means that the riot of Demetrius the silversmith took place in a theatre under reconstruction.

The first theatre here dates from the city of Lysimachus, and many features of the original building were incorporated into the Roman structure. Among these is the ingenious design of the *cavea*, or seating area, capable of holding 25,000 people: each successive range of seating up from the stage is pitched more steeply than the one below it, thereby improving the view and acoustics for spectators in the upper seats. Among other modifications, the Romans enlarged the stage, pitched it towards the audience, and built a three-story decorative stage wall behind it, improving the acoustics even more.

The Great Theatre is still used for performances, though it was closed at the time of writing for further restoration.

Behind the Great Theatre is Mt Pion, which bears a few traces of the **ruined city walls** of Lysimachus.

Sacred Way From the theatre, walk south along the marble-paved Sacred Way, also called the Marble Way. Note the remains of the city's elaborate water and sewer systems beneath the paving-stones, and the ruts made by wheeled vehicles (which were not permitted along the Arcadian Way). The large, open space to the right (west) of the street, once surrounded by a colonnade and shops, was the **commercial agora** (3 BC) or marketplace, heart of Ephesus' business life, presently under restoration.

On the left as you approach the end of the street is an elaborate **brothel** with a rich mosaic of the Four Seasons in the main hall; the heads of Winter and Autumn are still in good condition.

The Sacred Way ends at the **Embolos**, or 'central Ephesus,' with the Library of Celsus and the monumental Gate of Augustus to the right (west), and Curetes Way heading east up the slope.

Library of Celsus Gaius Julius Celsus Polemaeanus was the Roman governor of Asia Minor early in the 2nd century AD. In 110, after the governor's death, his son, Consul Gaius Julius Aquila, erected this library in his father's honour; so says an inscription in Latin and Greek on the side of the building's front staircase. Celsus was buried under the west side of the library, where he rests to this day.

The library held 12,000 scrolls in niches around its walls. A one-metre gap between the library's inner and outer walls protected the valuable books from extremes of temperature and humidity. Though it now stands alone, the library was originally built between other buildings, and architectural legerdemain was used to make it look bigger than it is: the base of the façade is convex, adding height to the central elements; and the central columns and capitals are larger than those at the ends.

The niches on the façade held statues (now in Vienna's Ephesus Museum) representing the Virtues: Arete (Goodness), Ennoia (Thought), Episteme (Knowledge) and Sophia (Wisdom). The library was restored with the aid of the Austrian Archaeological Institute.

To the right of the library, the **Gate of Augustus**, also called the Gate of Mazaeus and Mithridates, leads into the 110-metre-square commercial agora where food and craftwork items were sold. The monumental gate, dedicated to the honour of the Emperor Augustus, his wife and son-in-law, was apparently a favourite place for Roman ne'er-do-wells to relieve themselves, as an informal inscription curses 'those who piss here'.

Curetes Way As you head up Curetes Way, a passage on the left (north) leads to the **public toilets**, design demonstrating function unmistakably. These posh premises were for men only; the women's were elsewhere. In the **well** nearby, right next to the brothel, was found the famous figure of Priapus (now in the Ephesus Museum in Selçuk) with the penis of his dreams.

You can't miss the impressive **Temple of Hadrian**, on the left, in Corinthian style, with beautiful reliefs in the porch and a head of Medusa to keep out evil spirits. It was dedicated in 118 AD to Hadrian, Artemis and the people of Ephesus, but greatly reconstructed in the 4th century.

Across the street is a row of 10 shops from the same period, fronted by an elaborate 5th-century mosaic.

On the right side of Curetes Way across from the Temple of Hadrian, excavation and restoration work is still in progress on the **Yamaç Evleri** (hill-side houses). Several of the larger, grander houses with fine mosaics, frescoes and marble work are periodically opened to visitors. If you have the opportunity, be sure to see the rare **glass mosaic** in a niche off the atrium of one of the houses.

Further along Curetes Way, on the left, is the **Fountain of Trajan**, who was Roman emperor from 98 to 117 AD. A huge statue of the emperor used to tower above the pool; only the feet remain.

Curetes Way ended at the **Gate of Hercules**, constructed in the 4th century AD, a two-storey gate with reliefs of Hercules on both main pillars.

To the right is a side street leading to a colossal temple dedicated to the Emperor Domitian (81-96 AD), which now serves as the **Museum of Inscriptions**, which may or may not be open when you visit.

Up the hill on the left (north) are the very ruined remains of the **Prytaneum**, a municipal hall; and the **Temple of Hestia Boulaea**, in which the perpetual flame was guarded. Finally you come to the **Odeum**, a small 1400-seat theatre dating from 150 AD used for lectures, musical performances and meetings of the town council. Its lower seats, of marble, show something of the magnificence of the original.

To the east of the Odeum are the **Baths of Varius** and, farther east, the East Gymnasium and the Magnesia Gate, of which virtually nothing remains.

PAMUCAK

About seven km west of Selçuk (three km west of the highway junction with the Kuşadası and Seferihisar roads) lies Pamucak (PAH-moo-jahk) beach, a long wide crescent of dark sand. It's crowded with free campers and Turkish families on summer weekends, and mostly deserted except for litter thereafter.

Places to Stay

The shady *Dereli Motel* (☎ (232) 892 3636, fax 892 6547), to the left as you come to the

Meryemana

Legend has it that the Virgin Mary, accompanied by St Paul, came to Ephesus at the end of her life, circa 37-45 AD. Renaissance church historians mentioned the trip, and it is said that local Christians venerated a small house near Ephesus as Mary's.

In the 19th century a German woman named Catherine Emmerich (1774-1824) had visions of Mary and of her surroundings at Ephesus. When Lazarist clergy from İzmir followed Emmerich's detailed descriptions, they discovered the foundations of an old house in the hills near Ephesus; a tomb, also described by Emmerich, was not found.

In 1967 Pope Paul VI visited the site, where a chapel now stands, and confirmed the authenticity of the legend. A small traditional service, celebrated by Orthodox and Muslim clergy on 15 August each year in honour of Mary's Assumption into heaven, is now the major event here. To Muslims, Mary is Meryemana, Mother Mary, who bore İsa Peygamber, the Prophet Jesus.

The site is now a Selçuk municipal park; there is no regular dolmuş service, so you'll have to hitch, rent a taxi (about US$10 per car to Meryemana and back) or take a tour. The park is seven km from Ephesus' Lower (northern) Gate, or 5.5 km from the Upper (southern) Gate, and nine km from Selçuk, up steep grades. The views of Ephesus, Selçuk, Ayasoluk Hill, and the surrounding countryside are wonderful along the way. Entry to the site costs US$2.

Along the approach to the house are signboards explaining its significance in various languages. The house is usually busy with pilgrims, the devout and the curious. A small restaurant and snack stand provide meals at fairly moderate prices. If you're travelling on a budget, bring picnic supplies and enjoy lunch on your own in the shady park. ■

beach, has double or twin-bedded motel-style rooms with bath, facing the beach (US$35) or the land (US$30); slightly more comfortable rooms in bungalows cost US$40 a double. The whole place could do with a bit more maintenance, but it does offer a restaurant, food shop, camping area (US$11 for a tent, more for a caravan or camper van), and that lovely deep shade.

Beyond the Dereli to the south is the *Selçuk Belediyesi Halk Plajları*, the municipal beach and camping ground. The rate is US$6 for up to four people in a tent. There are showers and a snack shop, and you can use the services at the adjoining Dereli.

Inland from the beach 250m is the four-star, 150-room *Otel Tamsa* (☎ (232) 892 1190, fax 892 2771), Çorak Mevkii, Pamucak, an ageing tour-group hotel. Though the exterior has all the charm of a barracks, the interior is comfortable enough at US$45/60 a single/double during the high-summer season.

Getting There & Away

There are regular minibuses from Selçuk and Kuşadası in summer; hitching is easy during the hot months as well. Be sure to find out when the last minibus departs from the beach; it may leave well before sunset.

ŞİRİNCE

Eight km east of Selçuk up in the hills, in the midst of grapevines, peach and apple orchards, lies Şirince (population 800). The old-fashioned stone-and-stucco houses have red-tile roofs, and the villagers, who were moved here from Salonica and its vicinity during the exchange of populations (1924) after WWI, are ardent fruit farmers. They make interesting grape and apple wines. Locals regale you proudly with the story that in Ottoman times, when populated mostly by Greeks, the village was called Çirkince ('ugliness'), but that it was changed to Şirince ('pleasantness') shortly after they arrived. They'll also admit that a century ago it was much larger and more prosperous, the economic focus for seven monasteries in the hills around.

Stroll the winding streets, peek at the Byzantine churches and monasteries, walk in the hills, and haggle with local women for lace, their idle-hours handiwork. If a local woman invites you to inspect her 'antique house', you can be sure there will be lace for sale on display. Mostly the invitations are genuine, despite one reader's report of having been charged an outrageous amount for a 'welcoming' glass of tea.

Places to Stay & Eat

The minibus from Selçuk drops you at the centre of town in front of the restaurants. The *Köy Restaurant* and *Sultanhan Cafe* have the best shade and views, and specialise in village dishes such as mantı (Turkish ravioli), gözleme (thin pastry folded several times over a filling), yayık ayran (churned yogurt and spring water), and ev şarabı (home-made wine).

There are several pensions. The simple ones, some of them nameless, are roughly like Mrs Naciye Çatal's *Şirin Pansiyon* (☎ (232) 898 3167; follow the signs), offering clean beds in waterless rooms for US$8 a double.

Fancier places – restored village houses – include the German-run *Erdem Pansion* (☎ (232) 898 3430; in İzmir (232) 481 49 28) and the picturesque *Şirince Evleri* (☎ in İzmir (232) 421 0796, fax 421 0796), with cleaned-up charm and comforts for US$22 for a bed, US$5 for breakfast.

Getting There & Away

Three or four minibuses run daily between Selçuk and Şirince for US$0.60. The last minibus back to Selçuk may leave by mid-afternoon.

BELEVİ

North and east of Selçuk nine km on the İzmir highway is the village of Belevi, and about two km east of the village, just to the side of the new İzmir-Aydın otoyol, stands the **Belevi Mausoleum** (Belevi Mezar Anıtı), a large ancient funerary monument resting on a base of about 30 sq metres cut from the limestone bedrock. The roof was decorated with lion-griffins (now in the Ephesus Museum at Selçuk and in İzmir's Archaeological Museum), and the interior held a large sarcophagus with a carved effigy of its occupant; the sarcophagus is now in the museum in Selçuk. Archaeologists are not certain who built this great tomb. It may have been the Seleucid ruler Antiochus II Theos (261-246 BC), or it may have been the work of the Persian invaders a century or more earlier.

Just west of the mausoleum is a tumulus, or burial mound, thought to date from the 4th century BC, but little remains.

KUŞADASI

On the Aegean coast 20 km from Selçuk is Kuşadası (koo-SHAH-dah-suh, Bird Island). A seaside resort town with a population of 50,000, it is, like Selçuk, a base for excursions to the ancient cities in the vicinity (Ephesus, Priene, Miletus, Didyma), to Altınkum beach and Dilek Milli Park (a national park), and even inland to Aphrodisias and Pamukkale.

Many cruise ships on the Aegean islands circuit stop at Kuşadası so passengers can tour Ephesus and haggle for trinkets in Kuşadası's bazaar. Package-tour travellers arrive to stay in one of the hundreds of new hotels for a week of sun. The town centre is all shops and *işportacılar*, itinerant pedlars and touts ready to sell you anything and everything. The pleasant, easy atmosphere which made it popular in the 1970s is long gone, even though Kuşadası still has some businesses serving the farmers, beekeepers and fishers who still make up an ever-dwindling portion of the town's population.

Kuşadası gets its name from a small island, now connected to the mainland by a causeway, called Güvercinada, or Güvercin Adası (Pigeon Island). You can recognise it by the small stone fort which is the tiny island's most prominent feature.

History

The natural port here may have been in use several centuries BC, and was probably known to the Byzantines, but modern Kuşadası's history begins in medieval times when Venetian and Genoese traders came here, calling it Scala Nuova. Two centuries after the Ottoman conquest in 1413, Öküz Mehmet Paşa, vizier and sometime grand vizier to sultans Ahmet I and Osman II, ordered the building of the Kaleiçi mosque and hamam, the city walls, and the caravanserai in order to improve Kuşadası's prospects as a trading port with Europe and Africa.

Useful for exporting agricultural goods, Kuşadası was also an important defensive port along the Ottoman Aegean coast. In 1834 the little fortress on Güvercinada was restored and improved. It maintained its modest trade, farming and fishing economy and its quiet character until the tourism boom of the 1980s turned it into a brash resort.

Orientation

Kuşadası's central landmark is the Öküz Mehmet Paşa Kervansarayı, an Ottoman caravanserai which is now a hotel. It's 100m inland from the cruise-ship docks, at the intersection of the waterfront boulevard, Atatürk Bulvarı, and the town's main street, a pedestrian way named Barbaros Hayrettin Caddesi. Named for the great Ottoman admiral, this street goes inland (south-east) from the caravanserai.

Just beyond the PTT on the north side of Barbaros Hayrettin Caddesi, a narrow passage leads to the Öküz Mehmet Paşa mosque and the Kaleiçi Hamamı (Turkish bath). At the little stone tower that was once part of the town's defensive walls, Barbaros Hayrettin Caddesi crosses Sağlık Caddesi and changes names to become Kahramanlar Caddesi, lined with shops and restaurants. Turn left onto Sağlık Caddesi to explore Kuşadası's market and the old Kaleiçi neighbourhood of narrow streets, little restaurants and pensions. Turn right to find raucous Barlar Sokak (Bars Street), and pensions up on the hillside overlooking the harbour.

The little mosque about 100m along Kahramanlar Caddesi, called the Hacı Hatice

Hanım Camii (Hanım Camii for short), is a convenient landmark.

The bus and dolmuş station is more than one km east of the caravanserai on the bypass road.

Information

The Tourism Information Office (☎ (256) 614 1103, fax 614 6295), on İskele Meydanı, is down by the wharf where the cruise ships dock, about 100m west of the caravanserai. Hours are officially from 8.30 am to 7 pm daily in July and August, 8.30 am to 6 pm in May, June, September and October, and Monday to Friday from 8.30 am to 5.30 pm off season, all with a lunch-break from noon to 1 pm, but these hours are not strictly observed.

Banks with ATMs are on Barbaros Hayrettin Caddesi (Akbank, Garanti, Yapı Kredi, Ziraat).

The PTT is on Barbaros Hayrettin Caddesi near the caravanserai, and it changes money as well.

Kuydaş (☎ (256) 614 1828), İnönü Bulvarı 8/B, has a good selection of English-language books on Turkey, as well as novels, newspapers and periodicals.

Kuşadası has a government-run hospital (☎ (256) 614 1026) and many private doctors and dentists.

Kuşadası's postal code is 09400.

Beaches

After a stroll through the caravanserai and out to Güvercinada, you'll want to find the beaches. You can swim from the rocky shores of Güvercin Adası and its causeway, but **Yılancı Burnu**, the peninsula less than one km to the south, is more enticing. Or catch the Şehiriçi (in-town) dolmuş to the northern beach near the yacht marina or the far north past the Kuştur holiday village to the beach opposite the Tur-Yat Mocamp.

Kuşadası's most famous beach is **Kadınlar Denizi** (Ladies' Sea), 2.5 km south of town, served by dolmuş minibuses bearing that name and running along the shore road. Kadınlar Denizi is a small beach crowded by big hotels and woefully inadequate for the crowds in high summer, when the hotel pool is often more inviting. The coast south of Kadınlar Denizi has several more small beaches, each backed by its ranks of big hotels.

There's also **Pamucak** (see earlier), 15 km to the north, served by dolmuşes from Kuşadası's otogar in high summer; at other times you must change at Selçuk to a Pamucak dolmuş, or get out at the Pamucak road and walk three km.

Turkish Baths

Kuşadası's hamams are of the un-Turkish New Age type, allowing men and women to bathe at the same time, at inflated prices. The cost is US$15 for everything, an outrageous amount by Turkish standards.

The Belediye Hamamı (☎ 614 1219) is up the hill behind the Akdeniz Apart-otel; take the street which goes along the left side of the hotel. Kaleiçi Hamamı (☎ 614 1292) is just west of the Öküz Mehmet Paşa mosque.

Places to Stay

Prices for rooms in Kuşadası are highest in July and August (as quoted below), about 20% lower in June and September, and up to 50% lower in other months. Only a few places remain open from November to March.

Five-star hotels are on the outskirts. In the centre are small, moderately-priced hotels and cheap pensions. The rule of thumb is the same for any seaside resort: the farther you go inland (away from the sea), the cheaper the room.

Places to Stay – bottom end

Cheap pension rooms can be pleasant or stark. Most have sinks, a few have private baths. The price for a double ranges from US$18 to US$24 in season.

Pension touts await you at the otogar and ferry dock, and taxi drivers want to take you to a lodging which pays them a commission. The cheapest pensions and hotels are farther inland, and can be difficult to find on your own, so you may have to trust in the touts; many are in fact helpful. But say goodbye at the first sign of improper dealing to avoid being ripped off. Among Kuşadası pension owners are a small number of sleazy characters, so it's good to size a pension up carefully before staying there. The tourism officials at the otogar are helpful, but may try to book you in a hotel charging more than you want to spend.

There are several convenient clusters of pensions and small hotels near the centre; here's how to find them. Walk up Barbaros Hayrettin Caddesi, turn right towards the Akdeniz Apart-otel, and take Aslanlar Caddesi, the road on the right side of the Akdeniz. This takes you into the neighbourhood called Camiatik Mahallesi, which has a dozen pensions and inexpensive hotels.

Aslanlar Caddesi *Hotel İzmirli* (☎ (256) 614 4861), on Aslanlar Caddesi near the Hotel Akdeniz, is right in the thick of things, but if you choose your room carefully it can be serviceable. Rooms cost US$20/24/28 a single/double/triple, breakfast included.

Follow the signs to the family-run *Pansiyon Golden Bed* (☎ (256) 614 8708), Aslanlar Caddesi, Uğurlu 1 Çıkmazı 4, on a quiet little cul-de-sac not far from the centre.

Some rooms have balconies and sea views, and there are excellent views from the roof terrace. Rooms with shower cost US$20 a double with breakfast.

Farther uphill on Aslanlar Caddesi past the Hotel Flash, look for the *Hotel Ada* (☎ (256) 614 9559) and nearby the very simple but cheap *Pansiyon Su* (☎ (256) 614 1453), Aslanlar Caddesi 13, with basic waterless rooms for US$8 per person.

Kıbrıs Caddesi At the top of the slope, Kıbrıs Caddesi goes downhill on your right to the *Özhan Pansiyon* (☎ (256) 614 2932), Kıbrıs Caddesi 5, very central and normally quiet, with a nice roof terrace with bar and – occasionally – pension-sponsored belly-dance parties. Rooms with shower cost US$14/20 a single/double; breakfast costs extra, but is pleasant on the terrace.

Bezirgan Sokak Back up at the top of the hill, turn right and follow Bezirgan Sokak, looking for signs to the *Pansiyon Dinç* (☎ (256) 614 4249), Mercan Sokak – small, simple, and cheap at US$16 a double, breakfast included, in a waterless room. Past the Hotel Stella are several more, including the *King Pansiyon* (☎ (256) 614 3128), *Enişte Pansiyon* (☎ (256) 614 2171) and *Pansiyon Hasgül* (☎ (256) 614 3641), all in a quiet area, some with sea views.

Güzel Sokak At the top of Aslanlar and Kıbrıs Caddesis, instead of turning right onto Bezirgan Sokak, if you turn left you'll be on Güzel Sokak. Two blocks along is the 15-room *Hülya Pension* (☎ (256) 614 2075), İleri Sokak 39 near Güzel Sokak, which charges US$8 per person in a room, slightly less if you roll out your own sleeping bag on a bed on the roof. Some rooms have sinks or private showers. Laundry is done for an additional fee; cheap, good meals are available, or you may use the kitchen yourself.

Farther inland, *Pansiyon Sympathy* (☎ (256) 614 4388), Güvercin Sokak, is run by a smiling dynamo of a woman who provides good, cheap meals in a rooftop dining room as well as clean, cheap lodgings. Rates are from US$12/18 a single/double in summer; meals cost extra.

Şefik Pension (☎ (256) 614 4222), Camiatik Mahallesi, Doğan Sokak 11, is similar, at comparable rates, with good food and friendly family proprietors.

Camping North of the centre about one km, inland from the yacht marina, are three decent camping areas. Best is *Önder Camping* (☎ (256) 614 2413, fax 614 2946), open all year, with lots of facilities: tennis, swimming pool, laundry, and a good restaurant (open from March to October only). If the Önder is full, the adjoining *Yat Motel & Camping* takes the overflow.

Tur-Yat Mocamp, several km north of these on the shore just before the Tusan Hotel, is a larger camping ground open from mid-April or late May until mid to late October. Right across the road from a favoured beach, it charges US$8 for two in a tent. Motel rooms cost US$36/42/50 a single/double/triple, breakfast and dinner included.

Places to Stay – middle

Mid-range hotels are scattered throughout the town, with some inland from the yacht marina, some on the pension streets of Aslanlar and Kıbrıs Caddesis and Bezirgan Sokak, and many more farther inland along Kahramanlar Caddesi.

In Kaleiçi, just off Barbaros Hayrettin Caddesi opposite the caravanserai is Cephane Sokak (JEHP-hah-neh) and the *Bahar Pansiyon* (☎ (256) 614 1191, fax 614 9359), Cephane Sokak 12, a charming inn with a façade full of balconies and flower boxes, and a rooftop restaurant. The 13 rooms offer a step up in comfort, and also in price, at US$20/32 a single/double, breakfast included. The Bahar is closed from November to February.

Also right in the centre is the 22-room *Hotel Aynalı* (☎ (256) 614 4582), PTT Sokak 6 (walk north one block on the little street by the PTT), a modern building with old Turkish wood trim. Many rooms have balconies, all have baths, and breakfast is included in the price of US$32 a double.

Walk up Aslanlar Caddesi, which mounts the slope to the right of the Akdeniz Apart-otel, to find the *Hotel Flash* (☎ (256) 614 3806, fax 614 4225), Aslanlar 70-A, across from the Hotel Ada. Popular with groups, it has a nice swimming pool and bar, and charges from US$30 to US$38 a double, breakfast included.

Turn right onto Bezirgan Sokak to find the two-star, 22-room *Hotel Stella* (☎ (256) 614 1632, 614 3787), Bezirgan Sokak 44. It's a tidy, airy place with fabulous views of the town and the harbour; friendly and personable management; and bright, modern rooms priced at US$55 a double with shower, breakfast included.

About one km north of the centre is another group of moderately priced lodgings on İstiklal Sokak.

Hotel Köken (☎ (256) 614 1460, fax 614 5723), İstiklal Sokak 5, is the standard Turkish two-star: rooms with private baths for US$36, breakfast included.

Next door to the Köken is the Yunus Pension, and beyond that the 20-room *Çidem Pansiyon* (chee-DEHM) (☎ (256) 614 1895), İstiklal Sokak 9, a clean and cheerful place with single rooms for US$22 to US$26, doubles for US$28 to US$34; cheaper rooms have sinks, more expensive rooms have private showers.

The nearby *Hotel Akman* (☎ (256) 614 1501), İstiklal Caddesi 13, is a tidy if sterile little two-star, 46-room place open from mid-March to the end of October. It is used by tour groups, which enjoy the small swimming pool. Some rooms have bathtubs, and all rooms are priced at US$28/36 a single/double, breakfast included.

Facing the sea, only a few hundred metres north of the caravanserai on Atatürk Bulvarı, are several modern hotels offering a convenient location and comfortable rooms for moderate prices. The three-star *Otel İlayda* (☎ (256) 614 3807, fax 614 6766) has 40 rooms with bath (and many with sea-view balconies) for US$45/60 a single/double. *Otel Derici* (☎ (256) 614 8222, fax 614 8226), nearby at Atatürk Bulvarı 40, also has three stars, and 87 comfortable rooms (some with sea views) at rates of US$50 a double with breakfast.

Places to Stay – top end

The *Hotel Kısmet* (☎ (256) 614 2005, fax 614 4914), Akyar Mevkii, just north of the yacht marina perched on a little peninsula, is the best place to splurge a bit. Though relatively small (100 rooms), it is perfectly sited, well run and carefully maintained, and has the feel of a posh private club. Indeed, there are no signs displaying its name – it gets enough custom by word of mouth. Rates are US$100/135/155 a single/double/triple, breakfast included.

I wish I could recommend the refurbished Ottoman Öküz Mehmet Paşa Kervansaray at the centre of town, now called the *Hotel Kervansaray* (or Club Caravansérai; ☎ (256) 614 4115, fax 614 2423). But the interior is ruined with a plethora of tourist shops, and there is loud music in the courtyard till midnight some nights. The rate for the small stone rooms is US$50/65 a single/double, breakfast included.

The coast to the north and south of Kuşadası is crowded with huge, gleaming five-star hotels for the package-holiday trade. Rooms for single travellers cost from US$95 to US$125 a double in summer.

South of the centre on Kadınlar Denizi are comfortable hotels priced from US$50 to US$100 a double. These include the five-star, 250-room *İmbat Oteli* (☎ (256) 614 2000, fax 614 4960), and the much cheaper three-star *Martı Oteli* (☎ (256) 614 3650, fax 614 4700), an older 112-room place that offers a superb location and good value for money.

Five km south of the centre beyond Kadınlar Denizi at Yavansu Mevkii, the five-star *Onur Hotel* (☎ (256) 614 8505, fax 614 3727) is perched on a cliff right above the sea, offering 330 luxury rooms and full facilities.

Places to Eat

In summer, Kuşadası's restaurant prices are higher even than Selçuk's, which were already higher than İstanbul's. At least most restaurants post prices prominently so that you can do some comparison shopping.

Places to Eat – bottom end The cheapest food is in the low-budget pensions mentioned above. Ask about pension meals when you book a room. For other cheap meals, you must search well inland and find places patronised mostly by locals.

The restaurants on Sağlık Caddesi between Kahramanlar Caddesi and İnönü Bulvarı tend to be patronised more by Turks and are consequently cheaper than many others. Check prices at the *Konyalı* at No 40 and nearby shopfront places.

Walk south on Sabucali Sokak off Sağlık Caddesi to the Hotel Karasu and Gündoğdu Restaurant and turn right. The row of small grills facing the Municipal Wedding & Meeting Hall (Belediye Nikah ve Toplantı Salonu) specialises in the regional favourite, çöp şiş, bits of grilled meat on bamboo skewers. Prices at each – *Gamali, Ortaklar* etc – are displayed, and tend to be around US$2.50 per portion.

The once cheap grills off Kahramanlar Caddesi next to the Hacı Hatice Hanım Camii are now little restaurants serving lamb and chicken grills for US$4.50 to US$6.

Places to Eat – middle The town's prime dining location is on the waterfront by the fishers' harbour, but there is so much competition that prices are not much higher than those further inland. Meat grills priced at US$4.50 inland may cost US$5 here, but it's worth the extra for the view. Just be careful to get the price on any seafood you order, as it will be priced by the market and can be quite expensive. A full fish dinner with wine at the *Toros Canlı Balık* (☎ 614 1144), *Kâzım Usta'nın Yeri* (☎ 614 1226) or *Diba* (☎ 614 1063) may cost from US$15 to US$25 per person.

The big surprise in resorty Kuşadası is the *Restaurant Ada*, on Güvercin Adası, which has good food at low prices right on the water. It's almost too good to last.

There are numerous atmospheric places to eat in Kaleiçi, the old section behind the PTT. Some on Cephane Sokak, such as the *Avlu Restaurant* at No 15, have outdoor tables and lowish (for Kuşadası) prices for soups and stews. A favourite grill on this street is the *Öz Urfa Kebapçısı* (☎ 614 6070), strong on roast meats, with dishes from US$4.50 to US$5.50. Otherwise, there are dozens more, some advertising (in English) 'a complete English breakfast' for US$5.

Places to Eat – top end *Sultan Han Restoran* (☎ 614 3849), Bahar Sokak 8, also in Kaleiçi, is one of several large old caravanserais in Kaleiçi with lots of carved wood detail and local crafts. Food is offered in great variety, including fish and Turkish meat choices, a smattering of continental dishes, good mezes and traditional Turkish sweets. Some evenings there's a belly-dancer. Lunch and dinner are served daily from 11 am to 11 pm, for US$14 to US$20 per person.

Entertainment

Much of Kuşadası's nightlife is aimed at specific national groups. Barlar Sokak near the Akdeniz Apart-otel is choked with Olde English-style 'pubs' and Deutsches 'bierstuben' where patrons suffer excesses of jollity in pseudo-familiar surroundings. The quieter, classier bars are in Kaleiçi's narrow streets. Wander around to find *Olive*, the *Jazz Club*, *She*, and newer places. Most have dusky courtyards, cushy upholstered seats/benches, drinks, conversation and hip music.

Out on Güvercinada, the little fort is usually let to disco organisers. Even if the latest incarnation is not to your liking, the walk out to the island and back is quite pleasant.

Things to Buy

Kuşadası has the full range of Turkish crafts and arts: onyx, meerschaum, leather clothing and accessories, copper, brass, carpets and jewellery. If you're going elsewhere, save your shopping for later as almost any place will be cheaper. If you must shop here, do it before or after the cruise ships are in port, as prices are higher then and dealers ruder.

Getting There & Away

Air Top Air (☎ (252) 313 0626) runs a daily flight between Selçuk and İstanbul (except Wednesday and Saturday) for US$68, but archaeological officials hope to close down Selçuk airport, claiming that the aircraft noise, vibration and pollution damage the ancient structures.

Bus & Dolmuş Şehiriçi (intracity) minibuses frequently run from the otogar to the centre, and up and down the coast within the town all day in summer. Kadınlar Denizi minibuses go from the town centre along the shore road to that beach. For either, the fare is US$0.40.

Kuşadası's otogar is at the far southern end of Kahramanlar Caddesi on the bypass highway. Direct buses leave for several far-flung points in the country, or you can transfer at İzmir. Several companies have ticket offices on İnönü Bulvarı (see map). When you purchase a ticket, try to ascertain if it is indeed a direct coach: your 'bus to Priene' may turn out to be a minibus to Söke, where you must await a minibus to Priene.

Bodrum – 151 km, two hours, US$8; frequent buses in summer
Didyma – see Söke
İzmir – 95 km, 1½ hours, US$3; Elbirlik buses every 30 minutes from 6 to 8 am, then every 20 minutes till 9 pm in summer
Menderes airport – 80 km, 1¼ hours, US$2.75; take an Elbirlik İzmir bus and ask to be let off at the airport
Miletus – see Söke
Pamukkale – 220 km, three hours, US$8; some direct buses, or change at Denizli
Priene – see Söke
Selçuk – 20 km, 30 minutes, US$1.25; minibuses run frequently in summer, with the last minibus departing from Selçuk at 8.30 pm, and from Kuşadası at 9 pm
Söke – 20 km, 30 minutes, US$1.25; frequent minibuses, especially on Wednesday (Söke's market day). From Söke's otogar, transfer to minibuses for Güllübahçe (Priene), Balat (Miletus), or Yenihisar (for Didyma (Didim) and Altınkum beach).

Minibus Tours In summer, minibus drivers organise tours to various sites in the region for one flat fee, usually about US$20 per person. The tours may cost a bit more than normal dolmuş and bus fare, but save you the time you'd spend waiting on the road to hitch or find an onward minibus. When booking the tour, organise your group to put pressure on the driver to allow sufficient time at each site – an hour at each. Often the drivers will try to rush you through.

In spring and autumn, tours to Priene, Miletus and Didyma may run on Wednesday, Saturday and/or Sunday, or only when a group can be gathered.

Minibus drivers at the Kuşadası bus station also run tours to Ephesus and Meryemana for about US$15 per person.

Boat – Samos Any travel agency in Kuşadası will sell you a ticket for a boat to Samos. You can go over for the day and return in the evening, or go there to stay. Boats depart from each port, Samos and Kuşadası, at 8.30 am and 5 pm daily in high summer and about four times weekly in spring and autumn. Service is usually suspended in winter except for special excursions. The trip costs US$30 one-way, US$35 same-day round trip, or US$55 for a round-trip ticket good for a year. You may have to surrender your passport for immigration processing the evening before you travel. Some agencies discount these tickets, so ask, and flash your student card if you have one.

You can book through Diana Travel Agency (☎ (256) 614 3859, fax 614 3170), at the foot of Kıbrıs Caddesi behind the Tourism Information Office, or Azim Tour (☎ (256) 614 4635, fax 614 5479), Liman Caddesi Yayla Pasajı. These agencies also handle tickets for car ferries to Greece and Italy.

DİLEK NATIONAL PARK

Thirty km south of Kuşadası the Dilek peninsula juts westward into the Aegean, almost touching the island of Samos. West of the village of Güzelçamlı the land has been set aside as Dilek Milli Parkı, a nature reserve with some areas for day visitors; no camping is allowed. The mountain slopes here are clad in pines, the wildlife is abundant, the air clean, the sun bright.

The park is open daily from 8 am to 6 pm for US$0.50 per person, US$2.50 per car.

Approaching Dilek from Kuşadası or Söke, the road passes through the village of Davutlar and, seven km farther west, **Güzelçamlı**. The latter, a sleepy village a few years ago, is now backed by thousands of holiday villa/condominiums. Among the ranks and rows of summer flats are several small hotels of two and three-star rating.

It's two km from Güzelçamlı to the national park entrance, then another km to **İçmeler Köyü**, a protected cove with a small but beautiful beach, lounge chairs and umbrellas, a restaurant and picnic area.

Three km beyond İçmeler Köyü an unpaved road goes off to the right, downhill one km to **Aydınlık beach**, a pebble-and-sand strand about 800m long with surf, backed by pines, and served by a small café. (If you continue another 1.2 km on the main road you'll come to the far entrance to the same beach.)

Less than one km farther along is a jandarma post. Another km brings you to **Kavaklı Burun**, another sand-and-pebble surf beach 500m to the right of the road. As at Aydınlık, there is another entrance to the beach at the far end, another km along. West of that is a military zone, entry forbidden. It's 8.5 km back to the park entrance.

Getting There & Away

You can walk the three km from Güzelçamlı to İçmeler Köyü in about 30 minutes. Otherwise, without your own transport you must rely on dolmuşes from Kuşadası and Söke (45 minutes, US$1.50). They run from 8 am to dusk in summer, especially on weekends, and usually run all the way to the far end of Kavaklı Burun. It's a good idea to leave the park not too long after mid-afternoon, as the later dolmuşes fill up quickly.

PRIENE, MILETUS & DIDYMA

South of Kuşadası lie the ruins of three very ancient and important settlements well worth a day trip. Priene occupies a dramatic position overlooking the plain of the River Menderes (formerly Meander). Miletus preserves a great theatre, and Didyma's Temple of Apollo is among the world's most impressive religious structures. Beyond Didyma is Altınkum Beach, good for an after-ruins swim off season.

Priene

Priene was important around 300 BC when the League of Ionian Cities held its congresses and festivals here. Otherwise, the city was smaller and less important than nearby Miletus, which means that its Hellenistic buildings were not buried by Roman buildings. What you see in Priene is mostly what one saw in the city over 2000 years ago.

The setting is dramatic, with steep Mt Mykale rising behind the town, and the broad flood plain of the River Menderes spread out at its feet.

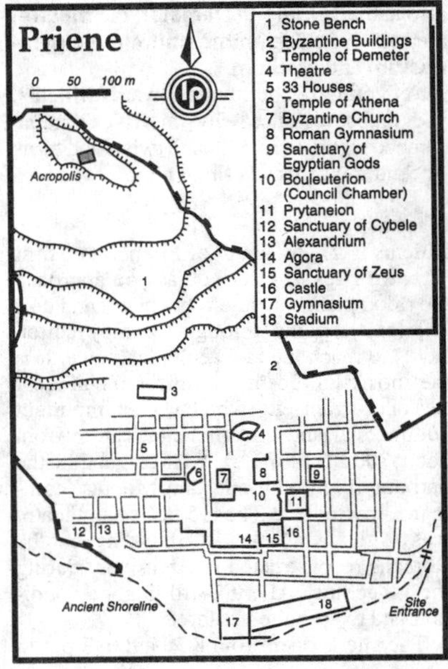

As you approach the archaeological zone, you'll come to a shady rest spot in a romantic setting: water cascades from an old aqueduct next to the *Şelale Restaurant* (☎ (256) 547 1009), where you can get a cool drink or hot tea, make a telephone call or have a meal. The *Han Restaurant* competes fiercely with the Şelale. There are several smaller, cheaper restaurants as well. The simple *Priene Pension & Camping* (☎ (256) 547 1249) can provide a bed if necessary, but it'd be better to move on.

The site at Priene is open from 8.30 am to 7 pm daily in summer (to 5.30 pm in winter) for US$2.50.

Priene was a planned town, with its streets laid out in a grid (the grid system originated in Miletus). Of the buildings which remain, the **bouleuterion** (city council meeting place) is in very good condition. The five standing columns of the **Temple of Athena**, designed by Pythius of Halicarnassus and looked upon as the epitome of an Ionian temple, form Priene's most familiar landmark; the view from here is the best. Look also at the **Temple of Demeter**, the **theatre**, the ruins of a **Byzantine church**, the **gymnasium** and **stadium**.

As you gaze southward towards Miletus, you realise at once why this river's name came to signify a river which twists and turns (meanders) across its flood plain.

Miletus

Miletus is 22 km south of Priene. Its **Great Theatre** rises to greet you as you approach the flood plain's southern boundary and turn left (east), riding through swampy cotton fields to reach the archaeological zone. It is the most significant building remaining of this once-grand city, which was an important commercial and governmental centre from about 700 BC till 700 AD. After that time the harbour filled with silt, and Miletus' commerce dwindled. The 15,000-seat theatre was originally a Hellenistic building, but the Romans reconstructed it extensively during the 1st century AD. It's still in good condition and exciting to explore.

The site is open from 8.30 am to 7 pm in summer (to 5.30 pm in winter), for US$2.50. The **Milet Müzesi** (Miletus Museum), about a km south of the theatre, is open from 8.30 am to 12.30 pm, and 1.30 to 5.30 pm, for US$2, but hardly worth it. Across the road from the Great Theatre is a small *restaurant* where you can get snacks and beverages and a shady grove where you can enjoy them.

A **Seljuk caravanserai**, 100m south of the ticket booth, has been restored and converted to shops, but no shopkeepers had moved in at the time of writing.

Climb to the top of the theatre for a view of the entire site, with several groups of ruins scattered about, among them a **stadium**; three **agoras**, northern, western and southern; the **Baths of Faustina**, constructed upon the order of Emperor Marcus Aurelius' wife; and a **bouleuterion** between the northern and southern agoras.

To the south of the main group of ruins, nearer to the museum, is the **İlyas Bey Camii** (1404), a mosque dating from the Emirate

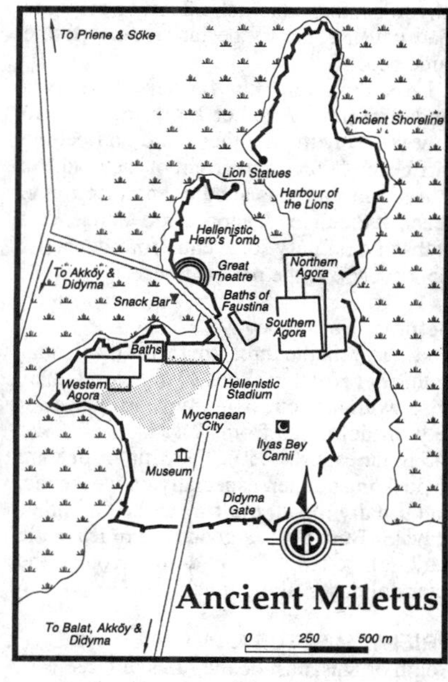

period. After the Seljuks but before the Ottomans, this region was ruled by the Turkish emirs of Menteşe. The mosque's doorway and the mihrab inside are worth noticing, and the picturesque neglect of the site is a welcome change from the swept and burnished tourist precincts.

From Miletus, head south again to Akköy (4.5 km), Yenihisar and Didyma, 14 km beyond Akköy. Transportation may be infrequent in these parts, and it may take some time to reach Akköy by hitchhiking. South of Akköy there is more traffic, however, and most of it goes past Didyma to Altınkum Beach.

Didyma

Called Didim in Turkish, this was the site of a stupendous temple to Apollo, where lived an oracle as important as the one at Delphi. The temple and the oracle have been important since very early times, but the great temple you see is the one started in the late 4th century AD. It replaced the original temple, which was destroyed in 494 BC by the Persians, and the later construction which was completed under Alexander the Great.

The Temple of Apollo was never finished, though its oracle and its priests were hard at work until, after 1400 years of soothsaying, Christianity became the state religion of the Byzantines and brought an end to pagan practices.

When you approach Didyma today, you come into the town of **Yenihisar**, which has spread at a cancerous rate in the last few years and has engulfed both Altınkum, the beach to the south, and Didim, formerly the Ottoman Greek town of Yeronda. Restaurants amidst the tourist shops across the road from the temple entrance provide drinks and meals at tourist prices, and carpet shops gush forth their touts at the approach of each new tour bus. Admission is from 8.30 am to 7 pm in summer (to 5.30 pm in winter), for US$2.50.

Ancient Didyma was not a town, but the home of a god. People did not live there, only priests. I assume that the priests, sitting on the temple treasure (which was considerable) had a pretty good life. The priestly family there, which specialised in oracular temple management, originally came from Delphi.

Temple of Apollo The temple porch held 120 huge columns, the bases of which are richly carved. Behind the porch is a great doorway at which the oracular poems were written and presented to petitioners. Beyond the doorway is the cella (court), where the oracle sat and prophesied after drinking from the sacred spring. We can only speculate on what that water contained to make someone capable of prophesies. The cella is reached today by a covered ramp on the right side of the porch.

In the temple grounds are fragments of its rich decoration, including a striking head of Medusa (she of the snakes for hair). There used to be a road lined with statuary which led to a small harbour. The statues stood there for 23 centuries but were then taken to the British Museum in 1858.

Places to Stay & Eat Though Altınkum has hundreds of lodgings, there are two good pensions right next to the temple. The *Oracle Pension* (☎ (256) 813 5503) is perched above the temple precinct to the south, with close-up views of the marble pile. If you don't stay here (US$10/18/20 a single/double/triple for bathless rooms), at least come for a cool drink on the terrace for the view.

Just around the corner from the temple, to the south on the Altınkum road, *Medusa House* (☎ (256) 813 4491) is a restored stone village house with a lovely rear garden. Rooms share baths and cost US$22 a double, breakfast included. Though only steps away from the temple, it has no temple view.

Altınkum Beach

Four km south of Didyma through the town of Yenihisar is Altınkum (Golden Sand) Beach, a resort visited mostly by Turkish families who patronise the typical assortment of little restaurants, pensions and hotels rated from no stars to three stars. Most lodgings – and especially the cheapest ones – are booked solid in summer. At a pinch, go west from the access road and look at the several small pensions which stand a block inland from the beach. A better plan, though, is to forget Altınkum unless you come off season.

Getting Around

If you start early in the morning from Kuşadası or Selçuk, you can get to the archaeological sites of Priene, Miletus and Didyma by dolmuş, returning to your base at night. If you have a car, you can see all three sites and have a swim and be back by mid-afternoon.

Minibus Tours Minibus drivers at the Selçuk bus station organise tours to Priene, Miletus, Didyma and Altınkum Beach during good weather in summer. The tour should take a whole day: the minibus departs from the bus station between 8.30 and 9.30 am, spends an hour at Priene, 1½ hours at Miletus, 2½ hours at Didyma and its museum, and about 1½ hours at Altınkum Beach before returning to Selçuk between 5.30 and 6.30 pm. These days, however, the drivers often hope to get in two trips a day, cutting these times in half, which is really not enough.

The cost is between US$18 and US$25, depending upon how many people participate. Lunch is not normally included in this price. It's a good idea to reserve your seat in advance, if possible.

If you want to do this trip yourself, begin by catching a dolmuş to Söke from Kuşadası (20 km) or Selçuk (40 km), then another onward to Priene.

When you've finished at Priene, wait for a passing dolmuş or hitchhike across the flat flood plain to Miletus (22 km). The dolmuş may bear a sign saying 'Balat' (the village next to Miletus), 'Akköy', a larger village beyond Balat, or 'Yenihisar'.

From Miletus, catch transport to Akköy or, if you can, something going all the way to Yenihisar (Didyma and Altınkum). If you do it all by dolmuş the fares will total about US$10.

SÖKE

The modern bus and dolmuş station in this transport town is divided into separate bus and dolmuş sections. From the bus side of the station, Söke municipal buses depart for İzmir every hour on the half-hour until 4 pm for US$3.50. Others head east to Denizli and Pamukkale, south to Bodrum and to Muğla (for Marmaris).

The dolmuş side of the station serves vehicles going to the following towns:

Altınkum Beach – 61 km, US$2.50
Aydın – 55 km, US$2.25 (the provincial capital on the way to Aphrodisias, Denizli and Pamukkale)
Balat – 35 km, US$1.75 (the village near Miletus)
Davutlar – 13 km, US$1.25 (on the way to Dilek National Park)
Didyma – 56 km, US$2
Güllübahçe – 14 km, US$1 (the village next to Priene)
Güzelçamlı – 22 km, US$1.50 (near Dilek National Park)
Kuşadası – 20 km, US$1.25
Milas – 82 km, US$3 (on the way to Bodrum)

Aphrodisias & Pamukkale Region

Hot calcium-laden mineral waters burst from the earth to run through a ruined Hellenistic city before cascading over a cliff at Pamukkale (pah-MOO-kah-leh, Cotton Fortress), the spa 220 km due east of Kuşadası. As the water cools, the calcium precipitates and clings to the cliffs, forming snowy white travertines, waterfalls of white stone, which give the spa its name. Nearby are the ruins of Laodicea, one of the Seven Churches of Asia.

On the way from Selçuk or Kuşadası to Pamukkale you can make several detours to significant archaeological sites, including the hilltop city of Nyssa about 100 km east of Kuşadası, and, about 150 km east of Kuşadası, Aphrodisias, one of Turkey's most complete and elaborate archaeological sites.

As you begin your trip you may pass through the ruins of Magnesia ad Meander, which lie on the road between Söke and Ortaklar. This ancient city is not really worth a stop, but the fragments of wall easily visible from the road are certainly impressive. From Ortaklar to the provincial capital of Aydın it's 33 km.

AYDIN

Framed by the mountains of Aydın Dağı to the north and Menteşe Dağı to the south, Aydın (population 120,000, altitude 64m) is at the centre of the agriculturally rich Menderes river valley. Olives, figs, cotton, grain and fruit grow in abundance. The valley has always been an important natural travel route, which today includes an east-west highway and the railway to Denizli, Burdur and Isparta.

Aydın was formerly Tralles, which flourished during Roman times. Its most famous son was perhaps the architect Anthemius of Tralles who, at the order of the Emperor Justinian and with the help of Isidore of Miletus, designed and built between 532 and 537 AD the great church of Sancta Sophia in Constantinople. During the War of Independence Aydın was occupied by the invading Greek forces for several years, and burned to the ground on their departure. Being at the centre of an earthquake zone has not helped Aydın's ancient buildings much either. What you see today is mostly modern.

Orientation & Information

The otogar is on the main highway a few hundred metres west of a large traffic roundabout which marks the beginning of Adnan Menderes Bulvarı. The centre of town is one km north of the highway along Adnan Menderes Bulvarı. At the centre, marked by the main square and a park, are various hotels, the PTT and train station.

The Tourism Information Office (☎ (256) 225 4145, fax 212 6226) is on the traffic roundabout on the main highway just east of the otogar. It's helpful and has an excellent map. Aydın's postal code is 09000.

Things to See

Though Aydın retains a good number of **Ottoman mosques**, they are in somewhat distant neighbourhoods and not really worth seeking out unless you're doing a close study of Ottoman religious architecture. Have a look at the **Süleyman Bey Camii** (1683), between the train station and the park right on the main square, designed by one of Sinan's apprentices.

The **Archaeology Museum** is 750m north-west of the main square (follow the signs), open from 9 am to noon and 1.30 to 5 pm for US$1. There are finds from Aphrodisias, Didyma, Miletus, Priene and Tralles, including good statues of Athena and Nike, and a fine bust of Marcus Aurelius.

Places to Stay & Eat

Just north of the main square are several hotels which will do nicely for a night. Perhaps the best value for money is the *Hotel Kabaçam* (☎ (256) 212 2794), Hükümet Bulvarı, 11 Sokak 2, where comfortable rooms with private shower cost US$14/18 a single/double. Across the street is the *Hotel Vardar*, somewhat cheaper but certainly less comfortable.

The *Hotel Baltacı* (☎ (256) 212 1321), Gazi Bulvarı, 3 Sokak (a bit farther up the hill from the Kabaçam, then bear right), charges about the same as the Kabaçam, but is not as nice.

The 28-room *Orhan Hotel* (☎ (256) 225 1713, fax 225 1781), Gazi Bulvarı 63, and the 30-room *Otel Özlü* (☎ (256) 225 3371), Adnan Menderes Bulvarı 71, both offer two-star comforts for slightly more than the Kabaçam, but the Özlü can be fairly noisy.

The best place in town is actually out of town on the road to Muğla. It's the four-star *Turtay Hotel* (☎ (256) 213 3003, fax 213 0351), with 70 air-con, satellite TV-equipped rooms priced at US$38/48 a single/double. The hotel offers private helicopter and aeroplane service as well.

The centre of the city has the usual good collection of small kebap and take away restaurants at your service.

Getting There & Away

Bus Buses run frequently to Denizli, Pamukkale, Kuşadası, Selçuk or İzmir, where you may have to change for other destinations.

Train Three daily trains connect Aydın with Denizli, Selçuk, Menderes airport and İzmir. See those sections for details.

NYSSA

East of Aydın, you are deep in the fertile farming country of the Büyük Menderes river valley. Cotton fields sweep away from the road in every direction. During the cotton harvest in late October, the highways are jammed (dangerously so) with tractors hauling wagons overladen with the white puffy stuff. Other crops prevalent in the valley, all the way to Denizli, are pomegranates, pears, citrus fruits, apples, melons, olives and tobacco.

Heading 31 km east from Aydın brings you to the town of Sultanhisar and, three km to the north uphill, ancient Nyssa, set on a hilltop amid olive groves. You'll have to walk or hitch to the site, as there is no public transport. When you reach the ruins you'll find public toilets, a soft-drink stand, and a guard who will charge you US$1.50 admission during daylight hours. The guard will show you around the site if you wish; a tip is expected.

The major ruins here are of the **theatre**, and a 115-metre-long **tunnel** beneath the road and the parking area which was once the main square of the ancient city. A five-minute walk up the hill along the road and through a field brings you to the **bouleuterion**, which has some nice fragments of sculpture.

What you will remember about Nyssa, however, is the peacefulness and bucolic beauty of its site, very different from tourist metropolises such as Ephesus. The walk back down to Sultanhisar and the highway is very nice in late afternoon.

Though Sultanhisar has a few simple eateries, there are no real hotels. The İzmir-Denizli trains stop in town, and the highway carries many east-west buses.

NAZİLLİ

Nazilli (NAH-zee-lee, population 100,000 altitude 87m), 14 km east of Nyssa and Sultanhisar, is a market town and the transfer point for a trip to Aphrodisias. The otogar is just north of the main highway, one block west of the main traffic roundabout. The train station is south of the highway.

Places to Stay & Eat

Unfortunately, Nazilli has no cluster of cheap little hotels around its otogar, as one might expect, though there are a few small places near the train station. The new two-star, 40-room *Hotel Metya* (☎ 256) 312 8888, fax 312 8891), in Karaçay Mahallesi at 92 Sokak 10, is a few steps west of the otogar across from the Shell fuel station. It was the best hotel in town at the time of writing, charging US$18/28 a single/double for a bath-equipped room and breakfast.

Go north 200m from the main traffic roundabout on the highway east of the otogar to reach the comfortable three-star, 54-room *Nazilli Ticaret Odası Oteli* (Chamber of Commerce Hotel; ☎ (256) 313 9678, fax 313 9681), Hürriyet Caddesi. Quite decent rooms with bath and balcony cost US$16/26 a single/double, breakfast included. There's a restaurant and bar of course, and also a decent pastry shop adjoining the hotel.

There are several little eateries in the bus station area.

Getting There & Away

Bus Nazilli is the local transportation hub, with buses to and from İzmir and Selçuk about every 45 minutes or less in the morning and afternoon, but infrequent in the evening.

One stops at Nazilli on the way to or from Aphrodisias, probably to change buses or to stay in Nazilli's hotels, which are better than anything in Karacasu, 42 km south of Nazilli near Aphrodisias.

Details of some other daily services from Nazilli follow:

Ankara – 545 km, eight hours, US$15; several buses
Antalya – 360 km, six hours, US$11; several buses
Bodrum – 225 km, four hours, US$8; several buses
Denizli – 65 km, one hour, US$2.50; very frequent buses and dolmuşes
İstanbul – 600 km, 12 hours, US$22; several buses
İzmir – 170 km, 2½ to three hours, US$5; very frequent buses
Konya – 505 km, eight hours, US$8; several buses
Kuşadası – 150 km, 2½ hours, US$5; several buses
Pamukkale – 85 km, 1½ hours, US$2.50; several buses
Selçuk – 130 km, 1½ hours, US$5; buses at least every hour

Train The three trains running daily between Denizli and İzmir stop at Nazilli. See the Denizli, Selçuk and İzmir sections for details.

APHRODİSİAS

The city's name quickly brings to mind 'aphrodisiac'. Both words come from the Greek name for the goddess of love, Aphrodite, called Venus by the Romans. Aphrodite was many things to many people. As Aphrodite Urania she was the goddess of pure, spiritual love; as Aphrodite Pandemos she was the goddess of sensual love, married to Hephaestus but lover also of Ares, Hermes, Dionysus and Adonis. Her children included Harmonia, Eros, Hermaphroditus, Aeneas and Priapus, the phallic god. All in all, she was the complete goddess of fertility, fornication and fun.

You come to Aphrodisias from Nazilli by way of the town of **Karacasu** (KAH-rah-jah-soo) surrounded by tobacco fields, fig trees and orchards. Besides farming, Karacasu is famous for its potters, who work with the local reddish-brown clay, firing it in 30 wood-fired kilns. To see the potters at work, ask to be directed to the *bardakçı ocakları.*

History

Excavations have shown the acropolis of Aphrodisias to be not a natural hill but a prehistoric mound built up by successive settlements beginning in the Early Bronze Age (2800-2200 BC). From the 8th century BC, the temple at Aphrodisias was famous and a favourite goal of pilgrims for over 1000 years, and the city prospered. But under the Byzantines the city changed substantially: the steamy Temple of Aphrodite was transformed into a chaste Christian church, and ancient buildings were pulled down to provide building stones for defensive walls (circa 350 AD).

The town, diminished from its former glory, was attacked by Tamerlane on his Anatolian rampage in 1402 and never recovered. The Turkish village of **Geyre** sprang up on the site sometime later. In 1956 an earthquake devastated the village, which was rebuilt to the west at its present location, allowing excavations to be more easily carried out at the site. The pleasant plaza by the big plane tree in front of the museum was the main square of pre-1956 Geyre.

Preliminary explorations of Aphrodisias were carried out by French and Italian archaeologists early in this century. After the earthquake of 1956, US and Turkish archaeologists began to resurrect the city. They found a surprisingly well-preserved stadium, odeum and theatre. The National Geographic Society (USA) supported some of the excavation and restoration. From 1961 to 1990 the work at the site was directed by Professor Kenan T Erim of New York University. His book, *Aphrodisias: City of Venus Aphrodite* (1986), tells the story of his work. After his death, Professor Erim was buried at the site he had done so much to reveal and explain.

Museum

The site and museum at Aphrodisias, 13 km past Karacasu, are open from 9 am to 6.30 pm in summer, 9 am to 5 pm in winter. Admission costs US$3 to the ruins, and the same again to the museum. No photography is permitted in the museum, and you are also prohibited from photographing excavations in progress here. Signs in the car park advise that no camping is allowed; they're afraid of antiquity thieves.

During Roman times Aphrodisias was home to a famous school for sculptors who

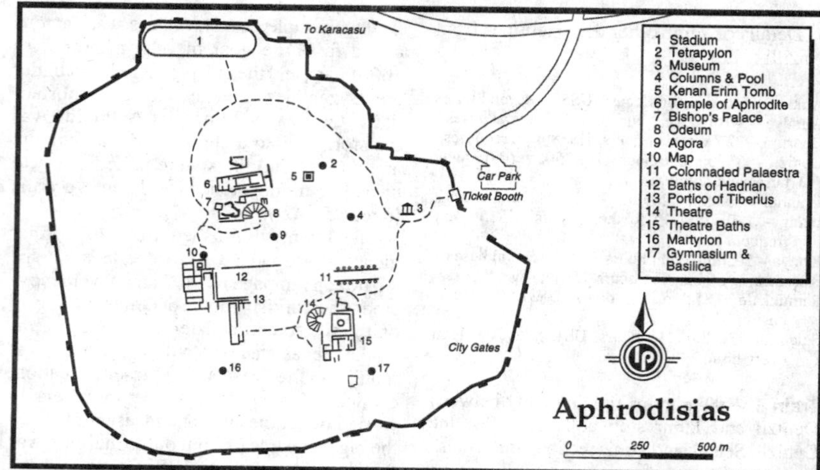

were attracted by the beds of high-grade white and blue-grey marble two km away at the foot of Babada' mountain. The statuary in the museum reflects the excellence of their work. Note especially the 'cult statue of Aphrodite, second century' and the 'cuirassed statue of an emperor or high official, second century, signed by Appolonius Aster'. The 'portrait statue of Flavius Palmatus, governor of the province of Asia', looks like a man with big problems. Did they make his head that small on purpose, or as an insult?

The Ruins

Follow the path to the right as you come from the museum. Most of what you see is from no earlier than the 2nd century AD.

The first site you pass, on your left, is an unmarked collection of serpentine **columns** in a murky pool. Farther along on the left is the **Tetrapylon**, or monumental gateway, which greeted pilgrims as they approached the temple of Aphrodite. The tomb of Professor Erim is just south-west of it.

The footpath next leads you towards the well-preserved **stadium**, off to the right, with most of its 30,000 seats still in useable condition.

Back to the main path, continue to the **Temple of Aphrodite**, completely rebuilt when it was converted into a basilica church (circa 500 AD): its cella was removed, its columns shifted to form a nave, and an apse added at the eastern end. It's now difficult to picture the place in which orgies to Aphrodite were held. Near the temple-church is the **Bishop's Palace**, dating from Byzantine times.

Just south of the Bishop's Palace is a side path eastward to the beautiful marble **odeum,** preserved for millennia in a bath of mud.

South of the Bishop's Palace and the odeum was Aphrodisias' main **agora**, once enclosed by Ionic porticoes but now little more than a grassy field. Next the path leads you to the **Baths of Hadrian**, five large **galleries** and a **colonnaded palaestra** or playing field, and the grand **Portico of Tiberius**.

The white marble **theatre** is virtually complete. South of it was a large baths complex.

Antiocheia

On the road between the main highway and Karacasu you may notice signs pointing the way to Antiocheia; you turn north at the centre of the village of Başaran, 18.3 km north-west of Karacasu. From Başaran it's one km to the impressively sited ruins of this ancient hilltop city. The ruins are extensive but in very bad condition, and totally unexcavated and unrestored. If you'd like to see what the archaeologists see on the day they begin their fieldwork, come and have a look at Antiocheia.

If you have your own vehicle, you can return to the Nazilli-Denizli highway, six km to the north, by continuing past Antiocheia across the intensely fertile flood plain of the Büyük Menderes river and through the farming village of **Azizabat**, which has some very fine fieldstone walls and houses. You regain the highway at a point 5.6 km east of the Karacasu turn off, 21 km east of Nazilli. Turn right for Denizli.

Places to Stay

Nazilli has the nearest two and three-star hotels, Karacasu has a few emergency lodgings, but there are a few suitable places near Geyre as well, all of which offer the option of camping.

Half a km before coming to the ruins from Karacasu you'll spot *Chez Mestan* (☎ (256) 448 8046), Afrodisias, Karacasu, Aydın, a house with an airy, shady front porch on the left-hand side of the road. Mestan Bey is Turkish; his wife, French. Simple rooms equipped with sinks and hand-held showers (but not toilets) cost US$10/12 a single/double, breakfast included. Meals on the front porch cost around US$4. They have an area set aside for camping as well.

The proprietors of Chez Mestan have opened a simple, modern hotel a half-km back towards Karacasu: the *Aphrodisias Hotel* (☎ (256) 448 8132, fax 448 8422), where rooms with shower, breakfast included, cost US$18/26.

Nearer the ruins is the *Belle Vue Pension*, 200m up from the crossroads closest to the ruins. It's a simple village house which may or may not be receiving visitors when you arrive. Rates are as at Chez Mestan.

Nine km from Geyre back towards Karacasu in the village of Dandalaz is the similar *Elmas Pension & Restaurant*.

In the town of Karacasu, the *Otogar Moteli*, on the upper floor of the bus station, is strictly for emergencies.

Places to Eat

Besides at *Chez Mestan*, you can get simple meals in Karacasu at the *Köseoğlu Restaurant* and at the *Öztekin* on the main street. A cut above the rest is the *Bonjour Restaurant* at the main traffic circle. Fancier restaurants, patronised mostly by coach tour groups, are to be found along the road between Karacasu and Nazilli. If you stop at one of these, you'll get better service if you arrive an hour before or after a group.

Getting There & Away

Bus There are a few direct buses a day between Karacasu and İzmir (210 km, 3½ hours, US$10) and Selçuk (130 km, two hours, US$8.50). If you don't get one of these, take a bus from İzmir, Selçuk, Ortaklar, Aydın or Denizli to Nazilli, and from there a dolmuş to Geyre, the village 13 km beyond Karacasu and right next to the ruins. If you can't find a dolmuş to Geyre or Aphrodisias, take one to Karacasu. Then take a dolmuş, hitch a ride or hire a taxi (US$10 round trip) in Karacasu for the final 13 km to Geyre and the ruins. You should be able to hitch easily in summer.

Minibus Tours Several bus companies, including Pamukkale and Kamil Koç, operate special minibuses in summer, departing from Pamukkale town at 10 am on the 1½-hour trip to Aphrodisias, returning at 3 pm, thus leaving you ample time to explore the ruins and have a picnic lunch. The cost is US$10 per person. The minibus is a special service for those based in Pamukkale who want to visit Aphrodisias, and it does not stop to take on or discharge passengers in Denizli.

Car Aphrodisias is 55 km from Nazilli, 101 km from Denizli and 38 km off the east-west highway.

DENİZLİ

Denizli (deh-NEEZ-lee, population 250,000, altitude 354m) is a prosperous and bustling agricultural city with some light industry as well. It is also noisy, dusty and smoky, but it has a number of hotels and restaurants in all price ranges, which are of interest if accommodation at Pamukkale is full.

Orientation & Information

The train station is on the main highway near the roundabout with the statue of a rooster, only one block west of the bus station, a short distance west of the three-point traffic roundabout called sügen by which one goes to Pamukkale 19 km to the north.

Delikli Çınar Meydanı, the city's main square, is two km south of the train station and the bus station.

Denizli's main Tourism Information Office (☎ (258) 264 3971, fax 264 7621) is at Atatürk Caddesi 8, Ufuk Ap, 2nd floor, office 4. A smaller office (☎ (258) 261 3393) is in the train station, but it is often inexplicably closed.

Denizli's postal code is 20100.

Places to Stay – bottom end

Behind the otogar is the district named Topraklık Mahallesi, with many small numbered streets.

The tidy *Yetkin Pansiyon* (☎ (258) 265 1266), Halk Caddesi, 452 Sokak 13, has 16 rooms and is on a quietish side street between İstasyon Caddesi and the otogar, a five-minute walk away. The old building has been spruced up with paint and carpeting, and the guest rooms have neat tiled showers. Rates are US$14 a double in a room with a shower, breakfast included.

The *Euro Hotel & Pension* (☎ (258) 263 5536), Gündoğdu Mahallesi, Atatürk Caddesi 94, is about 10 minutes' walk east of the otogar (look for the little signs) on a main boulevard. If you phone them they'll have someone come and pick you up. Rooms can cost as little as US$4 per person with shower, and are quite clean.

Most of Denizli's pensions are in Deliktaş Mahallesi, about two km (a 25-minute walk) from the bus station on the east side of the highway to the south of the Üçgen Çarşısı.

Best known is the *Denizli Pansiyon* (☎ (258) 261 8738), 1993 Sokak 14; signs point the way. All rooms have private showers and toilets and cost US$15 a double in summer, cheaper off season; breakfast costs another US$2 per person. The pension has a courtyard with a fountain and lots of fruit trees, and it's quiet; there's space for camping, too. The owner, Süleyman Can (pronounced 'john'), also sells carpets; he'll sometimes shuttle you to and from the bus station in his car. His wife cooks delicious Turkish meals for around US$3 each.

A block away from the Denizli Pension is the similar *Favorite Pension* (☎ (258) 261 6500, on 1975 Sokak; several others are nearby as well.

Places to Stay – middle

The two-star, 84-room *Otel Laodikya* (☎ (258) 265 1506, fax 261 5512), right behind the otogar, is new and comfortable, offering great value with air-con, TV-equipped rooms priced at US$30/42 a single/double, though I was quoted a figure considerably lower when I haggled a bit. The hotel has a restaurant and bar.

Otel Ben-Hur Yıldırım (☎ & fax (258) 263 3590), 632 Sokak 3, has 44 rooms, rates two stars, and will rent you a bath-equipped (perhaps with air-con) room for US$28, breakfast included. Have your room without breakfast if you like.

Otel Subaşıoğlu (☎ (258) 264 9207, fax 264 9215), across the highway from the train station, rates three stars and charges US$14/30 for a single/double with bath and breakfast.

Also here is the two-star *Otel Seza* (☎ (258) 264 6844, fax 262 4630), Halk Caddesi 6, which is older, but its 28 bath-equipped rooms cost substantially less: US$16/24 a single/double. Have a look at the roof bar in the evening.

Up the hill from the train station along İstasyon Caddesi are several more hotels, including the three-star, 60-room *Halley Oteli* (named for the comet) (☎ (258) 261 9544, fax 263 5218); and the two-star, 30-room *Keskinkaya Oteli* (☎ (258) 264 9938,

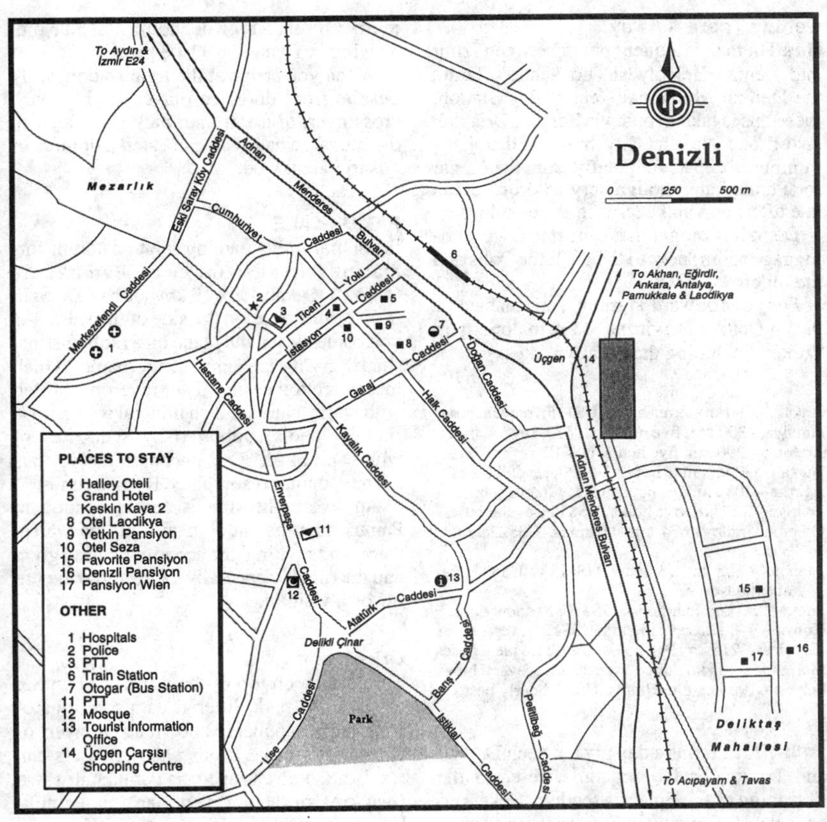

fax 263 3564), İstasyon Caddesi 83, at similar prices, with the same noise problem.

Places to Stay – top end

Grand Hotel Keskin Kaya 2 (☎ (258) 263 3565, fax 261 1488), İstasyon Caddesi 11, just a block from the station, is the best in town, boasting four stars, a garage, and 111 air-con rooms, all with shower/baths and satellite TV. Rates are US$40/55 a single/double – exceptional value for money.

Places to Eat

Denizli's bus station has several inexpensive restaurants, including the *Doyuran Kafeteryası* ('filling-up'), serving kıymalı pide (flat bread topped with ground lamb) for US$1.50. I recommend this because they bake the bread and make up the pide fresh to your order. The *Self-Servis Hamburg Restaurant* is open long hours, and is good for ready-made meals such as soups, stews and salads. Two plates, with bread and drink cost around US$3.

Right behind the bus station at the northwest corner of the Hotel Yıldırım is the *Özlem Lokantası*, another cheap dining possibility.

Getting There & Away

Bus There are frequent buses between İzmir and Denizli Belediyesi Oto Santral Garajı, the Denizli Municipal Central Bus Station; these buses take a route via Selçuk, Ortaklar, Aydın and Nazilli. City buses and dolmuş minibuses depart frequently from the otogar for Pamukkale, though service drops off in late afternoon and ceases in the evening.

Denizli's otogar has an *emanetçi* (left-luggage room) next to the PTT, the Polis and the toilets.

For your onward journey, you can catch a bus in Denizli for virtually any major city in Turkey, including these daily routes:

Ankara – 480 km, seven hours, US$15; frequent buses
Antalya – 300 km, five hours, US$10; several buses
Bodrum – 290 km, five hours, US$10; several buses
Bursa – 532 km, nine hours, US$20; several buses
Eğirdir – 208 km, 3½ hours, US$9; frequent buses
Fethiye – 280 km, five hours, US$10; several buses
Göreme/Ürgüp – 674 km, 11 hours, US$22; a few buses
İstanbul – 665 km, 13 hours, US$13 to US$24; frequent buses
İzmir – 250 km, four hours, US$10; frequent buses
Konya – 440 km, seven hours, US$13; several buses
Kuşadası – 215 km, 3½ hours, US$8; frequent buses
Marmaris – 185 km, three hours, US$7; several buses
Selçuk – 195 km, three hours, US$7; hourly buses

Train Three trains a day ply between Denizli and İzmir; for the schedule, refer to the beginning of the Ephesus section. Tickets go on sale at Denizli station an hour before departure.

The *Pamukkale Ekspresi* is a nightly train between Denizli and İstanbul via Afyon hauling sleeping, couchette and Pullman cars, departing from İstanbul (Haydarpaşa) at 5.30 pm and arriving in Denizli the next morning at 7.27 am. Departure from Denizli is at 6 pm, arriving in İstanbul (Haydarpaşa) at 8.35 am the next morning. A 1st/2nd-class seat ticket costs US$12/9; sleeping compartments range from US$35 for one person to US$80 for three people.

There is also a daily *mototren* (motor train) between Denizli and Afyon, departing from Denizli at 7.30 am for a five-hour journey. From Afyon departure is at 5.55 pm, arriving in Denizli at 11.08 pm.

When you arrive at the train station, walk out the front door, go out to the highway, cross over, turn left and walk one block to the otogar, where you can catch a dolmuş or bus to Pamukkale.

PAMUKKALE

From afar, the gleaming white calcium formations (travertines) of Pamukkale (pah-MOO-kah-leh), 19 km north of Denizli, form a white scar on the side of the ridge. As you come closer, they take on a more distinct shape, giving credence to the name, which means 'cotton castle.' The travertines, filled with warm, calcium-rich mineral water, form shallow pools supported by stalactites of white and black. This enchanting place has been a popular resort since Roman times.

An overnight stay is recommended at Pamukkale: the site is beautiful, the waters warm and inviting, the accommodation good and the ruins – especially the restored theatre – worth visiting.

Orientation

The plateau on top of the travertines within the national park, littered with the ruins of Roman Hierapolis, is known as Örenyeri or Ören Mevkii (the Ruins District). Cars can reach the south entrance via Pamukkale town (two km), or the north entrance via Pamukkale or Karahayıt. It's a short walk from the south entrance *(güney girişi)* to the centre of Örenyeri, but 2.5 km from the north entrance *(kuzey girişi)*.

Among the travertines are several motels, a municipal bathing establishment with various swimming pools, and the extensive ruins of the Roman spa city of Hierapolis.

At the base of the travertines to the west, outside the park, is Pamukkale town (Pamukkale Kasabası), once a farming village, now a fully-fledged town with dozens of lodging and dining places.

About five km to the west of the travertines is the village of Karahayıt, centre for most of the area's luxury hotel development.

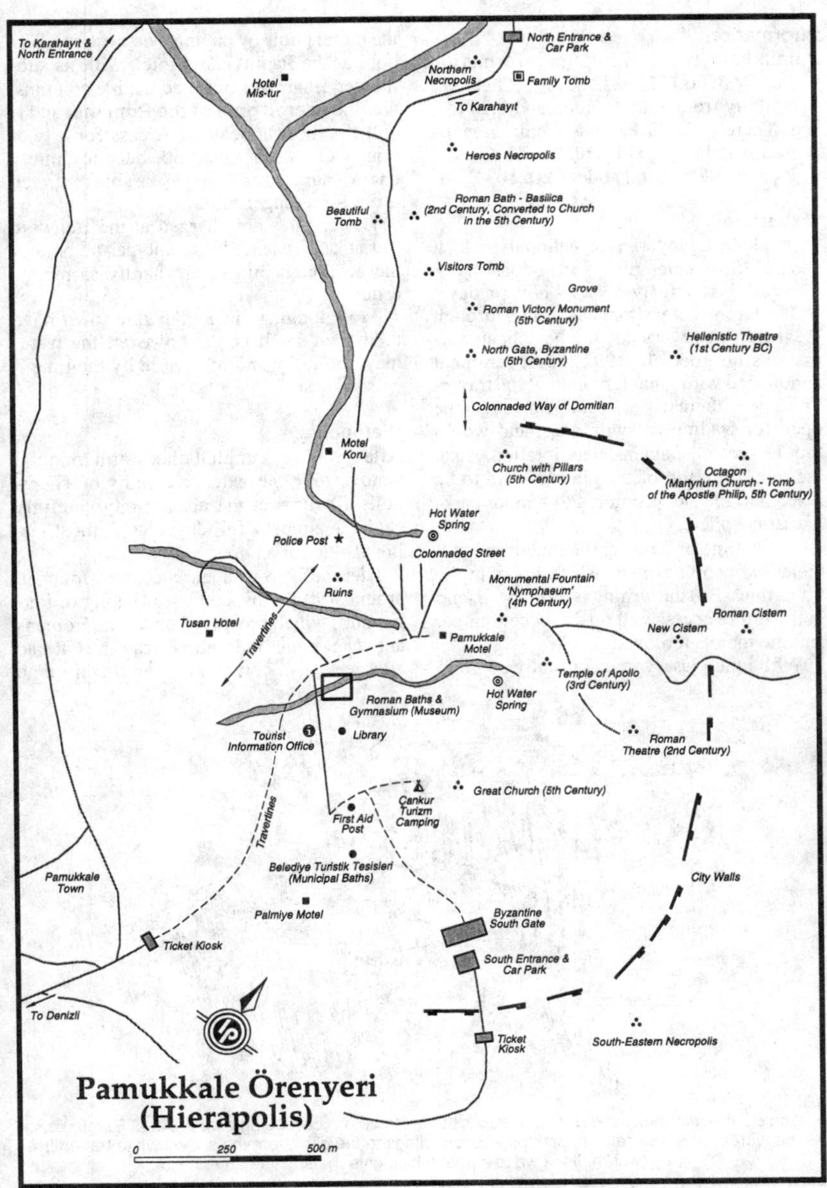

To Karahayıt & North Entrance
North Entrance & Car Park
Northern Necropolis
Family Tomb
Hotel Mis-tur
To Karahayıt
Heroes Necropolis
Roman Bath - Basilica (2nd Century, Converted to Church in the 5th Century)
Beautiful Tomb
Visitors Tomb
Grove
Roman Victory Monument (5th Century)
Hellenistic Theatre (1st Century BC)
North Gate, Byzantine (5th Century)
Colonnaded Way of Domitian
Motel Koru
Church with Pillars (5th Century)
Octagon (Martyrium Church - Tomb of the Apostle Philip, 5th Century)
Hot Water Spring
Police Post
Colonnaded Street
Ruins
Monumental Fountain 'Nymphaeum' (4th Century)
Tusan Hotel
Travertines
Pamukkale Motel
New Cistern
Roman Cistern
Temple of Apollo (3rd Century)
Roman Baths & Gymnasium (Museum)
Hot Water Spring
Tourist Information Office
Library
Roman Theatre (2nd Century)
Great Church (5th Century)
First Aid Post
Çankur Turizm Camping
Travertines
Beledlye Turistik Tesisleri (Municipal Baths)
Pamukkale Town
City Walls
Palmiye Motel
Byzantine South Gate
Ticket Kiosk
South Entrance & Car Park
To Denizli
Ticket Kiosk
South-Eastern Necropolis
Pamukkale Örenyeri (Hierapolis)
0
250
500 m

Information

Pamukkale has a Tourism Information Office (☎ & fax (258) 272 2077) at Örenyeri, open daily from 8 am to noon and 1.30 to 7 pm. There's also a PTT, souvenir shops, a museum and a first aid post.

Pamukkale's postal code is 20210.

Travertines

Pamukkale Örenyeri is a national park. It costs US$4 to enter, plus US$1 to park a car. The park is reputedly open 24 hours a day.

The throngs of visitors who tramp through the travertines every day do the delicate formations no good. In 1992 the government announced with great fanfare that the travertine pools themselves would no longer be open for wading or swimming, and would thus be protected against deterioration. Also, the motels on top of the plateau were to be razed and the site promoted to a more park-like atmosphere.

At the time of writing, the motels are still there and people still splash and play in the travertines. But the writing is on the wall, and in the future access will no doubt be limited, and the motels removed.

While they last, you can usually swim in the motel pools by paying a day-use fee. The pool at the Pamukkale Motel, with its submerged fragments of fluted marble columns, was the **sacred pool of the Romans**, and is still the most appealing. A pass for a two-hour swim costs US$4.50, but they rarely check your pass so you may be able to stretch it out for a longer time.

Lower rates are charged at the Belediye Turistik Tesisleri, the municipal baths, but these, though bigger, are hardly as picturesque.

Most lodgings in Pamukkale town have their own small pools, however, the water may be murky and lukewarm by the time it gets to these.

Hierapolis

After you've sampled the warm mineral waters, tour the extensive ruins of Hierapolis. To inspect the ancient city carefully can take almost a full day, though most visitors settle for an hour or two.

Hierapolis was a cure centre (founded around 190 BC by Eumenes II, king of Pergamum) which prospered under the Romans and even more under the Byzantines. It had a large Jewish community and therefore an

Hot calcium-laden mineral waters burst from the earth before cascading over a cliff at Pamukkale. As the water cools, the calcium precipitates and clings to the cliffs, forming snowy white travertines (waterfalls of white stone) which give the spa its name.

early Christian church. Earthquakes caused disaster a few times, and after the one in 1334 the people decided it was actually an unhealthy spot to live in and moved on.

Perhaps the centre of Hierapolis was the sacred pool, now the swimming pool in the courtyard of the Pamukkale Motel. If the motel is torn down as planned, perhaps the pool will again be visible as it was to the ancients. The city's **Roman baths**, parts of which are now the **Pamukkale Museum**, are in front of the Pamukkale Motel. The museum is open from 8.30 am to noon, and 1.30 to 5 pm, for US$1.25.

Near the museum is a ruined **Byzantine church** and the foundations of a **Temple of Apollo**. As at Didyma and Delphi, the temple had an oracle attended by eunuch priests. The source of inspiration was an adjoining spring called the Plutonium, dedicated appropriately to Pluto, god of the underworld. The spring gives off toxic vapours, lethal to all but the priests, who would demonstrate the gas' powers to visitors by throwing small animals and birds into it, which would promptly die.

To find the spring, walk up towards the Roman theatre but enter the first gate in the fence on the right, then follow the path down to the right about 30m. To the left and in front of the big, block-like temple is a small subterranean entry closed by a rusted grate and marked by a sign reading 'Tehlikelidir – Zehirli Gaz' (Dangerous – Poisonous Gas). If you approach and listen, you can hear the gas bubbling up from the waters below. Note that the gas is still deadly poisonous. In the years before the grate was installed there were several fatalities among those with more curiosity than sense.

The **Roman theatre**, capable of seating more than 7000 spectators, is in excellent condition, having been carefully restored by Italian stonecutters in the 1970s. A **Hellenistic theatre** in a greater state of ruin is several km to the north up the hill.

The **colonnaded street** still has some of its paving and columns intact. Once the city's main north-south commercial axis, it was bounded at its ends by monumental archways. The ruins of the **Arch of Domitian** are at the northern end.

For a health spa area, it has a surprisingly large **necropolis** (cemetery), extending several km to the north, with many striking, even stupendous, tombs.

Karahayıt

Five km to the north of Pamukkale is the village of Karahayıt (KAH-rah-hah-yuht), which has no spectacular travertines but boasts deep red iron-rich mineral waters. You can get cured (and stained red) at any of several small family pensions and camping places here, patronised mostly by ageing locals in search of the fountain of youth.

In recent years Karahayıt has been the building site of choice for the large and lavish hotels which cater to the tour-group trade. The dolmuş from Denizli to Pamukkale usually continues as far as Karahayıt, five km from the centre of Örenyeri.

Special Events

In late May or early June, the Pamukkale Festival brings spectators to Hierapolis' restored Roman theatre for musical and folkloric performances.

Places to Stay

The Turkish government, in league with UNESCO and the World Bank, plans to raze the motels on top of the ridge at Pamukkale. When they do, all the available lodgings will be in Pamukkale town and Karahayıt.

On weekends you may find the pensions and motels at Pamukkale full, and may have to seek lodgings in Denizli. To avoid the crush, come during the week, or very early on Friday or Saturday, and preferably in spring or autumn, not high summer.

Prices vary greatly according to the season, being highest in midsummer. In general, the inexpensive places to stay are in Pamukkale town, moderate places are at Örenyeri, and the new luxury hotels are at Karahayıt.

Pamukkale Town The town at the base of the ridge is filled with little family pensions, some more elaborate and expensive than others. Many have little swimming pools, often oddly shaped and filled with the calcium mineral water – cool by the time it gets here – and shady places to sit, read, sip tea or have a meal. If rooms are available, you will have no problem finding one, as pension owners will crowd around your bus as it arrives and importune you with offers. Those with rooms available after the mêlée will intercept you as you walk along the road into the village.

A walking tour of some of the better places to stay follows.

Right at the entrance to Pamukkale town, just off the highway, is the *Hotel Konak Sade* (☎ (258) 272 2002, fax 272 2175), the first lodging place in the village, opened more than 25 years ago. It's an old village house decorated with Turkish carpets, kilims and copperware. The shady rear garden holds a small swimming pool surrounded by tables and chairs; the view of the travertines from here is the best around. The 32 rooms are simple, but with private baths. You pay US$30 a double with breakfast.

Motels are squeezing out some cheap pensions as the demand for accommodation grows. The 58-room *Yörük Motel* (☎ & fax (258) 272 2073), just a short walk down the hill in the village centre, is nice. Guest rooms are on two levels, surrounding a courtyard with swimming pool. Balconies allow you to sit outside and enjoy the sun while watching the swimmers. The restaurant is often busy with tour groups. Double rooms with shower, breakfast included, cost US$25/35 a single/double in summer.

Walk past the Yörük and turn left to find the *Fatih Motel* (☎ (258) 272 2054), a great bargain. Smaller and slightly less fancy, it has an even quieter situation, though the pool is smaller and murkier. The price is the best part: US$18 a double, breakfast included.

Continue along the road past the Fatih, and turn left on İnönü Caddesi for the *Kervansaray Pension* (☎ (258) 272 2209), which offers rooms with shower for US$18, a swimming pool, and a friendly family atmosphere. It's been a favourite for years.

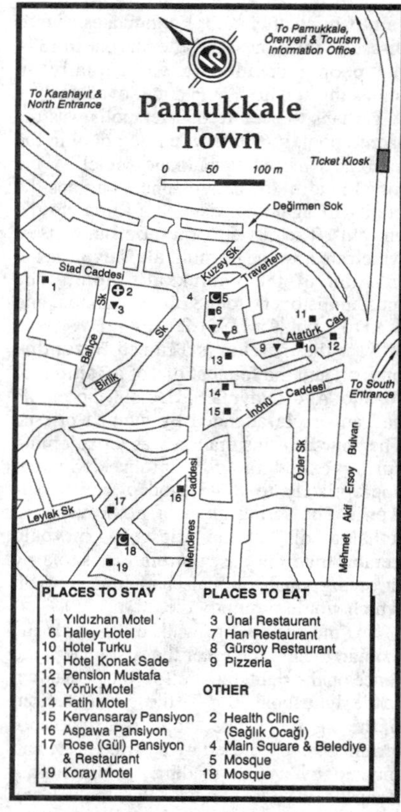

If the Kervansaray is full, go back to Menderes Caddesi and the next place along is the *Aspawa Pansiyon* (☎ (258) 272 2094), which is modern, friendly, and priced similarly.

Four hundred metres farther along is Rifat Durmuş's *Koray Otel* (☎ (258) 272 2300, fax 272 2095), an excellent choice. Away from the noise and bustle, it is well kept, friendly, and filled with plants. A double room with shower costs US$18. For US$10 more you get breakfast and dinner as well. If you call and let them know you've arrived at Denizli Otogar, a hotel car will come and pick you up.

Halley Hotel (☎ (258) 272 2204), next to the mosque in the town centre, has a few plain, clean rooms for US$12 a double without running water, or US$18 a double for the newer 'motel-style' rooms with nice tiled showers.

Hotel Turku (☎ (258) 272 2181) is fancier, with tidy rooms with private showers, a pool, and tasty meals in the dining room, but charges slightly higher prices (about US$25 a double). *Pension Rose* (☎ (258) 272 2289), also called the Gül Pansiyon (the translation), has a small camping area as well as cheap rooms. The *Arkadaş Pansiyon* (☎ (258) 272 2183, fax 272 2589) has been recommended by several readers.

Camping There are several camping grounds along the road between Denizli and Pamukkale. There is also the small *Çankur Turizm Camping* at Örenyeri, behind the Belediye Turistik Tesisleri swimming pools, though it's usually full every day in high season. Shady sites for tents and camper vans cost US$6 a double. Little A-frame shelters nearby cost a bit more.

Örenyeri As motels amidst the ruins at Pamukkale may not last long, if you plan to stay here, make reservations in advance to be sure the establishment is still in existence.

Pamukkale Motel (☎ (258) 272 2024, fax 272 2026) is the one with the garden swimming pool littered with broken marble columns that you see in photographs so often. With its column-studded pool, the Pamukkale Motel is in demand, though it is hardly luxurious. Rooms with a bath cost US$55/75 a single/double, breakfast and dinner included.

The three-star, 47-room *Tusan Hotel* (☎ (258) 272 2010, fax 272 2059) was the first comfortable motel here, and still commands premium prices of US$65/80 for a single/double with breakfast and dinner.

The *Hotel Mis-tur* (MEESS-toor; ☎ (258) 272 2130, fax 272 2013) is another middle-range place to stay. It is at the northern end of 'motel row', a 10-minute walk from the centre of Örenyeri. Its odd beehive rooms produce unnerving echoes, but it's well kept and attractive, with live entertainment around the pool most evenings. Rates are US$40/58 a single/double, breakfast included.

At the *Palmiye Motel* (☎ (258) 272 2014, fax 272 2018) you can choose from several styles of accommodation. The older rooms (Nos 101 to 129) are arranged so that you have your own individual section of swimming pool right near your room, with a magnificent view of the valley. Newer rooms (Nos 130 and up) do not share this fabulous valley view, but rather surround a big swimming pool. All are simple Turkish-style motel rooms, comfortable but fairly basic. In the busy summer season the motel, with one of the best situations on the ridge, can get away with charging US$50 a double for a room around the main pool, or US$75 for a room with an individual pool. Breakfast and dinner are included in these prices.

The conveniently located 130-room *Motel Koru* (☎ (258) 272 2020, fax 1023) is the largest lodging place here, with a big, beautiful swimming pool and pleasant gardens. It's a mecca for bus tours, and always seems to be thronged with groups settling in for a good feed. The air-con rooms with shower cost US$40/60 a single/double. Service to individual travellers may suffer as a result of the groups.

Karahayıt Four km north of Pamukkale Örenyeri and one km south of Karahayıt village are a few pensions, including the *Selçuklu* and the *Osmanlı*, but most lodgings are in the dozen new four-star hotels aimed at the tour-group market. The 69-room *Kur-Tur Motel* (☎ (258) 271 4117, fax 263 0818) rates three stars.

The four-star, 225-room *Club Polat's Hotel* (☎ (258) 271 4111, fax 271 4092), opened in 1988 and so has more established gardens and good guest rooms in two-storey sugar-cube-white blocks. Doubles cost US$80, breakfast included.

Similar four-star accommodations are available at the 230-room *Colossea Hotel Termal* (☎ (258) 271 4156, fax 271 4250);

the 210-room *Ergür Hotel* (☎ (258) 271 4170, fax 271 4146); the 158-room *Pam Hotel* (☎ (258) 271 4140, fax 271 4097) as well as the 208-room *Hierapolis Thermal Hotel* (☎ (258) 271 4105, fax 271 4816).

Places to Eat – bottom end

The inexpensive places (and they're not all that cheap for what you get) are at the bottom of the ridge in Pamukkale town. Most of the pensions serve meals, and I recommend that you take a room with breakfast and dinner included. Chances are very good that your pension will serve you better food, with larger portions at lower prices, than any of the eateries in the village.

The famous *Pizzeria* on the main street between the highway and the Yörük Motel was built to resemble a Pizza Hut in Australia, in which its builder worked for several years. Don't expect a shiny plastic fast-food place; this one's far more 'Turkish villagey', with prices to match, and excellent fresh pizza. The upper deck gives you a view with your meal. *Pizzaland* next door is also good, though the food is a bit more bland.

On top of the ridge there is a pide restaurant and a café selling soft drinks, with tables overlooking the travertines, but at prices somewhat higher than those in the valley. You'd be well advised to pack a picnic before you climb the ridge from Pamukkale town.

Places to Eat – middle

All of the motels at Örenyeri have dining rooms, mostly geared to tour groups. In Pamukkale town, try the *Gürsoy Restaurant*, facing the Yörük Motel on the main street. With its small, shady front terrace, it's great for people-watching. A three-course meal with drink costs about US$5. Similarly priced is the popular *Han Restaurant*, facing the main square. The menu has many popular dishes (grills for US$2.75 to US$3.75), and all prices are posted.

The *snal*, below the square, has less of a view and simpler décor, but is significantly cheaper, with set-price meals for US$3.50 and US$4.50. The *Mustafa Restaurant*, at the top of the hill near the main road, advertises vegetarian food.

For a drink, try the *Harem Restaurant & Bar*, on the main street, with a good view of the foot traffic.

Getting There & Away

Bus In summertime, Pamukkale has a surprising number of direct buses to and from other cities. Many of these buses are continuations of the Denizli service. Companies serving the town with direct buses include Kamil Koç, Köseoğlu, Pamukkale and Paklale. For distances and prices, see the Denizli section.

At the time of writing the town had no proper otogar. Ticket offices are near the junction of the highway and the town's main street.

Municipal buses make the half-hour trip between Denizli and Pamukkale every 45 minutes or so, more frequently on Saturday and Sunday, for US$0.50; the last bus runs at 10 pm in summer, probably around sunset in other seasons. Dolmuşes go more frequently, running until about 11 pm in summer, and faster, and charge US$0.60.

Car If you're driving from Aphrodisias and Nazilli, you might want to know that there's a shortcut to Pamukkale. About 600m after you pass the exit sign from Sarayköy ('Sarayköy' with a red diagonal stripe through it), there is a narrow road on the left going to Pamukkale via the villages of Sığma (SUH-mah), Akköy and Karahayıt. The road is not well marked, so you should ask directions for Pamukkale in each village. If enough people ask directions, the locals might erect signs.

Taxi A taxi between Denizli and Pamukkale costs about US$8, but don't take one until you're *sure* the bus and dolmuş have stopped for the day, which is what you're liable to hear from every taxi driver.

LAODİKYA

Laodicea was a prosperous commercial city at the junction of two major trade routes running north to south and east to west. Famed for its black wool, banking and medicines, it had a large Jewish community and a prominent Christian congregation. It is one of the Seven Churches of Asia mentioned in the New Testament Book of Revelation. Cicero lived here a few years before he was put to death at the request of Marc Antony.

To reach the ruins of Laodikya, you will need a car, a taxi, a hired minibus, or good strong legs. Head north towards Pamukkale from the Üçgen, the large traffic roundabout near Denizli's bus station. Take the left turn marked for Pamukkale, and then almost immediately (just before the village of Korucuk) another left marked for Laodikya.

From this point it is just over three km to the edge of the archaeological site, or just over four km from Laodikya's most prominent theatre. There are actually several routes to the ruins, but this one takes you through a little farming village; the road is unmarked, so ask, or when in doubt, go to the right. You should soon come to a railway level crossing; on the other side of the tracks, the ruins are visible. (Another route leaves the main road closer to Pamukkale, and brings you to the theatre first.)

At present there is no guard at the site, no fee and no appointed visiting hours, so you can come anytime during daylight hours.

Though the city was a big one, as you see by the ruins spread over a large area, there is not much of interest left for the casual tourist. The **stadium** is visible, but most of the cut stones were purloined for construction of the railway. One of the **two theatres** is in better shape, with many of its upper tiers of seats remaining, though the bottom ones have collapsed. Unless you have a car or are interested in church history, you can bypass Laodikya.

AK HAN

While you're digging about out here, consider taking a look at the Ak Han (White Caravanserai), a marble Seljuk Turkish caravan 'motel' just one km past the Pamukkale turn off from the main road. (Heading north from the Üçgen in Denizli, don't take the Pamukkale road, but continue in the direction marked for Dinar for one more km.) The caravanserai is set just off the highway on the left as you come down the slope of a hill. Somewhat neglected these days, the caravanserai awaits preservation, but it is still in quite marvellous shape considering that it dates from the early 1250s.

South Aegean

The south-western corner of Anatolia is mountainous and somewhat isolated. In ancient times this was the Kingdom of Caria, with its own indigenous customs and people, who later took on a veneer of Hellenic civilisation. Later, Christian anchorites (hermits) sought out the mountains and lake islands of Caria to be alone, and to escape the invading Arab armies. Ottoman sultans used the mountainous region to exile political troublemakers in Bodrum, secure in the belief that they could raise no turmoil from such a remote spot.

Your goal is probably Bodrum, the seacoast town in which sleek yachts are anchored in twin bays beneath the walls of a medieval crusaders' castle. Along the way are a number of ancient cities and temples worth stopping to see.

SÖKE TO MİLAS

The 86-km ride from Söke, near Selçuk and Kuşadası, to Milas need take only 1¼ hours if you go nonstop. But there are so many interesting detours and stops to make that it may take you several days.

About 29 km south of Söke there is a turn off, on the right, for Akköy (seven km), Miletus and Didyma, described above. Soon afterwards, the highway skirts the southern shore of **Bafa Gölü** (Bafa Lake). The lake was once a gulf of the Aegean Sea, but became a lake as the sea retreated. Thirteen km beyond the Akköy turn off are several restaurants, motels and camping areas, most prominently the *Turgut*.

Four km farther along (heading south-east) is a small island bearing traces of a ruined Byzantine monastery, and just beyond it is *Ceri'nin Yeri*, a restaurant serving sea bass, eel, carp and grey mullet which find their way into the lake to spawn. Ceri'nin's has a few pension and motel rooms, and a camp site as well. Sometimes you can arrange for a tour by boat to Latmos.

Latmos

At the south-eastern end of the lake is a settlement named Çamiçi, from which a paved road on the left is marked for **Kapıkırı**, 10 km to the north, though it's actually less than nine km. You will have to hike or hitch unless you can catch one of the infrequent dolmuşes.

At the end of the road, in and around the village of Kapıkırı (population 350), are the ruins of Herakleia ad Latmos. Behind the village is **Beşparmak Dağı**, the Five-fingered Mountain (1500m), named for its five peaks. This was the ancient Mt Latmos.

History Latmos is famous because of Endymion, the legendary shepherd boy. As the story goes, the handsome Endymion was asleep on Mt Latmos when Selene, the moon goddess, fell in love with him. The myths tend to differ in regard to what happened next, though you can easily imagine. It seems that Endymion slept forever, and Selene (also called Diana) got to come down and sleep with him every night. Selene somehow saw to the care of his flocks, and on he slept. No more to report. When the male lead sleeps through, it makes for a short play.

This area, ringed by mountains, was one of refuge for Christian hermits during the Arab invasions of the 8th century AD, which accounts for the ruined churches and monasteries. The monks reputedly thought Endymion a Christian saint because they admired his powers of self-denial, though catatonia seems more the word for it.

Things to See As you enter the village in summer (at other times they don't seem to bother), you may be asked to pay an admission fee of US$1.50. Bear right at the ticket booth, pass the Herakleia Restaurant & Camping, which has fine lake views, and you come to the Agora Restaurant. Park here and explore on foot.

A path behind the car park leads westward up to the **Temple of Athena**, on a promontory overlooking the lake. Also from the car park, paths lead eastward to the **agora**, and then several hundred metres through stone-walled pastures and across a valley to the unrestored **theatre**. The theatre is oddly sited, with no spectacular view; it's badly ruined. Its most interesting feature is the several rows of seats and flights of steps cut into the rock. You will also see many remnants of the **city walls** dating from 300 BC.

Much of the fun of a visit to Latmos is to observe real Turkish farming village life, as you will when you walk about this relatively untouristed spot. Beehives dot the fields, and camomile flowers *(papatya)* grow wild by the roadsides in spring and summer.

When you're finished in the village, follow the road down to the lake, past the **Endymion Temple** built partly into the rock, the ruins of a **Byzantine castle** and the city's **necropolis**.

Down at the lakeside, near the ruins of a Byzantine church, are several small restaurants for fish (if they've caught any that day), including the *Zeybek*, *Kaya* and *Selene*. All offer camping and boat tours of the lake as well. There's a small beach of coarse white sand. Just offshore is an 'island' which may be reached from the shore on foot as the level of the lake sometimes falls. Around the island's base are foundations of ancient buildings.

Places to Stay & Eat Several pensions with restaurants have sprung up in recent years, including the clean *Agora Pansiyon* (☎ & fax (252) 543 5445), charging US$15 for a waterless double (clean shared baths). Included in the price is a village breakfast: fresh eggs, local butter and honey (no packets). The *Herakleia Pansiyon* is similar. Of the camping areas, the *Herakleia* seems the best, though the less well-kept lakeside sites have the advantage of their position.

Euromos

About 15 km past Bafa Lake and one km south of the village of **Selimiye**, keep your eyes open for the picturesque **Temple of Zeus**, on the left-hand side of the road in the midst of what was once the city of Euromos. The Corinthian colonnades set in green olive groves seem too good to be true, like a Hollywood set of a classical scene. Once there was a town here, but now only the temple remains. But it's enough, and well worth a stop.

First settled in the 6th century BC, Euromos held a sanctuary to a local deity. With the coming of Greek, then Roman, culture, the local god's place was taken by Zeus. Euromos reached the height of its prosperity between 200 BC and 200 AD. Emperor Hadrian (117-38 AD), who built so many monuments in Anatolia, is thought to have built this one as well. From the several columns which remain unfluted, it appears that the work was never really finished.

The site is open from 8.30 am to 5 pm (to 7 pm in summer) for US$1.50. There are no services except soft drinks sales.

If you're interested in ruins, you can explore the slopes around to find other bits of the town. Look north-east (more or less towards İzmir) and find the big stone fortification walls up on the hillside. Climb up to them through the olive groves, go over the wall, and continue at the same altitude (the path dips a bit, which is OK, but don't climb higher). After 100m you'll cross another stone wall and find yourself on flat ground which was the stage of the ancient **theatre**. It's badly ruined now, with olive trees growing among the few remaining rows of seats. Besides the theatre, the town's **agora** is down by the highway to the north of the temple, with only a few toppled column drums to mark it.

The city of Milas is about 12 km south of Euromos, but before you come to this city, there are other places to visit.

Iasos

A sleepy Aegean fishing village built amidst the tumbled ruins of an ancient city: this description was once true of Iasos, but tourism has near spoiled its charm. Now as you enter this well-sited village you are greeted with a view of unfinished concrete villas going to ruin.

About four km south-east of Euromos (eight km north-west of Milas) is a road on the right (west) marked for **Kıyıkışlacık** (Iasos), about 18 km to the south-west over a twisting road. The Turkish name means 'Little Barracks on the Coast', but Iasos was in fact a fine city set on its dramatic perch several centuries before Christ. Earliest settlement may date from the Old Bronze Age, and may have included a civilisation much like the Minoan one on Crete.

As you approach the village, past the visually unfortunate villas the road forks. The right fork leads to a **museum** holding the village's most interesting ruin, a monumental Roman tomb; the left fork leads to the port, up over the hill and along the coast.

Iasos was built on a hill at the tip of a peninsula framed by two picture-perfect bays. Excavations have revealed the city's bouleuterion and agora, a gymnasium, a basilica, a Roman temple of Artemis Astias (190 AD) and numerous other buildings besides the prominent Byzantine fortress.

Today the hill above the port is covered with ruins, including a walled acropolis-fortress (admission costs US$1 if there's anyone there to collect it). Olive groves surround the town, somehow taking purchase in the rocky soil, and reach nearly to its centre. South-west of the hill on the bay is a small yacht harbour. Fishing smacks crowd the quay, and a handful of small pensions and restaurants cater to travellers who want to get away from it all for a few days. Have çipura (gilt head bream), if it's in season, at the *Iasos Deniz Restaurant*, right down on the water, or at the *Yıldız*, just up the hill.

Of the pensions, the *Cengiz* and *Zeytin* are clean and modern, with fine views and simple rooms for US$15 a double. As one reader of this guide wrote in a letter, 'If god is an artist, he surely painted the view out my window in Iasos.'

Boats come over to Iasos from Güllük to the south (see following) in summer, ferrying tourists and visiting beaches accessible by water; there are no good beaches in Iasos proper.

Labranda

Labranda was a sanctuary to Zeus Stratius, controlled for a long time by Milas. There may have been an oracle here. It's known that festivals and Olympic games were held at the site. Set into a steep hillside at 600m elevation in an area from which the ancient city of Mylasa and the modern town of Milas took their water supplies, Labranda today is surrounded by fragrant pine forests peopled by beekeepers. Late in the season (October) you can see their tents pitched in cool groves as they go about their business of extracting the honey and rendering the wax from the honeycombs. It's a beautiful site, worth seeing partly because so few people come here – yet.

The junction for the road to Labranda is 12 km south of Euromos, just before Milas. It's 14 km to the site: the first six km are paved and fast to travel on, the remaining eight km are on a rough, slow but scenic road deep in dust which winds tortuously up into the mountains. In rainy weather (October to April) the road turns to a slough of mud that may require 4WD. The village of Kargıcak is eight km along the way, and though you may be able to get a dolmuş from Milas to Kargıcak, that leaves six km to walk. Hitching is possible but not at all reliable, particularly later in the day. A taxi from Milas charges about US$22 for the trip to the site and back.

Labranda was a holy place, not a settlement. Worship of a god at this site had been going on by the 7th century BC, and perhaps long before. The site seems to have been abandoned circa 1000 AD. Today there is no settlement here either, just a caretaker who will welcome you, have you sign the guest book and show you around the site; he speaks only Turkish, with a few words of other languages, but the site is well marked.

The great **Temple of Zeus** honours the god's warlike aspect (Stratius, or Labrayndus, 'Axe-bearing'). Two men's religious gathering places, the **First Andron** and the **Second Andron**, are in surprisingly good condition, as is a large 4th-century **tomb** of fine construction, and other buildings. The ruins, excavated by a Swedish team in the early part of this century, are interesting, but it is the site of the sanctuary which is most impressive. The view over the valley is spectacular.

MİLAS

Milas (MEE-lahs, population 35,000, altitude 46m) is a very old town. As Mylasa, it was capital of the Kingdom of Caria, except during the period when Mausolus ruled the kingdom from Halicarnassus (now Bodrum). Today it is an agricultural town and has many homes in which carpets are woven by hand.

Orientation

Approaching Milas from the north-west, you pass Milas' new otogar one km (along 19 Mayıs Bulvarı) before coming to Labranda Bulvarı to the left; to the right (along İnönü Caddesi) the road is marked 'Şehir Merkezi' (City Centre). It's another km to the centre of town at the park (Milas Belediye Parkı).

Milas' postal code is 48200.

Things to See

Coming into town from the otogar, watch for signs pointing to the right for the Belediye and, opposite, turn to the left for the **Baltalı Kapı**, or 'Gate with an Axe'. Cross a small bridge and look to the left to see the well-preserved Roman gate, which has marble posts and lintel and Corinthian capitals. The eponymous double-headed axe is carved into the keystone on the north side.

Return to the road and continue south past the forgettable **museum**, bearing right to the traffic roundabout, in the centre of which is a marble scale model of the Gümüşkesen

monumental tomb next to the shady Milas Belediye Parkı.

Continue straight on for three blocks, turn right, then turn again at Gümüşkesen Caddesi to reach the tomb, 1.4 km from the roundabout on a hill west of the centre.

The **Gümüşkesen** ('That which cuts silver' or, construed as Gümüşkese, 'silver purse') is a Roman monumental tomb dating from the 1st century AD, thought to have been modelled on the great Tomb of Mausolus at Halicarnassus. As in the Mausoleum, Corinthian columns here support a pyramidal roof, beneath which is a tomb chamber, which you can enter. A hole in the platform floor allowed devotees to pour libations into the tomb to quench the dead soul's thirst.

The tomb enclosure, in a little park, is usually open. If he's around, the guardian will charge you the US$1.25 admission fee and allow you to climb a ladder up to the tomb platform. The view of the city is good.

You might also want to see some of Milas' fine mosques, especially the **Ulu Cami** (1378) and **Orhan Bey Camii** (1330), built when Milas was the capital of the Turkish principality of Menteşe. The larger, more impressive **Firuz Bey Camii** (1394) was built shortly after Menteşe became part of the new and growing Ottoman Empire.

Places to Stay

Otel Arıcan (☎ (252) 512 1215), next to the Hacı İlyas Camii (and, alas, its minaret), has cheap rooms for US$9 a double without bath, or US$12 with private shower. *Hotel Akdeniz* (☎ (6131) 2217), across the street, is a distant second choice. The Yeni Hamam, across Hacı İlyas Sokak from the Otel Arıcan, fills the need for a Turkish bath.

Altogether better is the *Hotel Çınar* (☎ & fax (252) 512 2102), Kadıağa Caddesi 52, which offers much more congenial accommodation, with a lobby one flight up. Take a room at the back as front rooms may be noisy. Rates are US$12 for a double, US$15 for twin beds, with private bath and breakfast.

Hotel Turan (☎ (252) 512 1342), Cumhuriyet Caddesi 26, has better prices for comparable rooms, about US$2 cheaper per person.

Otel Sürücü (☎ (252) 512 4001, fax 512 4000), on Atatürk Bulvarı more or less across from the statue of Atatürk, is just slightly more comfortable, with bigger rooms than the Çınar or Turan, at slightly higher prices: US$14/20 a single/double, with breakfast. The lobby is grander and some rooms have TV. There's no lift, though.

Places to Eat

The town's culinary offering runs to pide and not much more. The market area has several pidecis where a pide and soft drink sell for US$1.75, including the locally-esteemed *Pamukkale Pide Salonu* on Menteşe Caddesi. The Otel Arıcan has its own *Arıcan Bolu Lokantası* with soups, stews and kebaps. Eat early (before 7 pm), as these few places don't stay open late.

BEÇİN KALE & ÖREN

Three km south of Milas is an intersection: right to Bodrum, left to Ören, Muğla and Marmaris. Turn left and there's a road on the right marked for Ören, 50 km along where the road ends at the Gulf of Gökova.

Just over one km along the Ören road at Beçin, a road on the right is marked with a black-on-yellow sign for Beçin, a **Byzantine fortress** later pressed into service by the Turkish emirs of Menteşe. The fortress is open from 8 am to dusk (US$1), but there is not a lot to see inside. Less than 500m on are remnants of the Menteşe settlement (dating from the 14th century), including the Kızıl Han caravanserai, Orhan Bey Camii, and the Ahmet Gazi tomb and medrese.

Ören has been slow to lose that tranquil atmosphere which was once common to villages along the Turkish coasts. The village actually consists of two parts. Inland from the beach is the centre, with its PTT, shops, and old Ottoman houses set amidst the **ruins of the ancient city of Keramos** (or Ceramus), which flourished from the 6th century BC until at least the 3rd century AD. The **beach** is the centre of visitor interest, however.

The sand-and-pebble beach is one km long and draws Turkish holiday-makers from the big cities. They come for stays of a week, two weeks or more in the village's few cheap lodgings. If you bother to travel the 50 km to the village, you too will want to stay more than a night.

Places to Stay & Eat

If you plan to stay in high summer, come early in the morning to find a room, or call ahead and reserve one. Among cheap lodgings, try the *Karya Oteli* (☎ (252) 532 2115), the *Otel Göksu* (☎ (252) 532 2112) or the *Hotel Marçalı* (☎ (252) 532 2063), with double rooms for US$15. *Yıltur Motel* (☎ (252) 532 2108), at the eastern end of the beach, is a bit cheaper but simpler. For more comfort there's the *Hotel Salihağa* (☎ (252) 532 2138) and the *Keramos Motel* (☎ (252) 532 2065), which also has a camping ground. Ören also has a few restaurants to serve its transient population.

Ören to Gökova

An unpaved country road climbs steeply out of Ören for 10 km heading east for Gökova.

The next 20 km of road rises and falls with the land through back-country farming villages. The final 25 km is a gentle descent through the Mediterranean coast's characteristic pine forests, with beehives lining the road much of the way.

GÜLLÜK

Turn right at the intersection three km south of Milas, and another 15 km brings you to the road on the right for Güllük, a mining port and minor seaside resort town which retains a semblance of 'authentic' daily life.

Eight km west of the highway through olive groves, Güllük is spread along three bays. The road brings you, along with a steady stream of bauxite ore trucks, to the central bay and the centre of the town, where the ore is loaded onto waiting ships. Fishing boats are moored south of the ore dock, and beyond them more fishing craft are built in the traditional way at simple open-air boat yards. Though there is a yacht mooring, the harbour is mostly for working vessels.

Güllük is a working town with a sideline in tourism, and therein lies its attraction. There is sufficient accommodation and other services but none of the hassle encountered in hyper-resorts such as Kuşadası, Marmaris or Bodrum. If you'd like a few days in a traditional Turkish seaside town with swimming and ruins nearby, Güllük will do.

Orientation & Information

The bay to the left (south) of the central one is monopolised by a Türk Petrol company resort; to the right, the northern bay is lined with posh summer villas. The north bay is the best for swimming, but in fact there is no beach here. Day-excursions by boat to Iasos and nearby beaches can be arranged from the restaurants along the waterfront.

Places to Stay & Eat

A few Ottoman-era buildings survive in the centre, including the fine house now inhabited by Tekel and, north of it, a stone han and a warehouse, the latter fronted with restaurants including the *Çiçek, Kosova, İlayda* and *Eski Depo*, all of which post prices, serve alcohol, have good sunset water views, and can arrange boat excursions for you. The *Poseidon Restaurant*, on the upper floor of a building across from the central park, is a bit more refined. Just inland on the market square (the market begins at dawn on Friday) is the cheaper *Barış Pide Pizza Kebap Salonu*.

As for lodgings, the *Gökçe Pansiyon* (☎ (252) 522 2994; follow the signs) is simple but adequate at US$12 a double. The *Kordon Motel* (☎ 522 2356), behind the small bust of Atatürk just south of the aforementioned restaurants, has balconied sea-view rooms for about the same price, and its own restaurant.

Of the middle-range hotels, the three-star, 36-room *Kont Hotel* (☎ (252) 522 2427, fax 522 2426), on the hillside on the south side of the central bay, is well located. All rooms have balconies with sea views, and private baths, for US$22 a double. There's also a swimming pool.

The real value for money is at the138-room, four-star *Labranda Corinthia Hotel* (☎ (252) 522 2911, fax 522 2009), where a private beach, large swimming pool and two tennis courts are yours along with very comfortable TV and minibar-equipped rooms for US$40/55 a single/double.

Getting There & Away

Dolmuşes run to Güllük from Milas, and also from the village of Koru, on the highway a few km north of the Güllük turn off.

BODRUM

The road to Bodrum (population 25,000) winds through pine forests, finally cresting a hill to reveal a panorama of Bodrum with its striking crusader castle.

Bodrum owes its fame to a man long dead and a building long disappeared. It is, however, the South Aegean's prettiest resort, with a yacht harbour and a port for ferries to the Greek island of Kos.

The man long dead is King Mausolus, and the building is his tomb, the Mausoleum, but Bodrum has many other attractions. Most striking is the Castle of St Peter in the middle of town, guarding twin bays now busy with yachts. Palm-lined streets ring the bays, and white sugar-cube houses, now joined by ranks of villas, crowd the hillside. Yachting, boating, swimming, snorkelling and scuba diving are prime Bodrum activities. Daytime diversions include boat or minibus trips to nearby secluded beaches and villages, or over to the Greek island of Kos. At night, Bodrum's famous discos throb, boom and blare at will, keeping much of the town awake until dawn. Both Turkish and foreign visitors complain about the ear-splitting cacophony, but the local attitude seems to be, 'If you wanted peace and quiet, why did you come to Bodrum?'.

Bodrum's economy is now dedicated to tourism, though in winter there is a bounteous citrus crop (especially tangerines). A few sponge-fishing boats survive as well.

History

Following the Persian invasion, Caria was ruled by a satrap named Mausolus (circa 376-353 BC), who moved the capital here from Mylasa and called this town Halicarnassus. After the satrap's death, his wife undertook construction of a monumen-

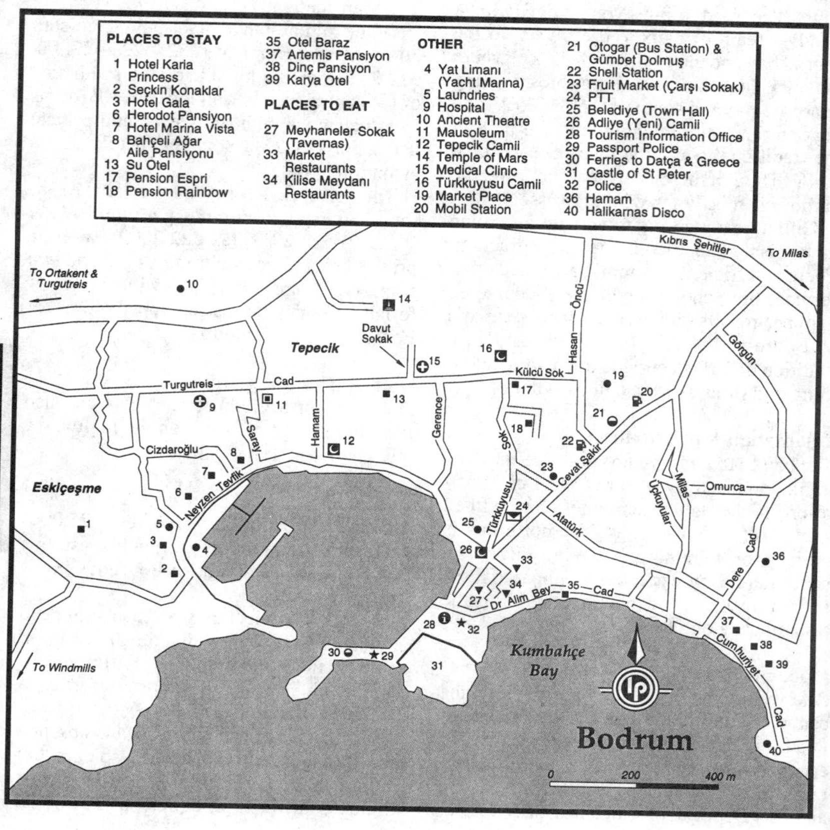

tal tomb which Mausolus had planned for himself. The Mausoleum, an enormous white-marble tomb topped by a stepped pyramid, came to be considered one of the Seven Wonders of the World. It stood relatively intact for almost 19 centuries, until it was broken up by the crusaders and the pieces used as building material in 1522.

Bodrum's other claim to fame comes from Herodotus (?485-?425 BC), the 'Father of History', who was born here. Herodotus was the first person to write a comprehensive 'world history', and all other histories in western civilisation are indebted to his work.

Orientation

The bus station is several hundred metres inland from the water, on Cevat Şakir, the main street into the centre. Walk down from the bus station towards the castle, and you will come to a small white mosque called the Adliye Camii (AHD-lee-yeh jah-mee, Courthouse Mosque), or Yeni Cami. Turn right, and you'll be heading west on Neyzen Tevfik Caddesi towards the Yat Limanı (Yacht Marina), past various restaurants and the quieter pensions; turn left and you will go through the bazaar, then walk along Doktor Alim Bey Caddesi, which later becomes Cumhuriyet Caddesi, past the noisier hotels and pensions. The array of lodgings continues all the way around the bay, then along the shore of another bay farther on.

Go straight on towards the castle and you'll be walking along Kale Caddesi, the tourist axis of Bodrum, lined with boutiques selling clothing, carpets, souvenirs and trinkets. At the end of Kale Caddesi, beneath the castle walls, is Oniki Eylül Meydanı (12 September Square), also called İskele Meydanı (Dock Square), the main plaza. It has the Tourism Information Office, customs office, teahouses and, along the wharf, day-excursion boats.

Bodrum's postal code is 48400.

Information

Tourist Offices The Tourism Information Office (☎ (252) 316 1091, fax 316 7694) is on İskele (Oniki Eylül) Meydanı. Summer hours are Monday to Friday from 8 am to 8 pm, Saturday from 9 am to noon and 3.30 to 7.30 pm, closed on Sunday. The staff are helpful, with bus and ferry schedules and accommodation lists. Several bus and ferry companies have ticket offices nearby.

Laundry The yachters don't have hotel staff to do their laundry, so the town's most convenient laundry places are near the yacht marina. The Minik and Neyzen laundries are on Neyzen Tevfik Caddesi to the right of the Hotel Gala. To wash and dry a full load in their machines costs US$6.

Market There is a fresh vegetable and fruit market just north of the otogar.

Castle of St Peter

When Tamerlane invaded Anatolia in 1402, throwing the nascent Ottoman Empire off balance for a time, the Knights Hospitaller, or Knights of St John of Jerusalem, based on Rhodes took the opportunity to capture

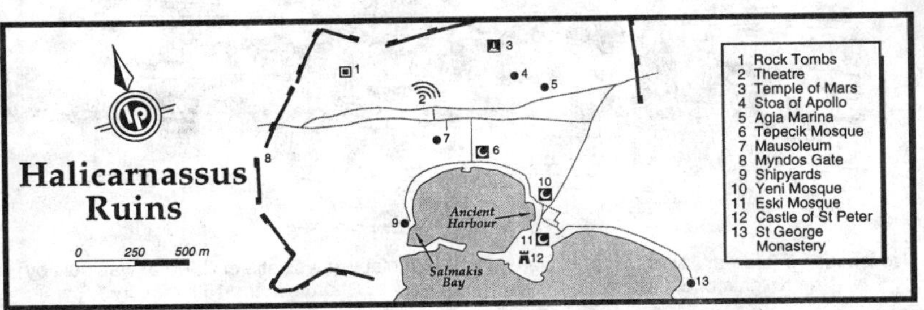

Bodrum. They built the Castle of St Peter, and it defended Bodrum (not always successfully) until the end of WWI.

The castle now holds Bodrum's famous **Museum of Underwater Archaeology.** Hours are from 8.30 am to 6 pm (closed Monday), but the exhibit halls close from noon to 1.30 pm for staff lunch. Admission costs US$3; students pay half-price. The **Glass-ship Wreck Hall** is open from Tuesday to Friday only, for an additional US$1.75. Signs are in Turkish and English. The maps of the castle posted here and there, and the directional signs, are not always clear or helpful, and construction often changes walking routes.

Walk up the stone ramp into the castle past crusader **coats of arms** carved in marble and mounted in the stone walls. Keep an eye out for bits of marble taken from the ancient Mausoleum.

The ramp leads to the castle's main court, centred on an aged ivy-covered tree.

To the left are **exhibits of amphorae** and other artefacts recovered from the waters of south-western Turkey.

At a small stall, a **potter** demonstrates the techniques used to make pottery centuries ago.

The courtyard café, amidst displays of Greek and Roman statuary, provides a shady resting-place for those who've already climbed the stone towers.

The former chapel here is being fitted with an exhibit featuring a full-sized reconstruction of the stern half of a **7th-century eastern Roman ship** discovered off Yassıada by a University of Pennsylvania team between 1961 and 1964. Visitors can walk the decks, stand at the helm, look below decks at the cargo of wine, and peek into the galley where the cook prepared meals for the crew.

Follow the path on the left side of the chapel to ascend to the towers past flocks of pigeons, roosters, and the occasional peacock. Halfway up the ramp is the **glass-ship wreck exhibit**, open Tuesday to Friday only for an additional charge of US$1.75. As you enter, look for the castle-like dovecote on the castle wall beyond.

Discovered by a sponge diver in 1973 and excavated from 1977 to 1979 by Professor George Bass of Texas A&M University and his international team of marine archaeologists, the 16-metre-long, five-metre-wide ship sank in 1025 while carrying a cargo of 25 tons of commercial glass between Byzantine and Fatimid ports. It is the oldest shipwreck ever discovered.

Farther up in the castle, the **Snake Tower** is under renovation. The **German Tower** is closed as well, but you can climb up to the ramparts nearby for fine views of the town.

Descend past the Ottoman toilets to the **Gatineau Tower** and the **dungeons** beneath. Over the inner gate is the inscription *Inde deus abest* (Where god does not exist). The dungeon was used as a place of confinement and torture by the Knights of St John from 1513 to 1523. A sign warns that the

Now housing Bodrum's Museum of Underwater Archaeology, the Castle of St Peter was built by the Knights of St John of Jerusalem who captured Bodrum in the 15th century.

exhibits of torture implements might not be suitable for most children. Indeed, they're enough to give adults bad dreams.

The **English Tower** was built during the reign of King Henry IV of England, and bears his arms above the entrance to the uppermost hall, now fitted out as a medieval refectory. The standards of the Grand Masters and their Turkish adversaries hang from the walls, suits of Turkish chain mail, authentic crusader graffiti carved into the stones (especially prominent in the window niches), and long wooden tables at which you can sit and have a glass of wine for US$1 – cheaper than in the town below – while listening to recordings of Carmina Burana, lute music, or other pseudo-medieval strains.

The **Uluburun Wreck Exhibit Hall** is under construction and not yet open.

Within the **French Tower**, the highest point in the castle, are the remains and sarcophagus of **Queen Ada**, a Carian princess *(Karyalı prenses)* whose intact tomb was discovered by Turkish archaeologists in 1989. The exhibit is open Tuesday to Friday from 10 am to noon and 2 to 4 pm. Only eight visitors are admitted to the small rooms at any one time; you may have to wait a bit.

The princess, who died sometime between 360 and 325 BC at about age 40, was of the Hecatomnid dynasty, probably the sister of Satrap Mausolus and the wife of Idreus. She was buried with her jewellery, including gold crown, necklace, bracelets, rings, and an exquisite wreath of gold myrtle leaves. Using modern reconstruction techniques, British experts at Manchester University made a model of the princess' face as she may have looked in life: she now greets you at the far end of the exhibit.

Mausoleum

Though most of the Mausoleum is long gone, the site is worth a visit.

In a handsome gallery here, archaeologists have arranged models, drawings and documents to give you an idea of why this tomb was among the Seven Wonders of the (ancient) World. It's a few blocks inland from Neyzen Tevfik Caddesi. Turn near the little white Tepecik Camii on the shore of the western bay, then left onto the road to Turgutreis Caddesi, following the signs.

The site is open every day from 8 am to 5 or 6 pm; though officially closed on Monday, you can usually get in by asking at the little grocery shop across the street. Admission costs US$1. Most labels and documents are in English as well as Turkish; a few are in French.

The site has pleasant gardens, with the excavations to the right and the exhibition galleries to the left. Exhibits include bits of sculpted marble found at the site, a model of Halicarnassus at the time of King Mausolus, a model of the Mausoleum and its precincts, and various diagrams and plans.

Written descriptions taken from ancient documents (1581) tell the alarming story: The Knights Hospitaller from Rhodes discovered the Mausoleum, largely buried and preserved by the dust of ages. They uncovered it, admired it for a while, then went back to the castle for the night. During the night, pirates broke in and stole the tomb treasures, which had been safe as long as the Mausoleum was buried. The next day the knights returned and broke the tomb to pieces for use as building stone. Some of the bits were pulverised to make lime for mortar. They used these materials to repair their castle in anticipation of an attack by Süleyman the Magnificent. They knew he would attack, and they knew they would lose and have to abandon the castle, but they saw the effort as a holding action. So the Mausoleum was sacrificed to the honour of a crusader military order.

In the large exhibition room is a copy of the famous frieze found in the castle walls; the original is now in the British Museum. Four fragments of the frieze here are original, having been discovered more recently.

In the archaeologists' hole itself there is little to see: a few pre-Mausolean stairways and tomb chambers, the Mausolean drainage system, the entry to Mausolus' tomb chamber, a few bits of precinct wall and some large, fluted, marble column drums.

Theatre

The theatre, behind the town up on the hillside by the bypass road, is cut into the rock of the hillside. The view is splendid, the traffic on the busy road noisy and smelly.

Boat Excursions

Dozens of yachts are moored along Neyzen Tevfik Caddesi on the western bay, and most have sales agents who will try and cajole you into taking a day trip. Most boat excursions depart at 10 or 11 am, return at 4.30 or 5 pm and cost US$6.

Here's a typical itinerary. First you sail to **Karaada** (Black Island) due south of Bodrum, where there are **hot springs** issuing in a strong current from a cave. Swimmers here rub the orange mud from the springs on their bodies, hoping for some aesthetic improvement. After a half-hour stop at Karaada, the boat makes for the coarse sand-and-pebble beach at **Ortakent Yalısı**, due west of Bodrum. There's a lovely little cove here with a few beach-front restaurants, small pensions and camping areas, but big hotels nearby as well.

After Ortakent, the boat sails to the 'Aquarium', a small cove deserted except for other excursion boats. The water is beautifully clear, and the idea is that you'll see lots of fish, but much of the time the boating and swimming activity scares the fish away. After the Aquarium, it's back to Bodrum.

Special Events

The Bodrum Festival is held annually during the first week in September. Lodgings may be especially crowded then.

Places to Stay

In high summer, especially on weekends, Bodrum can fill up with holiday-makers. Try to arrive early in the day to find a room. The Tourism Information Office may be able to help you find a room if space is tight.

Places to Stay – bottom end

North of the western bay are narrow streets harbouring good little pensions. These tend to be quieter than those on the eastern bay because they are farther from the nuclear-powered Halikarnas Disco. Pensions charge from US$15 to US$24 a double for rooms in high summer. Some rooms have private facilities, some include breakfast in the price. Off season, prices drop, and the breakfast which cost extra in season may now be included in the price.

Türkkuyusu Sokak This street with a tongue-twister name starts just north of the Adliye Camii and goes north past several good, cheap, convenient pensions. All have shady courtyards good for sitting, sipping and jotting notes. In general, the farther you walk along Türkkuyusu, the cheaper the rooms.

Sevin Pansiyon (☎ (252) 316 8361), Türkkuyusu Caddesi, Gencel Çıkmazı 12, is bare but friendly, close to the centre yet set back from the street. Rooms cost US$24 a double, breakfast included. The *Melis Pansiyon* (☎ (252) 316 1487), at No 50, is a second-best, at the same price.

The *Şenlik Pansiyon* (☎ (252) 316 6382), at No 115, is right on the street and a bit pricey at US$28 a double, but behind it (down the same narrow alley) is the family-run *Sedan Pansiyon* (☎ (252) 316 0355), officially at Türkkuyusu 121. The Sedan's courtyard, shaded by grapevines heavy with fruit in August, connects two buildings. In the newer, double rooms with shower cost US$20; in the older, waterless doubles are US$15.

Signs on Türkkuyusu point right to Gencel Çıkmazı, a narrow alley harbouring the *Pension Rainbow* (☎ (252) 316 5170), which is quiet and charges US$20 for waterless doubles; breakfast costs extra.

Otel Espri (☎ (252) 316 1129), Türkkuyusu 98, on the corner of Külcü Sokak, has a swimming pool, a bougainvillea-shaded terrace, and 40 rooms with bath costing US$38 a double, breakfast included.

Neyzen Tevfik Caddesi Menekşe Çıkmazı is a narrow alley which begins between Neyzen Tevfik 84 and 86. At its very end are two nearly identical plain, quiet, modern

TOM BROSNAHAN

TOM BROSNAHAN

Top: Yachting, boating, swimming and diving are among Bodrum's primary attractions.
Bottom: Warm calcium-laden waters cascade over the cliffs of Pamukkale, near Denizli, forming travertines topped by natural wading pools.

TOM BROSNAHAN

TOM BROSNAHAN

TOM BROSNAHAN

Top: At the centre of historic Antalya is the Roman harbour, now the yacht marina.
Bottom Left: Amidst the pines of this dramatic valley lie the ruins of the Lycian city of Olimpos.
Bottom Right: Many historic houses in Kaleiçi (Old Antalya) are under restoration.

pensions, the *Yenilmez* (☎ (252) 316 2520) at No 30, and the *Menekşe* (☎ (252) 316 0537) at No 34. Both have rooms with showers for US$20. Off season, breakfast is included.

Farther east, the *Toker Pansiyon* (☎ (252) 316 1874), Gerence Sokak 18, is fairly plain but convenient to the waterfront for US$20 a double without bath, breakfast extra.

Ataer Pansiyon (☎ (252) 316 5357), Neyzen Tevfik 102, is just east of the Tepecik Camii, back from the street, with doubles for US$24, breakfast included.

Still in business after three decades, the *Herodot Pansiyon* (☎ (252) 316 1093) rents rooms with private shower for US$22 a double with breakfast. Front rooms have views of the marina, but may suffer from street noise. There's a pleasant café in front.

Set back from the street at the end of a passage near the Herodot is the *Bahçeli Ağar Aile Pansiyonu* (☎ (252) 316 1648), with quiet rooms for US$20 a double.

Eastern Bay In my experience, pensions on the eastern bay are priced identically to those on the western, but are less friendly and subject to disco noise. If you want to be in the midst of the nightlife, look on Rasathane Sokak, a narrow alley beginning between Cumhuriyet Caddesi 147 and 149. The *Berlin Pansiyon* (☎ (252) 316 2524) has rooms with shower; the neighbouring *Durak* (☎ (252) 316 1564) has rooms with or without. The nearby *Evin* (☎ (252) 1312), is swathed from top to bottom in bougainvillea, but tends to smell of drains.

The narrow streets eastward harbour a few more pensions.

Camping Some of the smaller villages on the peninsula such as Bitez Yalısı and Ortakent Yalısı have campsites. There are more on the peninsula's north shore.

Places to Stay – middle

Western Bay Best is the charming *Su Otel* (☎ (252) 316 6906, fax 316 7391), Turgutreis Caddesi, 1201 Sokak, at the end of a cul-de-sac. Decorated with local crafts and an abundance of bougainvillea, rooms overlook a courtyard with a central swimming pool. It's an oasis of quiet and charm. Rooms cost US$30/55 a single/double, buffet breakfast included. With only 30 beds, it's often full; reserve if you can. Follow the street opposite the Tepecik Camii, turn right at the 'T' intersection, and walk several hundred metres following the signs.

Seçkin Konaklar (☎ (252) 316 1351, fax 316 3336), Neyzen Tevfik Caddesi 246 facing the marina, has multi-bed apartments sleeping up to six persons, and is often busy with tour groups. Doubles cost US$50.

Next door is the two-star *Hotel Gala* (☎ (252) 316 2216, fax 316 1910), nothing fancy, but not unreasonable at US$27/35 a single/double with shower, breakfast included. The guest rooms are simple and small.

Eastern Bay The two-star *Otel Baraz* (☎ (252) 316 1857, fax 316 4430), Cumhuriyet 70, is open all year, and right on the water. Its 24 rooms with shower are US$35/40 a single/double, breakfast included.

Farther east along Cumhuriyet Caddesi are three comparable places in a row facing the narrow beach (the water's a bit murky, though). The *Artemis Pansiyon* (☎ (252) 316 2530, fax 316 2907), at No 117, has 22 rooms priced identically to those at the Baraz.

A few steps east, the *Karya Otel* (☎ (252) 316 1535, fax 316 4814), at No 127, charges US$38 a double because its front rooms are double-glazed against the noise, and have ceiling fans and TVs.

The 16-room *Dinç Pansiyon* (☎ (252) 316 1141, fax 316 2051), at No 129, near the Artemis, is similar to the Artemis.

Gümbet Other lodging possibilities are to be found at Gümbet, the bay to the west of Bodrum over the hills. Dolmuşes (US$0.50) run regularly from Bodrum's otogar.

Places to Stay – top end

Bodrum has lots of luxury accommodation on the outskirts. If you prefer to stay closer to the centre, try the five-star *Hotel Karia Princess* (☎ (252) 316 8971, fax 316 8979),

Canlıdere Sokak 15. The 58 rooms have air-con, satellite TV, minibars, and king-size beds imported from France. Facilities include a marble-walled Turkish bath, sauna, fitness room, tennis court, a large swimming pool, casino, even two private hotel yachts. Posted rates are US$120/160 for a single/double with breakfast, but discounts are often available.

The five-star *Hotel Marina Vista* (☎ (252) 316 0356, fax 316 2347), Neyzen Tevfik 226, faces the marina with 84 rooms, lots of marble, two pools and many other services, for US$90/120 a double, breakfast included.

Places to Eat

You will have no trouble finding places to eat, but because many of the restaurants are seasonal, with inexperienced part-time staff, food and service are often mediocre. In July and August, prices are double those of İstanbul, but at least prices are usually available for inspection before you sit down.

Restaurants open and close all the time in Bodrum. Those described below are mostly dependable long-established ones.

Places to Eat – bottom end

Off season you should have no problem. For very cheap eats, buy a dönerli sandviç (dur-nehr-LEE sahn-DVEECH, sandwich with roast lamb) for less than US$2 at a streetside büfe. Look for the words in the window.

In July and August, the cheapest food is at simple local eateries well inland, without menus in English and German. Most serve no alcohol.

Türkkuyusu Caddesi *Buğday* ('Wheat', ☎ 316 2969), at No 72, is a 60s-style vegetarian restaurant serving whole food, herbal teas and freshly-squeezed juices on a shady craft-filled terrace. Tofu appetisers cost US$1, vegetarian salads US$2, and big plates of stir-fry under US$3. Let's hope it survives and prospers.

East of Adliye Camii In the grid of small market streets just east of the Adliye Camii are several restaurants which serve döner kebap and pizza that's not bad. *Babadan, Ziya'nin Yeri* and *Üsküdarlı* are patronised by locals as well as foreigners, and serve plates of döner for about US$2.75, beer for US$1.30. Around the corner from Üsküdarlı by the Garanti Bankası is the *Sakallı Köfteci,* ('Bearded Meatball-Maker'), serving full meals of grilled lamb meatballs, salad, bread and a drink for US$4, but no booze.

Just east of the bazaar is Hilmi Uran Meydanı, called Kilise Meydanı (Church Square) by locals; it once had an Orthodox church on its east side. The *Nazilli, Şahin,* and *Karadeniz* all serve cheap pide (US$2.50 to US$3.75), pizzas and kebaps.

For cheap breakfast or lunch, try the *Yunuslar Karadeniz Börekçisi*, just east of the Karadeniz Restaurant at the eastern edge of Kilise Meydanı on Taşlık Sokak. Peynirli börek (flaky pastry with cheese) costs US$1.50 a serving in the morning. (There's a grander branch of this börekçi on Dr Alim Bey.) At the end of Taşlık Sokak, *Aslan Usta'nin Çorba Salonu* serves cheap soups and kebaps mostly to locals.

For a sweet, try lokma, the traditional Aegean fritters, light balls of deep-fried dough dipped in syrup and sold in a paper cone for under US$1. The *Şahboylum Lokmacısı* at Cumhuriyet 49 has them, as does the *Ladin Patisserie* at Cumhuriyet 61-63. The Ladin is also good for böreks, pastries, puddings, fruitcups and other light fare. All prices are marked.

Cevat Şakir Caddesi Just inland from the Adliye Camii are branches of the Emlak and Halk banks. Walk between them to find the *Edirne Ciğer & Köfte Evi*, serving cheap fried liver and grilled köfte.

Inland along Cevat Şakir Caddesi, the *Sakallı Restaurant* at No 6, opposite the Türkiye İş Bankası, has outdoor tables, grills and stews. Traffic can be noisy, but you need pay only about US$4 for a meal.

Farther along Cevat Şakir are several more little grill shops where locals eat; some are open for lunch only. Food for picnics is available at the fruit market just south of

Çarşı Sokak and the Shell station, and in the shops behind the fruit.

Places to Eat – middle

Meyhaneler Sokak Walk from the Adliye Camii along Kale Caddesi towards İskele Meydanı and turn left just after the Tütünbank into a narrow alley shaded by vines, crowded with long rows of wooden tables, and cooled by ceiling fans hanging from the vines. This is Meyhaneler Sokak (Taverna St), and on summer evenings the mixed crowd of locals and foreigners is jolly without being raucous. The half-dozen restaurants – *Erkal, No 7 Osman, Ibo, Ayaz, Farketmez* etc – all serve alcohol and a varied menu of Turkish and continental dishes. Look at a few menus, find a seat, meet your neighbours, and get into the scene. The bill for a long dinner with drinks might be from US$12 to US$18, perhaps more if you have fish. You can come for lunch as well.

Western Bay Neyzen Tevfik Caddesi has several good places and all serve alcohol. *Mauzolos* is a modest but long-established place with a simple indoor dining room (used in winter), and a seaside open-air dining area across the street. Meat dishes are priced from US$3.50 to US$5.50, and the fish, though more expensive, is usually good.

Amca, at No 78, has a breezy 2nd-floor terrace with good views, and prices better than most places on the eastern bay. A main course, sweet and drink cost under US$10.

Amphora (☎ 316 2368), Neyzen Tevfik 164, across from the marina, has streetside tables and several interior dining rooms in an old stone commercial building. Turkish carpets add colour, and bits of seafaring equipment provide visual interest. Start with a selection of mezes (US$1.50 to US$2 each) and go on to grilled meat or fish (US$4 to US$10).

Eastern Bay Adliye Sokak runs inland off Cumhuriyet opposite a break in the buildings which allows access to the sea. *Pierre Loti*, at Adliye Sokak 5, in an old stone house, has a pretty courtyard and set-price French-style table d'hôte three-course meals priced from US$8 to US$35. A la carte, main course steak and chicken dishes cost US$18 to US$22.

Choice (☎ 316 7184), behind Cumhuriyet 143, has the requisite steaks and chicken (US$6 to US$10), but also Kirgiz mantı (ravioli) as a starter for US$3.50.

Sunny's Grill, Cumhuriyet 149, advertises a dinner of a half-chicken, chips and a beer for US$5. Inland on Rasathane Sokak, *Sunny's Restaurant* (☎ 316 0716) has a Turkish and continental menu on which most main courses (chicken Kiev, steak and kidney pie) cost US$8; vegetarian plates are less. Dining is in a nice courtyard.

Places to Eat – top end

The restaurants along Dr Alim Bey Caddesi are among Bodrum's priciest. Some have pleasant seaside dining areas. In high summer, a full meal with drinks would cost US$25 to US$30 per person. In May, June, September and October when Bodrum restaurants are competing for custom, you can do better on price.

Kocadon Restaurant (☎ 316 3705, fax 316 5338), Neyzen Tevfik Caddesi 160, is the place for a romantic dinner. Sheltered from the street by atmospheric old stone houses, a quiet courtyard is filled with soft music and lighting. Try the revived Ottoman dishes, such as Hünkar Beğendi (grilled şiş kebap over buttery aubergine purée). Dinner for two with a bottle of wine should cost around US$25 or US$30 per person. It's open daily in summer from 8 pm to midnight.

Entertainment

In summer, bars are everywhere, opening and closing with revolving-door frequency. Most are on the eastern bay along Dr Alim Bey/Cumhuriyet, or in narrow alleys off it, or in Gümbet. Most are empty until around 10 pm, after which the currently-favoured places fill up. Local drinks (beer, rakı, Turkish gin and vodka) are always significantly cheaper than foreign liquor.

İskele Meydanı is a good place to sit, sip a beer and watch the passing parade. The *Kale Café*, just past the western entrance to the castle, has boat and water views, and drinks and food at prices a bit below most.

Just inside the castle walls at the western entrance, the *Bodrum West Cafeteria*, run by the Ministry of Culture, has drinks at lowish prices (US$1 for beer) and an atmospheric setting. The castle is closed in the evening, but the caf, remains open.

On the western bay, the *Heaven Bar* next to the Kocadon restaurant draws a diverse crowd, and is one of the few bars in the area.

Staff at the famous *Halikarnas Disco*, on the eastern bay at the end of Cumhuriyet Caddesi, look you up and down for proper trendy dress and take a cover charge of between US$8 to US$12 (the latter on weekends) before admitting you to Turkey's classiest, loudest and most presumptuous disco. Inside it's like a Hollywood set, with a laser light show some evenings.

The throbbing heart of the disco scene these days is at Gümbet, over the hill to the west. Clubs line the shore, and are packed in summer.

Getting There & Away

Air The closest air service to Bodrum is at Imsık, 30 km to the north along the İzmir road. The nearest large airports to Bodrum are at İzmir, 220 km away, and Dalaman (near Fethiye), 220 km away.

Turkish Airlines (☎ & fax (252) 373 5780) operates two flights daily between Imsık and İstanbul in summer for US$90 one-way, and two flights to and from Ankara for US$80.

Bus As usual, Bodrum's bus service is frequent and far flung. Companies serving the Bodrum bus station include Aydın Turizm, Hakiki Koç, Kamil Koç, Karadeveci, Kontaş, Pamukkale and Varan. Here are some services; there are lots of others as well:

Ankara – 785 km, 13 hours, US$22; a dozen buses daily
Antalya – 640 km, 11 hours, US$22; one bus daily
Dalaman – 220 km, four hours, US$12; six buses daily
Fethiye – 265 km, 4½ hours, US$14; six buses daily
Gökova – 135 km, 2½ hours, US$10; Marmaris bus, then a dolmuş or hitch
İzmir – 250 km, four hours, US$9; buses at least every hour in summer
İstanbul – 830 km, 14 hours, US$18 to US$26; hourly buses in summer
Kaş – 400 km, six hours, US$12; Fethiye bus, then change
Konya – 750 km, 12 hours, US$24; one bus daily
Kuşadası – 151 km, 2½ hours, US$9; buses every half-hour in summer
Marmaris – 165 km, three hours, US$8; hourly buses in summer
Ören – 95 km, two hours, US$8; bus to Milas and change
Pamukkale – 310 km, five hours, US$13; two direct buses daily
Trabzon – 1565 km, 28 hours, US$34; one bus daily

Boat Ferries leave Bodrum's western bay for Datça, Didyma and Knidos, and to the Greek islands of Kos and Rhodes. For information and tickets contact Bodrum Express Lines (☎ (252) 316 1087, fax 313 0077), or the Bodrum Ferryboat Association (☎ (252) 316 0882, fax 313 0205), on the docks past the western entrance to the castle.

To Didyma Ferries depart Bodrum on Wednesday and Friday mornings at 7.30 am in summer on the one-hour voyage to Didyma (US$13 round trip); the return leg departs Didyma at 4 pm.

To Knidos On summer Sunday mornings, boats (1½ hours, US$22.50 one-way, US$29 same-day round trip) and hydrofoils (45 minutes, US$32 round trip, lunch included) leave Bodrum for Knidos, returning in the afternoon.

To Datça Hydrofoils (35 minutes) and car-and-passenger ferries (1½ to two hours) operate daily from May to September between Bodrum and Datça for US$12 round trip. The ferry actually docks at Körmen on the peninsula's northern coast, from which Datça is a 10 to 15 minutes' drive south; bus transport to Datça is included in your fare.

To Kos Hydrofoils (20 minutes) and ferries (50 minutes) carry passengers and cars across to Kos daily from May to September. Buy tickets (US$22.50 one-way, US$29 same-day round trip) at least a day in advance. Limited ferry service (usually two or three days per week, weather permitting) continues right through the winter.

To Rhodes Hydrofoils (two hours) depart Bodrum for Rhodes at 8.30 am on Monday and Thursday from May to September. The return trip departs Rhodes at 4 pm. Buy tickets (US$45 one-way, US$50 same-day round trip) from Bodrum Express a day in advance.

BODRUM PENINSULA

The volcanic landscape of the Bodrum peninsula is one of high hills, dramatic rock outcrops and surprising marine panoramas. It comes as a surprise to see so much traditional life in the midst of booming touristic modernisation, but in a few peninsula villages you may still see local women wearing the traditional *şalvar* (pantaloons) and white headscarves. Donkeys laden with sticks for fuel plod stubbornly to the domed, beehive-shaped earthen ovens still used to bake bread and roast mutton. But many of the distinctive white-domed stone cisterns *(gümbet*, 'dome') are falling to ruin, having been superseded by the ubiquitous tank trucks supplying *kullanma su* ('utility water'), not for drinking.

Several of the peninsula's beach villages are good for day trips. If you've come to stay for a while, you might even move your base from Bodrum.

Dolmuşes depart from Bodrum's bus station frequently to all of these points in high summer. Fares are rarely more than US$1. Off season, be aware of departure times for the last minibus back to Bodrum.

Southern Shore

The narrow beach at **Gümbet**, backed by scores of hotels and pensions, is only a five-km, 10-minute ride from Bodrum; or you can walk to Gümbet in about 45 minutes over the hills west of the yacht marina. The water is not all that clean, but it's crowded daily in summer nevertheless.

West of Gümbet, past the next peninsula, are the bays of **Bitez Yalısı, Ortakent Yalısı**, and **Yahşi Yalısı**, backed by white hotels, pensions, camping grounds and resort villas, and offering small but good beaches and services. At Bitez Yalısı there's a windsurfing school.

From Ortakent and Yahşi beaches you must travel inland via Gürece to continue your circuit of the peninsula, as there is not yet a coastal road west of Yahşi.

Karaincir, a similar cove with a beach, hotels, a few pensions and a holiday village, and **Akyarlar**, 30 km from Bodrum, are worth a day trip if you're staying a long time in Bodrum. The scenery can be dramatic. Akyarlar is a pretty village, formerly inhabited by Ottoman Greeks, with a narrow beach, several little pensions and hotels and a small yacht and fishing port. Holiday villas crowd the hillsides above.

Western Shore

Following the coastal road west and north from Akyarlar brings you to **Akçabük**, where there is another cove and beach. North of Akçabük all the way to Turgutreis the coast is covered in holiday villages.

Turgutreis The newly developed town of Turgutreis (toor GOOT-reh-yeess), 20 km west of Bodrum, might be called 'Son of Bodrum', a junior version of the main thing. The great Turkish admiral Turgut Reis (died 1560) was born here. (A monument to him stands south of the town on the shore.) There is a strip of beach, numerous hotels, pensions, and restaurants. Dolmuşes (US$0.70) run frequently from Bodrum, depositing you at the main square right on the beach.

Kadıkalesi From Turgutreis, a road leaves the highway about a km inland and goes north 3.5 km to Kadıkalesi, a village with a narrow but partly protected beach, several small pension-restaurants, a disused church in fair condition, and the inevitable holiday villages.

Gümçşlük To the north of Kadıkalesi three km by road (two km along the beach and over

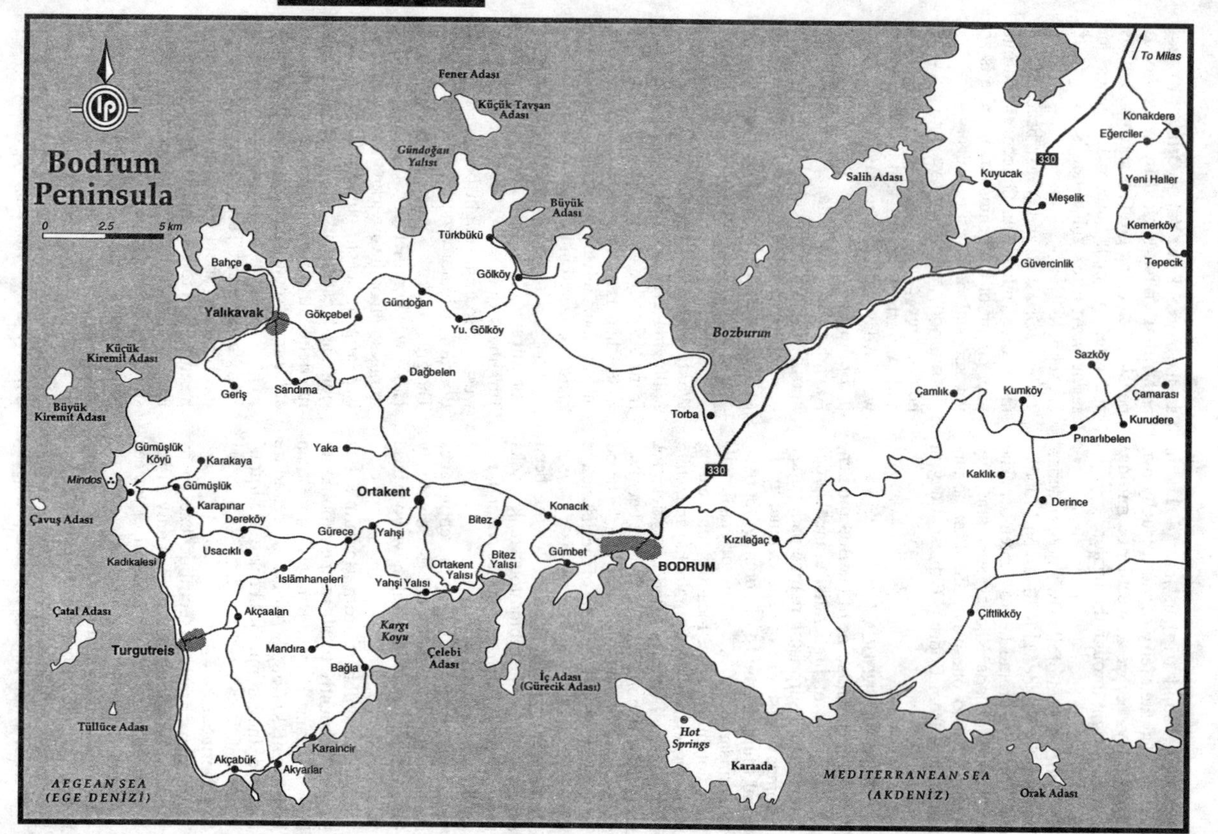
Bodrum Peninsula
0
2.5
5 km
To Milas
330
Konakdere
Eğerciler
Yeni Haller
Kemerköy
Tepecik
Kuyucak
Meşelik
Güvercinlik
Salih Adası
Fener Adası
Küçük Tavşan Adası
Gündoğan Yalısı
Büyük Adası
Türkbükü
Gölköy
Gündoğan
Yu. Gölköy
Gökçebel
Bahçe
Yalıkavak
Bozburun
Küçük Kiremit Adası
Büyük Kiremit Adası
Geriş
Sandıma
Dağbelen
Torba
Sazköy
Çamlık
Kumköy
Çamarası
Kurudere
Pınarlıbelen
Kaklık
Derince
Gümüşlük Köyü
Karakaya
Mindos
Gümüşlük
Karapınar
Yaka
Ortakent
Dereköy
Çavuş Adası
Gürece
Yahşi
Bitez
Konacık
Kızılağaç
Kadıkalesi
Usacıklı
Gümbet
BODRUM
Bitez Yalısı
Ortakent Yalısı
İslâmhaneleri
Yahşi Yalısı
Çiftlikköy
Çatal Adası
Akçaalan
Kargı Koyu
Çelebi Adası
Turgutreis
Mandıra
Bağla
İç Adası
(Gürecik Adası)
Hot Springs
Tüllüce Adası
Karaincir
Akçabük
Akyarlar
Karaada
AEGEAN SEA
(EGE DENİZİ)
MEDITERRANEAN SEA
(AKDENİZ)
Orak Adası

the hills) is Gümüşlük, which can be reached by direct dolmuş from Bodrum (US$1). Vehicles are banned from the village, which is no more than a hamlet on the shore of a fine small natural harbour protected by high headlands. The waterfront is lined with restaurants, their tables, each with its *fesleğen* (basil plant), ranged along the water under shady vines. On the rocky islet south of the hamlet, the ruins (some underwater) of ancient **Mindos** are amusing to explore during a swim. The beach on the village's south side is long and generally uncrowded; swimming in the village centre is from wooden platforms extended out into the water. The sea, though weedy in places, is suitable for swimming.

Gümüşlük is perhaps the best goal for a day trip from Bodrum. Come for a day of swimming and climbing on the headlands, with lunch on the shore; or come for an afternoon swim and stay for a sunset dinner (US$12 to US$20 per person). The restaurants, all with excellent sea, island and sunset views, post their prices and start to fill up an hour before sunset. The last dolmuş back to Bodrum departs at midnight. At other times of the year, keep track of the schedule. You may want to go before the last dolmuş, which might be overfilled.

In the off season, Gümüşlük is a haven of peace and quiet, a sleepy place with enough small pensions and restaurants to provide for the few visitors who seek it out.

Northern Shore

The northern shore of the peninsula is the least developed.

On the north-western corner of the peninsula, 18 km from Bodrum, is **Yalıkavak**, with several old windmills, a village square with taxis, teahouses, tractors, farmers and other evidence of normal Turkish life. Though there are several moderately-priced hotels on the outskirts, look for the cheap pensions in town.

Arrayed along a perfect little bay, 17 km north of Bodrum, is the village of **Gölköy**, a 'Gümüşlük without the ruins'. Family pensions accommodate most arrivals, though there is also the little *Sahil Motel* with pretty gardens, and fancier hotels on the outskirts. Wooden boat docks serve the fishing boats; the boat owners will also take you out for short excursions if you wish.

About 1.5 km around the point from Gölköy is **Türkbükü**, another village with a few modest pensions and motels, a PTT and a few simple restaurants and shops for the yachters who anchor in its harbour.

Aegean Hinterland

The Aegean coast is Turkey's foremost tourist mecca. The cities farther inland, in the Aegean hinterland, have less appeal for the casual holiday visitor, but plenty to offer the adventurous traveller. As everywhere in Turkey, the history of these hinterland cities is involved and eventful. Unlike the Aegean coast towns, however, the inland cities offer the interested visitor a look at real Turkish daily life and culture, without the overheated prices of the resorts.

For most travellers, Balıkesir is a transit point with enough interest to fill your few hours there. Eskişehir, 150 km south of Bursa, is Turkey's meerschaum mining centre. The soft white stone is artistically carved into bracelets, earrings, necklaces, cigarette holders, and of course meerschaum pipes. A short detour of 90 km south-east of Eskişehir brings you to Kütahya, its neighbourhoods of historic houses sheltering Turkey's faïence.

Afyon, the centre of government-controlled opium production, is famous for its clotted cream and Turkish delight (lokum). Denizli is an industrial city and transit point for the famous spa at Pamukkale. Eğirdir, near Isparta, has its bits of history but most visitors go for its setting at the edge of a vast lake.

BALIKESİR

The triangular province of Balıkesir includes coastline on both the Marmara and Aegean seas, and a mountainous eastern region bordering on Kütahya. Its namesake capital city (population 200,000, altitude 147m) is of less interest than its overt tourist centres: the resort town of Erdek and the railhead town of Bandırma on the Sea of Marmara, and the Aegean coastal resorts at Akçay, Edremit, Ören and Ayvalık. There are historic hot springs at Gönen, used since Roman times. At Sındırgı, 63 km south of Balıkesir town, the famous Yağcıbeydir Turkish carpets are woven by descendants of early Turkish nomads who came to this area from central Asia.

The city of Balıkesir is at least 5000 years old, and was known as Palaeokastron to the Romans and Byzantines. Though there are a few old buildings in Balıkesir, including the **Zağanos Paşa Camii** (1461), the **Yıldırım Camii** (1388), the **Umur Bey Camii** (1412) and the **Karesi Bey Türbesi** (1336), this is not really a touristic town. No doubt you will just be passing through on the bus or train.

For answers to questions, contact the Tourism Directorate (☎ (266) 241 1820, fax 244 7271), Dumlupınar Mahallesi, Anafartalar Caddesi, Sayar İşhanı 42/5.

There are numerous cheap hotels near the otogar. The one-star, 22-room *İnanöz Hotel* (☎ (266) 241 4265), Garaj Karşısı, is just opposite, offering rooms with bath for US$10/ 14 a single/double. The two-star *İmanoğlu Hotel* (☎ (266) 241 7144), Örücüler Caddesi 18, has 36 rooms with baths priced at US$20/27 a single/double. Best in town is the three-star, 57-room *Kervansaray Hotel* (☎ (266) 241 1635, fax 241 4861), Cumhuriyet Alanı, Akıncılar Caddesi, on the main square, charging a bit more.

AEGEAN TURKEY

ESKİŞEHİR

Though first settled by the Phrygians 3000 years ago, Eskişehir ('Old City', population 500,000, altitude 788m) is today a modern city despite its name. The scant ruins of Graeco-Roman Dorylaeum, which earlier occupied this place, lie mostly beneath modern buildings.

This has always been an important transit point in the natural routes from north, south, east and west. Railway locomotives manufactured here haul trains throughout Turkey, some of them laden with the products of Eskişehir's other industries: cement, sugar, textiles and more. The crack and whoosh of fighter jets announces a major air force base on the outskirts, though the quieter Anatolia University (Anadolu sniversitesi) is here as well.

Dusty in summer and muddy in winter, the unremarkable city centre is brightened by a riverside promenade with streetside cafés, and a bustling market. Be sure to try the local nuga helvası (nougat), on sale at the many confectioners' shops in the otogar.

Orientation & Information

The city centre is easily negotiated on foot. Hotels, restaurants, banks and other services are not too far from the train station, which is north-west of the centre, but the new otogar is on the outskirts by the sugar factory; take bus No 13.

The provincial authorities sponsor the local Tourism Information Office (☎ (222) 230 17 52, fax 230 3865), in the Vilayet (provincial government headquarters) at İki Eylül Caddesi 175, which has little to offer beyond a basic map.

Meerschaum Mining Villages

Those truly fascinated by meerschaum may want to visit the mining villages of **Sepetçi Köyü** and **Kozlubel**. Sepetçi, obviously more prosperous than its neighbours with its tidy white houses with windows trimmed in blue, has recently changed its name to Beyaz Altın (White Gold) in honour of its most valuable commodity. There are poultry and grain farmers here as well, but 85% of the village's wealth comes from meerschaum.

There are no services in the village, but if you ask for Mr Bülent Girgin, he will take you to his prominent carving workshop at the eastern edge of the village, and even show you a mining pit *(lületaşı ocağı)* farther east if you wish.

Transport can be difficult without your own vehicle. Ask at the otogar for the minibus to Yakakayı, which sometimes proceeds beyond its primary destination to

Meerschaum

Most tourists pass through Eskişehir on the bus or the train, but those who stop are usually looking for meerschaum (German for 'sea foam', *lületaşı* in Turkish). This soft, light, porous white stone, a hydrous magnesium silicate called sepiolite by mineralogists, is mined at numerous villages east of Eskişehir, including Başören, Karahöyük (Karatepe), Kemikli, Kozlubel Köyü, Nemli, Sarısıva, Sepetçi Köyü, Söğütçük and Yarmalar. Eskişehir has the world's largest and most easily accessible deposits, though meerschaum is also found near Madrid in Spain, in France's Seine-et-Marne, in the Crimea, in Kenya, and in the US states of Pennsylvania, South Carolina and Utah.

Miners are lowered into vertical shafts which penetrate the meerschaum beds to depths from 10 to 150m. The miners fill buckets with heavy mud, which is hauled to the surface, dumped and sluiced, revealing rough chunks of meerschaum. It's dark, dirty, dangerous work. There are no veins where large blocks can be cut. The larger the chunk, the higher its value.

Though once pulverised and used as tooth powder, meerschaum is now used for carving. While the stone is still wet and as soft as soap, carvers in the villages and in Eskişehir work it into fanciful shapes and decorative objects, most of which are exported. Block meerschaum was also exported until 1979, when someone figured out that to export the material was to export the carving jobs as well. Now it is illegal to export block meerschaum. Prayer beads, necklaces, belts, earrings, baubles and cigarette-holders are common items, but the most popular item by far is the meerschaum pipe.

A good carver can make about four pipes a day. More elaborate pieces can take a week. Meerschaum pipes are valued because the strong, light, porous material smokes cool and sweet, drawing off the burning tobacco's heat and some of the tar. Devoted meerschaum smokers wear special gloves while smoking to protect their prized pipes from tarnish by skin oils. With time, a coddled pipe will take on an even nut-brown patina that is highly valued by devotees.

You can view carvers at work and buy their art in Eskişehir Monday to Saturday from 9 am to about 7 pm at Işık Pipo (☎ (222) 323 8702), Sakarya Caddesi, Konya İşhanı 12/17; and Pipo Burhan Yücel, both in the city centre near the Büyük Otel. Burhan Yücel also has a shop in the collection of shops beneath the otogar. ■

Sepetçi. If you have wheels, drive north-east from Eskişehir on the road to Alpu as far as Çavlum (18.5 km), then turn left (north) and go via Kızılcaören, Yakakayı and Gündüzler to Sepetçi/Beyaz Altın (40 km) and, six km beyond it, to Kozlubel.

Special Events

The International White Gold Festival is held in Eskişehir and surrounding villages in the third week in September. Meerschaum (the 'white gold') is celebrated with art, photo and craft exhibitions, football (soccer) matches, musical performances and folk dances.

Places to Stay

There's no problem finding a good, convenient room at the right price. You're probably best off staying right near the otogar as the hotels in the city centre are even noisier.

The main street running north-south in front of the otogar is Yunusemre Caddesi. Come out of the otogar, turn left, and the street on the otogar's south side is Asarcıklı Caddesi. *Otel Beşik* (☎ (222) 231 2843), Asarcıklı Caddesi, Sanayi Sokak 1-F, is clean, proper and cheap at US$5/8 a single/double without running water.

The two-star *Emek Otel* (☎ (222) 231 2940), Yunusemre Caddesi, adjoins the otogar on its north side. Though well worn, it's serviceable and friendly. Rooms with bath cost US$12/16 a single/double; breakfast costs US$1.75 more.

Across Yunusemre Caddesi from the otogar are three more two-star hotels: older but cheaper, the 35-room *Otel Dural* (☎ (222) 233 1347) at No 97, charging US$14 a double with sink, US$18 with private shower; the *Soyiç Hotel* (☎ (222) 230 7190) at No 101, newer and very friendly, charging US$24 for a double with bath; and the 35-room *Porsuk Otel* (☎ (222) 231 5005), at No 103, among the newer ones in this area and quite comfy at US$26 a double.

In the city centre at the confluence of İnönü, Cengiz Topel, Sakarya, Muttalip and Sivrihisar Caddesis (in the district called Köprübaşı) are two more hotels. *Eskişehir Büyük Otel* (☎ (222) 231 6800, fax 234 6508), Sivrihisar Caddesi 40, is an older three-star place charging US$28 a double with bath and breakfast. Avoid the noisy front rooms.

The one-star, 45-room *Otel Şale* (☎ (222) 231 4743), İsmet İnönü Caddesi 17/1, across the street from the prominent Ordu Evi (ask for that to find the hotel) above the Tütünbank, is central but quite noisy. It charges US$12/17 for a single/double room with shower.

Places to Eat

For a quick, good, cheap kebap, leave the otogar, cross Yunusemre Caddesi and walk along the polluted river to the *Uğurlu Lokanta ve Kebap Salonu* (☎ 12 09 38), where soup, pilav and etli nohut (chickpeas with lamb in a tomato sauce), bread and water cost only US$2.25. It's quieter here than at the kebap places on Yunusemre Caddesi.

Getting There & Away

As Eskişehir is an important stop on the İstanbul-Ankara line, there is frequent train service to those cities throughout the day and night. (See the introductory Getting Around chapter for information on the major train services.)

The otogar, on the outskirts, may be reached by city bus 13. Bus service is equally convenient and includes the following services:

Ankara – 230 km, 3¼ hours, US$10; hourly
Bursa – 155 km, 2½ hours, US$7; hourly
İstanbul – 310 km, 4½ hours, US$12; hourly
Konya – 420 km, six hours, US$17; several direct buses, or change at Afyon
Kütahya – 91 km, 1¼ hours, US$4; hourly

KÜTAHYA

Spread beneath the walls of an imposing hilltop fortress in the midst of hill country, Kütahya (population 150,000, altitude 949m) is a small city famous for the manufacture of coloured tiles. An hour's ride away is the Temple of Zeus at Aizanoi, among the best-preserved Roman temples in Anatolia.

History

No-one knows for sure when Kütahya was founded; its earliest known inhabitants were Phrygians. In 546 BC it was captured by the Persians, and then saw the usual succession of rulers, from Alexander the Great to the kings of Bithynia and the emperors of Rome and Byzantium, who called the town Cotyaeum.

The first Turks to arrive were the Seljuks, in 1182. They were later pushed out by the crusaders, but they returned to found the Emirate of Germiyan (1302-1428), with Kütahya as its capital. The emirs cooperated with the Ottomans in nearby Bursa, and, upon the death of the last emir, his lands were incorporated in the growing Ottoman Empire. When Tamerlane swept in at the beginning of the 15th century, he upset everyone's applecart, made Kütahya his headquarters for a while and then went back to where he came from.

As an Ottoman province, Kütahya settled down to tile-making. After Selim I took Tabriz in 1514, he brought all of its ceramic artisans to Kütahya and İznik, and set them to work. The two towns rivalled one another in the excellence of their faïence.

After the collapse of the 1848 Hungarian revolution, the great leader Lajos Kossuth fled to the Ottoman Empire, where he was given refuge and settled in Kütahya for a short time. His house is now a museum.

Today Kütahya makes tiles and prospers. Faïence is used everywhere – on façades of buildings, in floors and walls, and in unexpected places. Every year scholars come here from many countries to attend the International Faïence & Ceramics Congress. The Dumlupınar Fuarı, held each year in the fair grounds of the same name not far from the

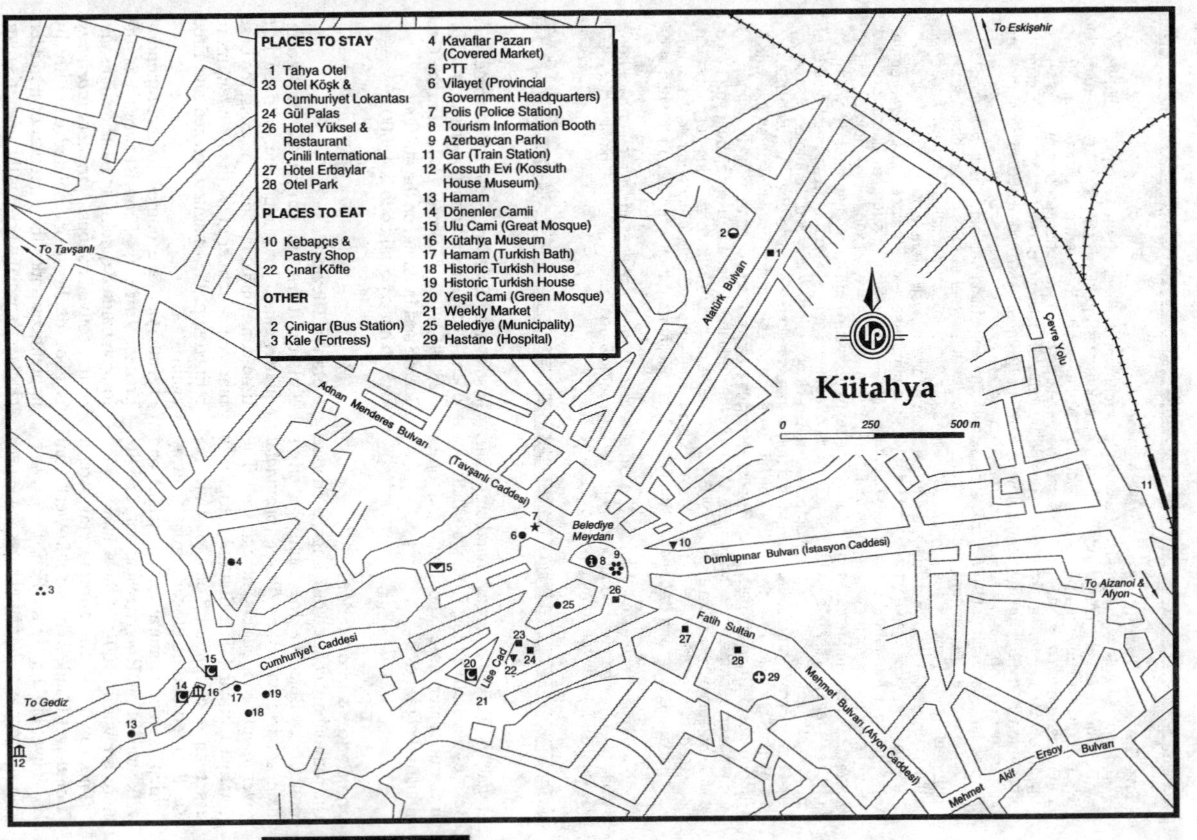

AEGEAN TURKEY

The Battle of Dumlupınar

The decisive battle of the Turkish War of Independence was fought in the vicinity of Kütahya.

During the Turkish War of Independence, Greek armies intent on claiming Ottoman lands for Greece pushed inland from İzmir, occupied Kütahya and threatened the fledgling Turkish republican government at Ankara. Twice the Greek advance was checked by the Turks at the village of İnönü, north-east of Kütahya, but the invading forces finally broke through, took Eskişehir and Afyon, and made them strong points in a defensive line that stretched 500 km from the Sea of Marmara to the valley of the Menderes (Meander) River.

Since the beginning of WWI, Turkish soldiers had been fighting defensive battles. In the Battle of the Sakarya, the longest pitched battle in history, the Greek armies had been fought to a standstill, with many casualties on both sides. The republican capital at Ankara had been successfully defended. But now the time had come for a Turkish offensive.

Plans for the offensive were carried out with the utmost secrecy. In place of calling a regular staff meeting, Mustafa Kemal (Atatürk) got all his generals together at a football game, so spies would never suspect that high-level consultations were under way. Troops were moved at night, under cover of darkness, resting by day beneath trees and in houses, away from the prying eyes of Greek reconnaissance flights. Small troops of soldiers were sent out to raise great clouds of dust to simulate larger troop movements. The Greek occupiers were so lulled into complacency that many of the commanders attended a dance in Afyon on the evening of 25 August 1922.

At first light the next morning, the Turkish forces began a bold and risky counterattack, with a thunderous barrage of artillery. The Turkish generals directed their troops from the front lines, not from observation points in the rear. By 9.30 am, the Turkish forces had taken all but two of their hilltop objectives, breaking through the Greek defences along the valley of Dumlupınar, due south of Kütahya, near the highway from İzmir to Afyon. They followed up quickly and relentlessly on this advantage, driving the enemy soldiers just as quickly from their second and third lines of defence.

In the battle for the valley, half of the Greek expeditionary force was annihilated or captured, while the other half was soon beating a hasty retreat towards İzmir. The Dumlupınar victory (30 August 1922) was the turning point in the war. ■

otogar, is Turkey's largest handicraft fair. Besides decorative tiles, Kütahya's factories turn out water pipes, conduits and other industrial ceramics.

Orientation & Information

The roundabout centred on a huge, tiled vase fountain is Belediye Meydanı, the city's main square, with the Vilayet (provincial government headquarters) here as well. The Kütahya Çinigar ('Tile-Station', otogar) is less than one km north-east of Belediye Meydanı; go out the otogar's front gateway (which is tiled, naturally), turn right and walk straight on. Hotels, restaurants and tile shops are within 100m of the square.

The town's main commercial street, Cumhuriyet Caddesi, runs south-west from the Vilayet building to the PTT.

In summer an information kiosk in the park just east of Belediye Meydanı is sometimes open. The tourism ministry office (☎ (274) 223 1962) is on Fuatpaşa Caddesi in the Özel İdare Sitesi building, on the 4th floor.

Kütahya's postal code is 43000.

Kütahya Tilework

Kütahya tiles are composed of kaolin, quartz, chalk, clay and sand. Refined in a time-consuming, laborious process, the base material is covered with an even more refined slip, then painted, glazed and fired again.

Kütahya ware comes in three general grades. *Turist işi* ('tourist work') is the lowest, painted quickly to basic designs and sold to souvenir shops. *Normal* or *fabrika işi* is good quality work painted carefully by apprentices under the direction of a master. *Özel işi* ('special work') is the master's own, often signed. Painting a single özel plate can take four or five days.

Kütahya has about 50 faïence ateliers of greater or lesser size producing plates, vases and other decorative tableware, flat tiles for wall mounting, and many other objects. The designs are mostly floral, geometric, or of Kuranic inscriptions.

You can find Kütahya pottery in any souvenir shop in Turkey, but the shops scattered around Belediye Meydanı have the widest selection of the best work. Each pottery has its authorised shop. Besides the expected tourist stuff, shops have fine mid-range pieces in a surprising variety of designs, and a small number of masterworks for connoisseurs.

The sons of Ahmet Şahin (see boxed story), Faruk Şahin and Zafer Şahin, are also master *çinicis*, as is Zafer Bey's son Ahmet Hürriyet Şahin. But Ahmet Hürriyet Şahin's wife, Nurten Şahin, is an acknowledged master çinici of the first rank, even though she had never painted a tile before her marriage. Look for their work from the former Işıl Çini atelier, their present work from Metin Çini, and that of other masters such as Ali Özker and İhsan and İbrahim Erdeyer of Süsler Çini, and Hakkı Ermumcu and Mehmet Gürsoy of İznik Çini.

If you're really into pots, ask at a shop to visit its factory. This should be easy to arrange with a bit of notice.

Kütahya Museum

Follow the signs from Belediye Meydanı 750m along Cumhuriyet Caddesi to the

Kütahya Faïence

The Kütahya *çini* (coloured tile, faïence) industry was founded in the late 14th century, and given a boost in the early 16th century when Sultan Selim I brought expert tile-makers here from his newly-conquered city of Tabriz in Persia. It thrived until the cataclysm of WWI, which resulted in the closure of all the city's pottery ateliers except two. One of these was run by David Ohannessian, an Ottoman Armenian. When he was called to Jerusalem to repair the tiles in the famous Dome of the Rock, he took a team of Kütahya's best artisans. Instead of returning, they established a traditional Turkish faïence industry in Jerusalem, where it thrives today.

That left one working atelier in Kütahya whose master, Hafız Mehmet Emin, died in 1922. Luckily, he had a skilled and inspired apprentice named Ahmet Şahin (born 1907) who, with another young and enthusiastic tile-maker named Hakkı Çinicioğlu, worked to keep the traditions of Kütahya tile-making alive. Though still tenuous in 1950, the Kütahya faïence industry has since grown to include some 50 ateliers.

From the beginning Ahmet Şahin insisted on creating coloured tiles of the highest standards of artisanship and aesthetics. Though he is master of every part of the complicated and laborious process of producing underglaze painted composite body ware, Şahin is renowned mostly as a designer. His patterns for the designs and calligraphy used on Kütahya faïence fill nine trunks. About 70% of all Kütahya designs are his, or derived from his designs.

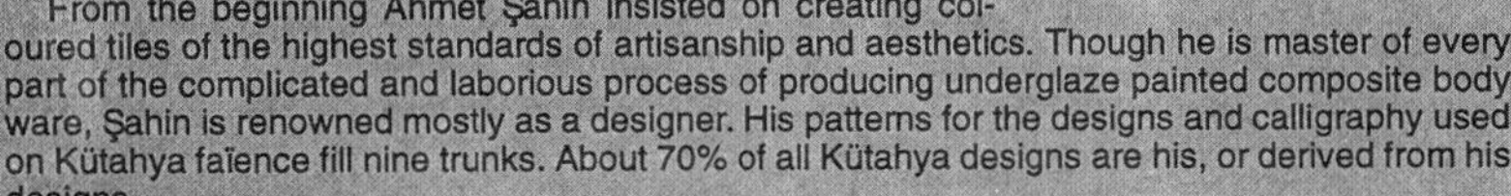

The art of faïence is very Turkish. In Europe or America, the artist is conceived as a rebel or gadfly, challenging the standards and beliefs of society in a quest for novelty and originality. In traditional Turkish art – as in the art of America's Shaker communities – the artist's role is to affirm the unity and harmony of Allah's creation by producing beautiful objects: each work of art is a prayer, a tribute to God and a gift to one's fellow humans. Each motif, flower, pattern or Koranic inscription is laden with significance and tradition. Though change and innovation are possible, they are attempted only after deep reflection and in a creative – not an iconoclastic – spirit. It is an art of continuity, of community, not of iconoclasm or egotism. ■

Kütahya Müzesi, open from 8 am to noon and 1.30 to 5.30 pm, closed Monday; admission costs US$1. The collection is the usual, from Chalcolithic to Ottoman, including finds from the precincts of the great Temple of Zeus at Aizanoi (see later in this chapter). The building, however, is the Vacidiye Medresesi, built by Umur bin Savcı of the princely family of Germiyan in 1314. Nicely restored, it has a fine central dome, now closed by a glass light, over a marble pool.

Great Mosque & Bazaar

The Ulu Cami (1410), adjoining the Vacidiye Medresesi, has been restored several times, including in our century. It's surrounded by Kütahya's colourful bazaar, in which you might stumble upon the **Kavaflar Pazarı**, a 16th-century market building; the **İshak Fakih Camii** (1434) and the **İmaret Mescidi** (1440), a former medrese.

Kossuth Evi

Walk around behind the Ulu Cami and follow the signs to the Kossuth Evi (Kossuth House), also called the Macar Evi (Hungarian House), 250m more or less straight on up the slope; look for the house on the left, marked by plaques in Turkish and Hungarian.

Lajos Kossuth (1802-94) was a prominent member of the Hungarian parliament. In 1848, chafing at Hapsburg rule from Vienna, he and others rose in revolt, declaring Hungary an independent republic in 1849. When Russian troops intervened on the side of the Austrians, he was forced to flee, was welcomed to the Ottoman domains, and lived in Kütahya in 1850-51.

His house, with its perfectly preserved kitchen, dining room, bedroom, and office, is open from 8 am to noon and 1.30 to 5.30 pm, closed on Monday; admission costs US$1. This is how upper-class Kütahyans lived in the mid-19th century.

Kütahya Fortress

The kale is reachable by a steep path from the neighbourhood of the Ulu Cami, or by a road which winds around the hill and approaches the top from the far side (follow black-on-yellow signs reading 'Döner Gazino').

Built originally by the Byzantines, the castle was restored and used by their successors, the Seljuks, the emirs of Germiyan, and the Ottomans.

The bulky remains of dozens of cylindrical towers in the walls, though badly ruined, make it easy to imagine that this was a formidable obstacle to any conquering army.

Tea gardens with splendid views and, in the castle keep (donjon), the cylindrical restaurant nightclub (Döner Gazino) reward you for the climb.

Places to Stay

Hotel Yüksel (☎ (274) 212 0111), Belediye Meydanı 1, is the cheapest place in the centre. It's a well-worn hostelry charging US$6.50/9 a single/double without shower. The *Otel Köşk* (☎ (274) 216 2024), Lise Caddesi 1, offers simple double rooms with sinks for US$9 or US$12 with shower. The *Otel Park* (☎ (274) 216 2310), Afyon Caddesi 20, is for emergencies.

The *Gül Palas* (☎ (274) 216 1759, fax 216 2135), Belediye Meydanı, is the city's old standard, renovated entirely in 1995 with the inevitable tiles used throughout. Comfortable if small rooms with private shower cost US$22/28 a single/double, breakfast included.

The three-star, 42-room *Hotel Erbaylar* (☎ (274) 223 6960, fax 216 1046), Afyon Caddesi 14, has good service and rooms with shower priced at US$30/35 a single/double, breakfast included. Some rooms have TVs and minibars.

The three-star *Tahya Otel* (☎ (274) 224 3071, 224 3074), on Atatürk Bulvarı across from the Çinigar, is the town's best, with 35 bath-equipped rooms priced at US$30/35 a single/double, breakfast included. The 52-room *Hotel Bakır Sözer* (☎ (274) 212 3338), Çinigar Caddesi, on the south side of the otogar, is a distant third-best.

Places to Eat

Çınar Köfte, Lise Caddesi 7, near the Otel

Köşk, serves köfte, soup, salad, bread and beverage for US$4 or less.

Beside the Gül Palas is the *Cumhuriyet Lokantası*, a dependably good eatery serving three-course meals for under US$8.

The *Restaurant Çinili International* (☎ 216 3879), Afyon Caddesi 2, a white-tablecloth place only a few steps from the vase fountain on Belediye Meydanı, specialises in İskender (Bursa) kebap (US$2.50, though it's inauthentic). The nearby *Meshur İskender Kebap Salonu*, Afyon Caddesi 6, may be better.

On the north-east side of Belediye Meydanı across Dumlupınar Bulvarı and Fatih Caddesi are several other good kebapçıs and a pastry shop. For fresh fruit, vegetables and picnic supplies, browse the open-air market one block south up the hill on Lise Caddesi.

Getting There & Away

The Kütahya Çinigar bus station has an emanet (left luggage/checkroom). Because Kütahya is a provincial capital, its otogar supports fairly busy traffic. Here are details on bus trips from Kütahya to:

Afyon – 100 km, under two hours, US$5; many buses daily
Aizanoi – see Çavdarhisar
Ankara – 315 km, five hours, US$10; a dozen buses daily
Antalya – 375 km, eight hours, US$17; a few buses daily in summer, fewer in winter
Bursa – 190 km, three hours, US$9; a dozen buses daily
Çavdarhisar – 60 km, one hour, US$2.75; take a Gediz or Emet minibus and get out at Çavdarhisar
Eskişehir – 91 km, 1¼ hours, US$3.50; very frequent buses daily
İstanbul – 355 km, six hours, US$13; a dozen buses daily
İzmir – 385 km, six hours, US$13; a dozen buses daily
Konya (via Afyon) – 335 km, five hours, US$15; several direct buses, or change at Afyon

AİZANOİ (ÇAVDARHİSAR)

Aizanoi (or Aezani), 60 km south-west of Kütahya, is the site of Anatolia's best-preserved Roman temple. The **Temple of Zeus** (or Jupiter) dates from the reign of Hadrian (117-38 AD), and was dedicated to the worship of Zeus and also the Anatolian fertility goddess Cybele (Artemis, Diana).

Hours are officially from 9 am to noon and 1 to 5 pm, but in fact there is no fence and the guard, Mr Nazim Ertaş, will find you after you arrive to sell you a ticket for US$1. He will also take you down to the sanctuary of Cybele beneath the temple and open the locked gate so you can see the goddess' special prayer place.

The temple stands on a broad terrace built to hold it, and which served as the temple precinct. Like some ancient Hollywood set, the north and west faces of the temple have their double rows of columns intact, but the south and east rows are fallen in a picturesque jumble. The three columns at the north-east corner were toppled by the disastrous Gediz earthquake of 1970, but have since been re-erected. The cella (interior) walls are intact enough to give you a good picture of the whole. On the north-west edge of the temple precinct is a wire enclosure holding some of the best bits of sculpture found at the site.

From the height of the temple you can survey the surrounding gardens and fields to see bits of the other Roman and Byzantine ruins, including the easily identifiable but badly ruined **amphitheatre** 800m to the north. Elsewhere in the town and surrounding fields and orchards are ruins of the main **baths** (off to the north-west); smaller baths with some surviving mosaics (near the minaret); a **stadium** between the temple and the amphitheatre; and an **old Roman bridge**.

Getting There & Away

The town of Çavdarhisar (population 4100) is on the Kütahya-Uşak road. Take a Gediz or Emet minibus from Kütahya Çinigar (one hour, US$3), which will follow the Afyon road for 10 km, then turn right (west) on the road marked for Aezani, Uşak and Gediz for another 50 km. The Temple of Zeus is 800m north-west of the Kütahya-Uşak road along the road to Emet.

Çavdarhisar has a few *eateries* (mostly for

pide), across from the marketplace north-east of the crossroads. You may be able to get permission to camp somewhere at the edge of the village, but there are no facilities except at the fuel stations and the toilets at the temple. If you have questions, ask at the Belediye, at the main crossroads in the town centre.

The best way to visit Aizanoi from Kütahya is to start early in the morning and bring a picnic to eat at the ruins. When you arrive in Çavdarhisar, ask about return mini-buses to Kütahya or onward minibuses to Gediz (37 km) and Uşak (65 km more), from whence you can easily catch a bus to Afyon, Ankara, Denizli/Pamukkale, İzmir, Konya or Manisa.

MİDAS ŞEHRİ

The rock-hewn monuments at Midas Şehri, midway between Afyon and Eskişehir, are the most impressive ones left to us from the civilisation of the Phrygians. If you have your own transport, it's worth a half-day detour to see them. It's best done in the early morning, the only time when sunlight bathes the Midas Tomb at Midas Şehri. Without your own wheels, you must have an intense interest in things Phrygian as public transport can be slow and uncertain.

What archaeologists call Midas Şehri is in the village of **Yazılıkaya** ('inscribed rock'), 72 km north of Afyon or 107 km south of Eskişehir, not to be confused with the Yazılıkaya at the Hittite capital of Boğazkale, east of Ankara.

Midas Tomb

Most prominent of the works in Midas Şehri is the so-called Midas Tomb, a 17-metre-high relief carved into the soft tufa (type of stone) representing the façade of a temple covered in geometric patterns. At the centre near the base of the façade is a niche where an effigy of the Anatolian fertility goddess Cybele would be displayed during festivals. Inscriptions in the Phrygian alphabet, one bearing the name of Midas, decorate the façade. A small **museum**, which you pass on the walk up to the Midas Tomb, holds a few finds from the site, and diagrams. A portion of the ancient road, visible from the wagon-wheel ruts worn into the rock, connects the museum with the Midas Tomb.

Beside the Midas Tomb is a later rock-cut 'monastery', with tombs beneath.

The Phrygians

The Phrygians emigrated from Thrace to central Anatolia around 1200 BC. They spoke an Indo-European language, used an alphabet similar to the Greek, and established a kingdom with its capital at Gordion, 106 km west of Ankara (see the Central Anatolia chapter). Phrygian culture was based on that of their neighbours the Greeks, but with strong Neo-Hittite and Urartian influences.

The Phrygians are credited with having invented the frieze, embroidery, and numerous musical instruments including cymbals (for which Turkey is still famous), double clarinet (aulos), flute, lyre, syrinx ('pan-pipes') and triangle.

The Phrygian Empire flourished under its most famous king, Midas (c 725-675 BC), one of many Phrygian monarchs to have that name, until the empire was overrun by the Cimmerians (676-585 BC).

Phrygian art and culture endured, flourishing from around 585 to 550 BC, when the rock-cut monuments at Midas Şehri – the most impressive Phrygian monuments extant – were carved. The area was later ruled by the Lydian kings from Sardis, and still later by the kings of Pergamum.

Phrygian art, executed in ceramics, wood, mosaics, metal and rock, is vigorous, spirited and original, and seems to have influenced later Greek vase painters in the Aegean's Cyclades islands.

The Phrygians' most notable exports seem to have been metal objects, textiles, slaves and the names of their kings: Midas and Gordios. Several kings bore these names, and archaeologists have found it difficult to solve the mystery of which Midas was which. ■

A few hundred metres to the west is Little Inscribed Rock (Küçük Yazılıkaya), another 6th-century BC rock-hewn cult monument which was never completed.

A walk around the base of the plateau, and a climb to the acropolis atop it, reveals more tombs, altars and ceremonial niches. The site guardian will take you on a walking tour for a tip. About 150m south of the Midas Tomb on the plateau's east side, a rock-hewn stairway decorated with reliefs of figures leads to the acropolis atop the 30-metre-high plateau. Here there are signs of a rock-hewn throne-altar, defensive walls, and other stairways leading down into the rock to a well.

Nearby Phrygian Sites

Another Phrygian cult temple is at **Arezastis**, about one km away on the Seyitgazi road.

Even more Phrygian rock carvings are to be found east and south of Midas Şehri along the roads and side-roads to Afyon. Heading west from Midas Şehri along unpaved roads, the village of **Kümbet** (17 km) has a Selüuk tomb *(kümbet)* and a Phrygian shrine with a relief of a lion (Aslanlı Mabet).

Two km west of Kümbet is the Seyitgazi-Afyon road (03-78), narrow but paved. Go south towards Afyon 21 km to an unpaved road on the right (west) marked for the **Göynüş Vadisi**, a valley of tufa outcrops bearing several phrygian reliefs, including Aslantaş (a relief of a lion), Yılantaş (a snake) and Maltaş (a sheep). Continue along the poor, unpaved road to İhsaniye (or go back to the Afyon road), go south to the hot-springs town of **Gazlıgöl** (14 km), then north-west to İhsaniye (16 km) via road 03-77). From İhsaniye take the unpaved road north towards Döğer (13 km) to reach other Phrygian carvings at **Kapıkayalar** and **Arslankaya**. The carving at Arslankaya is of Cybele with a lion at either side.

About five km south of the Göynüş Vadisi turn on the way to Gazlıgöl and Afyon is a turn on the left (east) at Kayahan for **Ayazinköyü**, the site of an ancient rock-hewn settlement called Metropolis. The village, five km east of Kayahan, is set amidst Cappadocia-like rock formations of soft tufa which have been hollowed out to make dwellings, storerooms and churches. The state of preservation of these troglodyte dwellings, and the decoration in the churches, is not nearly as good as in Cappadocia's Göreme valley, but is worth a look if you won't get as far as Cappadocia. There are a few minor Phrygian lion reliefs as well.

Getting There & Away

Transport is not easy by bus, dolmuş or train. You will almost certainly have to hitch rides at some point – and these roads have little traffic. Plan to spend the whole day on this excursion.

With your own vehicle, transport is easy enough, and you can visit most of these sites in less than a day. The best access road to Midas Şehri is the paved, one-lane road approaching from the east via Çifteler.

From Eskişehir Take a bus or dolmuş south to Seyitgazi, then ask. There may be a dolmuş south from Seyitgazi via Şükranlı and Çukurca to Yazılıkaya along the paved road. If not, take something bound for Gazlıgöl or Afyon along road 03-78, get out at the Kümbet turn, and hope to hitch a ride, or expect a long walk along the unpaved road eastward.

If you're driving, it's faster to take the Ankara highway (E90) east for 37 km to the turn south for Mahmudiye and Çifteler. At Çifteler, 60 km south-east of Eskişehir, turn right (west) on the one-lane macadam road for Gököüeköyü and Yazılıkaya, another 36 km along.

From Ankara Follow the Eskişehir highway (E90/D220) west via Polatlı. At Kaymaz, 31 km west of Sivrihisar, turn left (south) for Çifteler, and follow the directions as from Eskişehir (above).

From Afyon If you're driving, head due north from Afyon following signs for Organize Sanayi Bölgesi, Gazlıgöl and Seyitgazi, then follow the guidance given above under 'Nearby Phrygian Sites'.

Dolmuşes from Afyon go as far as Gazlıgöl and perhaps İhsaniye, where you will probably have to change for onward rides. A few trains can take you to İhsaniye and Döğer; after visiting Arslankaya and Kapıkayalar, you'll probably find it easiest to return to Afyon by dolmuş.

AFYON

Formerly called Afyonkarahisar (The Black Fortress of Opium), this workaday agricultural and carpet-weaving town (population 100,000, altitude 1021m), capital of the province of the same name, hardly lives up to its sinister moniker.

The eponymous fortress stands atop the massive rock in the historic centre of town, and this is still an important region for producing legal opium for legitimate pharmaceutical use. But today the opium – more than a third of the world's legal crop – is grown by the 'poppy straw' method, which is easier to police and control. The young plants are cut down before the narcotic sap begins to flow, and the 'straw' is processed in special government-operated factories.

Afyon is also important to the marble-cutting industry, with numerous marble factories on the outskirts.

It's a pleasant enough place to stop, though you're unlikely to see many other tourists, which may be why the town's hotels are sub-standard.

Opium is legally produced for pharmaceutical use in Afyon. Young poppy plants are cut before the sap flows, and 'poppy straw' is processed in government-operated factories

History

As with so many Anatolian towns, Afyon's history starts some 3000 years ago. After occupation by the Hittites, Phrygians, Lydians and Persians, Afyon was settled by the Romans and then the Byzantines, who called the town Akroenos, and later Nikopolis. Following the Selçuk victory at Manzikert (Malazgirt) in 1071, Afyon passed into the control of the Selçuk Turks. The important Selçuk vizier Sahip Ata took direct control of the town, and it was called Karahisar-i Sahip even through Ottoman times (1428-1923).

During the War of Independence, Greek expeditionary forces occupied the town during their push towards Ankara. During the Battle of the Sakarya, in late August 1921, within earshot of Ankara, the republican armies under Mustafa Kemal (Atatürk) stopped the invading force in one of the longest pitched battles in history. The Greek forces retreated and dug in for the winter near Eskişehir and Afyon.

On 26 August 1922 the Turkish forces began their counteroffensive, achieving complete surprise and advancing rapidly on the startled Greek army. Within days Kemal had set up his headquarters in Afyon's Belediye building, and had surrounded half of the Greek army at Dumlupınar, 40 km to the west. The Battle of the Commander-in-Chief, as it was to be known, destroyed the Greek expeditionary army as a fighting force, and sent its survivors storming towards İzmir, where they would flee to ships waiting in the harbour.

Orientation & Information

The main square, called Hükümet Meydanı, is east of the citadel, at the intersection of Ordu Bulvarı and Milli Egemenlik (usually called Bankalar) Caddesi. You'll know it by its fountain. About 250m south of it is another traffic roundabout, the starting point for Ambar Yolu (which goes north-east two km to the otogar) among other streets.

Almost everything important is on or just off Bankalar Caddesi between the two traffic roundabouts, including the PTT, several hotels, restaurants, and the local hamam.

The train station is two km from the centre, at the north-eastern end of Ordu Bulvarı. Minibuses connect both the gar (train station) and the otogar (bus terminus) to the centre.

The Tourism Information Office (☎ (272) 213 5447, fax 213 2623) is in the Hükümet Konağı (provincial government headquarters) on the 2nd floor, office 228. Opening hours are from 9 am to 5 pm Monday to Friday.

Afyon's postal code is 03000.

A Walking Tour

A few hours' walk, best done in the morning, will show you Afyon's attractions.

Start at the **İmaret Camii**, just south of the traffic roundabout at the southern end of Bankalar Caddesi, the major mosque in the centre. Built on the orders of Gedik Ahmet Paşa in 1472, it has an interesting design which shows the transition from Selçuk to Ottoman style. The spiral-fluted minaret is decorated with blue tiles in imitation of Selçuk style. The entrance on the eastern side is like an eyvan, or large niche, which leads to a main sanctuary topped by two domes, front and back, a design also to be seen in the early Ottoman capitals of Bursa and Edirne. A shady park with fountain provides a peaceful refuge from bustling Bankalar Caddesi. The mosque's medrese, now the city's **Ethnographic Museum**, is on the west side; its hamam (still in use) is nearer to the busy traffic roundabout.

Walk north along Bankalar Caddesi to Hükümet Meydanı, named for the neighbouring **Hükümet Konağı**, or provincial government headquarters. The Hükümet Konağı used to be the building facing the dramatic black Victory Monument (Zafer Anıtı; 1936). Today the government resides in a modern building beside the old one, and the former headquarters is the **Victory Museum** (Zafer Müzesi), with exhibits relating to the battles of the War of Independence which were fought nearby.

From Hükümet Meydanı opposite the Hotel Oruçoğlu, walk south-west up Millet (or Uzunçarşı) Caddesi, lined with confectioners' shops *(şekerleme)*, several short blocks to the small park in front of the Ot Pazarı Camii, where the kaymak-makers sell their wares in the early morning hours. Turn right and follow the main road (Köprübaşı and Camii Kebir Caddesis) uphill, looking for a 'Polis' sign on the left-hand side. Turn left at the sign and walk up the steps one block to the **Mevlevihane Camii**.

This was the site of the Afyonkarahisar Mevlevihanesi, or dervish meeting-place, dating from Selçuk times (13th century). Sultan Veled, son of Celaleddin Rumi, the founder of the Mevlevi (Whirling Dervish) order, established Afyon as the second most important Mevlevi centre in the empire. The present mosque, with twin domes, a pyramidal roof above its courtyard and a rather church-like aspect, dates only from 1908, when it was built on the orders of Sultan Abdülhamid II. It's usually locked except at prayer times.

Continue walking up the main road to the square **Ulu Cami**, or Great Mosque (1273), about 1100m from Hükümet Meydanı. The Ulu Cami is among the most important extant examples of the Selçuk architectural style which called for brick walls and a roof supported by carved wooden columns and beams. Note the green tiles on the minaret. Unless you come just after prayer time, you may have to ask around for the *bekçi* (custodian) to let you in.

On your walk to the Ulu Cami you will doubtlessly have noticed the many old **Ottoman houses** in this neighbourhood. Those in some other cities (Kütahya, for example) are in better repair, but Afyon has an interesting variety of styles in its domestic architecture.

Across the street from the Ulu Cami, a lane marked by a sign ('Kale – City Castle') leads up towards the rock and its fortress. At the end of the lane is the first of some 700 steps to the summit, 226m high.

Despite its eventful history (or perhaps because of it), the **citadel** holds little to see in the enclosure itself. The first fortress here is thought to have been built by the Hittite king Mursil II circa 1350 BC, and elaborated upon by every conqueror ever since. The views, however, are spectacular.

Archaeology Museum

Afyon's modern museum is almost two km south-east of Hükümet Meydanı along Kurtuluş Caddesi, the continuation of Bankalar Caddesi, near the intersection with İnönü Caddesi. Though closed for renovations at the time of writing, the museum is normally open from 9 am to noon and 1.30 to 5.30 pm for US$1. The Roman collection is particularly good.

Places to Stay

Afyon's hotels are old, dowdy, overpriced and often full.

Otel Mesut (☎ (272) 212 0429), Dumlupınar 2 Caddesi 5, on the north side of the PTT a half-block east of Bankalar Caddesi, offers perhaps the cheapest presentable accommodation at the very centre. Rooms, priced at US$14/20/28 a single/ double/triple with shower, are beat-up and somewhat depressing, but will do for a night. There are several even cheaper hotels farther along this street.

Otel Afyon Palas (☎ (272) 212 7429), Dumlupınar 15, one street north of the Mesut and just around the corner from the Otel Oruçoğlu, is cheap and quietish, charging US$7/10 a single/double in waterless rooms.

The two-star, 57-room *Otel Oruçoğlu* (☎ (272) 212 0120, fax 213 1313), Bankalar Caddesi, facing Hükümet Meydanı on the corner of Ordu Bulvarı, is well used but serviceable, with a decent dining room on the top floor. Rooms with private shower cost US$16/23/33 a single/double/triple.

Hotel Ece (☎ (4272) 215 2323, fax 215 6265), Ordu Bulvarı 2, around the corner, is a 39-room, nominally two-star place charging US$16/23/33 a single/double/triple, but open to haggling if business is slow. It's the best place in town at the time of writing, but that's not saying a lot.

For four-star comforts you must head out of Afyon on the Kütahya road 14 km to the *Termal Resort Oruçoğlu Hotel* (☎ (272) 251 5050, fax 251 5060), where one of the 216 comfy rooms can be had for US$45/65 a single/double.

Places to Eat

The little street named Ziraat Bankası Geçidi, across Bankalar from the Hotel Oruçoğlu just south of Hükümet Meydanı, has a good assortment of eateries, including the *Narin, Arzu* and *Doyum* restaurants and the *Zümrüt Etli Pide Salonu*. The first three are good for cheap, simple, filling meals (US$3 to US$4), including, of course, kaymak on your sweet. The pide salonu is cheaper still.

The *İkbal Lokantası* at Millet (Uzunçarşı) Caddesi 21, a half-block south-west of Hükümet Meydanı, was founded in 1956, and has a loyal if dwindling clientele. It's an interesting period piece which is worth trying for the old-time atmosphere. A full meal need cost no more than US$6 to US$8.

The best meals are in the top floor dining room of the *Hotel Oruçoğlu* on Bankalar Caddesi.

Don't forget to pop into one of the local şekerleme (confectioners' shops) for a taste of Afyon's famous lokum. Usually there are free samples to be had (point to something and say *Deneyelim!*, 'Let's try it!'). Cost for a half-kg is between US$1.50 and US$2, depending upon the type.

You can leave your sweets purchase until the last minute, as there are numerous şekerleme at Afyon otogar. I like the shop called Ogaş (pronounced 'oh-gosh'), as much for the name as for the lokum.

Getting There & Away

Afyon is on the inland routes connecting İstanbul with Antalya and Konya, and İzmir with Ankara and the east, so bus traffic is heavy. Trains will take you to Eskişehir, İstanbul, İzmir, Konya and Kütahya (see the introductory Getting Around chapter for details).

Bus Details of daily bus services follow:

Ankara – 260 km, four hours, US$10; buses at least hourly
Antalya – 300 km, five hours, US$14; frequent buses passing through
Eskişehir – 191 km, three hours, US$8; hourly buses
Isparta – 165 km, three hours, US$8; several buses
İstanbul – 455 km, eight hours, US$17; hourly buses
İzmir – 340 km, 5½ hours, US$15; hourly buses
Konya – 235 km, 3¾ hours, US$10; several buses
Kütahya – 100 km, 1½ hours, US$5; hourly buses
Pamukkale – 240 km, four hours, US$11; several buses

ISPARTA

Famous for its kilims, carpets and *attar* (rose oil), Isparta (population 125,000, altitude 1035m) is at an important highway junction on the way east to the pretty lakeside resort town of Eğirdir (36 km). But of the several cities in the Aegean hinterland, Isparta has the least to hold your attention.

The surrounding countryside is quite beautiful, however, as Isparta lies in the midst of the Aegean hinterland's lakes region. The play of tectonic plates long ago resulted in depressions which, when filled with water, became the lakes of Burdur, Eğirdir, Beyşehir and others.

Isparta's sandy soil is well suited to the growing of roses for oil. In the late 19th century, rose varieties were brought from Bulgaria and established here. Each year on 20 May the rose harvest begins. The attar produced is mostly exported to France.

Orientation & Information

The main square, Kaymakkapı Meydanı, is a traffic roundabout near the Otel Bolat. The otogar is 1.5 km away; the train station, a bit farther.

The local Tourism Information Office (☎ (246) 218 4438, fax 212 1065) is on the 3rd floor of the Hükümet Konağı (provincial government building). It is open from 9 am to 5 pm Monday to Friday.

Isparta's postal code is 32000.

Things to See

Should you have to spend some time here, stop in at the **Ulu Cami** (1417) and the **Firdevs Bey Camii** (1561) with its neighbouring **bedesten**, the latter two buildings attributed to Mimar Sinan. The **Archaeology Museum** on Kenan Evren Caddesi, is open from 8.30 am to 6 pm for US$1.

Also, wander in to the huge **Halı Saray** (Carpet Palace) on Mimar Sinan Caddesi. On four days each week, quantities of fine Isparta carpets are auctioned off to dealers and anyone else with the money to buy them.

Places to Stay & Eat

Mimar Sinan Caddesi is the hotel street, with a half-dozen lodging-places to choose from. Scattered amongst the hotels are intercity bus ticket offices.

Best of the cheapies is the *Hotel Yeni Gülistan* (☎ (246) 218 4085), Mimar Sinan Caddesi 31, charging US$12 for a double room with shower. The *Café Mega* near it does a good piliç döner for only US$2 a large portion.

The central three-star, 60-room *Otel Bolat* (☎ (246) 223 9001, fax 218 5506), Demirel Bulvarı 71, has about the best rooms in town and posts rates of US$40/55 a single/double, breakfast included, but lowers them to US$38 a double when not busy.

The two-star *Otel Erkoç* (☎ (246) 218 1505, fax 212 1313), a few steps north of the Bolat, is acceptable, with bath and TV-equipped doubles for US$25. A few steps from the Erkoç is the popular *Başkent Döner Pide ve Kebap Salonu*, a moderately-priced eatery. Its name is its menu.

Among the city's newest hotels is the three-star, 41-room *Hotel Artan* (☎ (246) 232 5700, fax 218 6629), Cengiz Topel Caddesi 12/B, on a quietish street behind the PTT. Rooms with shower and TV cost US$32, breakfast included. From the Firdevs Bey Camii, walk downhill from the fountain along the pedestrian way. Several small beer halls, good for an evening's thirst-quencher, are on this street as well.

Getting There & Away

Living up to its reputation as a transfer point, Isparta's otogar, 1.5 km from the main traffic roundabout in the centre, has daily buses to many destinations, including:

Afyon – 175 km, 2½ hours, US$6; frequent buses
Antalya – 175 km, two hours, US$6; hourly buses
Denizli – 175 km, 2½ hours, US$6; several buses
Eğirdir – 36 km, 30 minutes, US$1.50; minibuses every half-hour
İzmir – 425 km, seven hours, US$17; several buses
Konya – 270 km, four hours, US$11; frequent buses

EĞİRDİR

Eğirdir (pronounced eh-YEER-deer; population 18,000, altitude 950m) enjoys a beautiful situation on the road from Konya to the Aegean, near the southern tip of Lake Eğirdir (Eğirdir Gölü). It is Turkey's fourth-largest lake, covering 517 sq km, with an average depth of 12m and a maximum depth of 16.5m. On the hillside by the road into town from Isparta is a large Turkish army commando base, the commando slogan emblazoned in gigantic letters on the talus slope above: 'We're commandos: strong, brave, and ready' *(Komandoyuz, Güçlüyüz, Cesuruz, Hazırız)*. On their day off, their blue berets are a common sight in town.

In Lydian times the highway was the Royal Road, the main route between Ephesus and Babylon, and Eğirdir was a beautiful and convenient place to stop, so the town prospered.

Today the town, clinging to the base of the steep slopes of Davras Dağı (2635m), serves something of the same purpose. Travellers on their way to or from Konya stop for a day or two to enjoy views of the lake, dine on its fish, and generally relax in one of the pensions on the small island – now connected to the shore by a causeway – which stands a short distance out into the lake. The town is proud of its carpet and kilim weaving, mostly carried out by descendants of the Yörük nomads, and of its apple orchards and rose gardens, but really what it does best is relax the visitor.

History

Founded by the Hittites, Eğirdir was taken by the Phrygians circa 1200 BC, and was later ruled by the Lydians, captured by the Persians, and conquered by Alexander the Great, followed by the Romans. Its Roman name was Prostanna, and documents from the period hint that it was large and prosperous, but no excavations have been done at the site, which now lies within a large military reservation.

In Byzantine times, as Akrotiri ('steep mountain'), it was the seat of a bishopric. With the coming of the Turks, it became first a Selçuk city (circa 1080-1280), then the capital of a small principality covering the lakes region and ruled by the Hamidoğulları (1280-1381). Most of the historic buildings in town date from the Selçuk and Hamidoğulları periods. The Ottomans took control in 1417.

Under the Turks, Akrotiri was transformed into Eğridir, a word which carries meanings of 'crooked' and 'wrong'. In the 1980s, however, public relations caught up with Eğridir and the town officially changed its name to Eğirdir, a word which instead carries pretty references to spinning, sweet flag (a flower), and propolis (a sticky sap used by bees in hive-building).

Orientation & Information

Eğirdir stretches along the lakeshore for several km. Its centre is on a point of land jutting into the lake, marked by the statue of Atatürk, the historic Hızır Bey Camii, Dündar Bey Medresesi, the otogar, and most other important buildings. The Hotel Eğirdir is at the northern side of the town centre. The police station and PTT are in between the Hotel Eğirdir and the Tourism Information Office.

A few hundred metres north-west of the centre, the kale (fortress) rises at the beginning of the isthmus and causeway which leads to the Yeşilada peninsula, 1.5 km north-west of the otogar. Many of the town's good cheap pensions are on Yeşilada, or around the kale's crumbling walls. The train station is three km from the centre of town on the Isparta road.

The Tourism Information Office (☎ (246) 311 4388, fax 312 2098) is at 2 Sahil Yolu 13, 600m north-west of the otogar on the

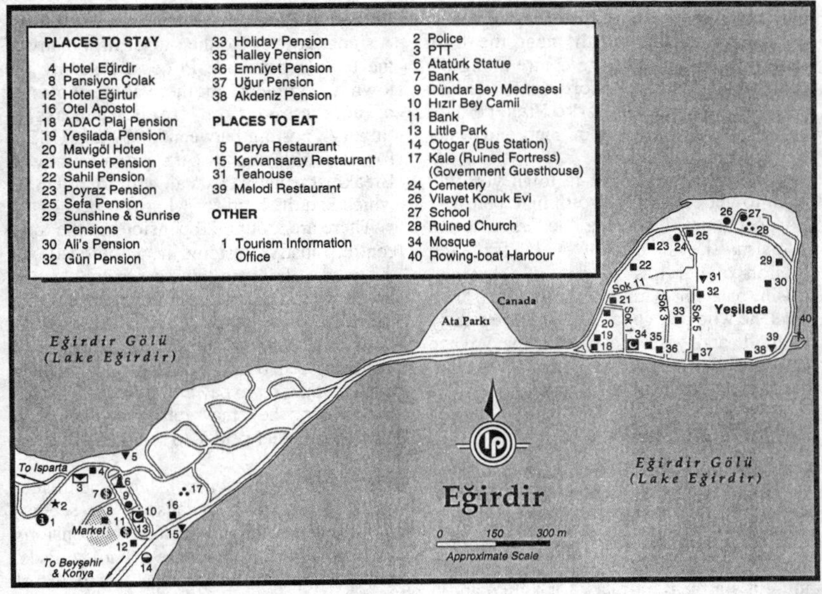

shore road towards Isparta. Hours are 8.30 am to noon and 1.30 to 6 pm, closed weekends.

Eğirdir's postal code is 32500.

Things to See

You can see Eğirdir's sights on a walking tour in an hour or two. Start at the centre.

The **Hızır Bey Camii** is a Selçuk construction built as a warehouse in 1237, but restored as a mosque in 1308 by Hızır Bey, the Hamidoğulları emir. Note especially the finely carved wooden doors, and the bits of blue tile still to be seen on the minaret. Otherwise, the mosque is quite simple, with a clerestory above the central hall. The tiles around the mihrab are new work.

Facing the mosque is the **Dündar Bey Medresesi**, a theological school built first by the Selçuk sultan Alaeddin Keykubat as a caravanserai in 1218, but converted to a medrese in 1285 at the order of Felekeddin Dündar Bey, the Hamidoğulları emir. It was last restored in 1979, and is now filled with shops. You can enter by the door near the **Atatürk statue**, but the grand main portal is the one facing the mosque. Note the Kufic inscription around the doorway, translated on a sign into Turkish and fractured English.

A few hundred metres out towards Yeşilada, the massive but crumbling walls of the **kale** rise above the beach. Its foundations may have been laid on the order of Croesus, the 5th-century king of Lydia. It was restored by successive rulers, including the Byzantines, Hamidoğulları, Seljuks and Ottomans. Near one of its walls is the **tomb of Devran Dede**, a local Muslim mystic.

Beaches & Boat Tours

The best beaches are out of the centre – Yeşilada has no real beaches to speak of. All of the following beaches have facilities such as changing cabins and food stands or restaurants. **Belediye Plajı** is less than one km from the centre on the Isparta road in the district called Yazla. **Altınkum Plajı** is several km farther north, near the train station, three km from the centre along the Isparta road. Yet farther north (about 11 km) on the road to Barla is **Bedre Plajı,** perhaps the best of all – 1.5 km of sand and water with adequate facilities.

As soon as you arrive in town you will begin to get offers for two things: pensions and boat tours. Choosing the first is often choosing the second as well, for each pension owner has a boat or a brother, cousin, or a son with a boat, or a deal with someone who has a boat. Offerings are fairly standard, and your pleasure in the voyage may depend more upon the force of the wind that day than on the boat or owner.

Excursions

When the citizens of Eğirdir take an outing, they usually go 25 km south to **Lake Kovada National Park** (Kovada Gölü Milli Park), the small (40 sq km) lake filled by the runoff from Eğirdir Gölü. Noted for its flora and fauna, it's a pleasant place for a hike and a picnic. Beyond the lake on the Çandır road are the Çandır canyons.

Taxi tours to Lake Kovada, including a three-hour wait while you enjoy the scenery, leave from the bus station and cost US$24 per carload. You may also want to try hitching on a Sunday in summer, when locals make excursions. You may be able to camp on the lakeshore.

Another excursion is to **Zından Caverns** (Zından Mağarası), 30 km to the south-west, one km north of the village of Aksu across a fine Roman bridge. The one-km-long cave has Byzantine ruins at its mouth, lots of stalactites and stalagmites, and a curious room dubbed the Hamam. Bring a torch if you plan to explore more than superficially. Taxis will take you here on a tour from the Eğirdir otogar for US$24 per carload.

Special Events

Eğirdir celebrates its apples and fish during the first week of September each year with the Golden Apple & Silver Fish Festival.

Places to Stay

A signboard next to the otogar lists many of the town's pensions. Prices are set by the town government, but there are four classes of accommodation, from 3rd class to 'luxury', costing between US$9 and US$16 for a double room with private shower. Breakfast usually costs an additional US$2, which is quite high for what you get.

There are around 20 pensions in the town centre, mostly clustered near the castle. In the bazaar streets to the west of the Atatürk statue are some typical small hotels, but they are not as pleasant as the many pensions.

Eğirdir pension owners, especially those on Yeşilada, seem biased against single travellers. Even if you offer to pay the double rate for just one person, they may refuse because there won't be another person to sell meals to.

Yeşilada Yeşilada, the 'island' peninsula, which is preferable because of the scenery and ambience, has more than 16 pensions. As of this writing there are no noisy discos and few importunate carpet sellers to disturb the island's tranquillity. But Yeşilada is adapting rapidly to tourism, simple pensions are becoming small hotels, and those banes of Turkish travel can't be far behind.

As you come onto the island, walk straight ahead with the sea on your right. *Halley Pension* (☎ (246) 311 3625) charges US$9 for its rooms. The two front rooms upstairs have balconies and showers. The Halley serves meals as well.

Closest in quality to the Halley is the *Uğur Pension* (☎ (246) 311 2212). Its lakeview rooms have balconies and private showers.

Some of the most pleasant pensions are at the far end of the island. *Sunrise Pension* (☎ (246) 311 3032) offers excellent lake views and doubles with bath for US$13. Breakfast, taken on the tidy front garden terrace, is included. Adjoining the Sunrise is the very similar *Sunshine Pension.*

Akdeniz Pension (☎ (246) 311 2432), also called the Mediterranean Sea (the translation of Akdeniz), has a garden in front and a little restaurant, and friendly family proprietors. *Sahil Pension* (☎ (246) 311 2167) is among the newer ones, and very clean. Top-floor rooms have nice woodwork ceilings. A waterless double costs US$8.

Perhaps the most charming traditional pension (but without water views) is Mustafa and Ayşe Gökdal's *Sefa Pension* (☎ (246) 311 1877), a very homy, traditional village house. Though retired, Ayşe Hanım works hard to keep it tidy, and Mustafa provides a warm welcome. Remove your shoes as you enter, in the old-fashioned way. Rooms cost US$9 a double without water.

Ali's Pension (☎ (246) 312 2547) is a family-run place that's cheap and good, at US$8 for a double without running water.

Near the Castle As you pass the kale on your way out to Yeşilada, look up to the left to see the *Fulya Pension* (☎ (246) 311 2175), among the best in town with its roof terrace, restaurant and panoramic views. Double rooms with shower and breakfast cost US$12. Down the hill from the Fulya is the five-room, friendly and family-run *Çetin* (☎ (246) 311 2154). Rates are US$6/9/14 a single/double/triple for rooms, some with fine lake views. Breakfast and dinner are served. Other places nearby include the *Kale*, the *Mehtap* (Moonlight, ☎ (246) 311 1517) and the *Eğirdir* (☎ (246) 311 2033), 'where you live just like one of the family'.

Hotels Cheapest is the very central *Pansiyon Çolak* (☎ (246) 311 4069), behind the Hotel Barla across the street from the minaret of the Hızır Bey Camii. Though named a pension it's a hotel by construction, charging US$7 for a double room with shower.

The central three-star, 51-room *Hotel Eğirdir* (☎ (246) 311 4992, fax 311 4219), 2 Sahil Yolu 2, is the tour-group favourite, with comfortable rooms for US$30 a double, breakfast included. Cheaper is the nearby *Hotel Eğirtur* (☎ (246) 312 3700, fax 311 5598), Güney Sahil Yolu 2, opposite the otogar, offering rooms with shower for US$20. Newest of all is the two-star, 27-room *Otel Apostol* (☎ (246) 311 5451, fax 312 3533), Atayolu 7, on the left just as you leave the otogar heading out to Yeşilada. Cheerful rooms, some with lake views, cost US$30 a double, breakfast included. Check out the view from the rooftop terrace.

Places to Eat

On Yeşilada, many pensions have their own restaurants. You may also want to try the *Melodi Restaurant*, next to the Akdeniz Pension at the tip of the island, where every dish except the fish fillet seems to cost US$1. There are good lake views from the dining room.

In the centre, the *Derya Restaurant*, across the street from the Hotel Eğirdir, is the class act, with outdoor tables set by the water, and a pleasant indoor dining room as well. Full meals range from US$4 to US$10. Also grand for this town is the *Kervansaray Restaurant* (☎ 311 6340) opposite the Otel Apostol on the lakeshore.

For cheaper kebapüıs, look in the narrow bazaar streets on the opposite side of the Atatürk statue. The *Halil İbrahim Sofrası* behind the Hotel Barla and near the Pansiyon Çolak serves Anadolu ev yemekleri (Anatolian home cooking), meaning the more traditional Turkish dishes, at low prices.

Getting There & Away

By bus is the easiest and fastest way of travelling to and from Eğirdir. Though there are trains to the spur which come in from the İzmir-Aydın line via Isparta, they are not frequent or fast. If there is no bus leaving soon for your destination, hop on a minibus to Isparta and catch a bus there. Details of some services from Eğirdir follow:

Ankara – 457 km, seven hours, US$15
Antalya – 186 km, 2½ hours, US$8
Denizli – 203 km, three hours, US$8
Isparta – 36 km, 30 minutes, US$1.50; minibuses every half-hour
İstanbul – 638 km, 11 hours, US$24
İzmir – 418 km, seven hours, US$15
Konya – 236 km, four hours, US$10
Nevşehir – 443 km, eight hours, US$19

SAGALASSOS

The setting of Sagalassos, about 40 km due south of Isparta on the Antalya road, is dramatic: an ancient city perched on a treeless plateau backed by the sheer rock of ragged mountains. If you have your own wheels and are passing nearby, it's worth taking the seven-km drive north from the modern town of Ağlasun along a narrow but paved road to visit the site. Travelling by bus, you'd be better advised to pass it by as buses can be infrequent and there is no accommodation or restaurant food in Ağlasun.

Founded by a warlike tribe of the 'People from the Sea', Sagalassos became an important Pisidian city second only to Antioch in Pisidia. Archaeologists are still at work on excavations. If these are followed by restoration, Sagalassos will be an impressive site indeed. As it is, the site is a broad field of mostly undifferentiated rubble, though there is a prominent theatre, and a temple with two walls standing. The baths are being restored – slowly.

Mediterranean Turkey

The southern coast of Turkey is delightful: a succession of scenic roads, interesting villages and picturesque ancient ruins. Only a few decades ago parts of this coast could only be explored with a sturdy vehicle, pack animal or boat. Now, new highway construction has changed all that and you can drive easily from Marmaris, where the Aegean and Mediterranean seas meet, to Antakya, near the Syrian border, enjoying the countryside rather than battling against it.

For all its beauty, most of the coastline is still relatively undeveloped. Instead of a Riviera with miles of hotels, Mediterranean Turkey consists of a succession of small settlements separated by miles of rocky coastline, with the occasional sweep of beach.

The most idyllic way to explore the coast is in a private yacht – not as outrageously expensive a proposition as you might imagine. While yachts chartered in the Greek islands may cost over US$100 per person per day, you can charter a beautiful wooden *gulet* (yacht) in Turkey in spring or autumn for as little as US$40 to US$70 per person per day, meals included. These meals, cooked by the crew, will include fish and octopus pulled fresh from the blue waters, with herbs gathered along the shore. There's more information on yacht chartering in the Marmaris section.

If time is short you could see the coast from Marmaris to Alanya pretty well in a week, but it's much more relaxing to take longer.

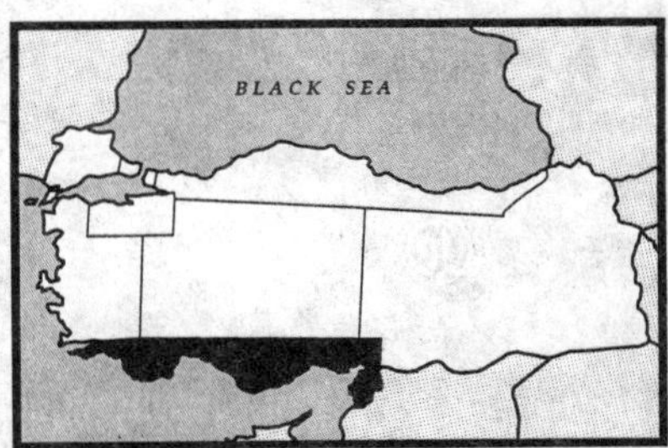

Highlights

- Boat trip to Kekova and Kale...or any other Blue Voyage
- Walking through the Saklıkent Gorge
- Exploring the ruins at Xanthos or Pnara
- Lazing on Patara beach
- Boat ride through the reedbeds of Dalyan to İztuzu
- Climbing through the mountainside ruins of Termessos
- Roman mosaics in the Antakya Museum
- Strolling the winding streets of Kaleiçi (Old Antalya)

Getting There & Away

Air The airport at Dalaman, 120 km east of Marmaris and 50 km west of Fethiye, is used mostly for charter flights from abroad, and services operated by İstanbul Airlines. In summer there are also daily flights to and from İstanbul, and at least weekly nonstop flights to Tel Aviv and Zürich by Turkish Airlines.

İstanbul Airlines has nonstop flights once a week between Dalaman and Amsterdam, Berlin, Cologne (Köln), Düsseldorf, Frankfurt, Hamburg, Hannover, İstanbul, Leipzig, Linz, London, Lyon, Mulhouse, Munich, Nürnberg, Paris, Stuttgart, Tel Aviv and Vienna.

For detailed information on land transport from Dalaman to other points on the Mediterranean coast refer to the Dalaman section.

The other south coast airports are at Antalya and Adana.

Bus Your coastal explorations will be by bus, car or hired yacht. With the yacht and car you travel at your own pace. There may be only a few buses a day between points. As with most parts of Turkey, service dwindles and disappears in the late afternoon or early

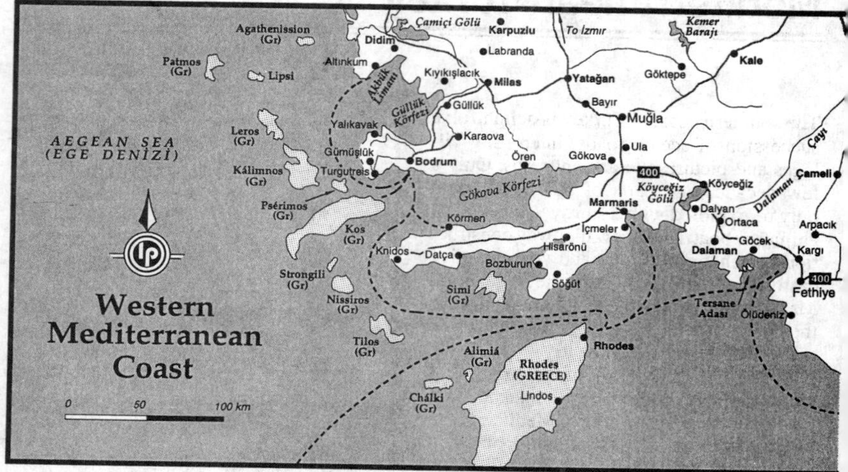

evening, so do your travelling early in the day and relax in the evening. With fewer buses it's all the more important to buy your reserved-seat tickets a day or so in advance.

Train There is no rail service south of Söke, Denizli and Isparta; trains do run from Ankara to Adana and Mersin, however. See the sections on Ankara and Adana for details.

BODRUM TO MARMARİS

The trip from Bodrum takes you back to Milas, then up into the mountains. The land is rich and heavily cultivated, with vast fields of sunflowers and frequent colonies of beehives. In the warm months beekeepers set up stands by the side of the road to sell jars of the translucent, golden, delicately pine-scented honey for which the region is famous.

Stratonikea

Just west of Yatağan at Eskihisar are the ruins of Stratonikea. It was founded under the Seleucids, important under the Romans, and are now threatened by a huge open-cut mine producing soft coal (lignite, *linyit*). Bits of ruin are visible from the road as you pass through, but you must follow the signposted road one km down to the abandoned former village of Eskihisar to reach the centre of Stratonikea.

Especially if you have picnic supplies, it's worth a stop as there are two ruined settlements here: the Roman city, and the ghost village of Eskihisar, abandoned as the mine tailings crept ever nearer.

Of Stratonikea, bits of the walls and gates, gymnasium and tomb survive, hidden in the grass and scrub and extending up the slope to the other side of the highway.

The abandoned Turkish village has houses of beautiful stonework, and a remarkable absence of modernity: no wires, commercial signs or cars. There is one building, on the shady former village square, maintained and used as a tea house, which may not be open. At the end of the village road another stone house is the museum/storehouse for archaeological finds from the site. (Admission costs US$1, but is not worth it.) Otherwise, Eskihisar is a museum village of Turkish rural life a century ago.

Muğla

This small, pleasant, obviously prosperous city (population 50,000, altitude 625m) is the

capital of the province of the same name, which includes the tourist centres of Bodrum and Marmaris. Muğla, set in a rich agricultural valley, prides itself on having had Turkey's first female *vali* (governor), and on a low unemployment rate, equal to Japan's, at about 3%. Though tourism and farming are Muğla's sources of wealth, the most common occupation here is that of bureaucrat.

History First settled around 1200 BC, Muğla was known as Alinda until Seljuk times. Captured by the Turkish emirs of Menteşe in 1261, it was seized by the Ottomans in 1390, but was returned to Menteşe control by the victorious Tamerlane in 1402. Mehmet the Conqueror regained control for the Ottomans in 1451. It seems to have been called Mabolla, Mobella or Mobolia in later Ottoman times.

Orientation The centre of Muğla is Cumhuriyet Meydanı, the traffic roundabout with the statue of Atatürk. Everything you may need is within walking distance: the otogar a few blocks south-west, the PTT 500m north-west along Recai Güreli Bulvarı, and the bazaar and historic quarter 500m due north along Kurşunlu Caddesi.

Information The Tourism Information Office (☎ (252) 214 3127) is on the north-west side of Cumhuriyet Meydanı, right at the centre.

Muğla's postal code is 48000.

Things to See Go north along Kurşunlu Caddesi from Cumhuriyet Meydanı to the **Kurşunlu Cami**, built in 1494 and repaired in 1853. Its minaret and courtyard were added in 1900. Nearby is the **Ulu Cami** (1344), dating from the time of the Menteşe emirs, though 19th-century repairs have rendered its pre-Ottoman design almost unrecognisable.

Continue walking north into the tidy **bazaar**, its narrow lanes jammed with artisans' shops and dotted with little cookshops (very basic restaurants). Proceed up the hillside to see Muğla's **Ottoman-era houses**, some still in good condition. Centuries ago there was a small fortress at the top of the hill, but now not a stone remains.

The **Vakıflar Hamamı**, on the corner of Tabakhane and Orgeneral Mustafa Muğlalı Caddesis, was built in 1258, is still operating, and has a separate women's entrance.

Places to Stay – bottom end Follow Tabakhane Caddesi into the bazaar to find the *Doğan Pansiyon* (☎ (252) 214 3960), above a *kiraathane* (coffee house) half a block from the Ulu Cami. It's simple and cheap at US$8 for a double room with no basin, shower or toilet. Equally basic and cheap is the *Muğla Pansiyon* (☎ (252) 212 0340), Saatli Kule Caddesi 78, entered through a shop front.

Otel Tuncer (☎ (252) 214 8251), Saatli Kule Altı, Kütüphane Sokak 1, is a long block north-east of the Kurşunlu Cami (follow the signs). It's relatively clean, fairly quiet, and well priced at US$11 a double with sink, US$13 a double with private shower.

Otel Zeybek (☎ (252) 214 1774, fax 214 3156), Turgut Reis Caddesi 5, two short blocks west of the Kurşunlu Cami, is older and a bit noisier, charging US$12/15/16 for a double with sink/shower/shower and toilet.

Walk east on Orgeneral Mustafa Muğlalaı Caddesi several blocks to the *açık pazar yeri* (marketplace), look to your left (north) and you'll find the *Hotel Saray* (☎ (252) 214 1594), among the town's newer hotels. Good, clean, newish rooms with shower and views of the marketplace go for US$12/17 a single/double.

Places to Stay – middle The 48-room *Hotel Yalçın* (☎ (252) 214 1599, fax 214 1050), Garaj Caddesi 7, is Muğla's best value-for-money lodging, half a block north-west of the otogar on a quiet street. Though three decades old, it is well maintained, charging US$14/24 a single/double for a comfortable room with shower, breakfast included.

The three-star *Hotel Petek* (☎ (252) 214 1897, fax 214 2421), Marmaris Bulvarı 27, 400m east of Cumhuriyet Meydanı, is the best choice for single travellers. Its smaller single rooms, aimed at business travellers, cost only US$12, while doubles are US$28, breakfast included.

Muğla's fanciest – and the only hotel in the area with swimming pool, hamam and sauna – is the four-star *Hotel Grand Brothers* (☎ (252) 212 2700, fax 212 2610), one km west of Cumhuriyet Meydanı along the Yatağan-İzmir highway. Run by the same people who own the Petek and the Saray, it is seldom even busy, and staff are usually willing to discount the posted rates of US$54/70 a single/double.

Places to Eat The bazaar holds numerous köfte grills, pide makers and ready food eateries. The *Kısmet Lokantası*, opposite the Otel Tuncer's street, serves tas kebap (meat and vegetable stew) and pilav for US$3, with a soft drink. Right next to the Otel Zeybek, the *Altın Sofra Kebap Salonu* is the best in the neighbourhood, with full meals for US$5.

The *Hotel Yalçın* has a terrace restaurant noted for its good food, service, and availability of alcoholic beverages. You can spend as little as US$5 or as much as US$10 here.

Just south of the market is a big office building called the Orgeneral Mustafa Muğlalı İşhanı, and on its north-east side are two fancy places, the *İmren Restaurant* and the *Bulvar Restaurant*. Both have indoor and outdoor seating, and a good meal at either should cost no more than US$5 to US$8.

Getting There & Away Muğla's tourist importance means its otogar is a busy one, with fairly frequent buses to all major destinations in the region. For points along the Mediterranean coast east of Marmaris, you may have to take a bus to Marmaris and change there to an eastbound bus. Details of some services follow:

Aydın – 100 km, 1¾ hours, US$5
Bodrum – 110 km, two hours, US$5.50
Dalaman – 86 km, 1½ hours, US$5
Denizli – 130 km, two hours, US$5.50
İzmir – 265 km, 4½ hours, US$10
İstanbul – 875 km, 14 hours, US$24
Köyceğiz – 57 km, one hour, US$3
Marmaris – 55 km, one hour, US$3

Gökova

Thirty km north of Marmaris the road comes over the Sakar Geçidi (Sakar Pass, at 670m) to reveal breathtaking views of Gökova bay, before descending by switchbacks into a fertile valley.

At the base of the hill, signs point the way right (west) to the village of Akyaka, often called Gökova after the beautiful bay. This little resort village is built on a hillside which descends to a little sand beach by a river mouth. Much favoured by British holidaymakers, Gökova has many small pensions, as well as hotels rating from two to four stars.

About 700m beyond the village of Akyaka is an *orman piknik yeri* (forest picnic ground), and another 500m beyond that is the port hamlet of İskele. The tiny beach at the end of a small cove is served by a few basic restaurants.

From the base of the hill at the Gökova turn-off, the Marmaris road crosses the floor of the broad river valley beside a magnificent double row – over two km in length – of great eucalyptus trees. (The old highway went right between the trees; the new one bypasses

The Lycians

Ancient Lycia extended along the Mediterranean coast roughly from Köyceğiz in the west to Antalya in the east. The Lycians first crop up in history when Homer records their presence during an attack on Troy in the *Iliad*. It is thought they may have been descendants of an Anatolian tribe called the Luvians. A matrilineal people with their own language, the Lycians lived in city-states, 23 of which formed the Lycian Federation to make communal decisions about 'foreign affairs'.

By the 6th century BC the Lycians had come under the loose control of Persia. In the 5th century BC the Athenians briefly drove the Persians out of Lycia which became part of the Delian Confederacy. All too soon, however, the Persians were back in charge, followed in turn by Alexander the Great, the Ptolemies, the Romans and the Rhodians. During this period the Lycians abandoned their own language in favour of Greek.

In the 2nd century BC Lycia was governed by the Pergamene kings. When the last of them died without an heir, he bequeathed Lycia to the Romans who incorporated it in their province of Asia. In spite of this nominal loss of independence, the Lycians seem to have continued their own way until, in 42 AD, the resurgent Lycian League made the unwise decision not to support Brutus, leading to the destruction of Xanthos.

In 43 AD the Romans joined Lycia to adjacent Pamphylia as a single province, a union that survived until the 4th century. Lycia never again regained its independence, succumbing in turn to invading Arabs and Turks.

The most obvious reminders of Ancient Lycia are the monumental sarcophagi littering the Mediterranean coast and the rock-cut tombs, sometimes resembling temples, high up on the hillsides at Dalyan, Xanthos, Fethiye, Kaş and Myra. At Letoön there are ruins of a huge temple built by the Lycian Federation to commemorate Leto, their supreme deity. Fethiye Museum also contains a trilingual stele which was used to decipher the Lycian language. ■

them on the west side.) At the far end of the trees the road ascends into the hills again before coming down into Marmaris.

MARMARİS

The once-sleepy fishing village of Marmaris (MAHR-mahr-ees) is situated on the marvellous natural harbour where Lord Nelson organised his fleet for the attack on the French at Abukir in 1798. The setting may still be glorious but the pretty old part of town around the harbour and castle is all but lost now in the sprawl of identikit concrete hotels, pensions and restaurants trailing off to the west. If it's an idyllic little resort town you're looking for, take only a brief look at Marmaris, then rush on to Datça.

Less cosmopolitan than Kuşadası, and lacking Bodrum's fine castle or Side's impressive ruins, Marmaris does still have Turkey's largest and most modern yacht marina and is consequently the country's busiest yacht-charter port.

Once the 'in' place for Turkey's rich and famous, Marmaris has recently taken a dive downmarket in pursuit of the cheap mass market British package holiday-maker. In summer the town's resident population of about 16,000 swells to between 150,000 and 200,000, and that's without the day trippers from Rhodes who – ignoring the dire warnings of Greeks that Turkey is expensive, unfriendly and dangerous – come over to find just the opposite.

Orientation

From the otogar head due south through the bazaar for 500m to reach İskele Meydanı, the harbourside plaza with the Tourism Information Office. The area immediately behind and above the Tourism Information Office is a conservation area with some of Marmaris's few remaining old buildings including a small fortress (now a museum).

Inland from İskele Meydanı stretches the shopping district, much of it a pedestrianised covered bazaar.

South and east of İskele Meydanı is the upmarket Netsel Marina and shopping mall. Hacı Mustafa Sokak, otherwise known as

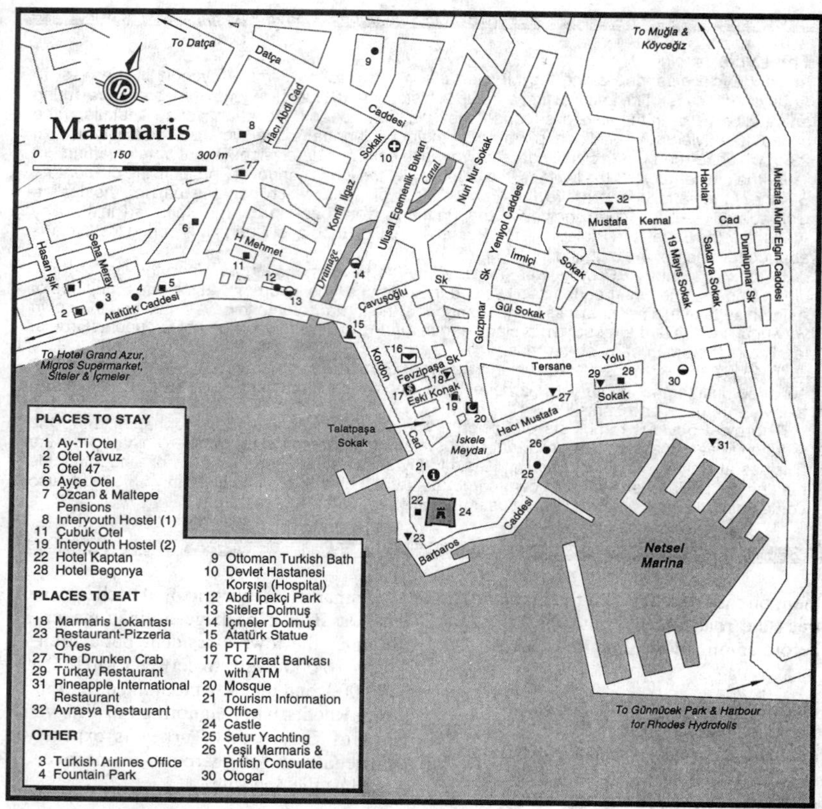

Bar Street, runs down from the bridge to the bazaar. Action here keeps going until the early hours.

The waterfront road heading north-west from İskele Meydanı starts out as Kordon Caddesi and then becomes Atatürk Caddesi at the landmark equestrian statue of Atatürk. Heading inland from here is the wide Ulusal Egemenlik (National Sovereignty) Bulvarı, the unofficial dividing line between 'old' Marmaris (to the east) and 'new' Marmaris (to the west).

A few hundred metres west of the Atatürk statue is Abdi İpekçi Park, with park benches and children's playground equipment shaded by palms. Yet another few hundred metres south-west is Fountain Park, with its namesake fountain and bits of ancient columns and statues.

Uzunyalı, a beach district full of hotels, pensions and tourist restaurants, is two to three km west of İskele Meydanı, and İçmeler, another beach resort area, is eight km south-west of it. The area immediately inland from Uzunyalı is a badly planned, haphazardly developing wasteland, full of small pensions and dirt-track roads, which extends northwards as far as Armutalan.

TOM BROSNAHAN

TOM BROSNAHAN

Top: Yacht sails near Uğurlu, Mediterranean Turkey.
Bottom: Kız Kalesi fortress, in the Mediterranean near Silifke, dates from Crusader times.

TOM BROSNAHAN

TOM BROSNAHAN

Top: The Anıt Kabir (Ataturk's mausoleum) stands at the centre of modern Ankara both physically and spiritually.
Bottom: Turkey's first republican parliament building in Ankara, Central Anatolia.

One km to the south-east is the new harbour for ferries to Rhodes and Günnücek, a forest park reserve.

Information

The Tourism Information Office (☎ (252) 412 1035) is at İskele Meydanı 39. Opening hours are from 8 am to 7.30 pm every day in summer, 8 am to noon and 1 to 5 pm Monday to Friday in winter.

Marmaris's postal code is 48700.

Money & Post Some of the exchange booths at the wharf, next to the tourism office, stay open on summer evenings and weekends when other banking facilities are closed. The TC Ziraat Bankası facing the harbour has an ATM dispensing foreign exchange. The PTT is open until 6 pm but the phones are accessible 24 hours a day.

Bookshops The Net Bookshop in Haçı Mustafa Sokak sells the *Turkish Daily News* and a limited range of second-hand books. For other foreign-language newspapers find the PTT and then walk one block farther into the bazaar. Turn right and look for a kiosk on the right.

British Consulate The consulate is at Barbaros Caddesi 118, facing the harbour. It's open Monday to Friday from 9.30 am to noon and 2.30 to 5 pm (except Friday) in summer.

Beaches

There's a narrow beach along the Kordon, and better, cleaner ones out of town, although they're all small. The better beaches are near the fancy hotels. Still others can be reached by excursion boat.

Fortress Museum

The small castle on the hill behind the tourism office was built during the reign of Sultan Süleyman the Magnificent. The sultan massed 200,000 troops here for the attack and seige of Rhodes, defended by the Knights of St John, in 1522. The fortress is now a museum open from 8 am to noon and 1 to 5 pm daily; admission costs US$1. Exhibits are predictably nautical, historical and unexciting, though the building itself and the views are nice. To reach it, follow the signs to the Panorama Bar from the harbour end of the bazaar.

Menzilhane

Behind and to the left of the tourism office is the stone *menzilhane*, an Ottoman 'pony express' way-station also built by Sultan Süleyman the Magnificent in 1545, its appearance ruined by souvenir shops.

Turkish Baths

A new 'Ottoman' bath for tourists has opened off Datça Yolu across from the government hospital (Devlet Hastanesi Karşışı). In addition to the usual accoutrements of a Turkish bath, this one boasts a sauna and alarmingly cold 'shock' pool. It's open from 8 am to 11 pm daily and charges a hefty US$11 for a bath, including assisted wash, massage and drink afterwards. If you find the massage too cursory, you can have a 20-minute massage with baby oil for another US$7. The bath is mixed and all the masseurs are male but it's all very clean and professional, so no one should have any qualms about using it – except over the cost!

The older Turkish bath in the bazaar is still open daily and charges an all-inclusive US$9, still steep by non-Marmaris standards but a snip compared with US$18!

Atatürk Statue

The equestrian statue of Atatürk at the foot of Ulusal Egemenlik Bulvarı provides a quick lesson in Turkish civic history. Plaques on the plinth bear the sayings 'Türk Öğün Çalış Güven' (Turk! Be Proud, Work, Trust) and 'Ne Mutlu Türküm Diyene' (What joy to him who says, 'I am a Turk'). Both sayings were meant to dispel the feeling of inferiority towards Europeans suffered by Ottoman Turks. Another plaque bears the words 'Egemenlik Ulusundur' (Sovereignty belongs to the Nation), Atatürk's assertion that the Turkish people, and not the imperial House of Osman, were in charge of the country's destiny. Yet another reads 'Vatan Sana Minettardır' (Your Country is Grateful to You). The final plaque in this statuary history lesson reads 'İzindeyiz' (We Follow in Your Footsteps) – the 'footsteps' being Atatürk's, of course.

Boat Excursions

Besides the daily boats and hydrofoils to Rhodes, numerous boats along the waterfront offer day tours of the harbour, its beaches and islands. Summer departures are usually at 9 am. Before deciding on your boat talk to the captain about where the excursion goes, what it costs, whether lunch is included and, if so, what's on the menu. A day's outing usually costs around US$15, much less in off-season when boats also leave later in the day.

The most popular daily excursions are to Dalyan and Kaunos or to the bays around Marmaris. In the latter case beware an extended lunch stop at Amos Bay where the only eating options are extremely expensive. Pack a picnic or hang on until you get to Turunç Bay and more choice.

You can also take longer, more serious boat trips to Datça and Knidos, well out along the hilly peninsula west of Marmaris.

Blue Voyages

Between the world wars, writer Cevat Şakir Kabaağaç lived in Bodrum and wrote an account of his idyllic sailing excursions along Turkey's Carian (southern Aegean) and Lycian (western Mediterranean) coasts, an area completely untouched by tourism at the time. Kabaağaç called his book *Mavi Yolculuk* (Blue Voyage), a name now co-opted for any cruise along these shores.

Marmaris is a good place to charter a gulet (a graceful Turkish wooden yacht) to explore the coastline. There are several ways to do this. If you don't want to do the crewing yourself and can get a party of up to 16 people together, you can charter a gulet complete with skipper and cook. Out of season, chartering the whole boat is likely to cost around US$700 per day, with the price rising to US$1250 in the high season. Obviously, the more people to share the costs, the less each individual will have to pay.

If you're not able to put together a large enough group of people to charter the entire boat, you can still opt for a cabin charter where you just pay for the berths you use.

Finally, experienced sailors can opt for a bareboat charter where you do the crewing (and cooking) yourself. To hire a bareboat for one week in low season will cost about US$1770 (shared among six people). In high season expect a price closer to US$2200. Extra charges for one-way journeys, employing a skipper, cleaning up at the end of the voyage etc can bump up the price even more.

For more information on yachting and lists of yachts and brokers, contact the Marmaris International Yacht Club (☎ (252) 412 3835), PO Box 132, 48700 Marmaris. You can usually book through a yacht broker or travel agency near your home. If not, contact Yeşil Marmaris (☎ (252) 412 1033), Barbaros Caddesi 118 (PO Box 8), 48700 Marmaris. For bareboat charters, contact Setur Yachting (☎ (252) 412 6530), Barbaros Caddesi 231, 48700 Marmaris.

Learning to Dive

There are several places in Marmaris where you can learn to dive on short courses for between US$30 and US$58, depending on the time of year. Look for the Marmaris Diving Centre on a boat moored near the tourist office. There are several others nearby.

Festivals

The Marmaris Yacht Festival is usually held in the second week in May. Though this is a private convention for yacht owners and brokers, anyone interested in yachts will enjoy seeing all the boats in the harbour and marina. Race Week, at the end of October, provides another chance to see the harbour full of yachts in full sail. For information, contact the Marmaris International Yacht Club (☎ (252) 412 3835), PO Box 132, 48700 Marmaris.

Places to Stay

Although Marmaris has several hundred hotels and pensions, the cheaper places are being squeezed out by the relentless rise in the number of hotels serving package holiday-makers. The cheapies that remain may be fairly central but very often they're also fairly noisy too. There are several moderately priced hotels a short walk from İskele Meydanı. Most of the really expensive hotels are well around the bay from the town, some as far out as İçmeler (see below).

Places to Stay – bottom end

The Tourism Information Office should be able to help you locate one of the few remaining *ev pansiyonlar* (home pensions), where you rent a room in a private home for perhaps US$8 to US$12 a double depending on facilities. Some rooms have three and four beds – good for families. At quiet times of year you may be met at the otogar by people offering rooms in ev pansiyonlar. Bear in mind that the families renting these rooms out are unlikely to speak anything other than Turkish.

Walk from İskele Meydanı along the shore road until you see the Abdi İpekçi Park and the Çubuk Otel on the right-hand side. Walk through the park and inland one block to 97 Sokak to find these pensions: the *Altun* at 97 Sokak 3, the *Taşkın* at 97 Sokak 4, the *Erdel* at 97 Sokak 7, the *Cihan* (☎ (252) 412 4312) at 97 Sokak 14, and the Etem at 97 Sokak 16.

For the night owls of Hacı Mustafa Sokak, there's a handy small pension right in the street, the *Günel* (☎ (252) 412 4676), at the otogar end with rooms for US$10. There's a laundry more or less opposite. Quieter would be the pension in the Karaduman Apartment building in 36 Sokak (☎ (252) 412 8332), on the right as you walk down to the bazaar from the otogar. Beds here cost US$5 each.

For more conventional pensions, walk from Abdi İpekçi Park westward in front of the Çubuk Otel. Turn right at the second street, walk down past the Ayçe Otel and cross a footbridge to reach the *Maltepe Pension* (☎ (252) 412 1629), with beds for US$10 a head. The bigger *Özcan Pension* (☎ (252) 412 7761) next door charges similar prices but gets very mixed reviews.

Keep walking inland from the Maltepe, cross the road and look for the *Interyouth Hostel* (☎ (252) 412 6432), Kemeraltı Mahallesi, İyiliktaş Mevkii (Eski Pazar Yolu). This newly renovated building offers beds in dormitory rooms for US$5, a roof-terrace bar, laundry, restaurant, baggage storage room, and free hot showers. There are also 'pension' rooms for US$11 a double here.

But the battle for the backpacker's dollar is hotting up. This original *Interyouth Hostel* has been joined by a second hostel (☎ (252) 412 3687) deep in the bazaar at Tepe Mahallesi, 42 Sokak 45 which has cheekily co-opted the same name. Neither is ideally situated – the original in Marmaris' dreary back streets, its newer rival in the noisy bazaar. A dorm bed in the new place costs US$6, a bed in a double nearer US$8.

A few small hotels survive right near İskele Meydanı. Have a look at the *Hotel İmbat* (☎ (252) 412 1413), Kemeraltı Eski Çarşı Sokak 30, with very plain but clean double rooms for US$12 without facilities, US$14 with shower. Also here is the *Otel Karaaslan* (☎ (252) 412 1867), Kemeraltı Eski Çarşı Sokak 36, charging the same prices for similar rooms. Some top-floor rooms have good water views. Both these places are likely to be noisy.

About two km west of the centre is Uzunyalı, its shore lined with four and five-star hotels. The area inland from these palaces is still being developed and there are many smaller, cheaper hotels. Take a minibus to Uzunyalı, get out at the Hotel Karacan, walk inland, and you should be able to find good lodgings for under US$20 a double with private shower.

Alternatively, you could take a Siteler-Turban minibus from the centre via Uzunyalı to its final stop at the Turban Tatil Köyü (Turban Holiday Village). Just east of this luxury complex there are several small hotels patronised mostly by Turkish families: *Birol Motel* (☎ (252) 412 1054), *Yüzbaşı Otel* (☎ (252) 412 2762), *Sembol*

Motel (☎ (252) 412 1356), *Panorama Motel* (☎ (252) 413 1958) and *Tümer Hotel* (☎ (252) 412 4413). Rooms in these places are often available for under US$20 a double, with bath.

Camping Camping areas are disappearing as the building boom races on. *Berk Camping* (☎ (252) 412 4171), just east of the previously mentioned Turban Tatil Köyü, has tent sites, little cabins and all services for about US$4 per person (more for the cabins). There's also camping in Günnücek Park, a forest park one km south-east of the otogar.

Places to Stay – middle

If you're in Europe and planning to stay more than a few days in a middle-grade Marmaris hotel in summer, check the price of package holidays on sale through travel agencies before booking. The market is so competitive that these may work out cheaper than buying a flight and then booking the room yourself. In peak season, many of the hotels and pensions are block-booked to the tour operators anyway and it would be hard to book privately, especially for just the odd night.

In the very centre of Marmaris, on the waterfront near the tourist office, is the *Hotel Kaptan* (☎ (252) 412 1251) where doubles with shower and breakfast cost US$27.

The *Hotel Begonya* (☎ (252) 412 4095, fax 412 1518), Hacı Mustafa Sokak 71, is an unexpected find in Marmaris. A stone house built to traditional design, it has a courtyard filled with plants and birdsong. The simply decorated rooms are equipped with tiled showers. Prices are US$35/45/55 a single/double/triple, including one of the best breakfasts in Turkey. Unfortunately, noise from the bars in neighbouring Bar Street goes on into the small hours, detracting somewhat from its charm. The Begonya closes in winter, and is often full in high summer.

A block inland on the western side of Abdi İpekçi Park is the *Çubuk Otel* (☎ (252) 412 6774), Atatürk Caddesi, Konti Sokak 1. Done out in the standard Turkish-Mediterranean idiom of white stucco and varnished pine trim, the hotel's six floors of rooms are tidy, simple and less noisy than the more expensive hotels right on Kordon Caddesi on the harbour. Prices for singles/doubles are US$27/33, breakfast and shower included.

Around the corner at Çam Sokak 4, is the *Ayçe Otel* (☎ (252) 412 3136, fax 412 3705). Small, quiet and comfortable, this is a welcoming place with a swimming pool, one of central Marmaris' better choices. Rooms rent for US$27/38.

On Atatürk Caddesi a bit farther west is the three-star *Otel 47* (kirk-yeh-DEE) (☎ (252) 412 1700, fax 412 4151), Atatürk Caddesi 10, a fairly lavish place for this district with a streetside restaurant, shops and comfortable air-con rooms with balconies overlooking the bay for US$40/50 including breakfast.

Otel Yavuz (☎ (252) 412 2937, fax 412 4112), farther west along Ataturk Caddesi has three-star comforts, 55 rooms and a small swimming pool on top of the building. Your room (with bath) may well have a balcony with a view of the bay. Depending on season the price is US$30 to US$41 a single or US$40 to US$52 a double for B&B.

Around the corner from the Yavuz and inland one block at Hacı Selim Sokak 27, is the *Ay-Ti Otel* (☎ (252) 412 3056) offering clean rooms in a convenient location for US$33/42.

On Uzunyalı beach, two km west of the centre, are many more hotels offering greater comfort at higher prices. *Otel Yunus* (☎ (252) 412 1799, fax 412 3877) is right on the waterfront and does a double with breakfast for US$50. Other possibilities nearby include the *Yeşil Hurma Oteli* (☎ (252) 412 6778), 100m farther north, the *Green Hotel* (☎ (252) 412 1861) and the *Sun Gezgin* (☎ (252) 413 3818).

Places to Stay – top end

Of Marmaris' several five-star hotels, best in terms of location is the 285-room *Hotel Grand Azur* (☎ (252) 412 8201, fax 412 3530), Kenan Evren Bulvarı 11 in Uzunyalı, three km west of the centre. The circular lobby with blue-veined marble floors and fluted columns sets a classic mood. A full range of services, facilities and activities keep guests happy...and so it should for US$222 a double in summer, including half-board. There's a casino in the grounds.

Places to Eat

Marmaris has something in the region of 3000 eating places so you certainly won't starve. There are concentrations of restaurants all along the harbour, along Kordon Caddesi and out along the shore to Uzunyalı, with more places to eat in the bazaar and along Hacı Mustafa Sokak. Small restaurants open, operate and go out of business at an alarming rate. The following suggestions merely scratch the surface.

Places to Eat – cheap

For the very cheapest fare, head for the bazaar and the streets beyond it looking for untouristy, local Turkish places selling pide, kebaps and ready food. Find where the farmers eat and you'll save 40% on the price of your meal.

Ayyıldız Lokantası, between the *menzilhane* and the mosque in the bazaar, has been dependably good for more than a decade. A meal of chicken kebap, bulgur pilav, salad and drink costs about US$7.50.

Fevzi Paşa Caddesi, the street with the post office, is closed to vehicles and in fine weather several restaurants along the street set tables outdoors. The *Marmaris Lokantası* gets the local vote here and does a tasty İskender kebap for US$4. Pop into the nearby *Hemşin Patisserie* for coffee and a cake afterwards. The *Yeni Liman Restaurant* is also good and cheap, with full meals for US$8 to US$10, as is the *Öz 49* where an İskender kebap costs US$4.

Near Abdi İpekçi Park, walk inland on the street between the park and the Çubuk Otel, and look on the left for *Altun Mantı ve Kebap Salonu*, specialising in cheap kebaps and mantı (Turkish ravioli). Keep walking down this street to the end, and turn right. Up at the far end on the left is *Aslan Usta'nın Yeri*, a small place where kebaps cost from US$4.50 to US$6, and breakfast goes for US$4.

The *Avrasya Restaurant* offers some of the best food and value for money in town. A filling main course and drink will cost you about US$5. Alcohol is not served, but that won't matter after the first bite. To find it turn right out of the otogar and right again before the bridge. Keep going until the end of the road and you'll see it on the left.

Hacı Mustafa Sokak (Bar Street) harbours all sorts of possibilities for cheap eating from filled baked potatoes through to pizzas. *Beyoğlu Café-Bar* has cheap fish meals for US$7.50. *Pizza Napoli* offers tasty, filling pizzas for around US$6.

Places to Eat – more expensive

Hacı Mustafa Sokak also has several more interesting dining places; you'll find something you like if you stroll along it in early evening. The *Türkay Restaurant* (☎ (252) 412 0741) at Mustafa Sokak 107, near the Hotel Begonya, does international cuisine at international prices; count on US$30 without alcohol. Farther down, *The Drunken Crab* (☎ (252) 412 3970), in what was once a stone-built family house, offers seafood in a friendly ambience for less than you'll pay along the waterfront. Alongside the tried and tested favourites, you'll find more unusual fish dishes just crying out to be sampled.

Waterfront restaurants to the east of the tourism office have pleasant outdoor dining areas but prices are inevitably higher than inland and the extra pays for the setting rather than the quality of the food. Assume you'll spend between US$10 and US$20 per person for a full meal with wine. Scattered among the standard seafood places, look for the trendy *Café Mistral* with live jazz music nightly and for *Fellini's* which does good pasta. Farther along towards the yacht harbour, the *Restaurant-Pizzeria O'Yes* is modern, pleasant and a bit cheaper, but often filled with tour groups.

In the Netsel Marina shopping mall the *Pineapple International Restaurant* boasts an international menu, a formal dining room and open-air tables, but prices are no worse than along the seafront and the food is considerably better. A full dinner with wine or beer will cost around US$15 to US$20.

Entertainment

Marmaris may not yet have a disco to march Bodrum's Halikarnas, but Hacı Mustafa Sokak (aka Bar Street) nevertheless boasts a plentiful supply of bar-discos, several of them outdoors, which keep the music pumping until the early hours. *The Back Street* has live music in a garden setting most nights and attracts a young crowd, or *Davy Jones's Locker* opposite, which is the 'in' place with the sailing fraternity. *Bar C'est Ça* nearby is a rhythm and blues bar.

Farther out on Atatürk Caddesi the bigger discos feature belly dancers and other such inducements.

Amid all the bars churning out western music you might think there was no room for anything traditionally Turkish, but head down to the yacht harbour and hunt out *Ezgi Bar* which has live Turkish music nightly and draws rapturous Turkish audiences.

Finding somewhere for a quiet drink is a tall order but my favourite place for a sundowner is the *Panorama Bar* with views that more than justify its name. To find it, follow the signs from the kale end of the bazaar.

Things to Buy

Marmaris has several shops selling the excellent local honey in jars priced from US$2 to US$4, or in larger tins for US$5 to US$10. Well worth visiting is Nur-Bal, Fevzi Paşa Caddesi 9-C, one block inland from the PTT on the same side of the street. A few steps farther inland, on the opposite side, Hobim ('My Hobby'), Fevzi Paşa Caddesi 8-D, sells honey, alongside Turkish delight and other traditional Turkish sweets.

Because the boats from Rhodes bring hordes of shoppers on day trips, Marmaris merchants stock everything: onyx, leather clothing and accessories, carpets, jewellery, crafts, Turkish delight, meerschaum pipes and baubles, sandals, apple tea powder, copper and beach-wear. Look out for bootleg cassettes at good prices too.

Getting There & Away

Air A small airport is being built at Ula, 40 km north of Marmaris. When finished, it will be able to receive aircraft seating up to 50 passengers. The region's principal airport is at Dalaman, 120 km east of Marmaris. İstanbul Airlines (☎ (252) 412 1443), Kenan Evren Bulvarı 88/A Siteler, has nonstop flights once a week between Dalaman and Amsterdam, Berlin, Düsseldorf, Frankfurt, Hannover, İstanbul, Linz, London, Munich, Paris, Stuttgart, Tel Aviv and Vienna.

In summer there are daily flights between Dalaman and İstanbul and Ankara by Turkish Airlines (☎ (252) 412 3751), Atatürk Caddesi 50-B.

Airport buses operated by Havaş and Marmaris Belediyesi serve Turkish Airlines' flights using Dalaman. Buses depart from the Turkish Airlines office on Atatürk Caddesi about three hours before flight departure. Alternatively, catch a regular bus to Dalaman, then take a taxi to the airport. For more information on land transport to and from Dalaman, refer to the Dalaman section.

Bus Marmaris' otogar is just north-west of the Netsel Marina, 500m north of İskele Meydanı. There are also convenient bus company ticket offices for Pamukkale, Kamil Koç, Uludağ and Metro on Ulusal Egemenlik Bulvarı, near the equestrian statue of Atatürk.

In summer, buses roll in and out of town all day long, but in winter services drop to what's required by a small farming town. Destinations include:

- Adana – 1025 km, 20 hours, US$32; change buses at Antalya
- Ankara – 780 km, 13 hours, US$22; a dozen buses daily in summer
- Antalya – 590 km, nine hours, US$14; a few buses daily
- Bodrum – 165 km, three hours, US$6.50; hourly buses in summer
- Dalaman – 120 km, 2½ to three hours, US$5 to US$6; hourly buses in summer
- Datça – 75 km, 1¾ hours, US$3.75; hourly buses in summer
- İstanbul – 900 km, 15 hours, from US$15; a dozen buses daily in summer

İzmir – 320 km, six hours, US$10; hourly buses in summer
Fethiye – 170 km, four hours, US$6.50; hourly buses in summer
Kaş – 305 km, five hours, US$8; several buses daily
Köyceğiz – 75 km, 1½ hours, US$2.75; at least nine buses daily in summer
Muğla – 55 km, one hour, US$2; frequent buses and dolmuşes
Pamukkale – 185 km, three hours, US$5.75; via Muğla and Tavas, several buses daily

Boats – to/from Rhodes Hydrofoils operate to Rhodes daily in summer, taking 45 minutes to reach Rhodes Town. Tickets cost US$41 one way, US$44 same-day return and US$56 open-date return. Buy your ticket at any travel agency in Marmaris (you'll see them along the Kordon) at least a day in advance. Entering Turkey from Rhodes on a one-way ticket you'll have to pay a US$10 port tax. When returning from Rhodes to Turkey, you will have to buy a new visa if you've stayed overnight but not if you went on a day trip.

In high summer boats also run to and from Rhodes three times a week, taking 2½ hours for the voyage. Turkish boats depart from Marmaris in the morning, returning from Rhodes in the late afternoon; Greek boats depart from Rhodes in the morning, returning from Marmaris in the late afternoon. Some of these ferries are capable of carrying cars as well as passengers. Most places selling hydrofoil tickets also sell boat tickets (US$30 one way, US$33 same-day return, US$44 open-date return) and these too must be booked at least a day in advance.

At other times of the year there may be fewer boats but you can depend on at least two a week except during stormy weather. No doubt because of the fraught state of relations between Greece and Turkey, the business of getting on and off the boats is drawn out and tedious. You may need to stand in line for a good hour just to board.

Getting Around

Dolmuşes (US$0.30) run frequently around the bay, beginning just inland from the Atatürk statue on Ulusal Egemenlik Bulvarı and going to Uzunyalı (three km), Turban-Siteler (four km) and İçmeler (eight km).

Several places along Kemal Seyfettin Elgin Bulvarı rent out bikes and motorbikes. The smallest motorbike will cost about US$38 a day, a bicycle more like US$11.

İçmeler

Once a separate fishing village, İçmeler, eight km west and south around the bay, is now little more than a beach suburb of Marmaris. However, it feels a much classier place, not least because it has been better planned, with wide tarmacked roads and completed buildings. There are even ramps on the kerbs to help people in wheelchairs get about.

These days İçmeler is nearly as popular with package holiday-makers as Marmaris itself so there's not a lot of cheap accommodation. The same advice applies as with Marmaris; if you're travelling from Europe, consider booking a package to take advantage of the tour operators' bulk buying power.

Most of the places to eat in İçmeler mirror the choices in Marmaris. However, in the hills two km above town, Mesut Akdeniz has created the *Turkish House Bar & Restaurant* (☎ (252) 455 3300), a pretty place where you can eat in a garden or in a restaurant decorated with kilims and handicrafts. Nor are the prices unreasonable: şiş kebap for US$6, köfte for US$5. The stuffed bear is a more dubious ornament. Villagers shot it 15 years ago when it was raiding their beehives. In summer you can get there in the tractor-pulled trailer that hauls people between Marmaris and İçmeler.

To get to İçmeler catch a dolmuş (US$0.30) just inland from the Atatürk statue in Marmaris. In summer they run until 1 am. After that you'll have to take a taxi for about US$10. Alternatively take a dolmuş ferry from near İskele Meydanı for US$2. These ferries run hourly between 10 am and 6 pm in summer.

REŞADİYE & DARAÇYA PENINSULAS

A narrow, mountainous finger of land stretches westward from Marmaris for about

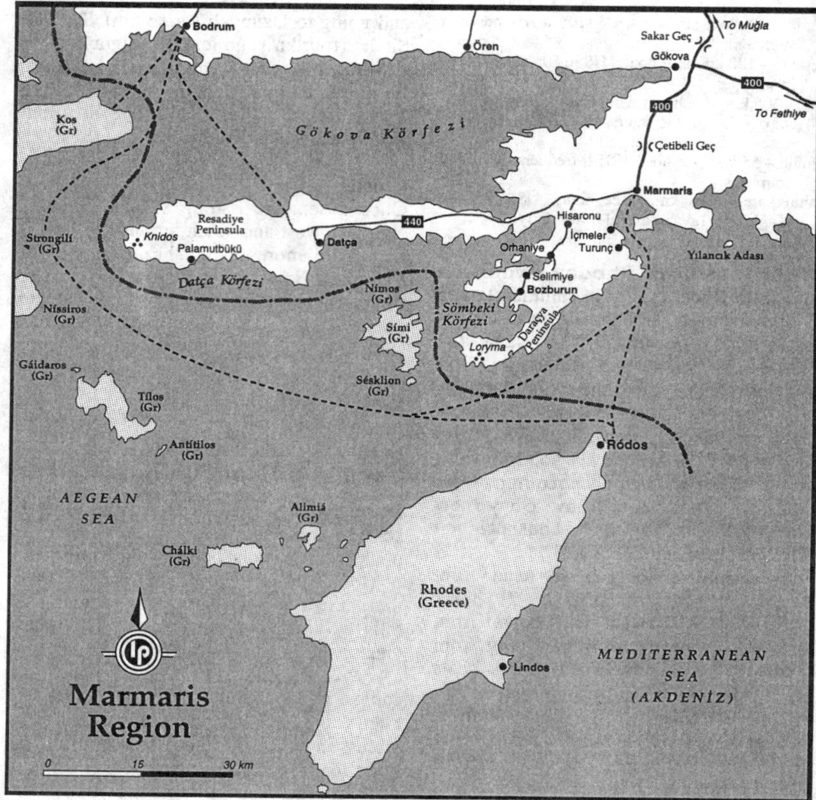

100 km into the Aegean between the Greek islands of Kos and Rhodes. Known in ancient times as the Peraea, it is now called the Reşadiye Peninsula, Datça Peninsula or Hisarönü; its southern branch is known as the Daraçya or Loryma peninsula, with the ruins of the ancient city of Loryma at its southern tip.

Until recently, access to the peninsula was mostly by sea as the road was primitive and slow. Now a paved, though twisting, road stretches from Marmaris westward beyond Reşadiye and Datça, and visits are possible by land as well. Besides the joy of sailing near the peninsula's pine-clad coasts and anchoring in some of its hundreds of secluded coves, visitors come to Reşadiye to explore Bozburun, a small fishing village 56 km south-west of Marmaris; Datça, a fast-growing resort town about 75 km west of Marmaris; and the hamlet and ruins of Knidos, the ancient city of the great sculptor Praxiteles, 35 km west of Datça.

Leaving Marmaris by road, you immediately climb into the mountains of the peninsula. After about 20 km the road divides. Go straight on for Datça and Knidos, turn left (south) for Bozburun.

The Road to Bozburun

At the time of writing, the seaside village of Bozburun was a perfect antidote to the tourist madness of Marmaris. Fishing and farming still employ most villagers, though some work in bars and shops set up to serve the yachters who drop anchor in Sömbeki bay. Though there's no good beach, there are rocks from which to swim, many interesting walks in the surrounding countryside, and excursions to be made by boat.

The road into Bozburun is being widened and improved. When it can handle large buses, the village will be utterly altered.

Travelling two km south from the main road from Marmaris brings you to the village of Hisarönü **Orhaniye**, set on a beautiful bay, is eight km farther along. You might want to stop for a meal here at the *Gület*, *Kadir* or *İskele* restaurants. There are also a couple of small pensions; the *Palmiye* (☎ (252) 486 8254) gets rave write-ups for its food. If the Marmaris touts haven't put you off carpets completely, you can also visit the Turgut Köyü Carpet Weaving Centre (☎ (252) 486 8113) near Orhaniye.

Nine km south of Orhaniye is an intersection with roads to Bayır and Bozburun. Follow the Bozburun road to reach the village of **Selimiye**, on its own lovely bay facing an islet topped by bits of ancient ruin. Selimiye has many pleasant cheap restaurants supplying the yachters, and also the *Emre Motel*, renting singles/doubles with shower for US$10/14. Old village houses are being rebuilt as villas; hotels and pensions will follow, and the apartment buildings can't be far behind.

Bozburun

From Selimiye the road deteriorates into dirt track until, after 12 km, you reach Bozburun, with a few small pensions and restaurants, a PTT and shops offering exchange facilities.

Things to Do Bozburun is not known for its beaches, but you can swim from the rocks by the *ilkokul* (primary school) south-east of the bust of Atatürk.

At the moment there are not enough tourists to justify regular excursion boats but you can charter private vessels to explore the surrounding bays.

Places to Stay Bozburun's simple pensions charge from US$4.50 to US$9 per person, depending upon season and demand.

In town the *Keskin Pension* (☎ (252) 456 2255), next to the big Akvaryum Yacht Club restaurant, has beds for US$4. The *Başçavuşun Yeri* (☎ (252) 456 2365), next to Sergeant's Restaurant and near the Atatürk bust, charges marginally more.

The pensions along the shore from the Atatürk bust are quieter, and have better sea views. First along the shore is the well-kept *Yılmaz Pension* (☎ (252) 456 2167), with nice views, priced at US$4 per person without bath. Just beyond it is the welcoming *Nail Pension* (nah-YEEL; ☎ (252) 456 2134), similar to the Yılmaz down to the chairs and tables on its porch from where you can enjoy views of the bay.

There are several more pensions along this beach, and finally the *Motel Pembe Yunus* (☎ (252) 456 2154), 250m beyond the *ilkokul*. Though not much fancier than a pension, the Pembe Yunus (Pink Dolphin) has a roof terrace for sunning and dining, and the inimitable Ms Fatma Doğanyılmaz as a manager. Fatma Hanım will rent you one of her clean but basic, shower-equipped rooms for US$10/18 a single/double, breakfast and dinner included.

Places to Eat Of the restaurants, *Sergeant's Restaurant*, next to the Atatürk bust, is among the cheapest, though *Kayika* and *Roguish Osman's Place* on the main promenade are more popular. Classiest is the upper-storey terrace restaurant of the *Akvaryum Yacht Club*. Meals for around US$5 are available at all of these places.

Getting There & Away Minibuses leave Bozburun for Marmaris (US$3) at 6.30 and 11 am and 12.30 pm. Return trips from Marmaris are in the afternoon, the last being at 7 pm. Services are most frequent in summer. At other times of year day trips from Marmaris can be tricky.

There are also minibuses to Orhaniye from Marmaris, and to Selimiye from Bozburun.

Datça

About 50 km past the Bozburun turn-off is Reşadiye, where a left (south) turn heads for Datça, while the main road continues westward to Knidos.

Orientation Once a small port village, Datça is slowly overflowing onto the surrounding hillsides. The main street, İskele Caddesi, runs downhill from the main road, passing several teahouses, restaurants and the PTT before arriving at the tourist information office and a small roundabout. Immediately before the roundabout, Bruxelles Caddesi on the right has several small pensions.

After the roundabout İskele Caddesi forks left and runs to Turgut Özal Meydanı, the main square with a marketplace and bus station. From there it continues to the harbour, with a cluster of small pensions off on the left, finally running out at the end of a short peninsula, once an island called Esenada. Just after the main square, Kargı Yolu turns right, skirts Taşlık Plajı and climbs up the hill, past the New Castle disco.

Some buses drop you at the otogar on the main road, next to the jandarma post. If that happens, come out onto the main road, turn right and follow the main road round until you see the signs for Şehir Merkezi. It's about a km from the otogar to the main square.

Datça has two small beaches: Kumluk Plajı, tucked away behind the shops on İskele Caddesi, and Taşlik Plajı, running west from the end of the harbour.

Information Datça's Tourism Information Office (☎ (252) 712 3163) is next to the main square and keeps a list of all the accommodation options. It's open daily from May to October but closes at weekends in winter.

Things to See Datça has no specific sights but it's a pretty place to hang around and relax. With its fine yacht-filled harbour, it's a bit like a smaller, quieter version of Marmaris.

In the summer there are daily excursion boats to Knidos and to the Greek island of Simi, with less frequent boats to Kos and Rhodes too.

Datça's nightlife certainly can't match Marmaris' but that's not to say it's dead at night. Apart from the New Castle disco in Kargi Yolu, there are also three very noisy bars at the town end of the harbour and the rather more restrained *Eclipse Bar* at the peninsula end.

Places to Stay – bottom end Datça has about 50 small pensions with a total of perhaps 400 or 500 beds costing around US$3 to US$5. Among the quieter pensions are the *Karaoğlu* (kah-RAH-oh-loo; ☎ (252) 712 3079) and the *Huzur* (☎ (252) 712 3052), both on a bluff above Kumluk Plajı. The Huzur has a pleasantly shady breakfast terrace, the Karaoğlu a garden café. Other quiet places include *Aşkın Pansiyon* (☎ (252) 712 3406) and *Pansiyon Şahin* (☎ (252) 712 3273), both in Bruxelles Caddesi. On İskele Caddesi itself the *Tuna Pansiyon* (☎ (252) 712 3931) has comfortable twin rooms with bath and balcony for US$11. Rooms at the back with sea views are particularly good value.

If you prefer a small hotel to a pension try the *Esenada Oteli* (☎ (252) 712 3579), almost at the end of the main street, out on the peninsula. Though it's next door to the town's only fancy hotel, the Esenada charges only US$8/12 for a double/triple room without running water. If there's no-one at reception, ask in the Çimen Kardeşler clothing shop next door.

The *Deniz Motel* (☎ (252) 712 3038), facing the main square, charges US$13 for a double room with bath and breakfast.

Camping If you walk along Taşlık Plajı on the eastern bay you'll come to Camping Ilıca where camping costs US$3 in high season, less in low. There are also a few wooden bungalows with beds for US$6 and a restaurant and picnic area.

Off the main road to Marmaris, *Surf Camping* (☎ (252) 712 2355) is on a stretch of beach good for windsurfing.

Places to Stay – middle Datça's prettiest hotel, the *Hotel Club Dorya* (☎ (252) 712 3593, fax 712 3303), is in İskele Mahallesi out on the peninsula at the end of the main street, amid lovely gardens. There's a pool at the front and swimming off the rocks at the back. Rooms with bath and perhaps a view cost US$33/$45 a single/double, including breakfast.

At the eastern end of Kumluk Plajı, the Datça *Öğretmen Evi* is a bit of an eyesore but sometimes has pleasant modern rooms with views for US$20 a double.

The three-star *Hotel Mare* (☎ (252) 712 3211), Yanık Harman Mevkii, is a 50-room hotel near the Club Datça. It has comfortable rooms with tiled showers and balconies with sea views for US$33/42 a single/double. It also has a pretty circular swimming pool. The beach is only metres away.

The *Club Datça* (☎ (252) 712 3378), İskele Mahallesi, is a 95-room holiday village. It's pretty pricey at US$53 a double but offers lots of water-sports facilities.

Places to Eat As usual in a harbour town, food prices rise the closer you get to the water. Breakfast, for example, costs less than US$2 in town, rising to nearer US$4 by the harbour.

The harbour is ringed with fish restaurants where you should expect a meal to cost at least US$15. Near the harbour on İskele Caddesi, the *Taraça* and the *Küçük Ev* don't look much from the street, but have nice terraces offering lovely harbour views. On the quayside the *Sunrise Café Bar* offers all sorts of breakfasts, all of them good if none of them cheap. Looking down on the quayside is the very popular and rather cool *Kristina Bistro* which serves pizza, lasagne and chicken curry for moderate prices. Their nonalcoholic fruit cocktails go down a treat too.

Set apart from the other restaurants is the *Yasu Restaurant & Bar* in Kargı Yolu where you can eat chicken in ginger or garlic or beef fillet at taverna-style tables overlooking the harbour. A meal here will cost a good US$10.

On Kumluk Plajı, the *Dutdibi Pide Salonu* is run by friendly people and does good, cheap food with beach views. *Temel Büfe* nearby will do you a filling breakfast for under US$2, while the neighbouring *Example Restaurant* will rustle up something vegetarian if you ask.

İskele Caddesi also has several restaurants where you can eat without worrying about the bill. *Kemal Restaurant* boasts home-cooked dishes including vegetarian options but is closed on Sundays. The *Mandalina Restaurant* is another possibility for a cheap pide supper.

Getting There & Away In summer there are hourly buses to Marmaris during the day (75 km, 1¾ hours, US$3), and you can change there for a bus to other destinations. There are also daily buses to İzmir and Muğla, and overnight services to Ankara and İstanbul.

Boat There are often boat excursions to Datça from Marmaris and sometimes you can buy a one-way ticket.

During the summer months, the Bodrum Ferryboat Association (☎ (252) 316 0882) operates scheduled ferry services between Bodrum and Datça. Ferries leave Bodrum on Saturdays at 9 am, returning from Datça at 5 pm. Tickets are on sale in the office opposite Turgut Özul Meydanı (☎ (252) 712 2143). The ferry actually departs from Körmen, about a 15-minute ride due north of Datça on the peninsula's northern coast but there are *servis* bus connections with the town centre.

Hydrofoils for Bodrum also leave Datça daily, except Sunday in summer, at 12.30 and 6 pm; they leave Bodrum at 11.30 am and 5 pm. Tickets are sold all around Datça but for more information phone ☎ (252) 712 3656. The fare is US$11 one-way or US$16 return; a car costs US$22.

For boats to the Greek islands and Knidos, ask in the harbour.

Knidos

At Knidos, 35 km west of Datça at the very tip of the peninsula, are ruins of a prosperous port city dating from about 400 BC. The Dorians who founded it were smart: the winds change as one rounds the peninsula and ships in ancient times often had to wait at Knidos for good winds...as they sometimes have to today also. This happened to the ship carrying St Paul to Rome for trial.

Being rich, Knidos commissioned the great Praxiteles to make a large cult statue of Aphrodite to go in a circular temple within sight of the sea. The statue, said to be the sculptor's masterpiece, has been lost, though copies or derivative versions exist in museums in Munich, New York and Rome.

The ruins aside, Knidos consists of a tiny jandarma post with a telephone for emergencies, a single restaurant unimaginatively called *Restaurant*, some unpleasant toilets and a repository for artefacts found on the site (no entry). Overnight stays in the village are not allowed, so there are no facilities. You can swim in the bays from wooden piers, but the beaches are several km out of town. The nearest PTT is in Çeşme Köyü, the last village you pass through on the road to Knidos from the village of Palamutbükü where excursion boats often stop for lunch (of the scattering of restaurants here the *Merhaba* along the beach is cheaper than the *Liman* close to where the boats dock).

The Ruins The ruins of Knidos are scattered along the three km at the end of a peninsula occupied only by goat herds and the occasional wild boar. The setting is dramatic: steep hillsides terraced and planted with groves of olive, almond and fruit trees rise above two picture-perfect bays in which a handful of yachts rest at anchor.

Few of the ancient buildings are easily recognisable, but you can certainly appreciate the importance of the town by exploring the site. The guardian will show you around for a small tip. Don't miss the ruins of the temple of Aphrodite and the theatre, the 4th century BC sundial and the fine carvings in what was once a Byzantine church.

Getting There & Away Since there's no dependable minibus service, the trip to Knidos must be made by private car, taxi (about US$45 for a day trip from Datça) or boat. A ferry departs from Datça in summer at 9 am for a day trip to Knidos, returning at 5 pm and charging US$8 per person. At other times of year, ask in the harbour about excursions to Knidos. They also tend to leave around 9 to 9.30 am and return in early evening and cost about US$11 a head.

EASTWARD TO KÖYCEĞİZ

Leaving Marmaris and heading north, the road climbs into mountains with beautiful panoramas and fertile valleys. At the end of that two-km-long double row of eucalyptus trees is a highway junction where you turn right towards Köyceğiz and Fethiye. Along the way are fields of cotton and tobacco, orchards of fruits and nuts, and cool pine forests buzzing with honey bees. At Kadırga and Günlük there are forest picnic areas.

KÖYCEĞİZ

Less than 50 km east of the turn-off from the Muğla-Marmaris road lies quiet, pretty Köyceğiz (population 6500), a small town at the northern end of the large Köyceğiz Gölü, which connects with the Mediterranean Sea via the stream Dalyan Çayı. The main attraction here is the lake itself – broad, beautiful and serene. Except for its small (but growing) tourist trade, Köyceğiz is a farming and fishing town. Among the goods produced here are citrus fruit, olives, honey and cotton. This region is also famous for its liquidambar trees, the sort which produced precious that petrified gum ages ago. The government is now sponsoring large-scale reafforestation projects to replant the hillsides with liquidambar evergreens.

Orientation

The otogar and local hospital are near the highway turn-off. To reach the waterfront, head south past a roundabout and then along tree-lined Atatürk Bulvarı for two km, passing the new precinct with the Belediye, Adliye and Hükümet Konağı on the right.

You'll come to the main square with the inevitable bust of Atatürk and then to a small mosque right by the waterfront. Kordon Boyu, the road skirting the lake, is lined with restaurants and small pensions.

Information

The Tourism Information Office (☎ (252) 262 4703), opposite the mosque on the square's eastern edge, stocks a simple map.

Things to Do

Stroll along the lakeshore promenade past the pleasant town park, an imaginative children's playground, shady tea gardens and several restaurants. If there's not much activity on the lake, you may see the fish jump.

When you get restless you can take a boat excursion from the promenade to the **Sultaniye Kaplıcaları** or thermal baths, 30 km by road or eight nautical miles across the lake on the southern shore. The hot mineral waters are rich in calcium, sulphur, iron, nitrates, potassium and other mineral salts and are said to be good for skin complaints and rheumatism; temperatures sometimes reach 40°C. Admission costs US$0.50, and you should allow an hour if you plan to bathe in the mud, let it dry, and wash it off.

Other than the hot baths, you can take boat trips to Dalyan and the Kaunos ruins, and to bays along the Mediterranean coast. For details see the Dalyan/Kaunos section following.

Bicycles are for rent next to the mosque.

Places to Stay – bottom end

There are a few pensions on Atatürk Bulvarı and around the main square but they won't let you appreciate Köyceğiz's pretty gardens and peacefulness. Continue down to the waterfront and you'll find lots of other possibilities prominently signposted.

Opposite the mosque is the *Çiçek Restaurant & Pension* (☎ (252) 262 3038), an old-fashioned building recently fixed up with white stucco and Ottoman-style lattice window screens and decorated with handicrafts and carved wood. Wooden tables outside allow you to dine in the fresh air. The high-ceilinged rooms are sparsely furnished, but come equipped with anti-mosquito devices. Baths and showers are down the hall, and are primitive but serviceable. Rates are US$6 a head.

If you head east along the waterfront you'll come to several pleasant, quiet pensions. The charming *Sarıkonak* (☎ (252) 262 1030) offers B&B in simple rooms in an old house with a pretty garden facing the lake for US$8 per person. Farther along, the brash new *Kordonboyu Pansion* (☎ (252) 262 3993) has attractive, modern rooms surrounding a pool for just US$6 a head. This place is big enough to handle groups so prices are likely to rise once it gets established.

Cutting inland and following the signs you'll come to the welcoming *Oba* set in more lovely gardens in Gülpınar Mahallesi (☎ (252) 262 4181). It charges US$7 per person which includes use of a kitchen and private car park.

Walking west along the shore you'll come to *Pansiyon Beyaz Konak* (☎ (252) 262 4893), a simple, modern building with double rooms renting for US$15 with shower. Inland a block from the Beyaz Konak (400m west of the main square) is the *Özbek Pension* (☎ (252) 262 2840), set in yet more lovely gardens, with doubles for US$12 in summer. Near here there's also the *Fulya Pansiyon* (☎ (252) 262 2301) charging marginally more.

Camping One km west of the mosque along the shore is *Anatolia Camping* (☎ (252) 262 4750), a forest camping ground among liquidambar trees, with a small beach nearby.

Places to Stay – middle

Turn right at the mosque for the two-star, 32-room *Hotel Özay* (☎ (252) 262 4300), Kordonboyu 11, a pleasant modern place with a small pool in front surrounded by shady vine-covered arbours. Rooms have private showers, small balconies with partial lake views, and cost US$30 for a double in the tourist season, breakfast included.

Farther along in the same direction (west) is the two-star *Hotel Kaunos* (☎ (252) 262 4288, fax 262 4836), Cengiz Topel Caddesi 37, where the 40 rooms have private showers and balconies overlooking the placid lake. In front of the hotel is a pretty terrace where you can relax and enjoy the view. There's a restaurant and bar as well. Rates are US$30 a double, breakfast included.

Even farther west and inland a few blocks is the new *Evceğiz Otel* (☎ (252) 262 2343, fax 262 2342), Ulucami Mahallesi, Ali İhsan Kalmaz Caddesi, which advertises itself as *çok çok ekonomik*. The nice atmosphere, friendly welcome and clean, comfortable rooms make the price, US$12 a double with shower, excellent value.

Places to Eat

As always, the market area has the cheapest eats. Try *Meşhur Ali Baba Pide Salonu*, on the east side of the main park, for good cheap Turkish pizza. The *Nokta Pide Salonu* and the *Penguen Pide Salonu* are nearby.

The lakeshore is lined with pricier outdoor fish restaurants. To the east you could try the *Çinaraltı* while to the west the *Şamdan*, next to the Star Pension, does good fish and grills.

Getting There & Away

Most buses will drop you at the Köyceğiz otogar on the outskirts of town. Unless you fancy a two-km walk to the lake, you'll need to take a dolmuş from there to the smaller central bus station west of the main street behind the Kamil Koç bus company office.

Kamil Koç runs 14 buses daily to Marmaris (75 km, 1½ hours, US$2.75), and 17 to Fethiye (95 km, two hours, US$3). Pamukkale has about a dozen buses to Marmaris, even more to Fethiye. It also offers one daily night bus to İstanbul and one to Ankara. Köyceğiz Minibüs Kooperatifi operates frequent minibuses to Marmaris, Muğla (57 km, one hour, US$2), Ortaca (for Dalyan, 20 km, 25 minutes, US$1), and Dalaman (34 km, 40 minutes, US$1.50).

DALYAN/KAUNOS

Pretty little Dalyan is an increasingly popular holiday destination, especially with Germans. On top of those who choose to stay here, summer afternoons see a positive armada of motorised excursion boats from Marmaris and Fethiye carving a path through the reedbeds of the Dalyan Çayı on their way to the ruins of ancient Kaunos and the beach at İztuzu. Above the river the weathered façades of Lycian rock tombs gaze silently down on all this activity. Fortunately no one has been allowed to slap any high-rise buildings on the riverbank yet, so Dalyan just about hangs on to its charm.

Orientation

It's 13 km from the highway at Ortaca to Dalyan's centre by the mosque and the towering post office building. Minibuses stop just behind the main square where the routine statue of Atatürk is overshadowed by a less routine one of turtles mating.

To the north along the riverbank are the requisite bars and, inland from them, pensions, hotels and restaurants. To the south most of the town's better hotels and pensions are along Maraş Caddesi, which runs for one km south and ends at the riverbank.

Information

Dalyan's Tourism Information Office (☎ (252) 284 4235) is behind the boat cooperative kiosk on the riverbank. It's open Monday to Thursday in summer from 9.30 am to noon and from 2.30 to 6 pm.

There is a Sağlık Ocağı (medical clinic) near the Hotel Dalyan, south of the centre.

Dalyan's postal code is 48840.

Boat Excursions

Every day in summer excursion boats leave the quayside at 10 am to cruise to Köyceğiz Gölü and the Sultaniye hot springs and mud baths, the ruins of Kaunos, and the beach at İztuzu on the Mediterranean coast. Inclusive tickets cost US$5 a head.

If you can organise a small group, it may be more economical to hire an entire passenger boat which holds from eight to 12 people.

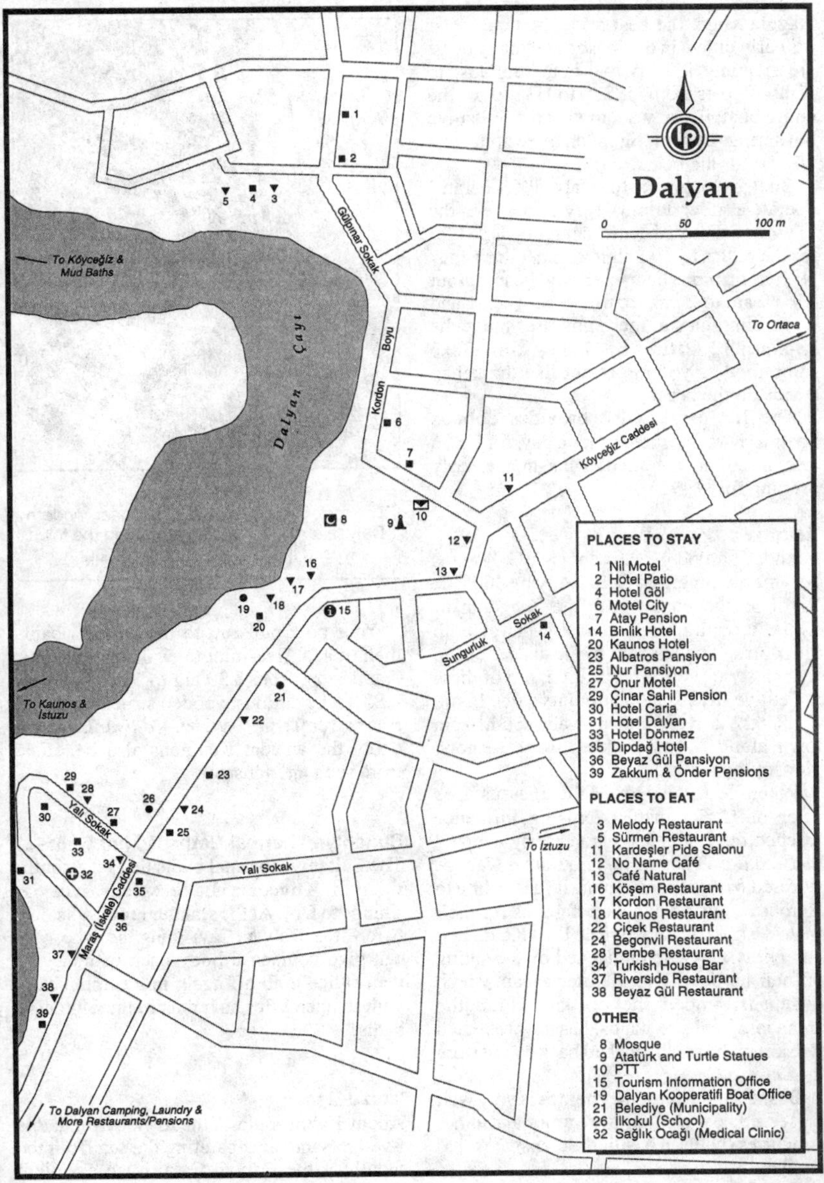

Dalyan

0 50 100 m

To Köyceğiz & Mud Baths
To Ortaca
To Kaunos & Iztuzu
To Iztuzu
To Dalyan Camping, Laundry & More Restaurants/Pensions

Dalyan Çayı
Gülpınar Sokak
Kordon Boyu
Köyceğiz Caddesi
Sungurluk Sokak
Yalı Sokak
Maraş (İskele) Caddesi

PLACES TO STAY

1 Nil Motel
2 Hotel Patio
4 Hotel Göl
6 Motel City
7 Atay Pension
14 Binlik Hotel
20 Kaunos Hotel
23 Albatros Pansiyon
25 Nur Pansiyon
27 Önur Motel
29 Çınar Sahil Pension
30 Hotel Caria
31 Hotel Dalyan
33 Hotel Dönmez
35 Dipdağ Hotel
36 Beyaz Gül Pansiyon
39 Zakkum & Önder Pensions

PLACES TO EAT

3 Melody Restaurant
5 Sürmen Restaurant
11 Kardeşler Pide Salonu
12 No Name Café
13 Café Natural
16 Köşem Restaurant
17 Kordon Restaurant
18 Kaunos Restaurant
22 Çiçek Restaurant
24 Begonvil Restaurant
28 Pembe Restaurant
34 Turkish House Bar
37 Riverside Restaurant
38 Beyaz Gül Restaurant

OTHER

8 Mosque
9 Atatürk and Turtle Statues
10 PTT
15 Tourism Information Office
19 Dalyan Kooperatifi Boat Office
21 Belediye (Municipality)
26 İlkokul (School)
32 Sağlık Ocağı (Medical Clinic)

Haggle to get the best price, particularly if it's early or late in the season and many boats are standing idle. A two-hour tour just to Kaunos costs from US$30 to US$40 for the entire boat; if you want to visit the Sultaniye hot springs as well, figure on three hours and US$50 for the boat.

Boats belonging to the Dalyan Kooperatifi operate a 'river dolmuş' service between the town and İztuzu beach, charging US$1.75 for the return trip. In high summer there may be five or more boats per day, heading out from 9 am to 2 pm, returning between 1 and 6 pm. (In high summer minibuses make the 13-km run to İztuzu by land as well.) Take some food as you might not like the kebap stands on the beach.

The Kooperatif also provides dolmuş boats to Kaunos, three times a day, for US$6 return, and to the mud baths in the early evening for US$2.

The rock-cut tombs at Kaunus, near modern Dalyan, are in Lycian style, though the town was in the ancient kingdom of Caria.

Kaunos

Founded around the 9th century BC, Kaunos became an important Carian city by 400 BC. Right on the border with the Kingdom of Lycia, its culture reflected aspects of both kingdoms. The **tombs**, for instance, are in Lycian style (you'll see many more of them at Fethiye, Kaş and other points east). If you don't take a river cruise, walk south from town along Maraş Caddesi to get a good view of the tombs.

When Mausolus of Halicarnassus was ruler of Caria, his Hellenising influence reached the Kaunians, who eagerly adopted that culture. Though of good size, Kaunos suffered from endemic malaria; according to Herodotus, its people were famous for their yellowish skin and eyes. The Kaunians' prosperity was also threatened by the silting of their harbour. The Mediterranean, which once surrounded the hill on which the archaeological site stands, has now retreated five km to the south, pushed back by silt from the Dalyan Çayı.

Besides the tombs, the **theatre** is very well preserved; parts of an **acropolis** and other structures (baths, a basilica, defensive walls) are nearby.

Your boat pulls up to the western bank, then it's a five-minute walk to the site. Admission, from 8.30 am to 5.30 pm, costs US$1. The curious wooden structures in the river are **fishing weirs** *(dalyanlar)*. No doubt the ancient Kaunians also benefited from such an industry.

Sultaniye Thermal Baths & Mud Baths

The Sultaniye thermal baths lie to the southwest of Köyceğiz Lake (see Köyceğiz, Things to Do). At the smaller mud baths, just before the Dalyan Çayı joins the lake, you can give yourself a body pack of mud and then sluice it all off again in a sulphur pool with temperatures as hot as in the Sultaniye baths.

İztuzu Beach

About 13 km south of the town by road, this five-km sandbar separating the sea from the mouth of the Dalyan Çayı, is an excellent swimming beach with some camping possibilities. A parking fee of US$1 is charged.

The beach is important as one of the last nesting sites in the Mediterranean of the loggerhead turtle. Special rules to protect the turtles are in force and should be respected.

Places to Stay

Once known for its many cheap *ev pansiyonlar* (house pensions), Dalyan is fast repositioning itself upmarket. Rooms are being given plumbing, pensions are being razed to make way for hotels and hotels are acquiring swimming pools. At present, however, there are still good lodgings in all price ranges. Most of the town's accommodation is south of the centre along Maraş Caddesi. The road continues for just over one km before ending at the riverbank, where there are several restaurants and a camping ground.

Places to Stay – bottom end

There are several pensions in the centre, but the ones along Maraş Caddesi to the south are quieter, and some have views of the river and the rock-cut tombs. In general, the farther south you walk, the quieter the pensions become. Prices are generally US$7 per person in waterless rooms, US$9 to US$10 with a private shower. Cheap hotels are usually priced from US$18 to US$22 for a double with shower.

In the town centre, the prominent *Atay Pension* (☎ (252) 284 2639) across from the mosque has a convenient location and rooms on the second and third storeys for US$8 a head, but beware of minaret noise. Round the corner on Kordon Boyu the *Motel City* (☎ (252) 284 3482) comes recommended by readers. It has a roof terrace and public areas decked out in marble and pine with kilims on the walls. Rooms at the back cost US$14,

Turtle Alert

A few years ago Dalyan's İztuzu Beach shot to world fame when a threat to one of the last Mediterranean nesting sites of *Caretta caretta*, the loggerhead turtle, was identified.

The loggerhead turtle (*deniz kaplimbağa* in Turkish) is a large flat-headed reptile, reddish brown on top and yellow-orange below. An adult can weigh up to 130 kg.

Between May and September the female turtles come ashore at night to lay their eggs in the sand. Using their back flippers they scoop out a nest about 40 cm deep, lay between 70 and 120 white ping-pong-ball-like eggs and then cover them over again. If disturbed the females may abandon the nests and return to the sea.

The eggs incubate in the sand for 50 to 65 days and the temperature at which they do so determines the sex of the ensuing young: below 30 degrees celcius all the young will be male; above 30 degrees they will be female. At a steady 30 degrees an even mix of the sexes will hatch out.

As soon as they're born (at night when it's cool and fewer predators are about), the young turtles make their way towards the sea, drawn, it is thought, by the moonlight. If hotels and restaurants are built too close to the beach, their lights can confuse the youngsters, leading them to move up the beach towards danger instead of down it to the sea and safety. So when it was discovered that developers wanted to build a hotel right on the beach there was an outcry which eventually lead to the plans being quashed.

At the same time rules were introduced to protect the turtles. Although the beach is still open to the public during the day, night-time visits are prohibited from May to September. A line of wooden stakes on the beach indicate the nest sites and visitors are asked to sunbathe behind them to avoid disturbing them. It's particularly important not to leave any litter on the beach which could hurt the turtles.

The loggerhead turtle also nests on the beaches at Dalaman, Fethiye, Patara, Kale, Kumluca, Tekirova, Belek, Kızıot, Demirtaş, Gazipaşa and Anamur and in the Göksu delta.

A second larger species of sea turle, *Chelonia mydas*, the hard-shelled green turtle, also nests in Turkey, at Kazanlı, Akyatan and Samandağ, along the east Mediterranean coast. Hunting of these turtles for their flesh (for turtle soup) and eggs has reduced their numbers to danger point. ■

those at the front (with the river views) US$18.

The *Kaunos Hotel* (☎ (252) 284 2057), between the mosque and the river bank, is certainly convenient, but it's well past its prime and the US$19 room tag seems steep for what you get.

There are more simple lodgings to the north of the centre past the Melody and Sürmen restaurants but they have no views to speak of. *Hotel Patio* (☎ (252) 284 2214) is clean and new, as is the *Nil Motel* (☎ (252) 284 2383), charging US$18 a double with shower.

Walking south along Maraş Caddesi, you'll come to the *Albatros Pansiyon* (☎ (252) 284 3287) which has no views and a bar pumping out live music in front. *Nur Pansiyon* (☎ (252) 284 2007), across from the ilkokul (primary school) is similar. The *Aktaş* (☎ (252) 284 2042) is on the water, however, with views of the river and tombs; all rooms have showers. Despite its name, the *Sahil* (shore), (☎ (252) 284 2187), actually has two locations, one on the water and one inland.

Dipdağ Hotel (☎ (252) 284 2401) is near the corner of Maraş Caddesi and Yalı Sokak, a short street running to the river. The spacious rooms have showers, and cost US$33 a double. By the time you read this there should also be a pool. Even so there are newer, nicer places at the same price on the street to the river.

Turn right towards the water at the Dipdağ. Here on Yalı Sokak you'll find the 35-room *Hotel Dönmez* (☎ (252) 284 2107, fax 284 2201). Bath-equipped hotel rooms with ceiling fans cost US$33 a double, and there's a roof terrace with bar and pool. The neighbouring *Hotel Caria* (☎ (252) 284 2075) has big, cool rooms for US$22 a double. Buffet meals can be eaten on a roof terrace with terrific views.

Onur Hotel, down and across the street, is a welcoming family run place with clean rooms for US$14/16 a single/double and an attractive roof bar. Readers have thoroughly enjoyed staying here. At the end of Yalı Sokak on the shore is the pleasant *Çınar Sahil Pension* (☎ (252) 284 2117), with a shady terrace from where you can gaze at the river.

Keep heading south along Maraş Caddesi and you'll pass yet more cheap pensions, including the *Zakkum* and the *Önder* next door to each other and charging US$7 a head. Even farther south, follow the signs to the new *Kilim Pansiyon* (☎ (252) 284 2253), decorated, as you'd expect, with kilims and with some of the biggest rooms in Dalyan for U$22 a double. There's a ramp for wheelchair access too.

Camping Camping sites are being squeezed out by the building boom, but going south along Maraş Caddesi you'll eventually come to *Dalyan Camping*, with just running water and toilets.

Places to Stay – middle

The *Hotel Göl* (☎ (252) 284 2096, fax 284 2555) is squeezed in between the Melody and Sürmen restaurants on the riverbank to the north. There's a pool at the front and the setting is very attractive. Rooms here cost US$20/30 a single/double, and there's one ground-floor room available.

The *Hotel Dalyan* (☎ (252) 284 2239, fax 284 2240) is at the end of Yalı Sokak – go around the corner and it's on the right. Set on a point of land at a bend in the river, an emerald carpet of lawn surrounds comfortable, modern facilities priced at US$88 a double, breakfast included. There are only 20 rooms and it's often filled by German tour groups, so reserve ahead if you can.

In Sungurluk Sokak, down from the Belediye, is the three-star *Hotel Binlik* (☎ (252) 284 2148, fax 284 2149) with comfortable air-con rooms set around two pools. Singles cost from US$40 to US$55, doubles from US$50 to US$65 depending on season.

About one km north of the centre in the midst of farmers' fields is the three-star, 42-room *Antik Hotel* (☎ (252) 284 2136, fax 284 2138), a modern place with rooms grouped around a nice swimming pool. It's an obvious choice for those with their own transport, charging US$35 for a double, breakfast included.

Places to Stay – top end

Dalyan now has one four-star hotel, the *Asur Oteli* (☎ (252) 284 3232, fax 284 3244). Although it's a km south of the centre at the end of Maraş Caddesi, this is a superb place, designed as a collection of 32 single-storey octagonal units round a big pool by the award-winning architect Nail Çakırhan. The rooms are quite small, but they all have air-con and come with mini bars, TVs and all mod cons. Prices are high at US$82 to US$114 depending on season, so look to see if any tour operators are offering competitively priced packages before booking.

Places to Eat

Café Natural is in a small kiosk facing the main square and serves döner kebap and toasted sandwiches. Prices are good, just US$4.50 for İskender kebap and a fresh orange juice. The *No Name Café* nearby looks as if it should be expensive but isn't. Pizzas here cost about US$5. Turn down Köyceğiz Caddesi for the *Kardeşler Pide Salonu* for even cheaper food.

The big open-air *Çiçek Restaurant*, on Maraş Caddesi, south of the centre, is dependably good and cheap for everything from breakfast to full evening meals. Farther down, the *Beyaz Gül* does outdoor grills on the riverbank. Opposite is the *Han Bar* where you can eat gözleme and mantı, Turkish versions of crêpes and ravioli respectively. Keep going right down the road and you'll come to the pleasant *Caretta Caretta Restaurant*, also on the riverbank, where you can sample octopus salad for US$4.50 as well as mullet, bream or whatever has been the catch of the day.

Facing a terrace leading down to the river at the centre of town are three nice semi-open-air restaurants: the *Köşem Restaurant, Kordon Restaurant* and *Kaunos Restaurant.* The prices and situations are nearly identical, with breakfast priced at under US$2, meat-based meals for US$5 to US$8, fish for slightly more.

North of the centre, try the *Sürmen* and *Melody*, both of which have excellent views of the river and town from their riverbank locations. A full fish dinner costs from US$10 to US$12.

The *Denizatı*, Dalyan's longest-lived restaurant, specialising in fish, has moved farther along the river. *Servis* boats from the quayside will take you there.

For atmospheric drinking duck into the small Turkish house opposite the Dipdağ Hotel. Here you can drink in a shady garden in summer or by an open fire in winter.

Getting There & Away

Every day in summer minibuses leave Dalyan at 10 and 11 am for Marmaris, Muğla and Fethiye and at 10 am for Göcek. Otherwise you usually need to take a minibus to Ortaca (US$0.30) and change to another bus there. The minibuses leave Dalyan and Ortaca every 15 minutes during the day in summer, but the last one to Dalyan is at 7 pm, even earlier in winter.

At Ortaca otogar you can connect with buses to Köyceğiz and Dalaman. You can sometimes catch buses to more distant points at the highway in Ortaca. If not, take a minibus to Dalaman (23 km, 30 minutes, US$0.30) and change there.

Getting Around

Mountain bikes and motorbikes can be rented from Kaunos Moto opposite the post office (PTT Karşişi, ☎ (252) 284 2816), or from Akhan in Maraş Caddesi (☎ (252) 284 3802). Expect to pay about US$7 a day for a bike, US$50 for a motorbike.

DALAMAN

This agricultural town (population 16,500) was quite dozy until the regional airport was built on the neighbouring river delta. Now it stirs whenever a jet arrives, before slumping back to sleep again as in the past. Most visitors pass straight through, and bus connections are good. If you need to stay the night, Dalaman has a reasonable selection of hotels.

Orientation

It's 5.5 km from the airport to the town, and another 5.5 km from the town to the east-west highway. The road connecting the highway with the airport is called Kenan Evren Bulvarı. A large mosque marks its junction with the town's main street, Atatürk Caddesi. Atatürk Caddesi is about 500m long, running east from Kenan Evren Bulvarı, with banks, shops and simple restaurants. The bus station, served by the Pamukkale, Aydın and Köseoğlu companies, is near the junction of Evren Bulvarı and Atatürk Caddesi. The PTT is a block north on Atatürk Caddesi.

Places to Stay

The well kept *Otel Hafızoğlu* (☎ (252) 692 5078), on Meltem Sokak, one block south of the bus station across Atatürk Caddesi, charges US$17/27/31 a single/double/triple for its standard one-star rooms with bath.

Most of the other places to stay are spread out along Kenan Evren Bulvarı which doesn't get enough traffic to be very noisy.

The cheapest choice is the *Dalaman Pansiyon* (☎ (252) 692 5543), 200m south of the traffic roundabout near the bus station, where a double room with bath costs US$11 without bath and US$13 with.

The two-star *Hotel Meltem* (☎ (252) 692 2901), farther down on the same side of the road, has 28 rooms with bath, a restaurant and bar, and charges US$22/27 a single/double.

Staying on the same side of the road, the *Airport Hotel Sevilen* (☎ (252) 692 2451, fax 692 2452) is just a bit farther south towards the airport. Its 39 rooms with private shower and air-con cost US$40 a double, breakfast included.

Across the road is the best place in town, the new *Hotel Dalaman Park* (☎ (252) 692 3156, fax 692 3332), with restaurant, bar, lifts, and a huge swimming pool. Impressive though it is, this is hardly the most atmospheric place to stay, so the prices (US$65/85) seem ridiculously optimistic. Still, if you're after comfort to recover from a late-night flight...

You can also camp in the shade of fragrant pines in the *Belediye Koru Parkı* (Municipal Forest Park), 300m north of the otogar along Kenan Evren Bulvarı.

Getting There & Away

In summer, several bus companies pick up passengers from immediately outside the airport. At other times you may need to get a taxi into Dalaman for around US$7 to US$9.

At Dalaman's small otogar you can buy tickets to many destinations. All routes north and east pass through either Muğla or Fethiye. Details of some services follow:

Antalya – 345 km, seven hours, US$9 (coastal route)
Bodrum – 201 km, 3½ hours, US$9
Denizli – 221 km, four hours, US$7
Fethiye – 50 km, one hour, US$2
Göcek – 23 km, 30 minutes, US$1
Gökova – 80 km, 1½ hours, US$2
İstanbul – 966 km, 16 hours, US$24
İzmir – 356 km, six hours, US$10
Kalkan – 131 km, three hours, US$6
Kaş – 160 km, 3½ hours, US$7
Köyceğiz – 34 km, 40 minutes, US$1.50
Marmaris – 120 km, 2½ to three hours, US$3
Muğla – 91 km, 1½ hours, US$2
Pamukkale – 240 km, 4½ hours, US$8 (take the cheaper bus to Denizli, then a cheap city bus or minibus)
Selçuk – 285 km, 5¼ hours, US$9

DALAMAN TO FETHİYE

The highway east of Dalaman winds through mountains cloaked in fragrant evergreen forests, also with many liquidambar trees, before reaching Fethiye 50 km to the south-east. The bends make the road slow to drive on but the beauty of the scenery helps make up for that. In places work to straighten out the bends is in progress.

Göcek

About 23 km east of Dalaman a road on the right (south) turns off to Göcek, a delightful village on a bay at the foot of the mountains. Yachts stop in the harbour and fishing boats ply their trade. Near the village is a wharf from which chromium ore and forest products are shipped out.

Orientation Buses drop you at a petrol station on the main road then it's a one km walk to the centre. Minibuses drive right down to beside the main square with the inevitable bust of Atatürk and a collection of small restaurants, laundries and a PTT with money-changing facilities. The square aside, Göcek mainly consists of the road running alongside the harbour which is lined with restaurants and pensions.

Things to Do Göcek is really a place for relaxing. There's only a fairly scrubby beach at the west end of the quayside, although you can take a '12 Island Cruise' to beaches on nearby islands. The Göcek Club Marina boasts a Turkish bath of the modern variety which you can use for US$13.

There are some excellent places to shop for souvenirs, including Bazaar Anatolia (☎ (252) 645 1768) which sells glorious brightly coloured wall hangings, belts and bedcovers imported from Türkmenistan. These are collector's items and priced accordingly.

Places to Stay In general beds cost US$6 a head in sparsely furnished but clean rooms, usually with shower. At the west end of the harbour the *Başask Pansiyon* has connecting rooms with four beds for US$22, ideal for families. The *Pınar* is fairly new and clean, with lovely views from its terrace. The neighbouring *Çelik* and the *Taştepe* farther to the east are even simpler. Because the pensions are mixed in with the bars your nights may not be as quiet as you'd expect though.

Boats ferry campers out to *Park Wall Bay Camping* which has some tents already in place. There you can windsurf and water-ski or visit nearby Lycian, Roman and Byzantine ruins.

In the hills above Göcek accommodation with a difference is provided at *Huzur Vadisi*, a settlement of felt *yurts* (nomadic tents). Phone ☎ (252) 645 2429 for more details.

Places to Eat Göcek has plenty of places to eat along the waterfront but some of them cater for the yachting fraternity and are quite pricey. The *Blue Bar & Restaurant* does fish kebaps for US$9 and a plate of mixed mezes for six people for US$15. The *Nanai Restaurant-Bar* has meat dishes for about US$10 each. You eat them in cool, trendy surroundings. For something cheaper but less atmospheric, head inland to the main square.

Getting There & Away Dolmuşes from Fethiye run to Göcek several times daily, and frequently on summer weekends. In summer there is also one minibus a day from Dalyan at 10 am. There are also excursion boats from Marmaris, Dalyan and Fethiye.

Küçük Kargı & Katrancı

At Küçük Kargı, 33 km east of Dalaman, a forest picnic area has a camping place and beach. Two km farther east at Katrancı is another picnic and camping spot with a small restaurant, on a beautiful little cove with a beach. It's a farther 18 km to Fethiye.

FETHİYE

Fethiye (FEH-tee-yeh, population 25,000) is a very old town, with few old buildings. An earthquake in 1958 levelled the town, leaving very little standing. Most of what was left were tombs from the time when Fethiye was called Telmessos (400 BC).

Fethiye's inner bay is an excellent natural harbour, protected from storms by the island Şövalye Adası. The much larger outer bay has 11 more islands. Beaches are good here, and even better at nearby Ölüdeniz, one of Turkey's seaside hot spots. The Fethiye region has many interesting sites to explore, including the ghost town of Karmylassos, just over the hill (see Kayaköy, later in this chapter).

Orientation

Fethiye's otogar is two km west of the centre of town, with a separate garage for minibuses one km nearer the centre. Mid-range and top-end hotels are near the centre, but most inexpensive pensions are either east of the centre near the minibus station, or west of the centre overlooking the yacht harbour.

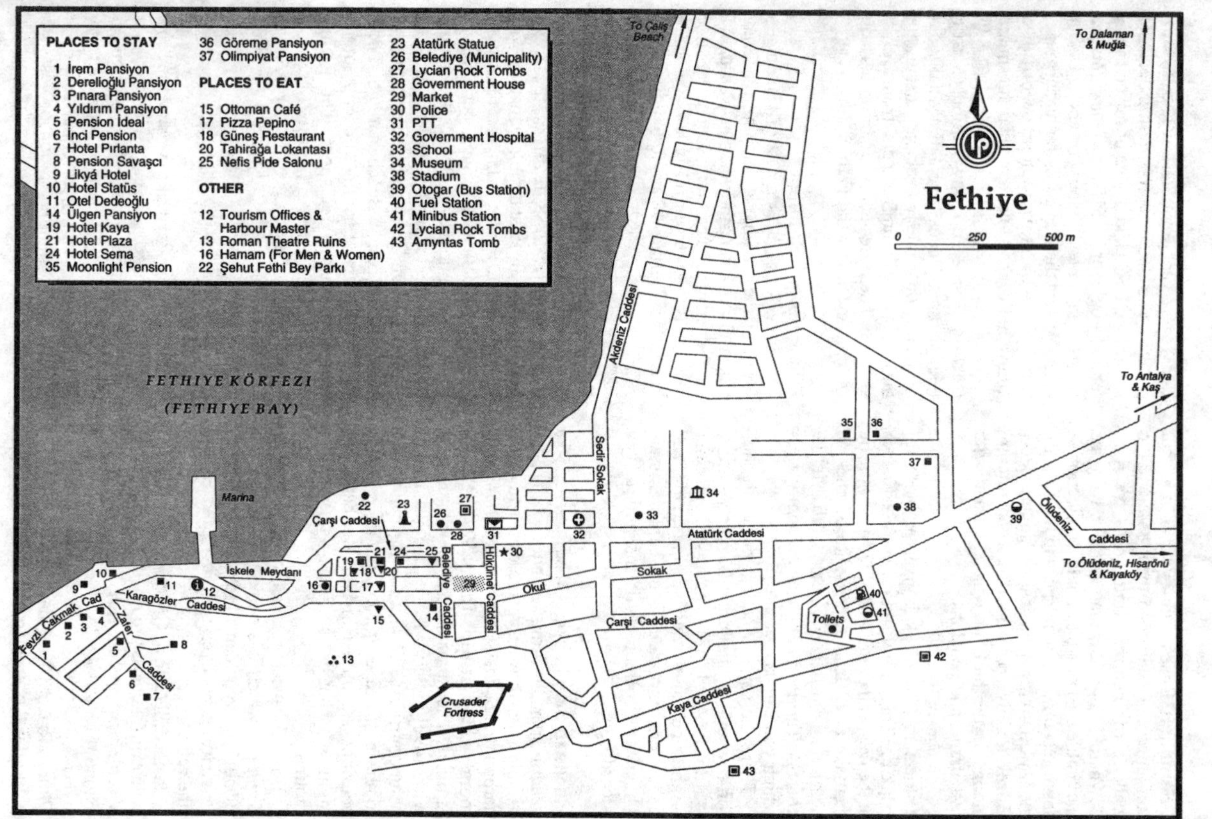
PLACES TO STAY
1 İrem Pansiyon
2 Derelioğlu Pansiyon
3 Pınara Pansiyon
4 Yıldırım Pansiyon
5 Pension İdeal
6 İnci Pension
7 Hotel Pırlanta
8 Pension Savaşçı
9 Likyá Hotel
10 Hotel Statüs
11 Otel Dedeoğlu
14 Ülgen Pansiyon
19 Hotel Kaya
21 Hotel Plaza
24 Hotel Sema
35 Moonlight Pension
36 Göreme Pansiyon
37 Olimpiyat Pansiyon
PLACES TO EAT
15 Ottoman Café
17 Pizza Pepino
18 Güneş Restaurant
20 Tahirağa Lokantası
25 Nefis Pide Salonu
OTHER
12 Tourism Offices & Harbour Master
13 Roman Theatre Ruins
16 Hamam (For Men & Women)
22 Şehut Fethi Bey Parkı
23 Atatürk Statue
26 Belediye (Municipality)
27 Lycian Rock Tombs
28 Government House
29 Market
30 Police
31 PTT
32 Government Hospital
33 School
34 Museum
38 Stadium
39 Otogar (Bus Station)
40 Fuel Station
41 Minibus Station
42 Lycian Rock Tombs
43 Amyntas Tomb
Fethiye
0
250
500 m
To Dalaman & Muğla
To Çalış Beach
To Antalya & Kaş
To Ölüdeniz, Hisarönü & Kayaköy
Ölüdeniz Caddesi
Akdeniz Caddesi
Sedir Sokak
Atatürk Caddesi
Sokak
Çarşı Caddesi
Kaya Caddesi
Okul
Hükümet Caddesi
Belediye Caddesi
Crusader Fortress
Toilets
İskele Meydanı
Karagözler Caddesi
Zafer Caddesi
Fevzi Çakmak Cad
Marina
FETHIYE KÖRFEZI
(FETHIYE BAY)

Dolmuşes run to the centre along Fethiye's main street, Atatürk Caddesi.

The all-important beach at Ölüdeniz is 15 km south of Fethiye. For full information see the Ölüdeniz section.

Information

Fethiye's otogar is one where you're likely to be hassled, so it's worth knowing that there's a hotel reservation office right there which can help you better than the touts.

Fethiye's Tourism Information Office (☎ (252) 614 1527), open from 8 am to 7 pm daily in summer (from 8 am to 5 pm in winter), is on İskele Meydanı next to the Dedeoğlu Hotel, near the yacht harbour. The staff will help you with lodgings and inexpensive yacht charters. Next door is the office of the Fethiye Turizm Derneği (Fethiye Tourism Association), a local group which can also provide helpful information.

Fethiye's postal code is 48300.

Money There are several banks for changing money along Atatürk Caddesi. Many of the shops here will also change money for you. Additionally, there are several exchange booths. However, some readers have written to say that the rate quoted and what you actually get may not always be the same thing. Beware in particular, places apparently offering much higher rates than their neighbours.

Ancient Telmessos

Throughout the town you will notice curious Lycian stone **sarcophagi** dating from around 450 BC. There's one sarcophagus near the PTT, and others in the middle of streets or in private gardens; the town was built around them. All were broken into by tomb robbers centuries ago, of course.

Carved into the rock face behind the town is the so-called **Tomb of Amyntas** (350 BC), a Doric temple façade carved in the sheer rock face. It's open from 8 am to 7 pm for US$1, and is very crowded at sunset in summer, the most pleasant time to visit. Other smaller tombs are near it, off to the left. Follow the signs from the otogar or take a taxi for a look at the tomb and the fine view of the town and bay.

Behind the harbour as you turn up Liman Caddesi to the Yasmin Bar you'll see the recently excavated remains of a **theatre** dating from Roman times.

On the hillside behind the town, just north of the road to Kayaköy, notice the ruined tower of a **crusader fortress** constructed by the Knights of St John on earlier foundations dating back to perhaps 400 BC.

Fethiye Museum

Fethiye's museum is open from 8.30 am to 5 pm (closed on Monday) and charges US$1 for admission. The most interesting exhibits are some small statues and votive stones (the so-called 'Stelae of Graves' and 'Stelae of Promise') and the trilingual stele (Lycian-Greek-Aramaic) from Letoön, which helped with deciphering the Lycian language. King Kaunos gave money to do some good work in honour of the gods, and the trilingual stele described his benefaction.

Archaeological Sites

You can arrange to take a boat or minibus tour to some of the archaeological sites and beaches along the nearby coasts. Standard tours are those which go west to Günlük (Küçük Kargı), Pınarbaşı, Dalyan and Kaunos, and east to Letoön, Kalkan, Kaş, Patara and Xanthos. See those sections for details on the sites and bear in mind that it will often be cheaper just to take a minibus direct to the site.

Beaches

Five km north-east of the centre is **Çalış**, a wide swath of beach several km long solidly lined with uninspiring hotels and pensions. Once very popular, it's now overshadowed by nearby Ölüdeniz (see later). If you want to stay for more than a day or so, it will almost certainly be cheaper to book through a European tour operator. Dolmuşes depart for Çalış from the minibus garage throughout the day.

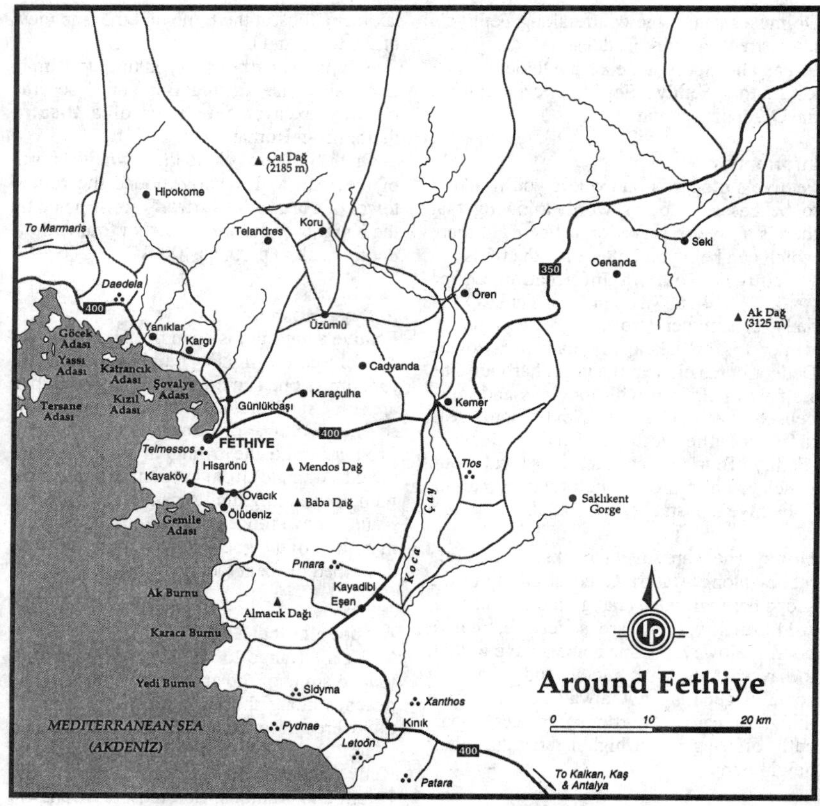

12-Island Cruise

Be sure to sign up for the 12-island tour, a boat trip around Fethiye Bay which takes most of a day (from 9 am to 6 or 7 pm) and costs between US$6 and US$8 per person. Any hotel or travel agency can sign you up, or ask around at the harbour.

A normal tour visits **Şövalye Adası**, an island at the mouth of the inner bay, with a beach and restaurant; **Gemile**, with the unrestored ruins of an ancient city; **Katrancı**, offshore from the beach of the same name to the west of Fethiye; **Göcek**, opposite the town 27 km west of Fethiye; and the **islands** named Kızılada, Tersane, Domuz, Yassıcalar, Delikli, Şeytanlı, and Karacaören.

Scuba Diving

European Divers, a scuba-diving company founded by two Welshmen, offers day trips for US$55, including two dives and lunch. The diving is well organised and visibility is excellent, though the seabed is somewhat littered and overfishing (and dynamite fishing) has robbed the area of much of its marine life. If you don't have a diver's certificate, you can take a certification course for US$300. Other Fethiye dive companies include the Fethiye Diving Centre and Divers' Delight on Fevzi Çakmak Caddesi.

Places to Stay

Fethiye has a good selection of budget and mid-range lodgings, but little in the way of luxury. Most of the better places are block-booked by European tour operators in summer and you may well get a better deal by buying a package rather than trying to book for yourself.

Places to Stay – bottom end

Fethiye has several dozen small, downtown hotels and almost 100 small pensions so you're sure to find suitable cheap lodgings. Pension owners with vacant rooms await your bus at the otogar.

East of the Centre There's a cluster of pensions near the stadium. To find them walk straight down the road heading north from the minibus station.

Near the stadium, *Göreme Pansiyon* (☎ (252) 614 6944), Dolgu Sahası, Stadyum Yanı 25, is run by the friendly, helpful Mrs Duvarcı who lived in London for a while and speaks English. B&B in spotless rooms costs US$10/16 a single/double. In 1996 Mrs Duvarcı will be adding some cheaper dormitory beds as well.

Across the road from the Göreme is the similar *Moonlight Pension* (☎ (252) 614 2178) where clean, simple rooms with balcony cost US$7.50 a head.

Turn right and follow the signs for the *Olimpiyat Pansiyon* (☎ (252) 614 3444), Stadyum Yanı, Yergüz Caddesi 48, which is run by Mr Osman Toklu and has big, clean rooms for US$14 a double, breakfast included.

West of the Centre The main concentration of pensions near the centre is west of the Tourism Office, up the hill behind the Likya Hotel in the district called 1. Karagözler Mahallesi: look for the 'pansiyon' signs. Some places provide rooms with shower, but most rooms are waterless and cost from US$7 to US$9 per person; breakfast usually costs another US$1. Most of these pensions close in winter.

Walking along Fevzi Çakmak Caddesi, you'll come to the *Yıldırım* (☎ (252) 614 3913); the *Pınara* (☎ (252) 614 2151); *Derelioğlu* (☎ (252) 614 5983); and *İrem* (☎ (252) 614 3985).

Up the steep hill behind these places on Zafer Caddesi (follow signs for the Hotel Pırlanta) are several excellent choices, including the *Pension İdeal* (☎ (252) 614 1981), Zafer Caddesi 1, with a fine terrace overlooking the bay. All rooms have showers and cost US$12/18 a single/double in season, breakfast included.

Farther uphill on the right is the friendly *İnci Pension* (☎ (252) 614 3325), with clean, shower-equipped rooms for US$10/14 a single/double. On the left, follow signs to the *Pension Savaşcı* (☎ (252) 614 6681) which charges US$15/24 for rooms with spectacular harbour views.

The Centre If you want a simple, central hotel try the *Hotel Kaya* (KAH-yah) (☎ (252) 614 2469), Cumhuriyet Caddesi 6, next to the Güneş Restaurant a block inland from the main road on a narrow market street. Graced with a wonderful jasmine vine on its façade, the Kaya charges US$7 for a bed in a simple room with private shower. Expect a bit of noise though.

The *Ülgen Pansiyon* (☎ (252) 614 3491), up a flight of steps off Çarşı Caddesi, is a good central pension. Convenient to everything in the centre, it also offers fine views, and charges only US$7/12 in friendly surroundings.

Places to Stay – middle

The rather forlorn two-star *Otel Dedeoğlu* (☎ (252) 614 4010, fax 614 1707), İskele Meydanı, next to the Tourism Information Office, has 41 rooms with sea views and private bathrooms priced at US$13/26, breakfast included. The roof terrace is its best feature.

In town at the intersection of Çarşı and Atatürk Caddesis stands the *Hotel Sema* (☎ (252) 614 1015, fax 614 1015) with beds for US$9 a head. To judge from the exterior, you could be forgiven for thinking it had closed. Much perkier is the new *Hotel Plaza* (☎ (252) 614 9030, fax 614 1070) across the road which charges US$16/22.

Near the yacht marina is the 40-room *Hotel Likya* (☎ (252) 614 2233, fax 614 3100), 1. Karagözler Mahallesi. Its older rooms open onto the sea and Fethiye's most pleasant gardens, and cost US$44/61/92 for singles/doubles/triples, breakfast included. The Likya has a swimming pool and a Chinese restaurant.

The two star, 27-room *Hotel Statüs* (☎ (252) 614 1068), near the Hotel Likya and the pensions on Fevzi Çakmak Caddesi, offers good views across the marina and bay, but the rooms with the best views may suffer from noise from the disco below. Rooms cost US$18/22.

The nominally four-star *Hotel Pırlanta* (☎ (252) 614 4959, fax 614 1686), 1. Karagözler Mevkii, is up the hill from the Hotel Likya. Many of its 72 rooms with bathrooms and balconies have wonderful water views. Rates are US$33/55.

Places to Eat

There's no shortage of places to eat in Fethiye but you should always ask prices – at least for the main course, and especially for fish – before you order. If you haven't ordered something don't let waiters put it on your table. If they do, ask *Bedava mı?* (Is it free?) It rarely is. Check your bill carefully for errors too.

Cheap For really cheap fare in Fethiye you must go off the beaten path to where the workers eat – no English menus, no fancy tablecloths. Head east along Atatürk Caddesi, past the PTT, and look for the small *İlhas* and *Ankara* kebap shops. There are also a few cheap places clustered around the minibus station.

Among the least expensive restaurants in the bazaar is the *Tahirağa Lokantası* on Carşı Caddesi which always has good selections of ready food as well as numerous kebaps; alcohol is served and you could get away with from US$5 to US$7 for a meal. Around the corner on Tütün Sokak is the *Rifat Tuna Lokantası*, which is a bit quieter. Also nearby is *Nefis Pide Salonu* which serves cheap pide, and more: soup, şiş kebap, bread and a soft drink only costs about US$3.

Near the steps leading up to the Ülgen Pansiyon is *Pizza Pepino* which serves tasty pizzas under a shady vine for reasonable prices; a good vegetarian pizza costs US$6. A pond separates it from the *Paspartur Pool Café* which also does pizzas on a menu featuring standards like köfte for US$4. While you eat you can watch the ducks who live in the pond and who boast such shockingly un-Turkish names as Lady Diana, Mike and Arnold Schwarzenegger.

More expensive At the heart of the bazaar area – and gradually taking it over, it seems – is the *Güneş Restaurant*, partly outdoors, partly indoors and popular with tour groups because of its size. There's a good range of meat and fish dishes and cold starters here, and prices aren't bad either (chicken kebap for US$5, for example), but service can be slow.

For atmosphere, try the *Yacht Restaurant*, facing the yacht harbour right by the Hotel Likya. The outdoor tables are very pleasant, the service polite, and the food quite good. A fish dinner might cost about US$12, drinks included. Turkish music and dancing might come as a free extra. Another good choice is the *Rafet Restaurant* on the waterfront.

The *Happy Chinese Restaurant* at the Hotel Likya makes a pleasant change, with tables set out by the water. Expect to spend about US$15 per person for good, if not absolutely authentic, Chinese cuisine.

Places to Drink

Up above the harbour Liman Caddesi boasts several bars. Towards the end of the street an old house has been converted into the *Yasmin Bar* with idiosyncratic 'classical' decoration and an odd mix of music...everything from opera to contemporary pop. This has found favour with readers of this guide although locals prefer the *Yes Bar* in Cumhuriyet Caddesi in the bazaar.

Immediately opposite Pizza Pepino in the bazaar is the *Ottoman Café* where you can get coffee (and a water pipe) in an attractively decorated old house with dervish music crooning in the background.

Getting There & Away

Bus The mountains behind Fethiye force transport to go east or west and for many destinations you must change at Antalya or Muğla. There are, however, buses eastward along the coast at least every two hours in summer. Bus fares along this stretch of coast tend to be higher than usual as the passengers are mostly tourists. The highways in this region are being improved, with new routings, wider curves and more gentle grades. These improvements shorten highway distances and decrease travel times.

The otogar, two km east of the centre, handles services to main destinations like İstanbul, Ankara, Antalya and Alanya. Another garage closer to the centre handles the minibus traffic to intermediate-distance destinations like Kaş and Kalkan.

Some approximate times and distances include:

Antalya – 295 km, seven hours, US$12 *(sahil,* 'coastal route'); 222 km, 4½ hours, US$8 *(yayla,* 'inland route')
Dalaman – 50 km, one hour, US$2
Demre – 155 km, 3½ hours, US$5
Denizli – 290 km, 5½ hours, US$8
Kalkan – 81 km, two hours, US$2.75
Kaş – 110 km, 2½ hours, US$3
Letoön – 60 km, 1½ hours, US$2
Marmaris – 170 km, four hours, US$6.50
Muğla – 150 km, three hours, US$6
Ölüdeniz – 15 km, 25 minutes, US$1
Pamukkale – 309 km, six hours, US$10
Patara – 75 km, two hours, US$2.75
Pınara – 52 km, one hour, US$1.75
Tlos – 40 km, one hour, US$1.75
Xanthos (Kınık) – 65 km, 1½ hours, US$1.75

Boat In high summer a hydrofoil service operates between Rhodes (Greece) and Fethiye on Tuesdays and Thursdays. A one-way ticket costs US$47, a day return US$71 and an open return US$93. Travel agencies in town can book tickets but will need your passport 24 hours in advance.

Getting Around

Minibuses ply the one-way system along Atatürk Caddesi and up Çarşı Caddesi to the otogar all day. There's a fixed charge of US$0.20 however far you go. A taxi from the otogar to the pensions east of the centre will cost more like US$5.

ÖLÜDENİZ

Ölüdeniz (eur-LUR-deh-neez, Dead or 'Calm' Sea) is not dead like its biblical namesake. Rather, it's a very sheltered lagoon completely hidden from the open sea. The scene as you come down from the pine-forested hills used to be absolutely beautiful – in the distance open sea, in the foreground a peaceful lagoon bordered by forest, in the middle a long spit of perfect sandy beach – but has been marred by thoughtless development. This discordant note is struck almost as soon as you leave Fethiye, with huge ugly billboards – at least one of them placed by a British tour operator – obtruding on what would otherwise be lovely views.

Nowadays Ölüdeniz has a reputation for its party atmosphere. Don't come here in August expecting the tranquillity the posters in the tourist offices might imply.

Orientation

As you approach Ölüdeniz, the road passes through the characterless village of Ovacık. Just beyond Ovacık a right turn leads to Hisarönü, little more than a dormitory for the hordes flown in by the package tour operators. The main road descends towards the beautiful swath of beach. Haphazard development begins several km inland from the seashore, and terminates with a jumble of makeshift camping areas and rentable shacks overlooking the free, public, Belcekız Plajı (beach).

The beach is very much the centre of things. To your right, on the road from Fethiye, you pass a jandarma post, a PTT and the entrance to the Ölüdeniz Tabiat Parkı,

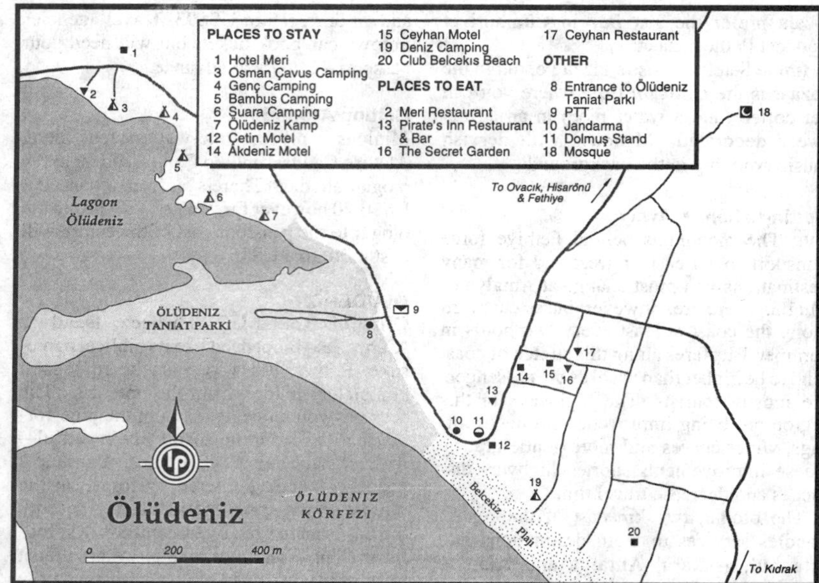

with a pay beach (US$0.50) winding round the lagoon. This stretch has been laid out with paths, showers, toilets and makeshift cafés. The road continues behind the park to several camping grounds and the Hotel Meri high above the lagoon.

To your left as you arrive the beach promenade is closed to traffic and backed with restaurants and 'camps' with small cabins, usually full in high season. Behind these cabin camps sprawl an ever-growing number of small and not so small hotels.

At the east end of the beach the road climbs up a slope and clings to the mountainside for two km before descending to Kıdrak Orman Parkı (Kıdrak Forest Park), with the most beautiful camping facilities of all.

Things to See & Do

Explorations of the coast and Butterfly Valley, as well as watersports and paragliding are amongst the things to see and do.

Excursions Throughout the summer excursion boats set out to explore the coast, charging roughly US$11 for a day trip including lunch. A typical excursion might take in Gemile Beach, the Blue Cave, Butterfly Valley and St Nicholas Island, with time for swimming as well. Some readers have not thought this trip good value for money. If you want to snorkel, ask how much equipment will be available before booking.

Butterfly Valley Although you can get to Butterfly Valley, home of the unique Jersey Tiger butterfly, on a tour, you might prefer to spend the night there, in which case boats leave Ölüdeniz daily at 11 am and 2 and 6 pm, charging US$10 return. Once there, you can spend the night in a treehouse platform, where beds cost US$3 a head, and eat at the beach café. Alternatively a path winds up a cliff to a house where better food is available. Unfortunately this path is treacherous. Someone was killed in a fall in 1992, and someone else was badly hurt by a stone dislodged from on high by a goat.

Sports You can rent water-sports equipment on the main beach. Several agencies offer tandem paragliding flights from a 1900m cliff for US$100 a thrill. Parasailing comes much cheaper at a mere US$35 a time.

Places to Stay – bottom end

These days Ölüdeniz is so much package-holiday territory that those on a tight budget will be scrabbling around to find somewhere suitable. Fortunately there are plenty of campsites, most of them offering fixed tents and cabins for those who don't want the trouble of carting the equipment around with them.

Pensions & Hotels Most of Ölüdeniz's hotels have their sights firmly fixed on package holiday-makers but there are one or two smaller places as well. The *Ceyhan Motel* (☎ (252) 616 6027), two blocks back from the beach, has beds for US$9 a head in a pretty bougainvillea-draped building with a garden restaurant immediately opposite. The *Çetin Motel* (☎ (252) 616 6393), closer to the beach, is pricier at US$22 a double but has camping facilities for much less.

If you can't find anything in your price range near the beaches, head back two km up the access road to the junction with Hisarönü. On the right-hand side of the road are a cluster of traditional, family run pensions – the *Mutlu*, the *Demet* and the *Üstün* – where beds will be more affordable. The *Üstün* is newest and furthest from the road, so likely to be quietest. At first sight Hisarönü looks even less likely to turn up any cheap beds than Ölüdeniz itself. However, look out for the *Ata*, *Hermes* and *Herodot* pensions and you may be lucky.

A reader also recommended the *Favalya Pension* up in the hills; during the summer the owners send a minibus down to the Çetin Bar in Ölüdeniz every evening at 6 pm to pick guests up. They're dropped back again in the morning at 9.30 am.

Camping Ölüdeniz's camp sites are very popular (sometimes too popular) places to stay in the summer. Those behind Belcekız Plajı are likely to be noisier than those around the lagoon.

The road to the Hotel Meri winds past five camping areas: *Ölüdeniz Kamp* (☎ (252) 616 6024), *Suara* (☎ (252) 616 6100), *Bambus* (☎ (252) 616 6988), *Genç Camping* (☎ (252) 616 6047) and *Osman Çavuş Camping*. Most of these places have a few fixed tents, sites for your own tent and small wooden cabins. Most also have restaurants; the menu at the Bambus is particularly impressive. Expect to pay about US$5 for a tent for two (US$7 if it's a site tent) and from US$9 for a cabin.

Beyond Belcekız Plajı one of the most popular camping areas is *Deniz Camping* (☎ (252) 616 6012) which has a big restaurant, a book exchange and the popular Buzz's Bar.

Places to Stay – middle

At the end of the road winding round the lagoon stands the two-star *Hotel Meri* (☎ (252) 616 6060, fax 616 6456), with 75 rooms tumbling down the hillside amid pretty gardens. The views from many of the rooms, especially those at the top, are magnificent. A major refit should see a lift installed and all the rooms fitted with air-con, fridges and satellite TV for the 1996 season. Rooms cost US$65/90/120 a single/double/triple with half-board. The hotel has its own beach and seaside restaurant.

At the far end of Belcekız Plajı there's an even flashier place, the *Club Belcekız Beach* (☎ (252) 616 6009, fax 616 6448) whose Mexican-pueblo design will no doubt displease as many people as it delights. Rooms here have cool tiled floors, modern decor and fabrics, pleasant bathrooms and small terraces. There's a huge pool, a Turkish bath and several dining areas. Rooms here don't come cheap, at US$66 a double (virtually the same for single occupancy), but you might get a better deal through a tour operator.

Places to Eat

The *Çetin* and *Deniz* restaurants, facing Belcekız beach, seem to be the most popular places to eat out, but they are interspersed with lots of snack places where you can eat more cheaply. You can also save a bit of money by walking inland along the access road to the *Pirate's Inn Restaurant & Bar* which, because it is 100m from the beach, has lower prices.

Just back from the beach next door to the Ceyhan Motel is *The Secret Garden*, a pleasant restaurant hidden away in dense foliage. Meals may not be particularly cheap here but they will be enjoyable.

Getting There & Away

In summer minibuses leave Fethiye for Ölüdeniz roughly every 15 minutes. Some of them also drop off in Hisarönü.

Kayaköy (Karmylassos)

Called Levissi for much of its history, this town of 2000 stone houses just beyond Hisarönü was deserted by its mostly Ottoman Greek inhabitants after WW I and the Turkish War of Independence. The League of Nations supervised an exchange of populations between Turkey and Greece, with most Greek Muslims coming from Greece to Turkey, and most Ottoman Christians moving to Greece. The people of Levissi, most of whom were Orthodox Christians, moved to the outskirts of Athens and founded Nea Levissi there.

As there were far more Ottoman Greeks than Greek Muslims, many of the towns vacated by the Ottoman Greeks were left unoccupied after the exchange of populations. Kayaköy, as it is called now, has only a handful of Turkish inhabitants.

With the tourism boom of the 1980s, a development company wanted to restore Kayaköy's stone houses and turn the town into a holiday village. Scenting money, the local inhabitants were delighted, but Turkish artists and architects were alarmed, and saw to it that the Ministry of Culture declared Kayaköy, or Kaya as it's called locally, a historical monument, safe from unregulated development.

There are now plans for careful restoration of the town, and its use as a venue for cultural presentations.

Two churches are still prominent: the Kataponagia in the lower part of the town, and the Taxiarkis farther up the slope. Both retain some of their painted decoration and black and white pebble mosaic floors.

In summer there are hourly minibuses from Fethiye to Kaya (half an hour trip, US$1). Alternatively it's about an hour's walk downhill through pine forest from Hisarönü. It's a steep slope so you might want to get the minibus back up again. There's also a marked trail to Ölüdeniz which should take two to 2½ hours (eight km)...although some readers have taken much longer!

If you want to stay at Kaya (a pleasant and certainly quieter alternative to staying in Hisarönü or Ölüdeniz) there's the *Çavuşoğlu Motel* (☎ (252) 616 6749) with a big swimming pool right where the minibus drops you off. Simple rooms here cost US$18 a double with bath and breakfast.

Following the road on you'll pass the rather isolated *Selçuk Pension* and arrive at the delightful and welcoming *Villa Rhapsody Pension* (☎ (252) 616 6551) where beds in comfortable modern rooms with balconies cost US$27 a head. There's a pool here too, set in a gorgeous garden.

FETHİYE TO KAŞ

This portion of the Lycian coast, sometimes called the Lycian Peninsula because it extends well south into the Mediterranean, is littered with the remains of ancient cities. With your own transport you can visit as many of these as you like by making a few short detours. Without a car you can still make your way to many of them by dolmuş or bus, with perhaps a bit of a hike here and there.

The highways in the Lycian peninsula are rapidly being improved which sometimes means changes in their routings. Keep this in mind as you travel to the sites described below.

Tlos

Tlos was one of the oldest and most important cities in ancient Lycia. Its prominence is matched by its promontory, as the city has a dramatic setting high on a rocky outcrop. As you climb the winding road to Tlos, look for the fortress-topped **acropolis** on the right. What you see is Ottoman-era work, but the Lycians had a fort in the same place. Beneath it, reached by narrow paths, are the familiar **rock-cut tombs**, including that of Bellerophon, a pseudo-temple façade carved into the rock-face which has a fine bas-relief of the hero riding Pegasus, the winged horse. You can reach the tomb by walking along a stream bed, then turning left and climbing a crude ladder.

The **theatre** is 100m farther up the road from the ticket kiosk, and is in excellent condition, with most of its marble seating intact, though the stage wall is gone. There's a fine view of the **acropolis** from here. Off to the right of the theatre (as you sit in the centre rows) is an ancient **Lycian sarcophagus** in a farmer's field. The **necropolis** on the path up to the fortress has many stone sarcophagi.

The site is open daily from 8 am to 5 pm for US$1. One of the men at the ticket kiosk will offer to be your guide (for a tip), which is a good idea if you want to see all the rock-cut tombs.

A meal of trout in garlic sauce, salad, bread and a cold drink will cost you US$6 at the *Café Tlawa Restaurant* opposite the site. Simple rooms are available here in an emergency, or you could try the *Mountain Lodge* or *Cağrı Pension* back down the road to the highway. With your own transport you could press on for another two km to the lovely *Yaka Park Restaurant* (☎ (252) 638 2011), where tables cascade down the hillside, shaded with plane trees and cooled with running water. The bar counter here has a channel cut into it along which trout swim so visitors can tickle them. How much the trout enjoy this experience is open to question, of course.

Getting There & Away The easiest way to get to Tlos is to take a dolmuş from Fethiye to Saklıkent. This passes within 4 km of the site. It would be a stiff walk because the road climbs steadily uphill but you might be able to get a lift or negotiate with the driver to drop you off. This should get easier when the road is tarmacked, supposedly in 1996. Driving, follow the signs to Saklıkent from Kayadibi and watch for the yellow ancient monument sign on the left.

Saklıkent Gorge

Another 12 km after the turn-off to Tlos you will come to the spectacular Saklıkent Gorge cut into the Akdağlar. The gorge is 18 km long and so steep and narrow that the sun doesn't penetrate so the water is icy-cold, even in summer. You approach the gorge along a wooden boardwalk above the river which opens out into a series of wooden platforms where you can buy and eat trout suspended above the water. From there you wade across the river, hanging onto a rope, and then continue into the gorge proper, sometimes walking in mud, sometimes in the water. Plastic shoes can be hired for US$0.50, a worthwhile investment if you're going to get the most out of the walk.

The gorge is open daily from 8 am to 5 pm for US$2. Get there in summer by taking a dolmuş from Fethiye. It takes three-quarters of an hour to get there, past lovely fields of cotton, and costs US$1.50. If there's no direct minibus, take one to Kayadibi and change. Alternatively you can sign up for an excursion from Fethiye, Kaş or Kalkan.

Back on the highway heading south towards Kaş, the road takes you up into fragrant evergreen forests and down into fertile valleys. You'll see herds of sheep and goats (and a few cattle) along the road near the villages. The road is windy and the journey somewhat slow.

Pınara

Some 46 km south-east of Fethiye, near the village of Esen, is a turn-off (to the right) for Pınara, which lies another six km up in the mountains. Infrequent minibuses from Fethiye (one hour, US$1.75) drop you at the start of the Pınara road, and you can walk six km to the site, or bargain with the driver to take you all the way. (Note: the highway is being improved, and may have been rerouted by the time you arrive.)

The road winds through tobacco and cornfields and across irrigation channels for over three km to the village of Minare, then takes a sharp left turn to climb the slope. The last two-plus km are extremely steep and rough, and not all cars can make it. If you decide to walk make sure you stock up on liquids first. There's a café at the foot of the slope and nothing after that.

At the top of the slope is an open parking area, and near it a cool, shady spring with refreshing water. The guardian will probably appear and offer to show you around the ruins, and it's as well to take up the offer as the path around the site (which is always open) is not easy to follow. You should probably tip the guardian if you have a tour.

Pınara was among the most important cities in ancient Lycia but, although the site is vast, the actual ruins are not Turkey's most impressive. Instead it's the sheer splendour of the isolated setting which makes the journey so worthwhile, the new toilet block providing the one jarring note.

The sheer column of rock behind the site, and the rock walls to its left, are honeycombed with **rock-cut tombs**, to reach any of which would take several hours. Other **tombs** are within the ruined city itself. The one called the Royal (or King's) Tomb has particularly fine reliefs, including several showing walled cities. Pınara's **theatre** is in good condition, its **odeum** and **temples** of Apollo, Aphrodite and Athena (with heart-shaped columns) badly ruined.

The village at **Esen**, three km south-east of the Pınara turn-off, has a few basic restaurants.

Sidyma

About four km from Esen, a rough dirt road running off for 12 km to the left leads to Sidyma. The ruins are not spectacular. If you've seen all the other Lycian cities and are simply aching for more, then take the time to visit Sidyma. Otherwise, press onward.

Letoön

Seventeen km south of the Pınara turn-off is the road to Letoön. The turn-off is on the right-hand (south-west) side near the village of Kumluova. (Dolmuşes run from Fethiye via Esen to Kumluova. Get out at the Letoön turn-off.) Turn right off the highway, go 3.2 km to a T-junction, turn left, then right after 100m (this turn-off is easy to miss) and proceed one km to the site through fertile fields and orchards, and past greenhouses full of tomato plants. If you miss the second turn you'll end up on the main square of the village. There are no services as this is still a farming village largely unaffected by tourism.

When you get to the ruins (open daily from 8.30 am to 5 pm), a person selling soft drinks and admission tickets (US$1) will greet you.

Letoön takes its name and importance from a large shrine to Leto, who according to legend was loved by Zeus. Unimpressed, Zeus' wife Hera commanded that Leto spend an eternity wandering from country to country. According to local folklore she spent much of this enforced holiday time in Lycia, becoming the Lycian national deity. The federation of Lycian cities then built this impressive religious sanctuary to worship her.

The site consists of three **temples** side by side: to Apollo (on the left), Artemis (in the middle) and Leto (on the right). The Temple of Apollo has a nice mosaic showing a lyre and a bow and arrow. The **nymphaeum** is permanently flooded (and inhabited by frogs), which is appropriate as worship of Leto was somehow associated with water. Nearby is a large Hellenistic **theatre** in excellent condition.

Xanthos

At Kınık, 63 km from Fethiye, the road crosses a river. Up to the left on a rock outcrop is the ruined city of Xanthos, once the capital and grandest city of Lycia, with a fine **Roman theatre** and **Lycian pillar tombs** with Lycian inscriptions. Dolmuşes run here from Fethiye and Kaş, and some long-distance buses will stop if you ask.

It's a short walk up the hill to the site which can be visited during daylight hours. For all its importance and grandeur, Xanthos had a chequered history of wars and destruction. Several times, when besieged by clearly superior enemy forces, the city was destroyed by its own inhabitants. You'll see the **theatre** at once, with the **agora** opposite. Despite Xanthos's importance, the **acropolis** is now badly ruined. As many of the finest sculptures and inscriptions were carted off to the British Museum in 1842, many of the inscriptions and decorations you see today are copies of the originals. French excavations in the 1950s have made Xanthos well worth seeing, however.

After visiting the main site, cross the road and follow the path behind the toilets for more Lycian tombs in a quiet, pretty setting.

Patara

Heading east again, after seven km you'll reach the turn-off on the right for Patara where the ruins come with a bonus in the form of a wonderful white sand beach some 50m wide and 20 km long.

Patara was the birthplace of St Nicholas, the 4th-century Byzantine bishop who later passed into legend as Santa Claus. Before that, Patara was famous for its temple and oracle of Apollo, of which little remains.

These days Patara attracts a partying crowd, so don't be fooled by its size into thinking you're going to a particularly quiet resort.

Orientation Look for the Patara turn-off just east of the village of Ovaköy; from here it's 3.5 km to the village of Patara and another 1.5 km to the ruins. The beach is another one km past the ruins and some dolmuşes will continue down there. So far, fortunately, the development of hotels, pensions and restaurants has been restricted to the village.

The Ruins Admission to the ruins and beach costs US$1. Patara's ruins include a triple-arched **triumphal gate** at the entrance to the site with a **necropolis** with several **Lycian tombs** nearby. Next are the **baths** and a much later **basilica**.

The good sized **theatre** is striking because it is half-covered by wind-driven sand, which seems intent on making a dune out of it. Climb to the top for a good view of the whole site.

There are also several other **baths**, two **temples** and a **Corinthian temple** by the lake, although the swampy ground may make them difficult to approach. Across the lake is a **granary**. What is now a swamp was once the city's harbour. When it silted up in the Middle Ages, the city declined.

The Beach The beach is simply splendid. You can get there by following the road past the ruins, or by turning right at the Golden Pension and following the track which heads for the sand dunes on the other (western) side of the archaeological zone. It's about a 30-minute walk. Sometimes you can hitch a ride with vehicles passing along the main road.

Be sure to bring footwear for crossing the 50m of scorching sand to the water's edge, and also something for shelter as there are few places to escape the sun. If you don't have your own shelter, rent an umbrella on the beach for US$2.

Behind the beach the *Patara Restaurant* provides shade and sustenance, and there's a wooden shack selling kebaps on the sand. You might prefer to bring a picnic. The beach closes at dusk as it is a nesting ground for sea turtles. Camping is prohibited.

Places to Stay – bottom end Patara has grown quickly and somewhat chaotically in recent years, and now has lodgings in all price ranges.

The best known of the cheap pensions is the *Golden Pension & Restaurant* (☎ (242) 843 5162), right in the village centre, with 15 rooms – six with private shower, nine without – and a restaurant on the roof. The charge for a double room with shower is US$15 in season, slightly less in the off season. The owner, Muzaffer Otlu, speaks some English and French and is very friendly. He also owns the *Hotel Patara Viewpoint* (☎ (242) 843 5022), high up on the hill above the road leading to the ruins. Rooms there are newer and classier and so cost that bit more. On the road leading to the village there are a cluster of newish cheapies: the *Flower*, *Rose* and *Akay*. Longer established pensions here include the *St Nicholas* (☎ (242) 843 5024) and the *Sisyphos* (☎ (242) 843 5043), charging about the same as the Golden.

Turn right into the village and continue up the hill by the *Eucalyptus Pension* (☎ (242) 843 5076) to the *Topaloğlu* (☎ (242) 843 5030) for cheaper beds...around US$11 a double.

Turn right past the PTT for the *Patara Motel*, a newer building with double rooms with shower for US$18 to US$20 in season, almost half-price in the off season. Continue up this road towards the Hotel Beyhan Patara for five more modern 'pensions' (actually small hotels), the *Sülo, Apollon, Zeybek 1, Jet* and *Zeybek 2*, charging US$18 a double, breakfast included. Some rooms have fine views.

Camping In the village, there are several camping grounds which are relocated frequently as construction pushes them from one lot to the next.

Places to Stay – middle Up on the hillside to the left as you enter the village are several hotels and lots of holiday villas. The *Hotel Delfin* (☎ (242) 843 5215) has standard Turkish hotel rooms with shower and balcony, a terrace restaurant and pool. The *Hotel Xanthos* (☎ (242) 844 2124), higher on the hill above the Delfin, also has a swimming pool and tennis court.

Right by the road junction leading to the beach is the *Ekizoğlu Motel* (☎ (242) 843 5045) where basic double rooms with bath and breakfast cost US$16.

Patara's best hotel is the three-star *Hotel Beyhan Patara* (☎ (242) 843 5098, fax 843 5097), high up on the hill to the west of town. The building itself may be a standard ugly block but it's set in pretty gardens, and facilities include a tennis court, hamam, sauna, sundecks, two restaurants, an exercise room, and 132 air-con rooms priced at US$40 for a double, breakfast included. Although this looks a peaceful situation, the hotel has five bars and is popular with tour groups so be sure to specify if you want a quiet room.

Places to Eat Most of the hotels and some of the pensions (including the Golden and the Patara Viewpoint) have restaurants. Others open and close by the month, it seems. The *Florya Restaurant*, near the Golden Pension, has good food and reasonable prices at about US$4 for a full meal – as do the *Maestro* and the *Antalya*. Some village shops sell stale packaged food. The *Patara Market* seems to have the edge on freshness.

Getting There & Away A small airport is being built inland from Patara and Kalkan, and may soon have service by small 'commuter' aircraft.

Dolmuşes run at least five times a day – and in high summer more than a dozen times a day – to Patara from Fethiye and Kaş. They tend to fill up so you should make careful arrangements for getting there and back; buy your tickets in advance to ensure a seat.

If you take a bus, be warned that it may drop you on the main road 3.5 km from Patara village.

In summer there are daily night buses to İstanbul, Ankara and Nevşehir.

KALKAN & KAŞ

Just past Patara are Kalkan and Kaş, two very popular, small, if steadily growing, holiday resorts. Of the two Kalkan has the more upmarket reputation. There you can often stay in attractively designed and decorated buildings but eating out and nightlife options are relatively limited. In Kaş you'll find yourself staying in a modern building of little architectural distinction but there are plenty of good places to eat. Nightlife, especially on the eastern side of town, can be pretty lively in summer. Kaş also boasts some excellent shops where you can buy handicrafts and fabrics from all over Turkey.

In recent years, both resorts have suffered from the tendency of large British tour operators to dump their unsold capacity at bargain prices, landing mass market tourists in places not really suited to their needs. This has had the effect of forcing prices down but has also lead to problems with street drinking etc.

Kalkan

About 11 km east of the Patara turn-off (81 km east of Fethiye, 26 km west of Kaş) the highway skirts Kalkan, a fishing village formerly occupied by Ottoman Greeks and called Kalamaki, but now completely devoted to tourism. Discovered a decade ago by intrepid travellers in search of the simple, cheap, quiet life, this perfect Mediterranean village soon boasted a yacht marina, then some modern hotels, and now a vast holiday village complex (the Hotel Patara Prince and Club Patara) covering an entire hillside to the south.

Since 1989 the Kalkan Foundation (Kalkan Vakfı), an association of public officers and private individuals, has been working to preserve the town's architecture, ambience and environment.

Orientation Kalkan is built on a hillside sloping down to the bay, and you'll find yourself trekking up and down it all day. Coming in from the highway, the road zigzags down to a central parking lot with a taxi rank, bus offices, the PTT and banks. It then enters the main commercial area and descends the hill as Hasan Altan Caddesi or 6 Sokak. The Kalkan Han hotel is one street above on Süleyman Yılmaz Caddesi (or 7 Sokak), though most of the other small hotels and restaurants line the terraces below the shopping area, all the way down to the harbour's edge.

More hotels and pensions can be found straggling out around the east of the bay.

Kalkan doesn't have a tourist information office, although travel agencies about town are very helpful.

Kalkan's postal code is 07960.

Places to Stay – bottom end Although cheap pensions are vanishing in favour of hotels suitable for the package holiday market, there are still quite a few relatively cheap places to stay right in the centre of Kalkan and in prime positions on the waterfront.

On the main shopping street, Mehmet Özalp, proprietor of the *Özalp Pansiyon* (☎ (242) 844 3486), charges US$9/13 for his good, modern rooms with shower and balcony. Some are tiny, others larger. There's a popular restaurant on the ground floor.

The nearby *Çelik Pansiyon* (☎ (242) 844 2126), Yalıboyu 9, more or less across from the Kalkan Han, is a standard simple pension charging US$9/16 a single/double, breakfast included. Continue along the road to the end for the *Holiday Pension* or up the hill across the street for the *Gül Pansiyon* (☎ (242) 844 3099), both more primitive and slightly cheaper.

Farther down towards the harbour, the *Akın Pansiyon* (☎ (242) 844 3025) has some waterless rooms on the top floor priced at US$17 a double; rooms lower down with private showers cost US$22, breakfast included. The *Akgül* (☎ (242) 844 3270) close by is similar.

Çetin Pansiyon (☎ (242) 844 3094), in the southern part of town, is out of the central bustle, quieter, and done in traditional style. Rooms cost US$16 a double. The nearby *Altan Pension* (☎ (242) 844 1044) is similarly charming with vine-covered wooden balconies.

Deren Motel (☎ (242) 844 3256) is a new building a bit out of the way on the hillside north of the centre but the views from its vine-covered terrace are spectacular, and it's quieter here. It's worth the short walk and rooms cost US$12 a double.

Places to Stay – middle Right in the heart of things the *Kalkan Han* (☎ (242) 844 3151), on 7 Sokak, used to be one of the most atmospheric places to stay. Built to resemble an old village house, it was decorated with stone and wood, local handicrafts and Turkish carpets. Unfortunately renovation is taking longer than anticipated, so you should check before showing up. Rates were US$38/55 a single/double, breakfast included.

On the road winding down past the

mosque to the harbour is the *Daphne Pansiyon* (☎ (242) 844 3380), nicely decorated with kilims and carpets, and with good reading lights in the bedrooms. You pay US$16/32 a single/double, including breakfast on a pleasant roof terrace where dinners are sometimes served too.

The *Balıkçı Han* (☎ (242) 844 3075), is another house designed to look like an older building, with stone fireplaces, red-tiled floors, and panels of coloured faïence in the walls. Some rooms have brass beds. Rooms with private shower cost US$27 a double, breakfast included. Keep going along this street right to the east end for *Balıkçı Han 2* (☎ (242) 844 3280), just as nicely decorated but in a quieter position.

Almost hidden beneath its veil of bougainvillea is the *Patara Pansiyon* (☎ (242) 844 3076), a lovely old stone house with views from the roof terrace. Rooms cost US$16/22 a single/double with shower and breakfast.

Out towards the west is *Hotel Diva* on Cumhuriyet Caddesi (☎ (242) 844 3175, fax 844 3139), a small new hotel built to look like an old village house, with vine-covered trellises shading the roof terrace and 17 comfy rooms with bath for US$20 to US$30 a double, breakfast included. The neighbouring 25-room *Hotel Dionysia* (☎ (242) 844 3681), under the same management, is equally comfortable.

The three-star *Hotel Pirat* (☎ (242) 844 3178, fax 844 3183) started out by adding an unwelcome six storeys to the village skyline and has now dumped a Disney vision of Kalkan's old houses around a swimming pool immediately above the harbour. Together these two sections offer 136 comfortable, modern rooms, 50 of them air-con, for US$45/63 a single/double, breakfast included. Service here is reputed to be exceptionally good.

There are several other good hotels in town, including the stylish *Oasis* (☎ (242) 844 3215), out to the west on Cumhuriyet Caddesi, with rooms for US$44/55 a single/double around a plant-filled atrium. Cut off from the rest of Kalkan (and not linked to it by public transport; take a taxi) are the three-star *Club Patara* (☎ (242) 844 3210) on the hillside to the south and the neighbouring architecturally splendid five-star *Patara Prince* (☎ (242) 844 3338, fax 844 3337). The latter in particular is thoroughly swish and snooty. Don't venture near it if you're not in the Porsche class.

Places to Eat Smaller than Kaş, Kalkan has fewer eating places to choose from and those it does have can be pricey because of their yachting clientele. However, choose carefully and you can still have a pleasant and not overly expensive meal.

In the commercial district at the top of the town, the *Smile Restaurant* is still relatively cheap, with meals for US$4 to US$6. The *Merkez Café* can also run you up snacky meals and delicious fruit juices without requiring a second mortgage. The *Köşk* in the town centre, on the other hand, has become more expensive, although it does offer fine views from its terrace seating area.

Farther south along Hasan Altan Caddesi (6 Sokak) from the Köşk, the *Alternatif Restaurant*, on an upper-storey terrace, offers tempting meals like tuna pasta, steak pie and broccoli mornay but a full meal could well cost US$10.

For food in a 'Turkish' setting, with tables at floor level and lots of kilims, head for *Belgin's Kitchen* where you can sample traditional dishes like mantı and çiğ börek (a filled pastry tube). The quality of the food doesn't always live up to the promise of the setting though.

Down on the waterfront by the marina are numerous restaurants which are fun to patronise in the evening, but tend to be expensive. To the east are the *Yakamoz, Korsan* and *Lipsos*; to the west, *İlayda, Han* and *Pandora*, with the *Shang Hai* Chinese restaurant incongruously tagged on at the end. Off-season, pick the one that's busiest. In season, you may have to grab a seat where you can find one. Expect to spend from US$15 to US$18 for a meal with wine or beer.

Getting There & Away Minibuses connect Kalkan with Fethiye (US$2) and Kaş (US$1) throughout the day in summer. There are also regular minibuses to Patara for the beach.

Kalkan to Kaş

Eighty-seven km from Fethiye is Kaputaş, a striking mountain gorge crossed by a small highway bridge. The plaques each side of the bridge commemorate four road workers who were killed during the dangerous construction of this part of the highway. Below the bridge is a perfect little sandy cove and beach, accessible by a long flight of stairs. A dolmuş from Kalkan will take you there in summer for US$0.50.

A short distance past Kaputaş, the Blue Cave (Mavi Mağara) lurks beneath the highway, marked by a sign. Look out for boats bringing tourists for a glimpse of this Turkish Capri.

Kaş

Fishing boats and a few yachts in the harbour, a town square with tea-houses and restaurants in which one can hear half a dozen languages spoken, inexpensive pensions and hotels, classical ruins scattered about: this is Kaş (KAHSH, population 5000), the quintessential Turkish seaside town.

Kaş is not popular because of its beaches – they are small, pebbly and some are a good way out of town – but is pleasant in itself and makes an ideal base for boat excursions to several fascinating spots along the coast.

Life centres on the town square by the harbour, with its tea-houses, restaurants, mosque, police station and shops.

A well-preserved ancient theatre is about all that's left of ancient Antiphellus, which was the Lycian town here. Also, on the sheer rock mountain wall above the town are a number of Lycian rock tombs, which are illuminated at night.

Orientation The otogar is just off the highway, a few hundred metres uphill from the town centre. Descend the hill, passing multitudinous signs to small pensions, to the harbour and mosque and turn left to reach the main square, Cumhuriyet Meydanı, and the tourist information office. İbrahim Serin Caddesi strikes north to the PTT and a bank with an ATM dispensing foreign exchange, while Uzun Çarşı Caddesi cuts north-west past lovely shops in restored wooden houses to a Lycian sarcophagus. Beyond the main square over the hill are more hotels and a small pebble beach.

Turning right at the mosque onto Yazar Yazıcı Caddesi takes you to the hospital, theatre and camping ground.

Information The Tourism Information Office (☎ (242) 836 1238) is on the main square. The staff speak English and have numerous handouts on local lodgings and sights.

Kaş' postal code is 07580.

Antiphellus Ruins Walk up the hill on the street to the left of the Tourism Information Office to reach the **Monument Tomb**, a Lycian sarcophagus mounted on a high base. It is said that Kaş was once littered with such sarcophagi but that over the years most were broken apart to provide building materials.

The **theatre**, 500m west of the main square, is in very good condition and was restored some time ago. Over the hill behind the theatre is the **Doric Tomb**, cut into the hillside rock in the 3rd century BC. You can also walk to the rock tombs in the cliffs above the town, but as the walk is strenuous go at a cool time of day.

Excursions Several standard excursions will take you along the coast for cruising and swimming. No matter which you take, check to see whether lunch is included in the price. If you're watching your budget you may prefer to pack a picnic or to pick your own place to eat when you reach the midday stop.

One popular excursion is to Kekova and Üçağız, about two hours away by boat, where there are several interesting ruins (see Kekova/Üçağız below). The cost is from US$7.50 to US$11 per person.

You can also visit Kastellorizo (Meis Adası in Turkish), the Greek island just off the coast and visible from Kaş, either returning to Kaş in the evening, or perhaps using it as a base to enter Greece and go on to other islands. If you want to do this, the travel agency making the arrangements will need your passport 24 hours in advance. The fare to Kastellorizo is likely to be about US$22.

Other standard excursions go to the Blue Cave, Patara and Kalkan or to Liman Ağzı, Longos and several small nearby islands. There are also overland excursions to the Saklıkent Gorge and villages farther inland.

For a three-day (two-night) yacht cruise along the coast, expect to pay about US$100 per day for the entire boat.

Places to Stay As you step out of the bus a swarm of hawkers will descend on you, pressing you to patronise their particular pension. You could ask questions about price and facilities, and then follow them home, but most of the town's lodgings are within a five or ten-minute walk.

Places to Stay – bottom end The cheapest pensions charge from US$5 or US$6 per bed in high season, but prices are more like US$8

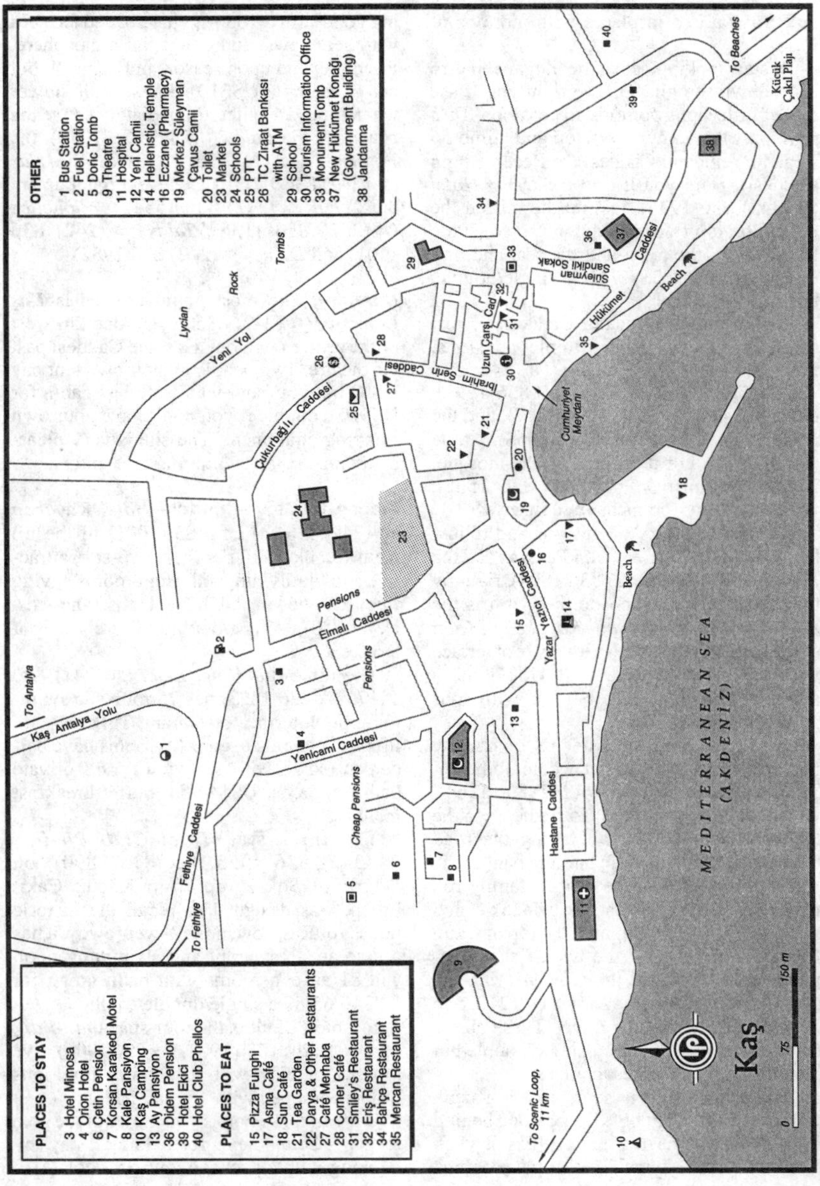

Kaş

PLACES TO STAY

3 Hotel Mimosa
4 Orion Hotel
6 Çetin Pension
7 Korsan Karakedi Motel
8 Kale Pansiyon
10 Kaş Camping
13 Ay Pansiyon
36 Didem Pension
39 Hotel Ekici
40 Hotel Club Phellos

PLACES TO EAT

15 Pizza Funghi
17 Asma Café
18 Sun Café
21 Tea Garden
22 Darya & Other Restaurants
27 Café Merhaba
28 Corner Café
31 Smiley's Restaurant
32 Eriş Restaurant
34 Bahçe Restaurant
35 Mercan Restaurant

OTHER

1 Bus Station
2 Fuel Station
5 Doric Tomb
9 Theatre
11 Hospital
12 Yeni Camii
14 Hellenistic Temple
16 Eczane (Pharmacy)
19 Merkez Süleyman Çavus Camii
20 Toilet
23 Market
24 Schools
25 PTT
26 TC Ziraat Bankası with ATM
29 School
30 Tourism Information Office
33 Monument Tomb
37 New Hükümet Konağı (Government Building)
38 Jandarma

To Antalya
Kaş Antalya Yolu
Fethiye Caddesi
To Fethiye
Yenicami Caddesi
Elmalı Caddesi
Pensions
Cheap Pensions
Çukurbağlı Caddesi
Yeni Yol
Lycian Rock Tombs
İbrahim Serin Caddesi
Uzun Çarşi Cad
Süleyman Sandikli Sokak
Hükümet Caddesi
Cumhuriyet Meydanı
Yazar Yazıcı Caddesi
Hastane Caddesi
To Scenic Loop, 11 km
Beach
Beach
To Beaches
Kücük Çakıl Plajı
MEDITERRANEAN SEA (AKDENİZ)
0 75 150 m

MEDITERRANEAN TURKEY

or US$10 a bed in places with more comforts.

To start looking, leave the otogar and turn right down the hill. On the right you'll see lots of little signs pointing to pensions. Turn right past the Limyra pension and climb 56 steps to Yenicami Caddesi (or Recep Bilgin Caddesi). Here you'll find the *Orion Hotel* (☎ (242) 836 1938), just up the hill on the right. The top floor is a quiet terrace with a fine view of the town and the sea, and tidy rooms go for US$13/22 a single/double, breakfast included.

Farther along Yenicami Caddesi, or just off it, are many other simple pensions, including the *Akkın Pansion* (☎ (242) 836 1232), the *Anı Motel* (☎ (242) 836 1791), *Hilal Pansiyon* (☎ (242) 836 1207), and the *Melisa Pansion* (☎ (242) 836 1068). At the (southern) end of the street, by the mosque, is the *Ay Pansiyon* (☎ (242) 836 1562), where the front rooms have sea views.

Turn right at the Ay Pansiyon and follow the signs to the quieter *Çetin Pension* and the *Pansiyon Kale* (☎ (242) 836 1094), right by the theatre ruins. Opposite the Çetin is the slightly pricier *Korsan Karakedi Motel* (☎ (242) 836 1887) with a lovely roof terrace with bar. Rooms here cost US$13/17 a single/double but may be full with tour groups in peak season.

On the other (eastern) side of town many more pensions offer similar accommodation. Try the pleasant *Koştur* (☎ (242) 836 1264), which readers have liked. To find it go to the PTT and turn up the hill along the road between the Corner Café and the bank.

There are a few more simple, family run pensions in Süleyman Sandıkçı Sokak which you reach by turning right at the top of Uzun Çarşı Caddesi behind the Lycian sarcophagus. Here you'll find the *Golden Pansiyon* (☎ (242) 836 1085), the *Didem* (☎ (242) 836 2694), the *Kösk* and the *Layla*. These places charge around US$9/13 a single/double but wouldn't be the quietest choices.

Over the hill to the south-east is Küçük Çakıl Plajı (Small Pebble Beach), and behind it, along with the big hotels (Ekici, Club Phellos), a row of small, newer places offering good simple rooms, vine-shaded terraces with sea views, and congenial atmosphere. Prices depend upon season and demand, but can go as low as US$10 a double with shower when times are quiet. Immediately above the beach try the *Lale* (☎ (242) 836 1074), the *Patara* (☎ (242) 836 1328) or the *Nur* (☎ (242) 836 1203). One level higher up are the *Cemil* (☎ (242) 836 1554), *Antiphellos* (☎ (242) 836 1136), *Talay* (☎ (242) 836 1101) and *Defne* (☎ (242) 836 1932).

Camping The most popular place is *Kaş Camping* (☎ (242) 836 1050), one km west of the centre out along Hastane Caddesi past the theatre. Two people in their own tent pay US$3 but you can rent a waterless cabin for US$10 a double if you don't have your own camping equipment. The site is very pleasant, with a small swimming area and bar.

Places to Stay – middle *Hotel Kayahan* (☎ (242) 836 1313, fax 836 2001), up the hill from Küçük Çakıl beach, is two-star, attractive and family run, with front rooms having fine sea views. All have baths, and cost US$28/30 a single/double. There's a roof terrace as well.

The three-star *Hotel Ekici* (☎ (242) 836 1417, fax 836 1823) has 75 rooms, a swimming pool, terrace restaurant, Turkish bath, lifts and central air-con. All rooms have balconies (some with sea views) and private baths, and cost US$44/54, buffet breakfast included.

The three-star *Hotel Club Phellos* (☎ (242) 836 1953, fax 836 1890), on Doğruyol Sokak, up from Küçük Çakıl beach, was designed to recall the historic houses of Kaş, now mostly swept away. It has a nice airy restaurant and swimming pool, and 81 air-con rooms with bath, going for US$40/65/80 a single/double/triple.

Flashiest of all is the four-star *Aqua-Park Hotel* (☎ (242) 836 1901, fax 836 1906), five km out of Kaş, with 106 fairly luxurious rooms equipped with TV and fridge.

With all these hotels you may well be able to get a better deal, for a longer stay, by booking with a package tour operator. Also bear in mind that they will be block-booked to these same operators for much of the summer.

Places to Eat For breakfast, snacks, pastries and puddings, the *Noel Baba Pastanesi* on the main square is a favourite, and best for people-watching when its outdoor tables are in shade. Also very popular is the *Corner Café*, at the PTT end of İbrahim Serin Caddesi, where you can get juices for US$1, yoghurt with fruit and honey for US$1.50 and a vegetable omelette for US$1. Immediately opposite is the *Café Merhaba*, run by two women, and offering a choice of home-made cakes to eat with coffee or juice. You can buy your foreign-language newspapers here to read while you're tucking in. At the harbour end of this same street look out for a hole-in-the-wall bakery dispensing hot pide and other snacks from breakfast time onwards.

In the centre of Kaş, five much-patronised restaurants suitable for lunch or dinner occupy an awning-shaded passage running between the waterfront and the marketplace. Closest to the water is the *Aslı Ocakbaşı* Then comes the longer established *Derya Restaurant*, where many dishes are set out for you to choose from. A lunch or dinner consisting of several plates of mezes should cost no more than US$4. Farther along are the *Orkinos*, *Eva Kent* and *Baba'nın Yeri*, so similar that it's difficult to tell where one stops and the next begins.

Out towards the east end of the harbour, the *Mercan* is noted for its waterfront location and its seafood. Choose a fish, have it weighed, get the price, then say 'evet' if you want it, or 'hayır' if you don't. A fish dinner with mezes and wine can cost from US$12 to US$16 per person.

Just back from the main square is the *Eriş*, with shady pseudo-rustic tables in front. Prices are not bad, but the food is good and the atmosphere makes it very popular in the evenings. Right next door is *Smiley's Restaurant*, a brasher but popular place serving pizza or seafood meals for around US$3 to US$6.

Up behind the Lycian sarcophagus it's also worth looking out for the *Bahçe Restaurant*, set, as its name suggests, in a garden with an excellent selection of cold mezes to choose from. Also in a garden setting amid banana plants and swaths of morning glory is the pricier *Kalamar Restaurant*, a seafood place in the centre of things at the harbour end of İbrahim Serin Caddesi.

Heading west from the Merkez Süleyman Çavus Camii, delicious pizzas are served under shady vines at *Pizza Funghi*, just up Yazar Yazıcı Caddesi, near the Yalı Pension. Service here is excellent too. The tiny *Asma Café*, tucked away to the right behind the mosque, also receives the local seal of approval for its salad lunches and pleasant ambience.

Finally, no visit to Kaş would be complete without dropping in on the *Sun Café*, at the end of the quay behind the central mosque. You'll find lower prices for drinks elsewhere but certainly not a more attractive setting to sup them in.

Getting There & Away Most tourists arrive and leave Kaş by bus.

Air A small airport is to be built inland from Patara and Kalkan, and this would serve Kaş with small-aircraft flights as well. For the time being, most tourists are bused in from Dalaman airport to the west.

Bus Most buses in and out of Kaş are handled by the Pamukkale, Kaş Turizm and Kamil Koç companies. Some daily services include:

Antalya – 185 km, four hours, US$6; frequent buses
Fethiye – 110 km, 2½ hours, US$3; frequent buses and dolmuşes
Kalkan – 29 km, 35 minutes, US$1; frequent minibuses
Patara – 36 km, one hour, US$2; regular dolmuşes

For other destinations you normally have to travel to Fethiye or Antalya and connect with onward services there.

ÜÇAĞİZ/KEKOVA

Fourteen km east of Kaş you will see signs for a turn-off right to Kekova. A 19-km drive along a paved road brings you to the village of Üçağız, the Lycian Teimiussa, in an area of ancient ruined cities, some of them partly submerged in the Mediterranean's waters. This area is regularly visited by day-trippers on boats and yachts from Kaş and Kalkan but you could also stay overnight.

Declared off-limits to development, Üçağız remains a relatively unspoilt Turkish fishing and farming village in an absolutely idyllic setting, on a bay amidst islands and peninsulas. The old houses, many white-washed, are of local stone rather than breeze block and the largest building is the modern *ilkokul* (primary school). Cows and chickens wander the streets, villagers lift sacks of carob beans down to the town wharf, and fisherfolk repair their nets on the quay as yachts glide through the harbour. Village girls sell hand-printed scarves *(yazmalar)* with handmade lace borders, while village women sit outside making lace and doing embroidery.

Here and there are remnants of ancient Lycian tombs. Near the Koç Restaurant in particular, look for two Lycian sarcophagi (one of them in the shape of a house) and a rock-cut tomb.

For the time being, Üçağız slumbers in between boat visitations. A few carpet shops have already opened, however, and the discos can't be far behind.

Orientation

The village you actually enter is Üçağız ('Three Mouths'; that is, entrances to the harbour), the ancient Teimiussa. Across the water to the east is **Kale**, a village on the site of the ancient city of Simena, accessible by boat. South of the villages is a larger harbour called **Ölüdeniz** (not to be confused with the famous beach spot near Fethiye), and south of that is the channel entrance, shielded from the Mediterranean's occasional fury by a long island named Kekova.

Places to Stay & Eat

Üçağız's small pensions charge around US$7 to US$11 per person.

Heading west, the *Onur Pansiyon* has simple rooms with solar-heated water, some overlooking the harbour. There's an agreeable waterfront dining area and terrace and you're allowed to use the fridge. It's immediately opposite the stylish *Fisherman's Inn* bar.

Continuing west, a good choice would be the *Likya* (☎ (242) 874 2090), where clean rooms with showers and balconies cost about US$11 a head. Nearby is the *Huzur* (☎ (242) 874 2031) and village end.

On one side of the Koç Restaurant is the *Flower Pension*, on the other the *Gözde* (☎ (242) 874 2168). The *Koç Restaurant* itself is popular with boat tours and does a pleasant lunch buffet with plentiful fish for US$5. If that doesn't take your fancy there are half a dozen little eateries on the waterfront, including the *Kordon, Liman, Hassan's* and *Kekova*, all charging around US$4 or US$5 for a meal.

You can camp on the western outskirts at *Kekova Camping* and there's a small store selling groceries in the village centre, opposite an information booth, open in high summer.

Boat Excursions

Boats from Üçağız will take you on a tour of the area lasting from one to 1½ hours. Chartering an entire boat costs around US$10 to US$16, but haggle as prices are negotiable. Although the water is very clear some readers have thought it worth paying a bit extra to sail past the 'sunken city' ruins in a glass-bottomed boat.

Kale

Tours from Kaş normally arrive in Üçağız and then proceed to Kale to see the **ruins of ancient Simena** and the **medieval Byzantine fortress** perched above the picture-perfect hamlet. Within the fortress a little **theatre** is cut into the rock and nearby are **ruins** of several temples and public baths, several sarcophagi and Lycian tombs;

the **city walls** are visible on the outskirts. It's a delightfully pretty spot, accessible by motorboat from Üçağız (10 minutes) or on foot (one hour).

Places to Stay & Eat Kale has a couple of pensions, including the delightfully sited *Mehtap Pansiyon* (☎ (242) 874 2146), high on the hill with spectacular views over the harbour and a sunken Lycian tomb. Beds cost US$8 in waterless rooms. Nearer the harbour there's also the *Kale Pansiyon* (☎ (242) 874 2111) with beds for US$7. The harbourside restaurants, the *Simena*, *Café Ankh* and *Kale*, tend to be pricey because of their yachting clientele.

Getting There & Away

Occasional minibuses link Kaş to Üçağız in winter, but services in summer are sometimes nonexistent. If there's no bus and you don't want to take an excursion you could get a taxi as far as Üçağız and then take a taxi boat to Kale for US$5 each way. In summer there's also a water taxi direct from Kaş; Kaş tourist office has the details.

Coming from Demre, motorboats can be chartered at the western beach, called Çayağzı, for US$30; sometimes it's possible to buy one place in the boat for a one-way journey for about US$3. You may be able to do this from Kaş as well.

Boat Tours Given the difficulty of getting to Kekova by public transport most people end up taking a boat tour of the area from Kaş or Kalkan. A standard boat excursion might start by heading for Üçağız, passing **Kekova Adası** (Kekova Island, also called Tersane). Along the shore of the island are Byzantine foundations and ruins, partly submerged in the sea, and called the Batık Şehir, the Sunken City. Signs say 'No Skin-Diving Allowed', indicating that this is an archaeological zone and the authorities are afraid of antiquity theft. The boat stops in a cove so you can swim and perhaps explore the ruins on land. Afterwards you head for lunch in Üçağız and then on to Kale, passing **sunken Lycian tombs** just offshore. There's usually about an hour to explore Kale and climb up to the eponymous castle. On the way back to Kaş there should be time for another swim.

Tours generally leave at 10 am and charge around US$8 per person.

KYANEAI

From the main highway at the Kekova turn-off, it's eight km east and south to the turn-off for Kyaneai, two km off the highway, where a few barely distinguishable ruins stand amid the houses and paddocks of a farming hamlet. A track starts in the town and leads three km uphill to the main part of this ancient city, founded in Lycian times, which flourished under the Romans and was the seat of a bishop during the Byzantine era. It was abandoned in the 10th century.

The site has some interesting tombs, and traces of other buildings, but the rough terrain and undergrowth make exploration difficult. This is one for dedicated antiquities buffs who enjoy having little-visited sites to themselves.

DEMRE

Winding past rocky, scrubby terrain from Kaş, the road descends from the mountains to a fertile river delta, much of it covered in greenhouses. Demre (DEHM-reh), 40 km east of Kaş, was the Roman city of Myra (the name comes from myrrh) and by the 4th century was important enough to have its own bishop (one of them St Nicholas, later immortalised as Santa Claus). Several centuries before that, St Paul stopped here on his voyage to Rome.

Though Myra had a long history as a religious, commercial and administrative town, Arab raids in the 7th century and the silting of the harbour led to its decline. Today that same silting is the foundation of the town's wealth. The rich alluvial soil supports the intensive greenhouse production of flowers and vegetables.

Orientation

Demre sprawls over the alluvial plain. At the centre is the main square, near which are several cheap hotels and restaurants. The street going west from it to the Church of St Nicholas is Müze Caddesi (also called St Nicholas Caddesi). Going north is Alakent Caddesi, which leads two km to the Lycian rock tombs of Myra. PTT Caddesi (also called Ortaokul Caddesi) heads east to the post office and the town's best hotel. The street going south from the square passes the otogar (100m) and continues to a cluster of cheap hotels (800m) across from the *ilkokul* (primary school), near the junction with the road to Antalya.

Five km west of the centre is Çayağzı beach, with several places to camp for free and several which charge a small amount. This was called Andriake in Roman times, an important entrepôt for grain on the sea route to Rome. The great granary built by Hadrian (finished in 139 AD) still stands, off to the south of the road.

Church of St Nicholas

The Church of St Nicholas ('Noel Baba' in Turkish) was first built in the 3rd century, and became a Byzantine basilica when it was restored in 1043. Later restorations sponsored by Tsar Nicholas I of Russia in 1862 changed the building even more. More recent work by Turkish archaeologists was designed to protect it from deterioration.

Not vast like Aya Sofya, nor brilliant with mosaics like İstanbul's Chora Church, the Church of St Nicholas at Demre is, at first, a disappointment. What redeems it is the venerable dignity lent it by its age and the stories which surround it.

Admission to the church (open 8 am to 5.30 pm daily) is overpriced at US$3, half-price for students.

Myra

Two km inland from Demre's main square lie the ruins of Myra, with a striking honeycomb of rock-hewn **Lycian tombs** and a well-preserved **Roman theatre**. Climb the ladders for a closer look at the tombs, which were thought to have been carved to resemble Lycian houses, wood beams and all. Around to the left as you climb is a tomb topped by a deathbed scene; there are other reliefs to discover as well.

Admission costs US$1; hours are from 8 am to 5.30 pm, till 7 pm in summer.

Taxi drivers in town will offer to take you on a tour, and can turn quite nasty if you decline, but the walk from the main square only takes about 20 minutes and the site is fairly self-explanatory.

Places to Stay

Demre doesn't have much accommodation. About 300m north of the main square on the way to the Myra rock tombs is the pretty basic *Noel Pansiyon* (☎ (242) 871 2304), with rooms for US$6/10 a single/double. Since the road is quite busy, expect some noise. More inviting is the *Kent Aile Pansiyon* (☎ (242) 871 2042), in a garden farther down towards the tombs. Right beside the tombs is the small, basic *Likya Pension*.

Three more hotels are less than one km south of the main square near the junction

Santa Claus

The legend of Father Christmas (Santa Claus; Noel Baba in Turkish) is said to have begun in Demre when a 4th century Christian bishop, later St Nicholas, gave anonymous gifts to dowryless village girls. He would drop bags of coins down the chimneys of their houses, and this 'gift from heaven' would allow them to marry, which is perhaps why he is the patron saint of virgins. He went on to become the patron saint of sailors, children, pawnbrokers, Holy Russia, and others.

St Nicholas' fame grew, and in 1087 a raiding party from the Italian city of Bari stole his mortal remains from the church. They missed a few bones which are now in Antalya Museum.

To judge from the carvings on its top, what is touted as St Nicholas' tomb in Demre church is more likely to be that of a Byzantine couple. ■

with the highway to Antalya: the *Kekova Pansiyon* (☎ (242) 871 2804), the *Otel Topçu* (☎ (242) 871 2200) and the *Kıyak Otel* (☎ (242) 871 2092). All these places charge around US$6/9. The Kekova is clean and friendly and has good bathrooms. Excellent buffet meals are on offer too.

On PTT Caddesi is the *Hotel Simge* (☎ (242) 871 3674, fax 871 3677) which charges US$13/20 with balcony, bathroom and breakfast but needs a bit of updating. Keep going down the road for the two-star *Grand Hotel Kekova* (☎ 242) 871 3462), Demre's newest, best and probably quietest with comfortable, modern rooms for US$13/22.

Places to Eat

The food from the little restaurants near the main square *(Çınar* and *Şehir)* and along Müze Caddesi between the square and the church (the *İpek* in particular) can fill you up perfectly adequately. Readers have also enjoyed eating at the *Likya Restoran*, right by the beach three km out of Demre on the Antalya road.

ÇAĞILLI & GÖKLİMAN

Heading east from Demre towards Antalya, you'll eventually come to Çağıllı, a small cove with a nice pebble beach overlooked by the highway. At Gökliman, another four km east, a longer, wider beach is good for a swim stop.

FİNİKE

Thirty km farther along the twisting mountain road is Finike (FEE-nee-keh, population 7000), the ancient Phoenicus, now a sleepy fishing port and way-station on the tourist route. Most of the tourists are Turks who have built ramshackle dwellings on the long pebble beach to the east of the town. The beach looks inviting but parts of it are polluted and insects can be a problem at certain times of year.

About 10 km inland from Finike are the ruins of ancient Limyra, not really worth the effort unless you're out to see every ancient town along the coast. Arycanda, 35 km north along the Elmalı road, is well worth seeing with its dramatic setting and many well-preserved buildings, but requires a special excursion. Finike itself is uninteresting and not worth making a special stop for.

Places to Stay

Since the demise of the *Kale Pansiyon*, the only architecturally distinguished place in town, you could try heading for the *Paris Pansiyon* (☎ (242) 855 1488), up a terrifying flight of steps, 200m west of the otogar. Beds here cost just US$6 including breakfast.

Another possibility for the same price would be the welcoming *Şendil Pansiyon* (☎ (242) 855 1660), signposted from near the old Kale Pansiyon on the west side of town.

In the market district behind the Belediye are several inexpensive hotels, including the *Hotel Bahar* (☎ (242) 855 2020), the friendly *Hotel Bilal* (☎ (242) 855 2199), and the older *Hotel Sedir* (☎ (242) 855 1183) at Cumhuriyet Caddesi 37. All these charge around US$9/17 single/double with shower, breakfast included. The brand-new *Engin Hotel* (☎ (242) 855 3040) on the main road through town is similar.

Baba Camping, three km east of Finike centre, is on the landward side of the very wide highway; *Karaca Camping*, two km farther east, is cheaper, simpler, and on the beach side.

FİNİKE TO KEMER

As you leave Finike the highway skirts a sand-and-pebble beach which runs for about 15 km. Once past the long beach the road transits **Kumluca** (population 17,000), a farming town surrounded by citrus orchards and plastic-roofed greenhouses, worth visiting on Fridays for its lively market. A few small pensions can put you up in an emergency.

After Kumluca the highway winds back up into the mountains with an especially good panorama about 28 km from Finike. Three km later you enter **Beydağları Sahil Milli Parkı,** the Bey Mountains Coastal National Park.

Olimpos/Çıralı

Midway between Kumluca and Tekirova two roads lead down from the main highway towards the villages of Çavuşköy and Çıralı, to Adrasan beach, and to the ruins of ancient Olimpos and the site of the Chimaera, all set within the glorious Bey Mountains Coastal National Park. Unless you have your own transport, you should take the road signposted 'Olimpos-Çıralı-Yanartaş/Chimaera 7 km' which will bring you straight down to Çıralı village and its plentiful pensions, all within walking distance of the Olimpos ruins and the Chimaera. Coming from Kumluca, this will be the second turn-off signposted to Olimpos; coming from Antalya it will be the first.

If you take the Çavuşköy turn-off it will be 11 km to the village.

The Ruins of Olimpos Though a very ancient city, the early history of Olimpos is shrouded in mystery. We know that it was an important Lycian city by the 2nd century BC, and that the Olympians worshipped Hephaestos (Vulcan), the god of fire. No doubt this veneration sprang from reverence for the mysterious Chimaera, an eternal flame which still springs from the earth not far from the city. Along with the other Lycian coastal cities, Olimpos went into a decline in the 1st century BC. With the coming of the Romans in the 1st century AD, things improved, but in the 3rd century AD pirate attacks brought impoverishment. In the Middle Ages the Venetians, Genoese and Rhodians built fortresses along the coast (bits of which still remain), but by the 15th century Olimpos had been abandoned.

Today the site is fascinating, not just for its ruins (which are fragmentary and widely scattered amidst the thick verdure of wild grapevines, flowering oleander, bay trees, wild figs and pines), but for its site, just inland from a beautiful beach along the course of a stream which runs through a rocky gorge. The stream dries to a rivulet in high summer, and a ramble along its course, listening to the wind in the trees and the songs of innumerable birds, is a rare treat, with never a tour bus in sight.

The site is effectively open all the time but during daylight hours a custodian awaits to relieve those wishing to climb to the acropolis of US$1. There's a car park at the non-beach end of the site.

The Chimaera From Çıralı, follow the track marked for the Chimaera (Yanartaş, 'burning rock' in Turkish) three km along a valley to a car park, then climb up a mud track for another 20 to 30 minutes to the site.

The Chimaera, a cluster of spontaneous and inextinguishable flames which blaze from crevices on the rocky slopes of Mt Olimpos, is the stuff of legends. It's not difficult to see why ancient peoples attributed these extraordinary flames to the breath of a monster – part lion, part goat and part dragon. Even today, they have not been explained.

Gas seeps from the earth, and bursts into flame upon contact with the air. The exact composition of the gas is unknown, though it is thought to contain some methane. Though the flames can be extinguished now by being covered, they will reignite when uncovered. In ancient times they were much more vigorous, being easily recognised at night by mariners sailing along the coast.

In mythology, the Chimaera was the son of Typhon. Typhon was the fierce and monstrous son of Gaia, the earth goddess, who was so frightening a being that Zeus set him on fire and buried him alive under Mt Aetna, thereby creating the volcano. Typhon's offspring, the Chimaera, was killed by the hero Bellerophon on the orders of King Iobates of Lycia. Bellerophon killed the monster by aerial bombardment – mounting Pegasus, the winged horse, and pouring molten lead into the Chimaera's mouth.

Places to Stay & Eat As you arrive in Çıralı you will cross a small bridge where a few taxis wait to run people back up to the main road. Continue across the bridge and you'll come to a junction in the road disfigured with innumerable signboards. Right by the junction is the *Moonlight Pension*. Go straight on for the pensions nearest to the path up to the Chimaera. Turn right for the pensions closest to Adrasan beach and the Olimpos ruins.

When you reach the beach, a string of pensions runs off to the east. Amongst them are the *Barış, Sahil* and *Bizim Cennet*, all charging US$4 or US$5 per person. Keep walking westwards for the small and friendly *Rüya Pansiyon* (☎ (242) 825 7055), tucked away behind a school, and for the *Blue Blue Pansiyon* (☎ (242) 825 7013) whose friendly proprietor speaks excellent English. The *Florya Pension* trumpets its healthy food as a selling point.

Walking along the beach towards the Olimpos ruins you'll come to the delightful *Olympos Lodge* (☎ (242) 825 7171, fax 825 7173), PO Box 38, Çıralı, a beautiful lodge and villas set amidst citrus orchards and well-tended gardens very near the beach. The management is German, everything is well maintained, and the price, at US$56/78 a single/double, breakfast included, is well worth a splurge.

In summer there are plenty of small beach restaurants serving up simple kebap meals but most close by the end of October.

Heading away from the beach towards the Chimaera you'll come to the small *Karakuş* pension on the right, then to the *Grand Aygün Pension* (☎ (242) 825 7185), and then to the classy *Çıralı Pansiyon* (☎ (242) 825 7122), actually a hotel, with balconied rooms with big bathrooms for US$14 a double, including a good breakfast in the adjacent *Star Restaurant*. Just past it on the right, hidden in lovely gardens, is the *Azur Hotel and Restaurant* (☎ (242) 825 7072) where comfortable modern rooms cost US$30/40 a single/double. Even farther along is *Green Point Caravan & Tent Camping* which readers have recommended (always bearing in mind that there's nothing to stop you camping for free along the beach and making use of the simple restaurant facilities there).

If you decide to stay in Çavuşköy instead of Çıralı there are still plenty of choices, including the *Atıcı Motel & Pension*, the *Çizmeci Hotel*, the *Gelidonya Pension*, *Yasemin Motel*, and the *Koreli Motel*. Rates vary from US$5 per person to US$24 a double, depending on the place and the season.

Along the road leading from Çavuşköy to the Olimpos ruins there are several rustic restaurants which allow camping as well. *Kadir's Restaurant & Free Camping* tends to get the most attention because of its tree-houses, available for just US$2.50 a head in summer only. Nearer to the car park are the *Atalay* and *Vadi* pension-restaurants, *Kadir's Bungalows*, and *Hasan's Restaurant & Free Camping*.

Getting There & Away Unless you have your own transport getting to Olimpos is tricky because no dolmuşes run to Çıralı, the most obvious place to base yourself. Buses plying up and down the main road linking Antalya and Fethiye will drop you at either of the road junctions leading to Çıralı or Çavuşköy. For the time being the taxis wait in hope at the Çavuşköy turn off, but an 11 km run down will work out pretty pricey. If you wait at the Çıralı junction instead, a taxi will no doubt pass by eventually (the charge for the 7 km run down should be about US$7), or you can try hitching.

In summer boats run from Adrasan beach to Demre and Kaş.

On Friday there are dolmuşes from Çıralı to Kumluca market.

Tekirova

About 13 km north-east of Olimpos is the turn-off for Tekirova, a resort area with several large luxury hotels, including the *Grand Otel Phaselis* (☎ (242) 825 4070), and a number of small pensions and camping grounds.

Phaselis

Three km north of the Tekirova turn-off, 12 km before the turn-off to Kemer, is a road marked for Phaselis, a ruined Lycian city two km off the highway on the shore. Shaded by soughing pines, the ruins of Phaselis are arranged around three small perfect bays, each with its own diminutive beach. The ruins are not particularly exciting, and are all from Roman and Byzantine times, but the setting is incomparably romantic.

The site is open from 7.30 am to 7 pm in summer for US$1. One km from the highway is the entrance to the site, with a small modern building where you can buy soft drinks, snacks and souvenirs, use the WC, and visit a one-room museum. The ruins and the shore are another km farther on. The nearest accommodation is in Tekirova.

KEMER

Kemer (population 10,000), 103 km from Demre, 12 km north of Phaselis and 42 km south-west of Antalya, is a burgeoning beach holiday resort with its face turned to the rough, rocky beaches of the Mediterranean and its back to the steep, pine-clad Beydağları (Bey Mountains). It was designed as a holding tank for planeloads of sun-seeking charter and group tours, and built to a government master plan. For most non-package holiday-makers it has little to offer. Passing through, you can stop for a meal and a look at the Yörük Parkı, an outdoor ethnological exhibit. Accommodation is available in all price ranges, should you want to stay, but most of the bigger places will be block-booked to tour operators throughout the summer.

Orientation

Liman Caddesi, the main street, is a typically narrow Turkish noise-canyon lined with white hotels, palm trees, banks and cafés, where you must run the gauntlet of a string of leather, jewellery and carpet shops. At the end of the main street to the north is the large yacht marina and dry-dock; to the south is a peaceful cove with a beautiful crescent of sand-and-pebble beach backed by emerald grass and fragrant pine trees. Stands here rent equipment for parasailing, water-skiing and windsurfing. Motorboat excursions run from the beach as well.

The otogar is on the north-western edge of town.

Information

The Tourism Information Office is in the Belediye Binası (municipal building) (☎ (242) 814 1537, fax 814 1536).

Kemer's postal code is 07980.

Yörük Parkı

On a promontory north of the cove beach is Kemer's Yörük Parkı, an ethnographic exhibit meant to introduce you to some of the mysteries of the region. Local nomads *(yörüks)* lived in these black camel-hair tents now furnished with carpets and grass mats. Typical nomad paraphernalia includes distaffs for spinning woollen yarn, looms on which Turkish carpets are being woven, musical instruments and churns for butter and ayran. Among the tents, in the shade of the pines, are little rustic tables with three-legged stools at which a 'nomad girl' will serve you refreshments and snacks.

Keep walking through the park and you'll emerge above the cove. The view is very pretty from here. At night, Antalya, to the north, is a long string of shore lights in the distance.

Places to Stay

Kemer's lodgings mainly cater to the package-holiday trade but a few cheaper places still manage to cling on. One of the longest established and most congenial of them is the *King Pension* (☎ (242) 814 1039), also called the King's Garden Pension, north-east of the otogar. The rooms, set round a garden, are fairly basic but comfortable enough; the location is quiet; and the owners (she's English, he's Turkish) very congenial. The popular restaurant attached to the pension has now been supplemented by one on the beach itself. In high season, rates for double rooms with shower are US$40, breakfast and dinner included. Off-season you can get B&B for US$20. Camping costs US$6 in a double tent. To find the King Pension, turn right out of the otogar, cross the main road and follow the signs.

If the King's prices are too high for you, cross the channel outside and walk back towards the otogar. You'll come to the

Portakal Pansiyon (☎ (242) 814 4701) where beds cost a more standard US$7.

Other cheap pensions and camping grounds abound in this neighbourhood. *Overland Camping* is one km north of the centre. Perhaps the nicest camping place is *Kındılçeşme Kamp Alanı*, operated by the forestry service, 3.5 km north of Kemer centre along the old highway. Set amidst fragrant pines at the edge of the sea, it's often fully booked in summer.

Kemer's hotels tend to be overpriced if you're not on a package tour. They range from the two-star *Ambassador Hotel* (☎ (242) 814 2626, fax 814 2606), Liman Caddesi 10, (US$45 a double), to the four-star 60-room *Otem Oteli* (☎ (242) 814 3181, fax 814 3190), Yat Limanı Karşısı, facing the yacht marina (US$60/88 a single/double).

Getting There & Away

Approaching Kemer from Fethiye, Kaş and Kalkan, you're likely to find yourself dropped off on the main highway, two km from the otogar. A taxi fare, if you don't want to walk or wait for a dolmuş will be about US$2. From the otogar, dolmuşes run nonstop between Kemer and Antalya all day. There are also several dolmuş runs daily to Tekirova and Phaselis.

BELDİBİ

North of Kemer, the old Antalya highway follows the shoreline more closely than the new highway, farther inland. About 12 km north of Kemer is the centre of Beldibi, another planned resort area. The beach here is stones, not even pebbles, but the water is clear, the pines cool and the mountain backdrop dramatic.

Most of the lodgings here are elaborate resort hotels and holiday villages, the best of which is the *Ramada Renaissance Resort Hotel* (☎ (242) 824 8390, fax 824 3256), PO Box 654, Antalya. With spacious pine-studded grounds, numerous restaurants, a casino, swimming pools, Turkish bath, water and other sports facilities, and 341 luxury air-con rooms and suites, it's a marvellous place to unwind. Rates range from US$65 to US$145, depending on the room and the season but rooms are heavily booked in summer, so try and plan ahead.

ANTALYA

Antalya (population one million, altitude 38m) is the chief city on Turkey's central Mediterranean coast. Agriculture, shipping, light industry and tourism have made Antalya boom during the past few decades, and this mostly modern Mediterranean city is still growing at a fast pace.

Rough pebble beaches (several km from the centre to east and west) provide for the seaside crowd, and the commercial centre provides necessities. Though Antalya has a historic Roman-Ottoman core, the ancient cities on its outskirts – Perge, Aspendos, Side, Termessos, Phaselis, Olimpos – offer more to see in the way of historic buildings. Antalya is a good base from which to visit them.

History

This area has been inhabited since the earliest times. The oldest artefacts found in the Karain caves, 25 km from Antalya, have been dated to the Palaeolithic period. Antalya as a city, however, is not as old as many other cities which once lined this coast but it is still prospering while the older cities are dead. Founded by Attalus II of Pergamum in the 1st century BC, the city was named Attaleia after its founder. When the Pergamene kingdom was willed to Rome, Attaleia became a Roman city. Emperor Hadrian visited here in 130 AD and a triumphal arch (Hadrianüs Kapısı) was built in his honour.

The Byzantines took over from the Romans. In 1207 the Seljuk Turks based in Konya took the city from the Byzantines and gave Antalya a new version of its name, and also its symbol, the Yivli Minare (Grooved Minaret). After the Mongols broke Seljuk power, Antalya was held for a while by the Turkish Hamidoğulları emirs. It was later taken by the Ottomans in 1391.

During WWI the Allies made plans to divide up the Ottoman Empire, and at the end

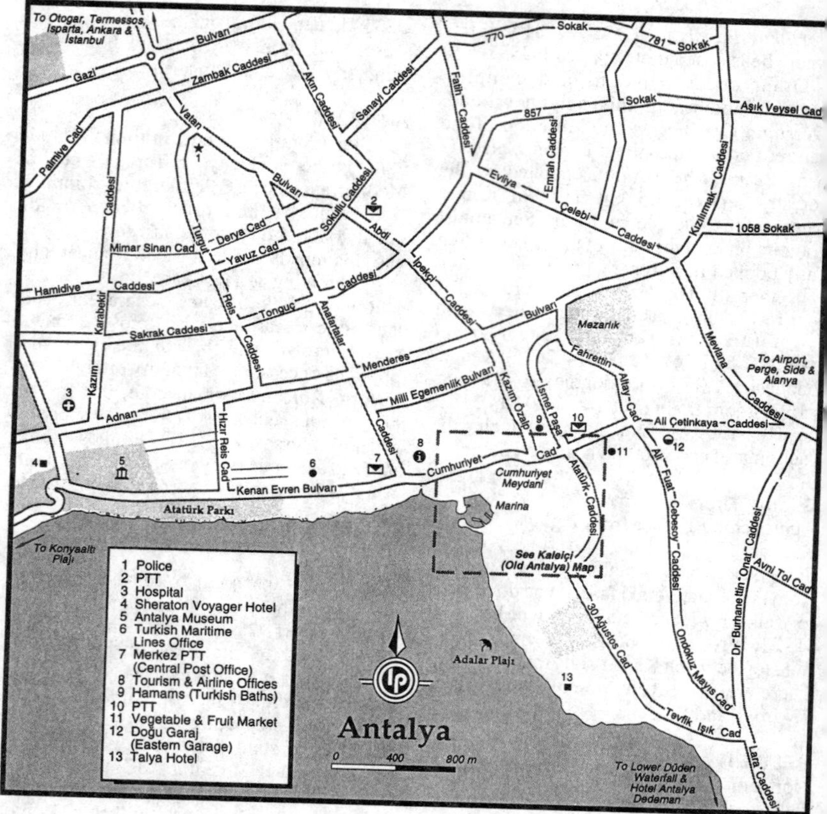

of the war they parcelled it out. Italy got Antalya in 1918, but by 1921 Atatürk's armies had put an end to all such foreign holdings in Anatolia.

Though always a busy port (trading to Crete, Cyprus and Egypt), Antalya has grown explosively since the 1960s because of the tourism boom. Its airport, the busiest on the Turkish Mediterranean, funnels travellers to the whole coast and beyond.

Orientation

At the centre of the historic city is the Roman harbour, now the yacht marina. Around it is the historic district called Kaleiçi ('Within the Fortress') of Ottoman houses sprinkled with Roman ruins. Many of the graceful old houses have been restored and converted to restaurants, pensions and small hotels – some simple, some quite luxurious.

Around Kaleiçi, outside the Roman walls, is the commercial centre of the city. Antalya's central landmark and symbol is the Yivli Minare (yeev-LEE mee-nah-reh, the Grooved Minaret), a monument from the Seljuk period which rises near the main square, called Kale Kapısı (Fortress Gate), marked by an ancient stone clock tower *(saat ulesi).* The broad plaza with the bombastic questrian statue is Cumhuriyet Meydanı Republic Square).

From Kale Kapısı, Cumhuriyet Caddesi goes west past the Tourism Information Office and Turkish Airlines office, then changes names to become Kenan Evren Bulvarı, which continues several km to the Antalya Museum and Konyaaltı Plajı, a pebble beach 10 km long, and now partly sullied by industrial development.

North-west from Kale Kapısı, Kazım Özalp Caddesi, also called Şarampol Caddesi, is a pedestrian way for several blocks before reverting to carrying vehicular traffic. Antalya's small bazaar, which seems to be mostly jewellery shops, is east of Kazım Özalp Caddesi.

East from Kale Kapısı, Ali Çetinkaya Caddesi goes to the Doğu Garajı (Eastern Garage), a mustering point for eastbound minibuses, then onward to the airport (10 km), Perge, Aspendos, Side and beyond. Atatürk Caddesi goes south-east from Ali Çetinkaya Caddesi, skirting Kaleiçi through more of the commercial district to the large Karaali Parkı before heading for Lara beach (12 km from the centre), lined with hotels and pensions.

A *çevreyolu* (ring road or bypass) named Gazi Bulvarı carries long-distance traffic around the city centre. The new bus station, opened early in 1996, is four km from the centre on the D 650 highway to Burdur, Ankara and Istanbul.

Information

There are two Tourism Information Offices, reputedly open from 9 am to 5.30 pm (5 pm on Saturday and Sunday in summer). The regional directorate (☎ (242) 247 0541, fax 247 6298) is on Mermerli Sokak in Kaleiçi, Ahiyusuf Camii Yanı, next to the Ahi Yusuf mosque, across the street from the Hotel Aspen.

The other, less convenient office (☎ & fax (242) 241 1747) is at Cumhuriyet Caddesi 91. It's 600m west of Kale Kapısı on the right-hand side in the Özel İdare Çarşısı building (the same building as Turkish Airlines). This building is after the big jandarma headquarters but before the pedestrian bridge over the roadway. Look for 'Antalya Devlet Tiyatrosu' emblazoned on it.

Antalya's postal code is 07100.

Banks The Yapı Kredi Bankası office at the southern end of Kazım Özalp Caddesi, just off Kale Kapısı, has a cash machine (Tele 24) connected to the major networks, including VISA, MasterCard, Eurocard, Cirrus and Plus Systems. Other banks, including Akbank, are a short distance north along Kazım Özalp, as are several currency exchange houses, including Süreyya Döviz, Tolunaylar Döviz, Görkem Döviz, etc.

Bookshops Try the Owl Bookshop, Barbaros Mahallesi, Akarçeşme Sokak 21, in Kaleiçi. The owner, Kemal Özkurt, stocks old and new books in English, French, German and Turkish.

Consulates Britain's honorary consulate (☎ (242) 247 7000) is at Kızılsaray Mahallesi, Dolaplıdere Caddesi, Pırıltı Sitesi, 1st floor.

The Swedish consulate (☎ (242) 248 9060, fax 241 5222), is at Konyaaltı Bulvarı 78.

Yivli Minare & the Bazaar

Start your sightseeing at the Yivli Minare, just downhill from the clock tower. The handsome and unique minaret was erected by the Seljuk sultan Alaeddin Keykubat I in the early 13th century, next to a church which the sultan had converted to a mosque, and which is now the **Fine Arts Gallery** (Güzel Sanatlar Galerisi) with changing exhibits. To its north-west is a Whirling Dervish (Mevlevi) tekke (monastery) which probably dates from the 13th century, and nearby are two **tombs**, that of Zincirkıran Mehmet Paşa (1378) and the lady Nigar Hatun.

The view from the plaza, taking in Kaleiçi, the bay and the distant ragged summits of the Beydağları (Bey Mountains), is spectacular. Teahouses behind Cumhuriyet Meydanı and the Atatürk statue offer the opportunity to enjoy the view at leisure.

Kaleiçi (Old Antalya)
Go down Uzun Çarşi, the street by the clock tower. On the left is the **Tekeli Mehmet Paşa Camii**, built by the Beylerbey (Governor of Governors) Tekeli Mehmet Paşa. No inscription dates the building, which was repaired extensively in 1886 and 1926. Note the beautiful Arabic inscriptions in the coloured tiles above the doors and windows.

Wander farther into Kaleiçi, now a historic zone protected from modern development. Many of the gracious old Ottoman houses have been restored, then immediately converted to pensions, hotels or, inevitably, carpet shops.

Roman Harbour The Roman harbour at the base of the slope was restored during the 1980s and is now used for yachts and excursion boats. It was Antalya's lifeline from the

Kaleiçi (Old Antalya) is now a historic zone protected from modern development. Many of its old Ottoman houses have been restored.

2nd century BC up until late in this centur when a new port was constructed about 1 km west of the city, at the far end c Konyaaltı beach. Today it's lined with re taurants, tavernas and shops. Day-excursio boats tie up here and tout for passengers.

A normal tour of the nearby coast take 4½ or five hours, visits the lower Düde waterfall, islands in the gulf, and beaches fo a swim, includes lunch, and costs US$14 t US$20 person.

Kesik Minare & Korkut Camii In the easter reaches of Kaleiçi is the **Kesik Minare** (Cu Minaret), a stump of a minaret which marks the ruins of a substantial building. Built originally as a 2nd-century roman temple, it was converted in the 6th century to the Byzantine Church of the Virgin Mary. Destroyed during the Arab raids of the 7th century, it was repaired and converted to a mosque by the Seljuks in the 9th century. When Antalya fell to the Christian king of Cyprus, Peter I in 1361, it became a church again, but reverted to a mosque under Sultan Beyazid II's son Prince Dede Korkut (1470-1509). It served the neighbourhood's Muslim population until 1896, when it was mostly destroyed by fire, including the wooden superstructure of its minaret.

Gates and walls prevent entry, but it's possible to see bits of marble decoration in Roman and Byzantine styles from a walk around.

Hıdırlık Kulesi At the south-western edge of Kaleiçi, on the corner with Karaali Parkı, rises the Hıdırlık Kulesi, a 14-metre-high tower in the ancient walls which dates from the 1st century AD, and may have been used as a lighthouse.

Hadrian's Gate & Karaali Park
Down Atatürk Caddesi is Hadrianüs Kapısı, (Hadrian's Gate; also called Üçkapılar, the Three Gates) erected during the reign of that Roman emperor (117-38). The monumental marble arch, which now leads to Kaleiçı, is

et in a shady little park in the midst of the ity.

Farther along Atatürk Caddesi towards the ea is Karaali Parkı, a large, attractive, lower-filled park good for a stroll and for views of the sea. Sunset, the prettiest time, is when most Turks come here to stroll.

Antalya Museum

Antalya's large and rich museum, Antalya Müzesi, is in the western part of town, just over two km from the Yivli Minare, reached by bus along Cumhuriyet Caddesi. Ask the driver: *Müzeye gider mi?* (mur-zeh-YEH gee-DEHR mee?), 'Does this go to the museum?'. The collections include fascinating glimpses into the popular life of the region, with crafts and costume displays as well as a wealth of ancient artefacts. Opening hours are from 9 am to 5 pm, closed Monday. Admission costs US$2.

The exhibits, most of them labelled in English as well as Turkish, start with fossils, proceed chronologically through the Stone and Bronze ages (in which Turkey is especially rich in artefacts) and continue through the Mycenaean, classical and Hellenistic periods. The Gods Gallery has statues of 15 classical gods from Aphrodite to Zeus, some of them very fine. Among the exceptionally good smaller objects are jewellery, vases, glass items and statuettes. The Tomb Room is also quite good.

The museum has a small collection of Christian art, including a room for icons which also contains a few of the bones of St Nicholas. There are also several sections of mosaic pavement.

The collection continues through Seljuk and Ottoman times, with costumes, armour, calligraphy, implements, faïence, musical instruments, carpets and saddlebags. The ethnographic exhibits are fascinating and include a fully furnished nomad's tent, a room with a carpet loom from a village home and several rooms from a typical Ottoman household.

A shady patio has tables where you can sit and have a cool drink or hot tea.

Festivals

Antalya is famous in Turkey for its Golden Orange Film Festival (Altın Portakkal Filim Festivali), held in late September or early October, and the Mediterranean Song Festival (Akdeniz Şarkı Festivali), a performance contest held immediately afterwards. Hotels are more heavily booked during the festivities.

Places to Stay

Antalya has hundreds of lodging places in all price ranges. Undoubtedly the most interesting area to stay in is Kaleiçi, which has simple, basic pensions, comfortable and charming mid-range 'boutique' hotels, and luxurious restored mansion hotels.

Kaleiçi's pensions and small hotels fall into three categories. Cheapest are the run-down old houses and new breeze-block buildings, which may or may not have charm, – and private facilities – but which charge from US$12 to US$16. Next come the houses renovated in the old style, most with lots of charm, private bathrooms, and rates of US$16 to US$34. Finally come the 'boutique' hotels, one or more adjoining houses perfectly restored and lavishly furnished, perhaps with a swimming pool, costing from US$60 to US$100 and up. Surprisingly, you don't get much more guest room for US$100 than you do for US$30.

Places to Stay – bottom end

Kaleiçi The most direct route to Kaleiçi's pensions is through Hadrian's Gate. Walk through the gate, bear left around the Urartu Rug Store and you're on Hesapçı Sokak which goes south-west past the Kesik Minare all the way to the cliffs above the sea. In general, the farther you go along Hesapçı Sokak, the cheaper the pensions and the better the room availability.

In the quarter called Barbaros Mahallesi, near the corner of Hesapçı and Hamit Efendi sokaks are four pensions, including the *Hasbahçe Pension* (☎ (242) 248 5367), Hesapçı Sokak 7-9, an old house renting rooms for US$14 a double with shower.

There are more and better choices farther along.

Turn left at Kandiller Ceçidi to find the tidy *Erkal Pansiyon* (☎ (242) 241 0757, fax 244 0159), Kandiller Geçidi 5. Clean, quiet and well-located, it rents double rooms with shower and fan for US$16, breakfast included.

Turn right onto Kocatepe Sokak then bear left around the mosque to find the *Adler Pension* (☎ (242) 241 7818), Civelek Sokak 16, which, being unrestored, is among the cheapest pensions in the neighbourhood at US$10/16 a single/double, with shared baths.

Turn left onto Akarçeşme Sokak and walk two blocks to the *Bahar Aile Pansiyon* (☎ (242) 248 2089), Akarçeşme Sokak 5, an unrestored and frankly unattractive house with the advantage of low prices (for US$12 a double) for simple, clean, waterless rooms. The showers are clean, tiled and fired by gas, not the sun.

Farther along Hesapçı Sokak are more pensions in the Kılınçaslan Mahallesi neighbourhood.

Garden Pansiyon (☎ (242) 247 1930), Zafer Sokak 16 (or Hesapçı Sokak 44 – it's on the corner), has a garden and seven rooms with bath for US$18 a double; the showers could be cleaner. A few older rooms without bath go for half that price. Unfortunately, a minaret is very close and loud.

Go north-west along Zafer Sokak to Hıdırlık Sokak and turn left to find the *Erken Pansiyon* (☎ (242) 247 6092), Hıdırlık Sokak 5, a well-preserved (not restored) Ottoman house of dark wood and white plaster. Double rooms with private showers cost US$25 with breakfast.

The *Pansiyon Dedekonak* (☎ (242) 247 5170), Hıdırlık Sokak 13, is full of character, very well kept, and a good choice at US$16/26 a single/double.

Down past the Kesik Minare (Cut Minaret), on and off Hesapçı Sokak, are many more pensions.

The *Sabah Pansiyon* (☎ (242) 247 5345), Hesapçı Sokak 60/A, has 16 rooms with shower from US$16 to US$18 a double, or US$10 a double for the rooms with share[d] bath. Single females may not feel comfort[able] able here.

There is a concentration of good, chea[p] pensions on Hesapçı Geçidi and Zeyti[n] Çıkmazı, a block and a half from the Sabah. Best is the *Hadriyanüs Pansiyon* (☎ (242) 244 0030), Kılınçarslan Mahallesi, Zeytin Çıkmazı 4/A-B, an old house fronting on to a refreshingly green walled garden. The owners are friendly and charge US$14/20 for a single/double room with shower, breakfast included. Other possibilities in this area include the *Tamer*, the *White Garden*, and the somewhat drab *Anatolia*.

At the south-western end of Hesapçı Sokak are a half-dozen pensions which, being somewhat out of the way, may be willing to haggle over the price. The *Saltur Pansion* (☎ (242) 247 62 38), on the corner of Hesapçı and Hıdırlık sokaks, has a nice garden and overlooks verdant Karaali Parkı. It charges US$15 for a double with shower and breakfast. The *Bermuda* and *Senem* across the street are other good bets.

The *Hıdırlık Pansiyon* (☎ (242) 247 4746), Hıdırlık Sokak 56, has a sea-view terrace, rooms with private shower, and lowish prices of US$18 a double, breakfast included.

A few doors down at Hıdırlık Sokak 35, the *Keskin Pansiyon* (☎ (242) 241 2865) is two converted houses (one built to look old). All rooms have baths, some have sea views, all come with breakfast and rent for US$17 in summer. Watch out for the smell of drains here.

Off Kazım Özalp (Şarampol) Caddesi

Until 1996, Antalya's otogar was mid-way along Kazım Özalp Caddesi, and there were several small hotels to serve travelers nearby. By and large these places offer less comfort than do those in Kaleiçi, and not much of a price advantage, but if Kaleiçi is booked solid, you may have to look here.

Just a block east of Kazım Özalp Caddesi is the quaint old *Otel Süngül* (☎ (242) 241 1408), Tahıl Pazarı, 459 Sokak 3. A real traditional old Turkish marketplace hotel ith friendly management in a stone building, the Süngül charges US$10 for double rooms with shower. The *Nas* across the street is also worth a look. The nearby *Kaya Oteli* (☎ (242) 241 1391), 459 Sokak 12, is newer and modern, but a bit expensive for what you get.

Camping It's expensive (US$8 per tent) and inconvenient. The *Parlar Mocamp*, 14 km north on the Burdur highway (D 650), is designed for caravans and RVs, but there are tent sites as well. Stopping a bus for transport to and from the city can be a problem.

Camping Bambus (☎ (242) 321 5263), on the road to Lara Plajı, is similar but even more expensive, with modern facilities and a beach.

Places to Stay – middle

Kaleiçi The *Ninova Pension* (☎ (242) 248 6114), Hamit Efendi Sokak 9, is an artistically restored house with a peaceful garden renting double rooms for US$32, breakfast included.

The *Atelya Pension* (☎ (242) 241 6416, fax 241 2848), Civelek Sokak 21, is a beautifully restored stone house with a vine-shaded garden on a quiet street. All rooms have private baths and there's a bar. Room rates are US$18/26 a single/double, breakfast included – excellent value.

For nice but slightly cheaper rooms, walk a few steps farther to the *Pansion Mini Orient* (☎ & fax (242) 244 0015), Civelek Sokak 30, an old house nicely restored but still simple. The four double and six triple rooms grouped around the small courtyard all have tiny private facilities, and there's a cosy dining room for meals. Prices in summer are US$22/30/40 for a single/double/triple, with reductions in the off season.

The *Hodja Pansiyon* (☎ (242) 248 9486, fax 248 9485), Hesapçı Sokak 37, is newish and clean, renting double rooms with shower for US$30, breakfast included. The nearby *Abadotel Pansiyon* (☎ (242) 247 6662, fax 248 9205), Hesapçı Sokak 52, is similar in its comforts and price.

The *Turistik Frankfurt Pansiyon* (☎ (242) 47 62 24), Hıdırlık Sokak 17, is a restored house with white plaster walls, bright honey-coloured wood trim on door frames and lattice-covered windows, and German-Turkish management. A little marble fountain burbles in the courtyard. It's pleasant, and excellent value at US$28/38 a single/double in high summer for a room with shower, a good breakfast included. It's often full.

Kazım Özalp Caddesi If you must have a modern hotel, try the three-star, 54-room *Maryot Hotel* (☎ (242) 247 4807, fax 247 4805), Elmalı Mahallesi, Kazım Özalp Caddesi 69, where well-equipped rooms cost US$40 a double, breakfast included.

Places to Stay – top end

Kaleiçi Old Antalya has some excellent charming 'boutique' hotels.

The *Villa Perla* (☎ (242) 248 9793, fax 241 2917), Hesapçı Sokak 26, has lots of character, and a tiny swimming pool in the midst of the well-regarded restaurant. Rooms cost US$35/45 with private shower and breakfast.

The *Hotel Alp Paşa* (☎ (242) 247 5676, fax 248 5074), Hesapçı Sokak 30-32, has been aggressively restored into a posh Ottoman dream of comforts, from its hamam and courtyard swimming pool to its suites with whirlpool baths. Doubles with bath and breakfast cost US$70, and are very comfortable.

The more luxurious places are ranged along Mermerli Sokak, just to the east of the yacht harbour.

Tütav Türk Evi Otelleri (☎ (242) 248 6591, fax 241 9419), Mermerli Sokak 2, is three beautifully restored Ottoman houses with 20 guest rooms, all done in late Ottoman Baroque décor with lots of gold leaf and Turkish carpets. There's a small octagonal swimming pool, and the sunset-view terrace café-bar overlooks the yacht harbour and the mountains beyond. All rooms have private baths and air-con, and cost US$65/95 a single/double, breakfast included.

Just down the street is the *Marina Hotel* (☎ (242) 247 54 90, fax 241 1765), Mermerli Sokak 15, managed by Kuoni of Switzerland. This Ottoman mansion has opulent decoration, air-con, TV, mini bars and direct-dial phones, as well as a swimming pool and courtyard garden café, but no lift. Depending on room size and view, the cost is US$85 to US$130 a double, breakfast included.

The four-star *Hotel Aspen* (☎ (242) 247 0590, fax 241 3364), Mermerli Sokak 16-18, across from the tourism office, is a perfect gem of a hotel, beautifully restored with bevelled glass, marble and gilt. The 36 rooms and four suites have air-con, satellite TV, mini bars and all the comforts. Indulge yourself in the swimming pool, Turkish restaurant and bar, and sauna. This is the best in Kaleiçi. Rates are US$95/120, breakfast included.

Big Luxury Hotels Without doubt, Antalya's most prestigious and luxurious address is the five-star, 409-room *Sheraton Voyager Antalya* (☎ (242) 243 2432, fax 243 2462), 100 Yıl Bulvarı, at the western end of Kenan Evren Bulvarı, eastern end of Konyaaltı beach, about 2.5 km west of Kale Kapısı. All the five-star services are here, a strikingly modern and appealing buildi with lavish terraced gardens. Rooms co from US$180 to US$210 a single, US$2 to US$260 a double, with breakfast.

Closer to the centre, the best local effort the five-star *Talya Hotel* (☎ (242) 248 680 fax 241 5400), Fevzi Çakmak Caddesi 30, modern 204-room place overlooking the se For US$135 a single or from US$165 US$200 a double, you get a modern air-co room, swimming pool, tennis court, restauran bar and other services. Staff can be stuffy.

Near Lara beach the best address is th five-star *Hotel Antalya Dedeman* (☎ (242 321 7910, fax 321 3873), Lara Yolu, next t the Antalya Aquapark, a high-rise propert of the Turkish chain with 482 rooms perche on a cliff overlooking the beach. Prices are reasonable at US$90 to US$110 a single US$120 to US$160 a double.

Flavours of Antalya

Antalya is renowned among Turks for its fruit jams and preserves, which come in a surprising array of flavours. Stroll to the corner of Cumhuriyet and Atatürk Caddesis and have a look in the shop windows. Here are some of the flavours:

- Bergamot (bergamot)
- Çilek (strawberry)
- Greyfurut (grapefruit)
- Gül (rose)
- Incir (fig)
- Karpuz (watermelon)
- Kayısı (apricot)
- Kiraz (cherry)
- Limon (lemon)
- Limon çiçeği (lemon blossom)
- Patlıcan (aubergine/eggplant)
- Portakal (orange)
- Turunç (Seville orange) ■

Places to Eat

In the Centre The closer you get to the harbour, the more expensive the food gets.

Go to the intersection of Cumhuriyet and Atatürk Caddesis and find the little street (parallel to Atatürk Caddesi) called Eski Sebzeciler İçi Sokak. The name means 'the Old Inner Street of the Greengrocers' Market'. The narrow street is now shaded by awnings and lined with little restaurants and pastry shops, many of which have outdoor tables. It's now quite touristy, but still enjoyable if you're careful not to let yourself be cheated.

The food is kebaps, mostly the ever-popular döner kebap, but you'll also find Antalya's speciality, tandır kebap – mutton baked in an earthenware pot buried in a fire pit; it's rich, flavourful and greasy, served on a bed of fresh pide with vegetable garnish. It's sold by weight so you can have as many grams as you like. A normal portion is 150g *(yüz elli gram)*, a small portion 100g *(yüz gram)*. A full meal costs anywhere from US$4 to US$8; ask prices before you sit down.

On my last visit I had 150g of döner kebap, *soslu* (with sauce), and a glass of ayran for US$4 at *Azim Döner ve İskender Salonu* (☎ (242) 241 6610) at No 6.

The little pedestrian-only street parallel to and just south-west of this one, 2 İnönü Caddesi, is developing into an eating-street as well.

The *Surkent Restaurant*, just around the corner from the Tekeli Mehmet Paşa Camii, has cheap lahmacun and fresh pide. The nearby *Sultanyar Restaurant* has a few shady outdoor tables, similar pide, and more substantial meals as well, but equally low prices yielding meals under US$4. The *Pasha Pide Kebap Salonu* facing the Sultanyar is similar.

The clientele at the *Şehir Ocakbaşı Restaurant* (☎ (242) 241 5127), not far from Kale Kapısı, is mostly locals, not tourists. In fine weather streetside tables are set up. First, the waiter rolls up a cart with dozens of mezes, from which you choose. With drinks, you can make a meal of mezes; or you can order a kebap. Food is not expensive, but the drinks are dear, so ask prices. A full meal with drinks should cost no more than US$10, and is usually less. To find the restaurant, from Kale Kapısı cross Cumhuriyet Caddesi to its northern side. More or less parallel, and just a few more steps up a rise to the north, is Birinci Sokak (written '1 Sokak' on street signs). Turn left on Birinci Sokak and look down the second street on the right to see the restaurant.

Just around the corner (inland) from the Şehir is the cheaper *Can İnegöl Köftecisi*, a small grill where you can eat for under US$4.

One goes to the *Hisar Restaurant* (☎ (242) 241 5281), Tophanealtı, more for the view than the food. Diners peer out from old vaulted stone chambers within the retaining wall behind Cumhuriyet Meydanı to the harbour and the sea beyond. Prime tables are on narrow terraces fastened to the walls. The cuisine is Turkish and a three-course meal with wine or beer should cost only US$10 to US$14 per person, unless you have the expensive and disappointing specialty, shrimp casserole (kalamar güveç). Come early for lunch (noon) or dinner (from 6 to 7 pm) if you want to get one of the tables with the view. To get to the restaurant walk from the Atatürk statue to the edge of the cliff and find the flight of stairs descending to the harbour.

Kaleiçi Kaleiçi has many small restaurants, mostly catering to foreign tourists with continental-style menus. *Villa Perla* (☎ 248 9793), in the pension of the same name at Hesapçı Sokak 26, is well regarded, with tables out in a verdant courtyard. Have the Caucasian şaşlık (skewered meat and vegetables) for US$7, or the chicken shish kebap for less. Full meals may be had for US$10 to US$16.

The *Sim Restaurant* on Kaledibi Sokak is small and simple, and when tables are set out in the street it's pleasant. Full meals cost US$6 to US$11.

A prime restaurant area is the junction of Balık Pazarı and Mermerli Banyo sokaks right by the large Atatürk Ortaokulu (school). *Barbaros Restaurant*, opposite the school, has a big garden, many shady tables, freshly squeezed orange juice, and a variety of grilled meats.

Walk along Balık Pazarı Sokak to Uzun Çarşı Sokak to find more restaurants, including the *Favorit*, *Sunset* and *Café Alba*, all on shaded terraces above the street. Prices are posted prominently.

Deeper into Kaleiçi, the *Kırk Merdiven* (Forty Steps) across from the Tütav Türk Evi Otelleri, has a Euro-Turk menu featuring mushroom soup and various continental-style grills served on a vine-shaded terrace. Your bill might come to US$14 per person for dinner here.

Kazım Özalp Caddesi Another place to look for good, cheap restaurants – these are mostly patronised by Turks – is Kazım Özalp (Şarampol) Caddesi. Just a few steps up Kazım Özalp from Kale Kapısı on the left-hand side is the entrance to a bare courtyard and the *Parlak Restaurant* (☎ (242) 241 6553), an old Antalya standby for grills. The impressively long grill pit belches smoke generated by its load of skewered chickens and lamb kebaps. Talk and rakı flow freely, and the evening passes quickly. If the décor is too basic (there is none), escape to the aile salonu on the left. A full meal of meze, grills and rakı costs from US$8 to US$12 a person. The neighbouring *Plaza Fast Food* is the sanitised version of the Parlak.

Farther along Kazım Özalp Caddesi on the

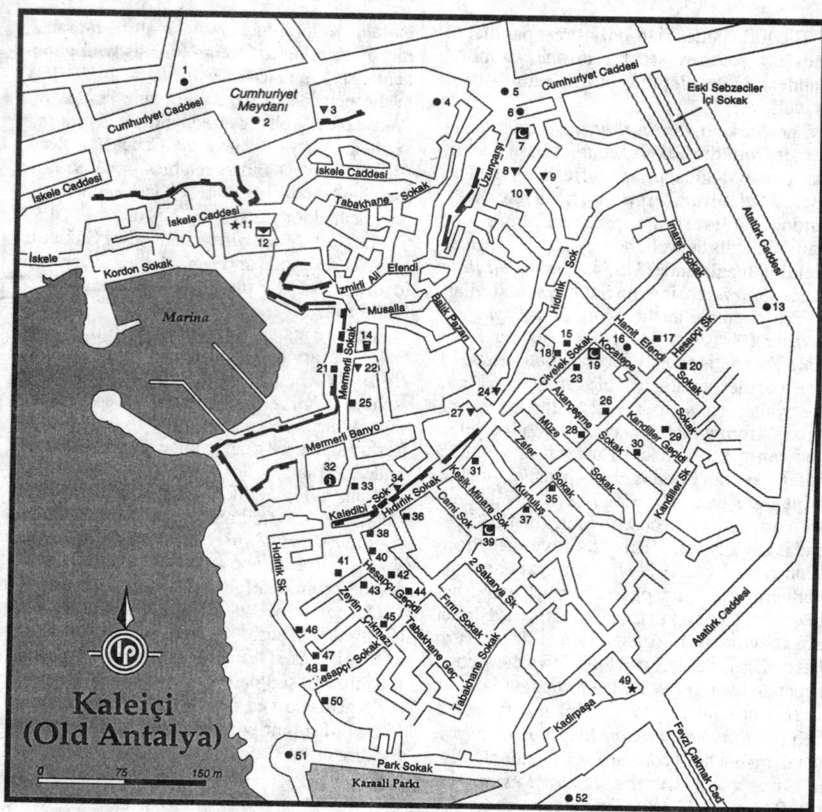

left-hand side is the *Topçu Kebap Salonu* (☎ 241 1616), another plain place famed for its kebaps. Good, simple, cheap and clean, it offers İskender kebap (Bursa-style döner) for US$2.25.

Entertainment

Long dinners are the rule. Kaleiçi and the yacht harbour have numerous bars and lounges good for drinks and conversation. Many visitors find that their pension owners – particularly in the cheaper places – organise evenings of singing, dancing and storytelling.

The Voice Bar, just uphill from the Tütav Türk Evi Otelleri, has live entertainment – usually an acoustic guitarist – many summer evenings.

Getting There & Away

Air The Antalya airport is 10 km east of the city centre on the Alanya highway. Turkish Airlines (☎ (242) 243 4384, fax 248 4761), Cumhuriyet Caddesi 91, in the same building as the Tourism Information Office, has several nonstop flights daily in summer to/from İstanbul and at least one from Ankara. There are also nonstops to Amman, Lefkoşa

PLACES TO STAY

15 Adler Pension
17 Ninova Pension
18 Pansion Mini Orient
20 Hasbahçe Pension
21 Tütav Türk Evi Otelleri
23 Atelya Pension
25 Marina Hotel
26 Villa Perla
28 Hotel Alp Paşa
29 Erkal Pansiyon
30 Bahar Aile Pansiyon
31 Erken Pansiyon
33 Hotel Aspen
35 Garden Pansiyon
36 Pansiyon Dedekonak
37 Hodja Pansiyon
38 Turistik Frankfurt Pansiyon
40 Anatolia Pension
41 Hadriyanüs Pansiyon
42 White Garden Pansiyon
43 Tamer Pansiyon
44 Abadotel Pansiyon
45 Sabah Pansiyon
46 Keskin Pansiyon
47 Hıdırlık Pansiyon
48 Bermuda Pension
50 Saltur Pansion

PLACES TO EAT

3 Hisar Restaurant
8 Surkent Restaurant
9 Sultanyar Restaurant
10 Pasha Pide Kebap Salonu
22 Kırk Merdiven
24 Favorit, Sunset & Café Alba Restaurants
27 Barbaros Restaurant
34 Sim Restaurant

OTHER

1 Government House
2 Atatürk Statue
4 Yivli Minare (Grooved Minaret)
5 Kale Kapısı
6 Saat Kulesi (Clock Tower)
7 Tepedelenli Ali Paşa Camii
11 Tourism Police
12 PTT
13 Hadrian's Gate
14 Voice Bar
16 Sefa Hamamı (Turkish Bath)
19 Mosque
32 Tourism Information Office
39 Kesik Minare & Korkut Camii
49 Police
51 Hıdırlık Kulesi (Tower)
52 Belediye (Municipality)

(Nicosia), London, Tel Aviv and Zürich at least weekly.

İstanbul Airlines (☎ (242) 243 3892, fax 243 3894; at the airport ☎ (242) 330 3070, fax 330 3071), Anafartalar Caddesi 2, Selekler Çarşısı 82, has nonstop flights at least weekly between Antalya and Brussels, Cologne, Copenhagen, Düsseldorf, Frankfurt, Graz, Hamburg, Hannover, İstanbul, İzmir, Lefkoşa (Nicosia), Linz, Lyon, Malpenza, Paris, Salzburg, Stuttgart, Tel Aviv and Vienna. Discounts are offered to families (10%), youth (aged from 12 to 24, 25%) and Golden Agers (60 years and over, 25%).

Bus Antalya's new otogar (bus station), replacing the old one on Kazım Özalp (Şarampol) Caddesi, is four km north of the centre on the northern edge of the city. Taxis and dolmuşes connect it with the centre at Kale Kapısı.

For minibuses to places east of Antalya (such as Perge, Aspendos, Manavgat, Side and Alanya) go to the Doğu Garajı, a staging area 600m east of Kale Kapısı along Ali Çetinkaya Caddesi. The minibus to Lara Plajı leaves from the Doğu Garajı.

Destinations served from Antalya include:

Adana – 555 km, 11 hours, US$12 to US$15; a few buses daily

Alanya – 115 km, two hours, US$4; hourly buses in summer

Ankara – 550 km, 8 hours, US$15 to US$17; frequent buses daily

Denizli (Pamukkale) – 300 km, five hours, US$8; several buses daily

Eğirdir – 186 km, 2½ hours, US$6

Fethiye – 295 km, seven hours, US$12 (sahil or coastal route); 222 km, 4½ hours, US$ 8 (yayla, inland route); several buses daily on each route

Göreme/Ürgüp – 485 km, 11 hours, US$20; several buses daily in summer

İstanbul – 725 km, 12 hours, US$14 to US$22; frequent buses daily

Kaş – 185 km, four hours, US$7.50; at least four buses daily

Konya – 365 km, six hours, US$12; several buses daily on two routes, the longer via Isparta, the faster and prettier via Akseki

Marmaris – 590 km, nine hours, US$14; a few buses daily

Side/Manavgat – 65 km, 1½ hours, US$3; very frequent buses and dolmuşes in summer

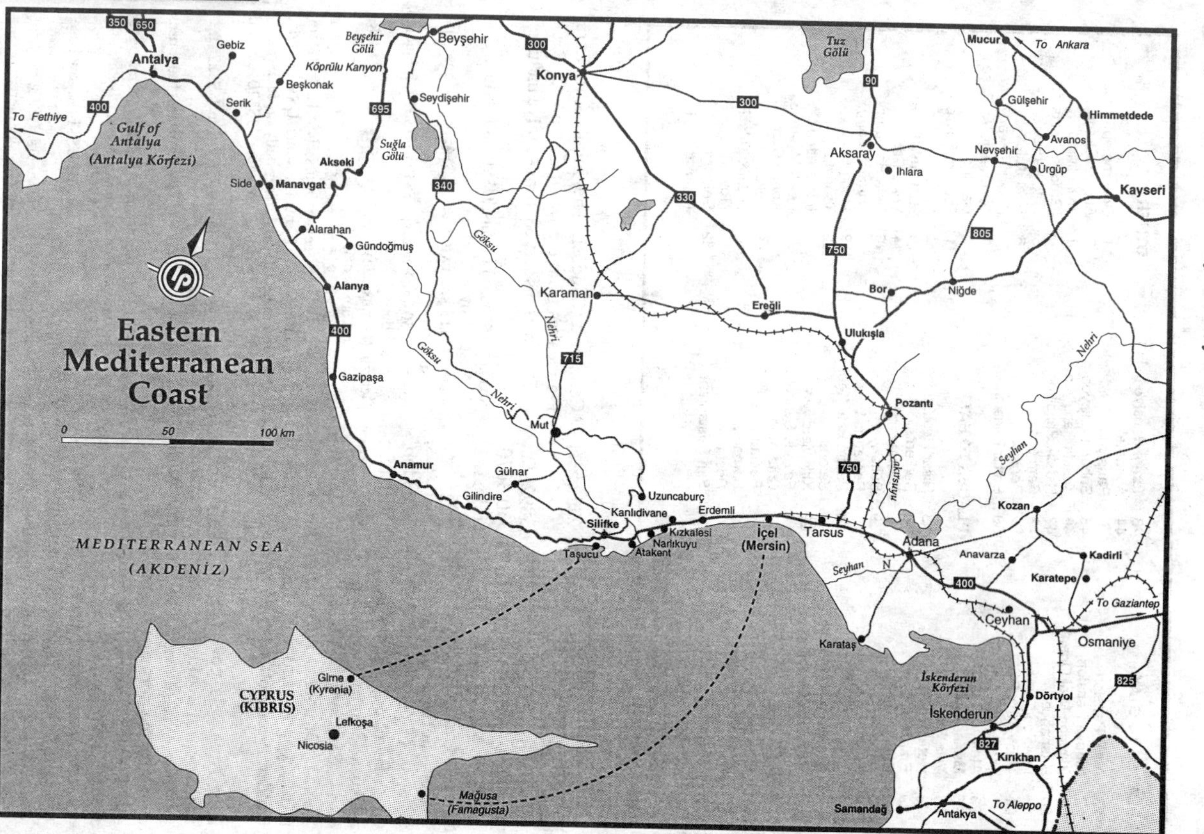
Eastern Mediterranean Coast
0
50
100 km
MEDITERRANEAN SEA
(AKDENİZ)
Gulf of Antalya
(Antalya Körfezi)
CYPRUS
(KIBRIS)
Girne
(Kyrenia)
Lefkoşa
Nicosia
Mağusa
(Famagusta)
İskenderun Körfezi
Tuz Gölü
Beyşehir Gölü
Suğla Gölü
Köprülu Kanyon
Göksu
Nehri
Göksu Nehri
Çakırsuyu
Seyhan
Nehri
To Ankara
To Fethiye
To Gaziantep
To Aleppo
Antalya
Gebiz
Serik
Side
Manavgat
Beşkonak
Alarahan
Akseki
Gündoğmuş
Alanya
Gazipaşa
Anamur
Gilindire
Gülnar
Mut
Taşucu
Silifke
Kanlıdivane
Uzuncaburç
Atakent
Narlıkuyu
Kızkalesi
Erdemli
İçel
(Mersin)
Tarsus
Adana
N
Karataş
Ceyhan
Anavarza
Kozan
Karatepe
Kadirli
Osmaniye
Dörtyol
İskenderun
Kırıkhan
Antakya
Samandağ
Pozantı
Ulukışla
Bor
Niğde
Ereğli
Karaman
Konya
Beyşehir
Seydişehir
Aksaray
Ihlara
Nevşehir
Ürgüp
Avanos
Gülşehir
Mucur
Himmetdede
Kayseri
350
650
400
695
340
300
715
330
90
750
805
827
825

AROUND ANTALYA

You can use Antalya as a base for excursions to Olimpos and Phaselis, Termessos, Perge, Aspendos and Side, but you might find it easier to visit Olimpos and Phaselis on your way to or from Kaş, and Perge and Aspendos on your way to Side. With your own car you can stop at Termessos on your way north or west to Ankara, Denizli/Pamukkale, Eğirdir, İstanbul or İzmir.

Travel agencies in Antalya operate tours to all of these sites. For instance, a half-day tour to the Düden waterfalls (Düden Şelalesi) and Termessos costs US$25 per person and is perhaps a bit rushed – there's a lot to see at Termessos.

A full-day tour to Perge, Aspendos and Side costs almost US$50. Or you can organise your own transport. If you can scrape together a party of four or five people you can negotiate with a taxi or minibus driver for a private excursion. The private taxi method is especially pleasant and useful for getting to Termessos, and is a lot cheaper than taking an organised tour.

Beaches

Antalya's reputation as a tourist centre is built not on its own beaches, but on those not far away, like Side's. Antalya's Konyaaltı beach to the west is pebbly, shadeless and relatively cheerless. Lara Plajı, to the east, is much better, but access is restricted and fees are charged. For a real beach holiday, spend your time at Side, Alanya or Patara.

Düden Waterfalls

The Upper Düden Falls, less than 10 km north of the city centre, can be reached by dolmuş from the Doğu Garajı. Within view of the falls is a nice park and teahouse. This can be a relaxing spot on a hot summer afternoon, but avoid Düden on summer weekends when the park is crowded.

The Lower Düden Falls are down where the stream Düden Çayı, meets the Mediterranean at Lara Plajı. Excursion boats include a visit to Lower Düden Falls on their rounds of the Gulf of Antalya. See Boat Excursions in the Antalya section for details.

Termessos

High in a rugged mountain valley 34 km inland from Antalya lies the ruined city of Termessos. The warlike Termessians, a Pisidian people, lived in their impregnable fortress city and guarded their independence fiercely. Alexander the Great was fought off in 333 BC, and the Romans accepted Termessos as an independent ally, not as a subject city in 70 BC.

Start early in the day as you have to walk and climb a good deal to see the ruins. Though it's cooler up in the mountains than on the shore, the sun is still quite hot. Take good shoes, a supply of drinking water, and perhaps a picnic lunch. Make this visit in the morning and spend the afternoon at the beach.

The Termessos archaeological site is open daily from 8 am to 7 pm (until 5.30 pm in winter); admission costs US$2.50, half-price for students.

At the agora are the remains of a small

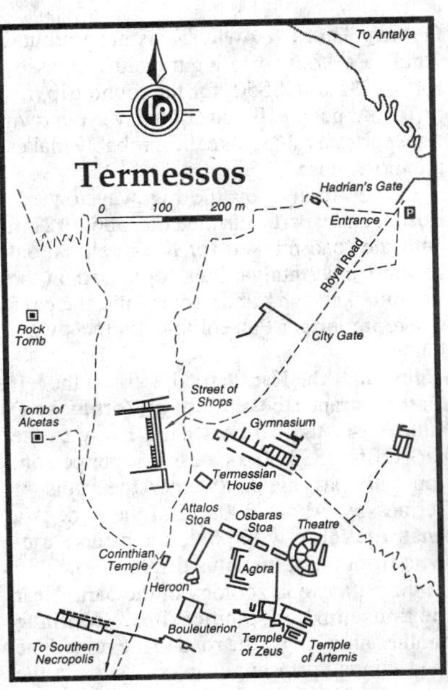

Temple of Hadrian, now little more than a doorway. Head up the path to the **city gate**, the impressive **theatre** (the best preserved building here) with its spectacular view, **gymnasium**, a **Corinthian temple** and the **upper city walls**.

Your goal is the **necropolis** *(mezarlık)* at the very top of the valley, three km up from the agora. It's a hike but the necropolis is a fantastic sight and the mountain vistas are breathtaking. As you toil upward you'll notice a wire running alongside the path. It goes to a fire tower at the top of the valley, where a man sits, drinks tea, smokes cigarettes, reads newspapers and keeps a lookout for fires.

The necropolis is impressive – a vast field of huge stone sarcophagi tumbled about by earthquakes and grave-robbers. The scene is reminiscent of medieval paintings portraying the Judgement Day, when all tombs are to be cast open. Most famous of the tombs here is that of Alcatus, a successor general of Alexander's, with fine reliefs on its façade.

Getting There & Away Taxis hang around Antalya's otogar offering trips to Termessos for US$35 to US$50, for the round trip, for up to four people. If you don't have your own transport, travelling like this probably makes the most sense.

Leave Antalya by the highway towards Burdur and Isparta, turning after about 12 km onto the road marked for Korkuteli. About 25 km from Antalya, look for a road on the right marked for Karain (nine km), the cave where important Palaeolithic artefacts were found.

Just after the Karain road, look on the left for the entrance to **Güllükdağı (Termessos) Milli Parkı,** the national park. Entry to the park costs US$3.50 for a car, 75c per person; you will pay again to enter the ruins of Termessos. About 800m into the park is a small **museum** with photographs and artefacts from the ruins, plus displays touching on the botany and zoology of the park. Near the museum are picnic sites. Continue another nine km up the road to the ruins. The road winds up through several gates in the city walls to the lower agora, the largest flat space in this steep valley. From here you must explore the ruins on foot.

Termessos to Denizli

If your itinerary takes you north from Termessos towards Denizli, you pass through Korkuteli and Tefenni, two undistinguished farming towns on the Anatolian Plateau. But onward, near Yeşilova, is Salda Gölü, a beautiful lake with a few simple camp sites and restaurants with signs in German.

Kurşunlu Şelalesi

About seven km east of Antalya and the same distance north from the Antalya-Aksu highway is Kurşunlu Şelalesi (Leaded Waterfall), a shady park set in a pine forest with a waterfall and pool. It's a good place to get away from the noise and activity of Turkish cities, except on weekends, when the city folk move here. Opening hours are from 8 am to 5.30 pm; admission costs US$0.35.

Bring a picnic (there are lots of tables), then follow the *geziyolu* (scenic trail) down the steps to the pool and the falls, actually a number of rivulets cascading down a rock wall festooned with ferns, vines and moss.

Perge

Perge (PEHR-geh), 15 km east of Antalya just north of the town of Aksu, is one of those very ancient towns. Greek colonists came here after the Trojan War and probably displaced even earlier inhabitants. The city prospered under Alexander the Great and the Romans but dwindled under the Byzantines before it was abandoned. The ruins are open from 8 am to 6 pm in summer; admission is US$2.50.

The substantial remains of a great theatre, stadium, huge Hellenistic and Roman gates and an impressive colonnaded street are worth seeing. At the acropolis, on a rise behind the other ruins, there is nothing much to see. For a fine view of the site climb to the top of the theatre.

Getting There & Away A visit to Perge can be included in the trip eastward to Aspendos

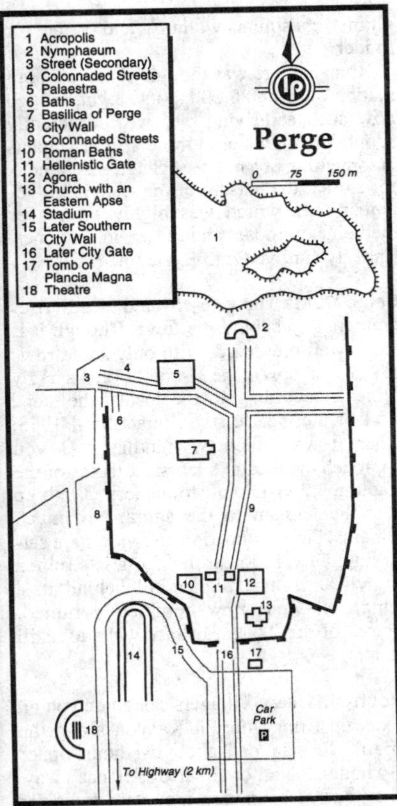

and Side, doing it all in a day if you're pressed for time. Leave early in the morning.

Dolmuşes leave for Aksu from the Doğu Garajı (Eastern Garage) or, better still, get an Aksu Belediyesi bus from the otogar. Ride the 13 km east from Antalya to Aksu and the turn-off for Perge, then walk (20 to 25 minutes) or hitch the remaining two km north to the ruins.

Sillyon

Seven km east of Perge and Aksu, a road on the left (north) is marked for Gebiz and Sillyon. Set on a mesa usually visible from the highway, Sillyon was a thriving city when Alexander the Great came through in the 4th century BC. Unable to take the city, the conqueror passed it by.

Sillyon offers little to the casual visitor. Bits of the ruined theatre, gymnasium and temple remain, but most of the ruins were destroyed by a landslide in 1969. The greatest curiosity here is an inscription in the Pamphylian dialect of ancient Greek, a unique example of this otherwise little-seen language.

Getting There & Away The ruins, near the village of Asar Köyü, are difficult to reach without your own vehicle. Despite the sign reading 'Sillyon 8 km' on the highway, it is farther: 7.2 km to a road on the right marked for Sillyon, then 2.2 km to another right turn (unmarked). Go 900m and bear left, then another 100m, and turn left at a farm. The ruins are clearly visible one km farther along.

Aspendos

The land east of Antalya was called Pamphylia in ancient times. The Taurus Mountains (Toros Dağları) form a beautiful backdrop to the fertile coast, rich with fields of cotton and vegetables. Concrete irrigation troughs radiate like spider webs through the lush agricultural land.

Aspendos (Belkis) lies 47 km east of Antalya in the Pamphylian plain. Go as far as the stream Köprüçayı, and notice the old Seljuk humpback bridge. Turn left (north) along the western bank of the stream, following the signs to Aspendos. The great theatre is less than four km from the highway. About 200m before it is the *Şato Wien Restaurant* (☎ (242) 735 7319), a good place for lunch. Opening hours for the archaeological site are from 8 am to 7 pm daily in summer; admission is US$2.

What you see here remains from Roman times, though the history of the settlement goes back to the Hittite Empire (800 BC). In 468 BC the Greeks and Persians fought a great battle here (the Greeks won, but not for long). Under the Romans, during the reign of Marcus Aurelius (161-80 AD), Aspendos got its theatre.

There are many fine Hellenistic and Roman theatres in Anatolia but the one at Aspendos is the finest of all. Built by the Romans, maintained by the Byzantines and Seljuks, it was restored after a visit by Atatürk. A plaque by the entrance states that when Atatürk saw the theatre he declared that it should be restored and used again for performances and sports.

Purists may question the authenticity of the restorations, but more than any other, the theatre at Aspendos allows the modern visitor to see and feel a true classical theatre: its acoustics, its lighting by day and night, and how the audiences moved in and out. Don't miss it.

Facing the theatre from the car park, a path to the right of the theatre is marked for Theatre Hill, which takes you up above the theatre for the stunning view. Follow the 'Aqueduct' fork in the trail for a good look at the remains of the city's aqueduct, and of the modern village to the left of it.

Other ruins of a stadium, agora and basilica offer little to look at. Follow the aqueduct trail along the ridge to reach them.

Getting There & Away From the Doğu Garajı take a minibus which passes by the Aspendos turn-off, then walk (45 minutes) or hitch the remaining four km to the site. Often there are taxis waiting at the highway junction to shuttle you to Aspendos.

Selge & Köprülü Kanyon

High in the mountains north of the lush Mediterranean littoral, about 44 km from the Antalya-Alanya highway, a Roman bridge spans the picturesque canyon of the Köprü Irmağı (Bridge River, anciently called the Eurymedon). Above it in the mountain fastness, less than 12 km away, are the ruins of the Roman city of Selge, scattered amidst the stone houses of the Turkish village of Altınkaya (Zerk, altitude 1050m) in a forest of Mediterranean cypresses. The setting, high in this mountainous country, is spectacular. The local people make their living cultivating wheat, corn, barley, apples, plums, chestnuts, walnuts, and vetch for fodder.

Roman Selge was thought to have a population of some 20,000 at its height, though how such a thriving city was sufficiently supplied with water in these arid mountains is something of a mystery. Selge was famous for storax, the balsam of the Asiatic liquidambar tree, which was highly prized for medicinal purposes and for use in perfumes. The city survived into Byzantine times.

Selge Ruins The vine-covered theatre rises dramatically behind the town. Though it is fairly well preserved, with only some rows of seats collapsed, the rest of the city is badly ruined. According to the locals, the stage wall of the theatre stood intact until 1948, when it was felled by lightning. As you approach the theatre's left side, traces of the stadium are visible off to the left. Climb up past the hamam to the agora. Not much remains, but the situation and views are satisfying. On a hill near the agora is a ruined church and, on a higher hill behind it, a temple of Zeus now completely ruined. Traces of the 2.5 km of city walls are still visible.

Mountain Hikes Villagers can guide you on hikes up from Köprülü Kanyon along the original Roman road, about two hours up, or 1½ hours down, for about US$10 each way. They can also arrange mountain treks for groups to Bozburun Dağı (2504m) and other points in the Kuyucuk range, with a guide, *katırcı* (muleteer) and *yemekçi* (cook) for about US$50 per day.

Canoe & Raft Trips Medraft (☎ (242) 248 0083, fax 242 7118), Cumhuriyet Caddesi 76/6, Işık Apt, Antalya, operates daily multi-person raft and two-person inflatable 'canoe' trips in summer along the Köprülü River in Köprülü Kanyon.

The company's buses pick you up at your hotel in the morning and drive you to the river. You paddle about 15 km downstream, stopping on the way for a picnic lunch. Buses return you to your hotel late in the afternoon.

The price per person is US$50 (half-price for children aged under 13 years), which includes lunch, insurance, guides and equipment.

Places to Stay At the time of writing there was little in the way of accommodation, though a request for a *misafir odası* (guest room) will sometimes produce a bed in a village house at a low price. There is camping farther down the valley. Altınkaya will not develop much because there is a shortage of water; the village's meagre supply is now brought from many km away. There is camping in the national park (see below).

Getting There & Away Köprülü Kanyon and Selge are included in some tours run from Antalya, Side and Alanya for about US$25 per person. If you'd rather do it independently, the one daily minibus departs from Altınkaya in the morning for Serik (1½ hours, $4) on the Antalya-Alanya highway, returning to Altınkaya in the evening. Thus you must plan to spend the night in the mountains, or haggle for a return fare, if you take the minibus.

With your own vehicle, you can make the visit in a half-day, though it deserves more time. About six km east of the Aspendos road (48 km east of Antalya) along the main highway, a paved road on the left (north) is marked for Beşkonak, Selge and Köprülü Kanyon Milli Parkı (Bridge Canyon National Park).

The road is paved and travelling is fast for the first 32 km. About four km before the town of Beşkonak, an unpaved road on the left is marked for Selge (22 km). The shorter route is straight on through Beşkonak. From the end of the paved road in Beşkonak, it's 6.5 km to the canyon and the graceful old arched Oluk bridge. Erosion by wind and water has sculpted the surrounding rock into fantastic shapes. Cross the bridge, ignore the road on the right marked for Selge and continue 600m past the Selge turn-off to the second bridge, named Böğrüm. Nearby is a pine-shaded camping ground, and two km farther along the unpaved road is the *Kanyon Pansion ve Camping*, a tidy place for lodging and meals right by the river.

Retrace your steps to the unpaved road marked for Altınkaya (or Zerk), the modern Turkish names for Selge, and climb 11.7 km from the canyon bridge to the village.

When you enter the village, local children will urge you to park next to refreshment stands which charge a parking fee. You can ignore the fee, or have one of them show you around for a tip.

SİDE

Cleopatra and Mark Antony chose Side (SEE-deh, population 18,000) as the spot for a romantic tryst, and today lots of Turkish couples follow their example. Side has everything: a km of fine sand beach on either side of the settlement, good Hellenistic ruins, an excellent little museum and a Turkish village.

It is perhaps too good. In recent years Side has been overrun in summer by tourists, mostly from Ankara but also from Germany and the UK. During the tourist season even moving down the streets can be difficult. The quaint main street is now lined with carpet and clothing shops, some with air-conditioners roaring and venting their hot blasts into the street. If you dislike crowds and shopping, you may want to avoid Side entirely in high summer, and lower your expectations in spring and autumn.

History

Ancient Side's great wealth was built on piracy and slavery. Many of its great buildings were raised with the profits of such dastardly activities. Slavery flourished only under the Greeks and was stopped when the city came under Roman control.

No-one knows where Side got its name, though it probably means 'pomegranate' in some ancient Anatolian language. The site was colonised by Aeolians around 600 BC but by the time Alexander the Great swept through, the inhabitants had abandoned much of their Greek culture and language.

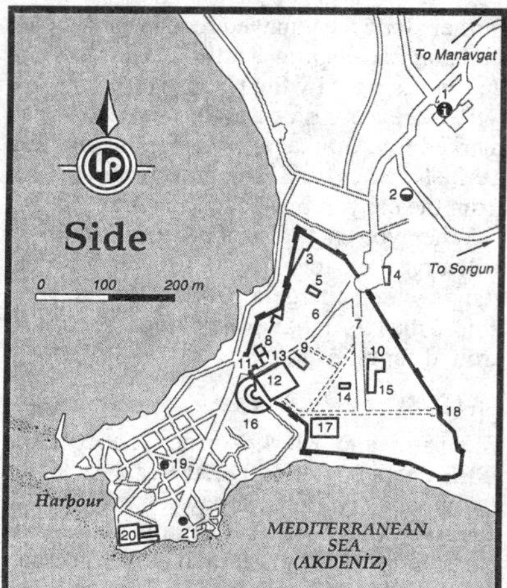

1 Tourism Information Office
2 Otogar (Bus Station)
3 Aqueduct
4 Nymphaeum
5 Houses
6 Colonnaded Street
7 Colonnaded Street
8 Baths
9 Houses
10 Basilica
11 Triumphal Arch
12 Round Building & Agora
13 Museum
14 Baptistry
15 Bishop's Palace
16 Theatre
17 Main Agora
18 South-eastern Gate
19 Baths
20 Temples
21 Nymphaeum

After the period of piracy and slave-trading, Side turned to legitimate commerce and still prospered. Under the Byzantines it was still large enough to rate a bishop. The Arab raids of the 7th century AD diminished the town, which was dead within two centuries, but it revived in the late 19th century under the Ottomans.

Orientation

Side is three km south of the east-west highway. The road to the village is littered with trashy signs and billboards and is dotted with little hotels and pensions, often bearing signs which read 'Boş Oda Var' (Rooms Available). The road passes through the archaeological zone and past the museum, beneath an arch and around the theatre. In high season you will not be allowed to drive a car into the village proper from 2 pm to 1 am. You must pay a fee and park in the car park outside the village, before the ruins. Visitors are shuttled to the centre on a *tramvay*, which in Side means a seat-filled wagon hauled by a tractor.

Side's otogar is near the Tourism Information Office, about one km from the village centre, on the road in from Manavgat.

Information

The Tourism Information Office (☎ (242) 753 1265, fax 753 2657) is on the outskirts of the village near the otogar, around one km from the village centre.

Side's postal code is 07330.

The Ruins

Side's impressive ruins are an easy walk from the village. Look first at the **theatre**, one of the largest in Anatolia, with 15,000 seats. Originally constructed during Hellenistic times, it was enlarged under the Romans.

Next to the theatre and across the road from the museum is the **agora**. The **museum** is built on the site of the Roman baths. It has a very fine small collection of statuary and reliefs. Opening hours are from 8 am to 5.15 pm daily; admission costs US$2.

To the east, between these buildings and the Hellenistic city walls, lie a **Byzantine basilica** and some foundations of Byzantine houses. Down at the edge of the eastern beach is another agora.

At the very southern tip of the point of land upon which Side lies are two temples, the **Temple of Athena** and **Temple of Apollo**, which date from the 2nd century AD. Who knows that Cleopatra and Mark Antony didn't meet at exactly this spot? Though they met (in 42 BC) before these great columns (some of limestone, newly erected) were standing, might they not have sat in earlier marble temples to enjoy one of Side's spectacular sunsets? Long after their meeting, the Byzantines constructed an immense basilica over and around the temple sites. Parts of the basilica walls remain.

Wandering among these marble remains at dusk is one of the finest things to do here.

Boat Excursions

Boats cast off from Side's waterfront each day in summer at about 10 am for seven-hour sailing, sightseeing and swimming excursions. The cost is about US$25 per person, lunch included; US$38 if you go as far as Alanya.

Manavgat & Seleukeia in Pamphylia

Manavgat, the larger town, five km to the north and east of Side, is a farmers' market and commercial town, with good shopping for souvenirs.

Four km north of central Manavgat is Manavgat's **waterfall** (Manavgat Şelalesi), a series of small falls in a shady park with teahouses, snack shops and restaurants around. It's a favourite resort on hot summer days. Admission costs US$0.35.

Two km north of the waterfall the road crosses a bridge over a stream. To the left is a fine old five-arched Ottoman bridge built next to a bastion which appears to be much older. Another km along are the remains of the Roman aqueduct which brought water from Dumanlı to Side.

Two km past the Ottoman bridge a road on the left is signposted for **Seleukeia**, seven km. Follow the road through the village of Şıhlar, with many old fieldstone houses, some with bits of columns incorporated into the walls. The paved road stops at Şıhlar; turn right at the mosque and take the road (unmarked) opposite the minaret. It's over three km to the ruins atop the hill along a very bad road, which may be impassable for low-slung cars at some times of year, but the walk is pleasant. There are no services whatsoever at the site, so bring some water if you walk.

The ruins, scattered amidst soughing pines in a beautiful and easily defensible hilltop location, include baths, a necropolis, a bouleuterion (small theatre), a temple and many unidentified buiuldings, all badly ruined. Most impressive is the large **market hall**, but in fact one comes here mostly for the beauty of the site and the feeling of antiquity as other, far more impressive ruins are more easily accessible from Side.

Seleukeia in Pamphylia was founded during Hellenistic times, and this hilltop city was thought to be it. But the recent discovery of an inscription here in both Greek and the language of ancient Side (which predated Alexander the Great) makes it more likely that this was the city of **Lyrbe**, though the modern signs still say Seleukeia.

Places to Stay

You may have difficulty finding a room in high summer so try to arrive early in the day. Before May and after early October you should have no problem finding the lodgings you want, but the 'tourist season' lasts from April to October these days. Prices are highest from June to September, slightly lower in April, May and October, and much lower in winter at the few places which remain open.

Places to Stay – bottom end

In the village proper, little pensions abound. There are dozens to choose from and your choice is dictated by availability as much as price. Prices depend upon season, demand, facilities, and even your nationality, and range from US$14 to US$18 for double rooms with running water; some have private showers.

Start your pension search in either of two general areas. First, walk down the main street several blocks and turn left (east). As you comb the town for good lodgings look for little signs which say 'Boş Oda Var' (Room Available). Some readers of this book have enjoyed the *Çiğdem*, and the small wooden bungalows (shared showers only) at the *İkimiz* (☎ (242) 753 2322), Mercan Sokak 18, for US$14 a double. *Heaven's Gate Pension* also has cheap triple rooms with toilet and shower. The *Morning Star, Pension Başak, Martı* (mahr-TUH) and *Türköz* are other favourites.

For the other pension area, walk down the main street until about two blocks from the waterfront, turn right, then left to find the *Şen Pansiyon*, a simple place on a quiet street not far from the water. My favourite in Side is the *Hanımeli Pansiyon* (☎ & fax (242) 753 1789), just beyond the Şen. It's a beautiful old stone house, nicely restored, surrounded by gardens scented by jasmine. It's quiet, full of character, and reasonably priced at US$24 a double with shower and breakfast.

Camping There are small, simple camping grounds on roads going to motels on the western beach; names and management seem to change from year to year.

Places to Stay – middle

Near the Köseoğlu Hotel is the *Sidemara Motel* (☎ (242) 753 1083), not far from the eastern beach. Double rooms with private shower go for US$34 to US$38, breakfast included.

Side has a few comfortable motels on its western beach, among which the best is the *Motel Side* (☎ (242) 753 1022). Close to the village, attractive and with a pretty patio restaurant, the motel charges US$30 for a double room, breakfast and dinner included.

Other motels along the western beach are reached by a road going west, outside the antique city walls. Lodgings here include the *Subaşı Motel* (SOO-bah-shuh) (☎ (242) 753 1215, 753 1047), one of the first places you come to along this road. The location is good as it's only a 15-minute walk to the village, and the motel's rooms (with balconies) face east and west to take full advantage of beach views, sunrises and sunsets. Two people pay US$42 for a double room with bath and breakfast. If the Subaşı is full, the nearby *Temple Motel* (☎ (242) 753 1119, 753 1414) is the place to check next. It's considerably cheaper at US$22 a double but is not right on the beach.

Many other three-and four-star hotels are along the western beach.

Places to Stay – top end

Side has scores of four and five-star hotels along its western beach. A convenient one is the five-star, 154-room *Hotel Asteria* (☎ & fax (242) 753 1830, fax 753 1830), about three km north-west of the village proper, on the western beach. Set on a rise overlooking the beach and the sea, the hotel's extensive grounds have swimming pools, sunning areas, bars and cafés, and lots of equipment for water sports. Each comfortable room has a small terrace; ask for a room with an eastern sea view. Rates are US$100/140 for a single/double in high summer, breakfast included.

Places to Eat

When looking for a pension, ask about cooking facilities. Most places have them and this allows you to make substantial savings. At the larger hotels you may be required to buy at least two meals a day, so the food problem is solved that way whether you like it or not. As for cheap restaurants, there aren't any. The names, prices, staff and quality of food change every season.

The cheapest food is pizza, served in many places. For a full restaurant, try *Bademaltı* (☎ 753 1403), at the top of the main street on the way to the theatre. The selection of dishes is good, and prices are reasonable (for Side), at US$5 to US$8 for a full meal.

For a gratifying lunch or romantic dinner try the very pleasant *Afrodit (or Aphrodite) Restaurant* (☎ 753 1171) at the beach end of the main street. A large place with lots of garden-terrace dining tables, the Afrodit usually has a selection of mezes and salads, as well as fish. To eat lightly and cheaply, order three or four meze plates with bread and a drink. If you go for fish, remember to ask prices. The average meal costs around US$12 per person.

The *Altın Balık Restaurant* ('Golden Fish'), on the east side of the main street on the waterfront, was a favourite during my last visit. The *Agora*, on what used to be

Side's main square many years ago, has fine water views as well.

Soundwaves Restaurant, beside the Otel Pamphylia, has a terrace surrounded by tall grasses, a woody pine interior, soft lighting, and a different menu: garlic prawns, honey-baked chicken, and onion steak, along with some Turkish standards. Full meals cost from US$10 to US$20 per person, drinks included.

Konak Restaurant, down at the waterfront to the left, is popular as well, and costs about as much as the aforementioned Bademaltı.

For drinks, snacks and perhaps a fondue in the evening, drop by the *Liman Bar* and the *Appolo'nun Bar*, just west of the temples (walk down the main street to the water and turn left). A woody décor, soft classical music, and good views of the water set the mood. Drinks cost from US$1.50 to US$3 and up. Go there for sunset.

Getting There & Away

Side, 75 km east of Antalya, is so popular as a resort that it has its own direct bus service to Ankara, İzmir and İstanbul. The numerous buses which run along the coast between Antalya and Alanya will drop you in Side or in Manavgat, the town on the highway. From Manavgat dolmuşes frequently travel the four km down to the shore.

Alanya – 63 km, 1¼ hours, US$3; frequent buses and dolmuşes in summer
Antalya – 65 km, 1¼ hours, US$3; very frequent buses and dolmuşes in summer
Konya – 296 km, 5½ hours, US$10; no direct buses from Side, but you can catch one in Manavgat or at the junction with D 695, 12 km east of Manavgat.

NORTH TO KONYA

About 12 km east of Manavgat (50 km west of Alanya) a highway heads north up to the Anatolian Plateau and Konya (280 km) via Akseki, curving through beautiful mountain scenery. The once-narrow and curvy road has been much improved, making it now the preferred route to Konya from this part of the Mediterranean coast. The route via Antalya and Isparta takes seven hours from Side.

EAST TO ALANYA

The journey from Manavgat to Alanya is 63 km and takes slightly over an hour by bus. The coastal highway skirts good **sandy beaches** virtually the whole way to Alanya. Hotels, holiday village and government rest camps line the beach much of the way. On the landward side you see the occasional bit of aqueduct or the foundations of some old caravanserai or baths.

About 23 km west of Alanya you pass İncekum (Fine Sand) and Avsallar. At İncekum is the **İncekum Orman İçi Dinlenme Yeri** (Fine Sand Forest Rest Area) with a camping ground in a pine grove near the beach. Thirteen km before Alanya notice the **Şarapsa Hanı,** a Seljuk caravanserai. Another one, the **Alarahan**, is accessible (nine km) by a side road heading north.

ALANYA

The Seljuk Turks built a powerful empire, the Sultanate of Rum (ROOM, Rome), which thrived from 1071 to 1243. Its capital was in Konya, but its prime port was Alanya. Several great structures remain from Seljuk times.

Like Side, Alanya (ah-LAHN-yah, population 200,000) occupies a point of land flanked by two great sweeping beaches. Once a sleepy agricultural, fishing and tourist town, Alanya was heavily affected by the tourism boom of the late 1980s. With its wide swath of sandy beach stretching 22 km eastward from the town, it has become Turkey's mini-Miami, with a similar clutter of high-rise towers and resort hotels, lots of carpet-shop touts and high prices. It's now a favourite destination of European package holiday groups and those in search of furnished flats near the beach. Most of its charm has been buried in the process. If you want sun and beach, Alanya has it. If you want more than beach, look elsewhere.

Orientation

The bus station (otogar) is on the coastal highway (Atatürk Caddesi) three km west of the centre. It is served by city buses which

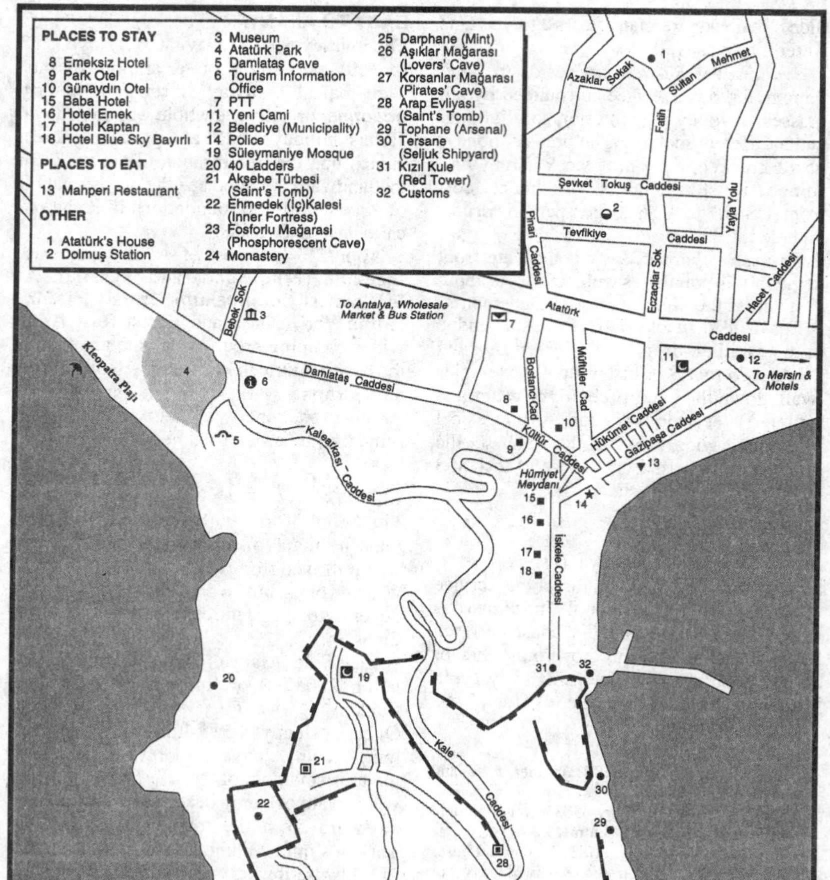

Central Alanya

PLACES TO STAY

8 Emeksiz Hotel
9 Park Otel
10 Günaydın Otel
15 Baba Hotel
16 Hotel Emek
17 Hotel Kaptan
18 Hotel Blue Sky Bayırlı

PLACES TO EAT

13 Mahperi Restaurant

OTHER

1 Atatürk's House
2 Dolmuş Station
3 Museum
4 Atatürk Park
5 Damlataş Cave
6 Tourism Information Office
7 PTT
11 Yeni Cami
12 Belediye (Municipality)
14 Police
19 Süleymaniye Mosque
20 40 Ladders
21 Akşebe Türbesi (Saint's Tomb)
22 Ehmedek (İç)Kalesi (Inner Fortress)
23 Fosforlu Mağarasi (Phosphorescent Cave)
24 Monastery
25 Darphane (Mint)
26 Aşıklar Mağarası (Lovers' Cave)
27 Korsanlar Mağarası (Pirates' Cave)
28 Arap Evliyası (Saint's Tomb)
29 Tophane (Arsenal)
30 Tersane (Seljuk Shipyard)
31 Kızıl Kule (Red Tower)
32 Customs

Azaklar Sokak
Sultan Mehmet
Fatih
Şevket Tokuş Caddesi
Tevfikiye Caddesi
Yayla Yolu
Pinari Caddesi
Eczacılar Sok
Hacet Caddesi
Atatürk Caddesi
To Antalya, Wholesale Market & Bus Station
To Mersin & Motels
Bebek Sok
Kleopatra Plajı
Damlataş Caddesi
Bostancı Cad
Müftüler Cad
Hükümet Caddesi
Gazipaşa Caddesi
Kültür Caddesi
Kalearkası Caddesi
Hürriyet Meydanı
İskele Caddesi
Kale Caddesi
MEDITERRANEAN SEA (AKDENİZ)
Cilyarda Burnu
0 200 400 m

take you into town every half-hour for US$0.60.

Alanya, having gone from a small town to a 20-km-long city almost overnight, has no real traditional main square or civic centre. The centre – such as it is – lies inland (north) from the promontory which bears the roaming walls of the citadel. Scattered in this central area are the PTT, Tourism Information Office and museum. The closest thing to a main square is Hürriyet Meydanı, a nondescript, wide traffic junction at the northern end of İskele Caddesi.

Development inland is limited by the slopes of the confining Taurus range, so the city sprawls east and west along the coast. The ranks of beach hotels don't thin out until you reach the districts of Mahmutlar and Kargıcak, 15 km east of Alanya centre.

Information

The Tourism Information Office (☎ (242) 513 1240, fax 513 5436), Çarşı Mahallesi, Kalearkası Caddesi, is at the north-western foot of the promontory, near the museum (Alanya Müzesi) and Damlataş cave. City buses to the top of the promontory depart from the office about every hour.

Alanya's postal code is 07400.

Seljuk Sites

As Alanya gets very hot and humid in summer, early morning is the best time for sightseeing; spend the afternoon at the beach.

Walk down to the harbour for a look at the **Kızıl Kule** (Red Tower), constructed in 1226 during the reign of the Seljuk sultan, Alaeddin Keykubad I, by a Syrian Arab architect. The five-storey octagonal tower, now restored to its former glory and outfitted as an ethnographic museum, was the key to Alanya's harbour defences. The tower/museum is open from 8 am to noon, and 1.30 to 5.30 pm (closed on Monday) for US$2.

Climb the 78 steps to the top of the battlements for five views of the harbour and the town. Past the tower, out towards the sea, a path leads to the old **Seljuk Tersane**, or shipyard (1228).

Fortress

Alanya's most exciting historical site is of course the Kale (fortress) on top of the promontory, reached by hourly city buses from the Tourism Information Office. Otherwise it's a very hot one-hour walk (three km), or take a taxi (US$5); with your own car you can drive right up to the fort.

The ancient city was enclosed by the rambling wall (1226) which makes its way all around the peninsula. At the top is the **Ehmedek Kapısı**, the major portal into the enclosure. From the İç Kale (inner fort or keep) you get a panoramic view of the peninsula, walls, town and great expanses of coastline backed by the blue Taurus Mountains. The İç Kale holds ruins of a Byzantine church, cisterns and storerooms.

Admission to the İç Kale is from 8 am to 5.30 pm daily, and costs US$2, half-price for students.

Atatürk's House

Atatürk visited Alanya on 18 February 1935 when he was president of the republic, and spent the night in a house on Azaklar Sokak, off Fatih Sultan Mehmet Caddesi. His stay here has little historical importance, but the owner of the house, Mr Rifat Azakoğlu, left it to be preserved as a museum. By visiting the house you will learn little about Atatürk, but much about the lifestyle of a well-to-do Turkish family in provincial Alanya during the 1930s.

Opening hours are from 8.30 am to noon, and 1.30 to 5.30 pm (closed on Monday); admission costs US$0.50. Among the attractions of the house is a paucity of visitors; you may have it to yourself. The kitchen is fully equipped with period utensils, and the bedrooms upstairs have period furnishings.

Museum

Alanya has a tidy little museum on the west side of the peninsula, near the Tourism Information Office. It's open daily from 8 am to noon and 1.30 to 5.30 pm; admission costs US$1.50. Exhibits span the ages from Old Bronze through Greek and Roman to Ottoman. Don't miss the Ethnology Room at the back, with a fine assortment of kilims (woven mats), *cicims* (embroidered mats), Turkish carpets, wood and copper-inlay work, gold and silver, and beautifully written and illuminated religious books.

Damlataş Cave

One hundred metres seaward from the Tourism Information Office is the entrance to Damlataş (Dripping-stone), a cave noted for its moisture-laden air. The stalactites do indeed drip, encouraged by the heavy-breathing exhalations of troops of curious tourists. If you have heart problems, the heavy atmosphere may be dangerous for you. In any case, it's hardly a world-class thrill. Admission costs US$1, from 10 am to 5 pm daily.

Boat Excursions

You can hire a boat for a coastal tour around the promontory, during which you'll approach several caves, including those called Aşıklar Mağarası (the Lovers' Cave), Korsanlar Mağarası (Pirates' Cave), Fosforlu Mağarası (Phosphorescent Cave), as well as Kleopatra Plajı (Cleopatra's Beach) on the west side of the promontory. To hire the entire boat for a short tour of one hour costs about US$17; for the long tour of 2½ hours, US$27. A boat can take seven or eight passengers.

By the way, Damlataş and Cleopatra's Beach are accessible on foot from the western side of the promontory, not far from the museum and the Tourism Information Office.

Places to Stay

Alanya has hundreds of lodging-places, most of them designed for and catering to group visitors and those in search of self-catering flats ('apartotels'). Indeed, group tours and short-term rentals offer the best prices for lodging in these hotels, and they are often filled to capacity.

On your own, the best plan is to arrive by early afternoon at the latest and to spend an hour or two looking for a suitable room at a good price.

Places to Stay – bottom end

The cheapest pensions are out of the centre near the otogar. Descend from your bus and follow the signs, or go with a pension owner who approaches you as you leave your bus. Among the best is the *Alaiye Pansiyon* (☎ (242) 247 5731), Elmalı Mahallesi, Milli Egemenlik Caddesi, 4. Sokak 42.

In the centre, the few small hotels and pensions rent rooms for about US$14 to US$18 a double. At the *Baba Hotel* (☎ (242) 513 1032), İskele Caddesi 6, uninspiring beat-up rooms cost US$13/16 a double without/with shower. Some upper storey rooms have sea views. The *Alanya Palas* (☎ (242) 513 1016) next door is similar.

Hotel Emek (☎ (242) 512 1223), İskele Caddesi 12, a few steps farther along toward the Red Tower, charges US$18 a double for better rooms.

Inland one block from the Baba Hotel is the *Çınar Otel* (☎ (242) 512 0063), Hürriyet Meydanı 6, on the plaza just north of the Kuyularönü mosque. Very basic rooms rent for US$9/12 a double without/with shower. *Günaydın Otel* (☎ (242) 513 1943), Kültür Caddesi 26/B, one long block inland from the hotels along İskele Caddesi, provides reliably enjoyable accommodation at US$12/22 a single/double, breakfast included. *Hotel Mehtap* (☎ (242) 511 0289), Müftüler Caddesi 6, in the market area at the centre, is cheap and well-located, though beat-up, with rooms for US$12/15 a double without/with shower.

Places to Stay – middle

I prefer small hotels in the centre of the town as they allow you to walk easily to restaurants and attractions.

The three-star, 45-room *Hotel Kaptan* (☎ (242) 513 4900, fax 513 2000), İskele Caddesi 62, near the Red Tower, has water-view, air-con singles for US$40, doubles for US$55, breakfast included.

A block closer to the Red Tower is the *Hotel Blue Sky Bayırlı* (☎ (242) 513 6487, fax 513 4320), with 54 shower-equipped rooms, many with nice balconies overlooking the town and the bay. Prices are similar to those at the Kaptan. Also here, the *Dolphin Harbour Apart Hotel* (☎ (242) 513 2996, fax 512 2835), İskele Caddesi 88, rents apartments (flats) for US$32 to US$40 per day, single or double, but you must reserve in advance as it is often full.

On Hürriyet Meydanı at the northern end of İskele Caddesi, the *Park Otel* (☎ (242) 513 1675, fax 513 2589), Eski PTT Caddesi 6, gets away with charging US$45 a double for its rooms because it has a swimming pool. The *Emeksiz Hotel* (☎ (242) 513 6675) across the street is more modest and less expensive.

Hotel Sunny Hill (☎ (242) 511 1211, fax 512 3893), Çarşı Mahallesi, Damlataş Mevkii, Sultan Alaaddin Caddesi 3, clings to the hillside above the tourism office. It's a prime example of the three-star group hotel, with a beautiful swimming pool, terrace restaurant and bar, and comfortable rooms (some with views) for US$32/48 a single/double, breakfast included. Half board (breakfast and dinner) rates are also available.

Places to Eat

Alanya is another of those towns where the waiters are liable to bring you expensive dishes you didn't order. If you don't want them, be sure they're taken away. Then make sure they don't reappear on your bill.

The cheapest meals are to be found in the narrow streets of Alanya's bazaar, in the centre of town on the eastern side of the promontory, away from the water. Lots of the little market eateries style themselves 'İnegöl Köftecisi', and serve cheap grilled meatballs and salad for US$4 or so. In fine weather, streetside tables are set up.

Vitamin Corner, a small stand in the bazaar, serves fresh-squeezed fruit and vegetable juices.

Many of these places are patronised mostly by tourists, but if you search you may find one which serves mostly Turks. I found the *İmren Kebap Salonu* (☎ (242) 511 5167), in a little courtyard entered at Hayati Hanım Sokak 22/C. I had kuru fasulye (beans in tomato sauce), salad, pilav, bread, soft drink and tea for US$4. Another is the *Gaziantep Başpınar Kebap ve Lahmacun Salonu*, inland a bit from the eastern end of the row of water-view restaurants.

On the waterfront promenade are several restaurants with attractive terraces looking out towards the sea. The *Mahperi Restaurant* (☎ (242) 513 1099) is one of long standing, serving at this location for more than 30 years. Seafood is the speciality, of course, but it also does a good chicken shish kebap (US$4.50). The others in this row – *Kordon, Yönet, Marina* and *Alanya* are similar, with prices posted prominently.

Entertainment

Each district – indeed, each hotel – in this sprawling city has its own collection of bars, tavernas, discos and jazz clubs. The ones in the centre change ownership and approach frequently.

At present, the most interesting is perhaps the *Telephone Café-Bar* just east (downhill) from Hürriyet Meydanı. Besides caffeinated and alcoholic beverages, the café features telephones from which you can make long-distance calls 'at the same rates as from the PTT', that is, without horrendous hotel surcharges.

Getting There & Away

Bus Much of Alanya's bus traffic travels via Antalya and you may find yourself switching buses there. When the Manavgat to Beyşehir road is finally widened and straightened you can expect to find direct buses between Alanya and Konya, making the 340-km trip in about six hours. Travel times and distances to other northern cities (Ankara, Nevşehir/Ürgüp) will be shortened by about three hours also.

Compared to the rest of Turkey, traffic is sparse eastward around the 'bulge' of Anamur. Few buses originate in Alanya so you have to rely on passing buses having empty seats, which they don't always have, so make your departure arrangements as far in advance as possible. Also keep in mind that the road eastward is mountainous and curvy and therefore takes a good deal longer to traverse than you might think from looking at the map.

Some destinations include:

Adana – 440 km, 10 hours, US$18; eight buses daily in summer
Anamur – 135 km, three hours, US$6; several buses daily in summer
Antalya – 115 km, two hours, US$4; hourly buses in summer
İstanbul – 840 km, 17 hours, US$23; several buses daily, more from Antalya
İzmir – 660 km, 12 hours, US$20; via Antalya
Kaş – 300 km, seven hours, US$14; via Antalya
Konya – 320 km, 6½ hours, US$16 (Akseki – Beyşehir route)
Marmaris – 700 km, 11½ hours, US$20; via Antalya
Mersin – 375 km, 8½ hours, US$16; eight buses daily in summer
Silifke – 275 km, seven hours, US$12; eight buses daily in summer
Ürgüp – 590 km, 10 hours, US$22 (Akseki – Beyşehir – Konya route)

Boat – to Cyprus You can make arrangements in Alanya to catch a ferry to northern Cyprus. Boats leave from Taşucu, just south-west of Silifke, 265 km east of Alanya. At Alanya's otogar you can make a boat reservation and also buy a ticket for the very early morning bus from Alanya to the ferry docks. For more information on these boats, see the Taşucu section.

Getting Around

Dolmuşes shuttle frequently along the coast in both directions to transport passengers from the outlying hotel areas to the centre.

ALANYA TO SİLİFKE

From Alanya you may want to head north to Konya, Cappadocia and Ankara. The eastern Mediterranean coast has a few sights worth seeing, but the cities of Mersin, Tarsus, Adana and İskenderun have very little to hold your interest. Agriculture, commerce and shipping, not the tourist trade, are their reasons for being.

From Alanya to Silifke is 275 km along a twisting road cut into the cliffs which rise steeply from the sea. Every now and then the road passes through the fertile delta of a stream, planted with bananas (as at Demirtaş) or crowded with glass greenhouses. Views of the sea and the occasional stretch of pine forest break the monotony of the drive, but there's little else to look at until Anamur.

This region was called Cilicia by the ancients, a somewhat forbidding part of the world because of the mountains. Anyone wanting to conquer Cilicia had to have a navy, as the only practicable transport was by sea. Pirates preyed on coastal shipping from the hidden coves along this stretch of coast. In the late 1960s the government completed the good paved road from Alanya to Silifke.

Anamur

Anamur (population 42,000), at the southernmost point along the Turkish coast, is near the ruined Byzantine city of Anamurium, which you should see, south-west of the town on the beach. To the east of the town are two crusader castles, the Mamure Kalesi and the Softa Kalesi, also worth a look. Each of these points of interest has a beach close by.

Orientation The town centre is to the north of the highway (one km to the main square). The otogar is at the junction of the highway and the main street. To reach the beach, head east from the otogar a short distance and turn right (south) at the signs; the beach is two km south of the highway (four km from the main square) in the district called İskele (dock).

The castle (Mamure Kalesi) is seven km east of the town centre. The ruins of Byzantine Anamurium are 8.5 km west of the centre.

Anamurium Approaching Anamur from the west and down from the Cilician mountains, the highway finally reaches some level ground and a straight section. At this point, six km from the main square in Anamur, a road on the right (south) is marked for the ruins. Another 2.5 km brings you past fields and through the ruins to a dead end at the beach. There is no regular dolmuş service to the ruins; you will probably have to take a taxi.

Founded by the Phoenicians, Anamurium

flourished through the Roman period. Its Golden Age may have been around 250 AD, after which it lost some importance, but nothing like what it was about to lose. When the Arab armies stormed out of Arabia in the 7th century they raided and pillaged this coast, including Anamurium. Despite its mighty walls and remote location, the city fell. It never recovered from the devastation and no-one was interested in settling here afterwards.

Had new settlers come, they doubtless would have torn down these old buildings and used the cut stones to build their own houses, stores, wharves and bridges, as they did everywhere until this century. Anamurium escaped this pillage and today it is an authentic Byzantine ghost town, with dozens of buildings perched eerily on this rocky hillside above an unsullied pebble beach. Churches, aqueducts, houses and defensive walls stand silent and empty, their roofs caved in but their walls largely intact. It's quite surprising that Anatolia's earthquakes did so little damage.

Anamurium's **baths** are well-preserved, even to some of the wall decoration; many of the tombs in the **necropolis** have traces of decoration as well.

Mamure Kalesi Seven km east of Anamur, just off the highway, stands the moat-girdled Mamure Kalesi, a maze of crenellated walls and towers with one foot in the Mediterranean.

There has been a fortress at this point since the Romans built one in the 3rd century AD, but the present structure dates from the time of the crusades when it was used by the crusader rulers of Cyprus, and later (13th century) the Karamanoğlu emirs.

The Ottomans took over in the middle of the 14th century and kept the castle in good repair until the empire ended this century. The fortifications, with crenellated walls and towers, are very impressive.

You can visit every day from 8 am to 5 or 6 pm; admission costs US$1.50.

Softa Kalesi Heading east from Anamur, 2.8 km past the Mamure Kalesi, is a yacht marina, and four km east of the harbour the town of **Bozyazı**, a town spread (like Anamur) on a fertile alluvial plain backed by rugged mountains. Eastward across the plain, clearly visible as you travel, is the Softa Kalesi, surrounded by the little hamlet of **Çubukkoyağı**. As you leave Bozyazı, a road on the left (north, inland) is marked for the Softa Kalesi, perched on top of its rocky crag and looming over the highway, but the road doesn't go all the way to the top; take care, you must clamber up the last bit amidst snakes and scorpions.

This castle, built by the Armenian kings who ruled Cilicia for a short while during the crusades, is now fairly ruined inside but the walls and situation are still quite impressive. From the Softa Kalesi it's 20 km west back to Anamur, or 140 km east to Silifke.

Places to Stay There are cheap pensions and camping grounds near each of the three points of interest.

Anamurium On the road to ancient Anamurium you pass the *Alper Pension* and the *Anamuryum Pension & Restaurant*, open in summer only. Down on the beach (bear left at the Alper Pension and go 650m) is the fancy *Anamuryum Mocamp* for campers. Prices are the standard US$4 to US$6 per person, depending upon season and demand.

Mamure Kalesi Just across the road from the Mamure Kalesi is the *Mamure Pension*, a tidy place which is handy but suffers from road noise. To the east of the castle in the next 1.5 km are lots more little pensions, including the very tidy *Ak Pansiyon*, charging US$15 a night, breakfast included. Staying at one of these places allows you to visit the castle and take a swim from the same base. Exactly 1.5 km east of the castle is the *Dikilitaş – Alpullu Orman İçi Dinlenme Yeri*, a forest camping ground operated by the General Directorate of Forests. The cost is US$3 for a tent, US$5 for a caravan, plus US$1 per person. There is a fine sandy beach just below.

Softa Kalesi On the little cove beneath the Softa Kalesi, called Bozyazı, are several little pensions, some condominiums and the two-star *Alinko Motel* (☎ & fax (324) 851 3998). The four-star *Vivanco Hotel* (☎ (324) 851 4200, fax 851 2291) is here as well.

İskele (Beach) Down at Anamur beach, called the İskele (dock) district, are numerous pensions and hotels ranged along İnönü Caddesi, the main waterfront street.

The *Star Pansiyon* (☎ (324) 816 4605), on İnönü Caddesi, is covered in morning glories, has a shady front terrace restaurant and a rooftop terrace with water views, and shower-equipped rooms renting for US$12 a double.

Other inexpensive lodgings are the prominent *Otel Meltem* opposite the park, at similar prices, and the *Hotel Şimşek*, offering double rooms with shower for US$30.

The three-star, 70-room *Hermes Hotel* (☎ (324) 814 3950, fax 814 3995), is Anamur's best, charging US$30/44 a single/double, breakfast included. The hotel has a swimming pool, and is only steps from the beach. The *Anemonia Hotel* (☎ (324) 814 4000, fax 814 1443) nearby is similar.

Town Centre In the town of Anamur itself the *Hotel Saray* (☎ (324) 813 1191), Tahsin Soylu Caddesi, near the Otel Alahan, is simple and cheap, with cleanish rooms for US$14 a double.

The two-star *Otel Anahan* (☎ (324) 813 3511, fax 813 1045), Tahsin Soylu Caddesi 109, is fairly simple. It has 30 fairly comfortable rooms (with balcony and private shower) reached by a marble staircase (no lift), a restaurant and a café-bar. It's one km east of the main square, 1.5 km from the otogar, and almost three km from the beach.

Places to Eat Many pensions provide meals, as do the hotels and motels. A few metres south of the main square is the *Bulvar Restaurant*: nothing fancy, but it provides food.

The best dining is along the waterfront in İskele, where a row of restaurants just east of the park, opposite the Hotel Hermes, specialises in seafood. Best of the lot is the *Astor*, with a palm-shaded seaside terrace and fish dinners for US$8 to US$14.

Getting Around Anamur is spread out and somewhat difficult to get around if you haven't got your own transport. To get to Anamurium, ask at the bus station; sometimes drivers going a longer distance will drop you at the crossroads, from where it's 1.5 km to the archaeological zone entrance. A taxi will run you out to the ruins, wait for an hour, and take you back into town for US$6 to US$8.

During the summer there are sometimes dolmuşes between İskele and Anamur centre, and you may also be able to hitch here. East of Anamur the transport situation brightens as there are frequent dolmuşes to Bozyazı from the Anamur otogar. You can use these to visit the Mamure Kalesi, the Softa Kalesi and the eastern beach.

East to Silifke

From Anamur it's 75 km to Aydıncık and 160 km to Silifke. The highway winds up into the mountains again, and then winds on and on, occasionally dipping down to another alluvial valley with its requisite farming or beach village and semi-tropical crops in greenhouses. If you'd like to climb into the mountains and see yet another medieval castle, turn left (north) three km south-west of Aydıncık and head up towards **Gülnar** (25 km) for a look at the **Meydancık Kalesi**, which has stood here in one form or another since Hittite times.

East of Aydıncık the highway passes through these towns, among others: **Yeşilovacık**, on the sea with a nice beach and several hotels and government rest camps; **Akdere**, in a valley separated from the sea by a high ridge of mountains; **Boğsak**, with the *Boğsak Motel* (☎ (324) 741 4450) and *Boğsak Camping* above the beach, and a few small pensions as well; and **Akçakıl**, just past a small ruined castle called the Liman Kalesi.

After interminable curves and switchbacks the highway finally comes down from the cliffside to the Cilician Plain, the fertile littoral at the foot of the Taurus Mountains which stretches from Silifke to Adana. Before coming to Silifke proper, you pass its port of Taşucu, from where ferries and hydrofoils depart for northern Cyprus.

Taşucu

Taşucu (TAHSH-oo-joo), the port of Silifke, lives for the ferries. Hotels put up voyagers, and car ferries and hydrofoils take them to and fro across the sea.

Orientation & Information The main square by the ferry dock has a PTT, a customs house, a Tourism Information Office (☎ (324) 741 4234), various banks, currency exchange offices, shipping offices and restaurants. It's only a few dozen metres south of the highway. The village bazaar is east of the main square. The beach, backed by a waterfront street (Sahil Yolu) and several good pensions, extends east of the docks area.

Places to Stay About the cheapest place to stay is the *Işık Otel* (☎ (324) 741 4026), on Atatürk Caddesi, an old waterfront building facing the main square with rooms for US$10 a double without running water. It's right next door to a *pavyon* (Turkish nightclub) and may be noisy.

The *Hotel Fatih* (☎ (324) 741 4125) is better. It's on the highway behind the Gümrük only metres from the square. Rooms have private showers, little balconies and prices of US$18/26/34 a single/double/triple, though you can haggle them down out of season. There's a restaurant as well.

The *Yuvam Pansiyon* (☎ (324) 741 4101) is on the hillside by the highway, overlooking the otogar and dock area, and might therefore be a bit noisy, though it's certainly convenient.

The better pensions are 500 to 1000m east of the docks along the beach. Try the *Tuğran Pansiyon* (☎ (324) 741 4493), Sahil Yolu 3, on the opposite (east) side of the park from the otogar. Clean, cheerful rooms with private shower and perhaps a sea view cost US$14. The nearby *Holmi Pansiyon* (☎ (324) 741 2321) is similarly priced.

The *Lades Motel* (☎ (324) 741 4008) has seen better days: its rooms are in dire need of renovation, but staff are friendly, there's a swimming pool and a restaurant with fine sea views. Rooms, also with fine views, cost US$20/30 a single/double, breakfast included.

A few hundred metres west of the Lades is a large five-star hotel which was closed at my last visit, but which should be open by the time you arrive.

Places to Eat The *Denizkızı Restaurant*, opposite the bust of Atatürk in the main square, is the locals' favourite at lunch and dinner time, and is fairly cheap. The *İstanbul Restaurant* next to the otogar is a popular choice with travellers awaiting the boat, with its sea-view terrace. The *100. Yıl Restaurant* on the main square is about the best, but a bit more expensive, with full meals for US$6 to US$12. For the cheapest meals, pick up a pide at the *Gaziantep Lahmacun ve Pide Salonu* for less than US$2.

Getting There & Away Passenger boats to Kyrenia (Girne, northern Cyprus) depart from Taşucu, 11 km west of Silifke's otogar.

Several companies run fast 'sea-buses' *(deniz otobüsü)* and hydrofoils *(uçandeniz otobüsü)* between Taşucu and Kyrenia, selling tickets from offices in Taşucu's main square. Note that you may be required to purchase a new Turkish visa when you re-enter Turkey from northern Cyprus. Sometimes you'll be let through if your old visa still has time on it, but in theory these are only 'single entry' visas. Yes, it's a rip-off.

Typical are the boats run by Ermal Denizcilik (☎ (324) 741 4782, fax 741 4211), Atatürk Caddesi. Their hydrofoils depart Taşucu and Kyrenia at 11 am daily on the 1½ to two-hour voyage at a cost of US$15 one-way, US$28 round trip. Fergün Express (☎ (324) 741 2323, fax 741 2802) also has 11 am departures, with the return leaving Kyrenia at 2 pm. Turkish Maritime Lines (Denizyolları; ☎ (324) 741 4785) has slow passenger services on the MV *Ayvalık* departing at midnight, Sunday through Thursday, and returning from Kyrenia at noon, Monday through Friday.

For the car ferry, passenger tickets cost less but the trip is longer. Ertürk (☎ (324) 741 4033, fax 741 4325), with its main office in Çeşme, west of İzmir, operates the MF *Ertürk 1*, with a capacity of 400 passengers and 20 cars, departing Taşucu at midnight on Sunday through Thursday, arriving in Kyrenia the next day at 7.30 am. From Kyrenia the ferry departs at noon on Monday through Friday, arriving in Taşucu at 4 pm. Tickets cost US$14 each way per driver or passenger, and US$65 per car. In Kyrenia, call Ertürk at ☎ (081) 52308 or 53784.

Fergün (☎ (324) 741 2323, fax 741 2802) runs the MF *Fatih* car ferry, departing Taşucu at midnight, returning from Kyrenia at 11.30 am, on the same days as Ertürk's ferry.

Getting Around Dolmuşes run between Taşucu and Silifke's otogar frequently throughout the day. The Silifke station is not the otogar proper, but a fuel station across the road from it.

SİLİFKE

Silifke (population 50,000) is the ancient Seleucia, founded by Seleucus I Nicator in the 3rd century BC. Seleucus was one of Alexander the Great's most able generals and founder of the Seleucid dynasty which ruled Syria after Alexander's death.

Silifke's other claim to fame is that Emperor Frederick I Barbarossa (1125-90), while leading his troops on the Third Crusade, drowned in the river near here – an ignominious end for a soldier.

A striking castle dominates the town from a Taurus hillside and promises good sightseeing. To many people, however, Silifke is just a place to catch the bus to Mersin, Adana or Konya.

Orientation

The bus station is near the junction of highways to Alanya, Mersin and Konya. From the bus station into the centre of the town is exactly one km along İnönü Bulvarı; halfway along you pass the Temple of Jupiter.

The town is divided by the Göksu River, called the Calycadnus in ancient times. Most of the services are on the southern bank of the river, including the bus station. Exceptions are the Tourism Information Office, several hotels and the dolmuş to Uzuncaburç, which are on the river's northern bank. By the way, Menderes Caddesi is often called Mut Caddesi by locals.

Information

Silifke's Tourism Information Office (☎ (324) 714 1151, fax 714 5328), is at Veli Gürten Bozbey Caddesi 6, a few steps north of Atatürk Caddesi and the Hotel Çadır. The helpful staff speak some English, French and German, and have interesting material on Silifke and its history.

Things to See

The **fortress** on the hill dates from medieval times. From the hilltop you can gaze down at the **Tekir Ambarı**, an ancient cistern some 46m long, 23m wide and 12m deep, carved from the rock. A circular stone staircase provides access to what was an important feature of the ancient city's water supply. To get to the Tekir Ambarı from the junction of İnönü and Menderes Caddesis, walk up the hill on the street to the left of the Emlak Kredi Bankası.

Perhaps the most striking ruin in Silifke is that of the **Temple of Jupiter**, which dates from the 2nd or 3rd century AD.

The **Archaeological Museum** is not far from the bus station, and includes a large number of Hellenistic coins and several mosaics, among many other exhibits from the area's deep and eventful past.

The town's mosques include the **Ulu Camii**, originally constructed by the Seljuks but much modified, and the **Reşadiye Camii**, an Ottoman work. The **stone bridge** across the river, which you cross to reach the Tourism Information Office, was originally built in Roman times.

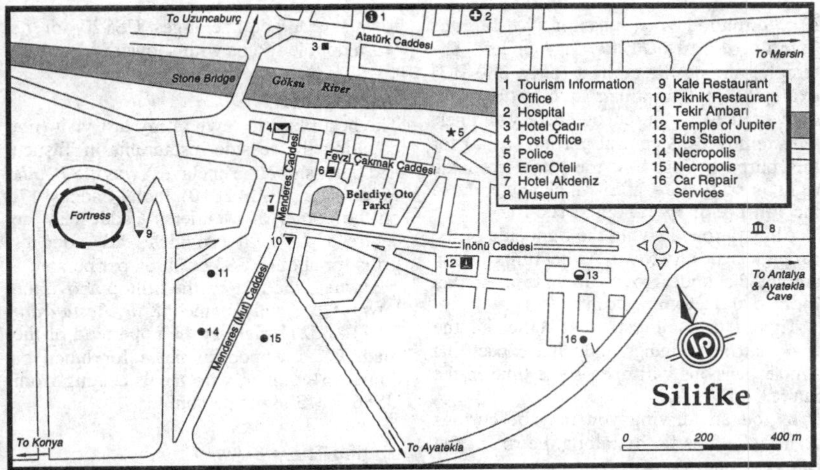

Cave of St Thecla

Another site of interest for those up on their biblical lore is the cave of St Thecla. The saint (Ayatekla in Turkish) is known as St Paul's first Christian convert. She was also the first woman to be threatened with death for the young faith. An outcast from family and society, legend has it that she retreated to a cave outside present-day Silifke, where she pursued good works, particularly healing the sick. The Byzantines built a church over the cave in her honour in 480 AD.

The site is four km from the otogar in Silifke, south past the museum, then to the right up a narrow road. Rubble from the Byzantine settlement is scattered over a large area. Ruins of the basilica and a nearby cistern are evident, but the entrance to the cave is not. As soon as you arrive (probably by taxi or on foot), a guardian will appear, sell you a ticket (US$1) and unlock the iron gate to the cave. In it are several vaulted chambers, some arches and columns. It's exciting if you are a fan of the saint.

Uzuncaburç

The ancient temple-city of Olbia, 28 km north of Silifke, was renamed Diocaesarea in Roman times and is now called Uzuncaburç. The place began its history (as far as we know) as a centre of worship to Zeus Olbius. It was ruled by a dynasty of priest-kings, who also managed the ceremonies in the large temple and arranged for the burial of many devout visitors, some of them quite wealthy.

You can take a dolmuş to the site, but then you have the problem of getting back to Silifke – dolmuşes are not frequent. You might decide to find a few other explorers and hire a taxi (from US$6 to US$8 for the car, for the round trip, waiting time included).

Because it was a holy place, many people wanted to be buried near it, and you will see lots of curious **tombs** on your detour into the mountains. Only eight km up the road from Silifke you encounter the first group of tombs, and at 8.7 km the **Twin Monument Tombs** (Çifte Anıt Mezarları) in the village of Demircili, plainly visible from the road. Turn right at 22.7 km and proceed through a lovely pine forest to the archaeological site, almost six km on. Entry costs US$2. A village child will find you and sell you a ticket.

From the car park you enter the site along

a colonnaded way, passing the famous **Temple of Zeus Olbius** on your left. The temple, among the earliest (circa 300 BC) examples of Corinthian architecture, was converted to a church by the Byzantines, who removed its central portion (cella) for this purpose. Just past the temple, on the right, is a **city gate**, after which you come to the **Temple of Tyche** (circa 100 BC).

Along a road leaving the right side of the car park is the **city tower**. Other ruins hidden among the undergrowth include a Roman **theatre** and a **temple tomb**.

There is a small restaurant at the site, the *Burç*, but no lodgings, though I expect that simple pensions will open some time in the future.

If you are driving you may be curious about what lies farther along the road. You can continue via Kırobası to Mut and to Konya. Winding up into the forests you may pass huge stacks of logs cut by the Tahtacılar, the mountain woodcutters who live a secluded life in the forest.

About 40 km before coming to Mut the road skirts a fantastic limestone **canyon** which extends for a number of km. High above in the limestone cliffs are **caves** which seem to have been inhabited at one time or another. The land in the valleys here is rich and well-watered, exploited by diligent farmers. The air is cool, clean and sweet.

Places to Stay

Most of the area's accommodation is at Taşucu, 11 km west of Silifke. In Silifke proper the hotels are much more modest.

The 27-room *Hotel Akdeniz* (AHK-deh-neez) (☎ (324) 714 1285), Menderes Caddesi 96, is at the western end of İnönü Caddesi. Simple but presentable, it charges US$12 for a double with private shower.

The nearby *Eren Oteli* (☎ (324) 714 2059), in a quiet location north of İnönü Caddesi, charges US$11/16 for a single/double room with private shower.

Across the river on the north side, the *Hotel Çadır* (☎ (324) 714 3535, fax 714 1244), Gazi Mahallesi, Atatürk Caddesi 16, which currently can boast of being this town's best hotel, charges US$20 for its worn double rooms with shower.

Places to Eat

The best place in town at my last visit (not counting the seaside restaurants in Taşucu and other shoreline enclaves) was the *Piknik Restaurant* (☎ 714 2810), İnönü Caddesi 17, on the corner of Menderes Caddesi in the centre of town. It provides ready food or grills for about US$3 or US$4 per person.

Up near the fort on the hilltop above the town is the aptly named *Kale Restaurant* (☎ 714 1521), right at the upper end of the road. It's a wonderful place for lunch or dinner in summer, with meals costing from US$6 to US$8 per person.

Getting There & Away

Being at the junction of the coastal highway and the road into the mountains and up to the plateau, Silifke is an important transportation point with good bus services.

Dolmuşes to Taşucu for the Cyprus ferries depart about every half hour from a Mobil fuel station across the highway from the bus station.

The highway east from Silifke to Adana is well travelled by buses. The Silifke Koop company buses depart for Adana about every 20 minutes throughout the morning and afternoon and will stop to pick you up on the road should you be visiting one of the many archaeological sites east of town.

Some other likely destinations include:

Adana – 155 km, two hours, US$4; 14 buses daily
Alanya – 275 km, six hours, US$8; a dozen buses daily in summer
Ankara – 520 km (via Konya), eight hours, US$12; five buses daily
Antalya – 390 km, nine hours, US$12; a dozen buses daily in summer
Kızkalesi – 20 km, 30 minutes, US$1.50; three buses per hour
Konya – 260 km, 4½ hours, US$8; frequent buses daily
Mersin – 85 km, two hours, US$3.50; three buses per hour
Narlıkuyu – 23 km, 30 minutes, US$1.50; three buses per hour
Ürgüp (via Mersin) – 400 km, 6½ hours, US$12; several buses daily (change at Mersin)

SİLİFKE TO ADANA

East of Silifke the Cilician Plain opens to an ever-widening swath of arable land which allowed civilisation to flourish. The ruins come thick and fast until Mersin, where modern commerce and industrialisation take over.

Atakent

Atakent (Susanoğlu) is a holiday village 16 km east of Silifke with a nice little beach backed by a million holiday flats. With all the condos for well-to-do Mersinli and Adanalı vacationers, there's little room for the passing traveller. The four-star, 108-room *Altınorfoz Banana Hotel* (☎ (324) 722 4211, fax 722 4215) has surprisingly reasonable rates of US$45/55 a single/double.

Narlıkuyu

The village of Narlıkuyu, on the seashore three km east of Atakent, has a few seaside restaurants, a little shop for snacks and necessities, a water pump, a little pension and the remains of a Roman bath (4th century AD) with a fine mosaic of the Three Graces – Aglaia, Thalia and Euphrosyne. Admission to the museum which protects the mosaic costs US$1. The fish restaurants here are good but surprisingly expensive; a little tea garden and kebapçı serves meals for less.

Caves of Heaven & Hell

Inland from Narlıkuyu, a road winds two km north-west up the mountainside to the Caves of Heaven & Hell (Cennet ve Cehennem).

This limestone coast is riddled with caverns but the Cennet (jeh-NEHT) is among the most impressive. According to legend, this may be the Korykos cave in which the gigantic half-human, half-animal monster Typhon held Zeus captive, though the king of the gods later emerged victorious in this battle between good and evil.

To enter the cave, pass the cluster of drinks stands and descend by the path of some 450 steps to the cavern mouth. Along the way notice the strips of cloth and paper tied to twigs and tree branches by those who have come to this 'mystical' place in search of cures. The bits of cloth and paper are reminders to a saint or spirit that a supplicant has asked for intercession.

At the mouth of the cave are the ruins of a small 5th-century Byzantine church dedicated to the Virgin. The cave is not lit so the immense mouth is about as far as you can go without a light or a guide.

About 75m east of Cennet is Cehennem (jeh-HEHN-nehm), or Hell, a 120m deep sinkhole reached by a ladder. Local legend holds this to be one of the entrances to the underworld.

Kızkalesi

The striking castle offshore, about 20 km east of Silifke at ancient Korykos, is called the **Maiden's Castle** (Kızkalesi). Though massive, it seems to float on the blue waves. Another, ruinous, is near it on the shore, and was linked to the sea castle by a causeway in ancient times. Today, strong swimmers can make it out to the Maiden's Castle (about 150m) alone; for the rest of us, boats leave frequently from the shore in summer.

These two edifices account for many legends, but historically the castles were built by the Byzantines and later extensively rebuilt in the 1200s by the Armenian kings of Cilicia with the support of the crusaders. The throne of Cilicia passed through two Armenian dynasties in the 1300s before being taken by Peter I of Cyprus while the Mamelukes of Egypt took the rest of Armenian Cilicia to the east.

The castles, and good beach, are served by the small but growing resort town of Kızkalesi, with a few restaurant streets, some pensions and hotels and camping areas. The clientele is a mixture of Turks and foreigners in-the-know, with a contingent of Yanks from İncirlik Air Base near Adana, so prices remain relatively low. The *BP Mocamp* is a comfortable, if pricey, place to camp.

Kanlıdivane

East of Kızkalesi the Cilician Plain is littered with a continuous expanse of ruins, some fairly grand, others now no more than fields of cut limestone. About three km east of

Kızkalesi at Ayaş are the extensive but mostly badly ruined remains of ancient Elaiussa-Sebaste, a city whose foundations date from at least the early Roman period, and perhaps even the Hittite.

Some 8.5 km east of Kızkalesi at Kumkuyu is the road to Kanlıdivane, and four km north of the highway are the ruins of ancient Kanytelis. The ancient city, founded in Hellenistic times, occupies a vast site around limestone caverns. As you ride into the hills the ruins, mostly dating from Roman and Byzantine times, become more extensive.

Kanytelis thrived through Byzantine times, as can be seen by several Greek churches and inscriptions. Its extensive necropolis (cemetery) has many Roman tombs built in the form of miniature temples.

Viranşehir

A few km west of the centre of Mersin at Mezikli is a road on the right (south) to Viranşehir, the ancient Soles or Pompeiopolis. Two km down the road is a row of Corinthian columns in a field, while in the distance is part of an aqueduct; all date from the 3rd century AD.

MERSİN

Mersin (mehr-SEEN, population 1.5 million), capital of the province of İçel, is a modern city built half a century ago to give Anatolia a large port conveniently close to Adana and its agriculturally rich hinterland. It has several good hotels in each price range and can serve as an emergency stop on your way through. Ferries from Mersin serve the Turkish Cypriot port of Famagusta (Gazimagosa).

Example of a Corinthian capital. The Corinthian order is the slenderest and most ornate of the three Greek architectural orders, and was much used by the Romans.

Orientation

The centre of sprawling Mersin is Gümrük Meydanı, the plaza which bears the modern Ulu Cami mosque and, on its east side, the four-star Mersin Oteli. Across the coastal highway from the mosque is a more readily recognisable landmark: a large Toyota car dealership.

Information

The Tourism Information Office (☎ & fax (324) 231 6358) is by the entrance to the docks, east of the park, at Yenimahalle, İnönü Bulvarı, Liman Giriş Sahası. Next to the office is the stop for buses to Mezitli and Viranşehir (see above).

Mersin's postal code is 33000.

Banks Currency exchange offices *(döviz)* and banks are clustered around Gümrük Meydanı and the Ulu Cami. Look for signs for Fırat Döviz and Kiraz Döviz. The Yapı Kredi Bankası, with its well-connected cash machines, is a block north of the Mersin Oteli.

Places to Stay – bottom end

Unfortunately, hotels near the bus station tend to be in the middle range. For a good cheapie, you'll have to trek into the centre. The place to look first for a cheap or medium-priced hotel is Soğuksu Caddesi, one block west of the Ulu Cami, then north.

Hotel Hitit (☎ (324) 231 6431), Soğuksu Caddesi 12, across from the old municipal market, rents doubles with private showers for US$12. The nearby *Hotel Savran* (☎ (324) 232 4473), Soğuksu Caddesi 46, is even cheaper.

Hotel Side (☎ (324) 231 1773) Soğuksu Caddesi 27, is overpriced at US$22 a double.

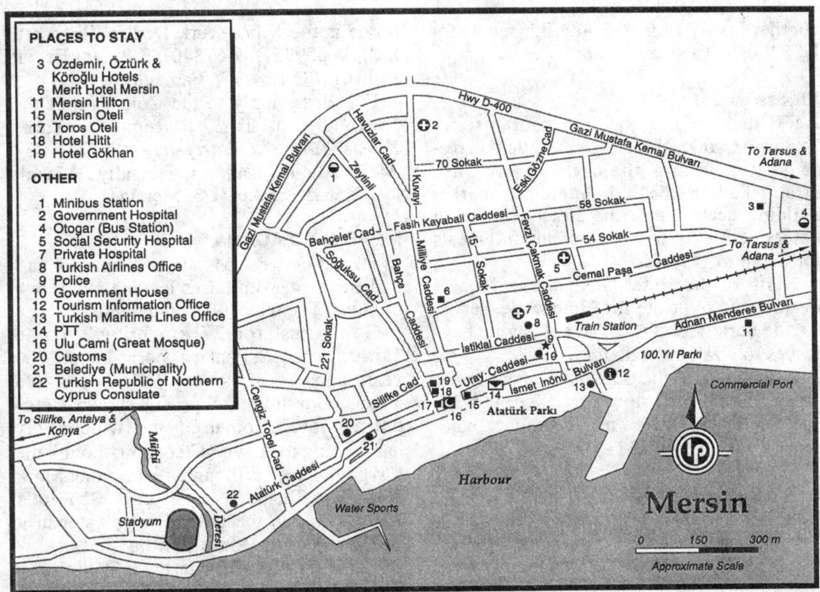

Much better value is the *Toros Oteli* (☎ (324) 231 2201, fax 237 8554), Atatürk Caddesi 33, a hundred metres west of the Ulu Cami, which rents good double rooms with shower and TV for US$20.

Places to Stay – middle

Soğuksu Caddesi has one or two middle-range choices, including the modern two-star, 28-room *Hotel Gökhan* (☎ (324) 231 6256, fax 237 4462), at Soğuksu Caddesi 20. Rates of US$30/40 a single/double are posted, but I was quoted US$30 for a double with TV, mini bar and private bath, breakfast included.

At least 10 hotels are right outside the otogar gates, most of them two-star places charging a uniform US$22 for a double room with private bath and breakfast. These include the *Özdemir Hotel* (☎ (324) 231 5740, fax 233 4747), 852 Sokak 12; the *Öztürk Hotel* (☎ (324) 233 9318); and the *Hotel Köroğlu* (☎ (324) 231 2176). The cheaper hotels in this area tend to rent rooms by the hour.

Places to Stay – top end

The four-star *Mersin Oteli* (☎ (324) 238 1040, fax 231 2625), Gümrük Meydanı 112 at the seaward end of Kuvayi Milliye Caddesi, is down on the waterfront just a few steps east of the Ulu Cami. Its 98 air-con rooms have comfortable beds, private bath, mini bar, telephone and balcony, and have been renovated recently. Rates are posted at US$70/105/125 for a single/double/triple, but reductions to half price are not uncommon.

For luxury, there's the five-star *Merit Hotel Mersin* (☎ (324) 336 1010, fax 336 0722), Kuvayi Milliye Caddesi 165, with 249 rooms in Mersin's tallest building – yes, that immense one which towers above all else. The *Mersin Hilton* (☎ (324) 326 5000, fax 326 5050), Adnan Menderes Bulvarı, right by the docks on the waterfront, is another luxury choice. Both offer rooms for US$100/140 a single/double.

Places to Eat

As with hotels, so with restaurants: try Soğuksu Caddesi first. Several little fish restaurants, among them the *Agora*, are established in the old municipal market building across from the Hotel Hitit, with outdoor tables in fair weather and full meals for US$5 to US$10.

North of the Hotel Gökhan, the *Kervan Restaurant*, opposite the Hotel Side, serves a wide variety of dishes, and alcoholic beverages to wash them down.

A bit fancier is the *Café Me-Ga*, just to the south, in a restored stone house. Grilled fish and white wine make a good dinner here, usually for under US$11.

Getting There & Away

Bus From Mersin's otogar, on the eastern outskirts of the city, buses depart for all points, including up to the Anatolian Plateau through the Cilician Gates. Distances, travel times and prices are similar to those from Adana, 70 km to the east on a fast four-lane highway.

Ferry – to/from Cyprus Turkish Maritime Lines (☎ (324) 233 9858 for reservations; 231 2536 for the ticket office) operates the MF *Yeşilada* car-ferry service to Famagusta (Mağusa or Gazimagosa, mah-GOH-sah) in Cyprus from Mersin all year. Ferries depart from Mersin at 10 pm on Monday, Wednesday and Friday arriving in Famagusta the next day at 8 am. Departures from Famagusta are at 10 pm on Tuesday, Thursday and Sunday, with arrival in Mersin the next day at 8 am.

Fares for the trip between Mersin and Famagusta range from US$25 for a Pullman chair to US$65 per person for a luxury cabin; mid-range cabins rent for US$35 per person. The fare for a car is US$80. Children aged six years and under sail free, those seven to 12 for half price.

Tickets are sold on the first floor of the Liman (harbour) building. The Famagusta office is the Kıbrıs Türk Denizcilik Şirketi Ltd, (☎ 65995, fax 67840), 3 Bülent Ecevit Bulvarı (PO Box 37), Famagusta.

For visas, apply to the Consulate of the North Cyprus Turkish Republic *(Kuzey Kıbrıs Türk Cumhuriyeti)* (☎ (324) 237 2482) Ataturk Caddesi, Hamidiye Mahallesi, Karadeniz Ap 71/3, Mersin.

MERSİN TO ADANA

Transport between Mersin and Adana is fast and frequent, with buses leaving every few minutes. There are even some trains.

Going east for 27 km brings you to **Tarsus**, where St Paul was born almost 2000 years ago. There is very little left of old Tarsus. Bus tour groups are shown **Cleopatra's Gate**, a Roman city gate which really has nothing to do with Cleopatra, though the Egyptian queen is thought to have met Mark Antony in Tarsus. There is also **St Paul's Well**, a hole in the ground with water in it and remnants of **Roman baths**.

Three km east of Tarsus the E 90 highway heads north through the Cilician Gates, a narrow gap in the Taurus Mountains, to Ankara, Nevşehir and Kayseri.

ADANA

Turkey's fourth largest city, Adana (AH-dah-nah, population 1.6 million), is commercial. Its wealth comes from local industry, the traffic passing through the Cilician Gates, and from the intensely fertile Çukurova, the ancient Cilician Plain deposited as silt by the rivers Seyhan and Ceyhan.

Adana has grown rapidly and chaotically since the middle of this century. Though the local people take pride in their modern city, outsiders see it as an overgrown village, an unplanned, disorderly adolescent metropolis, with much noise and confusion but little charm. The constant high temperature and humidity from May through October do little to boost its limited appeal.

Most likely you will find yourself in Adana because it has an airport, a train station, a large otogar, and good hotels. Its few sights are just enough to fill the few hours between transport in and transport out.

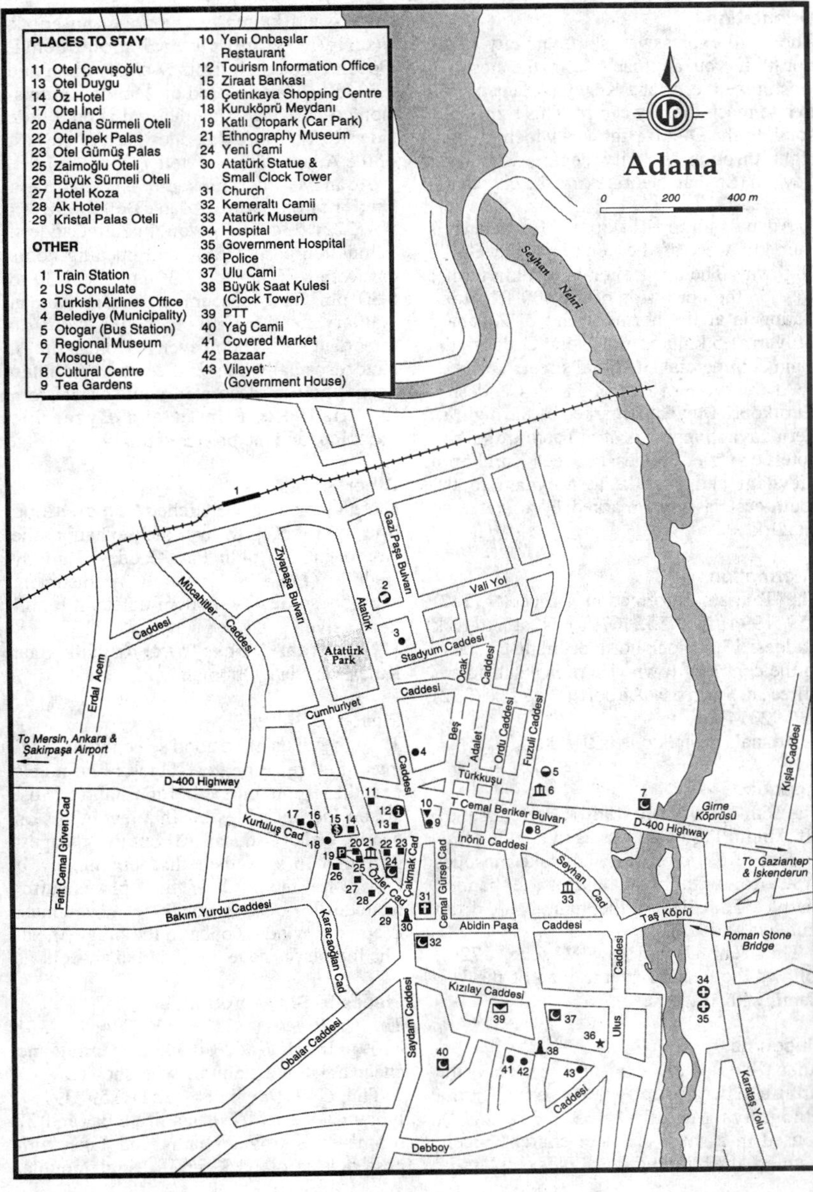

MEDITERRANEAN TURKEY

Orientation

The E 90 expressway skirts the city to the north. If you approach from the north or west, take the Adana Küzey (Adana North) exit to reach the city centre. This brings you south to the D-400 Highway which ploughs right through the city centre. The river Seyhan (Seyhan Nehri) skirts the city centre to the east.

Adana's airport (Şakirpaşa Havaalanı) is four km west of the centre on the D-400 Highway. The bus station is two km farther west on the north side of the 400. The train station is at the northern end of Ziyapaşa Bulvarı, 1.5 km north of İnönü Caddesi, the main commercial and hotel street.

At the western end of İnönü Caddesi is Kuruköprü Meydanı, marked by the highrise Çetinkaya shopping centre. There are several hotels on Özler Caddesi between Kuruköprü Meydanı and Küçüksaat Meydanı to the south-east, a plaza marked by a statue of Atatürk.

Information

The Tourism Information Office (☎ (322) 359 1994, fax 352 6790) is at Atatürk Caddesi 13, a block north of İnönü Caddesi, in the centre of town. There is a subsidiary office at Şakirpaşa Airport (☎ & fax (322) 436 92314).

Adana's postal code is 01000.

Mosques

The 16th-century **Ulu Cami** (Great Mosque), off Abidin Paşa Caddesi, is in a style reminiscent of Syria or the Mameluke mosques of Cairo, with black and white banded marble. The tiles in the mihrab are from Kütahya and İznik.

The Yeni Cami (New Mosque, 1724), follows the general square plan of the Ulu Cami, with 10 domes.

Museums

Adana has a little gem of a museum, the **Adana Ethnography Museum** (Adana Etnoğrafya Müzesi; ☎ (322) 352 2417), housed in a small crusader church. Nicely restored, the building now holds displays of carpets and kilims, weapons, manuscripts, inscriptions and funeral monuments. Opening hours are from 9 am to noon and 1.30 to 5.30 pm, closed on Monday; admission costs US$1. The museum is on a little side street off İnönü Caddesi, just to the east of the Adana Sürmeli Oteli.

Adana's other museum is the **Adana Regional Museum** (Adana Bölge Müzesi; ☎ (322) 234 3856), on Fuzuli Caddesi. Admission costs US$2, and opening hours are from 8.30 am to 12.30 pm and 1.30 to 5.30 pm. The museum is rich in Roman statuary as the Cilician Gates were an important transit point even in Roman times. Note especially the 2nd-century **Achilles sarcophagus**, decorated with scenes from the Iliad; the Roman and Byzantine **mosaics**, and the bronze statuary.

Other Sights

Have a look at the 16-arched **Roman stone bridge** (Taş Köprü) over the Seyhan, at the eastern end of Abidin Paşa Caddesi. Built by Hadrian (117-138), repaired by Justinian, and now sullied by modern traffic, it is still impressive.

The **Great Clock Tower** (Büyük Saat Kulesi) is a late Ottoman work.

Places to Stay

Though Adana has a good selection of lodgings in all price ranges, there are no hotels near the airport, otogar or train station. Most are on İnönü Caddesi, with a few others on nearby Özler Caddesi. All but the cheapest post high prices, then discount hugely if they're not busy. All of these places suffer from traffic noise, especially when you must keep your window open in the muggy heat. The top places have half-hearted air-con.

Places to Stay – bottom end

The *Öz Hotel* (☎ (322) 351 7844, fax 351 8209), İnönü Caddesi 34, is central and cheap at US$12 a double with shower.

The *Otel Duygu* (☎ (322) 359 3916), İnönü Caddesi 14/1, has a lift, a bar and 27 rooms with private baths and fans with posted rates of US$35/60 a single/double, but I was quoted US$14/20. Nearby, the two-star, 50-room *Otel İpek Palas* (☎ (322) 351 8741, fax 351 8745), İnönü Caddesi 103, charges US$18/28 for singles/doubles with private bath and ceiling fan.

Adjoining the İpek Palas is the rock-bottom *Otel Gümüş Palas* (☎ (322) 351 4175), hardly a 'silver palace' with rooms for US$4.50/6.75 a single/double, but it's central, and the rooms have sinks.

On Özler Caddesi, which joins İnönü Caddesi at Kuruköprü Meydanı, are several other bottom-end hotels.

The *Ak Hotel* (☎ (322) 351 4208, fax 352 3878), Özler Caddesi 43, just north-west of the roundabout with the statue of Atatürk, is homy and comfortable, with rooms for US$8.50 a double without private shower, US$12 with. A few steps closer to the roundabout, the *Kristal Palas Oteli* (☎ (322) 351 2335), Özler 19, is even cheaper at US$6.50/10 a single/double with shower (as it should be for what you get).

Across from the posh Zaimoğlu Oteli (see following), the two-star, 60-room *Hotel Koza* (☎ (322) 352 5857, fax 359 8571), Özler Caddesi 103, posts prices of US$40/50/60 a single/double/triple, but I was quoted prices exactly half as much.

Places to Stay – middle

The 94-room *Otel İnci* (☎ (322) 435 8234, fax 435 8368), Kuruköprü Meydanı, Kurtuluş Caddesi, offers the best value for money: four-star comforts right in the centre for US$60/80 a single/double.

The *Otel Çavuşoğlu* (☎ (322) 351 1350), Ziyapaşa Bulvarı 115, Atilla Altıkat Köprüsü Yanı, is at the southern end of the overpass which spans the D-400 Highway. Rated at two stars, the Çavuşoğlu has a restaurant, bar, and 29 decent rooms with bath for US$35/50 a single/double. Discounts are readily granted if the hotel's not busy.

Also good value for money is the four-star, 10-room *Adana Sürmeli Oteli* (☎ (322) 351 7321, fax 351 8973), İnönü Caddesi 142, with singles for US$65, doubles for US$80, but discounts are usually (and readily) available. Many rooms have baths. Its sister establishment behind it, the five-star, 210-room *Büyük Sürmeli Oteli* (bew-YEWK sewr-meh-LEE) (☎ (322) 352 3600, fax 352 1945), is slightly fancier for US$80/110.

Best in town is the 77-room *Zaimoğlu Oteli* (zah-EEM-oh-loo) (☎ (322) 351 3401, fax 351 6811), Özler Caddesi 72, between the two Sürmeli hotels. The price for a room with air-con, TV, mini bar and bath is US$90/120. Waver and they'll work with you to discover face-saving reasons for a slight discount: a 'corporate' or 'university' rate, for instance.

Places to Eat

The local speciality is Adana kebap, minced lamb mixed with hot pepper, squeezed on a flat skewer (see the fingermarks?) then charcoal-grilled. It's served with sliced purple onions dusted with fiery paprika, handfuls of parsley, a lemon wedge and flat bread.

For decades the favoured city-centre restaurant has been the *Yeni Onbaşılar Restaurant (yeh-NEE ohn-bah-shuh-LAHR)* (☎ (322) 351 4178), on Atatürk Caddesi just south of D-400 Highway, opposite the Tourism Office (enter on the south side). With virtually no competition, service and food are mediocre, but they do serve alcohol and prices aren't bad. Adana kebap, a salad and a big Efes beer comes to less than US$5. Don't tip; they add a presumptuous 20% *garsoniye.*

Otherwise, İnönü Caddesi and its side streets have numerous small kebaperies and even a few *birahanes* (bars). The *Üç Kardeşler Lokanta ve Kebap Salonu* (☎ (322) 351 7314), to the right of the Adana Sürmeli Oteli, is small and bright, with good kebaps, spectacular hummus, friendly service and low prices, but only soft drinks.

Getting There & Away

As an important transfer point for centuries, Adana is served by all means of transport.

Air Turkish Airlines (☎ (322) 453 7247, fax 435 7047), Stadyum Caddesi 32, operates daily nonstop flights between Adana and

Ankara (one hour) and İstanbul (1½ hours). There are also at least weekly flights to and from Amsterdam, Frankfurt, İzmir, Jeddah, Hannover, Munich and Nicosia (Lefkoşe), Cyprus.

An airport bus runs between the airport (☎ (322) 435 9186) and the Turkish Airlines office (US$2), meeting all Turkish Airlines flights. A taxi into town costs about US$4.

İstanbul Airlines (☎ (322) 454 3806, fax 458 3719), Atatürk Caddesi, Büyükşehir Belediyesi Yanı, Uğurlu Pasajı, Asma kat 101, has four nonstop flights weekly between Adana and İstanbul, and at least one weekly to Ankara, Cologne, Düsseldorf, Frankfurt and Münich.

Bus Adana's large otogar is active, as you might imagine, with direct buses to everywhere. Some daily services include:

Adıyaman (for Nemrut Dağı) – 370 km, six hours, US$10; seven buses per day, two of these go on to Kahta for an extra US$1
Alanya – 440 km, 10 hours, US$18; eight buses in summer
Ankara – 490 km, 10 hours, US$16; frequent buses
Antalya – 555 km, 12 hours, US$20; a few buses
Diyarbakır – 550 km, 10 hours, US$16; several buses
Gaziantep – 220 km, four hours, US$7.50; several buses
Haleb (Aleppo, Syria) – 300 km, 12 hours, US$30; at least one bus
Kayseri – 335 km, 6½ hours, US$12; several buses
Konya – 350 km, 6½ hours, US$12; frequent buses
Malatya – 425 km, eight hours, US$14; a few buses
Nevşehir (Cappadocia) – 285 km, 5½ hours, US$10; several buses
Şanlıurfa – 365 km, six hours, US$11; several buses
Van – 950 km, 18 hours, US$24; at least one bus

Train The façade of the Adana Gar (☎ (322) 453 3172), north of İnönü Caddesi at the northern end of Ziyapaşa Bulvarı, is decorated with pretty faïence panels. Trains depart six times daily for Mersin via Tarsus, a 75-minute trip.

Adana is served by three express trains which make their way up onto the Anatolian Plateau.

The *Erciyes Ekspresi* departs for Kayseri each evening at 5.30 pm, arriving at midnight. Departure from Kayseri is at 4.40 am, arriving in Adana at 10.46 am. One-way tickets cost US$4/5 for 2nd/1st class.

The *Çukurova Ekspresi* departs from Adana each evening at 7.15 pm for Ankara, arriving at 8.05 am. Departure from Ankara is at 8.10 pm, arriving at 8.18 am. One-way tickets cost US$10 for a seat, US$12 for a couchette, US$25/42/60 for a single/double/triple sleeping compartment.

The *Toros Ekspresi* departs from Adana each evening at 11.30 pm, going via Ankara to İstanbul (Haydarpaşa), arriving at 9.25 pm. Departure from İstanbul is at 9 am, arriving at 6 am. One-way tickets cost US$12/9 in 1st/2nd class; or US$26/46/64 for a single/double/triple sleeping compartment.

ADANA TO ANTAKYA

The very eastern end of the Turkish Mediterranean coast surrounds the Bay of İskenderun and includes the cities of İskenderun and Antakya, in the province of Hatay. Inland from the bay are ruins of a very old Hittite city at Karatepe, and a later Roman one (Anazarbus). On the road are several medieval fortresses. Dolmuşes from Adana run to the town of Kadirli, beyond Anazarbus and before Karatepe. You should be able to reach Anazarbus (by dolmuş and then hitchhike a short way) without too much trouble; you may want to stay the night in Kadirli. Hitching from there to Karatepe is not easy. If you have your own transport this detour is a breeze.

Yılankale

About 45 minutes (35 km) east of Adana is the **Snake Castle** (Yılankale), a fortress perched on a hilltop 2.5 km south of the highway. Built by Armenians and crusaders in the 12th or 13th century, it is said to have taken its name from a serpent which was once entwined in the coat of arms above the main entrance (today you'll see a king and a lion, but no snake); other versions have it that this area was once full of snakes. If you have the time, feel free to drive or walk up and have a look around. It's about a 20-minute climb over the rocks and up to the highest point in the fort. There are no services here, no guardian and no admission charge.

To see Anazarbus (Anavarza) and Karatepe, make a detour north and east just after the Snake Castle. About 37 km east of Adana is an intersection marked on the left (north) for Kozan and Kadirli, on the right (south) for Ceyhan. Take the Kozan/Kadirli road.

Anazarbus (Anavarza)

When the Romans moved into this area around 19 BC they built this fortress city on top of a hill dominating the fertile plain. They called it Caesarea ad Anazarbus. Later, when the Roman province of Cilicia was divided in two, Tarsus remained the capital of the west, and Anazarbus became capital of the east. In the 3rd century AD Persian invaders destroyed the city along with a lot of others in Anatolia. The Byzantine emperors rebuilt it and in later centuries, when earthquakes destroyed it several times, they rebuilt it again.

The Arab raids of the 8th century gave Anazarbus new rulers and a new Arabicised name, Ain Zarba. The Byzantines reconquered and held it for a brief period, but Anazarbus was an important city at a strategic nexus, and other armies came through and took it, including those of the Hamdanid princes of Aleppo, the crusaders, a local Armenian king, the Byzantines again, the Turks and the Mamluks. The last owners didn't care about it much and it fell into decline in the 15th century. Today it's called Anavarza.

The Road to Anazarbus From the D-400 Highway follow the Kozan/Kadirli road north to the village of Ayşehoca, where a road on the right is marked for Anavarza/Anazarbus, 4.5 km to the east. If you're in a dolmuş or bus you can get out here and usually hitch a ride pretty easily with a tractor or truck.

At a T-junction you come upon a large **triumphal arch** in the city walls. Through the gate was the ancient city, now given over to crops and pasture, with not much to see. If you turn left, after walking 650m you'll reach the remains of an **aqueduct**, several arches of which are still standing. Sometimes there's a gypsy camp set up around them.

Turn right at the T-junction and a 200-metre walk brings you to a little private **'open-air museum'** on the right-hand side of the road. Bits of column and sarcophagi are set in the garden, and an ancient pool has a nice **mosaic** of the goddess Thetis (Nereid), a sea nymph.

To reach the impressive **fortress** on the hilltop dominating the old city and the plain, you can traipse across the fields to a rock-cut stairway, or continue past the open-air museum for several km to a defile cut in the hill. An unpaved road leads through the cut to the far side of a hill, where a farmer's track along the base provides access to the **necropolis**. Ascent of the hill is much easier on this side. Inside are the ruins of a church.

The village of Anavarza has no services though you can get a glass of hospitality tea or a cool drink of water. As the flow of visitors increases, there will probably be some simple eateries and perhaps a pension. If you have camping equipment you can probably find a place to set up camp here.

Heading onward to Karatepe, return the 4.5 km to Ayşehoca and the road north to Çukurköprü and Kozan.

Karatepe-Aslantaş National Park

Now officially called the **Karatepe-Aslantaş Müzesi** (Black Hill-Lion Stone Museum), this site has been inhabited for almost 4000 years. The extant ruins date from the 13th century BC when this was a summer retreat for the neo-Hittite kings of Kizzuwatna (Cilicia), the greatest of whom was named Azitawadda.

From its forested hilltop, the Karatepe-Aslantaş Milli Parkı (national park) overlooks the **Ceyhan Gölü** (Lake Ceyhan), an artificial lake used for hydroelectric power and recreation, and has a camping ground as well as an archaeological site.

The park access road takes you two km to the car park, near picnic tables, charcoal grills and tent camping sites. From the car park it's a five-minute, 400-metre walk uphill through the forest to the hilltop archaeological zone. A building above the car park has toilets, and there are soft drinks for sale. Entry to the park costs US$0.25 per person, US$0.75 for a car (US$1 on weekends). A tent camping site costs US$2, a caravan (RV) site US$2.25. Entrance to the Hittite ruins, open from 8 am to sunset, costs an additional US$1.50 per person. If the guardian takes you on a tour of the site (a good idea), a tip is in order.

The Hittite remains here are significant. The city was defended by walls one km long, traces of which are still evident. Before arriving at the south gate there is a **lookout** giving a fine view of the lake, which was dammed and filled during the 1980s.

The southern entrance to the city is protected by four lions and two sphinxes and lined with fine reliefs showing a coronation or feast complete with sacrificial bull, musicians and chariots. Across the hill at the north gate the lions are even scarier (from an evil spirit's point of view, that is) and the reliefs are even sharper as the stones were buried for centuries and thus protected from weathering. The eyes in the volcanic lion statue are of white stone, held in by lead.

There are inscriptions in Hittite script; a very long one, with a Phoenician translation, was discovered here and deciphered, which is how we know the history of the city.

Continue past the north gate and bear left to make a circle of the hilltop, ending back at the guard's shed.

Getting There & Away Karatepe-Aslantaş may be approached from several directions.

From Osmaniye From the centre of Osmaniye, road 01-08 north-west is signposted for the Karatepe-Aslantaş Müzesi (34 km). Follow the road (and the signs), turning right and crossing a dam at Cevdetiye, then through the village of Kesmeburun to Hierapolis-Castabala, 15 km from Osmaniye. About 10 km beyond Hierapolis-Castabala, a road on the left is marked for Karatepe (9 km).

From Anazarbus (Anavarza) via Kadirli
From Anazarbus head north on road 817 via Ayşehoca to Naşidiye/Çukurköprü, where the road divides. The left is marked for Kozan and Feke, the right for Kadirli. Take the right fork.

Kadirli

Kadirli (population 55,000), 20 km east of Çukurköprü, is a farming town with a useful little bazaar, a few small restaurants and hotels. The *Aktürk Lokantası*, facing the shady park with the teahouses in the centre, is simple, cleanish, cheap and good.

It's 21 km from Kadirli to Karatepe through pretty hill country given over to farms and evergreen forests. The gravel road is easily passable in dry weather, but a bit uncertain after heavy rains. Hitchhiking is very chancy. You might have an easier time hitching if you approach from the south, taking a bus from Adana to Osmaniye, then a dolmuş towards Tecirli and Kadirli and hitchhiking the last 8.6 km to Karatepe; or you can hire a taxi or minibus in Osmaniye to take you round.

Hierapolis Castabala

Fifteen km north of Osmaniye and 19 km south of Karatepe (see above) are the ruins of Hierapolis Castabala, set in the midst of cotton fields. A castle (kale) tops a rocky outcrop above the plain about a km east of the road. Admission to the site, which is open during daylight hours, costs US$0.75. You can see everything here in about two hours.

Hierapolis Castabala, which was flourishing during the Hellenistic period, was later the capital of a little semi-independent principality paying tribute to Rome. Unfortunately one of its kings, Tarcondimotus I, unwisely sided with Antony in his struggle with Octavian and was defeated at the great sea battle of Actium in 31 BC. Though he was followed by Tarcondimotus II, the dynasty died out in the 1st century AD, as did the city in early Byzantine times.

From the ticket-seller's shed, walk along the **colonnaded street**, some of its columns still bearing Corinthian capitals, past a badly ruined **temple** and **baths** on the right-hand side. Keeping the kale on your left, walk past the rock outcrop to the **theatre**, also badly ruined. Beyond it to the south in the fields is a ruined Byzantine basilica. Farther along the same path is a **spring** *(çeşme)* and, in the ridge of rocks farther on, some **rock-cut tombs**. As you cross the fields, note the profusion of snails, both spiral and caracol, clinging to plants.

The kale has a road cut straight through the rock *(kaya kesiği)*, and good views from the summit.

Toprakkale

At a point 72 km east of Adana the highway divides, skirting the **Earth Castle** (Toprakkale), built of dark volcanic stone about the same time as the Snake Castle. The access road up to the fortress turns off from the westward branch of the highway (Adana to İskenderun); it's 600m to the fortress walls, then a few minutes' easy walk into the ruins.

Issos

At the time of writing, the E 98 expressway had been finished as far south as Erzin. If you follow the older road (817), eight km south of Toprakkale just east of Erzin, you'll notice a long **aqueduct** in the fields to the right, a remnant of the ancient city of Issos.

Payas

At Payas, also called Yakacık, 35 km south of Toprakkale, look for the inconspicuous signs in the centre of town (north of Payas' big steel factory) pointing the way (right, west) to the Cinkale Kervansaray, one km towards the sea.

The huge Ottoman **Sokullu Mehmet Paşa Kervansaray** was built for the grand vizier of Süleyman the Magnificent and Selim II in the 1570s. Opening hours are from 8 am to 4 or 5 pm daily. It's an elaborate complex of courtyards, Turkish baths, mosque, medrese and covered bazaar – a fortified city in what was then a recently conquered (1516) and still hostile territory. Parts of it look positively Burgundian, and it may be that Sokullu Mehmet Paşa's architects, who worked under the guidance of Sinan's school, may have restored and expanded the ruins of a crusader church.

Next to the caravanserai is the **Cin Kalesi**, or Fortress of the Genies, a restored bastion protected by a moat now filled with fig trees. The main gate is a double-bend defensive one which leads to a grassy interior now used as pasture for cattle. The ruins of a small mosque are the only other item of interest. If you walk around the outside of the castle walls you can descend to the moat by means of a stone subterranean stairway at the moat's westernmost point and pick figs.

Farther along down the tarmac road from these two buildings is another little **fortress** with a bent-gate entrance, a keep and gun ports, and there's the ruins of yet another fortress down by the water's edge. You can wander into all three forts at any time of day.

After Payas the road is lined with factories for making steel, cement, fertiliser and the like, all taking advantage of the historic port of İskenderun, 22 km to the south.

İskenderun

İskenderun (population 170,000), 130 km east of Adana, was founded by Alexander the Great in 333 BC and once bore the name Alexandretta, of which İskenderun is a translation. It was the most important port city on this part of the coast until Mersin was developed in the 1960s, but it has retained its importance as a port. Its importance increased during the 1980s with the opening of the oil pipeline from Iraq, and the shutting down of that pipeline during the Persian Gulf War of 1991.

İskenderun was occupied by the English in 1918, turned over to the French in 1919, and included under the French Protectorate of Syria as the Sanjak of Alexandretta. Atatürk reclaimed it for the Turkish Republic (with French acquiescence) in 1938, as he knew it would be of great strategic importance in the coming war (WWII).

There is nothing to hold you in İskenderun as it is just a sailors', brokers' and shippers' town. If you must stop, however, there are several good places to stay in this clean and pleasant city.

Orientation The seashore is on the north side of the city centre. Turn left (south) near the train station to reach the minibus station and the otogar, two buildings a block apart. Turn right (north) from the highway and follow Osman Gazi Caddesi, a wide avenue, to Atatürk Bulvarı, the waterfront boulevard, with its hotels, banks and restaurants. The main square, on Atatürk Bulvarı between Şehit Pamir and Ulu Cami Caddesis, is marked by a pretentious patriotic statue *(Abide*, ah-BEE-deh, monument) on the waterfront. Most of the town's lodgings are on Şehit Pamir Caddesi within a few blocks' walk of the Abide.

Information The Tourist Information Office (☎ (326) 614 1620, fax 613 2879), is at Atatürk Bulvarı 49/B, 100m west of the Abide. Staff are quite helpful.

İskenderun's postal code is 31200.

Places to Stay Two blocks inland from Atatürk Bulvarı and the Abide is the modest *Kavaklı Pansiyon* (☎ (326) 617 4608), Şehit Pamir Caddesi, 52 Sokak 14, a basic but adequate place with friendly staff, a lift, and rooms with running water for US$8/12 a single/double.

Hotel Açıkalın (☎ (326) 617 3732), Şehit Pamir Caddesi 13, is clean and central, with doubles for US$13; with shower for US$15.

Nearby, the *Hotel Altındişler* (☎ & fax (326) 617 1011), Şehit Pamir Caddesi 11, is a step up in quality at US$20 for a double with shower and TV. A bit more comfortable is the nearby *Hotel İmrenay* (☎ (326) 613 2117), Şehit Pamir Caddesi 5, at US$18/27 a single/double with shower.

The *Hataylı Oteli* (☎ (326) 614 1590, fax 617 8751), Osman Gazi Caddesi 2, four blocks east of Şehit Pamir Caddesi and one block inland, has 60 rooms with private baths for US$16/35 a single/double, breakfast included.

Best in town is the three-star, 35-room *Hotel Cabir* (☎ (326) 612 3391, fax 612 3393), Ulucami Caddesi 16, a block east of Şehit Pamir Caddesi, with comfortable doubles with shower for US$40, breakfast included.

Places to Eat The town's best is the big *Saray Restaurant*, a few blocks west of the Tourism Office on Atatürk Bulvarı. For cheaper meals, stroll along the narrow lane which runs between Şehit Pamir Caddesi at the Hotel Açıkalın, and Ulucami Caddesi at the Hotel Cabir. The street has a half-dozen cheap restaurants serving kebaps, stews, pide, etc at vine-shaded tables. The simple *Bahar Lokantası* is good for cheap stews (US$1), the *Yeni Lokanta* a bit fancier, with a separate room in which to serve its renowned döner kebap (US$2).

South of İskenderun

Past İskenderun the road winds uphill towards Antakya, 60 km away, through the town of Sarımazı (10 km from İskenderun) to Belen, the town at the head of a gorge 15 km south of İskenderun. Belen looks to be an old settlement, and indeed it is, as archaeological excavations nearby have unearthed evidence of settlements dating back to the time of Hammurabi, king of Babylon.

At 147 km from Adana the road passes over the Belen Pass (Belen Geçidi, altitude 740m) and then descends to the vast, flat, fertile Amik Plain, the source of Antakya's prosperity.

ANTAKYA

Antakya (population 150,000), also called Hatay (HAH-'tie'), was, until 1938, Arabic in culture and language. Many people still speak Arabic as a first language, Turkish as the second. The reason to visit Antakya is to see the marvellous Roman mosaics in the Antakya Museum (closed Monday). You can also visit 'the world's first cathedral', a cave-church in which, it is said, St Peter preached and the term 'Christian' was first used.

History

This is the ancient Antioch ad Orontes, founded by Seleucus I Nicator in 300 BC.

Before long it had a population of half a million. Under the Romans it developed an important Christian community (out of its already large Jewish one), which was at one time headed by St Paul.

Persians, Byzantines, Arabs, Armenians and Seljuks all fought for Antioch, and the crusaders and Saracens battled for it as well. In 1268 the Mameluks of Egypt took the city and wiped it out. It was never to regain its former glory.

The Ottomans held the city until Muhammed Ali of Egypt captured it in his drive for control of the empire (1831), but with European help the Ottomans drove their rebellious vassal back. The French held it as part of their Syrian protectorate until 1939. Atatürk saw WWII approaching and wanted the city rejoined to the republic as a defensive measure. He began a campaign to reclaim it, which came to fruition by means of a plebiscite shortly after his death.

Orientation

The Asi River (the ancient Orontes) divides the town. The modern district is on the west bank, with the PTT, government buildings and museum circling the traffic roundabout named Cumhuriyet Alanı; the Büyük Antakya Oteli, best in town, is just up the street.

The older Ottoman town on the eastern bank is the commercial centre, and has most of the hotels, restaurants and services, especially along Hürriyet Caddesi. The bus station (Santral Garajı) is a few blocks north-east of the centre, on the east bank. Surrounding these services is the sprawling bazaar.

Information

The provincial Tourism Information Office (☎ (326) 216 0610) is less than two km north of the PTT, on the western bank at a traffic roundabout. It's open from 8 am to noon and 1.30 to 6.30 pm daily.

Antakya Archaeological Museum

The Antakya Archaeological Museum (Arkeoloji Müzesi) is the prime reason for journeying all the way to Antakya. Admission costs US$2.50; opening hours are Tuesday to Sunday from 8.30 am to noon and 1.30 to 5 pm, closed Monday. Most labels are in English and Turkish. Photography (no flash or tripod) is permitted for a fee.

The first four 'salons' in the museum (Salons I to IV) are filled with Roman mosaics – and what mosaics! Photographs show how they looked in situ, and the tall, naturally lit exhibit rooms show them off well. Seasonal themes, fishing, hunting, war and mythological subjects are all astonishingly well portrayed using little coloured stone chips. Many of these mosaics came from Roman villas at the seaside and in the suburban resort of Daphne (Harbiye).

Salon V holds exhibits of artefacts recovered from the *tells* (mounds) at Açana and Cüdeyde. The pair of lions serving as column pediments, dating from the 8th century BC, are especially good.

Salon VI has Roman and Byzantine coins, statues, pots, glassware and tools, some dating from the Eski Tunç Devri II (Second Old Bronze Age, 2600-2500 BC). The cuneiform inscriptions are from the Açana excavations.

Cave-Church of St Peter

On the north-eastern outskirts of town, three km from the centre, is the **Senpiyer Kilisesi** or grotto Church of St Peter, open from 8 am to noon and 1.30 to 6 pm (closed Monday). Admission is free. If you buy a souvenir from the stand inside the gate, proceeds go to the upkeep of the church.

Tradition has it that this cave was the property of St Luke the Evangelist, who was from Antioch, and that he donated it to the burgeoning Christian congregation as a place of worship. Saints Peter and Paul lived in Antioch for a few years, and are thought to have preached here. When the Crusaders marched through, they constructed the wall at the front, and a narthex.

Traces of fresco and mosaic can still be seen, and mass is still celebrated here each Sunday from 3 to 4.30 pm. For further information, contact the Capuchins at the Katolik

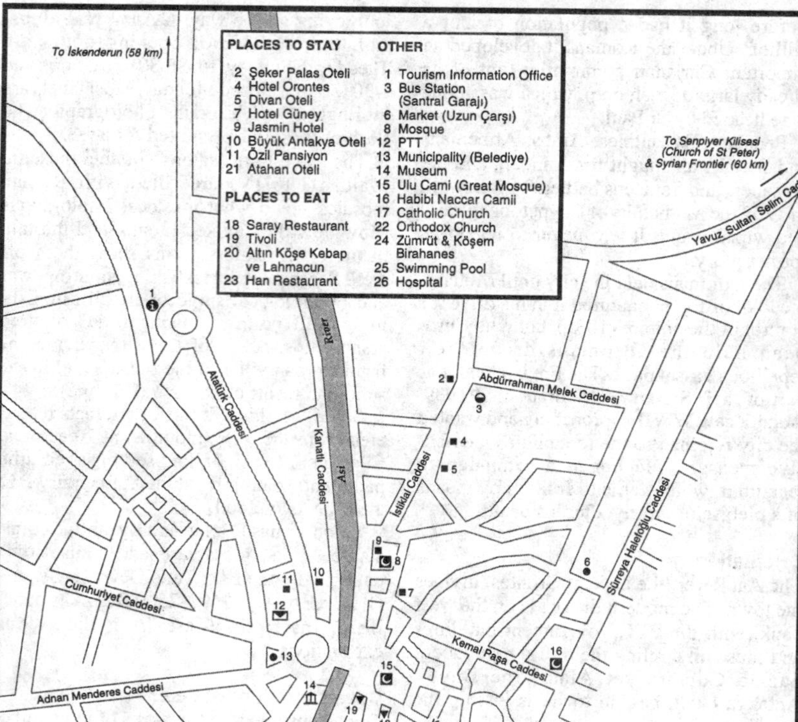

Antakya

PLACES TO STAY

2 Şeker Palas Oteli
4 Hotel Orontes
5 Divan Oteli
7 Hotel Güney
9 Jasmin Hotel
10 Büyük Antakya Oteli
11 Özil Pansiyon
21 Atahan Oteli

PLACES TO EAT

18 Saray Restaurant
19 Tivoli
20 Altın Köşe Kebap ve Lahmacun
23 Han Restaurant

OTHER

1 Tourism Information Office
3 Bus Station (Santral Garajı)
6 Market (Uzun Çarşı)
8 Mosque
12 PTT
13 Municipality (Belediye)
14 Museum
15 Ulu Cami (Great Mosque)
16 Habibi Naccar Camii
17 Catholic Church
22 Orthodox Church
24 Zümrüt & Köşem Birahanes
25 Swimming Pool
26 Hospital

To İskenderun (58 km)
To Senpiyer Kilisesi (Church of St Peter) & Syrian Frontier (60 km)
Yavuz Sultan Selim Cad
Abdürrahman Melek Caddesi
Atatürk Caddesi
Kanatlı Caddesi
Asi River
İstiklal Caddesi
Sürreya Halefoğlu Caddesi
Cumhuriyet Caddesi
Kemal Paşa Caddesi
Adnan Menderes Caddesi
Kutlu Sokak
Gündüz Caddesi
Kurtuluş Caddesi
İnönü Caddesi
Hürriyet Caddesi
To Habibi Naccar Cave
To Samandağ (29 km)
Vali Ürgen Bulvarı
Trajan Aqueduct
To Syrian Frontier (60 km)
0 0.5 1 km

Kilisesi (Catholic Church, ☎ (326) 215 6703), Kurtuluş Caddesi, Kutlu Sokak 6, who have cared for the Church of St Peter since 1846. The Orthodox liturgy is performed Sunday at 8 am in summer, 8.30 am in winter.

From the garden in front of the church there is a fine view of the city. Note the many vine-shaded roof terraces, which is where Antakyan families go in the evening to catch whatever breeze there is. On the high mountain to the south-east are remnants of the long **city walls** and, at the summit, a badly ruined **acropolis**.

There is no bus. You can walk easily, if it's not too hot, in about half an hour, north-east along İstiklal Caddesi and Kurtuluş Caddesi. A sign on the right side of the road marks the turning. A taxi charges US$2 each way.

Daphne (Harbiye)

Dolmuşes run frequently from Antakya's bus station to the hill suburb of Harbiye, the ancient Daphne, nine km to the south; there are less frequent city buses as well. Through a modern residential area and up the hill you come to the **waterfall** on the right (west), just past the Hotel du Liban. Walk down into the wooded valley, which is usually full of Antakyalı vacationers enjoying the cool shade, the little tea gardens (each with a scratchy-sounding cassette player), and the rivulets, pools and falls of cooling water.

Past Harbiye, 42 km farther on, is the **Yayladağı Yazılıtaş Orman Piknik Yeri**, a forest picnic spot near some **ancient inscriptions**. Along the way the road passes near the village of **Sofular**, next to which is a **crusader castle**.

Samandağ

Dolmuşes and Samandağ city buses (Samandağ Belediyesi) run frequently to this seaside suburb 28 km away, following Gündüz Caddesi past the Archaeological Museum and over the mountains to the sea.

Samandağ itself is uninspiring, but go six km north along the beach to Çevlik to see the ruins of **Seleucia ad Piera**, in ancient times Antioch's port town. Dolmuş service is not regular to Çevlik so talk your dolmuş driver into continuing to Çevlik for a small additional fare. Several restaurants here by the sea offer meals in pleasant surroundings; there are a few simple pensions as well. The water, for swimming, is not the cleanest.

Seleucia's ruins are not much to look at but a nearby feat of Roman engineering is quite interesting. During its heyday, Seleucia lived daily with the threat of inundation from the stream which descended the mountains and came through the town. To remove the threat, Roman emperors Titus and Vespasian ordered their engineers to dig a diversion channel around the town. This they did. From the car park in Çevlik, ascend the steps to the **Titus ve Vespasiyanus Tüneli**, pay the US$1 admission fee and a guide will accompany you up the hillside, along the channel and through a great gorge. At the upper end of the channel is an inscription dating the work.

Places to Stay – bottom end

Closest to the bus station is the stark, dour *Şeker Palas Oteli* (☎ (326) 215 1603), İstiklal Caddesi 79. Its dingy rooms, at US$4/6 for singles/doubles without water, are for emergencies.

Much better, but a distance away, is the *Özil Pansiyon* (☎ (326) 215 1009, 213 2035), Atatürk Caddesi 5, directly across from the towering Büyük Ankara Oteli. This family run pension caters mostly to local students, but accepts tourists as well at US$2.50 per person in waterless but clean rooms.

Walking south on İstiklal Caddesi from the bus station, a few blocks brings you to the *Jasmin Hotel* (☎ (326) 212 7171), İstiklal Caddesi 14, above the Garanti Bankası. The US$12 double rooms here are a step up, though baths are still shared.

The one-star *Divan Oteli* (dee-VAHN) (☎ (326) 215 1518), İstiklal Caddesi 62, offers the best value for money near the bus station, with 23 serviceable rooms with showers priced at US$15/22/28 a single/double/triple, but I was quoted a price of

US$13 a double when I asked. There are no fans but the cross-ventilation is fairly good.

Hotel Güney (☎ (326) 214 9713, fax 215 1778), İstiklal Sokak 28, is one narrow street east of İstiklal Caddesi. Big, bright and bare, with fresh paint all round, it serves mostly Turkish families who spend US$10 for a double without shower, US$14 with. The neighbouring Hotel Dinçkan should be avoided as it rents rooms by the hour.

First along Hürriyet Caddesi is the *Hotel Saray* (☎ (326) 214 9001, fax 214 9002), Hürriyet Caddesi 3, above the Saray Restaurant. Clean, decently kept rooms with showers go for US$13/18 a single/double.

Places to Stay – middle

The one-star, 28-room *Atahan Oteli* (☎ (326) 214 2140, fax 215 8006), Hürriyet Caddesi 28, was once the best in town, but is now a distant third-best, with rooms somewhat overpriced at US$23/31 for singles/doubles, but adequate – and air-con.

Hotel Orontes (☎ (326) 214 5931, fax 214 5933), İstiklal Caddesi 58, is new, shiny, comfortable, and the best mid-range choice at US$24/34 a single/double for its 35 air-con rooms, some with river views.

The best in town is the four-star, *Büyük Antakya Oteli* (☎ (326) 213 5860, fax 213 5869), Atatürk Caddesi 8, with 72 air-con rooms, some with river views. Rooms have TVs, baths, and prices of US$70/100 a single/double, which is a bit much for what you get – and they don't accept credit cards. They have a closed garage as well.

Places to Eat

The strong Syrian influence reaches deep into Antakya's cuisine. Handfuls of mint and wedges of lemon accompany many kebaps. Hummus, rare elsewhere in Turkey, is readily available here. Many main courses and salads are dusted with fiery pepper. If this isn't to your taste, ask for yours *acısız* (Ah-juh-SUHZ, without hot pepper). For dessert, try the local specialty, künefe, a circular cake of fine shredded wheat laid over a dollop of fresh, mild cheese, floated on a layer of sugar syrup, topped with chopped walnuts and baked. It's best when hot from the oven.

There are, as usual, many small, cheap eateries near the otogar, in this case lining the İstiklal Caddesi side.

Tivoli (☎ 214 7726), at the eastern end of the bridge and the beginning of Hürriyet Caddesi, is a convenient landmark. Antakya's gilded youth come here to see and be seen in air-conditioned comfort (mostly in the large dining room upstairs), and to consume fast food, espresso and cappuccino. A döner burger, pomfrit (fried potatoes) and drink costs US$3. Have your döner served dürüm-style, rolled up in flat village bread. The pastries look luscious.

Hürriyet Caddesi is lined with restaurants. Most have tiny street-level rooms, with larger dining rooms one flight up.

A few steps down Hürriyet Caddesi, the *Saray Restaurant* usually has a good selection of dishes and a modern salon to eat them in. Full meals can be had for US$2 to US$3.50.

Altın Köşe Kebap ve Lahmacun, on the opposite side near the Atahan Hotel, is good for a light lahmacun (pizza) lunch at a low price.

Perhaps the best all-round choice is the *Han Restaurant* (☎ 215 8538), Hürriyet Caddesi 19/1. Go upstairs to either of the large, pleasant open-air terraces and order their good döner kebap, served with flat peasant bread, chopped parsley and pepper-dusted sliced red onions. They make an exceptionally good künefe here; tell them early in the meal that you'll want it for dessert. A full meal of döner, salad, künefe and a beer comes to US$7.

If drink is more important than food, try the *Zümrüt* or the *Köşem*, two birahanes down at the southern end of Hürriyet Caddesi, where local men come to sip and talk sports and politics. There are other birahanes on Hürriyet as well.

Getting There & Away

Bus Dolmuşes run frequently from Antakya's bus station to Harbiye (nine km, 15 minutes), Samandağ (28 km, 35 minutes) and the Turco-Syrian border stations at

Reyhanlı (for Aleppo) and Yayladağ (for Lattakia and Beirut) throughout the day. Antakya city buses run to and from Harbiye and Samandağ.

Antakya bus station also has direct buses to most western and northern points (Ankara, Antalya, İstanbul, İzmir, Kayseri, Konya), most going via Adana and up through the Cilician Gates. There are also direct buses to major cities in neighbouring countries; travel times to these cities do not include border-crossing formalities, which may add several hours to the trip. Have your visas in advance to hasten formalities.

Daily buses from Antakya serve the following destinations:

Adana – 190 km, 2½ hours, US$5; very frequent buses
Amman (Jordan) – 675 km, 10 hours, US$28
Damascus (Syria) – 465 km, eight hours, US$20
Gaziantep – 200 km, four hours, US$8; frequent buses
Haleb (Aleppo, Syria) – 105 km, four hours, US$12; several buses
Şanlıurfa (Urfa) – 345 km, seven hours, US$14; several direct buses, or change at Gaziantep, from where buses go east to Urfa every half-hour

To/From Syria Syrian visas are not normally issued at the border, but this depends partly upon your nationality and partly upon current regulations. If you plan to travel to Syria and other Middle Eastern countries, plan ahead and obtain the necessary visas in your home country, in İstanbul or in Ankara.

At the border you are no longer required to change the equivalent of US$100 into Syrian currency at the official exchange rate, currently only 25% of the black-market rate.

To/From Israel Now that peace is dawning tentatively in the Middle East, it's possible to travel between Jerusalem and İstanbul by bus for around US$100, well below the equivalent airfare.

Until there is direct correspondence between Israeli and Syrian roads and bus companies, the route is through Jordan: cross via the Allenby/King Hussein Bridge to Amman; you may have to stay two days for your transit visa for Syria. Proceed from Amman to Damascus (Karnack Bus Company). From Damascus, take another Karnack bus to the border at Idlib/Hatay. The border crossing takes about two hours. From Antakya, transfer to a bus for any destination in Turkey.

Central Anatolia

When nomadic Turkish shepherds moved into Anatolia around the year 1100, they found a land which reminded them of central Asia: semi-arid, rolling steppe covered with grass, perfect for their flocks. Mountains and great lakes (some of them salt) broke up the vast expanse of steppe. By the numerous streams, marked with rows of tall and spindly poplars, the nomads gradually settled down to establish villages.

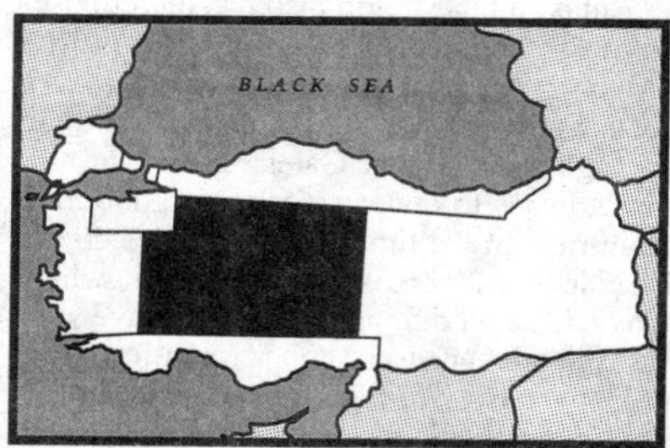

Highlights

- Staying in a restored Ottoman house in Safranbolu
- Visiting the Mevlâna Museum in Konya
- Walking through the Ilhara Gorge
- Exploring the Cappadocian valleys, especially Göreme
- Ankara's Museum of Anatolian Civilisations
- Hittite-spotting in Hattuşaş
- Staying in a rock-cut room in Cappadocia
- Trying not to get lost in the underground city of Kaymaklı or Derinkuyu

In spring, Central Anatolia is a sea of wild flowers. Great swaths of vivid colour run across the spare landscape in an annual extravagance born of the spring rains. Days are pleasantly warm and nights chilly. In summer the rain disappears and the Anatolian Plateau is hotter and drier, never humid like on the coasts. As you ride across Anatolia in summer, you will see the dark red of newly ploughed furrows, the straw yellow of wheat, the grey and green bands of sandstone in a rock-face. Winter is cold and rainy, with numerous snow falls. The snow is not surprising, for the plateau has an average altitude of 1000m.

The first impression of Central Anatolia as a vast emptiness dotted with oases of civilisation is deceptive. The armies of a dozen empires have moved back and forth across this 'land bridge' between Europe and Asia; a dozen civilisations have risen and fallen here, including the very earliest established human communities, which date from 7500 BC. Crumbling caravanserais scattered along the modern highways testify to rich trade routes which flourished for several millennia.

Today, Central Anatolia is still flourishing. Wheat and other grains, apples, cabbages, melons, potatoes, sugar beets, tomatoes and many other crops are grown in the dry soil, and flocks of sheep finish off the grass. Ankara, Turkey's capital city, is a sprawling urban mass in the midst of the semi-desert; Konya and Kayseri, fuelled by the wealth of agriculture and light industry, are growing at a remarkable pace. Modern at first glance, with wide boulevards, apartment blocks and busy traffic, each city has at its heart an old town, perhaps a fortress dating from Roman times, and sometimes even a few foundations dating from the dawn of civilisation.

Ankara

The capital of the Turkish Republic, Ankara (AHN-kah-rah, population three million, altitude 848m), was once called Angora. The fine, soft hair *(tiftik)* on Angora goats became an industry which still thrives. Today, Ankara's prime concern is government. It is

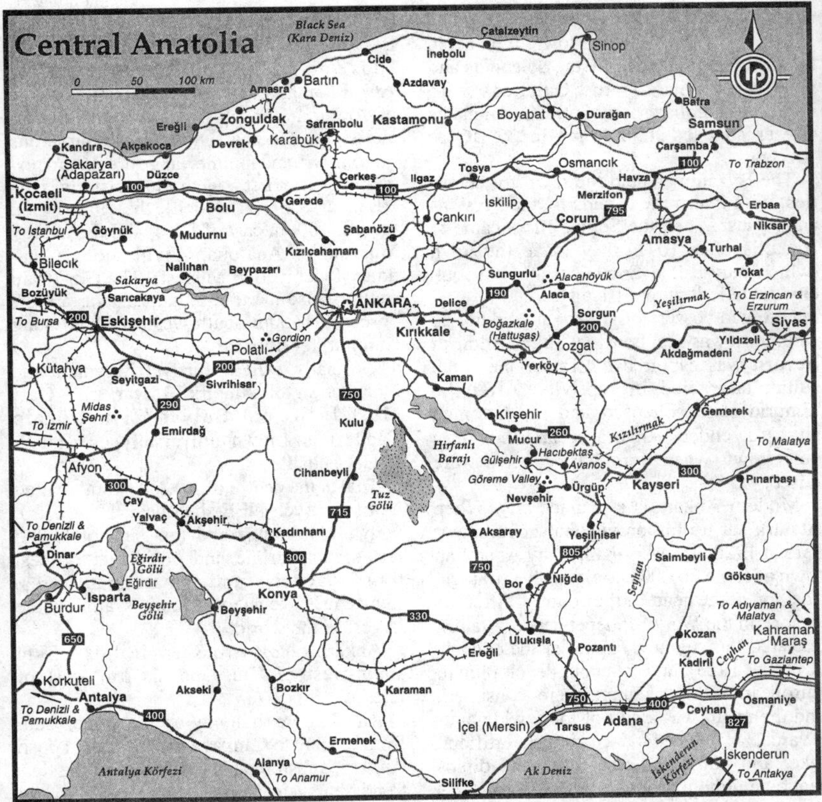

a city of ministries, embassies, universities, medical centres and some light industry. Vast suburbs are scattered on the hillsides which surround the centre; and most are filled by country people who have moved here in search of work and a better life.

Until recently, the principal heating fuel was a soft brown coal called lignite which produces thick, gritty smoke. During the season when heating is used (between 15 October and 15 April), Ankara's air was always badly polluted, but now a pipeline brings clean-burning natural gas to Ankara from Russia. Air quality is expected to improve dramatically as the city converts to this superior fuel. But natural gas will not prevent car-exhaust pollution, which is as bad in Ankara as in any other large, car-dependent city.

Ankara has several significant attractions, but you should be able to tour them all in 1½ to two days, or even a day if you're in a hurry.

History

It was the Hittites who named this place Ankuwash before 1200 BC. The town prospered because it was at the intersection of the north-south and east-west trade routes. After the Hittites, it was a Phrygian town, then taken by Alexander, claimed by the Seleucids and finally occupied by the Galatians who invaded Anatolia around 250 BC. Augustus Caesar annexed it to Rome in 25 BC as Ankyra.

The Byzantines held the town for centuries, with intermittent raids by the Persians and Arabs. When the Seljuk Turks came to Anatolia after 1071, they made the town (which they called Engüriye) into a Seljuk city but held it with difficulty.

Ottoman possession of Angora did not go well, for it was near here that Sultan Yıldırım Beyazıt was captured by Tamerlane – the sultan later died in captivity. After the Timurid state collapsed and the Ottoman civil war ended, Angora became merely a quiet town where long-haired goats were raised.

Modern Ankara is a planned city. When Atatürk set up his provisional government here in 1920, it was a small, dusty Anatolian town of some 30,000 people, with a strategic position at the heart of the country. After his victory in the War of Independence, Atatürk declared this the new capital of the country (October 1923), and set about developing it. European urban planners were consulted, and the result was a city of long, wide boulevards, a forested park with an artificial lake, and numerous residential and diplomatic neighbourhoods. From 1919 to 1927, Atatürk did not set foot in the old imperial capital of İstanbul, preferring to work at making Ankara the country's capital city in fact as well as in name.

For republican Turks, İstanbul is their glorious historical city, still the centre of business and finance, but Ankara is their true capital, built on the ashes of the empire with blood and sweat.

Orientation

The main boulevard through the city is, of course, Atatürk Bulvarı, which runs from Ulus in the north to the Presidential Mansion in Çankaya, six km to the south.

The old city of Ankara, dating from Roman times and including the Hisar (fortress), is near Ulus Meydanı, called simply Ulus (oo-LOOSS), the centre of 'old Ankara', marked by a large equestrian statue of Atatürk. The most important museums and sights are near Ulus, as are numerous bottom-end and middle-range hotels and restaurants. The first goal of most visitors is the Hisar, or Kale (KAH-leh), the citadel atop the hill 1000m east of Ulus, and the nearby Museum of Anatolian Civilisations (Anadolu Medeniyetleri Müzesi). The *Gar* (train station), also the terminus for Havaş airport buses, is 1400m south-west of Ulus along Cumhuriyet Bulvarı.

Officially called Hürriyet Meydanı, the intersection of Atatürk Bulvarı and Gazi Mustafa Kemal Bulvarı/Ziya Gökalp Caddesi is known universally as Kızılay (KUH-zuh-'lie').

This is the centre of 'new Ankara', called Yenişehir (yeh-NEE-sheh-heer, New City), with middle-range and top-end hotels and restaurants, airline and bus ticket offices, travel agencies and department stores. Yenişehir's Kocatepe Camii is among the largest in the world.

Ankara's *otogar* (bus terminal) is 6.5 km south-west of Ulus and six km west of Kızılay.

Kavaklıdere, halfway up the slope south from Kızılay to Çankaya, is the heart of posh Ankara, a fashionable district of embassies, trendy bars, smart shops, and the Hilton and Sheraton hotels.

At the southern end of Atatürk Bulvarı up in the hills is Çankaya, the residential neighbourhood which holds the Presidential Mansion (Cumhurbaşkanlığı Köşkü) and many of the most important ambassadorial residences. The prominent landmark here is the Atakule, a tall office tower and shopping complex with a bulbous top visible throughout the city.

Information

Tourist Offices The Ministry of Tourism has established a free telephone information service in Ankara on ☎ (900) 344 7090. There are tourism offices at Ankara's otogar

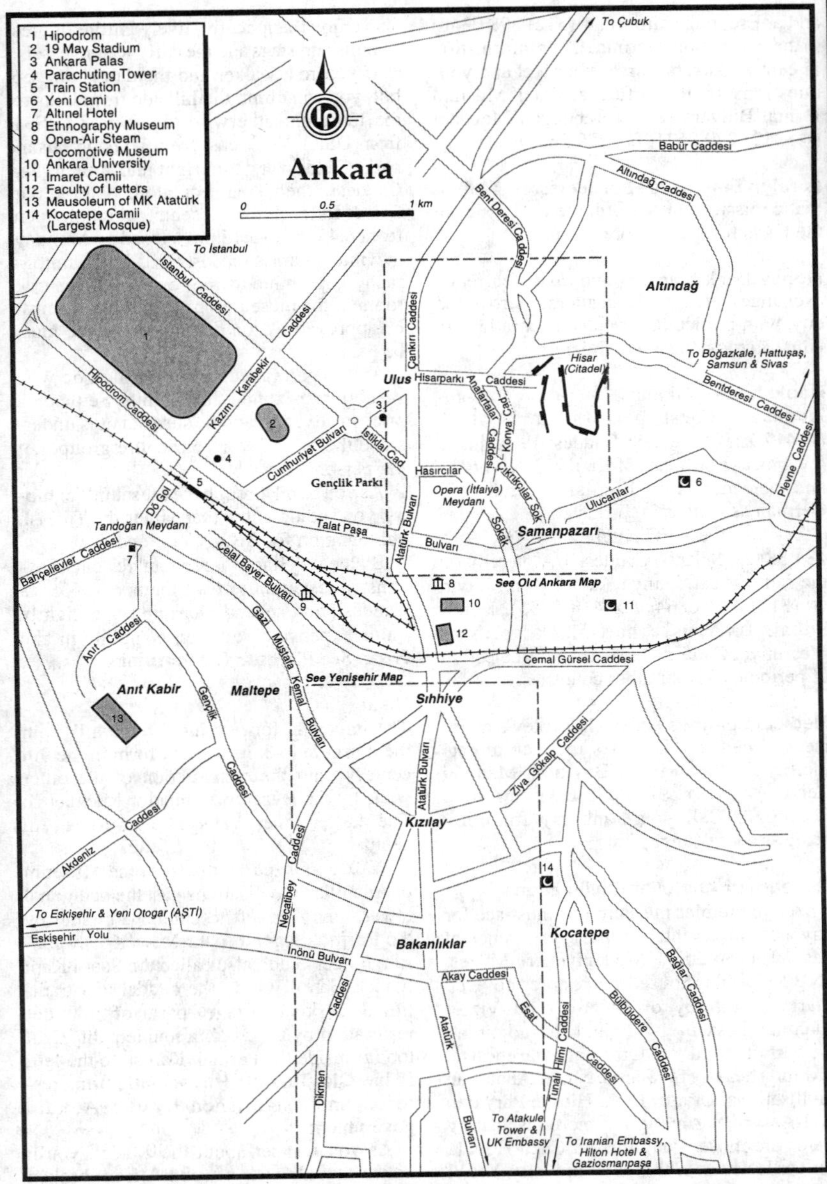
Ankara
0
0.5
1 km
1 Hipodrom
2 19 May Stadium
3 Ankara Palas
4 Parachuting Tower
5 Train Station
6 Yeni Cami
7 Altınel Hotel
8 Ethnography Museum
9 Open-Air Steam Locomotive Museum
10 Ankara University
11 İmaret Camii
12 Faculty of Letters
13 Mausoleum of MK Atatürk
14 Kocatepe Camii (Largest Mosque)
To Çubuk
Babür Caddesi
Altındağ Caddesi
Bent Deresi Caddesi
To İstanbul
İstanbul Caddesi
Caddesi
Kazım Karabekir
Hipodrom Caddesi
Altındağ
Çankırı Caddesi
Ulus
Hisarparkı
Caddesi
Anafartalar Caddesi
Konya Cad
Hisar (Citadel)
To Boğazkale, Hattuşaş, Samsun & Sivas
Bentderesi Caddesi
Plevne Caddesi
Cumhuriyet Bulvarı
İstiklal Cad
Hasırcılar
Çıkrıkçılar Sok
Gençlik Parkı
Opera (İtfaiye) Meydanı
Ulucanlar
Dö Gol
Tandoğan Meydanı
Talat Paşa
Bulvarı
Atatürk Bulvarı
Sokak
Samanpazarı
Bahçelievler Caddesi
Celal Bayer Bulvarı
See Old Ankara Map
Gazi Mustafa Kemal Bulvarı
Anıt Caddesi
Cemal Gürsel Caddesi
See Yenişehir Map
Anıt Kabir
Maltepe
Sıhhiye
Gençlik Caddesi
Ziya Gökalp Caddesi
Atatürk Bulvarı
Kızılay
Akdeniz Caddesi
Necatibey Caddesi
To Eskişehir & Yeni Otogar (AŞTİ)
Eskişehir Yolu
İnönü Bulvarı
Bakanlıklar
Kocatepe
Akay Caddesi
Esat Caddesi
Bağlar Caddesi
Bülbüldere Caddesi
Tunalı Hilmi Caddesi
Caddesi
Atatürk Bulvarı
Dikmen
To Atakule Tower & UK Embassy
To Iranian Embassy, Hilton Hotel & Gaziosmanpaşa

and at Esenboğa airport (☎ (312) 398 0348) in the international terminal. For information in central Ankara, direct your feet and your questions to the office at Gazi Mustafa Kemal Bulvarı 121, at Tandoğan Meydanı (☎ (312) 229 2631, fax 229 3661).

Foreign Embassies For addresses of diplomatic missions in Ankara, see Embassies in the Facts for the Visitor chapter.

Money Bank branches and *döviz* (currency exchange) offices are scattered across the city, with particularly rich concentrations in Ulus, Kızılay and Kavaklıdere.

Bookshops Ankara's long-time foreign-language bookshop is Tarhan Kitabevi (☎ 417 2550), Selanik Caddesi 19/A, just a few blocks north-east of Kızılay. It has books and periodicals in English, French and German as well as in Turkish.

Try also the ABC Kitabevi (☎ 433 2962, 434 3842), Selanik Caddesi 1/A, nearby on the same street. Dünya Aktüel Basın Yayın (☎ (312) 418 6864, fax 418 9155), Konur Sokak 10/A, is a half-block north of Meşrutiyet Caddesi and has a good selection of periodicals from other countries.

Medical Services Ankara is Turkey's major medical centre. The city's most up-to-date facility is the private Bayındır Medical Centre (☎ (312) 287 9000), Eskişehir Yolu, Söğütözü. Call your embassy for other health-service suggestions.

Museum of Anatolian Civilisations

Ankara's premier museum is a must-see for anyone with an interest in Turkey's ancient past. The Anadolu Medeniyetleri Müzesi (☎ 324 3160) is housed in a restored covered market, built by order of Grand Vizier Mahmut Paşa in 1471, and the adjoining Kurşunlu Han, an Ottoman warehouse. Exhibits heavily favour the earlier Anatolian civilisations: Urartu, Hatti, Hittite, Phrygian and Assyrian. Among the more fascinating items are those brought from Çatal Höyük, the earliest known human community. You'll also enjoy the graceful, lively Hittite figures of bulls and stags and the early water vessels.

If you're a walker and the day is not too hot, you can climb the hillside from Ulus to the museum; otherwise take a taxi (US$1 from Ulus). Walk east from Ulus on Hisarparkı Caddesi and turn right into Anafartalar Caddesi, then bear left along Çıkrıkçılar Sokak to reach the museum, which is open from 8.45 am to 5.15 pm, closed on Monday in winter; admission costs US$2.50. Photography is permitted (free) only in the central room of the museum; in other rooms it must be approved by the director and a fee must be paid.

You may be approached by a guide who will offer to explain the exhibits. Settle on a price in advance, and be sure that it is understood the price is for your entire group, not per person.

As you stroll through the museum's exhibits, you should know that MÖ is the Turkish abbreviation for BC.

By the way, there are several decent, inexpensive restaurants down the hill on Konya Caddesi, and several charming but slightly more expensive restaurants uphill in the Hisar. See Places to Eat for details.

Hisar

The imposing fortress just up the hill from the museum took its present form in the 9th century with the construction of the outer walls by the Byzantine emperor Michael II. The earlier inner walls date from the 7th century.

Walk up Gözcü Sokak from the Museum of Anatolian Civilisations past the octagonal tower, then turn left to enter the citadel by the **Parmak Kapısı** (pahr-MAHK kah-puh-suh, Finger Gate), also called the Saatli Kapı (Clock Gate). Within the citadel is a traditional Turkish village, parts of it under restoration by the Ankara municipality. Not too far inside the Parmak Kapısı, to the left, is the **Old Turkish House Museum**, restored and established by the Ankara government.

As you wander about the citadel, you'll notice that all sorts of rubble, from broken

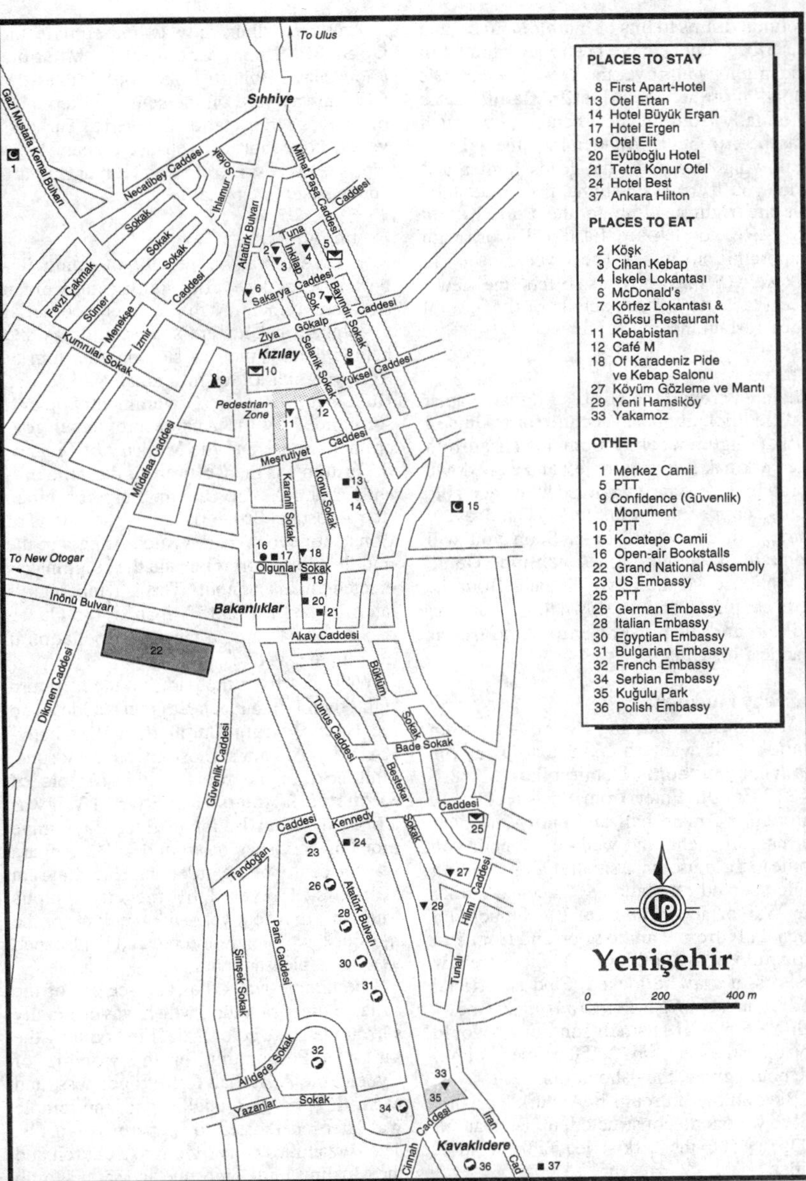
PLACES TO STAY
8 First Apart-Hotel
13 Otel Ertan
14 Hotel Büyük Erşan
17 Hotel Ergen
19 Otel Elit
20 Eyüboğlu Hotel
21 Tetra Konur Otel
24 Hotel Best
37 Ankara Hilton
PLACES TO EAT
2 Köşk
3 Cihan Kebap
4 İskele Lokantası
6 McDonald's
7 Körfez Lokantası & Göksu Restaurant
11 Kebabistan
12 Café M
18 Of Karadeniz Pide ve Kebap Salonu
27 Köyüm Gözleme ve Mantı
29 Yeni Hamsiköy
33 Yakamoz
OTHER
1 Merkez Camii
5 PTT
9 Confidence (Güvenlik) Monument
10 PTT
15 Kocatepe Camii
16 Open-air Bookstalls
22 Grand National Assembly
23 US Embassy
25 PTT
26 German Embassy
28 Italian Embassy
30 Egyptian Embassy
31 Bulgarian Embassy
32 French Embassy
34 Serbian Embassy
35 Kuğulu Park
36 Polish Embassy
Yenişehir
0
200
400 m
To Ulus
Sıhhiye
Kızılay
Bakanlıklar
Kavaklıdere
To New Otogar
Pedestrian Zone
Gazi Mustafa Kemal Bulvarı
Necatibey Caddesi
Ihlamur Sokak
Mithat Paşa Caddesi
Atatürk Bulvarı
Fevzi Çakmak
Sümer
Menekşe
İzmir
Kumrular Sokak
Tuna
İnkılap
Sakarya Caddesi
Bayındır Sokak
Ziya Gökalp Caddesi
Selanik Sokak
Yüksel Caddesi
Müdafaa Caddesi
Meşrutiyet Caddesi
Karanfil Sokak
Konur Sokak
Olgunlar Sokak
İnönü Bulvarı
Akay Caddesi
Dikmen Caddesi
Güvenlik Caddesi
Tunus Caddesi
Büklüm Sokak
Bade Sokak
Bestekar Sokak
Kennedy Caddesi
Tandoğan
Paris Caddesi
Şimşek Sokak
Alidede Sokak
Yazanlar Sokak
Hilmi Caddesi
Tunalı
Cinnah Caddesi
Iran Cad

column drums to bits of marble statuary and inscribed lintels, have been incorporated in the mighty walls over the ages. The citadel's small mosque, the **Alaettin Camii**, dates originally from the 12th century, but much has been rebuilt. Wander into the village, following any path that leads higher and soon you'll arrive at a flight of concrete stairs on the right leading to the **Şark Kulesi** (SHARK koo-leh-see, Eastern Tower), with panoramic city views. The tower at the north, **Ak Kale** (White Fort), also offers fine views. See Places to Eat for details of the several good restaurants in the Hisar.

Bazaar

The area around the Hisar's Parmak Kapısı has traditionally been a centre for trading in tiftik (Angora wool). Exiting the Hisar from the Parkmak Kapısı, turn left and walk down through the bazaar area, lined with vegetable stalls, copper and ironmongers and every variety of household item. Soon you will come to the Seljuk-built **Aslanhane Camii** (Lionhouse Mosque), which dates from the 13th century. Continue down the hill on Can Sokak and turn right into Anafartalar Caddesi for Ulus.

Railway Museums

Rail enthusiasts passing by Ankara's train station will want to have a look at the **Railway Museum** (Demiryolları Müzesi, ☎ 310 3500). Enter from the street, walk through the main hall and out to the platforms, turn right, and walk along until you come to the museum, a small station building which served as Atatürk's residence during the War of Independence. It's supposedly open daily from 9 am to noon and from 1 to 5 pm (closed on holidays). As there are few visitors, it may be locked. Find an official and request, *Müzeyi açarmısınız?* (mew-zeh-YEE ah-CHAR-muh-suh-nuhz, 'Would you open the museum?'). If the time is within the hours given, they should oblige.

Beyond the museum is Atatürk's private railway coach, constructed in Breslau in 1935, a gift to the Turkish leader from Adolf Hitler.

Ankara's other railway museum is the **Open-Air Steam Locomotive Museum** (Açık Hava Buharlı Lokomotif Müzesi), a vast railway yard on the south-western side of Ankara's train station devoted to Turkey's varied collection of well-used steam locomotives. Access is from Celal Bayar Bulvarı, and is best done by taxi.

Roman Ankara

Roman Angora was a city of some importance, and several significant Roman structures remain. At the north-east corner of the square in Ulus are some buildings and behind them is the first stop on your tour of Roman Ankara. Set in a small park called Hükümet Meydanı (Government Square), surrounded by the Ankara provincial government house and the Ministry of Finance & Customs, is the **Column of Julian** (Jülyanüs Sütunu). The Roman Emperor Julian (the Apostate, 361-63), last of the scions of Constantine the Great, visited Ankara in the middle of his short reign and the column was erected in his honour. Turkish inhabitants later dubbed it Belkız Minaresi, the Queen of Sheba's Minaret, a fanciful appellation if ever there was one.

Walk east from the park, up the hill; turn right, then left to reach Bayram Caddesi and the **Hacı Bayram Camii** (hah-JUH bahy-RAHM), Ankara's most revered mosque, built next to the ruins of the **Temple of Augustus & Rome**. Hacı Bayram Veli was a Muslim saint who founded the Bayramiye order of dervishes in around 1400. Ankara was the centre of the order and Hacı Bayram Veli is still revered by the city's pious Muslims. In recent years the precincts of the mosque have been reordered and landscaped to make a pleasant park.

The temple walls that you see are of the cella, or inner sanctum, which was originally surrounded by a colonnade. First built by the kings of Pergamum for the worship of Cybele, the Anatolian fertility goddess, and Men, the Phrygian phallic god, the temple was later rededicated to Emperor Augustus. The Byzantines converted it to a church and the Muslims built a mosque and saint's tomb

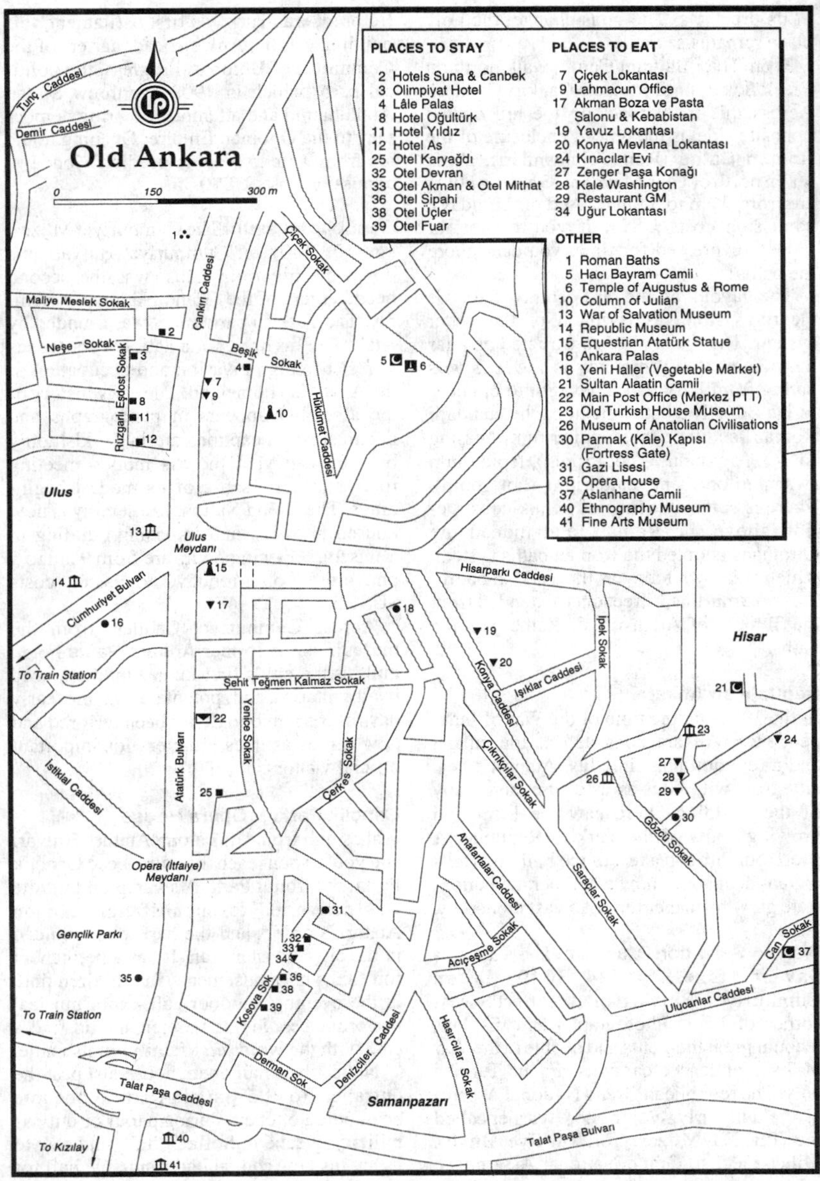
Old Ankara
0
150
300 m
PLACES TO STAY
2 Hotels Suna & Canbek
3 Olimpiyat Hotel
4 Lâle Palas
8 Hotel Oğultürk
11 Hotel Yıldız
12 Hotel As
25 Otel Karyağdı
32 Otel Devran
33 Otel Akman & Otel Mithat
36 Otel Sipahi
38 Otel Üçler
39 Otel Fuar
PLACES TO EAT
7 Çiçek Lokantası
9 Lahmacun Office
17 Akman Boza ve Pasta Salonu & Kebabistan
19 Yavuz Lokantası
20 Konya Mevlana Lokantası
24 Kınacılar Evi
27 Zenger Paşa Konağı
28 Kale Washington
29 Restaurant GM
34 Uğur Lokantası
OTHER
1 Roman Baths
5 Hacı Bayram Camii
6 Temple of Augustus & Rome
10 Column of Julian
13 War of Salvation Museum
14 Republic Museum
15 Equestrian Atatürk Statue
16 Ankara Palas
18 Yeni Haller (Vegetable Market)
21 Sultan Alaatin Camii
22 Main Post Office (Merkez PTT)
23 Old Turkish House Museum
26 Museum of Anatolian Civilisations
30 Parmak (Kale) Kapısı (Fortress Gate)
31 Gazi Lisesi
35 Opera House
37 Aslanhane Camii
40 Ethnography Museum
41 Fine Arts Museum
Tunç Caddesi
Demir Caddesi
Çiçek Sokak
Çankırı Caddesi
Maliye Meslek Sokak
Neşe Sokak
Rüzgarlı Eşdost Sokak
Beşik Sokak
Hükümet Caddesi
Ulus
Ulus Meydanı
Hisarparkı Caddesi
Cumhuriyet Bulvarı
İpek Sokak
Hisar
To Train Station
Şehit Teğmen Kalmaz Sokak
Konya Caddesi
Işıklar Caddesi
Yenice Sokak
Atatürk Bulvarı
Çerkes Sokak
Çıkrıkçılar Sokak
İstiklal Caddesi
Gözcü Sokak
Anafartalar Caddesi
Saraçlar Sokak
Opera (İtfaiye) Meydanı
Gençlik Parkı
Açıçeşme Sokak
Can Sokak
Ulucanlar Caddesi
To Train Station
Kosova Sok
Denizciler Caddesi
Hasırcılar Sokak
Derman Sok
Talat Paşa Caddesi
Samanpazarı
Talat Paşa Bulvarı
To Kızılay

in its precincts. The gods change, the holy place remains sacred.

From Hacı Bayram Camii, walk north on Çiçek Sokak until it meets Çankırı Caddesi. Across this main road, up the hill on the opposite side, is the fenced enclosure of the **Roman Baths** (Roma Hamamları), about 400m north of Ulus Meydanı. Opening hours are from 9 am to 5 pm (closed on Monday); admission costs US$1. If you're short of money or pressed for time, you can ignore the baths.

The layout of the 3rd-century baths is clearly visible, as is much of the water system. The baths were constructed on a far more ancient city mound, its lowest layers dating from Phrygian times (8th to 6th centuries BC). The baths included the standard Roman facilities: the apoditerium (dressing room), frigidarium (cold room), tepidarium (warm room) and caldarium (hot room). There is some evidence of Seljuk construction above the Roman, and indeed the Ottomans adopted the Roman baths system, which is known today as the Turkish bath.

A column-lined street once extended from the Temple of Augustus & Rome past the baths.

Republican Ankara

In the 1920s, at the time of the War of Independence, Ankara consisted of the citadel and a few buildings in Ulus. Atatürk's new city grew with Ulus as its centre, and many of the buildings here saw the birth and growing pains of the Turkish Republic. A short tour through a few of the buildings tells a great deal about how a democratic nation-state grew from the ruins of a vast monarchy.

War of Salvation Museum The Kurtuluş Savaşı Müzesi (☎ 324 3049) is on Cumhuriyet Bulvarı on the north-west corner of Ulus. Photographs and displays recount great moments and people in the War of Independence; captions are in Turkish only. The republican Grand National Assembly held its early sessions here (earlier called the TBMM Müzesi for Türkiye Büyük Millet Meclisi, Grand National Assembly). Before it was Turkey's first parliament, this building was the Ankara headquarters of the Committee of Union & Progress, the political party which in 1909 overthrew Sultan Abdülhamid and attempted to bring democracy to the Ottoman Empire. Opening hours are from 9 am to 5 pm (closed on Monday); admission costs US$0.35.

Republic Museum The Cumhuriyet Müzesi (☎ 310 7140), on Cumhuriyet Bulvarı just down the hill from Ulus, was the second headquarters of the Grand National Assembly. The Turkish parliament was founded by Atatürk in his drive for a national consensus to resist foreign invasion and occupation of the Anatolian homeland. The early history of the assembly appears in photographs and documents; all captions are in Turkish only but you can visit the assembly's meeting room and get a sense of its modest beginnings. The Grand National Assembly is now housed in a vast and imposing building in Yenişehir. Opening hours are from 9 am to 5 pm, closed on Monday; admission costs $US0.35.

Across Cumhuriyet Caddesi from the museum is the former **Ankara Palas** hotel, built as the city's first luxury lodging, used by dignitaries and potentates in the early days of the republic. It has been restored and now serves as guest quarters for important official visitors.

Gençlik Parkı & Opera House

Walk south from Ulus along Atatürk Bulvarı and you'll soon reach the entrance to Gençlik Parkı, the Youth Park. A swamp on this site was converted to an artificial lake on Atatürk's orders and the park was included in the city's master plan. It has a permanent fun fair with amusements for children and, in the evening, outdoor cafés with musical performances. Single women should find a café with the word *aile* (family) in its name.

Notice the small opera house just past the entrance to the park. Atatürk became enamoured of opera during a tour of duty as military attaché in Sofia (1905), and saw to it that his new capital had a suitable hall for performances as well. The opera has a full season, beginning in autumn. The new Atatürk Cultural Centre will no doubt supplant the quaint old opera house as the preferred venue for operatic productions.

Ethnography & Fine Arts Museums

The Ethnography Museum (Etnografya Müzesi, ☎ 311 9556) is perched above Atatürk Bulvarı, to the east of the boulevard and south of Ulus past Gençlik Parkı. Walk up Talat Paşa Bulvarı to reach it. Hours are from 8.30 am to 12.30 pm, and 1.30 to 5.30 pm (closed on Monday); admission costs US$1.25.

The building, which once housed Atatürk's offices, is a white marble post-Ottoman structure (1925) with an equestrian statue of the great man in front. Upon entering you confront a marble slab with an inscription which translates: 'This is the place where Atatürk, who entered into eternity on 10-xi-1938, lay from 21-xi-1938 until 10-xi-1953', after which his body was transferred to the just-completed Anıt Kabir (see below).

The museum's collection is wide-ranging and well chosen, with especially rich exhibits of *hattat* (Islamic calligraphy) and woodwork. The Sünnet Odası (Circumcision Room) is furnished in the sumptuous style of the Ottoman nobility. Weapons, metalwork, costumes, embroidery and musical instruments are represented as well.

Next door to the Ethnography Museum is the **Painting & Sculpture Museum** (Resim ve Heykel Müzesi), in the building which once served as headquarters for Atatürk's nation-building Turkish Hearths organisation. If you have an intense interest in the modern development of Turkish painting – or an hour to really murder – stroll through the galleries picking out the Ottoman-era scenes of Osman Hamdi, the forceful strokework of Hikmet Onat (1882-1977), the pseudo-primitive scenes of village life by Turgut Zaim (1906-1974), and the vigorous work in several styles of Bedri Rahmi Eyüboğlu, who was also an accomplished poet. If you've come this far, don't miss the paintings by those who inspired Ottoman painting: hanging on the left side of the main staircase are works by Aivazovsky, Keresagin and Zonaro.

The museum is open from 9 am to noon and 1 to 5 pm (closed on Monday); admission is free.

Ulus Markets

Ulus is the city's shopping epicentre, with huge crowds every day and long lines at the ATM cash machines.

Walk up the hill on Hisarparkı Caddesi out of Ulus and turn right at the first traffic signal onto Susam Sokak; a Ziraat Bankası will be on your right. Bear left, then turn left and on your right will be Ankara's **Yeni Haller**, or Vegetable Market, a good place for buying supplies or photographing colourful local life.

Behind the Vegetable Market, on Konya Caddesi, is the **Vakıf Suluhan Çarşısı**, a restored *han* with lots of clothing shops, a café, toilets and a free-standing small mosque at the centre of its courtyard.

Anıt Kabir

Atatürk's mausoleum (☎ 231 7975), called the Anıt Kabir (ah-NUHT-kah-beer, Monumental Tomb), stands on top of a small hill in a green park about two km west of Kızılay along Gazi Mustafa Kemal Bulvarı. If you saw Ankara from the Hisar or the terrace of the Ethnography Museum, you've already admired from a distance the rectangular mausoleum with squared columns around its sides on the hill.

A visit to the tomb is essential when you visit Ankara. Opening hours are from 9 am to 12.30 pm and 1.30 to 5 pm (4 pm in winter) every day; admission is free.

Walking along Gazi Mustafa Kemal Bulvarı from Kızılay, you can take a shortcut by turning left onto Maltepe Sokak. This becomes Erdönmez Sokak and then meets Gençlik Caddesi. Turn right onto Gençlik Caddesi, then left onto Akdeniz Caddesi and you'll see the back entrance to the park. You may not be allowed to enter by the pedestrian gate, but past it is the car exit road and you can enter there.

Should you take a taxi to the Anıt Kabir's main entrance, from Tandoğan Meydanı up Anıt Caddesi, you'll see the mausoleum as it is meant to be approached. Up the steps from the car park you pass between allegorical statues and two square kiosks; the right-hand kiosk holds a model of the tomb and photos of its construction. Then you pass down a long monumental avenue flanked by Hittite stone lions to the courtyard.

To the right as you enter the courtyard, beneath the western colonnade, is the **sarcophagus of İsmet İnönü** (1884-1973), Atatürk's close friend and chief of staff, a republican general (hero of the Battle of İnönü, from which he took his surname), diplomat, prime minister and second president of the republic.

Across the courtyard, on the east side, is a **museum** which holds memorabilia and personal effects of Atatürk. You can also see his official automobiles, several of which are US-made Lincolns.

As you approach the tomb proper, the high-stepping guards will jump to action. Past the colonnade, look left and right at the gilded inscriptions, which are quotations from Atatürk's speech celebrating the 10th anniversary of the republic (in 1932). As you enter the tomb through its huge bronze doors, you must remove your hat (if you don't, a guard will remind you that this is correct protocol). The lofty hall is lined in red marble and sparingly decorated with mosaics in timeless Turkish folk designs. At the northern end stands an immense marble **cenotaph**, cut from a single piece of stone. The actual tomb is beneath it.

The Anıt Kabir was begun in 1944 and finished in 1953. Its design seeks to capture the spirit of Anatolia: monumental, spare but beautiful. Echoes of several great Anatolian empires, from the Hittite to the Roman and Seljuk, are included in its design. The final effect is modern but timeless.

Presidential Mansion

At the far southern end of Atatürk Bulvarı in Çankaya is the Presidential Mansion (Cumhurbaşkanlığı Köşkü). Within the mansion's beautiful gardens is the **Çankaya Köşkü**, or Çankaya Atatürk Müzesi. This quaint chalet was Atatürk's country residence, set amid vineyards and evergreens. In the early days of the republic it was a retreat from the town, but now the town spreads beyond it. Visits to the mansion's gardens and grounds and to the museum are permitted on Sunday afternoons from 1.30 to 5.30 pm, and on holidays from 12.30 to 5.30 pm, free of charge. Bring your passport.

Take any Çankaya-bound bus or taxi to the far southern end of Atatürk Bulvarı, where you will find an entrance to the grounds of the Presidential Mansion. Tell the bus or taxi driver that you want to go to the Çankaya Köşkü (CHAHN-kah-yah kursh-kur). At the guardhouse, exchange your passport for an identity badge, leave your camera, and a guide will accompany you to and through the museum.

The house is preserved as Atatürk used it, with décor and furnishings of the 1930s. You enter a vestibule, then turn right into a games room, complete with tables for billiards and cards (the British ambassador was a favourite card partner). The next room is a green (Atatürk's favourite colour) parlour. The large dining room at the back of the house has its own little nook for after-dinner coffee, cigars and brandy.

Upstairs is a formal office, the bedroom and bath, another work room and the library (note the many books in foreign languages).

Downstairs again, to the left of the vestibule is a reception room for dignitaries.

Places to Stay

Ulus has numerous bottom-end and middle-range hotels. Yenişehir has good middle-range hotels. The top-end hotels are in Kavaklıdere.

Places to Stay – bottom end

Near Ulus İtfaiye Meydanı, also called Opera Meydanı, on the east side of Atatürk Bulvarı across from the opera house, is the centre of the cheap hotel district. To find it, ask anyone to point the way to Gazi Lisesi (GAH-zee lee-seh-see), the renowned high school on the east side of the square.

The *Otel Devran* (☎ (312) 311 0485), Tavus Sokak 8, is an older building, well used, but with nice touches such as marble staircases, brass trim and little chandeliers. Doubles cost US$16 with shower, US$18 with bath.

The two-star, 49-room *Otel Akman* (☎ (312) 324 4140), Tavus Sokak 6, next to the Devran, is in sore need of renovation. Until it gets it, its rates of US$14/20 a single/double with shower will be too high. The much better-kept *Otel Mithat* (☎ (312) 311 5410), adjoining the Akman at Tavus Sokak 2, is a better choice with shower-equipped doubles for US$18.

The *Otel Sipahi* (☎ (312) 324 0235), Kosova Sokak 1, is old and dingy but serviceable in a pinch, and certainly cheap at US$10 for a double with sink, US$13 with shower. A few steps further down the street, the *Otel Üçler* (☎ (312) 310 6664), Kosova Sokak 7, is clean and proper, if very simple, with waterless rooms for US$10 a double.

Perhaps the best value on the street is at the brightly-painted *Otel Fuar* (☎ 312) 312 3288), Kosova Sokak 11, where US$10 gets you a decent double room and sink, with showers down the hall.

On the northern side of Ulus are several other good choices.

The *Lâle Palas* (☎ (312) 312 5220), Hükümet Meydanı, Telgraf Sokak 5, is a bit of old Ankara with its marble and brass trim, faded grace and welcome quiet. Doubles with sink cost US$12, with private shower US$17.

Cross to the western side of Çankırı Caddesi and down the slope to Soğukkuyu Sokak to find more quiet hotels. The old but clean *Hotel Suna* (☎ (312) 324 3250), Soğukkuyu Sokak 6, charges US$14 for a quiet double room with sink, US$17 with shower. The neighbouring *Canbek* is similar, if a bit more expensive.

Also here is the *Olimpiyat Hotel* (☎ (312) 324 3331), Rügarlı Eşdost Sokak 18, with more modern, comfortable rooms for just slightly more: US$18 for a double with shower, a few dollars more with TV as well.

Walk south along Rügarlı Eşdost Sokak from the Olimpiyat past the new Hotel Oğultürk and turn left (east) to find the older but still serviceable one-star *Hotel As* (☎ (312) 310 3998, fax 312 7584), Rüzgarlı Sokak 4, with double rooms for US$17/21 with sink/shower.

Readers of this guide have recommended the *Hotel Kale* (☎ (312) 311 3393), Anafartalar Caddesi, Alataş Sokak 13, where clean rooms with hot water cost US$10 a double.

Near Kızılay The *Otel Ertan* (☎ (312) 418 4084), Selanik Caddesi 70, Kızılay 06640, a half-block south off Meşrutiyet Caddesi, is the best bet, especially for single women. On a quiet street, with a grape arbour and flowers in the front, it has rooms with shower for only US$14/21 a single/double; a few single rooms without baths on the top floor are tiny and unappealing but priced at only US$12. Don't confuse the modest Ertan with the adjoining three-star Hotel Büyük Erşan.

Places to Stay – middle

Near Ulus Compared to middle-range hotels in Yenişehir, those near Ulus offer similar comfort for less money, with the advantage of being within walking distance of the Hisar and museum.

There are nearly a dozen two-and three-star hotels north of Ulus on the west side of Çankırı Caddesi, but most are hopelessly noisy. For the quiet ones, go one street west of Çankırı Caddesi to Rüzgarlı Eşdost Sokak and the new three-star *Hotel Oğultürk* (☎ (312) 309 2900, fax 311 8321), Rüzgarlı Eşdost Sokak 6. Its boldly modern architecture contrasts sharply with the general workaday look of the modest street. The 54 rooms and five suites, most with TV and minibar, are comfortable at US$26/40, breakfast included.

Hotel Yıldız (☎ (312) 7581, fax 312 7584), Rüzgarlı Eşdost Sokak 4, adjoining the Oğultürk to the south, is an equally comfortable and new three-star, 60-room hotel with rooms at about the same price.

South-east of Ulus on the way to Opera (İtfaiye) Meydanı, the older two-star *Otel Karyağdı* (☎ (312) 310 2440, fax 312 6712), Sanayi Caddesi, Kuruçeşme Sokak 4, is quiet and still serviceable, though a bit overpriced at US$45 a double, breakfast included. They're ready to haggle if business is slow.

Near Kızılay Several good hotel choices are on quiet tree-shaded streets south-east of Kızılay in the district called Bakanlıklar. All have rooms with private bath and TV, and many have air-con and minibars as well. Most will drop prices a bit when not busy, especially if you plan to stay for more than one night.

The three-star, 52-room *Eyüboğlu Hotel* (☎ (312) 417 6400, fax 417 8125), Karanfil Sokak 73, 06640 Bakanlıklar, is shiny and proper, offering comfortable, quiet rooms for US$45/60.

The two-star, 40-room *Otel Elit* (☎ (312) 417 4695, fax 417 4697), Olgunlar Sokak 10, 06640 Bakanlıklar, at Karanfil Sokak, is shaded by trees, and is steps away from Olgunlar Sokak's used books stalls. Rooms of moderate comfort cost US$55 a double, breakfast included.

The simple one-star, 56-room *Hotel Ergen* (☎ (312) 417 5906, fax 425 7819), Karanfil Sokak 48, near Olgunlar Sokak, has a terrace café and charges only US$30/42 for rooms with bath.

The three-star *Otel Büyük Erşan* (☎ (312) 417 6045, fax 417 4943), Selanik Caddesi 74, 06640 Bakanlıklar, has 90 standard rooms on a quiet street for a reasonable US$40 a double.

Places to Stay – top end

For dignified, well-located four-star accommodation at decent prices, try the *Hotel Best* (☎ (312) 467 0880, 468 1122, fax 467 0885), Atatürk Bulvarı 195, 06690 Kavaklıdere, across the street from the US Embassy. Rates are US$75/104, breakfast included. Advance reservations are usually necessary.

The *Tetra Konur Otel* (☎ (312) 419 2946, fax 417 4915), Konur Sokak 58, 06640 Kızılay, has four-star comforts and understated elegance on a quiet street for US$100 a double, with prices reduced for longer stays.

The *Ankara Hilton* (☎ (312) 468 2888, fax 168 0909), Tahran Caddesi 12, 06700 Kavaklıdere, has 327 plush rooms and suites on 16 floors near Çankaya and the embassies. The hotel's bold, modern architecture uses traditional Anatolian coloured stone, brass, glass and lots of greenery. Rates are from US$160 to US$210 a single, US$180 to US$230 a double.

The 311-room *Sheraton Ankara Hotel & Towers* (☎ (312) 468 5454, fax 467 1136), Noktalı Sokak, 06700 Gaziosmanpaşa, is a landmark cylindrical high-rise which towers above this pleasant residential quarter. Views from the upper-floor rooms in the Sheraton Towers section are superb. Rates are from US$160 to US$210 a single, US$180 to US$230 a double.

If you plan to stay more than a day or two, consider renting a fully-furnished short-term apartment at the *First Apart-Hotel* (☎ & fax (4) 425 7575), İnkilap Sokak 29, 06650 Kızılay, a small modern building on a quiet back street three blocks east of Kızılay. Each of the 15 comfortable apartments has two bedrooms, living/dining room, bathroom and fully equipped kitchen, direct-dial phones, colour TVs and furnishings equal to those in a three or four-star hotel. The official rate per apartment for one to four persons is US$110, but I was quoted a reduced rate of US$75 per day for a one-week stay.

Places to Eat – bottom end

İtfaiye (Opera) Meydanı In the midst of the İtfaiye Meydanı hotels is the *Uğur Lokantası* (☎ 310 8396), Tavus Sokak 2, next to the Otel Mithat, specialising in Turkey's regional lamb kebaps. Expect to spend between US$3.50 and US$5 for a full meal here.

Near Ulus North of Ulus along Çankırı Caddesi, the left-hand (west) side of the street has several big, bright restaurants featuring rotisserie chicken, and serving other dishes as well; many serve beer.

On the east side of Çankırı, the brightly-coloured, amusingly-named *Lahmacun Office* specialises in Arab-style pizza, and has Turkish and Italian varieties as well. You can tuck in here for around US$5.

The most refined choice is the long-time favourite *Çiçek Lokantası* (chee-CHEK) (☎ 311 5997), Çankırı Caddesi 12/A, a half-block north of the square on the right-hand side. Dine next to the little havuz (pool, fountain) in the dining room amidst the tables with white tablecloths. Soup, kebap, salad and drink comes to US$6 to US$8.

Several restaurants are midway between Ulus Meydanı and the Museum of Anatolian Civilisations on Konya Caddesi, about two blocks south of Hisarparkı Caddesi. The *Yavuz Lokantası* (☎ 311 8508), Konya Caddesi 13/F, is the more expensive, specialising in seafood (but the kebaps are more trustworthy), and serving alcohol. Cheaper, but booze-less, is the *Konya Mevlana Lokantası* (☎ 324 5092), on the corner of Konya and Şan Sokaks, with good döner kebap for US$2.

Walk south on the east side of Atatürk Bulvarı and turn into the second courtyard to find the *Akman Boza ve Pasta Salonu*, Atatürk Bulvarı 3. Breakfasts, light lunches (sandwiches, omelettes etc) and pastries are not cheap, but in part you're paying for the pleasant garden setting. Boza, the fermented millet drink, though traditionally a winter favourite, is served all year here. Expect to spend from US$4 or US$5 for a light lunch, less for tea and pastry.

Right above the Akman Boza is *Kebabistan* (Kebap-Land, ☎ 310 8080), a family-oriented kebap and pide parlour serving fresh, cheap pide (US$1.25 to US$2) and kebaps (US$2 to US$3) all day, every day. There's a newer, more modern branch of Kebabistan near Kızılay, but the food's better here in the original location.

You can escape the noise and fumes of the city in Gençlikı Park and seek out the wistfully-named *Sahil Lokantası* (Shore Restaurant), on the northern side of the lake near the open-air theatre called the Muhsin Ertuğrul Açık Hava Tiyatrosu. The Sahil has shaded tables by the lakeside, and inexpensive mezes (US$1.25) and kebaps (US$2.50).

Near Kızılay The streets north of Ziya Gökalp Caddesi and east of Atatürk Bulvarı are closed to motor vehicles and lined with places to eat and drink. Cheap, filling snacks such as balık-ekmek ('fish-bread', a fried-fish sandwich) and dönerli sandviç (döner kebap in bread) sell for about US$1.25. Selanik Sokak north of Ziya Gökalp Caddesi is the best for cheap kebaps, with dozens of places to choose from.

South of Yüksel Caddesi, Selanik Sokak turns into a café-pastry shop scene, with a row of streetside cafés drawing the capital's gilded youth. *Café M* (☎ 419 3665), Selanik 40-42, serves excellent kazandibi and decent coffee and tea. Pastry or pudding and a beverage should cost no more than US$2. Also check out the Selanik incarnation of the *Akman Boza ve Pasta Salonu* at No 44, and the neighbouring *Rest-Out*, yet another café.

Sakarya Caddesi is parallel to and one block north of Ziya Gökalp Caddesi. Walk along Sakarya Caddesi to the big Sakarya Süper Marketi, the ground floor of which is devoted to snack stands. Just to the right of the market are more snack stands (try the *Otlangaç)* selling İstanbul Çiçek Pasaj-style fried mussels on a stick, Bodrum lokması (sweet fritters), kuzu kokoreç (grilled sheep's intestines) and similar treats.

For good kebap in a sit-down place, find *Cihan Kebap* (☎ 133 1665), Selanik Caddesi 3/B, between Sakarya and Tuna Caddesis. A full meal with soup, bread and kebap costs from US$3 to US$4.

South of Yüksel Caddesi is the Kızılay branch of *Kebabistan* (☎ 417 2222), Karanfil Sokak 15/A, across the street from the Hotel Melodi. The outdoor tables are pleasant. Döner kebap with yoghurt, salad and a soft drink costs less than US$3.

Even nicer is the nearby *Of Karadeniz Pide ve Kebap Salonu* (☎ 425 7815), Karanfil Sokak 63, across the street from the

Hotel Elit. The shady vine-covered terrace, complete with tinkling fountain, is a welcome oasis for a meal of soup, kebap and salad for less than US$3.50.

For those who need a Big Mac fix, there's a *McDonald's* (☎ 431 5956) at Atatürk Bulvarı 89, just north of Kızılay on the east side of the boulevard. A plain burger costs just over US$1, but as usual the combo meals (cheeseburger, drink and fries for US$2.25) provide the best value for money.

Places to Eat – middle

Citadel (Hisar) Within the citadel walls several old houses have been converted to atmospheric restaurants. Come here for lunch after a visit to the Museum of Anatolian Civilisations, or for a special dinner. All are open every day from 11 am to midnight, and all serve alcoholic beverages.

The historic restaurant trend was begun at the *Zenger Paşa Konağı* (☎ 311 7070), Doyran Sokak 13, and it is still the best of the lot. A virtual museum of old-time Ankara with a dining room on top, the Zenger's cuisine is Ottoman and fiercely authentic – even to the extent of having local women knead, roll and bake the wafer-thin village bread before your eyes. Try gözleme (folded, fried pastry with cheese, meat or vegetable filling), mantı (Turkish ravioli), and köfte or şiş kebap served on a hot tile. Full meals cost US$8 to US$12. The views from the dining room are spectacular, the several museum rooms drenched with atmosphere.

If you go through the Parmak Kapısı and walk straight on for several hundred metres you will come to the *Kınacılar Evi* (☎ 311 1010), Kalekapısı Sokak 28, on the right. This lofty Ottoman konak (mansion) is popular with tour groups, serving Ottoman and modern Turkish cuisine in gracious old salons decorated in 19th-century style. Try the çerkez tavuğu (chicken in walnut sauce), or the chicken and vegetable casserole. Full meals cost from US$8 to US$15 per person, drinks included. There's an open-air café at the back.

Restaurant GM (☎ 312 6903, 310 8041), Doyuran Sokak 3, features a south-eastern Turkish menu à la Gaziantep, with spicy kebaps and moderate prices of US$7 to US$14 for a meal.

Kale Washington (☎ (311 4344), Doyuran Sokak 5-7, has the highest prices and least authentic Ottoman atmosphere of the lot. The menu is Turkish-style continental, which means such things as şatobriyan (chateaubriand), böf stroganof, and chicken Kievsky. Meals tend to cost US$10 to US$20 all in, except if you order the outrageous brochette-grilled shrimp for US$35.

Near Kızılay The place to look for good, moderately priced food near Kızılay is along Bayındır Sokak, to the east of Atatürk Bulvarı and south of Ziya Gökalp Caddesi.

Köşk (☎ 432 1300), İnkilap Sokak 2 at Tuna Caddesi, is a veritable kebap palace at unbeatable prices. This huge two-storey eatery blazes with light, shining crystal and burnished brass, fountains playing. Elaborate kebaps, pides and lahmacuns cost only US$2.50 to US$4.50.

You can't go wrong at the *Körfez Lokantası* (keur-FEHZ, 'gulf') (☎ 131 1459), Bayındır Sokak 24, a half-block north of Ziya Gökalp Caddesi. Dining rooms are starkly plain; the terrace is preferable in good weather. Fish is the speciality for around US$4 to US$7, but there are many kebaps priced under US$4. Your meal comes with plenteous lavahş, freshly made flat unleavened village bread.

Next door to the Körfez is the *Göksu Restaurant* (☎ 431 2219), Bayındır Sokak 22/A, a longstanding favourite with much fancier surroundings, diligent service, and Turkish and continental cuisine. Have the filet mignon: good quality at a moderate price.

Another good seafood place with a taverna-style atmosphere is *İskele* (☎ 433 3813), Sakarya Caddesi, Bayındır Sokak 14/C. Start with fried mussels or a shrimp casserole (karides güveçi), and go on to grilled or poached fish, and you'll pay from US$10 to US$12, wine or beer included. İskele is closed on Sunday.

Kavaklıdere Kavaklıdere, the posh residential district up the hill towards Çankaya, has a good assortment of restaurants. Take a bus south (uphill) along Atatürk Bulvarı and get out at Kuğulu Park next to the Polish Embassy (Polonya Büyükelçilik), then walk east one short block to Tunalı Hilmi Caddesi, the district's main commercial street.

Yakamoz (☎ 426 3752), Tunalı Hilmi Caddesi 114/J 2-3, right at the edge of Kuğulu Park, is a big, busy place specialising in seafood. The best deal is the table d'hôte menu with drinks for US$14 per couple. Ordering à la carte, seafood plates cost around US$4 or US$5.

For a look at the district's other restaurants, stroll north (downhill) along Tunalı Hilmi, turning left onto Bestekar Sokak.

Black Sea cookery is the speciality at *Yeni Hamsiköy* (☎ 427 7576), Bestekar Sokak 78, off Tunalı Hilmi at Bülten Sokak. The garden terrace, open in fine weather, is the place to try hamsi (fresh anchovies) served in omelettes, dolmas or corn bread; there's also kara lahana (black cabbage) and other Black Sea specialities. The food and service are excellent, and prices are moderate at US$10 or so per person, beer, wine or rakı included.

Just up the street on Bülten Sokak (between Bestekar and Tunalı Hilmi), *Köyüm Gözleme ve Mantı* (☎ 426 4148) is decorated in a Turkish village theme. The specialities are gözleme, the fried folded pastry filled with cheese, meat or vegetables; and mantı, or Turkish ravioli. A full meal with drinks should cost no more than US$7 or US$8 per person.

For a romantic dinner with low lights and soft music, seek out *Villa* (☎ 427 0838), Boğaz Sokak 13, on a quiet residential street up the hill behind the Sheraton. The menu is what Ankara diners consider 'exotic', which is to say lots of dishes with mushrooms and cheese. They have pizzas as well. Dinner for two with drinks won't be much more than US$20.

Entertainment

Most visitors don't hang around in Ankara long enough to get deep into the nightlife. However, it's easy enough to find an evening's amusement.

Beer Gardens, Gazinos & Teahouses For drinks and talk Turkish-style, head for Kızılay and Bayındır Sokak between Sakarya Caddesi and Tuna Sokak. The street is lined with Turkish beer gardens, among them *Forza*, which usually has live Turkish pop music, beers for little more than US$1.25, and food as well.

Another good venue for drinks and conversation is Gençlikı Park, just west of Opera Meydanı. Walk around the lake to the fountain pool on its west. On the southern side of the pool are Turkish-style gazinos with live entertainment, drinks and food at low to moderate prices; on the northern side are mostly teahouses which vie with one another to advertise the lowest-priced beer.

Bars & Discos The posh bar-lounge-jazz club scene is in Kavaklıere, Gaziosmanpaşa and Çankaya. From Kuğulu Park in Kavaklıdere, go north on Tunalı Hilmi Caddesi one block to Bilir Sokak and turn right to find *Jazz Time*, Bilir Sokak 4/1, which usually has live Turkish pop or folk artists, and, behind it, the quieter *Gitanes* bar. Local drinks are the standard US$2.50 for rakı or gin and tonic, about US$1.50 for beer.

Çengel Café (☎ 426 1851), Noktalı Sokak 8/1, directly opposite the entrance to the Sheraton, is a bit more upscale and popular with a young, well-heeled crowd. It can get very busy on weekends.

For dancing, head for the *Airport Disco* (☎ 488 7781), Şili Meydanı, one block west of Kuğulu Park across Atatürk Bulvarı and up the hill. Entry costs US$5, after which local drinks are about US$2.50, imported drinks twice that much.

Cinema Several cinemas show recently-released western films, usually in the original language with Turkish subtitles. Look for these venues: *Akün Sineması* (☎ 427 7656), Atatürk Bulvarı 227 in Kavaklıdere; the *Kavaklıdere* (☎ 426 7379) at Tunalı Hilmi Caddesi 105, and the

Metropol (☎ 425 7478), at Selanik Caddesi 76 in Kızılay.

Opera, Ballet & Symphony Beginning in the autumn and running through until spring, Ankara has regular seasons of opera, ballet, symphony and chamber music, often with visiting foreign artists. The performances, though not of a standard to win rave reviews in New York, Paris or Rome, are enthusiastically done, and tickets are ridiculously low in price – usually around US$4 to US$6.

Among the most active sponsors of symphony, chamber music and classical recitals is Bilkent University (☎ 266 4539), which announces its events in the *Turkish Daily News*, as do other sponsors.

Getting There & Away

In Turkey, all roads lead to Ankara.

Air İstanbul's Atatürk airport is the country's major international airport, but Ankara's Esenboğa airport (☎ (312) 398 0000), 33 km north of the city centre, has good domestic connections.

Turkish Airlines (THY, ☎ (312) 312 4900 for information, 309 0400 for reservations, fax 312 5531) has offices at Atatürk Bulvarı 167/A, Bakanlıklar. Most THY flights require a stop or a change of aircraft in İstanbul.

İstanbul Airlines (☎ (312) 432 2234, 431 0920, fax 431 1632), Atatürk Bulvarı 83, Kızılay, has many nonstop flights.

Most one-way fares from Ankara on THY cost between US$70 and US$100; İstanbul Airlines' fares are somewhat lower. Here is a list of nonstop flights in summer; many more flights are available via connection in İstanbul. All flights are by THY unless otherwise noted, and all schedules are subject to change:

Adana – daily
Amsterdam – Monday, Friday and Saturday; Thursday (İstanbul Airlines)
Antalya – daily; Saturday (İstanbul Airlines)
Batman – daily
Berlin – Tuesday, Thursday, Friday, Saturday, Sunday
Bodrum – Friday and Sunday
Cologne – Tuesday, Wednesday, Friday, Saturday, Sunday; Thursday (İstanbul Airlines)
Copenhagen – Thursday (İstanbul Airlines)
Dalaman – Friday and Sunday
Diyarbakır – one or two daily
Dusseldorf – Tuesday, Wednesday, Thursday, Friday, Saturday; Tuesday, Wednesday, Friday (İstanbul Airlines)
Elazığ – daily except Saturday
Erzincan – Tuesday, Thursday and Saturday
Erzurum – twice daily
Frankfurt – Wednesday (İstanbul Airlines)
Gaziantep – daily
Hamburg – Friday (İstanbul Airlines)
Hannover – Friday (İstanbul Airlines)
İstanbul – a dozen flights daily; Tuesday, Wednesday, Thursday, Saturday (İstanbul Airlines)
İzmir – six or more flights daily; Friday (İstanbul Airlines)
Jeddah – Wednesday and Sunday
Kars – daily
Malatya – daily
Munich – Tuesday, Thursday, Friday, Saturday; Thursday (İstanbul Airlines)
Muş – daily except Thursday
Nicosia (Lefkoşa) – daily
Paris – Wednesday, Friday and Sunday
Samsun – Monday and Friday
Siirt – Wednesday and Saturday
Sivas – Wednesday and Friday
Stuttgart – Tuesday, Thursday, Friday and Saturday; Thursday (İstanbul Airlines)
Şanlıurfa – Monday, Wednesday, Friday and Sunday
Trabzon – daily
Van – twice daily; Tuesday and Thursday (İstanbul Airlines)
Vienna – Wednesday, Friday, Saturday, Sunday
Zurich – Friday

Other international airlines sometimes have flights to Ankara, or connections with Turkish Airlines' flights at İstanbul. The addresses of offices in Ankara follow:

Aeroflot
Cinnah Caddesi 114/2, Çankaya (☎ (312) 440 9874)
Air France
Atatürk Bulvarı 231/7, Kavaklıdere (☎ (312) 467 4400)
Alitalia
Emek İşhanı, 11th floor, Kızılay (☎ (312) 425 3813)
British Airways
Atatürk Bulvarı 237/29, Kavaklıdere (☎ (312) 467 5557)
KLM
Atatürk Bulvarı 127, 3rd floor, Bakanlıklar (☎ (312) 417 5616)

Lufthansa
İran Caddesi 2, Kavaklıdere (☎ (312) 436 6156, 467 5510)
Sabena World Airlines
Tunalı Hilmi Caddesi 112/1, Kavaklıdere (☎ (312) 467 2535)
Singapore Airlines
Tunalı Hilmi Caddesi, Bülten Sokak 17/3, Kavaklıdere (☎ (312) 468 4670)
Swissair
Cinnah Caddesi 1/2A, Kavaklıdere (☎ (312) 468 4846)

Bus Every city or town of any size – and even the occasional village – has direct buses to Ankara. From İstanbul there is a bus to Ankara at least every 15 minutes throughout the day and late into the night.

Ankara's gigantic bus terminal is known by many names including Yeni Terminal, Yeni Otogar, Yeni Garaj, and AŞTİ (for Ankara Şehirlerarası Terminalı İşletmesi). It's five km due west of Bakanlıklar and the Grand National Assembly building, on Bahçelerarası Caddesi (Konya Devlet Yolu) just north of İsmet İnönü Bulvarı (Eskişehir Yolu).

The terminal follows the traditional airport plan with departure gates on the upper level and arrivals on the lower. A huge airport-style tote board lists departures and arrivals, but as these are not organised beyond time (ie alphabetically by company or destination), the board is of limited use in determining when the next bus will depart for your desired destination, although it does tell you which gate *(peron)* your bus departs from.

As Ankara has many buses to all parts of the country, it is often sufficient to arrive at the otogar, baggage in hand, and ask around at the ticket desks for the next bus out.

Here are translations of some of the more prominent signs:

Alış Veriş	Shopping
Ankaray	Regional Train
Bekleme Yerleri	Waiting Areas
Gelen Yolcu Katı	Arrivals Level
Giden Yolcu Katı	Departures Level
İlk Yardım	First Aid Station
Kayıp Eşya	Lost & Found
Şehiriçi Servis	Local Shuttle Buses

Numerous bus companies maintain ticket offices near Kızılay on Ziya Gökalp Caddesi, Gazi Mustafa Kemal Bulvarı, İzmir Caddesi and Menekşe Sokak. Several premium bus companies, including Varan and Ulusoy, have their own terminal facilities near the otogar. The Varan ticket office (☎ (312) 417 2525) is south of Kızılay on the east side of Atatürk Bulvarı. Details of some services from Ankara follow:

Adana – 490 km, 10 hours, US$13 to US$16; frequent buses daily
Amasya – 335 km, five hours, US$9; frequent buses daily
Antalya – 550 km, 10 hours, US$17; frequent buses daily
Bodrum – 785 km, 13 hours, US$20; a dozen buses daily
Bursa – 400 km, 6½ hours, US$11; hourly buses
Denizli (Pamukkale) – 480 km, seven hours, US$12; frequent buses
Diyarbakır – 945 km, 13 hours, US$20; several buses daily
Erzurum – 925 km, 15 hours, US$23; several buses daily
Gaziantep – 705 km, 12 hours, US$20; frequent buses daily
İstanbul – 450 km, six hours, US$9 to US$20; virtual shuttle service
İzmir – 600 km, 8½ hours, US$14.50 to US$20; buses at least every hour
Kayseri – 330 km, five hours, US$8; very frequent buses daily
Konya – 260 km, 3½ hours, US$8; very frequent buses daily
Marmaris – 780 km, 13 hours, US$22; a dozen buses daily in summer
Nevşehir – 285 km, 4½ hours, US$8; very frequent buses daily
Samsun – 420 km, eight hours, US$14; frequent buses daily
Sivas – 450 km, eight hours, US$13; frequent buses daily
Sungurlu (for Boğazkale) – 175 km, three hours, US$4; hourly buses
Trabzon – 780 km, 12 hours, US$24; several buses daily

You can also buy through tickets to Damascus (Şam) for US$50, Tehran for US$65, and to other eastern destinations.

Train Train service is good between the Ankara Garı (☎ (312) 310 6515, 311 4994) and several major cities. See the Getting Around chapter for a description of train travel and the top trains, and the Getting There & Away sections of the İstanbul and İzmir chapters for descriptions of train service between Ankara and İstanbul or İzmir. The top trains – *Başkent Ekspresi, Fatih Ekspresi, Mavi Tren, Ankara Ekspres* – are quite good. Here are some notes on other trains serving Ankara – prices and schedules are subject to change.

Çukurova Ekspresi The *Çukurova Ekspresi* departs Ankara daily at 8.10 pm hauling one-class coaches, couchette cars and sleeping cars to Adana (arrives 8.18 am). The return trip departs from Adana at 7.15 pm, arriving in Ankara at 8.05 am. One-way tickets between Ankara and Adana or Mersin cost US$10/12 in a coach/couchette. Fares in a sleeping compartment cost US$24/42/58 for one/two/three persons.

Doğu Ekspresi The *Doğu* (doh-OO, east) is scheduled to arrive in Ankara from İstanbul at midnight, and depart from Ankara at 10.40 am for Kayseri, Sivas, Erzincan, Erzurum (arrives 1 pm) and Kars (arrives 5.45 pm) daily, but it usually falls behind schedule. A one-way 1st/2nd-class ticket from Ankara costs US$11/7.75 to Erzincan, US$14/9.50 to Erzurum, and US$16/11 to Kars. To travel from Ankara to Kars in a sleeping compartment costs US$30/52/66 for one/two/three persons.

Karaelmas The one-class 'Black Diamond' runs daily at 7.55 am to the Black Sea coal-mining centre of Zonguldak, arriving at 7.10 pm, for US$5. The return trip departs from Zonguldak at 9.20 am, arriving in Ankara at 8.08 pm.

Vangölü/Güney Ekspresi The *Vangölü Ekspresi* and *Güney Ekspresi* share a common route from İstanbul (daily at 8 pm) via Ankara (arrive 5.05 am, depart 6.50 am) to Sivas, Malatya and Elazığ Junction. East of the junction, the train continues on Tuesday, Thursday and Sunday as the *Vangölü* (Lake Van) *Ekspresi* to Tatvan and Monday, Wednesday, Friday and Saturday as the *Güney* (Southern) *Ekspresi* to Diyarbakır and Kurtalan (east of Diyarbakır).

These trains haul sleepers and 2nd-class coaches. A one-way 1st/2nd-class ticket from Ankara costs US$15/10.50 to Tatvan, US$13/10 to Diyarbakır. The fare in a sleeping car is from US$30/52/72 for one/two/three people.

Getting Around

The Airport Esenboğa airport is 33 km north of the city. Havaş airport buses, US$3.50, are supposed to depart from the forecourt of the Gar 1½ hours before domestic flight times, and 2¼ hours before international flight times. They may leave sooner if they fill up, however, so claim your seat on the bus at least two hours before flight time. Minimum check-in time at the airport for any flight is 45 minutes before departure time.

A separate Havaş bus operates about every hour between the otogar (AŞTİ) and the airport, at an identical fare.

When your flight arrives in Ankara, claim your luggage and board the Havaş bus as it will depart for the city within a half-hour after the flight has landed and there may not be another bus for several hours depending upon flights. Taxis between the airport and the city cost about US$20.

The Otogar City bus No 198 departs the arrivals level of the bus terminal headed for the Gar and Ulus; bus No 623 goes via Kızılay to Gaziler. Your bus company may have a *şehiriçi servis* (shuttle minibus) to take you to the company's central office; ask.

When the Ankaray suburban railway line is completed, there will be a station right in the otogar, and trains will take you to Kızılay.

A taxi between the otogar and the train station costs about US$2.75, about US$3.25 to Ulus or Kızılay.

The Gar The train station is about 1.25 km

south-west of Ulus and three km north of Kızılay. Any bus or dolmuş headed north-east along Cumhuriyet Bulvarı (straight out the station door) will take you to Ulus. Many buses headed east along Talat Paşa Caddesi, which runs past the station, go to Kızılay and Kavaklıdere; look on their signboards for your destination. It's about one km from the station to Opera Meydanı's hotels; any bus headed east along Talat Paşa Caddesi will drop you within a few hundred metres of them if you ask for Gazi Lisesi, the high school nearby.

Bus Ankara is served well and frequently by an extensive bus and minibus network. Signboards on the front and side of the bus are better guides than route numbers. Many buses marked 'Ulus' and 'Çankaya' ply the entire length of Atatürk Bulvarı. Those marked 'Gar' go to the train station; those marked 'AŞTİ' or one of the otogar's other names (see above) will drop you off there. To go from the train station to the bus terminal, walk north-east on Cumhuriyet Bulvarı (towards Ulus) for 400m to the stadium gate and take a Balgat dolmuş (US$0.75).

City bus tickets cost US$0.40 and can be bought from little ticket kiosks at major bus stops or from shops and vendors displaying a sign reading 'EGO Bilet Bayii' or 'EGO Bileti Satılır', or some other phrase with 'EGO Bilet' in it.

Metro Construction is well under way on Ankara's metro system. The first line will run from Kızılay north-west via Sıhhiye, Maltepe and Ulus to Batıkent, a distance of 14.6 km. The station at Kızılay will also serve the Ankaray, the city's new east-west suburban rail system. Construction is scheduled for completion by 1996, but the inevitable delays will no doubt carry it towards or beyond the year 2000.

Car See the Getting Around chapter for details on hiring cars. Do not rent a car to drive around Ankara, and if you have a car, park it and use public transport. Traffic patterns seem whimsically illogical, local drivers delight in speed, danger and chaos, and signs are woefully inadequate.

If you plan to hire a car and drive beyond Ankara, there are many small local companies, and the major international firms have offices at Esenboğa airport and in the city centre. Details of some of these follow:

Avis
: Tunus Caddesi 68/2, Kavaklıdere (☎ (312) 467 2313)

Budget
: Tunus Caddesi 39/A, Kavaklıdere (☎ (312) 417 5952, 427 8071, fax 425 9608)

Europcar
: (National, Interrent, Kemwel) Küçükesat Caddesi 25/C, Bakanlıklar (☎ (312) 418 3430, 418 3877, fax 417 8445)

Hertz
: Akay Caddesi, Kızılırmak Sokak 1/A, Bakanlıklar (☎ (312) 418 8440)

Thrifty
: Köroğlu Caddesi 65/B, Gaziosmanpaşa (☎ (312) 436 0505, 436 0606)

Taxi The drop rate is US$0.50 and an average trip costs from US$2 to US$3 during daylight hours, 50% more at night. The lower fare would be for a trip from the otogar or train station to Ulus; the higher fare, to Kızılay or Kavaklıdere.

GORDION

Gordion, the capital of ancient Phrygia, lies 106 km west of Ankara in the village of Yassıhöyük. Archaeological teams from the University of Pennsylvania have been excavating the 80 mounds at the site since 1950, and have uncovered 18 different levels of civilisation from the Bronze Age to Roman times.

History

The site, formerly a Hittite town, was occupied by the Phrygians as early as the 9th century BC, and soon afterwards became their royal capital. Although destroyed during the Cimmerian invasion, Gordion was later rebuilt, only to be conquered by the Lydians and the Persians in turn. Alexander the Great came through and cut the Gordian

The Hittites

Before this century little was known about the Hittites, a people who commanded a vast Middle Eastern empire, conquered Babylon, and challenged the Egyptian pharaoes over 3000 years ago. Aside from a few written references to them in the Bible and Egyptian chronicles, there were few clues to their existence until 1834 when the French traveller Charles Texier stumbled on the ruins around Boğazkale.

In 1905 excavations began at the site of Hattuşaş, the Hittite capital of Boğazkale. The digging produced notable works of art, most of them now preserved in Ankara's Museum of Anatolian Civilisations. Also brought to light were the Hittite state archives, written in cuneiform on thousands of clay tablets. From these tablets, historians and archaeologists were able to construct a history of the Hittite Empire.

Speaking an Indo-European language, the Hittites swept into Anatolia around 2000 BC, conquering the Hatti from whom they borrowed both their culture and name. They established themselves at Hattuşaş, the Hatti capital, and in the course of a millennium enlarged and beautified the city. From about 1375 to 1200 BC, Hattuşaş was the capital of a Hittite Empire which, at its height, incorporated parts of Syria too.

The Hittites worshipped over a thousand different deities but among the most important were Teshub, the storm god, and Hepatu, the sun goddess. The cuneiform tablets revealed a well-ordered society with more than 200 laws. The death sentence was prescribed for bestiality whilst thieves got off more lightly provided they paid their victims compensation.

From about 1250 BC the Hittite Empire seems to have gone into a decline, its demise hastened by the arrival of the Phrygians. Only the city-states of Syria survived until they, too, were swallowed by the Assyrians. ■

Knot in 333 BC, and the Galatian occupation of 278 BC put an end to what was left of the city. (For more on the Phrygians, see 'Midas Şehri' in the Aegean Turkey chapter.)

Acropolis

Excavations have yielded a wealth of data on these civilisations, but the 8th-century BC acropolis itself, across the road from a fuel station on the near side of the village as you approach, is not particularly exciting for the casual visitor.

The lofty main or Phrygian Gate, on the city's west side, was approached by a six-metre-wide ramp. Within the fortified enclosure were four megara, or large square halls, from which the king and his priests and ministers ruled the empire. Coloured mosaics found in the second megaron are now on display outside the site museum near the royal tomb.

Royal Tomb

In 1957 the Penn team discovered intact the tomb of a Phrygian king buried here sometime between 750 and 725 BC. The Royal Tomb *(Midas Tümülüsü)* is across the road from the museum *(müze)*, two km beyond the city mound on the far side of Yassıhöyük village. The undisturbed tomb is actually a gabled 'cottage' of pine surrounded by juniper logs, built then buried beneath a tumulus 60m high and 300m in diameter.

The archaeologists carefully drilled into the tumulus from above to determine the placement and composition of the tomb, then tunnelled in from the side. In the tomb was found the body of a 61 to 65-year-old man, 1.59m tall, surrounded with burial objects, but no weapons or jewellery of silver or gold. Although the occupant's name is unknown, both 'Gordius' and 'Midas' are good bets, as most Phrygian kings seem to have been called one or the other.

The tunnel and tomb entrance are modern; there was no such entrance in ancient times. The tomb, the oldest wooden structure ever found in Anatolia, and perhaps in the world, is open daily from 8 am to 5 pm, as is the nearby museum. Admission to the tomb and museum costs US$1.75.

Museum
The museum across the road from the tomb is built in the form of a megaron. Outside, beneath a sheltering roof, are mosaics moved from the second megaron. Inside the museum are collections from the Bronze Age (3000-2000 BC), Hittite period (2000-1000 BC), and Phrygian and Hellenistic times (1000-330 BC), especially bone pins (*fibulae*), whistles, decorations and arrowheads. The best objects are now in the Museum of Anatolian Civilisations in Ankara.

Getting There & Away
Gordion is 106 km west of Ankara, or 18 km west of Polatlı on the E90/D200 Ankara-Eskişehir highway, then north 12 km to the village of Yassıhöyük. Though the main railway line passes within a km of the site, the nearest station is at Polatlı (reachable more easily by bus), from which dolmuşes run occasionally, or you can hire a taxi. For the best chance of getting a dolmuş get to Polatlı early in the morning. Several tour agencies in Ankara run organised tours to Gordion as well.

South Central Anatolia

KONYA
Standing alone in the middle of the vast Anatolian steppe, Konya (population 510,000, altitude 1016m) is like some traditional caravan stopping-place. The wind-swept landscape gives way to patches of greenery in the city, and once in town you forget the loneliness of the plateau. In recent years Konya has been booming. The bare-looking steppe is in fact good for growing grain and Konya is the heart of Turkey's very rich 'bread-basket'. Light industry provides jobs for those who are not farmers.

Much of the city was built within the last 10 years but the centre is very old. No-one knows when the hill in the centre of town, the Alaettin Tepesi, was first settled but it contains the bones of Bronze Age men and women.

Plan to spend at least one or two full days in Konya, but avoid Monday as the museums will be closed. If your interest in Seljuk history and art takes wing you could easily spend even longer. As it often takes half a day to reach Konya, and another half-day to get

Gordian Knot & Golden Touch
The Phrygians left us two enduring legends.

The first is of King Midas, who showed hospitality toward Silenus, chief of the satyrs, and was rewarded by the god with a wish – anything he desired. Midas asked that everything he touch turn to gold. Granted his wish, at first he was delighted to be able to turn common objects into precious ones. But he discovered to his shock that the food he picked up to eat also turned to gold, and that he was in danger of starvation. He pleaded to the god to relieve him of the golden touch, and was told to bathe in the Pactolus stream, which he did. The sands of the Pactolus supposedly turned to gold, and gold dust continued to be found there in abundance for centuries afterwards.

The second is of the Gordian Knot. Legend says that during a period of civil unrest, a man named Gordius, his wife and his son Midas arrived at the site of Gordion in a wooden peasant's cart. An oracle had declared that the ruler who would save Phrygia from its turmoil would arrive in such a cart, and so Gordius was immediately proclaimed king of Phrygia, with Midas as his successor. Subsequent rulers took the names Gordius and Midas in succession.

The cart which had brought Gordius and his family to glory was enshrined in a temple, and an oracle foretold that whoever could untie the knot of cornel bark which bound the pole to the yoke of the cart would be the ruler of all Asia.

Alexander the Great arrived at Gordion in 333 BC, intent on the conquest of Asia, and attempted to untie the knot. Frustrated, the impetuous youth cut it with his sword, and went on to conquer all of Asia anyway. ■

away again, you should figure on spending at least two nights in a hotel here.

It's important to remember that Konya is a favourite with devout Muslims and a fairly conservative place; nine out of 10 women have their heads (and everything else) covered. Perhaps because of this, travellers may be hassled, especially lone women. Take special care not to upset the pious, and look tidy when you enter mosques and the Mevlâna Museum. If you visit during the holy month of Ramazan, don't eat or drink in public during the day as a courtesy to those who are fasting. (For Ramazan and other religious dates see The Calendar section of the Facts for the Visitor chapter.)

Note that the dervishes only dance during the Mevlâna Festival in December (see Special Events, following).

History

The city has been here a very long time and Çatal Höyük, 50 km to the south, has claims to being the oldest known human community, dating back to 7500 BC.

The Hittites called Konya 'Kuwanna' almost 4000 years ago but the name has changed over the years. It was Kowania to the Phrygians, Iconium to the Romans and then Konya to the Turks. Under the Romans, Iconium was an important provincial town visited several times by saints Paul and Barnabas, but its early Christian community doesn't seem to have been very influential.

Konya's heyday was during the 13th century, when it was capital of the Seljuk Sultanate of Rum, the last remnant of an earlier Seljuk empire. The Seljuk Turks ruled a powerful state in Iran and Iraq, the Empire of the Great Seljuks, during the 11th century. Omar Khayyam was their most noted poet and mathematician. But Great Seljuk power was fragmented in the early 12th century, and various parts of the empire became independent states. One of these states was the Sultanate of Rum, which encompassed most of Anatolia and had Konya as its capital from about 1150 to 1300. In that period, the Seljuk sultans built dozens of fine buildings in an architectural style decidedly Turkish, but with its roots in Persia and Byzantium.

Orientation

The city centre is the hill Alaettin Tepesi, crowned with a great Seljuk mosque and surrounded by the city's best Seljuk buildings. From the hill, Alaettin Caddesi goes south-east 500m to Hükümet Alanı (Government Plaza, also called Konak), with the provincial and city government buildings, the main PTT and a vast underground gold jewellery market. Most of the banks have branches in or around Hükümet Alanı.

East of Hükümet Alanı the boulevard changes name to become Mevlâna Caddesi and continues another 500m to the Tourism Information Office and the Mevlâna (Whirling Dervish) Museum, Konya's prime attraction.

Hotels are located along Alaettin/Mevlâna Caddesi and near the Mevlâna Museum. The otogar is 3.5 km due north of the centre, connected with it by regular minibuses. The *istasyon* (train station) is about three km due west.

Information

Konya's official Tourism Information Office (☎ (332) 351 1074) is at Mevlâna Caddesi 21, across the square from the Mevlâna Museum. Opening hours are from 8.30 am to 5 pm, Monday to Saturday in summer. The staff speak English, French and German. Across the street, the Konya Kültür ve Turizm Derneği (Konya Culture & Tourism Association; ☎ (332) 351 8288) can help with information about the dervishes if your Turkish is good. Otherwise, there's a kiosk in the Mevlâna Museum selling books and cassettes.

Konya's postal code is 42000.

Seljuk Turkish Architecture

Central Konya forms Turkey's best 'outdoor museum' of Seljuk architecture. While the buildings themselves are often starkly simple on the outside, the main portal is always grand and imposing, sometimes huge and wildly Baroque. The interiors are always

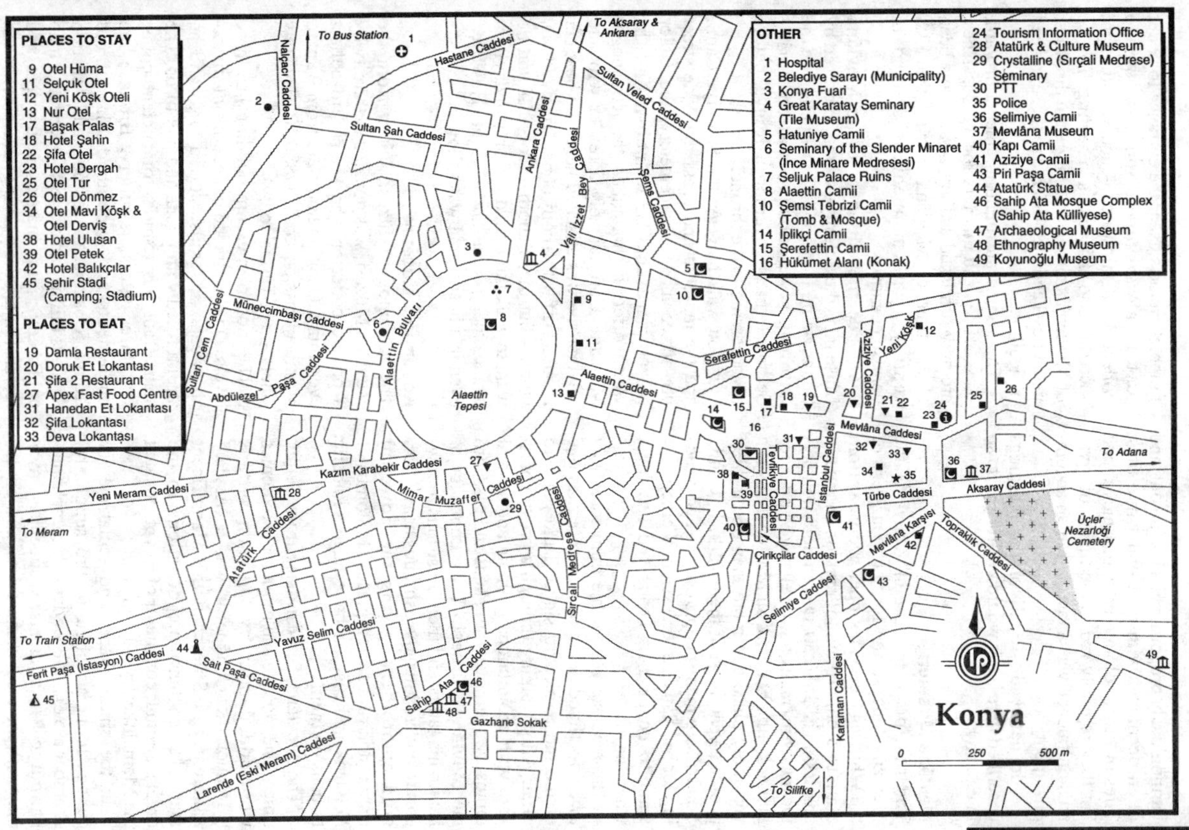
Konya
PLACES TO STAY
9 Otel Hüma
11 Selçuk Otel
12 Yeni Köşk Oteli
13 Nur Otel
17 Başak Palas
18 Hotel Şahin
22 Şifa Otel
23 Hotel Dergah
25 Otel Tur
26 Otel Dönmez
34 Otel Mavi Köşk & Otel Derviş
38 Hotel Ulusan
39 Otel Petek
42 Hotel Balıkçılar
45 Şehir Stadi (Camping; Stadium)
PLACES TO EAT
19 Damla Restaurant
20 Doruk Et Lokantası
21 Şifa 2 Restaurant
27 Apex Fast Food Centre
31 Hanedan Et Lokantası
32 Şifa Lokantası
33 Deva Lokantası
OTHER
1 Hospital
2 Belediye Sarayı (Municipality)
3 Konya Fuari
4 Great Karatay Seminary (Tile Museum)
5 Hatuniye Camii
6 Seminary of the Slender Minaret (İnce Minare Medresesi)
7 Seljuk Palace Ruins
8 Alaettin Camii
10 Şemsi Tebrizi Camii (Tomb & Mosque)
14 İplikçi Camii
15 Şerefettin Camii
16 Hükümet Alanı (Konak)
24 Tourism Information Office
28 Atatürk & Culture Museum
29 Crystalline (Sırçali Medrese) Seminary
30 PTT
35 Police
36 Selimiye Camii
37 Mevlâna Museum
40 Kapı Camii
41 Aziziye Camii
43 Piri Paşa Camii
44 Atatürk Statue
46 Sahip Ata Mosque Complex (Sahip Ata Külliyese)
47 Archaeological Museum
48 Ethnography Museum
49 Koyunoğlu Museum
To Bus Station
To Aksaray & Ankara
To Adana
To Meram
To Train Station
To Silifke
Nalçacı Caddesi
Hastane Caddesi
Sultan Şah Caddesi
Ankara Caddesi
Vali İzzet Bey Caddesi
Sultan Veled Caddesi
Şems Caddesi
Müneccimbaşı Caddesi
Sultan Cem Caddesi
Abdülezel Paşa Caddesi
Alaettin Bulvarı
Alaettin Tepesi
Alaettin Caddesi
Serafettin Caddesi
Aziziye Caddesi
Yeni Köşk
Mevlâna Caddesi
Tevfikiye Caddesi
İstanbul Caddesi
Türbe Caddesi
Aksaray Caddesi
Üçler Nezarloğı Cemetery
Kazım Karabekir Caddesi
Mimar Muzaffer Caddesi
Yeni Meram Caddesi
Atatürk Caddesi
Sırcali Medrese Caddesi
Çirikçilar Caddesi
Mevlâna Karşısı
Topraklık Caddesi
Selimiye Caddesi
Yavuz Selim Caddesi
Ferit Paşa (İstasyon) Caddesi
Sait Paşa Caddesi
Sahip Ata Caddesi
Gazhane Sokak
Karaman Caddesi
Larende (Eski Meram) Caddesi
0
250
500 m

harmoniously proportioned and laid out, and often decorated with blue and white tiles. Tiles of other colours are sometimes found but they're rarely red as the fusing of vivid reds on faïence was a later Ottoman accomplishment.

You can walk to all of the buildings described here but it would be tiring to do so in one day.

Mevlâna Museum

The first place to visit in Konya is the Mevlâna Müzesi, the former monastery of the Whirling Dervishes, open every day from 9 am to 5 pm (10 am to 5 pm on Monday); admission is US$0.50. On religious holidays the museum (really a shrine) may be open for longer hours. For Turkish Muslims, this is a very holy place and more than one million people a year, most of them Turkish, visit it. You will see many people praying and pleading for Mevlâna's intercession. Women may want to cover their heads and shoulders when they enter.

The monastery is visible from some way away, its fluted dome of turquoise tiles one of the most splendid sights Turkey has to offer. After walking through a pretty courtyard with an ablutions fountain and several tombs, you remove your shoes and pass into the **Mevlâna Türbesi**. The sarcophagi of Rumi, his father and their illustrious followers are covered in velvet shrouds heavy with gold embroidery, giving the powerful impression of a sacred place. The tombs of Mevlâna and his son have huge symbolic turbans on them.

The Mevlâna Türbesi dates from Seljuk times. The mosque and room for ceremonies were added later by Ottoman sultans (Mehmet the Conqueror was a Mevlevi adherent and Süleyman the Magnificent made large charitable donations to the order). Selim I, conqueror of Egypt, donated the Mameluke crystal lamps.

In the small chapel and semahane (or dance floor) attached to the sepulchral chamber are exhibits of dervish paraphernalia: musical instruments, vestments, prayer mats, illuminated manuscripts and ethnographic artefacts. Near the entrance look out for the big *Nisan tası* or April bowl, used to collect April rainwater which was thought sacred and so efficacious in healing. The tip of Mevlâna's turban was dipped in the water in the bowl and then offered to those in need of healing.

The rooms surrounding the courtyard, once offices and quarters for the dervishes, are now furnished as they would have been at the time of Mevlâna (during the 13th century), with mannequins dressed in dervish costumes.

Outside the entrance to the Mevlâna Museum is the **Selimiye Camii**, endowed by Sultan Selim II in 1567. Construction on the Ottoman-style mosque started during Selim's term as governor of Konya, before his accession to the throne.

If you walk between the Selimiye Camii and the museum and cross the wide street you'll see a verdant cemetery, the **Üçler Mezarlığı** (urch-LEHR meh-zahr-luh) which offers a shortcut to the Koyunoğlu Museum. Unfortunately a reader wrote to say that she was attacked here (she beat her assailant off with a copy of her *Lonely Planet* guide – but that's another story). If you do want to walk through, do so only in daylight when other people are in sight. However, even in a headscarf I was followed.

Koyunoğlu Museum

The Koyunoğlu Müzesi, 750m from the Mevlâna Müzesi, was donated to the city by a private collector who seemed to collect everything. Opening hours are from 9 am to 5 pm; admission costs US$0.50. The few labels are in Turkish only.

The modern museum building has three levels. Downstairs are collections of minerals, weapons, fossils, stuffed birds and an atrium filled with plants and live birds. The main floor has exhibits of ancient coins, sculptures, glass, jewellery, Bronze Age implements and a photo display of old Konya. Upstairs, the ethnographic section displays kilims and carpets (one bears a map of Turkey); illuminated manuscripts and Korans; miniature paintings and clocks; and

19th-century clothing, bath clogs, weapons, household items, coffee sets, musical instruments, embroidery and needlework.

Next door to the museum is the **Koyunoğlu Konya Evi**, a delightful old-fashioned house which shows how a Konyalı family lived a century ago. Leave your shoes at the carved wooden door, put on sandals as all Turks used to do and inspect the small ground-floor room with its silk carpet. There is another, smaller salon on the ground floor as well. Upstairs the rooms are traditionally furnished with lots of carpets, kilims, low benches, pillows, a fine tray-table and lots of turned wood. The picture is of the museum's founder.

Alaettin Mosque

Except for the Mevlâna Museum, many of Konya's principal sights are near the Alaettin Tepesi, or Aladdin's Hill, at the western end of Alaettin Caddesi. The hill's eastern slopes are set with tea gardens and the ancient Alaettin Camii (mosque) is right on the top.

The mosque of Alaeddin Keykubat I, Seljuk Sultan of Rum from 1219 to 1231, is a great rambling building designed by a Damascene architect in the Arab style and finished in 1221. Over the centuries it was embellished, refurbished, ruined and restored. It has only just reopened after yet more intensive restoration.

While the exterior is fairly plain, the interior is a forest of old marble columns surmounted with recycled Roman and Byzantine capitals, with a fine, carved wooden pulpit (1156) and a marble prayer niche surrounded by blue tiles. In the courtyard, restorers discovered the graves of eight Seljuk sultans.

You can visit the mosque from 8.30 am to 6 pm, but remember that it's still a place of worship and leave your shoes at the door.

On the north side of the Alaettin Tepesi, the scant **ruins of a Seljuk palace** are protected by a concrete shelter.

Great Karatay Seminary

The Büyük Karatay Medresesi, now called the Karatay Müzesi, is a Seljuk theological seminary just north of the Alaettin Tepesi. It houses Konya's outstanding collection of ceramics and tiles and is open from 9 am to noon and from 1 to 5 pm (closed Monday). Admission costs US$1.

The school was constructed in 1251-52 by the emir Celaleddin Karatay, a Seljuk diplomat and statesman, and has a magnificent sculpted marble doorway.

Inside, the central dome and the *eyvan* contain masterpieces of Seljuk light and dark blue tilework, interspersed with snatches of white and black. The Kufic-style Arabic inscription around the bottom of the dome is the first chapter of the Koran while the triangles below are decorated with the stylised names of the prophets (Muhammed, Jesus, Moses and David) and of the four caliphs who succeeded Muhammed.

Notice the curlicue drain for the central pool: its curved shape made the sound of running water a pleasant background noise in the quiet room where students studied.

The museum's tile collection includes interesting coloured ones from the Seljuk palace on Alaettin Tepesi and from the Palace of Kubadabad near Beyşehir Lake. Compare these with the later Ottoman tiles from İznik.

The Great Karatay Seminary (Büyük Karatay Medresesi) is a Seljuk theological seminary which houses Konya's ceramic and tile collection.

Seminary of the Slender Minaret

On the western side of Alaettin Tepesi is the Seminary of the Slender Minaret (İnce Minare Medresesi), now the Museum of Wood & Stone Carving. This religious school was built in 1264 on the order of Sahip Ata, a powerful Seljuk vizier, who may have been trying to outdo the patron of the Karatay Medresesi, built only seven years earlier.

Don't enter the building immediately, for half of what you came to see is the elaborate doorway with bands of Arabic inscription running up the sides and looping overhead which is far more impressive than the small building behind it. The minaret beside the door gave the seminary its popular name of 'slender minaret'. Over 600 years old, most of the very tall minaret was knocked off by lightning in 1901. Needless to say the latest restorative efforts included installation of a lightning conductor.

Inside, many of the carvings in wood and stone feature motifs similar to those used in the tile and ceramic work. You'll quickly see that the Seljuks didn't let Islam's famous condemnation of images of creatures with souls (humans and animals) stand in the way of their art. There are plenty of images of birds (the Seljuk double-headed eagle, for example), men and women, lions and leopards here. The eyvan in particular contains two delightful carvings of Seljuk angels with distinctly Mongol features.

The Seminary of the Slender Minaret is open the same hours as the Great Karatay Seminary and admission costs US$1.

South of Alaettin Tepesi

Several other Seljuk monuments lurk in a warren of streets to the south of the city.

Not far from Alaettin Tepesi on Ressam Sami Sokak is another Seljuk seminary, the **Crystalline Seminary** (Sırçalı Medrese), now a museum of funerary monuments named after its tiled exterior. Sponsored by a Seljuk vizier, construction was completed in 1242.

As always, the portal is grand and highly decorated. The inscriptions on the gravestones inside, done in a variety of Arabic scripts, are often very fine. Symbols of rank – headgear, usually – served to tell the passer-by of the deceased's role in life.

Konya's small but interesting **Archaeological Museum** is a few blocks south along Ressam Sami Sokak, in the grounds of the Sahip Ata Mosque Complex (Sahip Ata Külliyesi) which, besides the mosque, includes a dervish monastery and Turkish bath. The entire complex was finished in 1283. Note especially the portal to the mosque with its tiled minaret and prayer niche.

The museum contains several fine Pamphylian sarcophagi decorated with lively carvings, including the Labours of Hercules. Opening hours are from 9 am to noon and from 1 to 5 pm. Admission costs US$1.

Not far from the Sahip Ata Külliyesi is the city's small **Ethnography Museum**, open the same hours as the Archaeological Museum. Admission costs US$1.

Other Mosques & Tombs

Dotted about town are other buildings of interest. The **Şemsi Tebrizi Camii**, containing the 14th-century tomb of Rumi's spiritual mentor, is just north of Hükümet Alanı, not far from Alaettin Caddesi. The **Aziziye Camii** (1874) is a work of Ottoman late Baroque in the bazaar; it's the one with twin minarets bearing little sheltered balconies. The **İplikçi Camii** (1202) on Alaettin Caddesi is perhaps Konya's oldest mosque, built on orders of the Seljuk vizier Şemseddin Altun-Aba. The **Şerefettin Camii**, off Mevlâna Caddesi near Hükümet Alanı, was constructed in 1636.

The Bazaar

Konya's market area is behind the modern PTT building and is divided up in very medieval fashion – here a section for plastic flowers, there one for teapots, here another for coils of rope. Keep walking and you should come to the covered **Melik Hatun Çarşısı**, near the Azizye Camii. Stalls here sell some truly wonderful pungent local cheeses.

Excursions

Çatal Höyük The Neolithic site at Çatal Höyük, 50 km south-east of Konya, is touted as the world's oldest human community. The 13 layers of the tumulus date from 6800 to 5500 BC. When excavated by British archaeologist James Mellaart in and after 1958, the mound yielded houses with wall paintings, human bones, and crude baked earthenware mother-goddess figurines. Most of the finds are now in Ankara's Museum of Anatolian Civilisations, so there's little to see at the site today. However, excavations have recently restarted and are expected to uncover many more treasures.

To get there without your own car, take a dolmuş to Çumra and then hire a taxi for the last 10 km.

Gökyurt Konya may be well south of central Cappadocia but the landscape at Gökyurt (50 km south-west of Konya) is reminiscent of what you'll see in Güzelyurt or Ihlara: gorges with medieval churches cut into the rockface. Without a car it's not easy to get there but Mustafa Sarıoğlan at the Yeni Köşk Hotel in Konya may be able to help you arrange something.

Sille Nine km north-west of Konya is the pretty village of Sille with an old stone bridge and medieval frescoes rotting away in the barns. You can get there by bus from Konya.

Special Events

The Mevlâna Festival is held in mid-December, culminating on the 17th, the anniversary of Mevlâna's 'wedding night' with god. The festival features numerous performances of

Whirling to Ecstasy

The Mevlevi worship ceremony, which traditionally takes place on a Monday evening ('Tuesday morning' in Islamic thinking), is a ritual dance, or *sema*, representing union with God.

The dervishes enter, dressed in long white robes with full skirts which represent their shrouds. Over them they wear voluminous black cloaks symbolising their worldly tombs; their tall conical red felt hats represent their tombstones.

The ceremony begins with a chant by the *hafız*, a celebrant who has committed the entire Koran to memory. He intones a prayer for Mevlâna and a verse from the Koran. A kettledrum booms out, followed by the breathy, plaintive song of the *ney*, or reed flute.

The sheikh (*şeyh*), or master, bows, then leads the dervishes in a circle round the hall. As they pass the sheikh's ceremonial position at the head of the hall, they bow to one another. After three circuits, the dervishes drop their black cloaks to symbolise their deliverance from the cares and attachments of this world. One by one, arms folded on their breasts, they approach the sheikh, bow, kiss his hand, receive instructions whispered in their ears, then spin out onto the floor as they relinquish the earthly life to be reborn in mystical union with God.

The male choir and the orchestra of small drums (*bendir*), gourd viol (*rebap*) and bow (*kemançe*), and open-tube reed flute (ney) begin the music, and the dervishes unfurl their arms and begin to whirl.

By holding their right arms up, palms upwards, they receive the blessings of heaven which are communicated to earth by holding their left arms down, palms downwards. Pivoting on their left heels, the dervishes whirl ever faster, reaching ecstasy with a blissful expression. As they whirl, they form a 'constellation' of revolving bodies which itself slowly rotates. The dance master walks among them to make sure each dervish is performing the ritual properly. After about 10 minutes, they all stop and kneel down. Then, rising, they begin again. The dance is repeated four times, with the sheikh joining the last circuit. The whirling over, the hafız again chants poetical passages from the holy book.

The breathy, haunting music of the ney is perhaps the most striking sound during the ceremony. Each musician 'opens' (makes) his own instrument from a carefully chosen length of bamboo-like reed, burning the fingerholes to a mathematical formula. The ney is thought to have its own soul, and 'opening' it allows the soul to come out in its music. ■

the *sema*, or Mevlevi rite. Tickets are sold, and should be bought, well in advance. Contact the Tourism Information Office or the Konya Culture & Tourism Association for information. Reserve your hotel room in advance as well. If you can't make it to the festival, you can still see the İstanbul dervishes perform in the Galata Mevlevihanesi near Tünel Meydanı on the last Sunday of each month.

Places to Stay – bottom end

The first street to the right (south) as you walk along Alaettin Caddesi from Alaettin Tepesi is Karahüyüklü Sokak, and on it is the *Nur Otel* (☎ (332) 352 0397), an old-fashioned cheapie with pretty basic rooms for US$7/10 a single/double. Unless you're too tired to press on you can do better than this.

A much better choice for the same money might be the *Hotel Ulusan* (☎ (332) 351 5004), immediately behind the PTT and clearly signposted. Rooms here are also simple but there's a homely atmosphere which might suit lone women in particular. Nearby in the midst of the bazaar at Çıkrıkçılar İçi 40 is the tidy *Otel Petek* (☎ (332) 351 2599), squeezed in between a shop selling helva and another selling nuts and dried fruit. Clean, simple rooms with shower cost US$9/11 without breakfast, a little less without the showers. The top-floor breakfast room offers panoramic view of the bazaar and all the way up to the Mevlâna Müzesi.

On a quiet street south of Mevlâna Caddesi (opposite the Töbank) and west of the Mevlâna Museum is the *Otel Mavi Köşk* (☎ (332) 350 1904), Bostan Çelebi Sokak 13, also charging US$9/11 for rooms with shower. There are several rooms with three or four beds, good for families or small groups. Next door is the even nicer *Otel Derviş* (☎ (332) 351 1688) where, for the same price, you get simple but clean, modern rooms with towels supplied. The lobby isn't bad either.

In the narrow street beside the tourist office look out for the *Çatal Aile Pansiyonu* (☎ (332) 351 4981) where a kilim-decorated lobby leads to more simple rooms for US$7 a head. A block away from the tourist office is the *Otel Dönmez* (☎ (332) 351 5561), Eşarizade Sokak 2, where some rooms at the front overlook the Mevlâna Müzesi. Don't expect them to be quiet, though. A little further along Eşarizade Sokak is the *Otel Tur* (☎ (332) 351 9825), with very basic bare-bulb double and triple rooms, overpriced at US$20 a double with private shower but no breakfast. You can often haggle the price down. If it's full the *Hotel Konya* right next door is similar.

Look for signs off Mevlâna Caddesi to the *Yeni Köşk Oteli* (☎ (332) 352 0671), Yeni Aziziye Caddesi, Kadılar Sokak 28, run by Mr Mustafa Sarıoğlan. Clean, tidy and fairly quiet, it features rooms with private showers for US$12/16 a single/double, a basement breakfast room and a car park.

Near the Otogar *Hotel Sema 2* (☎ (332) 233 2557) is right next to the otogar and gets so much trade its carpet is all but worn away. The 33 rooms priced at US$11/22 for a single/double with sink, including breakfast, would be OK if you arrive late or need to make an early start from the otogar.

Much pricier is the three-star *Özkaymak Park Oteli* (☎ (332) 233 3770, fax 233 5974), across the park from the otogar, with simple rooms with shower for US$45/65.

Camping You can camp at the *Şehir Stadı*, the sports complex just east of the train station on İstasyon Caddesi.

Places to Stay – middle

City Centre If you can afford to pay more, take a look at the 82-room *Selçuk Otel* (☎ (332) 353 2525, fax 353 2529), near Alaettin Tepesi. Modern and conveniently located just north of Alaettin Caddesi, it rents air-conditioned rooms with bath and TV for US$50/75 a single/double. But one reader has mentioned noise and lax housekeeping.

Just off Alaettin Bulvarı, near the ruins of the Seljuk palace, is the new three-star *Otel Hüma* (☎ (332) 350 6618, fax 351 0244), another good choice, its architecture designed to mimic that of the nearby Alaettin Camii. Rooms here are also bright and modern, with minibars and TVs. Prices are slightly lower, at US$40/60. Set dinners in the restaurant cost another US$7.

The one-star *Başak Palas* (bah-SHAHK pah-LAHS) (☎ (332) 351 1338), Hükümet Alanı 3, facing the provincial government building midway along Alaettin Caddesi, is an older place with 40 renovated rooms. Rooms with sinks only (hot and cold water) cost from US$18/25, and from US$25/33 with private bath. Try haggling if it's not busy.

Hotel Şahin (☎ (332) 351 3350, fax 351 9782), Hükümet Alanı 6, right in the centre on the main street, is an older hotel but the rooms have been updated and equipped with TVs and minibars. The ones facing the busy street are inevitably quite noisy. Prices are US$28/46 with shower but no breakfast.

Just east of Hükümet Alanı, the tidy two-star, 31-room *Şifa Otel* (☎ (332) 350 4290, fax 351 9251), Mevlâna Caddesi 11, provides decent rooms with private shower at US$35/50, breakfast included.

Nearby is the three-star *Hotel Sema* (☎ (332) 350 4623, fax 352 3521) at Mevlâna Caddesi 15. Popular with tour groups, this place has comfortable rooms with showers for US$40/50 without breakfast. It's attached to the Sema 2 Restaurant.

The three-star, 100-room *Hotel Dergah* (☎ (332) 351 1197, fax 351 0116), Mevlâna Meydanı 19, very near the tourist office, is convenient but overpriced at US$36/58 for rooms with private bath. The rooms at the front have views of the Mevlâna Museum across the square, but are also subject to street noise.

Hotel Balıkçılar (☎ (332) 3510 9470, fax 352 3259), Mevlâna Karşısı 1, is right across the street to the south-west of the Mevlâna Müzesi. Its 48 three-star rooms all have air-con, minibars and TV sets, and cost US$50/71 a single/double. The quieter rooms are at the back, but some of those at the front have views of the Mevlâna Müzesi.

Places to Eat

Konya's speciality is fırın kebap, a rich, fairly greasy joint of mutton roasted in an oven. The city bakers also make excellent fresh pide topped with minced lamb, cheese or eggs, but in Konya pide is called etli ekmek (bread with meat). Dürüm (roll) is thin flat bread topped with a filling, then rolled up. This being a conservative, religious town few places other than hotel restaurants serve alcohol.

There are a couple of cheap places charging from US$1 to US$3 for a full meal on and around Çırıkçılar Caddesi in the bazaar, behind the PTT. Go past the PTT Telefon Müdürlüğü, turn right, and you should spot them. The *Çağlar Lokantası* has lots of ready-prepared dishes as well as etli ekmek; the upstairs aile salonu may be more pleasant than the downstairs room. Nearby is the *Özlem Lokantası* serving börek, etli ekmek and other simple dishes.

Locals swear by the *Damla Restaurant*, near the Hotel Şahin. In a dark, smoky room with the atmosphere of a teahouse, men (mostly) tuck into a wide range of cold mezes, and fish and meat main dishes. A meal is likely to cost upwards of US$7. For something cheaper, turn the corner onto İstanbul Caddesi for the *Doruk Et Lokantası*, where there's a range of kebaps including fırın. It's a clean, cheerful place with an upstairs aile salonu. A meal will probably cost about US$4.

The *Hanedan Et Lokantası*, Mevlâna Caddesi 2/B, at the south-eastern end of Hükümet Alanı, is famous for its meat dishes. Clean and bright, it's open every day and serves excellent fresh pide, döner kebap, köfte and vegetable dishes. Full meals cost from US$3 to US$5.

The *Çatal Lokantası* (chah-TAHL), just behind the Tourism Information Office, is a simple kebap place which serves good food at low prices. A full lunch or dinner shouldn't come to more than US$4. On Bostan Çelebi Sokak near the Köşk and Derviş hotels, look for the *Öztemel Konya Fırın Kebap Salonu*, specialising in the local oven kebap. Your meal is unlikely to cost more than US$4.

The bright, airy *Deva Restaurant*, Mevlâna Caddesi 3, across from the Hotel Dergah, serves an assortment of Turkish dishes including tandır kebap. With salad, bread and soft drink a meal might cost US$3 or so.

Nearby is the popular *Şifa Lokantası* (shee-FAH, health), Mevlâna Caddesi 30, only a short stroll from the Mevlâna Museum. Its modern if simple dining room does fırın kebap and a cold drink for US$4. The *Şifa 2* immediately opposite can round off the meal with baklava and tea for US$2.

The *Konya Mutfağı* (Konya Kitchen, ☎ 352 8547), Akçeşme Mahallesi, Topraklık Caddesi 66, across from the Akçeşme İlkokulu school, is in a restored house just a few minutes' walk from the Hotel Balıkçılar, down towards the Koyunoğlu Museum. Service is polite, the ambience and menu are traditional and fine, and yet prices are still well below US$8 per person.

Just in case you run away with the idea that nothing ever changes in Konya, walk round Alaettin Bulvarı to find the *Apex Fast Food Centre*, a McDonald's in all but name!

Getting There & Away

Air Turkish Airlines (☎ (332) 351 2000) has an office at Alaettin Caddesi 22, Kat 1/106, on the north side of the street not far from Alaettin Tepesi. There are no scheduled services from the airport at present.

Bus Konya's otogar is 3.5 km from the city centre at Hükümet Alanı (Konak). To get to the centre take a minibus from the rank outside the otogar. Some of the minibuses continue to Mevlâna Meydanı, next to the Tourism Information Office and the Mevlâna Museum.

Details of some bus services follow:

Adana – 350 km, 6½ hours, US$7; frequent buses
Adıyaman (Nemrut Dağı) – 720 km, 16 hours, US$11; change at Adana
Aksaray – 140 km, 2½ hours, US$4.50; frequent buses
Alanya – 480 km, 10 hours, US$8; change at Silifke or Antalya
Ankara – 260 km, 3½ hours, US$5; frequent buses
Antalya – 365 km, six hours, US$12; several buses daily on two routes, the longer via Isparta, the faster and prettier via Akseki
Bursa – 500 km, 8½ hours, US$10; several buses daily
Denizli (Pamukkale) – 440 km, seven hours, US$7; several buses daily
İstanbul – 660 km, 12 hours, US$12; frequent buses
İzmir – 575 km, eight hours, US$8; buses at least every two hours
Nevşehir (Cappadocia) – 226 km, 3½ hours, US$5; several buses daily
Silifke – 218 km, four hours, US$5; frequent buses
Side – 296 km, 5½ hours, US10; no direct buses to Side; take one to Manavgat

Train There is no direct rail link across the plateau between Konya and Ankara. The best way to make this journey is by bus. Between İstanbul (Haydarpaşa) and Konya you can ride either the *İç Anadolu Mavi Tren* (Inner Anatolia Blue Train) or the *Meram Ekspresi*. The *İç Anadolu Mavi Tren* departs from İstanbul (Haydarpaşa) daily at 11.15 pm and arrives in Konya the next day at 12.35 pm. In the reverse direction, the train departs from Konya at 8.10 pm, arriving at Haydarpaşa at 9.05 am. A one-way ticket costs US$10, or US$12 in a couchette. This train continues beyond Konya to Karaman, arriving at 2.25 pm; departure from Karaman for Konya and İstanbul is at 6.20 pm.

The *Meram Ekspresi* departs from İstanbul (Haydarpaşa) at 6.40 pm, arriving in Konya the next morning at 8.10 am. Departure from Konya is at 4.35 pm, arriving at Haydarpaşa at 6.30 am. A one-way ticket costs US$9 in 2nd class, US$10 in a couchette.

City buses, running at least every half-hour, connect the train station with the centre of town. If you take a taxi from the train station to Hükümet Alanı, it will cost about US$2.

Getting Around

As most of the city centre sights are easily reached on foot, you only need public transport to get to the bus and train stations. Konya's efficient system of minibuses does this well; a run from the otogar to the centre costs just US$0.25. The new tram runs from the otogar to Alaettin Bulvarı but doesn't continue down Alaettin Caddesi.

SULTANHANI

The highway between Konya and Aksaray crosses quintessential Anatolian steppe: undulating grassland, sometimes with mountains in the distance. Along the way, 110 km from Konya and 45 km from Aksaray, is the village of Sultanhanı, which has one of several Seljuk hans bearing that name. This Sultanhanı is 100m from the highway and can be visited on any day in summer from 7 am to 7 pm for US$1. It was constructed in 1229, during the reign of the Seljuk sultan Alaettin Keykubat I, restored in 1278 after a fire (when it became the largest han in Turkey) and restored again and reroofed 20 years ago. Don't miss the wonderful carved portal, the raised-up central *mescid* and the huge *ahır*, or stable, at the back.

The Sultanhanı is just past a school, all of whose pupils seem intent on begging for *bon-bons*, pens and cash. Please don't encourage them.

Immediately opposite the Sultanhanı, the *Sultan Restaurant & Kafeterya* offers a complete touristic service: restaurant, toilets, exchange facilities, shops, stamps, phone cards, somewhere to leave your bag while you look round...all this and a smile too! Nearby is the *Kervansaray Pansiyon & Camping* (☎ (382) 242 2008) with beds for US$7. Its owner has a car and may be willing to organise excursions to the Acı Gölü crater lake and to see the flamingoes on Tuz Gölü. The nearby *Sultan Pansiyon* (☎ (382) 242 2393) is similar. Walk 800m down the road, passing through the village centre, to find the *Kervan Pansiyon, Restaurant & Camping* (☎ (382) 242 2325).

To reach the han, take a Sultanhanı Belediyesi bus from Aksaray otogar. Alternatively catch a Konya bus and ask to be dropped off. To be sure of a seat on to Konya afterwards, make a reservation in Aksaray and ask to be picked up on the main road. The fare should be about US$1 and the journey takes three-quarters of an hour.

AKSARAY

Aksaray (population 92,000, altitude 980m) is another of those farming towns with little to offer tourists beyond a bed and a meal, although you can probably amuse yourself well enough if you have an hour to spare. Aksaray also makes a good base for visits to Ihlara and Güzelyurt.

It's 500m from Aksaray's otogar to the main square, with its nicely restored government buildings; to get there, leave the otogar and take a sharp left.

Aksaray's postal code is 51400.

Things to See

The **Zinciriye Medresesi** dates from Seljuk Turkish times, when it was built by the local dynasty of Karamanoğulları emirs. Since then it has been restored several times. Although it's now the local museum, with displays of pots and inscriptions arranged around the courtyard and in the rooms, it's the building itself which is interesting since it served as a theological college and a han as well. To find it, walk downhill past the Toprak hotel, turn right, and walk one short block further on.

The older part of town along Çerdiğin Caddesi (also called Nevşehir Caddesi) has some **old stone houses** and a curious **brick minaret** built in 1236 and leaning at a pronounced angle. Inevitably a nearby sign touts it as the 'Turkish Tower of Pisa'.

Places to Stay – bottom end

If you need somewhere to stay in transit there are a couple of good options very close to the otogar. To find them cross the road immediately outside the otogar and take the first left. The *Hitit Pansion* (☎ (382) 213 1996), Kılıçaslan Mahallesi, is an apartment house turned into a pension 'alla turka'. You remove your shoes and put on clean slippers when entering. The lobby is decorated with carpets, kilims, low couches *(sedir)* and pillows. The guest rooms upstairs are bare and waterless but the front ones are large and have balconies. Bathrooms down the hall are small but tiled and clean. Rooms cost US$5.50/10 a single/double. The nearby *Aksaray Pansion* is plainer but clean, with identical prices.

Aksaray also has several real cheapies

across the market square behind the Vilayet (government building) on the main square. The *Toprak Oteli* (☎ (382) 213 1308) is cheapest of all at US$3/4.50, but it's decidedly seedy. The *Mutlu Oteli* (☎ (382) 213 1073), round the corner in Kızılay Caddesi, is marginally better.

If you're camping, head for the *Ağaçlı Turistik Tesisleri*, a luxury camping ground at the main highway intersection, where you can pitch your tent or park your camper van for US$3, plus the same amount again for each person in your party.

Places to Stay – middle

The *Otel Yoğuran* (☎ (382) 213 5490), 3 Nolu Hükümet Caddesi, is in the midst of the bazaar a half-block from the Vilayet building. It's among the city's newer and more interesting places to stay because of its location. Rooms with private shower cost US$13/22, breakfast included.

Two other reasonable places face each other in Kızılay Caddesi. The two-star *Otel Tezcanlar* (☎ (382) 213 8482, fax 215 1234) has pleasant rooms brightened up with artificial plants and with spacious bathrooms for US$9/15 with breakfast. Immediately opposite, the one-star *Çakır İpek Oteli* (☎ (382) 213 7053) is similarly comfortable but slightly cheaper at US$7 a head without breakfast.

Right on the main square next to the modern Hacıbektaş Kurşunlu Camii is the new *Otel Yuvam* (☎ (382) 213 2025). Minaret and traffic noise might make the US$14/22 prices seem a bit steep but they're certainly negotiable out of season.

The top place in town is the *Ağaçlı Turistik Tesisleri* (Ağaçlı Touristic Establishments) (☎ (382) 213 4910, fax 213 4914), Ankara-Adana Asfaltı, Nevşehir Kavşağı, at the main highway intersection with the roads to Nevşehir and Niğde. If you have a car, the two motels set in green, shady gardens here might be convenient. The *Melendiz Motel* charges US$35/45, breakfast included. The *Ihlara Motel* charges a bit less, US$30/40. There's also a cafeteria, a more formal restaurant, gift shops, swimming and wading pools and a fuel station.

Places to Eat

Except in the better hotels, Aksaray has only simple restaurants. The best place to look is behind the Vilayet building, near the cheap hotels, where you'll find the *Çardak Okey Salonu* and *Aksaray Restaurant*, both serving tasty if simple meals for under US$3. Just off the main square, near the Hacıbektaş Kurşunlu Camii, there's also the *Kent Lokantası* with a good selection of meat dishes.

Getting There & Away

There are direct buses from Aksaray to Ankara (230 km, 4½ hours), Nevşehir (65 km, 1½ hours), Niğde (115 km, two hours) and Konya (140 km, 2½ hours). There are also sporadic dolmuşes in summer to Ihlara Köyü (45 km, one hour, US$0.50), the starting point for visits to the Ihlara valley, to Güzelyurt and to Sultanhanı.

IHLARA (PERİSTREMA)

Forty-five km south-east of Aksaray is Ihlara, at the head of the Peristrema gorge, a remote valley which was once a favourite retreat of Byzantine monks. Dozens of painted churches, carved from the rock or built from the local stone, have survived but this wildly beautiful place is still less touristy than Göreme.

The hike along the 16 km gorge, following the course of the Melendiz Suyu stream all the way from Selime to Ihlara village, is wilder and more exciting than touring the well-trodden paths amidst the rock-hewn churches at Göreme. Start early in the day and you'll enjoy the trip more, particularly in the height of summer.

Things to See

The scenery on this trip, especially on the descent into the gorge, is as wonderful as the ancient churches themselves. Allow a full day for seeing Ihlara. If you're coming out from Aksaray, the drive will also take some time.

On the rim of the gorge near Ihlara village there's a modern complex with restaurant, souvenir shop and ticket booth. You can buy

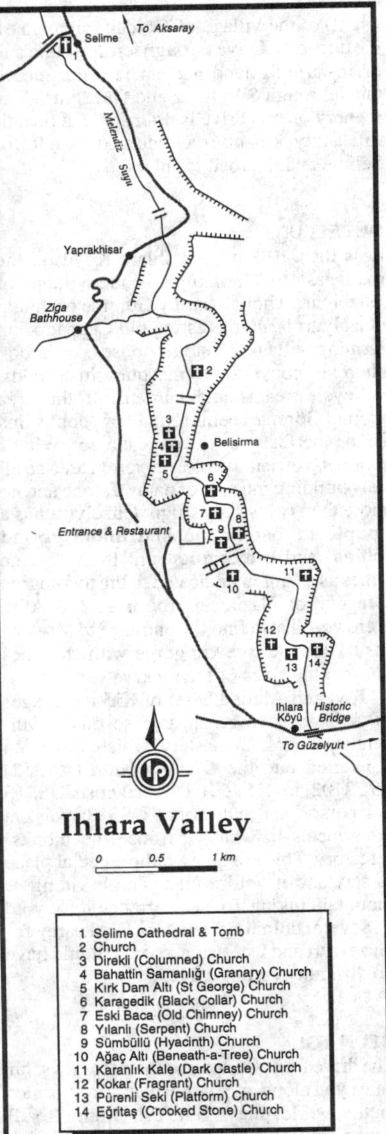

a ticket here for US$2 and enter the gorge any time between 8.30 am and 5.30 pm.

A very long flight of stairs leads down to the floor of the gorge and it will take several hours to find and visit the various churches there. Although there are a few simple eateries in the gorge itself, you might want to pack a picnic or at least take snacks and drinks.

Signs mark the **churches** along the way. The most interesting, with the best paintings, are the Yılanlı Kilise, Sümbüllü Kilise, Kokar Kilise and Eğritaş Kilisesi. Farther down the valley are the Kırk Dam Altı Kilise, Bahattin Samanlığı Kilise, Direkli Kilise and Ala Kilise. Several of the churches, notably the Çarıklı, Elmalı and Karanlık, are closed because of the risk of structural damage.

Places to Stay

You can stay in Ilhara village itself at the *Star Pansiyon*, tucked away at the far end. Waterless rooms here cost US$6 a head, but you wake to the sound of the river running past the verandah and are within easy reach of the village shops and cafés. If you're walking along the gorge from Selime you'll also emerge right by your accommodation, an advantage if you're tired.

There are newer places, with better facilities if less atmosphere, on the roads above the gorge. The *Pension Anatolia* (☎ (382) 453 7439) is on the road running between the village and the entry to the gorge. Beds with baths cost US$6 a head, or you can camp in the grounds for US$2. This place is often full with Dutch, Belgian or American groups.

Several more small pensions line the road from Ihlara village to Aksaray. The *Akar Pansiyon* (☎ (382) 453 7018) is in a pleasant modern building and has clean rooms with bath for US$9 a double. The shop downstairs sells picnic ingredients and there's a restaurant behind. The *Bişginler Ihlara Pansiyon* next door is marginally cheaper and has received good reports from readers. The *Pansiyon Famille* (☎ (382) 453 7098) across the road is a good deal more basic and yet charges slightly more.

You can camp at the entry to the gorge: US$3 for a tent, plus US$1.50 per person.

In Belisırma Köyü, midway along the gorge, you'll find the *Aslan Camping & Pansiyon* (☎ (451) 213 3780), with six beds in pre-erected tents which rent for US$5 a double. There's also a small *ev pansiyon* in the village (☎ (451) 213 2429), with tiny, waterless rooms for US$6 including a breakfast. The house itself is not particularly pretty but staying there would give you a glimpse of rural life.

Places to Eat

The restaurant at the rim entry to the gorge has a spectacular view, but a limited, not especially good menu. A full meal still costs around US$6 or US$7. Simple eateries operate in the village *(Mehmet Işık's Restaurant)* and the valley (two along the trail, one in Belisırma Köyü) during the summer months.

Getting There & Away

Bus The rim entry to the gorge is 1.5 km from the village of Ihlara Köyü, 45 km from Aksaray and 95 km from Nevşehir. Ihlara Belediyesi buses run several times daily from Aksaray's otogar, charging US$0.50 one-way. Tour companies in Göreme are often happy to agree on a one-way fare to leave you in the valley, usually after a visit to Derinkuyu underground city.

Car If you have a car, your visit is made much easier. From the main Aksaray to Nevşehir highway, turn south (right, if you're coming from Aksaray) at a point 11 km east of the intersection of the Ankara to Adana and Aksaray to Nevşehir highways. After making this turn, go about 23 km to another right turn marked for Ihlara Vadisi. The road passes through Selime village, with numerous rock-hewn buildings, and then three km farther on it runs through Yaprakhisar; both villages are dramatically surrounded by rock and marked by Göreme-style fairy chimneys. After another 13 km you come to Ihlara Köyü, where you turn left to reach the entrance at the rim of the gorge.

To get to Ihlara from Derinkuyu (52 km), proceed south towards Niğde, but turn west (right) at the village of Gölcük (signs mark the turn-off). Drive through fertile potato and grain-farming land and up into the mountains through Sivrihisar and Güzelyurt. The scenery on this drive is dramatic and beautiful. Sixty km after Gölcük, turn left for Selime and the road to Ihlara.

GÜZELYURT

Less than 10 km from Ihlara Köyü on the road east to Derinkuyu is the village of Güzelyurt. Though hardly Göreme or Ihlara, Güzelyurt is an interesting old Cappadocian farming village of stone houses, orthodox churches converted to mosques, lush fields, valleys, streams and gardens. If the area around Göreme seems too full of people, this is the perfect place to escape to. What's more, it's officially a conservation area so all new building must be of natural stone and no more than two storeys high. Güzelyurt has a couple of barely touched **underground 'cities'** and a **mosque** built in Byzantine times as a church dedicated to the theologian Gregory of Nazianzus (born in 330 AD). Here you'll also find the entrance to **Monastery Valley**, a five km gorge with churches cut into the sides of the rock.

Tovi and Ahmed Diler of Kirkit Voyages in Avanos have taken a lease on a 19th-century Greek monastery which has been converted into the *Otel Karballa* (☎ (382) 451 2102, fax 451 2107). B&B costs US$13 per person and half-board US$18; you eat your meals in what was once the monks' refectory. This is a quiet, rather special place to stay and if you're interested in riding or mountain biking Tovi can arrange it for you.

Several dolmuşes a day leave Aksaray for Güzelyurt and vice versa, so you should have no difficulty getting there.

UZUN YOL

The drive from Aksaray or Ihlara to Nevşehir takes you along one of the oldest trade routes in the world, the Uzun Yol (Long Road) which linked Konya, the capital of the Seljuk Sultanate of Rum, with its other great cities

(Kayseri, Sivas and Erzurum) and ultimately with the birthplace of Seljuk power in Persia.

Following the Long Road today takes you past the remains of several hans, including the impressive and well-preserved **Ağızkarahan** (1243) on the south side of the road about 13 km east of Aksaray, open daily from 7 am to 6 pm for a small fee; the 13th-century **Tepesidelik Hanı** (also called the Öresin Hanı) on the south side about 20 km east of Aksaray; and the 12th-century **Alay Hanı**, badly ruined, on the north side of the highway about 33 km east of Aksaray. All are marked by signs.

Cappadocia

Cappadocia, the region between Ankara and Malatya, between the Black Sea and the Taurus Mountains, with its centre at Kayseri, was once the heart of the Hittite Empire, later an independent kingdom, then a vast Roman province mentioned several times in the Bible.

Today the name survives to describe one of Turkey's most visited tourist areas, the moonscape around the town of Ürgüp and the Göreme Valley. Since the name doesn't appear on official road maps, you'll need to know that 'Cappadocia' is the area bordered by Kayseri in the east, Aksaray in the west, Hacıbektaş to the north and Niğde to the south.

For all its seeming barrenness, the mineral-laden volcanic soil is very fertile and Cappadocia today is a prime agricultural region with many fruit orchards and vineyards. Little wineries experiment with the excellent grapes, sometimes with pleasant results. Irrigation schemes should greatly increase the productivity of the region. Another source of wealth is carpet-making, but these days tourism is Cappadocia's industry par excellence. People come from all over the world to visit the Göreme open-air museum, to explore the rock-hewn churches and dwellings in surrounding valleys, to gaze on the fairy chimneys and to plumb the depths of the underground cities at Derinkuyu and Kaymaklı.

History

The history of Cappadocia began with the eruptions of three volcanoes (Erciyes Dağı near Kayseri, Melendiz Dağı near Niğde, and Göllüdağ between them), as much as 10 million years ago. The eruptions spread a thick layer of hot volcanic ash over the region which hardened into a soft, porous stone called tufa.

Over aeons of geological time wind, water and sand erosion wore away portions of the tufa, carving it into elaborate and unearthly shapes. Boulders of hard stone, caught in the tufa and then exposed by erosion, protect the tufa directly beneath from further erosion. The result is a column or cone of tufa with a boulder perched on top, whimsically called a *peribaca*, or 'fairy chimney'. Entire valleys are filled with these formations, many of them amusingly phallic in appearance.

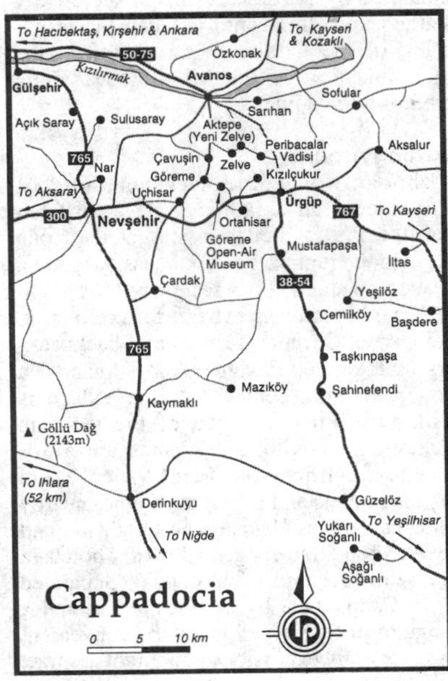

The tufa was easily worked with primitive tools and the inhabitants learned early that sturdy dwellings could be cut from it with a minimum of fuss. A cave could be carved out very quickly and, if the family expanded, more easy carving could produce a nursery or storeroom in next to no time.

When invaders flooded across the land bridge between Europe and Asia, Cappadocians went underground, carving elaborate multi-level cave cities beneath the surface of the earth and only coming to the surface to tend their fields.

When Christianity arrived in Cappadocia, its adherents found that cave churches, complete with elaborate decoration, could be carved from the rock as easily as dwellings. Large Christian communities thrived here and their rock-hewn churches became a unique art form. Arab armies swept through in the 7th century but the Christians retreated into their caves again, rolling stone wheel-doors across the entrances.

Many of the caves and villages were inhabited by the descendants of these early settlers until this century, when the crumbling of the Ottoman Empire forced the reorganisation of the Middle East along ethno-political lines.

Getting Around

Although you could see something of Cappadocia on a lightning day trip from Ankara, it's far better to stay at least one night in the region. You could easily spend a week here and still not see everything.

The most convenient bases for exploration are Ürgüp, Göreme (favourite of backpackers and budget travellers) and Avanos, a pottery-making centre. Göreme village is within walking distance of the Göreme Valley, and Ürgüp and Avanos are a 10-minute ride from the Göreme Valley. There are also hotels and pensions in other nearby villages such as Uçhisar and Ortahisar, and several good mid-range and luxury hotels in Nevşehir, the provincial capital. Separated from Cappadocia by around 70 km and a range of hills, Kayseri is not the convenient base for daily excursions you might assume.

NEVŞEHİR

Nevşehir (NEHV-sheh-heer, population 55,000, altitude 1260m), the provincial capital, is a dreary modern town where the Cappadocian moonscape is not much in evidence. Nonetheless, it's an important transfer point so you're almost bound to pass through it at some point. It's also a useful base for getting to the underground cities at Kaymaklı and Derinkuyu.

Orientation & Information

Atatürk Bulvarı, the main street, changes its name to become Yeni Kayseri Caddesi along its eastern reaches on the way to Göreme. The main north-south road, Lale Caddesi, intersects with Atatürk Bulvarı at the centre of the town, near the tourist information office. The new otogar is one km north of the centre on the road towards Gülşehir.

The Tourism Information Office (☎ (384) 213 3659), on Atatürk Bulvarı just east of the main intersection, is open every day in summer from 8.30 am to noon and from 1 to 5.30 pm. Staff are well informed and helpful.

Nevşehir's postal code is 50000.

Things to See & Do

There is little to see or do in Nevşehir proper except perhaps to visit the Monday **market** or climb up to the **citadel** to enjoy the view and be importuned into buying some of the locally handmade lace.

Have a look at the **Nevşehirli İbrahim Paşa Külliyesi**, the mosque complex uphill from the Hotel Lale. Sultan Ahmet III's grand vizier İbrahim Paşa (1662-1730), sometimes called Damat İbrahim, was a great builder, having supplied his sovereign with many romantic palaces and lodges in İstanbul. He was one of the first great men of the empire to have been influenced by European fashions. He was born in humble conditions in the village of Muşkara, and when he became rich and famous he returned to his village to found a new city (*nev*, new; *şehir*, city). Along with his New City, İbrahim founded this mosque complex (1726), consisting of the mosque, a seminary, a school, a library, a water fountain and a hamam. The mosque and hamam are still in business. Bath hours at the hamam are from 7.30 am to 9 pm. Wednesday is officially for women but female tourists are welcome any time.

The **Nevşehir Müzesi** is one km out along Yeni Kayseri Caddesi on the road to Göreme and Ürgüp. Opening hours are from 8 am to noon and from 1 to 5 pm, closed Monday; admission is US$1. The arrangement is the familiar one: an archaeological section with Phrygian, Hittite and Bronze Age pots and implements, then Roman, Byzantine and Ottoman articles; and an ethnographic section with costumes, tools, manuscripts and jewellery.

Places to Stay

Since Nevşehir is so uninviting, you're unlikely to want to stay here. However, buses sometimes dump you off here late at night or early in the morning. In peak season if you arrive late you may also think it wiser to spend a night in Nevşehir than to head on and risk finding everything full.

Places to Stay – bottom end

From the main intersection at the city centre, walk uphill on Atatürk Bulvarı past the Aspava Restaurant and Hotel Şems, and turn left at the next street, Belediye Caddesi. Walk along the road two short blocks to find a long-time favourite, the *Hotel Lale* (☎ (384) 213 1797), just west of the intersection with Lale Caddesi. The rooms with bath are quite comfortable for what you pay: US$11/19 a single/double.

Back on Atatürk Bulvarı the one-star, 25-room *Hotel Şems* (☎ (384) 213 3597), above the Aspava Restaurant, is newish, nice and reasonably priced at US$7/12. Rooms at the front of the hotel may be noisy.

Continue west along Atatürk Bulvarı and you will come to several small cheap hotels on the left-hand side which are badly affected by street noise. The *İpek Palas Oteli*

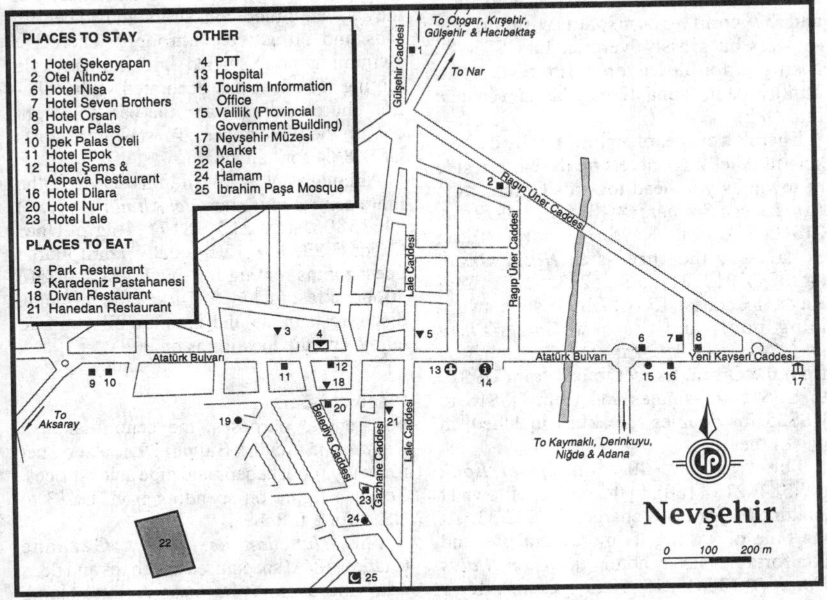

(☎ (384) 213 1478) charges US$2.50/5 with washbasin. A short distance uphill from the İpek Palas is the similar *Bulvar Palas* (☎ (384) 213 11695), which rents clean waterless rooms at the same rates. Neither of these, and especially not the İpek Palas, is especially suitable for lone women.

Camping None of the camping places along the Ürgüp road are outstanding; rates are generally US$2 per person, with another US$2 or so for a tent or caravan. Follow the signs to Ürgüp and shortly after leaving Nevşehir you will come to the *Dinler Turizm Mocamp*, behind a Türk Petrol station. Rates are about US$3 per adult, almost as much again for a tent or vehicle. The nearby *Koru Mocamp* has drawn a few complaints from readers.

Places to Stay – middle

Only 100m south of the otogar is the three-star *Hotel Şekeryapan* (☎ 384) 212 8184, fax 213 4051), Gülşehir Caddesi 8, with a lift and 37 comfy rooms, all with private showers, but grossly overpriced at US$50/80 a single/double, even with restaurant, Turkish bath, sauna, terrace bar and lounge thrown in.

There's a cluster of architecturally depressing middle-range hotels on the eastern side of town, as you head towards Göreme: the *Hotel Seven Brothers* (☎ (384) 213 4979, fax 213 0454), Yeni Kayseri Caddesi, Tusan Sokak 25; the three-star *Hotel Orsan* (☎ (384) 213 2115, fax 213 4223), Yeni Kayseri Caddesi 15, which boasts a swimming pool; and the new *Hotel Dilara* (☎ (384) 212 6052, fax 213 2739), across from the Orsan. Expect to pay from US$10 to US$15 for singles and from US$18 to US$25 for doubles, breakfast included, in any of them.

The two-star, 60-room *Hotel Epok* (☎ (384) 213 1168), in the middle of town at Atatürk Bulvarı 39, charges US$22/33. At the time of writing its more attractive and comfortable sister hotel, the *Şehir Palas Hotel* (☎ (384) 213 5329), Camii Kebir Caddesi 41, was closed. It might be worth checking to see if it has reopened.

Places to Stay – top end

About three km east of the centre on the Ürgüp road stands the big five-star, 350-room *Kapadokya Dedeman Hotel* (☎ (384) 213 9950, fax 213 5092). It's hardly a pretty building but the guest rooms have all the luxury accoutrements, including air-con, TVs and minibars. Two restaurants, four bars, two swimming pools, Turkish bath, sauna, courts for volleyball, basketball and tennis – it's all yours for US$75/110/150 a single/double/triple. The hotel is often busy with tour groups.

Another one km along the Ürgüp road, at the turn off for Göreme and Uçhisar, is the *Country Club Kapadokya Lodge* (☎ (384) 213 9945, fax 213 5092), a love-it-or-loathe-it pink and beige ziggurat of a building designed by Turkish architect Tuncay Çavdar. Rooms have relatively small windows to suggest a cave existence, but they have all mod cons: TVs, music centre, fans and attractive bathrooms. There's a swimming pool shaded with nomad-style tenting. The lobby is decorated with imitation church frescoes and the bar is straight out of the Flintstones. To stay here costs US$48/64 for half-board.

Although not as lavish in its services, the more central four-star *Otel Altınöz* (☎ (384) 213 5305, fax 213 2817), Ragıp Üner Caddesi 23, has 120 equally comfortable guest rooms renting for much less: US$50/70, breakfast included. Turkish bath, sauna, disco, restaurants and bars are all yours to enjoy, and the location is quiet.

Places to Eat

For general purposes, the central *Aspava Restaurant*, Atatürk Bulvarı 29, is a good bet for ready food, kebaps and pide at low prices. You can figure on spending from US$3 to US$4 for a full meal.

The *Hanedan Restaurant*, Gazhane Caddesi 18/A, specialises in kebaps and does a thriving takeaway business. A plate of lamb kebap, a salad and a glass of ayran costs less than US$3. It closes in the evening, though.

The *Park Restaurant*, across Atatürk Bulvarı from the Hotel Epok and up the hill through the park, is where Nevşehir's movers and shakers come in the evening to have a drink and talk politics, sport and business. Waiters quietly bring plate after plate of meze, grilled meat or chicken, various soups and stews and a few desserts. A full meal costs from US$6 to US$7. There's a pleasant tea garden at the front.

Getting There & Away

Bus Nevşehir's new Adnan Menderes Terminali handles both bus and dolmuş services for the area, although you can usually flag down the dolmuşes outside the tourist office as well. Here are details for several popular destinations:

Adana – 285 km, 5½ hours, US$7; several buses daily
Aksaray – 65 km, 1½ hours, US$2.50; frequent minibuses and buses
Ankara – 285 km, 4½ hours, US$8; several buses daily
Denizli (Pamukkale) – 665 km, 10 hours, US$14; one bus daily
İstanbul – 725 km, 10 to 12 hours, US$15 to US$20; a few buses nightly
Kayseri – 105 km, 2½ hours by bus, 1½ hours by minibus, US$2.50; very frequent buses and minibuses
Konya – 226 km, 3½ hours, US$6; several buses daily
Yozgat (via Kayseri) – 300 km, five hours, US$6

UNDERGROUND CITIES

For sheer fascination and mystery, you could hardly beat the underground cities south of Nevşehir along the road to Niğde: Kaymaklı, 20 km south of Nevşehir; Mazıköy, 10 km east of Kaymaklı; and Derinkuyu, 10 km south of Kaymaklı.

Some archaeologists date the earliest portions of these underground cities to Hittite times 4000 years ago. Martin Urban, a German archaeologist, says they were occupied by at least the 8th and 7th centuries BC. The ancient Greek historian Xenophon mentions underground dwellings in Cappadocia in his *Anabasis*.

In time of peace the people of this region lived and farmed above ground, but when invaders threatened they took to their troglodyte dwellings where they could live safely (if not always happily) for up to six months.

Kaymaklı

The countryside around Kaymaklı has no enchanting fairy chimneys or sensuously carved valleys, yet the stone is the same soft volcanic tuff which allowed early residents to develop the real estate cheaply.

At Kaymaklı, an unprepossessing farming village of white houses and unpaved streets, an unimpressive little cave in a low mound leads down into a maze of tunnels and rooms carved four levels deep into the earth.

Little arrows guide you into the cool depths. (Space yourself to travel in a gap between larger groups.) As you go down, it's like entering a huge and very complex Swiss cheese. Holes here, holes there, 'windows' from room to room, paths going this way and that, more levels of rooms above and below. Without the arrows and the electric wires, it would be fearfully difficult to find the way out again. If you wander off along another passage, separated from the group by only a few metres, you can hear what they say, you can converse with them, but you can't find your way back to them! Suddenly a foot comes into view and you realise that they're on the next level, almost above your head!

Signs of the troglodyte lifestyle are everywhere: storage jars for oil, wine and water, communal kitchens blackened by smoke, stables with mangers, incredibly deep wells. Soon it's easy to believe that tens of thousands of people could have lived here happily year-round, deep within the earth. It's even suspected that there were underground passages which connected Kaymaklı with its sister city of Derinkuyu, 10 km away, though the tunnels have yet to be excavated.

From the highway, follow the signs which indicate a left (east) turn, or ask for the Yeraltı Şehri (YEHR-ahl-tuh shehh-ree, Underground City). The entrance is one block east of the highway and it's open from

8 am to 5 pm (6.30 pm in summer) every day; admission costs US$2.50.

Mazıköy

Just north of the turn off for Kaymaklı's Yeraltı Şehri is another turn off east marked for Mazıköy Yeraltı Şehri, 10 km along. Nestled in a valley enclosed by the now-familiar sheer rock cliffs is the village of Mazıköy, with its central town square. Buy your ticket here (US$2) whenever there's anyone around, then head for the entrance just off the town square.

On top of the valley wall is a **necropolis** with slot-like graves. A guide will probably show you the stone shelter supposedly used for the *güvercin postası* (carrier-pigeon mail service).

At the time of writing the village has few services, but you can get simple meals and beds now, and fancier ones will follow.

Derinkuyu

Its name means 'deep well', and this underground city, 10 km south of Kaymaklı, has larger rooms arrayed on eight levels. Prices and opening times are the same as at Kaymaklı. When you get all the way down, look up the ventilation shaft to see just how deep you are – not for claustrophobics!

Derinkuyu has several restaurants near the main square. There's also the Hotel Ali Baba, and others, though once you've seen the underground city there's little reason to stay. You might have a look at the **mosque**, obviously built as a church, and the large **monastery church** (in good condition, complete with bell tower) on the main road just 100m south of the turn off for the underground city.

Getting There & Away

Board a Kaymaklı or Derinkuyu Belediyesi bus or minibus at the otogar in Nevşehir; they depart every 30 minutes or so and charge US$1.50 for the ride. Buses to Niğde also travel the same road.

Many of the day trips out of Göreme, Ürgüp and Avanos visit one of the underground cities. This is an easy way to visit them in summer, but means they can become horribly crowded.

NİĞDE

Niğde (NEE-deh, population 95,000, altitude 1216m), 85 km south of Nevşehir, was built by the Seljuks. Backed by snowcapped mountains, it's a farming centre with a small but fine selection of historic buildings, including a mosque built by the Mongols. East of the town is the ancient rock-hewn monastery of Eski Gümüşler, with the best-preserved paintings in Cappadocia.

Orientation & Information

İstasyon Caddesi is the main axis of the commercial district, bounded by Atatürk Meydanı (sometimes called Hükümet Meydanı), the main traffic roundabout at its west end, and a hill bearing the lofty *saat kulesi* (clock tower), kale (fortress) and Alaeddin Camii (largest mosque) near its east end. The marketplace is beneath the clock tower; Thursday is market day.

The otogar is one km north-east of İstasyon Caddesi, the train station one km south-east. Look on and near Atatürk Meydanı for hotels, restaurants and shops, and on aptly-named Bankalar Caddesi for banks.

The Tourism Information Office (☎ (388) 232 3393, fax 232 2326), İstiklal Caddesi, Vakıf İş Hanı 1/D, just off the main square, is open daily except Sunday from 8.30 am to noon and from 1.30 to 5.30 pm.

Mosques & Museum

The **Alaeddin Camii** (1223), a Seljuk work on the hill with the fortress and clock tower, is the town's grandest mosque. But the Süngür Bey Camii at the foot of the hill by the marketplace is, for me, the city's most interesting building.

Built by the Seljuks but restored by the Mongols in 1335, the **Süngür Bey Camii** is a curious and affecting blend of architectures. The embellished windows at ground level differ in style one from another. On the upper storey, blind lancet arches take the place of windows. The rose window above the north window bears a six-pointed 'Star

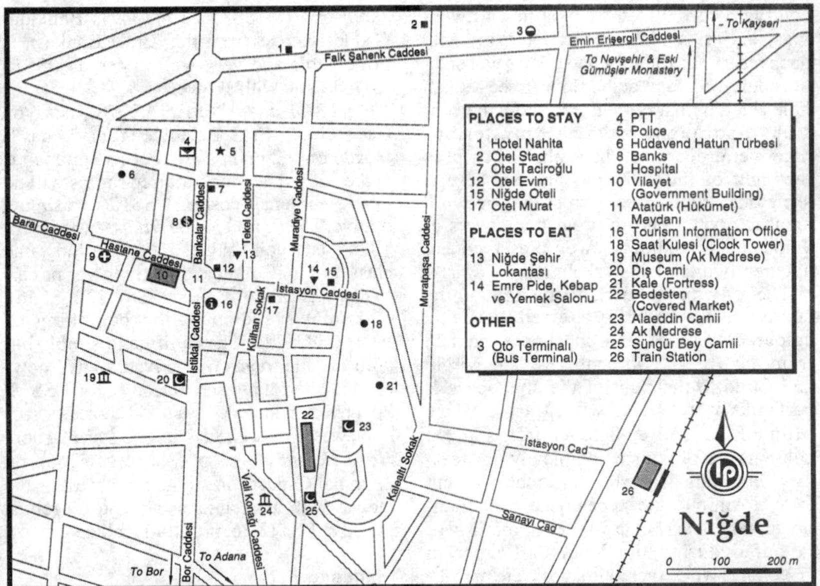

of David', a motif used elsewhere in the building. The big, stolid, square doors are finely carved.

Recent restorations have done wonders for the exterior stonework but have filled the interior with ugly reinforced concrete which breaks the spell cast by this ancient work. Even so, look at the north galleries, a conglomeration of architectural styles, and the mihrab, wonderfully carved and almost Chinese in appearance.

The **Ak Medrese** (1409) is now the town's museum, where pride of place is given to the mummy of a blonde nun discovered in the 1960s in the Ihlara Valley, and thought to be 1000 years old. Also take a look at the **Hüdavend Hatun Türbesi** (1312), a fine example of a Seljuk tomb; and the **Dış Cami**, an Ottoman mosque with a carved mimber inlaid with mother-of-pearl.

Eski Gümüşler Monastery

It's 10 km east from the clock tower in Niğde to the rock-hewn monastery of Eski Gümüşler.

On Hwy 805 east of the town centre, a Mobil station marks the intersection of roads west (to Niğde) and east to Eski Gümüşler (ess-KEE gur-mursh-LEHR), 4.75 km away (follow the signs). Gümüşler Belediyesi minibuses run between the village and Niğde's otogar. You can also hitch to the site.

The village of Gümüşler is in the midst of rich apple orchards which in October yield mountains of fruit. Bagged and boxed, the apples change the town landscape until the trucks come.

The monastery of Eski Gümüşler, discovered in 1963, is open daily in summer from 9 am to noon and from 1.30 to 6.30 pm; from October to May from 8 am to noon and 1 to 5 pm. The gates are normally locked, but the guardian will have seen you coming and will follow with the key. Admission costs US$1.50.

Through a rock-cut passage is a large

courtyard surrounded by rock-hewn dwellings, crypts, a kitchen and refectory with deep reservoirs for wine and oil. As you enter the courtyard, look at the floor to see a small hole fitted with a propeller to show the constant updraught from the mysterious nine-metre-deep shaft beneath. The crypt to the right of the entry passage has several skeletons still in place. Across the courtyard another crypt, beneath protective covers of wood and glass, holds a well-preserved and apparently undisturbed skeleton.

The lofty main church, to the right off the courtyard, has the best-preserved Byzantine coloured frescoes in Cappadocia, painted from the 7th to 11th centuries. The Virgin and Child to the right of the altar-space is particularly affecting, with Mary given a Mona Lisa smile. The church's great columns are of course completely unnecessary, but were left when the rock was cut away to mimic the appearance of a traditional temple. The cross-hatch motif was favoured during the Iconoclastic period (725- 842) when sacred images were prohibited and artists resorted to geometrics, a preference soon picked up by Islam.

Sultan Marshes Bird Paradise

Well over 250 species of birds visit the Sultansazlığı Kuş Cenneti (Sultan Marshes Bird Paradise), 60 km north-east of Niğde (80 km south-west of Kayseri), east of the Kayseri-Niğde highway south of Yeşilhisar. Though little developed for tourism, bird-fanciers may want to explore the marshes and seek out the observation tower at Ovaçiftlik, on the road to Yahyalı. It offers good views across the marshy lake Eğri Göl, and a little museum with exhibits on the local bird life. Birds you may encounter include cranes, eagles, herons, spoonbills and storks. North of Eğri Göl is Yay Gölü, a lake noted for its populations of flamingos.

Places to Stay

The *Otel Stad* (☎ (388) 213 7866), Terminal Caddesi 6, one short block west of the otogar, charges US$14 for a double with shower.

The other hotels are in the centre. *Otel Taciroğlu* (☎ (388) 213 3047), Bankalar Caddesi across from the Ziraat Bankası, is presentable and very well priced at US$15 for a double with shower.

Otel Murat (☎ (388) 213 3978), İstasyon Caddesi 46, Eski Belediye Yanı 5, has a façade on the main street but its entrance is at the back. The much-abused rooms will do in an emergency, costing US$10/15 a single/double. The nearby *Niğde Oteli* (☎ (388) 213 1826), İstasyon Caddesi 83, is in the same class, but may quote a slightly lower price.

Otel Evim (☎ & fax (388) 232 3536), Hükümet Meydanı at the beginning of İstasyon Caddesi, has a lift, and simple but comfortable rooms with private baths (showers and short tubs) and balconies for US$18/26, breakfast included – a good choice.

Newest and swellest is the one-star, 60-room *Hotel Nahita* (☎ & fax (388) 232 5366), on Terminal Caddesi one long block west of the otogar, with a restaurant, bar, and 60 rooms priced at US$18/26, breakfast included.

Places to Eat

Fancy dining is not Niğde's strong suit. Try one of the small eateries on İstasyon Caddesi, such as the *Emre Pide, Kebap ve Yemek Salonu*, the name of which is its menu. They have stews most days at lunch, kebaps in the evening, and pide anytime. The bill for a quick meal rarely tops US$3. The *Birtad*, on the other side of İstasyon adjoining the Hotel Murat, is stronger on kebaps.

The *Niğde Şehir Lokantası*, hidden away north of İstasyon, is an alternative, and there are others in the narrow side streets. For pastanes (pastry-shops), look along Bankalar Caddesi, where they vie with the banks to take your money.

Getting There & Away

Niğde's otogar has buses to most nearby destinations, but perhaps only one or two per day. There is frequent service to Adana (205 km, 3½ hours, US$6), Aksaray (115 km, two hours, US$3.50), Kayseri (130 km, 1½ hours, US$3.50) and Konya (250 km, 3½ hours, US$8).

Service to Nevşehir (85 km, 1½ hours) is

fast and frequent, with minibuses departing from the otogar every hour on the hour from 5 am to 6 pm.

CAPPADOCIAN VALLEYS

East of Nevşehir, the rolling terrain is sandy. After a few km the panorama of Cappadocia begins to unfold: distant rock formations become visible as the so-called fairy chimneys, and valleys with undulating walls of soft volcanic ash fall away from the road. In the distance, the gigantic snow-capped peak of the volcano, **Erciyes Dağı** (Mt Aergius), floats above a layer of cloud.

No matter where you base yourself, moonscape valleys with painted churches and troglodyte dwellings will draw your attention. The Göreme Valley is the most famous of these, but nearby Zelve is less touristy, and the valleys at Soğanlı even less so.

The most popular bases for exploring the Cappadocian Valleys are Göreme, Uçhisar, Ürgüp and Avanos. In summer, getting between these places is relatively straightforward, but at other times of year you will usually have to use Nevşehir as a connecting point. While there are convenient dolmuş services between Nevşehir and Ürgüp, public transportation to the valleys and villages south of Ürgüp is not as frequent as one might like.

Tours organised by local travel agencies allow you to see all the sights cheaply and conveniently, but often dump you in a carpet or souvenir shop in the middle of nowhere for two hours. The tour company gets as much as 30% commission on everything you buy but the tea is free and the 'shopping' can be a rest from walking in the sun. Ask around for a company which doesn't have the enforced shopping stop.

To hire a taxi or minibus, with driver, for a full-day tour of all Cappadocia, starting at Ürgüp or Nevşehir, costs from US\$50 to US\$80. Alternatively, you can rent a bicycle, moped or motorbike to help you get about. If you have more time than money, plan to walk and hitch through the region, a wonderful way to tour, though it can be tiring in the hot sun.

However you go, wear flat shoes for climbing the metal-rung ladders and stairways, and take a torch (flashlight) if you have one. Refreshments, snacks and light meals are available at all of the valleys.

GÖREME

Göreme, set among towering tufa cones and honeycomb cliffs and surrounded by vineyards and fields, is a magical place and deservedly popular with backpackers.

Once a sleepy farming village named Avcılar, Göreme grew explosively during the 1980s as Turkey's tourism boom swept over it. Nowadays it's chock-a-block with pensions, camping grounds, restaurants and tour agencies. It's the prime place for budget travellers because the beds and meals are cheap and good and the sights are within walking distance. The Göreme Open-Air Museum is just 1.5 km to the south-east.

Life in Göreme is an odd mixture of the modern and the ultra-conservative, with veiled women in the traditional baggy *salvar* trousers rubbing shoulders with scantily-clad tourists throughout the summer. Not altogether surprisingly this mixture doesn't always work and in recent years there have been a couple of incidents, one of them serious, in the valleys. Sad though it is to say it, women should probably think carefully about walking in them alone, even in daylight.

Orientation & Information

Buses and minibuses drop you off at an eyesore of an otogar-cum-shopping mall with an office detailing all the local accommodation and several travel agencies where you can change money. Immediately in front of the otogar is the main Nevşehir to Avanos road, with a cluster of eating places. Beside and behind the otogar dry canal beds cut through the village, with pension options leading off on either side.

Göreme's postal code is 50180.

Things to See

Göreme village is dominated by a single cone into which a **columned rock temple**

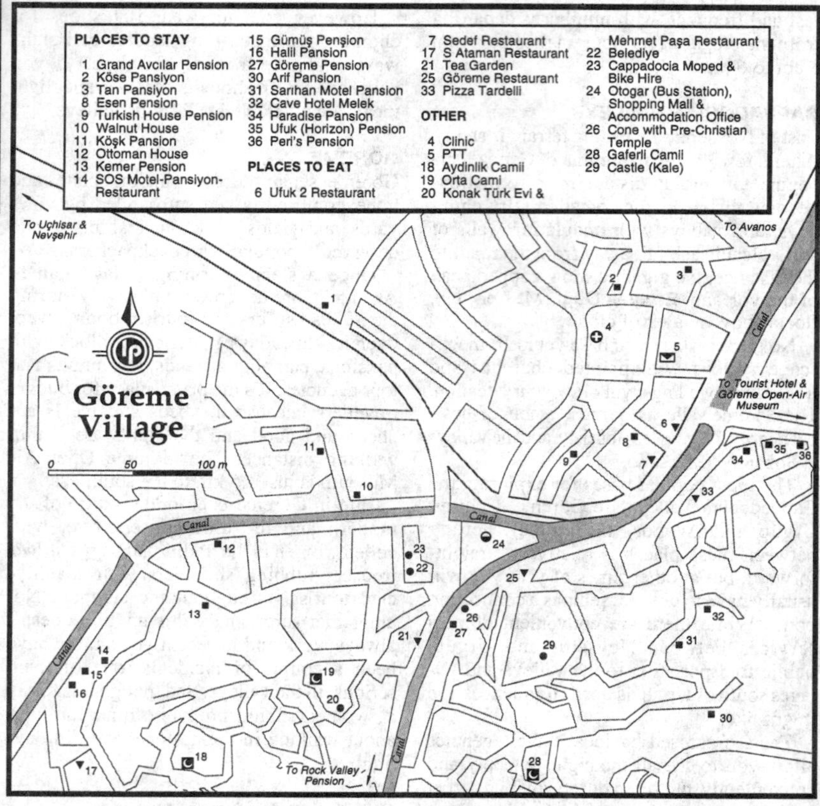

or grave was cut in pre-Christian times. Although the bottoms of the columns have fallen away, this is still a striking landmark.

The marvellous stone **Konak Türk Evi** (Turkish Mansion House, 1826), hidden in the maze of cobbled streets to the east of the village, has two beautifully decorated rooms: the Selamlık (men's room) and Haremlik (women's room). The frescoes on the walls were apparently created by the artist responsible for the paintings in the dining room of İstanbul's Topkapı Palace. It was once owned by the Ottoman Mehmet Paşa. Plans exist to turn the Konak Türk Evi into an Ottoman Museum, with admission fees going towards conservation of other village buildings. In the meantime the house serves as Göreme's most distinctive restaurant (see below).

Göreme Valley

Of all the Cappadocian valleys, Göreme's is the most famous, and rightly so. The entrance to the **Göreme Açık Hava Müzesi** (Göreme Open-Air Museum) is just one km uphill from the centre of the village, past the modern Tourist Hotel. The site is open from 8.30 am to 5.30 pm (4.30 pm in winter) and admission costs US$5 (students US$2). Parking for cars costs US$1; for motorcycles and mopeds it's about US$0.40. Try and get to the valley early in the morning in summer and space yourself between tour groups; when lots of people crowd into one of these little churches they block the doorway, which is often the only source of light.

It's easy to spend most of the day walking the paths here, climbing stairways or passing through tunnels to reach the various monastery churches with their wonderful, primitive 11th and 12th-century **frescoes**. In between churches, the utter improbability of the landscape floods over you: the lovely, soft textures in the rock, the fairytale cave dwellings, the spare vegetation growing vigorously from the stark but mineral-rich soil.

Walking into the valley from the entrance, you come first to the **Rahibeler Manastırı**, or Nun's Convent, a large plain room with steps up to a smaller domed chapel with frescoes. Across the way is the similar Monk's Monastery. From this point you can follow a loop path around the valley in either direction. Here are the main sights you come to if you walk clockwise, although the path also winds past various vistas and unmarked churches.

The **Çarıklı Kilise**, or Sandal Church, is named for the footprints marked in the floor opposite the doorway. One of the best frescoes shows Judas' betrayal (in the arch over the door to the left). Near the Sandal Church a small unmarked chapel has a fresco of a man on horseback – St George, no doubt.

The **Karanlık Kilise**, or Dark Church, among the most famous and fresco-filled, has only just been reopened after extensive restoration. The church took its name from its former condition when it had very few windows. The lack of light preserved the vivid colour of the frescoes which, among others, include scenes of Christ as Pantocrator, Christ on the cross and his betrayal by Judas. Beneath the Dark Church is a **refectory** with tables and benches cut right from the rock. Another smaller nameless church here retains a rock-cut iconostasis.

Göreme's Karanlık Kilise (Dark Church) contains well-preserved frescoes of Christ as Pantocrator, Christ on the cross and Judas' betrayal of Christ. The preservation of the frescoes is attributed to the lack of light in the church.

The **Yılanlı Kilise**, or Snake Church, has frescoes on part of the vault. On the left wall, St George and St Theodore attack the dragon yet again. Look out, too, for paintings of Constantine the Great and his mother Helena holding the True Cross.

The **Barbara Kilise**, or Church of St Barbara, has such plain decoration that it has sometimes been attributed to the iconoclastic period (725-842) when images were outlawed. However, it is unlikely that any of the churches here are as old as that. Instead, it is likely that simple designs of crosses and geometric motifs were drawn by the resident monks until more elaborate frescoes could be painted over them. There are a few fairly worn frescoes of the Virgin Mary and St Barbara as well. On the right three more chapels have carved crosses in the apse and primitive line drawings.

The **Elmalı Kilise**, or Apple Church, has a stunning display of frescoes. There are eight small domes and one large one, and lots of well-preserved paintings. Where's the apple? Some say the Angel Gabriel, above the central nave, is holding it. At the time of writing, a crack in the wall may cause the church to be closed for a time.

St Basil, the last church on the loop, has rather disappointing frescoes.

Outside the enclosure and back down the hill towards Göreme is the **Tokalı Kilise**, or Buckle Church, among the biggest and finest of the Göreme churches, with frescoes telling the stories of Christ's miracles. Don't miss the chapel downstairs. If a guardian is not on duty and the gate to the church is locked, ask someone to open it and turn on the lights (*ışıklar*, uh-shuk-LAHR).

Farther down the hill and along the road to Göreme are many less impressive but also less visited churches. Signs point the way to the **Nazar Kilise** (Church of the Evil Eye) and the **Saklı Kilise** (Hidden Church), which are worth seeing.

Organised Tours

Competition for tour groups is fierce but not

A Future for Göreme?

Given Cappadocia's astounding landscape, it's hardly surprising that it's now one of Turkey's top tourist honeypots, attracting an estimated one million visitors in 1995 alone. Many of those visitors were passing through on whistlestop coach tours, but a fair proportion chose to stay, especially in the hotels and pensions of the Avanos-Ürgüp-Göreme triangle.

All well and good, one might think, and certainly there are plenty of locals who have done very nicely out of tourism and would be reluctant to see any reduction in visitor numbers.

Unfortunately, the Cappadocian landscape is a fragile one, its beauty small-scale and easily damaged by thoughtless development...of which there are only too many instances. No one arriving at Göreme bus station, for example, could be anything but shocked that such an eyesore could have been dumped there. Nor do they have to walk far to discover hotels and pensions, the crude non-design of which seems to stick two fingers up at the very scenery they are supposed to celebrate.

The insults to the landscape are many: four and more-storey hotels; village outskirts defaced with rusting signboards; valley rims lined with stalls selling nutcrackers in the shape of a woman's body; road-widening projects that can only drag in yet more coaches; the list goes on.

It's not just tourism that is leading to the degradation of Cappadocia. Until comparatively recently many of the cones, caves and rock-cut houses were still lived in by villagers. Over the centuries repeated carving coupled with natural erosion has weakened some of the structures and the Disaster Relief Directorate has now declared many of these dwellings unsafe. Many villagers would, in any case, prefer to live in more 'modern' homes, and so slowly the old buildings are being left to collapse in favour of characterless blocks better suited to towns.

In theory, people need planning permission before they can tear down old houses or build new ones. However, in the past the law appears to have been better observed in the breach than in the observance. There are signs that things may be tightening up: in 1995 one pension-owner was supposedly awaiting jail for painting over a fresco 'because tourists like clean white walls'; while a notorious eyesore hotel on the Ürgüp-Nevşehir road was said to be facing closure.

Time may already have run out for Avanos, Ürgüp and Uçhisar but enough still remains of Göreme's charm to make it worth fighting for.

What can you do? Well, when choosing a place to stay you could take into account its impact on the environment (and that includes those signs on the outskirts). You could make it plain that you would be prepared to put conserving the landscape above immediate thoughts of saving money on your trip. You could show in your dress and behaviour that you care about the local culture and way of life.

Nico Leyssen at the Melek Hotel is trying to set up a 'Save Göreme Campaign'. Talk to him or any one of the many locals who fear that if things continue the way they have been their lovely village will soon be barely distinguishable from the outskirts of Nevşehir. ■

perhaps as overwhelming as in Ürgüp. Several readers have recommended Turtle Tours (☎ (384) 271 2388) across the road from the bus station. Hiro Tour (☎ (384) 271 2542), actually in the bus station, is also good.

At the beginning and end of the season the range of tours thins out, but most days someone is going to Ihlara and the underground cities. At the height of the season there will also be trips to Soğanlı and Mustafapaşa. Expect to pay around US$22 for a day tour by minibus inclusive of lunch. To save arguments later, check whether any visits to carpet shops or onyx factories appear on the itinerary. Most of the pensions either operate their own tours or work with one of the travel agencies.

Rainbow Ranch (☎ (384) 271 2413), uphill on the way to the Cave Hotel Melek, rents out horses for US$13 for two hours.

The most luxurious way to see the valleys must be on a sunrise hot-air balloon ride, organised out of the Kapadokya Lodge (☎ (384) 213 9945, fax 213 5092). The balloon company picks you up from your hotel to join the flight and returns you again afterwards. Flights last roughly 1¼ hours, but the price is a pretty horrifying US$250. Probably because it's so pricey it's by no means certain that the balloons will continue to fly.

Places to Stay

These days Göreme has 60-plus pensions whose owners have formed a co-operative with an office in Göreme bus station. Head straight there and you'll be guided to the pension of your choice without hassle or deception. The co-operative agrees prices at the start of the season so wherever you go you should get quoted the same rates: US$3.50 for a dorm bed, US$4.50 for a bed in a waterless room and US$7 for private facilities. A very few places charge more than this. Many pensions also have areas where you can camp for even less money.

Many people want the romance of staying in a tufa cone but few of these have private bathrooms. Rooms cut into the volcanic tufa are also a bit claustrophobic, although they're far cooler than rooms in modern buildings. Some of the pensions are cut into the rock-face, so you can get a feel for cave-living in more spacious surroundings.

If you're coming to Göreme in May or October, make sure you pack some warm clothes since it gets very cold at night and most pension owners will delay putting the heating on for as long as possible.

Places to Stay – bottom end

Backpackers have always been keen on *Köse Pansiyon* (☎ (384) 271 2294), up a side turning near the PTT. It's run by Mehmet and Dawn Köse and has an eight-bed dorm with mattresses on the floor as well as comfortable bedrooms with balconies and showers. Dinners in the evening cost US$4.50 and there's always one vegetarian and one meat option. Dawn runs a book swap scheme and keeps a visitor's book filled with travel tips rather than adulatory comments. If you're around Cappadocia at Christmas and are happy to muck in with preparations, she also organises Christmas dinner with all the trimmings.

Close to the Köse, the *Tan Pansiyon* (☎ (384) 271 2445), operated by Göreme's assistant mayor, offers clean doubles with shower in a modern building. Guests can use the kitchen facilities and there's a 'servis' car to pick up anyone weighed down with baggage.

Another place very popular with backpackers is Mustafa Yelkalan's *Rock Valley Pension* (☎ (384) 271 2153), well up the valley from the village centre – follow the bed of the dry canal to find it. As well as the standard double rooms, there's a four-bed dorm in a stone-vaulted room, a laundry service and a restaurant here.

On the road leading to the Göreme Open-Air Museum you'll find the *Paradise Pansion* (☎ (384) 271 2248) and the *Ufuk (Horizon) Pension* (☎ (384) 271 2157), both of them recommended by readers of this guide. *Peri's Pension* (☎ (384) 271 2136) has also received good reports. Rooms in fairy chimneys stand on one side of a pretty flower-filled courtyard and there's also an inviting bar in a chimney. Meals here are thoroughly enjoyable too.

For panoramic views of the valley it would be hard to beat the *Arif Pansion* (☎ 384) 271 2361), high up on the south-east side of town with several rock-cut rooms. Just below it the similarly quiet and comfortable *Sarıhan Motel Pansion* (☎ (384) 271 2216) also has good views of the town and rock-cut rooms. It boasts central heating as well, useful when the nights grow nippy towards the end of the season.

To the south-west the *Kelebek Pension* (☎ (384) 271 2531) has more spectacular views from its terrace. Unusually it also has a room in a cave chapel with a fresco cross on the ceiling. There's a nice cave bar with a rock fireplace and sedir seating. The five-bed dorm is nicely decked out with kilims. Some readers have not found this place as welcoming as they had hoped, though.

Close by is the *SOS Motel* (☎ (384) 271 2134), with some rooms carved from the rock. Guests can use the kitchen to cook meals which can then be eaten on a terrace with yet more panoramic views. Halfway back down to the valley floor is the *Kemer Pension* (☎ (384) 271 2013), another homy, family-run place with rock-cut rooms and a terrace.

On the valley floor below the SOS is the simple *Halil Pansion* (☎ (384) 271 2030), with more rooms carved right from the rock. Almost next door is the similar *Gümüş* (☎ (384) 271 2438), with a pretty garden and a small rock-cut bar.

Facing the SOS on the opposite side of the dry canal bed is the modern *Köşk Pansion* (☎ (384) 271 2233) in a quiet position well away from the bars. Some of the bedrooms boast spectacular cone views, as does the terrace. Guests can use the cooking facilities.

Heading back to the centre from the Köşk you'll come to the brand-new *Walnut House* (☎ (384) 271 2235), with six comfortable rooms designed with ceiling vaults to emulate the local architecture. There's a cosy, kilim-filled lobby too.

On the road heading to Uçhisar the *Grand Avcılar Pension* (☎ (384) 271 2301) is officially Göreme's youth hostel. However, it's in a pretty uninspiring building and charges the same as the other pensions so there's not much to gain by staying here.

Camping Several readers have recommended *Dilek Camping*, 50m along the road to Göreme Open-Air Museum. The facilities are clean, the staff friendly, and there's a swimming pool to relax in after a hot hike-filled day. The price for a tent and two people is US$4. *Berlin Camping* beside it is similar.

Places to Stay – middle

For more comforts at marginal extra cost, try the *Cave Hotel Melek* (☎ & fax (384) 271 2463), 150m uphill from the main street. You enter a small multi-level courtyard, then a village-style lounge with low seats and a fireplace adjoining the dining room. Guest rooms, in the buildings or carved into the tufa, cost US$10 a waterless double and US$16 a double with private shower, breakfast included.

Just past the Indigo carpet shop and owned by the same people, Ömer Tosun and Ruth Lockwood, is the new, and somewhat controversial, *Ottoman House* (☎ (384) 271 2616) which boasts luxury at affordable prices: US$9 a head without breakfast. Marble steps lead off a comfortable lobby to pleasant modern rooms with pretty quilts and photographs of Cappadocia on the walls. In the basement both the restaurant and the Harem Bar are densely decorated with carpets, kilims, old costumes and other handicrafts. Set dinners here cost US$7 a head. The roof terrace offers fine views of the valley...although at the cost of spoiling the view from some of the pensions behind!

Places to Stay – top end

At the end of the road running past the Ottoman House is the *S Ataman Hotel* (☎ (384) 271 2310, fax 271 2313) created out of a 200-year-old stone building. All the 13 rooms here are beautifully and individually decorated with carpets and handicrafts but boast all the mod cons (TV, fridge, hair-drier etc) as well. There's a basement disco and bar and a restaurant with a good reputation (see below). Half-board costs US$70/100 a single/double. By the time you read this, 35 new rooms should have opened on the far side of the existing ones. They will no doubt continue the high standards of the old ones, although their external design has upset some of the locals.

On the road to the Göreme Open-Air Museum, just past the Peri Pension, is the three-star *Turist Hotel* (☎ (384) 271 2430, fax 271 2011), a modern building which does at least keep its head down. Rooms here are comfortable if not particularly distinguished and cost US$35/50/60 a single/double/triple.

Places to Eat

Most Göreme pensions provide good, cheap meals. The town's eateries also generally serve wine and beer.

The *Sedef Restaurant*, on the main Ürgüp-Avanos road, offers good, reasonably-priced meals and cheerful service. A few steps farther along, moving away from the centre, the *Ufuk 2 Restaurant* even attracts the locals, always a good sign.

Immediately behind the otogar is the *Göreme Restaurant*, which is decorated with kilims and carpets and has some tables at floor level. Some nights there's live music too. You must take your shoes off and leave them by the door. Unfortunately when I visited the food was only so-so and the service nothing to write home about.

Göreme's most distinguished eatery is the *Mehmet Paşa Restaurant* (☎ & fax (384) 271 2463) in the Konak Türk Evi, with an open-air terrace, several charming dining rooms and a bar. The menu lists a mixture of Turkish, Ottoman and continental specialities. Expect to spend from US$8 to US$15 for a full meal. Unfortunately, Nico Leyssen who restored this place has had endless problems with the authorities and as a result the restaurant is not always open. To find it, follow the signs uphill opposite the big cone with the columns cut into it in the village centre.

The *S Ataman Restaurant* (☎ (384) 271 2310, fax 271 2313), up the valley behind the village, is clearly aimed at the bus-tour clientele who arrive frequently and abundantly, but provides good food and service in pleasant surroundings. The rock-hewn dining rooms are decorated with Turkish crafts. A full meal with drinks will probably cost from US$6 to US$10 per person.

Getting There & Away

Göreme's otogar may be ugly but at least it's relatively hassle-free. Minibuses leave here every half-hour in summer for Nevşehir where you can connect with services all round the country.

From Göreme itself there are frequent daily services to Ankara (US$8) and Kayseri (US$2.50). There are also night buses to İstanbul (US$14), Marmaris (US$18), Kuşadası (US$17) and Bodrum (US$18).

A warning is needed about so-called direct bus services to Göreme. Several readers have complained that they bought what they thought were direct tickets to Göreme, only to find themselves dumped in Nevşehir in the early hours. Even normally reputable companies have been known to do this. Unless you book with the Göreme or Nevtur bus companies, it might be best to assume you're going to have to change in Nevşehir.

Getting Around

There are several places to hire mountain bikes, mopeds and motorcycles, usually for around US$6 a day for a bike and US$13 for a scooter. Since Göreme doesn't have any petrol stations and the rental companies will hike fuel prices, fill up the tank in Nevşehir before returning the bike. You must leave your passport as a security deposit.

ÇAVUŞİN & ZELVE

From Göreme, the Avanos road leads north four km to Çavuşin, with its **Church of John the Baptist** near the top of the cliff which rises behind the village. A half-km north of the village, along the road, is the **Çavuşin Church** (look for the iron stairway).

A side road from Çavuşin heads up another valley five km to Zelve, which is almost as rich in churches and strange panoramas as Göreme, but much less well organised. Halfway along the road are groupings of curious 'three-headed' fairy chimneys near a row of souvenir stalls. If you're walking from Göreme, a footpath starts from Çavuşin and saves you a few km to the road junction, but it is more difficult walking on the path than on the road; take your pick.

Zelve was a monastic retreat. The valleys here don't have as many impressive painted churches, though you should see the few marked by signs.

The **Balıklı Kilise**, or Fish Church, has fish figuring in one of the primitive paintings, and the more impressive **Üzümlü Kilise** (Grape Church) has obvious bunches of grapes. Look also for the **Değirmen** (mill). Unfortunately, erosion continues to destroy the structures in the valley, and some parts may be closed because of the danger of collapse. There are also some sections included in tours which involve walking in pitch dark and scrambling down a frightening ladder. Take a torch/flashlight and be prepared.

Zelve's opening hours are from 8.30 am to 5.30 pm (4.30 pm in winter) and admission costs US$2. There are restaurants and tea gardens just outside.

VALLEY OF THE FAIRY CHIMNEYS

From Zelve, go 400m back down the access road and turn right on a paved road marked for Ürgüp. After two km you'll come to the village of **Aktepe** (Yeni Zelve), where you'll find the *Yörem Restaurant* with simple Turkish food at simple prices. Bear right, follow the Ürgüp road further uphill and, after less than two km, you'll find yourself in the Valley of the Fairy Chimneys (Peribacalar Vadisi).

Though many Cappadocian valleys boast collections of strange volcanic cones, these are the best-formed and most thickly clustered. Most of the rosy rock cones are topped by flattish, darker stones of harder rock. These dark cap-stones sheltered the cones from the rains which eroded all the surrounding rock, a process known to geologists as differential erosion.

If you continue to the top of the ridge, you will find yourself on the Avanos-Ürgüp road, with Avanos to the left, Ürgüp to the right.

UÇHİSAR

Uçhisar, seven km east of Nevşehir and four km south-west of Göreme, is dominated by the Kale, a tall rock outcrop riddled with tunnels and windows, and visible for miles around. Now a tourist attraction (open from 8 am to sunset for US$1), it provides panoramic views of the Cappadocian valleys and countryside. There's also an exhibition of photographs of Cappadocia taken by local photographer İrfan Ölmez whose images of Cappadocia in the snow adorn local postcard-stands.

There's less to see and do in Uçhisar than in Göreme or Ürgüp, but that also means there are fewer tourists except in the immediate vicinity of the Kale. There's a pleasant walk to Göreme along the signposted **Dovecote Valley** (Güvercinlik Vadisi) where the rockface is riddled with holes cut to attract nesting pigeons and their valuable fertiliser-providing droppings.

Places to Stay & Eat

Uçhisar has its own collection of pensions, hotels and restaurants, many especially popular with French tourists. In general if you want to stay here you have two choices: head east from the main square for modern places overlooking the Pigeon Valley, or west for places cut into the rock and cones.

Heading east, right by the main square on the edge of Güvercinlik Vadisi is the *Pension Méditerranée* (☎ (384) 219 2210), fairly fancy but with fabulous views, a nice roof restaurant and beds for US$13 including breakfast. The nearby *Villa Motel Pansion* (☎ (384) 219 2089), beside the PTT, is a pleasant enough building but lacks views. So does the friendly *Erciyes Pension* (☎ (384) 219 2090) which makes up for it with a lovely garden full of apple and walnut trees. Beds in clean rooms here cost US$7.

Beyond these pensions is the much

swisher *Kaya Otel* (☎ (384) 219 2007), a Club Med hotel carved into the volcanic tufa and with fabulous views. Even if you don't stay here you can use the magnificently sited outdoor swimming pool for US$3. The Kaya closes from October to March. Its *Bindallı Restaurant* (☎ (384) 219 2690) is Uçhisar's best, offering a magnificent lunch buffet for US$7. Beyond the Kaya Otel is the *Başaran Pension* (☎ (384) 219 2222) which advertises its 'vue superbe sur la vallée des pigeons'. Clean simple rooms cost US$13 a double including breakfast.

Heading west from the main square the road turns downhill through the old village of Uçhisar. Here you'll find *La Maison du Rêve* (☎ (384) 212 2199), with three storeys of rock-cut rooms, each with a sweeping terrace. The *Buket Pansiyon* (☎ (384) 219 2490) has several very nice cave rooms with interesting features and a cave dining room where guests eat together in the evening. Beds here cost US$7 a head. You can also organise a donkey excursion, with a picnic thrown in, for US$22.

Le Jardin des 1001 Nuits (☎ (384) 219 2293) has been created out of a cluster of cones so that all the rooms are different and there are all sorts of nooks and crannies to sit and soak up the glorious views. Beds vary in price, with the cheapest costing US$9 and the most expensive US$22. Nearby is the *Kaya Pension* (☎ (384) 219 2441), with a lovely plant and kilim-filled lobby and a big terrace. Readers have liked this place where beds cost US$9 including breakfast.

Getting There & Away

There are regular Uçhisar Belediyesi buses from Nevşehir, or you can take the half-hourly Nevşehir bus from Göreme and get out at the road junction for Uçhisar.

ORTAHİSAR

The village of Ortahisar, about three km south-east of the Göreme Valley, is near the intersection of the Nevşehir to Ürgüp and Göreme roads. A Cappadocian farming village at heart, Ortahisar's main claim to fame is its **kale**, an 18-metre-high rock used as a fortress in Byzantine times and a great place to come for sunset panoramas. From Ortahisar you can also hike to various lesser churches in the surrounding countryside, especially in the Pancarlık Valley.

Ortahisar's postal code is 50650.

Places to Stay

There are limited accommodation choices in the village centre, 1.5 km from the main road intersection. Try the basic *Gümüş* (☎ (384) 343 3123) on the street by the PTT which charges US$6/11 a single/double, or the nearby, and even more basic, *Dönmez*.

Continue up the hill past the PTT and turn left for the *Hotel Burcu* (☎ (384) 343 3800, fax 384 3500), which has 49 motel-style rooms around a courtyard (soon to be a swimming pool). Rooms are comfortable, with immaculate bathrooms, but they're fairly pricey at US$20/33.

On the outskirts of town heading towards Nevşehir is the modern *Hotel Yeni Yükseller* (☎ (384) 343 3450, fax 343 3451). It charges US$15 a head, but for this you get a swimming pool, comfy bath-equipped room, and a good restaurant.

Also out on the outskirts, right at the Göreme turn off on the Ürgüp-Nevşehir road, is the four-star, 252-room *Hotel Lapis Inn* (☎ (384) 343 3470, fax 343 3480), an eyesore built without planning permission on a scale completely out of keeping with its setting. Although it's undoubtedly a comfortable place to stay, it is contributing to the visual degradation of the area and so is best avoided. You may not have the choice for much longer anyway. Rumour has it that it will have to be taken down again in the near future.

Getting There & Away

There are regular Ortahisar Belediyesi buses from Nevşehir otogar.

ÜRGÜP

Twenty-three km east of Nevşehir and seven km east of Göreme Valley is the town of Ürgüp (population 11,000, altitude 1060m), at the heart of the Cappadocian wonderland.

In recent years Ürgüp has grown enormously and at first sight it's easy to dismiss it as just another modern town. Look more closely, however, and you'll discover something of the older lifestyle still clinging on amid the cones and rock formations to the west.

Because of the volcanic soil, sufficient water and abundant sunshine, the town is surrounded by a rich landscape of grain fields, vineyards and clusters of beehives.

Orientation & Information

The otogar is just behind the main street, Kayseri Caddesi, which is sprinkled with antique shops, carpet shops and restaurants. To find the older part of town, go west along Kayseri Caddesi to the main square and then climb the hill heading north-west towards Göreme. On the left you'll see an arched building. Walk through it for a part of Ürgüp where many buildings are made of the local tawny limestone with a pronounced grain and some have fine carved stone doorways, lintels and corbels.

The unusually helpful and well informed Tourism Information Office (☎ (384) 341 4059) is at Kayseri Caddesi 37, down the hill from the main square behind a tea garden and open every day from 8 am to 6 pm (8 pm in summer). The town's uninspiring museum, open daily from 8 am to 5 pm, is right next door. Admission costs US$1.

Ürgüp has far too many travel agencies competing for too little business. Most of them are clustered round the otogar and several are staffed by seriously unpleasant young men. One that has been recommended for quality rather than cheapness is Argeus (☎ (384) 46688, fax 341 5207) in İstiklal Caddesi behind the hamam. Depending on what you want, they can help with bicycling, walking and riding holidays as well as with day tours.

Turkish Bath

Overlooking the main square is the Tarihi Şehir Hamamı, a historic building (1902) of uncertain provenance which looks as though it may once have been a small church. Today it is a thoroughly touristy hamam with touristy prices: US$6 for a bath. Men and women are admitted together, which never happens in traditional hamams.

Wine Festival

The abundant sunshine and volcanic soil of Cappadocia are excellent for viticulture, resulting in delicious sweet grapes. Several small local wineries have carried on the Ottoman Greek tradition of making wine from Cappadocia's grapes. Ürgüp puts on a wine festival and tasting during the first week in June, when you can sample the products of small wineries such as Turasan, Duyurgan Bağcılık and Yemenici, and the large quasi-governmental Tekel, during the festival at special events. Contact the Tourism Information Office for details.

Several wines are available anytime; try Turasan's Peribaca light red, Duyurgan's dry white Algan, the hearty red Cappadocia from Mustafapaşa, or Tekel's Ürgüp white and Çubuk red, both quite cheap. Tekel has a *satış yeri* (sales point) on Fabrika Caddesi across from the Ürgüp Oteli.

Places to Stay – bottom end

Ürgüp has many pensions in which you can get a bed in a clean but spartan room for about US$3 to US$5 per person. These cheap pensions and hotels are clustered west of the otogar along İstiklal Caddesi and east of it in the quarter called Sivritaş Mahallesi.

İstiklal Caddesi runs from behind the Turkish bath. Turn down a side street just past the Hotel Cappadoce for the delightful *Hotel Elvan* (☎ (384) 341 4191), Dutlu Cami Mahallesi, Barbaros Hayrettin Sokak 11, run by Ahmet and Fatma Bilir. Rooms are arranged around a small courtyard; some are carved from the stone, with vaulted ceilings and wall niches. All are well kept, with tidy tiled showers and plenty of hot water. There's a very attractive lounge with carpets and sedirs and a roof terrace with panoramic views. Prices are US$10/21/25 a single/double/triple; breakfast costs an extra US$2 per person.

Continue up the hill for the *Hotel Asia Minor* (☎ (384) 3414645, fax 341 4520),

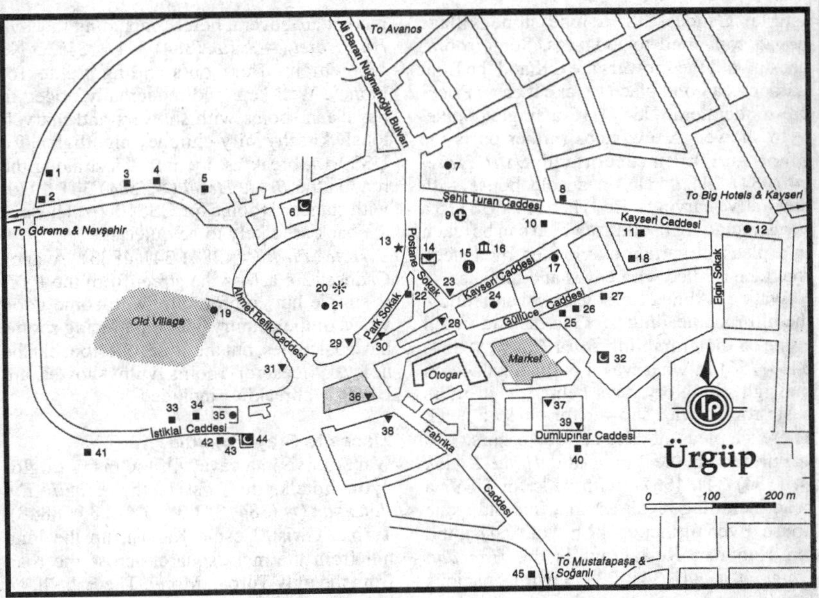

PLACES TO STAY

1 Esbelli Evi Pansiyon
2 Hotel Surban
3 Hanedan Hotel & Restaurant
4 Hotel Konak
5 Born Hotel
8 Göreme Şato Pansiyon
10 Büyük Almira Hotel
11 Hotel Anatolia
18 Eren Hotel
22 Hotel Park
25 Hotel Kuzey
26 Sarıhan Pansiyon
27 Merkez Hotel Pension
33 Hitit Hotel
34 Hotel Asia Minor
40 Yeni Hitit Hotel
41 Hotel Alfina
42 Hotel Elvan
45 Taşsaray Hotel

PLACES TO EAT

23 Tea Garden
28 Ürgüp Restaurant
29 Sofa Restaurant
30 Merkez Pastanesi
31 Han Çirağan Restaurant
36 Şömine Café & Restaurant
37 Cappadocia Restaurant
38 Uğrak Restaurant
39 Kent Restaurant & Kardeşler Pizza Restaurant

OTHER

6 Mosque
7 Altıkapılı Türbesi
9 Hospital
12 Bridge over Damsa Stream
13 Police
14 PTT
15 Tourism Information Office
16 Museum
17 Ürgüp Ilçesi Hükümet Konaği
19 Arch to Old Village
20 Temenni Hill Viewpoint
21 Kılıçarslan Türbesi
24 Belediye
32 Mosque
35 Tarihi Şehir Hamamı
43 Arğeus Tours
44 Mosque

İstiklal Caddesi 38, a nice stone village house converted to lodgings. Some rooms are tiny but the showers are OK and the front garden is a good place to take it easy. Prices are moderate at US$11/16 a single/double, with shower. A few steps further on is the plant and kilim-decorated *Hitit Hotel* (☎ (384) 341 4481), in an old house with decorative carvings. Beds here cost US$15 a head, including breakfast which can be taken in a pleasant garden overlooked by a steep rockface riddled with caves and tunnels.

Walk up Ahmet Refik Caddesi and follow the hill road heading for Göreme and you'll come to the crumbling *Born Hotel* (☎ 384) 341 4756) in what was a pasha's palace on the right. Its glory days behind it, it offers basic rooms with shower for US$5 a head. There's a pleasant cave bar downstairs.

Further up the hill is the *Hotel Konak* (☎ (384) 341 4667), with beds for US$7 a head including breakfast in a fine old stone house. Even further up the hill tucked behind the Hanedan Restaurant is the *Hanedan Hotel* (☎ (384) 341 2317) with spacious rooms, some of them rock-cut, for the same US$7 a head. Either of these hotels would be a good choice.

Güllüce Sokak, the street south of Kayseri Caddesi, has many of the real cheapies, charging US$5/10 for a waterless single/double room. Coming from the centre, you first reach the *Hotel Kuzey* (☎ (384) 341 4874), then the *Sarıhan Pansiyon* (☎ (384) 341 2264) and then the *Merkez Hotel Pension* (☎ (384) 341 2746).

The *Hotel Anatolia* (☎ (384) 341 4487), on Kayseri Caddesi one block north of the Merkez Hotel Pension, is a similarly priced place that's a favourite with backpackers despite the road noise.

If they're open, the *Göreme Pansiyon* and *Hotel Şato* (☎ (384) 341 4146) are two halves of the same building just off Kayseri Caddesi. A homy, quiet place decorated with lots of carpets and kilims, its rooms are fairly cool in summer. They cost US$12/18 a single/double, but the owner is often ready to agree to a lower rate.

On Dumlupınar Caddesi south of the market are several hotels, including the *Yeni Hitit Hotel* (☎ & fax (384) 341 3131), at No 47, which offers outstanding value for money. Well-kept and moderately priced, it has clean rooms with showers and marvellously kitschy fairy-chimney nightlights, for US$9/14, breakfast included. Just along the road is the *Belde Hotel* (☎ (384) 341 4970) with standard rooms for US$10/16. Those at the back are likely to be quietest.

Hotel Park (☎ (384) 341 4883), Avanos Caddesi 20, across the street from the PTT, is simple but comfortable, with some good views of the countryside. East-facing rooms have balconies, but the street out front can be noisy. Prices for rooms with shower are US$9/14, breakfast included.

Places to Stay – middle

Want to live in a cave? Of the many troglodytic hotels, the best is the *Esbelli Evi Pansiyon* (☎ (384) 341 3395, fax 341 8848), Turban Girişi, Çeşme Karşısı, up the long hill from the main square, across the road from the ugly Turban Motel. The Esbelli, an old village house cut into the rock, has been lovingly restored and now boasts rooms with modern baths, a sun deck-terrace, two lounges, and modern kitchen and laundry facilities at your disposal. Several of the rooms, including the one for honeymooners, have fine iron bedsteads. One room is in what was once a rock-cut kitchen complete with soaring chimney. Another would be ideal for families, with a big double bed, a single and a cot. Rates are US$45/55 a single/double, excellent breakfast included.

The *Hotel Alfina* (☎ (384) 341 4822, fax 341 2424), on İstiklal Caddesi, a 10-minute walk back up the hill from the otogar, also has 32 comfortable rooms hewn from the volcanic rock (the cutter's tool marks are still visible). There's a pleasant terrace restaurant so you can escape from your cave-person existence now and then. The price, at US$29/41, is hardly prehistoric, but how many times do you get the chance to live in a cave? This place is not for claustrophobes, though, and some find the external architecture unsympathetic.

Hotel Surban (☎ (384) 341 4603, fax 341 2025), Yunak Mahallesi, PO Box 55, is uphill on the road towards Nevşehir near the Hanedan Restaurant. New and comfortable, it offers value for money: good rooms with bath for US$14/22, breakfast in a rock-cut basement thrown in.

At İmran Mahallesi, Güllüce Sokak 1, is the new three-storey *Eren Hotel* (☎ (384) 341 3115) which has clean rooms with small balconies and quilts on the beds for US$17/29, breakfast included. Rooms at the back are likely to be quietest.

The comfortable, tawny sandstone *Taşsaray Hotel* (☎ (384) 341 2344), Mustafapaşa Caddesi 10, is 400m from the otogar. Prices for rooms with bath and balcony are moderate at $42 a double with shower, breakfast included.

Places to Stay – top end

Right in town on Kayseri Caddesi just past the museum is the 101-room four-star *Büyük Almira Hotel* (☎ 384) 341 8990, fax 341 8999) with a swimming pool, shop, restaurant and bar. Comfortable, modern, air-con rooms with TVs and fridges cost US$50/75 a single/double.

Ürgüp's other fancy hotels are one to two km out of town along Kayseri Caddesi. Best of the lot is the four-star, 230-room *Perissia Hotel* (☎ (384) 341 2930, fax 341 2524), PO Box 68. The hotel's square, box-like buildings set amid gardens echo the local architecture, but provide all the luxuries, including swimming pools, restaurants, bars, and a disco. Rooms cost US$67/90/125 a single/double/triple, breakfast included.

Places to Eat – bottom end

An Ürgüp speciality is kiremit kebap, a large patty of minced lamb or chicken baked on a clay tile. The tile draws off some of the grease and keeps the meat hot after it's served. Other strange ways of cooking lamb, such as saç kavurma (sizzling bits of lamb on a steel parabola like an inverted wok) are also popular here.

In a converted han in the main square is the *Sofa Restaurant* with a fine selection of mezes and main courses in an atmospheric setting – you eat looking up at a cone riddled with more holes than a Swiss cheese. The *Cappadocia Restaurant*, with a few outdoor tables and many more indoor, fairly attentive service and decent three-course meals for around US$4 or US$5, is in the street running up beside the market to Dumlupınar Caddesi.

For cheaper meals continue to Dumlupınar Caddesi. The *Kardeşler Pizza Restaurant* specialises in good cheap pide (for as low as US$0.90) and kebaps. A vegetarian kebap costs US$4. The drearier *Kent Restaurant*, more or less across the street from the Yeni Hitit Hotel, has saç kavurma and kiremit kebap for less than US$2. Both these restaurants serve breakfast.

On Fabrika Caddesi, near the entrance to the otogar, is the *Uğrak Restaurant*, with a few outdoor tables on the busy street corner and full meals for US$3.

For pastries and sweets, the *Merkez Pastanesi* on the main square is the best in town. A large glass of tea and a portion of cake cost around US$1.

Places to Eat – middle

The town's most prominent place is the *Şömine Cafe & Restaurant*. Right on the main square, its high terrace provides outdoor tables to supplement those inside. Ürgüp-style kebaps baked on tiles are a speciality, but several readers have found them less than tasty. Grilled meats cost from US$2 to US$4, full meals with drinks from US$8 to US$12.

The *Han Çirağan Restaurant* is at the far end of the main square in an old stone house behind a vine-covered garden. In summer you can dine outside in a pleasant small courtyard. The menu offers a welcome change from the standard kebaps and ready foods, listing some regional dishes. Main courses cost around US$4, a bottle of wine from US$4 to US$5.50.

Hungry for fish? That's the speciality at the *Hanedan Restaurant*, uphill from the centre on the road to Nevşehir. Make sure to ask the price first though; full meals cost upwards of US$12 or so. This place is popular with groups so it might be as well to make a reservation (☎ (384) 341 4266).

Getting There & Away

Bus and minibus services are frequent and convenient in high summer with less frequent services in winter. Details of some daily services follow:

Adana – 308 km, six hours, US$8; one bus
Ankara – 308 km, five hours, US$8; at least seven buses in summer
Antalya – 485 km, 11 hours, US$14; at least one bus in summer
İstanbul – 748 km, 11 hours, US$14; at least two buses
Fethiye – 780 km, 14 hours, US$18; at least one bus in summer
Kayseri – 80 km, 1½ hours, US$2; hourly minibuses from 7 am to 7 pm
Konya – 250 km, four hours, US$6; at least three buses in summer
Nevşehir – 23 km, 30 minutes, US$0.40; minibuses every half-hour
Pamukkale – 690 km, 11 hours, US$15; at least one bus in summer

Note that there's a Turkish Airlines bus to run people directly to Kayseri airport for US$4.

Getting Around

Minibuses run the tourist circuit hourly each day from June to September, departing from Ürgüp for the Göreme Valley, Göreme village, Zelve, Avanos etc. You can hop on and off anywhere around the loop, but each ride costs US$0.40.

The major international car companies – Avis, Europcar (National), Hertz and Interrent – all have franchisees with offices near Ürgüp's main square, within one block of the otogar. For more details on renting cars, see the introductory Getting Around chapter.

Agencies in town rent bicycles, mopeds and motorcycles at prices similar to those given in the Göreme section.

In summer it's usually fairly easy to hitchhike as well.

MUSTAFAPAŞA

Called Sinasos when it was an Ottoman Greek town before WWI, Mustafapaşa is today the relatively undiscovered gem of Cappadocia, a quiet village with lovely old stone-carved houses, several minor rock-cut churches and a growing selection of places to stay.

As you approach from Ürgüp (five km) you will reach a large central reservation with a non-functioning fountain. A shop here doubles up as a tourist office of sorts and there's a signboard indicating the whereabouts of the **rock-cut churches** in the vicinity. There's a 19th-century **medrese** with a fine carved portal (including stone columns that swivel) to the south-west. Follow the road round and you'll come to Cumhuriyet Meydanı, the centre of the village with the habitual bust of Atatürk and several tea shops.

Places to Stay & Eat

Mustafapaşa has a couple of cheapie pensions on the road leading to St. Nicholas' monastery. The *Atasoy Pension* (☎ (384) 353 5378) has simple shower-equipped rooms with beds for US$5, including breakfast. The *Monastery Pension* next door is similar.

To the east as you come into town from Ürgüp is the *Hotel Pacha* (☎ (384) 353 5331) in a restored Greek house with flower-filled courtyard and top-floor terrace with lovely views. Shower-equipped rooms here can accommodate two to four people and cost US$6 a head, including breakfast.

Another pleasant choice would be the *Hotel Cavit* (☎ (384) 353 5186), run by a retired army officer. For US$7 per person per day you get a family-style welcome and breakfast of fresh milk from the cow and home-made fruit preserves from the orchard. It's on the southern side of town as you head out to Soğanlı.

But Mustafapaşa's best hotel is undoubtedly the *Otel Sinasos* (☎ (384) 353 5009, fax 353 5435), to the west as you come into town from Ürgüp. Here bedrooms are in a modern extension to an old Greek house and come attractively decorated, with all mod cons. But the real gem is the *restaurant* in the old house itself, with its wonderful painted wooden ceilings painstakingly restored and a balcony overlooking a lovely garden. Rooms here cost US$16/32 a single/double, well worth a splurge.

Getting There & Away

Mustafapaşa Belediyesi buses leave Ürgüp for Mustafapaşa every hour. A brief stop in Mustafapaşa is also included in many day trips to Soğanlı.

SOĞANLI

This valley, about 35 km south of Ürgüp via Mustafapaşa and Güzelöz, is much less touristy than Göreme or Zelve. Indeed in recent years the number of visitors to Soğanlı has actually diminished, probably because it's on the road to nowhere. It's a beautiful and interesting place to explore, and unless your visit coincides with one of the day trips from Göreme you may well have it to yourself.

The valleys of **Aşağı Soğanlı** (Lower Onion Valley) and **Yukarı Soğanlı** (Upper Onion Valley) were, like Göreme and Zelve, largely monastic. Turn off the main road and proceed five km to the village, where signs point out the **Tokalı Kilise**, or Buckle Church, on the right, reached by a steep flight of worn steps, and the **Gök Kilise**, or Sky Church, to the left across the stream bed. Follow the signs, walk up the stream bed 50m, then go up on the left to the church. The Gök is a twin-nave church, with the two naves separated by columns, ending in apses. The double frieze of saints is badly worn.

At the point where the valleys divide, the villagers have posted a billboard map indicating the other churches by number. The ticket office is also here. The village square is to the left, backed by the *Cappadocia Restaurant*, toilets, a tea shop and a line of women selling knitted gloves and socks, and the dolls for which Soğanlı is supposedly famous. Just in front of the ticket office is the *Soğanlı Restaurant* with tables set under shady trees and good food at reasonable prices. At the moment there's nowhere to stay in the village itself.

Of the churches, one of the most interesting is No 4, the **Karabaş** (Black Head), in the right-hand valley and covered in paintings showing the life of Christ, with Gabriel and various saints. A pigeon in the fresco shows local influence. Pigeons were very important to the monks, who wooed them with dovecotes cut in the rock. The dovecote across from the Karabaş Kilise has white paint around its small window entrances to attract the birds; the sides of the entrance are smoothed so the birds cannot alight, but must enter. Inside, a grid of poles provides roosting space for hundreds of birds which dump manure by the kg onto the floor below. The monks gathered the manure, put it on the grapevines and got the sweetest grapes and the best wine for miles around. In the yard between the church and the dovecote is a refectory, with tandoor ovens in the ground (note the air-holes for the fires). The monks lived apart but dined communally.

Also in the right-hand valley, across the stream bed and high on the far hillside, are No 5, the **Kubbeli & Saklı** (Cupola & Hidden churches). The Kubbeli is interesting because of its unusual Eastern-style cupola. The Hidden Church is just that: hidden from view until you get close to it.

Farthest up the right-hand valley is No 6, the **Yılanlı** (Snake Church), its frescoes deliberately painted over with black paint, probably to protect them. You can still make out the serpent to the left as you enter.

The churches are open from 8.30 am to 5.30 pm and there's an admission fee of US$1.

Getting There & Away

It's not easy to get to Soğanlı by public transport. Buses run from Ürgüp to Mustafapaşa and no further, so you could try to hitch from there, or take a taxi. The easiest way to get there, of course, is to sign up for a day tour costing roughly US$22.

AVANOS

North of Göreme, on the banks of the river Kızılırmak, lies Avanos (AH-vah-nohs, population 12,000, altitude 910m), once called Venessa, another potential base for exploring the Cappadocian valleys. Like Ürgüp,

Avanos is coyer about revealing its charms than Göreme, but head up into the old village behind the central square and you'll find lovely old stone houses, some of them decorated with ancient motifs – an almost rural setting inside a small town. Be grateful too for what you're seeing because if it hadn't been for the sterling efforts of certain locals most of these buildings would have been ripped down in favour of a 'modern' holiday village in the 1970s.

Modern Avanos is famous for its pottery. The town's workshops still turn out pots, ashtrays, lamps, chess sets and other utensils and souvenirs moulded from the red clay of the Kızılırmak, or Red River, as they have been doing in many cases for several centuries. Most of these workshops welcome visitors who would like to find out about pottery or even try their hand at it.

If you're not staying overnight, Avanos is still a good place for lunch or a çay break. There are banks, a PTT, pensions, hotels, restaurants, pharmacies and other such necessities.

Orientation & Information

Most of the town is on the north bank of the river, with Atatürk Caddesi providing the main thoroughfare, but several pensions (and most of the ugly modern hotels) are to the south. The otogar is also south of the river, although many of the dolmuşes also stop outside the PTT to the north, across from the main square, distinguished by a large statue of a potter. There's a Tourism Information Office (☎ (384) 511 4360) in the otogar; the otogar turns into a marketplace on Friday.

Avanos' postal code is 50500.

Things to See

In the main square is a marvellous **monument**. Made entirely of red clay pottery, it shows an amazingly lifelike potter at work. Below it is a scene depicting a woman and a girl weaving a Turkish carpet – another traditional Avanos craft. On the left side is a bearded, shorts-clad, camera-touting tourist holding a bunch of grapes and laughing while standing on a huge pair of hands. At the back of the monument a woman sits on a donkey with a child peering out of a saddlebag. On the right side is a self-portrait of the monument's creator, H Ömer Taşkın, who finished the work in 1974.

Several of the **pottery workshops** welcome visitors and even sponsor pottery classes. To find them, go behind the pottery monument and turn right just after the Şanso-Panso restaurant. Along this street are several potteries, on the way to the Panorama Pension. Other potteries are scattered throughout the town; look for Chez Efe on Atatürk Caddesi near the Kirkit Pension.

The town's **hamam** in Orta Mahalle, west of the Sofa Hotel on the riverbank, was built at the end of the 1980s with tourists in mind. Named the Alaaddin Turkish Bath (☎ (384) 511 5036), it is a Disneyfied version of the real thing, using local sandstone and red tiles for the roof. A bath with all the works costs US$9. In summer this place is very popular with tour groups.

Yellow Caravanserai The Seljuk-era Sarı Han is signposted six km east of Avanos. It was restored in the late 1980s, and is now open as a museum from 9 am to 1 pm and 2 to 6 pm every day, for US$1. The elaborate Seljuk portal, with a small mosque above it, is, as usual, quite impressive. Inside, there's the standard layout with a large court where animals were loaded and unloaded, and a great hall where people and animals could escape the weather. If you climb to the top of the walls, try to ignore the liberal use of concrete in the restoration.

Özkonak Underground City North of Avanos is the village of Özkonak, beneath which is a small version of the underground cities to be seen at Kaymaklı and Derinkuyu, with the same wine reservoirs, air shafts, rolling stone doors, grindstones etc. It's not nearly so dramatic or impressive as the larger ones, but is much less crowded. The town's muezzin originally found it in his garden.

In the old days, things were very casual here and the muezzin would show you round himself. These days, however, you'll find the

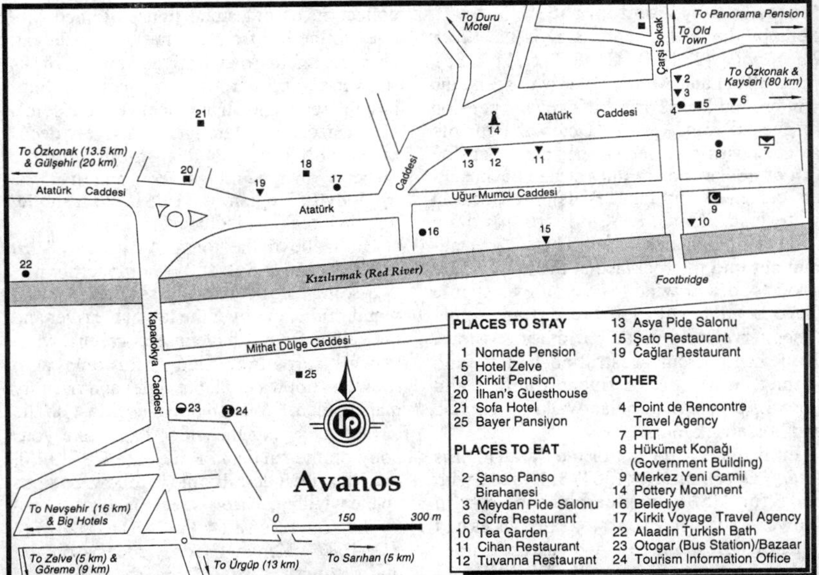

standard ticket booth, alongside a row of toilets and a couple of cafés and souvenir shops. The site is open from 8 am to 5.30 pm; admission costs US$1. Take a jumper or jacket and a torch (flashlight) if you have them. Some of the passages and tunnels from room to room require you to bend almost double.

The easiest way to get there is on one of the dolmuşes from Avanos to Özkonak (30 minutes, US$0.20). Özkonak is a straggley village without a clear centre so you'll need to watch out for the sign to the Yeraltı Şehri (underground city). It's on the left immediately opposite the Petrol Ofisi as you come in from the Kayseri road. From there it's about 500m to the car park.

Organised Tours

Avanos has several travel agencies offering excursions and tours to other parts of Cappadocia. Kirkit Voyages, run by the owners of the Kirkit Pension, can arrange walking, biking, rafting, canoeing and horse-riding as well as the more usual guided tours. To hire a horse for a day would cost about US$20; a mountain bike is around US$13. They can also arrange longer tours. Another company worth trying is Point de Rencontre, on the corner of the main square.

Special Events

Avanos is a handicrafts town and its citizens sponsor the annual Avanos Elsanatları Festivalı (Avanos Handicrafts Festival) for three days in late August.

Places to Stay

Avanos has a couple of excellent pensions and several perfectly serviceable ones, as well as one good central hotel and an ever-growing number of concrete monstrosities catering to the package holiday trade. At the cheaper end of the market places seem to open and close with frightening rapidity. The Tourism Information Office should have an up-to-date list.

Places to Stay – bottom end

Perhaps the best place to stay is the *Kirkit Pension* (☎ (384) 511 3148, fax 511 2135), run by Tovi and Ahmet Diler who spend the winter months in Paris, but open the pension to guests from April to October. Four old stone houses have been turned into a pension full of nooks and crannies where backpackers can meet and chat. Beds cost US$6 in waterless rooms, US$8 in rooms with shower, breakfast included. There's a restaurant cut into the rockface at the back where good food and wine (as you'd expect in a place popular with the French) are sometimes served up with ad hoc music sessions. Tovi, who is an Australian-Israeli, and Ahmet, who speaks fluent English and French, organise popular walking, bicycle and horseback tours.

Immediately in front of the Sofa Hotel is *İlhan's Guesthouse* (☎ (384) 511 4828), with beds for US$6 in pleasant rooms with showers. Some have old stone fireplaces and other features. There's a breakfast terrace with river views. İlhan speaks English.

Another low-price favourite is *Panorama Pension* (☎ (384) 511 1654), a five-minute walk (250m) uphill through the back streets of the old town, with impressive views from the terrace. There are 18 rooms sleeping from two to four persons; bed and breakfast costs from US$4 to US$8, depending upon the room and whether or not it has a private shower.

The *Nomade Pension* (☎ (384) 511 4832), on the left as you walk up into the old village, is another hardy perennial place to stay although the rooms are nothing to write home about.

Right on the edge of the otogar is the strange *Bayer* (☎ (384) 511 4287), originally built as an apartment building with shop (now the lobby) below and rooms above. If you arrive late or need to make an early start this could be handy. Otherwise there are better places.

Places to Stay – middle

The *Sofa Hotel* (☎ (384) 511 4489, fax 511 5186), Köprübaşı, Venessa Oteli Yanı, is a collection of old stone houses joined into one, up the hill from the traffic roundabout near the main road bridge. Several of its shower-equipped rooms are partially built into the rock, and all are nicely kept. There's also a sizeable restaurant, attractively decorated with kilims and cushions and the owner's own paintings. You can live the troglodytic life here for US$15/20 a single/double, breakfast included.

High above the town stands the *Duru Motel* (☎ (384) 511 4005), a modern white two-storey block with a grassy terrace and wonderful views over the town, the river and the valley. Rooms have insect screens, wall-to-wall carpeting, tiled bathrooms with showers (hot water all the time) and friendly management. You can have breakfast on the terrace, enjoying the view, then bake your body on the sundeck. Prices are US$13/20, breakfast included. To find it, follow the signs up the winding, narrow street to the top.

The *Hotel Zelve* (☎ (384) 511 4524, fax 511 4687), Kenan Evren Caddesi, on the main square across from the Hükümet Konağı (Sub-province Government House) is pleasant and modern, with kilims in the lobby and functional guest rooms with bath going for US$10/20 a single/double, buffet breakfast included.

Across the bridge on the road to Göreme are a number of three and four-star hotels, intended for the group trade but available to individual travellers as well. These include the four-star, 84-room *Hotel Altınyazı* (☎ (384) 511 2010), the four-star, 178-room *Hotel Yıltok* (☎ (384) 511 2313), and the three-star, 46-room *Hotel Palansaray* (☎ (384) 511 4044). The latest addition is the ugly four-star *Avrasya Otel* (☎ (384) 511 5181) which was yet to get into its stride at the time of writing. With all these hotels, you're likely to get a better deal booking through a tour operator.

Places to Eat

For simple meals, the *Cihan Restaurant* (jee-HAHN) on the main square is a popular ready-food and broiled-chicken place open for all three meals, and usually full. Lunch or dinner might cost US$3 or US$4. The *Sofra Restaurant*, Hükümet Konağı Karşısı, next to the Hotel Zelve and facing the government building, is similar.

The *Tuvanna* is slightly fancier and more expensive, with şiş kebap and small beefsteaks priced from US$3 to US$5, full meals from US$8 to US$12.

Şanso-Panso Birahanesi, on the right up the slope of the main square behind the pottery monument, serves Efes Pilsen beer and food and is the closest thing Avanos has to a taverna. Its speciality is güveç, beef mixed up with potatoes, tomatoes, garlic, paprika and cumin and baked in the oven (US$2.50). Also here is the *Meydan Pide Salonu*, to the left of the Point de Rencontre travel agency, serving cheap pide at outdoor tables. There's another good, cheap pide place, the *Tafana Pide Salonu*, Kenan Evren Caddesi 47, a block to the south, nearer to the river.

Further up Atatürk Caddesi, near Kirkit Voyage, is the *Çağlar Restaurant* which serves mantı for US$2 and has an especially pretty aile salonu.

Along the river, south of the main square, are the *Çalı Piknik Restaurant*, serving trout, and the *Şato Restaurant*, in a mock castle with food for around US$8 to US$10 per person, drinks included.

For dinner and entertainment, try the *Dragon Restaurant*, 1.5 km west of the Hotel Sofa along the Gülşehir road. Popular with tour groups, this cave-club provides food and drink, as well as Turkish folk and belly-dancing most summer evenings. Expect to spend a total of about US$20 for the entire evening.

For pastries, there's the *Aytemur Pastanesi*, near the Tuvanna, where one of the special banana rolls and a large glass of tea costs under US$1.

Getting There & Away

Avanos Belediyesi buses travel the route from Avanos via Çavuşin, Göreme and Uçhisar to Nevşehir every 30 minutes in summer from 6.45 am to 6.15 pm, for US$1. In winter there will still be services to Nevşehir and Ürgüp, if not to Göreme.

GÜLŞEHİR

Some 23 km west of Avanos is Gülşehir (population 8500). It has several unimpressive rock formations on the outskirts: **Karşı Kilise**, or St John Church; an unexcavated underground city; and **Açık Saray**, rock formations with a few insignificant churches. In the centre of the village stands the **Karavezir Mehmet Paşa Camii & Medrese** (1778), an Ottoman mosque and its college (now a library).

Gülşehir has two good hotels, one of them the three-star Swiss-run *Kepez Hotel* (☎ (384) 411 3163, fax 411 3639), the crenellated building on the flat-top hill in the centre of town. The Kepez is attractively built of local sandstone. Rooms have marble floors and showers, with the heating in the floor, and reading lights specially designed by the hotel's owner and builder. There are spectacular views from the restaurants. It costs US$26 per person to stay here, breakfast and dinner included.

Hotel Gülşehir (☎ (384) 411 3028), on the northern outskirts by the river, is a three-storey building where airy, decently furnished rooms with bath are officially priced at US$45/95 a single/double, breakfast included. There's a swimming pool and a restaurant. A new road is being built immediately in front of the hotel. It remains to be seen how much noise it produces.

Getting There & Away

Buses from Nevşehir to Ankara pass through Gülşehir, but are often already full when they arrive in Nevşehir. If that is the case, go out of Nevşehir otogar and wait on the main road for the hourly Gülşehir Belediyesi minibus (30 minutes, US$0.40).

HACIBEKTAŞ

Hacıbektaş (population 8000) is on the north-western outskirts of the Cappadocian region, 27.5 km west of Gülşehir. It's famous not for its churches or troglodyte dwellings, but as the home of Hacı Bektaş

Veli, founder and spiritual leader of the Bektaşi order of dervishes.

Things to See

There's only one thing to see really, the **Hacı Bektaş Monastery**, officially called the Hacıbektaş Müzesi, open from 8.30 am to 12.30 pm and 1.30 to 5 pm, closed on Monday. Admission costs US$1. Plaques are in Turkish, with some in English. Though it's called a museum, you should remember that it is a sacred place.

Several rooms are arranged as they might have been when the dervishes lived here, including the **Aş Evi**, or kitchen, with its implements, and the **Meydan Evi**, where novice dervishes were inducted into the order. Other rooms display musical instruments, costumes, embroidery, turbans and other artefacts of the order, as well as relevant old photographs.

Remove your shoes before stepping inside the **saint's tomb** in the garden at the far end of the building, as this is a place of prayer.

Needless to say, the area immediately in front of the monastery is awash with stalls selling Lourdes-style religious paraphernalia.

Places to Stay & Eat

If you're planning a visit in August around the time of the annual pilgrimage, you'll need to plan well ahead as accommodation is very limited.

Across the street from the monastery is a market and shopping complex, and the simple *Hotel Hünkar* (☎ (384) 411 3344), with clean rooms and telephone-style showers for US$6/12 a single/double. It's right next door to the *Sila Restaurant*.

Out on the Ankara road, one km from the monastery, is the *Hotel Cem* (☎ (384) 411 2414), a pleasant three-storey hotel with 26 modern rooms priced at US$17/22 a single/double, breakfast included.

Getting There & Away

Buses from Nevşehir to Ankara pass through Hacıbektaş. Alternatively you can pick up a Kırşehir Belediyesi minibus from Gülşehir (one hour, US$1) which also passes through. The last bus back to Nevşehir leaves at 5 pm.

Hacı Bektaş Veli & the Bektaşi Sect

Born in Nishapur in Iran at some time in the 13th century, Hacı Bektaş inspired a religious and political following that blended aspects of Islam (both Sunni and Shiite) with Orthodox Christianity. During his life he is known to have travelled around Anatolia and to have lived in Kayseri, Sivas and Kırşehir but eventually he settled in the hamlet which grew after his death into the small town of Hacıbektaş.

Although not much is known about Hacıbektaş himself, the book he wrote, the *Makalât*, describes a mystical philosophy which was less austere than mainstream Islam. In it he laid out a four-stage path to enlightenment (the 'Four Doors'). During the first stage the dervish came to know the difference between right and wrong. In the second they prayed constantly. In the third they came to understand God's love. During the fourth and final stage they arrived at an understanding of reality through constant awareness of God and through self-effacement.

Though often scorned by mainstream Islamic clerics, Bektaşi dervishes attained considerable political and religious influence in Ottoman times. Along with all the other dervishes they were outlawed in 1925.

The Bektaşi spiritual philosophy developed in the borderlands between the Turkish and Byzantine empires, where guerrilla fighters from both sides had more in common with one another than they had with their sovereigns in Konya or Constantinople. Their liberal beliefs caught on with the common people, and Bektaşi ideas are still important in Turkish religious life today.

Every August, in what has been described as a 'mini haj', up to 500,000 believers descend on the saint's tomb in Hacıbektaş. So complete has been his rehabilitation that these days politicians try to muscle in alongside the singing and dancing with speeches claiming the great man for their own beliefs. ■

KIRŞEHİR

Midway along the road from Ankara to Cappadocia lies Kırşehir (population 75,000, altitude 978m), an ancient city, now a provincial capital with a few old buildings and several cheap, basic hotels. Kırşehir was famous in Ottoman times as the centre of the mystical Ahi (Akhi) brotherhoods, the Muslim equivalent of the Masonic lodges. The Ahi brotherhoods were founded in the 14th century as secret religious societies among members of the crafts guilds, particularly the tanners' guild. Their political power grew to a point where sultans had to reckon with them. The founding father and inspiration for the Akhi brotherhoods was Ahi Evran (1236-1329), a tanner whose family came from Horasan. He lived and died in Kırşehir and his tomb is a Muslim place of pilgrimage.

Orientation & Information

The city centre is Cumhuriyet Meydanı, the main traffic roundabout with an ugly modern clock tower. Almost everything you'll need is within a five-minute walk of here. The main commercial street running out of the square is Ankara Caddesi, with the PTT a few steps along it. Hotels, restaurants and the Ahi Evran Türbesi are a short walk farther along Ankara Caddesi. The Cacabey Camii is on the opposite side of Cumhuriyet Meydanı from Ankara Caddesi.

The otogar is 1.5 km south of town. Local buses stop rather more conveniently within 100m of Cumhuriyet Meydanı.

The Tourism Information Office, Cumhuriyet Meydanı, Aşık Paşa Caddesi, is right in the city centre but the chances of finding it open are minimal.

Kırşehir's postal code is 40000.

Things to See

The **Ahi Evran Camii ve Türbesi**, or Ahi Evran Mosque and Tomb, also called the Ahi Evran Zaviyesi (Dervish Lodge), are simple stone structures, obviously very old. Pilgrims in their 'Friday best' are usually crowded into the small rooms in prayer.

Just off the traffic roundabout is the **Cacabey Camii** (JAH-jah-bey), built by the Seljuk Turks in 1272 as a meteorological observatory and theological college and now used as a mosque. The brown and white stonework draws the eye and there's a wonderful portal too.

The **Alaettin Camii** dates from Seljuk times as well. You may also see a number of tombs dating from the 14th century.

Places to Stay & Eat

The *Otel Anadolu* (☎ (386) 213 1826), Ankara Caddesi 20, across the main street from the Ahi Evran Camii, has well-worn rooms with bath for US$6/9 a single/double. The neighbouring *Otel Banana* (☎ (386) 213 1879) is virtually identical.

Going upmarket, the new three-star *Terme Hotel* (☎ (386) 212 22404), Terme Parkı, on the outskirts of town near the Terme Kaplıcaları hot springs, provides Kırşehir with 132 bath-equipped rooms at US$35/46 for a single/double, a Turkish bath, and a swimming pool. Follow the signs to find it. There's also the *Otel Kervansary*, conveniently positioned on the highway as you turn into town.

As for meals, places on Ankara Caddesi can fill this need as well. *Meşhur Kebap 49*, with doner kebaps for US$2, is more or less opposite the Otel Banana, while the *Sofra Lokanta* is down an alley beside the Banana. In the street behind the Banana look out also for the cheaper *Yeniler Pide Salonu*.

KAYSERİ

Once the capital of Cappadocia, Kayseri (KAHY-seh-ree, population 425,000, altitude 1054m) is now a booming farm and textile centre. In the shadow of Erciyes Dağı (Mt Aergius, 3916m), the sleepy, conservative town surrounding the ancient black citadel became a bustling city of modern, apartment-lined boulevards during the 1980s. These two aspects of Kayseri aren't completely comfortable together, and something remains of old Kayseri's conservative soul. After 9 pm, for example, you'll be hard pressed to find a restaurant open.

Much has changed in Kayseri in recent

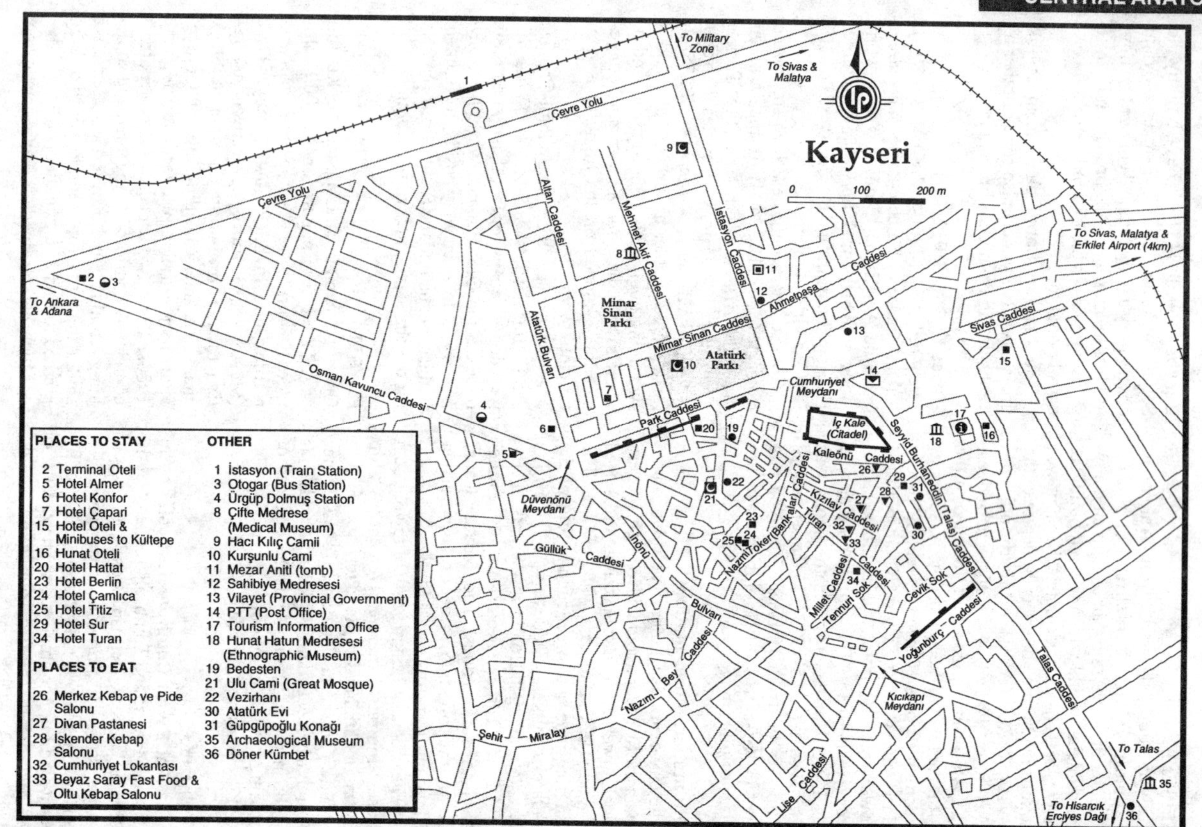
Kayseri
0
100
200 m
To Military Zone
To Sivas & Malatya
To Sivas, Malatya & Erkilet Airport (4km)
To Ankara & Adana
To Talas
To Hisarcık Erciyes Dağı
Çevre Yolu
Altan Caddesi
Mehmet Akif Caddesi
İstasyon Caddesi
Ahmetpaşa Caddesi
Mimar Sinan Caddesi
Mimar Sinan Parkı
Atatürk Parkı
Atatürk Bulvarı
Osman Kavuncu Caddesi
Park Caddesi
Cumhuriyet Meydanı
İç Kale (Citadel)
Kaleönü Caddesi
Seyyid Burhaneddin (Talas) Caddesi
Sivas Caddesi
Düvenönü Meydanı
Güllük Caddesi
İnönü Bulvarı
Nazmi Toker (Bankalar) Caddesi
Kızılay Caddesi
Turan Caddesi
Millet Caddesi
Tennuri Sok
Cevik Sok
Yoğunburç Caddesi
Talas Caddesi
Kıcıkapı Meydanı
Nazım Bey Caddesi
Şehit Miralay
Lise Caddesi
PLACES TO STAY
2 Terminal Oteli
5 Hotel Almer
6 Hotel Konfor
7 Hotel Çapari
15 Hotel Öteli & Minibuses to Kültepe
16 Hunat Oteli
20 Hotel Hattat
23 Hotel Berlin
24 Hotel Çamlıca
25 Hotel Titiz
29 Hotel Sur
34 Hotel Turan
PLACES TO EAT
26 Merkez Kebap ve Pide Salonu
27 Divan Pastanesi
28 İskender Kebap Salonu
32 Cumhuriyet Lokantası
33 Beyaz Saray Fast Food & Oltu Kebap Salonu
OTHER
1 İstasyon (Train Station)
3 Otogar (Bus Station)
4 Ürgüp Dolmuş Station
8 Çifte Medrese (Medical Museum)
9 Hacı Kılıç Camii
10 Kurşunlu Cami
11 Mezar Aniti (tomb)
12 Sahibiye Medresesi
13 Vilayet (Provincial Government)
14 PTT (Post Office)
17 Tourism Information Office
18 Hunat Hatun Medresesi (Ethnographic Museum)
19 Bedesten
21 Ulu Cami (Great Mosque)
22 Vezirhanı
30 Atatürk Evi
31 Güpgüpoğlu Konağı
35 Archaeological Museum
36 Döner Kümbet

years. The town used to be notorious for its irritatingly persistent and omnipresent carpet sellers. However, since the Gulf War and PKK terrorism effectively ended the throughput of visitors to Eastern Turkey, things have become much quieter. You can still buy a carpet if you want to, but you are unlikely to be persecuted by touts. Indeed, the cannier operators have found new ways to sell their wares which are much less dependent on the hard sell.

If you're passing through en route to Cappadocia, take a few hours to tour Kayseri, meet some of the very hospitable Kayserilis, and visit the many wonderful Seljuk buildings and the bazaar. Those heading east might want to see the sights, spend the night, and get an early start the next morning. There are also two superb Seljuk caravanserais north-east of the city, off the Sivas road.

History

This was Hittite country, so its history goes way back. The first Hittite capital, Kanesh, had also been the chief city of the Hatti people. It's at Kültepe, 20 km north-east of Kayseri, off the Sivas road. There was probably an early settlement on the site of Kayseri as well, though the earliest traces which have come to light are from Hellenistic times.

A crusader. The crusades, or 'holy wars', were a series of military expeditions between the 11th and 13th centuries undertaken by Christians to recapture the Holy Land from the Muslims.

Under the Roman emperor Tiberius (14-37 AD), the town received its name, Caesarea, and later became famous as the birthplace of St Basil the Great, one of the early Church Fathers. Its early Christian history was interrupted by the Arab invasions of the 7th century and later.

The Seljuks took over in 1084 and held the city until the Mongols' arrival in 1243, except for a brief period when the crusaders captured it on their way to the Holy Land.

After Kayseri had been part of the Mongol Empire for almost 100 years, its Mongol governor set up his own emirate (1335) which lasted a mere 45 years. It was succeeded by another emirate (that of Kadı Burhaneddin), then captured by the Ottomans (seized during the Ottoman interregnum by the Karamanid emirs), later taken by the Mamelukes of Egypt, and finally conquered by the Ottomans again in 1515, all in just over 100 years.

Orientation & Information

The black-walled citadel at the centre of the old town just south of Cumhuriyet Meydanı, the huge main square, is a good landmark. Another convenient point of reference is Düvenönü Meydanı, 350m west of the citadel along Park Caddesi. Mimar Sinan Parkı, a vast expanse north of Park Caddesi, has some of the city's most outstanding Seljuk buildings.

The train station is at the northern end of Atatürk Bulvarı, over a half km north of Düvenönü Meydanı. Kayseri's otogar is over one km north-west of the citadel (750m north-west of Düvenönü Meydanı) along Osman Kavuncu Caddesi.

The very helpful Tourism Information Office (☎ (352) 222 3903) is right beside the Hunat Mosque and Seminary, and is open from 8.30 am to 5.30 pm daily in summer (closed on weekends in winter).

Kayseri's postal code is 38000.

Citadel

The citadel (hisar or İç Kale), which has been

restored and turned into a shopping bazaar, was built by Emperor Justinian in the 6th century, and extensively repaired by the Seljuk sultan Keykavus I around 1224. In 1486, the Ottoman sultan, Mehmet the Conqueror, made further repairs. With Erciyes Dağı looming over the town, it's not surprising that the hisar should be made of black volcanic stone.

Hunat Mosque & Seminary

Kayseri has several important building complexes which were founded by Seljuk queens and princesses. East of the hisar is a complex which includes the Hunat Hatun Camii (1228), built by the wife of the Seljuk sultan Alaettin Keykubat, plus the tomb of the lady herself, and a Turkish bath (separate sections for men and women).

Next to the mosque is the Hunat Hatun Medresesi (1237), now Kayseri's **Ethnographic Museum** open from 8 am to 5 pm; admission costs US$1. Displays inside include ceramics and faïence, weapons, glassware, kitchen utensils, coins, costumes for both men and women, and a mock-up of a nomadic tent site. You can also visit Lady Hunat's tomb, an octagonal room with a high-domed ceiling. The tomb also contains the remains of her grandchild and of an unknown other. Remove your shoes before entering the room.

Sahibiye Seminary

The Sahibiye Medresesi, on the north side of Cumhuriyet Meydanı, dates from 1267 and has an especially beautiful Seljuk portal. It's now used as a book bazaar, with booksellers' shops stocked mostly with Turkish titles and with photographs of flora and fauna supposedly growing with the Arabic character for Allah on their body.

Lead-Domed Mosque

You can spot the Ottoman-style Kurşunlu Cami by its lead-covered dome, unusual in old Kayseri, north of Park Caddesi and west of Cumhuriyet Meydanı and Atatürk Parkı. Also called the Ahmet Paşa Camii after its founder, it was completed in 1585 following plans possibly drawn by the great Sinan, but certainly influenced by him.

Twin Seminaries

Two adjoining religious schools, the Gıyasiye ve Şifaiye Medreseleri, are sometimes called the Çifte Medrese or the Twin Seminaries. Set in the midst of Mimar Sinan Parkı north of Park Caddesi, they were founded as the bequest of the Seljuk sultan Giyasettin I Keyhüsrev and his sister Gevher Nesibe Sultan (1165-1204), who was the daughter of the great sultan Kılıçaslan. Today the twin medreses have been restored, and serve as a **museum of medical history** for Erciyes University.

Princess Gevher Nesibe Sultan is entombed in a chamber on the right side of the courtyard as you enter; a mescit (prayer-room) is above. Topping the mescit outside is a Seljuk-style dome surrounded by an inscription in Arabic which instructs the medrese's administration to accept medical students and patients into the seminary without regard to religion: Muslim, Jew and Christian were to study and be healed side by side.

A doorway on the left side of the courtyard leads to the medical section, which gives fascinating insights into the medical practices of the 13th-century Seljuks. Look out for a replica of an original stone carving of snakes (symbols of medicine and healing since ancient times) and the Seljuk *çark-ı felek* (wheel of fortune), which determined someone's fate in life and presumably their chances of recovering from disease.

The **Ameliyathane** (Operating Room) has a hole in the ceiling which acted as a 'spotlight' on the patient during operations (presumably Seljuk doctors only operated on sunny days). In the **Akıl Hastanesi** (Mental Hospital) is a suite of tiny cells for mental patients, who were kept one to a cell if violent, an unbelievable four to a cell otherwise.

The central heating system for the hamam, combined with an insulating layer of earth on top of the roof, kept the entire medical side of the building warm during Kayseri's sometimes frigid winters. (The rooftop earth was used to grow vegetables and fruits to feed the patients. After it was removed during restoration, water penetrated the ceilings below, and caused the plaster to flake. The Seljuks knew more about preservation than we do.)

The **Sertabib Başhekim Odası** (Head Doctor's Room) has been furnished in Ottoman style with wood panelling, sedirs and Turkish carpets. As often as not it's kept locked, though.

The museum is open from 8 am to noon and 1 to 5 pm, closed on Monday and Tuesday; admission costs US$1. Most of the signs explaining Seljuk medical practices are in Turkish only which is rather disappointing, as is the state of many of the exhibits.

Hacı Kılıç Mosque

North of the Çifte Medrese on İstasyon Caddesi is the mosque (1249) of the Seljuk vizier Abdülgazi, called the Hacı Kılıç Camii, with some very fine Seljuk architectural detail, especially in the doorways.

Great Mosque

Kayseri's Ulu Cami is near Düvenönü Meydanı. It was begun in 1142 by the Danışmend Turkish emirs and finished by the Seljuks in 1205. Despite all the repair and 'restoration' over the centuries, it's still a good example of early Seljuk style.

Bazaar

West of the hisar, east of Düvenönü Meydanı and south of Park Caddesi is Kayseri's energetic bazaar, which is definitely worth exploring. Set at the intersection of age-old trade routes, Kayseri has been an important commercial centre for millennia. Its several Ottoman covered markets have recently been beautifully restored.

The **Bedesten**, built in 1497 on orders from Mustafa Bey, was first dedicated to the sale of textiles, but now sells all sorts of things. The **Vezirhanı** was constructed in 1727 on the orders of Damat İbrahim Paşa, and now houses shops selling wool and cotton on the ground floor and carpets on the upper. The **Kapalı Çarşı** (Covered Bazaar) was built in 1859, restored in 1988, and now has 500 shops selling necessities (including huge quantities of gold jewellery) to local people. Look out also for the Pamuk Han or cotton bazaar.

Seljuk Tombs

Among Kayseri's other Seljuk archaeological treasures are several distinctive tombs. The **Döner Kümbet** (deur-NEHR kewm-beht), or Revolving Tomb, is about one km south-east of the hisar along Talas Caddesi. Though it doesn't (and never did) revolve, its cylindrical shape suggests turning, and as you view its marvellous and elaborate Seljuk decoration (1276), you will at least revolve around it. Nearby is another, the 14th-century **Sırçalı Kümbet**, which used to be covered in coloured tiles and topped by a pyramidal roof.

Archaeological Museum

The city's Archaeological Museum is near the Döner Kümbet. It houses the finds from Kültepe, site of ancient Kanesh, including the cuneiform tablets which told historians much about the Hittite Empire. Hittite, Hellenistic and Roman statuary, plus exhibits of local ethnography, help to make it worth a visit. Opening hours are from 8 am to noon and from 1 to 5 pm daily except Monday; admission costs US$1.

Historic Houses

Just south-east of the citadel is the wonderful **Güpgüpoğlu Konağı**, a fine stone mansion dating from the 18th century, now opened as a museum. The Sofa (main hall), kitchen, Selamlık (men's quarters) and Haremlik (women's and family quarters) have been decorated in period style, and the fine woodwork on the ceilings and walls beautifully restored. It's open daily from 8 am to 5 pm in summer for US$1.

Near the Güpgüpoğlu Konağı is the **Atatürk Evi**, the house where Atatürk stayed when he visited Kayseri. Two rooms are sporadically open as a museum.

Kültepe (Kanesh-Karum)

Appropriately named 'Hill of Ashes' in Turkish, this archaeological site 20 km north-east of Kayseri was originally settled around 4000 BC. The town of Kanesh came to prominence during Old Bronze times (around 2500-2000 BC) when Zipani, king of Kanesh, joined an alliance of Anatolian kings against the powerful king of Akkadia (Mesopotamia), Naram Sin.

By around 1850 BC, Kanesh was the most powerful kingdom in Anatolia. The neighbouring Assyrian commercial centre of Karum, specialising in metals, was among the oldest and richest bazaars in the world. Then a great fire destroyed Kanesh-Karum. It was rebuilt and by around 1720 BC was the Hittite city of Nisa, capital of King Anitta who conquered the pre-Hittite rulers of Hattuşaş (Boğazkale) and made that a Hittite city.

The size and height of the mound is the most impressive thing about the site, showing that ancient Kanesh-Karum was indeed an important city, but signs warn you not to go near the excavation trenches, so there is little to see. The custodian is also liable to dog your every footstep. The best finds are in the Archaeological Museum in Kayseri. It's only really worth coming out here if you're very interested in the Hittites, although on a clear day there are stunning uncluttered views of Mt Erciyes from the top of the mound.

About 600m beyond Karum is the farming village of **Karahöyük**, a cluster of old stone houses near a graveyard of rough-cut tombstones, providing a glimpse of real country life.

To get to Kültepe take a Bünyan bus or minibus from Sivas Caddesi (30 minutes, US$0.50). Eighteen km along, just before a BP fuel station (café, toilets), a road to the left is marked for 'Kültepe Kaniş Karum'. Just over two km from the main road is the site marked 'Kültepe Kaniş' and, 200m farther along, 'Karum'.

Caravanserais

North and east of Kayseri are several beautiful restored Seljuk caravanserais which anyone interested in Seljuk architecture will want to see.

You can get to Sultan Han quite easily by taking a Sivas bus and hitching from the road junction, but Karatay Han is a taller order without your own transport since it's 15 km from the main Malatya to Kayseri highway. Haggle with a taxi driver for an excursion to both hans, and you will probably end up with a figure of US$20 to US$30 for the entire car.

Sultan Han The Sultan Han is on the old Kayseri to Sivas highway, 45 km north-east of Kayseri and about one km off the new highway. Besides being a fine example of the Seljuk royal caravan lodging, it has been beautifully restored so it's easy to appreciate the architectural fine points. The han was finished in 1236; restoration was carried out only a few decades ago. Don't let the locked gate worry you. Shortly after your car draws up, a boy will come running with the key and a booklet of tickets; admission costs US$1. Opening hours are supposedly from 9 am to 1 pm and from 2 to 5 pm (till 7 pm in summer), closed Monday, but in fact the han is open whenever the guardian can be found.

Tour the inside, noticing particularly the elegant snake motif on the little mosque's arches. Climb up to the roof, but don't neglect a walk around the exterior as well. Note the lion-faced water spouts on the walls, and the plain towers of varying design.

Karatay Han If you have time, continue to the Karatay Han, in a Turkish village now well off the beaten track. The Karatay Han, built in 1240 for the Seljuk vizier Emir Celaleddin Karatay, was once on the main east-west trade route. It was restored in the 1960s, and is yet another fine example of high Seljuk art.

From the Sultan Han, head back towards Kayseri and take the turn off south or east to Bünyan. Pass through Bünyan heading towards Malatya, and after about 30 km take the road on the right for Elbaşı. Four km beyond Elbaşı is Karatay. (Coming from

Malatya, look for a turn-off marked 'Karatay Han, 10 km' about 35 km west of Pınarbaşı.)

Erciyes Dağı

Erciyes Dağı, or Mt Aergius (3916m), as it was known in Roman times, is an extinct volcano 26 km south of Kayseri. It is one of Turkey's few **ski centres**, with a chairlift, beginners' lift, and a ski lodge, the *Kayak Evi* (Ski House, ☎ (352) 342 2031) with 100 beds.

Frequent minibuses go as far as Hisarcık (14 km) but you must hitch or take a taxi (US$10) for the last dozen or so km to Tekir Yaylası (2150m) and the ski lodge where equipment can be rented.

Though fairly good for skiing (for Turkey), Erciyes is rather inhospitable to hikers. Short walks can be made from the ski lodge, but longer treks require planning, good equipment and a guide. For full information, see Lonely Planet's *Trekking in Turkey*.

Places to Stay – bottom end

You won't get much cheaper than the *Hunat Oteli* (☎ (352) 432 4319), Zengin Sokak 5, behind the Hunat Mosque and near the Tourism Information Office. It's a convenient, quiet but very basic place with waterless rooms priced at US$5/8 a single/double. The proprietor is thoroughly avuncular but some single women would find this a daunting pitstop.

One block away from the Vezirhanı is the *Hotel Berlin* (☎ (352) 222 4368), Maarif Caddesi, Yeni Han Çıkmazı 12. On a quiet dead-end street, it offers beds for US$5 each, but once the bazaar has closed down this can be a spooky area to walk in.

There are a couple of other rock-bottom cheapies, the *Meydan* and the *Hisar*, on Osman Kavuncu Caddesi opposite the posh Almer but they lack any sense of location.

Hotel Sur (SOOR) (☎ (352) 222 4367), Cumhuriyet Mahallesi, Talas Caddesi 12, is conveniently positioned and offers rooms with more furnishing than usual. Those on the street side have windows but are liable to be noisy; those on the inside have no windows but will be quieter. Singles/doubles cost US$14/20 with private shower. To find it, walk south-east along Talas Caddesi from the citadel, with a remnant of the city walls and the Sivas Kapısı (Sivas Gate) on your right. Turn right through a gap in the wall, then right again, and you'll see the hotel.

The two-star *Hotel Turan* (too-RAHN) (☎ (352) 222 5537, fax 231 1153), Millet Caddesi, Turan Caddesi 8, is an old faithful which has served travellers for many decades. Some of the spacious rooms have bathtubs instead of showers. They usually cost US$13/20 but the staff are ready to haggle if business is slack. There's a terrace on the roof and a carpet shop off the pleasant lobby.

In the bazaar is the tidy and fairly quiet *Hotel Çamlıca* (CHAHM-luh-jah, ☎ (352) 231 4344), Bankalar Caddesi, Gürcü Sokak 14, with serviceable rooms priced at US$16 a double with washbasin, US$18 with shower. From the Divan Pastanesi (see Places to Eat), turn right off Millet Caddesi and take the third street on the left, Nazmi Toker Caddesi, known to the locals as Bankalar Caddesi (Banks St), for obvious reasons. After you come to an intersection, walk one block more along the curving street to the hotel.

Hotel Titiz (☎ (352) 222 5040, fax 222 5542), Maarif Caddesi 7, just down the street from the Çamlıca, is modern, clean and presentable at US$15/27 a single/double with private shower. Some rooms have TVs.

Finally, on Park Caddesi overlooking the Kurşunlu Mosque, there's the 20-year-old *Hotel Hattat* (☎ (352) 222 6558) with serviceable rooms with showers and balconies for US$15/22/29 a single/double/triple.

Places to Stay – middle

Kayseri has several good new hotels around Düvenönü Meydanı. The two-star, 44-room *Hotel Çapari* (☎ (352) 222 5278, fax 222 5282), Donanma Caddesi 12, is hidden away on a quiet back street just one block north-east of Düvenönü Meydanı. All rooms have private bath and TV, and cost US$17/24/30 a single/double/triple, breakfast included.

Hotel Konfor (☎ (352) 320 0184, fax 336 5100), Atatürk Bulvarı 5, is a few dozen metres north of Düvenönü Meydanı on the left. Attractively modern, its rooms are comfy and well located, and cost about the same as those at the Çapari.

Facing Düvenönü Meydanı on its southwest corner is Kayseri's best, the three-star *Hotel Almer* (☎ (352) 320 7970, fax 320 7974), Osman Kavuncu Caddesi. Very comfortable rooms equipped with TV, minibar and air-con cost US$28/34 a single/double, breakfast included.

Next to the otogar is the faded but nominally one-star *Terminal Oteli* (TEHR-mee-NAHL) (☎ (352) 330 1120), Osman Kavuncu Caddesi 176, with 21 rooms for US$17 a double with private shower, US$15 a double with just a washbasin.

Places to Eat

Kayseri boasts a few special dishes, among them pastırma, salted, sun-dried veal coated with çemen, a spicy concoction of garlic, red peppers, parsley and water. It takes about a month to prepare, has a very strong flavour, tends to stick in your teeth and rules your breath despotically for hours afterwards, but once you acquire the taste you look forward to returning to Kayseri. The darker the pastırma, the longer it has been allowed to age. Many shops in the centre sell it.

Other Kayseri specialities include sucuk (soo-JOOK), a spicy sausage; salam (sah-LAHM), Turkish salami; tulum peynir (too-LOOM pehy-neer), hard cheese cured in a goatskin; and bal (BAHL), honey. Apart from pastırma, few of these things appear on restaurant menus, so you must buy them for a picnic.

The *İskender Kebap Salonu*, Millet Caddesi 5 by the citadel, one floor above street level, has been serving good Bursa-style döner kebap for several decades. It has a pleasing view of the busy street, and low prices of about US$3 to US$4 for a meal of kebap, ayran and salad. The general dining room is one flight up, the aile salonu up another one.

Nearby is the *Merkez Kebap ve Pide Salonu*, with similar fare, including fresh pide, while the nearby *Cumhuriyet Lokantası* is a good choice for ready food or roast chicken.

The *Divan Pastanesi* is a good, fancy pastry shop on Millet Caddesi a block south of the citadel, on the corner of Mevlevi Caddesi. Have their şam fıstıklı baklava (many-layered flaky pastry sweet with pistachio nuts) and a large glass of tea for about US$1.50. There's a second branch in Sivas Caddesi.

Further along Millet Caddesi, near the Hotel Turan, is the *Beyaz Saray Fast Food ve Oltu Kebap Salonu*. Normally the words 'fast food' are enough to dampen any appetite, but in this case there's no need to worry. The Beyaz Saray does a wide range of dishes, from soups to pizzas and kebaps, but its speciality is oltu kebap which is roasted on a horizontal spit and then served up on a skewer; it's fatty but makes a change and costs about US$4. Another plus is the on-site pastahane so you can round the meal off nicely with a cake. Families love this place.

As ever, the bazaar has numerous good, cheap eateries.

Getting There & Away

Air Turkish Airlines connects Kayseri's Erkilet airport with İstanbul by daily nonstop flights. Buy your tickets at the THY office (☎ (352) 222 3858) at Sahibiye Mahallesi, Yıldırım Caddesi 1. At the time of writing, there was no air service to Ankara. An airport bus (US$1.50) connects the city with Erkilet airport. Catch the bus 1¼ hours before flight departure time, or be at the airport at least 30 minutes before the scheduled departure time. Local bus No 2 also runs to the airport from Atatürk Caddesi.

Bus Being at an important north-south and east-west crossroads, Kayseri has lots of bus services. To get to the citadel from the otogar, walk out of the front of the otogar, cross the avenue and board any bus marked 'Merkez'

(Centre), or take a dolmuş marked 'Şehir'. A taxi to the citadel costs US$2.

The otogar has a PTT, shops and cafés. Details of some services follow:

Adana – 335 km, 6½ hours, US$6; several buses daily
Ankara – 330 km, five hours, US$6; hourly buses
Gaziantep – 371 km, 6½ hours, US$8; several buses daily
Kahramanmaraş – 291 km, five hours, US$6; several buses daily
Malatya – 354 km, six hours, US$7; several buses daily
Nevşehir – 105 km, 2½ hours by bus US$2; very frequent buses and minibuses
Sivas – 200 km, 3½ hours, US$5; frequent buses daily
Ürgüp – 80 km, 1½ hours, US$2.75; hourly minibuses from 7 am to 7 pm

Train Several daily trains connect Kayseri with Ankara and points east; see the Ankara section for details. Both the *Vangölü/Güney Ekspresi* and the *Doğu Ekspresi* stop at Kayseri in the early hours of the morning, while the *Çukurova Ekspresi* leaves for Ankara at 1 am.

The train between Kayseri and Malatya takes 10 hours, if it's on time; the bus is much quicker. There are no good train connections north to the Black Sea; better to take a bus, or the train to Sivas, then an onward bus to Samsun.

To get into town from the train station, walk out of the station, cross the big avenue and board any bus heading down Atatürk Bulvarı to Düvenönü Meydanı.

North Central Anatolia

The region north-east of Ankara and north-west of Sivas has a little of everything: ancient Hittite ruins, gritty industrial cities, graceful old Ottoman towns, mountain scenery and plains. Most travellers stop in this region on their way to somewhere else. Heading for the Black Sea coast, it's worth seeing Tokat, and Çorum can provide lodgings if your itinerary demands it. But a few destinations are worth excursions in themselves: the well-preserved Ottoman town of Safranbolu, the Hittite ruins at Boğazkale, near Sungurlu; and the historic city of Amasya, situated in a dramatic river gorge.

SAFRANBOLU

For many years Safranbolu (population 25,000, altitude 350m) was a closely guarded secret: a small town of well-preserved Ottoman houses hidden in the hill country 250 km north of Ankara. Turkish architects, painters and photographers knew about it and exploited its artistic potential but only the most adventurous travellers wandered through it, often by accident, on their way to the Black Sea coastal town of Amasra. Safranbolu's charms have now been discovered, but not yet over-exploited. The town, 10 km north of the grim steel-manufacturing city of Karabük, is not on the most heavily travelled tour bus routes and you must still make a special effort to get here. Once you do, however, you'll enjoy walking along the narrow, twisting cobbled lanes and seeing traditional trades and crafts practised just as they were in Ottoman times.

History

The settlement founded here between 2000 and 1500 BC was subject to the usual conquest, rule, exploitation and enjoyment by Hittites, Paphlagonians, Persians, Lydians, Romans and Byzantines. Under the Turks, the rulers were the Danışmends, Seljuks, Çobanoğlus, Çandaroğlus and Ottomans. During the 17th 3century, the main Ottoman trade route between Gerede and the Black Sea coast passed through Safranbolu, bringing commerce, prominence and wealth to the town. Wealthy patrons established caravanserais, mosques and Turkish baths. Safranbolu produced many men and women who were successful in commerce and government, and who shared their success with their birthplace by endowing charitable foundations.

During the 18th and 19th centuries Safranbolu's wealthy families built spacious mansions of sun-dried mud bricks, wood and stucco. The families of the surprisingly large

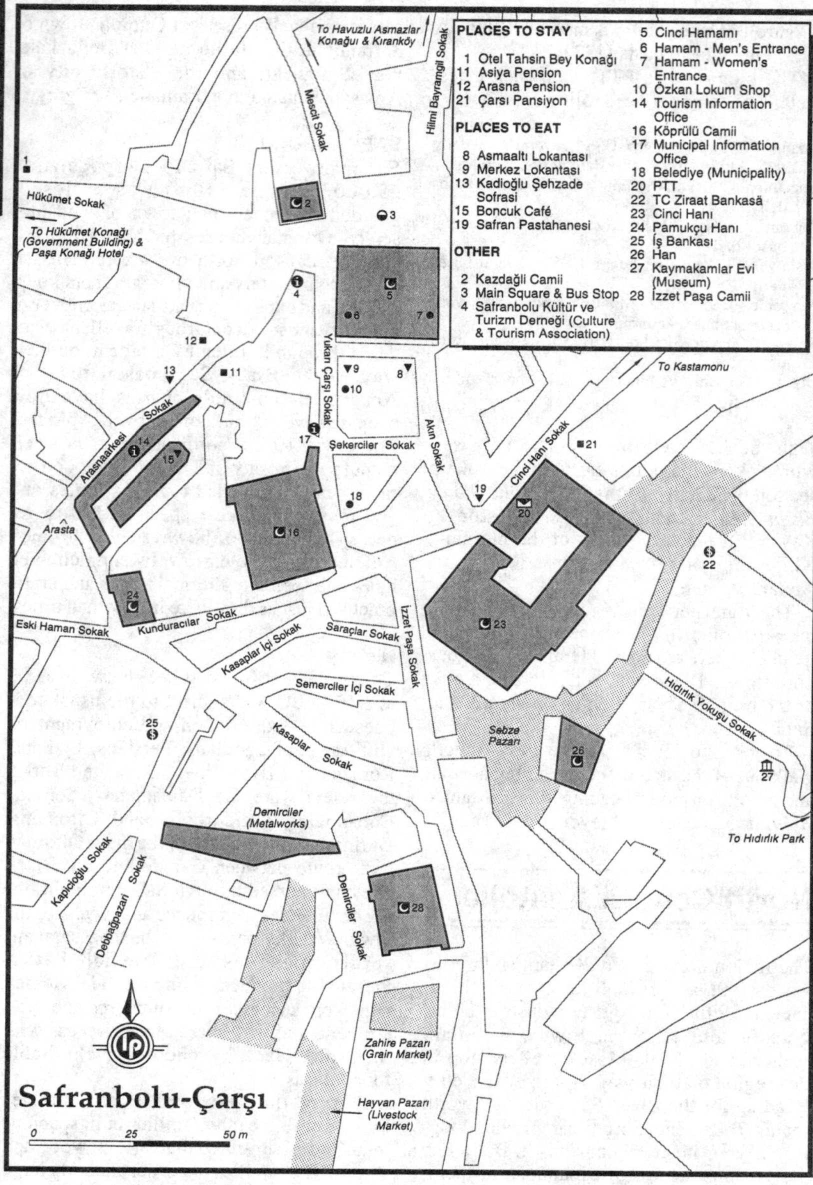
PLACES TO STAY
1 Otel Tahsin Bey Konağı
11 Asiya Pension
12 Arasna Pension
21 Çarsı Pansiyon
PLACES TO EAT
8 Asmaaltı Lokantası
9 Merkez Lokantası
13 Kadioğlu Şehzade Sofrasi
15 Boncuk Café
19 Safran Pastahanesi
OTHER
2 Kazdağli Camii
3 Main Square & Bus Stop
4 Safranbolu Kültür ve Turizm Derneği (Culture & Tourism Association)
5 Cinci Hamamı
6 Hamam - Men's Entrance
7 Hamam - Women's Entrance
10 Özkan Lokum Shop
14 Tourism Information Office
16 Köprülü Camii
17 Municipal Information Office
18 Belediye (Municipality)
20 PTT
22 TC Ziraat Bankasā
23 Cinci Hanı
24 Pamukçu Hanı
25 İş Bankası
26 Han
27 Kaymakamlar Evi (Museum)
28 İzzet Paşa Camii
To Havuzlu Asmazlar Konağıı & Kıranköy
Mescit Sokak
Hilmi Bayramgil Sokak
Hükümet Sokak
To Hükümet Konağı (Government Building) & Paşa Konağı Hotel
Yukarı Çarşı Sokak
Arasnaarkesi Sokak
Arasta
Şekerciler Sokak
Akın Sokak
Cinci Hanı Sokak
To Kastamonu
Eski Haman Sokak
Kunduracılar Sokak
Kasaplar İçi Sokak
Saraçlar Sokak
İzzet Paşa Sokak
Semerciler İçi Sokak
Kasaplar Sokak
Sebze Pazarı
Hıdırlık Yokuşu Sokak
To Hıdırlık Park
Demirciler (Metalworks)
Kapıcıoğlu Sokak
Debbağpazarı Sokak
Demirciler Sokak
Zahire Pazarı (Grain Market)
Hayvan Pazarı (Livestock Market)
Safranbolu-Çarşı
0 25 50 m

population of prosperous artisans built less impressive but similarly sturdy, harmonious homes, and a surprising number of these buildings survive today. During the 19th century about 20 to 25% of Safranbolu's population were Ottoman Greeks, most of whom moved to Greece during the great exchange of populations following WWI. Their principal church, dedicated to St Stephen, has been restored as Kıranköy's Ulu Cami (Great Mosque).

Safranbolu is a very popular destination with Turkish tourists at weekends and over public holidays. If you must visit at those times, try and make reservations in advance.

Orientation

Coming via Karabük, you arrive in Kıranköy, the modern part of Safranbolu, arrayed along the ridge of a hill and formerly called Misaki Milli by its Ottoman Greek inhabitants. If you continue uphill from the traffic roundabout you will reach the section called Bağlar (baa-LAHR), with its centre at Köyiçi, which has many interesting old houses.

Turn right (south-east) at the roundabout and go 1.7 km, down the hill, up the other side and down again to reach the centre of Old Safranbolu (Eski Safranbolu), the section called Çarşı (Market). On Saturday a busy market does in fact take place in the main square, marked by the Kazdağlı Camii (1779). There are a few modern hotels in Kıranköy, but most of what there is to see is in Eski Safranbolu and Bağlar.

Information

Çarşı has two tourist offices. The government Tourism Information Office (☎ (372) 712 3863) is 100m from Çarşı's main square in the arasta (collection of Ottoman-style shops) formerly occupied by Safranbolu's cobblers. English and German are spoken.

There is also an information office sponsored by the Safranbolu Culture & Tourism Association (Kültür ve Turizm Derneği; ☎ (372) 712 1047) just off Çarşı's main square on Arasta Sokak, marked by signs.

Safranbolu's postal code is 67700.

Historic Architecture

In Ottoman times, prosperous residents of Safranbolu maintained dual households. In winter they occupied their town residences in Çarşı, situated at the meeting-point of three valleys and protected from the winter winds. During the warm months they moved to summer houses amidst the vineyards of Bağlar ('Vines'). After the iron and steel works at Karabük was established in 1938, modern houses built by factory staff encroached on the old neighbourhoods of Bağlar.

Some of the largest houses had interior pools which, though big enough to be swimming pools, were not used as such. The running water cooled the room and gave a pleasant background sound. The best and most accessible example of this is the **Havuzlu Asmazlar Konağı** (Mansion with Pool), now operated as a hotel by the Turkish Touring & Automobile Association. See Places to Stay for details.

Several historic houses have been restored and as time goes on and funds allow, more places are being saved from deterioration. To see inside a house, head for the **Kaymakamlar Evi**, open from 8.30 am to noon and 1.30 to 5 pm (closed on Monday). Unfortunately, while the lack of interior furnishings may be authentic, without the people to fill the empty space the rooms seem lifeless and dull. The US$0.30 entry fee probably doesn't even cover the cost of the blue plastic bags you have to put on over your shoes to look around. On the ground floor old farm implements, an old telephone switchboard and a *çıkrık* (spinning wheel) are displayed in the area once reserved for storage and stabling animals. Otherwise, there's little specific to look at.

Other Historic Buildings

Çarşı's most famous and imposing structure is the large stone **Cinci Hanı** (1645), a caravanserai presently being converted into a three-star hotel. Right by Çarşı's main square is the **Cinci Hamamı,** built along with the Cinci Hanı and still in service, with lots of creamy marble and glass dome lights which let in dramatic rays of sunshine. There are separate baths for men (Erkekler Kısmı) and women (Kadınlar Kısmı); the women's section may look closed but if you ask someone will probably open it for you. It's a great place to come clean for between US$2 and US$4 depending on what extras you choose.

The large **Köprülü Mehmet Paşa Camii** (1662), by the arasta with the Tourism Information Office, is presently under restoration. The **İzzet Paşa Camii** (1796) was restored in 1902-03.

The **arasta** used to be where the shoemakers worked but they have now moved into the surrounding streets, leaving the little wooden shops to the souvenir sellers. Here you can buy fabrics from all around Turkey but at prices up to twice what you would pay for them in their place of origin.

Walk uphill past the Kaymakamlar Evi to reach **Hıdırlık**, the so-called kale, which was never a fortress despite its modern bits of crenellated wall. On top of the hill is a park offering excellent views of the town, and two türbes (tombs) dating from the 19th century. Peek through the windows of the locked tomb of Ahmet Lütfi and you'll see a mountain of coins left by the faithful.

Safranbolu did have a real citadel but its last remnants were removed early this century to make way for the ornamented **Hükümet Konağı** (government building) on the hilltop across the valley.

Safranbolu's traditional character is now protected by regulation. Indeed, UNESCO has dubbed the old town a World Heritage Site, on a par with Florence in Italy and Bath in England. Efforts are also being made to preserve the artisans' shops and trades. Most of the active shops and workshops line the streets south of the Cinci Hamamı and the Köprülü Camii.

Bağlar has many wonderful old houses, but they are much more spread out and at the time of writing were not organised for viewing. The situation might have changed by the time you arrive.

Excursion to Yörük Köyü

Another, smaller, less renowned village of old houses is Yörük Köyü (which translates oxymoronically as 'Nomad Village'), 11 km east of Safranbolu along the Kastamonu road. The people of the village grew rich, somewhat surprisingly, on making bread and some of the houses are truly enormous. Ask around and someone may take you to see the old village *çamaşırlık*, or laundry, with arched hearths where the water was heated in cauldrons and a huge stone table, rather like the *göbektaşı* in a hamam, for the actual scrubbing.

Yörük Köyü has a traditional tea-house and a weekends-only café selling ayran, baklava and gözleme. Otherwise tourism has hardly touched the village. It's best to get there with your own transport. Failing that, you'll need to haggle with a Safranbolu taxi driver to take you there, wait for an hour or so while you explore the village, then return. This will cost between US$10 and US$14 depending on your bargaining skills.

If you have your own car, there's an excellent restaurant, *Çevrik Köprü* (☎ (372) 737 2119), on the right side of the road just before the turn off for Yörük Köyü. Here you can tuck into juicy kuyu kebap in shady gardens with fountains and pools.

Places to Stay – bottom end

More places to stay have recently opened in the Çarşı part of town, which means you're unlikely to have to stay in less atmospheric Kıranköy.

The *Çarşı Pansiyon* (☎ (372) 725 1079) is a small, friendly place in Babasultan Mahallesi, not far from the Cinci Hanı. Rooms with private baths come with low-level beds, sedirs, carpets and pretty curtains for US$7 (breakfast included). If you want hot water, just ask the proprietor in advance. There's also a small café here.

There are two other small pensions in restored houses closer to the arasta: the *Arasna* and the *Asiya*. Both will do you a bed for about US$7 in simple Ottoman style. The Arasna has live music on Friday and Saturday nights when an early night might be out of the question.

In Kıranköy, at İnönü Mahallesi, as you

head down towards Çarşı from the roundabout, you'll find the *Konak Pansiyon* (☎ (372) 725 2485), overpriced at US$8.50 a head considering its position. If all else fails the *Zalifre Pansiyon* (☎ (372) 712 0530) in Cumhuriyet Caddesi, also in Kıranköy, charges US$4 per person but you will stay upstairs in a grim modern block, and share the floor with the HQ of the Safranbolu branch of the Refah Partisi.

Places to Stay – middle

The classiest lodgings in Safranbolu are undoubtedly at the *Havuzlu Asmazlar Konağı* (☎ (372) 721 2883, fax 712 3824), Mescit Sokak, enclosed behind high walls 400m uphill from Çarşı's main square, opposite the turn off for the Bartın-Zonguldak road. On the left as you enter you'll see the fine pool which gives the house its name, right in the centre of the main room, surrounded by low sofas and small brass-tray tables at which guests take tea and have breakfast.

The 11 guest rooms are beautifully furnished with brass beds, sedirs, brass tables and kilims; rooms 14, 15, 20 and 21 upstairs are the nicest. Bathrooms are minuscule and sound-proofing is at a minimum but these are minor inconveniences. Overflow rooms in a house across the road are cheaper but much less atmospheric.

Bearing in mind the prices you pay for 'Ottoman' comfort in İstanbul, the *Havuzlu* represents an excellent opportunity to pamper yourself without breaking the bank: it charges US$22/31 a single/double.

Two other more recently converted Çarşı houses offer similar, if slightly less stylish, accommodation to the Havuzlu. The *Tahsin Bey Konağı* (☎ (372) 712 6062) is at Hükümet Sokak 50, the *Paşa Konağı* at Çeşme Mahallesi, just 50m further up the road and to the left. Both offer light, airy rooms with built-in cupboards, plastered fireplaces and other points of interest. The Tahsin Bey has good views from some rooms, the Paşa Konağı a secluded garden and rather eerie bar. In both cases some of the bathrooms are inside cupboards with high doorsteps which might trouble some guests. Check before agreeing to take your room. Prices at both places are US$20/29 a single/double.

If you need to stay in Kıranköy, the fanciest place there is the two-star, 30-room *Uz Otel* (☎ (372) 712 1086, fax 712 2215), newly built to resemble an old Safranbolu house. Restaurant and shower-equipped guest rooms are yours for US$19/33 a single/double, breakfast included. Anywhere else this would be a good deal. In Safranbolu, of course, it's let down by being in the wrong part of town.

Places to Eat

Çarşı New places to eat are rapidly opening up in Çarşı, although as yet none have latched on to banana pancakes and milk shakes. Amongst the older places favoured by the locals are the *Merkez Restaurant*, plain, clean and typical, with three-course meals for US$2.50. Next door is the *Özkan*, a beautiful old sweets shop. Near the arasta, the *Boncuk Café* is one of the town's most congenial places, a modern Safranbululu's conception of what an 'antique' café should be. Here you can watch gözleme being made. To sample it will cost you about US$1.50. Opposite the Cinci Hanı the friendly *Safran Pastahanesi* makes a very congenial place to stop for breakfast or a cake.

Near the arasta, the newer *Kadıoğlu Şehzade Sofrası* has lots of attractive indoor dining rooms plus a courtyard round a fountain. You can get pide here but the house speciality is kuyu kebap, made by enclosing lamb in an underground pit where it is grilled in its own juice over a wooden fire. Kebap, salad and a drink will set you back about US$6.

The vast basement restaurant of the *Havuzlu Asmazlar Konağı* has marble floors and an arched fireplace. The menu lists such Ottoman delights as mıklama (fried eggs, tomatoes, spinach, ground lamb, onions and pastırma) and gözleme but they may only be available when the hotel is busy. Otherwise it's şiş kebap. Portions are large and prices moderate: less than US$8 for soup, salad, main course and beer.

Kıranköy Besides the Uz Otel's good restaurant, you can try the *Çelik Palas Restaurant* next door, which has a pleasant terrace. *İmren Lokumları* is famous locally for its lokum (Turkish delight), and has another branch in Çarşı's arasta, near the tourist office.

Getting There & Away

There are a few direct buses to Safranbolu but most drop you at Karabük's grimy otogar. Minibuses ply up and down the road outside to run you the last 10 km to Kıranköy (US$0.50). Ulusoy has regular daily services to İstanbul, İzmir and Ankara and picks up passengers from Çarşı as well as Kıranköy.

If you're driving, exit from the Ankara-İstanbul highway at Gerede and head north, following signs for Karabük.

You could also reach Safranbolu by taking the Ankara-Zonguldak train (*Karaelmas*) and getting out at Karabük.

Getting Around

Every 30 minutes or so throughout the day local buses (US$0.40) roll along the route from Çarşı's main square over the hills to Kıranköy and up to the Köyiçi stop in Bağlar.

KASTAMONU

Heading on from Safranbolu to Ankara or the Black Sea you may need to stop in Kastamonu, a small town of 50,000 people which is nonetheless an important transport connecting point. There's not much specifically to linger for, although you might be interested in the small museum, the castle and the assorted ancient market buildings. There's a reasonable range of places to stay and the chance to sample cheeses and puddings you may not have encountered elsewhere. You can also make a side trip to see one of Turkey's finest surviving wooden mosques in the village of Kasaba.

History

As a result of its position, Kastamonu has had as chequered a history as many central Turkish towns. Archaeological evidence suggests there was settlement here as far back as 2000 BC, but the Hittites, Persians, Macedonians and Pontic kings all left their mark. In the 11th century the Seljuks descended, followed by the Danışmends. In the late 13th century the Byzantine emperor John Comnenus tried to hold out here but the Mongols and the Ottomans soon swept in and by 1459 Kastamonu was secured as an Ottoman town.

More recently, Kastamonu played an unexpected role as the town Atatürk chose to launch his hat reforms from in 1925 (see boxed story in Facts about the Country).

Orientation

Kastamonu's small otogar is on the west side of the city centre, as you come in from Samsun or Sinop. It's about one km from the centre, reachable by dolmuş or taxi (US$1.50).

A stream runs in a channel through the centre of the town. The road along its north bank is Yalçın Caddesi, which becomes Plevne Caddesi as it reaches the centre and then Atatürk Caddesi. The road along the south bank is Kışla Caddesi, which becomes Cumhuriyet Caddesi towards the centre.

The centre of town is Cumhuriyet Meydanı with an imposing Valilik building and statue of Atatürk. This is where you'll find the PTT, the tourism information kiosk and local bus stops.

Just to the west of Cumhuriyet Meydanı the stream passes under a truncated stone bridge. To the south side a road leads to Nasrullah Meydanı and the bazaar.

Information

A tourist information office-cum-souvenir shop is conveniently positioned right in front of Cumhuriyet Meydanı. In theory it's open daily from 9 am to 10 pm and some English and German is spoken. It sells a town plan for US$2.

Kastamonu's post code is 37200.

Kastamonu Museum

About 100m east of Cumhuriyet Meydanı

along Cumhuriyet Caddesi is the Kastamonu Arkeoloji ve Etnoğrafya Müzesi, open daily except Monday from 8.30 am to 4.30 pm for US$1. It's housed in the attractive building where Atatürk announced his planned headgear reforms on 30 August 1925.

There's the usual mildly depressing collection of dusty Roman and Byzantine relics, including a gruesome sarcophagus opened to reveal the skeleton inside still with a full head of hair. Upstairs, look out for some of the wood blocks used to make the printed cloths on sale around here and for some fine carved wood and horn spoons. Amongst the costumes on display, a couple of fezzes are more interesting when you know the history of the building.

If the custodian doesn't immediately offer, ask him to unlock the **Atatürk Salonu** on the ground floor so you can see the photos of the 1925 visit. Some were taken in İnebolu and show his entourage looking silly in hats with turned-up brims. Two days later they are marching into Kastamonu looking much more confident in their Panamas. There are also assorted quotations from Atatürk's speech, but in Turkish only which is a great shame.

Historic Buildings

Kastamonu is dominated by its **kale**, built on a rock above the town. Parts of it date back to Byzantine times, but most of what you see belongs to the later Seljuk and Ottoman reconstructions. A family still lives inside the castle so you should be able to get in at most reasonable times. It's a steep one-km climb up through the streets of the old town and you'll be rewarded with fine views of the town's roofs. Otherwise, you can appreciate the outline of the walls better from down below.

Nasrullah Meydanı is dominated by the Ottoman **Nasrullah Camii** and the fine double fountain in front of it. The area immediately south of Nasrullah Meydanı is filled with old market buildings, several of them still in use. The modern-day bazaar takes place in and around the **Karanlık Bedesten**, the **Balkapanı Hanı** and the **İsmail Bey Hanı** (1466) which was restored in 1972 to provide workshops. Wander down any of the side streets in this area and you'll come across old hamams, fountains and other buildings.

Excursion to Kasaba Köyü

The tiny village of Kasaba, 17 km from Kastamonu as the crow flies, is an unlikely place to find one of the finest wooden mosques still surviving in Turkey. The **Mahmudbey Camii** was built in 1366. Externally there is nothing other than the unusually lovely wooden doors to suggest there is anything special about this mosque. Get the *hoja* to unlock it, however, and you'll find a stunning interior, with four painted wooden columns, a wooden gallery and fine painted ceiling rafters. The mosque has been restored and is currently carpetless (which doesn't exempt you from the duty of removing your shoes).

To get to Kasaba, take a minibus to Daday from Kastamonu otogar and ask to be let off at Subaşı (US$0.50). From there it's another three km to Kasaba. If there's no sign of a lift, walk through Subaşı and out the other side, bearing right when the road forks and walking through the village of Göçen. After Göçen the road is signposted 'Mahmudbey Camii' on the right. In the village you'll see a bridge on the right. The mosque is the second alongside the stream.

Places to Stay

Kastamonu's hotels are clustered around Belediye and Cumhuriyet Caddesis, right in the centre of town.

One of the cheapest is the *Ilgaz Oteli* (☎ 366) 212 4217), on Belediye Caddesi, which has very basic waterless rooms for US$4/7 a single/double. A couple of doors along the *Otel Hâdi* (☎ 366) 214 1696) is twice as expensive and has rooms with private showers. It's a cheerful enough place, although the bedroom decor is rather odd and the bathrooms only so-so.

Nearby on Cumhuriyet Caddesi the *Otel İdrisoğlu* (☎ (366) 214 1757) has a dingy lobby but serviceable rooms with private bath for US$7 per person. Street-facing rooms could be noisy though. A few doors away is the altogether cheerier *Ruganci Otel* (☎ (366) 214 9500, fax 212 4343) which has pretensions to stylish décor in the bedrooms. For US$12/17 you get TV and breakfast here too. The same warnings about noise would apply.

Just off Nasrullah Meydanı at Banka Sokak 10 is the *Otel Selvi* (☎ (366) 214 1763). Rooms here are averagely comfortable although in need of modernisation, but some on the top floor have good views of the castle. Beware of doors with glass panels that let hallway light in. Prices are supposedly US$7/12 but bartering can bring reductions.

Kastamonu's best is undoubtedly the two-star *Otel Mütevelli* (☎ (366) 212 2020, fax 212 2017) at Cumhuriyet Caddesi 10, across the road from Cumhuriyet Meydanı. The good, clean rooms manage to escape the standard Turkish blanket bed covering, and although the price might seem a bit high (US$17/26/30 a single/double/triple) there are lots of extras like a decent restaurant and bar.

Places to Eat

Across the road from the Otel Hâdi is an alleyway with several small restaurants; the *Ender* here does saç kavurma, while the *Uludağ Pide ve Kebap Salonu* on the corner serves more standard fare. The *Merkez Lokantası*, south of the Otel Selvi, stays open later than most other places, although you're liable to be served tepid food after 7 pm.

In Cumhuriyet Caddesi, near the Otel Mütevelli, is the cheerful *Ömür Pastanesi* where you can sample tavuk göğsü, a dessert made from milk, rice and chicken.

Across the other side of the stream, Plevne Caddesi has several beerhouses, including the *Kervan Saray Bira Salonu* and the *Agora Birahanesi*, the closest thing in appearance to an English pub that you'll find in central Turkey.

Given Kastamonu's lack of exciting eateries, you might want to make up a picnic, in which case it's worth dropping into the *Kaptan Şarküteri*, as you turn from Cumhuriyet Caddesi into Nasrullah Meydanı. Here you'll find a wide range of Turkish cheeses from Kars, Urfa, Van and Erzincan, as well as honey from Erzurum and plentiful olives.

Getting There & Away

Kastamonu's small otogar offers regular departures for Ankara, Samsun and İstanbul. To get to Sinop you usually have to travel via Boyabat. There are hourly departures for Karabük (two hours, US$3), with some buses continuing to Safranbolu. Minibuses for İnebolu and Cide also leave from the otogar.

BOYABAT

Heading for the Black Sea from Kastamonu you may need to transit in Boyabat (1½ hours, US$2), a small town with a large brick-making industry. Boyabat's otogar is just off Adnan Menderes Bulvarı, the main road through town. Chances are you'll be passing through, but with an hour or so to spare, go out of the otogar and turn right along the highway towards a road bridge. Just to the left of the bridge you'll find a pleasant pine-tree-shaded tea garden to while away the time. From the bridge itself there's a fine view of Boyabat's **castle**, built to guard a prominent gorge. Beneath the bridge are some unexpectedly clean toilets.

Alternatively, leave the otogar, cross the highway and cut through any of the breaks in the shops to find the **bazaar** behind. Interspersed amid the shops are some fine old timber buildings. You'll also see women wearing a white, black and red headscarf that looks like an Indian bedspread, called a *pita*.

If you need to spend the night here, come out of the otogar, turn right towards the bridge, cross the highway and turn left following the sign marked 'Şehir'. Just past the PTT on the right you'll find the *Merkez Oteli* (☎ 368) 315 1119) with very basic rooms at US$4 a head. There are several places to eat opposite the otogar but none are going to win any prizes for their cuisine.

The road north from Boyabat passes through some stunning forested scenery, zigzagging up to 1370m, so that it takes 2½ hours to reach Sinop.

SUNGURLU

Going east from Ankara to the Hittite cities of Boğazkale and Alacahöyük takes you through Sungurlu, where you must change buses and may want to stay the night. A commercial and farming town 175 km (three hours) east of Ankara, Sungurlu has nothing to detain you except its transport and minimal lodging services. There is no otogar. Buses and minibuses drop you on the highway or in the centre of town.

Orientation

The town centre (Şehir Merkezi), 500m off the main highway, is marked by an old clock tower next to a fountain facing a platform surmounted by the usual statue of Atatürk. Minibuses to Boğazkale depart from north of this square. Don't let the taxi drivers tell you that the minibuses don't run on Sunday; they do.

Places to Stay & Eat

Sungurlu seems to have given up the unequal battle to persuade people to stay and now has just two hotels, representing extreme ends of the market. *Otel Ferhat* (☎ (364) 311 8067), near where the minibuses for Boğazkale stop and around the corner from the Türkiye Vakıflar Bankası, has tiny, tattered rooms. A waterless double costs US$7 and there are even cheaper singles where you'd have trouble fitting yourself and your bag in at the same time. The *Günay Pide ve Kebap Salonu* next door serves good fresh Turkish pizza cheaply.

Otherwise, you'll have to go for the *Hitit Motel* (☎ (364) 311 8042, fax 311 3873), one km east of the commercial square, on the Ankara-Samsun road. Its position is rather off-putting and the sign can be hard to spot, squeezed in as it is between the Petrol Ofisi fuel station and the Renault garage. Hard though it is to believe, Prince Charles stayed here in May 1992 while on a private birdwatching trip to Turkey. Really, this should be a good choice, with 23 rooms on two floors set amid pretty gardens around a swimming pool (usually empty). The restaurant has good food and service, the guest rooms have private showers and balconies looking onto the grounds, and prices are quite reasonable: US$19/29/39 a single/double/triple, less if it's not full with groups. However, it can seem rather soulless when empty. In the restaurant, expect to spend from US$5 to US$7 per person for lunch or dinner, drinks included.

Getting There & Away

Buses leave Ankara's otogar hourly, heading for Sungurlu. Frequent minibuses also come from Çorum (US$1.50) and bigger buses from Samsun, Amasya, Artvin and all points east.

Getting away from Sungurlu, you can catch a Boğazkale Belediyesi minibus operated by the village (US$0.50) for the 30-km, 40-minute ride to Boğazkale, or pay slightly more and take a minibus. Minibuses run throughout the day, with the last run departing from Boğazkale at 5.30 pm, and from Sungurlu at 6 pm.

To hire a taxi or minibus for a tour of Boğazkale and Alacahöyük is likely to cost about US$30 for the entire car, about twice as much for a 15 to 20-person minibus.

BOĞAZKALE & THE HITTITE CITIES

The village of Boğazkale (or Boğazköy) lies 200 km east of Ankara off the highway to Samsun and is well worth visiting as the site of Hattuşaş, the Hittite capital. Nearby is Yazılıkaya, an open-air Hittite religious sanctuary with fine rock carvings. Boğazkale also makes a possible base for a visit to Alacahöyük, site of yet more impressive Hittite ruins.

Orientation

Boğazkale (population 2500), 30 km south-east of Sungurlu, has several hotels, camping grounds and restaurants, a couple of tea-houses and a few shops selling essentials. Basically a small farming village, it experienced a mini tourism boom in the late 1980s when several new hotels were built. Since then, however, it has had difficulty recovering from the double blow of the Gulf War and the PKK onslaught and you're unlikely to find it overcrowded.

Coming from Sungurlu, you enter the village opposite the Aşikoğlu Motel. From there it's just 100m south to the museum.

Coming from Yozgat, you follow a road which sweeps over the mountains from the south-east and skirts the eastern part of the archaeological zone. There's a fine view of the ruined city from this road.

South of the village, up on the hillside, sprawl the extensive ruins of Hattuşaş. It's exactly one km from the Aşikoğlu Motel to the ticket kiosk, and another 2.5 km up the hillside to the farthest point, the Yerkapı (Earth Gate), along the road which loops through the ruins. The separate site of Yazılıkaya is about three km uphill from the ticket kiosk along another road.

Boğazkale Museum

The little museum in the town (open from 8 am to 5.30 pm, US$1) has a large topographical map of the site, and some Hittite artefacts worth seeing: fascinating cuneiform tablets, signature seals, arrows and axeheads, a saw, and whimsically shaped pots and vessels. High on the walls around the museum are large photographs of the site and Hittite objects during excavation. The few Byzantine crosses come from a later church on the site. There's some German labelling. The toilets here must be some of the best kept in Turkey.

Hattuşaş

Hattuşaş was once a great and impressive city, well defended by stone walls over six km in length. Today the ruins consist mostly of reconstructed foundations, walls and a few rock carvings, but there are several more

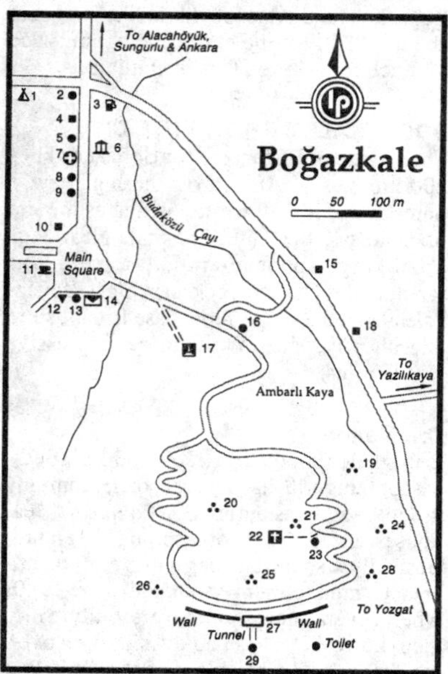

PLACES TO STAY

1 Camping Ground
4 Aşikoğlu Turistik Moteli
10 Hattuşas Restaurant & Pansiyon
15 Başkent Restoran, Pansiyon & Camping
18 Kale-Burg Motel

PLACES TO EAT

11 Tea House
12 Bakery

OTHER

2 Jandarma
3 Petrol Station
5 Adliye
6 Museum
7 İlçe Sağlık Ocağı (Clinic)
8 Ortaokal
9 İlkokul
13 Belediye
14 PTT
16 Tickets
17 Büyük Mabed (Great Temple)
19 Büyük Kale
20 Sarıkale
21 Nişantaş
22 Site of Byzantine Church
23 Watering Trough
24 Güney Kale
25 Yenicekale
26 Aslanlıkapı
27 Yerkapı
28 Kral Kapı
29 Postern

interesting features, including a tunnel and some fine hieroglyphic inscriptions preserved in situ. The site itself is strange, almost eerie, exciting for its ruggedness and high antiquity rather than for its extant buildings or reliefs. Chances are that you'll share it with the skylarks for much of the day.

The road looping around the entire site of Hattuşaş (not including Yazılıkaya) is five km long, from the ticket kiosk all the way around and back. The walk itself takes at least an hour, plus time spent exploring the ruins, so figure on spending a good three hours here. You might want to take some water with you, and start early in the day before the sun is too hot; there's little shade along the way.

Hattuşaş is open from 8 am to 5 pm, with a theoretical break for lunch from noon to 1.30 pm; in practice it's impossible to completely enclose a site this size and you are unlikely to be prevented from getting in. Admission costs US$2 and the ticket is valid for Yazılıkaya as well.

The following description assumes you do the loop in an anticlockwise direction.

The first site you come to, 300m up (south-west) from the ticket kiosk, is the **Büyük Mabed**, or the Great Temple of the storm god, a vast complex that's almost a town in itself, with its own water and drainage systems, storerooms and ritual altars. It dates from the 14th century BC and seems to have been destroyed in around 1200 BC.

About 350m south past the Great Temple, the road forks; take the right (west) fork and follow the winding road up the hillside. On your left in the midst of the old city you can see several ruined structures fenced off from the road, including the **Sarı Kale** which may be a Phrygian fort on Hittite foundations.

From the fork in the road it's about one km uphill to the **Aslanlı Kapı**, or Lion Gate, which has two stone lions defending the city against all comers. The city's defensive walls have been restored along the ridge which allows you to appreciate the scope of the construction effort that took place almost 4000 years ago.

Continue another 700m up to the top of the hill and you'll find the **Yer Kapı** or **Sfenksli Kapi** (Earth or Sphinx Gate), once defended by two great sphinxes, who are now domesticated in the museums of İstanbul and Berlin. The most interesting feature here is the long, 70-metre **tunnel** running beneath the walls to a **postern** on the southern side of the hill. As the true arch was not discovered until much later, the Hittites used a corbelled arch, two flat faces of stones leaning towards one another. Primitive or not, the arch has done its job for millennia, and you can still pass down the tunnel as Hittite soldiers did, emerging from the postern. Your reward is a WC, off to the left at the base of the slope. Climb back up to the Yer Kapı by either of the **monumental stairways** placed on either side of the wide stone glacis beneath the walls. Once back on the top, enjoy the wonderful view from this highest point, sweeping down over Hattuşaş, Boğazkale and beyond. Below you you'll see the **Yenice Kale**, where Hittite engineers transformed the very uneven site into a plain on which to build their structures.

Another 600m eastward down the slope brings you to the **Kral Kapı**, or King's Gate, named after the regal-looking figure in the relief carving. The one you see is an obvious copy, as the original was removed for safekeeping to the Ankara museum. Actually, the figure is not a king at all, but the Hittite war god.

Heading downhill again you'll come to the **Nişantaş**, a rock with a long Hittite inscription cut into it, in sore need of conservation. Immediately opposite a path leads up to the recently excavated **Güney Kale**, or Southern Fort, and to what may have been a royal tomb with fine hieroglyphics and human figures carved into another tunnel-shaped structure.

The ruins of the **Büyük Kale**, or Great Fortress, are 800m downhill from the Kral Kapı. This elaborate fortress also held the royal palace and the Hittite state archives. The archives, discovered in 1906, contained a treaty between Hittite monarch Hattusili III and Egyptian pharaoh Ramses II written in cuneiform on a clay tablet. From the fortress it's just over one km back to the ticket kiosk.

Yazılıkaya

The Turkish name (yah-zuh-LUH kah-yah) means 'inscribed rock', and that's what you find at this site just under three km from Boğazkale. Follow the signs from the ticket kiosk. The road circles a hillock called Ambarlı Kaya, on top of which there were more Hittite buildings, before crossing a stream and climbing the hill past the Başkent restaurant, pension and camping ground (you might want to stop here for refreshments or lunch).

Yazılıkaya was always a naturalistic religious sanctuary open to the sky, but in later Hittite times (13th century BC) monumental gateways and temple structures were built in front of the **natural rock galleries**. It is the foundations of these late structures that you see as you approach from the car park.

There are two natural rock galleries, the larger one to the left, which was the empire's sacred place, and a narrower one to the right, which was the burial place of the royal family. In the large gallery, the low reliefs of numerous conehead gods and goddesses marching in procession indicate that this was the Hittites' holiest religious sanctuary. Of the Hittites' 1000 gods, fewer than 100 are represented here.

Alacahöyük

There's less to see at Alacahöyük, a very old site settled from about 4000 BC, 25 km north of Boğazkale. As at the other Hittite sites, movable monuments have been taken to the museum in Ankara, though there is a small site museum, and a few worn sphinxes and good bas-reliefs have been left in place.

To get there, leave Boğazkale heading north-west on the Sungurlu road, and after 13.5 km turn right at the road marked for Alaca and Alacahöyük. (Coming from Sungurlu, turn left about 11 km after turning onto the Boğazkale road.) Go another 11.5 km and turn left for Alacahöyük, nine more km along.

At the time of writing there was no dolmuş service. The villagers apparently prefer to get rides with trucks which charge less than the minibus drivers. If you don't fancy copying them, reckon on about US$22 to US$25 to get a taxi or minibus to take you to the ruins and back to Boğazkale. Coming from Sungurlu or Yozgat you should be able to get a dolmuş as far as the town of Alaca, 18 km from Alacahöyük, but from there you must hitch.

Alacahöyük is now a farming hamlet with a humble main square on which stands a fountain, a PTT, a souvenir shop, a bakery and a modest grocery shop. The museum is right by the ruins, and both are open from 8 am to noon, and from 1.30 to 5.30 pm, closed on Monday. The admission fee for everything is US$1. In the **small museum** you can inspect tools used in the excavations, and finds from the Chalcolithic and Old Bronze ages. A handy ant-farm-style glass case shows the stratigraphy of Alacahöyük's 15 layers of history. Note also the Hitit Çağı Banyo Teknesi, a Hittite-Age bathtub. Upstairs there's an ethnographic section, which many people find more absorbing than the ancient potsherds.

At the ruins, signs are in Turkish and English. The **monumental gate**, with its lions guarding the door and its very fine reliefs down in front, is what you've come to see. The reliefs show storm-god-worshipping ceremonies and festivals with musicians, acrobats, priests and the Hittite king and queen. Off to the left across the fields is a **secret escape tunnel** leading to a postern as at Hattuşaş.

Leaving Alacahöyük, signs for Sungurlu lead you seven km out to the Sungurlu-Çorum highway by a road not shown on many maps. Turn left (south-west) for Sungurlu (27 km), right for Çorum (42 km) and Samsun (210 km). There are frequent buses along the Sungurlu-Corum highway.

Places to Stay & Eat

Boğazkale's hotels and pensions charge a fairly standard US$7/12 a single/double and most of them only open from April to October. This is a pleasant place to spend the odd night or so, with such noise as there is coming from honking geese, crowing cockerels and braying donkeys. However, the outsize new mosque does its best to shatter the peace!

If you want to be at the heart of Boğazkale's limited action, a good first choice is the 23-bed *Hattuşaş Restaurant & Pansiyon* (☎ (364) 452 2013), on the main square in the village, renting simple but spacious rooms. It's well located so you can easily walk to the museum and to Hattuşaş, and Ahmed, the friendly proprietor, speaks good English. The restaurant, popular with the locals, is pleasingly decorated with old kilims and other artefacts. The pansiyon is open all year round.

The 25-room *Aşikoğlu Turistik Moteli* (ah-SHEEK-oh-loo) (☎ (364) 452 2004), also within easy walking distance of the museum and shops, is open from mid-March to November. Simple double rooms with sink and shower (no toilet) cost US$18 – but the price goes up and down depending on who's asking, and when. The hotel also has a capacious restaurant with acceptable food for around US$5 or US$6 a head. Not surprisingly, it's popular with such tour groups as still come here. At the back a pretty basic *camping ground* charges US$5 for a caravan and US$3 for a tent.

Up the hill, one km from the museum on the road to Yazılıkaya and Yozgat, is the *Başkent Restoran, Pansiyon & Camping* (☎ & fax (364) 452 2037), Yazılıkaya Yolu Üzeri, with 18 motel-style rooms with twin beds and showers. To camp here costs around US$4. The restaurant, with its white laminate tables, dark wood trim and red tile roof is pleasant, and has good views of the ruins.

Just 400m farther up the hill along the Yazılıkaya road is the *Kale-Burg Motel* (☎ (364) 452 2189), which looks fancier than it actually is. Very simple double rooms with showers cost the standard US$7/12. The camping ground is primitive, but there's a *restaurant* here as well. *Atilla Camping* (☎ (364) 452 2101) is just over one km west of the Aşikoğlu Motel on the Sungurlu road. There's a *restaurant* with music and belly dancing in the evenings, but the camping ground is rather far from the shops and there's little shade.

Getting There & Away

With your own car you can stop at Boğazkale on the way to the Black Sea coast at Samsun.

Relying on public transport, you're best off starting from Sungurlu from where there are regular buses and dolmuşes. From Yozgat it's much trickier (see below). If you want to head on to Cappadocia afterwards, the simplest way is to backtrack to Sungurlu and pick up a bus to Ankara either from the main highway or the otogar. In Ankara there will be easy onward connections.

If you don't want to hike around the ruins when you arrive in Boğazkale, you may be able to find a taxi to give you a tour for around US$10.

Boğazkale makes an easy day's excursion from Ankara and several tour operators offer tours for US$75 per person. Look for their advertisements in the *Turkish Daily News* or try Konvoy Tur (☎ (312) 426 7624, fax 467 4608), Atatürk Bulvarı 233/8, Kavaklıdere, Ankara; or Angel Tours (☎ (312) 436 1216, fax 437 6344), Gölgeli Sokak 27/16, Ankara.

YOZGAT

About 35 km south-east of Boğazkale and on the Ankara-Sivas highway is Yozgat (population 50,000, altitude 1301m), with those three things travellers need – hotels, restaurants and an otogar. Otherwise, it's an unprepossessing provincial capital founded by the Ottomans in the 18th century. The main highway is lined with modern Turkish waffle-front apartment buildings. In contrast is the **Nizamoğlu Konağı**, a 19th century Ottoman house converted to hold ethnographic exhibits.

Five km south of Yozgat is **Çamlık Milli Parkı** (Pine-Grove National Park).

Orientation

The old main road, a block north of the highway, is more pleasant than the highway, Ankara Caddesi. Walk two blocks north to reach the main square, Cumhuriyet Meydanı, with its old clock tower, Vilayet building, PTT, and an Ottoman building now serving as local army offices; the sultan's monogram is still emblazoned in the tympanum. The Büyük Cami (or Çapanoğlu Camii, 1778), one long block west of the clock tower, is a late Ottoman work. Yozgat's otogar is less than one km east of the main square, an easy walk. To find your way to the main square from the otogar, go back onto the main road and turn right.

Places to Stay

There are a couple of cheapies around the main square. The *Otel Hitit* (☎ (354) 211 1269), Cumhuriyet Meydanı, Sakarya Caddesi, has been almost worn out by long and frequent usage. Doubles with a sink cost US$7, and with a shower US$10. Across the other side of the square is the *Otel Villa* (☎ (354) 217 0981) which is even more basic, with beds in waterless rooms for US$5 a head. Slightly off the actual square, it could be quieter than the Hitit.

Up a notch is the fairly dowdy, nominally two-star, 44-room *Yılmaz Oteli* (☎ (354) 212 1107, fax 212 1991), Ankara Caddesi 3, on the highway in the middle of town. The rooms here, all with private shower, are clean and spacious if nothing out of the ordinary, but the additional services hardly justify the steep prices (US$20/40 a single/double); the restaurant has closed down and the bar can only rustle up soft drinks. There's a Turkish bath next door.

Places to Eat

Yozgat is not going to win any Michelin stars for its cooking. If you need to eat here, the *66 Restaurant*, in the street leading down to the highway from the clock tower, offers a good choice of kebaps. There's also the smaller *Beyaz Saray* on the corner of the same street where it meets the highway.

If you're just passing through, the otogar has a small *restaurant* and the usual range of snacks.

Getting There & Away

As with travelling to Sungurlu, getting to Yozgat is easy: just hop on a bus from the otogar in Ankara (220 km), Kayseri (250 km), or Sivas (230 km). For most other destinations, you must change buses at one of those cities. All three are a three-hour, US$6 ride from Yozgat.

If you want to get to Boğazkale, you'd be better off starting from Sungurlu since there are no direct buses from Yozgat. Five minibuses a day run from Yozgat to Alaca (the last leaving at 4 pm), whence you can hitch to Alacahöyük, or catch an onward minibus to Sungurlu and another to Boğazkale. If you arrive too late in the day to do this or are pushed for time, a taxi to Boğazkale should cost about US$15 to US$18. For a full tour around (the ride to the site, two hours to look around, and the return run to Yozgat), reckon on more like US$30 for the taxi.

ÇORUM

Set on an alluvial plain on a branch of the Çorum River, Çorum (population 120,000, altitude 801m) is an agricultural town and provincial capital. As with so many settlements in Turkey, its origins extend back into the mists of history. People have been living here for at least 4000 years.

You may have thought a chickpea was just a chickpea but that was before you came to Çorum, the chickpea capital of Turkey. The town's main street is lined with *leblebiciler* (chickpea roasters) and you'll see sacks of the chalky little pulses, all labelled with distinctions obvious to a chickpea dealer but not, perhaps, to anyone else. Turks love to munch leblebi (dry roasted chickpeas) while sipping rakı.

If you're travelling north or east by bus you may have to stop in Çorum. Given the lack of transport to Boğazkale from Yozgat and the shortage of accommodation in Sungurlu, it may also make a handy base for getting to the Hittite sites. Çorum has a small **Byzantine kale** on a hilltop, and a Seljuk mosque, the 13th-century **Ulu Cami** (Great Mosque). Most of its other old buildings are Ottoman, and there are some fine, if crumbling, old houses near the clock tower.

Orientation & Information

The clock tower marks the centre of Çorum, with the PTT, Belediye and tourist office all within 100m. The otogar is one km from the clock tower along İnönü Caddesi where there's a fair sprinkling of banks waiting to change your money. Off the clock tower end of İnönü Caddesi look out for Eğridere Sokak, a small street lined with shops selling gold jewellery. Several of them also offer exchange facilities.

Çorum Museum

About 400m from the otogar is the Çorum Müzesi (open from 8 am to 5.30 pm every day for US$1), with a small, mildly interesting collection of Hittite, Byzantine-Roman and Ottoman exhibits. Ethnographic exhibits cover Turkish life during the last century. If you're stuck for an hour or two in between buses, go out of the main entrance of the otogar, turn left, then left again at the traffic roundabout. The museum is in the copse of pines on the right-hand side at the next roundabout, across the street from the Turban Oteli.

Places to Stay – bottom end

Most hotels are along the main street (İnönü Caddesi) between the museum and the clock tower and there should be something to suit all budgets.

Otel Aygün (☎ (364) 213 364), not far from the museum and the Turban Oteli, is well past its prime but the rooms are reasonably clean and cheap at just US$6/8 a single/double with private shower. It's a great improvement on the grungy *Yılmaz Otel* (☎ (364) 213 1586) further along on the same side of the road, with beds from US$4.

Hotel Merih (☎ (364) 213 8379), facing the clock tower on İnönü Caddesi, is oldish but serviceable, with waterless singles/doubles for US$7/13, slightly more for private facilities.

Places to Stay – middle

The two-star *Hotel Kolağası* (☎ (364) 213 1971, fax 213 1556), İnönü Caddesi 97, is overpriced at US$14/23 for rooms with shower but it's clean and has a lift.

The *Turban Oteli* (☎ (364) 213 8517, fax 213 0612), near the museum and otogar, will never win any prizes for its architecture but it's a friendly, comfortable middle-range place with restaurant, hairdresser and handy shop for toiletries, postcards etc. Rooms with TV and private bath cost US$17/24 (less at quiet times).

Fancier is the new three-star *Çorum Büyük Otel* (☎ (364) 224 6092, fax 224 6094), unfortunately situated at İnönü Caddesi 90 on a hectic road junction as you come into town from Sungurlu but handy for the otogar. Spacious modern rooms with pleasant bathrooms cost US$22/35/45 a single/double/triple, and there are plenty of extras: two restaurants, an American bar (with alcohol), a billiards room, a TV lounge and a sauna.

Even more promising is the three-star *Hotel Sarıgül* (☎ (364) 224 2012, fax 224 0396), tucked away behind Gazi Caddesi at Azap Ahmet Sokak 18, near the Kültür Sitesi. It's 1.5 km from the otogar but otherwise pretty central and is done up in modern style, with bar, restaurant and Turkish bath. Comfortable rooms cost US$22/32 a single/double, but they're not used to foreigners yet.

Places to Eat

The liveliest place in town is the *Sevdalım Restaurant* (☎ (364) 212 8874) on İnönü Caddesi, more or less opposite the Turban Oteli. This is where the chickpea dealers gather to down beer and tuck into saç kavurma (wok-fried lamb), to an accompaniment of live music, sometimes abruptly cut off in favour of televised football. A meal here will cost you about US$4 or US$5. Groups frequent this place, so advance booking might be advisable. There's no aile salonu and lone women may feel conspicuous in the masculine atmosphere.

Otherwise, İnönü Caddesi offers plenty of other choices. The small *Karadeniz Lokantası* offers tandır kebap (pit-roasted lamb), and the *Özler Lokantası*, further up towards the clock tower, does good roast chicken. Across the street, the *Kılıçlar Kebap ve Pide Salonu* has a popular family room upstairs.

For more upmarket dining, head straight

for the *Büyük Otel*. The *restaurant* on the top floor of the Kültür Sitesi in Gazi Caddesi might be another good choice in the evenings.

Getting There & Away

Çorum, on the main Ankara-Samsun highway, has good bus connections. Details of some services follow:

- Alaca – 60 km, one hour, US$1; several minibuses daily
- Amasya – 95 km, 1½ hours, US$2; several buses daily
- Ankara – 242 km, 3½ hours, US$4 to US$6; frequent buses
- Kayseri – 274 km, four hours, US$7; several buses daily
- Samsun – 176 km, three hours, US$5; frequent buses
- Sungurlu – 70 km, one hour, US$1.50; very frequent buses
- Yozgat – 104 km, 1½ hours, US$4; several buses daily

AMASYA

Amasya (ah-MAHSS-yah, population 57,000, altitude 392m), capital of the province of the same name, was once the capital of a great Pontic kingdom. On the banks of the Yeşilırmak (Green River), surrounded by high cliffs, Amasya's dramatic setting adds interest to its numerous historic buildings: the rock-hewn tombs of the kings of Pontus, some fine old mosques, picturesque Ottoman half-timbered houses and a good little museum. Set away from the rest of Anatolia in its tight mountain valley, Amasya has a feeling of independence, self-sufficiency and civic pride. It's one of Turkey's most pleasant towns.

History

Despite seeming rather sleepy, Amasya has seen exciting times. It was a Hittite town, and was conquered by Alexander the Great. When his empire broke up, Amasya became the capital of a successor-kingdom ruled by a family of Persian satraps. By the time of King Mithridates II (281 BC), the Kingdom of Pontus was entering its golden age and dominated a large part of Anatolia.

During the latter part of Pontus' flowering, Amasya was the birthplace of Strabo (circa 63 BC to 25 AD), the world's first historian. Perhaps he felt constrained by Amasya's surrounding mountains, because he left home and travelled through Europe, west Asia and north Africa, and wrote 47 history and 17 geography books. Though most of Strabo's history books have been lost, we know something of their content because he was quoted by many other classical writers.

Amasya's golden age ended when the Romans decided it was time to take all of Anatolia (47 BC) and call it Asia Minor. After them came the Byzantines, who left little mark on the town, and the Seljuks (1075) and Mongols (early 14th century), who built numerous fine buildings which still stand. In Ottoman times, Amasya was an important base when the sultans led military campaigns into Persia. A tradition developed that the Ottoman crown prince should be taught statecraft in Amasya, and test his knowledge and skill as governor of the province. The town was also noted as a centre of Islamic theological study, with as many as 18 medreses and 2000 theological students in the 19th century.

After WWI, Mustafa Kemal (Atatürk) escaped from the confines of occupied İstanbul and came to Amasya via Samsun. Here he secretly met with several friends on 12 June 1919 and hammered out basic principles for the Turkish struggle for independence. The monument in the main square commemorates the meeting; other scenes depict the unhappy state of Turks in Anatolia before the War of Independence. Each year, Amasyalıs commemorate the meeting with a week-long art and culture festival beginning on 12 June.

Orientation

The otogar is at the north-eastern edge of town and the train station at the western edge. It's two km from either to the main square, marked by a statue of Atatürk and a bridge across the river. Most of the town (including the main square, the bazaar and the museum) is on the southern bank of the river. On the northern bank are various government and military offices, the tombs of

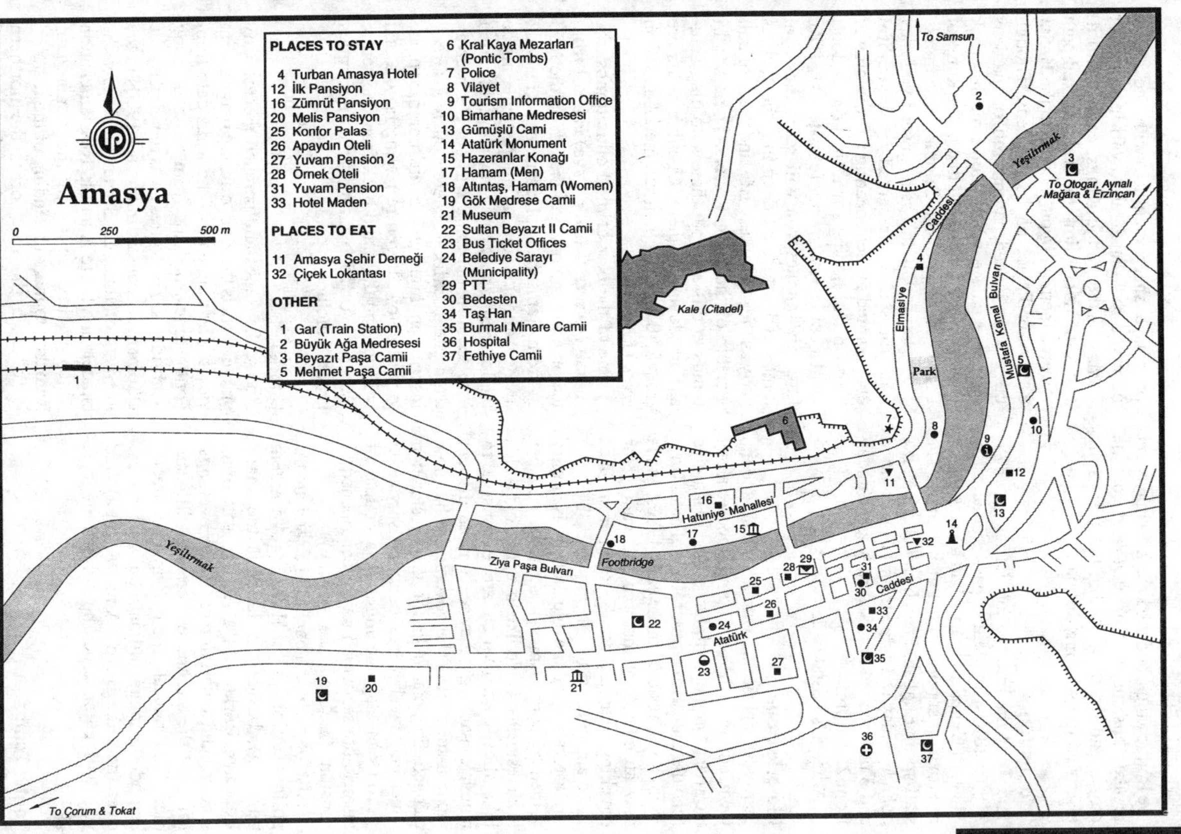
Amasya
0
250
500 m
PLACES TO STAY
4 Turban Amasya Hotel
12 İlk Pansiyon
16 Zümrüt Pansiyon
20 Melis Pansiyon
25 Konfor Palas
26 Apaydın Oteli
27 Yuvam Pension 2
28 Örnek Oteli
31 Yuvam Pension
33 Hotel Maden
PLACES TO EAT
11 Amasya Şehir Derneği
32 Çiçek Lokantası
OTHER
1 Gar (Train Station)
2 Büyük Ağa Medresesi
3 Beyazıt Paşa Camii
5 Mehmet Paşa Camii
6 Kral Kaya Mezarları (Pontic Tombs)
7 Police
8 Vilayet
9 Tourism Information Office
10 Bimarhane Medresesi
13 Gümüşlü Cami
14 Atatürk Monument
15 Hazeranlar Konağı
17 Hamam (Men)
18 Altıntaş, Hamam (Women)
19 Gök Medrese Camii
21 Museum
22 Sultan Beyazıt II Camii
23 Bus Ticket Offices
24 Belediye Sarayı (Municipality)
29 PTT
30 Bedesten
34 Taş Han
35 Burmalı Minare Camii
36 Hospital
37 Fethiye Camii
To Samsun
To Otogar, Aynalı Mağara & Erzincan
Yeşilırmak
Mustafa Kemal Bulvarı
Elmasiye Caddesi
Park
Kale (Citadel)
Hatuniye Mahallesi
Footbridge
Ziya Paşa Bulvarı
Atatürk Caddesi
To Çorum & Tokat

the Pontic kings, and the kale. You may want to take a bus, minibus, or taxi to and from the otogar and the train station, but everything else is within walking distance.

Information

The Tourism Information Office (☎ (378) 218 7428) is in Mehmetpaşa Mahallesi at Mustafa Kemal Bulvarı 27, in a kiosk on the riverbank just north of the main square. The staff speak English, French and German. It's open Monday to Friday from 10 am to noon and 3 to 7 pm, and on Saturday and Sunday from 2 to 7 pm.

Amasya's postal code is 05000.

Historic Houses

Start your sightseeing with a walk around the town, admiring the old Ottoman houses along the river. On the north bank, along Hatuniye Mahallesi, the **Hazeranlar Konağı** dates from 1865. It was restored in the early 1980s, and is now an ethnology museum and gallery for travelling exhibits, usually open from 9 to 11.45 am and 1.15 to 4.45 pm for US$1.

Restoration of the old houses is highly valued by some Amasyalıs. However, other local residents would like to replace old buildings they own (which are expensive to renovate) with what they see as more efficient modern structures. The government has now pledged financial help for their restoration which could weigh in favour of conservation.

You can stay the night in a couple of historic houses which have been opened as pensions (see the Places to Stay).

Also on the north bank of the river are the police station and Vilayet (government building); beside the latter is the shady **Belediye Parkı** with a tea and soft drink service, and entertainment some evenings. Many of the old houses here are still occupied. Walk beneath the railway line directly behind the huge military building on the river (near the Büyük Amasya Hotel), and you will enter a neighbourhood of such houses.

Pontic Tombs

Looming above the northern bank of the river is a sheer rockface with the easily observed rock-cut Kral Kaya Mezarları, or Tombs of the Pontic Kings, carved into it. Cross the river, climb the well-marked path towards them and you'll come to the **Kızlar Sarayı**, or Palace of the Maidens. Though there were indeed harems full of maidens here, the palace which stood on this rock terrace was not theirs but that of the kings of Pontus and later of the Ottoman governors.

As you follow the path upward you may find yourself accompanied by a youthful unappointed guide repeating a few words of German and hoping for a tip. If you don't want a guide, say *İstemez* (eess-teh-MEHZ). In a few minutes you will reach the royal tombs of Pontus, cut deep into the rock as early as the 4th century BC, and used for cult worship of the deified rulers. There are 14 tombs in this area but there's nothing actually inside any of them. Opening hours are from 8.30 am to 7 pm in summer. Admission costs US$0.50.

One of the best of the Pontic tombs, the **Aynalı Mağara** (Mirror Cave) is apart from the others, signposted to the left on the road in from Samsun, a pleasant one-km walk away. Although you can't hope to get inside the lofty entrance, you can walk right round it to see how the tomb was cut clean away from the rockface. There's also a Greek inscription high above the commonplace graffiti below. If you're feeling lazy, a taxi will run you there and back from the centre for about US$5, waiting time (not much needed) included.

Citadel

Above the tombs and perched precariously on the cliffs is the kale, offering magnificent views. The remnants of the walls date from Pontic times, perhaps from those of King Mithridates. The fortress was repaired by the Ottomans, and again in the late 1980s in the interests of tourism. Somewhat below the citadel on a ledge is an old Russian cannon which is fired during the holy month of Ramazan to mark the ending of the fast.

To reach the kale, cross the northern bridge near the Büyük Ağa Medresesi and follow the Samsun road for 850m to a street on the left marked 'Kale'. It's 1.7 km up the mountainside to a small car park, then another 15 minutes' steep climb to the summit, marked by a flagpole.

Amasya Museum

The small museum on Atatürk Caddesi is open from 8.30 to 11.45 am and from 1.15 to 5 pm (closed on Monday). Admission costs US$1. The collection includes artefacts from Pontic, Roman, Byzantine, Seljuk and Ottoman times, and the usual collection of kilims, costumes and weaponry.

Perhaps the most interesting exhibits are the wooden doors of the ancient Gök Medrese Camii, the carpets, and the strange baked-clay coffins. Upstairs, look out for the bronze figure of Teshup, the Hittite storm god, with pointed cap and huge almond-shaped eyes. In the museum garden is a Seljuk tomb, the **Sultan Mesut Türbesı,** containing some gruesome mummies dating from the Seljuk period which were discovered beneath the Burmalı Cami. Not for the squeamish.

Sights East & West of the Main Square

Across Atatürk Caddesi from the museum is the graceful **Sultan Beyazıt II Camii** (1486), Amasya's principal mosque, with a medrese, *kütüphane* (library) and sweet-scented garden.

West of the museum about a half km is the **Gök Medrese Camii** (GEURK meh-dreh-seh), or Mosque of the Blue Seminary, built in 1266-67 by the Seljuks. It has a wonderfully ornate doorway once covered in blue tiles. Near it are several Seljuk türbes, including the **Torumtay Türbesi** (1278), that of the man who founded the Gök Medrese Camii. The neighbouring Ottoman **Yörgüç Paşa Camii** dates from 1428.

East of the museum, across Atatürk Caddesi from the Kapalı Çarşı (Covered Market), is the **Taş Han** (1758), an Ottoman caravanserai still used by local traders and artisans. It was originally larger, but much of it has fallen into ruin. Behind it to the south is the **Burmalı Minare Camii,** or Spiral Minaret Mosque, a Seljuk construction (1237-47) with elegant spiral carving on the minaret, true to its name.

To the east of the main square and Atatürk's statue, perched on a rise, is the **Gümüşlü Cami** (Silvery Mosque) which was built in 1326. It was rebuilt in 1491 after an earthquake, in 1612 after a fire, and again in 1688, then added to in 1903, and restored yet again in 1988.

Sights North of the Main Square

North of the main square along the river are Amasya's other historic buildings. The **Bimarhane Medresesi** (Insane Asylum Seminary) was built by the İlkhanid Mongol governors of Amasya in 1308. The İlkhans were the successors to the great Mongol Empire of Ghengis Khan. Their architecture reflects styles and motifs borrowed from many conquered peoples. Today only the outer walls of the building stand, stabilised to prevent further deterioration. With the pretty garden in front, this place has a sort of brooding presence.

The large obtrusive building on the opposite bank of the river is an army recreation facility, contributing little to the town's beauty.

Next along the river is the pretty **Mehmet Paşa Camii,** an early Ottoman mosque (1486), which now serves as the girls' Koran study centre. The **Beyazıt Paşa Camii,** a few hundred metres north and just past the bridge, was finished in 1419 and bears many similarities to the famous early Ottoman Yeşil Cami in Bursa. Note especially the porch with marble arches in two colours of stone, the entranceway with gold and blue and the carved doors.

Across the river from the Beyazıt Paşa Camii is the **Büyük Ağa Medresesi** (Seminary of the Chief White Eunuch), built to an octagonal plan in 1488 by Sultan Beyazıt II's chief white eunuch, Hüseyin Ağa. Nicely restored, it still serves as a seminary for boys who are training to be *hafız* (theologians who have memorised the entire Koran). The medrese is not open to the public, but if the door is open you may peep in to see local boys at their Koranic studies.

On the southern bank of the river, Ziya Paşa Bulvarı is shady and cool with huge old plane trees. There's an early Ottoman **covered bazaar** (1483) or bedesten in the narrow streets of the market south of here.

Nearby Villages

Occasional buses run to villages in the surrounding hills, where villagers still make lovely striped kilims from sheep and goat's hair. At **Yassıçal** there's a pleasant *restaurant* (☎ (358) 241 6003) set around an artificial pool full of fish; you dine in wooden kiosks amid flowers. At the time of writing a hotel was under construction at the site and grandiose expansion plans even envisage an eventual ski run! You can get here easily at any time with your own transport but the last bus back to Amasya goes at 5 pm.

Further along the road, but without reliable bus links, are **Saraycık Köyü** and **Kaleköy**. Of the two, Kaleköy has the most interesting buildings (the eponymous castle, an old wooden mosque, and a crumbling hamam and stone laundry), but the villagers are moving away, so Saraycık is livelier.

In the villages surrounding Amasya, lovely striped kilims are still made from goats' hair.

You may be able to arrange a taxi excursion to some of these villages. Mr Ali Kamil Yalçın, proprietor of the İlk Pansiyon (see Places to Stay), may be able to advise on the possibilities.

Yedi Kuğular Gölü

About 15 km west of town is the recently made artificial Yedi Kuğular Gölü (Seven Swans Lake), a favourite stopping-place for birds on their spring and autumn migrations. Trees have been planted and when they mature this *kuş cenneti* (bird paradise) may be as welcoming to humans as to birds.

Places to Stay – bottom end

Amasya has one particularly inviting place to stay, the *İlk Pansiyon* (☎ (378) 218 1689, fax 218 6277), Gümüşlü Mahallesi, Hitit Sokak 1, by the river east of the Atatürk statue (follow the signs). Ali Kamil Yalçın is an architect who discovered the once grand but then dilapidated mansion of a one-time Armenian priest, rented it and restored it beautifully to its former grace and charm. The five light, airy, spacious salons are now fitted with beds and bathrooms, and offered to travellers for US$8 to US$21 a single, US$13 to US$29 a double, depending upon the room. Some rooms have three beds. There's one smaller, cheaper room with bath off a courtyard which provides a convivial setting (complete with cat and dog) for breakfast and dinner.

If the İlk Pansiyon is full (as it often is), try the *Yuvam Pension* (☎ (378) 218 1324, 12259), Atatürk Caddesi 24/5, on the main thoroughfare 2½ blocks south-west of the Atatürk statue on the north side of the street. There are actually two Yuvam pensions, one in a modern apartment building on Atatürk Caddesi, and the other, *Yuvam Pension 2*, in an old restored Amasya house, about 300m farther to the south-west (follow the signs uphill marked 'Hastane' and then turn right at the top). The old house, with its quiet garden, is preferable, but both are good choices at US$12 to US$16 a double. Ask about rooms at the *eczane* (pharmacy) at street level, which is where the Yeners are during the day.

Several readers have written to recommend the *Zümrüt Pansiyon* (☎ (358) 218 1769) in Hatuniye Mahallesi. The usual clean, simple rooms cost US$7 a head without bath, but the real plus of this place is the roof terrace with uninterrupted views of the Pontic Tombs, especially impressive when floodlit at night. It's just across the road from the Yıldız Hamam (men only).

Heading further west you'll find the new *Melis Pansiyon* (☎ (358) 212 3650), Hal Karşısı, Torumtay Sokak 135, close to the Gök Medrese. Bright, clean rooms with bath cost US$12/18 a single/double. The décor, while aspiring to Ottoman style, might be a little too precious for some tastes.

Amasya's other cheap lodgings are far less atmospheric. The mundane 31-room *Apaydın Oteli* (☎ (358) 218 1184), Atatürk Caddesi 58, is perhaps the most presentable, charging US$7/10 for a room with sink (cold water only). The common bathrooms have showers with electric-heater shower-heads but there's a Turkish-style splash bath as well.

The inaptly named *Konfor Palas* (kohn-FOHR, Comfort Palace) (☎ (358) 218 1260), Ziya Paşa Bulvarı 4, by the river, has 36 rooms with sinks and charges less: US$5/8. Some rooms have balconies looking onto the river but over an outdoor eating area so they could be noisy.

The similarly priced *Örnek Oteli* (☎ (358) 218 1108), Ziya Paşa Bulvarı 2, is across the courtyard, with eight basic rooms without baths.

Places to Stay – middle

The two-star *Büyük Amasya Hotel* (☎ (358) 218 4054, fax 218 4056), Herkiz Mahallesi, Elmasiye Caddesi 20, north of the centre near the Büyük Ağa Medresesi, is a small, fairly quiet 50-room hotel on the riverbank. It has a restaurant and bar with fine views of the river, and rooms with shower for US$14/20, breakfast included, but is often filled by tour groups.

On the main street across from the Yuvam Pension is the two-star *Hotel Maden* (☎ (358) 218 6050), above the Ford-Tofaş car showroom. It's newer than the Büyük Amasya Hotel, but also noisier and marginally more expensive.

About 28 km north of Amasya on the Samsun road, at Suluova, is the *Saraçoğlu Muzaffer Turistik Tesisleri* (Muzaffer Saraçoğlu's Touristic Installations; ☎ (358) 417 1010), a small highway motel and restaurant next to a fuel station. Rooms are simple but acceptable, though there is some highway noise. The price for a room with bath is from US$12 to US$18 a single, US$20 to US$26 a double.

Places to Eat

Look for small restaurants in the narrow market streets off the main square (the one with the statue of Atatürk), such as the *Çiçek Lokantası*, which is cheap and serviceable, with decent roast chicken and ready food.

The *Elmas Kebap ve Pide Salonu*, on the same street more or less behind the Hotel Apaydın, is similar, and stays open late in the evening.

There are many small kebapçıs north of the Yuvam Pension in the bazaar streets around the covered market. The *Beslen Kebap ve Pide Salonu*, Kocacık Çarşısı 18, has good food and friendly staff.

Ocakbaşı Aile Pide ve Kebap Salonu, in front of the Konfor Palas, is friendly enough and has outdoor tables where you can enjoy your freshly baked pide.

For tea in a pleasant garden setting, go to the Belediye Parkı, across the river from the main square, by the town hall.

For nicer dining at a higher price (from US$5 to US$8 for a full meal with drinks), go to the restaurant in the *Büyük Amasya Hotel*.

Foreign tourists are also welcome at the *Amasya Şehir Derneği*, in the dismal Öğretmen Evi building overlooking the river at the north end of the bridge opposite the main square. This is a quasi-private club with stark décor but good moderately priced food and drink. Amasya's prominent citizens come here to eat, drink, talk business and while away the evening.

Getting There & Away

Amasya is not far off the busy route between Ankara and Samsun, so buses are frequent. It is also on the railway line between Samsun and Sivas, but the daily trains are quite slow. Some bus companies (Amasyatur, Azimkar) maintain ticket offices on Atatürk Caddesi across from the Belediye building, just east of the Sultan Beyazıt II Camii. Details of some daily bus services follow:

Adıyaman (for Nemrut Dağı) – 650 km, 10 hours, US$12; one bus
Ankara – 335 km, five hours, US$7; very frequent buses
Çorum – 95 km, 1½ hours, US$3; at least eight buses
İstanbul – 685 km, 11 hours, US$22; a dozen buses
Kayseri – 405 km, eight hours, US$7; three buses
Malatya – 460 km, nine hours, US$8; five buses
Samsun – 130 km, 2½ hours, US$3; 10 buses
Sivas – 225 km, four hours, US$5; five buses
Tokat – 115 km, two hours, US$4; nine buses

There are also direct buses to Adana, Alanya, Antakya, Antalya, Bursa, Diyarbakır, Erzurum, Gaziantep, İzmir, Marmaris and Şanlıurfa.

TOKAT

Tokat (TOH-kaht, population 90,000, altitude 623m) is on the southern edge of the Black Sea region and shares in its fertility.

The town doesn't get many tourists, and those who do come usually have a quick look at the famous Gök Medrese and then leave, which is a shame since they miss the wonderful Latifoğlu Konağı, as excellent an example of a restored Ottoman house as you'll find in Turkey.

Anyway, Tokat is a fine place to spend a day or two. Half Ottoman and half modern, it's liberally sprinkled with crumbling ruins, many of them now below ground level. Between the 13th and 20th centuries Tokat's ground is thought to have risen by up to five metres as silt from the hills was carried down into the valley by rain and floods, and debris from earthquakes added to the accumulation.

History

Tokat's history is very long and involved, starting in 3000 BC and proceeding through the sovereignty of 14 states, including the Hittites and Phrygians, the Medes and the Persians, the empire of Alexander the Great, the kingdom of Pontus, the Romans, the Byzantines, the Turkish principality of Danışmend, the Seljuks and the Mongol İlkhanids.

By the time of the Seljuk Sultanate of Rum, Tokat was the sixth largest city in Anatolia and on important trade routes. The roads approaching the city are littered with great Seljuk bridges and caravanserais testifying to its earlier importance.

After the Mongols rushed in and blew away everyone's composure in the mid-13th century, their Ilkhanid successors took over, followed by a succession of petty warlords who did little for Tokat.

Under the Ottomans, who took the town in 1402, it resumed its role as an important trading entrepôt, agricultural town (the grapes are especially good) and copper-mining centre (the copper artisans have been famous for centuries). Significant non-Muslim populations (Greek, Armenian, Jewish) were in charge of the town's commerce until the cataclysm of WWI. There is still a small but active Jewish congregation here.

Orientation & Information

The town centre is the big open square named Cumhuriyet Alanı, where you will find the Vilayet, the Belediye, the PTT and the coyly named Turist Otel. A subterranean shopping centre has added lots of retail space without ruining the spaciousness of the square. Across the main street from the shopping centre is the Tarihi Ali Paşa Hamamı, an old Turkish bath studded with bulbous glass to let in sunlight.

Looming above the town is a rocky promontory crowned by the obligatory ancient fortress. Beneath it cluster the bazaar and the town's old Ottoman-style houses.

The main street, Gazi Osman Paşa Bulvarı, runs downhill from the main square

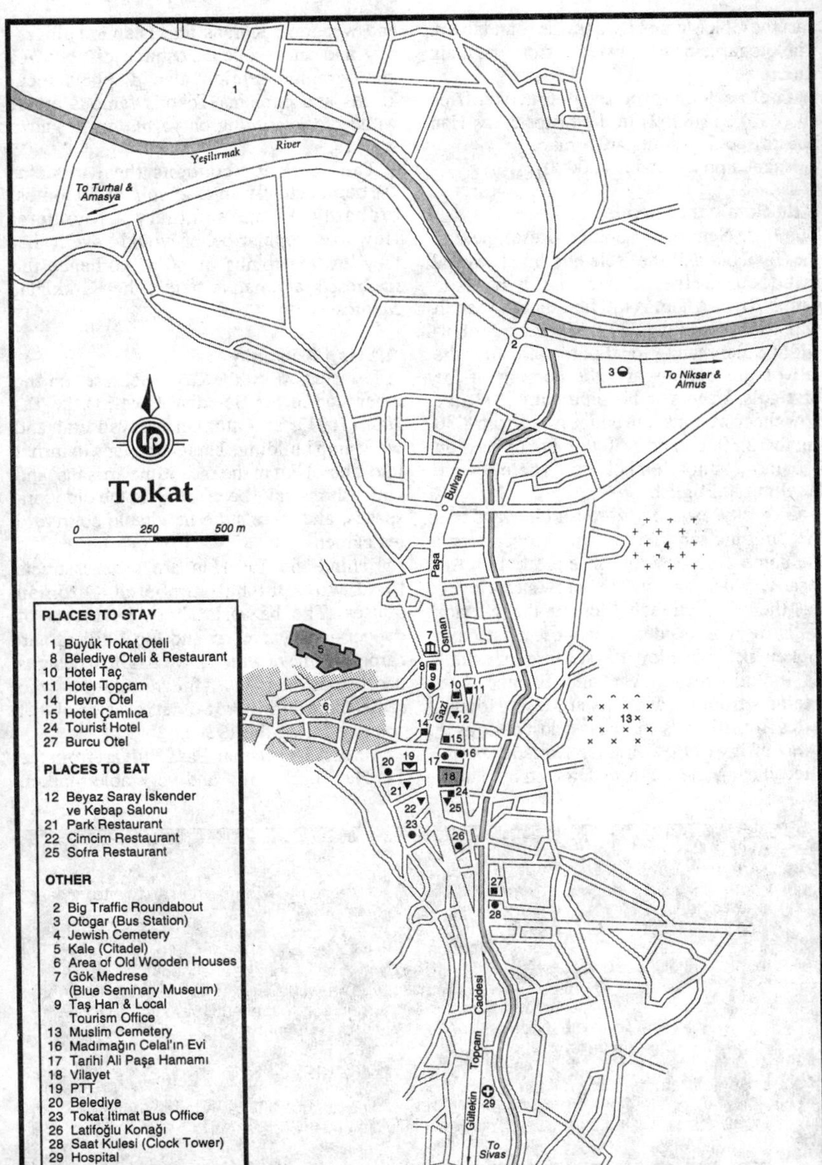
Tokat
0
250
500 m
Yeşilırmak
River
To Turhal & Amasya
To Niksar & Almus
Bulvarı
Paşa
Osman
Gazi
Topçam
Caddesi
Gültekin
To Sivas
PLACES TO STAY
1 Büyük Tokat Oteli
8 Belediye Oteli & Restaurant
10 Hotel Taç
11 Hotel Topçam
14 Plevne Otel
15 Hotel Çamlıca
24 Tourist Hotel
27 Burcu Otel
PLACES TO EAT
12 Beyaz Saray İskender ve Kebap Salonu
21 Park Restaurant
22 Cimcim Restaurant
25 Sofra Restaurant
OTHER
2 Big Traffic Roundabout
3 Otogar (Bus Station)
4 Jewish Cemetery
5 Kale (Citadel)
6 Area of Old Wooden Houses
7 Gök Medrese (Blue Seminary Museum)
9 Taş Han & Local Tourism Office
13 Muslim Cemetery
16 Madımağın Celal'ın Evi
17 Tarihi Ali Paşa Hamamı
18 Vilayet
19 PTT
20 Belediye
23 Tokat Itimat Bus Office
26 Latifoğlu Konağı
28 Saat Kulesi (Clock Tower)
29 Hospital

past the Gök Medrese to a traffic roundabout. The otogar is nearby, two km from the main square.

There's a helpful local tourist office (☎ (356) 211 8252) in the historic Taş Han but its opening hours are erratic.

Tokat's postal code is 60000.

Blue Seminary Museum

The Blue Seminary (Gök Medrese), next to the Taş Han and the Belediye hotel several hundred metres down the hill from Cumhuriyet Alanı, is the first thing to see. It was constructed in 1277 by Pervane Muhineddin Süleyman, a local potentate, after the fall of the Seljuks and the coming of the Mongols. Used as a hospital until 1811, it's now the town museum and is open from 8.30 am to 12.30 pm and 1.30 to 5 pm (closed on Monday); admission is US$1. There's some labelling in English.

Gök (sky) is also a word for blue, and it is the building's blue tiles which occasioned the name. Very few of these are left on the façade, which is now well below street level, but there are enough tiles on the interior walls to give an idea of what it must have looked like in its glory days. Museum exhibits include Stone Age and Bronze Age artefacts from excavations at Maşat Höyük, relics from Tokat's churches (most curious is a wax effigy of the Christian Christina, martyred during the reign of Diocletian), tools and weapons, Korans and Islamic calligraphy and an excellent costume display. An ethnographic section also displays local kilims and explains Tokat's famous art of wood-block printing on *yazmalar*, or gauze scarves.

The seminary contains the **Kırkkızlar Türbesi**, actually an assembly of 20 tombs, probably of the seminary's founders. However, popular belief would have it that they are the tombs of 40 girls, hence the medrese's alternative name, the Kırkkızlar Medresesi.

Taş Han & Vicinity

A few steps from the Gök Medrese, on the other side of the Belediye Hotel, is the Taş Han (1631), an Ottoman caravanserai and workshop building. There are plans to turn it into a hotel but in the meantime artisans' and crafts shops have been set up in the old work spaces, and there's the inevitable courtyard tea garden.

Behind the Taş Han are bazaar streets lined with old half-timbered Ottoman houses. The bazaar's shops have lots of copperware, yazmalar and local kilims and carpets, some of which have Afghani designs because of the many Afghani refugees who settled here during the Soviet invasion of that country during the 1980s.

Across Gazi Osman Paşa Bulvarı from the Taş Han, in the fruit and vegetable market,

---

He Came, He Saw, He Conquered

It may come as quite a surprise to learn that Julius Caesar was near Tokat when he uttered those immortal words *Veni, Vidi, Vici* (I came, I saw, I conquered).

During the first century BC, Tokat lay within the kingdom of Pontus, which had held out against the Romans, indeed declared war against them, even after the rest of Anatolia had submitted.

In 47 BC, while Julius Caesar was distracted in Egypt, King Pharnake II launched an attack on the Roman provinces of Galatia, Armenia and Cappadocia with the intention of recreating the earlier Pontic kingdom of his ancestors. Caesar was forced to retaliate and marched on Zile with his army. At a site between the modern villages of Yünlü and Bacul on the Zile to Amasya road, the two armies confronted each other. During a fierce five-hour battle, Pharnake's army drove chariots with scythes fitted to their wheels against the Romans, but despite heavy losses Caesar's troops eventually triumphed.

He then sent the famous words back to Rome, landing latterday Tokat with the inevitable but cringe-making advertising slogan...'I came, I saw, I fell in love!' ■

TOM BROSNAHAN

TOM BROSNAHAN

Top: Ottoman houses along the Yeşilırmak River, Amasya, Central Anatolia.
Bottom: The famous 'moonscape' troglodyte dwellings of Göreme valley.

CHRIS BARTON

PAUL STEEL

Top: A monastery on a rocky outcrop below Hasan Dağı in Cappadocia, Turkey's most visited tourist area, which lies between the Black Sea and the Taurus Mountains.

Bottom: When invaders flooded across the land bridge between Europe and Asia, Cappadocians went underground, carving elaborate multi-level cave cities.

stands the **Hatuniye Camii** and its medrese, dating from 1485 during the reign of Sultan Beyazıt II.

Several hundred metres north down the hill from the Gök Medrese, on the same side of the street, look out for the portal of the **Sümbül Baba lodge of dervishes**, probably built in 1292 and now incorporated into a house. Another block further north is the octagonal **Sefer Paşa Mausoleum**, a Seljuk-style tomb dating from 1251. Beside it a road leads up to the kale, of which little remains but the fine view.

Tarihi Ali Paşa Hamamı

Go into any hamam in Turkey and ask the masseur where he came from and chances are he'll answer Tokat. So while in Tokat you should certainly not miss the chance to bathe in the wonderful Tarihi Ali Paşa Hamamı. These baths, with their breast-like glass bulbs to let in light, were built in 1572 for Ali Paşa, and have separate bathing areas for men and women. A simple bath costs US$2.

Historic Houses

On the main street south of Cumhuriyet Alanı stands the **Latifoğlu Konağı**, one of the most splendid 19th-century houses on view in Turkey. The house's large, gracious rooms are surrounded with low sedir sofas. In the bedrooms, bedding was taken up and stored in cabinets during the day, Asian-style. The most spectacular rooms are upstairs: the Paşa Odası (Pasha's Room) for the men of the house, and the Havuzbaşı room for the women. The light, airy upstairs hall would have been used in summer only as it was not heated.

It's open from 9 am to 12.30 pm and 1.30 to 5 pm (closed on Monday) for US$0.50. Enter through the garden on the north side.

Madımağın Celal'ın Evi, Tokat's other well-preserved old house, is one block down on the street to the east of the Tarihi Ali Paşa Hamamı. It contains wonderfully elaborate gold and green plasterwork and painted scenes of Topkapı Palace and Sultan Ahmet Mosque but is not open to visitors at the moment.

Sulu Sokak

The houses to the east of Gazi Osman Paşa were mainly owned by Tokat's wealthier citizens, but to the west you can find many streets of simpler but elegant houses. Take the street running west beside the Ali Paşa Camii in Cumhuriyet Alanı (it's signposted to the Bedesten) and you'll arrive in Sulu Sokak, which used to be Tokat's main thoroughfare before the Samsun-Sivas road was improved in the 1960s. The further along it you go, the more interesting it gets, with the crumbling remains of a bedesten and several medreses, türbes and mosques. At the western end of the road, smaller cobblestoned streets fan out in all directions. Here you can lose yourself amid wonderful old wooden houses, their upper storeys jutting at all angles to suit the geography of the street.

Excursions

Seventy km west of Tokat, **Zile** is near where Caesar battled Pharnaces and afterwards sent his famous one-liner – *Veni, Vidi, Vici* – back to Rome. The actual battle site was along the Amasya-Zile road. The town of Zile has a very old citadel, and mosques and hamams dating from the Danışmend, Seljuk and Ottoman periods.

Formerly Neocaesarea, **Niksar**, 54 km north-east of Tokat, was a city of the Pontic kings, then of the Romans. For 40 years after its conquest in 1077 by the Seljuk general Melik Ahmet Danışmend Gazi it was the capital of the Danışmend Turkish Emirate, and today preserves several rare examples of Danışmendid architecture, as well as many Ottoman works.

Forty-eight km to the west of Tokat and an easy break of journey between Amasya and Tokat, **Turhal** has an impressive citadel with a network of subterranean tunnels. It, too, was a Danışmendid town, and has several mosques, baths and other buildings to show for it.

The Roman city of Sebastopolis (today **Sulusaray**) lay 67 km south-west of Tokat, on the banks of the Çekerek river. Excavations here have produced extensive remains and there is now a museum with some fine mosaics. Getting to it without your own transport could be tricky, though, since it's 49 km off the main Tokat to Sivas road.

Places to Stay – bottom end

Among the cheapest places is the old *Belediye Oteli* (☎ (356) 214 9924), on Gazi Osman Paşa Bulvarı, which charges US$6/8 for a single/double with a sink, slightly more with shower and TV.

Across the main street in the bazaar, near the Hatuniye mosque, the *Hotel Topçam* (☎ (356) 211 0315) is as basic as Tokat gets but dirt-cheap at US$7.50 a double.

The situation improves as you move towards the centre. The *Hotel Taç* (☎ (356) 214 1331), in the İnci Vakıf İş Hanı building on Gazi Osman Paşa Bulvarı, opposite the Taş Han, charges US$6/7 for waterless rooms with peeling wallpaper. Those on the kale side have fine views.

The nearby 26-room *Hotel Çamlıca* (☎ (356) 214 1269), Gazi Osman Paşa Bulvarı 85, badly needs renovating but prices are only US$7/13 with cold-water sink or US$12/17 with hot water and private shower. Get a back room if you need peace and quiet. Across from the Çamlıca and Taç is the superior *Plevne Otel* (☎ (356) 214 2207), Gazi Osman Paşa Bulvarı 83, named for the great general's most famous battle. Posted prices for its rooms are slightly higher than for those at the Çamlıca and Taç but price reductions are usually offered.

Facing the Vilayet building, just off Cumhuriyet Alanı, is the one-star *Turist Otel* (☎ (356) 214 1610). The rooms with private showers are old but clean and serviceable, and the cosy lobby is decorated with bits of Roman, Byzantine and Seljuk stonework and local woven and embroidered crafts. Rooms cost US$12/16 with shower.

If you need somewhere near the otogar for a quick getaway, the two-star *Hotel Gündüz* (☎ (356) 211 1278), Gazi Osman Paşa Bulvarı 200, is one km away, suitable if a bit noisy at US$10/16 with bath. It's a 10-minute walk north of the main square.

Camping Tokat has no organised camping grounds, but you can camp at several recreation areas nearby, including Gümenek (the ancient town of Comana, nine km east); Almus, on the shores of the lake, 35 km east; Niksar Ayvaz hot springs; and Çamiçi forest, 53 km north-east.

Places to Stay – middle

The *Burcu Otel* (☎ (356) 212 8494), Gazi Osman Paşa Caddesi 48, 300m south of the main square and just north of the clock tower (1902), has quite comfortable rooms with private baths for US$11/20, breakfast included.

Despite its distance from the centre (three km from the main square), by far the best middle-range bargain in town is the four-star *Büyük Tokat Oteli* (☎ (356) 228 1661, fax 228 1660) in Demirköprü Mevkii, on the north-western outskirts. Its 60 rooms all have TVs and private baths with tubs, and cost only US$23/34/56 for a single/double/suite, breakfast included. These prices must certainly rise as the hotel's business increases. For now, enjoy the big swimming pool, Turkish bath, barber's shop and pastry shop at low rates. Both the restaurant and the pool have wonderful views thrown in.

Places to Eat

The local speciality is Tokat kebap: skewers of lamb, sliced potato and aubergine (eggplant) hung on rods and baked rather than grilled in a wood-fired oven. Tomatoes and pimentos (peppers), which take less time to cook, are baked on separate skewers. As the lamb cooks, it releases juices which baste the potato and aubergine.

The *Beyaz Saray İskender ve Kebap Salonu*, across the street from the Taş Han and the Belediye Hotel, is a simple split-level place with good Bursa-style döner kebap and a selection of grilled meats and salads. Meals for US$2 are easy to get, though you can spend a bit more.

Behind the Beyaz Saray, in the sebze halı (fruit and vegetable market) near the Hatuniye Camii, are little köfte and kebap shops with even lower prices. Try the *Cihan Lokantası* on the corner: you can find it easily if you walk straight out of the Taş Han, across Gazi Osman Paşa Bulvarı, down the alley and into the market. It's a bit fly-blown but very friendly.

Between the Taş Han and the Gök Medrese, the *Belediye Lokantası*, on the ground floor of the Belediye Hotel, is fancier than the hotel and has a vine-draped central courtyard. Expect to spend around US$3 or US$4. Heading north towards Cumhuriyet Alanı you'll pass the *Hacıbeyler Pide Salonu*, down a side alley with a few pavement tables.

The most pleasant place in town is the *Park Restaurant*, to the left of the Belediye on the main square. True to its name, dining tables here are set on terraces amidst evergreens and cooled (in spirit at least) by a tinkling fountain and pool. Come here for a meal or a relaxing glass of çay. A good feed costs from US$4 to US$6.

Just south of Cumhuriyet Alanı on the main street, on the way to the Latifoğlu Museum House, is the light, airy *Sofra Restaurant* with good meals for US$4 to US$7. The *Cimcim Restaurant* on the west side of the main street has gloomier décor but serves good fresh pide and beer to go with it. This is also the best place for Tokat kebap.

Getting There & Away

Bus Tokat's small otogar is not as busy as some, but buses still manage to get you where you want to go pretty easily. The better bus companies provide servis buses to ferry you into town. Otherwise, if you don't want to wait for the infrequent ordinary bus service, a taxi will cost about US$2 to the main square. To walk, go 400m west to the traffic roundabout, turn left (south) and it's just over one km to the cluster of hotels, 1.5 km to the main square. Several bus companies have ticket offices on the south side of the main square, saving you a trip to the otogar to buy onward tickets. Daily services from Tokat include:

Amasya – 115 km, two hours, US$3; about nine buses
Ankara – 440 km, eight hours, US$12; frequent buses
İstanbul – 800 km, 14 hours, US$18; several buses
Samsun – 245 km, 4½ hours, US$6; frequent buses
Sivas-105 km, two hours, US$4; frequent buses
Yozgat – 240 km, 4½ hours, US$6; hourly buses south to Yıldızeli, then hourly buses west to Yozgat

To/From Sivas From Tokat you can go east up to Kızıliniş Geçidi (Kızıliniş Pass, 1150m) then south into the Çamlıbel Dağları mountain range, up over Çamlıbel Geçidi (Çamlıbel Pass, 2038m), down again to Yıldızeli, then into Sivas. Along the way, you leave the lushness of the Black Sea littoral and enter the Anatolian Plateau with its dry red soil. For information on Sivas, see the Eastern Anatolia chapter.

Black Sea Coast

Turkey's Black Sea coast is a unique part of the country, lush and green throughout the year with plentiful rainfall, even in summer. Dairy farming, fishing and tea production are big industries, and there are bumper crops of tobacco *(tütün)*, cherries *(kiraz)* and hazelnuts *(fındık)*; during the summer roadsides are lined with hazelnuts laid out to dry in the sun.

You'll catch the occasional glimpse of crumbling old Ottoman houses of wood and plaster, but for the most part the towns of the Black Sea coast, especially those to the east, are conspicuous for their ugly brick and concrete construction.

The Black Sea coast is more popular with Turkish holiday-makers and those from the ex-Soviet republics than with westerners. Its waters are certainly chillier than those of the Aegean or the Mediterranean but can be refreshing nonetheless.

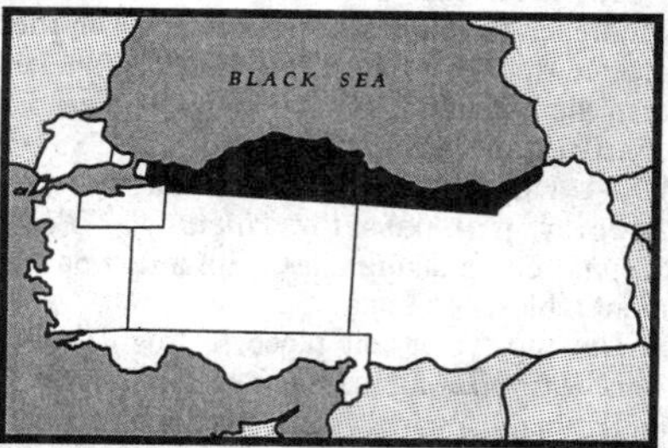

Highlights

- Cruising along the coast from İstanbul to Rize
- Dining in one of Amasra's fish restaurants
- Climbing up to Sumela Monastery
- Bathing in the Sekiz Direkli Hamam in Trabzon
- Seeing the Hemşin people in holiday mood in Ayder
- Trekking in the Kaçkar mountains
- Crossing into Georgia

History

The coast was colonised in the 8th century BC by Milesians and Arcadians, who founded towns at Sinop, Samsun and Trabzon. Later it became the Kingdom of Pontus. Most of Pontus' kings were named Mithridates, but it was King Mithridates IV Eupator who gave the Romans a run for their money in 88-84 BC. He conquered Cappadocia and other Anatolian kingdoms, finally reaching Nicomedia (Kocaeli/İzmit), which was allied with Rome. When the latter came to its defence, Mithridates pushed onward to the Aegean. The Roman response was hampered by civil war at home, but Rome's legions finally drove into Cappadocia and Pontus (83-81 BC), and Mithridates was forced to agree to a peace based on prewar borders.

In 74-64 BC Mithridates was at it again, encouraging his son-in-law Tigranes I of Armenia to seize Cappadocia from the Romans. He tried, but the Romans conquered Pontus in response, and forced Mithridates to flee and later to commit suicide. The Romans left a small client-kingdom of Pontus at the far eastern end of the coast, based in Trebizond (Trabzon).

The coast was ruled by Byzantium, and Alexius Comnenus, son of Emperor Manuel I, proclaimed himself emperor of Pontus when the crusaders sacked Constantinople and drove him out in 1204. His descendants ruled this small empire until 1461, when it was captured by Mehmet the Conqueror.

While Alexius was in Trabzon, Samsun was under Seljuk rule and the Genoese had trading privileges. But when the Ottomans came, the Genoese burned Samsun to the ground before sailing away.

After WWI, the Ottoman Greek citizens of this region attempted to form a new Pontic state with Allied support. Turkish inhabitants, disarmed by the Allied occupation authorities, were persecuted by ethnic Greek guerrilla bands which had been allowed to keep their arms. It was fertile ground for a revolt. Mustafa Kemal (Atatürk) used a bureaucratic ruse to escape from the sultan's control in İstanbul, and landed at Samsun on 19 May 1919. He soon moved inland to Amasya, and began to organise what would become the battle for independence.

Getting There & Away

Details and schedules are given in the Getting There & Away sections for individual towns but this summary should help with planning your travels along the Black Sea coast.

Air Turkish Airlines (THY) has daily nonstop flights between Trabzon and Ankara and İstanbul, and between Samsun and İstanbul. İstanbul Airlines flies between İstanbul and Trabzon on Monday, Tuesday, Wednesday and Sunday.

Bus Buses to and along the coast are fast, frequent and cheap. Ulusoy, the most prominent company, has normal, non-smoking, double-decker and luxury services between Trabzon and many other cities. It's quite easy to take the bus to Samsun from Bartin (130 km), Ankara (420 km), Kayseri (450 km) or Sivas (340 km).

Train The only passenger rail service to the Black Sea coast is the *Karaelmas* express which departs from Ankara daily at 7.55 am, arriving in Zonguldak at 7.10 pm. Departure from Zonguldak is at 9.20 am, with arrival in Ankara at 8.08 pm. The single fare is US$5.

Boat Turkish Maritime Lines operates car ferries on what amounts to a weekly mini-cruise service between İstanbul and Rize. Ships depart from İstanbul each Monday afternoon, calling at Sinop and Samsun on Tuesday, and at Giresun in the early hours on Wednesday, before arriving in Trabzon around 9.30 am and in Rize at lunch time. They then return to Trabzon to take on west-bound passengers and cars at dinner time. On Thursday the boat calls at Giresun, Samsun and Sinop, arriving back in İstanbul by mid-afternoon on Friday. The main problem with this service is that tickets sell out fast – well in advance in summer. If you're travelling Pullman or deck class you'll also have to endure pretty awful toilet facilities.

The five classes of cabin range from cheap 'E' class to deluxe 'A' class, and there are also aircraft-type Pullman reclining seats, the cheapest way to go. Some sample per person prices (in US$) to/from İstanbul follow:

Port	*Seat*	*Cheap Cabin*	*Deluxe Cabin*	*Car*
Sinop	$10	$12	$22	
Samsun	$11	$15	$25	$33
Giresun	$15	$19	$31	$38
Trabzon	$16	$22	$35	$45
Rize	$18	$25	$42	$53

The cruise is fun, but much of the time you will be travelling at night with no chance to appreciate the passing scenery. Food and drink on board tend to be expensive and not very good (breakfast costs US$3, lunch or dinner US$8, paid for with chits *(konsomasyon fişi)* bought from the purser), so pack your own supplies. Heading for Trabzon, there will be time to stock up in Samsun too. If you find the Pullman seat uncomfortable, stake out some deck space, roll out your sleeping bag, and spend the night beneath the stars. 'Deck class' may be the only option anyway if all the accommodation is full.

Getting Around

With the exception of Amasra, the Black Sea coast west of Sinop is difficult to get to and has little to offer at present. Its chief city, Zonguldak, is a gritty industrial centre and port town.

Access to the western coast is slow and sometimes difficult. East of Sinop, and especially east of Samsun as far as Trabzon, things pick up considerably. Although some upgrading is taking place near Samsun, the coast road is mainly single carriageway and has trouble coping with the volume of traffic, especially in summer. Frequent buses ply up and down though.

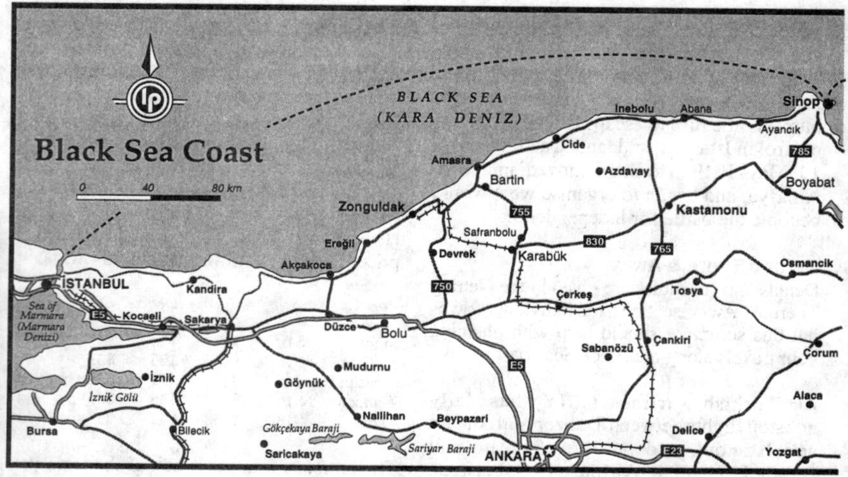

Between Amasra and Sinop there's some rolling beautiful coastline. The 116-km coast road between Sinop and Bafra also passes beautiful, unspoilt scenery, with fields of sunflowers and racks of drying tobacco to catch the eye in summer.

The 360-km ride from Samsun to Trabzon can be done in a day if you wish but the most attractive stretch of coast is between Ordu and Ünye where development has been kept to a minimum and there are several attractive small ports; coming from the west, it would be particularly worth pausing at Bolaman, Yalıköy, Mersin or Perşembe. You'll find campsites, tea gardens and fish restaurants at regular intervals along the way.

Beyond Trabzon, the scenery deteriorates into a sequence of ugly modern towns, built with complete disregard for the environment.

After taking in Trabzon's sights you can head up onto the plateau to Erzurum, or eastward along the coast through the tea plantations to Rize, Hopa and the Georgian border.

From Hopa you can climb into the mountains to Artvin in Anatolia's north-eastern corner, a region of exceptionally beautiful scenery described in detail in the Eastern Anatolia chapter.

AMASRA

Amasra (population 6700) is a pleasant coastal town in the shadow of a fortified promontory which juts out assertively towards the coastal sea lanes. This small fishing port is little visited by tourists, which adds to its charm. It's on the western Black Sea coast, 90 km north of Safranbolu (see the Central Anatolia chapter) and 100 km east of Zonguldak, and should not be confused with the similarly named inland city of Amasya 130 km south of Samsun.

If you're planning to visit out of season, be warned that many of the restaurants and hotels close at the end of October.

Orientation & Information

As you come into Amasra, you pass the museum on the left. Head straight on and you'll reach the eastern beach, which is mostly residential. Turn left at the park and follow Küçük Liman Caddesi around to Atatürk Meydanı (the main square), where most of the buses stop. Continue past the Çınar Pansiyon & Restaurant to find half a dozen small pensions and restaurants, plus the entrance to the citadel. On Tuesdays and Fridays a market is held next to the Belediye

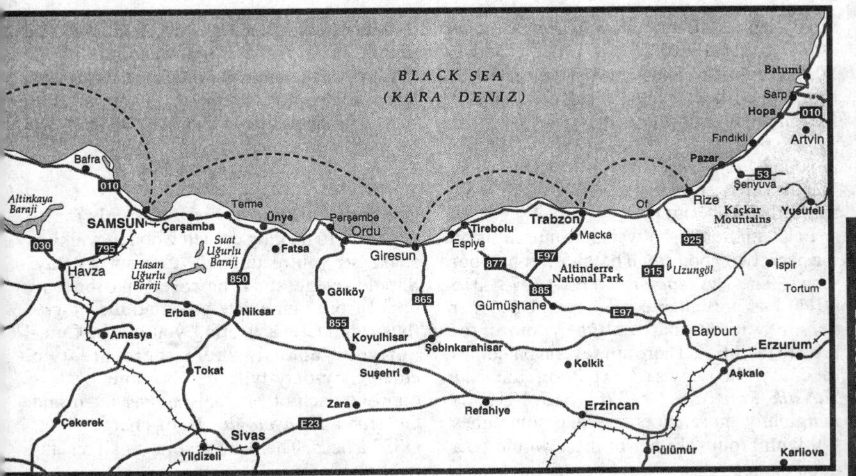

(Municipality) across the street from the Çınar. There's a small office here for the local Kültür ve Turizm Derneği (Culture & Tourism Association). The government tourist office, rarely open, is off to the east.

Amasra's postal code is 67570.

Citadel

Follow Küçük Liman Caddesi through several massive stone portals to reach the kale (citadel), the promontory fortified by the Byzantines when this small commercial port was known as Sesamos Amastris. The greater fortress seems to have replaced a smaller one erected against Russian adventurers around 861. Rented by the Genoese as a trading station in 1270, Amasra was taken by Mehmet the Conqueror in 1460 without a fight. During Napoleon's invasion of Ottoman Egypt in 1798, French traders doing business in Anatolia were gathered together and interned here for five years as potential enemy agents. Under Ottoman rule, Amasra lost its commercial importance to other Black Sea ports.

Much of the area within the citadel's walls is now residential. Make your way to the north-western outcrop to enjoy the views from a rocky meadow fragrant with wild figs, iris, bay, thistle, wild mint and sage.

Amasra Museum

The museum, on the seafront near the park, contains a fairly standard collection of Roman, Byzantine and Hellenistic odds and ends, together with some fine costumes and gold-embroidered bed linen. It's open daily except Monday from 9 am to 5.30 pm and admission costs US$1.

Handicrafts

Around town you'll see shops stuffed with turned-wood trinkets known as *ağaç biblo* (wooden bibelots). Amasra's woodworkers traditionally carved utilitarian objects like spoons, forks and spatulas, and these no-nonsense items are still easy to spot. But as cheap stainless steel and aluminium utensils have invaded their markets, carvers have switched to producing things like statuettes, lampshades and key rings, lacking the appeal of the traditional items.

Places to Stay

Many cheap hotels are on Küçük Liman Caddesi between the Belediye and the citadel gate. *Otel Pansiyon Belvü Palas* (☎ (378) 315 1237), Küçük Liman Caddesi 20, has two floors of clean, bare waterless rooms well kept by the resident family of Mehmet Ot. Sunset views are best from rooms 6, 7 and 8. The cost is US$5 per person. *Çınar Pansiyon* (☎ (378) 315 1018), Küçük Liman Caddesi 1, charges the same for fairly basic rooms.

In Çamlı Sokak, between the museum and the park, two good small hotels offer harbour views. The *Paşakaptan Oteli* (☎ (378) 315 1011) has presentable rooms for US$7 per person without bath, slightly more for private facilities. There are several balconies to enjoy the views. Next door, the *Nur Turistik Pansiyon* (☎ (378) 315 1015) is marginally more expensive and sometimes full with groups. Either of these would be a good choice.

Places to Eat

Amasra has several pleasant seafront fish restaurants, although you should reckon on paying US$6 to US$8 for a meal. Overlooking the main harbour is the upstairs *Çesm-i Cihan* fish restaurant. The *Çınar Restaurant*, across Küçük Liman Caddesi from the Belediye, has an outdoor terrace where you can dine beneath shady plane trees. The fish here is good, as is the börek, especially when it's piping hot. The *Mustafa Amca'nın Lokantası* next door advertises canlı balık (live fish) and is particularly popular at Sunday lunch time.

The nearby *Kupa Birahanesi* is a favourite local drinking place, but food is served as well.

For cheaper meals, *Köşem Pide ve Kebap Salonu*, inland near the park, serves decent-sized portions of good food for US$2 to US$4 for a full meal.

The shady park is the place to enjoy a cool drink or bracing glass of çay in either the *Café Kumsal* or the *Halikarnas Aile Çay Bahçesi*. The *Kumsal* serves pide and lahmacun too.

Getting There & Away

The town of Bartın, 10 km south of Amasra, is better served by transport than Amasra proper. From Ankara, Karabük, Safranbolu or Zonguldak, you will probably have to take a bus to Bartın, then change to a minibus to reach Amasra. From Safranbolu, it's 2½ hours by bus to Amasra.

Bartın

The town of Bartın is interesting only for its expertise in making carved wooden walking sticks so you're unlikely to want to stay. Should you get stuck, however, take the road uphill from immediately behind the *otogar* (bus terminal). It'll bring you out in Cumhuriyet Caddesi where there are two emergency-only-type hotels more or less opposite each other: the *Emniyet Oteli* and the *Hotel Kalaycıoğlu*. Both charge about US$2 a head. There are several small restaurants nearby too.

AMASRA TO SİNOP

Travelling the scenic coastal road from Amasra eastward to Sinop is slow-going, with mostly local point-to-point minibus services. If you have your own transport it's enjoyable to explore this relatively untouristed part of the coast, stopping for a swim at Bozköy beach west of **Çakraz**, to see the boat-wrights at work in the town of **Kurucaşile**, or for a rest in the pretty village of **Kapısuyu**.

İnebolu (population 8000) resembles Amasra in its splendid isolation, but has several hotels, pensions and restaurants to serve travellers.

West of İnebolu, **Abana** is a fast-growing resort with a decent beach. At Ayancık the road divides, with the left (northern) fork being the more scenic route to Sinop.

SİNOP

Sinop (SEE-nohp, population 25,000), on a promontory jutting into the Black Sea, is a natural site for a port, and has been one for millennia.

The town takes its name from the legend of Sinope, daughter of the river god Asopus. Zeus fell in love with her and, in order to win her heart, promised to grant her any wish.

Sinope, who didn't fancy marrying him, asked for eternal virginity. Outwitted, Zeus allowed Sinope to live out her days in happy solitude at the tip of the peninsula.

History

There is evidence of port life in and around Sinop since the first Chalcolithic settlements of around 4500 BC. Colonised from Miletus in the 8th century BC, its trade slowly grew and successive rulers – Cimmerians, Phrygians, Persians, the Pontic kings (who made it their capital), Romans and Byzantines – turned it into a busy trading centre. The Seljuks used Sinop as a port after taking it in 1214; but the Ottomans preferred to develop Samsun, which had better land communications.

On 30 November 1853, Sinop was attacked without warning by a Russian armada and the local garrison was overwhelmed with great loss of life. The battle of Sinop hastened the beginning of the Crimean War in which the Ottomans allied with the British and French to fight Russian ambitions in the Near East.

Orientation & Information

Sinop is at the narrow point of the peninsula, with the road continuing eastward beyond the town to beaches and land's end. The otogar is at the western entrance to the town by the fortified walls. From here the main street, Sakarya Caddesi, goes eastward through the centre 800m directly to the Sinop Valiliği (the provincial government headquarters), just north of which are the museum and the Temple of Serapis.

From the Valiliği, Atatürk Caddesi turns right (south) and descends the hill 250m past the clock tower and Belediye to the PTT, the prominent Hotel Melia-Kasım and the harbour. East of here the road leads along the shore three km to Karakum Plajı, a municipal beach.

Tourist information can be obtained from the trendy-looking Evim Café-Bar at Kıbrıs Caddesi 7/A (☎ (368) 261 7900) where some German is spoken. To find it from Kurtuluş Caddesi, take Denizciler Yolu, the road heading inland from opposite the PTT Evi. This becomes Kıbrıs Caddesi as it nears Sakarya Caddesi.

Sinop's postal code is 57000.

Fortifications

Open to easy attack from the sea, Sinop seems to have been fortified since earliest times but the existing walls are developments of those originally erected in 72 BC by Mithridates IV, king of Pontus. At one time the walls, some three metres thick, were over two km in length.

Across Sakarya Caddesi, south of the otogar, is a Seljuk building converted into a prison by the Ottomans in 1877 and still in use. On the northern side of the otogar down near the shore is an ancient bastion called the Kumkapı (Sand Gate). Another square tower looms above the harbour on the south side of town.

East of the centre almost at Karakum beach is the Paşa Tabyaları (Pasha Battery), a gun emplacement built to defend the town during the Crimean War.

Religious Buildings

In the town centre on Sakarya Caddesi stands the **Alaettin Camii** (1267), also called the Ulu Camii. It was constructed on the orders of Muinettin Süleyman Pervane, a powerful Seljuk grand vizier. The mosque has been repaired many times; its marble mihrab and mimber were added in 1429 by the local Candaroğlu emir.

Next to the Alaettin Camii is the **Alaettin Medresesi**, also called the Süleyman Pervane or Alaiye Medresesi, built in the late 13th century by the self-same Süleyman Pervane to commemorate the Seljuk conquest of Sinop.

Go eastward uphill from the Sinop Valiliği along Kemalettin Sami Paşa Caddesi to reach the **Balatlar Kilisesi**, a Roman temple converted to a Byzantine church in the 7th century. A few traces of frescoes are visible.

Farther uphill, one km from the Valiliği, is the **Cezayirli Ali Paşa Camii** (Mosque of Ali Pasha the Algerian). Inside is the **Seyit Bilal Türbesi**, or tomb of St Bilal, built for Emir

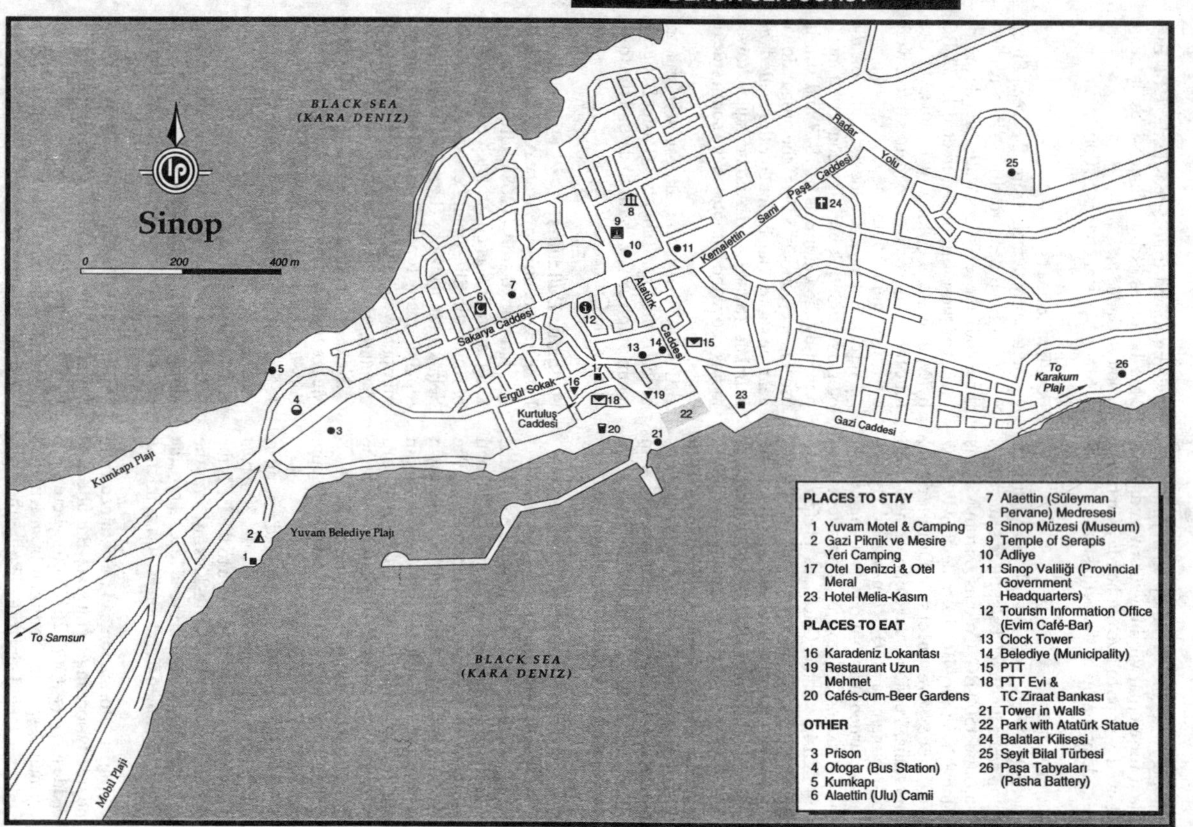
Sinop
0
200
400 m
BLACK SEA
(KARA DENIZ)
BLACK SEA
(KARA DENIZ)
Radar Yolu
Kemalettin Sami Paşa Caddesi
Atatürk Caddesi
Sakarya Caddesi
Ergül Sokak
Kurtuluş Caddesi
Gazi Caddesi
To Karakum Plajı
Yuvam Belediye Plajı
Kumkapı Plajı
Mobil Plajı
To Samsun
PLACES TO STAY
1 Yuvam Motel & Camping
2 Gazi Piknik ve Mesire Yeri Camping
17 Otel Denizci & Otel Meral
23 Hotel Melia-Kasım
PLACES TO EAT
16 Karadeniz Lokantası
19 Restaurant Uzun Mehmet
20 Cafés-cum-Beer Gardens
OTHER
3 Prison
4 Otogar (Bus Station)
5 Kumkapı
6 Alaettin (Ulu) Camii
7 Alaettin (Süleyman Pervane) Medresesi
8 Sinop Müzesi (Museum)
9 Temple of Serapis
10 Adliye
11 Sinop Valiliği (Provincial Government Headquarters)
12 Tourism Information Office (Evim Café-Bar)
13 Clock Tower
14 Belediye (Municipality)
15 PTT
18 PTT Evi & TC Ziraat Bankası
21 Tower in Walls
22 Park with Atatürk Statue
24 Balatlar Kilisesi
25 Seyit Bilal Türbesi
26 Paşa Tabyaları (Pasha Battery)

Tayboğa in 1297. Seyit Bilal, grandson of Hüseyin (who was a grandson of the Prophet Muhammed), was blown ashore here in the 7th century and put to death by the Byzantines.

Down near the harbour in the market area is the **Tersane Hacı Ömer Camii** (1903) formerly a Gothic church. Next to it is a touching monument, a fountain built in memory of the many Turkish soldiers who died in the surprise Russian attack of 1853. The fountain was built using the money recovered from the soldiers' pockets.

Museum & Temple

Just north of the Valiliği is the Sinop Müzesi, open from 8 am to 5.30 pm (noon to 5.30 pm on Monday, 9 am to 5 pm at weekends) for US$1. The collection spans Sinop's history from the Bronze Age to the Turkish War of Independence. A collection of 19th-century Greek Orthodox icons are reminders that the Black Sea coast was heavily populated by Ottoman Greeks until the War of Independence and the subsequent exchange of populations with Greece.

In the museum's garden are mosaics, tombstones and a few remains of an ancient **Temple of Serapis** (the Egyptian embodiment of Apollo) excavated in 1951.

Beaches

As you approach Sinop, turn right (south) a few hundred metres west of the otogar and prison and descend to the shore to find the Yuvam Belediye Plajı (municipal beach), a forest camping area, and the Yuvam Motel. On the north side of the peninsula near the Kumkapı is another small beach where the water is cooler.

Three km east of the harbour on the southern shore is Karakum beach, officially styled the Özel İdare Karakum Yüzgeç Tatil Köyü, with a pay beach of black sand, a restaurant, a nightclub and a nice camping ground with shady tent sites and electrical hook-ups.

Across the peninsula on the northern shore is Akliman, a long beach backed by forest and adjoined by the Hamsaroz fiord.

Places to Stay

Camping South-west of the otogar near the Yuvam Belediye Plajı are two camping grounds. At *Gazi Piknik ve Mesire Yeri*, 300m south-west of the main road, you camp in full shade with fine views of the sea and there are tables and benches, even a playground for the children. There's easy transport to the town centre along the main road. The charge of US$3 per site is rarely levied at slow times of the year.

Farther along the same road, 700m off the main road (two km west of the Valiliği), the *Yuvam Belediye Dinlenme Tesisleri* camping ground is fairly dismal, with shadeless sites with hook-ups, but has a reasonable restaurant with a shady terrace.

The camp sites at Karakum (☎ (368) 261 5117), 3.5 km east of the Valiliği along the southern shore, are pleasantly shady, with hook-ups, and cost about US$3 per site.

Hotels As a port town, Sinop has plenty of cheap hotels, mostly with posted rates of US$7/12 for a single/double without bath (US$10/17 with bath), although discounts are readily available out of season. Start looking by the harbour in and around Kurtuluş Caddesi, with the PTT Evi and Ziraat Bankası as landmarks.

Otel Denizci (☎ (368) 261 0904) and *Otel Meral* (☎ (368) 261 3100) are right across the street from the Ziraat Bankası. Of these two the Meral, with small, clean rooms, is probably the better choice although the glass-panelled doors let in corridor light infuriatingly. Round the corner from the Denizci, the *Karahan Oteli* (☎ (368) 261 0688) is in a courtyard which should cut down some of the street noise.

Yılmaz Aile Pansiyonu (☎ (368) 261 5752), at No 11 on the street just east of the PTT Evi, charges less (US$4.50 per person and US$1.25 for hot showers) but is friendly and lives up to its family reputation.

In İskele Caddesi, right beside the waterfront cafés, is the *Uğur Oteli* (☎ (368) 261 3742) where some of the otherwise unexceptional front rooms have pleasant harbour views. Watch out for noise here though.

The best place in town is the rather dingy two-star *Hotel Melia-Kasım* (☎ (368) 261 4210; fax 261 1625), Gazi Caddesi 49. It's 250m south of the Valiliği, just east of the harbour on the waterfront. The location is good, with sea views from many rooms, but the nuclear-powered nightclub may keep you up till all hours of the night. Rooms cost US$22/34 a double for land/sea views, breakfast included. If the navy's in town it could well be full.

At the time of writing the once-good *Hotel 117* in Rıhtım Caddesi was closed pending renovation. It may have reopened by the time you read this.

Places to Eat

If you're staying around Kurtuluş Caddesi, the *Karadeniz Lokantası* is handily positioned and serves breakfast, lunch and dinner at good prices, but without alcohol. Alternatively the nearby *Liman* is popular with visiting sailors of both sexes.

East of the PTT Evi along the waterfront are several open-air cafés-cum-beer gardens with shady terraces. This being a port, menus feature international dishes alongside the more usual Turkish ones. The *Barınak Café*, for example, can rustle up a hamburger, pizza, spaghetti or steak and eggs. Probably the best food and décor is at the *Restaurant Uzun Mehmet*, facing the end of the dock, but it lacks views of the boats which is a shame. Breakfast goes for less than US$2, although if you want your eggs hot you need to say so. Lunch or dinner will cost from US$4 to US$8, slightly more for fish.

After dinner you can drink tea in one of the many tea gardens lining the seafront.

Getting There & Away

Most of the services leaving Sinop's small otogar are heading for Ankara (nine hours) or Samsun (three hours), with some buses continuing to Trabzon (six hours). There's only one bus a day heading west for Inebolu and that's at 8 am. If there's no direct service heading for Kastamonu, take a minibus and change at Boyabat (2½ hours, US$2). To get to Safranbolu you'll need to take a bus to Karabük and change (six hours, US$3). There are no direct services to Amasra.

Getting Around

Dolmuşes (US$0.30) run through the town from the otogar in the west to Karakum on the south-eastern shore. A taxi to the otogar from Kurtuluş Caddesi costs about US$2.

SİNOP TO SAMSUN

On the Samsun road 116 km west of Sinop is **Bafra**, a town known as a centre of the Black Sea tobacco-growing region. There's no reason to stop, but if you need a meal there are numerous small restaurants on the main square near the Hükümet Konağı (government headquarters). A few rather forlorn hotels offer emergency lodging.

SAMSUN

Burnt to the ground by the Genoese in the 15th century, Samsun (sahm-SOON, population 300,000) has little to show for its long history. A major port and commercial centre, it's the largest city on the coast, a grim and often dusty place. There's little reason to stop here except to change buses, have a meal or find a bed.

Orientation & Information

The city centre is Cumhuriyet Meydanı (Republic Square), just north-west of a large park with an equestrian statue of Atatürk. Just south-east of the statue stands the Vilayet (provincial government headquarters). A handy landmark is the Hotel Yafeya on the north-west side of Cumhuriyet Meydanı.

The large building like a celestial ski jump on the waterfront is the new Kültür Sarayı. When it's finished it will host ballet, concerts, theatre performances and opera.

The train station is one km south-east and the otogar just over two km south-east of the centre along the shore road, Atatürk Bulvarı. Any city bus or dolmuş heading north-west through Samsun will drop you at Cumhuriyet Meydanı (US$0.30).

The Tourism Information Office (☎ (362) 431 1228) is beside the Archaeological

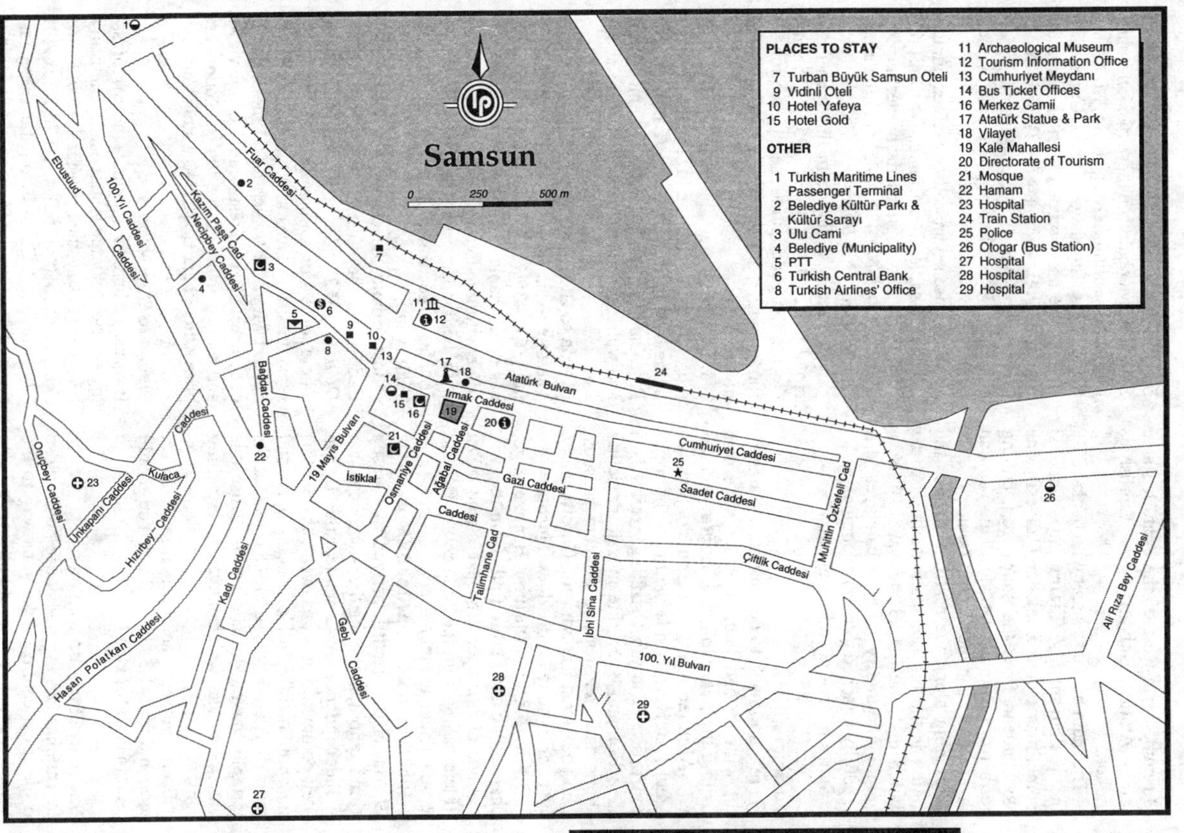

BLACK SEA COAST

Museum, north-west of the Atatürk statue across Atatürk Bulvarı. Some English is spoken.

The main business street with banks, PTT and restaurants is Kazım Paşa Caddesi (sometimes called Bankalar Caddesi), one block inland from the shore road, cutting north from Cumhuriyet Meydanı. You can change money at the Central Bank.

Running along the seafront towards the station is the big Lunapark funfair. At the station end you'll find the Vagon Café, a couple of gaudily painted carriages still hopefully attached to a steam engine.

Samsun's postal code is 55000.

Museums

There's not much to detain you in Samsun, but with an odd hour to spare it's worth visiting the **Arkeoloji ve Etnoğrafya Müzesi** (Archaeological Museum), just off Atatürk Bulvarı, beside the tourist information office. The most striking exhibit is a huge Romano-Byzantine mosaic depicting Thetis and Achilles and the four seasons, found nearby at Karasamsun. Unfortunately, the poor lighting hardly does it justice.

Other exhibits include Bronze Age, Chalcolithic and Hittite finds from the twin mounds at İkiztepe, a bronze statue of an athlete dating from the 2nd century BC and some wonderful embroidery.

Right next door is the **Atatürk Müzesi**. On 19 May 1919 Atatürk arrived in Samsun from İstanbul, preparing the way for the War of Independence. A statue near the Turban Oteli commemorates this event, as does this museum, mainly full of photographs and items of Atatürk's apparel. One look at his portable shaving kit and you'll realise this was not a man who believed in travelling light!

Both museums are open from 8 am to noon and from 1.30 to 5.30 pm. You should get into both for US$1.

Places to Stay – bottom end

Samsun has lots of good cheap hotels close to the town centre. Make your way to the Atatürk statue and Vilayet building just one block south-east of Cumhuriyet Meydanı. Stand midway between these two landmarks and walk inland along Kale Mahallesi towards the futuristic Merkez Camii. The streets here are crowded with cheap hotels like the *Otel Altay* (☎ (362) 431 6877), Meşrutiyet Sokak 5, a clean, friendly place charging US$9/11 a single/double without bath.

Nearby are several other choices, including the passable *Otel Sönmez* (☎ (362) 431 2669) with similar prices, the borderline *Otel Menekşe* (☎ (362) 431 9835), and the emergencies-only *Otel Bahar*.

Much the best choice in this area is the *Hotel Gold* (☎ (362) 431 1959), Orhaniye Geçidi 4, a good, quiet, clean place renting rooms with bath for US$12/18 a single/double.

If everything hereabouts is full, there are more cheap hotels around Gaziler Meydanı in the bazaar. Walk north-west along Kazım Paşa Caddesi, turn left after the Central Bank and walk several short blocks to get there.

Places to Stay – middle

The three-star, 96-room *Hotel Yafeya* (☎ & fax (362) 435 1131), Cumhuriyet Meydanı, has comfortable if somewhat noisy rooms, some with good views over the city. Rooms with bath cost from US$20/34 a single/double, larger suites with TV and minibar slightly more.

Just around the corner, on Kazım Paşa Caddesi, is the three-star, 46-room *Vidinli Oteli* (☎ (362) 431 6050, fax 431 2136) where some rooms are more like suites, with separate sitting areas and views over Cumhuriyet Meydanı (which could mean noise, of course). The roof restaurant has fine views and works of art on the walls. Rooms are pricey though, at US$27/40 a single/double.

Places to Stay – top end

It would be hard to imagine a more depressing exterior for what is supposedly Samsun's best place to stay, the four-star *Turban Büyük Samsun Oteli* (☎ (362) 431 0750, fax 431 0740) at Sahil Caddesi, on the shore just north of Cumhuriyet Meydanı. Inside things improve although signs of wear and tear are still obvious, and the décor is decidedly old-fashioned. If you're after a swimming pool or tennis court, this could be the place for you, but only the two suites rise to air-conditioning, despite the price tags of US$35 to US$39 for a single and US$50 to US$55 for a double (the higher prices are for sea views, but even these encompass the rusting TCCD track as well).

Places to Eat

The hotel areas also have lots of small, good restaurants. Look for the *Sila Restaurant* on the corner of Cumhuriyet Caddesi and Hürriyet Sokak, directly opposite the Vilayet. This is the most pleasant place near the park and offers meals for about US$4. A few steps back along Cumhuriyet Caddesi (towards the Hotel Yafeya), facing the park, are the *Ravza Restaurant*, which serves good meals and cheap lahmacun, and the adjoining *Zirve Pide ve Kebap Salonu*, another kebap, pide and lahmacun place. Next in this row, *Birtat Pastanesi* satisfies desires for sweets and puddings. You can sample aşure (Noah's Pudding) here. Alternatively continue towards Cumhuriyet Meydanı, stopping at the *Divan Pastanesi* for cakes and coffee outdoors.

On the corner of Irmak and Osmaniye Caddesis is the popular *Oba Restaurant*. Turn down Osmaniye Caddesi for the *Ovalı Restaurant*, where you can have wine or beer with your meal. There are lots more small places to eat around the Merkez Camii.

Ezgi Akçaabat Köfte Salonu at Kazım Paşa Caddesi 31 serves good cheap köfte and other dishes, and tends to be open over holidays and at breakfast time when other places are closed.

All the better hotels have their own restaurants. That at the *Büyük Samsun* is not overly expensive and has live entertainment in the evenings. There are set meals for US$10 or you can go à la carte.

Heading out of town, it's worth noting that the big *Terminal Café* at the otogar offers good food and friendly service and has nice clean toilets too.

Getting There & Away

Air Turkish Airlines has nonstop daily flights between Samsun and İstanbul for about US$80. Make your reservations at the Turkish Airlines office (☎ (362) 431 5065/3455), Kazım Paşa Caddesi 11/A.

Bus Samsun seems to offer at least one bus service per day to every important destination in Turkey, and very frequent buses to logical next destinations. Though there are daily trains between Samsun and Sivas, the train trip takes over 12 daylight hours, and is hardly worth it when the bus makes the same trip in about half the time. Details of some daily bus services follow:

Amasya – 130 km, 2½ hours, US$3; 10 buses
Ankara – 420 km, eight hours, US$16; frequent buses
Artvin – 615 km, 10 hours, US$10; several buses
Giresun – 220 km, four hours, US$6; frequent buses
İstanbul – 750 km, 12 hours, US$18to US$23; several buses
Kayseri – 530 km, nine hours, US$10; a few buses
Sinop – 168 km, three hours, US$3; several buses
Sivas – 345 km, 6½ hours, US$7; a few buses
Trabzon – 365 km, six hours, US$18; frequent buses
Yozgat – 275 km, 7½ hours, US$8; a few buses

Boat For details of the Turkish Maritime Lines car ferries between İstanbul and Trabzon, stopping at Samsun, see the beginning of this chapter. The Turkish Maritime Lines agent is Türer Alemdarzade (☎ (362) 445 1605) by the harbour.

We've also had reports of a ferry service between Samsun and Constanţa, Romania, by the *Eforie*.

Getting Around

Dolmuşes to the otogar ply Atatürk Bulvarı (look for signs saying 'Garaj'). City buses to the airport leave from the small bus depot near the tourist information office.

EAST TO TRABZON

Two of Anatolia's great rivers, the Kızılırmak and the Yeşilırmak, empty into the sea on either side of Samsun. The rivers have built up fertile deltas which are now planted with corn and tobacco crops amidst scenes of bucolic contentment. Each house has a lush lawn from its door to the roadway, and each lawn has its own fat cow.

The road is good and you can travel quickly between Samsun and Ünye. You might want to break your journey after 37 km at **Çarşamba** to examine an unusual wooden -framed and tile-roofed mosque.

Ünye

Ünye (EURN-yeh, population 46,000), a small port town amid hazelnut groves, is 95 km east of Samsun. Its biggest claim to fame is that the great Turkish mystical poet Yunus Emre, who wrote during the early 14th century, is thought to have been born here.

Seven km inland from the town along the Niksar road stands **Ünye Kalesi**, a fortress built by the Byzantines to protect this pass to the interior.

In the centre of Ünye, you might note that the Eski Hamam was once a church. It's open to men in the morning and women in the afternoon (US$2). You won't be able to miss the huge new Merkez Büyük Camii taking shape to the east of the main square.

Ünye's bus station is 500m south-east of the Atatürk statue in the centre.

Information The Tourism Information Office (no telephone) is beside the Belediye on the sea-facing side. Some staff speak English. Otherwise there's the usual stock of brochures.

Places to Stay As you approach Ünye coming from Samsun, the road skirts the beaches and passes a number of camping grounds, pensions and seaside motels, including the *Europa*, *Camping Derya* and *Altınkum*; more development is on the way.

The *Belediye Çamlık Motel* (☎ (452) 312 1333), in a pine forest on the shore just under two km west of Ünye, is well used but pleasantly situated and not overly expensive for what you get. A double room with bath and sea view costs US$16, or US$20 for a two-room suite with small kitchen.

The nearby *Pansiyon İpek Yolu* (☎ (452) 312 2643), a tidy, modern place on the shore nearby, is slightly cheaper. *Motel Kumsal* (☎ (452) 312 4490), farther west of the town, is also worth considering.

There are other small hotels in the town itself. Facing the Belediye is the new *Otel Burak* (☎ (452) 312 0186) which has clean, simple rooms with bath for US$6/12 a single/double. A few doors along is the equally new *Güney Otel* (☎ (452) 323 8406) where very pleasant rooms have natural wood fittings. Even some of the singles here are a fair size, and there's a roof terrace with good views. Prices are US$9 or US$12 a head depending on whether you have a bathroom.

Round the corner in Hükümet Caddesi is the older and more basic *Hotel Çınar* (☎ (373) 323 1148), charging US$4 per person.

The *Otel Kılıç* (☎ (452) 323 1224), Cumhuriyet Meydanı, Hükümet Yanı 4, is on the main square next to the government headquarters (Ünye İlçesı Hükümet Konağı). It provides good, clean, light rooms with showers for US$5/10/12 a single/ double/ triple. Some front rooms have balconies. Beware the minaret noise from the neighbouring Saray Camii, however.

Places to Eat Unusually, Ünye seems to have more jewellers and pharmacies than good eating places. Heading into town from the otogar you'll pass the big *Beyti Kebap Salonu* with the usual range of dishes for around US$2 to US$4. A block east of the main square there's also the *Terme Pide Evi* for something cheaper. The *Park Restaurant*, right on the seafront, has more atmosphere but is inevitably pricier.

Ordu

Riding eastward from Ünye, the road passes through **Bolaman**, with many fine (though dilapidated) wooden Ottoman houses, and then through the town of Perşembe.

Seventy km east of Ünye is Ordu (population 102,000), another fishing port with some nice old houses. When approaching the town from the west, you pass a small forest picnic spot *(orman piknik yeri)*.

Orientation & Information The centre of town is at the Atatürk bust by the Aziziye (Yalı) Camii, where there's a town plan on a signboard. The bazaar is just inland.

The otogar is 1.5 km east of the main square, but the dolmuş station for local routes is just east of the main square. You can buy bus tickets at offices a few steps inland from the mosque by the main square.

The Tourism Information Office (☎ (452) 223 1608) is conveniently situated on the ground floor of the Belediye, just east of the mosque on the main road. Rather unexpectedly, good English is spoken here.

Ordu's postal code is 52100.

Museum The Pasha's Palace & Ethnographic Museum (Paşaoğlu Konağı ve Etnoğrafya Müzesi) is 500m uphill from Ordu's main square past the Aziziye Camii. Follow signs reading 'Müze – Museum'.

This late 19th-century house, a pale yellow box decorated with wedding-cake trim, has a fairly tame ethnographic exhibit downstairs. The bedrooms, guest rooms and salon on the 1st floor, however, are fully furnished with period pieces, costumes and embroidery, and bring to life the Ottoman lifestyle of the 19th century. In the garden at the back, don't miss the old stone *ocakbaşı* for Ottoman banquets.

This is a gem of a place and it's a shame that it doesn't get more visitors. It's open from 8 am to 5 pm daily for US$0.50.

After visiting, follow the signs saying 'Boztepe' for fine views over the town.

Places to Stay & Eat *Otel Kervansaray* (☎ (452) 214 1330), Kazım Karabekir Caddesi 1, just east of the Aziziye Camii and inland from the dolmuş station, is old fashioned but serviceable, charging US$12 for a double room with shower. There's a clean restaurant on the ground floor.

Across the street from the Kervansaray, and a big step down in standard, is the *Otel Başar Palas* (☎ (452) 214 4165), charging from US$4. There are many similar places in the bazaar nearby.

The two-star, 39-room *Turist Otel* (☎ (452) 214 9115), Atatürk Bulvarı 134, is a bit noisy but moderately priced at US$12/20 a single/double without breakfast. The doubles are OK, but as usual if you get a single you may feel you've been overcharged.

Fancier and newer is the three-star *Belde Hotel* (☎ (452) 214 3987, fax 214 9398), several km west of Ordu on a promontory at Kirazlılimanı, charging US$25/35 a single/double for rooms with private bath, TV and minibar. There's a swimming pool as well.

A little further west and you come to the newest of the lot, the three-star *Hotel Balıktası.*

Foodwise, the *Merkez Lokantası* on the east side of the Aziziye Camii, right by the dolmuş station, fits the bill fairly cheaply. Ordu also has many small, clean eateries in the bazaar; the *Nur Café* near the PTT is very popular with women. For sea views, try the *Midi Restaurant* right on the seafront beside the car park.

Giresun

The town of Giresun (GEE-reh-SOON, population 68,000), 46 km east of Ordu, was founded some 3000 years ago. Legend has it that Jason and the Argonauts passed by on their voyage to the fabled kingdom of Colchis (Georgia), on the eastern shores of the Black Sea, in search of the Golden Fleece. The Argonauts supposedly stopped at a nearby island (Büyük Ada) where Amazon queens had erected a shrine to Ares, god of war.

After the Romans conquered the Kingdom of Pontus, they discovered that the locals had orchards full of trees bearing delicious little red fruit. One theory holds that the ancient name for the town, Cerasus, is the root for many of the names for the fruit – *cherry* in English, *cerise* in French, *kiraz* in Turkish – as well as for the town's modern name. Cherries are still important here 2000 years on.

You can see the ruins of a medieval castle (Giresun Kalesi) above the town. On the eastern side of the city, a disused Greek Orthodox church has been turned into the Şehir Müzesi (City Museum).

Seed of a Myth?

In ancient times what is now Georgia was known as Colchis. Greek myth relates how Jason and the Argonauts sailed there in search of a Golden Fleece, supposedly owned by the Colchian king Aeëtes. After many adventures along the coast of the Pontus Euxinus (the Black Sea), Jason was helped to acquire the Fleece by the king's sorceress daughter, Medea, whom he married.

Complete fantasy, you might think. However, it's likely that the myth grew out of folk memory of a 13th-century BC trading voyage during which sailors saw the Colchians laying fleeces in the river beds to gather alluvial gold. ■

Orientation & information The centre of Giresun is the Atapark on the main road. The Belediye (Municipality) is just inland from the park. The main commercial street is Gazi Caddesi, climbing steeply uphill from the Belediye. The bus station is four km west of the centre; if you're coming from the east and heading west, have the bus drop you at the Atapark. Bus companies have ticket offices near the Belediye.

Dolmuşes to Görele, Espiye and Tirebolu use a more convenient lot, one long block east of the Atapark on the main road. Those to Ordu stop on the main highway opposite the Atapark. The PTT is 500m uphill from the Belediye.

The Tourism Information Office (☎ (454) 216 4707) is in a kiosk in the Atapark. It's open from 9 am to 6 pm daily and has a city plan. Otherwise, the Müze can supply a range of brochures in indiscriminate languages.

The Turkish Maritime Lines office (☎ (454) 216 2382) is at Giresun Liman İşletmesi, Atatürk Bulvarı, Akgül Apartımanı 542/3.

Giresun's postal code is 28000.

Kalepark With time to kill in Giresun, the things to do are to eat hazelnuts and chocolate bars containing hazelnuts, and walk 1.5 km uphill to the Kalepark (Castle Park) which is perched on the steep hillside above the town. The beautiful shady park offers panoramic views of the town and the sea, tables for picnickers and tea-sippers, bosky groves for lovers, and barbecues for grillers. It's busy on weekends.

No public transport serves the park, so you must hike there. Walk inland uphill from the Atapark on Gazi Caddesi and turn left one block past the Otel Kit-Tur; this is a shortcut, not passable for cars. If in doubt, ask directions for the Vilayet or the Kale. The prominent mansion on the hillside above the minibus lot is the Vilayet, near a mosque which was obviously once a church.

City Museum The Şehir Müzesi, with its run-of-the-mill collection, is housed in the disused 18th-century Gogora church, 1.5 km around the promontory east of the Atapark on the main road. Perhaps the most interesting exhibits are old French photographs of turn-of-the-century Giresun. At the time of writing the museum was undergoing restoration.

The museum administration is housed in a lovely restored Ottoman building next door and there's a terrace in between which might or might not be serving cold drinks.

Festivals The grandly named International Black Sea Giresun Aksu Festival, held annually on 20 May, is a delightful legacy from pagan times. Traditionally celebrated by Ottoman Greeks on 7 May according to the Julian calendar (Gregorian, 20 May), the festival hails rebirth, fecundity and the coming of the new growing season. Locals say it dates back to the days of the Hittite fertility gods: Priapus, the phallic god; Cybele, the Anatolian earth-mother goddess; and other such worthies.

Festivities begin at the mouth of the Aksu creek, where participants pass through a trivet, then through seven double pieces and one single piece of stone to boats waiting at the shore. The boats sail around Büyük Ada while the voyagers cast pebbles representing the last years' troubles into the water. Returning to the town, everyone eats and drinks, and drinks some more.

Places to Stay – bottom end The *Hotel Bozbağ* (☎ (454) 216 1249), Arifbey Caddesi 8, is in a quiet location one block up the street from the Belediye. The spacious lobby/lounge has a TV, and the rooms are decently maintained and clean. Rates are US$5/8 a single/double without bath. Hot water is on in the evenings only. You pay the same but get less at the *Otel Kent* (☎ (454) 216 0457), Gazi Caddesi 6, next to the Bulut Döviz, uphill behind the Belediye on the main street.

Places to Stay – middle The two-star, 20-room *Hotel Çarıkçı* (☎ (454) 216 1026, fax 4578) at Osmana'a Caddesi 6, a half-block east of the Belediye, is a good choice. A building almost a century old has been carefully restored, and now provides perhaps the most comfortable rooms with private bath for US$17/26 a single/double, breakfast included. Attentive service is a plus and strong windows keep out most of the street noise.

Round the corner at Çapulacılar Sok 8 is the one-star *Er-Tur Otel* (☎ (454) 216 1757), another good choice, not least because it's new and the fittings haven't had time to wear out. For US$11/22 a single/double, it's certainly good value and probably quiet too.

The three-star *Otel Kit-Tur* (☎ (454) 212 0255, fax 212 3034) is at Arifbey Caddesi 2, two short blocks uphill from the Belediye along Gazi Caddesi. Modern rooms have TV, private bath and insect screens, but prices are steep at US$31/42 a single/double. A ludicrously small lift has space for just two people!

Once the town's best hotel, the two-star *Giresun Oteli* (☎ (454) 216 3017, fax 216 6038), on the Black Sea side of the highway to the east of the Atapark, now suffers from road noise. The rooms are perfectly acceptable at US$17/25, and breakfast served in the 6th floor restaurant with wonderful sea views is a bonus.

Places to Eat The *Deniz Lokantası*, next to the Belediye and the Ulusoy bus ticket office, is simple, cheap and open from early in the morning to late at night.

Directly behind the Hotel Bozbağ (on the other side of the block), on a street reserved for pedestrians, is the more modern but still cheap *Halil Usta Pide ve Kebap*. There are several other eateries on this street as well, and you can dine outdoors in fine weather.

Heading up Gazi Caddesi you'll find several bright, cheerful pastahaneler serving cakes, coffee and ice cream. Surrounding shops major in hazelnuts.

On Osmanağa Caddesi near the Hotel Çarıkçı several beer halls serve light meals and snacks.

Getting There & Away Frequent buses and minibuses shuttle between Trabzon and Giresun, taking about 2½ hours and charging about US$4. Buses and minibuses between Girseun and Ordu are similarly regular. The journey takes about an hour and costs about US$1.

Giresun to Trabzon

From Giresun it's another 150 km to Trabzon. Along the way, the road passes through several small towns, including **Espiye**, with the castle Andoz Kalesi, and the attractive town of **Tirebolu**, with a tree-lined shore drive (the highway) and two castles (the St Jean Kalesi and Bedrama Kalesi). Tirebolu has a Çaykur tea-processing plant, which signals your arrival in Turkey's tea country.

Just east of Tirebolu is a stretch of pebble beach. Take a Görele dolmuş to reach it.

Görele is the next town eastward, and after it is **Akçakale**, where you'll see the ruins of a 13th-century Byzantine castle on a little peninsula, marked by a prominent sign.

TRABZON

Immortalised in Rose Macauley's classic novel *The Towers of Trebizond*, the modern town of Trabzon is the largest port along

Eastern Turkey's Black Sea coast. Goods arrive here by sea and continue overland by road to Georgia, Armenia, Azerbaijan and Iran, a 20th-century commerce which has given Trabzon new life and a burgeoning population of 150,000 plus.

Modern Trabzon is thoroughly cosmopolitan. With the collapse of the Soviet Union and the opening of formerly closed borders, citizens of the Soviet Union's successor republics, particularly Georgia and Armenia, flooded into Turkey in search of a quick buck. They came to sell whatever they could bring from home, and to buy Turkish consumer goods unavailable in their own countries. With them came an influx of petty criminals and prostitutes, indiscriminately dubbed 'Natashas' by the Turks. The traders and prostitutes are still very much in evidence, but fortunately for Trabzon they have been followed by a new wave of Russian tourists, and several agencies catering to their needs have now opened up. You'll hear Russian spoken about town and see shop signs advertising in Cyrillic script. One or two restaurants have even added a Russian twist to their menus.

Nowadays the main reasons for visiting Trabzon are to see the medieval church of Aya Sofya; to poke around in the old town;

The Laz & Hemşin Peoples

The Kurds may scoop all the publicity but Turkey does have other minority peoples. The mountainous north-eastern corner of the country is home to two such groups: the Laz and the Hemşin. The Laz people mainly inhabit the valleys between Trabzon and Rize, the Hemşin those further to the east.

The Laz East of Trabzon you can hardly miss the Laz women in their vivid red and maroon striped shawls. Laz men are less conspicuous, although they were once amongst the most feared of Turkish warriors; for years black-clad Laz warriors were Atatürk's personal bodyguards.

The Laz are a Caucasian people who speak a language related to Georgian. There are perhaps 250,000 of them in Turkey today. It is believed that they originally lived along the coast of Georgia and were, perhaps, the people of Colchis who guarded the Golden Fleece of Greek myth. (The Turks claim that they were nomads who arrived with other Turkic groups from central Asia.) In the Middle Ages they were probably driven west by Arab invaders and settled in north-east Turkey where they became so assimilated that they eventually forgot not only where they had come from but also that they had been Christians until the 16th century.

Just as speaking Kurdish was prohibited until 1991, so was speaking Lazuri, a language which, until recently, had not been written down. Since the 1960s, however, a German, Wolfgang Feuerstein, has been working to preserve Laz culture. As part of that effort he has created an alphabet with Latin and Georgian characters. With the Kaçkar Working Group he is also compiling a Lazuri dictionary and a history of the Laz people. If his hope was to create a sense of Laz nationalism, there are small signs that his work may be bearing fruit: Lazuri words have appeared on placards at student demonstrations in İstanbul and a Laz pop band has had modest commercial success.

Today the Laz have a reputation for their business ability and many of them are involved either in the shipping or construction industries.

The Hemşin Hemşin women are even more eye-catching than Laz women although you're less likely to see them unless you make the ascent to Ayder in August. Even then many of the women, with their lovely leopard-print scarves tied over coin-draped black head-dresses, are simply returning to visit their old homes. Most villages in this area are fast losing their young people to the cities. There may be as few as 15,000 Hemşin people still living in the area.

Caucasians like the Laz, the Hemşin may have arrived in Turkey from parts of what is now the Republic of Armenia. Like the Laz they, too, were originally Christian and their relatively recent conversion could explain why they seem to wear their Islam so lightly. You won't see women cowering beneath veils or chadors in Ayder.

The Hemşin have a great reputation as bread and pastry-makers. These days many of the pastry shops in İstanbul, Ankara and İzmir are owned by Hemşin people. ■

to visit Atatürk's lovely villa on the outskirts; and to make an excursion through the alpine scenery to Sumela, a dramatic Byzantine monastery carved out of a sheer rock cliff. The modern town is bright, bustling and very pleased with itself although the traffic fumes and crowds of people, added to the humid air and overcast skies, can make it feel mildly oppressive in summer.

This being as football-crazy a city as any in Turkey, one of the finest streets is Trabzonspor Bulvarı, named after the cup-winning football team whose stadium stands alongside it. Its kerbstones are picked out in the team's blue and maroon colours.

History

Trabzon's recorded history begins around 746 BC, when colonists originally from Miletus (south of Kuşadası) came from Sinop and founded a settlement (Trapezus) with its acropolis on the *trápeza*, or 'table' of land above the harbour.

The town did reasonably well for 2000 years, occupying itself with port activities, until 1204 when the soldiers of the Fourth Crusade seized and sacked Constantinople, driving its noble families to seek refuge in Anatolia. The imperial family of the Comneni established an empire along the Black Sea coast in 1204, with Alexius Comnenus I reigning as the emperor of Trebizond. The Trapezuntine rulers became skilful at balancing their alliances with the Seljuks, the Mongols, the Genoese and others; it didn't hurt to be cut off from the rest by a wall of mountains either. Prospering through trade with Eastern Anatolia and Persia, the empire reached the height of its wealth and culture during the reign of Alexius II (1297-1330), after which it fell to pieces in 'byzantine' factional disputes. Even so, the Empire of Trebizond survived until the coming of the Ottomans in 1461.

When the Ottoman Empire was defeated after WWI, Trabzon's many Greek residents sought to establish a Republic of Trebizond echoing the old Comneni empire, but Atatürk's armies were ultimately victorious.

Orientation

Trabzon is built on a mountainside. The port is at the centre of town, with the ancient acropolis on the 'table' now occupied by the main square called Atatürk Alanı (or Meydan Park), rising to the west of it. Most government offices, airline offices, hotels and restaurants are in and around Atatürk Alanı. The Meydan Oto Parkı, just east of the İskender Paşa Camii, charges US$2 to US$3 per day for parking.

Many of Trabzon's most interesting sights are west of the square along Uzun Yol (oo-ZOON yohl, Long Road), also called Uzun Sokak.

Trabzon's otogar is three km east of the port on the landward side of the shore road. The airport is eight km east of the town. Buses bearing the legend 'Park' or 'Meydan' go to Atatürk Alanı.

Information

Tourist Office The Tourism Information Office (☎ (462) 321 4659), on Atatürk Alanı near Akbulut (Boztepe) Caddesi, is conveniently situated on the main square. Staff on duty at different times speak English, French or German but are not as helpful as they used to be. Next to it on Atatürk Alanı is the Turkish Maritime Lines agency (☎ (462) 321 7096).

Consulates There's a Georgian Consulate (☎ (462) 326 2226, fax 326 2296) at Gazipaşa Caddesi 20. Such is the hunger for dollars that getting a visa couldn't be easier. You hand over your money and a visa is usually issued on the spot without the need for form-filling or photographs. A single-entry visa costs US$30 (cash) and is valid for up to 30 days. A transit visa costs US$15, a multiple-entry visa US$90.

Trabzon also has a Russian Consulate (☎ (462) 326 2600) in Ortahisar Mahallesi, opposite the mosque. At the time of writing, however, visas were not being granted to most foreign nationals. If you want to visit Russia you should apply from your home country instead. However, the situation may

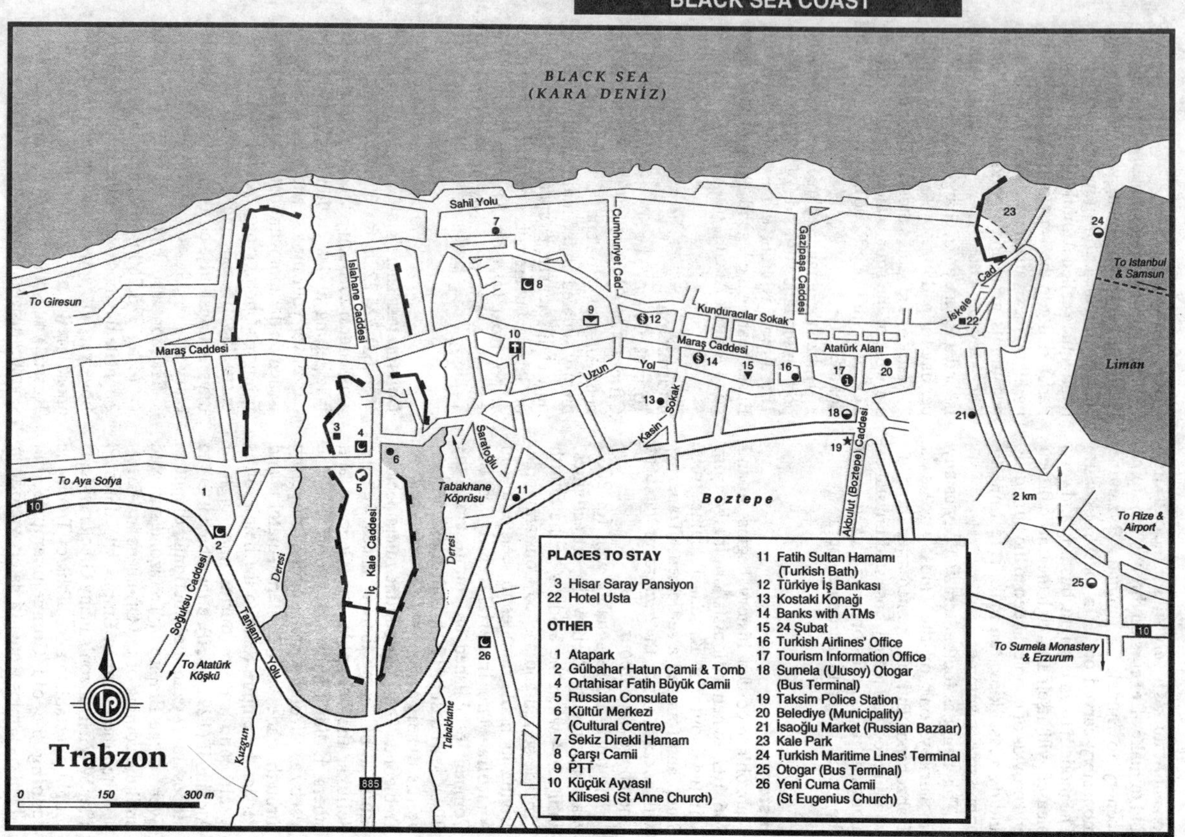
BLACK SEA
(KARA DENİZ)
Sahil Yolu
Cumhuriyet Cad
Gazipaşa Caddesi
Kunduracılar Sokak
Islahane Caddesi
Maraş Caddesi
Maraş Caddesi
Atatürk Alanı
Uzun Yol
Kasin Sokak
Akbulut (Boztepe) Caddesi
Saraftoğlu
Tabakhane Köprüsü
İç Kale Caddesi
Deresi
Deresi
Tanjant Yolu
Soğuksu Caddesi
Kuzgun
Tabakhane
İskele Cad
Liman
Boztepe
To Giresun
To Aya Sofya
To Atatürk Köşkü
To Istanbul & Samsun
To Rize & Airport
To Sumela Monastery & Erzurum
2 km
10
885
Trabzon
0
150
300 m
PLACES TO STAY
3 Hisar Saray Pansiyon
22 Hotel Usta
OTHER
1 Atapark
2 Gülbahar Hatun Camii & Tomb
4 Ortahisar Fatih Büyük Camii
5 Russian Consulate
6 Kültür Merkezi (Cultural Centre)
7 Sekiz Direkli Hamam
8 Çarşı Camii
9 PTT
10 Küçük Ayvasıl Kilisesi (St Anne Church)
11 Fatih Sultan Hamamı (Turkish Bath)
12 Türkiye İş Bankası
13 Kostaki Konağı
14 Banks with ATMs
15 24 Şubat
16 Turkish Airlines' Office
17 Tourism Information Office
18 Sumela (Ulusoy) Otogar (Bus Terminal)
19 Taksim Police Station
20 Belediye (Municipality)
21 İsaoğlu Market (Russian Bazaar)
23 Kale Park
24 Turkish Maritime Lines' Terminal
25 Otogar (Bus Terminal)
26 Yeni Cuma Camii (St Eugenius Church)

change in which case this place could become useful.

Money Most of the banks are along Maraş Caddesi. The Türkiye İş Bankası is a state-of-the-art place where cashing a travellers cheque is almost a pleasure! There are also several exchange offices along Maraş Caddesi. Most give better rates for cash than the banks, but some only accept dollars and marks. Esas Döviz accepts sterling, francs and several other currencies too. Other exchange offices can be found on the north side of Atatürk Alanı and in the bazaar.

Post Office The post office is on Maraş Caddesi, which extends west from Atatürk Alanı. For letters or cards there's also a handy booth in Atatürk Alanı.

Trabzon's postal code is 61000.

Newspapers The Büfe Güzel in Güzelhisar Caddesi often stocks the *Turkish Daily News*. If you don't see it, ask.

Atatürk Alanı

The heart of Trabzon's social life is Atatürk Alanı which has a fountain, a statue of Atatürk, tea gardens and lots of trees. In daylight it's a pleasant place to while away a few hours, with men and women, boys and girls going about their business or taking their leisure. At night, of course, it reverts to male-only territory.

Walking Tour

A pleasant way to get to grips with Trabzon's sometimes confusing topography is to go on a walking tour. The one described below starts at Atatürk Alanı and takes you right across the city to the Gülbahar Hatun Camii.

Set off from the İstanbul Airlines office at the north-west corner of Atatürk Alanı. Walk north along Gazipaşa Caddesi and turn left at the first street, Kunduracılar Sokak, which cuts through the **bazaar**. Keep going until you reach the **Çarşı Camii** (Market Mosque) which was restored recently.

Enter the mosque by the north door. On either side above the inner door, note the little 'dove temples', a fairly common feature of Ottoman architecture. The mosque's interior, adorned with crystal chandeliers, is rich in arabesques painted on domes and pillars, and trompe l'oeil 'stonework' painted on pillars and walls.

Just south-east of the Çarşı Camii is the **Taş Han** (or Vakıf Han), a collection of traders' and artisans' shops set around a courtyard entered by a portal from the street and reminiscent of the hans around İstanbul's Covered Bazaar.

A block south-west of the Çarşı Camii on Paşahamam Sokak is the **İskender Paşa Hamamı**, an ancient Turkish bath still in use by local men.

Walk west past the İskender Paşa Hamamı and turn left at the second street, Kazazoğlu Sokak, to reach busy Maraş Caddesi at the 19th-century Müftü İsmail Efendi Camii. Follow Maraş Caddesi uphill for one block and then turn right. The crumbling **church of St Anne** (Küçük Ayvasıl Kilisesi) is among the city's oldest buildings, having been built during the reign of Byzantine emperor Basil I in 884-85, with later renovations. Unfortunately, it's closed to visitors.

To reach the 13th-century **church of St Eugenius**, walk south to Uzun Yol, then right (west) to the Tabakhane Köprüsü, the bridge across the steep-sided Tabakhane ravine with the big Tabakhane Camii beside it. At the east end of the bridge, take Sarafoğlu Sokak uphill following the signs to the Fatih Sultan Hamamı. Cami Sokak is the first right, before the hamam, and half way up you'll see the old stones of the church-mosque on the right.

Tradition holds that Eugenius, an early Christian living here, raged against the priests of Mithra and was martyred. His skull was miraculously discovered on this spot shortly after the arrival of the Comneni imperial family, driven from Constantinople by the Fourth Crusade. St Eugenius is now the patron saint of Trabzon.

The church was built in the 13th century, but badly damaged in a fire in 1340, and modified during repairs. After Mehmet the Conqueror took the city in 1461, he per-

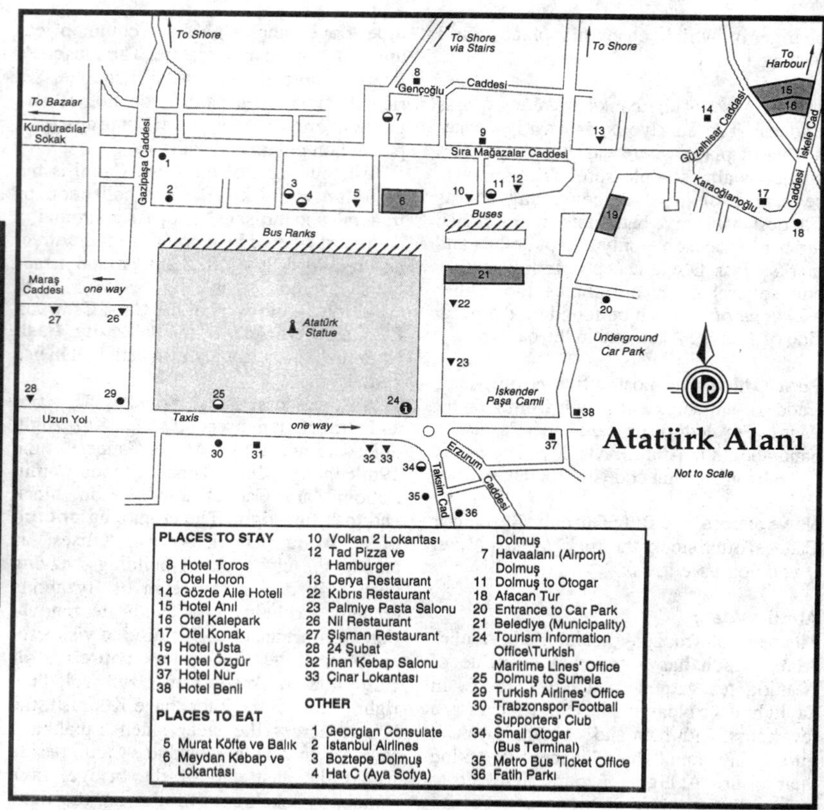

formed his Friday ablutions in the nearby baths, proclaimed the church a mosque, prayed there, and ordered the construction of the minaret.

The mosque's north door is often locked, but the east door, reached by the courtyard to the left, may be open if the *bekçi* (guardian) is about. The building is elegantly simple, lofty and light, with three parallel naves and a transversal topped by a cupola; its design is more easily visible as a mosque than it would have been with the elaborate interior decoration of a Byzantine church.

Cross the Tabakhane bridge westward on Uzun Yol and you're in Ortahisar (Middle Castle), so called from its position within the old city walls and halfway up the slope. Just up the slope is the **Ortahisar Fatih Büyük Camii**, formerly the Gold-Topped Church of the Virgin (Panaghia Chrysokephalos). The building you see dates mostly from the 13th century, the time of the Comneni Empire of Trebizond, though there was probably an earlier church here. It took its name, meaning 'Gold-Topped', from gold-plated copper cladding on the cupola, an affordable Comneni extravagance as this was the principal church for imperial ceremonies. The

Byzantine splendour of its decoration, however, has long since been replaced by depreciation of the church's architecture, though not of its interior furnishings.

Continue westward along Uzun Yol for several hundred metres and up the slope on the south side of the Atapark you'll find the **Gülbahar Hatun Camii**, built by Selim the Grim, the great Ottoman conqueror of Syria and Egypt, in honour of his mother Gülbahar Hatun in 1514. Gülbahar Hatun, a princess of the Comneni imperial family, was much loved for her charitable works, which she performed for the benefit of Christians and Muslims alike. Her tomb is the little building to the east of the mosque.

From the Gülbahar Hatun Camii, walk north-east across the street from the Atapark to a bastion in the restored **city walls**, marked with 'TC' for Türkiye Cumhuriyeti (Turkish Republic) and the *tuğra* (monogram) of Sultan Mehmet the Conqueror. Inside is the Zindan Restaurant (see Places to Eat).

On the east side, by the Atapark Kiraaathanesi, is the elaborate marble **Ottoman Abdullah Paşa Çeşmesi** fountain (1844).

The **Atapark** has pleasant tea gardens for refreshment after your long walk. Afterwards, dolmuşes (US$0.30) run from the north-west corner of the park by the Gülbahar Hatun Camii eastward along Uzun Yol to Atatürk Alanı.

If you walk back, pause to look at the wonderful **Kostaki Konağı,** a typical 19th-

The Natasha Syndrome

Until 1990, Turkey's borders with the Soviet Union were sealed. Then with the collapse of the Union and the liberation of the ethnic nation-states of Georgia, Armenia and Azerbaijan along the borders, there was a sudden influx of 'Russians' into north-eastern Turkey. First came the traders with an eye to a bargain, but they were soon followed by a flood of women who saw the potential for enriching themselves in Turkey's sexually conservative society.

Of course there's nothing new about prostitution in Turkey. Almost every town of any size has a brothel *(genelev)* on the outskirts where many a Turkish male has received his sexual initiation. It's a testimony to the popularity of these places that throughout the 1980s and early 1990s Turkey's single highest tax payer was Matild Manukyan, a Turkish-Armenian entrepreneur who, along with her fashion apparel enterprises, is also madam of a string of 32 brothels.

But brothels were always limited and tended to be contained to ghettos. The Russian women, in contrast, operate quite openly in the centre of towns, to such an extent, in fact, that it's increasingly hard to find a legitimate hotel in Trabzon, Rize, Pazar, Ardeşen, Hopa or Artvin.

With their bleach-blonde hair, halter-neck tops and mini skirts, the 'Natashas' – as they have been dubbed for obvious reasons – are virtual parodies of themselves. Venture into a *gazino* (nightclub) in any of the aforementioned towns and you'll see them in action, but don't expect to get away with your curiosity free of charge, especially if you're male.

Old-style Turkish brothels are controlled by the government and women working in them are required to undergo regular health checks. With the new-style arrangements, however, anything goes. Reliable condoms *(preservatif)* are readily available in pharmacies but the Turkish male is no better known for his readiness to wear one than his counterparts elsewhere. The 'Natashas' therefore represent a very obvious way for AIDS to get its teeth into Turkey.

Apparently some 'Natashas' look upon their young and attractive years as the time to make good money and save it up for later. One such immigrant told a Turkish newspaper reporter that she had a husband and children back home, and when she saved up enough capital she'd return and open a shop.

The influx of the 'Natashas' has caused consternation amongst Turkish call girls who work (illegally) outside the brothels. In 1995 a Turkish newspaper ran a story on two Turkish prostitutes who had been arrested in İstanbul. They had bleached their hair and learned a few words of Russian. When asked why, they answered, 'Are you kidding? We can charge three or four times as much! Turkish men think Natashas are "exotic" and think they know how to do different things than we do.' ■

century Trabzon town mansion a half-block south of Uzun Yol at Zeytinlik Caddesi 10. Sadly, work on turning it into a museum seems to have ground to a halt.

Boztepe

On the hillside south-east of the town centre is a lookout and the Boztepe Piknik Alanı with fine views of the city and the sea. In ancient times Boztepe harboured temples to the Persian sun god Mithra and to Apollo. Later the Byzantines built several churches and monasteries here, ruins of which still remain.

To get there from Atatürk Alanı, take a bus labelled 'Park-Boztepe Bld Dinlenme Tesisleri' or a Boztepe dolmuş (from beside the Halkbank on the north side of Atatürk Alanı). The route goes uphill 1.5 km to the local orthopaedic hospital, then another 700m to a forest with picnic facilities.

About three or four km up the hill, past the picnic area, are the ruins of the former **Kaymaklı Monastery**, boasting some fine frescoes. The monastery is now part of a farm and it's hard to find in the maze of hillside paths. The **Kiralı Monastery** is also signposted but one group of readers was allegedly attacked when they tried to visit it.

Aya Sofya Müzesi

The Aya Sofya Müzesi (Hagia Sophia or Church of the Divine Wisdom) is three km west of the centre on a terrace which once held a pagan temple. The site is above the coastal highway, reachable by city bus or dolmuş from Atatürk Alanı (look for a 'Hat C' (Route C) dolmuş on the lower side of the square).

Built between 1238 and 1263, the church was clearly influenced by Eastern Anatolian and Seljuk design, though the excellent wall paintings and mosaic floors follow the style of Constantinople. Tombs were built into the north and south walls. Next to the church, the gloomy bell tower was finished much later, in 1427. Nothing remains of the monastery that once stood here.

The church is now a museum, open from 8.30 am to 5 pm (closed on Monday in winter); admission costs US$1.

Atatürk Villa

The Atatürk Köşkü or Atatürk Villa ('Atatürk Pavilion' on some signs), accessible by city bus or dolmuş, is five km south-west of Atatürk Alanı, above the town with a fine view and lovely gardens. The white villa was designed in a Black Sea style popular in the Crimea, and built between 1890 and 1903 for the wealthy Trabzon banking family, the Karayannidis.

The family gave it up when Atatürk visited the city in 1924 although he only actually visited Trabzon and stayed here on three brief occasions, the last time in 1937. When he died in 1938 the villa, and all the rest of his estate, became national property. It's now a museum with various bits of Atatürk memorabilia, primarily photos of the great man in his plus-fours. There's a pleasant tea garden surrounded by hydrangeas at the back.

The villa and its well-kept gardens are open every day from 9 am to 5 pm (7 pm in summer); admission is US$0.50. To get there, take a city bus from the bus stop on the lower side of Atatürk Alanı. Buses depart at 20 minutes past the hour, passing the Gülbahar Hatun Camii along the way, and arriving at the villa 25 minutes later. Get off at the Atatürk Köşkü stop. The round trip costs US$0.30. Alternatively, there are regular dolmuşes from Atatürk Alanı.

Russian Bazaar

On the main highway due east of Atatürk Alanı at the bottom of the hill, a line of bus shelters has been turned into a flea market – the Russian bazaar or İsaoğlu Market. For US$0.30 you are admitted to the shelters, to find displays of hardware, toys, clothing, electric appliances, watches, crockery, household wares, car parts, cameras etc. Prices (and quality) are generally low, and haggling is essential, but there are a couple of handicrafts stalls worth tracking down.

Buses to Sarp and the Georgian border leave from outside the Russian bazaar.

Sekiz Direkli Hamamı

Of Trabzon's many hamams, one of the most enjoyable to visit is the Sekiz Direkli (Eight-

Pillared) Hamamı at the eastern end of the bazaar. The rough-hewn pillars are said to date back to Seljuk times, although the 'rest' area has all mod cons. The bath is open daily for men; women get their turn on Thursday between 8 am and 5 pm. To use the bath costs US$3. An assisted wash costs another US$1.50, a massage the same again. To find it, walk to the Çarşi Camii and then continue westwards until you see the signs.

Places to Stay – bottom end

Trabzon has no shortage of cheap hotels. The trouble is that most of them are filled with traders and prostitutes from the former Soviet republics (all indiscriminately called 'Russians' or 'Natashas' by the Trabzonlus) and with so much willing custom, there's little incentive to maintain standards.

Most of the cheapies are in the district called İskender Paşa Mahallesi, off the north-east corner of Atatürk Alanı on Güzelhisar Caddesi. You may not want to stay in a hotel which is really a thinly-disguised brothel, but that doesn't mean this area is dangerous or threatening, and there are usually plenty of police about in the evening. At the time of writing the following hotels seemed to be 'Natasha'-free zones but the situation can easily change.

Hotel Anıl (☎ (462) 321 9566), Güzelhisar Caddesi 10, has a flashy lobby and fairly clean rooms. Rooms with showers cost US$11/18.

The *Gözde Aile Hoteli* (☎ (462) 321 9579) in İskenderpaşa Mahallesi, just off Güzelhisar Caddesi, offers reasonable rooms with private sinks and showers but no toilet for about US$4 a head. This might be a good choice for lone women.

The *Hotel Toros* (☎ (462) 321 1212), Gençoğlu Sokak 3/A, has clean, if basic, rooms without running water for US$5 per bed, or US$6.75 per bed with private shower. It's behind the *Hotel Horon*. Be careful if you ask for a single. There has sometimes been confusion over pricing with singles being charged at double rates.

Hotel Benli (☎ (462) 321 1022), Cami Çıkmazı Sokak 5, is just off the eastern end of Atatürk Alanı, up the hill behind the Belediye and the İskender Paşa Camii. It's a family-run place but its small, rather smelly rooms rent for US$5/10 a single/double with sink, slightly more with shower. Facing it is the newer *Hotel Nur* (☎ (462) 321 2798) where spotless cell-like rooms cost much the same; the ones in the eaves that they're reluctant to let have fine views over the city to compensate for the lack of sink or space. It's a shame that the staff demand payment upfront which hardly makes for a welcoming arrival.

In the old city, right behind Ortahisar Camii, the *Hisar Saray Pansiyon* (☎ (462) 326 3162) is housed in an old Ottoman building with fine views into the ravine. Beds cost US$10 per person, but are often booked out to Russian tourist groups. If you can get one, rooms come with a curious mix of old and new décor.

Travellers are also welcome at the hostel of the *Sankta Maria Katolik Kilisesi* (☎ (462) 321 2192), Sümer Sokak 26. Built by French Capuchins in 1869 when Trabzon was a cosmopolitan trading port, the hostel offers clean simple rooms and the use of hot showers in exchange for a donation. You needn't be Catholic to stay here.

Places to Stay – middle

Trabzon has a couple of good hotels in the middle price range but no truly top-class hotels.

The two-star *Hotel Özgür* (☎ (462) 326 4703, fax 321 3952), Atatürk Alanı 29, has 45 rooms (all with bath or shower), most of which suffer from the traffic noise from the square. Rates are US$30/40/50 a single/double/triple.

The four-star *Hotel Usta* (☎ (462) 326 5700, fax 322 3793), Telgrafhane Sokak 1, across from the İskender Paşa Camii on the north-eastern corner of Atatürk Alanı in a fairly quiet yet convenient location, is currently the best in town, with 76 rooms, all with bath. It's often full with groups and has been known to boast some unpleasantly tip-greedy waiters. Services include a lift and car park. Rates are high at US$44/60 a single/double, breakfast included.

Perhaps the best bet is the newly-renovated, two-star *Otel Horon* (☎ (462) 321 1199, fax 321 6628) in Sıra Mağazalar Caddesi 125, which has comfortable modern rooms for US$30/40 a single/double and is far enough away from Güzelhisar Caddesi to be relatively quiet. If you get one of the purpose-built singles you might think the price a tad steep, but the doubles are very comfortable.

Places to Eat

Atatürk Alanı is more or less ringed with small restaurants. The following are tried and tested favourites.

Derya Restaurant, across from the Belediye on the north-east corner of Atatürk Alanı, has a good selection of ready food and serves a tasty İskender kebap. Full meals can be had for around US$3. Look also for the *Volkan 2* a few steps to the west. Close by is the *Tad Pizza ve Hamburger*, a reasonable approximation to a US-style pizza parlour. Pizzas cost from US$2.25 to US$3, burgers half that, but if you want the bun toasted you may have to ask.

Meydan Kebap Salonu, also nearby, is bright, hectic, crowded and noisy – a real human fuel-stop which serves a very tasty çevirme piliç (rotisserie chicken).

On the north side of Atatürk Alanı *Murat Balık Salonu* is a simple grill place specialising in fish. Prices depend upon what's in season, but uskumru (mackerel), which grills well, goes for US$1.50 to US$3 per fish, alabalık (trout) for more.

On the east side of the square the *Kıbrıs Restaurant* has a small, rather plain dining room at street level and a bigger one upstairs. Dishes include the Turkish classics, and a meal with a beer might cost from US$6 or US$8, more if you have fish. Further up this side the *Palmiye Pasta Salonu* sells excellent Laz böreği, flaky pastry sandwiched with confectioner's custard and sprinkled with icing sugar for US$1 a throw.

Across from the tourist office on the south side are the *İnan Kebap Salonu* and the *Çınar Lokantası*, both with a good selection of ready meals, best eaten fresh at lunch-time.

Şişman Restaurant (☎ (462) 322 3445), on Maraş Caddesi just west of the square, has a pleasant yazlık (open-air terrace) on the roof where alcohol is served with a range of mediocre food. Meals cost from US$5 to US$10 but service can be iffy. The *Nil Restaurant* on the corner of Maraş Caddesi does better food but without the views.

Leaving Ataturk Alanı, *24 Şubat*, along Uzun Yol, is a surprisingly westernised and friendly café decorated with wooden puppets and potted plants. Its excellent US$2 breakfasts include gözleme, a type of folded crêpe. Further down at Uzun Sokak 84/B the *Gelik Lokantası* serves a wide choice of food, including talaş, a pastry filled with meat, potatoes and vegetables. A meal here costs about US$3. Uzun Yol also has a number of shops selling hazelnuts, helva, lokum and pestil for those with sweet teeth.

For a bit of a blow-out, try the *Zindan Restaurant* (☎ (462) 322 3232) on the 1st and 2nd floors of a bastion in the city walls near the Gülbahar Hatun Camii. Meals here cost from US$6 to US$9 and afterwards there are fine views from the roof terrace.

Just as Americans hanker for apple pie and the British for fish & chips after a while away from home, so you can't keep a 'Natasha' from her potatoes and cabbage. Accordingly, down a few steps on the north side of Güzelhisar Caddesi you'll find *Hisar Kafeterya* which serves a range of 'Russian' cuisine.

If you want a beer without a meal, Trabzon boasts a number of basement *gazinos* of varying degrees of seediness. If you want a glimpse of a side of Turkey the tourist offices keep very quiet about, these could prove illuminating. Lone women would be unwise to go near them.

Getting There & Away

As the commercial hub of the eastern Black Sea coast, transport to and from Trabzon is easy by bus, air and sea. The Turkish-Georgian border crossing at Sarp has also reopened to travellers (see To/From Georgia under Hopa later in this chapter).

Air Turkish Airlines has daily nonstop flights between Trabzon and Ankara and İstanbul. The Turkish Airlines office (☎ (462) 321 1680) is on the south-west corner of Atatürk Alanı.

İstanbul Airlines also flies nonstop between İstanbul and Trabzon on Monday, Tuesday, Wednesday and Sunday, at fares lower than the competition. Its office (☎ (462) 322 3806; at the airport, 325 8026) is on the north-west corner of Atatürk Alanı at Kazazoğlu Sokak 9, Sanat İş Hanı.

Karadeniz Hava Yollari has a Wednesday-only service to Samsun for around US$22. Try Sarptur (☎ (462) 326 2496), Maraş Caddesi 35 for reservations.

Aeroflot (☎ (462) 326 2494) has an office on the 3rd floor of Maraş Caddesi 35. Provided you're in possession of a Russian visa they should be able to help you with reservations to Moscow.

Bus Trabzon's otogar, three km east of the port, is served by buses and dolmuşes running along the coastal road and up to Atatürk Alanı. The otogar has a left-luggage area, post office, restaurant, cafeteria, barber and simple shops.

In addition to its regular buses, Ulusoy operates especially good double-decker 'Neoplan' buses to the most popular destinations, including Ankara and İstanbul. You pay from 5 to 10% more for the added comfort. Details of some daily services follow:

Ankara – 780 km, 12 hours, US$15 to US$20; frequent buses
Artvin – 255 km, five hours, US$10; occasional buses
Erzurum – 325 km, six hours, US$10; several buses
Hopa – 165 km, three hours, US$5; half-hourly buses
İstanbul – 1110 km, 19 hours, US$20 to US$32; several buses
Kars – 525 km, 12 hours, US$15; change at Erzurum or Artvin
Kayseri – 686 km, 12 hours, US$24; several buses
Rize – 75 km, one hour, US$2; shuttle dolmuşes
Samsun – 365 km, six hours, US$6; frequent buses
Van – 745 km, 17 hours, US$19; a few buses, direct or via Erzurum

The otogar is haunted by a bull-like man who tries to part travellers from their money by rushing them onto buses which are just leaving and claiming they don't need a ticket. Don't hand over cash to anyone who's not behind a counter and certainly not without getting a ticket in return. This guy was even in a uniform on one occasion when he tried to hustle me.

Boat For information on the İstanbul, Samsun and Trabzon ferries, see the beginning of this chapter.

Karden Line ferries also operate between Trabzon and Sochi in Russia. Boats leave Trabzon on Monday and Thursday at 6 pm and return from Sochi on Tuesday and Friday at 6 pm. Cabin tickets (US$60) are available from Navi Tour (☎ (462) 326 4484), İskele Caddesi Belediye Dükkanları. At the time of writing most people had to have obtained a visa before leaving their home country to be able to use this service, but the situation may change.

Getting Around

The Airport The airport bus (US$1) leaves the Turkish Airlines office at the south-west corner of Atatürk Alanı for the airport 90 minutes before each scheduled Turkish Airlines flight. You can also take a Havaalanı ('Airport') dolmuş from a side street on the north side of Atatürk Alanı, near the Toros Hotel.

The Bus Station To reach Atatürk Alanı from the otogar, cross the shore road in front of the terminal, turn left, walk to the bus stop and catch any bus with 'Park' in its name; the dolmuş for Atatürk Alanı is marked 'Garajlar-Meydan'. A taxi between the otogar and Atatürk Alanı costs less than US$4.

Getting to the otogar, the easiest way is to catch a dolmuş marked 'Garajlar' from the north-east side of Atatürk Alanı.

Dolmuşes Dolmuşes departing from Atatürk Alanı will take you to most sights. Route descriptions are included with the previously mentioned sightseeing information. Regardless of where you're going, the fare should be about US$0.30.

Away from Atatürk Alanı beware of dolmuş drivers who suddenly claim they're driving private taxis. If the vehicle has 'taksi' written on the roof, it's a taxi; if it has a named destination, it's a dolmuş and that should be the end of it.

Tours Afacan Tur (☎ (462) 321 5804, fax 321 7001), İskele Caddesi 40/C, does reasonably priced trips to Sumela (daily, 10 am, US$3), Uzungöl (Saturdays, 9 am, US$10) and Ayder (Sundays, 8.30 am, US$8). If you're pushed for time these could be worth taking.

Sumela Monastery

The Greek Orthodox Monastery of the Virgin Mary at Sumela, 46 km south of Trabzon, was founded in Byzantine times and abandoned in 1923 after the creation of the Turkish Republic put paid to hopes of creating a new Greek state in this region. The monastery clings to a sheer rock wall high above evergreen forests and a rushing mountain stream. It's a mysterious, eerie place, especially when mists swirl among the tops of the trees in the valley below. Note that on Wednesday, when the ferry from İstanbul arrives in Trabzon, Sumela is crowded with cruise passengers. It's very busy over summer weekends too.

You reach Sumela via the Erzurum road. At Maçka, 30 km south of Trabzon, turn left for Sumela, also signposted as Meryemana, because the monastery was dedicated to the Virgin Mary.

About 3.5 km from Maçka (12.5 km from Sumela) is *Sumela Camping*, a stream-side camping ground. Another 2.5 km takes you through Coşandere village, where there's an old Ottoman humpback bridge and more camping possibilities in the grounds of the *Coşandere Restaurant*.

The road then winds into dense evergreen forests, following the course of a rushing mountain stream. Peasant houses looking like those in alpine central Europe are interspersed with more modern brick-built blocks. The road is subject to landslides, and may be impassable after heavy rains.

At the entrance to the national park you pay an admission fee of US$2.50 (US$1.25 students) to visit the monastery. To bring in a car costs another US$1. Opening hours vary with the amount of daylight, but are generally between 9 am and 6 pm.

At the end of the road you'll find a shady park with picnic tables and fireplaces by a roaring brook, a post office, a restaurant and several A-frame shelters for rent. (No camping is allowed in the park.)

The head of the trail up to the monastery begins in the picnic area. This trail is steep but easy to follow, and is the one most people use. A second trail begins farther up the valley. To get to it, follow the unpaved road behind the picnic area across two bridges until you come to a wooden footbridge over the stream on the right. This trail cuts straight up through the trees, past another small, abandoned church, and on busy days is likely to be much quieter than the one pointed out by the guides.

As you climb through forests and alpine meadows, catching occasional glimpses of the monastery above you, the air gets noticeably cooler. In all you'll ascend 250m in about 30 to 45 minutes. In autumn just before the snows arrive, a beautiful sort of crocus, called *kar çiçeği* (snowflower) blooms in the meadows.

The various chapels and rooms are mere shells or façades but have a good deal of fine **fresco painting**. Many of the paintings are the worse for wear, as bored shepherd boys used them as targets for pebble attacks and visitors scratched their names into them. In recent years, antiquity thieves and black marketeers have also been a problem.

Restoration work on the monastery is likely to continue for some years, rendering parts of the site a mess of scaffolding and closing other parts off altogether. The addition of a tea-house is also a dubious benefit, bringing in its wake the inevitable trail of empty snack packets and discarded drinks cans.

Getting There & Away The monastery is

easily visited from Trabzon. In summer, Ulusoy runs buses to Sumela, departing at 11 am from the town-centre terminal just uphill from the tourist office. The trip takes about 40 minutes and costs US$4. There are return buses at 2 and 3 pm.

Afacan Tours (☎ (462) 321 5804), İskele Caddesi 40/C, run daily tours to Sumela, departing at 10 am. They charge US$3 per person for transport and a cursory guided tour but tend to hustle visitors back down from the monastery and leave them at the restaurant for two hours. Perhaps the best thing to do is to check the time of the return journey and then let the guide know you can manage without them.

Dolmuşes leaving from opposite the Hotel Özgur in Atatürk Alanı charge US$20 for a carload of people there and back, but these days it's hard to rustle up enough people to make this an economic option.

TRABZON TO ERZURUM

Heading south into the mountains, you're in for a long but scenic ride. An extensive programme of road improvement is under way and the road is good as far as Torul but the widening of this ancient caravan route will cause traffic delays for years to come.

Carrying Liquids

The atmospheric pressure at sea level is much greater than it will be in the mountains. If you have a full water bottle in your pack at Trabzon, it will have burst or at least leaked by the time you reach Gümüşhane. If you're descending to Trabzon from Erzurum, your water bottle will collapse and leak due to the increase in pressure as you descend. It's best to carry liquid-filled containers with you as hand luggage and adjust the pressure as you travel.

Sights En Route

Along the highway south, you zoom straight to Maçka, 35 km inland from Trabzon. One and a half km north of Maçka the road tunnels straight through a dramatic rock formation of basaltic columns resembling California's Devil's Postpile or Ireland's Giant's Causeway; you may just catch a glimpse of it before disappearing into the dark. From Maçka, you begin the long, slow climb along a serpentine mountain road through active landslide zones to the breathtaking **Zigana Geçidi** (Zigana Pass) at an altitude of 2030m. The landscape is one of sinuous valleys and cool pine forests with dramatic light. Just before the pass there's a small restaurant, grocery and holiday village.

The dense, humid air of the coast disappears as you rise and becomes light and dry as you reach the south side of the **Doğu Karadeniz Dağları** (Eastern Black Sea Mountains). Along with the landscape, the towns and villages change: Black Sea towns look vaguely Balkan, while places higher up appear much more central Asian. Snow can be seen in all months except perhaps July, August and September.

Gümüşhane, about 125 km south of Trabzon, is a small town in a mountain valley with a few simple travellers' services, but not much to stop for except the scenery. By the time you reach **Bayburt**, 195 km from Trabzon, you are well into the rolling steppe and low mountains of the high Anatolian Plateau. A dry, desolate place, Bayburt has a big **medieval fortress** and simple travellers' services. The road from Bayburt passes through green, rolling farm country with stands of poplar trees and flocks of brown-fleeced sheep. Wayside stalls sell locally made *pestil*, sun-dried fruit pressed into sheets. In early summer wild flowers are everywhere.

Exactly 80 km west of Erzurum is the **Kop Geçidı** (Kop Pass) at an altitude of 2370m. A **monument** here commemorates the countless soldiers who lost their lives fighting for this pass under the most dire conditions during the War of Independence. A memorial ceremony is held annually on 15 May.

From Kop Pass, the open road to Erzurum offers fast, easy travelling.

EAST FROM TRABZON

Uzungöl

Fifty-six km east of Trabzon is the town

called Of. Go south 25 km up the Solaklı creek valley past the town of Çaykara, then another 16 km along a rough road to Uzungöl (Long Lake, altitude 1100m) to enjoy the mountain air and perhaps hike in the countryside.

Uzungöl is a popular destination for local people on weekend outings, so try and come midweek if you want to stay. In Uzungöl village right beside the lake is the *Özkan Otel ve Restoran* (☎ (462) 656 6197), a simple place with singles for US$10 and doubles for US$18. The more basic *Uzungöl Pansiyon* (☎ (462) 656 6129) is even closer to the water. Beyond the actual lake the *Sezgin Motel* (☎ (462) 656 6175) charges US$10 per person for half-board in pine cabins, with trout from the adjacent fish farm served up in the restaurant. The *İnan Kardeşler Tesisleri* (☎ (462) 656 6021) charges much the same and serves simple but delicious meals of local trout for around US$10. Both these places are very touristy at weekends and the surrounding haphazard development robs them of much setting.

At weekends you may be able to get a dolmuş direct from Trabzon to Uzungöl. Failing that, take a Rize-bound dolmuş to Of and then wait for another heading inland. Afacan Tours (☎ (462) 321 5804) at İskele Caddesi 40/C in Trabzon runs tours to Uzungöl every Saturday departing at 9 am. They're popular with locals but tend to focus more on lunch at the Sezgin than on seeing the best of the scenery. Tours cost about US$11.

Rize

Seventy-five km east of Trabzon, Rize (REE-zeh, population 52,000) is at the heart of Turkey's tea plantation area. Like most Black Sea towns, its architecture is mostly concrete but the steep hillsides above the town are thickly planted with tea bushes. The tea is cured, dried and blended here, then shipped throughout the country.

Arriving by boat in Rize, turn right at the harbour gate to walk into town (about one km), or flag down a dolmuş.

Rize's main sight is the **Çay Araştırma Enstıtüsü** (Tea Research Institute), 800m above town via the steep, sticky road behind the central mosque. Keep walking up till you come to a crossroads, then take the turn to the right that doubles back above you and keep climbing. A taxi from outside the mosque will run you there for US$1. The Institute's grounds are a tea garden set amid hollyhocks, roses and hydrangeas. The views are great, the tea even better. In summer you can sit out here until 10.30 pm.

Places to Stay There are plenty of reasonably priced hotels although all are in ugly modern blocks and many double up as brothels. One of the cheapest is *Otel Akarsu* above a kebab shop near the Şehir hamam; clean, simple bathless rooms cost about US$5 per person. The dingy *Otel Yalta*, off Çanakkale Caddesi (☎ (464) 217 1477), costs much the same and has some three and four-bedded rooms.

Up a notch, the *Otel Efes* in Atatürk Caddesi (☎ (464) 214 1111) has clean twins with bath for US$30; the nearby *Evin Otel* (☎ (464) 217 5911) is marginally cheaper.

For two-star comfort, try *Hotel Çay* (☎ (464) 213 1698) near the Russian bazaar or the *Otel Keleş* (☎ (464) 217 4612) in Palandöken Caddesi; both have lifts to rooms with TVs and private baths for around US$20/30 a single/double.

At the time of writing the four-star *Hotel Dedeman Rize* (☎ (464) 223 5344) was nearing completion on the western outskirts, too far from the centre to walk into town. When it opens, expect all the usual mod cons.

Places to Eat There are plenty of simple kebap and pide places along Cumhuriyet Caddesi. *Mis Kebap* and *Bekiroğlu Pide ve Kebap* are particularly good. For something classier try the *Muzë Kafeterya* in a restored Ottoman building up the hill behind the main post office. There you can join the local youth and dine on çizburger and çips (cheeseburger and chips), either on a terrace or in a room decorated with local handicrafts.

Getting There & Away The bus company

TOM BROSNAHAN

Top: Nomad's tent, Doğubeyazıt, Eastern Anatolia.
Bottom: The ruined fortress palace of İshak Paşa, outside of Doğubeyazıt retains much of its impressive decoration.

TOM BROSNAHAN

TOM BROSNAHAN

Top: The Balıklı Göl (carp pool) in Şanlıurfa provides a welcome respite from the heat.
Bottom: The great funerary statues atop Nemrut Dağı, between Malatya and Kahta, lost their heads to earthquakes.

ticket offices are on Cumhuriyet Caddesi. Minibuses to Trabzon (1½ hours, US$1) leave from out on the main highway to the west, those to Hopa (1½ hours, US$1) further to the east. The harbour for boats to İstanbul is even further out west.

KAÇKAR DAĞLARI

The Kaçkar Dağları is a mountain range in the north-east of Turkey with its highest point at **Mt Kaçkar** (3937m). The Kaçkars are increasingly popular for organised trekking trips of anything from one to 10 days. Provided you bring a tent, sleeping bag and good shoes you could even spend a month exploring the mountains and summer villages *(yaylalar)*. If you want to arrange a tour, a good person to talk to would be Adnan Pirikoğlu. Find him by asking at the *Pirikoğlu Aile Lokantası* in Ayder or by calling ☎ (464) 657 2021 or 655 5084.

For full information on hiking in the Kaçkar range, see Lonely Planet's *Trekking in Turkey*.

Çamlıhemşin

About 40 km east of Rize, just before Ardeşen, a road on the right is signposted for Çamlıhemşin (19 km), a village deep in the Kaçkar mountains. As you ascend into the mountains, you'll pass several absurdly picturesque ancient humpback bridges across the Fırtına Çay.

Çamlıhemşin has one basic hotel, the *Otel Hoşdere* (☎ (464) 651 7107), where the rooms are nothing much to write home about, even for US$4 a head. Still, if you're arriving in Ayder on a summer Saturday it's worth knowing there's this fallback if everything there is full.

The restaurant is a much better bet, with a wooden terrace over the river at the back which is popular with tour groups. Here it's worth sampling a Black Sea delicacy, *muhlama*, a sort of melted cheese soup eaten with thick corn bread. The trout, baked in butter with tomatoes and onions for US$4, is excellent.

Just beyond Çamlıhemşin the road forks and you'll have to decide whether to bear right (signposted Zil Kalesi) for Şenyuva or left (signposted Ayder Kaplıcaları) for Ayder.

Şenyuva

Five km from Camlıhemşin you'll find *Otel Doğa* (☎ (464) 651 7455) run by İdris Duman who speaks French and English. Simple rooms here often come with balconies overlooking the river, and there are two suites for up to six people, one with a double balcony. Beds cost US$6 each.

Another two km along the road is the *Sisi Pansiyon* (☎ (464) 653 3043), operated by Doris Güney, who organises treks into the nearby mountains. Beds in A-frame bungalows at the Sisi Pansiyon cost US$16, or you can camp with your own tent for a fraction of that. Sisi Pansiyon is in an idyllic setting, approached via a chair lift over the river. Use of a sauna cabin with river views is also thrown in. For a get-away-from-it-all break you could hardly better this.

The only snag with Şenyuva is the limited public transport. You may have to walk to and from Camlıhemşin, or catch a taxi for about US$4 each way. Because of this both Sisi Pansiyon and Otel Doğa offer half-board arrangements as well.

From Şenyuva the road continues past the ruins of Zilkale castle to **Çat** (1250m), a mountain hamlet used as a trekking base. There's one small hotel there, the *Cancık*, but it can only sleep up to 15 people.

Ayder

To get to Ayder from Camlıhemşin, turn left and cross a modern bridge, following the sign for Ayder Kaplıcaları. The road winds steadily upwards for 17 km, finally reaching Ayder (1300m), a *yayla* (high-pasture) village with two kaplıcalar (hot springs).

Unfortunately the same sort of thing is happening to Ayder as to Uzungöl: haphazard, often unsightly development, aimed mainly at the domestic tourism market. In August the village can hardly cope with the flood of tourists, especially at weekends when, despite the growing number of hotels, most places will be full by mid-afternoon.

Outside August you should have no problem finding a bed for about US$5.

Ayder gets more than its fair share of bad weather but if you're lucky and the sun's shining, even the ugly brick buildings will look quite tolerable and the mountain air, after the dust and fumes of Trabzon, will seem nothing short of miraculous.

Orientation The sign for Ayder is some way before you reach the actual village. With a car you'll have to pay a US$1 entrance fee.

Ayder itself is little more than one long street which crosses a ford and then continues to a picnic area cum campsite and car park in a meadow. Most of the hotels are on either side of this main street, although one or two require a deviation. There are a few small shops selling most essentials, as well as a bakery and a cake shop. Some readers have reported a shortage of bottled water. Certainly before leaving Ayder to walk in the hills you should make sure you have adequate supplies.

There's a minuscule PTT beside the ford but nowhere to change money.

Things to See & Do The main reasons to come to Ayder are to see the wonderful surrounding scenery, trek in the mountains and soak in the **kaplıcaları** (hot springs). The springs have recently been given splendid new bath-houses capable of handling 200 people per hour. The water inside reaches temperatures of 56°C (133°F) and is said to be good for ulcers, skin complaints, cuts and allergies. There are separate sections for men and women, open daily from 7 am to 8 pm and charging US$2 to US$7, depending on what you want done.

If you're in search of peace and quiet, you should certainly try and avoid visiting over August weekends when the main street virtually seizes up with traffic. On the other hand, if you're interested in seeing **Hemşin culture** in action, summer weekends could be the best time of all to come. Wander out into the meadow to the south of Ayder and you may find groups of Hemşin holidaymakers dancing a conga-like dance to the whining rhythm of the *tulum*, a bagpipe made out of a goatskin and played by many local men. Everywhere there will be women in their splendid head-dresses, which look slightly incongruous topping off cardigans, long skirts and trainers!

In summer, too, the Nazlı Çiçek restaurant hosts evening **music and dance sessions.** Forget any stories about 8 or 9 pm starts. You'll be lucky if the action kicks off much before 10.30 pm.

For information about trekking routes in the surrounding mountains see Lonely Planet's *Trekking in Turkey*.

Places to Stay All of Ayder's hotels are pretty basic, with prices reflecting that fact. Beds in waterless rooms usually cost between US$5 and US$7.

Coming in from the north, the first place you come to on the left is the *Otel Ayder* (☎ (464) 657 2039), with clean, simple rooms, some with nice views, well away from the village-centre traffic jams. There's a restaurant downstairs. Next on the left is the *Otel Pirikoğlu* (☎ (464) 657 2021) with pine beds in clean rooms. There's a kitchen for guests to use, and more pleasant mountain views.

A sign on the right points to a brick eyesore which is actually one of the better choices, the *Otel Yeşil Vadi* (☎ (464) 657 5051), where clean, simple rooms are more spacious than usual. The roof terrace is a good vantage point for studying Ayder.

Back on the main street the *Otel Merkez* (☎ (464) 657 2022) is as basic (and cheap) as they come but the toilets are smelly and the rooms are like cells.

Ayder's most visually distinguished hotel is the *Hotel Saray* (☎ (464) 657 2001), on the left on a bluff overlooking the ford. Inside, however, it's not much different to the others and the fact that the rooms open off a central area with TV could mean noisy nights. The terrace outside lets you watch the traffic chaos at the ford.

Don't let the *Ayder Hilton Hotel*'s name fool you. There's nothing remotely luxurious about this place (☎ (464) 657 2024), a large, unmissable building on the right just after you pass the ford.

Turn right behind the Hilton and ascend the steps beside the baths. There are a few more places down here, including the *Hotel Kervansaray*, the *Hotel Altıparmak* and the *Otel Çınar*, but the proximity of the mosque means they're unlikely to be quiet choices.

A path running up beside the Yıldırım Kafeterya leads to the *Hotel Kaçkar* (☎ (464) 657 2041) and yet more clean but simple rooms. The Hemşin women who run this place are a lot of fun but the washing facilities are pretty rudimentary. There are a couple of single rooms if you arrive late and the other places want to charge you for two beds.

Finally, continue past the baths and you'll come to *Otel Çağlayan*, a family-run place in a wooden building on the right. Here, at least, you'll get a quiet night.

Places to Eat Beside the ford are two prominent eating places: the *Nazlı Çiçek* and the *Otel Saray Et ve Balık Restoran*. The Nazlı specialises in trout and there are big tanks of fish by the entrance; two fish, some rice and a non-alcoholic drink will cost about US$4. For breakfast, they will rustle you up a pair of delicious fried eggs, with bread, cheese and a large tea for about US$1.50. The Saray restaurant serves alcohol and has a central grill where you can watch your köfte being prepared.

Another place to try for breakfast is the *Yıldırım Kafeterya*, which serves bread, honey, olives and elderly cheese.

Getting There & Away In summer dolmuşes make hourly runs between Pazar on the coast and Çamlıhemşin, in some cases continuing to Ayder. On summer Sundays the trickle of minibuses up to Ayder turns into a flood. Otherwise, passengers are mostly shoppers from the villages, so dolmuşes descend from the mountain villages in the morning and return from Pazar in early afternoon. One bus a day travels direct to Trabzon from Ayder, leaving at 4 pm.

Note that space in the minibuses is reservable, so if you want to leave over a weekend or on a Monday morning you'd do well to buy your ticket in advance from the Ayder Turizm booth above the ford.

Hopa

The easternmost of Turkey's Black Sea ports is Hopa (population 18,000), 165 km east of Trabzon. Once rather sleepy, Hopa has woken up to the potential of the traders and truckers battling to satisfy the appetites of the commerce-starved former Soviet republics. The town's growth has been chaotic, and Hopa has lost even the vestigial charm it once had. Only stop here if you must.

Sarp, 30 km to the east, is the border-crossing point for Georgia.

Places to Stay & Eat Most of Hopa's hotels are on the eastern side of the Sundura Çayı stream along the waterfront street called Orta Hopa Caddesi, but they're usually filled with Russian and Turkish truckers and traders, and suffer from constant truck noise. As in Trabzon and Artvin many have found it easier to fill their rooms an hour at a time, so you need to be wary of most of the cheaper places.

Best of the lot if your budget can stand it is the *Cihan Hotel* (jee-HAHN) (☎ (466) 351 4897, fax 351 4898), at Orta Hopa Caddesi 7, with clean, comfortable modern rooms for US$14/US$20 a single/double without breakfast. Also good is the one-star *Hotel Papila* (☎ (466) 351 3641, fax 351 2975), 200m east of the Cihan, charging US$17/22 for clean, if slightly dingier, rooms with shower.

The cheaper places are clustered around the PTT, 200m west of the Hotel Cihan. The *Hotel Devran* (☎ (466) 351 4091) charges US$4 a head for pretty basic rooms. Its next door neighbour, the *İmren*, looks more dubious.

On the outskirts and well away from truckers and/or 'Natashas' is the new three-star *Terzioğlu*.

Getting There & Away Direct buses from Hopa to Erzurum depart early in the morning. If you miss the direct bus, you can catch a later one to Artvin (1½ hours,

US$1.50), then an onward bus from Artvin. There are also regular minibuses to Rize and Trabzon (US$1 and US$4 respectively), as well as frequent minibuses for Sarp (US$1) and the Georgian border.

To/From Georgia The border between Turkey and Georgia (the former Soviet Socialist Republic of Georgia; Gürcistan in Turkish) at Sarp has been opened to foreigners. If you want to cross it, your starting point should be a visit to the Georgian Consulate in Trabzon to sort out a visa.

At 7 pm a bus leaves from beside the Russian bazaar to go to the Georgian seaside resort of Batumi. Since this will get you there in the middle of the night you may prefer to take a minibus to Rize or Hopa and pick up another one heading to Sarp. This part of the journey should cost about US$5. The potholed, dusty state of the road east of Hopa says a lot about past Turkish-Soviet relations although it is being gradually improved.

Leaving Turkey and entering Georgia is unproblematic and you can probably ignore half-hearted demands for dollars from the Georgian customs officials.

On the other side of the border taxis will be waiting to run you to Batumi for US$10. Ask to be dropped near the train station. There's a small 'hotel' (actually a family house with a few spare beds) nearby where you can stay for another US$4.

Only masochists catch the train on to Tbilisi (two to three days without electricity for lighting) but there are daily buses which do the run in eight hours for about US$5. Before setting out, though, it would be wise to check the current political situation.

Leaving Georgia to return to Turkey is more tricky. If you take a taxi back to the border and arrive alone you are at the mercy of the avaricious customs officers. On the other hand if you take the bus for collective protection, the bureaucracy involved can result in a four-hour delay.

On the Turkish side of the border most people will need to buy a new entry visa.

Eastern Anatolia

Eastern Turkey is a land of adventure where each event of the day seems to take on the character of some fabled happening. You might go to bed at night disappointed because Mt Ararat was covered in cloud. Early next morning the mountain will take you by surprise, intruding into your consciousness, shining in the sun outside your hotel window. Or you might be riding along a rough road and suddenly come upon the ruins of a medieval castle, not marked on any map, not described in any guidebook. Every day reveals some new notion of epic events.

The east is not as well developed as western Turkey. Instead of grain-harvesting machinery, you might come across farmers threshing and winnowing in the ancient manner.

The people are no less friendly than in other parts of Turkey but they are often more reticent and not, generally speaking, used to seeing and dealing with foreigners (except in the hotels and tourist offices). It may take a little more time for the friendliness of the adults to emerge, but not so with the children. Every single one will have to find out where you come from and what language you speak.

When travelling, be prepared for the distances. You may ride for hours to get from one town to the next. When you get to that town, there may not be many hotels to choose from. And the one you want – particularly if it's the best in town – may be fully booked. Travelling in eastern Turkey is certainly not as comfortable as it is in the west. But if you are adaptable and out for adventure, this is the place to find it.

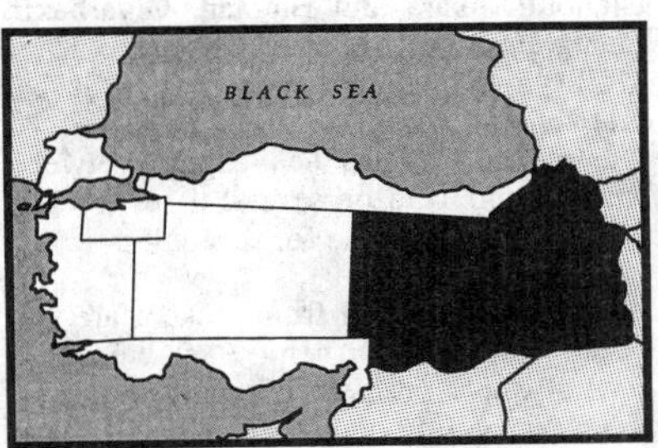

Highlights

- Getting lost in the Ottoman-era bazaars of Şanlıurfa
- Exploring the Seljuk ruins of Sivas and Divriği
- Driving through the Georgian valleys
- White-water rafting out of Yusufeli
- Visiting the İshak Paşa Sarayı in Doğubayazıt
- Seeing the ruins of Ani
- Being invited into one of Harran's ancient beehive mud houses
- Gazing at the sunset among the colossal statues atop Nemrut Dağı

Warning

As this guidebook goes to press, the Kurdish insurgency continues in portions of eastern Turkey. Travel is possible to many points in the region, and as the insurgency dies down (as seems to be happening), more of the region will become safe for travel. For now, travellers to the east should scrupulously observe the following rules:

- Contact your embassy or consulate in advance, ask about current conditions, tell them your plans and ask their advice.
- Travel only during daylight hours, only on major highways (or preferably by air), and restrict your stops to major cities, towns and sites.

Getting There & Away

Buses, as always, go everywhere; there are even direct buses to İstanbul from most large eastern cities such as Erzurum, Van and Diyarbakır. Though there are some trains, they're usually not as comfortable nor as fast as the buses.

Many visitors spare themselves the tedium (and, in some cases, danger) of a long bus ride to the east by flying to a major eastern city and bussing from there.

Air Turkish Airlines (THY) flies between İstanbul/Ankara and Batman, Diyarbakır, Elazığ, Erzincan, Erzurum, Gaziantep, Kars, Malatya, Muş, Şanlıurfa, Siirt, Sivas, Trabzon and Van.

İstanbul Airlines has flights between İstanbul and Trabzon several times weekly. Check with the airline for schedules.

Bus Services to and from Ankara are frequent. Routes running east-west are generally not a problem, but north-south services can be infrequent, so allow plenty of time and check departure schedules as soon as you can.

Train From Ankara via Kayseri there are three major eastern rail destinations: Erzurum, Kurtalan/Diyarbakır and Tatvan/Van. The Erzurum line goes on to Kars and in good times goes as far as the Armenian frontier, with a connecting train to Moscow. The Van line goes on to Iran, with a connection to Tabriz and Tehran. South of Elazığ, this line branches for Diyarbakır and Kurtalan.

For information on trains serving these routes, see Getting There & Away in the Ankara section of the Central Anatolia chapter.

Getting Around

The eastern mountains and high plateaux are subject to long and severe winters. I don't recommend travelling in the east except from May to September and preferably in July and August. If you go in May or September, be prepared for some quite chilly nights. A trip to the summit of Nemrut Dağı (2150m) should not be planned for early morning except in July and August. In other months the mountain top will be very cold at any time and bitterly cold in early morning. There may also be snow.

Most visitors touring this part of the country make a loop through it, starting from Amasya, Tokat, Kayseri, Trabzon, Adana or Antakya. Such a trip might follow one of the itineraries below.

From Amasya, Tokat or Kayseri, head via Sivas and Malatya to Adıyaman, then Kahta to see Nemrut Dağı, then either north-east to Erzurum, Doğubeyazıt, Kars and Artvin, or south to Şanlıurfa, via Mardin, to Diyarbakır for its ancient walls and mosques.

Starting from Adana or Antakya, go to Adıyaman and Kahta via Gaziantep. After seeing Nemrut Dağı, head south to Şanlıurfa, east to Mardin and north to Diyarbakır.

From Diyarbakır, head east through Bitlis and around the southern shore of Van Gölü (Lake Van), stopping to see the Church of the Holy Cross on the island of Akdamar, before reaching the city of Van. Then head north to Ağrı and east to Doğubeyazıt to see Mt Ararat and also the İshak Paşa Sarayı, the dramatic Palace of İshak Pasha.

From Doğubeyazıt head north to Kars to see the ruins of Ani, then to Erzurum. At Erzurum you can catch a plane westward, or toil through the mountains to Artvin, or head for the Black Sea coast at Trabzon, or start the return journey westward to Sivas and Ankara. This itinerary, from Kayseri or Adana to Van to Kars to Erzurum to Sivas, covers about 2500 km and would take an absolute minimum of 10 days to complete by bus and/or train. It's better to take two weeks or more.

Car Special warnings are in order for those driving in the east. Fuel stations are fewer, roads can be significantly worse, and Kurdish separatist activity must be taken into account.

Fill your fuel tank before setting out, carry bottled water and snacks, and expect the ride to be longer than you think. Try to do most of your travelling in the earlier part of the day, reaching your destination by mid-afternoon. Avoid driving in the evening or at night.

Roads in the extreme east of the country, and particularly in the north-east, are often riddled with potholes which break tyres and dent rims if hit at speed. When filled with rainwater it is impossible to judge the depth or damage capacity of the potholes. They occur at random in otherwise smooth roads, and necessitate slow driving even on good stretches.

The good news is that if you damage a tyre, even to the extent of gashing the side-wall open, a good Turkish *lastikçi* (tyre repairer) can probably fix it – unbelievable, but true.

As long as the Kurdish separatist unrest continues in the south-east there will be numerous military and police roadblocks. When you approach a roadblock, slow down and be sure you interpret the soldiers' signals correctly. When there is the slightest doubt about the signal, stop. If you misinterpret a signal and unintentionally run a roadblock, there may be serious consequences.

North-Eastern Anatolia

Mountainous and remote from the cosmopolitan atmosphere of Ankara and İstanbul, north-eastern Anatolia is a large slice of the 'real' Turkey, relatively unchanged by the tourist flood which swept over the western and central sections of Anatolia during the past decade.

As with much of Anatolia, cities and towns here date their existence in millennia rather than centuries. The Hittites, Romans, Persians, Armenians, Georgians, Arabs and Russians have all battled for control of these lands but this is Seljuk country *par excellence*. Sultans of the first Turkic empire in Anatolia (during the mid-1200s) built impressive mosques, medreses, caravanserais and baths in Sivas and Erzurum which shouldn't be missed by anyone interested in architecture. The beautiful mountain scenery and historic Armenian and Georgian churches of extreme north-eastern Anatolia (around Artvin and Kars) are among the most powerful attractions in this region. The mountain trekking in the Kaçkar range between Erzurum and Artvin is excellent.

The following description of north-eastern Anatolia moves from west to east, from Sivas via Divriği, Erzincan and Erzurum to Artvin and Kars.

SİVAS

The highway comes through Sivas, the railway comes through Sivas, and over the centuries dozens of invading armies have come through Sivas (population 225,000, altitude 1285m), often leaving the town in ruins in their wake. The Seljuks left perhaps the most obvious mark and the centre of town is liberally sprinkled with some of the finest Seljuk Turkish buildings ever erected.

Nowadays Sivas is fairly modern, with bicycle lanes along its main thoroughfare and even some kerbstone ramps. It doesn't immediately strike you as a place of high passions. Yet in 1993, in the wake of the furore over Salman Rushdie's *Satanic Verses*, an arsonist set fire to the Otel Madımak, where the late Aziz Nesin, the famous Turkish humorist (and agnostic), who had published parts of the book in Turkish, was attending a writers' conference. Thirty-seven people died in the blaze. Nesin, who was minding his own business, was accused of incitement to riot just because he was there. The abashed locals have as many theories about the arsonist (the CIA, the European Union) as there were deaths, but the likeliest suspects must remain Islamic fundamentalists.

History

The tumulus at Maltepe, near Sivas, shows evidence of settlement as early as 2600 BC. Sivas itself was probably founded by the Hittite king Hattushilish I around 1500 BC. Ruled later by the kings of Assyria, the Medes and the Persians, it came within the realms of the kings of Cappadocia and Pontus before being claimed by Rome. The Romans called it Megalopolis, which was later changed to Sebastea and shortened to Sivas by the Turks.

Byzantine rule lasted from 395 to 1075, when the city was taken by the Danışmend emirs. Danışmend rule was disputed by the Seljuks, and Sivas changed allegiance from one side to the other several times between

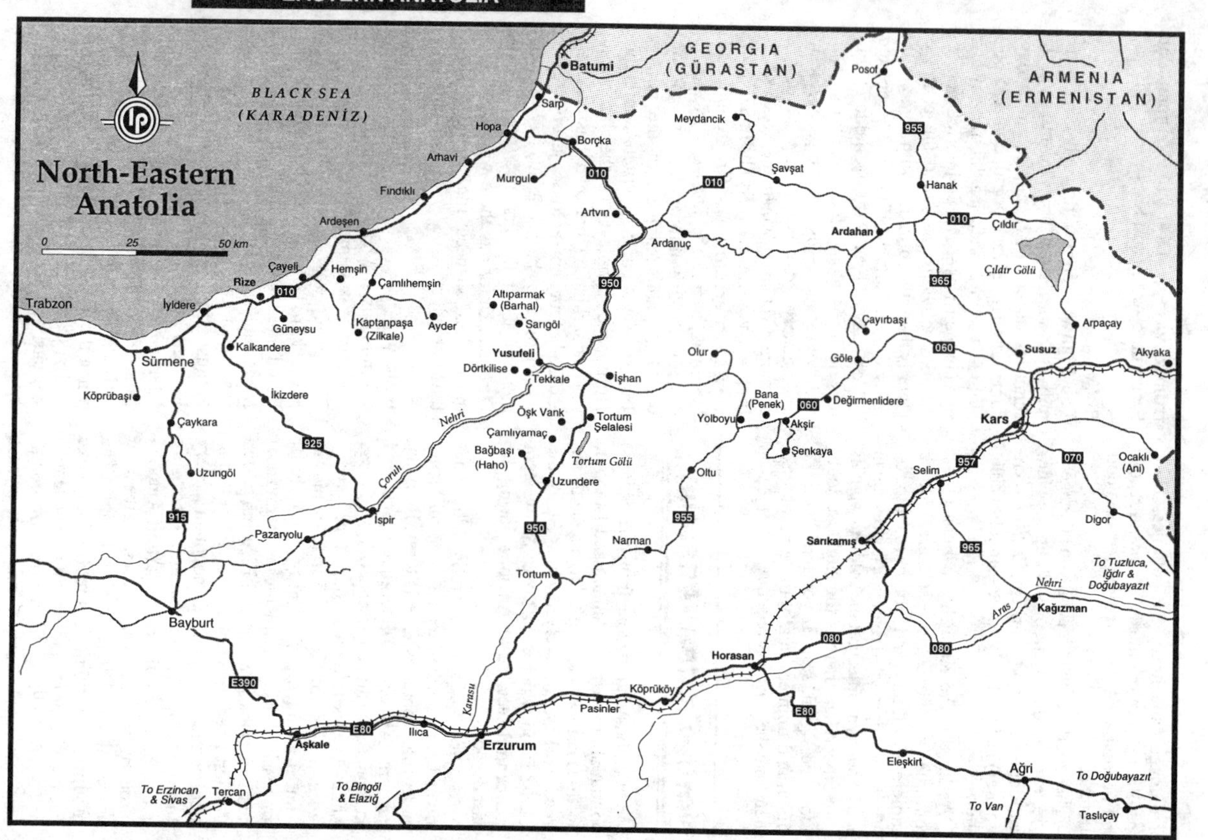
North-Eastern Anatolia
0
25
50 km
BLACK SEA
(KARA DENİZ)
GEORGIA
(GÜRASTAN)
ARMENIA
(ERMENİSTAN)
Batumi
Sarp
Hopa
Borçka
Meydancık
Posof
Arhavi
Murgul
Fındıklı
Artvin
Şavşat
Hanak
Ardeşen
Ardanuç
Ardahan
Çıldır
Çıldır Gölü
Çayeli
Hemşin
Çamlıhemşin
Rize
Trabzon
İyidere
Güneysu
Kaptanpaşa (Zilkale)
Ayder
Altıparmak (Barhal)
Sarıgöl
Çayırbaşı
Arpaçay
Susuz
Akyaka
Kalkandere
Sürmene
Yusufeli
Dörtkilise
Tekkale
Olur
Göle
İşhan
Köprübaşı
İkizdere
Bana (Penek)
Değirmenlidere
Kars
Öşk Vank
Tortum Şelalesi
Yolboyu
Akşir
Çaykara
Nehri
Çamlıyamaç
Bağbaşı (Haho)
Tortum Gölü
Şenkaya
Ocaklı (Ani)
Selim
Uzungöl
Oltu
Uzundere
Çoruh
İspir
Digor
Pazaryolu
Narman
Sarıkamış
To Tuzluca, Iğdır & Doğubayazıt
Tortum
Aras
Kağızman
Bayburt
Horasan
Köprüköy
Pasinler
Karasu
Ilıca
Aşkale
Erzurum
Eleşkirt
Ağrı
To Doğubayazıt
To Erzincan & Sivas
Tercan
To Bingöl & Elazığ
To Van
Taslıçay
955
010
950
965
060
070
957
925
915
080
E390
E80

1152 and 1175, when the Seljuks finally took it – until the Mongol invasion of 1243.

Even after the Mongols were succeeded by the İlkhanids, Sivas's travails weren't over. Taken by the Bey of Eretna in 1340, it succumbed to Tamerlane in 1400, and soon after (in 1408) to the Ottomans.

In more recent times Sivas gained fame as the location for the Sivas Congress, which opened on 4 September 1919. Atatürk came here from Samsun and Amasya, seeking to consolidate the Turkish resistance to Allied occupation and partition of his country. He gathered delegates from as many parts of the country as possible, and confirmed decisions which had been made at the earlier Erzurum congress. These two congresses were the first breath of the revolution and heralded the War of Independence.

Orientation

The centre of town is Konak Meydanı, in front of the attractive Vilayet Konağı (Provincial Government Headquarters). Near it are most of Sivas' important sights, hotels and restaurants.

The train station (Sivas Gar) is about 1.5 km south-west of Konak Meydanı along İnönü Bulvarı. If arriving by rail, walk out of the station to the bus stop on the station side of İnönü Bulvarı. Any bus running along this major road will trundle you to or from the station. If in doubt, just ask the driver, 'Konak?'. The bus station (Sivas Otogar) is over two km south-east of the centre.

Most of the sights are conveniently grouped in a pleasant park at Konak Meydanı. The Gök Medrese (Blue Seminary) is a short walk away.

There are several banks for changing money along Atatürk Caddesi. The main PTT and the bus company offices are here too.

Information

The Tourism Information Office (☎ (346) 221 3535, fax 222 2252) is on the ground floor of the Vilayet Konağı building, facing the main square. It's open Monday to Friday from 8.30 am to 6 pm. A little English and more German is spoken.

Sivas' postal code is 58120

Kale Camii

Heading down İnönü Bulvarı from Konak Meydanı, the first building you'll probably come to is the Kale Camii (1580), an Ottoman work constructed by Sultan Murad III's grand vizier Mahmut Paşa.

Bürüciye Medresesi

A few steps east of the Kale Camii, near the gazebo with an ablutions fountain on top and a toilet beneath, is the Bürüciye Medresesi, built in 1271 by Muzaffer Bürücirdi, who is entombed in it (inside, to the left, with the fine tilework). With a grassy courtyard, a blissfully quiet tea garden with tables and chairs, and *sedirs* (low sofas) in the *eyvans* (niche-like rooms), it's a wonderful place for a rest and refreshment. Historic carpets and kilims decorate the walls.

Şifaiye Medresesi

Across the park from the Bürüciye Medresesi is the Şifaiye Medresesi (İzzettin Keykavus Şifahanesi, Darüşşifa), a hospital medical school which ranks as one of the city's oldest buildings. It dates from 1217, when it was built for the Seljuk sultan İzzettin Keykavus I, whose architect used stylised sun/lion and moon/bull motifs in the decoration.

Look to the right (south) as you enter the courtyard to see the porch which was closed up and made into a tomb for Sultan İzzettin upon his death in 1219. Note the beautiful blue tilework and Arabic inscriptions.

The main courtyard has four eyvans, with sun and moon symbols on either side of the eastern one. It's now grassed over and surrounded by tea tables and leather, carpet and souvenir shops. In the centre stands a large coop of ornamental pigeons and a smaller cage in which a lone squirrel devotes its life to trying to escape. If you want to shop for Turkish souvenirs, this would be a good place to start looking.

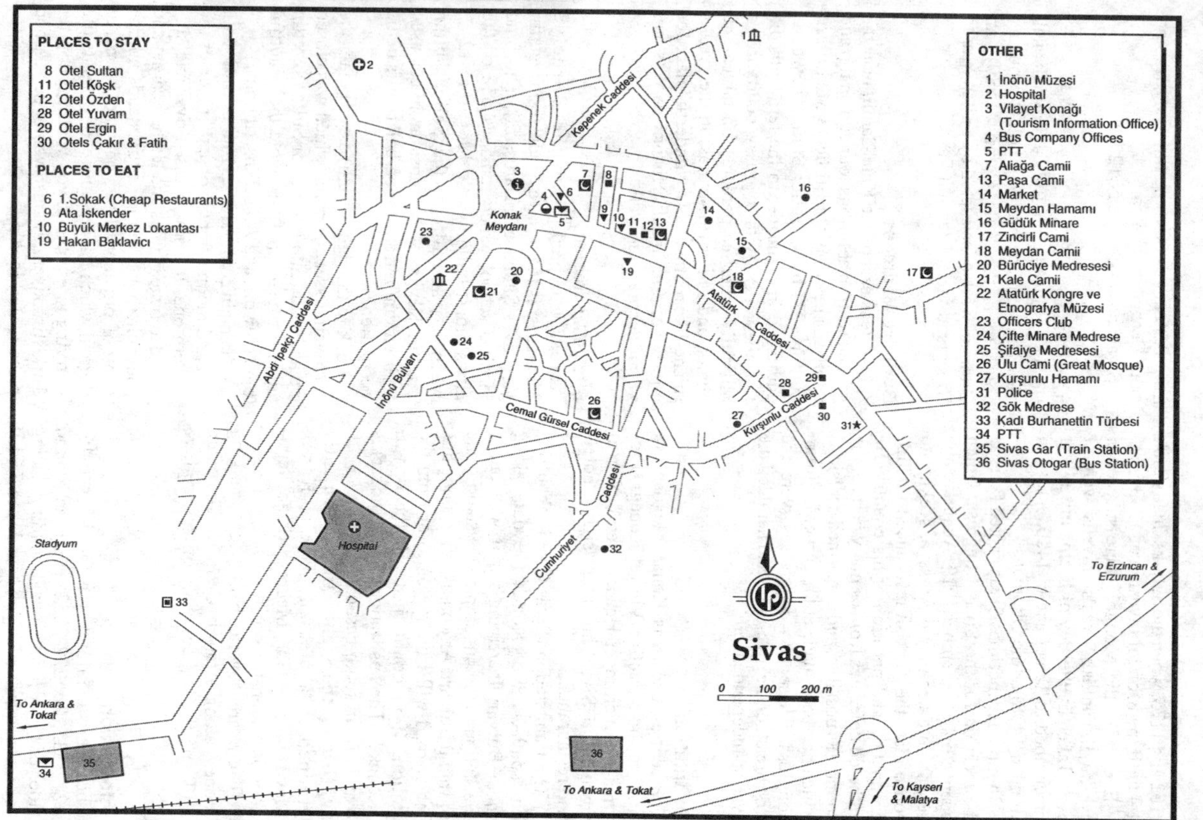
PLACES TO STAY
8 Otel Sultan
11 Otel Köşk
12 Otel Özden
28 Otel Yuvam
29 Otel Ergin
30 Otels Çakır & Fatih
PLACES TO EAT
6 1.Sokak (Cheap Restaurants)
9 Ata İskender
10 Büyük Merkez Lokantası
19 Hakan Baklavacı
OTHER
1 İnönü Müzesi
2 Hospital
3 Vilayet Konağı (Tourism Information Office)
4 Bus Company Offices
5 PTT
7 Aliağa Camii
13 Paşa Camii
14 Market
15 Meydan Hamamı
16 Güdük Minare
17 Zincirli Cami
18 Meydan Camii
20 Bürüciye Medresesi
21 Kale Camii
22 Atatürk Kongre ve Etnografya Müzesi
23 Officers Club
24 Çifte Minare Medrese
25 Şifaiye Medresesi
26 Ulu Cami (Great Mosque)
27 Kurşunlu Hamamı
31 Police
32 Gök Medrese
33 Kadı Burhanettin Türbesi
34 PTT
35 Sivas Gar (Train Station)
36 Sivas Otogar (Bus Station)
Kepenek Caddesi
Konak Meydanı
Abdi İpekçi Caddesi
İnönü Bulvarı
Atatürk Caddesi
Cemal Gürsel Caddesi
Kurşunlu Caddesi
Cumhuriyet Caddesi
Hospital
Stadyum
To Ankara & Tokat
To Ankara & Tokat
To Kayseri & Malatya
To Erzincan & Erzurum
Sivas
0 100 200 m

Çifte Minare Medrese

Directly opposite the Şifaiye Medresesi, the Çifte Minare Medrese (Seminary of the Twin Minarets) has, as its name states, a pair (*çift*) of minarets. Along with its grand Seljuk-style portal, that's about all it has, as the actual medrese behind the portal has long been ruined. Finished in 1271, it was commissioned by the Mongol-İlkhanid vizier Şemsettin Güveyni who ruled here. If you stand between the two opposing medreseler, you will be able to see clearly what a difference half a century made to the exuberance of Seljuk architecture.

Atatürk Congress & Ethnography Museum

North-west of the Kale Camii across İnönü Bulvarı is the Ottoman secondary school building which was the site of the Sivas Congress on 4 September 1919. Today it's the Atatürk Kongre ve Etnografya Müzesi, open from 8.30 am to noon and 1.30 to 5.30 pm (closed on Monday). Admission is free. The entrance is round the back of the building.

The ethnographical collection is pleasantly displayed on the ground floor and includes a fine selection of kilims and carpets, some magnificent embroidery, the old wooden doors from the Ulu Cami/Darüşşifa complex in Divriği, a 12th-century wooden *mimber* (pulpit) from the Kale Camii in Divriği and relics collected from dervish *tekkes* (monasteries) closed in 1925.

Upstairs, the Congress Hall is preserved as it was when the Sivas Congress met, with photos of the delegates touchingly displayed on old school desks. You can also see Atatürk's bedroom and the cable room which played a more important role in developments than you might imagine. The other displays (mainly photographs and documents) are captioned in Turkish only.

Ulu Cami (Great Mosque)

The town's other sights are south-east of Konak Meydanı along Cemal Gürsel and Cumhuriyet caddesis. To find them, walk to the southern end of the park and turn left (east) onto Cemal Gürsel Caddesi.

The Ulu Cami, or Great Mosque (1197), is Sivas' oldest building of significance. Built during the reign of Kutbettin Melikşah, it's a large, low room with a forest of 50 columns. The brick minaret was added in 1213. Though it's not as grand as the more imposing Seljuk buildings, it has a certain old-Anatolian charm.

Gök Medrese

Just east of the Ulu Cami, turn right (south) on Cumhuriyet Caddesi to reach the Gök Medrese, or Blue Seminary. It was built in 1271 at the behest of Sahip Ata, the grand vizier of Sultan Gıyasettin II Keyhüsrev, who funded the grand Sahip Ata mosque complex in Konya and many other buildings throughout the Seljuk realm.

The building's façade has been decorated with wild exuberance. Although built to the traditional Seljuk medrese plan, here the fancy embellishments of tiles, brickwork designs and carving cover not just the doorway, but the windows and walls as well.

The blue tilework gave the school its name, 'gök' (sky) being an old Turkish word for 'blue'.

At the time of writing the medrese was closed for restoration.

Places to Stay – bottom end

Sivas has one or two decent cheap hotels and any number of less decent ones. There are no hotels near the bus or train stations.

The inexpensive hotels in the first 500m south-east of Konak Meydanı along Atatürk Caddesi are uniformly drab and dingy, and expensive for what you get. *Otel Özden* (☎ (346) 221 1254), Atatürk Caddesi 21, is typical, with cleanish rooms but dodgy plumbing and ancient beds for US$11 a double with sink, US$16 a double with private shower. There's a lift, the management is friendly and the location is convenient, though noisy.

The better cheap hotels are 700m south-east of Konak Meydanı, at the junction of Atatürk and Kurşunlu caddesis.

Perhaps the best of the newer places in this

area is the *Otel Çakır* (☎ (346) 222 4526), which charges US$7/9 for a clean single/double with bath, including breakfast. It has a particularly pleasant lobby for relaxing in. The nearby *Otel Fatih* (☎ (346) 233 4313), Kurşunlu Caddesi 15, charges marginally more for similar standards.

Across the road from these two is the cheaper *Otel Yuvam* (☎ (346) 221 3349), where waterless singles/doubles cost just US$2 per person. Round the corner at Atatürk Caddesi 176, the friendly *Otel Ergin* (☎ (346) 221 2301) offers beds from US$4. Single women would probably be better off at the Çakır or Fatih.

Places to Stay – middle

Sivas' middle-range accommodation has been greatly reduced since the 1993 fire took out the Madımak (see introduction under Sivas earlier in this section). The remaining better hotels are 250m south-east of Konak Meydanı.

The *Otel Sultan* (☎ (346) 221 2986, fax 221 9346), Eski Belediye Sokak 18, across the street from the German consulate, has 30 restored comfortable double rooms. It's good value for US$23/42 a single/double with private shower (copious hot water) and breakfast, and it's quieter than most in Sivas.

The two-star *Otel Köşk* (KURSHK) (☎ (346) 221 1150, fax 223 9350) at Atatürk Caddesi 7 has a restaurant, a lift and 44 fairly noisy, but reasonably modern, double rooms priced at US$22/33 a single/double with private bath, bidet and TV. Buffet breakfast is included. Ask for a room at the back if you're a light sleeper.

Places to Eat

Sivas has plenty of good inexpensive places to eat. For a range of foods at the lowest prices, find 1. Sokak (Birinci Sokak) in Sularbaşı Mahallesi, behind the PTT just off the eastern side of Konak Meydanı. The Aliağa Camii is halfway up the slope, and below it are several small, cheap restaurants good for a quick feed for US$2 to US$4. The *Nimet* and *Anadolu* are the nicest, the Nimet having a particularly inviting upstairs *aile salonu* (room for families and single women). *Güleryüz Kebap* is the best for a variety of kebaps, including grills, İskender kebap and spicy-hot Adana kebap.

There are more cheap eating places where Atatürk Caddesi meets Eski Belediye Sokak. The *Ata İskender* has risen from the ashes of the Madımak and serves İskender kebap later in the day than most other places. There's also the *Hacı Kasimoğlu* and the smaller *Özlem Lokantası*.

Round the corner on Atatürk Caddesi, near the Hotel Köşk and beside the Pamukbank, is the spacious *Büyük Merkez Lokantası* serving a wide range of ready meals.

If you're staying in Kurşunlu Sokak, the *Bulvar Lokantası* on the corner with Atatürk Caddesi could save a walk back into the centre.

Across Atatürk Caddesi from the Hotel Köşk and down a bit towards the Merkez Camii is *Hakan Baklavacı*, where Sivas' youth gather in two upstairs rooms to eye one another warily and consume delicious baklava and other sweets for US$1 or so per portion.

For fancier meals with alcoholic beverages, you must resort to the dining room of the *Otel Köşk* (See Places to Stay – bottom end, earlier in this section).

Getting There & Away

As Sivas is on Turkey's main east-west highway and is also a north-south transit point, it is well served by rail and bus.

Bus Sivas' otogar, 2.2 km south of Konak Meydanı, is difficult to find if you're on foot. Likewise, it's difficult to walk from the otogar to Konak, so you'll probably end up taking a taxi (US$3). The otogar has its own PTT branch, a restaurant and pastry shop, a shoe repairs shop and an *emanetçi* (left-luggage room).

Bus traffic is intense in all directions, though many of the buses are passing through, so it's hard to know whether seats are available until they actually arrive. Details of some daily services follow:

Amasya – 225 km, four hours, US$6; five buses
Ankara – 450 km, six hours, US$8; frequent buses
Divriği – 175 km, 3½ hours, US$5; several buses, only one starting in Sivas
Diyarbakır – 500 km, eight hours, US$10; several buses
Erzurum – 485 km, nine hours, US$10; several buses
İstanbul – 900 km, 12 hours, US$15 to US$20
Kayseri – 200 km, 3½ hours, US$6; hourly buses
Malatya – 235 km, five hours, US$5; several buses
Samsun – 341 km, six hours, US$8; several buses
Tokat – 105 km, two hours, US$4; frequent buses
Yozgat – 224 km, four hours, US$5; frequent buses

Train Sivas is a main rail junction for both east-west and north-south lines. The two main east-west expresses, the *Doğu Ekspresi* and the *Güney/Vangölü Ekspresi*, go through Sivas daily. See the Ankara Getting There & Away section in the Central Anatolia chapter for details.

SIVAS TO DİVRİĞİ

At Divriği, 175 km south-east of Sivas, a ruined castle stands guard over two magnificent Seljuk buildings. Along the way at Balıklı Kaplıca is a medical curiosity.

Balıklı Kaplıca

On your way to Divriği, the uninteresting farm town of Kangal, east of the Sivas-Malatya road, offers no reason for you to stop. But 15 km east of Kangal at Balıklı Kaplıca (or Çermik) off the Divriği road is a curious – even bizarre – health spa for those with psoriasis. Sufferers from this disease, which causes itchy, unsightly patches on the skin, come to Balıklı Kaplıca ('Hot Spring with Fish') to relax in the pools of hot mineral water and let the resident fish nibble their scaly skin. The combination of the water and the fish is said to offer some relief, at least part of which must surely be comic relief.

Divriği

Divriği (DEEV-ree, population 25,000), a town hidden beyond a mountain pass (1970m high) in a fertile valley, is visited by relatively few tourists, foreign or Turkish. It's a typical old-fashioned Turkish mountain town with an economy based on agriculture. The narrow streets are laced with grapevines and paved in stone blocks, and its houses are still uncrowded by modern construction.

Uphill from the town centre stands the combined complex of the Ulu Cami (Great Mosque) and Darüşşifa (hospital). Both were founded in 1228 by the local emir Ahmet Şah and his wife, the lady Fatma Turan Melik. Beautifully restored and preserved, these remote buildings have been listed as world heritage sites by UNESCO.

Divriği has a few basic lodging places, some simple restaurants and banks. Given the scarcity of tourists, however, it might be a good idea to change whatever money you'll need in Sivas.

Ulu Cami Say 'Ulu Cami' (OO-loo jah-mee) to anyone in town and they'll point the way 250m up the hill along Ulu Cami Caddesi to the complex.

The northern portal of the Ulu Cami is stupendous, a sort of exuberant rococo Seljuk style, with geometric patterns, medallions, luxuriant stone foliage and intricate Arabic inscriptions bursting free of the façade's flatness in a richness that is simply astonishing. It's the sort of doorway which only a provincial emir, with more money than restraint, would ever dream of building. In a large Seljuk city, this sort of extravagance would have been ridiculed as lacking in taste. In Divriği, it's the wonderful, fanciful whim of a petty potentate shaped in stone.

The northern portal is really what you've come to see, although the north-western one has some fine work as well. The mosque's interior is very simple, with 16 columns and a plain mihrab, but you're unlikely to see it as it's kept locked outside prayer times.

Darüşşifa Adjoining the Ulu Cami is the hospital, equally plain and simple outside except for the requisite elaborate portal. Inside, eclecticism and odd ingenuity reigns: the floor plan is asymmetrical, the four columns all dissimilar. The octagonal pool in the court has a spiral run-off, similar to the one in Konya's Karatay Medresesi, which allowed the soothing tinkle of running water to break the silence of the room and soothe the patients' nerves. A platform raised above the main floor may have been for musicians who likewise soothed the patients with pleasant sounds.

The Darüşşifa is open from 8 am to 5 pm Monday to Friday, and is free of charge.

Seljuk Tombs As this was once an important provincial capital, you will notice several drum-like *kümbets*, Seljuk tombs, scattered about town. Ahmet Şah's tomb is near the Ulu Cami, as are several earlier ones dating from 1196 and another from 1240.

Kale Trailing down the sides of the hill dominating Divriği are the ruinous walls of its medieval castle, with the Kale Camii a solid but equally ruinous structure on the summit. Given the difficulty of getting onto a bus out of Divriği, you might want to explore at least some of the kale while you wait.

Places to Stay None of Divriği's three hotels are perfect, but of the three, the best is probably the *Belediye Oteli* (☎ (346) 418 1825), which, despite its makeshift air, will suffice for a night. Beds in so-so rooms with showers cost about US$4. Rooms at the back have balconies overlooking the kale ruins. There's a popular ground floor and terrace restaurant, and a large tea garden opposite. The noise from the restaurant and tea garden combined can be deafening but with luck it will stop around 11.30 pm.

The Belediye Oteli is along a side turning marked by a broken Pepsi sign on the left, off the main road into town. Ask to be dropped off, otherwise a taxi back from the otogar will cost about US$1.50.

The other two possibilities are on the main commercial street in the centre of town. The *Otel Ninni* (☎ (346) 418 1239) charges US$5 for a double room without water; the common shower and toilet, though reasonably clean, are down one floor from some of the rooms. You need to be feeling pretty desperate to go for the *Hotel Değer* next door.

Getting There & Away Getting to and from Divriği can be tricky, especially if you don't have a car. Although three or four daily buses run between Sivas and Divriği, all but one of them has come from Ankara or İstanbul, which means they are often already full when they get to Sivas. In the opposite direction, people book days ahead, so this too can be problematic. Only one bus a day actually starts its run in Sivas and that's at 4.30 pm; in the opposite direction it leaves Divriği at 7 am. The trip between Sivas and Divriği takes about 3½ hours and costs US$7. Divriği's bus station is on the highway southwest of the village.

If you're driving, note that there is no road onward towards Erzincan from Divriği, forcing you to backtrack.

Given these problems you might prefer to take a train, even though it will take longer than the bus. The rail line from Sivas to Erzurum passes through Divriği and you could continue eastwards to Erzurum (roughly 6½ hours away), though you may have to stay overnight in Divriği and catch a connection the next day. Divriği train station is about two km south of the Ulu Cami.

ELAZIĞ

Elazığ (EHL-lah-zuh, population 200,000, altitude 1200m) is a new town, only founded in the 19th century at a place called Mezraa.

In 1834 Sultan Mahmut II gave his vizier Reşit Mehmet Paşa the duty of reasserting Ottoman imperial control over the semi-independent provincial lords of the region. The paşa proclaimed Mezraa a provincial capital and installed an army garrison.

During the reign of Sultan Abdülaziz, its governor gave it the name of Mamuretülaziz, later shortened to Elaziz and, in republican times, to Elazığ. Today Elazığ is a farming centre and university town, though its importance as an entrepôt ended when the Keban Lake cut it off from main roads to the north and east. Viticulture is important; Tekel, the government spirits company, raises its big dark-red *öküzgözü* (ox-eye) grapes in the region.

If you need to stay for the night, plan to spend some time seeing the Urartian treasures in the archaeological museum and the ruins of ancient, earthquake-ruined Harput, five km north of Elazığ.

Orientation & Information

The city centre is Cumhuriyet Meydanı at the intersection of Bosna-Herzek Bulvarı (shown as İstasyon Caddesi on old maps) and Gazi and Hürriyet caddesis, near the İzzet Paşa Camii; turn left along Gazi Caddesi for Fırat Üniversitesi and right along Hürriyet Caddesi for Harput and the banks.

The Belediye and PTT are here, while the helpful Tourism Information Office (☎ (424) 212 3301) is at Bosna-Herzek Bulvarı 35 in the İl Halk Kütüphanesi (Provincial Library) building.

Elazığ's postal code is 23000.

Archaeology & Ethnography Museum

In the 1960s the creation of the Keban Dam (Keban Barajı), north-west of Elazığ, caused the flooding of the valleys to the north. Before the new lake was created, an archaeological rescue project excavated many likely sites and the artefacts uncovered are displayed in the Elazığ Archaeology & Ethnography Museum (Elazığ Arkeoloji ve Etnografya Müzesi) on the campus of Euphrates University (Fırat Üniversitesi) on the outskirts of the city. Among the most valuable finds were Early Bronze Age royal seals, gold jewellery and a cuneiform inscription from the time of Menua, king of Urartu.

You may have to hunt around for someone to open the museum and sell you a ticket for US$1. Given that this is a university museum it's a shame that the labelling is so perfunctory, both in Turkish and in English. Upstairs, carpets to make a Kayseri salesman weep with envy languish unlabelled and poorly lit.

To get to the museum take a bus marked 'Üniversite' from Hürriyet Caddesi. The campus is vast so don't try and walk it.

Harput

It was Harput, not Elazığ, which had the long, eventful history, effectively ending in the 19th century when it was ruined by earthquakes. Guarded by its photogenic castle, Harput was an important way-station on the Silk Road to and from China and India, but with the earthquake and the building of Elazığ its importance diminished.

Today, besides the castle, you can visit the Great Mosque (Ulu Cami), dating from the 1100s and thus one of the oldest in Anatolia, the Church of the Virgin Mary (Meryem Ana Kilisesi), and the Arap Baba Türbesi, a Seljuk work. There's also a small, thoroughly dusty museum and assorted other ruins scattered about. Pick up a plan at Elaziğ tourist office before you go. Take a minibus from Harput Caddesi (US$0.20) to get to Harput.

Places to Stay & Eat

Elazığ's places to stay are concentrated in and around Hürriyet Caddesi, which means they're central if not necessarily particularly quiet.

If you can afford it, the two-star *Beritan Hotel* (☎ (424) 218 4484, fax 212 7970), Hürriyet Caddesi 24, has 68 comfortable rooms with private baths going for US$27/44 a single/double. Otherwise there are cheaper places almost next door. Try the *Hotel Divan* (☎ (424) 218 1103) or the *Hotel Çınar)* (☎ (424) 218 1811), both of which have singles for US$6 and doubles for US$10, slightly more with private baths.

In Bakırcılar Sokak, off Bosna-Herzek Bulvarı, the *Otel Erdem* (☎ (424) 218 2212) has bathless rooms for US$9/15 a single/double, but could be quieter than the other cheapies.

If you're just passing through, it's worth noting that the *Kafeterya* in the otogar serves better than average food right through from a choice of breakfasts.

Getting There & Away

Elazığ's spacious otogar is three km east of

the centre. Dolmuşes will ferry you into the centre for less than US$0.10.

There are fairly frequent services to and from Diyarbakır (151 km, two hours, US$5), Erzurum (324 km, seven hours, US$15), Malatya (101 km, 1½ hours, US$3) and Mersin (585 km, 10 hours, US$11).

ERZİNCAN

Like other north-eastern Anatolian cities, Erzincan (EHR-zeen-jahn, population 100,000, altitude 1185m) is very old. Unlike other cities, however, Erzincan has little to show for its great age, as it lies at the heart of Turkey's earthquake zone.

In 1939 it was devastated by Turkey's worst earthquake this century when almost 33,000 people died. Other quakes, most recently in 1993, have left hardly anything of historical or architectural interest. What you see today is a modern farming town whose people await the next devastation with apparent nonchalance.

Earthquakes have effectively erased Erzincan's old street plan as well. The modern main street is broad and arrow-straight, lined with shops, hotels and restaurants.

Places to Stay & Eat

Should you need to stop, hotels along the main street can provide basic no-frills lodging. Several of the town's best hotels fell victim to the last quake, and the best is now the brand-new three-star *Büyük Erzincan Otel* (☎ (446) 223 7305), on the eastern outskirts. More convenient for a brief transit stop are the *Kılıçlar Oteli* (☎ (446) 212 1641) and the *Otel Karakaya* (☎ (446) 214 3673), more or less opposite each other within five minutes' walk of the otogar on Fevzipaşa Caddesi, Erzincan's main drag.

Given that your stay in Erzincan is likely to be brief, it's good to be able to report a pleasant, shady *çay bahçesi* (tea garden) and the *Sila Restoran* right beside the otogar (under reconstruction at the time of writing). For spit-roasted chicken, stroll out to the *Oba Restaurant* in Fevzipaşa Caddesi.

TERCAN

Midway on the age-old highway between Erzincan and Erzurum stands Tercan (TEHR-jahn, population 12,000, altitude 1475m), yet another ancient settlement with a momentous history. A town of farmers and herders, Tercan is set in a fertile river valley accented by huge rock outcrops to the south. Just west of the town, where the highway and railway cross the river, is an ancient stone bridge with most of its arches fallen.

Tercan houses the **Tomb of Mama Hatun** (Mama Hatun Türbesi), built between 1192 and 1202 and unique in Anatolian architecture. It's uphill through the town 250m off the highway next to the **Mama Hatun Kervansaray**.

The tomb proper is surrounded by a high, thick wall which you enter through a portal decorated with bands of unusual Kufic script. Inside, the circular wall is pierced by 12 eyvans in which lesser notables could be entombed; several cenotaphs indicate burials below. The south-west mihrab faces Mecca from this easterly location.

If the tomb is unlocked, climb the stairs to the right of the entrance portal to get a view of the tomb and the surrounding cemetery. The eight-lobed tomb proper stands in the centre of the circle, oriented to the points of the compass with the door to the south. Its roof resembles an umbrella. The space above the actual burial chamber is still used for prayers.

The neighbouring caravanserai is topped by a forest of chimneys. The western door, facing the town on the opposite side of the caravanserai from the tomb, is the one most likely to be open.

Though much repaired and rebuilt over the centuries, the caravanserai still exhibits some unusual features. Its long entry hall is lined with eyvans, leading to a singularly large eyvan across the courtyard from the entrance. Conical caps on the bastion tops are an odd feature. At the time of writing the entire complex was undergoing extensive restoration.

Should you need to stay the night, Tercan has two very small truck-stop hotels, the

Kervansaray and the *Calışkan*, out on the highway. There are simple restaurants as well.

ERZURUM

Erzurum (EHR-zoo-room, population 300,000, altitude 1853m) is the largest city on the Eastern Anatolian high plateau. It has always been a transportation centre and military headquarters, and is the command post for the defence of Anatolia from Russian and Persian invasion. Now it's assuming a new role as an eastern cultural and commercial city.

With its severe climate and sparse landscape, Erzurum lacks the colour and complexity of İstanbul or İzmir, but makes up for it with a rough frontier refinement. The orderly, modern, tree-lined boulevards provide a welcome contrast to the arid, almost lifeless appearance of the surrounding oceans of steppe.

It's also a city that seems to face in two directions at once: many more women wear a veil and a surprising number are in purdah; the old men go to prayer early and often. In contrast, Cumhuriyet Caddesi boasts a wide range of consumer durables and even a Wimpy. Since Erzurum is a university town, there are plenty of students whose opinions span the range of western capitalist and eastern Islamist ideas.

For tourists, Erzurum is a transfer point with air, rail and bus connections. But if you stay one or two nights, you'll be able to visit some fine Turkish buildings and a lively market area. You can also take an excursion to the Tortum Valley and the mountain village of Yusufeli on the way to Artvin.

History

During the Byzantine era Erzurum was called Theodosiopolis after the emperor who founded it on the ruins of an earlier settlement in the late 5th century. The powers in Constantinople had their hands full defending this town from Arab attack on several occasions. The Seljuks took it after the Battle of Manzikert in 1071, effectively opening Anatolia to Turkish settlement.

Being in a strategic position at the confluence of roads to Constantinople, Russia and Persia, Erzurum was conquered and lost by armies (in alphabetical order) of Arabs, Armenians, Byzantines, Mongols, Persians, Romans, Russians, Saltuk Turks and Seljuk Turks. As for the Ottomans, it was Selim the Grim who conquered the city in 1515. It was captured by Russian troops in 1882 and again in 1916.

In July 1919 Atatürk came to Erzurum to hold the famous congress which, along with the one at Sivas, provided the rallying cry for the independence struggle. The Erzurum Congress is most famous for determining the boundaries of what became known as the territories of the National Pact, those lands which would be part of the foreseen Turkish Republic. Atatürk and the congress claimed the lands which, in essence, form the present Turkish state and rejected claims to other formerly held Ottoman lands. The phrase at the time was, 'We want no more, we shall accept no less'.

Orientation

Although the old city of Erzurum was huddled beneath the walls of the kale, the new Erzurum, which has grown up around the old, has broad boulevards, traffic roundabouts and an open, airy feeling, part of which comes from the dry wind which blows constantly.

You can walk to everything in the centre (Old Erzurum), including the train station, but will need a taxi or bus to get to and from the otogar, the airport and one of the better hotels.

Besides the main otogar west of the centre, there is the Gölbaşı Semt Garajı on the north-eastern outskirts, with minibus services to points north and east.

In Old Erzurum, a convenient point of reference is Gürcü Kapı. Once the 'Georgian gate' in the city walls, it's marked by a chunky stone fountain at a traffic intersection 600m up the hill (south-east) from the train station.

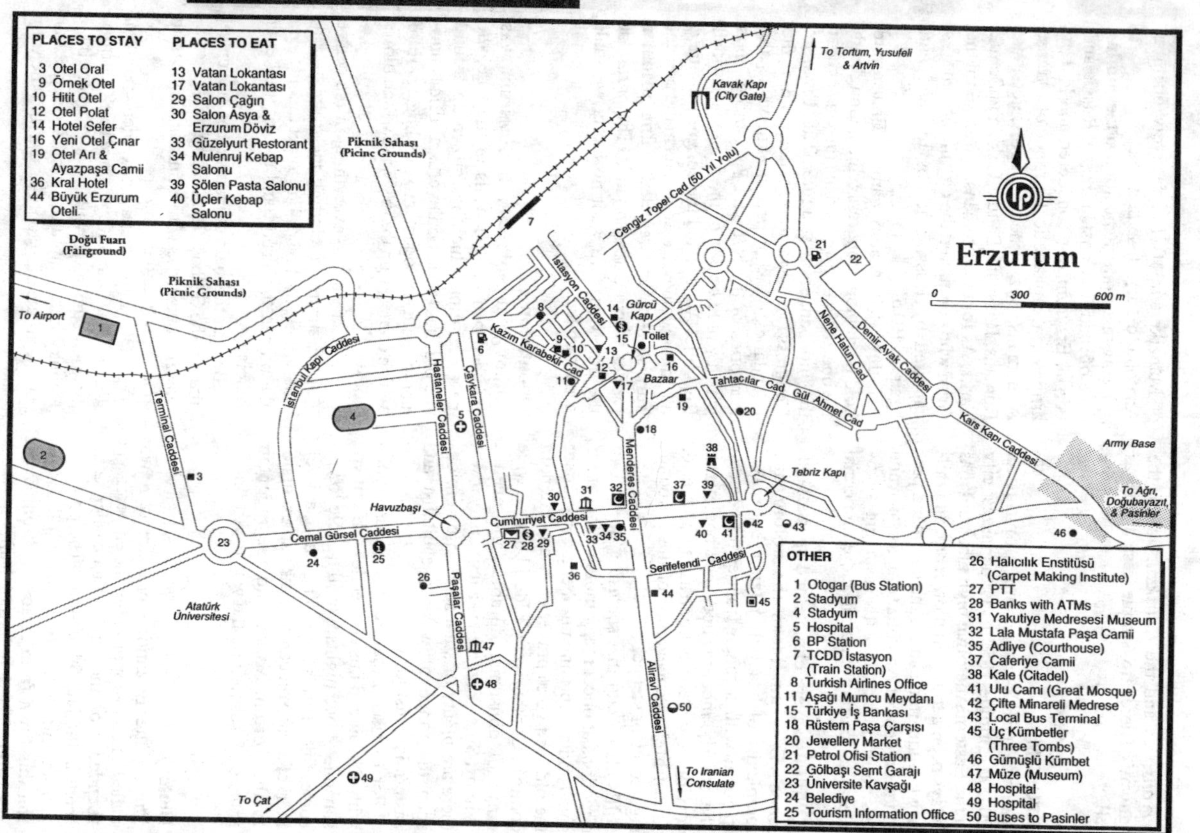
Erzurum
0 300 600 m
PLACES TO STAY
3 Otel Oral
9 Örnek Otel
10 Hitit Otel
12 Otel Polat
14 Hotel Sefer
16 Yeni Otel Çınar
19 Otel Arı & Ayazpaşa Camii
36 Kral Hotel
44 Büyük Erzurum Oteli
PLACES TO EAT
13 Vatan Lokantası
17 Vatan Lokantası
29 Salon Çağın
30 Salon Asya & Erzurum Döviz
33 Güzelyurt Restorant
34 Mulenruj Kebap Salonu
39 Şölen Pasta Salonu
40 Üçler Kebap Salonu
OTHER
1 Otogar (Bus Station)
2 Stadyum
4 Stadyum
5 Hospital
6 BP Station
7 TCDD İstasyon (Train Station)
8 Turkish Airlines Office
11 Aşağı Mumcu Meydanı
15 Türkiye İş Bankası
18 Rüstem Paşa Çarşısı
20 Jewellery Market
21 Petrol Ofisi Station
22 Gölbaşı Semt Garajı
23 Üniversite Kavşağı
24 Belediye
25 Tourism Information Office
26 Halıcılık Enstitüsü (Carpet Making Institute)
27 PTT
28 Banks with ATMs
31 Yakutiye Medresesi Museum
32 Lala Mustafa Paşa Camii
35 Adliye (Courthouse)
37 Caferiye Camii
38 Kale (Citadel)
41 Ulu Cami (Great Mosque)
42 Çifte Minareli Medrese
43 Local Bus Terminal
45 Üç Kümbetler (Three Tombs)
46 Gümüşlü Kümbet
47 Müze (Museum)
48 Hospital
49 Hospital
50 Buses to Pasinler
To Tortum, Yusufeli & Artvin
Kavak Kapı (City Gate)
Piknik Sahası (Picinc Grounds)
Cengiz Topel Cad (50 Yıl Yolu)
Doğu Fuarı (Fairground)
Piknik Sahası (Picnic Grounds)
To Airport
İstasyon Caddesi
Gürcü Kapı
Toilet
Kazım Karabekir Cad
Bazaar
Tahtacılar Cad
Gül Ahmet Cad
Nene Hatun Cad
Demir Ayak Caddesi
Kars Kapı Caddesi
Army Base
To Ağrı, Doğubayazıt, & Pasinler
Tebriz Kapı
İstanbul Kapı Caddesi
Hastaneler Caddesi
Çaykara Caddesi
Terminal Caddesi
Menderes Caddesi
Havuzbaşı
Cumhuriyet Caddesi
Cemal Gürsel Caddesi
Şerifefendi Caddesi
Paşalar Caddesi
Atatürk Üniversitesi
Aliravi Caddesi
To Iranian Consulate
To Çat

Modern Erzurum's main thoroughfare is Cumhuriyet Caddesi, renamed Cemal Gürsel Caddesi along its western reaches. The two parts of the street are divided at the centre by a traffic roundabout bearing a large statue of Atatürk, a pool and fountain and the name Havuzbaşı. It's almost two km from the otogar to the Havuzbaşı roundabout and three km from the otogar to the centre of town. The train station is 2.5 km from the otogar.

Erzurum's sights are conveniently grouped in the old part of town, within easy walking distance of one another.

Information

The Tourism Information Office (☎ (442) 218 5697) is inconveniently positioned on the south side of Cemal Gürsel Caddesi at 9/A, one block west of the Havuzbaşı traffic roundabout. Staff are friendly but speak very little English.

Erzurum's postal code is 25000.

Money Erzurum Döviz, on Cumhuriyet Caddesi just west of the Yakutiye Medresesi next to the big Inter-Erzurum Toyota showroom, changes cash (Deutschmarks and dollars only) daily from 10.30 am to 1 pm and 1.30 to 7.30 pm. Several banks will also change cash but are less keen on travellers' cheques. Türkiye İş Bankası changes cheques efficiently and without fuss. There's a branch just off Gürcü Kapı.

Iranian Consulate There's an Iranian consulate (☎ (442) 218 3876) in Erzurum off Aliravi Caddesi across from the Education Faculty (Eğitim Fakultesi Karşışı). It's open every day, except Friday, from 8 am to 1 pm and 2 to 4 pm; however, just to apply for a visa here will cost you US$50. Your application will be forwarded to Tehran and a month later may or may not be granted. If it isn't, you don't get your money back. If it is, you must then pay a proper visa fee. It makes more sense to apply for your visa from your home country before setting out.

Newspapers After 3 pm in the afternoon you can get copies of the *Turkish Daily News* in the Kültür Sarayı at Cumhuriyet Caddesi 30, opposite the Yakutiye Medresesi. It's usually kept behind the counter, so if you don't see it, ask.

Çifte Minareli Medrese (Twin Minaret Seminary)

At the eastern end of Cumhuriyet Caddesi is the Çifte Minareli Medrese (1253), or Twin Minaret Seminary, open every day from 8.30 am to 6 pm. Admission costs US$0.50.

The Çifte Minareli was built by Alaettin Keykubat II, son of the Seljuk sultan known for his many great building projects. Enter through the towering limestone portal topped by its twin minarets made of brick and decorated with small strips of blue tile. The main courtyard has four large niches and a double colonnade on the eastern and western sides. Stairways in each of the corners lead to the students' cells on the upper level.

At the far end of the courtyard is the grand 12-sided domed hall which served as the Hatuniye Türbesi, or Tomb of Huant Hatun, the sultan's daughter. Beneath the domed hall is a small room with ingenious vents to allow the light and air in. This may have been a *mescit* (prayer room) with a cenotaph, the actual tomb being beneath the floor.

Ulu Cami (Great Mosque)

Next to the Çifte Minareli is the Ulu Cami, or Great Mosque (1179). The contrast between the two buildings is striking: the Ulu Cami, built by the Saltuklu Turkish emir of Erzurum, is restrained but elegant, with seven aisles running north-south and six running east-west, resulting in a forest of columns. You enter from the north along the central aisle. Above the fourth east-west aisle a stalactite dome is open to the heavens. At the southern end of the central aisle are a curious wooden dome and a pair of bull's-eye windows.

Üç Kümbetler (Three Tombs)

To reach the Üç Kümbetler, a complex of three Seljuk tombs, walk south between the Çifte Minareli and the Ulu Cami until you come to a T-junction. Turn left then immediately right and walk a short block up the hill to the tombs, which are in a fenced enclosure on the right-hand side. The tombs are well decorated, the best being on the octagonal Emir Sultan Saltuk Türbesi, dating from the 12th century.

Erzurum Kale (Citadel)

The citadel, or kale, erected by Theodosius around the 5th century, is on the hilltop to the north of the Çifte Minareli and the Ulu Cami. Walk up the hill towards the curious old clock tower topped by a Turkish flag. The tower was built as a minaret in the time of the Saltuks but was later converted to its current time-keeping function. It stands by the entrance to the kale.

The kale walls harbour a few old cannons with Russian or Ottoman inscriptions, a disused prayer room and a light-up picture of Atatürk. Steep steps lead up to the rough top of the walls where there's a fine view, especially of the Çifte Minareli huddled beneath the surrounding mountains. This is an especially fine place to be at prayer time, with the call to prayer seemingly coming at you from all sides.

The view from the walls is impressive but this is not an experience for anyone inclined to vertigo. Alternatively you can climb the clock tower, preferably taking a torch with you. Open the cupboard doors at the top of the stairs and you'll find the clock which was made in Croydon, England, and given to the Ottomans by Queen Victoria in 1877.

Every July bouts of wrestling take place in front of appreciative audiences in the grounds of the kale.

The kale is open from 8 am to noon and 1.30 to 7.30 pm in summer; admission costs US$0.75.

Ottoman Mosques

Return to Cumhuriyet Caddesi, then head west and you will pass on the right the small Ottoman **Caferiye Camii**, constructed in 1645 upon the order of Ebubekiroğlu Hacı Cafer.

Cross at the busy intersection and you come to the **Lala Mustafa Paşa Camii** (1563) on the north-western corner. Lala Mustafa Paşa was a grand vizier during the golden age of the Ottoman Empire, and his mosque is a classical Ottoman work of the high period, possibly designed by Sinan or one of his followers.

Yakutiye Medresesi

Just west of the Lala Mustafa Paşa Camii is the Yakutiye Medresesi (Yakutiye Seminary), a Mongol theological seminary dating from 1310 and built by the local Mongol emir. Its portal copies the Seljuk style and is well worth inspection, especially for the lions on the sides. The minaret borrows from Seljuk architecture also. The türbe at the back was meant to be used as the emir's tomb but never was.

The seminary now houses the **Turkish & Islamic Arts & Ethnography Museum** (Türk – İslâm Eserleri ve Etnoğrafya Müzesi), one of Eastern Turkey's better museums, with a mock-up of the interior of an Ottoman dwelling and a display of carpets and kilims. The side rooms contain exhibits relating to the black amber jewellery trade, Seljuk ceramics, copperwork, weaponry, womens' clothing and much more. There's even a little tea room at the back. It's open from 8 am to noon and 12.30 to 5 pm, closed on Monday; admission costs US$0.50.

Erzurum Museum

The Erzurum Müzesi is several long blocks south-west of the Yakutiye Medresesi. Walk west along Cumhuriyet Caddesi to the Havuzbaşı roundabout, then turn left (south) and walk up the hill. The museum is just before the next intersection, on the left (east) side of the street. It's a 15-minute walk, or you can take any bus climbing the hill from Havuzbaşı.

Now that the museum's collection of ethnology has been moved into the Yakutiye Medresesi (see this section earlier), what's left here looks pretty sad. Cases at the back document the massacre and mass burial of the Muslim inhabitants of Yeşilyayla and Alaca Köyü by Armenian insurgents at the beginning of the century, but the labelling is only in Turkish.

Otherwise, the museum has some fragments of Seljuk tiles and Urartian pottery, some jewellery found in Hellenistic and Roman tombs and some impressive Trans-Caucasian pottery. In place of ethnology, the main room is now devoted to finds from digs at Büyüktepe Höyük and Sos Höyük, luckily labelled in English.

The museum is open from 8 am to noon and 12.30 to 5 pm, closed on Monday; admission costs US$1.

Bazaars

Erzurum's market areas are scattered through the old part of the city and it's easy to get lost in the narrow, winding streets. Start your wanderings at the Lala Mustafa Paşa Camii, then walk north along the street next to the mosque. You will pass the covered Rüstem Paşa Çarşısı, which is the centre for the manufacture and sale of black amber prayer beads. For a look at the shops go to the upper floor. Those around the courtyard do a good trade in black amber jewellery too.

Just down the street from the Rüstem Paşa Çarşısı is the small **Pervizoğlu Camii** (1715). Along Kavaflar Çarşısı Sokak you'll find many tinsmiths selling handmade cookers, heaters and samovars – all prized in a town renowned for its snow.

Fruit, vegetables and livestock are sold alongside craft goods in Turkey's markets.

Continuing downhill in the market district will bring you, finally, to İstasyon Caddesi, the street leading to the train station and the numerous hotels in this district.

The **Erzurum Hamamı** at the bazaar end of İstasyon Caddesi has been praised by many readers of this guide. Unfortunately, it's only open to men. Continue along the road winding past the kale, however, and you'll come to two small baths for women: the Hanım and the Kırkçeşme. Neither is brilliant, although the Hanım may be slightly cleaner.

Places to Stay – bottom end

Erzurum is a low-budget traveller's dream, with many very cheap places to stay not far from the town centre. As for the upper end, there are several comfortable three-star places but no hotels in the luxury class.

Erzurum's inexpensive lodging places are scattered throughout the old part of town and are especially thick along Kazım Karabekir Caddesi (KYAA-zumm kah-rah-beh-KEER), north-west of Gürcü Kapı, not far from the train station and the bazaar.

Otel Arı (☎ (442) 218 3141), Ayazpaşa Caddesi 8, is about average, with double rooms from US$6 to US$8. Your room may have a sink, or shower, or toilet, or a combination of these; in winter hot water is available on request. The hotel is right next to the Ayazpaşa Camii. From Gürcü Kapı, walk uphill along the street to the left of the Türk Ticaret Bankası ('Türkbank' on the sign) and when it widens into a square go left towards all those 'Avukat' signs.

Nearby is the well regarded, friendly *Yeni Otel Çınar* (☎ (442) 218 3580), Ayazpaşa Caddesi 18, which is a little more comfortable for similar prices: US$7 with sink, US$9 with shower for a double room. To find it, look for the Gürpınar Sineması (cinema) in the bazaar. The street opposite leads to the Çınar.

Beginning in Aşağı Mumcu Meydanı, the little square at the bazaar end of Kazım Karabekir Caddesi, walk north-west along the Kazım Karabekir Caddesi to find the 32-room *Hitit Otel* (☎ (442) 218 1204) at No 26. A room with sink costs US$8/11 a single/double, US$10/13 with private shower. Next door is the similarly priced *Örnek Otel* (☎ (442) 218 1203), with 35 rooms, all with private showers. The rooms are much like those in the other cheapies but some effort has been made to make the reception area look more interesting.

Better than either of these is the one-star *Otel Polat* (☎ (442) 218 1623) at Kazım Karabekir Caddesi 4. It's a step up in comfort and price, with a lift (no steps to the entrance), a family atmosphere, pretensions to modernity and 60 rooms, each with a bath, for US$7/10 a single/double.

Round the corner is the 36-room, two-star *Hotel Sefer* (☎ (442) 218 6714) on İstasyon Caddesi, near Aşağı Mumcu Meydanı. Convenient, but certainly not fancy, it charges US$10/15/18 a single/double/triple, including breakfast, and is popular with tour groups. The entrance is decrepit; the guest rooms are better.

Just off Cumhuriyet Caddesi, opposite the Yakutiye Medresesi and so in the heart of things, the *Kral Hotel* (☎ (442) 218 7783, fax 218 6973) at Erzincankapı 18 has much nicer rooms than the lobby might suggest for US$9/14 a single/double with shower and TV. Noise could be a problem though.

EASTERN ANATOLIA

Places to Stay – middle

Otel Oral (☎ (442) 218 9740, fax 9749), Terminal Caddesi 3, used to be the best hotel in the city but is starting to show its age. Its 90 two-star rooms all have showers or baths and cost US$36 to US$52. Front rooms (including the suites) suffer from street noise: in the warm months, when you need the windows open for ventilation, request a room at the back *(arka tarafta)*. The Oral's inconvenient location also forces you to go everywhere by taxi or minibus.

The 50-room, nominally three-star *Büyük Erzurum Oteli* (☎ (442) 218 6528, fax 212 2898), Aliravi Caddesi 5, is older than the Oral but has a more convenient location just up the hill from the Lala Mustafa Paşa Camii. The staff speak some English. The hotel is old fashioned and drab, and although the bedrooms are clean and pleasant they are, frankly, not much different from those in cheaper places. A single with bath is US$20, a double US$32.

Places to Stay – top end

The new three-star *Hotel Dilaver* at Aşağı Mumcu Caddesi Petit Meydanı (☎ (422) 235 0068, fax 218 1148) is currently Erzurum's most comfortable hotel. Rooms cost US$40/$60 a single/double, for which you get modern décor and fittings, TV, air-con, a mini bar and private bathroom. The top-floor restaurant offers splendid views over Erzurum.

Another new hotel is being built on Aliravi Caddesi and should be open by the time you read this. Standards and prices are likely to match the Dilaver's.

Places to Eat – bottom end

As with hotel prices, meal prices in Erzurum are low. Kebap places are, as usual, among the cheapest and best. One good place to eat near the Ulu Cami is *Üçler Kebap Salonu* at Cumhuriyet Caddesi, Osmanpaşa Sokak No 2. To find it, look for a sign and turn down the alley. Here you can get local kuşbaşı lamb kebaps (marinated in salt, oil and chili for several days) or the usual range of pides etc. There's an unusually attractive *aile salonu* at the back.

Just opposite the Akçay Otel on Kamil Ağa Sokak is the *Mulenruj Kebap Salonu* (that's 'Moulin Rouge'), where the main dining room is decorated with a fine 3D model of a hydroelectric power plant! Döner kebap, along with kuru fasulye (beans in tomato sauce), pilav and a soft drink comes to about US$3.50. Several other kebapçıs are within a few steps of the Mulenruj.

A stroll along Cumhuriyet Caddesi reveals several slightly fancier places. The *Salon Çağın* is near the traffic roundabout closest to the Yakutiye Medresesi, on the south side of the street. Clean, bright and cheery, it has very tasty food and on Sunday makes the house speciality, mantı (Turkish ravioli). If you can face it, they'll even do you a tripe soup for breakfast.

Across the street is the fancier *Salon Asya*. The menu includes a large variety of kebaps, including tereyağlı (with butter) and Bursa kebap. Meals cost from US$3 to US$4.

Several cafés and pastry shops on Cumhuriyet Caddesi are useful for a quick bite or breakfast. Best is the *Kılıçoğlu Baklavaları*, two doors west of the Salon Çağın. Bright and modern, it sells excellent buttery baklava with tea for US$1. *Patisserie Zirve*, farther west down the hill from the Salon Çağın, is good for pastry and tea or breakfast. Further east towards the Caferiye Camii is the *Şölen Pasta Salonu* which is popular for afternoon ice creams.

On Kazım Karabekir Caddesi, try the *Vatan Lokantası* opposite the Hotel Polat, a block behind the Hotel Sefer. The Vatan has an excellent selection of sulu yemek (ready food, mostly stews) at lunch. Full meals can be had for around US$3. There's a second branch round the corner on Menderes Caddesi.

Near the Hotel Dilaver, the *Rıhtım Restaurant* at Petit Meydanı No 36 serves good chicken and salads for around US$3 to US$5.

Places to Eat – middle

Erzurum's best, since 1928, is the *Güzelyurt Restorant* (☎ (442) 218 1514), directly facing the Yakutiye Medresesi across Cumhuriyet Caddesi. With soft lighting, quiet music, experienced black-clad waiters and alcohol, the Güzelyurt is the place where westernised business men come to dine after a hard day's toil. Have the house speciality, mantarlı güveç – a delicious casserole of lamb, pimientos, onions, tomatoes, mushrooms and cheese. It's big enough for two people if you've already had several appetisers. The bill shouldn't exceed US$5 to US$8 a head.

Getting There & Away

As eastern Turkey's main city, Erzurum is well served by all modes of transport.

Air Turkish Airlines (☎ (442) 218 1904) at 100 Yıl Caddesi, SSK Rant Tesisleri 24, near the north-western end of Kazım Karabekir Caddesi, has a daily flight from İstanbul via Ankara to Erzurum and back.

Bus The modern otogar, three km from the centre along the airport road, handles most of Erzurum's intercity traffic. It has a post office, barber, *emanet* (left luggage), shops and a restaurant. City bus No 2 passes by the otogar and will take you into town for US$0.20; a taxi is about US$2.

Details of some daily services from Erzurum's otogar follow:

Ankara – 925 km, 15 hours, US$17; several buses
Artvin – 215 km, four hours, US$5; several buses
Diyarbakır – 485 km, 10 hours, US$16; several buses
Doğubayazıt – 285 km, 4½ hours, US$8; five buses
Erzincan – 192 km, 2½ hours, US$5; frequent buses
İstanbul – 1275 km, 21 hours, US$20 to US$23; several buses
Kars – 205 km, 3½ hours, US$6; several buses
Sivas – 485 km, 7½ hours, US$10; several buses
Tortum – 53 km, one hour, US$2; several dolmuşes
Trabzon – 325 km, eight hours, US$8; several buses
Van – 420 km, 7½ hours, US$9; several buses
Yusufeli – 129 km, three hours, US$4; several dolmuşes

For Iran (if you already have your visa), take a bus to Doğubayazıt where you can catch a minibus to the Iranian frontier.

The Gölbaşı Semt Garajı, about one km north-east of Gürcü Kapı through the back streets, handles minibuses to towns to the north and east of Erzurum, including Ardanuç, Ardeşen, Arhavi, Çayeli, Fındıklı, Hopa, Pazar, Rize, Şavşat, Şelale, Tortum and Yusufeli. The Gölbaşı Semt Garajı can be difficult to find unless you take a taxi. Look for the Hotel Ersin and a Petrol Ofisi fuel station; it's behind the Petrol Ofisi station.

Train The Erzurum Garı is at the northern end of İstasyon Caddesi, 600m north of Gürcü Kapı and over a km from Cumhuriyet Caddesi. You can walk from the station to most hotels except the Oral. City buses depart from the station forecourt every half-hour and circulate through the city.

Erzurum has good rail connections with Ankara via Kayseri, Sivas, Divriği and Erzincan. The Doğu Express covers the distance between Erzurum and Ankara in about

25 hours – if it's on time. For details of trains serving Erzurum, see Getting There & Away in the Ankara section of the Central Anatolia chapter.

Getting Around

The airport bus (US$0.50) meets every flight and stops at the otogar on the way into town. For the trip back to the airport, it leaves the Turkish Airlines office 1½ hours before flight time. A taxi to or from the airport, 10 km from town, costs around US$5.

Hat 2 (Route 2), covered by city buses and minibuses, runs between the district of Yoncalık by the citadel westward along Cumhuriyet Caddesi as far as the otogar.

A taxi should cost less than US$3, no matter where you go in town.

AROUND ERZURUM

Excursion to the Georgian Valleys

Many visitors to Erzurum make an excursion northward into the Tortum Valley (Tortum Vadisi) to enjoy the dramatic mountain scenery and visit some of the old Georgian churches in farming villages. For details, see the following Georgian Valleys section.

Palandöken

Towering above Erzurum, 10 km to the south, is the new ski resort area of Palandöken where you can usually ski from November to mid-May. There are ski lifts and three levels of pistes.

To be close to the slopes you can stay in the big new four-star *Dedeman Hotel* (☎ (422) 316 2414, fax 316 3607). Alterna-

A Brief History of Georgia

The Georgian kingdom was founded in the Mingrelian lowlands and Caucasus Mountains at the eastern end of the Black Sea around the 4th century BC.

Georgia was independent until around 100 BC when King Mithridates VI of Pontus conquered it for a while. Dominated by Rome and the Persian Sassanids, the country was converted to Christianity by St Nino of Cappadocia in the mid-4th century.

The partly Armenian dynasty of the Bagratids had gained control of Georgia by the 6th century. Though they maintained good relations with the Byzantine patriarchs and emperors, Georgia was briefly captured and ruled by the Arabs in the early 8th century.

After the Arab invasion the Byzantine emperor was nominal ruler of the districts north of Erzurum (named Tao and Klarjeti in Georgian), but real power was in the hands of local Georgian princelings. One of them, King Ashot I Kuropalates, began creating a true Georgian kingdom, seizing territory from the Byzantines and Arabs and building churches – work continued by his successors David the Great and Bagrat III.

In the early 11th century, the Byzantines retook effective control of Tao and Klarjeti in an effort to stave off invasion by the Seljuk Turks. The Seljuks were not to be deflected, however, and Alp Arslan, sultan of the Great Seljuks of Persia, took Georgia and Armenia in 1064 on his way to the fateful defeat of the Byzantines at Manzikert (1071) which opened all of Anatolia to Turkish settlement.

The Great Seljuk State soon splintered into a welter of principalities, allowing King David II ('the Restorer') to reunite the Georgian lands under his rule.

David's great-granddaughter, Queen Tamara (1184-1213), or Thamar, was a master of statecraft and strategy, both military and political. Having greatly extended her kingdom's borders, she reigned over the flowering of medieval Georgian culture. Unfortunately for her country, she died just as the Mongol storm was gathering in the east.

The Mongols swept through Georgia in the 13th century, to be followed by Tamerlane in the 14th century. King Alexander I divided his kingdom into three for his sons which led to a more rapid decline in Georgia's fortunes. By 1555 much of the country had been partitioned between the Ottomans and the Persians.

Threatened by the Turks to the west and the Iranians to the east, the Georgian kings pledged their allegiance to the Russian tsar during the 18th century, but he was no less hungry for territory than his imperial neighbours. In 1801 King George XIII ended the history of the independent Georgian kingdom by abdicating in favour of the tsar, who took control. ■

tively you could stay in Erzurum and make the trip up daily.

Out of the skiing season there are only likely to be buses at weekends, and a taxi ride along the rough road to the hotel costs about US$8 one way. Public transport is most frequent during the winter festival in early April.

Visiting Pasinler

Pasinler Belediyesi buses shuttle frequently between Aliravi Caddesi and Pasinler, 38 km to the east. You can hop on one to make a day excursion to see the Hasankale fortress and to enjoy the Pasinler hot springs. Alternatively, you could stay in Pasinler and visit Erzurum to look round. For details, see Pasinler in the Erzurum to Kars section later in this chapter.

GEORGIAN VALLEYS

The mountainous country north of Erzurum towards Artvin was once part of the medieval kingdom of Georgia, and has numerous churches and castles to show for it. The trouble you take to see this region will be amply rewarded. The mountain scenery is at times spectacular, and the churches, which share many characteristics with Armenian, Seljuk and Persian styles, are interesting and seldom visited. If you happen to be passing in mid-June, the orchards of cherries and apricots should be in bloom – a special treat.

Getting Around

The small mountain villages in these valleys are a delight to explore, but public transport to and from most of them consists of a single minibus which heads down to Erzurum early in the morning for the market, returning in the afternoon. You can see much more if you have your own car. Failing that, try to find other travellers to share the cost and hire a taxi for a day's excursion from Erzurum, perhaps ending at Yusufeli, which you can use as a base for further exploration. Unless your bartering skills are especially acute, a taxi for a 12-hour excursion around the churches will cost about US$100. If you have time for only one or two churches, head for İşhan or Öşk Vank first.

Most of the villages can rustle up a glass of tea but food is a much taller order. There are a few restaurants along the main highway from Erzurum to Yusufeli and plenty of children hawk fruit by the roadside too. Otherwise, unless you're especially fond of dry biscuits, stock up on picnic foods before leaving Erzurum.

Bağbaşı (Haho)

About 25 km north of Tortum is a turn-off on the left (west), near a humpback bridge, to this village, called Haho by the Georgians. Go 7.5 km up the unpaved road through orchards and fields to the village. Stop at the Belediye and teahouse, and ask for the *kilise anahtarı*, or church key; a guide will probably accompany you for the last 600m up the road to the church, which is now the village mosque. The church, dating from the 10th century, is still in fairly good repair, thanks to its continued use for worship. The guide will show you several reliefs reminiscent of those at Akdamar.

Probably because this church is still in use, albeit as a mosque, it is not signposted as a monument from the highway. No doubt for the same reason, some restoration work has taken place here.

Öşk Vank

Another 15.5 km north of the Bağbaşı turn-off, in a wide valley with the river to the left (west) of the highway, is the road to Öşk Vank, seven km off the highway and up into the mountains. In winter, you must ford the river and wind up the road to the village, where you can't miss the big, impressive monastery church, built in the 10th century. Most of the roof is gone, but there are still traces of paintings, inscriptions and fine reliefs, both on the outside and on the inside columns. The *Coşkun Çay Evi* to the right of the church serves tea.

Tortum Gölü

West of Öşk Vank, the highway skirts the western shore of Tortum Gölü (Tortum Lake), which was formed by a landslide about three centuries ago. Note that the lake is a considerable distance from Tortum village.

The 48m Tortum Şelalesi (waterfall), in the grounds of the Türkiye Elektrik Kurumu (TEK), is worth seeing in winter when there's plenty of water. In summer, the meagre flow of water is diverted to the hydroelectricity plant. The lake makes a beautiful picnic spot, but if you arrive alone the guard at the gate to the TEK grounds may demand a US$6 admission fee. Accompanied by a Turk you should have no problem getting in free.

A few km west of the lake at Çamlıyamaç is a lookout across the valley, and the mountains to the Tortum Çayı river gorge cut through the banded rock. Children from the green oasis below will no doubt be on hand to sell you whatever fruit is in season in an area famous for its orchards.

İşhan

Heading north from the lake, take the road on the right marked for Olur and go six km (exactly 50 km from the Vank road) to a turn-off on the left for İşhan, marked by a sign reading 'İşhan Kilisesiğ'. This village is another six km up a steep, muddy road carved out of the mountainside and probably impassable in bad weather.

The mountain village is spectacularly sited, and the **Church of the Mother of God**, 100m past the village and down the hill, is wonderful. The front faces an open space, while the back nestles into the hillside. The church was built in the 8th century and enlarged in the 11th. There are some traces of fresco inside (vanishing fast – 20 years ago whole walls were covered in them), a horseshoe arcade in the apse and several reliefs on the exterior, including one of a lion battling a snake.

There are several other churches and castles to visit to the east of İşhan along the Olur road. For details, see under Yusufeli to Kars later in this section.

Return to the Olur road, go back the six km to the highway and then north towards Artvin. In the 8.5 km between the Olur and Yusufeli roads, the highway passes through a dramatic gorge, wild and scenic, with striking bands of colour in the tortured rock of the sheer canyon walls. The Yusufeli turn-off is at a place called Su Kavuşumu (Water Confluence), where the waters of the Tortum Çayı and the Oltu Çayı join the Çoruh Nehri (Çoruh River). From the turn-off, it's 10 km up the Çoruh Valley to the town.

Yusufeli

The swift Barhal Çayı rushes noisily through Yusufeli (population 4000, altitude 1050m) on its way to the Çoruh River nearby. Yusufeli is kept neat and tidy in the best tradition of alpine towns. The local people are friendly, and, now that they've got used to the idea, are rapidly warming up to the white-water-rafting business. The best months for this are May and June; by August the water is sinking too low.

Several of the hotels in town can arrange rafting trips for around US$18 for five hours; ask at the Barhal or Çiçek Palas for starters.

A short stroll reveals everything Yusufeli has to offer: Halim Paşa Caddesi, the main street; the Belediye facing the main market street next to the river; the three banks (İş, Ziraat and Halk); and the few small hotels and restaurants. The town hospital (Devlet Hastanesi) is on the road into the village.

Yusufeli's postal code is 08800.

Georgian Churches Yusufeli is a convenient base for visits to the churches at Barhal and Dörtkilise. At the time of writing there was a limited dolmuş service to these villages, but soon no doubt the drivers will wise up and offer day-long tours to these and other Georgian churches in the region.

Thirty-two km north-west of Yusufeli high in the mountains over an unpaved road, **Barhal** (officially called Altıparmak, altitude 1300m), preserves a fine 10th-century Georgian church long used as the village mosque. The church and the village's mountain setting are well worth the bumpy drive or two-hour dolmuş ride.

Thirteen km south-west of Yusufeli via Tekkale, **Dörtkilise** (Four churches) has another ruined 10th-century Georgian

EASTERN ANATOLIA

church and monastery. On the way there you'll pass the ruins of another church perched like an eyrie on top of a sheer rock. The main church is similar to, but older and larger than, the one at Barhal, and it takes less time and effort to see it. If you don't have a car, take a dolmuş towards Kılıçkaya or Köprügören and get out at Tekkale, then hike six km to Dörtkilise, bearing in mind that there is no sign for the church, which is high up amid the vegetation on the left-hand side of the road. If you do have a car, the road is pretty rough from Tekkale onwards.

Places to Stay Cross the footbridge from the town centre and follow the signs to find *Akın Camping* and *Greenpeace Camping*, both very simple and cheap.

The hotels are of the most basic type, most with just beds in waterless rooms. The official municipality room rates are about US$3/5.50 a single/double but outside the busiest months of May and June you should be able to barter them down.

One of the nicest places, the *Çiçek Palas Oteli* (☎ (466) 811 2393), is getting a refit which will reduce the number of rooms but will add private bathrooms to the remainder. Also reasonably clean and new is the *Hotel Barhal* (☎ (466) 811 3151) by the rickety suspension bridge over the river. Upstairs is the older *Hotel Aydın* (☎ (466) 811 2365) and opposite is the *Hotel Çoruh* with smelly toilets.

The *Hotel Hacıoğlu* (☎ (466) 811 2087) is apart from these hotels on Mustafa Kemal Caddesi, as is the *Hotel Çelik Palas* (☎ (466) 811 2507), right next to the mosque, where minaret noise will wake you at dawn.

Places to Eat On the far side of the river near the footbridge, the neighbouring *Mahzen Fıçı Bira* and *Kaçkar Fıçı Bira*, and the *Çınar Restaurant* facing them, are very pleasantly situated. Draught beer (fıçı bira) is a strong point, as are the balconies right over the river.

Mavi Köşk Et Restaurant, entered via an inconspicuous stairway opposite the Halkbank, is as posh as Yusufeli gets. Satin tablecloths, an elaborate (for Yusufeli) sound system and a TV add to its charm. Prices are about US$4 or US$6 for a meal, and alcoholic beverages are served.

The *Saray Lokantası* on the main street is the local cheap favourite for ready food at lunch, but can be hot and crowded at this time.

Getting There & Away Dolmuşes depart from Erzurum's Gölbaşı Semt Garajı several times daily for Yusufeli (130 km) and other towns and villages in the Georgian valleys.

Yusufeli to Kars

The scenic drive up the valley of the Oltu Çayı from Yusufeli to Olur is along a good paved road. The aptly named Taşlıköy (Stony Village), 22 km east of the İşhan turn-off, illustrates the rough living in this harsh if beautiful region: the low stone houses with sod roofs are built half into the earth to escape the rigours of the winter cold.

Just north-east of the Olur road, look over the bridge over the Gölbaşı to see a **ruined Georgian castle** perched on a rock spur, one of many in the region.

Continue south to Yolboyu, the junction with roads east to Bana (Penek) and Göle, and south to Oltu. At Yolboyu, **twin castles** on opposite sides of the stream guard this fertile valley, the eastern gateway to the mountainous region.

There's an even grander **citadel** at Oltu, south-west of Bana and 36 km south of the Olur castle.

Bana (Penek), 11 km east of Yolboyu, has a fine **7th-century Georgian church** set in a riverside meadow one km south-east of the road across the Penek Çayı. Though the church is worth a visit, access is difficult and only for the truly devoted Georgian church goer.

From the Bana church it's seven km north-east to the Şenkaya turn-off and another three km to the village of Akşir. About 17 km past Akşir in a particularly lush and narrow valley is Değirmenlidere village, a collection of **low stone houses** with wood portals – an eerie sight when unoccupied – which serve as summer quarters for transhumant herders.

At the upper end of Değirmenlidere, the road emerges from the mountain valleys and the countryside widens out into vast rolling steppe. The road surface deteriorates markedly here, the potholes slowing your vehicle's speed to a crawl. It doesn't improve until 30 km short of Kars. For information on Kars and Ani, see those sections later in this chapter.

ARTVİN

Artvin (ahrt-VEEN, population 20,000, altitude 600m) is the capital of the province bearing the same name. You can approach it from Yusufeli (75 km, 1¼ hours) or from Hopa on the Black Sea coast (70 km, 1½ hours). Sit on the right-hand side of the bus coming up from Hopa to get the best views.

If you come from Hopa, remember that any liquid-filled containers in your luggage will expand and leak as you ascend into the mountains. Keep these containers with you and open them periodically to adjust the atmospheric pressure.

The ride to Artvin via either route is wonderfully scenic. As you approach the town you will notice ruined medieval castles guarding the steep mountain passes. During the third week in June, the Kafkasör Yaylası, a pasture seven km from Artvin, becomes the scene of an annual festival, the Kafkasör Kültür ve Sanat Festivalı (Caucasus Culture & Arts Festival), with bull wrestling matches *(boğa güreşleri)* as the main event.

Given the town's spectacular mountain setting, it should be a much nicer place to spend a few days than it actually is. In fact Artvin is terribly two-faced, putting on a show of small-town respectability by daylight that rapidly gives way to something raunchier as the sun goes down. Artvin has been dubbed 'one large brothel'. There's a nightlife here to equal Trabzon's but not of a kind that would suit everyone.

Orientation & Information

Artvin is perched on a high hill which snakes its way upwards above a bend in the Çoruh River. It's little more than one steep street (İnönü Caddesi) and is easily negotiated on foot, except for the trip to and from the otogar.

İnönü Caddesi is lined with the government offices required of a provincial capital: the Valilik (Provincial Headquarters, also called Hükümet Konağı), the Belediye (Municipality), lots of banks etc. Most hotels are within a block or two of the Valilik.

Artvin's otogar is in Köprübaşı (sometimes called Çarşı), the riverside district at the foot of the hill. Minibuses (Artvin Belediyesi Halk Münübüsü, US$0.30) shuttle passengers between the town centre and the otogar at Köprübaşı. Alternatively, a taxi up will cost you about US$3.

Artvin's postal code is 08000.

Places to Stay

As in Trabzon, most of the cheap hotels have long since given up the unequal battle to make money out of tourism in favour of the easier pickings from prostitution. At the time of writing the following hotels are legitimate lodging places, but this is subject to change.

The *Şafak, Konak* and *Trabzon* are all dispiriting, even at US$2 a bed. Much better is the *Güven* (☎ (466) 211 1118), across İnönü Caddesi from the Valilik and down a few steps on Hamam Sokak. The lobby is not inspiring but the rooms, with hospital-style beds, are clean and simple, and cost from US$5 a head, with another US$1 for a shower. Two roof terraces offer mountain views. The Şehir Hamamı (Turkish bath) is only a few metres away, guaranteeing a good bath. It's basically for men but women can use it later in the day if they make a prior appointment.

One step up in price and 'comfort' is the *Hotel Kaşkar* (☎ (466) 212 3397), also in Hamam Sokak. The rooms here are also pretty simple (although some have huge TVs), but some have wonderful mountain views. Readers have written to recommend this place, but there are locals who insist your nights are likely to be disturbed. A single costs US$7, a double US$12.

Artvin's supposedly best hotel is the *Karahan Otel* (☎ (446) 212 1802) on İnönü Caddesi, although the entrance is actually up the hill on the opposite side of the building.

EASTERN ANATOLIA

The 48 shower-equipped rooms are pleasant enough, and much better than the old-fashioned lobby and dreary exterior might suggest. However, prices are nothing short of outrageous for what you get at US$22 a single and US$25 a double. The hotel is also very popular with tourist groups. Rooms with views are at the front of the hotel (ie not on the side you come in!).

The *Kafkasör Tatil Köyü Dağ Evleri* (Caucasus Holiday Village Mountain Chalets, ☎ (466) 212 5013) are simple lodgings near the Kafkasör meadow. Ask at the Karahan Otel about access.

Places to Eat

The Karahan Otel restaurant is one of Artvin's best but it's not cheap: breakfast costs US$4, a table d'hote dinner US$12.

A better choice might be the *Efkar Restaurant* at the foot of İnönü Caddesi where it turns to descend the slope. The *Efkar* boasts 'million dollar views' from its terrace, which is certainly a good place to take breakfast (US$2), surrounded by signs instructing you not to throw rubbish or cigarette butts over the balcony. It's in hot competition for passing trade with the *Nazar Restoran* below.

Another place where you can dine with fine views is the *Hanedan Restorant* (☎ (466) 212 7222) at İnönü Caddesi No 23. Get there early as there are only a few tables by the window and big groups like this place.

For cheaper fare, explore the upper reaches of İnönü Caddesi. *Talat Usta* at No 56 is good for döner kebap, and the nearby *Çınar Lokantası* for soups and stews.

For tea, pastries and light meals, try the *Akın* and the *Köşk*, across the street from one another, midway along İnönü Caddesi, near the big *Aile Çay Bahçesi*. The *Cennet Pastanesi* nearby serves luscious puddings in modern surrounds. Despite its promising name, the çay bahçesi is often packed with soldiers from the guardpost across the street.

Getting There & Away

The roads from Artvin to Hopa and Erzurum are fairly good, smooth and fast.

A few minibuses depart from Artvin in the morning and early afternoon for Yusufeli, Hopa and Rize, circulating through the upper town looking for passengers before descending to Köprübaşı and the otogar. Metro, Artvin Expres and As Turizm have ticket offices on İnönü Caddesi across from the Valilik as well as at the otogar.

Details of some daily services from Artvin follow:

Erzurum – 215 km, four hours, US$6; several buses and dolmuşes
Hopa – 70 km, 1½ hours, US$3; frequent dolmuşes
Kars – 270 km, five hours, US$7; two buses
Samsun – 577 km, eight or nine hours, US$13; one or two buses
Tortum – 91 km, 2½ hours, US$4
Trabzon – 255 km, five hours, US$6; frequent buses
Yusufeli – 75 km, 1¼ hours, US$3; several dolmuşes

Some buses coming from Erzurum and heading on to Hopa don't go into the otogar but drop you at the roadside at the very bottom of the hill. Dolmuşes from here take time to fill up, and the taxis waiting will charge about US$4 to run you to the top.

ARTVİN TO KARS

The most direct route between Artvin and Kars, a distance of 205 km, is via the old Georgian town of Şavşat. The road deteriorates east of Şavşat, so plan on taking more time for the journey than the distance alone might indicate. The southern road via Ardanuç is little more than a track; go via Şavşat. Both roads meet at Ardahan, then go on via Gölebert and Susuz to Kars.

If you have your own vehicle, start early from Artvin (or Kars) and plan to make an excursion to one of the Georgian churches within easy reach of the main road. Take some water and snacks, whether you go by bus or car. If you have your own car, it's a good idea to fill your fuel tank before setting out on this journey.

Ardanuç, on the southern route, boasts a large **Bagratid fortress**. The village of Bulanık is 14 km farther on, and the 10th-century **church of Yeni Rabat** is a few km off the main road.

On the road to Şavşat just after passing the

Ardanuç turn-off, look for a stone bridge and a sign to Hamamlı. This village, just over six km off the main road, boasts the fine 10th-century **Georgian church of Dolishane** (now a mosque). Back on the main road, another 12 km brings you to Pırnallı village and the trailhead for the 30 to 45-minute hike up to the 9th-century **Georgian monastery** and **church of Porta**.

Another **fortress** guards the western approach to Şavşat. From here you can make an excursion north via the Veliköy road for 10 km to Cevizli to see the 10th-century **monastery church of Tbeti**, in ruins but still beautiful in its setting.

After traversing the rough road east of Şavşat, the simple town of Ardahan seems an oasis of civilisation. There are a few very basic services, but you will want to press on to Kars for the night.

ERZURUM TO KARS

East of Erzurum the highway climbs into a landscape of wide vistas, rich irrigated fields and the inevitable flocks of cattle and sheep.

Pasinler

Some 38 km east of Erzurum, the **Hasankale fortress** dominates Pasinler (population 22,000, altitude 1656m) from its rock promontory. Much of the triple-walled fortress, reached by a block-paved street on the west side of the highway, is in good repair (some restored). It dates from the 1330s when the İlkhanid emir Hasan had it built. Extensive repairs were made later by the Akkoyunlu leader Uzun Hasan.

The town is conservative in the eastern way, with fiery-eyed, white-bearded men and many women completely enveloped by burlap-coloured chadors. Watch out for shops selling Hasankale lavaşı, the village's special metre-long thin loaves of bread.

Pasinler is famous in the region for its *kaplıcalar* (hot springs). From the main intersection next to the Belediye, cross the railway line, turn left and continue 800m to a bridge leading to the Hotel Kale. On either side of the bridge stand bathhouses for men and women. Those for women are open from 10.30 am to 7 pm, those for men for longer. To use them costs about US$1.

The highway and the rail line follow the broad flood plain of the Aras Nehri (Aras River) from Pasinler eastward 43 km to Horasan. In Köprüköy just before Horasan you may spot the **Çoban Köprü**, a 16th-century stone bridge designed, it is said, by the great Sinan.

At Karakurt, the road leaves the river valley to climb into the mountains through pine forests, passing one fertile mountain pasture after another on its way to Sarıkamış.

Places to Stay *Hotel Kale* (☎ (442) 661 3538) charges US$10/12 a single/double for a quiet but not especially inspiring room with shower. Until recently the hotel was owned by the Belediye. Now that it has been privatised the rooms could well improve. At the back of the hotel there are private cabins with their own plunge pools and massage areas. To hire a small cabin costs US$4 per hour. A large one costs US$8 an hour regardless of how many people share it. The restaurant here is of a much higher calibre than the rooms. A sizeable meal for two including alcohol would cost about US$15. Since the last half-hourly shuttle bus to Pasinler from Erzurum (US$0.50) goes at 10 pm in summer, bath-lovers could consider staying here instead of in Erzurum itself.

For more modest budgets, the *Hotel Park* (☎ (442) 661 3569), a block west of the Belediye in the market, is about the best cheap bet, with clean, simple rooms for US$5 per person. There are some four-bed rooms on the ground floor.

Sarıkamış

Sarıkamış (sah-RUH-kah-mush, population 22,000, altitude 2125m), a lumbering town 152 km east of Erzurum, has a small ski resort, a huge army base, a forestry headquarters and, on its eastern outskirts, a big shoe factory.

The army base and a stone monument on the eastern outskirts are poignant reminders of a military disaster. In December 1914, during the early days of WWI, the Ottoman

Third Army was encamped for the winter at Sarıkamış, defending this approach to Anatolia against an equal force of Russian troops. The egomaniacal Enver Paşa, effective head of the Ottoman war effort, ordered his troops to attack and push eastward – a disastrous tactic in midwinter. (Mustafa Kemal (Atatürk) was astounded and appalled when he heard of the order.) The Ottomans lost 75,000 troops to cold, hunger and casualties. The Russians counter-attacked and took Erzurum.

Places to Stay Sarıkamış has one hotel better than any found in Kars. Since there are frequent buses, you could consider staying here and taking day trips to Kars.

The *Turistik Hotel Sarıkamış* (☎ (474) 413 4176), Halk Caddesi 64, is in the centre of town, marked prominently by signs. Although the hotel is not fancy, the lobby is colourfully decorated with local carpets and animal skins, and the rooms are well kept and fairly cheerful. The dining room is quite serviceable. Rooms cost US$6/12 a single/double with bath and breakfast.

The *Çelik Palas*, near where the buses stop, is as basic as they come.

The *Sarıkamış Kayak Tesisleri* (Ski Facilities; ☎ (474) 413 4249) are four km west of the town centre marked by the Belediye building. From the Belediye, follow the signs 1.5 km to the railway line, cross it and continue past the ghostly shells of crenellated stone warehouse and factory buildings. Three km from the Belediye turn right by a crude brickyard and walk up the hill to the ski lift. The simple ski lodge *(kayak evi)* has accommodation. You may be able to find lodging here in summer (phone first), and certainly can in winter.

KARS

East of Sarıkamış, the highway climbs out of the lush mountain valleys and away from the evergreen forests to vast rolling steppe with mountains in the distance. It is in this sea-of-grass setting that you find Kars (population 80,000, altitude 1768m), a desolate agricultural and garrison town dominated by a permanently lowering sky and fierce, wet weather.

You will see lots of police and soldiers in Kars, and every one of them can tell you without hesitation the precise number of days he has yet to serve in Kars before he can go west to 'civilisation'. As for the locals, a harsh climate and a rough history has made them, for the most part, dour and sombre, though none the less welcoming once you speak to them. They're said to be descended from the Karsaks, a Turkish tribe which came from the Caucasus in the 2nd century BC and who gave their name to the town.

When the sun shines there are hints at what might have been, with fine pastel-coloured stone buildings slowly crumbling to dust. Otherwise Kars has a vaguely Wild West atmosphere, with men on horseback galloping along roads so potholed the taxis have to weave their way along them.

Dominated by a stark medieval fortress which is still used as part of the city's defences, Kars was a pawn in the imperial land-grabbing game played by Turkey and Russia during the 19th century. The Russians captured Kars in 1878, installed a garrison, and held it until 1920 and the Turkish War of Independence, when the republican forces retook it. One of the large mosques was obviously built as a Russian Orthodox church and many of the sturdier stone buildings along the main streets date back to the Russian occupation.

The main reason for coming to Kars is to visit Ani. While you're in Kars, however, there are a few others things well worth seeing.

Orientation

The Russians must have had great plans for Kars. They laid it out on a grandiose grid plan which, only now over a century later, is being completed. Nonetheless, almost everything in Kars except the train station and the museum is within walking distance. The new bus station is about 10 km to the west, but shuttle buses run to the old bus station in the town.

Information

The Kars Tourism Information Office

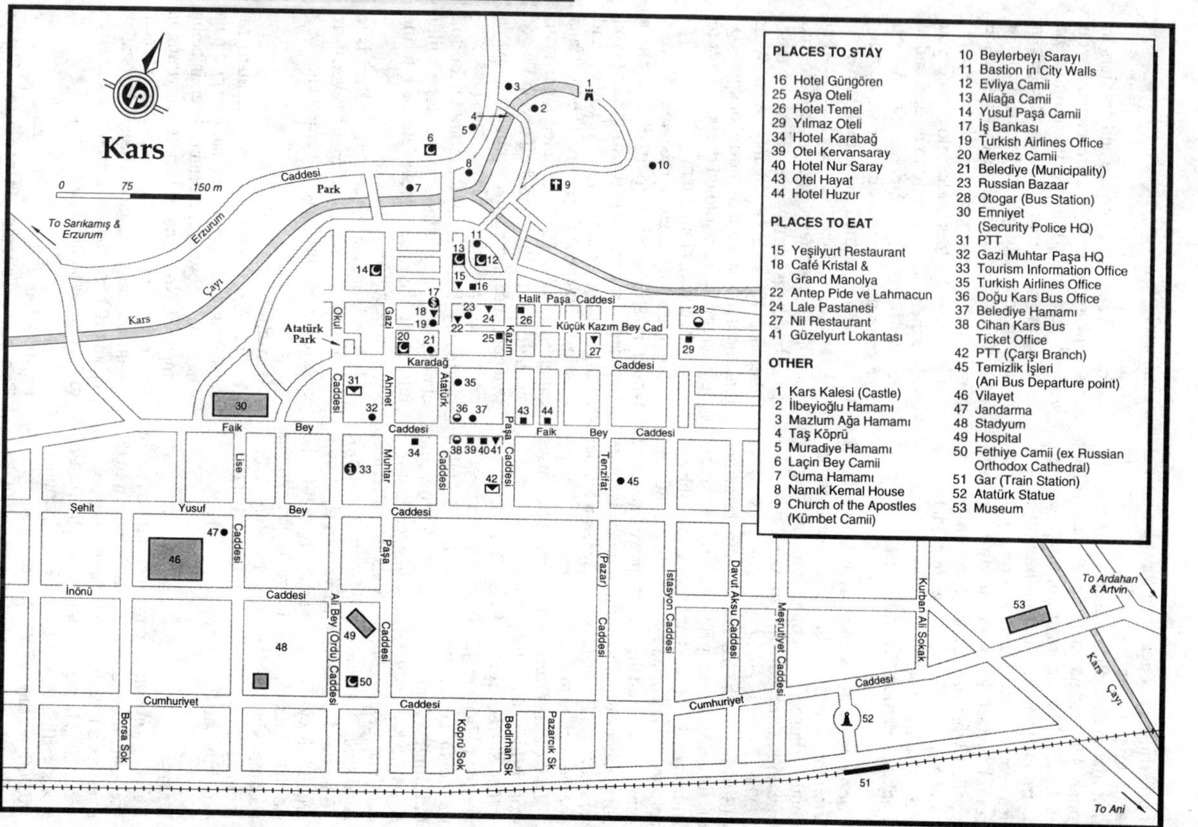
Kars
0
75
150 m
PLACES TO STAY
16 Hotel Güngören
25 Asya Oteli
26 Hotel Temel
29 Yılmaz Oteli
34 Hotel Karabağ
39 Otel Kervansaray
40 Hotel Nur Saray
43 Otel Hayat
44 Hotel Huzur
PLACES TO EAT
15 Yeşilyurt Restaurant
18 Café Kristal & Grand Manolya
22 Antep Pide ve Lahmacun
24 Lale Pastanesi
27 Nil Restaurant
41 Güzelyurt Lokantası
OTHER
1 Kars Kalesi (Castle)
2 İlbeyioğlu Hamamı
3 Mazlum Ağa Hamamı
4 Taş Köprü
5 Muradiye Hamamı
6 Laçin Bey Camii
7 Cuma Hamamı
8 Namık Kemal House
9 Church of the Apostles (Kümbet Camii)
10 Beylerbeyi Sarayı
11 Bastion in City Walls
12 Evliya Camii
13 Aliağa Camii
14 Yusuf Paşa Camii
17 İş Bankası
19 Turkish Airlines Office
20 Merkez Camii
21 Belediye (Municipality)
23 Russian Bazaar
28 Otogar (Bus Station)
30 Emniyet (Security Police HQ)
31 PTT
32 Gazi Muhtar Paşa HQ
33 Tourism Information Office
35 Turkish Airlines Office
36 Doğu Kars Bus Office
37 Belediye Hamamı
38 Cihan Kars Bus Ticket Office
42 PTT (Çarşı Branch)
45 Temizlik İşleri (Ani Bus Departure point)
46 Vilayet
47 Jandarma
48 Stadyum
49 Hospital
50 Fethiye Camii (ex Russian Orthodox Cathedral)
51 Gar (Train Station)
52 Atatürk Statue
53 Museum
To Ardahan & Artvin
Kars Çayı
To Ani
To Sarıkamış & Erzurum
Erzurum
Park Caddesi
Kars Çayı
Atatürk Park
Okul
Gazi Ahmet Muhtar Paşa Caddesi
Karadağ
Atatürk Caddesi
Halit Paşa Caddesi
Kazım
Küçük Kazım Bey Cad
Faik Bey Caddesi
Kazım Paşa Caddesi
Tenzifat
Lise Caddesi
Yusuf
Şehit
İnönü
Bey Caddesi
Kurban Ali Sokak
Meşrutiyet Caddesi
Davut Aksu Caddesi
İstasyon Caddesi
(Pazar) Caddesi
Paşa Caddesi
Ali Bey (Ordu) Caddesi
Cumhuriyet Caddesi
Pazarcık Sk
Bedirhan Sk
Köprü Sok
Borsa Sok
Cumhuriyet

(☎ (474) 223 2724), Ordu (also called Ali Bey) Caddesi 140, is open from 8.30 am to 5.30 pm daily in summer, closed weekends in winter. We have received many letters of complaint about this place and indeed its unprepossessing, green-painted exterior hardly inspires confidence. You will have to come here to get your permit to visit Ani. Otherwise, don't hold your breath for much useful information.

Money Several banks along Atatürk Caddesi advertise exchange facilities, although if you roll up with a travellers' cheque they are likely to look at you askance. Persevere and you should manage to cash it. As usual, the İş Bankası is a good bet. It charges a flat US$3 commission.

Kars Museum

Kars Müzesi is worth seeing. Opening hours are from 8.30 am to 5.30 pm, except on Monday, but with so little to do in Kars, the staff is usually on duty anyway. Admission costs about US$1.

There are exhibits from the Old Bronze Age, the Roman and Greek periods, and Seljuk and Ottoman times. Photographs show excavations at Ani and there are shots of Armenian churches in Kars province. Look out for a pair of carved doors from the town's main Orthodox church (now a mosque) and a Russian church bell from the time of Tsar Nicholas II (1894-1917).

Don't miss the ethnographic exhibits upstairs, as this area produces some very fine kilims, carpets and *cicims* (embroidered kilims). Costumes, saddlebags, jewellery, samovars and a home carpet loom complete the display. A curiosity designed for local consumption is the Katliam Bölümü (Genocide Section), a showcase displaying photos and documentation (all in Turkish) about the massacre of Muslims by Armenian forces in the early part of the century.

Behind the museum is the railway coach in which representatives of Russia's Bolshevik government and the fledgling Turkish Republic signed the protocol ending the Russian occupation and annexation of Kars in 1920.

Church of the Apostles

Although called the Drum-Dome Mosque (Kümbet Camii), the Church of the Apostles was actually built between 932 and 937 by the Bagratid king Abas. It was repaired extensively in 1579, when the Ottomans rebuilt much of the city, and the porches were added in the 19th century. The relief carvings on the drum are of the apostles.

Locked and slowly surrendering to weeds, the church would make an excellent museum if Kars ever develops enough of a tourist trade. For now, the only way to see the interior is to peek through the doors on the river side.

Stone Bridge

Near the church is the Taş Köprü (Stone Bridge), which dates from the 15th century. It was repaired in 1579 along with everything else in town, but was later ruined by an earthquake. In 1719 it was rebuilt in its present form by the local Karaoğulları emirs. Ruins of the Ulu Cami and a palace called the Beylerbeyı Sarayı nestle beneath the castle (kale) near the bridge.

Kars Castle

There has probably been a fortress at this strategic spot since earliest times, but records show that one was built by the Saltuk Turks in 1152 and torn down by Tamerlane in 1386. It was rebuilt upon the order of the Ottoman sultan Murat III by his grand vizier Lala Mustafa Paşa in 1579. Further repairs were made in 1616 and 1636, and the entire complex was rebuilt yet again in 1855.

The kale was the scene of bitter fighting during and after WWI. When the Russian armies withdrew in 1920, control of Kars was left in the hands of the Armenian forces which had allied themselves with Russia during the war. Civilians, whether Christian or Muslim, suffered oppression and worse when under the control of irregular troops of the opposing religion. As the slaughter of Christian Armenians occurred in some parts of eastern Turkey, there was also slaughter of Muslim Turks and Kurds around Kars until the republican armies took the kale.

Although Kars Kalesi is still an active military base, it's open free to visitors most afternoons. Take the road which passes the Church of the Apostles and the ruined palace known as the Beylerbeyı Sarayı. The huge sign dominating the kale is a quote from Atatürk: *Vatan Sana Minettardır* (Your Country is Grateful to You).

Historic Houses

The best example of a traditional Kars house is the **Gazi Muhtar Paşa Headquarters** on the corner of Faik Bey and Gazi Ahmet Muhtar Paşa caddesis. This stone house was used as an HQ by Gazi Ahmet Muhtar Paşa, commander of the Ottoman forces during the Russian war in 1877. Later a school, then for a while the tourist office (if only it still were), it is now not open for visits.

The other house with a history is not much to look at, but its former occupant, Namık Kemal (1840-88), played a significant role in the development of modern Turkey. Born in Tekirdağ, the son of the Sultan's court astronomer, he became a government translator. An interest in European society and philosophy led him to translate the works of Rousseau and Montesquieu, and then to expound a similar political philosophy in plays, essays, articles and poems.

Kemal advocated Turkey's adoption of European political, technical, economic and social advances, but did so in the context of devout Islam. He reinterpreted European progress for an Islamic context, adapted it to Islamic traditions, and made it more acceptable to traditional Muslims. Kemal's calls for 'freedom and fatherland' got him into trouble with the sultan. He died in internal exile on Chios, but his ideas were eagerly absorbed by the Young Turks and by Mustafa Kemal (Atatürk).

Turkish Baths

The Belediye Hamamı is on Faik Bey Caddesi, opposite the Hotel Kervansaray. The grungy Muradiye Hamamı at the citadel end of the Stone Bridge is for women only. Perhaps because of its cold climate, Kars has many other warm steamy baths as well.

Places to Stay

Kars' hotel line-up is as depressing as the town's weather, but at least most places are cheap. Electricity (and water) stops unexpectedly and frequently. Bear this in mind before stepping into a lift.

Places to Stay – bottom end

The best value for money is the *Hotel Temel* (☎ (474) 223 1376), Kazım Paşa Caddesi 4/A. Clean and relatively pleasant rooms, some with private shower and wild wallpaper, cost US$7/12 a single/double.

The *Hotel Güngören* (☎ (474) 212 0298, fax 223 1636), Halit Paşa Caddesi, Millet Sokak 4, is less than ten years old but already reflects hard use. Every room has a private bath with tub and shower, and there's an adjoining hamam and a grill restaurant. Rates are US$15/25 a single/double.

The 38-room *Otel Kervansaray* (☎ (474) 223 1990), Faik Bey Caddesi 124, is pretty basic. Double rooms come waterless or with sink for US$5, or with shower (but no toilet) for US$7; you can haggle for discounts if it's not busy. Rooms at the back are quieter. The Belediye Hamamı is right across the street. Next door to the Kervansaray, the *Hotel Nur Saray*, Faik Bey Caddesi 208, is even more basic.

One block east, the *Otel Hayat* (☎ (474) 223 4280), Faik Bey Caddesi 167, and the *Hotel Huzur* (☎ (474) 212 0687) at 171 are as basic as you can get for just US$2 a head.

The 30-room *Yılmaz Oteli* (☎ (474) 223 1074), Küçük Kazımbey Caddesi 14, near the bus station, was once the best in town but is now well past its prime, with filthy carpets and curtains. Beds with shower cost around US$6 per head. The Yılmaz's one lingering advantage is its proximity to the old otogar; to find it from the otogar, walk through a passage in the big building on the east side of the bus lot (the ticket offices are on the west side).

The 33-room *Asya Oteli* (☎ (474) 223 2299), Küçük Kazım Bey Caddesi 50, is

EASTERN ANATOLIA

grubby and run-down, but quiet. Rooms with shower go for US$4 a head.

Places to Stay – middle

Kars has one reasonably decent modern hotel, the three-star *Hotel Karabağ* (☎ (474) 212 2585, fax 223 3089) at Faik Bey Caddesi No 84. A single here costs US$35, a double US$45. The restaurant should be good once it gets into its stride but the likelihood of power cuts means you shouldn't place too much store by the TVs and fridges.

Groups tend to favour the 96-room (☎ (474) 212 3517, 223 7404), but its position two km south of central Kars detracts from its usefulness unless you have a car.

Places to Eat

Kars is noted for its excellent honey. Look out for the *Lale Pastanesi*, Halit Paşa Caddesi 166. Most of the day it sells just dry cakes and biscuits, but its kahvaltı (breakfast) is Kars honey and butter to spread on half a loaf of fresh bread, with tea or hot, sweet milk. Several shops along Halit Paşa Caddesi near the Temel and Güngören hotels also sell Kars honey and the local kaşar peynir ('kosher' mild yellow cheese). One such is the PŞ Mandıra at No 158, across from the Vakıfbank.

The *Güzelyurt Lokantası*, a few doors down from the Hotel Kervansaray on Faik Bey Caddesi, serves all three meals, including breakfast with Nescafé, but check prices before ordering as bills have a habit of mounting up.

Unexpectedly in a town so full of sheep and horses, the *Nil Restaurant*, not far from the Hotel Yılmaz, offers several meat-free dishes as well as the usual range of tasty stews. The *Otogar Restaurant*, upstairs from the otogar, is all right if you need a meal before getting on your bus.

Almost side by side on Atatürk Caddesi are the *Café Kristal* and the *Grand Manolya Restaurant ve Pastahane*. The Kristal is the brightest, most cheerful place in Kars and serves a wide range of ready meals: soup, rice, beans and a cold drink for about US$3. Afterwards you can get a coffee and a pastry in the Manolya. Just up the street, the *Antep Pide ve Lahmacun* is more traditional but does at least make an effort with its decor.

For ocakbaşı (open-grill) dining, try the restaurant at the Hotel Güngören.

Things to Buy

Kars carpets *(Kars halıları)* are coarse woven, with simple but bold patterns and colours. Many of the yarns used are undyed, retaining the natural colour of the fleece. There are several grades of carpets, and thus several price ranges. Once you've found a carpet you like and have agreed on a price per sq metre (haggle!), the carpet is measured, yielding the exact price.

These are not fine Turkish carpets, but they are sturdy and inexpensive, although heavy and bulky to carry home.

Getting There & Away

Bus Kars has two bus stations, the new one near the museum about 10 km from the centre, and the old one near the bazaar. Dolmuşes shuttle between the new otogar and the town centre.

The major company here is Doğu Kars, with ticket offices at both otogars and on Faik Bey Caddesi between Atatürk and Kazım Paşa caddesis, near the Hotel Kervansaray.

Details of some daily services follow:

Ankara – 1100 km, 18 hours, US$16; a few buses
Artvin – 275 km, 5½ hours, US$7; a few buses
Doğubeyazıt – 240 km, three hours, US$5; see note following
Erzurum – 205 km, 3½ hours, US$5; several buses
Sivas – 653 km, 12 hours, US$12; a few buses
Trabzon – 525 km, 12 hours, US$10; a few buses (change at Erzurum or Artvin)

For Ani (45 km, 50 minutes), see the transport notes in the following Ani section.

For Doğubeyazıt a special warning is in order. At the time of writing there are very few direct buses from Kars to Doğubayazıt. The usual way to get there is to take one bus to Iğdır then another to Doğubayazıt. The wait in Iğdır varies from minutes to hours which doesn't stop the Kars transport sharks from selling you 'direct' tickets to Doğubayazıt at premium prices. The ticket may indeed take you all the way from Kars to Doğubayazıt, but chances are when you reach Iğdır it will stop like all the rest and you will have to change.

Train One might hope that the Kars garı (train station) would be a 19th-century Russian architectural extravagance, but unfortunately it's a crumbling, characterless modern structure. A statue of Atatürk greets you as you approach, and a valiant old steam locomotive, mounted in front of the station, evokes a more romantic age of rail travel.

Two trains daily run out to the Armenian border at Doğu Kapı. The slow *Akyaka Postası* departs each Friday at 10.45 am for Ahuryan, just across the border in Armenia, returning to Kars at 6.05 pm each Tuesday.

Two trains shuttle daily between Kars and Erzurum. The *Karma* local train departs from Kars daily at 2.40 pm, arriving in Erzurum about six hours later (the bus takes 3½ hours). The *Doğu Ekspresi* departs from Kars daily at 7.10 am bound for Erzurum (about 5½ hours) and ultimately for İstanbul's Haydarpaşa station. A one-way ticket between Kars and Erzurum costs US$3 in 2nd class. Travelling to Ankara costs US$12, İstanbul US$17, with another US$2 for a couchette. Readers have reported waits of several days for booking couchettes.

ANİ

The ruined city at Ani, 45 km east of Kars, is striking. Its great walls, over a km in length, rise to challenge you as you drive across the wheat-covered plains and into the poor Turkish village of Ocaklı Köyü. Within the walls is a medieval ghost town set in grassy fields overlooking the deep gorge cut by the stream Arpaçay, which forms the boundary between the Turkish and Armenian republics.

During the Soviet period, Ani was within the 700m no-man's-land imposed by Moscow on the Turkish border. Visits to the ruins were governed by the strict terms of a protocol agreed between Moscow and Ankara. Today the mood is much more relaxed, although remnants of the past linger on in the bureaucracy involved in paying a visit.

History

Anahid, the Persian equivalent of the Greek goddess Aphrodite, was worshipped by the pagan Urartians and has left her name on this great city as Ani.

On an important east-west trade route and well served by its natural defences, Ani was selected by King Ashot III (952-77) as the site of his new capital in 961, when he moved here from Kars. His successors Smbat II (976-89) and Gagik I (990-1020) reigned over Ani's continued prosperity but after Gagik, internecine feuds and Byzantine encroachment weakened the Armenian state.

The Byzantines took over the city in 1045, then in 1064 came the Great Seljuks of Iran, then the Kingdom of Georgia and for a time local Kurdish emirs. The struggle for the city went on until the Mongols arrived in 1239 and cleared everybody else out. The nomadic Mongols had no use for city life, so they cared little when the great earthquake of 1319 destroyed much of Ani's beauty – not to mention infrastructure. The depredations of Tamerlane soon after were the last blow: trade routes shifted, Ani lost what revenues it had managed to retain and the city died.

Information

Since Ani stands so near the Armenian border, you must have permission from the Turkish authorities to visit it. The procedure for getting permission is reminiscent of the old Soviet-style 'make work' system. Start by filling in a form at the Kars Tourism Information Office. Then take it to be stamped at the Emniyet Müdürlüğü (ehm-nee-YEHT mew-dewr-lew, Security Directorate), two blocks west on Faik Bey Caddesi, where police officials will routinely approve your application. You should have little trouble getting the permit by yourself, even if you speak no Turkish. Only when you've got it can you trek out to the Kars Museum to buy a ticket (US$2); tickets are

not sold at Ani proper. The site is open from 8.30 am to 5 pm.

Touring the Ruins
Ocaklı Köyü, in the lee of the great walls, is a typical Kurdish-Turkish village: stone houses with sod roofs topped by TV aerials. You'll smell the distinctive aroma of burning *tezek*, cakes of dried dung used for fuel. There are a few snack and drinks stands but no other services. Village children will volunteer to guide you in exchange for tourist treats: coins, sweets, empty plastic water bottles, pens and cigarettes.

Enter the ruined city through the Alp Arslan Kapısı, a bent double gate named for the Seljuk sultan who conquered Ani in 1064.

Your first view of Ani is stunning: wrecks of great stone buildings adrift on a sea of grass, landmarks in a ghost city where once more than 100,000 people lived. Use your imagination to people the one and two-storey buildings which would have crowded the city's streets, with the great churches looming above them. Today birdsong is almost the only sound carried on the constant breeze, and the tangy scent of mint rises from underfoot as you walk.

The shepherds of Ocaklı Köyü pasture their flocks on the lush grass which grows on top of the undulating field of rubble from Ani's collapsed buildings. During your explorations, you're sure to be approached by someone wanting to sell you *eski para* (old coins) or perhaps a bit of coloured tile unearthed in the ruins.

Follow the path to the left and tour the churches in clockwise order.

Church of the Redeemer The Church of the Redeemer dates from 1034-36, but only half of the ruined structure is still standing, the other half having been destroyed by lightning in 1957.

Church of St Gregory (Tigran Honentz) Beyond the Redeemer church, down by the walls separating Ani from the gorge of the Arpaçay, is the Church of St Gregory (Tigran Honentz, 'The Illuminator'), called the Resimli Kilise (Church with Pictures) in Turkish. Named for the apostle to the Armenians, it was built by a pious nobleman in 1215, and is in better condition than most other buildings at Ani. Look for the frieze carved on the east and south exterior walls, as well as the frescoes inside depicting scenes from the Bible and Armenian church history.

Convent of the Virgins Follow the paths south-west and down into the Arpaçay gorge to visit the Convent of the Virgins (Kusanatz), enclosed by a defensive wall. The scant ruins of a bridge across the river are to the west.

Cathedral Up on the plateau again, the cathedral (Fethiye Camii) is the largest and most impressive of the churches. Ani cathedral was begun by King Smbat II in 987, and finished under Gagik I in 1010. Trdat

Mendet, the cathedral's architect, also oversaw repairs to the dome of Sancta Sophia in Constantinople, brought down in the earthquake of 989. Ani became the seat of the Armenian Catholicos (pontiff). As the grandest religious edifice in the city, it was transformed into a mosque whenever Muslims held Ani, but reverted to a church when the Christians took over. The cathedral demonstrates how Armenian ecclesiastical architecture emphasises height above all else: the churches are not long or wide so much as high – reaching towards heaven. In the case of Ani's cathedral, heaven comes right in – the spacious dome fell down centuries ago.

Menüçer Camii To the south-west of the cathedral are the ruins of the Menüçer Camii, which was created by the Seljuks in the late 1000s, probably by converting an earlier building to sacred purposes, or by using Armenian artisans who thought a mosque should look like a church. Some people climb the minaret, although it's debatable how wise this is.

Citadel South-west of the mosque across the rolling grass and beyond the ruined walls rises the İç Kale and, beyond that, the small church called the Kızkalesi, both of which are usually off limits. Obey the guards if they tell you not to venture here.

Church of St Gregory (Abughamrentz) On the west side of the city, the Church of St Gregory (Abughamrentz) dates from the mid-1000s and was built to plans by the same architect as the Church of the Redeemer.

Kervansaray The Church of the Holy Apostles dates from 1031, but the Seljuks added a portal after their conquest of the city in 1064 and used the building as a caravanserai, hence its name.

Church of St Gregory (Gagik I) North-west from the caravanserai, the Church of St Gregory (Gagik I) was begun in 998 to plans by the same architect as Ani's cathedral. Its ambitious dome, like that of İstanbul's Sancta Sophia, collapsed shortly after being finished, and the rest of the building is now also badly ruined.

Off to the north-west are the ruins of a Seljuk palace built into the city's defensive walls.

Getting There & Away

Transport to Ani was always a problem but the decline in tourism to the east has made a bad situation even worse.

The cheapest transport (US$1.25) is the municipal bus to Ocaklı which makes one run daily from Kars to Ani at 1 pm, departing from the Temizlik İşleri building on Pazar Caddesi between Faik Bey and Şehit Yusuf Bey caddesis. Unfortunately, this is of little use since there is no return service until next morning and you're not allowed to stay overnight at the site.

The only real alternative is to take a taxi or a dolmuş and this is where the shortage of visitors becomes such a pain. A taxi is likely to charge between US$29 and US$35, depending on your bargaining skills, fair enough if you're in a group but a hefty sum if you're on your own. If you decide to go ahead, make sure you agree a realistic amount of waiting time at the site. The taxi drivers will try to limit you to two hours and many visitors find this isn't enough.

Once you reach it, Ani is wonderful, so it's a great shame the procedures for visiting can't be made more user-friendly.

KARS TO IĞDIR & DOĞUBEYAZIT

To reach Doğubeyazıt and Mt Ararat, go south via Kağızman, Tuzluca and Iğdır (UH-duhr), a distance of 240 km. The road is badly potholed as far as Tuzluca, then improves considerably.

North of Kağızman, above Çamuşlu Köyü, the villagers can show you 12,000-year-old **rock carvings** *(kaya resimleri,* kah-YAH reh-seem-leh-ree). You'll also get a look at authentic village life. At Tuzluca, there are **salt caves** to visit.

From Tuzluca the road to Iğdır passes very near to the Armenian frontier, and is closed between dusk and sunrise. The army patrols the area to prevent border violations and smuggling, and if you are on that road at night they'll assume you're doing one or the other.

Maps indicate several ruined Armenian churches along this route. However, the authorities are not keen that you explore them and they are not signposted with the usual black-on-yellow signs, making them hard to find. For some, you need advance permission anyway and in the current tense security atmosphere of the east this is unlikely to be forthcoming. You can try approaching the Ministry of Culture in Ankara, but don't hold your breath waiting for the go ahead.

In Iğdır there are two good two-star hotels: the *Otel Latif* (☎ (476) 227 7837), on Karadağ Caddesi; and the even better *Otel K Yıldırım* (☎ (476) 227 9844, fax 227 7429) in Bağlar Mahallesi at Hürriyet Caddesi 42, beside a Fiat dealer. Both charge around US$10 a head. Coming in from the north you'll pass the cheaper *Otel Öztürk* (☎ (476) 227 0099) at Evrenpaşa, Caddesi 172. Rooms here are about half the price and some of the staff speak German.

AĞRI

The Turkish name for Mt Ararat is Ağrı Dağı, but the town of Ağrı (ah-RUH, population 65,000, altitude 1640m), 100 km west of the snow-capped peak, is a strong contender for the title of drabbest town in Turkey. There's a new otogar on the western outskirts with taxis waiting to ferry passengers into town. Once there, however, there's nothing to hold you bar the few very modest emergency-only hotels: the *Otel Can* and *Otel Salman*, within a block of the main crossroads in the town centre. You'd do better to head on to Doğubayazıt in the east or Erzurum in the west.

DOĞUBEYAZIT

It's only 35 km between the Iranian frontier and Doğubeyazıt (doh-OO-bey-yah-zuht, population 36,000, altitude 1950m), a town that is dusty in summer and muddy in winter, is pleasantly quiet after its bigger neighbours. A range of bare, jagged mountains tower above the town, while in front of it stretches a table-flat expanse of wheat fields and grazing land. On the far northern side of this flatness rises Mt Ararat (Ağrı Dağı, 5137m), an enormous volcano capped with ice and often shrouded in dark clouds. The mountain has figured in legends since time began, most notably as the supposed resting place of Noah's Ark.

Until recently Doğubeyazıt received a steady stream of western visitors, coming to see Mt Ararat (and perhaps look for Noah's Ark) and the İshak Paşa Sarayı, a fortress-palace-mosque complex perched on a terrace five km east of town. Sadly since 1991 the flow of tourists has virtually dried up, with unfortunate consequences for the local economy. Nowadays Doğubeyazıt is the starting point for the modern overland trail through Iran and Pakistan to India and thence to China. It's well worth coming, although you are likely to feel very conspicuous.

Orientation & Information

Doğubeyazıt is small and easily negotiated on foot. Called 'Dog Biscuit' by its admirers it has no Tourism Information Office, but Sanoz Tourism across the road from the otogar will be able to supply you with everything you need to know.

You can buy film for about US$3 a roll in the electrical market near the otogar. Much of what's on sale here has been smuggled across the border.

None of the three banks in town are currently enthusiastic about changing money, whether cash or travellers' cheques. If you run out of liras, you may have to resort to the gold shops or your hotel, where rates will be poor.

The postal code is 04400.

İshak Paşa Sarayı

Head east, five km from town, to get to İshak Paşa Sarayı. It's a pleasant walk, although you may feel rather isolated. At weekends dolmuşes often pass nearby; otherwise a taxi driver will want about US$5 for a return trip, waiting time included. Admission to the site costs US$2 and it's supposedly open from 8 am to 5 pm, but may close earlier in winter.

The building was begun in 1685 by Çolak

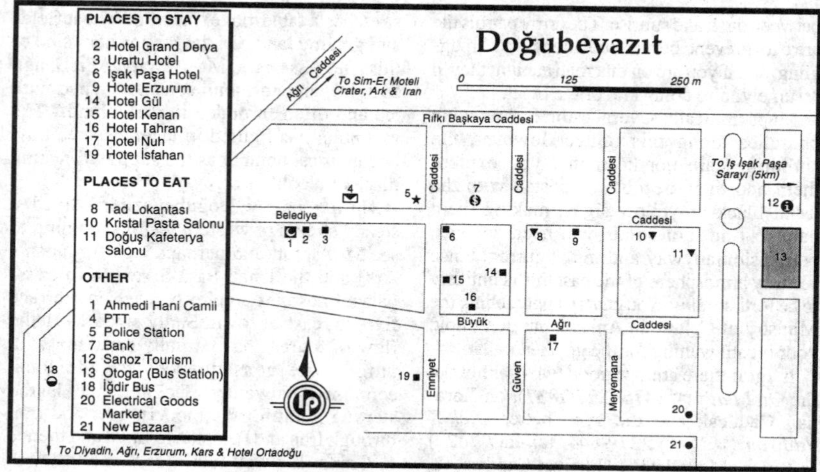

Abdi Paşa and completed in 1784 by his son, a Kurdish chieftain named İshak (Isaac). The architecture is an amalgam of Seljuk, Ottoman, Georgian, Persian and Armenian styles. A grand main portal leads to a large courtyard. The magnificent gold-plated doors which once hung here were removed by the Russians and now grace the Hermitage Museum in St Petersburg.

Although ruined, the 366-room fortress-like palace has many elements which are in good condition. The palace was once equipped with central heating and sewerage systems, and with running water. You can visit the mosque (which was used for prayers until about a decade ago) and the various palace rooms. Note especially the little türbe with fine relief work in a corner of the court.

In recent years the palace has been extensively restored (some would say rebuilt) and work will continue for some years to come. The end results may not please the purists, but the view across the palace at sunset is still spectacular.

Fortress & Mosque

Across the valley are a mosque, a türbe and the ruins of a fortress. The fortress foundations may date from Urartian times (from the 13th to 7th centuries BC), though the walls will have been rebuilt by whoever needed to control this mountain pass.

The mosque is thought to date from the reign of Ottoman sultan Selim I (1512-20), who defeated the Persians decisively near the town of Çaldıran, 70 km south of Doğubayazıt, in 1514, thus adding all of Eastern Anatolia to his burgeoning empire. He went on to conquer Syria and Palestine too.

Nearby stands an 18th-century striped türbe containing the grave of the popular Kurdish writer Ahmedi Hani.

The ruined foundations you see rising in low relief from the dusty plain are of Eski Beyazıt, the old city, probably founded in Urartian times circa 800 BC. Modern Doğubayazit is a relative newcomer, the villagers only moving from the hills to the plain in 1937.

Mt Ararat

Mt Ararat (Ağrı Dağı) has two peaks when seen from Doğubeyazıt. The left-hand peak called Büyük Ağrı (Great Ararat) is 5137m high, while Küçük Ağrı (Little Ararat) rises to about 3895m. The best time to view the mountain is within an hour or two of sunrise, before the clouds obscure it.

Until recently it was possible to get permission to climb Mt Ararat but at the time of writing the political problems in the east had put paid to this and the small agencies in town that used to specialise in arranging trips had all closed down. Even in good times, the mountain was regarded as dangerous: severe weather, ferocious sheep dogs, rock and ice slides, smugglers and outlaws could easily turn an adventure into a disaster. PKK guerrillas were the last straw as far as the government was concerned. The situation may change in the future. For more information on Mt Ararat see Lonely Planet's *Trekking in Turkey*.

Giant Crater

In 1920 a bit of celestial refuse arrived on earth about 35 km from Doğubeyazıt. The vast crater it created (supposedly 60m x 35m, making it the second largest in the world) has now been added to the regular circuit of things to see near Doğubeyazıt. To find it, head out towards the Iranian border. Four km before the border it's signposted as 'Meteor Çukuru.

Diyadin Hot Springs

Another good side trip is to the sulphur hot springs at Diyadin, where you can wonder at a spouting rock formation said to resemble the two Ararats and explore a river which flows into a cave. Afterwards you can bathe in one of the local swimming pools. Not all are very clean so it's best to make enquiries first. If you tip the guardian about US$3 you can get a pool to yourself.

Note that at the time of writing, security

The Search for Noah's Ark

The story of Noah's Ark, as related in Genesis Chapter Six, is one of the best known of all Bible stories. Deciding the world he had created was corrupt, God instructed Noah to build an Ark and fill it with one male and one female of each living animal. A great flood then swept the earth but, after 40 days, the Ark carried Noah and his family to safety. Afterwards the human and animal stock of the Ark repopulated the world. A similar story also appears in the pre-biblical Sumerian *Epic of Gilgamesh*.

In folk memory it has long been believed that the Ark came to rest on Mt Ararat in Eastern Turkey.

The Ark Mark One Over the years several people reported sighting a boat shape high up on the mountainside, and in 1955 an expedition brought back what was presumed to be a piece of wood from the Ark, found in a frozen lake. Later radio-carbon dating indicated that the wood dated back only to 450-750 AD. The most famous Ararat Ark-hunting expedition of all was organised by ex-US astronaut James Irwin in 1982 but even he was unable to bring back wholly convincing evidence.

The Ark Mark Two Since Irwin's expedition, the political situation in the east has put Mt Ararat out of bounds to Ark-seekers. Rather conveniently, then, another expedition in 1985 organised by American David Fusold 'discovered' the Ark on Musa Dağı, near the village of Üzengili, east of Doğubayazıt. The site custodian will point out an elongated oval shape in stone which is supposed to be the boat. He has a sheaf of papers, including a French report setting out at length the 'proof' that this is the true Ark. For those sceptics who're sure that the biblical Ark was wooden, it points out that the meaning of the Hebrew word usually translated as 'cypress wood' is actually uncertain. Whether that convinces you or not, probably depends on your level of cynicism.

Given the current state of security checks in the area, latterday Ark-spotters would probably do well to sign up for a tour out of Doğubayazıt. ■

around Doğubeyazıt was very tight, with frequent army checks on documentation. If you're heading for the Diyadin hot springs on your own you may well be turned back at the last checkpoint. If this happens, you can go back to the town and ask for permission at the army office there. In general you will make life easier if you sign up with a guide (see the following Tours section).

Tours

Given the security in operation around Doğubeyazıt, you may find it easier to take a tour to the outlying sights. Zafer Önay at Sanoz Tourism (☎ (472) 311 5736) opposite the otogar offers tours to İshak Paşa Sarayı, the supposed site of Noah's Ark, the Iranian border and the crater site for US$25 a head. Alternatively he will take you to the hot springs at Diyadin and to some of the Kurdish villages for the same price. These are good tours, and well worth the price for the information you'll pick up along the way.

Places to Stay – bottom end

Camping Just before you reach İshak Paşa Sarayı, you'll come to *Murat Camping* on the left-hand side of the road, where you can pitch a tent for about US$1. There's a tea garden here, and you're within easy walking distance of the palace. If it's open, the ugly *İshak Paşa Cafeteria*, overlooking the İshak Paşa Sarayı, allows travellers to roll out their sleeping bags in a room off the dining room for US$1.75 per person. Or there's *Isfahan Camping* down on the plain.

Hotels Doğubeyazıt has plenty of cheap hotels considering the shortage of tourists, but many of them are very basic indeed and women travelling alone may not feel comfortable in some of them. On the main street, several blocks from the Hotel İshak Paşa, is the *Hotel Erzurum* (☎ (472) 312 5080) on Belediye Caddesi where spartan waterless rooms go for around US$7. The carpets could do with a clean, as could some of the toilets. The *Saruhan Hotel* (☎ (472) 311 3097) next door is cheap (US$4 per person) and friendly, and in exchange for very basic accommodation offers good views of Mt Ararat or İshak Paşa Sarayı.

The tidy *Hotel Tahran* (☎ (472) 311 2223), Büyük Ağrı Caddesi 86, up the street from the big Hotel İsfahan, has acquired a reputation for hosting enthusiastic Muslims. It's simple but clean and charges US$8.50 for a double with private shower. *Hotel Gül* (☎ (472) 311 5176), Güven Caddesi 34, behind the Hotel Kenan in the next block, is similarly cheap, and similarly popular with religious Iranian tourists. Waterless doubles cost US$8, plus another US$1 for a bath.

There are three small hotels on Emniyet Caddesi, the street between the prominent İshak Paşa and İsfahan hotels. At the time of writing the *Hotel Kenan* (☎ (472) 311 5303) on Emniyet Caddesi was closed for restoration. When it reopens it may well have moved up a price bracket. The *Hotel İlhan* (☎ (472) 311 2085) has very basic accommodation in waterless rooms and charges US$5 a bed. The *Hotel Nur*, nearby, is similar.

Places to Stay – middle

Rising above Doğubeyazıt is the two-star *Hotel İsfahan* (☎ (472) 215 5139, fax 215 2044), Emniyet Caddesi 26, with five floors of rooms with showers costing US$25/38/46 a single/double/triple. It's comfortable, with lots of kilims and carpets in the lobby and lounge, as well as its own lift and car park.

The three-star, 125-room *Sim-Er Moteli* (SEEM-ehr; ☎ (472) 215 5601, fax 215 3413), PK 13, İran Transit Yolu, is a modern 130-room establishment five km east of town on the highway to Iran. This used to be one of Doğubeyazıt's best hotels, but although it's still quiet, with good views of the mountain, it's fallen on hard times since the Ararat trekking trade vanished and it shows. Rooms cost US$28/40 a single/double with shower, , and the set-price meal costs US$10. There's a 30% reduction on room rates for children.

The two-star *İshak Paşa Hotel* (☎ (472) 312 7036, fax 312 7644), Emniyet Caddesi 10, a block from the Hotel İsfahan at the intersection of Emniyet and Belediye caddesis, is simpler than the aforementioned hotels and lower in price. It has 21 rooms on four floors, each with tiled shower and balcony. There is a restaurant and bar, and rooms cost US$7/9 a single/double.

There's also the *Urartu Hotel* (☎ (472) 312 7695) with beds from US$22; however, some readers of this guide have not felt this was good value for money.

Places to Stay – top end

Given the paucity of tourists it's astonishing to find that two new expensive hotels have opened in town. Best is undoubtedly the three-star *Hotel Grand Derya* in Belediye Caddesi (☎ (472) 312 7531, fax 312 7833), right beside the Ahmedi Hani Camii, which has a pleasant modern reception area and first-floor lounge, complete with kilims and comfy chairs. Some of the rooms are more modern looking than others, but all are clean and well equipped. No air-con, alas. For the time being you can probably get away with paying about US$20 per person.

At No 65 Büyük Ağrı Caddesi is the three-star *Hotel Nuh* (☎ (472) 312 7232, fax 312 6910), where the terrace offers panoramic views of Mt Ararat and the palace. There's a private car park, a lift and constant hot water, and the rooms are clean and comfortable. Again, you can probably negotiate a room for about US$20 a head.

A third three-star hotel, the *Hotel Ortadoğu*, should have opened on Ağri Caddesi by the time you read this. Its prices are likely to mirror those of the Nuh.

Places to Eat

Belediye Caddesi has three or four kebapçıs, including the excellent *Tad Lokantası*, a bright, cheery place which does good chicken kebaps with pitta and salad for about US$3. The same people run the *Doğuş Kafeterya Salonu* near the otogar which will serve you a pleasant pide or a more substantial meal.

The restaurants in the established top hotels are good; those in the newer ones will no doubt meet the same standards in future.

The *Kristal Pasta Salonu* on Belediye Caddesi offers a Turkish breakfast for US$1 and afternoon tea and pastry for about the same price. You can hardly miss the mouth-watering displays of cakes and biscuits in the windows. Mind the treacherous steps to the aile salonu upstairs though.

Getting There & Away

Doğubeyazıt now has a proper otogar, but bus services are limited and mostly go via Erzurum or Iğdır. Details of (mostly daily) services follow:

Ankara – 1210 km, 18 hours, US$18; three buses
Erzurum – 285 km, 4½ hours, US$8; three buses
Iğdır – 51 km, 45 minutes, US$2; hourly dolmuşes
İstanbul – 1550 km, 22 hours, US$20; two direct buses
Kars – 240 km, three hours, US$5; a few buses
Van via Ağrı – 315 km, 5½ hours, US$6; several buses to Ağrı, change for Van

INTO IRAN

Provided you accept the cultural peculiarities of the Islamic Revolution, travel in Iran can be enjoyable since the people are mostly very friendly and helpful.

To visit or travel through Iran you must have a visa, theoretically obtainable from an Iranian embassy or consulate, but this may depend on the fluctuating currents of international relations.

It may take anywhere from a week to a month or more to obtain a visa and you may have to show a visa for the country you will enter when you leave Iran and a bus or airline ticket out of Iran. Be prepared for some Middle Eastern bureaucratic hassles. See the Visas & Embassies section in the Facts for the Visitor chapter, and contact your embassy in Ankara for details on current availability and requirements for visas.

Women contemplating making the crossing will first need to buy a *chador* (the all-encompassing black robe favoured by the Revolutionary Guards), available from Doğubeyazıt market for about US$18.

A dolmuş to the border at Gürbulak, 34 km east of Doğubeyazıt, should cost about US$1. The crossing here may take as little as one hour. You may be asked to pay an unofficial fee (ie a bribe) by the Iranian officials. The Bank Melli branch at the border changes cash (dollars or pounds) or travellers' cheques into Iranian rials (tomans). Even if it refuses Turkish liras, you may be able to change them at banks farther into Iran.

From the border you can take a taxi to Maku, then an Iran Peyma bus from Maku to Tabriz.

Note that there is a post office, a tourist office and a reasonable restaurant on the Turkish side of the border despite its off-putting, shades-of-war-torn-Beirut appearance.

South-Eastern Anatolia

Turkey's south-eastern region shares some characteristics with the north-east: its history is involved and eventful, its landscapes dramatic, and its tourist traffic much lighter than that on the congested Aegean and Mediterranean coasts. But apart from these things, the regions are dramatically different.

South-eastern Anatolia is mostly hot, dry country with elevations ranging from Şanlıurfa's 540m to Van's 1725m. The people are mostly Kurdish, and farming is their principal occupation. With the inauguration in 1992 of the gigantic Atatürk Dam, keystone of the vast South-east Anatolia Project (Güneydoğu Anadolu Projesi, GAP), this poor but fertile land began to get the water it needs to become the country's most abundant producer of crops.

GAZİANTEP

Known in Ottoman times as Aintab, the city of Gaziantep (population 650,000, altitude 843m) got its modern name from the heroism displayed by its citizens during the War of Independence.

Despite its remarkably long history, Gaziantep today is a large, modern city with only a few sights to interest visitors: the kale (citadel), two museums and some old houses.

Otherwise, it is the economic powerhouse of the south-east, surrounded by farmland and ringed by light industry (textiles, food processing etc). The longer the Kurdish troubles to the east continue, the richer Gaziantep will become as professionals, skilled workers, the rich and their capital flee to this haven of safety.

If you find it convenient to break your journey here, Gaziantep offers a range of hotels and far more baklava shops than you thought you'd see in a lifetime. The region is also known for excellent grapes and olives, for the soft Arabic 'pizza' called lahmacun (LAHH-mah-joon) and for pistachio nuts (about US$8 per kg in the shells; more without shells). This is the pistachio *(şam fıstığı*, SHAHM fuhss-tuh) capital of Turkey, growing, shelling, packing and shipping hundreds of tons each year.

History

Archaeologists have sifted through some of the dirt which forms the artificial hill beneath the kale, and have found prehistoric artefacts dating from Neolithic times (7000-5000 BC), but the history begins when small Proto-Hittite, or Hatti, city-states grew up between 2500 and 1900 BC.

Hittites and Assyrians battled for this region until it was taken by Sargon II, king of Assyria, in 717 BC. The Assyrians ruled for almost a century before being overcome by the Cimmerians, a Crimean people driven from their traditional lands by the Scythians. The Cimmerians swept through Anatolia destroying almost everything that lay in their path, setting an example that would be followed by numerous uncreative hordes which showed up in later history.

The Cimmerians cleared out and the Persians took over from 612 to 333 BC. They were followed by Alexander the Great, the Romans and the Byzantines. The Arabs conquered the town in 638 AD and held it until the Seljuk Turks swept in from the east in the 1070s.

With the crusades, Gaziantep's history perks up a bit, but most of the action and romance took place in Urfa. The crusaders didn't stay long before the Seljuks took over again, and Gaziantep remained a city of Seljuk culture, ruled by petty Turkish lords until the coming of the Ottomans under Selim the Grim in 1516.

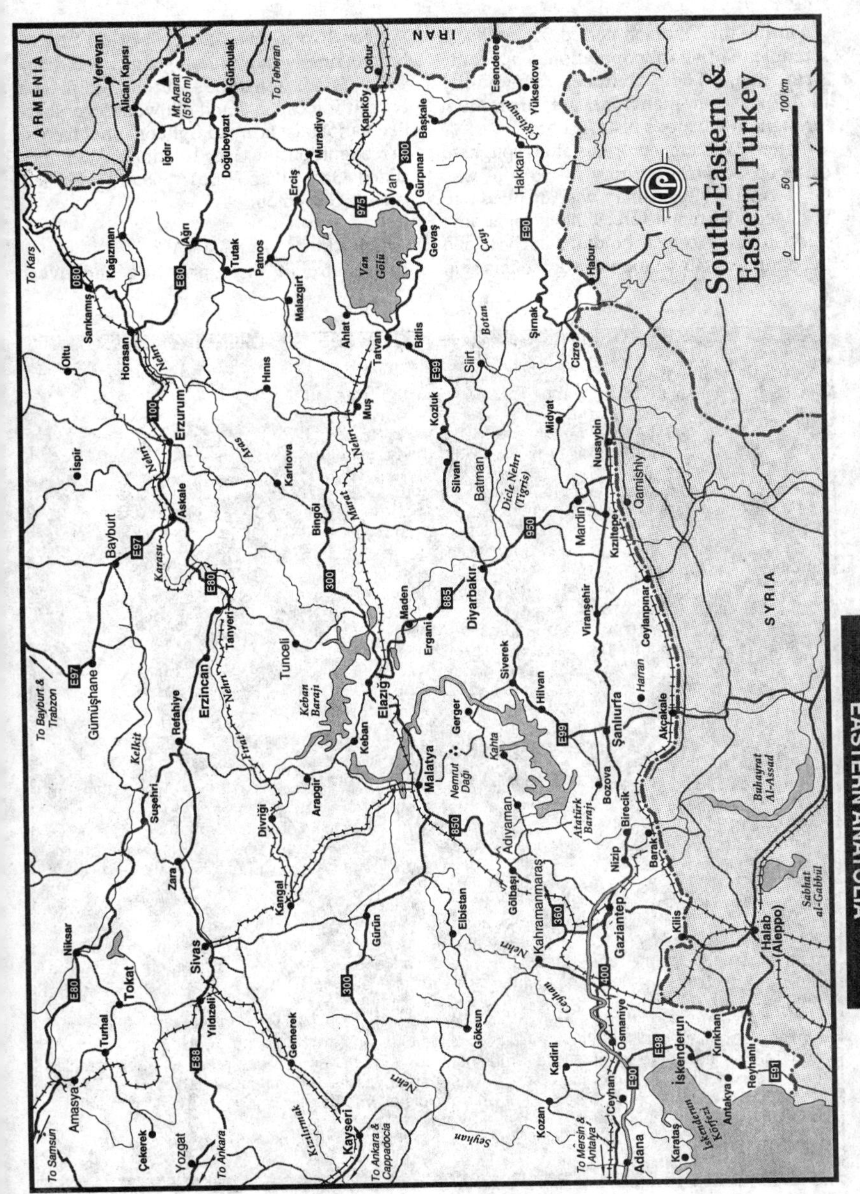
South-Eastern & Eastern Turkey
0
50
100 km
ARMENIA
IRAN
SYRIA
Yerevan
Alican Kapısı
Mt Ararat (5165 m)
Gürbulak
To Teheran
Qotur
Kapıköy
Esendere
Yüksekova
Çığlısuyu
Hakkari
Başkale
Muradiye
Doğubeyazıt
Iğdır
Kağızman
To Kars
Sarıkamış
Horasan
Oltu
Ağrı
Tutak
Patnos
Erciş
Van Gölü
Van
Gürpınar
Gevaş
Çayı
Malazgirt
Ahlat
Tatvan
Bitlis
Botan
Şırnak
Habur
Cizre
Siirt
Hınıs
Erzurum
Nehri
İspir
Aras
Karlıova
Muş
Murat
Kozluk
Midyat
Silvan
Batman
Dicle Nehri (Tigris)
Nusaybin
Qamishly
Askale
Bayburt
Karasu
Bingöl
Mardin
Kızıltepe
Diyarbakır
Maden
Ergani
Tunceli
Tanyeri
Erzincan
Gümüşhane
To Bayburt & Trabzon
Kelkit
Refahiye
Fırat
Keban Barajı
Keban
Elazığ
Siverek
Hilvan
Viranşehir
Ceylanpınar
Harran
Şanlıurfa
Akçakale
Gerger
Kahta
Nemrut Dağı
Malatya
Arapgir
Divriği
Suşehri
Zara
Kangal
Adıyaman
Atatürk Barajı
Bozova
Birecik
Nizip
Barak
Buhayrat Al-Assad
Sabhat al-Gabbül
Gölbaşı
Kahramanmaraş
Elbistan
Gürün
Gaziantep
Kilis
Halab (Aleppo)
Sivas
Niksar
Tokat
Turhal
Amasya
To Samsun
Çekerek
Yozgat
To Ankara
Yıldızeli
Gemerek
Kızılırmak
Kayseri
To Ankara & Cappadocia
Göksun
Ceyhan
Osmaniye
Kadirli
Kozan
Seyhan
To Mersin & Antalya
Adana
Ceyhan
İskenderun
Kırıkhan
Reyhanlı
Antakya
İskenderun Körfezi
Karataş
E80
E97
E80
E88
E90
E98
E91
E99
E90
100
080
300
975
950
885
850
360
400
300

During the Ottoman period, Antep had a sizeable Christian population, especially Armenians. Their churches, community buildings and mansions are prominent throughout the city's historic core.

After WWI, the victorious allies sought to carve up Ottoman territory as spoils of war. On 1 April 1920, Aintab was attacked and besieged by French forces intent on adding Turkish lands to their holdings in Syria and Lebanon. Aintab's nationalist defenders held out for 10 months, at a cost of 600 lives, before finally surrendering on 8 February 1921. Their tenacious defense kept the French forces busy and allowed the embattled nationalist army to fight on other fronts. In recognition, the Grand National Assembly added Gazi (War Hero) to the Turkicised Antep: Gaziantep.

Orientation

The centre of this sprawling and ever-

Kurdish Separatism

Turkey's Kurdish minority, numbering an estimated 10 million people, is dispersed throughout the country, with significant communities in the major cities. By some estimates there are nearly a million Kurds living in İstanbul alone. But only in the south-east do Kurds come close to constituting a majority of the regional population.

The Kurds of south-eastern Anatolia have complained for years that the taxes collected in this underdeveloped region went to Ankara but none of the money came back to them in the form of government investment or services. The GAP project is answering that complaint, and the south-east promises to become a very wealthy area indeed. Besides the exponential increases in crop yields and the amount of arable land, the vast new lakes formed by GAP will provide abundant new sources of hydroelectric power, as well as revenue from tourism and fish aquaculture.

The new wealth may temper – or aggravate – Turkey's decade-old Kurdish separatist movement.

Periodically through Ottoman and republican times, some Kurds in south-eastern and east-central Anatolia have dreamed of building a separate and independent Kurdish state, uniting the Kurdish minorities in north-western Iraq, eastern Turkey, northern Syria and north-western Iran.

In recent years the separatist movement has been led by the Kurdistan Workers Party, known as the PKK. The group's terrorist activity takes place mostly in south-eastern Turkey, but there have been attacks against Turkish troops and civilians in north-eastern Anatolia and even in such cities as Ankara, Antalya and İstanbul.

The violence between the Turkish authorities and the Kurdish separatists ebbs and flows, but in recent years the government forces seem to be gaining the upper hand. Human rights organisations in Turkey and abroad have criticised – sometimes bitterly – the Turkish army's harsh methods of subduing the rebellion. But it's generally acknowledged that – whatever right the Kurds may have to an airing of their complaints – the PKK is even worse when it comes to violence and coercion.

Thus the army has the support of the majority of the Turkish public. With so many young conscripts coming back from the east in body bags, Turkish parents are hardly inclined to support moderation against the rebels, even for the sake of innocent non-combatants. Some Turks claim (perhaps not seriously) that they'd support a separate Kurdish state in the east just to get rid of the trouble, but any Turkish president or prime minister who even so much as mentioned such a possibility would be out of office in a matter of days, if not hours.

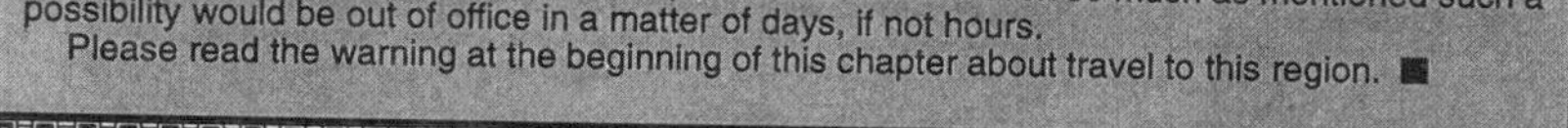

Please read the warning at the beginning of this chapter about travel to this region. ■

growing city is the intersection of Atatürk Bulvarı/Suburcu Caddesi and Hürriyet/İstasyon Caddesis, site of the Hükümet Konağı (Government Headquarters) and a large equestrian statue of Atatürk. Though the provincial government is now headquartered in a modern building to the north, locals (and, more importantly, dolmuş drivers) still call the place Hükümet Konağı. Hotels, restaurants, banks etc are here.

The Devlet Hastanesi (State Hospital), another useful landmark, is a few blocks past Hükümet Konağı on Hürriyet Caddesi.

Most hotels are within a block or two of the main intersection – an easy and pleasant walk. The museum is about half a km from here and the kale another half a km from the museum. The kale is on the high hill topped by a twin-minaret mosque.

The otogar is two km from the main intersection, accessible by frequent 'Devlet Hastanesi' minibus and less frequent city buses.

The train station is almost as far from the centre. Walk from the station to the first large intersection to catch the 'Devlet Hastanesi' minibus. A taxi to the centre costs about US$2.50.

Information

Gaziantep's Tourism Information Office (☎ (342) 230 5969, fax 234 0603), 100 Yıl Parkı İçi, Vilayet Konağı Arkası, is behind the new Gaziantep Valiliği (Provincial Government Headquarters) near the fairgrounds. Follow the signs to reach it.

The Akbank opposite the old Vilayet building in the centre has well-connected ATM's. Upstairs, Mr Ali Akif Boztoprak changes travellers' cheques with a smile.

Gaziantep's postal code is 27000.

Kale

The citadel was first constructed, as far as is known, by the emperor Justinian in the 6th century AD, but was rebuilt extensively by the Seljuks in the 12th and 13th centuries. The massive doors to the fortified enclosure may well be locked, but at least have a look at them. As you approach the kale bear right around the massive walls. Don't go through what appears to be an enormous stone gateway; this is actually the *fosse* (dry moat), straddled in ancient times by a drawbridge high above. Around to the right of the fosse you will come to a small mosque, opposite which is a ramp leading up to the citadel doors. If they're open, proceed across the wooden bridge which spans the fosse and into the kale.

The surrounding quarter is one of artisans' workshops, old stone houses and little neighbourhood mosques. Trucks for hire are gathered at one side of the kale, heirs to the ancient carters and teamsters.

Gaziantep Museum

The Gaziantep Müzesi (☎ 231 1171), next to the stadium on İstasyon Caddesi, is open from 9 am to 5.30 pm, and is closed on Monday. Admission costs US$1.25. Surrounded by the requisite sculpture garden, the museum holds something from every period of the province's history, from mastodon bones to Hittite figurines and pottery, Roman mosaics (three fairly good ones) and funeral stones complete with portraits of husband and wife, to an Ottoman ethnography room of kilims, carpets and furniture heavily worked in mother-of-pearl.

Old Mosques & Houses

A few blocks away from bustling Hükümet Konağı are neighbourhoods with old Ottoman houses and mosques of a distinctly Arabic cast.

Walk uphill from the Hükümet Konağı intersection on Kayacık Sokak past the Hotel Evin to the **Eyüboğlu Camii**. This Syrian-style mosque dating from the 14th century was extensively but unsensitively restored in 1947, and much of its original character sacrificed.

Walk farther uphill narrow Hanifioğlu Sokak, following the signs for the **Hasan Süzer Etnoğrafya Müzesi** (☎ 230 4721), a two-century-old Gaziantep stone house restored and opened as a museum of local ethnography. The museum is open daily

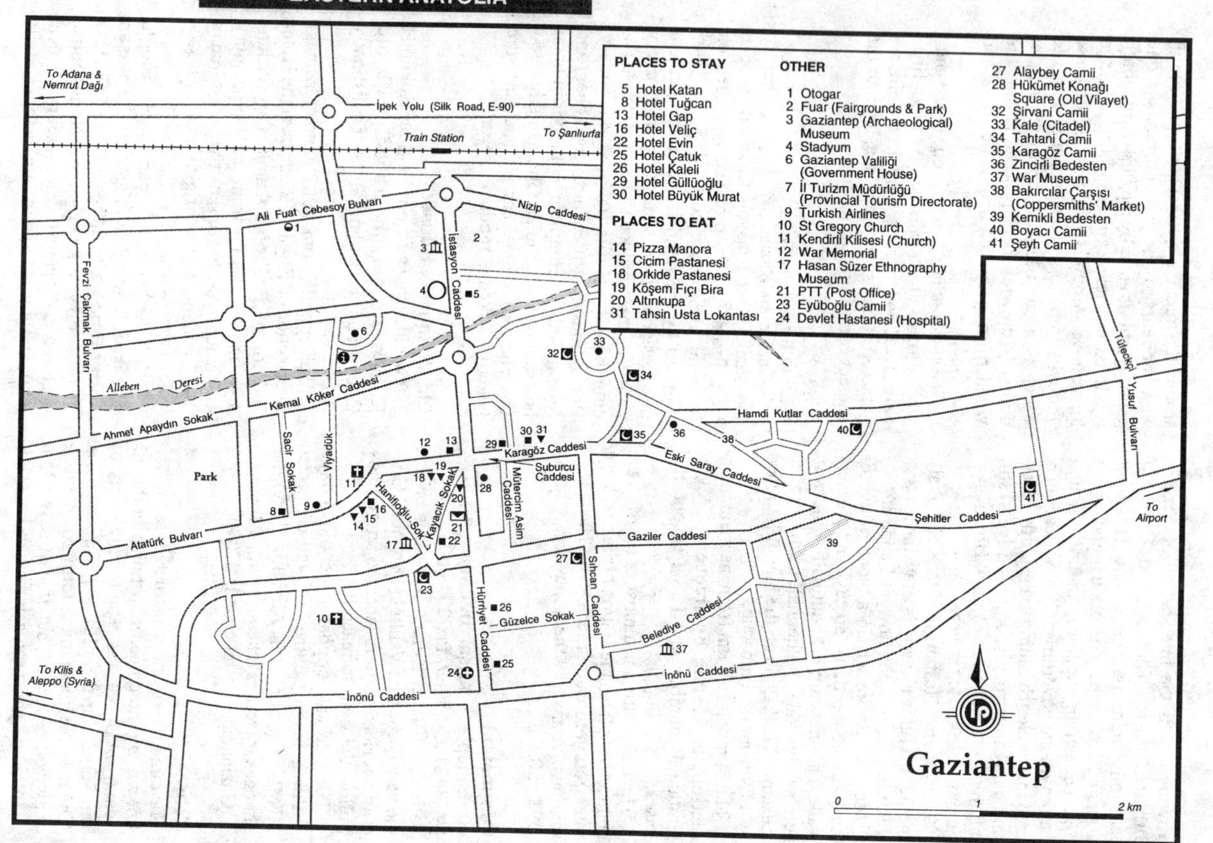
PLACES TO STAY
5 Hotel Katan
8 Hotel Tuğcan
13 Hotel Gap
16 Hotel Veliç
22 Hotel Evin
25 Hotel Çatuk
26 Hotel Kaleli
29 Hotel Güllüoğlu
30 Hotel Büyük Murat
PLACES TO EAT
14 Pizza Manora
15 Cicim Pastanesi
18 Orkide Pastanesi
19 Köşem Fıçı Bira
20 Altınkupa
31 Tahsin Usta Lokantası
OTHER
1 Otogar
2 Fuar (Fairgrounds & Park)
3 Gaziantep (Archaeological) Museum
4 Stadyum
6 Gaziantep Valiliği (Government House)
7 İl Turizm Müdürlüğü (Provincial Tourism Directorate)
9 Turkish Airlines
10 St Gregory Church
11 Kendirli Kilisesi (Church)
12 War Memorial
17 Hasan Süzer Ethnography Museum
21 PTT (Post Office)
23 Eyüboğlu Camii
24 Devlet Hastanesi (Hospital)
27 Alaybey Camii
28 Hükümet Konağı Square (Old Vilayet)
32 Şirvani Camii
33 Kale (Citadel)
34 Tahtani Camii
35 Karagöz Camii
36 Zincirli Bedesten
37 War Museum
38 Bakırcılar Çarşısı (Coppersmiths' Market)
39 Kemikli Bedesten
40 Boyacı Camii
41 Şeyh Camii
Gaziantep
0
1
2 km
To Adana & Nemrut Dağı
İpek Yolu (Silk Road, E-90)
Train Station
To Şanlıurfa
Ali Fuat Cebesoy Bulvarı
Nizip Caddesi
İstasyon Caddesi
Fevzi Çakmak Bulvarı
Alleben Deresi
Kemal Köker Caddesi
Ahmet Apaydın Sokak
Sacir Sokak
Viyadük
Park
Hanifioğlu Sok
Kayacık Sokak
Atatürk Bulvarı
Karagöz Caddesi
Suburcu Caddesi
Mütercim Asim Caddesi
Hamdi Kutlar Caddesi
Eski Saray Caddesi
Tüfekçi Yusuf Bulvarı
Şehitler Caddesi
To Airport
Gaziler Caddesi
Sıhcan Caddesi
Hürriyet Caddesi
Güzelce Sokak
Belediye Caddesi
İnönü Caddesi
To Kilis & Aleppo (Syria)

except Monday from 8 am to noon and 1 to 5 pm. Admission is US$0.75.

A central court *(hayat)* dressed in patterns of light and dark stone provides light and access to the rooms. Those on the ground floor were for service; those on the 1st floor made up the Selamlık, for male family members and their visitors; and those on the 2nd floor made up the Haremlik, for female family members and their visitors. Many of the rooms have been decorated according to their historic function: kitchen, bath and reception rooms (with nighttime bedding stored in the cupboards). Several of the rooms now hold local historical exhibits, including one showing Gaziantep's role in the War of Independence through photographs, documents and artefacts, such as old rifles, battle standards and decorations.

On the top floor in the Harem, one room holds life-size Madame Tussaud-style wax figures of the museum's ever-modest benefactor, Mr Süzer, currently owner of the Pera Palas Hotel in İstanbul, and his parents.

The Mesk Odası, a room set apart for the men's games, now holds an exhibit of a *tandır* (charcoal brazier or oven) set under a stone table covered with a *yorgan*, or cotton-filled quilt. This is the traditional means of winter warmth for humble country families: occupants would put their legs under the quilt to get the heat, and talk or play games on the quilted table above.

The Mesk Odası also holds a dresser that's an eye-popping example of *sedef*, or furniture worked with mother-of-pearl, a Gaziantep speciality.

Continue following Hanifioğlu Sokak downhill past the museum, jogging to right and left as necessary, looking at other old Gaziantep houses, and you will ultimately emerge on Atatürk Bulvarı just east of the Hotel Veliç. Turn right and walk 100m to reach Hükümet Konağı.

Places to Stay – bottom end

The *Hotel Güllüoğlu* (☎ (342) 232 4363), Suburcu Caddesi 1/B, provides about the best value for money at US$14/18 a single/double for a room with shower. Enter the hotel around the corner from the baklavacı on the side street. The neighbouring *Hotel Büyük Murat* (☎ (342) 231 8449, fax 231 1658), its unfortunate initials emblazoned proudly on its doors, is newer, and though prices displayed are higher, they usually preserve parity with the Güllüoğlu.

The 35-room *Hotel Veliç* (☎ (342) 231 1726), Atatürk Bulvarı 23, is the dowdiest of the three, charging identical prices.

There are cheaper rooms along Kayacık Sokak, a dingy lane of card rooms, beer halls and billiard salons. Pass the inappropriately-named *Gül Palas* (Rose Palace) and the *Emre* to reach the *Hotel Evin* (☎ (342) 231 3492), with dim lights and dour management charging US$8/11 for singles/doubles with shower.

Places to Stay – middle

All middle-range rooms are air conditioned.

Hotel Çatuk (☎ (342) 231 9480, fax 233 0043), Hürriyet Caddesi 27, just across from the Devlet Hastanesi, has rooms for US$14/25/36 a single/double/triple with shower.

Gaziantep's longtime favourite lodging is the three-star *Hotel Kaleli* (☎ (342) 230 9690, fax 230 1597), Hürriyet Caddesi, Güzelce Sokak 50, between the main intersection and the Devlet Hastanesi. The 70 rooms (US$16/20 a single/double, or US$30 a triple in a suite) are old-fashioned, which means spacious; those on the front have bathtubs, on the back, small showers. The rooftop restaurant is among the city's best.

The *Hotel Gap* (☎ (342) 220 3974, 234 2102), Atatürk Bulvarı 10, is very central, and quite fancy with its grand marble-paved lobby. The excellent new rooms cost US$38/42 a single/double, breakfast included. It has a car park as well.

Out by the museum and kale is the two-star, 42-room *Hotel Katan* (☎ (342) 230 6969, fax 230 8454), İstasyon Caddesi 58, opposite the stadium, at prices similar to those at the Gap.

Places to Stay – top end

The best place in Gaziantep is the five-star, 141-room *Tuğcan Hotel* (☎ (342) 220 4323, fax 220 3242), Atatürk Bulvarı 34 at Sacir Sokak, about 400m west of Hükümet Konağı. A room with all luxuries and especially elaborate toilet facilities costs US$100/115/130 a single/double/triple.

Places to Eat

Suburcu Caddesi and Atatürk Bulvarı hold an incredible number of shops selling baklava, pastries, cakes, kadayıf and other Turkish sweets. One would think the Gaziantеplis forget dinner and head straight for what comes after, but in fact the sprinkling of real-food restaurants belies that appearance.

Among the sweets shops, the most famous is *Güllüoğlu*, in the hotel of the same name (see the earlier Places to Stay – bottom end section). Its fame grew because of its şam fıstıklı baklava (with pistachios), but the shop serves many other varieties as well, including kaymaklı (with clotted cream). A 150g portion costs about US$1. You'll see the name Güllüoğlu on other shops, as later generations have taken up the art.

For the fanciest European-style cakes, pop into the *Orkide Pastanesi* (☎ 231 2277), Atatürk Bulvarı 7/A, just off the main intersection. For Turkish treats, the fanciest shop is *Cicim Pastanesi*, on Atatürk Bulvarı south of the Hotel Veliç.

For pre-baklava courses, there are many small kebapçıs and restaurants on and off Suburcu Caddesi. A modern choice is the *Tahsin Usta Lokantası* (☎ 220 8934), serving a variety of south-eastern kebaps but specialising in oven-baked lahmacun and pide (watch them being made at the back). The dining room is airy and bright. Meals cost US$2 to US$3; no alcohol is served.

Gaziantep's gilded youth congregate for pizza and burgers at *Pizza Manora* (☎ 232 9521), Atatürk Bulvarı 37/C. Though the atmosphere is upscale (and comfortable for single women travellers), prices are not bad at US$2.50 to US$4 for a one-person pizza.

For a more formal dinner with drinks, try the rooftop restaurant at the *Hotel Kaleli* on Hürriyet Caddesi. Though the setting is genteel, prices are moderate, and a full tuck-in with drinks costs only about US$6 to US$9 per person.

At the corner of Atatürk and Hürriyet is a shopping complex containing several licensed restaurants, the best of which is the *Altınkupa*. There's Turkish-style *şantöz* (chanteuse) entertainment some nights.

If it's just drink and snacks you're after, *Köşem Fıçı Bira* across Kayacık Sokak from the Altınkupa is about the most genteel birahane in the district, with a marble counter and a well-behaved clientele.

Getting There & Away

Air Turkish Airlines (☎ (342) 230 1565, 230 1567), Atatürk Bulvarı 30/B, near the Tuğcan Hotel, operates daily nonstop flights between Gaziantep's Sazgın airport (20 km from the centre), Ankara (one hour) and İstanbul (1¾ hours). An airport bus departs from the downtown office on Atatürk Bulvarı 90 minutes before flight time and costs less than US$2.

Bus The modern otogar is two km from the town centre and the bus service is frequent and far-reaching. Details of some daily services follow:

Adana – 220 km, four hours, US$7.50; several buses
Adıyaman & Kahta (Nemrut Dağı) – 210 km, four hours, US$8; several buses
Ankara – 705 km, 12 hours, US$20; frequent buses
Antakya – 200 km, four hours, US$8; frequent buses
Diyarbakır – 330 km, five hours, US$11; frequent buses
Mardin – 330 km, 5½ hours, US$12; several buses
Şanlıurfa – 145 km, 2½ hours, US$5.50; frequent buses

Train The *Toros Ekspresi* departs daily from İstanbul (9 am) and Gaziantep (4.05 pm), arriving in the opposite city about 30 hours later, having made stops in Ankara, Kayseri, Niğde and Adana. A one-way 1st/2nd-class ticket all the way costs US$15/10.50. The fare in a sleeping car is US$30/52/72 for one/two/three people.

An alternative is to take the overnight *Çukurova Ekspresi* from Ankara to Adana, and then proceed by bus.

GAZİANTEP TO ŞANLIURFA

The road from Gaziantep to Şanlıurfa is very hot in summer, yet the land is fertile, with fig orchards, olive trees, cotton and wheat.

At Nizip, there is a turn-off south for **Karkamış** (Carchemish), a neo-Hittite city which flourished around 850 BC, about the time Akhenaton occupied the throne of Egypt. Though Karkamış assumed the role of Hittite capital after the fall of Hattuşaş, there is little left to see, and you must see it with a military escort so you don't get shot at as a smuggler – it's hardly worth the trip.

At Birecik you cross the Euphrates River (Fırat Nehri). The town has a **ruined fortress**, rebuilt and used by the crusaders. In spring (March or April), the town holds a traditional festival in honour of the **bald ibis**, which used to winter here, but is now on the verge of extinction. Authorities had established an **ibis feeding and protection station** to give the birds meat and eggs, and even built wooden houses for them following plans provided by the Turkish Wildlife Protection Society and World Wildlife Fund.

As you head east, the land becomes rockier and less fertile. By the time you approach Şanlıurfa, the land is parched, rolling steppe roasting in the merciless sun. The landscape is changing, however, as the gigantic South-east Anatolia Project comes online, bringing irrigation waters to vast tracts of otherwise unarable land.

KAHRAMANMARAŞ

Formerly known as Maraş, the sonorous new name of this city (population 250,000, altitude 568m) was given to it in 1973 in honour of its role during the War of Independence. Maraş was occupied by French troops after WWI, and the populace showed such a fierce resistance to French rule that parliament – belatedly – added Kahraman (Heroic) to its traditional name half a century later.

The site of the city has moved repeatedly over the centuries, the present site having been chosen by the Dülkadır emirs during the 14th century. Wars and earthquakes have destroyed much of old Maraş, but if you need to stop for a meal or for the night you can spend a few hours pleasantly enough – and you will see very little indeed of other tourists.

Today Maraş is a modern city set where the agricultural plain meets the slopes of Ahır Dağı (Horse Mountain, 2301m). It's a farming centre with vast, rich crops of cotton and potatoes in the surrounding countryside. Copper working is also important. The Maraşlıs enjoy riding around on motorcycles with sidecars – convenient in this sunny, dry climate.

History

Marqasi was the capital of a principality which sprang up after the collapse of the Hittite Empire based at Boğazkale/Hattuşaş in 1200 BC. Destroyed by King Sargon of Assyria in the 8th century BC, it rose again under the Romans, who called it Germaniceia.

The Byzantines employed its citadel as an eastern defence-point against Arab invasion, but the Arabs took it (in 637) anyway. The Byzantines reclaimed it in later centuries, but while the Byzantines were dealing with the Seljuk invasion up north, control of Germaniceia passed in 1070 to an Armenian strongman named Philaterus. He ruled over a large kingdom briefly, until it was conquered by the crusaders and then returned to Byzantine control.

A succession of Kurdish, Seljuk and Turcoman emirs and sultans ruled the city until it was conquered by the Ottoman sultan Selim in 1515. Maraş had a significant Armenian population until the War of Independence, after which many from this community fled to neighbouring Syria or abroad.

Orientation & Information

The city's otogar is 100m to the west of the main highway on Azerbeycan Bulvarı. This major thoroughfare continues west 400m to the archaeology museum, and beyond it 900m to Kıbrıs Meydanı (Cyprus Square) in the heart of the business district. Many hotels are near Kıbrıs Meydanı, or along the 400m stretch of Atatürk Bulvarı which goes west from Kıbrıs Meydanı to the Ulu Cami (Great Mosque), an ancient building which marks the traditional centre of the city. There are no hotels near the otogar.

The train station (TCDD, or DDY, Gar) is at the foot of Cumhuriyet Caddesi, just east of the main highway, two km north-east of Kıbrıs Meydanı. There are no hotels, restaurants or other services nearby.

The Tourism Information Office (☎ (344) 212 6590, fax 223 0355) is off Azerbeycan Bulvarı at Yeşiltepe Sokak 2, TEK Bitişiği, Gölkari Apartımentı, 1st floor.

The postal code for Kahramanmaraş is 46000.

Historic Buildings

Start your walk around the **Ulu (Acemli) Camii**, built in a Syrian Arabic style in 1502, during the time of the Dülkadır emirate. Note especially its tall and unusual minaret, which has survived the depredations of earthquakes and invaders relatively intact. Across the park to the south-west is the recently restored tomb of the founders. The **Çukur Hamamı** Turkish bath is nearby as well.

The **citadel** (kale) to the south has been rebuilt and repaired over the centuries, and looks as if it has. There is nothing to see now but the gates and walls.

A few steps t the north is the **Taş Medrese**, a seminary dating from the 14th century. The **Taş Han** was the city's caravanserai.

South-west of the Ulu Camii up the wooded slopes is a neighbourhood of **old Ottoman houses**, some in good repair.

Kahramanmaraş Museum

The Kahramanmaraş Müzesi, 900m east of Kıbrıs Meydanı along Azerbeycan Bulvarı (400m uphill from the otogar), is open from 8 am to 5 pm (weekends from 9 am to 5 pm, Monday from 10 am to 1 pm). Admission costs US$1.25. Exhibit labels (when they exist) are usually in Turkish, with a few in English.

Exhibits include dinosaur bones found in the region and a dozen very fine Hittite stelae covered in fascinating, lively reliefs. An Assyrian border marker is covered in cuneiform inscriptions. Other exhibits cover every period from the Old Bronze and Hittite to Ottoman. The ethnographic section is rich in textiles, costumes of gold cloth, inlaid woodwork and beautiful local kilims.

Places to Stay & Eat

Because it is an agricultural trading centre, Kahramanmaraş has several comfortable two-star hotels right in the centre off Kıbrıs Meydanı.

Otel Kazancı (☎ (344) 223 4462, fax 212 6942), just uphill a few steps from Kıbrıs Meydanı, is perhaps the best: central, yet quiet, and charging US$28/45 for a single/double with bath and breakfast.

One block to the north-east is the cheaper but still quite good *Otel Büyük Maraş* (☎ (344) 223 3500, fax 212 8894), Milli Egemenlik Caddesi 7, charging only US$22/35 for a single/double with bath, breakfast included.

The noisier two-star, 80-room *Hotel Belli* (☎ (344) 223 4900, fax 214 8282), across Kıbrıs Meydanı from the two previously mentioned hotels, is somewhat older but still good, charging US$24/30 for a single/double with bath and breakfast.

Maraş is noted for several culinary specialties, among them saç kavurma, bits of lamb fried on a convex steel griddle; and külbastı, grilled lamb chops with çemen (cumin, the spice made from ground fenugreek seeds), red pepper and garlic. Most famous of all is 'hakiki Kahramanmaraş dövme dondurma' (authentic Maraş beaten ice cream), made with so much glue-like binder that it withstands the city's intense summer heat, can be displayed hanging on a hook like meat, and eaten with knife and fork. For a sample, try the elaborate *Yaşar Pastanesi* (☎ 225 0808), next to the Hotel Belli. The *Reyhanlıoğlu Restaurant* next door will do for a meal in a pinch.

Getting There & Away

Maraş shares the traffic which criss-crosses the region from Kayseri to Gaziantep and Adana to Malatya. Most of the bus services originate somewhere else, and may or may not have onward seats. Details of some daily services follow:

Adana – 190 km, 3½ hours, US$8; frequent buses
Adıyaman – 164 km, three hours, US$7; several buses
Antakya – 185 km, four hours, US$8; several buses
Gaziantep – 80 km, one hour, US$2; very frequent dolmuşes depart from beside the Hotel Kazancı on Kıbrıs Meydanı
Kayseri – 291 km, 5½ hours, US$10; several buses
Malatya – 226 km, 4½ hours, US$9; several buses

NEMRUT DAĞI

The Commagene Nemrut Dağı (NEHM-root dah-uh), not to be confused with a mountain of the same name on the shores of Lake Van, rises to a height of 2150m between the provincial capital of Malatya to the north and the town of Kahta in Adıyaman province to the south. It's part of the Anti-Taurus range.

The summit was formed when a petty, megalomaniac pre-Roman king cut two ledges in the rock, filled them with colossal statues of himself and the gods (his 'relatives'), then ordered an artificial mountain peak of crushed rock 50m high to be piled between them. The king's tomb may well lie beneath those tonnes of rock. Nobody knows for sure.

Earthquakes have toppled the heads from most of the statues, but many of the colossal bodies sit silently in rows, and the two-metre-high heads watch from the ground.

History

Nobody knew anything about Nemrut Dağı until 1881, when an Ottoman geologist making a survey was astounded to come across this remote mountaintop full of statues. Archaeological work didn't begin until 1953, when the American School of Oriental Research undertook the project.

From 250 BC onwards, this region was the borderland between the Seleucid Empire (which followed the empire of Alexander the Great in Anatolia) and the Parthian Empire to the east, also occupying a part of Alexander's lands. A small but strategic land, which was rich, fertile and covered in forests, it had a history of independent thinking ever since the time of King Samos circa 150 BC.

Under the Seleucid Empire, the governor of Commagene declared his kingdom's independence. In 80 BC, with the Seleucids in disarray and Roman power spreading into Anatolia, a Roman ally named Mithridates I Callinicus proclaimed himself king and set up his capital at Arsameia, near the modern village of Kahta Kalesi. Mithridates prided himself on his royal ancestry, tracing his forebears back to Seleucus I Nicator, founder of the Seleucid Empire to the west, and to Darius the Great, king of ancient Persia to the east. Thus he saw himself as heir to both glorious traditions. He married a Parthian princess.

Mithridates died in 64 BC and was succeeded by his son Antiochus I Epiphanes (64-38 BC) who, born of a Parthian mother, consolidated the security of his kingdom by immediately signing a non-aggression treaty with Rome, turning his kingdom into a Roman buffer against attack from the Parthians. His good relations with both sides allowed him to grow rich and to revel in delusions of grandeur. As heir to both traditions, he saw himself as equal to the great god-kings of the past. It was Antiochus who

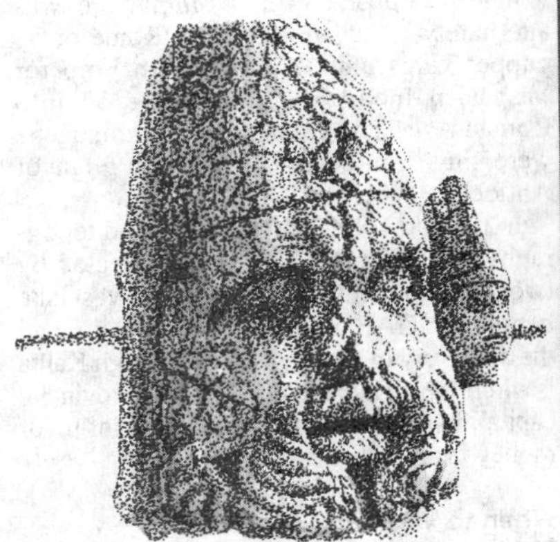

The colossal statues of the gods atop Nemrut Dağı, near Malatya, are an impressive sight. This head of Zeus is nearly two metres tall.

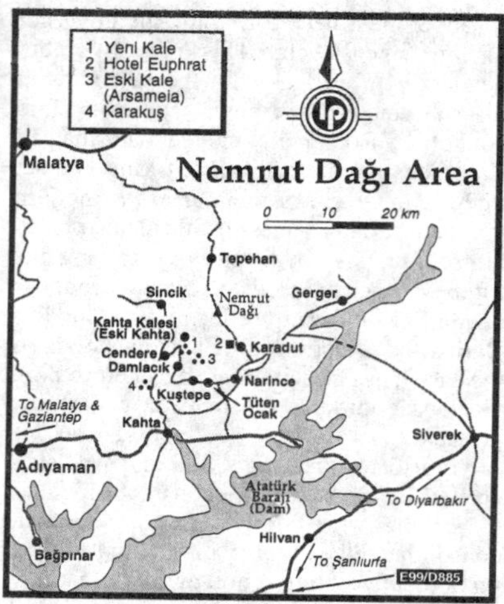

ordered that the fabulous temples and funerary mound be built on top of Nemrut.

Antiochus must have come to believe in his own divinity, for in the third decade of his reign he sided with the Parthians in a squabble with Rome, and in 38 BC the Romans deposed him. Commagene was alternately ruled directly from Rome or by puppet kings until 72 AD, when Emperor Vespasian incorporated it for good into Roman Asia. The great days of Commagene were thus limited to the 26-year reign of Antiochus.

In the late 1980s the economy and topography of this area were greatly affected by two developments: the filling of the vast lake behind the GAP project's Atatürk Dam, and the discovery of oil near Kahta. Though Kahta is where the oil is, it is Adıyaman, the provincial capital, which has benefited from an influx of money for building and development.

When to Visit

Plan your visit to Nemrut between late May and mid-October, and preferably in July or August. The road to the summit becomes impassable in the snow. Remember that at any time of year, even in the heat of summer when the sun bakes the valleys below, it will be chilly and windy on top of the mountain. This is especially true at sunrise, the coldest time of the day. Take warm clothing and a windbreaker on your trek to the top, no matter when you go.

Tour Bases

The traditional bases for the ascent up the southern slopes of Nemrut Dağı are the provincial capital of Adıyaman and the nearby town of Kahta, both covered in detail later in this section.

Distances among important points in the region are as follows:

Adıyaman to Kahta – 35 km
Adıyaman to Malatya – 190 km
Kahta to Nemrut – 70 km
Gölbaşı to Malatya – 121 km
Malatya to Nemrut – 110 km

Tours from Malatya

The northern road to the summit from Malatya via Tepehan can also be covered in a day, or with an overnight stay in the village of Büyüköz near the summit, where there are simple pensions and a basic but adequate hotel. By taking the Malatya route, visitors miss seeing the several sights along the Kahta-Nemrut road, such as Arsameia. The cost is about the same by either route (if you don't get ripped off). If you decide to go via Malatya, refer to the Malatya section later in this chapter.

Tours from Cappadocia & Şanlıurfa

It is possible to take minibus tours from Cappadocia to Nemrut. The tour from Cappadocia takes two days, costs about US$75 to US$100 and involves many hours of breakneck driving, but you may want to consider it if your time is limited. There are tours from Şanlıurfa as well, which take one very long day.

Adıyaman

The provincial capital of Adıyaman (ah-DUH-yah-mahn, population 130,000, altitude 669m) is the nearest city to the southern approaches of Nemrut Dağı. Now a boom oil town, Adıyaman is a gritty concrete wasteland stretched along several km of highway D 360, known locally as Atatürk Bulvarı. Its citizens are not particularly welcoming to foreign tourists.

The Tourism Information Office (☎ (416) 216 1008, fax 216 3840), Atatürk Bulvarı 184, is next to the PTT on Atatürk Bulvarı (D 360).

Adıyaman's postal code is 02100.

Places to Stay Hotel prices are high for what you get, and service standards low because, with the oil boom, it's a seller's market.

The three-star *Hotel Antiochos* (☎ (416) 216 3377, fax 213 8456), Atatürk Bulvarı 141, on the main road toward the eastern edge of town, was the newest and best at the time of writing, offering clean rooms with TV and breakfast for US$14/18 a single/double. There's a swimming pool as well.

The *Motel Beyaz Saray* (☎ (416) 216 2100), Atatürk Bulvarı 136, also called the *Beyaz Yılancı Pansiyon*, on the highway in the eastern part of town, has acceptable but unexciting rooms with shower for US$7/12/15 a single/double/triple.

The prominent 54-room *Bozdoğan Hotel* (☎ (416) 216 3999, fax 216 3630), on Atatürk Bulvarı near the western end of town, looks promising, but disappoints. For US$32/50 a single/double you get a dingy room without air-con or TV, a bathroom without a proper toilet seat, a restaurant with stained tablecloths and a murky swimming pool. Pay in advance; no credit cards accepted.

A short distance farther east along Atatürk Bulvarı at the junction with Turgut Reis Caddesi near the Vilayet is the two-star *Hotel Serdaroğlu* (☎ (416) 216 3331, fax 216 1554). It was closed at my last visit, with no news of when it might reopen.

Getting There & Away Adıyaman is served by frequent buses, but no flights or trains. Dolmuşes run between Kahta and Adıyaman (35 km, 30 minutes, US$1.75) throughout the day.

Kahta

The oil boom is changing the face of Kahta (population 45,000) rapidly. Once just a dusty little town with nothing to recommend it, it is now a dusty big town with nothing to recommend it.

The tourist office (☎ (416) 725 5007), on the main street near the Hotel Kommagene, is fairly helpful. The town's postal code is 02400.

Places to Stay For lodgings on the mountain, refer to the following description of the trip ascending Nemrut Dağı from Khata.

While hotels in Adıyaman are filled with oilies, Kahta's slightly cheaper 'motels' are often filled with bus-tour groups. Virtually any Kahta hotelier will expect you to participate in one of his minibus tours up Nemrut, and whatever bargain you get on the hotel room may be neutralised by the mark-up on the tour.

The cheapest of the pensions is the Anatolia Pension (☎ (416) 725 2479), Kahta Adıyaman 02400, run by Mr Orhan Kılıç and his family. Rooms cost US$8 a double. Breakfast (which costs extra) is served in the garden. It may only be open in summer.

Hotel Mezopotamya (☎ (416) 725 5112), on Mustafa Kemal Caddesi (the main road) on the western outskirts of Kahta, charges according to demand. Rooms with bath might cost anywhere from US$12 to US$20 a double, breakfast included. The same can be said for the *Hotel Nemrut Tur* (☎ & fax (416) 216 6967) directly opposite.

Next to the Mezopotamya is *Zeus Camping* (☎ (416) 725 5695, fax 725 5696), charging US$8 for a two-person site. A new hotel is under construction here as well.

At the junction with the Nemrut road is the *Hotel Kommagene* (☎ (416) 725 1092, fax 725 5548), PK 4, a converted house with flyscreens on the windows, and lots of Turkish carpets and kilims to lend atmosphere. It charges US$10/16 a single/double with bath for its much used and very basic rooms. The hotel has a bar and a camping area.

The *Nemrut Family Pension*, across the

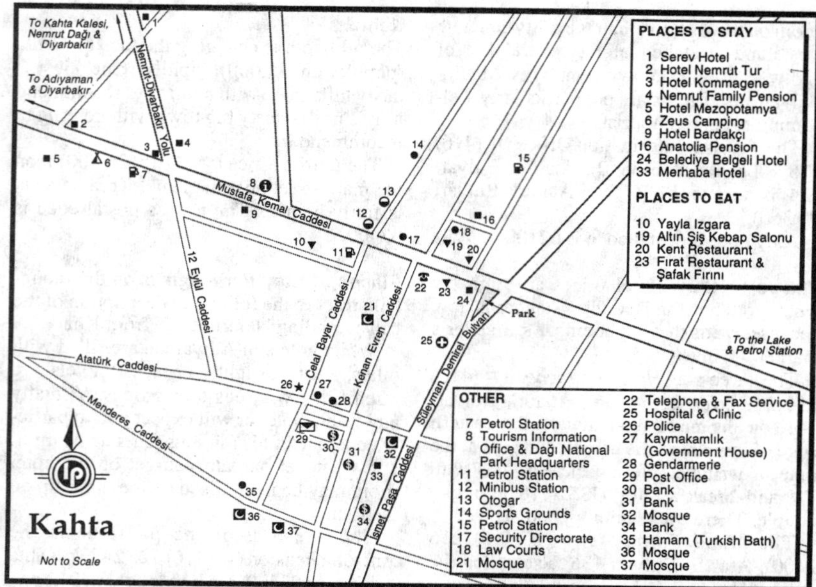

Nemrut road from the Kommagene, is an alternative to the motels at slightly lower prices.

The *Hotel Bardakçı* under construction on Mustafa Kemal Caddesi in the town centre hopes to get a four-star rating after it's finished.

Places to Eat The *Kent Restaurant*, on the north side of Mustafa Kemal Caddesi in the centre of town, has been here for years and still turns out decent, cheap fare at low prices. To the east is the similar *Özen*, and to the west the more modern *Yudum* (☎ 725 5245), Mustafa Kemal Caddesi 23. At any of these, two plates of food and a drink cost about US$3.50.

Getting There & Away Dolmuşes run between Kahta and Adıyaman (35 km, 30 minutes, US$1.75) throughout the day.

Two direct buses run daily between Kahta and Malatya (225 km, three hours, US$7); or change at Adıyaman.

The road east to Diyarbakır was flooded by the lake formed behind the Atatürk Dam. A slow, small and infrequent car ferry bridges the gap on the road east of Kahta to Siverek, but most buses circumvent the southern shores of the lake on new roads.

Should you decide to take the slow ferries eastward, you will enter that fabled cradle of civilisation, the watershed of the Tigris (Dicle, DEEJ-leh) and Euphrates (Fırat, fuh-RAHT) rivers. The partly submerged highway east from Kahta goes via Akıncılar and Çaylarbaşı to the east-west highway (53 km). Turn right (west) at the highway for Şanlıurfa, 70 km from the junction; or left (east) for 23 km to Siverek and another 116 km to Diyarbakır, a total distance of 192 km.

Ascending Nemrut Dağı from Kahta

Whichever way you go to the summit, you might want to pack a bottle of water and some snacks such as dried fruit, biscuits and nuts, as the round-trip journey can take between four and six hours and services along the way are limited. Plan on spending between one and 1½ hours driving (or riding) for the outward trip from Kahta to the summit. The return trip takes almost as long. Add to these two or three hours of sightseeing at the various sites.

Tour Scams In past years, Kahta earned quite a reputation as a rip-off town, but recently some citizens have been making significant efforts to improve its treatment of tourists.

Once known for their shady practices, Kahta's minibus and taxi drivers are now moving toward respectability. No longer do they remove the road signs on the road to Nemrut in order to make it difficult for tourists to get up the mountain in their own cars. Only now and then do they tell them that they won't be able to make it in their car, and they need to hire a minibus instead.

Even the old bait-and-switch game may soon go out of fashion. In this game, you'd agree with a minibus driver on a tour price and a departure time to get to the summit by sunrise. At the appointed time, the driver wouldn't appear, but another driver *just happened* to be waiting across the street from your hotel and would take you up for twice the price.

Let's hope that the 'new' Kahta continues to treat visitors with the kind of hospitality that's so easily found in other Turkish towns.

Minibus Tours The short tour (60 km, six hours, US$35 per group) takes you from Kahta to the summit, allows you about an hour there and stops at Eski Kale (Arsameia) on the way down to Kahta again.

The long or complete tour (eight hours, 70 km, US$45 per group) takes you to the summit, and on the trip down stops at Eski Kale, Yeni Kale (next to Kahta Kalesi) and Karakuş.

These prices are per group (not per person) for up to 10 in a minibus. Fares in a taxi are about US$12 less.

Though sunrise and sunset are popular times to be at the summit, either one condemns you to a long ride in the dark. I recommend going in the middle of the day when it's warmer and you can enjoy the scenery in both directions.

Private Car You can easily make the trip on your own using the map in this guidebook. Make sure you have fuel for at least 200 or 250 km of normal driving. Though the trip to the summit and back is only about 125 km, much of that will be driven in low gear, which uses more fuel.

Karakuş Highway D20360 marked for Nemrut Dağı Milli Parkı (Mt Nimrod National Park, nine km) and Sincik (36 km) leaves Kahta next to the Hotel Kommagene. Along the way this once purely agricultural landscape has become a busy oil field with nodding pumps, storage tanks and earthmoving equipment.

The Mt Nimrod National Park is entered at Karakuş, 10 km from Kahta, via a road to the left off the highway. The Karakuş hilltop, like that on Nemrut, is artificial, created to hold the graves of royal ladies of Commagene. A black eagle *(karakuş)* tops one of the several columns marking the site. The summit of Nemrut is clearly if distantly visible from Karakuş; it's the highest point on the horizon to the north-east.

Highway D 360 descends into the river valley to cross it. Follow the highway to go directly to the summit of Nemrut in the shortest possible time. For other sites, stay on the old road marked for Cendere and Kahta Kalesi.

Cendere & Kahta Kalesi Nineteen km from Kahta and five km before Kahta Kalesi, the road crosses the **Roman bridge** at Cendere, built in honour of Emperor Septimius Severus (194-211 AD), his wife and sons, long after Commagene had become part of Roman Asia. Of the four original columns (two at either end), three are still standing. Some historians think that the missing column was removed by one of the sons, Caracalla, when he murdered the other son, Geta, in 212.

As you leave the bridge, there should be a sign pointing to the right for Nemrut Dağı and Gerger; the road to the left is for Kahta Kalesi.

You approach Kahta Kalesi along the valley of a stream called the Kahta Çayı. Opposite the village are the ruins of a 14th-century Mameluke castle, now called **Yeni Kale** (yeh-NEE kah-leh, New Fortress), which you can explore. It bears some Arabic inscriptions; the Mamelukes were originally a Turkic people, but they were assimilated into Egyptian society.

Several decades ago the only way to reach the summit of Nemrut was to walk. You can still engage a guide in Kahta Kalesi to lead you up a trail to the summit if you like.

Eski Kale (Arsameia) About a km up the road from Kahta Kalesi, a road to the left takes you the two km to Eski Kale, the ancient Commagene capital of Arsameia. Admission costs US$1.25. Walk up the path from the car park and you'll come to a large stele with a figure (maybe female) on it. Further along are two more stelae, a monumental staircase and, behind them, an opening in the rock leading down to a cistern.

Another path leads from the first path to the striking stone relief which portrays the founder of Commagene, Mithridates I Callinicus, shaking hands with the god Heracles. Next to it is a long inscription in Greek and to the right is a tunnel descending through the rock. The locals will tell you the tunnel goes all the way to the valley floor below, though it has not yet been cleared of the centuries of rubble. Archaeologists believe it is a dead-end.

Above the relief on the level top of the hill are the foundations of Mithridates' capital city. The view is magnificent from here. If you stop at Arsameia on your way down from Nemrut, this is the perfect site for a picnic.

Eski Kale to Karadut Three km upward from Eski Kale is Damlacık.

The next settlements are Kuştepe (seven km), then Tüten Ocak (three km). After Narince the road becomes rougher and steeper. Another seven km east of Narince is a turn-off to the left marked for Nemrut, which you want to take; to continue straight on would take you to the village of Gerger.

Continue up the mountain five km to the hamlet of Karadut, which has a few small eateries and Mehmet Çınar's *Karadut Motel* renting rooms for US$4, and offering home-cooked meals as well. At the upper end of Karadut village is the *Karadut Kamping & Restaurant*. If you stay you'll have to take a minibus from Karadut to reach the summit. A passing minibus may charge US$2 or more; to rent an entire minibus for a trip to the summit and back to Karadut costs about US$20.

North of Karadut, the last half-hour's travel (12 km) to the summit is on a steep road paved in black basalt blocks and still fairly rough. There are two lodging places along the road. The 30-room *Hotel Euphrat* (☎ (416) 737 2175, fax 737 2179), 9.5 km from the summit, charges US$17 per person for bed, breakfast and dinner. The *Hotel Nymphaios* behind it (same phone) is similar. The *Zeus Motel*, a mountain inn seven km below the summit, has been closed for years.

At the Summit You're well above treeline when you climb the final ridge and pull into the car park at the summit. Just up from the car park is a building with toilets, and a café for snacks and hot tea, soft drinks and souvenirs. The staff runs a very basic pansiyon here for US$5 to US$7 per person with electric heat (so they say). The attendants don't seem to mind if you park a camper van in the car park overnight, or if you camp discreetly (remember: it's cold). This permissive attitude may change if lots of people camp at the same time.

Beyond the building is the pyramid of stones; it's a hike of less than one km (15 or 20 minutes) over the broken rock to the western temple. Sometimes donkeys are on hand to carry you, but this is not much help since staying on the donkey is almost as difficult as negotiating the rocks on your own. Admission to the archaeological site costs US$3.50.

Antiochus I Epiphanes ordered the construction of a hierothesium, or combination tomb and temple here:

I, great King Antiochus, have ordered the construction of these temples, the ceremonial road, and the thrones of the gods, on a foundation which will never be demolished...I have done this to prove my faith in the gods. At the end of my life I will enter my eternal rest here, and my spirit will join that of Zeus-Ahura Mazda in heaven.

Approaching from the car park, you see first the western temple and behind it the conical tumulus, or funerary mound, of fist-sized stones.

At the western temple, Antiochus and his fellow gods sit in state, though the bodies have mostly been tumbled down along with the heads. But at the eastern temple the bodies are largely intact, except for the fallen heads, which seem more badly weathered than the western heads. On the backs of the eastern statues are inscriptions in Greek.

Both terraces have similar plans, with the syncretistic gods, the 'ancestors' of Antiochus, seated in this order, from left to right: first is Apollo, the sun god – Mithra to the Persians, Helios or Hermes to the Greeks; next is Fortuna, or Tyche; in the centre is Zeus-Ahura Mazda; to the right is King Antiochus; and at the right end is Heracles, also known as Ares or Artagnes. The seated figures are several metres high; their heads alone, about two metres tall.

Low walls at the sides of each temple once held carved reliefs showing royal processions of ancient Persia and Greece, Antiochus' 'predecessors'. Statues of eagles represent Zeus.

The flat space next to the eastern temple, with an 'H' at its centre, is a helipad which accepts the arrival of the wealthy, the important and the fortunate. It stands on the site of an ancient altar. In the valley below, about three km from the summit, is the *Güneş Hotel*, of use mostly to those coming up Nemrut from Malatya. The Güneş charges US$18 per person for bed and breakfast, with supper and a hot shower included.

MALATYA

Going from Adıyaman via Gölbaşı to Malatya (mah-LAHT-yah, population 285,000, altitude 964m), the highway crosses the **Reşadiye Pass** (Reşadiye Geçidi; 1510m) and passes through a dramatic rock-bound gorge before descending to Malatya, a modern town grown large and rich on agriculture. This is the apricot *(kayısı)* capital of Turkey, and after the late-June harvest thousands of tonnes of the luscious fruit are shipped throughout the world. Almost as good are Malatya's cherries, which are harvested from early to mid-June. The citizens of Malatya celebrate the end of the harvest with an apricot festival in July.

Malatya offers an alternative way of approaching Nemrut Dağı. Otherwise its claim to fame is as the birthplace of İsmet İnönü (Atatürk's right-hand man and successor) and Mehmet Ali Ağca (who shot Pope John Paul II).

History

Malatya has stood at the crossroads of major trade routes since Neolithic times. There was an early Assyrian settlement here, and a Hittite one also. After the fall of the Hittite Empire, various city-states emerged, among them Milidia (or Maldia), a name preserved for over 3000 years and now pronounced Malatya.

The Assyrians and Persians conquered the city alternately, and later the kings of Cappadocia and Pontus did the same. In 66 BC Pompey defeated Mithridates and took the town, then known as Melita, and later as Melitene. The Byzantines, Sassanids, Arabs and Danışmend emirs held it for a time until the coming of the Seljuks in 1105. Then came the Ottomans (1399), the armies of Tamerlane (1401), the Mamelukes, the Dülkadır emirs and the Ottomans again (1515).

When the forces of Egypt's Mohammed Ali invaded Anatolia in 1839, the Ottoman forces garrisoned Malatya, leaving it in ruins upon their departure. Later the residents who had fled the war returned and established a new city at Malatya's present site.

Orientation

Malatya stretches for many km along İnönü/Atatürk Caddesi, its main street. Hotels, restaurants, banks and other services

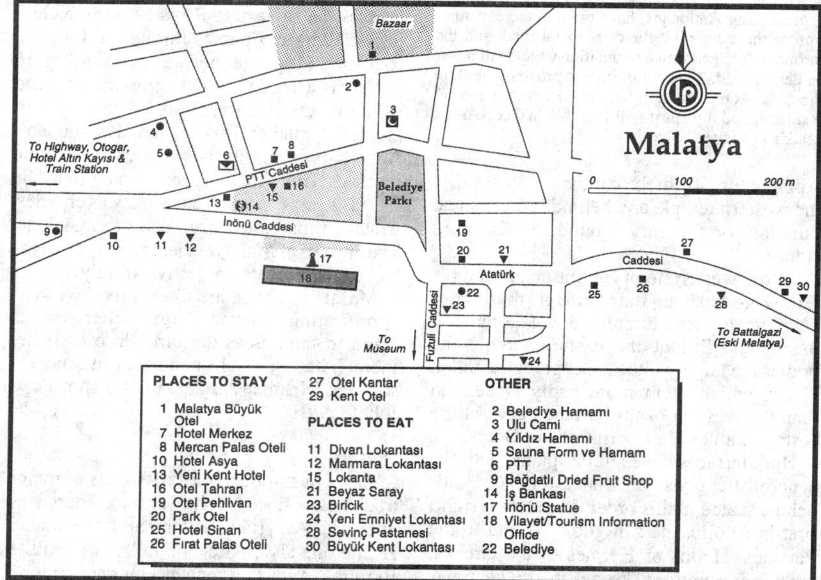

are near the main square with its statue of İnönü, the Vilayet building and the Belediye (Municipality) nearby. The Belediye Parkı, on the north side of İnönü Caddesi opposite the İnönü statue, is a convenient landmark.

A new otogar about six km west of the centre, just off the highway, may have come into use by the time you read this. If so, the old otogar will have become a terminal for dolmuş services which, at present, stop and start all over the place.

The train station *(istasyon)* is also on the outskirts, several km west of the centre. City buses and dolmuşes marked 'Vilayet' operate between the station and the centre.

Information

The Tourism Information Office (☎ (422) 323 3025) is on the ground floor of the Vilayet building and is open daily from June to October from 8 am to 5 pm. In winter it closes at weekends.

There is also a small tourist information office in the otogar, where a tourism official will be on hand to urge you to sign up for a tour to the top of Nemrut Dağı (for details see Tours to Nemrut Dağı later in this section).

Old Malatya

Eleven km north of the centre at Battalgazi are the remains of Old Malatya (Eski Malatya), the walled city inhabited from early times until the 19th century.

The modern Turkish village of Battalgazi has grown up in and around the ruined but still impressive **city walls** with their 95 towers. The walls have lost all their facing stone to other building projects, and apricot orchards now fill what were once city blocks, but it's easy to see that this was once a great city.

The **Ulu Cami** (1224), on the main square, is a Seljuk work dating from the reign of Alaettin Keykubat I. The **Silahtar Mustafa Paşa Hanı** (caravanserai) on the main square is a recently restored Ottoman work dating from the 17th century.

Bus No 3 or 4 to Battalgazi will take you there.

Malatya Museum

The Malatya Müzesi, open from 8 am to 5 pm (closed Monday), is almost a km from the centre. Walk down Fuzuli Caddesi and turn left and immediately right at the end. Admission costs US$1. There's some English labelling.

The collection covers everything from the Palaeolithic, Chalcolithic and Old Bronze Age through to Roman and Byzantine times, with finds from the excavations at Arslantepe and also from the Lower Euphrates Project, a rescue mission conducted by the Middle East Technical University (Ankara) and İstanbul University in the Euphrates valley before the Keban Dam flooded it in the 1960s. The ethnography section upstairs may or may not be open when you get there.

Bazaar

Malatya has a particularly vibrant bazaar which sprawls north from PTT Caddesi and the Malatya Büyük hotel. There's a large undercover area which is fascinating provided you're not too squeamish or concerned about fish rights, and an even livelier metal-working area where you must watch out for welders in the middle of the road. Souvenirs are thin on the ground, although you can pick up some fine baskets or packeted *mercimek* (lentils).

Hamams

The men-only Historical Municipal Bath with Sauna (Tarihi Saunalı Belediye Hamamı) faces the Malatya Büyük Otel. The modern Sauna Form ve Hamam and the Yıldız Hamamı are on a side street near the PTT. A small women's bath is tucked away behind the Belediye. A simple bath costs US$2, and more still if you have massages etc.

Tours to Nemrut Dağı

The tourist office organises minibus tours (daily from April to mid-October) which seem to be hassle free. Have your overnight gear with you and meet at the front door of the office at 11.30 am any day (even on weekends when the office is closed).

The minibus comes and picks you up at noon for the four-hour ride up Nemrut through dramatic scenery. The last 30 km of road is unpaved, but it goes right to the summit, closer than the road from Kahta. After enjoying the sunset for two hours, you descend two km to the *Güneş Hotel*, where you have dinner and spend the night. In the morning, you take the minibus to the summit for sunrise before returning to the hotel for breakfast, then to Malatya, arriving around 10 am.

The cost per person is US$22, including transport, dinner, bed and breakfast, and you pay another US$3.50 for admission to the national park. Some readers have negotiated a transport-only fare, and taken a sleeping bag and food to the summit with them. If you want to do this, remember that the mornings are freezing cold even in July.

If you prefer to descend via Kahta, hike across the summit to the car park and café building, and ask around for a minibus with an empty seat; or hitch a ride with a tourist going down to Kahta.

Places to Stay – bottom end

Malatya's quietest hotels tend to be the oldest ones with the least inviting rooms along PTT Caddesi. Conversely, the better rooms are mainly in the hotels along Atatürk Caddesi, where you'll need one at the back to escape the traffic noise.

For rock-bottom budgets there's the grubby *Mercan Palas Oteli* (☎ (422) 312 1570), PTT Caddesi 14, which charges just US$5 a double for waterless rooms. Women travelling alone might feel very conspicuous here. The *Merkez, Özer* and *Tahran* nearby are similar.

Noisier but more cheerful is the *Park Otel* (☎ (422) 321 1691) on Atatürk Caddesi across from the Belediye. Doubles here cost US$7 without a shower and US$9 with shower.

Otel Kantar (☎ (422) 321 1510), Atatürk Caddesi 81, has only bathless rooms, but the staff are friendly and a double room with sink costs US$7. The *Otel Pehlivan* (☎ (422) 321 2609), Cumhuriyet Caddesi 26, is run by the same people and costs the same.

On the opposite side of the road to the Otel Kantar is the old-fashioned *Fırat Palas Oteli* (☎ (422) 321 1241), Atatürk Caddesi 30, with doubles for US$6.

Readers have also recommended the *Hotel Asya* (☎ (422) 321 4717) on İnönü Caddesi. The rooms here are nothing special but are certainly cheap at US$4/6 a single/double with bath. The Asya's big plus is that its English-speaking owner Abuzer Fırat used to be a guide on Nemrut Daği and is a mine of useful information on how to do it properly. The Asya is often full so it might be wise to ring ahead.

Places to Stay – middle

Perhaps the best deal in town is the two-star, 52-room *Malatya Büyük Otel* (☎ (422) 321 1400, fax 321 5367), facing the Yeni Cami, a block north of the Belediye Parkı, which looks more expensive than it actually is. All the rooms have baths and some have TVs but rates can go as low as US$13/19 a single/double, breakfast included, when it's quiet. Despite its position in the bazaar this is likely to be one of the quieter places to stay.

The other star-rated hotels are on Atatürk Caddesi, east of the Vilayet. The one-star, 55-room *Hotel Sinan* (☎ (422) 321 2907) has eight floors, a lift and a bar, and charges from US$8/13 a single/double. The more expensive rooms have private baths and more amenities. Being right on the main street, the front rooms suffer from noise.

A bit farther east on the opposite side of the road is the one-star, 50-room *Kent Otel* (☎ (422) 321 2175, fax 312 2813) which charges US$13/16 a single/double, subject to haggling when it's quiet. The same people also own the *Yeni Kent Otel* (☎ (422) 321 1053, fax 324 9243) on PTT Caddesi where newer rooms justify higher prices: US$18 a single and US$24 a double. The décor is pleasingly modern (although the carpet stains are already accumulating), but you'd better ask for a room on the PTT (front) side to escape street noise. Breakfasts here are big enough to suit an apricot trader's stomach... and include apricots, of course!

Places to Stay – top end

The new four-star *Hotel Altın Kayısı* (☎ (422) 238 3232, fax 238 0083) is at the top of İstasyon Caddesi where it meets Buhara Bulvarı. Externally it's nothing to write home about, but inside the rooms are big and modern, with TVs, fridges and air-con. There's a restaurant and bar, and plenty of parking space at the front. The rather remote situation also ensures that it's quieter than other choices in the town centre. Singles here cost US$50, doubles US$70 and the three suites US$120.

Places to Eat

At PTT Caddesi 29 next to the Otel Tahran is *Lokanta*. It's clean, white and shiny bright, a modern, upmarket, proper place for Malatya's business community. The food is good and moderately priced; no alcohol is served.

On İnönü Caddesi across from the İş Bankası, the *Marmara* and *Güngör* restaurants specialise in fluorescent lighting, quick service and good, cheap food. The Marmara is most pleasant, but at either place you can fill up for US$3 or less.

On Atatürk Caddesi, near the Park Otel, the popular *Beyaz Saray* serves excellent İskender kebap for less than US$2. There's a choice of ready meals as well. A few doors uphill from the Kent Otel at Atatürk Caddesi 137 is the even more popular *Büyük Kent Lokantası*. It's excellent for soups and stews as well as döner kebap. Meals cost between US$3 and US$6.

Malatyans seem to have sweeter teeth than other Turks and the town positively creaks with tempting cake shops. One such is the *Sevinç Pastanesi*, opposite the Otel Kantar on Atatürk Caddesi, where gleaming showcases are stuffed with all sorts of sweet treats. Another is the *Biricik* on Fuzuli Caddesi which does Paris-quality coffee and cake for nothing like Paris-style prices. It's handily placed for a stop en route to or from the museum.

Yeni Emniyet Lokantası, south behind the

Belediye, is Malatya's old standby for drinking, eating and talking. The ground-floor dining room is a bit like a train station waiting room, but there's a nicer room upstairs and a roof terrace as well. Hundreds of bottles of rakı stand ready behind the bar. Food is good and service eager; meals cost from US$6 to US$10, more if you drink a lot.

Atatürk Caddesi is lined with dried-fruit shops selling baskets of apricots and other dried fruits with nuts and snacks, both sweet and salty.

Getting There & Away

Air Turkish Airlines (☎ (422) 321 1922), Kanalboyu Caddesi 10, Orduevi Karşısı, has one nonstop flight daily between Malatya's Erhaç airport and Ankara, with connections to İstanbul and İzmir. The airport bus costs US$1.50 and leaves the Turkish Airlines office 90 minutes before flight departure time.

Bus Malatya's new otogar is on the western outskirts of the city, but some services will continue to operate from the old otogar closer into town for some time yet. Dolmuş minibuses (US$0.25) run between the otogars and various points around the town centre.

Malatya bus services include daily trips to the following destinations:

Adana – 425 km, eight hours, US$7; a few buses
Adıyaman – 190 km, three hours, US$3; frequent buses
Ankara – 685 km, 11 hours, US$12; frequent buses
Diyarbakır – 260 km, four hours, US$6; frequent buses
Gaziantep – 250 km, four hours, US$5; a few buses
Elaziğ – 101 km, 1½ hours, US$2; a few buses
İstanbul – 1130 km, 18 hours, US$20; a few buses
Kahta – 225 km, three hours, US$3; two morning buses
Kayseri – 354 km, six hours, US$8; several buses
Sivas – 235 km, five hours, US$7; several buses

Train Malatya's station can be reached by dolmuş (US$0.25) or by 'İstasyon' city bus from the Belediye Parkı.

The city is served daily by express train from İstanbul (Haydarpaşa) and Ankara via Kayseri and Sivas. On Monday, Wednesday and Friday it's the *Vangölü Ekspresi* to Tatvan; on other days it's the *Güney Ekspresi*, heading east for Diyarbakır and Kurtalan. See Getting There & Away in the Ankara section of the Central Anatolia chapter for details.

There are also daily services to Elaziğ but these are likely to be slower than the bus. The 1st-class-only *Mavi Tren* to Ankara also passes through Malatya.

ŞANLIURFA

Dry, dusty and hot – this is the way Şanlıurfa (population 295,000, altitude 518m) appears at first glance. You may think, 'What importance could such a town in the middle of nowhere possibly have?'. When you get to know Urfa (as it's commonly called), you'll find that it's known for a shady park with several pools and great religious significance, a richness of agricultural produce, a cool and inviting labyrinthine bazaar, and its great historical importance.

Urfa gives a mixture of impressions. In the shadow of a mighty medieval fortress, grey-bearded men toss chickpeas into a pool full of sacred carp or gather at a cave said to be the birthplace of the patriarch Abraham. In the cool darkness of the covered bazaar, shopkeepers sit on low platforms in front of their stores, as was the custom in Ottoman times. The chatter of Turkish is joined by a babble of Kurdish and Arabic, with the occasional bit of English, French or German.

You must spend at least one night in Urfa and a full day, or at least a morning, to see the sights and get lost in the bazaar. You may also want to make an excursion south to Harran, the biblical town of beehive houses near the Syrian frontier.

History

The mysterious laws of geography ruled that this dusty spot would be where great empires clashed again and again over the centuries. Far from Cairo, Tehran and Constantinople, Urfa was nevertheless where the armies, directed from those distant capitals, would often meet. Urfa's history, then, is one of wreckage.

Urfa has been sizzling in the sun for a long time. It is thought that more than 3500 years ago there was a fortress on the hill where the kale now stands. Called Hurri (Cave) by the

Babylonians, the people built a powerful state by military conquest simply because they knew what a chariot was and how to use it in battle (few of their neighbours had heard of the chariot). But the Hittites finally got the better of the Hurrites, despite the latter's alliance with the Pharaohs of Egypt. Around 1370 BC, the Hittites took over. After the fall of Hattuşaş, Urfa came under the domination of Carchemish.

The alliance with Egypt produced an interesting cultural exchange. After Amenhotep IV (Akhenaton) popularised the worship of the sun as the unique and only god, a similar worship of Shemesh (the sun) was taken up here. Sun worship (one would think it might be shade worship instead!) was not just a religious belief, but a political posture. Thus Urfa defied the cultural, political and religious influence of the nearby Hittites, by adopting the customs of the Egyptians, who were a safe distance away.

After a period of Assyrian rule, Alexander the Great came through. He and his Macedonian mates named the town Edessa, after a former capital of Macedonia, and it remained the capital of a Seleucid province until 132 BC when the local Aramaean population set up an independent kingdom and renamed the town Orhai. Though Orhai maintained a precarious independence for four centuries, bowing only slightly to the Armenians and Parthians, it finally succumbed to the Romans, as did everyone hereabouts. The Romans did not get it easily, however. Emperor Valerian was badly defeated here in 260 AD and subsequent Roman rulers had a hard time over the centuries keeping the Persians out.

Edessa pursued its contrary history (witness the sun worship) by adopting Christianity at a very early time (circa 200 AD), before it became the official religion of the conquerors. The religion was so new that for Edessan Christians the liturgical language was Aramaic, the language of Jesus and not the Greek on which the church's greatness was built. Edessa, having pursued Christianity on its own from earliest times, had its own patriarch. It revelled in the Nestorian monophysite heresies as yet another way to thumb its nose at its faraway rulers, whose armies so often trooped through and flattened everything.

Edessa was at the outer edge of the Roman Empire near the frontier with Persia, and as the two great empires clashed, Edessa was shuttled back and forth from one to the other, as in a tug-of-war. In 533 AD the two empires signed a Treaty of Endless Peace which lasted seven years. The Romans and Persians kept at it until the Arabs swept in and cleared them all out in 637 AD. Edessa enjoyed three centuries of blissful peace under the Arabs, after which everything went to blazes again.

Turks, Arabs, Armenians and Byzantines battled for Edessa from 944 until 1098, when the First Crusade under Count Baldwin of Boulogne arrived to set up the Latin County of Edessa. This odd European feudal state lasted until 1144 when it was conquered by a Seljuk Turkish emir. The 'loss' of Edessa infuriated the pope, who called for the Second Crusade, which never set foot near Edessa and accomplished little except to discredit itself. But the Latin county made its mark in history by giving Europeans a look at Eastern architecture and some of what they saw turned up later in the Gothic style.

The Seljuk Turkish emir, from the Zengi family, was succeeded by Saladin, then by the Mamelukes. The Ottomans under Selim the Grim conquered most of this region in the early 16th century, but Edessa did not become Urfa until 1637 when the Ottomans finally took over.

As for its modern sobriquet, Urfa became Şanlıurfa (Glorious Urfa) a little more than a decade ago. Even since 1973, when Heroic Antep was given its special name, the good citizens of Urfa have been chafing under a relative loss of dignity. Now that their city is 'Glorious', the inhabitants can look the citizens of 'Heroic' Antep straight in the eye.

Orientation

Except for inside the bazaar, it is fairly easy to find your way around Urfa. You will see the fortress (kale) to the right (south) as you enter the town along the highway from

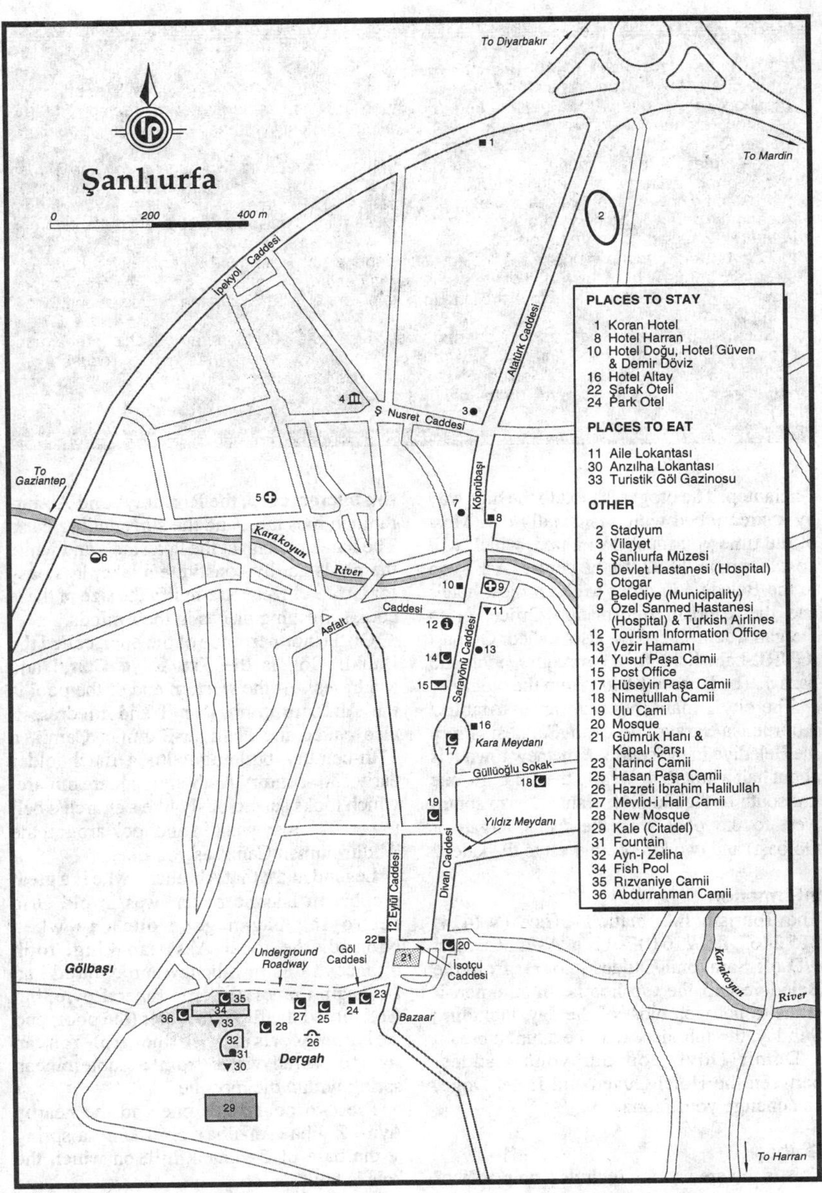

Şanlıurfa
0
200
400 m
To Diyarbakır
To Mardin
To Gaziantep
To Harran
İpekyol Caddesi
Atatürk Caddesi
Ş Nusret Caddesi
Köprübaşı
Karakoyun River
Asfalt Caddesi
Sarayönü Caddesi
Kara Meydanı
Güllüoğlu Sokak
Yıldız Meydanı
Divan Caddesi
12 Eylül Caddesi
Underground Roadway
Göl Caddesi
İsotçu Caddesi
Gölbaşı
Bazaar
Dergah
Karakoyun River
PLACES TO STAY
1 Koran Hotel
8 Hotel Harran
10 Hotel Doğu, Hotel Güven & Demir Döviz
16 Hotel Altay
22 Şafak Oteli
24 Park Otel
PLACES TO EAT
11 Aile Lokantası
30 Anzılha Lokantası
33 Turistik Göl Gazinosu
OTHER
2 Stadyum
3 Vilayet
4 Şanlıurfa Müzesi
5 Devlet Hastanesi (Hospital)
6 Otogar
7 Belediye (Municipality)
9 Özel Sanmed Hastanesi (Hospital) & Turkish Airlines
12 Tourism Information Office
13 Vezir Hamamı
14 Yusuf Paşa Camii
15 Post Office
17 Hüseyin Paşa Camii
18 Nimetulllah Camii
19 Ulu Cami
20 Mosque
21 Gümrük Hanı & Kapalı Çarşı
23 Narinci Camii
25 Hasan Paşa Camii
26 Hazreti İbrahim Halilullah
27 Mevlid-i Halil Camii
28 New Mosque
29 Kale (Citadel)
31 Fountain
32 Ayn-i Zeliha
34 Fish Pool
35 Rızvaniye Camii
36 Abdurrahman Camii

South-East Anatolia Project (GAP)

Urfa's character is changing as the South-East Anatolia Project (GAP) comes on line, bringing irrigation waters to large arid regions and generating enormous amounts of hydroelectricity for industry. Parched valleys have become fish-filled lakes and dusty villages are becoming booming market towns, factory cities or lakeside resorts.

The project is truly gigantic, greatly affecting eight provinces and two huge rivers, the Tigris and Euphrates. By the year 2005 when completion of the project is envisioned, 22 dams and 19 hydroelectric power plants will have been built. Three million hectares of land will be newly under irrigation. There will be new employment opportunities for 1.8 million people; per capita income in the region is expected to double.

The Atatürk Dam, keystone of the project, is capable of generating 8.9 billion kilowatt-hours of electricity annually from the runoff of the vast lake (817 sq km, 162m deep) which its construction created. One element in the project, the Urfa Irrigation Tunnel is, at 26 km, the longest such tunnel in the world.

Such a huge project, capable of enormous success, can also generate sizable problems, especially ecological ones. The change from dry agriculture to wet has already caused an explosion of infectious disease. Incidence of malaria has increased tenfold, and it is feared that diarrhoea and dysentery, already on the rise, will follow suit. ■

Gaziantep. The otogar is next to the highway by a stream bed which is usually dry. Most of the time you must take a taxi, which will cost less than US$2, to the centre. Ask to go to the Belediye in order to reach most hotels and the Tourism Information Office, or to Dergah (dehr-GYAH), also called Gölbaşı (GURL-bah-shuh), for the mosques, pools and bazaar. The latter is 1.5 km from the otogar.

The city's main thoroughfare is Atatürk/Köprübaşu/Sarayönü/Divan Caddesi. From the Belediye in the centre of the new town it is about half a km north-west to the museum, one km south to the Gümrük Hanı, 1.5 km south-west to the pool with the fish (Dergah or Gölbaşı) and two km south-west to the kale.

Information

The Tourism Information Office (☎ (414) 215 2467, fax 216 0170) is at Asfalt Caddesi 4/D off Sarayönü Caddesi, not far from the Belediye and the top hotels. In summer, it tends to be open most of the day, including Sunday, though there may be a lunch break.

Demir Döviz, on Sarayönü Caddesi between the Hotel Güven and Hotel Doğu, can change your money.

Gölbaşı

This is the area which includes the **pools of the sacred carp**, the Rızvaniye and Abdurrahman mosques, and the surrounding park. The name means 'at the lakeside', and while the pools hardly constitute a lake, it is easy for Urfa's citizens to amplify the size of these cool, refreshing places in their minds.

On the northern side of the pool, called the Balıklı Göl, is the **Rızvaniye Camii** and Medresesi. At the western end of the pool is the **Abdurrahman Camii** and Medresesi, also called the Halil ur-Rahman Camii, a 17th-century building with a much older early 13th-century Arab-style square minaret which looks suspiciously like a church's bell tower. You may walk in and look around the Abdurrahman Camii as you like.

Legend had it that Abraham, who is a great prophet in Islamic belief, was in old Urfa destroying pagan gods one day when Nimrod, the local Assyrian king, took offence at this rash behaviour. Nimrod had Abraham immolated on a funeral pyre, but God turned the fire into water (the pool) and the burning coals into fish (the carp). You can sip the sacred water from a subterranean spring within the mosque.

The two pools, this one and the nearby Ayn-i Zeliha (Anzılha), are fed by a spring at the base of Damlacık hill, on which the kale is built.

Local legend makers have had a field day with the fish in the pool, deciding that they are sacred to Abraham and must not be caught lest the catcher go blind. You can buy food for the fish from vendors at the poolside, even though signs say, 'In the interests of the fishes' health, it is requested that they not be fed'.

Instead of feeding the fish, take a seat at a shady table in one of the tea gardens and have a cool drink or bracing glass of çay to ward off the heat of the day. (Hot tea will make you perspire, thus cooling you down.)

Dergah

The area called Dergah, to the south-east of the pools and the park, is a complex of mosques and parks surrounding the **Prophet Abraham's Birth Cave** (Hazreti İbrahimğin Doğum Mağarası) in which, legend has it, the Prophet Abraham was born. There are separate entrances for men and women, as it is a place of pilgrimage and prayer. A new, large, Ottoman-style mosque stands to the west of the birth cave to supplement the smaller prayer places.

Next door to the birth cave is a complex of mosques and medreses called **Prophet Abraham, Friend of God** (Hazreti İbrahim Halilullah), built and rebuilt over the centuries as an active place of pilgrimage. To the east, on Göl Caddesi, is the **Hasan Paşa Camii**, an Ottoman work.

The **Mevlid-i Halil Camii** holds the tomb of a saint named Dede Osman.

All of these places are open for visits, but as they are places of prayer and worship, and this is a Muslim-conservative city, you should be neatly and modestly dressed, and should go quietly and decorously.

Fortress

Depending upon your reference source, the fortress on Damlacık hill was built either during Hellenistic times, or by the Byzantines or during the crusades or by the Turks. No doubt all are true, as one could hardly have a settlement here without having a fortress, and it was normal for fortresses to be built and rebuilt over the centuries. In any case, it is vast and can be reached by a cascade of stairs.

You enter between a pair of columns which local legend has dubbed the Throne of Nemrut after the supposed founder of Urfa, the biblical King Nimrod (Genesis 10: 8-10). Once inside the kale precincts, where there is little to see, you will confront the possibility of broiling in the sun while your fellow travellers are resting in the cool shade of the park by the pools.

Bazaar

Urfa's bazaar is less than 500m east of the pools. The first place to visit is the old

The bazaar at Şanlıurfa has changed little in several centuries. It reveals dozens of fascinating scenes from traditional life.

Gümrük Hanı, or customs depot, an ancient caravanserai. To the left (south) of the caravanserai courtyard is the **Kapalı Çarşı**, or covered bazaar, which has not changed much in several centuries, except for some of the products.

After you've visited the Gümrük Hanı, just wander. Urfa's bazaar reveals dozens of fascinating scenes from traditional life.

Mosques
Urfa's **Ulu Cami** (Great Mosque) on Divan Caddesi dates from 1170-1175. It's a Syrian-style building with a spacious forecourt and 13 eyvans opening onto a spacious forecourt with a tall tower topped by a clock with Ottoman numerals.

At Kara Meydanı, the square midway between the Belediye and Dergah, is the **Hüseyin Paşa Camii**, a late-Ottoman work built in 1849.

Şanlıurfa Museum
Up the hill to the west of the Vilayet building, off Atatürk Caddesi, is the Şanlıurfa Müzesi, open from 8.30 am to noon and 1.30 to 5 pm daily (on Monday from 1.30 to 5 pm only). Admission costs US$1.50. Exhibits are labelled in Turkish and English.

Renovations in 1988 brought marble floors, good lighting and attractive exhibits. Surrounding the museum in its gardens are various sculptures, and on the porch as you enter are several mosaics, but only one is worth a look. Inside, noteworthy artefacts include neolithic implements, Assyrian, Babylonian and Hittite relief stones, and other objects from Byzantine, Seljuk and Ottoman times. Large photos and diagrams explain the use of many otherwise inscrutable objects.

Upstairs is the ethnology section, which is interesting, but exhibit labels are in Turkish only.

Prophet Job's Site
Otherwise known as Eyüp Peygamber Makamı, Prophet Job's Site is off the Harran road and is marked by signs. Visit free at any time. Eyüp (Job), standard-bearer of the Prophet Muhammed, passed through Urfa with the Arab armies riding into Anatolia to attack Constantinople. Local legend holds that he became ill here, but was cured (or at least made to feel a bit better) by drinking water from a spring on the outskirts of town. The spring is now in a grotto next to a mosque within a walled grove of evergreens.

Places to Stay
Most hotels are near the Belediye. There are no lodgings near the bus station.

The *Hotel Güven* (☎ (414) 313 1700, fax 215 9391), Sarayönü Caddesi 133, is a small, simple family place with rooms renting for US$14/18 a double without/with private shower – a bit overpriced. The nearby *Doğu Hotel* is much cheaper at US$6/9/11 a single/double/triple with shower.

Near the Özel Sanmed Hastanesi you'll find more choices. The *Hotel İpek Palas* (☎ (414) 215 1546), Köprübaşı 4/B, has doubles for US$9.50/12 without/with private showers.

Just around the corner is the *Cumhuriyet Palas* (☎ (414) 313 4828), Köprübaşı 6, which is also quiet, but cheaper.

Between Dergah and the centre of town is the modern shopping district. Just off the main street in a quiet location is *Otel İstiklal*, Sarayönü Caddesi, Zincirli Kapı 4/E. It has a vine-shaded courtyard and a small terrace restaurant. Its cool, fairly quiet rooms and usually hot showers cost US$9 a double.

Hotel Altay (☎ (414) 215 1917, fax 215 9252), on Sarayönü Caddesi at Kara Meydanı opposite the PTT, offers good value with its double rooms with shower but no toilet for US$13, or with toilet for US$18. Doubles with just sinks are US$10.

Urfa's traditional favourite is the three-star *Hotel Harran* (☎ (414) 313 4743, fax 313 4918), on Köprübaşu Caddesi, directly opposite the Belediye. All 54 rooms have air-con and private bathrooms, and some have TVs and refrigerators. The hotel also has a terrace restaurant and a Turkish bath. Rates are US$20/38 a single/double, or US$50 for a double with bathtub.

The three-star, 54-room *Koran Hotel*

(☎ (414) 313 1809, fax 312 1737), İpekyolu Caddesi 13/A-B, on the main highway, is the Harran's competition. It's nice enough, with air-con, minibars and TVs in the rooms, but the location is inconvenient for walking to town. Rates are US$20/38 a single/double.

Places to Eat

Caution Be very careful with your choice of food in Urfa. With the dramatic increase in waterbourne pathogens joining the traditional germ-incubating heat, Urfa is a holiday resort for microbes. Be sure all food is freshly and fully cooked.

Specialities Urfa's culinary specialities include çiğ köfte (minced uncooked mutton), a sure-fire recipe for gastrointestinal disaster in this hot climate. Indeed, with the coming of large-scale irrigation from the GAP project, professors at Tigris University predict a significant increase in the incidence of dysentery, malaria and other 'tropical' diseases. You must be especially careful of what you eat here. Be sure stews are fresh and hot, or have fully cooked grills or safe foods such as yoghurt or pilav instead.

Other Urfa specialities include içli köfte (a deep-fried croquette with a mutton filling) and Urfa kebap (skewered chunks of lamb or minced lamb rissoles – broiled on charcoal and served with tomatoes, sliced onions and hot peppers).

Restaurants The *Güney Lokantası* (☎ 215 2237) at Köprübaşı 3/D near the Hotel İpek Palas has ceiling fans to keep the hot air moving and refrigerated cases to keep the drinks cold. The location keeps the noise at bay, and the chef fills his steam table with various stews, vegetable dishes, pilavs and soups each day. A simple meal costs from US$2 to US$3.

The *Aile Lokantası*, a garden restaurant on Sarayönü Caddesi south of the Özel Sanmed Hastanesi, is more pleasant, more comfortable for women and not much more expensive.

Perhaps the most pleasant place for an inexpensive meal is in the park at Gölbaşı. The *Turistik Göl Gazinosu, Lokanta & Aile Çay Bahçesi* (Touristic Lake Club, Restaurant & Family Tea Garden), next to the Balıklı Göl, has a family dining area, a video cassette player and a prohibition against alcoholic beverages. We had domatesli kebap (köfte grilled with chunks of tomato and served with chopped scallions, grilled hot peppers and huge flaps of flat village bread). With a tankard of cool ayran, the cost was US$4. Tea is cheap, Turkish coffee costs twice as much and soft drinks three times as much as tea.

The *Hotel Harran* is the best place to dine. Service is attentive and polite, the food is good, alcoholic beverages are served and the open-air terrace at the back of the hotel several floors up is pleasant. A dinner of tavuk şiş (chicken brochettes), mixed salad, bread and beer costs around US$8 to US$10.

Getting There & Away

Air Turkish Airlines (☎ (414) 215 3344, fax 215 2001) at Kaliru Turizm Seyahat Acentesi, Sarayönü Caddesi 74/A, Köprübaşı, has nonstop flights to and from Ankara on Monday, Wednesday, Friday and Sunday, with continuing service to İstanbul and İzmir.

Bus The otogar has a restaurant, pastry shop and a left-luggage depot. As it is on the main highway serving the south-east, Urfa has plenty of bus traffic but most buses are passing through, so you must take whatever seats there are. Details of some daily services follow:

Adana – 365 km, six hours, US$12; several buses
Ankara – 850 km, 13 hours, US$20; several buses
Diyarbakır – 190 km, three hours, US$8; frequent buses
Erzurum – 665 km, 12 hours, US$20; a few buses
Gaziantep – 145 km, 2½ hours, US$7; frequent buses
İstanbul – 1290 km, 24 hours, US$40; a few buses
Kahta (for Nemrut Dağı) – 375 km, four hours, US$10; a few buses to Adıyaman, change for Kahta
Malatya – 395 km, seven hours, US$15; a few buses
Mardin – 175 km, three hours, US$9; several buses
Van – 585 km, 10 hours, US$22; a few buses

Train Although Urfa is supposedly served by train, the station is at Akçakale on the Syrian frontier, 50 km south of the town. Therefore, Urfa is best reached by bus.

HARRAN

And Terah took Abram his son, and Lot the son of Haran his son's son, and Sarai his daughter in law, his son Abram's wife; and they went forth with them from Ur of the Chaldees, to go into the land of Canaan; and they came unto Harran, and dwelt there.

Genesis 11: 31

So says the Bible about Harran's most famous resident, who stayed here for a few years back in 1900 BC. It seems certain that Harran, now officially called Altınbaşak, is one of the oldest continuously inhabited spots on earth. Its ruined walls and Ulu Cami, its crumbling fortress and beehive houses give it a feeling of deep antiquity.

Harran's ancient monuments are interesting, though not really impressive. It is more the lifestyle of the residents that you may find fascinating. They live by farming and smuggling, and now await the wealth expected to come with the development of the South-east Anatolia Project.

History

Besides being the place of Abraham's sojourn, Harran is famous as a centre of worship of Sin, god of the moon. Worship of the sun, moon and planets was popular in Harran and at neighbouring Sumatar, from about 800 BC until 830 AD, although Harran's temple to the moon god was destroyed by the Byzantine emperor Theodosius in 382 AD. Battles between Arabs and Byzantines amused the townsfolk until the coming of the crusaders. The fortress, which some say was built on the ruins of the moon god's temple, was restored when the Frankish crusaders approached. The crusaders won and maintained the fortress for a while before they too moved on.

Things to See

Before even reaching the town you'll see the hill surrounded by crumbling walls and topped with ruined buildings. Besides the gates and city walls, the most impressive of the ruins, in which some good mosaics were found, is the **Ulu Cami**, built in the 8th century by Marwan II, last of the Umayyad caliphs. You'll recognise the square minaret (very un-Turkish) of the mosque.

On the far (east) side of the hill is the **fortress**, in the midst of the **beehive houses**. As soon as you arrive, children will run to you and crowd around, demanding coins, sweets, cigarettes, empty water bottles and ballpoint pens. Whether you hand out some of these treats or not, they'll continue their demands. Expect to have an escort as you tour the ruins.

Getting There & Away

If you have your own car, you must go to Harran. Without a car, you must decide whether the three to four-hour 100-km round-trip from Urfa should be done by taxi (US$35 to US$40 for the car and driver) or by minibus tour (US$5 to US$9 per person). If you're interested in the minibus tour, be advised that there are several tours in town and that not all give good service. Ask other travellers who have just taken the tour and see what they say. The minibus normally departs from Urfa at 9.30 am, returning at 1.30 pm from Harran.

While Harran is now officially called Altınbaşak, you will see signs in both names. Leave Urfa by the Akçakale road at the south-east end of town and go 37 km to a turn-off to the left (east). From there, it's another 10 km to Harran. As you approach the site you come to a jandarma post, across from which is a small restaurant, a camping ground and a souvenir shop. There is no accommodation in Harran, though this will no doubt change soon .

DİYARBAKIR

The Tigris (Dicle, DEEJ-leh) River flows by the mighty black walls of Diyarbakır (dee-YAHR-bah-kuhr, population 400,000, altitude 660m), often called Kara Amid ('Black Chief') by the Turks.

As with many Turkish cities, this one has grown beyond its ancient walls only in the last few decades. Farming, stock raising, some oil prospecting and light industry fuel the Diyarbakır economy.

It comes as a surprise that this city, set in the midst of a vast, rock-strewn plain, prides itself especially on its watermelons. A brochure published for the annual watermelon festival in late September states:

> In olden times, our watermelons had to be transported by camel as they weighed 90 or 100 kg. They were carved with a sword and sold in the market.

Nowadays the prize-winning melons at the festival weigh a mere 40 to 60 kg. To grow them, pits are dug in the rich soil by the river, and pigeon droppings mixed in for fertilizer.

Diyarbakır is more famous, perhaps, as the centre of the Kurdish separatist insurgency. Traditional life continues nonetheless. Many of the men wear the traditional baggy trousers, and older women have black head coverings which they gather in front as veils.

The narrow alleys and the mosques in the Arab style with black-and-white banding in the stone all add to the city's exotic aspect. The people, predominantly Kurds, tend to be taciturn and not particularly outgoing in their dealings with foreigners, and the street urchins can be annoying. In summer it's very hot.

History

Considering that Mesopotamia, the land between the Tigris and Euphrates valleys, saw the dawn of the world's first great empires, it's no surprise that Diyarbakır's history begins with the Hurrian Kingdom of Mitanni circa 1500 BC, and proceeds through domination by the civilisations of Urartu (900 BC), Assyria (1356-612 BC), Persia (600-330 BC), Alexander the Great and his successors the Seleucids.

The Romans took over in 115 AD, but because of its strategic position the city continued to change hands numerous times until it was conquered by the Arabs in 639 AD. Until then it had been known as Amida, but the Arabs settled it with the tribe of Beni Bakr, who named their new home Diyar Bakr, the Realm of Bakr.

The next few centuries were troubled ones for the city, as evidenced by its list of conquerors:

930 – The Hamdanids conquer it and fight off the Byzantines.

978-984 – The Buweyhids take Diyarbakır, but it soon falls to the Kurdish Marwanid dynasty.

1085 – A Seljuk Turkish dynasty, the Cüheyroğulları, takes over.

1093 – A Syrian Seljuk dynasty, the İnaloğulları, takes the city.

1142-1183 – The Seljukid Nisanoğulları take control.

1183 – The Artukid ruler Nurettin Muhammet reigns in the city.

1232 – The Ayyubids take control.

1240 – The Great Seljuks take it, only to lose it to the Ayyubids in 1257.

1259 – The Mongol emperor Hulagu Khan reconquers it and gives it back to the Seljuks.

1302 – Ghazan Khan takes it and yields it to the Mardin Artukids.

1394 – Tamerlane conquers Diyarbakır and gives control to Akkoyunlu Kara Yülük Osman Bey in 1401.

The Akkoyunlu (White Sheep Turkumans) ruler formed a pact with the Venetian Empire against the Ottomans, but was defeated by Mehmet the Conqueror in 1473. After 1497, the Safavid Dynasty founded by Shah Ismail took over Iran, putting an end to more than a century of Turkoman rule in this area.

The Ottomans came and conquered in 1515, but even then, Diyarbakır was not to know a lasting peace. Because it stands right in the way of invading armies from Anatolia, Persia and Syria, it saw many more tribulations. Being at the centre of the Kurdish insurgency today, true peace continues to elude it.

Orientation

Old Diyarbakır has a standard Roman town plan, with the rough circle of walls pierced by four gates at the north, south, east and west. From the gates, avenues travel to the centre and meet. Since Roman times, several sections of wall have been razed and a few new gates opened.

Except for these four major streets,

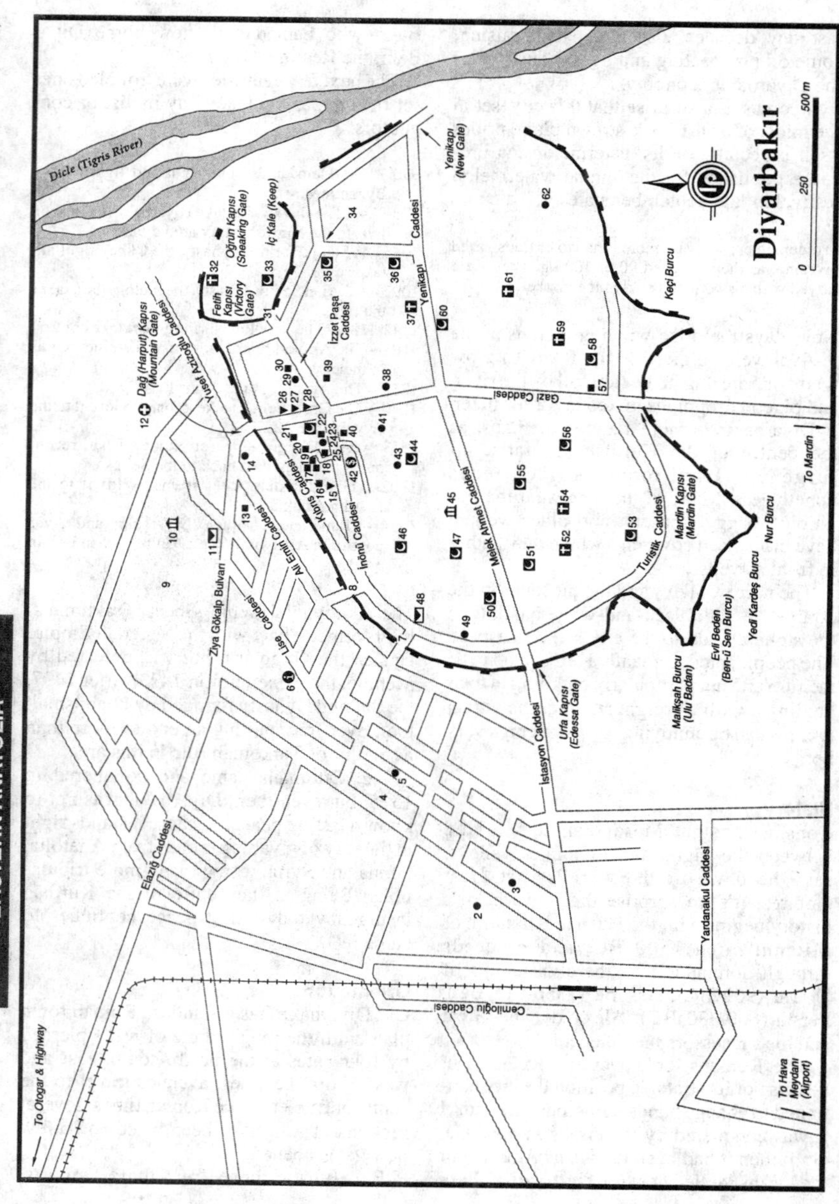
Diyarbakır
0 250 500 m
Dicle (Tigris River)
Oğrun Kapısı (Sneaking Gate)
İç Kale (Keep)
Fetih Kapısı (Victory Gate)
Dağ (Harput) Kapısı (Mountain Gate)
Yusuf Azizoğlu Caddesi
Yenikapı (New Gate)
Yenikapı Caddesi
İzzet Paşa Caddesi
Gazi Caddesi
Kıbrıs Caddesi
Ali Emiri Caddesi
İnönü Caddesi
Lise Caddesi
Melek Ahmet Caddesi
Turistik Caddesi
Keçi Burcu
Mardin Kapısı (Mardin Gate)
Nur Burcu
Yedi Kardeş Burcu
Evli Beden (Ben-ü Sen Burcu)
Malikşah Burcu (Ulu Badan)
Urfa Kapısı (Edessa Gate)
İstasyon Caddesi
Ziya Gökalp Bulvarı
Elazığ Caddesi
Yardanakul Caddesi
Cemiloğlu Caddesi
To Otogar & Highway
To Hava Meydanı (Airport)
To Mardin

PLACES TO STAY

13 Turistik Oteli
16 Hotel Uçak
17 Aslan Palas Oteli
18 Hotel Kaplan
19 Hotel Kristal
20 Hotel Güler
21 Hotel Dicle
23 Büyük Otel
25 Hotel Malkoç
30 Hotel Kenan
39 Demir Otel
40 Hotel Derya
57 Otel Büyük Kervansaray (Deliller Han)

PLACES TO EAT

15 Sarmaşık Sofra Salonu
26 Hanedan Lahmacun ve Pide
27 Antep Baklava ve Pasta
28 Sinan Lokantası

OTHER

1 Gar (Railway Station)
2 Radio TRT
3 Şehir Stadı (Stadium)
4 Cumhuriyet Parkı
5 Vilayet Konağı (Government Building)
6 Tourism Information Office
7 Hindi Baba Kapısı (Indian Father Gate)
8 Tek Kapı (Single Gate)
9 Fuar Sahası (Fairgrounds)
10 Archaeology Museum
11 PTT (Branch)
12 Devlet Hastanesi (Government Hospital)
14 Atatürk Statue & Selahaddin-i Eyubi Çarşısı (Dolmuş Station)
22 Nebi Camii
24 Turkish Airlines Office
29 Diyarbakır Tourism Association Office
31 Saray Kapısı (Palace Gate)
32 Church of St George
33 Hazreti Süleyman Camii
34 Dicle Kapısı (Tigris Gate)
35 Nasuh Paşa Camii
36 Fatih Paşa Camii
37 Keldanî Kilisesi, Surp Giragos Church
38 Hasan Paşa Hanı
41 Belediye (Municipality)
42 Aziz Döviz
43 Mesudiye Medresesi
44 Ulu Cami
45 Ziya Gökalp Museum
46 İskender Paşa Camii
47 Safa Camii
48 PTT (Main Post Office)
49 Balıklı Medresesi (Ayn Zülal)
50 Melek Ahmet Camii
51 Lala Bey Camii
52 Church of the Virgin Mary
53 Ali Paşa Camii
54 Kozma Greek Orthodox Church
55 Behram Paşa Camii
56 Hoca Ahmet Camii
58 Hüsrev Paşa Camii
59 Protestant Church
60 Kasım Padişah Camii (Dört Ayaklı Minare)
61 Armenian Catholic Church
62 Yıkık Hamam

Diyarbakır's street plan within the walls is a maze of narrow, twisting, mostly unmarked alleys. It's virtually impossible for a non-resident to find the way within any point in the maze without the help of a guide. Local boys will urge their services upon you, and you may have to use them to find many of the mosques, museums and churches hidden within the maze. Be sure to agree on a price in advance.

The train station is at the western end of İstasyon Caddesi. From the station, this street goes east to the Urfa Kapısı (OOR-fah kah-puh-suh, Edessa Gate), the city's eastern gate. Inside the walls, the continuation of İstasyon Caddesi is called Melek Ahmet Caddesi or sometimes Urfa Caddesi. To go downtown from the station (about 1.5 km), walk out the front door, go to the first big street and wait on the left (north-east) corner of the far side for a dolmuş going to the Dağ Kapısı (DAAH kah-puh-suh, Mountain Gate).

The otogar is north-west of the city where Elazığ Caddesi (also called Ziya Gökalp Bulvarı) intersects the highway. Travel along Elazığ Caddesi to the centre and you will pass the Turistik Oteli just before penetrating the walls at the Dağ Kapısı, the northern gate, also called the Harput Kapısı. From this gate, Gazi Caddesi leads to the centre. From the otogar, take a dolmuş to Dağ Kapısı, 3.5 km away. Don't let people tell you that there are no dolmuşes and that you must take a taxi.

Information

The Tourism Information Office (☎ (412) 221 2173, fax 224 1189) is in the Kültür Sarayı, 5th floor, office 28.

Most banks have branches on İnönü Caddesi. Aziz Döviz is a convenient currency-exchange house next to the Hotel Derya (closed Sunday). Diyarbakır's postal code is 21000.

The Walls

Although there were Roman and probably

earlier walls here, the present walls, almost six km in length, date from early Byzantine times (330-500 AD).

The historic names for the **gates** in the walls are the Harput Kapısı (north), Mardin Kapısı (south), Yenikapı (east) and Urfa Kapısı (west). The massive black basalt walls are defended by 72 bastions and towers, many of them gathered around the İç Kale (EECH-kaleh, citadel or keep) on the north-eastern corner, overlooking the Tigris. Of the gates, the Harput Kapısı or Dağ Kapısı is in the best condition.

Unfortunately, you must exercise caution during your walks on and along the walls as I have had a few reports of robbery attempts. It's best to go in a group, if possible.

Perhaps the most rewarding area of the walls to explore for inscriptions and decoration is the portion between the İç Kale and the Mardin Kapısı, going westward (away from the river). Start at the Mardin Kapısı near the Deliller Han, a stone caravanserai now restored as the Otel Büyük Kervansaray. Climb up to the path on top of the walls, walk along – dodging the television aerials mounted here for best reception – and you'll pass by the **Yedi Kardeş Burcu** (Tower of Seven Brothers) and **Malikşah Burcu** (Tower of Malikşah, also called Ulu Badan). The views of the city are good, and the bird's-eye vantage point allows you to see a lot of Diyarbakır's daily street life right below. You must descend at Urfa Kapısı, but you can climb up again on the opposite side of İstasyon Caddesi.

Mosques

Diyarbakır has many mosques, but the most interesting is the **Ulu Cami**, built in 1091 and extensively restored in 1155 after being damaged by fire. The mosque is rectangular in plan – Arab-style, not Ottoman. Its founder was Malik Şah, an early sultan of the Seljuks.

Across the courtyard from the Ulu Cami

Old Diyarbakır Houses

Diyarbakır's long and often violent history, its extremes of climate, and its melange of cultures have produced a distinctive domestic architecture.

Most old Diyarbakır houses are made of the familiar black basalt, sometimes with a wood frame superstructure. 'Female' (the lighter, more porous stone) is used to pave courtyards and build house walls so they remain cool in the heat. 'Male' (dense, fine-grained) stone is used for large public buildings such as mosques, hans and caravanserais.

Rubble walls hide most houses from the narrow passageways which serve as streets in the old quarters. Doorways are marked by neatly-cut ashlars, and often sheltered by small roofs from the hot sun and chill rain.

Within, the traditional house is divided into summer and winter quarters. The centre of the summer house is the eyvan, or arched room open on one side which faces the courtyard. Usually a fountain made of male basalt plays quietly at the centre of the shady eyvan. The sunny courtyard may have a pool and flower boxes. In summer the family moves high wooden platforms called *taht* (throne) into the courtyard for sleeping, making it possible to catch any wayward zephyr.

The traditional Islamic division into selamlık (the men's rooms) and haremlik (the women's) is supplemented by a room called the *mabeyn* ('interval') which joins the two. Floors may be of basalt or of *horasan*, a traditional mortar developed by the Persians several millenia ago, and used by the Romans and everyone since.

The larder *(serdap)* is in the basement; the upper floors are known as *çardak* (shelter). Kitchen, toilet, stables and even a private hamam (Turkish bath) might complete an elaborate house.

Among decorative elements, the most prominent is *cis* or *kehal*, a stencilled decoration done in colours. The best surviving example is in the Cahit Sıtkı Tarancı Culture Museum.

Several traditional houses are open to visit, including the Cahit Sıtkı Tarancı Cultural Museum in the city proper, the Atatürk Villa, 2.5 km to the south, and the Cihannüma Köşk on the eastern bank of the Tigris in Kavs Köyü. ■

is the Mesudiye Medresesi, now used as offices. Across Gazi Caddesi from these buildings is the **Hasan Paşa Hanı,** a caravanserai dating from the 16th century, now used by carpet sellers and souvenir vendors.

Black-and-white stone banding is a characteristic of Diyarbakır's mosques, many of which date from the reign of the Akkoyunlu Dynasty. One of these is the **Nebi Camii** (1530) at the main intersection of Gazi and İzzet Paşa/İnönü Caddesis.

The **Behram Paşa Camii** (1572), in a residential area deep in the maze of narrow streets, is Diyarbakır's largest mosque and is in a similar style. The **Safa Camii** (1532) is more Persian in style, with a grand and highly decorated minaret.

The **Kasım Padişah Camii** (1512) is also famous for its minaret, but it's the engineering that draws the interest – the huge tower stands on four slender pillars about two metres high, lending it the name Dört Ayaklı Minare or Four-Legged Minaret.

Atatürk Villa

The Atatürk Köşkü or Villa, traditionally known as the Seman Köşkü, dates from the 15th-century rule of the Akkoyunlu Turcoman dynasty. Located about 2.5 km south of the centre, it's among the most beautiful and best preserved of Diyarbakır's traditional houses.

Alternate courses of light and dark stone banding make for a dramatic effect. Inside, the eyvans on both the ground and upper floors, and its situation overlooking the Tigris, add to its grace and grandeur. The house, given to Atatürk by the city in 1937, was opened as a museum only two years later upon the great leader's death. It's now open from 8 am to noon and 1 to 5 pm, for US$0.75.

To get there, leave the city by the Mardin Kapısı and cross to the eastern side of the Tigris by the historic bridge.

Cahit Sıtkı Tarancı Museum

The poet Cahit Sıtkı Tarancı (1910-1956) was born in Diyarbakır in this house in the Cami-i Kebir district near the Ulu Cami. Built in 1820, the two-storey black basalt house's selamlık was later demolished; only the haremlik survives, surrounding the traditional courtyard.

The museum, open daily except Monday from 8 am to noon and 1.30 to 5 pm (US$1.50), contains some of the poet's personal effects and furnishings, exhibits detailing his life and work, and ethnographic displays from Diyarbakır and vicinity.

Ziya Gökalp Museum

Sociologist Ziya Gökalp (1876-1924) was a formative influence on the Turkish movement which strove to create a Turkish ethnic national identity to parallel the ethnic identities of Ottoman subject peoples such as the Greeks, Jews and Armenians. He is remembered today as an intellectual precursor of the Turkish republic.

His house in the Tacettin district is now a museum open daily except Monday from 8 am to noon and 1.30 to 5 pm for US$0.75. The exhibits dealing with his life and work are of interest mostly to Turks and Turcologists, but his graceful old house appeals to all.

Archaeology Museum

Diyarbakır's Archaeology Museum is in the Fuar Sahası (fairgrounds) off Ziya Gökalp Bulvarı. To get there, leave the old city through the Dağ Kapısı. Besides the usual archaeological and classical finds and the obligatory ethnological rooms, it has collections showing the accomplishments of the Karakoyunlu and Akkoyunlu, powerful tribal dynasties which ruled much of Eastern Anatolia and Iran between 1378 and 1502.

Churches

Among Diyarbakır's melange of peoples were numerous Christians including Armenians and Chaldaeans. The **Keldani Kilisesi** (Chaldaean Church) off Yenikapı Caddesi is still used by Christians of the Syrian rite (in communion with the Roman Catholic church).

The **Meryem Ana Kilisesi**, the Church of

the Virgin Mary, is a very old building still in use by Syrian Christians of the Orthodox rite – Jacobites or Monophysites, who refused to accept the doctrines laid down at the Council of Chalcedon in 451 AD (see the Mardin section, following).

Places to Stay – bottom end

Almost all the hotels are near the Dağ Kapısı on Kıbrıs and İnönü/İzzet Paşa caddesis, or in the narrow alleys connecting them. In the summer's heat, avoid hotel rooms just beneath the building's roof or rooms that get full late-afternoon sun.

The plain *Hotel Kenan* (☎ (412) 221 6614), İzzet Paşa Caddesi 24, is perhaps the best budget choice, with shower-equipped double rooms for US$7.50, and a hamam right in the hotel.

The *Hotel Malkoç* (☎ (412) 221 2975), İnönü Caddesi, Sütçü Sokak 6, is quieter and a step up in quality, charging US$8/11 a single/double with shower and TV. Next door is the drabber *Hotel Kaplan* (☎ (412) 221 3358, fax 224 0187), Sütçü Sokak 14, at slightly cheaper prices.

There are three hotels right on Kıbrıs Caddesi. The one-star *Hotel Dicle* (☎ (412) 223 5326), Kıbrıs Caddesi 3, right at Dağ Kapısı, may be a bit noisy, but is otherwise suitable at US$7.50/11 a single/double. West of it, the 29-room *Aslan Palas Oteli* (☎ (412) 221 1227), Kıbrıs Caddesi 21, is a bit cheaper, and gives you the choice of rooms without bath (US$8 a double), or with shower and TV (US$10). Finally, the *Hotel Uçak* (☎ (412) 221 1076), Kıbrıs Caddesi 31, is the cheapest at US$7.50 for a bathless double.

The one-star *Hotel Derya* (☎ (412) 221 4966), İnönü Caddesi 13, offers fairly good value at US$14/20 a single/double for its 28 rooms with shower. Renovations were under way at the time of writing.

The *Hotel Güler* (☎ & fax (412) 224 0294), Kıbrıs Caddesi, Yoğurtçu Sokak 7, offers excellent value for money: a quiet location, clean, attractive rooms and bathrooms, even TVs, for US$14/18 a single/double. If business is slow, they'll drop the price.

Second-best is the 30-room *Hotel Kristal* (☎ (412) 224 0297, fax 224 0187), Yoğurtçu Sokak 10, directly across the street, at similar prices.

Places to Stay – middle

Best in town is the veteran 57-room, three-star *Turistik Oteli* (☎ (412) 224 7550, fax 224 4274), Ziya Gökalp Bulvarı 7, a block north-west of the Dağ Kapısı. Built in 1953 but exceptionally well maintained, it has spacious public rooms and high-ceilinged guest rooms with air-con, refrigerators, TVs, balconies, and bathrooms with tubs. There's a swimming pool and terrace at the back, and guarded parking. Rooms cost US$30/45/55 a single/double/triple, breakfast included.

The most atmospheric lodging is the *Otel Büyük Kervansaray* (☎ (412) 228 9606, fax 223 7731), in the Deliller Han, a converted caravanserai on Gazi Caddesi next to the Mardin Kapısı in the city walls. Comfortable if simple rooms with bath in a historic building cost US$38/45 a single/double, breakfast included. There's a beautiful swimming pool in the rear courtyard. The front court, where the guest rooms are, is sometimes used as a nightclub, making sleep difficult.

The four-star, 58-room *Demir Otel* (☎ (412) 221 2315, fax 228 4300), İzzet Paşa Caddesi 8, has fairly good housekeeping but ineffective air-con for US$28/35 a single/double.

The nearby 75-room *Büyük Otel* (beur-YEURK, ☎ (412) 228 1295, fax 221 2444), İnönü Caddesi 4, is cheaper, with the trappings, but not really the comforts, of a luxury hotel. Rooms cost US$26/33 a single/double with bath.

Places to Eat

A stroll along Kıbrıs Caddesi from Dağ Kapısı westward will reveal several small, cheap places to eat, including the *Neşem Yemek Salonu*, to the right of the Hotel Dicle: clean, proper, with a selection of stews and grills, and an aile salonu for women and families. Three-course meals cost from US$2.50 to US$4. It's closed Sunday.

A bit farther along, *Büryan Salonu* (☎ 222 4372), Kıbrıs Caddesi 17, near the Hotel Aslan, is a similar place (also closed Sunday). Just beyond it, the *Sarmaşık Ocakbaşı* (☎ 228 3731), has a selection of dishes, but specialises in ocakbaşı grills, where you can sit right at the grill, watch the chef, and eat as he hands you the skewers. It's open on Sunday, and a shish kebab dinner costs about US$3 to US$5.

The air-conditioned *Sarmaşık Sofra Salonu* (formerly the Güneydoğu 21 Sofra Salonu, ☎ 224 2597), İnönü Caddesi 32/A, is the best place on this street, and convenient to the Derya and Büyük hotels.

Few Diyarbakır restaurants serve alcohol with meals, the exception being the *Sinan Lokantası* (☎ 221 1048), not far from Dağ Kapısı. Signs on the façade read (in English) 'Welcome to the best pleace (sic) in down town' and 'Friendly Pleace'. Meals (US$3 to US$7), and – in the heat of a Diyarbakır summer – cold Efes beer are served on the vine-shaded terrace one flight up.

The alternatives for a meal with wine or beer are the hotel restaurants, including those at the Hotel Dicle, Demir and Büyük.

Getting There & Away

Air Turkish Airlines (☎ (412) 221 2314, fax 224 3366), İnönü Caddesi 8, next to the Büyük Hotel, serves the city's Kaplaner airport with daily nonstop flights to and from Ankara, with connecting service to İstanbul. Additional flights to and from İstanbul on Monday and Friday are nonstop.

An airport bus (US$1) departs the city ticket office every two hours. A taxi to the airport costs about US$3.

Bus Many bus companies, including the large local firms such as Diyarbakır Seyahat and Diyarbakır Sur, have ticket offices in town on Kıbrıs or İnönü Caddesi or in other spots near the Dağ Kapısı. Minibuses to Mardin (US$3.50) depart not from the otogar but from the Selahaddin-i Eyubi Çarşısı, the modern market complex just outside the Dağ Kapısı. Details of daily services on the main routes follow:

Adana – 550 km, 10 hours, US$16; several buses
Ankara – 945 km, 13 hours, US$20; several buses
Erzurum – 485 km, 10 hours, US$16; several buses
Kahta (Nemrut Dağı) – 192 km, three hours, US$8; several buses
Malatya – 260 km, four hours, US$8; frequent buses
Şanlıurfa – 190 km, three hours, US$7; frequent buses
Sivas – 500 km, nine or 10 hours, US$16; several buses
Van – 410 km, seven hours, US$14; several buses

Train Train service to the south-east is neither speedy nor dependably on time, so you may prefer to take the bus.

Diyarbakır is connected with Ankara by the *Güney Ekspresi* which runs eastward on Monday, Wednesday, Friday and Saturday, departing from Ankara at 10.40 am, stopping at Kayseri and Sivas before arriving in Diyarbakır at 12.42 pm the next day. The train continues eastward to Batman and Kurtalan.

The return service from Diyarbakır departs at 1.35 pm on Monday, Wednesday, Friday and Sunday, arriving in Ankara at 4.10 pm the next day.

For ticket prices, see the Ankara section of the Central Anatolia chapter under Getting There & Away.

The *Güney Ekspresi*'s schedule connects with that of the *Anadolu Ekspresi*, allowing direct train travel between İstanbul and Diyarbakır via Ankara.

MARDİN

About 175 km east of Urfa and 100 km south of Diyarbakır is Mardin (mahr-DEEN, population 60,000, altitude 1325m), an odd and very old town crowned with a castle and a set of immense radar domes, all overlooking the vast, roasted Syrian plains.

There is a certain amount of smuggling trade with Syria (in sheep for example, which are much more expensive in Syria than in Turkey) and lots of Kurdish separatist activity, but other than that, Mardin sizzles and sleeps.

This town had a large Christian community and there are still a few Syrian Christian families and churches. On the outskirts is the monastery of Deyrul Zafaran in which Aramaic, the language of Jesus, is still used as the liturgical tongue.

Mardin is not particularly well equipped with hotels and restaurants, and is perhaps best visited on a day trip from Diyarbakır if you prize your comforts. Travelling on the cheap, it makes sense to take a bus from Urfa to Mardin, stay the night if you're in no hurry, then take a minibus north to Diyarbakır.

History

The history of Mardin, like that of Diyarbakır, involves disputes by rival armies over dozens and dozens of centuries, though now nobody cares. A castle has stood on this hill from time immemorial.

Assyrian Christians settled in this area during the 5th century. The Arabs occupied Mardin between 640 and 1104. After that, it had a succession of Seljuk Turkish, Kurdish, Mongol and Persian overlords until the Ottomans under Sultan Selim the Grim took it in 1517.

Orientation & Information

Perched on a hillside, Mardin has one long main street, Birinci Caddesi, running for about two km from the Belediye Garajı at the western end of town through the main square, Cumhuriyet Meydanı, to Konak, a small square with the Hükümet Konağı and military buildings at the eastern end.

Everything you'll need is along this street or just off it. City buses and intracity dolmuşes run back and forth along the street. If you are driving your own car, leave it in the car park at Cumhuriyet Meydanı and walk to the hotels and sights.

The Tourism Information Office (☎ (482) 212 1665, fax 212 3232) is on Cumhuriyet Meydanı at No 551.

Mardin's postal code is 47000.

Things to See

Around Town Dating from 1385, the **Sultan İsa Medresesi**, a seminary, is the town's prime attraction. Walk east from the main square to the Hotel Başak Palas, then left (north) up the stairs to a large and imposing doorway. The doorway is what you have come to see, as there is little to attract inside. The ancient building is used, in part, as a private residence.

The **Kasım Paşa Medresesi**, near the western end of town, below the main street, was built in the 15th century. You'll have to ask for guidance to find it.

The **Mardin Müzesi** (☎ 212 7797) is on Cumhuriyet Meydanı, and is open from 8.30 am to noon and 1 to 5 pm daily; admission is free. It holds bits of statuary, but you've really come to admire the building and the view across the vast plains towards Syria.

The ancient **Ulu Cami**, built in the 11th century, is an Iraqi Seljuk structure. It's south of the main street at Cumhuriyet Meydanı. As Mardin's history has been mostly one of warfare, the mosque has suffered consider-

Monophysites

In the 6th century, Jacobus Baradeus, bishop of Edessa (Urfa), had a difference of opinion with the patriarch in Constantinople over the divine nature of Christ.

The patriarch and official doctrine held that Christ had both a divine and a human nature. The bishop held that He had only one *(mono)* nature *(physis)*, that being divine. The bishop was branded a Monophysite heretic and excommunicated. He promptly founded a church of his own, which came to be called the Jacobite (or Syrian Orthodox) after its founder. During his lifetime he claimed to have consecrated 27 bishops and around 100,000 priests.

At the same time and for the same reason, the Armenian Orthodox Church, the Coptic Church in Egypt and the Ethiopian Church were established as independent churches.

In the case of the Jacobites, control from Constantinople was soon not a problem, as the Arabs swept in and took control, allowing the Monophysites to practice their religion as they chose. ■

ably over the centuries, particularly in the Kurdish rebellion of 1832.

Deyrul Zafaran In the rocky hills east of the town, six km along a good but narrow road, is the monastery of Mar Hanania, called Deyrul Zafaran. This means the Saffron Monastery in Arabic, a name which, legend says, was given because saffron crocuses were used in the mortar of the building. It was once the seat of the Syrian Orthodox patriarch. Though the patriarchate is now in Damascus, the monastery still has the modest trappings due to the patriarch and continues its charitable work of caring for orphans.

As you drive to the monastery, you will no doubt notice a hillside on which a motto has been written with white stones, 'Ne Mutlu Türküm Diyene' (What Joy to the Person Who Says, 'I am a Turk'). Atatürk originally uttered the phrase as part of his campaign to overcome the Turkish inferiority complex imposed by Europe and the USA. Here, though, it has a different significance, reiterating the government's commitment to the unity of the country against the efforts of Kurdish separatist groups.

The first sanctuary on this site, now included within the monastery, was dedicated to the worship of the sun. In 495 AD the first monastery was built. Destroyed by the Persians in 607, it was rebuilt, to be looted by Tamerlane six centuries later.

You can visit the monastery any day without prior arrangement. As there is no public transport you must take a taxi from the town centre, which will cost about US$8. Haggle for a set price to include the return journey and an hour's waiting time.

Enter the walled enclosure through a portal bearing a Syriac inscription. An Orthodox priest will greet you and hand you over to one of the orphans for a guided tour.

First comes the **original sanctuary**, an eerie underground chamber with a flat ceiling of huge, closely fitted stones held up as if by magic, without the aid of mortar. The guide says that this room was used ages ago by sun worshippers, who viewed their god rising through a window at the eastern end. A niche on the southern wall is said to have been for sacrifices.

The guide then leads you through a pair of 300-year-old doors to the **tombs of the patriarchs and metropolitans** who have served at Deyrul Zafaran.

In the chapel, to the left of the altar as you face it, is the **patriarch's throne**. It bears the names of all the patriarchs who have served since the monastery was refounded in 792. To the right of the altar is the **throne of the metropolitan**. The present **stone altar** was carved to replace a wooden one which burnt about half a century ago. The chapel is fairly plain and simple, but the primitive art is wonderful, especially the carved furniture and paintings. Services are said in Aramaic.

The next rooms on the tour hold several **litters** used to transport the church dignitaries, and also one of several **wells** in the monastery. In a small side room is a 300-year-old **wooden throne**. The **mosaic work** in the floor is about 1500 years old.

A flight of stairs takes you up to the suite of guest rooms, very simple accommodation for travellers and those coming for meditation. The **patriarch's suite**, a small, simple bedroom and parlour, are here. On the walls of the parlour are pictures of the patriarch (who lives in Damascus) with Pope John Paul II. Another picture shows an earlier patriarch with Atatürk.

As you leave the parlour, take a moment to enjoy the fine view of the mountains. Other monasteries, now in ruins, once stood farther up the slope. Some of the water for Deyrul Zafaran comes from near these ruins, through underground channels excavated many centuries ago.

At the end of the tour you may want to tip the guide. He'll refuse at first, but will probably accept when you offer a second or third time.

Places to Stay

All of Mardin's central hotels are basic and cheap. Few are pleasant. The better and more expensive hotels are on the outskirts.

East of Cumhuriyet Meydanı are several

small, modest hotels, such as the *Yıldız Oteli* (☎ (482) 212 1096), Birinci Caddesi 391, where plain rooms without plumbing will cost you US$4/6.50 for a single/double. The public showers have cold water only.

The *Hotel Bayraktar* (☎ (482) 212 1338) is on the main street facing Cumhuriyet Meydanı, with its other side overlooking the plains. The 50 rooms on eight floors all have showers and cost US$16 a double.

The *Hotel Başak Palas* and the even simpler *Hotel Şirin Palas* are on the main street beneath the Sultan İsa Medresesi.

On the outskirts near the highway, the three-star, 48-room *Bilen Otel* (☎ (482) 212 5568, fax 212 2575) has fairly comfortable rooms for US$18/26 a single/double with private shower.

Places to Eat

There are several small, very inexpensive eateries east of the town centre along the main street. Ask for prices when you order.

Getting There & Away

Several buses run daily from Urfa to Mardin. Minibuses run about every hour between Mardin's Belediye Garajı and Diyarbakır's Dağ Kapısı (Selahaddin-i Eyubi Çarşısı) for US$3.50. The 100-km journey takes about 1¾ hours.

BİTLİS

Travel eastward from Diyarbakır 88 km and you'll reach the town of Silvan from where it's another 22 km to Malabadi. Just east of here is the Batman Suyu, a stream spanned by a beautiful humpbacked **stone bridge** built by the Artukid Turks in 1146. It is thought to have the longest span (37m) of any such bridge in existence. With its engaging bend in the middle, it's truly a work of art. Restoration in 1988 has returned it to much of its former stateliness.

Another 235 km brings you to Bitlis (BEET-leess, population 45,000, altitude 1545m), an interesting but dusty and somewhat chaotic old town squeezed into the narrow valley of a stream. A **castle** dominates the town and a hump-backed bridge and another old bridge span the stream.

The **Ulu Cami** was built in 1126, while the **Şerefiye Camii** and **Saraf Han** (a caravanserai) date from the 16th century. The town was the capital of a semi-autonomous Kurdish principality in late Ottoman times.

Walnut trees surround the town and, in autumn, children stand by the highway with bags of nuts for sale.

Up the hill at the eastern side of the town, on the left (north) side of the road, is an old caravanserai, the **Pabsin Hanı,** built by the Seljuks in the 13th century. Often there are nomads camped near it, their sprawling black tents pitched beneath its crumbling walls.

It's only 26 km to Tatvan, a railhead and western port for lake steamers.

TATVAN

Tatvan is a crossroads town, built for and surviving on the commerce which moves through by road and rail. This includes the Turkish army, which is here to protect the country's eastern borders at the traditional invasion points from north, east and south.

The town, several km long and only a few blocks wide, is not much to look at and has only a few poor tourist services. However, its setting on the shores of an inland sea, backed by bare mountains streaked with snow, is magnificent.

You must pass through Tatvan, and you may even make it your base for explorations along the north-western shore of the lake, so here's what you need to know.

The Tourism Information Office (☎ (434) 827 6301, fax 827 6300), at Sahil Mahallesi, İşletme Caddesi 6, is by the lakeshore.

Nemrut Dağı

The mountain rising to the north of Tatvan is Nemrut Dağı, not to be confused with the one near Adıyaman and Malatya with the statues on top. This Nemrut Dağı (3050m) is an inactive volcano with a crater lake on its peak which is beautiful, clear and cold, and should be visited for the view or for a swim if you normally swim among icebergs. If not, there are hot springs as well. Nemrut is the volcano which dammed up the outflow of Lake Van, causing it to cover its present vast area of 3750 sq km, and to become highly alkaline.

In summer, dolmuşes make the run up the mountain (for around US$6 per person) if there are enough people interested. If you have your own transport, leave Tatvan by the road around the lake to the north marked for Ahlat and Adilcevaz. On the outskirts of Tatvan, look for a left turn near a Türk Petrol station, as this road will take you up the mountain.

Ahlat

Continue northward by car or dolmuş along the lakeshore for 42 km and you'll come to the town of Ahlat, famous for its Seljuk Turkish tombs and graveyard.

History Founded during the reign of Caliph Omar (581-644), Ahlat became a Seljuk stronghold in the 1060s. When the Seljuk sultan Alp Arslan rode out to meet the Byzantine emperor Romanus Diogenes in battle on the field of Manzikert (see the following Malazgirt section), he rode out from his base at Ahlat.

In following centuries, Ahlat had an extraordinarily eventful history – even by Anatolian standards – with emir defeating prince and king driving out emir. It's no wonder Ahlat is famous for its cemeteries.

Ahlat, and indeed this whole region, was conquered by the Ottomans during the reign of Süleyman the Magnificent in the 16th century. The fortress on the shore in Ahlat dates from that period.

Tombstones The tombstones are most commonly of grey or red volcanic tuff. The artistry of the Ahlat stonemasons is extraordinary, with intricate web patterns and bands of Kufic lettering. It is thought that Ahlat stonemasons were employed on other great stoneworking projects, such as the decoration of the great mosque at Divriği, near Sivas.

To the right (south) of the highway as you approach the town is **Ulu Kümbet**, the Great Tomb, now in the midst of a field near some houses. Across the highway from it is a little **museum**, and beyond the museum is a unique **Muslim cemetery** with stele-like headstones. Over the centuries, earthquake, wind and water have set the stones at all angles, giving the graveyard an unsettling and eerie look.

On the north-western side of the graveyard is the **Çifte Kümbet** (Twin Tomb) and **Bayındır Türbesi** (Bayındır Tomb), with a colonnaded porch and its own small prayer room.

Malazgirt

About 60 km north of Ahlat is Malazgirt (Manzikert), which is of immense importance in Turkish history. On 26 August 1071, the Seljuk Turkish sultan Alp Arslan and his armies decisively defeated the Byzantine emperor Romanus Diogenes and took him prisoner. The Byzantine defeat effectively opened Anatolia to Turkish migration and conquest.

The Seljuks established the Sultanate of Rum with its capital at Konya, and other nomadic Turkish tribes came from central Asia and Iran to settle here. A band of border warriors, following a leader named Osman, later spread its influence and founded a state which would become the vast Ottoman Turkish Empire. It all started here, in 1071, when the heir of the Caesars lost to a Turkish emir.

Adilcevaz

Twenty-five km east of Ahlat is the town of Adilcevaz, once an Urartian town but now dominated by a great Seljuk Turkish fortress, the **Kef Kalesi**, and the even greater bulk of **Süphan Dağı** (4434m).

Meltwater from the year-round snowfields on Süphan Dağı flows down to Adilcevaz, making its surroundings lush and fertile. As you enter town along the shore, the highway passes the nice little **Tuğrul Bey Camii**, built in the 13th century and still used daily for prayer. You can climb Süphan Dağı in summer. For details, see Lonely Planet's *Trekking in Turkey*.

Dolmuşes run between Adilcevaz and Van (Beş Yol) several times daily. If you continue around the lake, you will pass through **Erciş**, a modern town which covers settlements that date from Urartian times.

Places to Stay

Ahlat and Adilcevaz have a few small, cheap pensions. In Tatvan, the few cheap hotels – such as the *Otel Trabzon*, where rooms cost US$4/7 a single/double with washbasin – are very basic and well used, but so is the best hotel in town, the *Vangölü Denizcilik Kurumu Oteli* (☎ (434) 827 1777).

Hidden on the shore a short walk from the centre, the old stone building looks as though it is left from Ottoman times, though it may have been built to accommodate train passengers. It has a serviceable restaurant and the 23 drab, basic and old-fashioned rooms cost from US$15 to US$25 a double, some with private showers. Despite its lack of comforts, this is the best hotel in Tatvan, and is often fully booked with tour groups.

Getting There & Away

Tatvan's train station is about two km north-east of the centre along the road to Ahlat and Adilcevaz; there are infrequent city buses.

The *Vangölü Ekspresi* departs from Tatvan at 9.50 am on Tuesday, Thursday and Saturday bound for Ankara, arriving at 4.10 pm the following day. A one-way ticket from Tatvan to Ankara costs US$15/10.50 in 1st/2nd class. The fare in a sleeping car is US$30/52/72 for one/two/three people. Reserve your sleeping-car space well in advance.

Ferries operated by Turkish Maritime Lines cross the lake from Tatvan to Van on an irregular schedule – while there are supposed to be four boats per day, there often is only one. Don't believe the departure times you're told. You can make the 156-km journey o Van more quickly (two hours) by bus around the southern shore.

AKDAMAR

Between Tatvan and Van, the scenery is beautiful, but there is no reason to stop except at a point eight km west of Gevaş, where you *must* see the 10th-century **Akdamar Kilisesi**, or Church of the Holy Cross. One of the marvels of Armenian architecture, it is perched on an island in the lake. Motorboats ferry sightseers back and forth. You can also make this trip as an excursion from Van.

In 921, Gagik Artzruni, King of Vaspurakan, built a palace, a church and a monastery on the island, three km out in the lake. Little remains of the palace and monastery, but the church walls are in superb condition and the wonderful relief carvings on the walls are among the masterworks of Armenian art.

If you are familiar with biblical stories, you'll immediately recognise Adam and Eve, Jonah and the Whale, David and Goliath, Abraham about to sacrifice Isaac (but he sees the heaven-sent ram, with its horns caught in a bush, just in time), Daniel in the Lions' Den, Sampson etc.

The paintings inside the church are not in the best condition, but their vagueness and frailty seem in keeping with the shaded, partly ruined interior.

Getting There & Away

Dolmuşes run from Beş Yol in Van to Gevaş for US$2. Some of the dolmuş drivers have a racket whereby they take you to Gevaş, then set a high price for the remaining eight km to the boat dock for Akdamar. To beat this, agree on a price all the way to the dock (Akdamar İskelesi) before you board the dolmuş in Van.

Boats to the island (US$3 for the round trip) run about every 30 minutes if traffic warrants this, which it usually does in the warm months, especially on Sunday. If it doesn't, you may have to charter a boat for a special trip, for around US$25 to US$35. The voyage takes about 20 minutes and an admission ticket to the church costs US$1.

A fairly expensive *teahouse* and *camping area* are near the dock.

VAN

Almost 100 km across vast Lake Van (Van Gölü) from Tatvan lies Van (population 160,000, altitude 1727m), the eastern railhead on the line to Iran and the largest Turkish city east of Diyarbakır and south of Erzurum.

Van has several claims to fame. It was the Urartian capital city, and at the Rock of Van near the lakeshore are long cuneiform inscriptions. Van is also the market centre for the Kurdish tribes who live in the mountains of extreme south-eastern Turkey. An excursion to the south-east takes you past the ancient Urartian city at Çavuştepe and the craggy mountain fortress of Hoşap to Hakkari and Yüksekova, deep in the alpine scenery of the Cilo Dağı mountains.

History

The kingdom of Urartu, called Ararat in the Bible, flourished from the 13th to the 7th centuries BC. The Urartian capital, Tushpa, was near present-day Van. The Urartians were traders and farmers, highly advanced in the art of metalwork and stone masonry. They borrowed much of their culture, including cuneiform writing, from the neighbouring Assyrians, with whom they were at war more or less permanently. The powerful Assyrians never completely subdued the Urartians, but when the battle was joined by the several waves of Cimmerians, Scythians and Medes which swept into Urartu, the kingdom met its downfall.

After the downfall of Urartu, the region was resettled by a people whom the Persians called Armenians. By the 6th century BC the region was governed by Persian and Mede satraps.

The history of the Armenians is one of repeated subjugation to the rule of other peoples as they occupied a strategic crossroads at the nexus of three great empires in Syria, Persia and Anatolia. Tigranes the Great succeeded in gaining control of the kingdom from its Parthian overlords in 95 BC, but his short-lived kingdom was soon crushed in the clash of armies from Rome in the west and Parthia in the east.

In the 8th century AD, the Arab armies flooded through from the south, forcing the Armenian prince to take refuge on Akdamar Island. Unable to fend off the vast number of Arabs, he agreed to pay tribute to the Caliph. When the Arabs retreated, the Byzantines and Persians took their place, and overlordship of Armenia see-sawed between them as one or the other gained military advantage.

The next wave of invaders was Turkish. Upon defeating the Byzantines in 1071 at Manzikert, north of Lake Van, the Seljuk Turks marched in to found the Sultanate of Rum and were followed by a flood of Turkoman nomads. Domination of Eastern Anatolia by the powerful Karakoyunlu and Akkoyunlu Turkish emirs followed, and continued until the coming of the Ottoman armies in 1468.

During WWI, Armenian guerrilla bands intent on founding an independent Armenian state collaborated with the Russians to defeat the Ottoman armies in the east. The Armenians, former loyal subjects of the sultan, were looked upon as traitors by the Turks. Bitter fighting between Turkish and Kurdish forces on the one side and Armenian and Russian on the other brought wholesale devastation to the entire region and to Van.

The Ottomans destroyed the old city of Van (near the Rock of Van) before the Russians occupied it in 1915. Ottoman forces counterattacked but were unable to drive the invaders out, and Van remained under Russian occupation until the armistice of 1917. Under the Turkish Republic, a new planned city of Van was built four km east of the old site.

Orientation & Information

The highway passing between the town and the lake is the ancient Silk Road (İpek Yolu). In the city, the main commercial street is Cumhuriyet Caddesi, with banks, hotels, restaurants, the Turkish Airlines office and the tourism office. At the northern end of Cumhuriyet Caddesi, where it meets five other streets, is the square called Beş Yol (Five Roads), site of dolmuş and bus stops.

The city's bus station is on the north-western outskirts, just off the Silk Road.

The two train stations are the İskele İstasyon, or lakeside Dock Station, and the

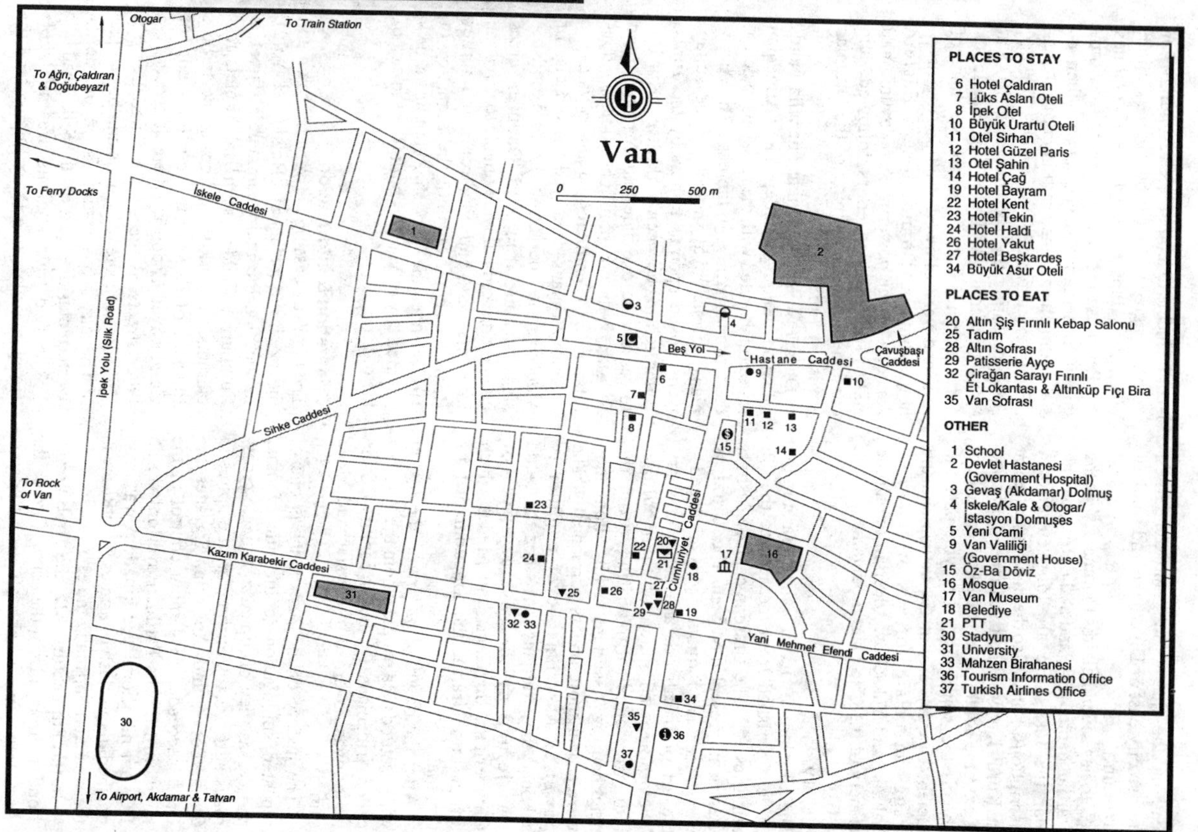
Van
0
250
500 m
PLACES TO STAY
6 Hotel Çaldıran
7 Lüks Aslan Oteli
8 İpek Otel
10 Büyük Urartu Oteli
11 Otel Sirhan
12 Hotel Güzel Paris
13 Otel Şahin
14 Hotel Çağ
19 Hotel Bayram
22 Hotel Kent
23 Hotel Tekin
24 Hotel Haldi
26 Hotel Yakut
27 Hotel Beşkardeş
34 Büyük Asur Oteli
PLACES TO EAT
20 Altın Şiş Fırınlı Kebap Salonu
25 Tadım
28 Altın Sofrası
29 Patisserie Ayçe
32 Çırağan Sarayı Fırınlı Et Lokantası & Altınküp Fıçı Bira
35 Van Sofrası
OTHER
1 School
2 Devlet Hastanesi (Government Hospital)
3 Gevaş (Akdamar) Dolmuş
4 İskele/Kale & Otogar/İstasyon Dolmuşes
5 Yeni Cami
9 Van Valiliği (Government House)
15 Öz-Ba Döviz
16 Mosque
17 Van Museum
18 Belediye
21 PTT
30 Stadyum
31 University
33 Mahzen Birahanesi
36 Tourism Information Office
37 Turkish Airlines Office
Otogar
To Train Station
To Ağrı, Çaldıran & Doğubeyazıt
To Ferry Docks
İskele Caddesi
İpek Yolu (Silk Road)
Sihke Caddesi
To Rock of Van
Kazım Karabekir Caddesi
Beş Yol
Hastane Caddesi
Çavuşbaşı Caddesi
Cumhuriyet Caddesi
Yani Mehmet Efendi Caddesi
To Airport, Akdamar & Tatvan

Şehir İstasyon (City Station). The City Station is north-west of the centre near the bus station, while the Dock Station is several km north-west on the shore.

Van Kalesi (the Rock of Van), the only significant sight, is about five km west of the centre.

The Tourism Information Office (☎ (432) 216 3675, 216 2018), with helpful staff, is at the southern end of Cumhuriyet Caddesi at No 127.

Van's postal code is 65000.

Van Museum

The Van Müzesi (☎ 216 1139) is open from 8 am to noon and 1 to 5 pm; though nominally closed on Monday, you may find it open. Admission costs US$1.25; no photography is allowed. The easiest access is via the passageway through the Belediye building on Cumhuriyet Caddesi.

The ground floor Urartian exhibits include jewellery, some with amber and coloured glass, cylindrical seals and pots from the Old Bronze Age (circa 5000 BC). The Urartu Süsleme Plakaları (Jewellery Breastplates) from the 9th to 7th centuries BC are particularly fine, as are the bronze belts. Another exhibit has *at gemleri* (horse bits) from the 9th and 8th centuries BC.

The ethnographic exhibits upstairs include local Kurdish and Turcoman kilims and a *sedir* (low couch), such as is found in village houses, covered with traditional crafts. The Katliam Seksiyonu (Genocide Section) is a grisly display of skulls, bones and bits of dress recovered from mass graves left from the Armenian massacres of Turks and Kurds at Çavuşoğlu and Zeve.

Rock of Van

'İskeleğ dolmuşes to the Rock of Van (Van Kalesi) depart from Beş Yol and cost US$1.50. Many people hitchhike, which is fairly easy, or walk the five km in less than an hour if it's not too hot.

On the north side of the rock is the **tomb** of a Muslim holy man which is visited frequently by pilgrims.

A stairway from the car park at the north-western corner leads to the top, where you can see the fortifications, including the **Sardur Burcu** (Sarduri Tower, 840-830 BC), with several cuneiform inscriptions in Assyrian praising the Urartian king Sarduri I.

On the south side is a narrow walkway with an iron railing leading to several **funeral chambers**, including that of King Argishti I (786-764 BC), cut from the rock. Before reaching these you pass a long **cuneiform inscription** which recounts the high points of Argishti's reign.

The view south of the rock reveals a flat space broken by the grass-covered foundations of numerous buildings. This was the site of **Tushpa**, an Urartian city which flourished almost 3000 years ago. The foundations you see, however, are those of the **old city of Van**, destroyed during the upheavals of WWI and the futile struggle for an Armenian republic in eastern Turkey. The sight is stunning – a dead city, buried as though in a grave, with only the **Ulu Cami** raising its broken minaret above the grass-covered rubble.

Lake Van (Van Gölü)

This highly alkaline lake was formed when the volcano named Nemrut Dağı (not the one with the statues) blocked its natural outflow. The water level is now maintained by evaporation which results in a high mineral concentration and extreme alkalinity: clothes washed in the lake come clean without soap.

In recent years evaporation has been insufficient, and the lake level has been rising, slowly flooding shoreline villages and bringing a plague of snakes and flies to those only slightly higher up.

Near Van the lake is polluted, but the beaches at Gevaş and Edremit are good for a swim. Don't go in if you have sunburn or open cuts or sores, as the alkaline water will burn them intensely.

Çavuştepe & Hoşap

A day excursion south-east of Van along the road to Başkale, Yüksekova and Hakkari takes you to the Urartian site at Çavuştepe,

25 km from Van, and the Kurdish castle at Hoşap (Güzelsu), another 33 km further along.

Old Tuşba Turizm (☎ (432) 216 4561), Posta Caddesi 9, operates full-day minibus tours to these sites as well as the Rock of Van and Akdamar, also allowing for a swim in the lake, for about US$25 per person. Departure is after breakfast and the minibus returns in the evening in time for supper.

To do it on your own, catch a bus heading to Başkale (US$5) and say you want to get out at Hoşap. After seeing the castle, hitch back to Çavuştepe, 500m off the highway, and then hitch or catch a minibus back to Van. Pack a lunch and water, and plan to be gone for the better part of the day as rides can be scarce.

Çavuştepe The narrow hill on the right side of the highway at Çavuştepe was once crowned with the fortress-palace Sarduri-Hinili, home of the kings of Urartu, built between 764 and 735 BC by King Sardur II, son of Argisti. Climb the hill to the car park, where there is a guardian to keep you from taking photos (excavations are still underway) and perhaps to show you what there is to see. No admission fee is being charged yet, and no drinks or refreshments are available at the site.

Climb the rocky hill to the temple ruins, marked by a gate of black basalt blocks polished to a high gloss. A few of the blocks on the left side of the doorway are inscribed in cuneiform. As you walk around, notice the cisterns for water and, at the far end where the palace once stood, the royal Urartian loo.

Hoşap Castle Back on the road, another half-hour's ride (33 km) brings you up over a hill and down the other side, where the castle Hoşap Kalesi stands perched and photogenic on top of a rocky outcrop. Beneath it is the village of Güzelsu, along a stream. On the left side of the road before the village is a badly ruined caravanserai or medrese. Cross the bridge into the village and follow the signs around the far side of the hill to reach the castle entrance.

The castle, built in 1643 by a local Kurdish chieftain, has a very impressive entrance portal in a round tower. A guardian is supposed to be on duty from 8.30 am to noon and 1.30 to 5 pm. The guardian will sell you a ticket for US$1 and let you walk up into the fortress via a passage cut through the rock. Many of the castle's hundreds of rooms are still clearly visible and the view is good. Across the valley are the remains of mud-brick defensive walls, now badly eroded and looking like a dinosaur's spine. Soft drinks are on sale at the castle entrance.

Places to Stay – bottom end

Camping *Kadembaş*, *Anatolia* and *Güney* camping grounds are at Edremit, 18 km south-west of Van. Gevaş, with its dock for boats to Akdamar, has two small camping grounds, the *Sahil* and *Ahtamara*. Facilities are primitive.

Hotels Van is well supplied with cheap hotels. Those in the bazaar to the west of Cumhuriyet Caddesi tend to be the cheapest; those to the east are slightly more expensive, but also cleaner and more comfortable.

Several hotels west of Cumhuriyet serve visiting farmers and traders, charging US$3.50 per person in rooms with sink and/or private shower. Among the better ones are the *İpek Otel* (☎ (432) 216 3033), Cumhuriyet Caddesi, Eski Hal Civarı, and the *Lüks Aslan Oteli* (☎ (432) 216 2469), Eski Hal Civarı. The 63-room *Hotel Kent* (☎ (432) 216 2404), Küçük Cami Civarı, charges a bit more for less.

Hotel Bayram (☎ (432) 216 1136, fax 216 5758), Cumhuriyet Caddesi 1/A, is less comfortable than its modern façade implies. Some of its 72 rooms have been fixed up a bit and cost US$4.50 a double with shower; others are unredeemed at US$3.50.

Hotel Güzel Paris (☎ (432) 216 3739, fax 216 6968), Hükümet Binası Yanı 20, on the south side of the Van Valiliği government headquarters, has acceptable rooms with shower in an excellent location for US$8/12 a single/double. The *Hotel Çağ* (☎ (432) 214 5712), Hastane 2 Caddesi 46, is similar.

Two short blocks down towards the lake

from Beş Yol, the *Hotel Çaldıran* (CHAHL-duh-RAHN, ☎ (432) 216 2718), Sıhke Caddesi, Büyük Cami Karşısı, has 48 well-used and somewhat noisy rooms priced at US$8/12 a single/double with private shower.

The 52-room *Hotel Tekin* (☎ (432) 216 3010, fax 216 1366), Küçük Cami Civarı, Nur Sokak 24, has an easily visible sign on its roof. Catering to country-town merchants, it charges US$9/14/20 a single/double/triple with private shower.

The modest one-star *Büyük Asur Oteli* (beur-YEURK ah-SOOR, ☎ (432) 216 8792, fax 216 9461), Cumhuriyet Caddesi, Turizm Sokak 5, has a restaurant, lift and 48 rooms in muted colours lit by fluorescence. Rooms cost US$9/14 a single/double with shower.

The two-star *Hotel Beşkardeş* (BEHSH-kahr-desh, ☎ (432) 216 1116, fax 216 6466), Cumhuriyet Caddesi 34, has 40 rooms (some noisy) with balconies, TVs and private showers priced at US$14/18 a single/double. The *Otel Şahin* (☎ (432) 216 3062, fax 216 3064), İrfan Baştuğ Caddesi 20, is similar in price, but quieter, with bathtubs in many of its two-star rooms.

Places to Stay – middle

The best hotel in town is the 75-room, three-star *Büyük Urartu Oteli* (☎ (432) 212 0660, fax 212 1610), Cumhuriyet Caddesi, Hastane Caddesi 60, across from the Devlet Hastanesi hospital. Van's most comfortable guest rooms, with private bath and TV, are priced at US$42/60 a single/double, but if you hesitate and make for the door, the price may drop, unless a group in residence is making the good rooms scarce.

The best value-for-money alternative to the Urartu is the three-star, 50-room *Otel Sirhan* (☎ (432) 214 3463, fax 216 2867), Cumhuriyet Caddesi, Hükümet Konağı Yanı, on the south side of the Van Valiliği provincial government headquarters, charging US$28 a double, breakfast included. Avoid rooms right above the nightclub.

Other choices include the three-star, 33-room *Hotel Haldi* (☎ (432) 214 0144, fax 216 1524), Yübaşıoğlu Caddesi 1, with posted prices of US$35/45 a single/double, though you will undoubtedly be quoted a lower price. The 64-room *Hotel Yakut* (☎ (432) 214 2832, fax 214 2833), Kazım Karabekir Caddesi, PTT Sokak 4, is cheaper, charging US$20/28 a single/double with private bath and perhaps a TV.

Places to Eat

Van specialities include otlu peynir, cheese mixed with the tangy herb geven otu *(gum tragacanth, Astragalus tragacantha)*, and Kürt köftesi (Kurdish köfte, also called kurutlu köfte), a meatless mixture of bulghur wheat and onions flavoured with mint, formed into balls and cooked. Though you may find Kürt köftesi in restaurants, otlu peynir is more often sold in grocery stores (bakkaliye). Van's normal restaurant fare is the now-familiar – indeed overly familiar – selection of kebaps.

A good all-round place is *Altın Sofrası* (☎ 216 4773) on Cumhuriyet Caddesi to the left of the Hotel Beşkardeş. The ground floor is a 'süpermarket'; the 1st floor a restaurant with stews and kebaps; 2nd floor is the aile salonu; 3rd floor is the pastryshop-café; and top floor is the women's pastryshop dining room.

Van Sofrası or 'Van Dinner-table' (☎ 216 5414), on Cumhuriyet Caddesi across from the tourism office, is the place to try Kürt köftesi and other local dishes. A full meal need cost no more than US$4 or US$5.

The *Altın Şiş Fırınlı Kebap Salonu*, or Golden Skewer Oven-Equipped Kebap Salon (☎ 216 2265), on Cumhuriyet Caddesi north of the PTT, is typical of the rest with a selection of cheap kebaps, including good döner (US$2) at lunchtime.

On Kazım Karabekir Caddesi, the *Çırağan Sarayı Fırınlı Et Lokantası* (☎ 214 4561) at No 49 is a similarly presentable kebapçı, as is the *Tadım* (☎ 212 2605) across the street. There are many more in the bazaar.

Van has a good selection of pastanes for cakes and sweet snacks at about US$1 per portion. *Patisserie Ayçe* on Kazım Karabekir Caddesi just west of Cumhuriyet Caddesi is the poshest. The *Güven Pastanesi* (☎ 216 6578), just north of the Vakıfbank on Cumhuriyet, is reliably good. The *Çavuşoğlu Pastanesi* (☎ 216 6578), Cumhuriyet Caddesi 19, is nice enough, but its dining room is below street level.

For alcoholic drinks with dinner you must patronise one of the better hotels. The *Büyük Urartu* is the most likely to have fresh food (in summer, at least). The *Hotel Haldi* has a roof terrace with good views which is set up as a restaurant if there's enough business to warrant the effort.

Entertainment

There's precious little nightlife in Van. For a beer, try *Altınküp Fıçı Bira* or Golden Mug Draught Beer (☎ 216 6779), Kazım Karabekir Caddesi 53, near the Çirağan Sarayı Lokantası. The nearby *Mahzen Birahanesi*, at the rear of Kazım Karabekir Caddesi 37, is subterranean as well as (expectedly) excluively male, making it doubly claustrophobic.

Things to Buy

Van's collection of handicrafts shops was decimated by the precipitous drop in tourist arrivals during the early to mid-1990s. Now that tourism has begun to return, you may again find shopkeepers stocking especially fine handwoven carpets, kilims and saddlebags which they buy from the Kurdish artisans in the hills.

Getting There & Away

As the 'capital' of the extreme south-east, Van has ready transport.

Air Turkish Airlines (☎ (432) 216 1241, fax 216 1768), Cumhuriyet Caddesi 196, in the Enver Perihanoğlu İş Merkezi building, has one daily nonstop flight to/from Ankara, and another to/from İstanbul; the Ankara flight meets connections for İstanbul and İzmir.

Bus Many bus companies maintain ticket offices at the intersection of Cumhuriyet and Kazım Karabekir caddesis, including Van Gölü, VanTur and Van Seyahat companies. They customarily provide *şehiriçi servis* minibuses to shuttle passengers to and from the bus station. Details of some, mostly daily, bus services follow:

Ağrı – 210 km, four hours, US$8; frequent buses
Ankara – 1250 km, 22 hours, US$32; frequent buses
Diyarbakır – 385 km, seven hours, US$14; several buses
Doğubeyazıt via Çaldıran – 185 km, five hours, US$12; direct dolmuş every few days; more frequent service planned
Doğubeyazıt via Erçiş, Patnos and Ağrı – 315 km, 5½ hours, US$12; several to Ağrı, then change for Doğubeyazıt
Erzurum – 410 km, 7½ hours, US$18; several buses
Hakkari – 205 km, four hours, US$9; several buses
Malatya – 580 km, 10 hours, US$22; several buses
Şanlıurfa – 555 km, 10 hours, US$20; a few buses
Tatvan – 144 km, three hours, US$6; frequent buses
Trabzon – 745 km, 17 hours, US$30; a few direct buses, most via Erzurum

Train The *Vangölü Ekspresi* from İstanbul and Ankara goes right on to the lake steamer at Tatvan and cruises across the lake daily. The train is so unreliable that there is no set schedule for the ferry: when the train comes, the ferry goes. If you go with it, take food, as only drinks are sold during the four-hour voyage.

On Sunday, Monday, Wednesday and Friday, trains depart from Van at 3 pm for the 101-km journey to the Iranian frontier at Kapıköy (just west of Qotur), arriving at 6.35 pm; the return journey runs on Monday, Tuesday, Thursday and Saturday departing from Kapıköy at 5.30 am, arriving in Van at 8.35 am. Fares are ridiculously low. This connection is not really very useful to international travellers.

On Wednesday the weekly Ankara-Tehran train, wistfully termed an express, passes through Van. Ask at the tourism office for the current schedule, such as it is.

Getting Around

An airport bus (US$1) meets each flight, and is advisable as the taxi fare for the short six-km ride is a high US$5. The bus departs the ticket office for the airport 1½ hours before each THY flight.

For dolmuşes to the Rock of Van (Kale),

the ferry dock (İskele), the Akdamar boat dock (Gevaş) and Adilcevaz on the lake's northern shore, go to Beş Yol at the northern end of Cumhuriyet Caddesi.

HAKKARİ

The mountain scenery is spectacular in Hakkari (hah-KYAH-ree, population 35,000, altitude 1700m), 210 km south of Van over a zig-zag road. However, this is a centre of the still-smouldering Kurdish insurgency. Foreign visitors are looked upon with suspicion by the police and army, and indeed it was still unsafe to venture here at the time of writing. If you reach Hakkari, you may find severely limited tourist services.

Buses depart from Van daily for Hakkari. At 112 km is Başkale, notable for its altitude (2450m). Yeni Köprü, at 160 km, is the point at which a road to the left goes to Yüksekova and the Esendere border post on the road to Iran – an alternative base for climbs into the mountains in better times, when political and military conditions allow.

Finally, 210 km from Van you arrive in Hakkari. If things have not changed since this writing, you will be escorted from the bus to a hotel by a security officer. The hotel might be the *Otel Ümit* for US$8 per room, or the two-star *Otel Şenler* for US$15/25 a single/double.

Climbing in the breathtaking mountains around Hakkari was not possible at the time of writing, but to enjoy the scenery you can take one of several daily buses to Yüksekova. Three basic hotels will accommodate you for US$3 to US$6 per person.

NORTH FROM VAN

If you're bound for Doğubeyazıt, you have a choice of routes. The traditional one is from Erçiş to Patnos and Ağrı. The alternative, Bendimahi-Muradiye-Çaldıran-Ortadirek, is more scenic and only 185 km long, though you must keep your passport handy for the several Turkish army checkpoints. The road's officially closed after 5 pm, however, as Turkish army patrols are on duty to stop smugglers.

Glossary

Here, with definitions, are some unfamiliar words and abbreviations you might meet in the text or on the road in Turkey:

acropolis – high city, hilltop citadel and temples of a classic Hellenic city
adliye – court house
agora – open space for commerce and politics in a classic Hellenic city
aile salonu – family room, for couples, families and single women in a Turkish restaurant
akaryakıt – liquid fuel, petrol (gasoline), diesel etc
Allah korusun – God protect me!
apse – semicircular recess for the altar in a church
araç çıkabılır – vehicles entering
arasta – row of shops near a mosque, the rent from which supports the mosque
askeri araç – military vehicle

banliyö – suburb(an)
bedesten – vaulted, fireproof market enclosure where valuable goods are kept
belediye – municipality/town hall
bouleuterion – place of assemby, council meeting-place in a classic Hellenic city

cami(i) – mosque
caravanserai – caravan palace, large fortified way-station for caravans
çarşı – market, bazaar
çeşme – spring, fountain
çevreyolu – ring road, bypass
cuneiform – wedge-shaped characters used in several ancient languages

dağ(ı) – mountain
Damsız Girilmez – 'No single males admitted' (Turkish nightclubs)
DDY – Devlet Demiryolları, (Turkish) State Railways; same as TCDD
deniz – sea
deniz otobüsü – hydrofoil
Denizyolları – Turkish Maritime Lines
dervish – member of mystic brotherhood, some (whirling) noted for frenzied dance
Dikkat! Yavaş! – Careful! Slow!
dinlenme parkı – (highway) rest area

eczane – chemist/pharmacy
eski – old (thing, not person)
eyvan – large recess, vaulted or domed, open to a courtyard

figure malzeme – gravel mound at roadside

gazino – Turkish nightclub (not for gambling)
geçit, -di – mountain pass
geniş araç – wide vehicle

hamam(ı) – Turkish steam bath
han(ı) – inn or caravanserai in a town or city
harabe(ler) – ruin(s)
harem – family/women's quarters of a residence (see also *selamlık)*
hazır yemek – food prepared and kept hot on a steam table
heyelan (bölgesi) – landslide (zone)
hisar – fortress, citadel; same as *kale*
hükümet konağı – government house
Hünkar Mahfili – sultan's special prayer-place in a mosque

imam – prayer leader, Muslim cleric
imaret(i) – soup kitchen for the poor
İşhanı – office building
iskele(si) – landing-place, wharf, quay

kale(si) – fortress, citadel; same as *hisar*
kapı(sı) – door, gate
kaplıca – thermal spring or baths
karayolları – highways
kat – storey (of a building)
Katma Değer Vergisi – Value Added Tax
kat oto parkı – multi-level parking garage

kervansaray(ı) – Turkish for caravanserai
kilim – napless woven wool mat
kilise(si) – church
konak, konağı – mansion, government headquarters
köprü – bridge
köşk(ü) – pavilion, villa
köy(ü) – village
kule(si) – tower
külliye(si) – mosque complex including seminary, hospital, soup kitchen etc
kümbet – vault, cupola, dome; tomb topped by this
küşet(li) – (railway carriage having) couchette(s), shelf-like beds

liman(ı) – harbour

Maaşallah – Wonder of God! (said in admiration or to avert the evil eye)
mağara(sı) – cave
mahalle(si) – neighbourhood, district of a city
medrese(si) – Muslim theological seminary
mescit, -di – prayer room, small mosque
meydan(ı) – public square, open place
meyhane – wine shop, tavern
mihrab – niche in a mosque indicating the direction of Mecca
mimber – pulpit in a mosque
minare(si) – minaret, tower from which Muslims are called to prayer
müezzin – cantor who sings the *ezan*, or call to prayer

narthex – enclosed porch or vestibule at the entrance to a church
nave – middle aisle of a church
necropolis – city of the dead, cemetery
nufüs – population

oda(sı) – room
odeon – odeum, small classical theatre for musical performances
okul taşıtı – school bus
otogar – bus station
otoyol – motorway, limited-access divided highway

pansiyon – pension, B&B, guesthouse
park yeri – car park
patika – trail, footpath
pazar(ı) – weekly market, bazaar
PTT – Posta, Telefon, Telğraf: post, telephone and telegraph office

rakım – altitude above sea level
Ramazan – Muslim lunar holy month

şadırvan – fountain where Muslims perform ritual ablutions
saray(ı) – palace
sarcophagus – a stone or marble coffin or tomb, especially one with inscription
sebil – public fountain or water kiosk
şehir – city; municipal
selamlık – public/male quarters of a residence (also see *harem*)
Seljuk – of or pertaining to the Seljuk Turks
sufi – Muslim mystic, member of a mystic (dervish) brotherhood
sürücü adayı – student (learner) driver

tatil köyü – holiday village
TCDD – Türkiye Cumhuriyeti Devlet Demiryolları, Turkish State Railways; same as DDY
tehlikeli madde – dangerous cargo
Tekel – government alcoholic beverage & tobacco company
tekke(si) – dervish lodge
TEM – Trans-European Motorway
TC – Türkiye Cumhuriyeti (Turkish Republic), which designates an official office or organisation
THY – Türk Hava Yolları, Turkish Airlines
tırmanma şeridi – overtaking lane
TML – Turkish Maritime Lines, Denizyolları
TRT – Türkiye Radyo ve Televizyon, Turkish broadcasting corporation
tuff, tufa – soft stone laid down as volcanic ash
tuğra – sultan's monogram, imperial signature
türbe(si) – tomb, grave, mausoleum

uzun araç – long vehicle

valilik, valiliği, vilayet – provincial government headquarters
vizier – high official

yalı – waterside residence
yasak bölge – forbidden zone
yayla – mountain pasture, usually used in summer only
yol(u) – road, way
yol onarımı – road repairs
yol yapımı – road construction

zaviye – dervish hostel

Historic Place Names

HISTORIC NAME	MODERN NAME
Adrianople	Edirne
Aintab	Antep, Gaziantep
Alexandretta	İskenderun
Amida	Diyarbakır
Anatolia	Anadolu
Angora	Ankara
Antioch	Antakya
Antioch-in-Pisidia	Yalvaç
Antiphellus	Kaş
Ararat, Mt	Ağrı Dağı
Asia Minor	Anadolu
Assos	Behramkale
Attaleia	Antalya
Black Sea	Karadeniz
Bosphorus	İstanbul Boğazı
Byzantium	İstanbul
Caesarea	Mazaca Kayseri
Cappadocia	Kapadokya (Nevşehir region)
Caria	Milas region
Chalcedon	Kadıköy
Cilicia	Silifke region
Constantinople	İstanbul
Dardanelles	Çanakkale Boğazı
Dorylaeum	Eskişehir
Edessa	Urfa, Şanlıurfa
Ephesus	Efes, Selçuk
Euphrates (River)	Fırat
Galatia	Ankara region
Gallipoli	Gelibolu
Halicarnassus	Bodrum
Harran	Altınbaşak
Hattuşaş	Boğazkale
Hellespont	Çanakkale Boğazı
Hierapolis	Pamukkale
Iconium	Konya
Ida, Mt	Kaz Dağı
Ilium	Truva
Ionia	İzmir region
Kanesh	Kültepe

HISTORIC NAME	MODERN NAME
Laodicea	Laodikya (Goncalı, Denizli)
Lycia	Fethiye region
Lydia	Manisa region
Magnesia-ad-Sipylum	Manisa
Meander (River)	Büyük Menderes
Mediterranean Sea	Akdeniz
Miletus	Milet
Mylasa	Milas
Myra	Demre, Kale
Nicaea	İznik
Nicomedia	Kocaeli (İzmit)
Nimrod, Mt	Nemrut Dağı
Olympus, Mt	Uludağ
Pamphylia	Antalya region
Paphlagonia	Sinop region
Pergamon, Pergamum	Bergama
Philadelphia	Alaşehir
Phocea	Foça
Phoenicus	Finike
Phrygia	Burdur region
Proussa, Prusa	Bursa
Sardis	Sart
Sebasteia	Sivas
Seleucia of Isauria	Silifke
Sesamos Amastris	Amasra
Sinope	Sinop
Smyrna	İzmir
Tarsus	Tarsus
Telmessos	Fethiye
Theodosiopolis	Erzurum
Thrace	Trakya
Thyatira	Akhisar
Tigris (River)	Dicle
Tralles	Aydın
Trebizond	Trabzon
Troy	Truva
Xanthos	Kınık

Index

MAPS

TEXT

Map references are in **bold** type.

THANKS

Thanks to the following people and many travellers from all over the world who took the time and trouble to write to us about their experiences in Turkey:

Eve Addis, Azhar Ali, Steven Allan, Lamond & Brian Allcock, Craig Allen, Jodie Allison, Kevin & Jennifer Alpert, Kit Althen, Gail & Allan Anderman, Elizabeth Anderson, Fiona Anderson, Morey & Fern Anderson, J Andrews & S Perkins, Konnie W Andrews, Louise Andrews, Richard Ansdell, Frank Armstrong, Magnus Arvidsson, Victor Ashe, Frank Ashworth, Bonnie Asnes, Hakan Ayaz, Beth Baer, Judy Baker, Eszter Balazs, Csaba Ban, Janina Bard, Edith Barry, Paul Bassett, Ross Bastiaan, Reinier Bax, Phyllis Becker, Kylie Beckhouse, David & Stewart Bell, S & J Bentley, Kristen Berger, Belig Berkoz, Geraldine Besson, Ian Bevis, Deborah Binder, Mrs B Bingham, Lindsay Bligh, Kami Bloom, Andris Blums, Nicole Boonstra, Dini Borst, Kees Breek, Gillian Breen, E G Brewitt-Taylor, Francoise Bringel, Clive Brown, Ian Brown, Mr & Mrs Brucken, Brenda & Clare Buckley, Trevor Burford-Reade, Sheena Burton, Tamsin & Patrick Bynne, Ilona Caldwell, Kevin Callaghan, John Campbell, Laura Campbell, Ian Carter, Joe Carter, Mary Caselli, Michelle Caudieau, Kate & Jeff Channing, Nina Charana & R Cromwell, Mr & Mrs Fred Charles, Mr & Mrs Chastang, Caroline Cheng, Alice Choyke, Louise Clarke, Paul & John Clifton, Richard Clifton, Alison Colebourn, Mark Coleman, John & Judy Collins, Wendy Conner, George Conder, Paul Coppin, Julie Cornwell, Tony Cotton, Kevin Coughlan, Judith Court, Gabrielle Cramp & Co, Ann & Lindsay Crawford, Seamans Crimmins, Terry Cringle, Maurice & Jane Croft, Jodi Crout, Vicki Crowe, Aldo D'astoli, Phil D'eath & Sarah Allsop, M Da Costa, Michel Dagonneau, Winthrop Dahl, Salih Dal, Heidi Dalhoff, Kimberley Daly, Jennifer & Steve Dalzell, Valerie Darling, Signe Davidsen, Kimee Davidson & Brian Bush, Keri Davis-Miller, Angela Davison, Tom De Clerck, Christian Delooder, Theodoros Dermentzogloy, Dan Devos, Joel Didomizio, Ms E Jane Doering, Greg & Pam Doman, Anthony Dore, Stephen Downes, Alan Drayton, Fam Drielsma, Cheryl Duchow, NA Duffield, Rifat Durmus, Dr Recep Efe, Erik & Roeline Efes, Arno Eijl, Dr & Mrs VS Ellis, Bryan Everts & Corinne Campbell, Elizabeth Farkas, Jeanne Feldman, Ann Fells, Hugh Finsten, Lucy Fisher, Ari & Ayelet Fleischer, Katherine Foley, Samantha Forrest, Eleanor Foster, B Francow, Sally Freudenstein, Andree Frieze, Danny Frisby-Griffiths, M J Furmston, Ann & Jim Gage, Nicola George, Liz & David Gillham, Rachel Gilmour, Tony Goddard & Kate Rantall, Elizabeth Godfrey, Joel L Goldschmidt, Mrs Patricia Gooding, Gabriel Gorenstein, C Grant, Jan Grant, Barbara Gray, Michael C Greenfield, Robert Greenwood, Erica Gregory, Bekir Gunay, Paul Gurtler, V Aykut Guzer, W Haelman, Susanne Hahleituer, Anne Haisley, Denyse Hale, Zac Hanscom, Barbie Harchy, Chris & Carol Harman, Ross Harper, John Harrison, Suzie Hawkridge, Phillipa Hay, Pat Haynes, Per Heggby, Philip Heinecke, Michelle Heinemann, Mary & Mark Henderson, Berend Hendriks, Miss Pam Herbert, Thomas Herbert, Pam Hersey, M Hertog-Sernoff, Christopher Hicks, Barry Hiern, Nancy Higbie, Derek Hill, Richard Hillam, Connie Hilton, Katy Hirschman, Sharyn Hocking, Simon & Helen Holliday, Diana Holsinger, Hans Hommels, Jeff Hopkins, Liza Hopkins, Joei Hossack, Lesley Houfe, Soren Houmoller, Wendy Hubbert, D Huchel & R Lewis, Shirley Hudson, Cathy Hughes, Denis Hughes, Kelly Hunt, Mehmet Irdem, Marion James, Jane & Rowdy, Brian Janeway, Graeme Janton, Philip Jarvis, Douglas Jasch, Tim Jeffreys, Charlotte Jensen, Sandra Johnson, Philip Jolly, Ron Jordon, Zinas Kanther, Dr Prabodh Karnik, Sally Kay, Ravi & Tal Kayatsky, Peter Kerby, Simone Kerrie, David Kinder, Tamara Kjar, Helaine Knickerbocker, Magda Konings, Mary Koopman, Edith Koopmans, Dawn Kose, Bobbi Kraham, Salman (Sammy) Kult, N Kwaja, Bill & Susan Lafferly, Jeri Lang, David Latchford, Mrs Chester Later, Nicole LeBlanc, Mr Lee, Tim Leffel & Donna Marcus, Rita Leghissa, Mrs Lois Lemehens, Hagar Leschner, Joseph & Yael Levy, Nancy Liddle, Adam Lillywhite, Ali Lilusan, Melissa Lindsay, Deirdre Linton, Louise Lister, Dr Keith Liyaragama, Julian Longley, Mark Love, Bernard Luckhurst, Patrick Lyons, Rene & Yolanda Maassen, S MacDonald, Katie Machin, K Machin & A Miles, Joanne Macicewske, Christina & Dennison MacKinnon, Iskele Mah, Julia Maiden, Bill Marshall, Graham Marshall, Chris & Denise Martin, Mrs P Mattinson, Lesley Mauders, Heather Maynard, Rob McCampbell, Mary McClarry, Margaret McConnell, M McConnell & B Harvey, Bryan McGee, Maria McKenzie, Tim McLaughlin, P Meister, Helen Meistrich, Marion & Ralph Melville, John Miraglia, Hiroko Miyagi, David Mordy, Susan Murray, Paul Myers, Carol Nelson, Scott Nelson, Ann Nevans, Dr AP Newton, Fiona Nicks, Zoe Nielsen, Annette Novotka, Douglas Oles, Ken Olver, Philip Orlick, Guri Osterberg, D Osterman & E Mayes, Asur Oteli, Pavlina Otmar, David Owen, Cahit Ozbek, Ercan Ozyurt, Joel Palombo, Isobel Palson, Tracy Perks, Syd Peters, H Phelan & R Thomas, Boudewijn Pieters, Sandy Polishuk, Juliet Pope, Thomas Porter, Susan Praeger, Barbara J Preston, Sonia Prior, Jane Rades, Gabriela Radulescu, TH Rainbolt, Janet Rees, Mr Howard Reid, A Kevin Reinhart, JA Reynolds, Malcolm Richardson, Kathreen Ricketson, Hazel Riggall, Betty Robinson, Ray Robinson, Angel Rodgers, Claudio Rodriguez, William Rollins, David Romano, Fiona Rooney, Inge Roose, Edward Rosenthal, Rein Rosestraten, Twan Rosmalen, Nathalie Roy, Ian Russell, Rod Russell, Bruce & Tara

Ryan, Conor Ryan, Justin Ryan, Dolores Rylee, Ali Sabah, Lester Saegenschnitter, Csaba Salamon, Paul Sargent, Amy Sarkiss, Bert & Joanne Schnitzer, Annemarie Schoorel, Dr AJG Schoots, Charlotte Scott, Mark Scott, Alan Scullard, Tom Seaman, Richard Selby, Adam Sellars, A Sevim, Alon Shalit, Erin Shaylor, David Shrall, C Simm & M Papoui, Alison Smith, Jary Smith, Louise J Smith, Melissa Snow, Adam Spreadbury, Jimmie Spulecki, Michelle Squires, Wim Staes, AJC Steenhoek, Donald Steinberg, Anneli Sterling, Mrs Joan Stokes, Polly Tafrate, Saim Tahir, Robert Talley, A Tam, Martine et Phug Taminh, Jon Tapscott, Julie Taylor, Roger Taylor, A Templeton, JE Terrell, Niall Thewlis, Priscilla Thorley, Mark Tippett, Andrew Tokeley, Tom K Tolk, Richard & Jean Toon, Halil Toparlak, Zolton Toth, Marion Tuchy, Eric & Maggie Turner, Mehmet Umur, Giorgio Usai, Eric Van den Broeck, Tony & Helga van der Lisdonk, Paul van Ingen, John & Brenda van Ness, Kasper van Ommen, Kari Vaughan, Paivi Vilppala, Yvan Volders, J Kramer Vreugdenhil, Florence Vuillet, Michael Walker, D Wallis, Shannon Ward, MJ Warren, Ravena Watson, Vance Weaver, Ian Webber, Duncan Webster, Tom Weingarten, Arndt Weishaupt, Rod Westcott, T Westley, Ben Wheeler, Pippa White, Saly Whitney, Steve Whittington, Vincent Wiers, Joanna Wilkinson, Wendy Wilkinson, Monique Willemse, Anna Williams, Elaine Williams, Joanne Williams, Martin & Eryl Williams, RF Williams, Martina Winn, E Winters, Tony Winters, Shirley Wise, Steve Witts & Sharon Walton, Robert Woodburn, Rhona Woodbury, Louise Woollett, Patrick Wullaert, Ayla Jean Yackley, Michal & Eran Yariv, Jane Yates, Stuart Young and Nalan Yuksel.

Warning & Request

Things change – prices go up, schedules change, good places go bad and bad places go bankrupt – nothing stays the same. So if you find things better or worse, recently opened or long since closed, please write and tell us and help make the next edition better.

Your letters will be used to help update future editions and, where possible, important changes will also be included in an Update section in reprints.

We greatly appreciate all information that is sent to us by travellers. Back at Lonely Planet we employ a hard-working readers' letters team of Julie Young and Shelley Preston in Australia, Sarah Long in the UK, Marina Bonnamy in France and Beth Eisler in the US to sort through the many letters we receive. The best ones will be rewarded with a free copy of the next edition or another Lonely Planet guide if you prefer. We give away lots of books, but, unfortunately, not every letter/postcard receives one.